Advancement of Mathematical Methods in Feature Representation Learning for Artificial Intelligence, Data Mining and Robotics

Advancement of Mathematical Methods in Feature Representation Learning for Artificial Intelligence, Data Mining and Robotics

Editors

Jianping Gou
Weihua Ou
Shaoning Zeng
Lan Du

MDPI • Basel • Beijing • Wuhan • Barcelona • Belgrade • Manchester • Tokyo • Cluj • Tianjin

MDPI

Editors
Jianping Gou
Southwest University
China

Weihua Ou
Guizhou Normal University
China

Shaoning Zeng
University of Electronic Science and Technology of China
China

Lan Du
Monash University
Australia

Editorial Office
MDPI
St. Alban-Anlage 66
4052 Basel, Switzerland

This is a reprint of articles from the Special Issue published online in the open access journal *Mathematics* (ISSN 2227-7390) (available at: https://www.mdpi.com/si/mathematics/Advancement_Mathematical_methods_Feature_Representation_Learning_Artificial_Intelligence_Data_Mining_Robotics).

For citation purposes, cite each article independently as indicated on the article page online and as indicated below:

LastName, A.A.; LastName, B.B.; LastName, C.C. Article Title. *Journal Name* **Year**, *Volume Number*, Page Range.

ISBN 978-3-0365-7262-8 (Hbk)
ISBN 978-3-0365-7263-5 (PDF)

Contents

About the Editors

Jianping Gou

Jianping Gou (Senior Member, IEEE) received a Ph.D. degree in computer science from the University of Electronic Science and Technology of China, Chengdu, China, in 2012. He was previously a Post-Doctoral Research Fellow with the University of Sydney. He is currently a Professor in the College of Computer and Information Science, College of Software, Southwest University, Chongqing, China. His current research interests include pattern classification and machine learning. So far, he has published over 100 papers in international journals or conferences, such as in IJCV, TNNLS, TII, TITS, T-CYB and TKDD. He is an academic editor of Scientific Programming, an editorial board member of Mathematics, a senior member of CCF, and a senior member of CSIG.

Weihua Ou

Weihua Ou received a Ph.D. degree in Information and Communication Engineering from Huazhong University of Science and Technology (HUST), China. Currently, he is a full Professor at the School of Big Data and Computer Science in Guizhou Normal University, Guiyang, China. His current research interests include cross-modal retrieval, deep learning, and image processing and computer vision. His research results mean he has published more than 70 papers in prominent journals and conferences, such as IEEE T-NNLS, IEEE T-MM, IEEE T-CSVT, PR, ICPR, and ICME. His publications have been cited in Google Scholar more than 1800 times; his H-Index is 23.

Shaoning Zeng

Shaoning Zeng received a B.S. degree and M.S. degree from Beihang University (BUAA), Beijing, China, in 2004 and 2007, respectively, and his Ph.D. degree in computer science in the Department of Computer and Information Science, Faculty of Science and Technology from the University of Macau in 2020. He is an Associate Professor at the Yangtze Delta Region Institute (Huzhou), University of Electronic Science and Technology of China. His research interests include computer vision, pattern recognition, machine learning, and deep learning for multimedia and image processing applications.

Lan Du

Dr Lan Du is a senior lecturer in Data Science and AI in the Faculty of IT, Monash University. His research interest lies in the joint area of machine/deep learning and natural language processing and their applications in different domains, such as public health, where he and his research team are developing cutting-edge NLP technologies for AI-enabled medical NLP. He is best known for his research work on learning and understanding the semantics of the free language texts as a leading Australian researcher in topic modeling.

mathematics

MDPI

Editorial

Preface to the Special Issue "Advancement of Mathematical Methods in Feature Representation Learning for Artificial Intelligence, Data Mining and Robotics"—Special Issue Book

Weihua Ou [1], Jianping Gou [2,*], Shaoning Zeng [3] and Lan Du [4]

1 School of Big Data and Computer Science, Guizhou Normal University, Guiyang 550025, China
2 College of Computer and Information Science, Southwest University, Chongqing 400715, China
3 Yangtze Delta Region Institute (Huzhou), University of Electronic Science and Technology of China, Huzhou 314006, China
4 Faculty of Information Technology, Monash University, Melbourne 3800, Australia
* Correspondence: goujianping@ujs.edu.cn

The feature representation learning is the basic task that plays an important role in artificial intelligence, data mining and robotics. With the recent rapid development of deep learning, many advanced methods have been proposed and have gained remarkable successes both in academia and in industry, such as auto-encoders, convolutional neural networks, generative adversarial networks, and so on. However, many questions remain unsolved. What makes one representation better than another? What are appropriate objectives for learning representations well? How can security and the algorithm be explained?

This special issue aims to highlight the latest results on the mathematical methods in feature representation learning for artificial intelligence, data mining and robotics, covering several recently reported methods.

The representation learning is the basic problem for computer vision. For example, the authors of [1] comprehensively reviewed the development of vehicle re-identification and revealed that representation learning plays a vital role in the vehicle re-identification. Furthermore, they classified the vehicle re-identification feature representation approaches into two parts: hand-crafted and deep learning based feature representations. In [2], semantic intelligent detection of vehicle color was studied under rainy conditions for jointly detaining and recognizing vehicle color. Specifically, the feature maps of the recovered clean image and the extracted feature maps of the input image are cascaded into the feature pyramid net (FPN) module to achieve joint semantic representation learning. Based on the YOLOX algorithm, works [3,4] proposed to learn representation features for high-performance head counting and garbage quantity identification, respectively.

Based on the fact that the low-level features contain small object information, while the high-level features contain accurate, large object information, the authors of [5] proposed an effective approach by integrating the characteristics of different stages on pedestrian detection. To explore the high-order information representation in vision tasks, the authors of [6] developed second-order spatial-temporal correlation filters for visual tracking, and the authors of [7] studied facial recognition via compact second-order image gradient orientations. In work [8], the authors proposed deep-learning based cyber & physical feature fusion for anomaly detection in industrial control systems.

In [9], discriminative multidimensional scaling based on pairwise constraints for a feature learning model was proposed considering both the topology of samples in the original space and the cluster structure in the new space. The authors of [10] proposed deep large-margin rank loss for feature learning for multi-label image classification. Ref. [11] proposed reinforcement learning-based representation approach for resource allocation in

Citation: Ou, W.; Gou, J.; Zeng, S.; Du, L. Preface to the Special Issue "Advancement of Mathematical Methods in Feature Representation Learning for Artificial Intelligence, Data Mining and Robotics"—Special Issue Book. *Mathematics* **2023**, *11*, 940. https://doi.org/10.3390/math11040940

Received: 4 February 2023
Accepted: 7 February 2023
Published: 13 February 2023

the elastic optical networks, and Ref. [12] presented a deep reinforcement learning based framework for gait adjustment for the patients suffer from physical disabilities.

Representation learning also plays an important role for the low-level image processing task. The authors of [13] studied blind image deblurring and proposed and learned an innovative sparse channel prior. The authors of [14] proposed a joint deep recovery model to efficiently address motion blur and resolution reduction simultaneously. The proposed multi-order attention mechanism comprehensively and hierarchically extracts multiple attention features and fuses them properly by drop-out gating. In [15], the authors reported an image aesthetic quality assessment and proposed a method that includes a representation learning step and a label propagation step. The authors of [16] developed a plug-and-play-based algorithm for mixed noise removal with the logarithm norm approximation model.

Since available source data are collected from related domains, multi-domain adaptation (MDA) has become increasingly popular. Although multiple source domains provide a significant amount of information, the processing of domain shifts becomes more challenging, especially in learning a common domain-invariant representation for all domains. In [17], due to the ambiguity of the category boundary, the authors proposed Dempster–Shafer evidence theory (DST) to reduce category boundary ambiguity and output reasonable decisions by combining adaptation outputs based on uncertainty. Inspired by generative adversarial networks (GANs), the authors of [18] proposed a novel adversarial domain adaptation method with an initial state fusion strategy followed by a domain similarity strategy based on information entropy. In [19], the authors adopt domain adaptation strategy to solve the remaining useful life (RUL) prediction caused by insufficient sample data of equipment under complex operating conditions. The authors of [20] proposed a geometric metric learning method for multi-output learning.

Sentiment classification is an important task in natural language processing. Traditional word-level vector representations provide the same representation for words that express different sentiment polarities in various domains. In [21], the authors proposed a dual-word embedding model considering syntactic information for cross-domain sentiment classification. The authors of [22] reported a graph convolutional network for aspect-based sentiment analysis considering the dependencies between words and the types of these dependencies simultaneously. The authors of [23] proposed a knowledge-enhanced dual-channel GCN for aspect-based sentiment analysis. In [24], the authors developed a triplet contrastive learning network to coordinate syntactic and semantic information for the domain of aspect-level sentiment classification. Works [25,26] show that the effectiveness of the knowledge enhanced sentiment feature learning for aspect-level the sentiment classification and hate speech detection. [27] studied the embedding representation learning for the uncertain temporal knowledge graph while [28] studied Tensor Affinity Learning for Hyperorder Graph Matching.

Some other representative works also show the importance of the feature representation learning. Such as, Ref. [29] studied the 3D reconstruction of self-rotating objects, Ref. [30] presented a fusion verification method cross-site scripting attacks. Ref. [31] proposed a novel feature transformation-based method to improve the robustness of adversarial example by transforming the features of data. Ref. [32] studied the requirement analysis for complex mechanical products scheme design, while Ref. Ref. [33] studied stability of switched systems with time-varying delays.

Briefly, this Special Issue received 65 submissions, 33 of which were published, including 32 research articles and 1 review article. All submissions covered topics from low-level vision feature learning to high-level semantic representation learning, including texts, images and videos from single domains to cross-domains. We believe that these will effectively boost the research on representation learning. We found the selection of papers for this Special Issue very inspiring and we thank the editorial staff and reviewers for their efforts and assistance during the process.

Author Contributions: Conceptualization, W.O., J.G., S.Z. and L.D.; methodology, W.O., J.G., S.Z. and L.D.; software, W.O., J.G., S.Z. and L.D.; validation, J.G., S.Z. and L.D.; formal analysis, J.G., S.Z. and L.D.; investigation, J.G., S.Z. and L.D.; resources, J.G., S.Z. and L.D.; data curation, J.G., S.Z. and L.D.; writing—original draft preparation, J.G., S.Z. and L.D.; writing—review and editing, J.G., S.Z. and L.D.; visualization, J.G., S.Z. and L.D.; supervision, J.G., S.Z. and L.D.; project administration, J.G., S.Z. and L.D.; funding acquisition, J.G., S.Z. and L.D. All authors have read and agreed to the published version of the manuscript.

Funding: This research received no external funding.

Conflicts of Interest: The authors declare no conflict of interest.

References

1. Zakria; Deng, J.; Hao, Y.; Khokhar, M.; Kumar, R.; Cai, J.; Kumar, J.; Aftab, M. Trends in Vehicle Re-Identification Past, Present, and Future: A Comprehensive Review. *Mathematics* **2021**, *9*, 3162.
2. Hu, M.; Wu, Y.; Fan, J.; Jing, B. Joint Semantic Intelligent Detection of Vehicle Color under Rainy Conditions. *Mathematics* **2022**, *10*, 3512. [CrossRef]
3. Zhang, Z.; Xia, S.; Cai, Y.; Yang, C.; Zeng, S. A Soft-YoloV4 for High-Performance Head Detection and Counting. *Mathematics* **2021**, *9*, 3096. [CrossRef]
4. Lin, J.; Yang, C.; Lu, Y.; Cai, Y.; Zhan, H.; Zhang, Z. An Improved Soft-YOLOX for Garbage Quantity Identification. *Mathematics* **2022**, *10*, 2650. [CrossRef]
5. Ding, Z.; Gu, Z.; Sun, Y.; Xiang, X. Cascaded Cross-Layer Fusion Network for Pedestrian Detection. *Mathematics* **2022**, *10*, 139. [CrossRef]
6. Yu, Y.; Chen, L.; He, H.; Liu, J.; Zhang, W.; Xu, G. Second-Order Spatial-Temporal Correlation Filters for Visual Tracking. *Mathematics* **2022**, *10*, 684. [CrossRef]
7. Yin, H.; Wu, X.; Hu, C.; Song, X. Face Recognition via Compact Second-Order Image Gradient Orientations. *Mathematics* **2022**, *10*, 2587. [CrossRef]
8. Du, Y.; Huang, Y.; Wan, G.; He, P. Deep Learning-Based Cyber&Physical Feature Fusion for Anomaly Detection in Industrial Control Systems. *Mathematics* **2022**, *10*, 4373.
9. Zhang, L.; Pang, B.; Tang, H.; Wang, H.; Li, C.; Luo, Z. Pairwise Constraints Multidimensional Scaling for Discriminative Feature Learning. *Mathematics* **2022**, *10*, 4059.
10. Ma, Z.; Li, Z.; Zhan, Y. Deep Large-Margin Rank Loss for Multi-Label Image Classification. *Mathematics* **2022**, *10*, 4584.
11. Tang, B.; Huang, Y.; Xue, Y.; Zhou, W. Deep Reinforcement Learning-Based RMSA Policy Distillation for Elastic Optical Networks. *Mathematics* **2022**, *10*, 3293. [CrossRef]
12. Li, A.; Chen, J.; Fu, Q.; Wu, H.; Wang, Y.; Lu, Y. A Novel Deep Reinforcement Learning Based Framework for Gait Adjustment. *Mathematics* **2023**, *11*, 178. [CrossRef]
13. Yang, D.; Wu, X.; Yin, H. Blind Image Deblurring via a Novel Sparse Channel Prior. *Mathematics* **2022**, *10*, 1238. [CrossRef]
14. Chu, Y.; Zhang, X.; Liu, H. Decoupling Induction and Multi-Order Attention Drop-Out Gating Based Joint Motion Deblurring and Image Super-Resolution. *Mathematics* **2022**, *10*, 1837. [CrossRef]
15. Zhang, X.; Zhang, X.; Xiao, Y.; Liu, G. Theme-Aware Semi-Supervised Image Aesthetic Quality Assessment. *Mathematics* **2022**, *10*, 2609. [CrossRef]
16. Liu, J.; Wu, J.; Xu, M.; Huang, Y. Plug-and-Play-Based Algorithm for Mixed Noise Removal with the Logarithm Norm Approximation Model. *Mathematics* **2022**, *10*, 3810. [CrossRef]
17. Huang, M.; Zhang, C. A Novel Multi-Source Domain Adaptation Method with Dempster Shafer Evidence Theory for Cross-Domain Classification. *Mathematics* **2022**, *10*, 2797. [CrossRef]
18. Huang, M.; Yin, J. Research on Adversarial Domain Adaptation Method and Its Application in Power Load Forecasting. *Mathematics* **2022**, *10*, 3223. [CrossRef]
19. Chen, W.; Chen, W.; Liu, H.; Wang, Y.; Bi, C.; Gu, Y. A RUL Prediction Method of Small Sample Equipment Based on DCNN-BiLSTM and Domain Adaptation. *Mathematics* **2022**, *10*, 1022. [CrossRef]
20. Gao, H.; Ma, Z. Geometric Metric Learning for Multi-Output Learning. *Mathematics* **2022**, *10*, 1632. [CrossRef]
21. Lu, Z.; Hu, X.; Xue, Y. Dual-Word Embedding Model Considering Syntactic Information for Cross-Domain Sentiment Classification. *Mathematics* **2022**, *10*, 4704. [CrossRef]
22. Yang, J.; Dai, A.; Xue, Y.; Zeng, B.; Liu, X. Syntactically Enhanced Dependency-POS Weighted Graph Convolutional Network for Aspect-Based Sentiment Analysis. *Mathematics* **2022**, *10*, 3353. [CrossRef]
23. Zhang, Z.; Ma, Z.; Cai, S.; Chen, J.; Xue, Y. Knowledge-Enhanced Dual-Channel GCN for Aspect-Based Sentiment Analysis. *Mathematics* **2022**, *10*, 4273. [CrossRef]
24. Xiong, H.; Yan, Z.; Zhao, H.; Huang, Z.; Xue, Y. Triplet Contrastive Learning for Aspect Level Sentiment Classification. *Mathematics* **2022**, *10*, 4099. [CrossRef]
25. Yu, H.; Lu, G.; Cai, Q.; Xue, Y. A KGE Based Knowledge Enhancing Method for Aspect-Level Sentiment Classification. *Mathematics* **2022**, *10*, 3908. [CrossRef]

26. Zhong, W.; Wu, Q.; Lu, G.; Xue, Y.; Hu, X. Keyword-Enhanced Multi-Expert Framework for Hate Speech Detection. *Mathematics* **2022**, *10*, 4706. [CrossRef]
27. Li, T.; Wang, W.; Li, X.; Wang, T.; Zhou, X.; Huang, M. Embedding Uncertain Temporal Knowledge Graphs. *Mathematics* **2023**, *11*, 775. [CrossRef]
28. Wang, Z.; Wu, Y.; Liu, F. Tensor Affinity Learning for Hyperorder Graph Matching. *Mathematics* **2022**, *10*, 3806. [CrossRef]
29. Li, Z.; Zhang, Z.; Luo, S.; Cai, Y.; Guo, S. An Improved Matting-SfM Algorithm for 3D Reconstruction of Self-Rotating Objects. *Mathematics* **2022**, *10*, 2892. [CrossRef]
30. Xu, H.; Hu, C.; Yin, H. Enhancing the Transferability of Adversarial Examples with Feature Transformation. *Mathematics* **2022**, *10*, 2976. [CrossRef]
31. Lu, J.; Wei, Z.; Qin, Z.; Chang, Y.; Zhang, S. Resolving Cross-Site Scripting Attacks through Fusion Verification and Machine Learning. *Mathematics* **2022**, *10*, 3787. [CrossRef]
32. Wang, T.; Li, H.; Wang, X. Extension Design Pattern of Requirement Analysis for Complex Mechanical Products Scheme Design. *Mathematics* **2022**, *10*, 3132. [CrossRef]
33. Liu, C.; Liu, X. Stability of Switched Systems with Time-Varying Delays under State-Dependent Switching. *Mathematics* **2022**, *10*, 2722. [CrossRef]

mathematics

Article

A Soft-YoloV4 for High-Performance Head Detection and Counting

Zhen Zhang [1], Shihao Xia [1], Yuxing Cai [1], Cuimei Yang [1] and Shaoning Zeng [2,*]

1 School of Computer Science and Engineering, Huizhou University, Huizhou 516007, China; zzsjbme@sjtu.edu.cn (Z.Z.); mr123zhang@gmail.com (S.X.); hzucyx@gmail.com (Y.C.); meikoyoung1024@gmail.com (C.Y.)
2 Yangtze Delta Region Institute, University of Electronic Science and Technology of China, Huzhou 313000, China
* Correspondence: zeng@csj.uestc.edu.cn; Tel.: +86-177-5723-7213

Abstract: Blockage of pedestrians will cause inaccurate people counting, and people's heads are easily blocked by each other in crowded occasions. To reduce missed detections as much as possible and improve the capability of the detection model, this paper proposes a new people counting method, named Soft-YoloV4, by attenuating the score of adjacent detection frames to prevent the occurrence of missed detection. The proposed Soft-YoloV4 improves the accuracy of people counting and reduces the incorrect elimination of the detection frames when heads are blocked by each other. Compared with the state-of-the-art YoloV4, the AP value of the proposed head detection method is increased from 88.52 to 90.54%. The Soft-YoloV4 model has much higher robustness and a lower missed detection rate for head detection, and therefore it dramatically improves the accuracy of people counting.

Keywords: head detection; YoloV4; NMS; soft-NMS; people counting

Citation: Zhang, Z.; Xia, S.; Cai, Y.; Yang, C.; Zeng, S. A Soft-YoloV4 for High-Performance Head Detection and Counting. *Mathematics* **2021**, *9*, 3096. https://doi.org/10.3390/math9233096

Academic Editor: Radu Tudor Ionescu

Received: 26 October 2021
Accepted: 28 November 2021
Published: 30 November 2021

1. Introduction

People counting is a process of counting the number of people in images. It is one of the most important features in a modern intelligent camera. Without this artificial intelligence technique, we have to manually count the number of people in the surveillance video. However, this is unacceptable due the fact that the scale of video data becomes larger and larger. What is worse, it is unlikely to have a precise count when the number of people is too large. For this reason, many automatic people counting methods have been proposed based on the detection of skin color [1], facial features [2], and pedestrians [3]. Nowadays, deep learning, image recognition, and other artificial intelligence (AI) technologies are continuously developing [4]. These intelligent technologies are gradually being applied in our daily life, e.g., face recognition [5] and human action recognition [6]. In typical places, like classrooms and shopping malls, pedestrians are easily blocked by other objects, which prevents a precise counting of people. The good news is that this problem happens relatively infrequently on head counting. A computer can be adapted to detect human heads and, in turn, count the number of people. For example, the people counting system can detect the head of the student's heads in the classroom, so that the teachers can know whether a student is absent or not. In another case, the number of people in a self-study room can be counted and fed back to the mobile phone in real-time by head detecting. In this way, the students can quickly know which self-study room still has available seats, avoiding spending lots of time and energy searching for an unoccupied space. Besides these, a shopping mall owner can analyze the laws of customer flow by detecting heads in each store, which helps them make appropriate marketing strategies. All of these demonstrate that high-performance head detection and counting is one of the most crucial techniques in modern AI systems and applications.

2. Related Work

As a fundamental technique of people counting, head counting belongs to target detection in computer vision. A lot of machine learning methods have been proposed for this task. The traditional machine learning target detection algorithms include AdaBoost based on Harr features [7], SVM based on Hog [8] and LBP [9] features, etc. The principle of these detection algorithms mainly depends on the traditional manually extracted features. The procedure usually includes extracting features from the images, then constructing a classifier for classification, and finally obtaining the targets. However, most of these traditional target detection algorithms cannot produce a high accuracy for real applications, neither have a good enough generalization ability.

Deep neural networks, on the other hand, have a much better performance in target detection. Hinton et al. published a deep neural network using RBM coding [10]. Since then, deep learning methods have dominated the implementation of target detection applications. Currently, deep target detection algorithms are mainly divided into three categories. The first one is the multi-stage algorithms such as R-CNN [11] and SPPNet [12]. Then, two-stage implementations like Fast R-CNN [13], Faster R-CNN [14], Mask R-CNN [15], and HyperNet [16] have shown very promising performance. However, the speed of these methods is not fast enough for real applications. Besides these, there are many one-stage algorithms including YoloV1 [17], YoloV2 [18], SSD [19], Retina-Net [20], AlignDet [21], CenterNet [22], FSAF [23], FCOS [24], and YoloV4 [25]. All of the above one-stage algorithms have a fast recognition speed, but the accuracy is far from high enough. There is still a gap to be filled. For this reason, our goal is to improve the YoloV4 model, which represents the current state-of-the-art, to create a high-performance head detection and counting model.

In the conventional YoloV4, non-maximum suppression (NMS) sets the score of adjacent detection frame (adjacent detection frame probably contains object) to 0, then the final output will not contain this detection frame, which caused the occurrence of missed detection. This is harmful in the head-counting application. Soft-NMS algorithm was proposed to attenuate the score of the adjacent detection frame rather than set it to 0 [26]. As long as the score of the adjacent detection frame is greater than the threshold, the final output will contain this detection frame. Inspired by the above inference, this paper proposes a novel head detection method based on YoloV4, which we call Soft-YoloV4 (the NMS in YoloV4 is replaced by Soft-NMS). We make the following novel contributions:

1. We reveal why the conventional YoloV4 model is prone to miss detection in the case of people's heads are blocked by each other;
2. We proposed a new head detection model (Soft-YoloV4) by improving YoloV4. The experiments in two datasets show that the number of people can be counted more accurately by Soft-YoloV4;
3. We compared the Soft-YoloV4 and other methods previously reported, which showed that the Soft-YoloV4 has a better performance and is more conducive to real applications.

The present paper is organized as follows. Section 2 introduces the algorithm design of Soft-YoloV4 and presents the acquisition of experimental data. The results of Soft-YoloV4 in a real application and the comparison of Soft-YoloV4 between other several methods are presented in Section 3. The conclusion is provided in Section 4.

3. Methods

3.1. NMS Algorithm

The YoloV4 model mainly consists of the following parts: CSPDarknet53 (the backbone features extraction network), SPP (the strengthened features extraction network), PANet, and Yolo Head [27]. When the size of the inputted picture is $416 \times 416 \times 3$, the architecture consisting of CSPDarknet53, SPP, PANet, and Yolo Head is shown in Figure 1.

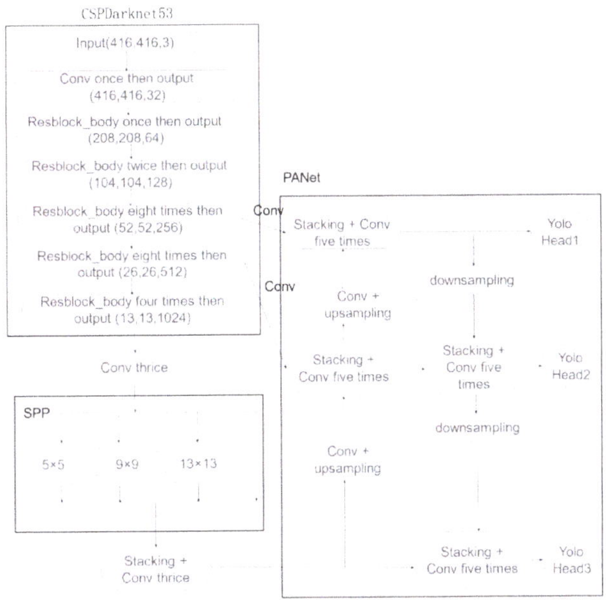

Figure 1. The architecture of YoloV4 network.

In particular, CSPDarknet53 mainly consists of a series of ResNet [28]. The detailed description can be found in the cspdarknet53 module in Figure 1.

Max-pooling in the SPP architecture mainly uses different pooling kernel sizes of $5 \times 5, 9 \times 9, 13 \times 13$. It pools the inputted feature layers and stacks each output. The Max-pooling process reduces the features and parameters of the result and keeps some invariance well, like rotation, translation, expansion, and others. The SPP architecture also increases the receptive field of the output unit nicely.

PANet was proposed by Shu Liu et al. [29]. This architecture makes full use of shallow and deep features. It obtains a more effective feature layer by fusing shallow features and deep features. In YoloV4, PANet is mainly used on three effective feature layers $(13, 13, 1024)$, $(26, 26, 512)$, $(52, 52, 256)$. By fusing the features in PANet, three effective feature layers are available in sizes of $52 \times 52 \times 128$, $26 \times 26 \times 256$, and $13 \times 13 \times 512$, respectively. Yolo Head has two convolution layers: the first layer is a 3×3 convolution, the second is a 1×1 convolution. For the case of Yolo Head1, the input of Yolo Head1 is $52 \times 52 \times 128$ feature layer, and $52 \times 52 \times 18$ feature layer is obtained after Yolo Head1 processing. Likewise, $26 \times 26 \times 18$ feature layer is obtained after Yolo Head2 processing, $13 \times 13 \times 18$ feature layer is obtained after Yolo Head3 processing. Finally, $52 \times 52 \times 18$, $26 \times 26 \times 18$, and $13 \times 13 \times 18$ feature layers will be the output of YoloV4.

In the original YoloV4 model, NMS is used to sift out the detection frame with the highest scores in the same category. However, the elimination mechanism of NMS is very strict, only considering the detection frame and its *IOU* (Intersection over Union), which easily leads to a missed detection. For example, a missed detection as an instance is shown in Figure 2:

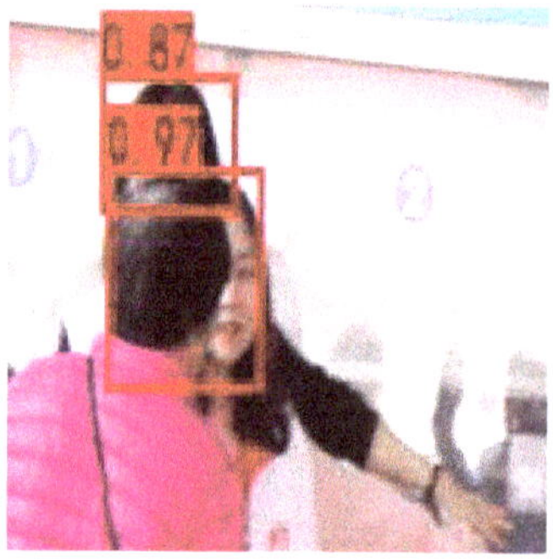

Figure 2. A missed detection happened using NMS.

There are three people in Figure 2. However, only two people were detected using NMS, which means a missed detection. Obviously, in a crowded occasion, using NMS algorithm to remove the redundant detection frames when people's heads are blocked by each other is likely to cause a missed detection.

In our improvement, the key step to achieve people counting is detecting people's heads. When there are too many people, their heads are easily blocked by each other. Therefore, we utilize Soft-NMS to replace NMS in the Soft YoloV4 model to fix the problem. Here, we have the following analysis.

3.2. Principle of Soft-NMS Algorithm

From a mathematical point of view, the mechanism of NMS to remove redundant frames can be expressed as:

$$score_i = \begin{cases} 0, IOU(M, b_i) \geq \text{threshould of } IOU \\ score_i, IOU(M, b_i) < \text{threshould of } IOU \end{cases} \quad (1)$$

where $score_i$ represents the score of the current detection frame. The best threshold of *IOU* we found is 0.5 after multiple debugging in the data set of this experiment.

In other words, for the detection frame with a higher *IOU* adjacent to one with the highest score, NMS will set the score of this frame to 0 and then remove it. It is very likely to cause a missed detection when in the situation shown in Figure 2. The mechanism of Soft-NMS to remove redundant detection frames can be expressed as:

$$score_i = score_i e^{-\frac{IOU(M,b_i)^2}{\theta}} \quad (2)$$

It means that Soft-NMS will not directly set the score of the detection frame with a higher *IOU* adjacent to the one with the highest score to 0. Instead, it penalizes the score. The multiplication of the score of the current detection frame and the weight function is to penalize this detection frame. We used the Gaussian function as the weight function: $e^{-\frac{IOU(M,b_i)^2}{\theta}}$ (θ is the parameter of the weight function. After debugging, the detection effect is the best when θ is 0.1). The higher overlap with the highest-score detection frame, the more severe the score of this detection frame decreases. Finally, only the detection frame with a score higher or equal to 0.5 remains. In this way, Soft-NMS can remove the redundant detection frame and reduce the missed detection rate as well. The flow chart of Soft-NMS is shown in Figure 3.

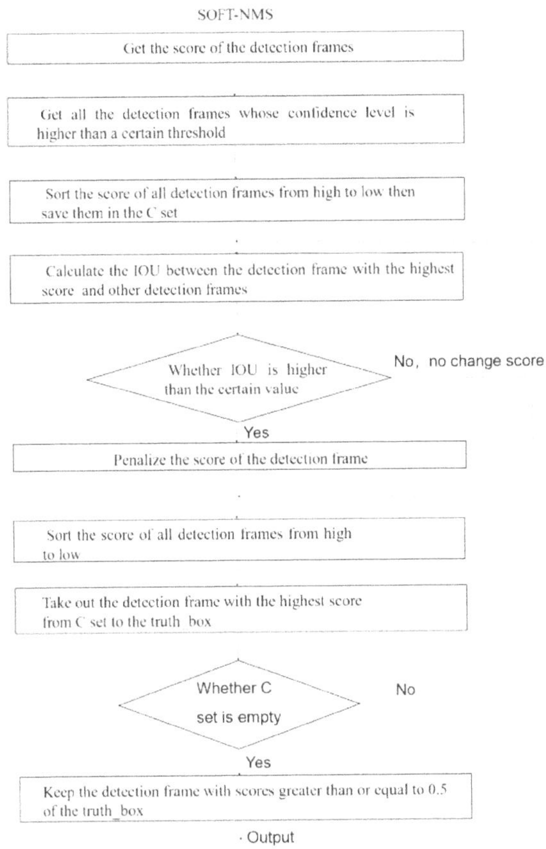

Figure 3. The flow chart of Soft-NMS.

In summary, the main idea of Soft-NMS is as follows. Firstly, it finds out all the detection frames which have a higher confidence level than a certain artificial-set confidence level from an image. The circumstance that the confidence level is lower than this certain confidence level means that there is no target object in the detection frame. Secondly, it processes the detection frames that belong to the same category. Finally, it establishes a set B and puts all the detection frames that belong to the same category into this set. The specific algorithm of Soft-NMS is as follows.

1. Sort the score of the detection frame in set B (this score indicates the probability that the position of the detection frame belongs to this category) from high to low, and choose the frame H with the highest score from the B set.
2. Traverse all the detection frames in set B, and calculate the IOU of each detection frame and the detection frame H with the highest score. Soft-NMS does not directly remove a detection frame from set B but makes a corresponding penalty for this detection frame to decrease the score. The higher the degree of overlapping with the detection frame with the highest score, the more severe the score of this detection frame decreases. Then saving the detection frame H into truth_box.
3. Return to 1. until the set B is empty, and finally, keep the detection frame with a score higher or equal to 0.5 in the truth_box as the output.

After processing Figure 2 by Soft-NMS, the detecting result is as shown in Figure 4.

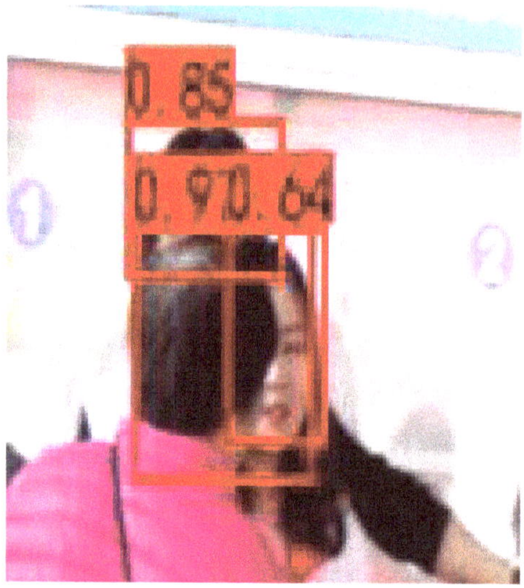

Figure 4. Soft-NMS processing, no missed detection.

4. Experimental Datasets and Evaluation Indexes

The experiments were conducted on two human heads data sets: Brainwash [30] and SCUT_HEAD [31]. The Brainwash data set contains 11,438 images, with a total of 81,975 human heads. The scene in this data set is a coffee shop, and the annotation method of the data set is not the Pascal VOC format. It needs to convert to the Pascal VOC annotation format. The SCUT_HEAD data set contains 4405 images with a total of 11,251 heads. Two data sets include lots of complex scenes, such as classrooms, cafes, daytime, night, and others.

For the case of Brainwash, the size of each image is 640 × 480, 300 images are selected randomly as the testing set, and 11,138 images as the training set. For the case of SCUT_HEAD, the size of each image is different, 141 images are selected randomly as the testing set, and 4264 images as the training set. The third dataset contains all images of A and B, 441 images are selected randomly as the testing set, and 15,402 images as the training set. For the YoloV4 model, the size of the input image is 416 × 416, so all images will be preprocessed, which means all images will be resized to 416 × 416 before being put into the YoloV4 model.

The indexes of the evaluation model in this experiment include the Precision value, the Recall value, and AP value [32]. The calculation of the Precision value and the Recall value are respectively represented by Formulas (3) and (4):

$$\text{Precision} = \frac{TP}{TP + FP} \quad (3)$$

$$\text{Recall} = \frac{TP}{TP + FN} \quad (4)$$

On the above formulas, TP means the prediction result is classified correctly into positive samples, FP indicates the wrong classification into positive samples, and FN represents the wrong into negative samples. The PR curve is the relationship between the Precision value and the Recall value. We can see the PR curve in Figure 5:

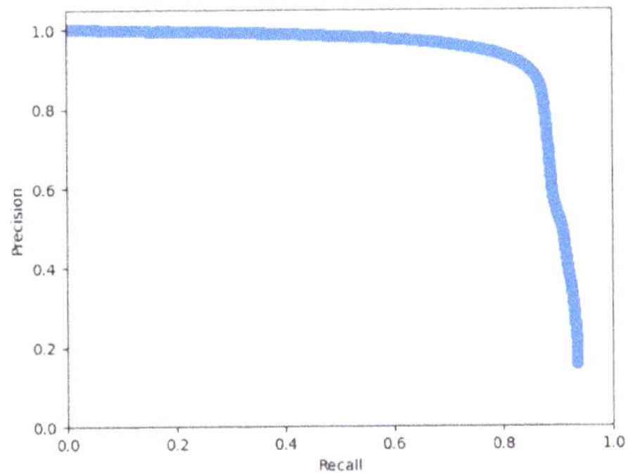

Figure 5. The PR curve.

AP is the area enclosed by the PR curve (the blue area). The higher the value of AP, the better the predictive ability of the model.

5. Results

5.1. Comparison of NMS and Soft-NMS

To verify the efficiency of the Soft YoloV4 model, the same prediction parameters and data sets (more than 400 complex images) are used for head detection in the YoloV4 model using NMS and Soft-NMS. Judging whether the recognition is accurate is based on whether there is a missed detection.

The AP value of the YoloV4 model before improvement is 88.52%, the Precision is 91.15%, and the Recall is 86.93%. When using Soft-NMS, the prediction result of the Soft YoloV4 model is improved, where the AP value is 90.54%, the Precision is 91.94%, and the Recall is 85.55%.

The comparison results on the third dataset between the YoloV4 model before and after improvement are shown in Table 1.

Table 1. The comparison results.

Model	AP/%	Precision/%	Recall/%
Original YoloV4	88.52	91.15	86.93
Soft YoloV4	90.54	91.94	85.55

After contradistinction and analysis, we can see that the AP value and the Precision value are improved compared with the original model. However, the Recall has declined. Soft-NMS remove the redundant detection frame by penalizing the score. There is an adjustable parameter θ in Formula (2). A large parameter θ will result in a smaller penalty, then the redundant detection frame may not be removed, which means the model may indicate that there are two objects although there is only one object. The reason why recall has declined is that the parameter θ is large. Recall or Precision cannot be used to evaluate the effect of the algorithm comprehensively, so the AP index is selected. The experiments proved that the AP value using Soft YoloV4 was higher than that using Original YoloV4, even though recall dropped a little. In this way, replacing NMS with Soft-NMS in YoloV4 is effective.

5.2. Comparison with State-of-the-Arts

The experiments include the following comparison methods: end-to-end people detection (abbreviated as ReInspect [30]), detecting heads using features refined net and cascaded multi-scale architecture (abbreviated as FRN_CMA [31]), target detection algorithm based on YoloV3 (abbreviated as YoloV3 [33]), and pedestrian head detection algorithm based on clustering and Faster RCNN (abbreviated as CFR-PHD [34]). All methods use the same evaluation index. The detection results of each method on the Brainwash data set and SCUT_HEAD data set are shown in Table 2.

Table 2. Experimental results obtained on Brainwash and SCUT_HEAD.

Methods	Brainwash (AP/%)	SCUT_HEAD (AP/%)
ReInspect	78.10	77.50
FRN_CMA	88.10	86.30
YoloV3	85.11	84.13
CFR-PHD	90.20	87.70
Soft YoloV4	92.29	91.70

According to the experiment results on the Brainwash data set and the SCUT_HEAD data set, our Soft YoloV4 algorithm improves detection performance compared to the above algorithms. On the Brainwash data set, the AP value dramatically increases. Compared to the ReInspect, FRN_CMA, YoloV3, and CFR-PHD algorithms, the improvements are 14.19%, 4.19%, 7.18%, and 2.09%, respectively. On the SCUT_HEAD data set, the improvements by the AP value are 14.20, 5.40, 7.57, and 4.00%. Therefore, the performance of our proposed improvement can be approved.

Here are three examples, as shown in the following Figures 6–8.

Figure 6. One example of people counting results. There are 33 people in the classroom, and it was predicted that there would be 33 people. The result is completely correct.

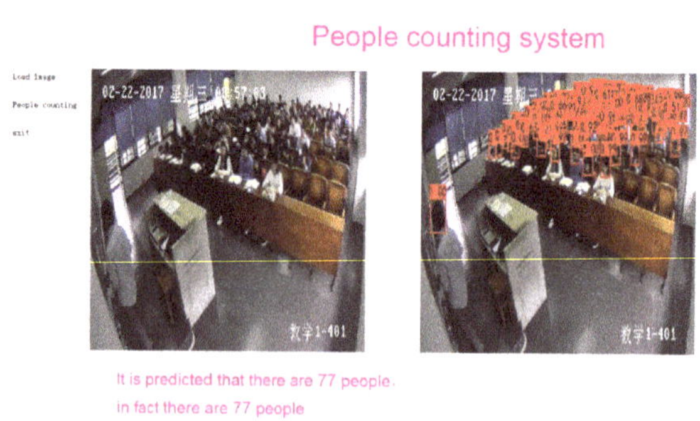

Figure 7. One example of people counting results. There are 77 people in the classroom, and it was predicted that there would be 77 people. The result is completely correct.

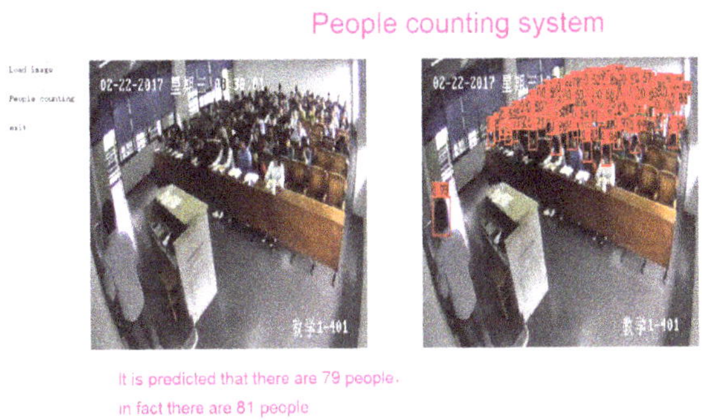

Figure 8. One example of people counting results. There are 79 people in the classroom, and it was predicted that there would be 81 people. The result is not completely correct.

The result in Figure 8 is not completely correct. With the increase of pedestrian density in a scene, the visibility of heads decreases with the increase of mutual occlusions, resulting in the decrease of head detection, as shown in Figure 8. The possible reason why the model cannot predict objects over heavily overlapped with others is that a detection frame only predicts an object rather than a set of correlated objects.

6. Conclusions

Compared with other target detection models, the Soft-YoloV4 model in this paper has a higher recognition accuracy and a better people counting effect. Soft-YoloV4 can be built on the server. By recognizing the images sent by the client, the server can return the specific number of people to the client. In this way, the number of people in the classroom can be counted conveniently and quickly, which helps teachers count the number of students, and students do not need to go to each classroom to check whether there is an available seat for them, and then quickly choose a self-study room.

This paper is still unable to accurately recognize the situation that the degree of blockage is too high. In the future, we can consider combining the human body model to determine whether there is a blockage in the detection frame. The network architecture of the target detection model is also too large. Although the accuracy is high, the detecting speed is relatively slow. The next step is to modify the network architecture of the model to speed up the recognition process without significantly decreasing the accuracy. KuralNet is a lightweight deep learning model that strikes a good balance between parameters and effectiveness [35]. In the KuralNet, the inverse residual block with deep convolution and frequency-doubling convolution can be used for signal processing to reduce the computational cost. Perhaps we can learn from this to reduce the complexity of Soft-YoloV4.

This paper proposes a head detection model by improving YoloV4 to count the number of people. By detecting people's heads, we have an improved version YoloV4 using Soft-NMS. In this way, the number of people can be counted more accurately and performance close to the requirement of real applications is obtained. The original YoloV4 model uses the NMS algorithm to remove redundant detection frames. The Soft-YoloV4 model uses the Soft-NMS algorithm. After comparative analysis, Soft-YoloV4 has a higher accuracy in head detection. The AP value of Soft-YoloV4 is 90.54%, 2.02% higher than the original YoloV4 model. Therefore, Soft-YoloV4 is more suitable for head detection on crowded occasions.

Author Contributions: Conceptualization, Z.Z. and S.Z.; Data curation, S.X.; Formal analysis, Z.Z., S.X., Y.C. and C.Y.; Funding acquisition, Z.Z.; Investigation, S.X.; Supervision, S.Z. All authors have read and agreed to the published version of the manuscript.

Funding: This research was funded by [Young innovative talents project of colleges and universities in Guangdong Province] grant number [2021KQNCX092]; [Doctoral program of Huizhou University] grant number [2020JB028]; [Outstanding youth cultivation project of Huizhou University] grant number [HZU202009].

Institutional Review Board Statement: Not applicable.

Informed Consent Statement: Not applicable.

Data Availability Statement: Data available in a publicly accessible repository that does not issue DOIs. Brainwash dataset and SCUT_HEAD dataset were analyzed in this study. Brainwash dataset can be found here [https://github.com/aditya-vora/FCHD-Fully-Convolutional-Head-Detector] (accessed on 30 November 2021). SCUT_HEAD dataset can be found here [https://github.com/HCIILAB/SCUT-HEAD-Dataset-Release] (accessed on 30 November 2021).

Conflicts of Interest: The authors declare no conflict of interest.

References

1. Tan, Y.L. Statistical Image Recognition Algorithm Based on Skin Color. *J. Huaihai Inst. Technol.* **2014**, *23*, 36–39.
2. Zhang, L. *Population Density Statistics Based on Face Detection*; Lanzhou University of Technology: Lanzhou, China, 2018.
3. Jin, Y.H. *Video Pedestrian Detection and People Counting*; Inner Mongolia University: Hohhot, China, 2018.
4. Zeng, S.; Zhang, B.; Gou, J. Learning double weights via data augmentation for robust sparse and collaborative representation-based classification. *Multimed. Tools Appl.* **2020**, *79*, 20617–20638. [CrossRef]
5. Rathgeb, C.; Dantcheva, A.; Busch, C. Impact and detection of facial beautification in face recognition: An overview. *IEEE Access* **2019**, *7*, 152667–152678. [CrossRef]
6. Li, W.; Nie, W.; Su, Y. Human action recognition based on selected spatio-temporal features via bidirectional LSTM. *IEEE Access* **2018**, *6*, 44211–44220. [CrossRef]
7. Zhang, C.L.; Liu, G.W.; Zhan, X.; Cai, H.; Liu, Z. Face detection algorithm based on new haar features and improved AdaBoost. *J. Chang. Univ. Sci. Technol. (Nat. Sci. Ed.)* **2020**, *43*, 89–93.
8. Tan, G.X.; Sun, C.M.; Wang, J.H. Design of video vehicle detection system based on HOG features and SVM. *J. Guangxi Univ. Sci. Technol.* **2021**, *32*, 19–23, 30.
9. Gu, W. Research on moving target detection algorithm based on LBP texture feature. *Off. Informatiz.* **2017**, *22*, 21–24.
10. Hinton, G.E.; Salakhutdinov, R.R. Reducing the Dimensionality of Data with Neural Networks. *Science* **2006**, *313*, 504–507. [CrossRef] [PubMed]
11. Girshick, R.; Donahue, J.; Darrell, T.; Malik, J. Rich feature hierarchies for accurate object detection and semantic segmentation. In Proceedings of the IEEE Conference on Computer Vision and Pattern Recognition, Columbus, OH, USA, 23–28 June 2014; pp. 580–587.
12. He, K.; Zhang, X.; Ren, S.; Sun, J. Spatial pyramid pooling in deep convolutional networks for visual recognition. *IEEE Trans. Pattern Anal. Mach. Intell.* **2015**, *37*, 1904–1916. [CrossRef] [PubMed]
13. Li, J.; Liang, X.; Shen, S.; Xu, T.; Feng, J.; Yan, S. Scale-aware fast R-CNN for pedestrian detection. *IEEE Trans. Multimed.* **2017**, *20*, 985–996. [CrossRef]
14. Ren, S.; He, K.; Girshick, R.; Sun, J. Faster R-CNN: Towards real-time object detection with region proposal networks. *IEEE Trans. Pattern Anal. Mach. Intell.* **2016**, *39*, 1137–1149. [CrossRef] [PubMed]
15. He, K.; Gkioxari, G.; Dollár, P.; Girshick, R. Mask r-cnn. In Proceedings of the IEEE International Conference on Computer Vision, Venice, Italy, 22–29 October 2017; pp. 2961–2969.
16. Kong, T.; Yao, A.; Chen, Y.; Sun, F. Hypernet: Towards accurate region proposal generation and joint object detection. In Proceedings of the IEEE Conference on Computer Vision and Pattern Recognition, Las Vegas, NV, USA, 27–30 June 2016; pp. 845–853.
17. Redmon, J.; Divvala, S.; Girshick, R.; Farhadi, A. You only look once: Unified, real-time object detection. In Proceedings of the IEEE Conference on Computer Vision and Pattern Recognition, Las Vegas, NV, USA, 27–30 June 2016; pp. 779–788.
18. Redmon, J.; Farhadi, A. YOLO9000: Better, faster, stronger. In Proceedings of the IEEE Conference on Computer Vision and Pattern Recognition, Honolulu, HI, USA, 21–26 July 2017; pp. 7263–7271.
19. Liu, W.; Anguelov, D.; Erhan, D.; Szegedy, C.; Reed, S.; Fu, C.Y.; Berg, A.C. Ssd: Single shot multibox detector. In Proceedings of the European Conference on Computer Vision, Amsterdam, The Netherlands, 11–14 October 2016; pp. 21–37.
20. Lin, T.Y.; Goyal, P.; Girshick, R.; He, K.; Dollár, P. Focal loss for dense object detection. In Proceedings of the IEEE International Conference on Computer Vision, Venice, Italy, 22–29 October 2017; pp. 2980–2988.
21. Chen, Y.; Han, C.; Wang, N.; Zhang, Z. Revisiting feature alignment for one-stage object detection. *arXiv* **2019**, arXiv:1908.01570.
22. Duan, K.; Bai, S.; Xie, L.; Qi, H.; Huang, Q.; Tian, Q. Centernet: Keypoint triplets for object detection. In Proceedings of the IEEE/CVF International Conference on Computer Vision, Seoul, Korea, 27–28 October 2019; pp. 6569–6578.
23. Zhu, C.; He, Y.; Savvides, M. Feature selective anchor-free module for single-shot object detection. In Proceedings of the IEEE/CVF Conference on Computer Vision and Pattern Recognition, Long Beach, CA, USA, 15–20 June 2019; pp. 840–849.

24. Tian, Z.; Shen, C.; Chen, H.; He, T. Fcos: Fully convolutional one-stage object detection. In Proceedings of the IEEE/CVF International Conference on Computer Vision, Seoul, Korea, 27–28 October 2019; pp. 9627–9636.
25. Bochkovskiy, A.; Wang, C.Y.; Liao, H.Y.M. Yolov4: Optimal speed and accuracy of object detection. *arXiv* **2020**, arXiv:2004.10934.
26. Bodla, N.; Singh, B.; Chellappa, R.; Davis, L.S. Soft-NMS—Improving object detection with one line of code. In Proceedings of the IEEE International Conference on Computer Vision, Venice, Italy, 22–29 October 2017; pp. 5561–5569.
27. Neubeck, A.; van Gool, L. Efficient non-maximum suppression. In Proceedings of the 18th International Conference on Pattern Recognition (ICPR'06), Hong Kong, China, 20–24 August 2006; Volume 3, pp. 850–855.
28. He, K.; Zhang, X.; Ren, S.; Sun, J. Deep residual learning for image recognition. In Proceedings of the IEEE Conference on Computer Vision and Pattern Recognition, Las Vegas, NV, USA, 27–30 June 2016; pp. 770–778.
29. Liu, S.; Qi, L.; Qin, H.; Shi, J.; Jia, J. Path aggregation network for instance segmentation. In Proceedings of the IEEE Conference on Computer Vision and Pattern Recognition, Salt Lake City, UT, USA, 18–22 June 2018; pp. 8759–8768.
30. Stewart, R.; Andriluka, M.; Ng, A.Y. End-to-end people detection in crowded scenes. In Proceedings of the IEEE Conference on Computer Vision and Pattern Recognition, Las Vegas, NV, USA, 27–30 June 2016; pp. 2325–2333.
31. Peng, D.; Sun, Z.; Chen, Z.; Cai, Z.; Xie, L.; Jin, L. Detecting heads using feature refine net and cascaded multi-scale architecture. In Proceedings of the 2018 24th International Conference on Pattern Recognition (ICPR), Beijing, China, 20–24 August 2018; pp. 2528–2533.
32. Zheng, L.; Shen, L.; Tian, L.; Wang, S.; Wang, J.; Tian, Q. Scalable person re-identification: A benchmark. In Proceedings of the IEEE International Conference on Computer Vision, Santiago, Chile, 7–13 December 2015; pp. 1116–1124.
33. Redmon, J.; Farhadi, A. Yolov3: An incremental improvement. *arXiv* **2018**, arXiv:1804.02767.
34. Zhang, J.; Chen, L.; Li, Z.; Wang, S.; Chen, Z. Pedestrian head detection algorithm based on clustering and Fast RCNN. *J. Northwest Univ.* **2020**, *50*, 971–978.
35. Ayala, A.; Fernandes, B.; Cruz, F.; Macêdo, D.; Oliveira, A.L.; Zanchettin, C. KutralNet: A portable deep learning model for fire recognition. In Proceedings of the 2020 International Joint Conference on Neural Networks (IJCNN), Glasgow, UK, 19–24 July 2020; pp. 1–8.

mathematics

MDPI

Review

Trends in Vehicle Re-Identification Past, Present, and Future: A Comprehensive Review

Zakria [1], Jianhua Deng [1,*], Yang Hao [2,*], Muhammad Saddam Khokhar [3], Rajesh Kumar [4], Jingye Cai [1], Jay Kumar [4] and Muhammad Umar Aftab [5]

1 School of Information and Software Engineering, University of Electronic Science and Technology of China, Chengdu 610054, China; zakria@uestc.edu.cn or zakria.uestc@hotmail.com (Z.); jycai@uestc.edu.cn (J.C.)
2 Institute of Applied Electronic (IAE), China Academy of Engineering Physics, Mianyang 621900, China
3 School of Computer Science and Communication Engineering, Jiangsu University, Zhenjiang 212003, China; muhammadsaddam@stmail.ujs.edu.cn or saddam_khokhar@hotmail.com
4 Yangtze Delta Region Institute (Huzhou), University of Electronic Science and Technology of China, Huzhou 313001, China; raja@uestc.edu.cn (R.K.); jay@std.uestc.edu.cn (J.K.)
5 Department of Computer Science, National University of Computer and Emerging Sciences, Chiniot-Faisalabad Campus, Chiniot 35400, Pakistan; Umar.aftab@nu.edu.pk
* Correspondence: jianhua.deng@uestc.edu.cn (J.D.); yhao@caep.cn (Y.H.)

Abstract: Vehicle Re-identification (re-id) over surveillance camera network with non-overlapping field of view is an exciting and challenging task in intelligent transportation systems (ITS). Due to its versatile applicability in metropolitan cities, it gained significant attention. Vehicle re-id matches targeted vehicle over non-overlapping views in multiple camera network. However, it becomes more difficult due to inter-class similarity, intra-class variability, viewpoint changes, and spatio-temporal uncertainty. In order to draw a detailed picture of vehicle re-id research, this paper gives a comprehensive description of the various vehicle re-id technologies, applicability, datasets, and a brief comparison of different methodologies. Our paper specifically focuses on vision-based vehicle re-id approaches, including vehicle appearance, license plate, and spatio-temporal characteristics. In addition, we explore the main challenges as well as a variety of applications in different domains. Lastly, a detailed comparison of current state-of-the-art methods performances over VeRi-776 and VehicleID datasets is summarized with future directions. We aim to facilitate future research by reviewing the work being done on vehicle re-id till to date.

Keywords: vehicle re-identification; license plate recognition; video surveillance; feature extraction

Citation: Zakria; Deng, J.; Hao, Y.; Khokhar, M.S.; Kumar, R.; Cai, J.; Kumar, J.; Aftab, M.U. Trends in Vehicle Re-Identification Past, Present, and Future: A Comprehensive Review. *Mathematics* **2021**, *9*, 3162. https://doi.org/10.3390/math9243162

Academic Editor: Aleksandr Rakhmangulov

Received: 23 October 2021
Accepted: 27 November 2021
Published: 8 December 2021

1. Introduction

Due to growing global population, commercial activities have been extensively increasing, which leads everyone to access road transportation as a source of mobility. Due to easy accessibility of road transportation system, traffic on roads is massively increasing that not only creates the problem of high traffic congestion but also a drastic increase in carbon dioxide emissions. Along with these issues, road accident risks and the overall transportation complexity increases as well. Therefore, a smooth transportation source and medium is always required for growing commercial activities. Furthermore, traffic management authorities are facing hectic challenges to maintain an undisturbed transportation system. Their task includes tracking the suspicious vehicle, handling traffic jam, and to check whether the vehicle is registered or not. Maintaining undisturbed transportation becomes harder when a large number of vehicles are on the roads.

1.1. Intelligent Transportation System

Transport is essential for the daily routine functioning of the economy and the society. Over the past few decades there is huge development, deployment, and growth in the transport system and have notable effect of development in society and daily life. Therefore, transportation should be redefined as ITS. Currently, not only mechanical and engineering fields are doing research and development for better transportation facility, but computer science related concepts are also playing major role for instance, artificial intelligence (AI), communication, machine learning (ML), internet and so many other emerging technologies.

Due to traffic problems in China, the average speed of vehicle has been decreased to 20 km/h, even in some areas between 7 and 8 km/h [1,2]. Such low speed of vehicles for a long time on roads is a threat for the natural environment of the world like exhaust emissions that deteriorate air quality. In order to deal traffic problems and alleviate the pressure of vehicles on roads, the governments are investing too much on research and ITS development. ITS based infrastructure strengthens the relationship between people, vehicles, and road networks.

ITS have the capability to enhance the performance of current transportation system and make it efficient, safe, comfortable as well as reduces harmful environmental consequences. ITS based real-time applications include electronic payment systems, traffic management systems, emergency vehicle pre-emption management system, advanced vehicle control systems, weather precautionary measures management system, and commercial vehicle operations. Applications of ITS now regularly deployed, such as closed-circuit television surveillance, automatic car parking, electronic toll collection, border control, and in-car navigation equipment. Therefore, an ITS is needed to analyze the recorded video, control, maintain and communicate to ground transport and improve mobility and manage problems efficiently. Furthermore, Figure 1 demonstrates the ITS based environment.

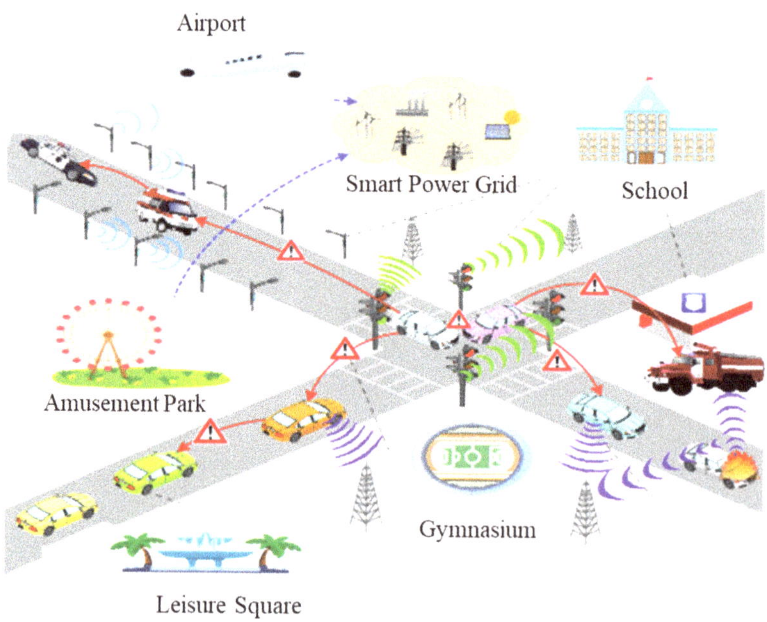

Figure 1. Depicts smart city and intelligent transportation system.

1.2. Video Surveillance

In metropolitan cities, cameras are widely adopted in numerous areas to monitor activities [3]; but most of the current video surveillance systems provides the facilities like capture, storage and distribute video, while leaves unwanted event detection task totally on human operators. Human operator-based monitoring of the surveillance system is not as efficient and a very labour-intensive task, as shown in Figure 2. It requires full visual attention by watching the video in control room and it is very difficult for single person as everyday tasks. Specifically, the ability to focus and react to occasionally occurring activities that require full attention. Furthermore, millions of hours of video data generated by multiple cameras over surveillance network require large number of operators for the task. It's almost infeasible, inefficient and costly to obtain real-time prevention.

Figure 2. Shows view of manually traffic monitoring at control room.

Due to digital cameras and the advent of powerful computing resources, automatic video analysis become possible and more and more common in video surveillance applications [4], thus reduces the labor cost. Practically, the objective of automatic video analysis for safety, security, and surveillance is to detect automatically unwanted events or situations that need security attention. Automated video analysis not only process the data faster but also significantly improve the ability to preempt incidents on time. Augmenting security staff with automatic processing increases their efficiency and effectiveness. For the posterior mode, searching a specific vehicle in hundreds of hours of camera recorded video footage needs large number of officers to do this task and takes a lot of time. Automated content-based video retrieval reproducing and assisting human analysis on recorded videos largely enhances forensic capabilities. Furthermore, the surveillance systems application's main goal is to develop intelligent systems that automate the human decision-making mechanism.

An important task to maintain a smooth transport system is to re-identify the specific vehicle that appeared in different cameras over the surveillance network. The vehicle re-id module in ITS should recognize same vehicle that appears in surveillance cameras installed in different geographical locations. Specifically, vehicle re-id can be treated as a fine-grained recognition problem [5,6] that identifies the subordinate type of input class. However, the vehicle re-id problem's granularity is much finer since the system should search specific targeted vehicle instead of the same vehicle model and type. Moreover, recently vehicle re-id gained more attention in research community because of various significant real-world applications. It is a difficult task to analyze the surveillance environment for effective vehicle identification. An example of practical environment can be seen in Figure 3, where surveillance cameras can be observed over roads and public places.

Figure 3. Illustrates the practical scenario of surveillance camera network.

1.3. Re-Identification

In a surveillance camera without overlapping vision, re-id is defined as a task to identify objects' captured images taken from different camera networks. It is used to know whether the object image captured by multiple surveillance cameras matches the same object or a different image of the object. Object re-id technology has a significant role in multi-object tracking, intelligent monitoring, and other fields. Recently, re-id gained extensive attention in the computer vision research community. The main application fields of an object re-id are vehicle re-id and person re-id.

Formally, re-id can be defined as a matching task. A targeted image (Query) is matched against a gallery set image (representing the previously captured images in the surveillance camera network). Thus, the query of re-identifying targeted image can be defined by its descriptor P, and it is formulated as:

$$T = arg_{T_i}\min D\ (T_i, Q), T_i \in \mathcal{T} \tag{1}$$

where $\mathcal{T} = \{T_1, \ldots, T_N\}$ is a gallery set of N image descriptors, and $D(,)$ represents the distance metric. Therefore, to solve above the re-id problem, it is important first to answer how we can represent targeted object using a descriptor to robust performance. Furthermore, rest of the paper investigates this topic.

Vehicle Re-identification: Similar to person re-id, vehicle re-id is also a demanding task in camera surveillance. Aim of vehicle re-id is to match vehicle images with already captured vehicle images over the camera network [7–9]. However, due to surveillance cameras on the roads for smart cities and traffic management, the demand to perform vehicle search from the gallery set is increased. Vehicle re-id is similar to several other applications, such as person re-id [10], behavior analysis [11], cross-camera tracking [12], vehicle classification [13], object retrieval [14], object recognition [15,16], and so on.

To understand designing the vehicle re-id system, we analyze how a person re-identifies the vehicle. A person re-identifies vehicle by keeping in mind some characteristics like unique feature, color, size etc., our brain and eyes are learned to detect and identify different objects, as shown in Figure 4 and how system identify vehicle is shown in Figure 5.

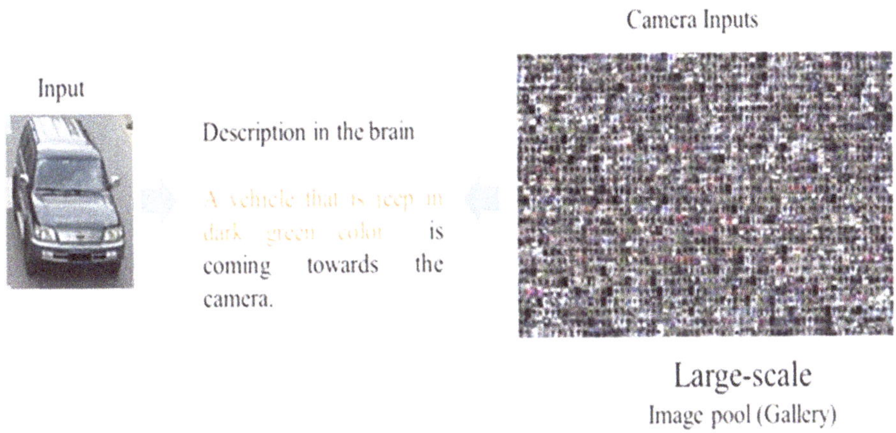

Figure 4. Shows how human re-identify vehicle?

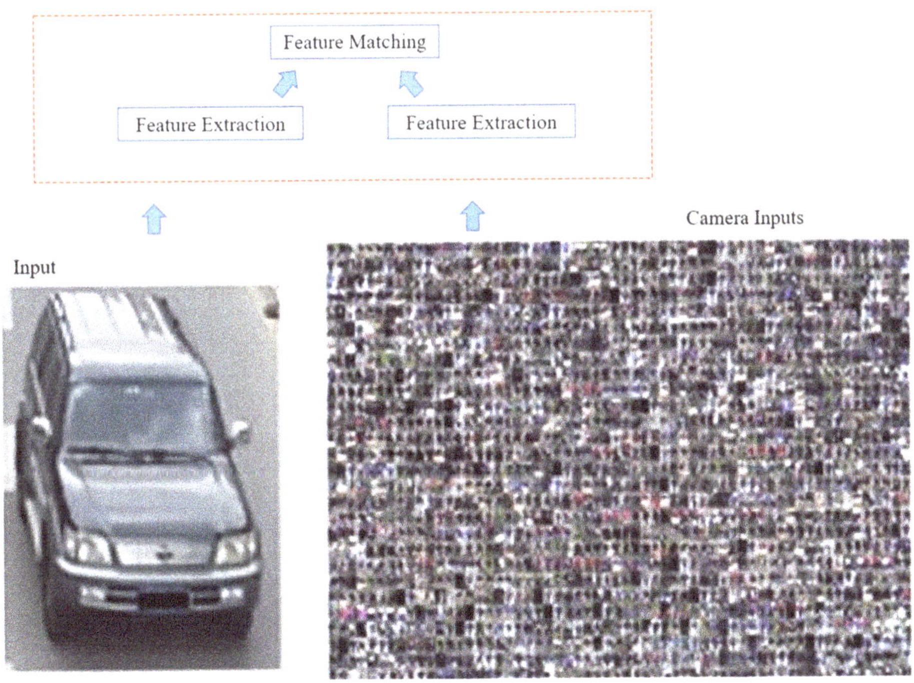

Figure 5. Illustrates how machine re-identify vehicle?

1.4. Vehicle Re-Identification Practical Application

There are many significant real-world applications where vehicle re-id system can be utilized and satisfies the great needs of our practical life. However, some major applications are briefly discussed as follows:

- Suspicious vehicle search: Most of the time terrorists use vehicle for their criminal activities and soon leave that spot on vehicles. It is very difficult to fast search suspicious vehicle manually from surveillance camera.

- Cross camera vehicle tracking: In vehicle race sports, some of the viewers on television wish to watch specific vehicle. With vehicle re-id system broadcaster can only focus on that specific vehicle when it comes in the field of view of surveillance camera network.
- Automatic toll collection: Vehicle re-id system can be used at toll gates to identify vehicle type like small medium and large and charge the toll rate accordingly. Automatic toll collection reduces delay and improves the toll collection performance by saving travelers time and fuel consumption.
- Road access restriction management: In big cities, heavy vehicles like trucks are not permitted in the daytime, or some of the vehicles with specific license plate number are permitted on specific days to avoid congestion in city or officially authorized vehicles can enter in city.
- Parking lot access: vehicle re-id system can be deployed at the gate of parking lot of different places like head offices, and residential societies. So only authorized vehicles are allowed to park.
- Traffic behavior analysis: Vehicle re-id can be used to examine the traffic pressure on different roads at different times, such as peak hours calculation or particular vehicle type behavior.
- Vehicle counting: System can be useful to count a certain type of vehicle.
- Speed restriction management system: Vehicle re-id system can be utilized to calculate the vehicle's average speed when it is crossing from two subsequent surveillance camera positions.
- Travel time estimation: Travel time information is important for a person who is traveling on road, it can be calculated when a vehicle is passing in between consecutive surveillance cameras.
- Traffic congestion estimation: By knowing the number of vehicles flow from one point to another point within a specific time period using vehicle re-id system, we can estimate traffic congestion at the common spot from where all vehicles may cross.
- Delay estimation: Specific commercial vehicle delay can be estimated after predicting traffic congestion on the rout that vehicle follows.
- Highway data collection: Highway data can be collected through surveillance cameras that are installed on roadsides and that data can be used for any purposes after processing and analyzing at the traffic control center.
- Traffic management systems (TMS): Vehicle re-id is an integral part of TMS, it helps to increase transportation performance, for instance, safe movement, flow, and economic productivity. TMS gathers the real-time data from the surveillance cameras network and streams into the Transportation Management Center (TMC) for data processing and analyzing.
- Weather precautionary measures: When specific vehicle is identified that may be affected by weather, then traffic management systems notify that vehicle about weather conditions like wind velocity, severe weather etc.
- Emergency vehicle pre-emption: If any suspicious vehicle is identified at any event or road then vehicle pre-emption system passes messages towards lifesaving agencies such as security, firefighters, ambulance, traffic police, etc. to reach in time and stabilize the scene. With this system, we can maximize safety and minimize response time.
- Access control: Vehicle re-id system can be implemented for providing safety and security, logging and event management. With the implementation of the system only authorized members can get an automatic door opening facility, which helps guards on duty.
- Border control: Vehicle re-id system can be adopted at different check posts to minimize illegal vehicle border crossing. Vehicle re-id system can provide vehicle and owner's information as it approaches security officer after identifying the vehicle. Commonly these illegal vehicles are involved in cargo smuggling.
- Traffic signal light: When the traffic light is red and any vehicle crosses stop line, the vehicle re-id system can be implemented to identify that vehicle for fine.

- Vehicle retrieval: In this case, re-id is associated with a recognition task. The specific query with a target vehicle is provided, and all the related vehicles are searched in the database. The re-id task is thus employed for image retrieval and usually provides ranked lists, similarly related items, and so on.

However, due to the vast range of practical applications that employ vehicle re-id system and to limit the scope of the paper, this review article mainly focuses only on vision-based methods. Moreover, it is very hard to cover all technologies for vehicle re-id in one survey paper but despite of that we have summarized the strengths and weaknesses of all technologies in Table 1. Therefore, this review article focuses on the use of vision-based approaches including, Appearance, license plate, contextual information etc. In last few years, there has been lack of comprehensive study of the overall problem and different solutions. This paper fills the gap by providing a detailed review covering main challenges, different approaches, and applicability. In addition, it provides the analysis and comparison of existing vehicle re-id methodologies. Aiming to facilitate other researchers, this review also provides the required information about the publicly available datasets and discusses several important research directions with under-investigated open issues to narrow the gap between the closed-world and open-world applications, taking a step towards real-world re-id system design.

Table 1. Summary of strengths and weaknesses of different vehicle re-id technologies.

Technology	Strengths	Weaknesses
Surveillance camera	Don't require the owner's cooperation. Low cost because usually cameras are installed on roadsides, so don't require additional charges to install.	Complex and unconstrained environment along with varied road topology affects the performance. Performance degrades due to dirt, snow, occluded image, blurry image, and sunshine, etc. The vehicle is identified only when it comes in the field of view of the camera.
Magnetic Sensor	Insensitive to bad weather like snow, fog, and rain. There is no privacy issue in magnetic sensors.	Complicated installation. Embedding magnetic sensor under carriageway after drilling hole. Identified only at the detection terminal.
Inductive loop	Provides different traffic parameters like speed, volume, headway, presence, and occupancy etc.	Installation of inductive loop technology requires metallic loops under the road. The vehicle is identified in the field-of-view of detection terminal.
GPS	Provides continuous vehicle information, such as space and time, to the control centre. 100% vehicle recognition rate.	Require owner's cooperation to install hardware in vehicle. Varying accuracies, minimal fleet penetration, and signal loss because of tunnels, trees, and tall buildings.

Two ways for writing surveys can be found in the object re-id literature; first way gives a deep insight into methodologies, whereas the second way covers the overall perspective related to the problem [17,18] This survey includes both methodologies and overall perspective of vehicle re-id literature. We also review the recent development of vision-based vehicle re-id along with other technologies. In addition, this survey draws a timeline to introduce important milestones for vehicle re-id, which can be seen in Figure 6.

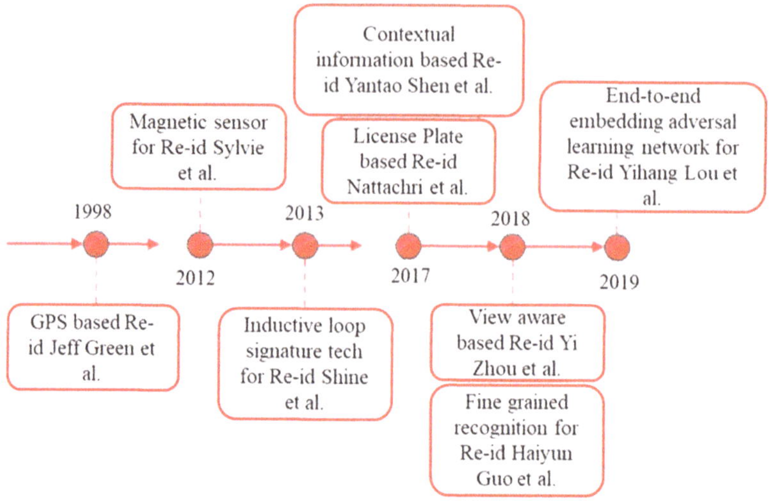

Figure 6. Milestones existing re-id approaches in the Vehicle re-id history.

The paper is organized in the following way. Sections 2–5 provide an overview of recent state-of-the-art proposed methodologies in various technologies. Section 6 presents a publicly available benchmark dataset that covers various real-world surveillance scenarios. Section 7 discusses the challenging problems in vehicle re-id. Section 8 sheds light on the evaluation measures for vehicle re-id. Section 9 analyzes and compares the experimental results of various approaches. Meanwhile, the last section concludes and discusses future work.

The main contributions of this review paper is summarized as follows:

- To the best of our knowledge, this is the first comprehensive review paper that covers computer vision-based methods for vehicle re-id tasks, with a different technological background of approaches for completeness such as, global positioning systems (GPS), inductive loop and magnetic sensors.
- Discusses various real-world applications of vehicle re-id in different domains including the intelligent transportation system.
- Comprehensive comparisons of existing methods on several state-of-the-art publicly available vehicle re-id datasets are provided, with brief summaries and insightful discussions being presented.
- Discusses the challenges in detail for designing an efficient vehicle re-id system and illustrates the recent trends and future directions.

2. Methods Used for Vehicle Re-Identification

Traditionally different traffic sensors are adopted to know the vehicle presence, volume, occupancy, and speed data. Nowadays, new sensor-based technology is adopted to get more information like origin-destination estimation, travel time and other travel information applications. Based on different technologies vehicle re-id approaches can be divided into six categories, as depicted in Figure 7.

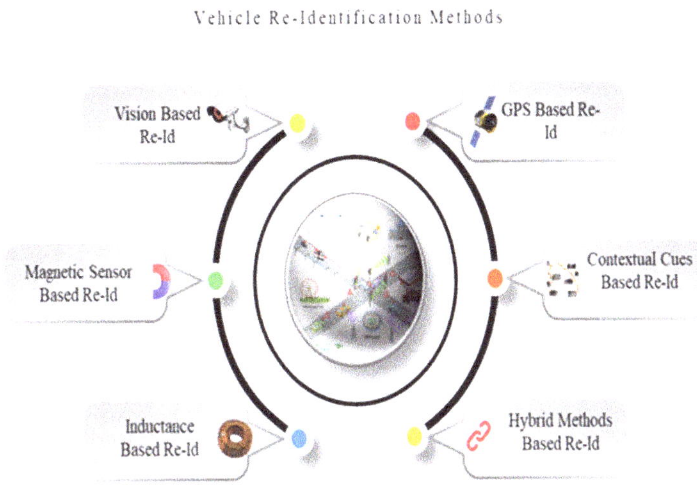

Figure 7. Shows vehicle re-id methods.

2.1. Magnetic Sensor-Based Vehicle Re-Identification

An electromagnetic field is used to detect the vehicle, when it crosses and it is used to provide occupancies, counts, and vehicle speed. However, vehicles are made up of metal. It disrupts the magnetic field, so magnetic signature regenerated by one vehicle is different from the other vehicle [19]. This approach helps in re-identifying a specific vehicle. Moreover, for ITS the Berkeley's company sells magnetic sensors with the name "Sensys Network" [20]. A straight-line re-id rat is 50%, and the approach reduces the magnetic signature peak value sequence for calculating the signature distance to prevent vehicle speed dependency [21]. For real-time vehicle re-id processing unit is associated to thousands of magnetic sensor nodes and a large number of magnetic sensors that generate massive data streams, and to deal with real-time data stream mining, high-performance FPGAs and low-performance microcontroller are used [22,23]. Sylvie Charbonnier et al. [24] studied various approaches for vehicle re-id by adopting vehicle tridimensional magnetic signature measured with sensor, when car passes sensor and changes in the magnetic field were induced and measured in three different directions like X, Y, Z. Rene O. Sanchez et al. [25] investigated vehicle re-id approaches by using wireless magnetic sensors and compares vehicle magnetic signatures to overcome the limitations of system while vehicle is stopped or moving slow at detection station.

2.2. Inductive Loop-Based Vehicle Re-Identification

Vehicle can be re-identified using inductive loops embedded in the road surface for the detection of vehicle. From those loops, a fingerprint is captured for every car passing by. The travel time can be determined when those fingerprints or certain aspects of them coming from different locations are compared with each other. Jeng and Chu [26] designed a real-time inductive loop signature-based vehicle re-id method named RTREID-2M. Inductive signature is used for vehicle re-id and much efforts have been done to utilize inductive loop signature technology. Inductive signature-based vehicle re-id algorithms identify specific vehicle at downstream detection station by matching the inductive signature at upstream detection station, considering that vehicle have same signature by crossing different loop detection stations [27]. Vehicle re-id researchers have proposed several algorithms like optimization, piecewise slope rate (PSR) matching [28], lexicographic and blind deconvolution [29], all these proposed approaches are for raw signature processing, signature feature extraction, and vehicle matching. R.J. Blokpoel [30] proposed an algorithm with different sizes of a single loop. Validation tests depict re-id rates up to 100%, when loops are identical to the similar type and 88% when compare between different types.

2.3. Global Positioning Systems-Based Vehicle Re-Identification

Global Positioning Systems (GPS) technology is an essential and valuable tool for ITS and traffic surveillance, because it provides positioning data for every single vehicle [31,32]. There are still some limitations in vehicle re-id using GPS like varying accuracy, minimal fleet penetration, and signal loss because of tunnels, trees, tall buildings, etc. GPS is adopted with vehicles to locate and get travel information along with longitude and latitude information and timestamp. GPS is special form of mobile sensing technology that enables the devices like GPS logger, GPS cellular phones, and smartphones moves with vehicles to get speed information and location continuously. However, different types of vehicles have different behaviors such as deceleration rates, acceleration, and speed variation. This encourages the author to adopt GPS technology for vehicle classification and re-id [33].

2.4. Vision-Based Vehicle Re-Identification

In computer vision, the aim of vehicle re-id is to identify specific vehicle that appeared over in multiple cameras network. The large surveillance camera network is deployed in different areas of public places like hospitals, parks, colleges, roads, and other areas. It is also difficult and tiresome job for security officers to track targeted or specific vehicle over multiple camera network manually. However, computer vision techniques can automatically re-id a vehicle and basic five main working steps are discussed below (shown in Figure 8).

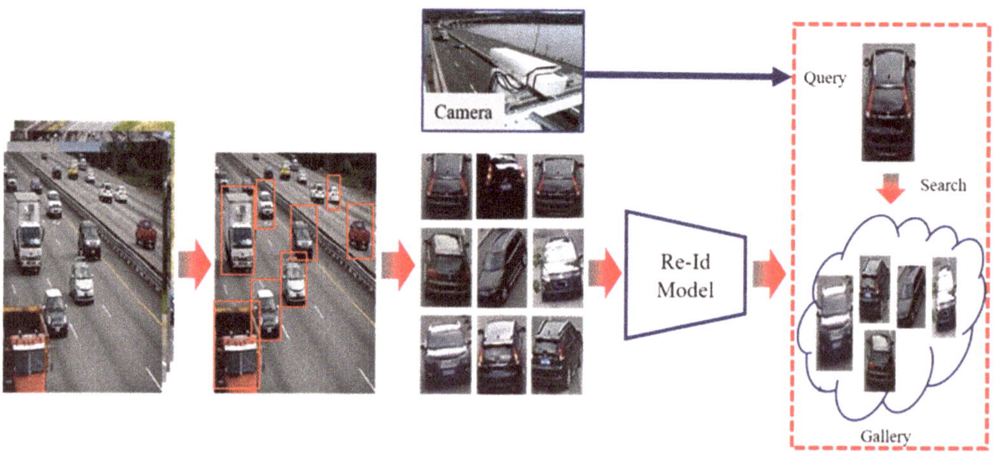

Figure 8. The flow of designing a practical vehicle re-id system, including five main steps.

- Step 1: Data Collection: For real-time video analysis raw videos from surveillance cameras is one of the key component. The cameras are fixed at different locations in an unconstrained environment [34].
- Step 2: Bounding Box Generation: It is very difficult almost impossible when we have large scale surveillance videos to extract vehicle image. We use a bounding box and it is obtained by vehicle detection technique [35].
- Step 3: Training Data Annotation: Data annotation is a process of labeling the videos or images of dataset with metadata. It is an indispensable step for vehicle re-id model training because each surveillance camera video recording is in a different environment.
- Step 4: Model Training: Model training is simply the task of learning discriminative features and good values for all the weights and the bias from previous annotated

vehicle videos or images of the dataset. It is a key step in vehicle re-id systems and a widely explored area in literature.

- Step 5: Vehicle Retrieval: Vehicle retrieval is a task of matching targeted vehicle (query image) over a gallery set.

3. Vision-Based State-of-the-Art Vehicle Re-Identification Approaches

Vision-based methods focus on examining robust feature representations to calculate the distance between features of two-vehicle images and vehicles with the same class have a low distance otherwise high. However, vehicle features are difficult to distinguish when a captured vehicle image consists of similar colors and pose. In this section gives an overview of recent works on computer vision-based methods for vehicle re-id problem, furthermore general approach for vision-based method is shown in Figure 9. Several impressive vision-based methods have been proposed to improve vehicle re-id performance either by modifying the existing DL architectures or designing a new deep neural network (DNN). Generally speaking, eight different techniques have been employed in this research area: (A) Feature representation for vehicle re-id, (B) Similarity metric for vehicle re-id, (C) Traditional machine learning-based vehicle re-id, (D) View-aware-based vehicle re-id, (E) Fine-grained visual recognition-based vehicle re-id, (F) Generative adversarial network-based vehicle re-id, (G) Attention mechanism, (H) License plate-based vehicle re-id.

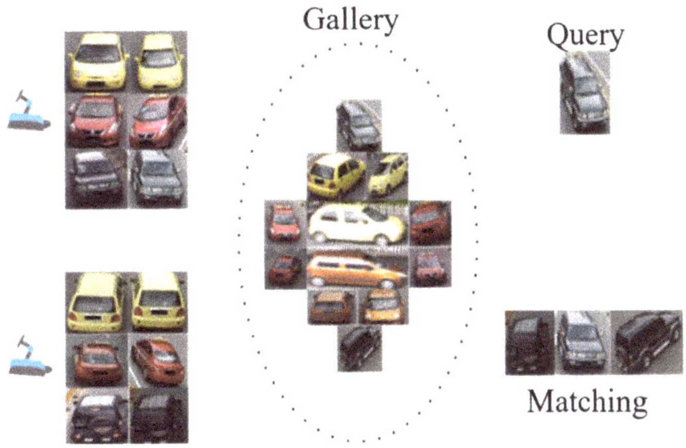

Figure 9. The vehicle re-id problem. given a Query, find the matching candidate in the gallery.

3.1. Feature Representation for Vehicle Re-Identification

Feature representation play vital role in progress of many different computer vision tasks. In this regard, vehicle re-id features representation approaches can primarily be classified into two parts: hand-crafted and deep learning features representations. Hand-crafted feature representations BOWCN [36], and LOMO [37] initially utilized in person re-id and then applied directly on vehicle re-id task. Some well-known deep learning-based feature representations such as GoogLeNet [38], VGGNet [39], AlexNet [40], and, ResNet [41] are used for vehicle re-id. The researcher also adopts these baseline models in their approaches for vehicle re-id. Such as, NuFACT [42] takes GoogLeNet [38], FACT [43] uses AlexNet [40], DRDL [44] utilizes VGGNet [39] to extract features of vehicles. Various type of loss functions are utilized to efficiently learn vehicle image discriminative feature representation to train deep learning-based model vehicle re-id; such as the deep joint discriminative learning (DJDL) [45] approach uses identification, and verification and triplet loss functions improved triplet convolutional neural network [46] uses classification and-oriented and triplet loss function to extract discriminative feature representation.

3.2. Traditional Machine Learning-Based Vehicle Re-Identification

In traditional machine learning (TML), we adopt feature engineering to artificially clean and refine data. However, previously proposed approaches are grouped into for robust features extraction and learning discriminative classifiers. In TML extracted features are directly computed from image pixels and it is low level feature representation. Moreover, TML-based algorithm design is expensive and difficult. Broadly, it consists of two steps feature extraction and feature classification. There are many algorithms proposed for low level feature extraction for instance speeded up robust features (SURF) [47], scale-invariant feature transform (SIFT) [48], and histogram of oriented gradient (HOG). After feature extraction different classifiers are applied, which are widely used in TML approaches such as linear regression, k-Nearest Neighbor (KNN) [49], logistic regression, support vector machine (SVM) [50], bayes classification [51], and decision tree [52]. The features extracted using SIFT are local features of the image, which maintains the scale scaling, invariance of rotation, and brightness variation. In addition, it also maintains a particular degree of stability to affine transformation, the viewing angle change, and noise.

Moreover, one of the feature descriptor adopted for targeted object detection in image processing is HOG. The large area of image features are formed by calculating the gradient direction histograms of its local regions. However, an overlapping local contrast normalization approach is adopted to improve the performance. Zapletal and Herout [53] utilize the color histogram and the HOG features with linear regression to re-id vehicle. Chen et al. [54] designed a method to re-id vehicles grid-by-grid with HOG features extraction for coarse search and further improves the result by utilizing histograms of matching pairs. In [55], vehicle re-id local variance measures are applied using local binary patterns and joint descriptors.

3.3. Similarity Metric for Vehicle Re-Identification

Performance of vehicle re-id can be improved by selecting appropriate distance matrices regardless of appearance representation. Distance metric learning approaches [56] are thoroughly studied in image retrieval and recognition tasks, in which matric space is defined in such a way that features that belong to same class are kept closer and different are at distant as shown in Figure 10. In the re-id task, image features are known as appearance descriptor. In this the learned distance matric in appearance space minimizes the distance for descriptor between same vehicles and maximizes distance for descriptor of different vehicles. As in various face recognition algorithms [57,58] uses Euclidean and Cosine distance matric to measure the similarity, and FACT [43] also utilizes Euclidean and cosine distance metrics to measure similarity between the pair of vehicle for re-id. Similarly, NuFact [42] utilizes the Euclidean distance to measure the similarity between the probe and gallery set vehicle images in discriminative null space [59]. Furthermore, deep relative distance learning (DRDL) [44] studied a two-branch convolutional neural network to covert the raw vehicle images into a Euclidean space, so that distance can be used directly to measure the similarity of two individual vehicles.

Pairwise constraints are required for matrix learning and it is done in supervised fashion. During the training features of appearance descriptor are in pair and labelled as positive and negative. It is totally depending on appearance descriptor whether it belongs to the same vehicle or different vehicle. Appearance descriptors are represented as $x_1, x_2, \ldots, x_n$, here n represents number of training instances and the dimensionality of every instance is represented by m. The aim of metrics learning is to learn distance metric and matrix $D \in \mathrm{R}_{\mathrm{mxm}}$ represents it; thus, the distance between pair of appearance descriptors x_i and x_j is as follows:

$$d(x_i, x_j) = (x_i - x_j)^T D(x_i - x_j) \tag{2}$$

$d(x_i, x_j)$ is a true metric only possible when matrix D is symmetric positive semi-definite. This issue is resolved by adopting convex programming as follows:

$$min_D \sum_{(x_i,x_j)\in Pos} \|(x_i - x_j)\|_D^2 \; s.t.D \geq 0, \; and \sum_{(x_i,x_j)\in Neg} \|(x_i - x_j)\|_D^2 \geq 1 \tag{3}$$

where Pos represents the positive label in training samples, and it is the appearance descriptor of the same vehicle, whereas Neg represents the negative label in training samples and it is the appearance descriptor of a different vehicle.

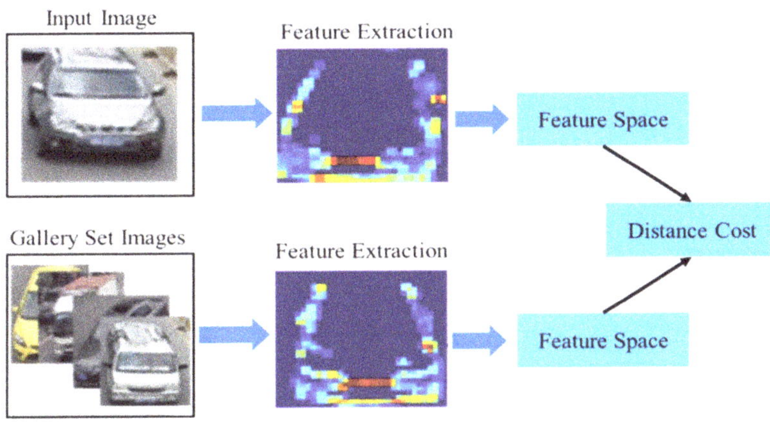

Figure 10. Vehicle re-id system based on metric-based methods.

3.4. Fine-Grained Visual Recognition-Based Vehicle Re-Identification

Vehicle re-id is fine-grained recognition task, and fine-grained vehicle recognition can be divided into two parts, representation learning model and part-based model. Many approaches are proposed [60] that utilize alignment and part localization for feature extraction of main parts and then those parts are compared for vehicle re-id. Xiao et al. [61] studied weakly supervised way in fine-grained domain using reinforcement learning to get discriminative parts of vehicle. In addition, Lin et al. [62] presents a bilinear architecture to get the pair of local features in which output descriptors of two networks are merged in an invariant way. Boonsim et al. [63] presents an approach for fine-grained recognition of vehicles at night. The authors utilize shape and lights of vehicle visible in night and relative position to identify model and make of a vehicle, which are visible from the front and rear side.

In fine-grained recognition, local region features are extracted from different points such as logo, annual inspection stickers, and decorations, to make system more efficient and robust various attributes of vehicles are also incorporated like color, model, and type information. For example, in different vehicles with similar global appearance in Figure 11, all the vehicles are different in each column. The differences between each vehicle are pointed out with red circles. From Figure 11 it can also be seen that the differences between similar global appearance vehicles lie in some local regions.

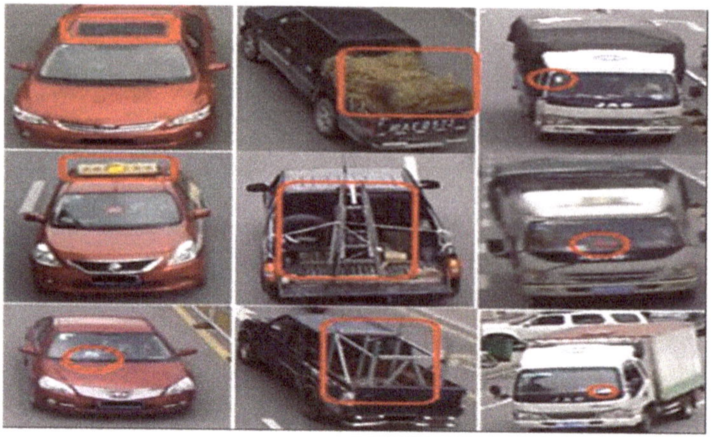

Figure 11. Shows vehicles that are same in global appearance but differentiated by local regions that are marked in red circle.

3.5. View-Aware-Based Vehicle Re-Identification

Most of the above discussed deep learning features [38,39,45] are general, and these learned features end at multiple fully connected layers. Despite that, all these approaches performance is not bad. But these approaches are not designed for a specific problem related to view point variation. It is a central challenge in vehicle re-id task. Vehicle re-id is closely related to person re-id, however, intra-class variation is a major problem in person re-id in which the same person looks different by changing viewpoint. Zhao et al. [64] designed a novel approach that achieved satisfactory results and the method was based on person body parts guided for re-id. Wu et al. [65] proposed a study with pose prior that made identification efficient and robust to viewpoint. Zheng et al. [66] proposed the pose box structure that generates the pose estimation after affine transformations. It is also challenging and crucial in vehicle re-id, because image viewpoint is the same as a consequence of vehicle rigid motion. Wang et al. [67] studied the orientation invariant feature embedding to solve the issue of viewpoint variation influence on vehicle re-id system. Prokaj et al. [68] proposed a pose estimation-based approach to handle multiple viewpoint problem. Yi Zhou et al. [69] studied uncertainty in the viewpoint of vehicle re-id system and designed end to end deep learning-based architecture on Long Short-Term Memory (LSTM) bi-directional loop and concatenated CNN, in this model author takes full advantage of LSTM and CNN to learn the different viewpoints of vehicle. And also, there are many more approaches are proposed to handle the view point variation issue in vehicle re-id such as adversarial bi-directional long short-term memory (LSTM) network (ABLN) [70], spatially concatenated convolutional network (SCCN) and CNN-LSTM bi-directional loop (CLBL) [69]. However, all these approaches need vehicle datasets. Every vehicle image is densely sampled camera viewpoints. Despite that, it is hard to gain in real-time camera surveillance systems. Therefore, there is still ample room for vehicle re-id by thoroughly considering viewpoint variations.

3.6. Generative Adversarial Network-Based Vehicle Re-Identification

GAN [71] is one of the hot technique in semi-supervised and unsupervised learning algorithms. It is proposed by Goodfellow by deriving backpropagation signals through a competitive process involving a pair of networks. GAN can be adopted in different applications, like style transfer, image synthesis, image super-resolution, semantic image editing, image super-resolution, classification and person/vehicle re-id. The GAN-based vehicle re-id flow is shown in Figure 12. At present, there have been many papers that adopt GAN to solve the problems of vehicle re-id. The existing datasets have low diversities and small scales, which leads to poor generalization performance on the trained models. To solve this problem. Generative Adversarial Network (GAN) in Object re-id is among the latest research trends in the deep learning approaches. GANs achieved significant performance in in many fields such as translation [72] and image generation [73]. Furthermore, recently GANs are also utilized for re-id problems (person re-id and vehicle re-id) [74,75]. Zheng et al. [76] proposed a method in which they used the DCGAN [73] with Gaussian noises to generate unlabeled person images before training. Wei et al. [77] studied a PT-GAN to minimize the domain gap by transferring person images between different styles. Zhou et al. [78] proposed GAN based model to solve cross-view vehicle re-id problem by generating vehicle images in different viewpoints. Lou et al. [74] designed a model to generate the same and cross-view vehicle images from original images to facilitate training model. Zhou et al. [78] proposed a conditional generative network to generate cross-view images from desired vehicle pairs.

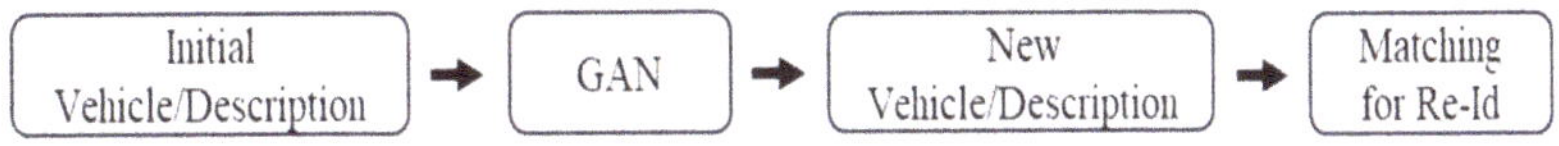

Figure 12. Vehicle re-id system based on GAN diagram.

Aihua et al. [79] proposed a framework that primarily comprises view transform and vehicle re-id model. The view transform model comprises of GAN to generate vehicle images in different views to overcome the viewpoint related issue. The vehicle re-id model consists of one backbone, three subnetworks, and one embedding network. The overall framework is illustrated in Figure 13.

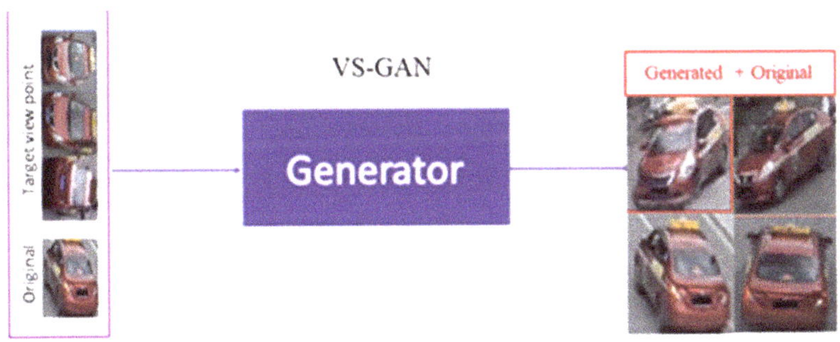

Figure 13. Overview of deep feature representations guided by the meaningful attributes.

3.7. Attention Mechanism

The neural networks at some extent imitate human brain actions in simple way. Attention Mechanism is also an effort to develop a technique that concentrate on selective thing/actions that are relevant to task and neglecting the others in neural networks. Currently, researchers are trying hard to design an efficient attention-based neural network for vision-related applications. Such as image classification [80], fine-grained image recognition [81], action recognition [82], and re-id [83]. The commonly followed strategy in these approaches is integrating a hard part selection subnet work or soft mask branch into the deep networks. Such as Zhao et al. [84] studied the part-localization CNN for predicting salient parts and features of these parts exploit for person re-id. Wang et al. [80] utilizes residual learning technique [41] to develop the Residual Attention unit for soft mask learning and gained significant image classification results. Though, only the soft pixel-level attention has very small participation in the performance of vehicle re-id task. It gives only global information like vehicle logo, annual inspection stickers, and personalized decorations. So, they presented joint learning framework for vehicle re-id in which both soft and hard level attentions are utilized Furthermore, Guo et al. [85] proposed a model with one trunk and two salient part branches for hard part level attention. Trunk branches extracts the global features of vehicle and salient branches extracts the features from vehicle head parts and windscreen. For soft pixel level attention residual attention modules are inserted into trunk and salient branches. Lastly, global and salient part features of vehicle are put to gather for effective feature representation with the supervision of multi-grain ranking loss for vehicle re-id task and complete framework is shown in Figure 14. Furthermore, comparison of different attention mechanism-based approaches are shown in Table 2.

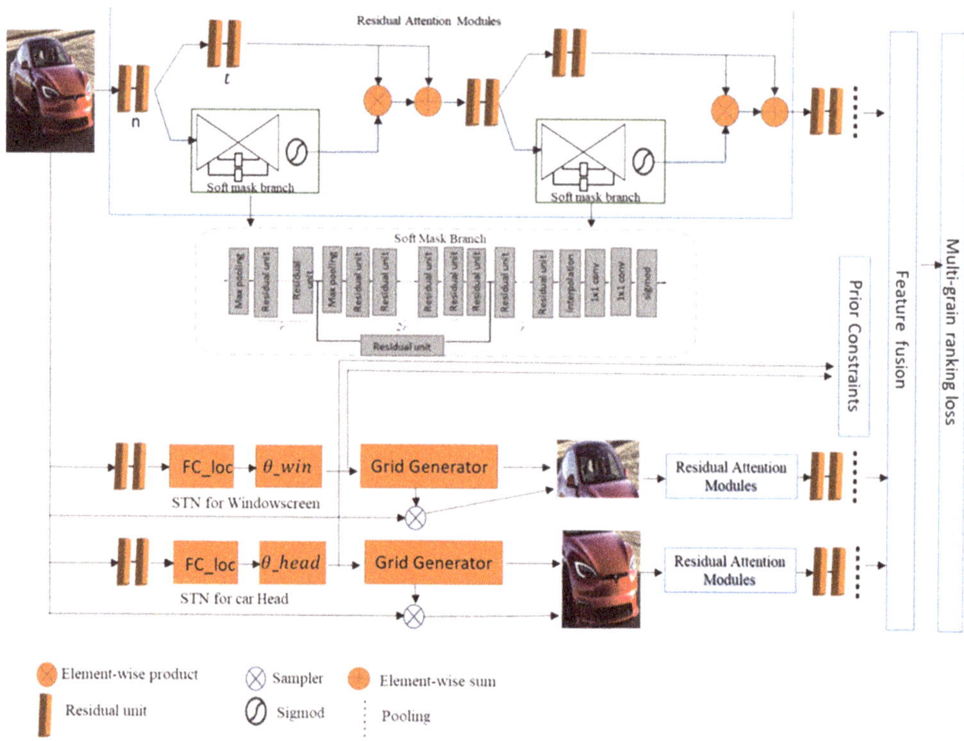

Figure 14. An overview of Two-level Attention network supervised by a Multi-grain Ranking loss (TAMR) structure.

Table 2. Comparison of different attention mechanism-based approaches.

Method and Reference	mAP%	Rank-1 (%)	Rank-5 (%)
RNN-HA [86]	56.80	74.79	87.31
SCAN [87]	49.87	82.24	90.76
AAVER [88]	61.18	88.97	94.70
PGAN [89]	79.30	96.50	98.30

3.8. License Plate-Based Vehicle Re-Identification

Vehicle re-id using license plate is simply the system's ability to automatically detect, extract, and recognize license plate characters automatically from vehicle image. License plate recognition (LPR) is a conventional method to identify a specific vehicle [90]. An automatic LPR system is mainly divided into two parts, first license plate detection and second, interpreting the vehicle license plate image into numerically readable form. There are many approaches proposed in past for LPR. However, it is still challenging due to some reasons like vehicle image is not captured perfectly, some characters may be occluded, illumination, variation in size of an image, camera distance and zooming. Li and Shen [91] studied a sequence labelling-based approach to recognize the vehicle license plate without character-level segmentation using recurrent neural networks (RNN). The input feature sequence to RNN is extracted using a nine-layer CNN. Super-resolution is also proposed to restore a license plate image to improve performance. Shi et al. [92] designed convolutional recurrent neural network (CRNN) for scene text recognition that incorporates feature extraction, transcription and sequence modeling into a unified framework. Moreover, Figure 15 shows the basic steps of license plate-based vehicle re-id.

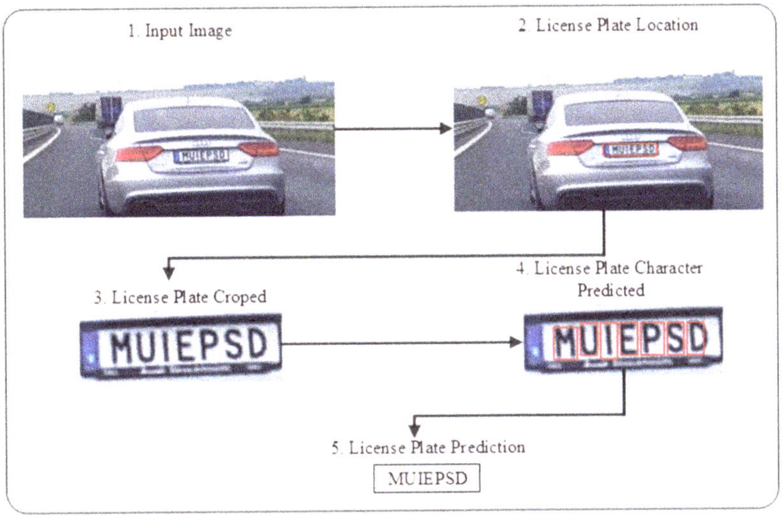

Figure 15. The flow of the license plate-based vehicle recognition.

4. Spatio-Temporal Cues-Based Vehicle Re-Identification Approaches

Introducing contextual information in vehicle re-id system can increase the efficiency and reduces irrelevant vehicle gallery images. As compared to person, for vehicle it is necessary to follow traffic rules for instance, practically vehicle follows speed limits, routes, and traffic lanes, so in this scenario vehicle moving in between different cameras at specific time and location helps a lot in vehicle re-id. Spatio-temporal cues are greatly examined for various objects association in surveillance camera network [93]. As in [94] concluded few key findings. Firstly, one specific captured vehicle in one camera cannot appear at more than one location at the same time. Secondly, along the time vehicle is moving continuously based on these finds, authors use location and time slots to eliminate irrelevant vehicle images from list as demonstrated in Figure 16. Ellis et al. [93] proposed approach that trains the model on temporal and topological transitions of trajectory data and is acquired from surveillance camera network. Loy et al. [95] presented a method for obtaining the spatio-temporal topology of surveillance camera network using multiple camera correlation analysis. Furthermore, time and location information is also exploited for vehicle re-id task. Liu et al. [96] studied a spatio-temporal affinity method for quantifying different pairs of vehicle images. Shen et al. [97] also introduces the spatio-temporal path data for vehicle re-id.

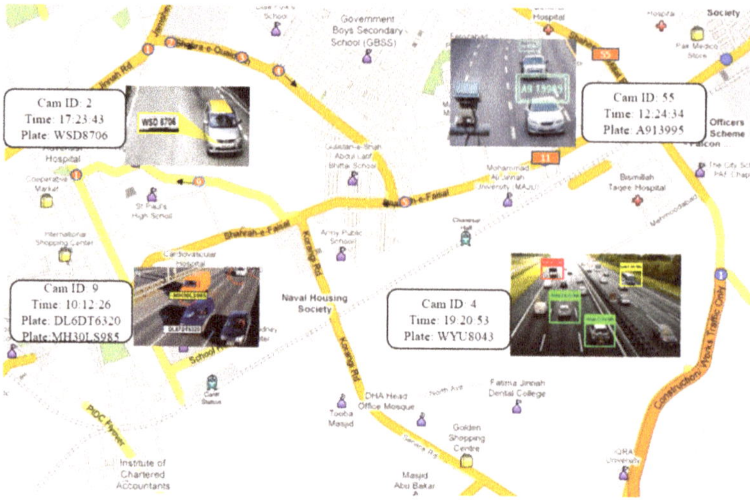

Figure 16. Depicts the spatio-temporal information.

5. Hybrid Methods-Based Vehicle Re-Identification

To further enhance the robustness and efficiency of vehicle re-id system researchers have proposed the approaches in which they combined the two or more different techniques, for instance Liu et al. [42] proposed a framework with name PROVID, in this framework author not only consider the visual appearance of vehicle for re-id system, but also exploits the license plate and spatio-temporal cues of vehicle as shown in Figure 17. Jiang et al. [98] studied vehicle re-id algorithm using appearance and contextual information, author examines the multiple attributes during training like vehicle model, color, and vehicle image features individual respectively and sort vehicles on the bases of spatio-temporal cues. Shen et al. [97] designed a two-step architecture, a pair of query vehicle images with contextual information and visual temporal path are produced using Markov Random Fields (MRF) chain model, and then the similarity score is generated.

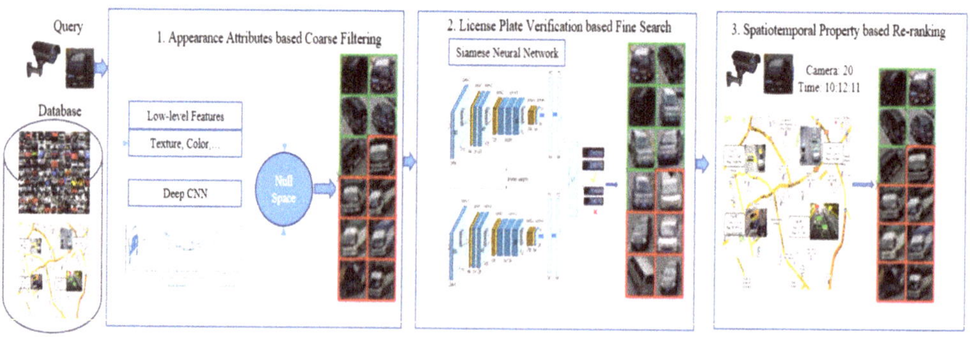

Figure 17. The architecture of the PROVID framework.

6. Vehicle Re-Identification Benchmark Datasets

Datasets are the key components to measure the performance of vehicle re-id system and should reflect the practical surveillance camera data. We cannot avoid some factors like occlusion, background clutter, change in illumination etc. to evaluate the approach [99]. However, multiple benchmark datasets are available, some well-known like VeRi-776,

VehicleID, etc. that are prepared by the research community to evaluate vehicle re-id techniques. Table 3 and Figure 18 lists the commonly used vehicle re-id dataset with attributes. Furthermore, a brief description of the most popular datasets is as follows:

Table 3. Characteristics of publicly available datasets.

S. No	Dataset	Year	Total No. of Images	No. of Vehicle Models	No. of Vehicles	No. of Viewpoints	No. of Cameras
1	VeRi-776 [43]	2016	50,000	10	776	6	18
2	PKU VehicleID [44]	2016	221,763	250	26,267	2	12
3	Vehicle-1M [100]	2018	936,051	400	55,527	……	……
4	BoxCars21k [35]	2016	63,750	148	21,250	4	……
5	VehicleReId [53]	2016	47,123	……	1232	……	……
6	CompCars [101]	2015	136,726	1716	……	5	……
7	VRIC [102]	2018	60,430	……	5622	……	60
8	VRID [103]	2017	10,000	10	1000	……	326
9	VERIWild [104]	2019	416,314	……	40,671	Unconstrained	174

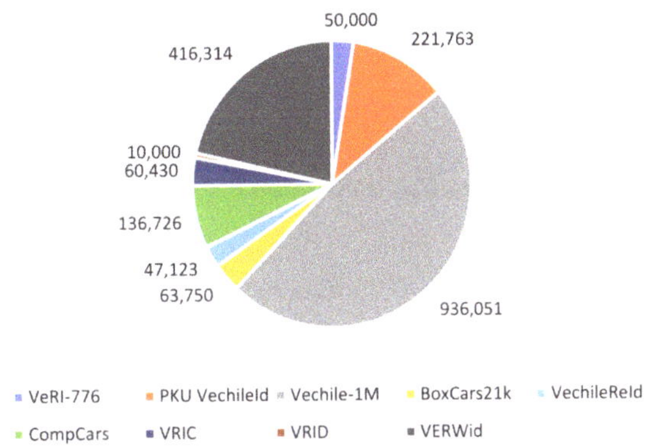

Figure 18. Depicts the number of total images per vehicle re-id dataset.

VeRi-776: [43] VeRi-776 is a publicly available vehicle re-id dataset, and often adopted by the computer vision researcher community. Dataset images are gathered in real scenario using surveillance cameras, and the total images in dataset are 50,000 of 776 different vehicles. Each captured vehicle images have 2 to 18 viewpoints with different resolution, occlusion, and illumination. Furthermore, spatio-temporal relations and license plate are annotated for all vehicles. To make dataset more robust, images are labelled with color, type, and vehicle model. In Figure 19 various types of vehicles from VeRi dataset are shown.

Figure 19. Depicts the sample images of VeRi-776 dataset.

PKU VehicleID: [44] VehicleID dataset is developed by Peking University with the funding of the Chinese national natural science foundation and national basic research program of China in the national engineering laboratory for video technology (NELVT). The vehicle dataset consists of 221,763 total images of 26,267 vehicles, and all the images are captured during daytime in a small town of China with multiple surveillance cameras with 10,319 vehicles model information i.e "Audi A6L", "MINI-cooper" and "BMW 1 Series" are labeled manually. In Figure 20 different vehicles from PKU vehicleID dataset are shown.

Figure 20. Depicts the sample images of PKU VehicleID dataset.

Vehicle-1M: [100] Vehicle-1M dataset is developed by the University of Chinese Academy of Sciences in the National laboratory of pattern recognition, Institute of Automation. This benchmark dataset contains 55,527 vehicles with 400 different vehicle models, and the total captured images are 936,051. Surveillance cameras capture all the images in China's town at day and night time and consist of a vehicle's rear and head view. Moreover, each image in this dataset is labeled with a model, make, and vehicle year. Images from Vehicle-1M are shown in Figure 21.

Figure 21. Depicts the sample images of vehicle-1M dataset.

BoxCars21k: [35] BoxCar116k dataset is developed using 37 surveillance cameras, and this dataset consists of total images 116,286 of 27,496 vehicles. For the preparation of dataset, 45 brands of the vehicle are used. Moreover, captured images of the vehicle in the dataset are in an arbitrary viewpoint, i.e., side, back, front, and roof. All vehicle images in the dataset are annotated with 3D bounding box, model make, and type. However, some sample images are shown in Figure 22.

Figure 22. Depicts the sample images of BoxCar21k dataset.

VehicleReId: [53] VehicleReId dataset provides 47,123 vehicle images and all these images are extracted from five different video shots by using two surveillance cameras, out of total images 24,530 vehicle image pairs are human annotated.

CompCars: [101] CompCars dataset consists of two types of image nature (1) Web-nature images (2) Surveillance-nature images. There are total of 136,726 web-nature images in which there are 163 car makers with 1716 car models. However, in surveillance-nature, the total car images are 50,000 that are captured from the front view. Samples of CompCars dataset are shown in Figure 23.

Figure 23. Depicts the sample images of CompCars dataset.

VRIC: [102] VRIC contains 5622 vehicles with 60,430 total images with different traffic road surveillance cameras and images captured at day and night. Images with different angles, viewpoints, occlusions and illuminations from VRIC dataset are depicted in Figure 24.

Figure 24. Depicts the sample images of VRIC dataset.

VRID: [103] This dataset contains total 10,000 images and specially developed for vehicle re-id with 326 surveillance cameras the VRID images were captured from 7 a.m. to 5 p.m. for one week. In the development of the dataset there are 1000 vehicles used with 10 commonly used vehicle models, and at least 10 times each vehicle is captured over a camera network in Guangdong city, China. Surveillance cameras have been fixed in a practical environment with arbitrary directions and angles; therefore, dataset images have various resolutions and poses distributed from 400 × 424 to 990 × 1134 pixels.

VERI-Wild: [104] Collects a large-scale vehicle re-id dataset in the unconstrained environment. For dataset development, an existing large CCTV system is utilized. It consists of 174 cameras across, recorded till one month (30 × 24 h). The CCTV cameras are spread over a large city consists of 200 km^2. The dataset includes 12 million vehicle raw images, and 11 volunteers cleaned the dataset for one month. After data cleaning and annotation, 416,314 vehicle images of 40,671 identities are collected. VERI-Wild dataset images with viewpoint changes, illumination variations, occlusion, and background variations are presented in Figure 25, and statistics are shown in Figure 26.

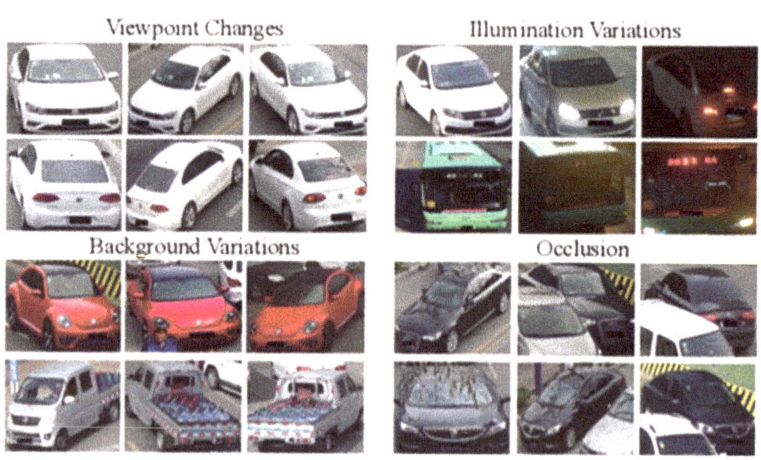

Figure 25. Depicts the sample images of VERI-Wild dataset.

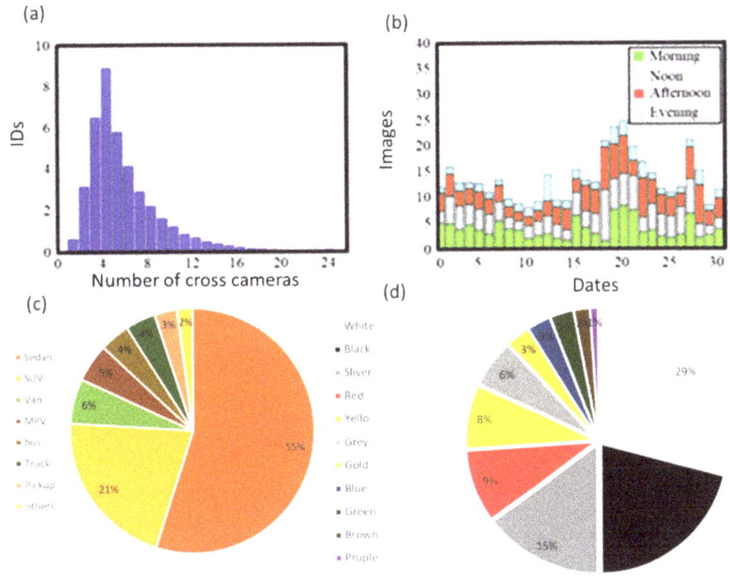

Figure 26. Illustrates the characteristics of VERI-Wild dataset. (**a**) The number of identities across multiple surveillance cameras; (**b**) Total number of IDs captured in different slots of each day; (**c**) Division of vehicle types; (**d**) Division of vehicle colors.

7. Challenges Regarding Vehicle Re-Identification

The vehicle re-id is among an essential and challenging task, and it is defined as, either any specific vehicle captured in one camera has already appeared over multiple camera network or not. With the increasing need for automated video analysis, the vehicle re-id receives increasing attention these days in the computer vision research community. Therefore, some key factor and their effects on performance are explained following.

- Insufficient data: For vehicle re-id systems each single image should match with gallery images, so it is very hard to get sufficient data for good model learning of each intra-class variability. However, it is also major challenge that dataset should reflect the real-world surveillance, currently, most of the datasets available are consists of non-overlapping views with a limited number of cameras; as a result, datasets have few viewpoints with unchanged regulation, and most of the publicly available datasets are consists of limited instances and classes that influence the performances.
- Inter-class similarity: This problem arises due to different automobile manufacturing companies have a similar visual appearance, as a result, two different make, model, and type of vehicles looks similar from rear or front side, as shown in Figure 27. [105,106].
- Intra-class variability: due to the unconstrained environment and viewpoint, the same vehicle looks different over different geographical locations of the surveillance camera network [107], as depicted in Figure 27.
- Pose and viewpoint variations: Due to the camera calibration, viewing angle and location on the roadside, captured vehicle image appearance varies, and the same vehicle looks different and different looks same. A learned model on the rear pose of a vehicle will probably fail to detect a vehicle's front, side pose. Furthermore, the effect of viewpoint change on vehicle is shown in Figure 28.

Figure 27. Demonstration of two main challenges in vehicle re-id. (**a**) Intra-class variance; (**b**) Inter-class similarity.

Figure 28. Images of the same vehicle taken from different cameras to illustrate the appearance changes.

- Partial occlusions: If some part of an input vehicle is hidden by any object or vehicle in congestion as result, some key discriminative parts are not visible and the matching fails probably. Moreover, due to these features generated by an occluded vehicle image is corrupted [108].
- Illumination changes: Vehicle captured images illumination varies surveillance camera to surveillance camera and surveillance camera scenes and also illumination changes on the same surveillance camera due to different time slots like day and night. The same vehicle observed in different lighting conditions can have a color difference on the appearance because of the unconstrained environment [109]. Vehicles lights also have an effect on image illumination, so vehicle appearance changes at different a period of time and multiple camera network [110].
- Resolutions variation: Changes in resolution in pair of same vehicle occurs because of camera calibration, and another factor is various old surveillance cameras with different heights are fixed on the roadside that give a different-resolution,
- Deformation: Due to load or accident, vehicle shape, and body changes.

- Background clutter: This problem occurs in vehicle re-id when the vehicle's color and image background is the same.
- Changes in color response: The color attribute is one of the key parameters in vehicle re-id, but surveillance cameras color response changes because of camera settings features [110].
- Lighting effects: Specular reflection and shadows of the vehicle body generate the noise in vehicle image feature descriptor. If vehicle shadow is larger, there are more chance of inconsistency and noise in feature descriptor. As compared to the practical environment in a controlled environment, the lights and specular reflections can be controlled; but practically, we cannot control shadows, and it is one of the major problems in extracting information from the vehicle image
- Long-term re-id: If the same vehicle is captured after a long time or captured at different locations, then there is a high possibility that the vehicle looks different shape wise due to extra carry load/object.
- Cross dataset vehicle re-id: In vehicle re-id systems training and testing of model is performed on same dataset, but it is practically infeasible, due to significant difference between training and testing data and model may not generalize well.
- Insufficient temporal data: Due to the absence of unconstrained environmental information in datasets, it is impossible to exploit temporal data. However, temporal information can play an important role in the performance of vehicle re-id system.
- Vehicle re-id system scalability: Scalability means the system can adapt to varying factors while maintaining the performance, such as storing large gallery sizes that are constantly increasing and computational devices that efficiently analyze data.
- Real-time processing: Practical applications require real-time video processing, and the time constraint is the main challenge in vehicle re-id systems.
- Data labeling: This is a common difficulty in the computer vision field. Training a good model robust to all variations in a supervised way couldn't be done without a sufficient amount of annotated data. For a large camera network, manually collecting and annotating the amount of data from each surveillance camera is expensive.
- A small number of images per identity for training: Since one vehicle may appear very limited times in a camera network, it's difficult to collect much data of one single vehicle. Thus, usually data is insufficient to learn a good model of each specific vehicle's intra-class variability.
- A large number of candidates in gallery set: A camera network may cover a large public space, like a parking lot. Thus, there can be a huge amount of candidate for a given re-id query, and the number of candidates increases over time. The computation for matching with a large gallery set becomes expensive.
- Camera setting: Due to different camera settings and features, the same vehicle image captured by different cameras shows color dissimilarities. There may also be some geometric differences. For example, the shape of a vehicle may be observed with varying aspect ratios.
- Computation: All the proposed methods are based on deep learning. The computation for the training step with back propagation is more expensive than classical methods. In most cases, a powerful GPU is advisable for training, and more computation and memory resources are thus necessary. In applications with real-time constraints and without GPU, a very deep network may not be suitable for inference.

8. Evaluation Metrics

In the re-id task, the target object's images are mostly aligned and cropped. However, the vehicle re-id task is same as the instance retrieval. Given the input image, the candidates with a similar input image in the gallery set are required to be placed in the top positions within a ranking list. To measure the performance of vehicle re-id approaches, the cumulative matching characteristics (CMC), curve HIT@1 and HIT@5 are commonly used by researchers. CMC curve provides the probability that an input image identity appears in a different-sized gallery set as shown in Figure 29. The cumulative number of correctly matched inputs is demonstrated based on the rank list in which inputs are re-identified. Moreover, HIT@1 is precision at rank-1 and HIT@5 is precision at rank-5. Rank is utilized to measure the matching score of test image to its own class, and higher value of rank indicates the improved performance of the system. Where the number of correctly re-identified input images in rank 1 is $q(i)$, the CMC value for rank i can be defined as:

$$CMC(i) = \sum_{r=1}^{i} q(r) \tag{4}$$

where r represents the rank index. CMC curve not only computes the rank-1 but also places the correctly matched images top ranks. Therefore, the CMC curve is a suitable option to describe the vehicle re-id performance of different approaches. Besides, CMC curves, if multiple ground truths for each query image in the gallery set are available, mean average precision (mAP) is used to measure the overall performance for vehicle re-id system. For the given query image, the average precision (AP) can be defined as:

$$AP = \frac{\sum_{k=1}^{n} P(k) \times G(k)}{Ngt} \tag{5}$$

where n is the number of test tracks and Ngt represents the number of ground truths. $P(k)$ shows the precision at cut-off k in the ranking lists. $G(k)$ equals 1 if the k-th match is true, otherwise 0. The mAP measures the overall performance of vehicle re-id system. Therefore, the mAP can be defined as:

$$mAP = \frac{\sum_{q=1}^{Q} AP(q)}{Q} \tag{6}$$

where Q denotes the number of queries.

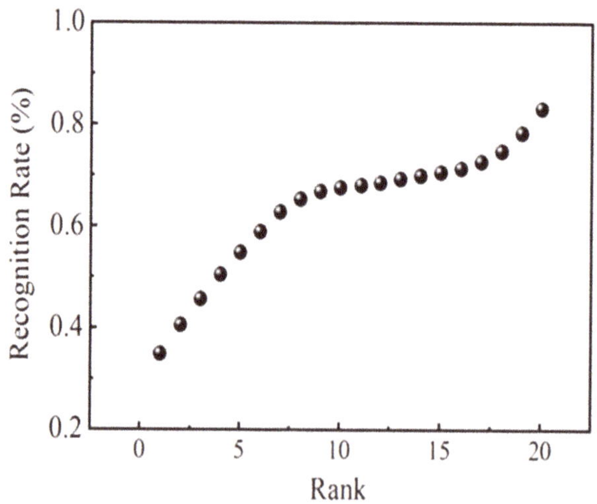

Figure 29. Cumulative matching characteristics (CMC) curve.

Another way by which vehicle re-id techniques performance can be evaluated is the confusion matrix. A confusion matrix consists of various columns and rows; it depends on the number of classes. It's diagonal represents the recognizing accuracy or true classification and off-diagonal express the misclassification.

9. Performance Comparison of Recently Proposed State-of-the-Art Approaches

The first phase in vehicle re-id is to decide whether the given vehicle image exists in the gallery set or not. In other terms, before considering for a similar match, the vehicle re-id system should have the capacity to decide whether the given vehicle probe image is a part of the gallery set or not. This approach is known novelty detection and it needs that vehicle re-id systems to have the ability to discard the miss-matched vehicle images. Usually in vehicle re-id systems, once the gallery set images are ranked in comparison with the given query image, the query image belongs to the gallery set if the similarity distance is higher than an operating threshold. We give a summary of the vehicle re-id mAP of some state-of-the-art methods including CMGN+Pre+Track [111], DF-CVTC [79], PROVID [42], and RAM [112] etc. on VeRi-776 dataset mentioned above. We have chosen VeRi-776 dataset for comparison because it is consisting of varying illumination, more viewpoints, and resolution. In short, this dataset fulfills most of the aspects of real-world camera surveillance data. The statistics about this dataset have been provided in Table 3.

However, Table 4 provides recently proposed state-of-the-art approaches on VeRi-776 dataset. For comparison, we measure the performances of each method in mAP, HIT@1 and HIT@5. From Table 4, and Figure 30 we can observe that mAP of different models is increasing during the years 2016 to 2020. As on VeRi-776 dataset from the years 2016 to 2020, the performances of state-of-the-art methods have improved from 12.76% to 85.20%, with an increase of 72.44%. Moreover, Figure 31 shows the CMC of different state-of-the-art approaches on VehicleID dataset with different test size.

Table 4. Performance analysis of some proposed approaches in state-of-art on VeRi-776.

Reference	Venue	Approach	mAP	HIT-1%	HIT5%
		Year 2020			
L. Xiangwei et al. [113]	Mobile Networks and Applications	JPFRN	72.86	93.14	97.85
Z. Aihua et al. [114]	Neural Computing and Applications	MSA	62.89	92.07	96.19
Q. Jingjing et al. [115]	Measurement Science and Technology	SAN	72.5	93.3	97.1
W. Honglie et al. [116]	Applied Sciences	LFASM	61.92	90.11	92.91
Z. Jianqing et al. [117]	IEEE Internet of Things	JQD^{3}Ns	61.30	89.69	95.17
Z. Hui et al. [118]	IEEE ITNEC	AAN+triplet +focal+range (Model-3	75.14	5.17	97.80
O. Daniel et al. [119]	IEEE Access	MidTriNet+UT	......	89.15	93.74
L. Sangroket al. [120]	CVPRW	StRDAN (R+S, best)	76.1	......	......
J. Zhu et al. [121]	IEEE TITS	QD-DLF	61.83	88.50	94.46
L. Xiaobin et.al. [122]	IEEE Trans. on Image Processing	GRF+GGL	00.61	0.89	0.95
		Year 2019			
A. A-Acevedo et al. [111]	IEEECVPR	CMGN+Pre+Track	85.20	96.60	......
F. Wu et al. [123]	Image Communication	SSL+re-ranking	69.90	89.69	95.41
S. Ahmed et al. [124]	IEEE ICIP	Mob.VFL-LSTM + Mob.VFL	59.18	88.08	94.63
G. Rajamanoharan et al. [125]	IEEE CVPR	MTML-OSG	68.3	92.0	94.2
P. Khorram et al. [88]	ArXiv	AAVER+ResNet-101	61.18	88.97	94.70
A. Zheng et al. [79]	ArXiv	DF-CVTC	61.06	91.36	95.77
Y. Lou et al. [74]	IEEE TIP	Hard-View-EALN	57.44	84.39	94.05
J. Hou et al. [126]	Neurocomputing	Baseline + MLL + MLSR	57.52	87.19	94.16
B. He et al. [127]	IEEE CVPR	Part-reg. discr. feature preserving	74.3	94.3	98.7
X. Zhong et al. [128]	ICMM	PGST+visual-SNN	69.47	89.36	94.40
R. Kumar et al. [107]	IJCNN	BS	67.55	90.23	96.42

Table 4. *Cont.*

Reference	Venue	Approach	mAP	HIT-1%	HIT5%
		Year 2018			
X. Liu et al. [42]	IEEE Trans. on Multimedia	PROVID	53.42	81.56	95.11
Y. Bai et al. [8]	IEEE Trans. on Multimedia	GS-TRE loss W/mean VGGM	59.47	96.24	98.97
J. Zhu et al. [129]	IEEE Access	JFSDL	53.53	82.90	91.60
Y. Zhou et al. [70]	IEEE WACV	ABLN-Ft-16	24.92	60.49	77.33
Y. Zhou et al. [69]	IEEE TIP	SCCN-Ft+CLBL-8-Ft	25.12	60.83	78.55
N. Jiang et al. [98]	IEEE ICIP	App +Color +Model + Re-Ranking	61.11	89.27	94.76
J. Zhu et al. [130]	MM Tools and Applications	VRSDNet	53.45	83.49	92.55
X. Liu et al. [112]	IEEE IME	RAM	61.5	88.6	94.0
D. Xu et al. [110]	ICIMCS	MTCRO	62.61	87.96	94.63
D. Sun et al. [131]	Springer ICBICS	ResNet-50 +GoogleNet,+ F.F via CSR	58.21	90.52	93.38
S. Teng et al. [87]	Springer PCM	Light_vgg_m+SCAN	49.87	82.24	90.76
Y. Zhou et al. [83]	CVPR	VAMI	50.13	77.03	90.82
Xiu-Shen et al. [86]	ACCV	RNN-HA (ResNet)	56.80	74.79	87.31
		Year 2017			
Y. Zhou et al. [78]	BMVC	XVGAN	24.65	60.20	77.03
Y. zhang et al. [46]	IEEE ICME	VGG+C+T	58.78	86.41	92.91
Z. Wang et al. [67]	ICCV	OIF+ST	51.4	92.35	......
Y. Shen et al. [97]	ICCV	Siamese-CNN-Path-LSTM	58.27	83.49	90.04
Y. Tang et al. [132]	IEEE ICIP	Combining Network	33.78	60.19	77.40
		Year 2016			
X. Liu et al. [43]	IEEE ICME	FACT	18.75	52.21	72.88
H. Liu et al. [44]	CVPR	VGG	12.76	44.10	62.63
X. Liu et al. [96]	ECCV	FACT + Plate-SNN + STR	27.77	61.44	78.78
L. Yang et al. [101]	CVPR	GoogLeNet	17.89	52.32	72.17

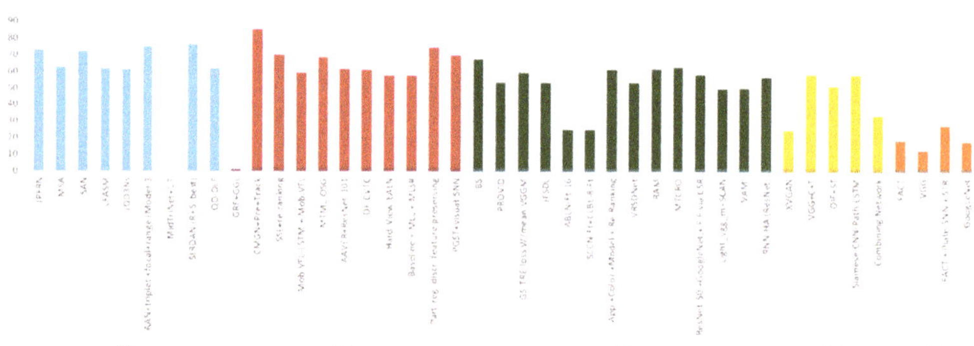

Figure 30. Demonstrates the performance comparison of different state of the art approaches.

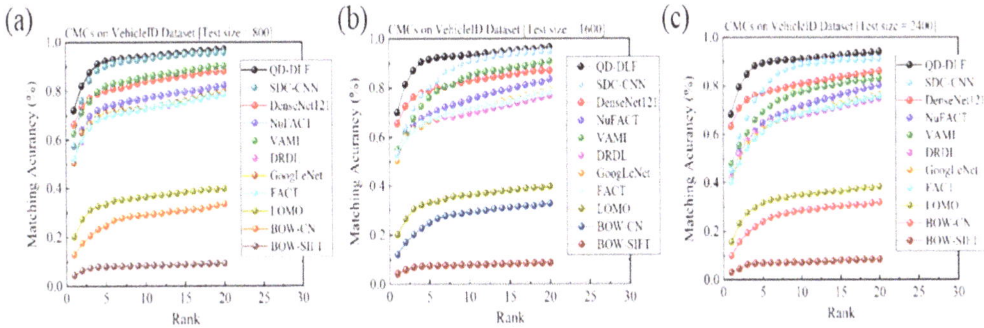

Figure 31. Demonstrates the performance comparison of different state-of-the-art approaches on VehicleID dataset. (**a**) Test size = 800; (**b**) Test size = 1600; (**c**) Test size = 2400.

10. Conclusions & Way Forward

Vehicle re-id is one of the most critical and challenging area in the ITS. Despite high significance, it is not well explored compared to a similar problem that is person re-id. In this review paper, the authors present recent advancements being done for vehicle re-id. Moreover, to draw a detailed picture of study, the authors discuss different vehicle re-id technologies, especially vision-based, including appearance, license plate, spatio-temporal, etc., along with the quantitative and qualitative comparison of different vision-based methods on VeRi-776 and VehicleID datasets. In addition, this review provides comprehensive synopses of publicly available benchmark datasets utilized for performance evaluation with a brief description of re-id evaluation techniques. This paper also presents applications as well as the main challenges of camera-based vehicle re-id such as complex and unconstrained environment, dirt, snow, occluded image, blurry image, and sunshine, etc., along with varied road topology that affects the performance.

There are many aspects of vehicle re-id that can be improved. In the future, a reader can explore possibilities to enhance the overall performance of vehicle re-id. Moreover, there is significant potential to extend the approach with some of the following concepts:

CNN works on edges, shapes, and original vehicle features, but the relationship between these features is not considered; hence, the model performance is often unsatisfactory when the vehicle image is rotated or captured with a different rotation. However, a recent capsule network [133] is introduced, which showed improved performance in handling different poses, orientations, and occluded objects.

Secondly, attention-based deep neural network models have gained encouraging results on various challenging tasks, including machine translation [134], caption generation [135], and object recognition [136]. However, attention-based neural network models are still not well investigated for vehicle re-id.

Lastly, due to the development of large-scale real-world data sets, the vehicle re-id system's performance is significantly increased. However, existing datasets offer a specific range of vehicle images with correlated data that causes over-fitting due to over-tuned parameters on specific data. Therefore, the system cannot efficiently generalize other data. A reader can develop large scale real-world surveillance vehicle datasets in an unconstrained environment with multiple views to enhance the training of the state-of-the-art approaches for performance improvement.

Concisely, Vehicle re-id is a demanding and challenging area with massive opportunities for improvement and research. This review paper attempts to provide an overview of the vehicle re-id problem, its challenges, and applications, and, simultaneously, present a way forward. We hope this paper will be valuable for anyone who wants to work in this area.

Author Contributions: Conceptualization, Z. and M.S.K.; methodology, Z., Y.H. and R.K.; software, J.D., and J.K.; writing—review and editing, M.U.A.; supervision, J.D. and J.C.; funding acquisition J.C. All authors have read and agreed to the published version of the manuscript.

Funding: This paper has been supported The National Key Research and Development Program of China (2017YFC0821505), Funding of Zhongyanggaoxiao ZYGX2018J075 and also supported by Sichuan Science and Technology Program 2019YFS0487.

Institutional Review Board Statement: Not applicable.

Informed Consent Statement: Not applicable.

Data Availability Statement: Not applicable.

Acknowledgments: I am grateful to my worthy supervisor as well as all the lab mates for their endless support.

Conflicts of Interest: The authors declare that they have no known competing financial interests or personal relationships that could have appeared to influence the work reported in this paper.

References

1. The Ministry of Transport of the People's Republic of China. *Annual Report of City Transportation Developmentin China*; The Ministry of Transport of the People's Republic of China: Beijing, China, 2010.
2. Chen, Z.; Fan, W.; Xiong, Z.; Zhang, P.; Luo, L. Visual Data Security and Management for Smart Cities. *Front. Comput. Sci. China* **2010**, *4*, 386–393. [CrossRef]
3. Cheng, K.; Khokhar, M.S.; Ayoub, M.; Jamali, Z. Nonlinear Dimensionality Reduction in Robot Vision for Industrial Monitoring Process via Deep Three Dimensional Spearman Correlation Analysis (D3D-SCA). *Multimed. Tools Appl.* **2020**, *80*, 5997–6017. [CrossRef]
4. Khokhar, M.S.; Cheng, K.; Ayoub, M.; Eric, L.K. Multi-Dimension Projection for Non-Linear Data Via Spearman Correlation Analysis (MD-SCA). In Proceedings of the 2019 8th International Conference on Information and Communication Technologies (ICICT), Karachi, Pakistan, 16–17 November 2019; pp. 14–18.
5. Qian, Q.; Jin, R.; Zhu, S.; Lin, Y. Fine-Grained Visual Categorization via Multi-Stage Metric Learning. In Proceedings of the IEEE Conference on Computer Vision and Pattern Recognition (CVPR), Columbus, OH, USA, 23–28 June 2014; IEEE: Piscataway, NJ, USA; pp. 3716–3724.
6. Cui, Y.; Zhou, F.; Lin, Y.; Belongie, S. Fine-Grained Categorization and Dataset Bootstrapping Using Deep Metric Learning with Humans in the Loop. In Proceedings of the IEEE Conference on Computer Vision and Pattern Recognition (CVPR), Boston, MA, USA, 7–12 June 2015; IEEE: Piscataway, NJ, USA; pp. 1153–1162.
7. Zhao, Y.; Shen, C.; Wang, H.; Chen, S. Structural Analysis of Attributes for Vehicle Re-Identification and Retrieval. *IEEE Trans. Intell. Transp. Syst.* **2019**, *21*, 723–734. [CrossRef]
8. Bai, Y.; Lou, Y.; Gao, F.; Wang, S.; Wu, Y.; Duan, L.-Y. Group-Sensitive Triplet Embedding for Vehicle Reidentification. *IEEE Trans. Multimed.* **2018**, *20*, 2385–2399. [CrossRef]
9. Deng, J.; Cai, J.; Aftab, M.U.; Khokhar, M.S.; Kumar, R. Visual Features with Spatio-Temporal-Based Fusion Model for Cross-Dataset Vehicle Re-Identification. *Electronics* **2020**, *9*, 1083. [CrossRef]
10. Wu, Y.; Lin, Y.; Dong, X.; Yan, Y.; Bian, W.; Yang, Y. Progressive Learning for Person Re-Identification with One Example. *IEEE Trans. Image Process.* **2019**, *28*, 2872–2881. [CrossRef] [PubMed]
11. Rasouli, A.; Kotseruba, I.; Tsotsos, J.K. Understanding Pedestrian Behavior in Complex Traffic Scenes. *IEEE Trans. Intell. Veh.* **2018**, *3*, 61–70. [CrossRef]
12. Chen, Z.; Liao, W.; Xu, B.; Liu, H.; Li, Q.; Li, H.; Xiao, C.; Zhang, H.; Li, Y.; Bao, W.; et al. Object Tracking over a Multiple-Camera Network. In Proceedings of the IEEE International Conference on Multimedia Big Data, Beijing, China, 20–22 April 2015; pp. 276–279.
13. Cai, J.; Deng, J.; Khokhar, M.S.; Umar Aftab, M. Vehicle Classification Based on Deep Convolutional Neural Networks Model for Traffic Surveillance Systems. In Proceedings of the 15th International Computer Conference on Wavelet Active Media Technology and Information Processing (ICCWAMTIP), Chengdu, China, 14–16 December 2018; pp. 224–227.
14. Arandjelovic, R.; Zisserman, A. Three Things Everyone Should Know to Improve Object Retrieval. In Proceedings of the 2012 IEEE Conference on Computer Vision and Pattern Recognition, Providence, RI, USA, 16–21 June 2012; pp. 2911–2918.
15. Khokhar, M.S.; Cheng, K.; Ayoub, M.; Rub, N.E. Data Driven Processing Via Two-Dimensional Spearman Correlation Analysis (2D-SCA). In Proceedings of the 2019 13th International Conference on Mathematics, Actuarial Science, Computer Science and Statistics (MACS), Karachi, Pakistan, 14–15 December 2019; pp. 1–7.
16. Yan, L.; Wang, Y.; Song, T.; Yin, Z. An Incremental Intelligent Object Recognition System Based on Deep Learning. In Proceedings of the 2017 Chinese Automation Congress (CAC), Jinan, China, 20–22 October 2017; pp. 7135–7138.

17. Saghafi, M.A.; Hussain, A.; Saad, M.H.M.; Tahir, N.M.; Zaman, H.B.; Hannan, M.A. Appearance-Based Methods in Re-Identification: A Brief Review. In Proceedings of the 2012 IEEE 8th International Colloquium on Signal Processing and its Applications, Malacca, Malaysia, 23–25 March 2012; pp. 404–408.
18. Doretto, G.; Sebastian, T.; Tu, P.; Rittscher, J. Appearance-Based Person Reidentification in Camera Networks: Problem Overview and Current Approaches. *J. Ambient. Intell. Humaniz. Comput.* **2011**, *2*, 127–151. [CrossRef]
19. Yi, D.; Lei, Z.; Li, S.Z. Deep Metric Learning for Practical Person Re-Identification. In Proceedings of the 2014 22nd International Conference on Pattern Recognition, Stockholm, Sweden, 24–28 August 2014; pp. 37–39. [CrossRef]
20. Kwong, K.; Kavaler, R.; Rajagopal, R.; Varaiya, P. A Practical Scheme for Arterial Travel Time Estimation Based on Vehicle Re-Identification Using Wireless Sensors. *Transp. Res. Part C Emerg. Technol.* **2009**, *17*, 586–606. [CrossRef]
21. Wang, R.; Zhang, L.; Sun, R.; Gong, J.; Cui, L. Easitia: A Pervasive Traffic Information Acquisition System Based on Wireless Sensor Networks. *IEEE Trans. Intell. Transp. Syst.* **2011**, *12*, 615–621. [CrossRef]
22. Sart, D.; Mueen, A.; Najjar, W.; Keogh, E.; Niennattrakul, V. Accelerating Dynamic Time Warping Subsequence Search with GPUs and FPGAs. In Proceedings of the 2010 IEEE International Conference on Data Mining, Sydney, NSW, Australia, 13–17 December 2010; pp. 1001–1006.
23. Tarango, J.; Keogh, E.; Brisk, P. Instruction Set Extensions for Dynamic Time Warping. In Proceedings of the 2013 International Conference on Hardware/Software Codesign and System Synthesis (CODES+ISSS), Montreal, QC, Canada, 29 September–4 October 2013; pp. 1–10.
24. Charbonnier, S.; Pitton, A.-C.; Vassilev, A. Vehicle Re-Identification with a Single Magnetic Sensor. In Proceedings of the 2012 IEEE International Instrumentation and Measurement Technology Conference Proceedings, Graz, Austria, 13–16 May 2012; pp. 380–385.
25. Sanchez, R.O.; Flores, C.; Horowitz, R.; Rajagopal, R.; Varaiya, P. Vehicle Re-Identification Using Wireless Magnetic Sensors: Algorithm Revision, Modifications and Performance Analysis. In Proceedings of the 2011 IEEE International Conference on Vehicular Electronics and Safety, Beijing, China, 10–12 July 2011; pp. 226–231.
26. Jeng, S.C.; Chu, L. Vehicle Reidentification with the Inductive Loop Signature Technology. *J. East. Asia Soc. Transp. Stud.* **2013**, *10*, 1896–1915. [CrossRef]
27. Sun, C.; Ritchie, S.G.; Tsai, K.; Jayakrishnan, R. Use of Vehicle Signature Analysis and Lexicographic Optimization for Vehicle Reidentification on Freeways. *Transp. Res. Part C Emerg. Technol.* **1999**, *7*, 167–185. [CrossRef]
28. Jeng, S.-T.; Tok, Y.C.A.; Ritchie, S.G. Freeway Corridor Performance Measurement Based on Vehicle Reidentification. *IEEE Trans. Intell. Transp. Syst.* **2010**, *11*, 639–646. [CrossRef]
29. Kwon, T.M. Blind Deconvolution of Vehicle Inductance Signatures for Travel-Time Estimation. In Proceedings of the 85th Annual Meeting of the Transportation Research Board, Washington, DC, USA, January 22–25 2006; Elsevier: Amsterdam, The Netherlands; pp. 1–12.
30. Blokpoel, R.J. Vehicle Reidentification Using Inductive Loops in Urban Areas. In Proceedings of the 16th ITS World Congress and Exhibition on Intelligent Transport Systems and Services, Stockholm, Sweden, 21–25 September 2009; pp. 1–7.
31. Kim, J.-H.; Oh, J.-H. A Land Vehicle Tracking Algorithm Using Stand-Alone GPS. *Control Eng. Pract.* **2000**, *8*, 1189–1196. [CrossRef]
32. Taylor, S.Y.; Green, J.; Richardson, A.J. *Applying Vehicle Tracking and Palmtop Technology to Urban Freight Surveys*; Transport Data Centre, Dept. of Transport NSW: New South Wales, Australia, 1998.
33. Sun, Z.; Ban, X. (Jeff) Vehicle Classification Using GPS Data. *Transp. Res. Part C Emerg. Technol.* **2013**, *37*, 102–117. [CrossRef]
34. Wang, X. Intelligent Multi-Camera Video Surveillance: A Review. *Pattern Recognit. Lett.* **2013**, *34*, 3–19. [CrossRef]
35. Sochor, J.; Spanhel, J.; Herout, A. Boxcars: Improving Fine-Grained Recognition of Vehicles Using 3-D Bounding Boxes in Traffic Surveillance. *IEEE Trans. Intell. Transp. Syst.* **2019**, *20*, 97–108. [CrossRef]
36. Zheng, L.; Shen, L.; Tian, L.; Wang, S.; Wang, J.; Tian, Q. Scalable Person Re-Identification: A Benchmark. In Proceedings of the 2015 IEEE International Conference on Computer Vision (ICCV), Santiago, Chile, 7–13 December 2015; IEEE: Piscataway, NJ, USA; pp. 1116–1124.
37. Liao, S.; Hu, Y.; Zhu, X.; Li, S.Z. Person Re-Identification by Local Maximal Occurrence Representation and Metric Learning. In Proceedings of the 2015 IEEE Conference on Computer Vision and Pattern Recognition (CVPR), Boston, MA, USA, 7–12 June 2015; IEEE: Piscataway, NJ, USA; pp. 2197–2206.
38. Szegedy, C.; Liu, W.; Jia, Y.; Sermanet, P.; Reed, S.; Anguelov, D.; Erhan, D.; Vanhoucke, V.; Rabinovich, A. Going Deeper with Convolutions. In Proceedings of the IEEE Computer Society Conference on Computer Vision and Pattern Recognition, Boston, MA, USA, June 7–12 2015; IEEE: Piscataway, NJ, USA; pp. 1–9.
39. Simonyan, K.; Zisserman, A. Very Deep Convolutional Networks for Large-Scale Image Recognition. *arXiv* **2014**, arXiv:1409.1556. [CrossRef]
40. Krizhevsky, A.; Sutskever, I.; Hinton, G.E. ImageNet Classification with Deep Convolutional Neural Networks. *Commun. ACM* **2017**, *60*, 84–90. [CrossRef]
41. He, K.; Zhang, X.; Ren, S.; Sun, J. Deep Residual Learning for Image Recognition. In Proceedings of the IEEE Conference on Computer Vision and Pattern Recognition (CVPR), Las Vegas, NV, USA, 27–30 June 2016; pp. 770–778.
42. Liu, X.; Liu, W.; Mei, T.; Ma, H. PROVID: Progressive and Multimodal Vehicle Reidentification for Large-Scale Urban Surveillance. *IEEE Trans. Multimed.* **2018**, *20*, 645–658. [CrossRef]

43. Liu, X.; Liu, W.; Ma, H.; Fu, H. Large-Scale Vehicle Re-Identification in Urban Surveillance Videos. In Proceedings of the 2016 IEEE International Conference on Multimedia and Expo (ICME), Seattle, WA, USA, 11–15 July 2016; pp. 1–6.
44. Liu, H.; Tian, Y.; Wang, Y.; Pang, L.; Huang, T. Deep Relative Distance Learning: Tell the Difference between Similar Vehicles. In Proceedings of the IEEE Conference on Computer Vision and Pattern Recognition (CVPR), Las Vegas, NV, USA, 27–30 June 2016; pp. 2167–2175.
45. Li, Y.; Li, Y.; Yan, H.; Liu, J. Deep Joint Discriminative Learning for Vehicle Re-Identification and Retrieval. In Proceedings of the 2017 IEEE International Conference on Image Processing (ICIP), Beijing, China, 17–20 September 2017; pp. 395–399.
46. Zhang, Y.; Liu, D.; Zha, Z.-J. Improving Triplet-Wise Training of Convolutional Neural Network for Vehicle Re-Identification. In Proceedings of the 2017 IEEE International Conference on Multimedia and Expo (ICME), Hong Kong, China, 10–14 July 2017; pp. 1386–1391.
47. Bay, H.; Tuytelaars, T.; Van Gool, L. Surf: Speeded up Robust Features. In *European Conference on Computer Vision*; Springer: Berlin/Heidelberg, Germany, 2006; pp. 404–417.
48. Lowe, G.D. Distinctive Image Features from Scale-Invariant Keypoints. *Int. J. Comput. Vis.* **2004**, *60*, 91–110. [CrossRef]
49. Guo, G.; Wang, H.; Bell, D.; Bi, Y.; Greer, K. KNN Model-Based Approach in Classification. In *OTM Confederated International Conferences "On the Move to Meaningful Internet Systems"*; Springer: Berlin/Heidelberg, Germany, 2003; pp. 986–996.
50. Gunn, S.R. Support Vector Machines for Classification and Regression. 1998. Available online: https://citeseerx.ist.psu.edu/viewdoc/download?doi=10.1.1.10.7171&rep=rep1&type=pdf (accessed on 10 May 1998).
51. Friedman, N.; Geiger, D.; Goldszmidt, M. Bayesian Network Classifiers. *Mach. Learn.* **1997**, *29*, 131–163. [CrossRef]
52. Quinlan, J.R. Induction of Decision Trees. *Mach. Learn.* **1986**, *1*, 81–106. [CrossRef]
53. Zapletal, D.; Herout, A. Vehicle Re-Identification for Automatic Video Traffic Surveillance. In Proceedings of the IEEE Conference on Computer Vision and Pattern Recognition Workshops (CVPRW), Las Vegas, NV, USA, 26 June–1 July 2016; pp. 1568–1574.
54. Chen, H.C.; Hsieh, J.-W.; Huang, S.-P. Real-Time Vehicle Re-Identification System Using Symmelets and HOMs. In Proceedings of the 2018 15th IEEE International Conference on Advanced Video and Signal Based Surveillance (AVSS), Auckland, New Zealand, 27–30 November 2018; pp. 1–6.
55. Cormier, M.; Sommer, L.W.; Teutsch, M. Low Resolution Vehicle Re-Identification Based on Appearance Features for Wide Area Motion Imagery. In Proceedings of the 2016 IEEE Winter Applications of Computer Vision Workshops (WACVW), Lake Placid, NY, USA, 10 March 2016; pp. 1–7.
56. Yang, L.; Jin, R. *Distance Metric Learning: A Comprehensive Survey*; Michigan State University: Michigan, MI, USA, 2006.
57. Sun, Y.; Wang, X.; Tang, X. Deep Learning Face Representation from Predicting 10,000 Classes. In Proceedings of the 2014 IEEE Conference on Computer Vision and Pattern Recognition, Columbus, OH, USA, 23–28 June 2014; pp. 1891–1898.
58. Sun, Y.; Wang, X.; Tang, X. Deep Learning Face Representation by Joint Identification-Verification. In Proceedings of the 27th International Conference on Neural Information Processing Systems (NIPS'14), Montreal, QC, Canada, 8–13 December 2014; pp. 1988–1996.
59. Zhang, L.; Xiang, T.; Gong, S. Learning a Discriminative Null Space for Person Re-Identification. In Proceedings of the 2016 IEEE Conference on Computer Vision and Pattern Recognition (CVPR), Las Vegas, NV, USA, 27–30 June 2016; pp. 1239–1248.
60. Shih, K.J.; Mallya, A.; Singh, S.; Hoiem, D. Part Localization Using Multi-Proposal Consensus for Fine-Grained Categorization. *arXiv* **2015**, arXiv:1507.06332.
61. Liu, X.; Xia, T.; Wang, J.; Yang, Y.; Zhou, F.; Lin, Y. Fully Convolutional Attention Networks for Fine-Grained Recognition. In Proceedings of the Thirty-First AAAI Conference on Artificial Intelligence (AAAI-17), San Francisco, CA, USA, 22 March 2016; pp. 4190–4196.
62. Lin, T.-Y.; RoyChowdhury, A.; Maji, S. Bilinear CNN Models for Fine-Grained Visual Recognition. In Proceedings of the IEEE International Conference on Computer Vision (ICCV), Santiago, Chile, 7–13 December 2015; pp. 1449–1457.
63. Boonsim, N.; Prakoonwit, S. Car Make and Model Recognition under Limited Lighting Conditions at Night. *Pattern Anal. Appl.* **2017**, *20*, 1195–1207. [CrossRef]
64. Zhao, H.; Tian, M.; Sun, S.; Shao, J.; Yan, J.; Yi, S.; Wang, X.; Tang, X. Spindle Net: Person Re-Identification with Human Body Region Guided Feature Decomposition and Fusion. In Proceedings of the IEEE Conference on Computer Vision and Pattern Recognition (CVPR), Honolulu, HI, USA, 21–26 July 2017; IEEE: Piscataway, NJ, USA; pp. 907–915.
65. Wu, Z.; Li, Y.; Radke, R.J. Viewpoint Invariant Human Re-Identification in Camera Networks Using Pose Priors and Subject-Discriminative Features. *IEEE Trans. Pattern Anal. Mach. Intell.* **2015**, *37*, 1095–1108. [CrossRef]
66. Zheng, L.; Huang, Y.; Lu, H.; Yang, Y. Pose-Invariant Embedding for Deep Person Re-Identification. *IEEE Trans. Image Process.* **2019**, *28*, 4500–4509. [CrossRef] [PubMed]
67. Wang, Z.; Tang, L.; Liu, X.; Yao, Z.; Yi, S.; Shao, J.; Yan, J.; Wang, S.; Li, H.; Wang, X. Orientation Invariant Feature Embedding and Spatial Temporal Regularization for Vehicle Re-Identification. In Proceedings of the IEEE International Conference on Computer Vision (ICCV), Venice, Italy, 22–29 October 2017; IEEE: Piscataway, NJ, USA; pp. 379–387.
68. Prokaj, J.; Medioni, G. 3-D Model Based Vehicle Recognition. In Proceedings of the 2009 Workshop on Applications of Computer Vision (WACV), Snowbird, UT, USA, 7–8 December 2009; pp. 1–7.
69. Zhou, Y.; Liu, L.; Shao, L. Vehicle Re-Identification by Deep Hidden Multi-View Inference. *IEEE Trans. Image Process.* **2018**, *27*, 3275–3287. [CrossRef] [PubMed]

70. Zhou, Y.; Shao, L. Vehicle Re-Identification by Adversarial Bi-Directional LSTM Network. In Proceedings of the 2018 IEEE Winter Conference on Applications of Computer Vision (WACV), Lake Tahoe, NV, USA, 12–15 March 2018; pp. 653–662.
71. Goodfellow, I.J.; Pouget-Abadie, J.; Mirza, M.; Xu, B.; Warde-Farley, D.; Ozair, S.; Courville, A.; Bengio, Y. Generative Adversarial Nets. In Proceedings of the International Conference on Neural Information Processing Systems, Montreal, Canada, 8–13 December 2014; MIT Press: Cambridge, MA, USA; pp. 2672–2680.
72. Deng, W.; Zheng, L.; Ye, Q.; Kang, G.; Yang, Y.; Jiao, J. Image-Image Domain Adaptation with Preserved Self-Similarity and Domain-Dissimilarity for Person Reidentification. In Proceedings of the IEEE Conference on Computer Vision and Pattern Recognition (CVPR), Salt Lake City, UT, USA, 18–23 June 2018; IEEE: Piscataway, NJ, USA, 2018.
73. Radford, A.; Metz, L.; Chintala, S. Unsupervised Representation Learning with Deep Convolutional Generative Adversarial Networks. *arXiv* **2015**, arXiv:1511.06434.
74. Lou, Y.; Bai, Y.; Liu, J.; Wang, S.; Duan, L.-Y. Embedding Adversarial Learning for Vehicle Re-Identification. *IEEE Trans. Image Process.* **2019**, *28*, 3794–3807. [CrossRef] [PubMed]
75. Ma, L.; Sun, Q.; Georgoulis, S.; Van Gool, L.; Schiele, B.; Fritz, M. Disentangled Person Image Generation. In Proceedings of the In Proceedings of the IEEE Conference on Computer Vision and Pattern Recognition (CVPR), Salt Lake City, UT, USA, 18–23 June 2018; IEEE: Piscataway, NJ, USA, 2018; pp. 99–108.
76. Zheng, Z.; Zheng, L.; Yang, Y. Unlabeled Samples Generated by Gan Improve the Person Re-Identification Baseline in Vitro. *arXiv Preprint* **2017**, arXiv:1701.077173.
77. Wei, L.; Zhang, S.; Gao, W.; Tian, Q. Person Transfer Gan to Bridge Domain Gap for Person Re-Identification. In Proceedings of the IEEE Conference on Computer Vision and Pattern Recognition (CVPR), Salt Lake City, UT, USA, 18–23 June 2018; IEEE: Piscataway, NJ, USA, 2018.
78. Zhou, Y.; Shao, L. Cross-View GAN Based Vehicle Generation for Re-Identification. In Proceedings of the British Machine Vision Conference, London, UK, 4–7 September 2017; BMVA Press: London, UK, 2017; pp. 1–12.
79. Zheng, A.; Lin, X.; Li, C.; He, R.; Tang, J. Attributes Guided Feature Learning for Vehicle Re-Identification. *arXiv* **2019**, arXiv:1905.08997.
80. Wang, F.; Jiang, M.; Qian, C.; Yang, S.; Li, C.; Zhang, H.; Wang, X.; Tang, X. Residual Attention Network for Image Classification. In Proceedings of the IEEE Conference on Computer Vision and Pattern Recognition (CVPR), Honolulu, HI, USA, 21–26 July 2017; IEEE: Piscataway, NJ, USA; pp. 6450–6458.
81. Fu, J.; Zheng, H.; Mei, T. Look Closer to See Better: Recurrent Attention Convolutional Neural Network for Fine-Grained Image Recognition. In Proceedings of the IEEE Conference on Computer Vision and Pattern Recognition (CVPR), Honolulu, HI, USA, 21–26 July 2017; IEEE: Piscataway, NJ, USA; pp. 4476–4484.
82. Sharma, S.; Kiros, R.; Salakhutdinov, R. Action Recognition Using Visual Attention. *arXiv* **2015**, arXiv:1511.04119.
83. Zhouy, Y.; Shao, L. Viewpoint-Aware Attentive Multi-View Inference for Vehicle Re-Identification. In Proceedings of the 2018 IEEE/CVF Conference on Computer Vision and Pattern Recognition, Salt Lake City, UT, USA, 18–23 June 2018; IEEE: Piscataway, NJ, USA; pp. 6489–6498.
84. Zhao, L.; Li, X.; Zhuang, Y.; Wang, J. Deeply-Learned Part-Aligned Representations for Person Re-Identification. In Proceedings of the 2017 IEEE International Conference on Computer Vision (ICCV), Venice, Italy, 22–29 October 2017; IEEE: Piscataway, NJ, USA; pp. 3239–3248.
85. Guo, H.; Zhu, K.; Tang, M.; Wang, J. Two-Level Attention Network with Multi-Grain Ranking Loss for Vehicle Re-Identification. *IEEE Trans. Image Process.* **2019**, *28*, 4328–4338. [CrossRef]
86. Wei, X.-S.; Zhang, C.-L.; Liu, L.; Shen, C.; Wu, J. Coarse-to-Fine: A RNN-Based Hierarchical Attention Model for Vehicle Re-Identification. In Proceedings of the 14th Asian Conference on Computer Vision, Perth, Australia, 2–6 December 2018, pp. 574–591.
87. Teng, S.; Liu, X.; Zhang, S.; Huang, Q. SCAN: Spatial and Channel Attention Network for Vehicle Re-Identification. In *Pacific Rim Conference on Multimedia*; Springer International Publishing: Cham, Switzerland, 2018; pp. 350–361.
88. Khorramshahi, P.; Kumar, A.; Peri, N.; Rambhatla, S.S.; Chen, J.-C.; Chellappa, R. A Dual-Path Model with Adaptive Attention for Vehicle Re-Identification. *arXiv* **2019**, arXiv:1905.03397.
89. Zhang, X.; Zhang, R.; Cao, J.; Gong, D.; You, M.; Shen, C. Part-Guided Attention Learning for Vehicle Re-Identification. *arXiv* **2019**, arXiv:1909.06023.
90. Qadri, M.T.; Asif, M. Automatic Number Plate Recognition System for Vehicle Identification Using Optical Character Recognition. In Proceedings of the 2009 International Conference on Education Technology and Computer, Singapore, 17–20 April 2009; pp. 335–338.
91. Li, H.; Shen, C. Reading Car License Plates Using Deep Convolutional Neural Networks and LSTMs. *arXiv* **2016**, arXiv:1601.05610.
92. Shi, B.; Bai, X.; Yao, C. An End-to-End Trainable Neural Network for Image-Based Sequence Recognition and Its Application to Scene Text Recognition. *IEEE Trans. Pattern Anal. Mach. Intell.* **2017**, *39*, 2298–2304. [CrossRef]
93. Ellis, T.; Makris, D.; Black, J.; Engineers, E. Learning a Multi-Camera Topology. In Proceedings of the Joint IEEE Workshop on Visual Surveillance and Performance Evaluation of Tracking and Surveillance (VS-PETS), Nice, France, 11–12 October 2003; pp. 165–171.

94. Wu, C.W.; Liu, C.T.; Chiang, C.E.; Tu, W.C.; Chien, S.Y. Vehicle Re-Identification with the Space-Time Prior. In Proceedings of the IEEE Computer Society Conference on Computer Vision and Pattern Recognition Workshops, Salt Lake City, UT, USA, 18–22 June 2018; IEEE: Piscataway, NJ, USA; pp. 121–128.
95. Loy, C.C.; Xiang, T.; Gong, S. Multi-Camera Activity Correlation Analysis. In Proceedings of the 2009 IEEE Conference on Computer Vision and Pattern Recognition, Miami, FL, USA, 20–25 June 2009; pp. 1988–1995.
96. Liu, X.; Liu, W.; Mei, T.; Ma, H. A Deep Learning-Based Approach to Progressive Vehicle Re-Identification for Urban Surveillance. In *European Conference on Computer Vision*; Springer: Cham, Switzerland, 2016; pp. 869–884.
97. Shen, Y.; Xiao, T.; Li, H.; Yi, S.; Wang, X. Learning Deep Neural Networks for Vehicle Re-Id with Visual-Spatio-Temporal Path Proposals. In Proceedings of the IEEE International Conference on Computer Vision (ICCV), Venice, Italy, 22–29 October 2017; pp. 1918–1927.
98. Jiang, N.; Xu, Y.; Zhou, Z.; Wu, W. Multi-Attribute Driven Vehicle Re-Identification with Spatial-Temporal Re-Ranking. In Proceedings of the 2018 25th IEEE International Conference on Image Processing (ICIP), Athens, Greece, 7–10 October 2018; pp. 858–862.
99. Jamali, Z.; Deng, J.; Cai, J.; Aftab, M.U.; Hussain, K. Minimizing Vehicle Re-Identification Dataset Bias Using Effective Data Augmentation Method. In Proceedings of the 2019 15th International Conference on Semantics, Knowledge and Grids (SKG), Guangzhou, China, 17–18 September 2019; pp. 127–130.
100. Guo, H.; Zhao, C.; Liu, Z.; Wang, J.; Lu, H. Learning Coarse-to-Fine Structured Feature Embedding for Vehicle Re-Identification. In Proceedings of the Thirty-Second AAAI Conference on Artificial Intelligence AAAI18, New Orleans, LA, USA, 2–7 February 2018; pp. 6853–6860.
101. Yang, L.; Luo, P.; Loy, C.C.; Tang, X. A Large-Scale Car Dataset for Fine-Grained Categorization and Verification. In Proceedings of the IEEE Conference on Computer Vision and Pattern Recognition (CVPR), Boston, MA, USA, 7–12 June 2015; IEEE: Piscataway, NJ, USA; pp. 3973–3981.
102. Kanacı, A.; Zhu, X.; Gong, S. Vehicle re-identification in context. In *German Conference on Pattern Recognition*; Springer: Cham, Switzerland, 2018; pp. 377–390. [CrossRef]
103. Li, X.; Yuan, M.; Jiang, Q.; Li, G. VRID-1: A Basic Vehicle Re-Identification Dataset for Similar Vehicles. In Proceedings of the 2017 IEEE 20th International Conference on Intelligent Transportation Systems (ITSC), Yokohama, Japan, 16–19 October 2017; pp. 1–8.
104. Lou, Y.; Bai, Y.; Liu, J.; Wang, S.; Duan, L.-Y. VERI-Wild: A Large Dataset and a New Method for Vehicle Re-Identification in the Wild. In Proceedings of the IEEE/CVF Conference on Computer Vision and Pattern Recognition (CVPR), Long Beach, CA, USA, 15–20 June 2019; pp. 3230–3238.
105. De Oliveira, I.O.; Fonseca, K.V.O.; Minetto, R. A Two-Stream Siamese Neural Network for Vehicle Re-Identification by Using Non-Overlapping Cameras. In Proceedings of the 2019 IEEE International Conference on Image Processing (ICIP), Taipei, Taiwan, 22–25 September 2019; pp. 669–673.
106. Cai, J.; Deng, J.; Aftab, M.; Khokhar, M.; Kumar, R. Efficient and Deep Vehicle Re-Identification Using Multi-Level Feature Extraction. *Appl. Sci.* **2019**, *9*, 1291. [CrossRef]
107. Kumar, R.; Weill, E.; Aghdasi, F.; Sriram, P. Vehicle Re-Identification: An Efficient Baseline Using Triplet Embedding. *arXiv* **2019**, arXiv:1901.01015. [CrossRef]
108. Zhu, J.; Zeng, H.; Lei, Z.; Liao, S.; Zheng, L.; Cai, C. A Shortly and Densely Connected Convolutional Neural Network for Vehicle Re-Identification. In Proceedings of the 2018 24th International Conference on Pattern Recognition (ICPR), Beijing, China, 20–24 August 2018; pp. 3285–3290.
109. Xu, D.; Lang, C.; Feng, S.; Wang, T. A Framework with a Multi-Task CNN Model Joint with a Re-Ranking Method for Vehicle Re-Identification. In Proceedings of the 10th International Conference on Internet Multimedia Computing and Service-ICIMCS'18, Nanjing, China, 17–19 August 2018; ACM Press: New York, NY, USA, 2018; pp. 1–7.
110. Frías-Velázquez, A.; Van Hese, P.; Pižurica, A.; Philips, W. Split-and-Match: A Bayesian Framework for Vehicle Re-Identification in Road Tunnels. *Eng. Appl. Artif. Intell.* **2015**, *45*, 220–233. [CrossRef]
111. Ayala-acevedo, A.; Devgun, A.; Zahir, S.; Askary, S. Vehicle Re-Identification: Pushing the Limits of Re-Identification. In Proceedings of the IEEE Conference on Computer Vision and Pattern Recognition (CVPR), Long Beach, CA, USA, 15–20 June 2019; IEEE: Piscataway, NJ, USA; 2019; pp. 291–296.
112. Liu, X.; Zhang, S.; Huang, Q.; Gao, W. RAM: A Region-Aware Deep Model for Vehicle Re-Identification. In Proceedings of the 2018 IEEE International Conference on Multimedia and Expo (ICME), San Diego, CA, USA, 23–27 July 2018; pp. 1–6.
113. Lin, X.; Zeng, H.; Hou, J.; Cao, J.; Zhu, J.; Chen, J. Joint Pyramid Feature Representation Network for Vehicle Re-Identification. *Mob. Netw. Appl.* **2020**, *25*, 1781–1792. [CrossRef]
114. Zheng, A.; Lin, X.; Dong, J.; Wang, W.; Tang, J.; Luo, B. Multi-Scale Attention Vehicle Re-Identification. *Neural Comput. Appl.* **2020**, *32*, 17489–17503. [CrossRef]
115. Qian, J.; Jiang, W.; Luo, H.; Yu, H. Stripe-Based and Attribute-Aware Network: A Two-Branch Deep Model for Vehicle Re-Identification. *Meas. Sci. Technol.* **2020**, *31*, 95401. [CrossRef]
116. Wang, H.; Sun, S.; Zhou, L.; Guo, L.; Min, X.; Li, C. Local Feature-Aware Siamese Matching Model for Vehicle Re-Identification. *Appl. Sci.* **2020**, *10*, 2474. [CrossRef]
117. Zhu, J.; Huang, J.; Zeng, H.; Ye, X.; Li, B.; Lei, Z.; Zheng, L. Object Reidentification via Joint Quadruple Decorrelation Directional Deep Networks in Smart Transportation. *IEEE Internet Things J.* **2020**, *7*, 2944–2954. [CrossRef]

118. Zhou, H.; Li, C.; Zhang, L.; Song, W. Attention-Aware Network and Multi-Loss Joint Training Method for Vehicle Re-Identification. In Proceedings of the 2020 IEEE 4th Information Technology, Networking, Electronic and Automation Control Conference (ITNEC), Chongqing, China, 12–14 June 2020; pp. 1330–1334.
119. Organisciak, D.; Sakkos, D.; Ho, E.S.L.; Aslam, N.; Shum, H.P.H. Unifying Person and Vehicle Re-Identification. *IEEE Access* **2020**, *8*, 115673–115684. [CrossRef]
120. Lee, S.; Park, E.; Yi, H.; Lee, S.H. StRDAN: Synthetic-to-Real Domain Adaptation Network for Vehicle Re-Identification. In Proceedings of the 2020 IEEE/CVF Conference on Computer Vision and Pattern Recognition Workshops (CVPRW), Virtual Conference, 14–19 June 2020; IEEE: Piscataway, NJ, USA; pp. 2590–2597.
121. Zhu, J.; Zeng, H.; Huang, J.; Liao, S.; Lei, Z.; Cai, C.; Zheng, L. Vehicle Re-Identification Using Quadruple Directional Deep Learning Features. *IEEE Trans. Intell. Transp. Syst.* **2020**, *21*, 410–420. [CrossRef]
122. Liu, X.; Zhang, S.; Wang, X.; Hong, R.; Tian, Q. Group-Group Loss-Based Global-Regional Feature Learning for Vehicle Re-Identification. *IEEE Trans. Image Process.* **2020**, *29*, 2638–2652. [CrossRef] [PubMed]
123. Wu, F.; Yan, S.; Smith, J.S.; Zhang, B. Vehicle Re-Identification in Still Images: Application of Semi-Supervised Learning and Re-Ranking. *Signal Process. Image Commun.* **2019**, 261–271. [CrossRef]
124. Alfasly, S.A.S.; Hu, Y.; Liang, T.; Jin, X.; Zhao, Q.; Liu, B. Variational Representation Learning for Vehicle Re-Identification. *arXiv* **2019**, arXiv:1905.02343v1. [CrossRef]
125. Rajamanoharan, G.; Kanacı, A.; Li, M.; Gong, S. Multi-Task Mutual Learning for Vehicle Re-Identification. In Proceedings of the The IEEE Conference on Computer Vision and Pattern Recognition (CVPR), Long Beach, CA, USA, 15–20 June 2019; IEEE: Piscataway, NJ, USA; pp. 62–70.
126. Hou, J.; Zeng, H.; Cai, L.; Zhu, J.; Chen, J.; Ma, K.-K. Multi-Label Learning with Multi-Label Smoothing Regularization for Vehicle Re-Identification. *Neurocomputing* **2019**, *345*, 15–22. [CrossRef]
127. He, B.; Li, J.; Zhao, Y.; Tian, Y. Part-Regularized near-Duplicate Vehicle Re-Identification. In Proceedings of the Proceedings of the IEEE Computer Society Conference on Computer Vision and Pattern Recognition (CVPR), Long Beach, CA, USA, 15–20 June 2019; IEEE: Piscataway, NJ, USA; pp. 3997–4005.
128. Zhong, X.; Feng, M.; Huang, W.; Wang, Z.; Satoh, S. Poses Guide Spatiotemporal Model for Vehicle Re-Identification. In *International Conference on Multimedia Modeling*; Springer International Publishing: Cham, Switzerland, 2019; pp. 427–440.
129. Zhu, J.; Zeng, H.; Du, Y.; Lei, Z.; Zheng, L.; Cai, C. Joint Feature and Similarity Deep Learning for Vehicle Re-Identification. *IEEE Access* **2018**, *6*, 43724–43731. [CrossRef]
130. Zhu, J.; Du, Y.; Hu, Y.; Zheng, L.; Cai, C. VRSDNet: Vehicle Re-Identification with a Shortly and Densely Connected Convolutional Neural Network. *Multimed. Tools Appl.* **2018**, *78*, 29043–29057. [CrossRef]
131. Sun, D.; Liu, L.; Zheng, A.; Jiang, B.; Luo, B. Visual Cognition Inspired Vehicle Re-Identification via Correlative Sparse Ranking with Multi-View Deep Features. In *International Conference on Brain Inspired Cognitive Systems*; Springer International Publishing: Cham, Switzerland, 2018; pp. 54–63.
132. Tang, Y.; Wu, D.; Jin, Z.; Zou, W.; Li, X. Multi-Modal Metric Learning for Vehicle Re-Identification in Traffic Surveillance Environment. In Proceedings of the IEEE International Conference on Image Processing (ICIP), Beijing, China, 17–20 September 2017; pp. 2254–2258.
133. Sabour, S.; Frosst, N.; Hinton, G.E. Dynamic Routing between Capsules. In Proceedings of the Proceedings of the 31st International Conference on Neural Information Processing Systems, Long Beach, CA, USA, 26 October 2017; pp. 3859–3869.
134. Bahdanau, D.; Cho, K.; Bengio, Y. Neural Machine Translation by Jointly Learning to Align and Translate. *arXiv* **2014**, arXiv:1409.0473.
135. Xu, K.; Ba, J.; Kiros, R.; Cho, K.; Courville, A.; Salakhutdinov, R.; Zemel, R.; Bengio, Y. Show, Attend and Tell: Neural Image Caption Generation with Visual Attention. In Proceedings of the 32nd International Conference on Machine Learning, Lille, France, 10 February 2015; pp. 2048–2057.
136. Ba, J.; Mnih, V.; Kavukcuoglu, K. Multiple Object Recognition with Visual Attention. *arXiv* **2014**, arXiv:1412.7755.

mathematics

Article

Cascaded Cross-Layer Fusion Network for Pedestrian Detection

Zhifeng Ding [1], Zichen Gu [2,*], Yanpeng Sun [1] and Xinguang Xiang [1]

1 School of Computer Science and Engineering, Nanjing University of Science and Technology, Nanjing 210023, China; dingzhifeng@njust.edu.cn (Z.D.); yanpeng_sun@njust.edu.cn (Y.S.); xgxiang@njust.edu.cn (X.X.)
2 INMAI Railway Technology Co., Ltd., Beijing 100015, China
* Correspondence: guzichen2018@rails.cn

Abstract: The detection method based on anchor-free not only reduces the training cost of object detection, but also avoids the imbalance problem caused by an excessive number of anchors. However, these methods only pay attention to the impact of the detection head on the detection performance, thus ignoring the impact of feature fusion on the detection performance. In this article, we take pedestrian detection as an example and propose a one-stage network Cascaded Cross-layer Fusion Network (CCFNet) based on anchor-free. It consists of Cascaded Cross-layer Fusion module (CCF) and novel detection head. Among them, CCF fully considers the distribution of high-level information and low-level information of feature maps under different stages in the network. First, the deep network is used to remove a large amount of noise in the shallow features, and finally, the high-level features are reused to obtain a more complete feature representation. Secondly, for the pedestrian detection task, a novel detection head is designed, which uses the global smooth map (GSMap) to provide global information for the center map to obtain a more accurate center map. Finally, we verified the feasibility of CCFNet on the Caltech and CityPersons datasets.

Keywords: pedestrian detection; machine learning; end-to-end; anchor-free; feature reuse

Citation: Ding, Z.; Gu, Z.; Sun, Y.; Xiang, X. Cascaded Cross-Layer Fusion Network for Pedestrian Detection. *Mathematics* **2022**, *10*, 139. https://doi.org/10.3390/math10010139

Academic Editors: Radu Tudor Ionescu, Jianping Gou, Weihua Ou, Shaoning Zeng and Lan Du

Received: 25 November 2021
Accepted: 22 December 2021
Published: 4 January 2022

1. Introduction

Pedestrian detection is a crucial but challenging task in computer vision and multimedia, which has been applied in various fields. The goal of pedestrian detection is to find all pedestrians in images and videos. Early detection methods [1–6] show that directly using the features of the backbone output is not conducive to the detection of small objects in the image. Recent detection methods show that obtaining high-resolution and high-quality feature representations is the key to improving detection results. As we all know, the low-level features of the backbone contain accurate small object information, while the high-level features contain accurate large object information. Therefore, how to more effectively integrate the characteristics of different stages has been the focus of research on pedestrian detection in recent years.

According to the feature detection method, we divide the feature fusion methods into FPN-like (Like Feature Pyramid Networks) methods and FCN-like (Like Fully Convolutional Networks) methods. The specific difference is that the FPN-like methods detects features of different scales separately, while the FCN-like methods only detects final feature after the fusion of features of different scales. The basic idea of the FPN-like methods is proposed by Single Shot MultiBox Detector (SSD) [2], and its main process is to detect objects in feature maps at different resolutions. However, SSD ignores the spatial information in the shallow feature map, and thus loses the information of small objects in the shallow feature. To improve the recognition performance of small objects, Feature Pyramid Networks (FPN) [7] combines high-level feature maps with strong semantic information and low-level feature maps with weak semantic information but rich spatial information. Some recent works have proposed some FPN-like methods [8–14]. In order to more effectively integrate features of different scales. However, these methods mainly focus on the features of adjacent stages in the feature fusion process, and the deep features containing rich semantic information gradually weaken during the top-down process. Therefore, high-level semantic information is lost when detecting shallow features, so that small objects in the image can not be effectively detected.

To avoid the shortcomings of FPN-like methods, some methods directly fuse features of different scales, and then only need to detect the fused features. The origin of this type of method comes from Fully Convolutional Networks (FCN) [15], which combines the features of different stages to obtain feature maps containing semantic information of different scales. In this paper, structures similar to FCN are collectively referred to as the FCN-like methods [15–24]. Compared with FPN-like methods, FCN-like methods have lower computational complexity and faster computational speed, while avoiding the situation that small objects can not be detected due to loss of high-level semantic information. These methods have the same weights for feature fusion at different scales in the feature integration process. In this case, the noise in the shallow features will directly affect the accuracy of the final feature. Previous work Semantic Structure Aware Inference (SSA) [25] proved that the information of small objects is not only in the shallow features, but there is also a small amount of small object information in the deep features. However, the noise information in the shallow network is huge, so how to reduce the impact of the noise information in the shallow features on the detection accuracy is a problem that has not been solved by the current FCN-like methods.

Toward this end, this work takes pedestrian detection as an example and proposes a novel Cascaded Cross-layer Fusion Network (CCFNet), which consists of backbone network, Cascaded Cross-layer Fusion module (CCF), and novel detection head. The basic process framework is shown in Figure 1. First, the CCF merges the features in different stages in the backbone to obtain the final feature map and then performs detection on the feature map. Different from the previous method, CCF uses deep features to denoise shallow features and then reuses deep features to increase the semantic information in the final feature map. To improve the running speed of the algorithm, CCFNet adopts the anchor-free method, based on the detection of pedestrian center points, does not generate anchor points and anchor boxes, and does not match multiple key points. In the detection head, we introduced the center map and global smooth map (GSMap) of the object respectively to reduce the impact of complex scenes and object crowding on the detection performance. Traditional anchor-free detection head only rely on scale map to solve the problem of *'where'* and *'how size'* the object is. This approach increases the difficulty of training the detector. Therefore, we first introduce the center map to undertake the task of *'where the object is'*, while the scale map only needs to undertake the task of *'how size the object is'*. The center map is obtained by convolution, so the center map is obtained by local feature inference. The finiteness of local features limits the accuracy of the center map, so we introduce global smooth map to provide global information for the center map. The specific process is shown in the detection head in Figure 1. Extensive experimental are conducted on the Caltech and CityPersons datasets. The superior performance of CFFNet for pedestrian detection is demonstrated in comparison with the state-of-the-art methods.

The main contributions of this work are summarized as follows:

(1) We propose a novel Cascaded Cross-layer Fusion module (CCF) to reduce the noise information in the shallow features through high-level semantic information, and at the same time reuse high-level semantic information to strengthen the high-level semantic information in the final feature map;
(2) The center map provides the confidence of each object center point, but the confidence is obtained from local information. Therefore, this paper proposes global smooth map to provide the center map with global information, thereby improving the accuracy of the center map;
(3) The feasibility of CCFNet is verified on the Caltech and CityPersons Datasets.

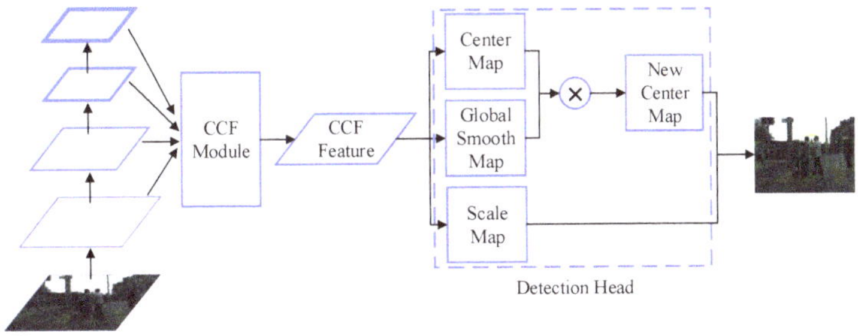

Figure 1. The overall structure of Cascaded Cross-layer Fusion Network (CCFNet). It includes two parts: CCF module and detection head. CCF cascades and reuses features to generate low-level feature maps with contextual semantic information. This feature map generates center map, scale map, and global smooth map through the detection head. And generate the new center map with global information by integrating center map and global smooth map. Finally, locate and mark the objects.

2. Related Work

2.1. Anchor-Base and Anchor-Free

The object detection model can be divided into anchor-based detection network and anchor-free detection network. The anchor-based detection network uses anchor points and anchor boxes to generate high-quality prediction regions, then classifies and regresses the prediction regions, which have high accuracy and can extract richer features. Such as Faster Regions with CNN Features (Faster R-CNN) [1], Cascade Regions with CNN Features (Cascade R-CNN) [26], SSD [2], You Only Look Once Version 2 (YOLOv2) [27], etc. However, anchor-base detection network requires manual intervention due to the number of anchor points and the large aspect ratio of the anchor box, which has disadvantages such as too many parameters and insufficient flexibility.

Therefore, people study methods that do not rely on anchor points and anchor boxes, this method is called the anchor-free detection network. The anchor-free detection network are divided into two types: anchor-free detection network based on key points and anchor-free detection network based on object center. The former generate an object bounding box through a set of predefined or self-learned key points (usually a set of corner points of the bounding box) to locate the object, such as CornerNet-Lite [28] and ExtremeNet [29], etc. The latter locates the object by calculating the distance from the object center to the four sides of the bounding box, such as Center and Scale Prediction (CSP) [23], CenterNet [30], etc. The anchor-free detection network based on object center is similar to the anchor-base detection network, but there is not need to generate a large number of anchor points to predict the bounding box, which improves the detection speed of the algorithm. Recently, Zhang et al. [31] proposed that the definition of positive and negative samples of the dataset is the fundamental difference between their performance. Therefore, CCFNet is also built with an anchor-free structure and has reached or even exceeded the accuracy anchor-base detection network.

2.2. FPN-like Methods

The main idea of FPN [7] is to build a top-down feature pyramid to fuse feature maps at different stages of the backbone, and to detect objects of different sizes on feature maps of different scales. This idea is used in different models, You Only Look Once Version 3 (YOLOv3) [8] obtains multi-scale information through multiple convolutions and repeated fusion of the features of the last three stages of the backbone. Adaptively Spatial Feature Fusion (ASFF) [9] adds attention structure based on YOLOv3, which realizes the selective use of the feature information of different stages by controlling the contribution degree of the features of other stages to the current feature. Bi-Directional Feature Pyramid Network (BiFPN) [11] realize adaptive control of the size of FPN by overlapping effective blocks in FPN multiple times. Recursive Feature Pyramid Network (Recursive-FPN) [12] uses recursive FPN to re-input the mixed multi-scale feature map to the backbone, extract the features again, and finally achieve extremely competitive performance. Multi-level Feature Pyramid Network (MLFPN) [13] proposes three modules, Feature Fusion Module (FFM1), Thinned U-shape Module (TUM), and Scale-wise Feature Aggregation Module (SFAM), to integrate semantic information and detailed information by overlapping feature maps multiple times. However, FPN-like methods not only need to fuse feature maps multiple times but also need to build detection head on feature maps of different output sizes to deal with objects of different sizes. Therefore, FPN-like has shortcomings such as a complex model and slow calculation speed.

2.3. FCN-like Methods

With the attention of anchor-free detection networks, the idea of FCN-like gradually shifted from the segmentation task to the object detection task. Different from the FPN-like methods, the FCN-like methods only outputs a feature map that integrates feature information of different scales to the detection head. FCN [15] uses deconvolution layer to upsample the feature map of the last stage of the backbone to restore it to the same size of the input image, thereby preserving the spatial information in the input image to classify each pixel in the feature map. In contrast, the reference [24] adopts a completely symmetrical structure, uses deconvolution to restore the image size, splices and fuses feature information of different scales according to the dimension of the feature map. However, its parameters are few and it is not suitable for large-scale detection or segmentation tasks. CornerNet [21] and CSP [23] use FCN to generate feature maps adapted to the detection head. FCN-like methods have fast calculation speed, but the feature information contained in feature maps of different scales is different. If two feature layers with a large semantic information gap are mixed through dimensionality reduction, a large amount of feature information will be lost, and small objects in the image will be lost.

The difference from the above is that CCF combines the advantages of FPN-like methods and FCN-like methods, and retains more low-level detailed information and high-level semantic information through feature reorganization. In addition, CCFNet also proposes global smooth map that enhances the global perception of the center map to deal with the problem of object occlusion.

3. Methods

This section will elaborate on the proposed Cascaded Cross-layer Fusion Network (CCFNet) for pedestrian detection by exploring the feature fusion and global dependencies.

3.1. Detection Network

The object detection network is usually divided into backbone network, neck, and detection head. The backbone network is responsible for extracting features from the image. A high-quality feature will significantly improve the ability of object localization. The neck is the hub connecting the backbone and detection head. It integrates the features obtained by the backbone network and then inputs the integrated features into the detection head. A high-quality neck can more fully integrate the high-level and low-level information of the image to improve the representation ability of the model. The detection head is responsible for classification and regression.

Most backbone networks [32–36] can be divided into five stages. With the deepening of the network stage, the resolution of the feature map is reduced at a rate of 2 times. In other words, the size of the feature map obtained in the last stage is 1/32 of the input image, which is not friendly to the small object. Previous work [37,38] proposed that the size of the feature map generated in the fifth stage of backbone should be kept at 1/16 of the input image, which can improve the detailed information in the deep feature map to increase the ability to detect small objects.

The input image $I \in R^{3\times H\times W}$ passes through each stage of the backbone network to obtain a set of feature maps $F = \{F_1, F_2, F_3, F_4, F_5\}$. The low-level feature maps generated in the previous stage have more detailed information, but it has a lot of noise. The high-level feature maps generated in later stages have more semantic information. The neck [13,19,39] will reprocesses the feature map set F of the backbone network to obtain feature map f_{det} suitable for the detection head. The detection head [1,40,41] is used to classify and locate the object on the feature map f_{det} output by the neck. In anchor-free detection network, the detection head is defined as $F_{det} = \{cls(f_{det}), regr(f_{det})\}$, $cls(\cdot)$ represents the classification branch that classifies the object by key points, $regr(\cdot)$ represents the regression branch that locates the object by scale.

3.2. Cascaded Cross-Layer Fusion Module

We combine the advantages of the FPN-like methods and the FCN-like methods, propose Cascaded Cross-layer Fusion module (CCF) to more effectively extract the feature information of the object. CCF uses deconvolution to change the scale of the deep feature map to fuse with the shallow feature map. CCF transfers the deep features to the shallow features in a top-down method, enriching the shallow features while removing noise. However, in this transfer process, the semantic information contained in the deep feature map will continue to be lost. Therefore, CCF supplements missing semantic information by reusing deep feature maps. In this way, the final feature map can not only retain the detailed information in the shallow feature map, but also have the semantic information in the deep feature map. Following [23,37], the final feature map size of CCF is $[H/4, W/4]$. It is worth noting that this is the same size as the feature map of the second stage. The specific implementation process is as follows:

As shown in Figure 2, CCF uses F_4 and F_5 as the source to deliver deep semantic information and denoise the shallow feature maps, because the feature maps generated in the fourth and fifth stages of the backbone network contain rich semantic information. In addition, to reduce the computational complexity of the network, the dimensions of F_4 and F_5 are reduced by 1×1 convolution to generate F_{c4} and F_{c5}. Finally, F_{c4} and F_{c5} are fused to obtain the feature map F_{s4}. F_{s4} retains the semantic information of F_4 and F_5 and continues to be used for subsequent transmission of semantic information. The fusion generation method of feature map F_{s4} can be expressed as:

$$\mathcal{F}_{s4} = Sum(F_{c4}, F_{c5}) \tag{1}$$

where $Sum(\cdot)$ indicates that the fusion method of F_{c4} and F_{c5} is the element-wise addition between the feature maps F_{c4} and F_{c5}.

The feature map F_{s4} will serve two purposes: (1) Regarding F_{s4} as a new source, it will fuse with the new receiver F_3 and continue to convey semantic information from the deep features map. Only the output features of the last two stages in the backbone have the same size. Therefore, it is necessary to perform deconvolution before fusing the shallow features to make it the same size as the previous layer. Therefore, the new source F_{s4} performs up-sampling through deconvolution to obtain a feature map F_{sd4} of the same size as F_{c3}. The process is as follows:

$$\mathcal{F}_{sd4} = DC(F_{s4}) \tag{2}$$

where $DC(\cdot)$ means 4×4 deconvolution. F_{sd4} will be used as the new source, and F_{c3} after dimensionality reduction of feature map F_3 will be fused to obtain F_{s3} according to Equation (1). F_{s3} will be used to transfer the semantic information and detailed information contained in the feature maps F_3, F_4 and F_5. (2) As mentioned before, in purpose (1), the semantic information of the deep feature map will continue to be lost, so the feature map F_{sd4} needs to be transformed into a feature map F_{d4} of size $[H/4, W/4]$ for feature reuse (Equation (2)). F_{d4} can retain the feature representation in the deep feature map.

To continue to transmit the semantic information from the deep feature map and retain the detailed information in F_3, the feature map F_{s3} is transformed to the same size as F_2 through deconvolution, and the resulting F_{sd3} will be used for subsequent operations (Equation (2)).

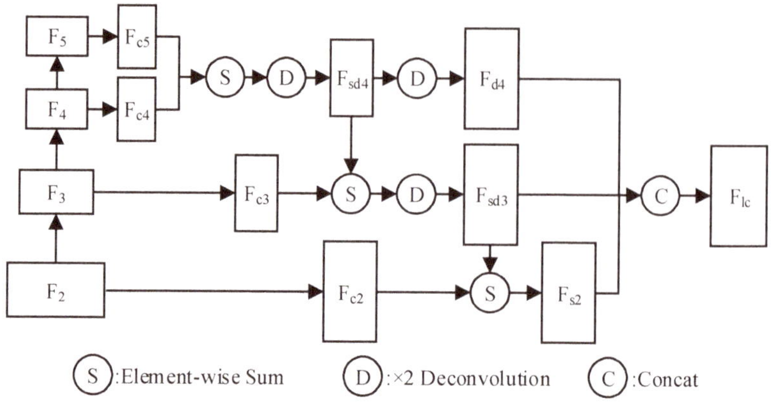

Figure 2. Cascaded Cross-layer Fusion Module (CCF).

The feature map F_3 only contains part of the detailed information, which is not enough to support the network to detect small objects, as shown in the ablation study (Section 4.3). Therefore, CCF refers to the feature map F_2 generated in the second stage, so that the final feature map input to the detection head has more detailed information. However, F_2 contains a lot of noise. CCF uses F_{sd3} containing depth semantics to denoise F_2. In other words, the feature map F_{c2} is obtained by reducing the dimension of F_2 through 1×1 convolution. F_{c2} and F_{sd3} are calculated by Equation (1) to get the feature map F_{s2}. It is worth noting that the size of F_{s2} is $[H/4, W/4]$. There is no need to perform additional processing on F_{s2}.

Finally, CCF merge all feature maps through $Concat(\cdot)$ to obtain a final feature map F_{lc} with rich detailed information and semantic information, F_{lc} can be expressed as:

$$\mathcal{F}_{lc} = Concat(F_{d4}, F_{sd3}, F_{s2}) \tag{3}$$

Following [7], CCF use 3×3 convolution after F_{lc} to reduce the aliasing effect produced in the process of deconvolution and feature fusion.

3.3. Detection Head

Our detection head contains center map, scale map, and global smooth map. Following CSP [23], the center map is equipped with gaussian heat map to locate the object, and scale map is used to determine the size of the object. Although the Gaussian heat map can reduce the weight of negative samples around the object center point, the center map only obtains local perception and lacks global perception. To this end, we add global smooth map, which is fused with the center map, and the generated new center map will have global perception. In addition, considering that the aspect ratio of the pedestrian will change with the change of the pedestrian state, we discarded the scale map that predicts the size of the pedestrian by only predicting the height and fixing the width. The scale map was modified to predict the height and width of pedestrians at the same time.

As shown in Figure 3, the detection head includes center map, global smooth map and scale map. They are all obtained by the feature map F_{lc} generated by CCF through different 1×1 convolutions. Then we use the global smooth map to modify the center map to obtain a more accurate new center map. Finally, the new center map and scale map are used to generate detection results. Optionally, the offset map can be added to the detection head to correct the position of the object.

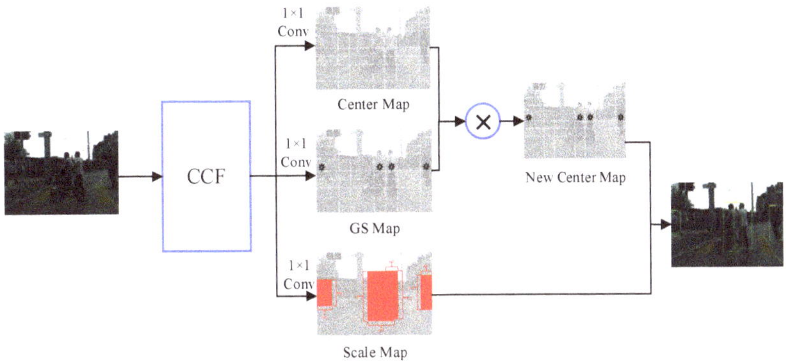

Figure 3. The overall architecture of the detection head mainly includes three map components, namely the center map, the scale map and the global smooth map (GSMap).

3.4. Loss Function

3.4.1. Center Loss

Combined with the global smooth map, the center loss is modified as follows:

$$\mathcal{L}_{center} = -\frac{1}{K}\sum_{i=1}^{W/4}\sum_{j=1}^{H/4}(s_{ij}f_{ij} + (1-s_{ij})b_{ij})log(1-p_{ij}) \quad (4)$$

where

$$\begin{cases} f_{ij} = gs_{ij}(1-p_{ij})^{\gamma} \\ b_{ij} = p_{ij}^{\gamma}(1-M_{ij})^{\beta} \end{cases} \quad (5)$$

from Equations (4) and (5), K is the total number of objects, W and H are the width and height of the input image respectively, s_{ij} represents the true label on the coordinates (i,j), p_{ij} represents the probability of the positive on the coordinates (i,j), gs_{ij} is global smooth confidence, M_{ij} is Gaussian heat map [23], f_{ij} and b_{ij} represent the foreground and background scores in the image, respectively.

3.4.2. Scale Loss

Calculate the scale map by SmoothL1 loss [42] to predict the error between the height and width of the object according to the ground truth. The details of scale loss as follows:

$$\mathcal{L}_{scale} = -\frac{1}{K}(\sum_{k=1}^{K} SmoothL1(h_k, \hat{h}_k) + \sum_{k=1}^{K} SmoothL1(w_k, \hat{w}_k)) \quad (6)$$

where h_k and $\hat{h}_k$ respectively represent the height of the prediction boxes of the network and the height of the ground truth of each positive, w_k and $\hat{w}_k$ respectively represent the width of the prediction boxes of the network and the width of the ground truth of each positive.

3.4.3. Total Loss

Optionally, if the offset map is added to correct the object position, the offset loss is:

$$\mathcal{L}_{offset} = -\frac{1}{K}(\sum_{k=1}^{K} SmoothL1(o_k, \hat{o}_k)) \quad (7)$$

where o_k represents the predicted offset of each positive and $\hat{o}_k$ represents the ground truth of each positive.

Therefore, the complete loss function is:

$$\mathcal{L} = \lambda_c L_{center} + \lambda_s L_{scale} + \lambda_o L_{offset} \quad (8)$$

where λ_c, λ_s, and λ_o are the weights of center loss, scale loss and offset loss, which is set to 0.01, 1 and 0.1 in this experiments. Although on the surface, our loss function is similar to the loss of many methods, from the details we can know that this is different.

4. Experimental Results

To evaluate the proposed CCFNet, we conducted comparative experiments on Caltech [43,44] and CityPersons [45]. In this section, we introduce the datasets and experimental setting, then verify the effectiveness of the model by the ablation study on the CityPersons dataset, and finally show the compare experimental results with state-of-the-art methods and visualize to verify the superiority of the CCFNet.

The details of each section are as follows: The Section 4.1 introduces the datasets and evaluation indicators of pedestrian detection. The Section 4.2 introduces the experimental setting. The ablation studies on the CityPersons dataset will be analyzed in the Section 4.3. In Section 4.4, the superiority and effectiveness of the model is verified by comparison with other methods on the Caltech and CityPersons datasets. In Section 4.5, visualize the detection results to further illustrate the superiority of CCFNet. Finally, in Section 4.6, we discuss all the experimental results.

4.1. Datasets

The Caltech dataset is about 10 hours of video data, divided into 11 subsets, of which 6 subsets are training sets and 5 subsets are test sets. We divided the video into RGB frames, the training set extracts one image for every 3 frames (total of 42,782 images) and the test set extracts one image for every 30 frames (total of 4024 images). It is observed in Figure 4a,b: the training set contains 5564 pedestrians and 4992 ignored regions, the test set contains 7596 pedestrians and 0 ignored regions.

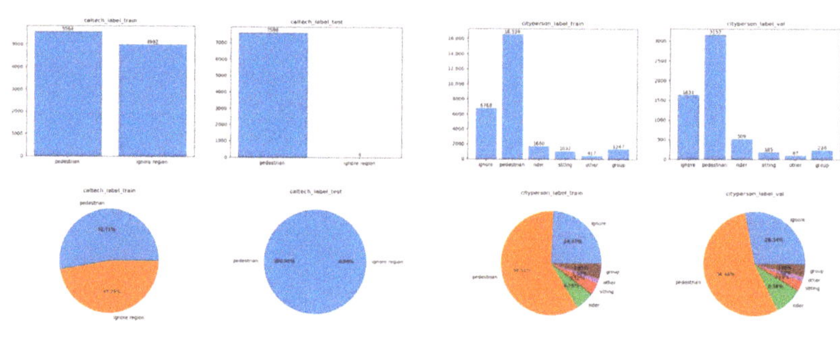

(a) Caltech_Train **(b)** Caltech_Val **(c)** Cityperson_Train **(d)** Cityperson_Val

Figure 4. The histogram and pie chart represent the distribution statistics of each category in the Caltech and CityPersons datasets. (**a**) represents the label distribution of the training set in the Caltech dataset. (**b**) represents the label distribution of the test set in the Caltech dataset. (**c**) represents the label distribution of the training set in the CityPersons dataset. (**d**) represents the label distribution of the validation set in the CityPersons dataset.

The CityPersons dataset is a subset of the Cityscapes dataset, it has a training set of 2975 images and a validation set of 500 images. From Figure 4c,d, we can clearly known that objects with 59.51% in the training set are marked as pedestrian labels. Objects with 24.37% are marked as ignore labels, including object height pixels less than 20, unclear object status, billboards, etc. Objects with 6.05% are marked as rider labels, Objects with 3.72% are marked as sitting labels. Objects with 1.50% are marked as other labels, including being held of the people. Objects with 4.85% belong to the group. It is worth noting that during the evaluation process, prediction boxes that match rider, sitting, other, ignored areas, etc. It will not be included in the error sample. The label distribution of the validation set is similar to the training set.

Following [44], we using Log-Average Miss Rate (MR^{-2}) as an evaluation indicator. It evaluates the False Positive Per Image (FPPI) of each image between $[0.01, 1]$. The Caltech dataset is evaluated on the Reasonable and Reasonable_Occ=Heavy subsets. The CityPersons dataset is evaluated on the Reasonable, Bare, Partial and Heavy subsets. The definition rules of subsets are shown in Table 1, where inf means infinity.

Table 1. Standards for dividing subsets of the pedestrian datasets.

Subsets	Height	Visibility
Reasonable	$[50, inf]$	$[0.65, inf]$
Bare	$[50, inf]$	$[0.90, inf]$
Partial	$[50, inf]$	$[0.65, 0.90]$
Heavy	$[50, inf]$	$[0, 0.65]$
Reasonable_Occ=Heavy	$[50, inf]$	$[0.2, 0.65]$

4.2. Experimental Setting

Unless otherwise specified, The construction of CCFNet follows mmdetection [46] and pedestron [47]. The experiment in this paper is run on a TITAN RTX. On the Caltech dataset, the batch size is set to 16, the initial learning rate is 2×10^{-4}, and the iteration is 20 epoch. On the CityPersons dataset, the batch size is set to 4, the initial learning rate is 2×10^{-4}, and the iteration is 150 epoch. Our experimental setup is based on [48,49].

4.3. Ablation Study

For CCF. To study the effective combination methods of the feature maps, we test the impact of different fusion strategies on model performance. CCF starts with the features of the second stage and keeps the final feature map size as $[H/4, W/4]$, which is consistent with the feature map size of the second stage. As shown in Table 2, s_n represents the feature map generated at the n-th stage of the backbone. It can be easily observed that the last model combines feature maps $\{s_2, s_3, s_4, s_5\}$ obtains the best performance. When s_2 is removed, that is, the combination way $\{s_3, s_4, s_5\}$ gets a poor result, which indicates that the lack of detailed information makes it impossible to accurately locate the object. When s_5 is removed, that is, the combination way $\{s_2, s_3, s_4\}$ also obtains a bad result, which shows that the semantics information contained in the deep features information is crucial. In summary, $\{s_2, s_3, s_4, s_5\}$ is the most suitable combination methods.

Table 2. Ablation study analysis of different combinations of multi-scale feature on the Citypersons dataset.

Feature Maps				Backbone	Reasonable	Bare	Partial	Heavy
s_2	s_3	s_4	s_5					
✓	✓	-	-	ResNet-50	29.4	22.8	26.9	67.0
-	✓	✓	-	ResNet-50	16.6	12.3	15.4	55.2
-	-	✓	✓	ResNet-50	15.5	10.3	15.4	56.3
✓	✓	✓	-	ResNet-50	16.3	12.4	15.3	54.4
-	✓	✓	✓	ResNet-50	15.4	10.8	14.6	53.7
✓	✓	✓	✓	ResNet-50	10.6	7.1	10.1	48.4

To verify the effectiveness of CCF, we use different neck to connect the backbone network ResNet-50 and the detection head [23], such as FPN [7], Augmented FPN (AugFPN) [50], Attention-guided Context Feature Pyramid Network (ACFPN) [51] and CSP [23]. As shown in the table 3, we can observe that compared with necks of other models, CCF has strong competitiveness in Reasonable, Bare and Partial subsets. In the Heavy subset, CCF is also better than part of the necks. Compared with FPN, CCF reuses the semantic information of deep feature maps to obtain more contextual information in the final feature map. In addition, CCF does not need to output multi-scale feature maps to detect objects. Compared with CSP, CCF removes the noise in the shallow feature map, and retains more detailed information by cascading.

Table 3. Ablation study of different neck module on the Citypersons dataset.

	Reasonable	Bare	Partial	Heavy
ResNet-50 + FPN	11.9	8.1	11.6	48.6
ResNet-50 + AugFPN	11.9	8.5	11.7	50.2
ResNet-50 + ACFPN	11.8	8.2	11.2	50.7
ResNet-50 + CSP	11.2	7.7	10.6	45.7
ResNet-50 + CCF	10.6	7.1	10.1	48.4

For GSMap. Table 4 shows the ablation study on GSMap. The Baseline contains neck and detection head. The neck contains the deconvolution of the fifth stage of ResNet-50 and the detection head contains center map and scale map. Baseline + GSMap means adding GSMap to the detection head. Baseline + GSMap means replacing the neck in the baseline with CCF. Baseline + CCF + GSMap uses CCF to replace the neck in the baseline and adds GSMap to the detection head. As shown in Table 4, we can be observed that adding GSMap separately based on the baseline increases the Reasonable subset by 0.7%, the Bare subset by 0.3%, the Partial subset by 0.8%, and the Heavy subset by 3.7%. If CCF and GSMap work at the same time, compared with baseline + CCF, each subset increases by 0.4%, 0.3%, 0.6% and 5.7%, respectively. This result shows that GSMap enhances the locating ability by making the center map have global feature information. Its performance is enhanced as the effective feature information increases.

Table 4. Ablation study of global smooth map on the Citypersons dataset.

	Backbone	Reasonable	Bare	Partial	Heavy
Baseline	ResNet-50	11.2	7.3	10.8	50.3
Baseline + GSMap	ResNet-50	10.5	7.0	10.0	46.6
Baseline + CCF	ResNet-50	10.6	7.1	10.1	48.4
Baseline + CCF + GSMap	ResNet-50	10.2	6.8	9.5	42.7

For Scale Prediction. Table 5 shows the impact of scale prediction on CCFNet. Following previous work [23], we set the three scale predictions of height, width and height + width. Compared with the predicted height, height + width increases by 0.6% on the reasonable subset and 4.5% on the heavy subset. Compared with the predicted width, height + width increases by 1.2% on the reasonable subset and 7.2% on the heavy subset. Simultaneously predicting the height and width of the object can further improve the performance of CCFNet. This result is attributed to predicting the height and width of the object at the same time, which can adapt to objects with different aspect ratios, rather than being limited to a certain aspect ratio. In addition, retaining more feature information is conducive to the prediction of object width. From the results of the heavy subsets, it can be concluded that predicting the height and width at the same time helps to deal with dense and overlapping objects.

Table 5. Ablation study of different definitions for scale prediction on the Citypersons dataset.

Scale Prediction	Backbone	Reasonable	Bare	Partial	Heavy
Height	ResNet-50	10.8	7.2	10.7	47.2
Width	ResNet-50	11.4	8.1	11.0	49.9
Height + Width	ResNet-50	10.2	6.8	9.5	42.7

4.4. State-of-the-Art Comparisons

Caltech Dataset: CCFNet compares some excellent methods in reasonable and Reasonable_Occ=Heavy subset. As shown in the Figure 5, CCFNet has 4.33% MR-FPPI on the Reasonable subset, which is 0.37% more advanced than the best method. On the Reasonable_Occ=Heavy subset, CCFNet has 43.21% MR-FPPI, which is also competitive. When the model is initialized on the CityPersons dataset, the performance of CCFNet has increased by 6.04%, surpassing other comparison methods. CCFNet uses feature cascading and reorganization to retain more contextual information, and improves the positioning ability of the center map through global smoothing graph.

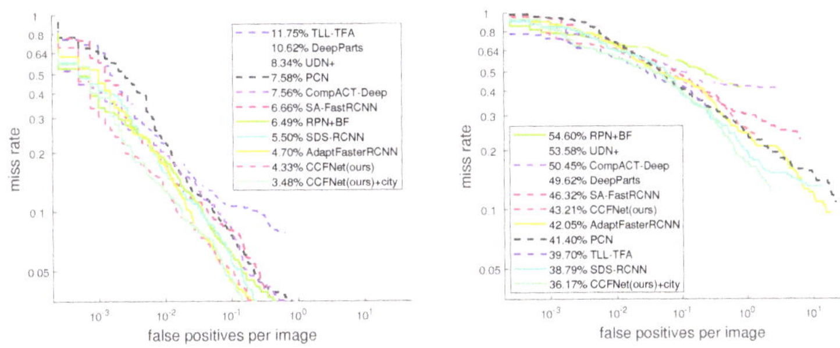

(**a**) Reasonable (**b**) Reasonable_Occ=Heavy

Figure 5. The results of various models on the Caltech dataset. (**a**) Compare with existing methods on Reasonable subset. (**b**) Compare with existing methods on the Reasonable_Occ=Heavy subset.

As shown in the Table 6, CCFNet also compares advanced algorithms, such as Repulsion Loss (RepLoss) [38] used to solve the occlusion problem and anchor-free detection network CSP, etc. In the reasonable subset, CCFNet achieved 4.3% MR-FPPI, which is 0.7% and 0.2% lower than that of RepLoss and CSP, respectively. In the Reasonable_Occ=Heavy subset, CCF has reached 43.2% MR-FPPI, which is an increase of 4.7% and 2.6% compared to RepLoss and CSP, respectively. This is an impressive improvement. When the model is initialized on the CityPersons dataset, CCFNet reaches 3.5% on a reasonable subset, and 36.2% on the Reasonable_Occ=Heavy subset. It is proved that CCFNet reuses high-level features in cascaded manner is effective.

Table 6. The results of various models on the Caltech dataset.

	Reasonable	**Reasonable_Occ=Heavy**
ALFNet [52]	6.1	51.0
MGAN [53]	6.8	38.2
HyperLearner [54]	5.5	48.7
RepLoss [38]	5.0	47.9
CSP [23]	4.5	45.8
CCFNet (ours)	4.3	43.2
ALFNet + city [23,52]	4.5	43.4
RepLoss + city [23,38]	4.0	41.8
CSP + city [23]	3.8	36.5
CCFNet + city (ours)	3.5	36.2

CityPersons Dataset: We verify the performance of CCFNet on CityPersons dataset, which contained reasonable, heavy, bare and partial subsets. The comparative experiment results as show in Table 7. MR^{-2} of CCFNet on the reasonable subset is 10.2%, on the bare subset is 6.8%, on the partial subset is 9.5%, and on the heavy subset is 42.7%. In the reasonable subset, CCFNet is 0.4% and 0.3% lower than Attribute-aware Pedestrian Detection (APD) [55] and Mask-Guided Attention Network (MGAN) [53], respectively.

In the heavy subset, CCFNet is increased by 7.1% and 4.5% compared with APD and MGAN, respectively. It can be seen that CCFNet achieved best performance beyond other comparison methods. It reflects the strong competitiveness of CCFNet.

Table 7. The results of various models on the CityPersons dataset.

	Backbone	Reasonable	Bare	Partial	Heavy
TLL [37]	ResNet-50	15.5	10.0	17.2	53.6
TLL + MRF [37]	ResNet-50	14.4	9.2	15.9	52.0
RepLoss [38]	ResNet-50	13.2	7.6	16.8	56.9
OR-CNN [56]	VGG-16	12.8	6.7	15.3	55.7
ALFNet [52]	ResNet-50	12.0	8.4	11.4	51.9
CSP [23]	ResNet-50	11.0	7.3	10.4	49.3
APD [55]	ResNet-50	10.6	7.1	9.5	49.8
MGAN [53]	VGG-16	10.5	-	-	47.2
CCFNet (ours)	ResNet-50	10.2	6.8	9.5	42.7

4.5. Visualization

To further illustrate the superiority of CCFNet, we visualized the detection results on the CityPersons dataset, as shown in Figure 6. The first line (a) represents the original image in the validation set of the CityPersons dataset. The second line (b) represents the ground truth. The third line (c) represents the visualization result of the CSP. And the fourth line (d) represents the visu.alization result of CCFNet. The visualization results of CSP and CCFNet rely on the same confidence.

To show the effectiveness of the CCFNet, we selected three images from different scenes to compared with CSP. The first image belongs to a crowded scene. The second image belongs to a simple scene containing small objects. The third image is a scene with low visibility, low exposure, and small objects. The visualization result as show in Figure 6. It can be seen that in the first image, CSP and CCFNet generate a large number of detection boxes, but CCFNet has fewer false detection boxes. In addition, CCFNet can better solve the problem of multiple detection boxes for one single object. From the second image, CSP and CCFNet have the problem of overlapping detection boxes, but CSP has extremely bad results. In contrast, CCFNet has better visualization. From the third image, CSP can detect small objects in the image, but it also gets a lot of objects that should not be detected. In contrast, CCFNet avoids this problem. Therefore, CCFNet not only has good performance, but its visualization results are also robust.

As shown in Figure 7, the first line (a) represents the original image in the validation set of the CityPersons dataset. The second line (b) represents the heat map of the ACFPN. The third line (c) represents the heat map of the CSP. And the fourth line (d) represents the heat map of CCFNet. We also selected the images of the three scenes for comparison. The three images respectively cover complex environments, crowded scenes, and general scenes. It can be seen that the highlight of ACFPN presents a discrete distribution, the highlight of CSP presents a concentrated distribution, and the highlight of CCFNet is multi-peak. The ACFPN can not distinguish which type of person belongs to, and can not cope with the crowded state of objects, this is related to the fact that ACFPN is a general object detection network. The CSP responds to certain backgrounds, which makes CSP a bad visualization result, even though it has a low error detection rate. The CCFNet will not over-respond to the background and can distinguish the categories of people, it not only has a lower error detection rate, but its visualization results are also more optimistic.

Figure 6. Visualization results of CCFNet and CSP do not limit the visibility of pedestrian objects. (**a**) Input the original image for the CityPersons dataset; (**b**) is the ground truth corresponding to (**a**); (**c**) is the visualization result of CSP; (**d**) is the visualization result of CCFNet.

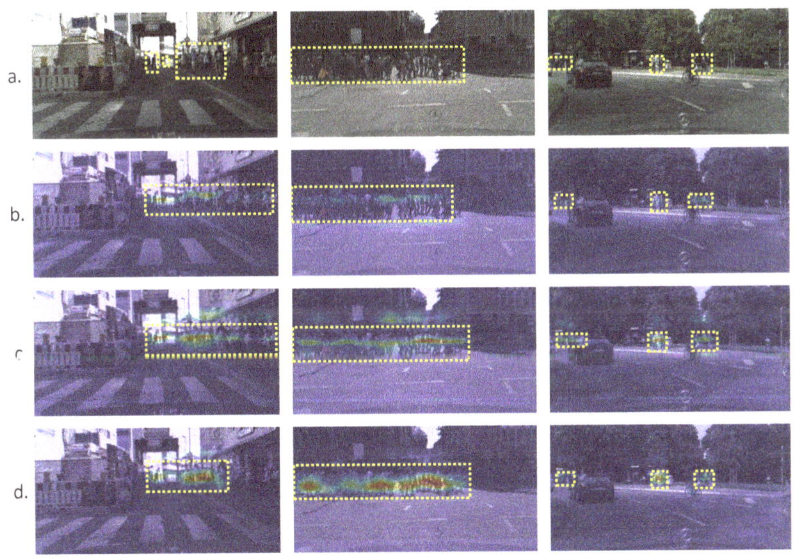

Figure 7. Visualization results of ACFPN, CSP, and CCFNet. (**a**) Input the original image for the CityPersons dataset; (**b**) is the visualization result of ACFPN; (**c**) is the visualization result of CSP; (**d**) is the visualization result of CCFNet.

4.6. Discussion

The proposal of CCFNet is influenced by the anchor-free object detection network. In the anchor-free network, how to make the neck effectively use the feature representation extracted by the backbone network will directly affect the performance of the detection head. Previous work [50,51] has achieved good performance in general object detection, but it can not be generalized to some special tasks, such as pedestrian detection.

Table 2 shows the ablation experiment of multi-scale features in the CCF module. By combining the feature maps of different stages, the optimal feature map combination is discussed. CCF reduces the noise in the shallow feature map by cascading and reusing deep semantic information, while retaining the semantic information lost due to dimensionality reduction operations. The purpose of this is to make the final feature map have more features.

Table 3 shows the comparative experiments between CCF and other necks. The previously proposed FPN-like methods and FCN-like methods achieve the most advanced performance in general object detection, but they are not suitable for pedestrian detection tasks. CCF module shows a very competitive performance.

Table 4 shows the ablation experiment of GSMap. The center map reduces the weight of negative samples through the Gaussian heat map, but does not change the shortcomings of convolution operation that can only obtain partial global information [57–59]. The proposal of GSMap can enable the center map to obtain more global information. In addition, according to the results of the heavy subset. It not only proves that the congestion problem between objects can not be completely solved by enhancing the semantic information in the feature map, but also requires additional modules for assistance, such as GSMap.

Table 5 shows the experiment of object scale prediction. The previous work only determines the size of the object by predicting the height [23,48]. We have proved through experiments that predicting the height and width of objects at the same time is the most suitable for CCFNet. In addition, this can also help cope with dense and overlapping problems.

Figure 5 and Table 6 show the comparative experiments of CCFNet with other advanced algorithms on the Caltech dataset. Table 7 shows the comparative experiments of CCFNet with other advanced algorithms on the Citypersons dataset. Their results prove the effectiveness of CCFNet.

5. Conclusions

In this paper, we proposed Cascaded Cross-layer Fusion module (CCF), which combines deep semantics and shallow details to obtain features, which will obtain more contextual semantic information. In order to cope with the situation of highly congested and severely occluded objects, we designed global smooth map (GSMap) and improved center loss function, which can effectively solve this problem at a small cost. Cascaded Cross-layer Fusion Network (CCFNet) can achieve better performance without relying on anchor points, multiple key points and complex post-processing. Finally, we conducted a large number of experiments on Caltech and CityPersons datasets to verify the superiority of CCFNet. Although the model introduces dimensionality reduction operations in the design process to reduce the computational complexity of the model, the final model still uses a large number of parameters that cannot meet the requirements of the real-time system. Therefore, designing an effective lightweight module is the focus of our next work.

Author Contributions: Formal analysis, Z.G., Y.S. and X.X.; methodology, Z.D. and Y.S.; project administration, Z.D.; validation, Z.G. and X.X.; visualization, Z.G and X.X.; writing–original draft, Z.D.; writing–review and editing, Z.G., Y.S. and X.X. All authors have read and agreed to the published version of the manuscript.

Funding: Not applicable.

Institutional Review Board Statement: Not applicable.

Informed Consent Statement: Not applicable.

Data Availability Statement: Not applicable.

Acknowledgments: Not applicable.

Conflicts of Interest: The authors declare no conflict of interest.

References

1. Ren, S.; He, K.; Girshick, R.; Sun, J. Faster r-cnn: Towards real-time object detection with region proposal networks. *Adv. Neural Inf. Process. Syst.* **2015**, *28*, 91–99. [CrossRef]
2. Liu, W.; Anguelov, D.; Erhan, D.; Szegedy, C.; Reed, S.; Fu, C.Y.; Berg, A.C. Ssd: Single shot multibox detector. *European Conference on Computer Vision*; Springer: Amsterdam, The Netherlands, 2016; pp. 21–37.
3. Lin, T.Y.; Goyal, P.; Girshick, R.; He, K.; Dollár, P. Focal loss for dense object detection. In Proceedings of the IEEE International Conference on Computer Vision, Venice, Italy, 22–29 October 2017; pp. 2980–2988.
4. Girshick, R.; Donahue, J.; Darrell, T.; Malik, J. Rich feature hierarchies for accurate object detection and semantic segmentation. In Proceedings of the IEEE Conference on Computer Vision and Pattern Recognition, Columbus, OH, USA, 23–28 June 2014; pp. 580–587.
5. Li, Z.; Tang, J.; Zhang, L.; Yang, J. Weakly-supervised Semantic Guided Hashing for Social Image Retrieval. *Int. J. Comput. Vis.* **2020**, *128*, 2265–2278. [CrossRef]
6. Redmon, J.; Divvala, S.; Girshick, R.; Farhadi, A. You only look once: Unified, real-time object detection. In Proceedings of the IEEE Conference on Computer Vision and Pattern Recognition, Las Vegas, NV, USA, 27–30 June 2016; pp. 779–788.
7. Lin, T.Y.; Dollár, P.; Girshick, R.; He, K.; Hariharan, B.; Belongie, S. Feature pyramid networks for object detection. In Proceedings of the IEEE Conference on Computer Vision and Pattern Recognition, Honolulu, HI, USA, 21–26 July 2017; pp. 2117–2125.
8. Redmon, J.; Farhadi, A. Yolov3: An incremental improvement. *arXiv* **2018**, arXiv:1804.02767.
9. Liu, S.; Huang, D.; Wang, Y. Learning spatial fusion for single-shot object detection. *arXiv* **2019**, arXiv:1911.09516.
10. Ghiasi, G.; Lin, T.Y.; Le, Q.V. Nas-fpn: Learning scalable feature pyramid architecture for object detection. In Proceedings of the IEEE Conference on Computer Vision and Pattern Recognition, Long Beach, CA, USA, 15–20 June 2019; pp. 7036–7045.
11. Tan, M.; Pang, R.; Le, Q.V. Efficientdet: Scalable and efficient object detection. In Proceedings of the IEEE Conference on Computer Vision and Pattern Recognition, Seattle, WA, USA, 13–19 June 2020; pp. 10781–10790.
12. Qiao, S.; Chen, L.C.; Yuille, A. Detectors: Detecting objects with recursive feature pyramid and switchable atrous convolution. In Proceedings of the IEEE Conference on Computer Vision and Pattern Recognition, Nashville, TN, USA, 20–25 June 2021; pp. 10213–10224.
13. Zhao, Q.; Sheng, T.; Wang, Y.; Tang, Z.; Chen, Y.; Cai, L.; Ling, H. M2det: A single-shot object detector based on multi-level feature pyramid network. *Aaai Conf. Artif. Intell.* **2019**, *33*, 9259–9266. [CrossRef]
14. Zhang, D.; Zhang, H.; Tang, J.; Wang, M.; Hua, X.; Sun, Q. Feature pyramid transformer. In *Proceedings of the European Conference on Computer Vision*; Springer: Amsterdam, The Netherlands, 2020; pp. 323–339.
15. Long, J.; Shelhamer, E.; Darrell, T. Fully convolutional networks for semantic segmentation. In Proceedings of the IEEE Conference on Computer Vision and Pattern Recognition, Boston, MA, USA, 7–12 June 2015; pp. 3431–3440.
16. Huang, L.; Yang, Y.; Deng, Y.; Yu, Y. Densebox: Unifying landmark localization with end to end object detection. *arXiv* **2015**, arXiv:1509.04874.
17. Zhu, Z.; Li, Z. Online Video Object Detection via Local and Mid-Range Feature Propagation. In Proceedings of the 1st International Workshop on Human-Centric Multimedia Analysis, Seattle WA, USA, 10–14 October 2020; pp. 73–82.
18. Li, Z.; Tang, J.; Mei, T. Deep collaborative embedding for social image understanding. *IEEE Trans. Pattern Anal. Mach. Intell.* **2018**, *41*, 2070–2083. [CrossRef]
19. He, K.; Zhang, X.; Ren, S.; Sun, J. Spatial pyramid pooling in deep convolutional networks for visual recognition. *IEEE Trans. Pattern Anal. Mach. Intell.* **2015**, *37*, 1904–1916. [CrossRef]
20. Zhou, H.; Li, Z.; Ning, C.; Tang, J. Cad: Scale invariant framework for real-time object detection. In Proceedings of the IEEE International Conference on Computer Vision Workshops, Venice, Italy, 22–29 October 2017; pp. 760–768.
21. Law, H.; Deng, J. Cornernet: Detecting objects as paired keypoints. In Proceedings of the European Conference on Computer Vision, Munich, Germany, 8–14 September 2018; pp. 734–750.
22. Li, Z.; Sun, Y.; Tang, J. CTNet: Context-based Tandem Network for Semantic Segmentation. *arXiv* **2021**, arXiv:2104.09805.
23. Liu, W.; Liao, S.; Ren, W.; Hu, W.; Yu, Y. High-level semantic feature detection: A new perspective for pedestrian detection. In Proceedings of the IEEE Conference on Computer Vision and Pattern Recognition, Long Beach, CA, USA, 15–20 June 2019; pp. 5187–5196.
24. Ronneberger, O.; Fischer, P.; Brox, T. U-net: Convolutional networks for biomedical image segmentation. In *International Conference on Medical Image Computing and Computer-Assisted Intervention*; Springer: Munich, Germany, 2015; pp. 234–241.
25. Sun, Y.; Li, Z. SSA: Semantic Structure Aware Inference for Weakly Pixel-Wise Dense Predictions without Cost. *arXiv* **2021**, arXiv:2111.03392.
26. Cai, Z.; Vasconcelos, N. Cascade r-cnn: Delving into high quality object detection. In Proceedings of the IEEE Conference on Computer Vision and Pattern Recognition, Salt Lake City, UT, USA, 18–23 June 2018; pp. 6154–6162.
27. Redmon, J.; Farhadi, A. YOLO9000: Better, faster, stronger. In Proceedings of the IEEE Conference on Computer Vision and Pattern Recognition, Honolulu, HI, USA, 21–26 July 2017; pp. 7263–7271.
28. Law, H.; Teng, Y.; Russakovsky, O.; Deng, J. Cornernet-lite: Efficient keypoint based object detection. *arXiv* **2019**, arXiv:1904.08900.
29. Zhou, X.; Zhuo, J.; Krahenbuhl, P. Bottom-up object detection by grouping extreme and center points. In Proceedings of the IEEE Conference on Computer Vision and Pattern Recognition, Long Beach, CA, USA, 15–20 June 2019; pp. 850–859.
30. Zhou, X.; Wang, D.; Krähenbühl, P. Objects as points. *arXiv* **2019**, arXiv:1904.07850.

31. Zhang, S.; Chi, C.; Yao, Y.; Lei, Z.; Li, S.Z. Bridging the gap between anchor-based and anchor-free detection via adaptive training sample selection. In Proceedings of the IEEE Conference on Computer Vision and Pattern Recognition, Seattle, WA, USA, 13–19 June 2020; pp. 9759–9768.
32. Simonyan, K.; Zisserman, A. Very deep convolutional networks for large-scale image recognition. *arXiv* **2014**, arXiv:1409.1556.
33. Pouyanfar, S.; Sadiq, S.; Yan, Y.; Tian, H.; Tao, Y.; Reyes, M.P.; Shyu, M.L.; Chen, S.C.; Iyengar, S.S. A survey on deep learning: Algorithms, techniques, and applications. *ACM Comput. Surv. (CSUR)* **2018**, *51*, 1–36. [CrossRef]
34. Adjabi, I.; Ouahabi, A.; Benzaoui, A.; Taleb-Ahmed, A. Past, present, and future of face recognition: A review. *Electronics* **2020**, *9*, 1188. [CrossRef]
35. Dong, S.; Wang, P.; Abbas, K. A survey on deep learning and its applications. *Comput. Sci. Rev.* **2021**, *40*, 100379. [CrossRef]
36. He, K.; Zhang, X.; Ren, S.; Sun, J. Deep residual learning for image recognition. In Proceedings of the IEEE conference on computer vision and pattern recognition, Las Vegas, NV, USA, 27–30 June 2016; pp. 770–778.
37. Song, T.; Sun, L.; Xie, D.; Sun, H.; Pu, S. Small-scale pedestrian detection based on topological line localization and temporal feature aggregation. In Proceedings of the European Conference on Computer Vision, Munich, Germany, 8–14 September 2018; pp. 536–551.
38. Wang, X.; Xiao, T.; Jiang, Y.; Shao, S.; Sun, J.; Shen, C. Repulsion loss: Detecting pedestrians in a crowd. In Proceedings of the IEEE Conference on Computer Vision and Pattern Recognition, Salt Lake City, UT, USA, 18–23 June 2018; pp. 7774–7783.
39. Liu, S.; Qi, L.; Qin, H.; Shi, J.; Jia, J. Path aggregation network for instance segmentation. In Proceedings of the IEEE Conference on Computer Vision and Pattern Recognition, Salt Lake City, UT, USA, 18–23 June 2018; pp. 8759–8768.
40. Yang, Z.; Liu, S.; Hu, H.; Wang, L.; Lin, S. Reppoints: Point set representation for object detection. In Proceedings of the IEEE International Conference on Computer Vision, Seoul, Korea, 27 October–2 November 2019; pp. 9657–9666.
41. Tian, Z.; Shen, C.; Chen, H.; He, T. Fcos: Fully convolutional one-stage object detection. In Proceedings of the IEEE International Conference on Computer Vision, Seoul, Korea, 27 October–2 November 2019; pp. 9627–9636.
42. Girshick, R. Fast R-CNN. In Proceedings of the IEEE International Conference on Computer Vision, Santiago, Chile, 7–13 December 2015; pp. 1440–1448.
43. Dollár, P.; Wojek, C.; Schiele, B.; Perona, P. Pedestrian detection: A benchmark. In Proceedings of the IEEE Conference on Computer Vision and Pattern Recognition, Miami, FL, USA, 20–25 June 2009; pp. 304–311.
44. Dollar, P.; Wojek, C.; Schiele, B.; Perona, P. Pedestrian detection: An evaluation of the state of the art. *IEEE Trans. Pattern Anal. Mach. Intell.* **2011**, *34*, 743–761. [CrossRef]
45. Zhang, S.; Benenson, R.; Schiele, B. Citypersons: A diverse dataset for pedestrian detection. In Proceedings of the IEEE Conference on Computer Vision and Pattern Recognition, Honolulu, HI, USA, 21–26 July 2017; pp. 3213–3221.
46. Chen, K.; Wang, J.; Pang, J.; Cao, Y.; Xiong, Y.; Li, X.; Sun, S.; Feng, W.; Liu, Z.; Xu, J.; et al. MMDetection: Open MMLab Detection Toolbox and Benchmark. *arXiv* **2019**, arXiv:1906.07155.
47. Hasan, I.; Liao, S.; Li, J.; Akram, S.U.; Shao, L. Generalizable Pedestrian Detection: The Elephant in the Room. In Proceedings of the IEEE Conference on Computer Vision and Pattern Recognition, Nashville, TN, USA, 20–25 June 2021; pp. 11328–11337.
48. Wang, W. Adapted Center and Scale Prediction: More Stable and More Accurate. *arXiv* **2020**, arXiv:2002.09053.
49. Krizhevsky, A. One weird trick for parallelizing convolutional neural networks. *arXiv* **2014**, arXiv:1404.5997.
50. Guo, C.; Fan, B.; Zhang, Q.; Xiang, S.; Pan, C. Augfpn: Improving multi-scale feature learning for object detection. In Proceedings of the IEEE Conference on Computer Vision and Pattern Recognition, Seattle, WA, USA, 13–19 June 2020; pp. 12595–12604.
51. Cao, J.; Chen, Q.; Guo, J.; Shi, R. Attention-guided context feature pyramid network for object detection. *arXiv* **2020**, arXiv:2005.11475.
52. Liu, W.; Liao, S.; Hu, W.; Liang, X.; Chen, X. Learning efficient single-stage pedestrian detectors by asymptotic localization fitting. In Proceedings of the European Conference on Computer Vision, Munich, Germany, 8–14 September 2018; pp. 618–634.
53. Pang, Y.; Xie, J.; Khan, M.H.; Anwer, R.M.; Khan, F.S.; Shao, L. Mask-guided attention network for occluded pedestrian detection. In Proceedings of the IEEE International Conference on Computer Vision, Seoul, Korea, 27 October–2 November 2019; pp. 4967–4975.
54. Mao, J.; Xiao, T.; Jiang, Y.; Cao, Z. What can help pedestrian detection? In Proceedings of the IEEE Conference on Computer Vision and Pattern Recognition, Honolulu, HI, USA, 21–26 July 2017; pp. 3127–3136.
55. Zhang, J.; Lin, L.; Zhu, J.; Li, Y.; Chen, Y.c.; Hu, Y.; Hoi, C.S. Attribute-aware pedestrian detection in a crowd. *IEEE Trans. Multimed.* **2020**, *23*, 3085–3097. [CrossRef]
56. Zhang, S.; Wen, L.; Bian, X.; Lei, Z.; Li, S.Z. Occlusion-aware R-CNN: Detecting pedestrians in a crowd. In Proceedings of the European Conference on Computer Vision, Munich, Germany, 8–14 September 2018; pp. 637–653.
57. Dosovitskiy, A.; Beyer, L.; Kolesnikov, A.; Weissenborn, D.; Zhai, X.; Unterthiner, T.; Dehghani, M.; Minderer, M.; Heigold, G.; Gelly, S.; et al. An Image is Worth 16x16 Words: Transformers for Image Recognition at Scale. *arXiv* **2020**, arXiv:2010.11929.
58. Zhang, D.; Zhang, H.; Tang, J.; Hua, X.S.; Sun, Q. Self-Regulation for Semantic Segmentation. In Proceedings of the IEEE International Conference on Computer Vision, Montreal, Canada, 11–17 October 2021; pp. 6953–6963.
59. Srinivas, A.; Lin, T.Y.; Parmar, N.; Shlens, J.; Abbeel, P.; Vaswani, A. Bottleneck transformers for visual recognition. In Proceedings of the IEEE Conference on Computer Vision and Pattern Recognition, Nashville, TN, USA, 20–25 June 2021; pp. 16519–16529.

mathematics

MDPI

Article

Second-Order Spatial-Temporal Correlation Filters for Visual Tracking

Yufeng Yu [1], Long Chen [1], Haoyang He [2], Jianhui Liu [3], Weipeng Zhang [4] and Guoxia Xu [5,*]

1 Department of Computer and Information Science, University of Macau, Macau 999078, China; yuyufeng220@163.com (Y.Y.); longchen@um.edu.mo (L.C.)
2 Department of Statistics, Guangzhou University, Guangzhou 510006, China; hoeyeungho@163.com
3 Jiangsu Province Key Lab on Image Processing and Image Communication, Nanjing University of Posts and Telecommunications, Nanjing 210003, China; 1864700023@e.gzhu.edu.cn
4 PLA Strategic Support Force, Beijing 450001, China; guagua_mitnick@163.com
5 Department of Computer Science, Norwegian University of Science and Technology, 2815 Gjovik, Norway
* Correspondence: gxxu.re@gmail.com

Abstract: Discriminative correlation filters (DCFs) have been widely used in visual object tracking, but often suffer from two problems: the boundary effect and temporal filtering degradation. To deal with these issues, many DCF-based variants have been proposed and have improved the accuracy of visual object tracking. However, these trackers only adopt first-order data-fitting information and have difficulty maintaining robust tracking in unconstrained scenarios, especially in the case of complex appearance variations. In this paper, by introducing a second-order data-fitting term to the DCF, we propose a second-order spatial–temporal correlation filter (SSCF) learning model. To be specific, the SSCF tracker both incorporates the first-order and second-order data-fitting terms into the DCF framework and makes the learned correlation filter more discriminative. Meanwhile, the spatial–temporal regularization was integrated to develop a robust model in tracking with complex appearance variations. Extensive experiments were conducted on the benchmarking databases CVPR2013, OTB100, DTB70, UAV123, and UAVDT-M. The results demonstrated that our SSCF can achieve competitive performance compared to the state-of-the-art trackers. When penalty parameter λ was set to 10^{-5}, our SSCF gained DP scores of 0.882, 0.868, 0.706, 0.676, and 0.928 on the CVPR2013, OTB100, DTB70, UAV123, and UAVDT-M databases, respectively.

Keywords: correlation filters; second-order fitting; visual tracking

MSC: 68T45

Citation: Yu, Y.; Chen, L.; He, H.; Liu, J.; Zhang, W.; Xu, G. Second-Order Spatial-Temporal Correlation Filters for Visual Tracking. *Mathematics* **2022**, *10*, 684. https://doi.org/10.3390/math10050684

Academic Editors: Jianping Gou, Weihua Ou, Shaoning Zeng and Lan Du

Received: 10 January 2022
Accepted: 17 February 2022
Published: 22 February 2022

1. Introduction

Visual object tracking is a fundamental problem in the field of computer vision, which has a wide range of applications in human–computer interaction, video surveillance, unmanned driving, and so on. The task of visual object tracking always suffers from the challenges of appearance variations, such as illumination variation, fast motion, out-of-plane rotation, and in-plane rotation. To deal with these challenges, various innovative trackers have been proposed and achieved significant progress in tracking performance and robustness. Among these tracking methods, discriminative-filter-based trackers [1–5] have received significant attention due to their competitive performance.

The standard discriminative-correlation-filter (DCF)-based tracker treats the filter learning as a ridge regression problem, and the objective function can be transferred to the frequency domain by the fast Fourier transform (FFT) for the solution. Bolme et al. [6] first learned the correlation filter to perform the target tracking task and proposed a minimum output sum of squared error (MOSSE) model. The MOSSE trains the filter by calculating the minimum actual and expected mean-squared errors of sequence images. Inspired by the MOSSE, Henriques et al. [7] considered that cyclic displacement could be used to replace random sampling to achieve dense sampling and proposed a theoretical framework to explore the effect of dense sampling. The proposed framework formulates a kernelized correlation filter to improve the tracking performance. Zhang et al. [8] adopted the Bayesian principle to build a spatial–temporal context model for tracking. However, these CF-based trackers only utilize single-channel features, which is not robust in the tracking scenarios with complex appearance variations. To tackle this issue, some CF-based methods [9–19] extract multiple features to learn the filters. The commonly used handcrafted features include the histogram of oriented gradients (HOG), color names (CNs), the local binary pattern (LBP), and scale-invariant feature transform (SIFT). These features describe the shape and color information of the targets. Trackers using multiple features are more robust to the fast movement and deformation variation of targets. For instance, Galoogahi et al. [17] employed multi-channel HOG descriptors in the frequency domain to extract HOG features for filter learning and proposed a multi-channel CF tracker (MCCF). Huang et al. [14] used hybrid color features to learn filters in which the compressed CN features and the HOG features based on the opponent color space were extracted, and principal component analysis was used to reduce the computational cost. Li et al. [12] integrated the raw pixel, HOG, and color label features into the DCF framework and presented an adaptive multiple feature tracker. Kumar et al. [19] exploited the LBP, color histogram, and pyramid of the histogram of gradients to model the object's appearance and developed an adaptive multi-cue particle filter method for real-time visual tracking.

Even though these DCF-based trackers using multi-channel features succeed to some extent, some aspects such as the redundancy of multi-channel features, the boundary effect, and data fitting have not been fully explored. To tackle these issues, many structural regularized DCF methods [20–26] have been presented. Zhu et al. [2] proposed an adaptive attribute-aware strategy to distinguish the importance of different channel features. Jain et al. [20] presented a channel graph regularized CF model by introducing a channel weighing strategy in which a channel regularizer was integrated into the CF framework to learn the channel weights. Xu et al. [22] proposed a channel selection scheme for multi-channel feature representations and adopted a low-rank approximation to learn filters in a low-dimensional manifold. In addition, many trackers propose a variety of strategies to solve the boundary effect. The SRDCF [23] incorporates a spatial regularizer into the DCF to deal with the problem caused by the periodic assumption. Li et al. [24] supplemented the temporal regularization term into the SRDCF tracker [23] and proposed a spatial–temporal regularization CF framework. To be specific, the STRCF integrates both temporal regularization and spatial regularization into the standard DCF model and can perform model updating and DCF learning simultaneously. As a result, the STRCF could be regarded as an approximation of the SRDCF with multiple samples and achieves better tracking performance than the SRDCF. The BACF [25] utilizes a cropping matrix to extract patches densely from the background and expands the search area at a low computational cost. Xu et al. [26] combined temporal consistency constraints and spatial feature selection to propose an adaptive DCF model in which the multi-channel filters can be learned in a low-dimensional manifold space. However, the aforementioned trackers only employ the first-order data-fitting information of the feature maps. In other words, such methods do not consider high-order data-fitting information for tracking.

On the basis of the above-mentioned analysis, we propose a novel CF-based tracker, the second-order spatial–temporal correlation filter (SSCF) learning model. We formulated our tracking algorithm by incorporating a second-order data-fitting term into the DCF framework, which helps to take full advantage of target features against surrounding background clutter. The main contributions of the SSCF are summarized as follows:

- We propose a new discriminative correlation filter model for visual tracking with complex appearance variations, unlike prior DCF-based trackers in which the first-order data-fitting information is only used. We incorporated the second-order data fitting and spatial–temporal regularization into the DCF framework and developed a more robust tracker;

- An effective alternating-direction method-of-multipliers (ADMM)-based algorithm was used to solve the proposed tracking model;
- Extensive experiments on the benchmarking databases demonstrated that our SSCF can achieve competitive performance compared to the state-of-the-art trackers.

The remainder of this paper is organized as follows. Section 2 introduces the related work. Section 3 describes the detailed mathematical formulation of the proposed model and introduces the optimization algorithm. Section 4 reports the experimental results and the corresponding analysis. Finally, Section 5 draws the conclusions.

2. Related Work

In this section, we review mainly three categories of tracking methods, including trackers based on target detection, trackers based on clustering, and channel-reliability learning trackers.

Since target detection techniques [27–29] have attracted wide attention in the computer vision field, many trackers based on target detection have been proposed. Guan et al. [30] proposed a joint detection and tracking framework for object tracking in which the detection threshold was adaptively modified according to the information fed back to the detector by the tracker. Zhang et al. [31] employed a faster recurrent convolutional neural network to extract the candidate detection areas and proposed a multi-target tracking algorithm. In [32], Liu et al. combined motion detection with correlation filtering and presented a new model for object tracking. The presented model determines the object position via the weighted outputs of motion detection and the tracker. Considering that the existing kernelized correlation filter tracking methods fail to identify occlusion, Min et al. [33] adopted a detector to assist the occlusion judgment and improve the tracking performance.

Clustering-based algorithms [34,35] have been commonly used in pattern recognition and computer vision, such as image segmentation [36] and patten classification [37]. Inspired by this, many researchers use clustering algorithms to improve the performance of object tracking. For instance, Keuper et al. [38] combined motion segmentation with object tracking and presented a correlation co-clustering model to improve the performance. In [39], Li et al. developed an intuitionistic fuzzy clustering model for object tracking. Specifically, the local information of the targets is incorporated into the intuitionistic fuzzy clustering to improve the robustness. Considering that DBSCAN clustering does not require the number of clusters, He et al. [40] employed a DBSCAN clustering-based track-to-track fusion strategy for multi-target tracking.

Recently, the idea of different weights distinguishing the importance of different components has been widely used in pattern classification [41,42] and face recognition [43]. Similarly, some DCF-based channel-reliability learning trackers have been proposed to deal with the problem of model degradation. Du et al. [44] argued that different channels have different contributions in the tracking process and proposed a joint channel-reliability and correlation-filter learning model. The proposed tracker assigns each channel a weight to distinguish the different importance. To exploit the interaction between different channels, Jain et al. [20] assigned similar weights to similar channels to emphasize important channels and developed a channel attention model. Li et al. [45] argued that the existing trackers do not consider the complementary information of different channels and proposed a channel-feature integration method. All channels of each feature share an importance map to avoid overfitting. In [46], the authors introduced channel and spatial reliability to the DCF framework and employed the reliability scores to weight the per-channel filter responses. The experiments showed that the channel weights were able to improve the tracking performance. These methods principally focus on overcoming model degradation by incorporating channel reliability and enhance the discriminative performance to some extent.

3. The Proposed Model

3.1. Objective Function Construction

As mentioned above, the existing DCF-based methods only utilize first-order data-fitting information and ignore high-order data-fitting information for tracking, which cannot take full advantage of target features against surrounding background clutter and suffer from the stability–plasticity dilemma. To deal with these issues, we built a second-order spatial–temporal correlation-filter learning framework. Specifically, we incorporated a second-order data-fitting term and spatial–temporal regularization into the DCF framework and formulated a robust model. The objective function is able to be formulated as below.

We first denote the dataset $\mathbb{S} = \{\mathbb{X}_t\}_{t=1}^{T}$, and each frame $\mathbb{X}_t \in R^{M\times N\times K}$ contains K feature maps with a size of $M \times N$. $\mathbf{Y} \in R^{M\times N}$ is the Gaussian-shaped label. Our aim was to learn a multi-channel convolution filter $\mathbb{F} \in R^{M\times N\times K}$ by minimizing the following objective function:

$$\begin{aligned} \min_{\mathbb{F}} \frac{1}{2}\left\|\sum_{k=1}^{K} \mathbf{X}_t^k * \mathbf{F}^k - \mathbf{Y}\right\|_F^2 + \frac{1}{2}\sum_{k=1}^{K}\|\mathbf{W}\cdot\mathbf{F}^k\|_F^2 \\ +\frac{\lambda}{2}\left\|\sum_{k=1}^{K} \mathbf{X}_t^k * \mathbf{F}^k * \mathbf{X}_t^k - \mathbf{Y}\right\|_F^2 + \frac{\mu}{2}\|\mathbb{F} - \mathbb{F}_{t-1}\|_F^2 \end{aligned} \tag{1}$$

where $*$ represents the convolution operator and $\cdot$ denotes the Hadamard product. $\mathbf{W}$ is the spatial regularization matrix, and $\mathbb{F}_{t-1}$ is the correlation filter used in the $t-1$-th frame. λ and μ are penalty parameters. The first term is the first-order data-fitting term, which is a generic formulation for learning the filter in DCF-based trackers. The second term is the spatial regularizer to solve the boundary effect. The third term is the second-order data-fitting term, which can be helpful to make full use of discriminative target features. The last term is the temporal regularizer to force the current frame filter close to the previous one, which helps to prevent the effect caused by the corrupted samples.

3.2. Optimization Algorithm

It can be noted that the objective function in Equation (1) is convex, and the minimization problem can be solved by the ADMM algorithm. To be specific, we introduced an auxiliary variable $\mathbb{G} \in R^{M\times N\times K}$ by restricting $\mathbb{F} = \mathbb{G}$ and constructed the augmented Lagrangian form of Equation (1) as:

$$\begin{aligned} L(\mathbb{F},\mathbb{G},\mathbb{S}) = \frac{1}{2}\left\|\sum_{k=1}^{K} \mathbf{X}_t^k * \mathbf{F}^k - \mathbf{Y}\right\|_F^2 + \frac{1}{2}\sum_{k=1}^{K}\|\mathbf{W}\cdot\mathbf{G}^k\|_F^2 \\ +\frac{\lambda}{2}\left\|\sum_{k=1}^{K} \mathbf{X}_t^k * \mathbf{F}^k * \mathbf{X}_t^k - \mathbf{Y}\right\|_F^2 + \frac{\mu}{2}\|\mathbb{F} - \mathbb{F}_{t-1}\|_F^2 \\ +\frac{\gamma}{2}\sum_{k=1}^{K}\|\mathbf{F}^k - \mathbf{G}^k\|_F^2 + \sum_{k=1}^{K} Tr((\mathbf{F}^k - \mathbf{G}^k)^T\mathbf{S}^k) \end{aligned} \tag{2}$$

where $\mathbb{S} = [\mathbf{S}^1, \mathbf{S}^2, \cdots, \mathbf{S}^K] \in R^{M\times N\times K}$ is the Lagrange multiplier and γ is the stepsize. Assuming $\mathbb{H} = \frac{1}{\gamma}\mathbb{S}$, Equation (2) can be written as:

$$
\begin{aligned}
L(\mathbb{F},\mathbb{G},\mathbb{H}) = & \frac{1}{2}\left\|\sum_{k=1}^{K}\mathbf{X}_t^k * \mathbf{F}^k - \mathbf{Y}\right\|_F^2 + \frac{1}{2}\sum_{k=1}^{K}\|\mathbf{W}\cdot\mathbf{G}^k\|_F^2 \\
& + \frac{\lambda}{2}\left\|\sum_{k=1}^{K}\mathbf{X}_t^k * \mathbf{F}^k * \mathbf{X}_t^k - \mathbf{Y}\right\|_F^2 + \frac{\mu}{2}\|\mathbb{F}-\mathbb{F}_{t-1}\|_F^2 \\
& + \frac{\gamma}{2}\sum_{k=1}^{K}\left\|\mathbf{F}^k - \mathbf{G}^k + \mathbf{H}^k\right\|_F^2
\end{aligned} \tag{3}
$$

The optimization problem can be divided into several subproblems as follows.

$$
\begin{aligned}
\mathbb{F}^{(l+1)} = & \arg\min_{\mathbb{F}}\left\|\sum_{k=1}^{K}\mathbf{X}_t^k * \mathbf{F}^k - \mathbf{Y}\right\|_F^2 \\
& + \left\|\sum_{k=1}^{K}\mathbf{X}_t^k * \mathbf{F}^k * \mathbf{X}_t^k - \mathbf{Y}\right\|_F^2 \\
& + \gamma\sum_{k=1}^{K}\left\|\mathbf{F}^k - \mathbf{G}^k + \mathbf{H}^k\right\|_F^2 + \mu\|\mathbb{F}-\mathbb{F}_{t-1}\|_F^2
\end{aligned} \tag{4}
$$

$$
\mathbb{G}^{(l+1)} = \arg\min_{\mathbb{G}}\sum_{k=1}^{K}\|\mathbf{W}\cdot\mathbf{G}^k\|_F^2 + \gamma\sum_{k=1}^{K}\left\|\mathbf{F}^k - \mathbf{G}^k + \mathbf{H}^k\right\|_F^2 \tag{5}
$$

$$
\mathbb{H}^{(l+1)} = \mathbb{H}^{(l)} + \mathbb{F}^{(l+1)} - \mathbb{G}^{(l+1)} \tag{6}
$$

Then, we can alternatively solve each subproblem as follows:

Solving $\mathbb{F}$: According to Parseval's theorem, the subproblem in Equation (4) can be formulated in the Fourier domain as:

$$
\begin{aligned}
& \arg\min_{\hat{\mathbb{F}}}\left\|\sum_{k=1}^{K}\hat{\mathbf{X}}_t^k\cdot\hat{\mathbf{F}}^k - \hat{\mathbf{Y}}\right\|_F^2 + \lambda\left\|\sum_{k=1}^{K}\hat{\mathbf{X}}_t^k\cdot\hat{\mathbf{F}}^k\cdot\hat{\mathbf{X}}_t^k - \hat{\mathbf{Y}}\right\|_F^2 \\
& + \gamma\sum_{k=1}^{K}\left\|\hat{\mathbf{F}}^k - \hat{\mathbf{G}}^k + \hat{\mathbf{H}}^k\right\|_F^2 + \mu\|\hat{\mathbb{F}}-\hat{\mathbb{F}}_{t-1}\|_F^2
\end{aligned} \tag{7}
$$

Here, $\hat{\mathbb{F}}$ represents the discrete Fourier transform (DFT) of $\mathbb{F}$. From Equation (7), it can be noted that the i-th row and the j-th element of $\hat{\mathbf{Y}}$ only depend on the i-th row and the j-th element of $\hat{\mathbb{F}}$ and $\hat{\mathbb{X}}_t$ across all K channels. Assume $v_{ij}(\mathbb{F})$ is a K-dimensional vector that contains the i-th row and the j-th elements of $\mathbb{F}$ along all K channels. Optimizing the problem in Equation (7) is equivalent to solving the following MN subproblems:

$$
\begin{aligned}
& \arg\min_{v_{ij}(\hat{\mathbb{F}})} \| v_{ij}(\hat{\mathbb{X}}_t)^T v_{ij}(\hat{\mathbb{F}}) - \hat{y}_{ij} \|_2^2 + \mu \| v_{ij}(\hat{\mathbb{F}}) - v_{ij}(\hat{\mathbb{F}}_{t-1}) \|_2^2 \\
& + \lambda \| (v_{ij}(\hat{\mathbb{X}}_t)\cdot v_{ij}(\hat{\mathbb{X}}_t))^T v_{ij}(\hat{\mathbb{F}}) - \hat{y}_{ij} \|_2^2 \\
& + \gamma \| v_{ij}(\hat{\mathbb{F}}) - v_{ij}(\hat{\mathbb{G}}) + v_{ij}(\hat{\mathbb{H}}) \|_2^2
\end{aligned} \tag{8}
$$

where $i = 1, \cdots, M$ and $j = 1, \cdots, N$.

Taking the derivative of Equation (8) with respect to $v_{ij}(\hat{\mathbb{F}})$ as zero, we have:

$$
v_{ij}(\hat{\mathbb{F}}) = (\mathbf{Q} + (\gamma+\mu)\mathbf{I})^{-1}\mathbf{z} \tag{9}
$$

Here, $\mathbf{Q} = v_{ij}(\hat{\mathbb{X}}_t)v_{ij}(\hat{\mathbb{X}}_t)^T + \lambda(v_{ij}(\hat{\mathbb{X}}_t)\cdot v_{ij}(\hat{\mathbb{X}}_t))(v_{ij}(\hat{\mathbb{X}}_t)\cdot v_{ij}(\hat{\mathbb{X}}_t))^T$ and $\mathbf{z} = v_{ij}(\hat{\mathbb{X}}_t)\hat{y}_{ij} + \mu v_{ij}(\hat{\mathbb{F}}_{t-1}) + \lambda(v_{ij}(\hat{\mathbb{X}}_t)\cdot v_{ij}(\hat{\mathbb{X}}_t)) + \gamma v_{ij}(\hat{\mathbb{G}}) - \gamma v_{ij}(\hat{\mathbb{H}})$.

Solving $\mathbb{G}$: From Equation (5), each element of $\mathbb{G}$ is able to be updated independently, and we adopted the same strategy as solving $\mathbb{F}$. Assume $v_{ij}(\mathbb{G})$ is a K-dimensional vector that contains the i-th row and the j-th elements of $\mathbb{G}$ along all K channels. Optimizing the problem in Equation (5) is equivalent to solving the following MN subproblems:

$$\arg\min_{v_{ij}(\mathbb{G})} w_{ij}^2 \parallel v_{ij}(\mathbb{G}) \parallel_2^2 + \gamma \parallel v_{ij}(\mathbb{F}) - v_{ij}(\mathbb{G}) + v_{ij}(\mathbb{H}) \parallel_2^2 \quad (10)$$

Taking the derivative of Equation (10) with respect to $v_{ij}(\mathbb{G})$ as zero, we have:

$$v_{ij}(\mathbb{G}) = (\mathbf{P}^T\mathbf{P} + \gamma\mathbf{I})^{-1}(\gamma v_{ij}(\mathbb{F}) + \gamma v_{ij}(\mathbb{H})) \quad (11)$$

where $\mathbf{P}$ is a diagonal matrix and each diagonal element is w_{ij}.

Updating $\mathbb{H}$: Let $v_{ij}(\mathbb{H})$ be a K-dimensional vector that contains the i-th row and the j-th elements of $\mathbb{G}$ along all K channels. In the $l+1$-th iteration of the ADMM, the Lagrange multiplier vector $v_{ij}(\mathbb{H})$ can be updated as follows:

$$v_{ij}(\mathbb{H})^{(l+1)} = v_{ij}(\mathbb{H})^{(l)} + v_{ij}(\mathbb{F})^{(l+1)} - v_{ij}(\mathbb{G})^{(l+1)} \quad (12)$$

The details of the optimization procedure can be seen in Algorithm 1.

Algorithm 1 SSCF algorithm

Input: Feature maps $\mathbb{X}_t$, Gaussian-shaped label $\mathbf{Y}$, previous correlation filters $\mathbb{F}_{t-1}$, spatial regularization matrix $\mathbf{W}$, initial values $\mathbb{G}^{(0)}$ and $\mathbb{H}^{(0)}$.
Output: Estimated correlation filters $\mathbb{F}$.
1: **repeat** Step 2–Step 5
2: Update $v_{ij}(\hat{\mathbb{F}})^{(l+1)}$ via Equation (9);
3: Update $v_{ij}(\mathbb{G})^{(l+1)}$ via Equation (11);
4: Update $v_{ij}(\mathbb{H})^{(l+1)}$ via Equation (12);
5: $l = l + 1$;
6: **Until** $v_{ij}(\hat{\mathbb{F}})$, $v_{ij}(\mathbb{G})$, $v_{ij}(\mathbb{H})$ have converged;
7: Obtain correlation filters $\mathbb{F}$ by applying the inverse DFT.

3.3. *Computational Complexity*

In this subsection, we discuss the computational complexity of the presented SSCF. As shown in Section 3.2, we divided the optimization problem into several subproblems. According to the Parseval theorem and the ADMM algorithm, the complexity of solving $\mathbf{F}$ is $O(KMN)$ in each iteration. Taking the DFT and inverse DFT into account, the computational complexity of solving $\mathbf{F}$ is $O(KMN\log(MN))$. Moreover, the complexity of subproblems $\mathbf{H}$ and $\mathbf{G}$ is $O(KMN)$. Suppose the number of iteration is T: the whole computational complexity of the proposed SSCF is $O(TKMN(\log(MN)+1))$. In view of this, the speed of our tracker is not fast.

4. Experiment Results and Analysis

This section provides the experiments to validate the superiority of the presented SSCF in target tracking. To evaluate the performance of the proposed model, we compared it with the state-of-the-art trackers, including spatially regularized discriminative correlation filters (SRDCFs) [23], kernelized correlation filters (KCFs) [47], spatial–temporal regularized correlation filters (STRCFs) [24], background-aware correlation filters (BACFs) [25], learning adaptive discriminative correlation filters (LADCFs) [26], discriminative scale space tracking (DSST) [48], the scale-adaptive with multiple features tracker (SAMF) [12], ECOHC [49], ARCF-HC [50], the MSCF [51], and AutoTrack [52]. These experiments were conducted on the CVPR2013 [53], OTB50 [54], OTB100 [54], DTB70 [55], UAV123 [56], and UAVDT-M databases [57].

In the experiments, our tracker was implemented using MATLAB R2017a on a computer with an i7-8700K processor (3.7GHz) with 48GB RAM. λ was set to 10^{-5}, and other parameters were set to the same values as the STRCF. The histogram of oriented gradients (HOG) features were used to conduct the comparative experiments. In addition, we followed the one-pass evaluation (OPE) protocol [53] to evaluate the performance of different trackers. The success and precision plots are reported based on the bounding box overlap and center location error. The AUC is the area under the curve of the success plot, and the distance precision (DP) is the percentage of the location errors within 20 px.

4.1. Results on the CVPR2013 Database

The CVPR2013 database contains 50 fully annotated video sequences with 11 different attributes, such as background clutter, low resolution, occlusion, and out of view. The overall performance, which is summarized by the success and precision plots, is listed in Figure 1. It can be observed that the proposed SSCF achieved the top-ranking results. The area under the curve (AUC) and distance precision (DP) scores were 0.681 and 0.882, respectively. Specifically, the AUC and DP scores of SSCF were higher by 1.2% and 0.9% than the STRCF. This indicates that incorporating the second-order data-fitting term is effective at improving the tracking performance.

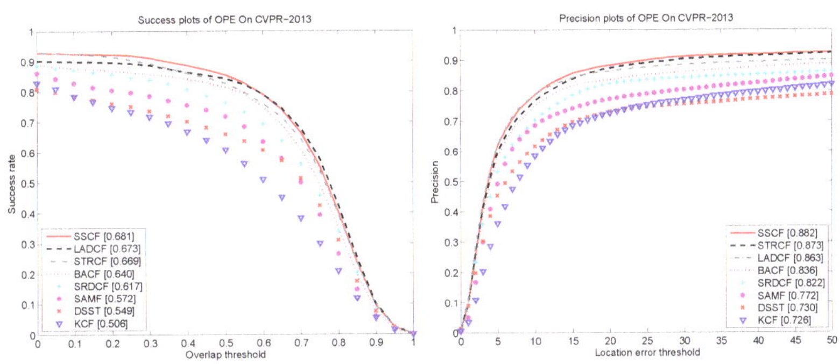

Figure 1. Success plots (**a**) and precision plots (**b**) of the proposed SSCF and other trackers on the CVPR2013 database.

To evaluate the robustness of the proposed SSCF on different attributes, we constructed subsets with different dominant attributes for the experiments. The 11 challenging factors were background clutter (BC), low resolution (LR), illumination variation (IV), motion blur (MB), out of view (OV), fast motion (FM), deformation (DEF), occlusion (OCC), out-of-plane rotation (OPR), scale variation (SV), and in-plane rotation (IPR). Table 1 shows the AUC and DP scores of the proposed SSCF and the other trackers on the 11 attributes on the CVPR2013 database. Despite not all scores of the proposed SSCF being the highest, our method achieved the best robustness. Especially for the AUC scores on the different attributes, our SSCF outperformed the other trackers, except LADCF.

4.2. Results on the OTB100 Database

OTB100 is a database containing 100 challenging video sequences, and these sequences consist of more than 28,000 fully annotated frames. The results of the success and precision plots for all trackers are shown in Figure 2. From the figure, the proposed SSCF outperformed all the competing trackers in its overall performance. Our tracker achieved 0.664 and 0.868 in terms of the AUC and DP scores, respectively.

We also provide the attribute-based evaluation to validate the robustness of our SSCF. The AUC and DP scores of all trackers on the 11 different attributes are reported in Table 2. From the DP scores listed in the table, the proposed SSCF outperformed all competing trackers on eight attributes. In terms of the AUC scores, our tracker performed better than the other trackers on seven attributes. On other attributes, the SSCF was among the top-three trackers. These results demonstrate that our SSCF is more robust than the other trackers.

Table 1. The area under the curve (AUC) and distance precision (DP) scores of the proposed SSCF and the other trackers on different attributes on the CVPR2013 database. The top-three methods on each attribute are denoted by different colors: red, blue, and green. That is, red represents the best performance, blue represents the second best, and green represents the third best (AUC/DP).

Attributes	DSST [48]	KCF [47]	SAMF[12]	SRDCF [23]	BACF [25]	STRCF [24]	LADCF [26]	SSCF
FM	0.413/0.485	0.435/0.559	0.460/0.568	0.541/0.691	0.583/0.766	0.572/0.697	0.591/0.728	0.604/0.754
BC	0.517/0.694	0.535/0.753	0.520/0.676	0.587/0.803	0.631/0.833	0.625/0.850	0.592/0.783	0.641/0.840
DEF	0.492/0.633	0.512/0.702	0.604/0.775	0.609/0.811	0.644/0.832	0.639/0.854	0.657/0.852	0.680/0.885
IPR	0.555/0.753	0.484/0.702	0.512/0.692	0.550/0.739	0.622/0.824	0.621/0.802	0.612/0.785	0.633/0.826
IV	0.551/0.711	0.477/0.699	0.498/0.655	0.557/0.727	0.600/0.788	0.599/0.779	0.599/0.752	0.630/0.799
LR	0.378/0.682	0.272/0.629	0.376/0.709	0.471/0.767	0.406/0.659	0.540/0.777	0.580/0.776	0.510/0.744
MB	0.433/0.504	0.462/0.589	0.428/0.507	0.560/0.719	0.609/0.790	0.566/0.681	0.579/0.702	0.626/0.778
OCC	0.523/0.690	0.499/0.724	0.598/0.816	0.610/0.815	0.612/0.797	0.646/0.854	0.673/0.869	0.673/0.872
OPR	0.529/0.723	0.485/0.710	0.549/0.749	0.586/0.796	0.620/0.822	0.651/0.863	0.657/0.850	0.667/0.875
OV	0.462/0.511	0.550/0.650	0.555/0.636	0.555/0.680	0.553/0.706	0.632/0.728	0.633/0.720	0.652/0.748
SV	0.546/0.738	0.427/0.679	0.507/0.723	0.587/0.778	0.584/0.765	0.647/0.836	0.649/0.821	0.639/0.823

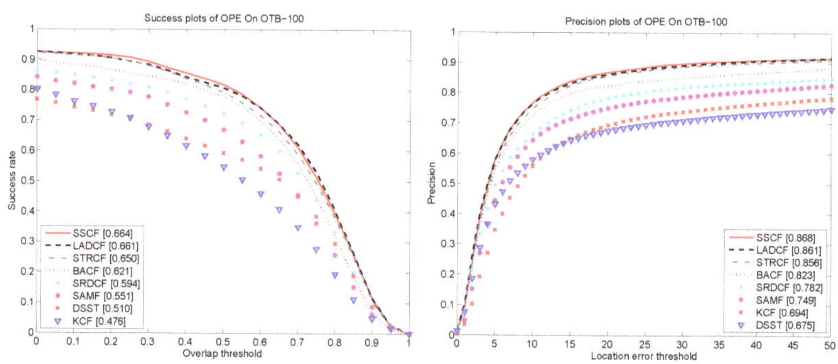

(a) (b)

Figure 2. Success plots (**a**) and precision plots (**b**) of the proposed SSCF and the other trackers on the OTB100 database.

Table 2. The area under the curve (AUC) and distance precision (DP) scores of the proposed SSCF and the other trackers on different attributes on the OTB100 database. The top-three methods on each attribute are denoted by different colors: red, blue, and green. That is, red represents the best performance, blue represents the second best, and green represents the third best (AUC/DP).

Attributes	DSST [48]	KCF [47]	SAMF [12]	SRDCF [23]	BACF [25]	STRCF [24]	LADCF [26]	SSCF
FM	0.439/0.540	0.457/0.617	0.502/0.649	0.586/0.749	0.600/0.791	0.617/0.780	0.625/0.790	0.635/0.803
BC	0.521/0.703	0.509/0.731	0.532/0.705	0.584/0.777	0.643/0.861	0.648/0.872	0.637/0.830	0.679/0.884
DEF	0.414/0.532	0.427/0.600	0.500/0.671	0.533/0.715	0.599/0.802	0.596/0.825	0.595/0.812	0.613/0.835
IPR	0.496/0.681	0.468/0.698	0.515/0.717	0.535/0.729	0.583/0.787	0.593/0.794	0.601/0.810	0.602/0.817
IV	0.551/0.709	0.468/0.699	0.524/0.697	0.600/0.770	0.632/0.821	0.640/0.819	0.649/0.808	0.666/0.833
LR	0.370/0.649	0.290/0.671	0.425/0.766	0.514/0.765	0.516/0.797	0.579/0.843	0.614/0.850	0.576/0.834
MB	0.458/0.551	0.456/0.594	0.519/0.648	0.580/0.739	0.590/0.762	0.637/0.797	0.646/0.807	0.672/0.845
OCC	0.447/0.587	0.442/0.626	0.536/0.722	0.551/0.719	0.576/0.743	0.606/0.797	0.644/0.830	0.638/0.827
OPR	0.466/0.637	0.447/0.665	0.530/0.728	0.542/0.729	0.584/0.785	0.619/0.836	0.632/0.838	0.632/0.850
OV	0.383/0.481	0.418/0.540	0.495/0.662	0.464/0.601	0.521/0.721	0.585/0.766	0.613/0.815	0.600/0.777
SV	0.468/0.638	0.400/0.642	0.498/0.713	0.562/0.746	0.571/0.769	0.632/0.842	0.636/0.836	0.634/0.843

4.3. Results on the OTB50 Database

Figure 3 lists the success plots comparing the presented method on OTB50 with the existing trackers. The overall performance is summarized in Figure 3a. It can be seen that the proposed SSCF had the best success rates. The success plots of all trackers on the 11 different attributes are shown in Figure 3b–l. The proposed SSCF outperformed the existing trackers on eight attributes, i.e., fast motion, background clutter, motion blur, illumination variation, in-plane rotation, occlusion, out-of-plane rotation, and out of view. Our SSCF incorporates the second-order data fitting and spatial–temporal regularization into the DCF framework to develop a robust tracking pattern. The tracking results of the SSCF on the other three attributes were among the top two. This also demonstrates the effectiveness and robustness of our tracker.

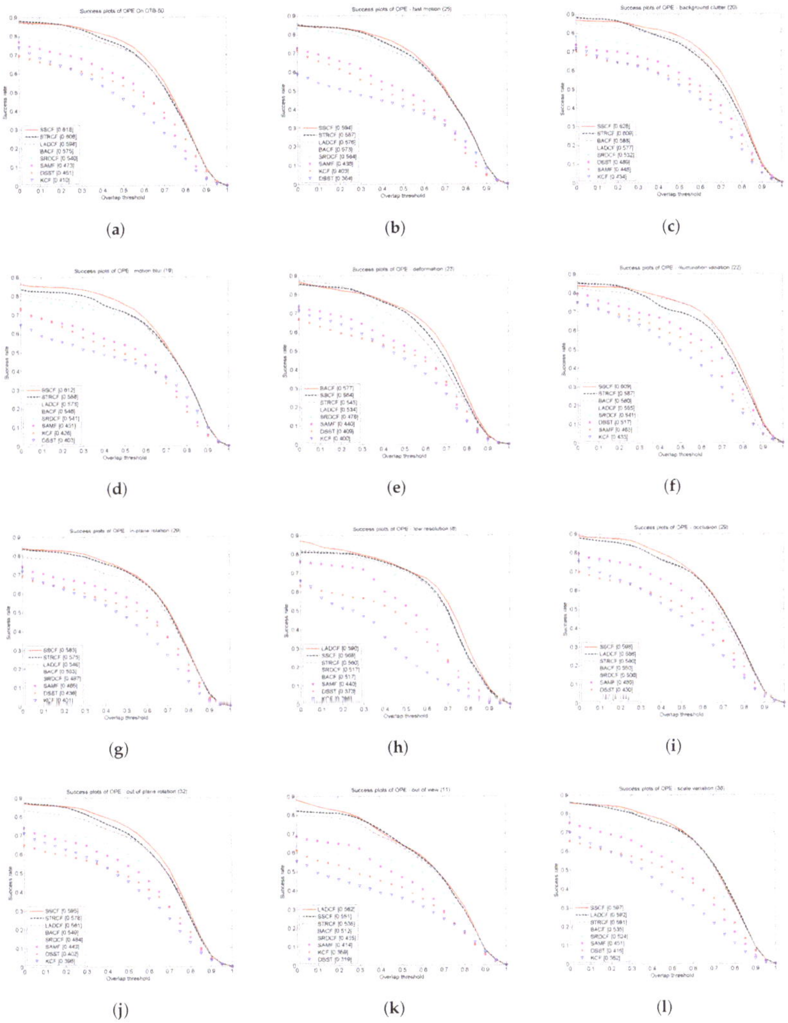

Figure 3. Success plots of the proposed SSCF and the other trackers on the OTB50 database. (**a**) Overall performance; (**b**–**l**) success plots on the 11 different attributes.

4.4. Results on the DTB70 Database

Figures 4 and 5 show the success plots and precision plots comparing the presented method on the DTB70 database with the existing trackers. The overall performance is summarized in Figures 4a and 5a. It is observed that our SSCF achieved the best results in the overall performance. The success plots and precision plots of all trackers on the 11 different attributes are shown in Figures 4b–l and 5b–l. Our SSCF outperformed the existing trackers on nine attributes except motion blur and low resolution.

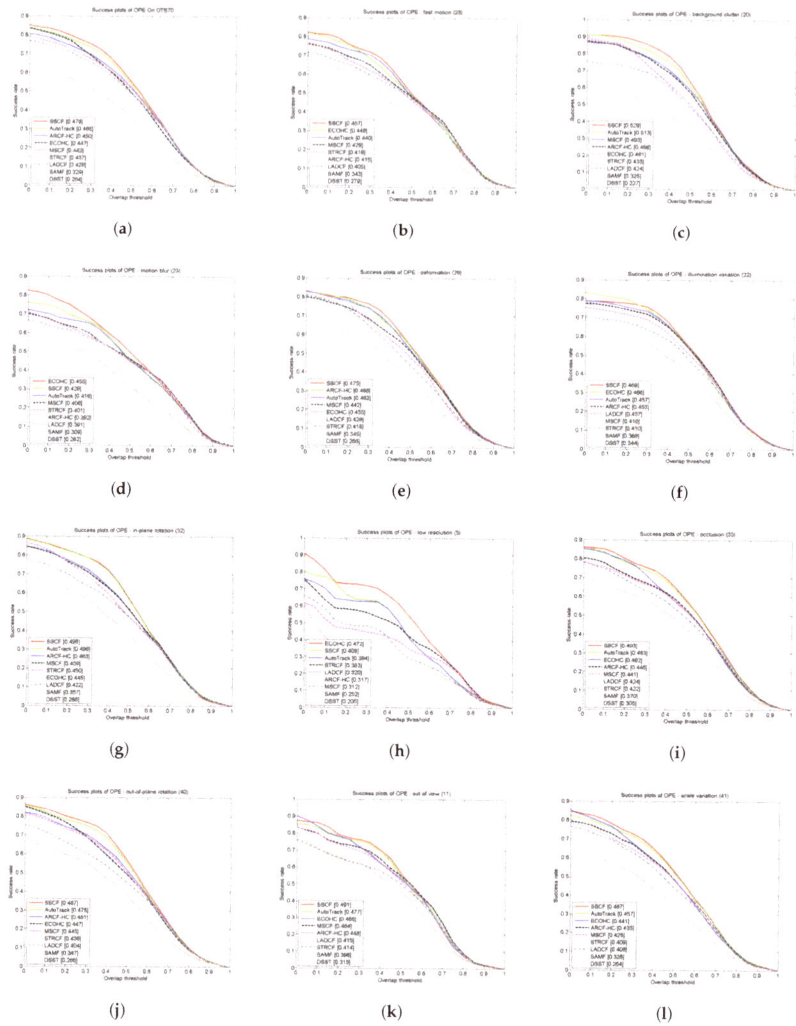

Figure 4. Success plots of the proposed SSCF and the other trackers on the DTB70 database. (**a**) Overall performance; (**b–l**) success plots on the 11 different attributes.

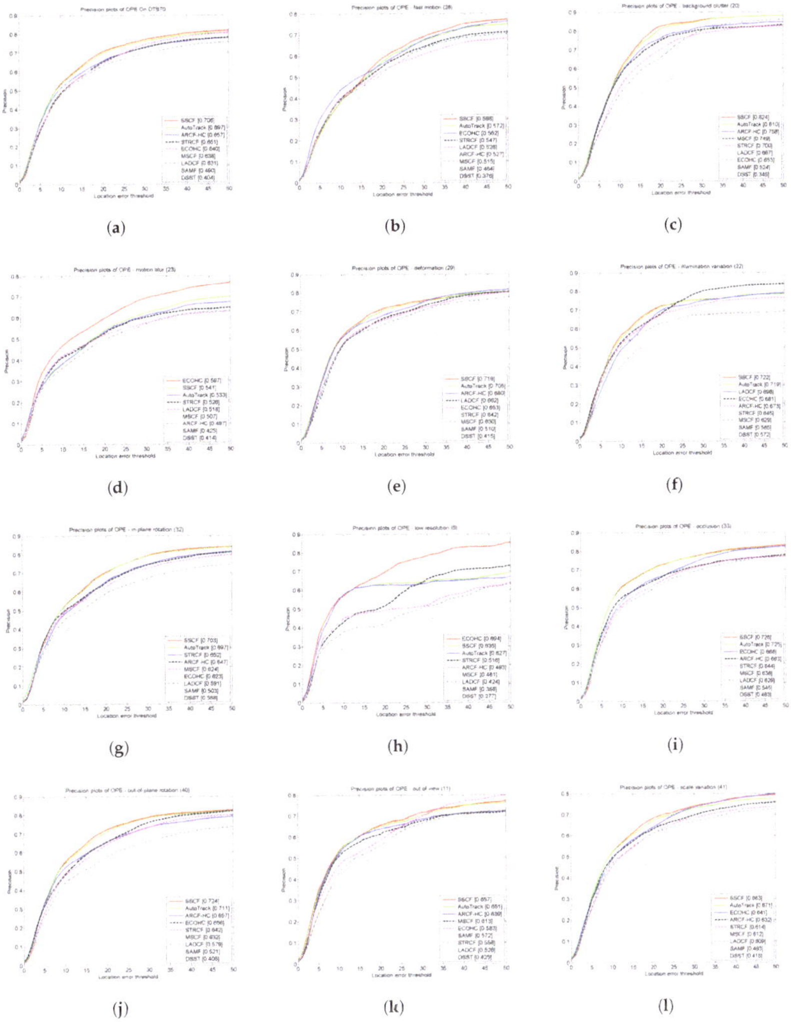

Figure 5. Precision plots of the proposed SSCF and the other trackers on the DTB70 database. (**a**) Overall performance; (**b**–**l**) precision plots on the 11 different attributes.

4.5. Results on the UAV123 Database

The UAV123 dataset contains 123 video sequences, which is the most commonly used and most comprehensive dataset for UAV tracking. The overall performance, which is summarized by success and precision plots, is listed in Figure 6. It can be observed that the proposed SSCF achieved the top-ranking results. The area under the curve (AUC) and distance precision (DP) scores were 0.479 and 0.676, respectively.

In order to visually show the performance of the proposed SSCF in the tracking process, we selected three different types of video sequences, namely person, boat, and car sequences, to conduct the experiments. As shown in Figure 7, each column corresponds to three frames of the images, and the images were randomly selected from the video sequences. The comparative methods were five trackers, including our SSCF, AutoTrack, the MSCF, the STRCF, and the LADCF, marked in green, red, blue, yellow, and orange, respectively. It can be seen that our SSCF always tracked the correct target and had the best performance. The STRCF and LADCF were not robust in tracking the small targets.

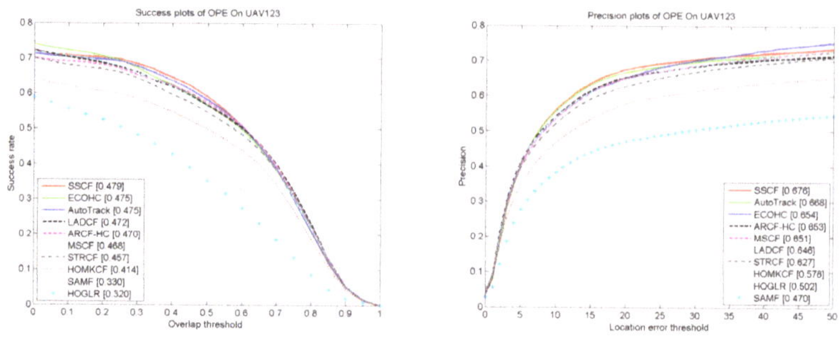

(**a**) (**b**)

Figure 6. Success plots (**a**) and precision plots (**b**) of the proposed SSCF and the other trackers on the UAV123 database.

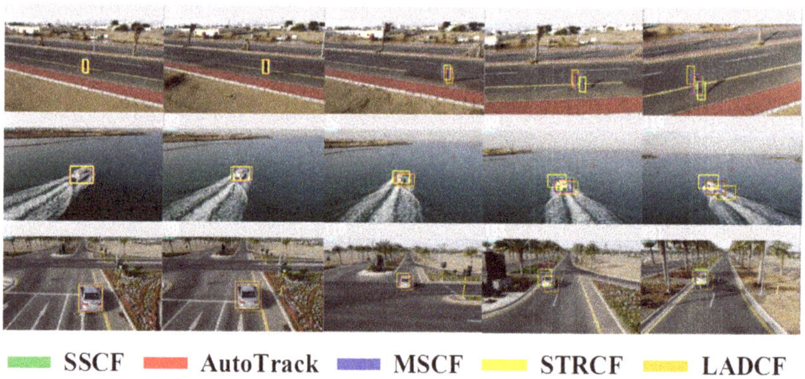

Figure 7. The qualitative analysis of different trackers on three video sequences.

4.6. Results on the UAVDT-M Database

In this section, we compare our SSCF with the existing methods on the UAVDT-M database. We also report the running speed of these methods. The running speed was measured in frames per second (FPS). Table 3 shows the comparison results. It can be observed that our SSCF achieved better performance than the existing trackers. The area under the curve (AUC) and distance precision (DP) scores were 0.667 and 0.928, respectively. However, It should be pointed out that the performance improvement of our tracker came at the expense of speed reduction.

Table 3. The area under the curve (AUC), distance precision (DP) scores, and FPS of the proposed SSCF and other trackers on the UAVDT-M database.

Methods	SSCF	AutoTrack [52]	MSCF [51]	STRCF [24]	ARCF-HC [50]	LADCF [26]	ECOHC [49]	DSST [48]
DP	0.928	0.917	0.913	0.904	0.902	0.895	0.891	0.878
AUC	0.667	0.655	0.642	0.625	0.636	0.614	0.602	0.530
FPS	3.8	65.4	37.6	9.3	15.3	18.2	15.9	100.7

5. Conclusions

In this paper, we proposed a new model called the second-order spatial–temporal correlation filter (SSCF) for visual object tracking. The SSCF is a DCF framework of combining the second-order data-fitting term and spatial–temporal regularization. To solve the proposed model, we divided the optimization problem into several subproblems and adopted the ADMM algorithm to solve each subproblem. By taking full advantage of the second-order data-fitting information, the SSCF becomes more discriminative and robust in addressing complex tracking situations. Extensive experiments on the benchmarking databases demonstrated that our SSCF can achieve competitive performance compared to the state-of-the-art trackers.

It can be noted that the presented SSCF achieved better tracking results than the existing trackers on most of the attributes, but it was not robust on a few attributes, such as low resolution and occlusion. Recently, occlusion-processing methods have been presented in face recognition such as occlusion dictionary learning [58,59] and the occlusion-invariant model [60]. Can these occlusion processing methods be used for object tracking with occlusion? If the answer is yes, how can we design a new model to enhance the performance? It also should be pointed out that the performance improvement of our tracker came at the expense of speed reduction. How to improve the running speed of our SSCF is an important problem. In addition, although the proposed SSCF achieved better results than the existing methods, the accuracy was not high when tracking small targets. Self-paced learning has been widely used in computer vision and machine learning [61]. Combining self-paced learning and filter learning could potentially yield better performance in tracking small targets. In future work, we will focus on these topics.

Author Contributions: Conceptualization, Y.Y. and G.X.; methodology, Y.Y. and G.X.; software, H.H. and J.L.; validation, L.C., H.H., W.Z. and G.X.; writing—original draft preparation, Y.Y.; writing—review and editing, Y.Y., L.C., J.L., W.Z. and G.X.; supervision, L.C. and G.X.; funding acquisition, L.C. All authors have read and agreed to the published version of the manuscript.

Funding: This work was supported in part by the Science and Technology Development Fund, Macau SAR (File no. 0119/2018/A3), in part by the National Natural Science Foundation of China under Grant 62006056, in part by the Natural Science Foundation of Guangdong Province under Grant 2019A1515011266, in part by National Statistical Science Research Project of China under Grant 2020LY090, and in part by Science and Technology Planning Project of Guangzhou under Grant 202102020699.

Institutional Review Board Statement: Not applicable.

Informed Consent Statement: Not applicable.

Acknowledgments: We greatly thank the Reviewers and Editors for the insightful comments and suggestions.

Conflicts of Interest: The authors declare no conflict of interest.

References

1. Yang, J.; Tang, W.; Ding, Z. Long-Term Target Tracking of UAVs Based on Kernelized Correlation Filter. *Mathematics* **2021**, *9*, 3006. [CrossRef]
2. Zhu, X.-F.; Wu, X.-J.; Xu, T.; Feng, Z.; Kittler, J. Robust visual object tracking via adaptive attribute-aware discriminative correlation filters. *IEEE Trans. Multimed.* **2021**, *24*, 1–13. [CrossRef]
3. Deng, C.; He, S.; Han, Y.; Zhao, B. Learning dynamic spatial–temporal regularization for uav object tracking. *IEEE Signal Process. Lett.* **2021**, *28*, 1230–1234. [CrossRef]
4. Yang, H.; Wang, J.; Miao, Y.; Yang, Y.; Zhao, Z.; Wang, Z.; Sun, Q.; Wu, D.O. Combining Spatio-Temporal Context and Kalman Filtering for Visual Tracking. *Mathematics* **2019**, *7*, 1059. [CrossRef]
5. Fang, S.; Ma, Y.; Li, Z.; Zhang, B. A visual tracking algorithm via confidence-based multi-feature correlation filtering. *Multimed. Tools Appl.* **2021**, *80*, 23963–23982. [CrossRef]
6. Bolme, D.S.; Beveridge, J.R.; Draper, B.A.; Lui, Y.M. Visual object tracking using adaptive correlation filters. In Proceedings of the 2010 IEEE Computer Society Conference on Computer Vision and Pattern Recognition, San Francisco, CA, USA, 13–18 June 2010; pp. 2544–2550.
7. Henriques, J.F.; Caseiro, R.; Martins, P.; Batista, J. Exploiting the circulant structure of tracking-by-detection with kernels. In Proceedings of the European Conference on Computer Vision, Florence, Italy, 7–13 October 2012; pp. 702–715.

8. Zhang, K.; Zhang, L.; Liu, Q.; Zhang, D.; Yang, M.-H. Fast visual tracking via dense spatio-temporal context learning. In Proceedings of the European Conference on Computer Vision, Zurich, Switzerland, 6–12 September 2014; pp. 127–141.
9. Wang, Y.; Luo, X.; Ding, L.; Wu, J.; Fu, S. Robust visual tracking via a hybrid correlation filter. *Multimed. Tools Appl.* **2019**, *78*, 31633–31648. [CrossRef]
10. Lukezic, A.; Vojir, T.; Cehovin Zajc, L.; Matas, J.; Kristan, M. Discriminative correlation filter with channel and spatial reliability. In Proceedings of the IEEE Conference on Computer Vision and Pattern Recognition, Honolulu, HI, USA, 21–26 July 2017; pp. 6309–6318.
11. Zhu, H.; Han, Y.; Wang, Y.; Yuan, G. Hybrid cascade filter with complementary features for visual tracking. *IEEE Signal Process. Lett.* **2021**, *28*, 86–90. [CrossRef]
12. Li, Y.; Zhu, J. A scale adaptive kernel correlation filter tracker with feature integration. In Proceedings of the European Conference on Computer Vision, Zurich, Switzerland, 6–12 September 2014; Springer: Cham, Switzerland, 2014; pp. 254–265.
13. Javed, S.; Mahmood, A.; Dias, J.; Seneviratne, L.; Werghi, N. Hierarchical spatiotemporal graph regularized discriminative correlation filter for visual object tracking. *IEEE Trans. Cybern.* **2021**. [CrossRef]
14. Huang, Y.; Zhao, Z.; Wu, B.; Mei, Z.; Gao, G. Visual object tracking with discriminative correlation filtering and hybrid color feature. *Multimedia Tools Appl.* **2019**, *78*, 34725–34744. [CrossRef]
15. Danelljan, M.; Hager, G.; Shahbaz Khan, F.; Felsberg, M. Adaptive decontamination of the training set: A unified formulation for discriminative visual tracking. In Proceedings of the IEEE Conference on Computer Vision and Pattern Recognition, Amsterdam, The Netherlands, 8–16 October 2016; pp. 1430–1438.
16. Zhu, H.; Peng, H.; Xu, G.; Deng, L.; Cheng, Y.; Song, A. Bilateral weighted regression ranking model with spatial–temporal correlation filter for visual tracking. *IEEE Trans. Multimed.* **2021**. [CrossRef]
17. Galoogahi, H.K.; Sim, T.; Lucey, S. Multi-channel correlation filters. In Proceedings of the IEEE International Conference on Computer Vision, Sydney, Australia, 1–8 December 2013; pp. 3072–3079.
18. Han, Y.; Deng, C.; Zhao, B.; Zhao, B. Spatial-temporal context-aware tracking. *IEEE Signal Process. Lett.* **2019**, *26*, 500–504. [CrossRef]
19. Kumar, A.; Walia, G.S.; Sharma, K. Real-time visual tracking via multi-cue based adaptive particle filter framework. *Multimed. Tools Appl.* **2020**, *79*, 20639–20663. [CrossRef]
20. Jain, M.; Tyagi, A.; Subramanyam, A.V.; Denman, S.; Sridharan, S.; Fookes, C. Channel graph regularized correlation filters for visual object tracking. *IEEE Trans. Circuits Syst. Video Technol.* **2021**, *32*, 715–729. [CrossRef]
21. Fu, C.; Xu, J.; Lin, F.; Guo, F.; Zhang, Z. Object saliency-aware dual regularized correlation filter for real-time aerial tracking. *IEEE Trans. Geosci. Remote. Sens.* **2020**, *58*, 8940–8951. [CrossRef]
22. Xu, T.; Feng, Z.-H.; Wu, X.-J.; Kittler, J. Joint group feature selection and discriminative filter learning for robust visual object tracking. In Proceedings of the IEEE International Conference on Computer Vision, Seoul, Korea, 27–28 October 2019; pp. 7950–7960.
23. Danelljan, M.; Hager, G.; Shahbaz Khan, F.; Felsberg, M. Learning spatially regularized correlation filters for visual tracking. In Proceedings of the IEEE International Conference on Computer Vision, Santiago, Chile, 7–13 December 2015; pp. 4310–4318.
24. Li, F.; Tian, C.; Zuo, W.; Zhang, L.; Yang, M.-H. Learning spatial temporal regularized correlation filters for visual tracking. In Proceedings of the IEEE Conference on Computer Vision and Pattern Recognition, Salt Lake City, UT, USA, 18–23 June 2018; 4904–4913.
25. Kiani Galoogahi, H.; Fagg, A.; Lucey, S. Learning background-aware correlation filters for visual tracking. In Proceedings of the IEEE International Conference on Computer Vision, Venice, Italy, 22–29 October 2017; pp. 1135–1143.
26. Xu, T.; Feng, Z.-H.; Wu, X.-J.; Kittler, J. Learning adaptive discriminative correlation filters via temporal consistency preserving spatial feature selection for robust visual object tracking. *IEEE Trans. Image Process.* **2019**, *28*, 5596–5609. [CrossRef]
27. Deng, L.; Zhang, J.; Xu, G.; Zhu, H. Infrared small target detection via adaptive m-estimator ring top-hat transformation. *Pattern Recognit.* **2021**, *112*, 1–9. [CrossRef]
28. You, X.; Li, Q.; Tao, D.; Ou, W.; Gong, M. Local metric learning for exemplar-based object detection. *IEEE Trans. Circuits And Systems Video Technol.* **2014**, *24*, 1265–1276.
29. Zhu, H.; Ni, H.; Liu, S.; Xu, G.; Deng, L. Tnlrs: Target-aware non-local low-rank modeling with saliency filtering regularization for infrared small target detection. *IEEE Trans. Image Process.* **2020**, *29*, 9546–9558. [CrossRef]
30. Guan, Y.; Wang, Y. Joint detection and tracking scheme for target tracking in moving platform. In Proceedings of the IEEE Radar Conference (RadarConf20), Florence, Italy, 21–25 September 2020; pp. 1–4.
31. Zhang, L.; Fang, Q. Multi-target tracking based on target detection and mutual information. In Proceedings of the Chinese Control and Decision Conference (CCDC), Kunming, China, 22–24 May 2020; pp. 1242–1245.
32. Liu, C.; Gong, J.; Zhu, J.; Zhang, J.; Yan, Y. Correlation filter with motion detection for robust tracking of shape-deformed targets. *IEEE Access* **2020**, *8*, 89161–89170. [CrossRef]
33. Min, Y.; Wei, Z.; Tan, K. A detection aided multi-filter target tracking algorithm. *IEEE Access* **2019**, *7*, 71616–71626. [CrossRef]
34. Ou, W.; Yu, S.; Li, G.; Lu, J.; Zhang, K.; Xie, G. Multi-view non-negative matrix factorization by patch alignment framework with view consistency. *Neurocomputing* **2016**, *204*, 116–124. [CrossRef]
35. Long, Z.Z.; Xu, G.; Du, J.; Zhu, H.; Yu, Y.F. Flexible subspace clustering: A joint feature selection and k-means clustering framework. *Big Data Res.* **2021**, *23*, 1–9. [CrossRef]

36. Mishro, P.K.; Agrawal, S.; Panda, R.; Abraham, A. A novel type-2 fuzzy c-means clustering for brain mr image segmentation. *IEEE Trans. Cybern.* **2021**, *51*, 3901–3912. [CrossRef] [PubMed]
37. Ayo, F.E.; Folorunso, O.; Ibharalu, F.T.; Osinuga, I.A.; Abayomi-Alli, A. A probabilistic clustering model for hate speech classification in twitter. *Expert Syst. Appl.* **2021**, *173*, 1–21. [CrossRef]
38. Keuper, M.; Tang, S.; Andres, B.; Brox, T.; Schiele, B. Motion segmentation amp; multiple object tracking by correlation co-clustering. *IEEE Trans. Pattern Anal. Mach. Intell.* **2020**, *42*, 140–153. [CrossRef]
39. Li, L.-Q.; Wang, X.-L.; Liu, Z.-X.; Xie, W.-X. A novel intuitionistic fuzzy clustering algorithm based on feature selection for multiple object tracking. *Int. J. Fuzzy Syst.* **2019**, *21*, 1613–1628. [CrossRef]
40. He, S.; Shin, H.-S.; Tsourdos, A. Multi-sensor multi-target tracking using domain knowledge and clustering. *IEEE Sens. J.* **2018**, *18*, 8074–8084. [CrossRef]
41. Gou, J.; Qiu, W.; Yi, Z.; Shen, X.; Zhan, Y.; Ou, W. Locality constrained representation-based k-nearest neighbor classification. *Knowl.-Based Syst.* **2019**, *167*, 38–52. [CrossRef]
42. Gou, J.; Ma, H.; Ou, W.; Zeng, S.; Rao, Y.; Yang, H. A generalized mean distance-based k-nearest neighbor classifier. *Expert Syst. Appl.* **2019**, *115*, 356–372. [CrossRef]
43. Yu, Y.-F.; Dai, D.-Q.; Ren, C.-X.; Huang, K.-K. Discriminative multi-layer illumination-robust feature extraction for face recognition. *Pattern Recognit.* **2017**, *67*, 201–212. [CrossRef]
44. Du, F.; Liu, P.; Zhao, W.; Tang, X. Joint channel reliability and correlation filters learning for visual tracking. *IEEE Trans. Circuits Syst. Video Technol.* **2020**, *30*, 1625–1638. [CrossRef]
45. Li, A.; Yang, M.; Yang, W. Feature integration with adaptive importance maps for visual tracking. In Proceedings of the Twenty-Seventh International Joint Conference on Artificial Intelligence, Stockholm, Sweden, 13–19 July 2018; pp. 779–785. [CrossRef]
46. Lukezic, A.; Vojir, T.; Ehovinzajc, L.; Matas, J.; Kristan, M. Discriminative correlation filter with channel and spatial reliability. *Int. Comput. Vis.* **2018**, *126*, 671–688. [CrossRef]
47. Henriques, J.F.; Caseiro, R.; Martins, P.; Batista, J. High-speed tracking with kernelized correlation filters. *IEEE Trans. Pattern Anal. Mach. Intell.* **2014**, *37*, 583–596. [CrossRef] [PubMed]
48. Danelljan, M.; Hager, G.; Khan, F.S.; Felsberg, M. Discriminative scale space tracking. *IEEE Trans. Pattern Anal. Mach.* **2016**, *39*, 1561–1575. [CrossRef] [PubMed]
49. Danelljan, M.; Bhat, G.; Khan, F.S.; Felsberg, M. ECO: Efficient Convolution Operators for Tracking. In Proceedings of the IEEE Conference on Computer Vision and Pattern Recognition, Honolulu, HI, USA, 21–26 July 2017; pp. 6638–6646.
50. Huang, Z.; Fu, C.; Li, Y.; Lin, F.; Lu, P. Learning aberrance repressed correlation filters for real-time UAV tracking. In Proceedings of the IEEE/CVF International Conference on Computer Vision, Seoul, Korea, 27 October–2 November 2019; pp. 2891–2900.
51. Zheng, G.; Fu, C.; Ye, J.; Lin, F.; Ding, F. Mutation Sensitive Correlation Filter for Real-Time UAV Tracking with Adaptive Hybrid Label. In Proceedings of the IEEE International Conference on Robotics and Automation, Xi'an, China, 30 May–5 June 2021; pp. 503–509.
52. Li, Y.; Fu, C.; Ding, F.; Huang, Z.; Lu, G. AutoTrack: Towards High-Performance Visual Tracking for UAV With Automatic Spatio-Temporal Regularization. In Proceedings of the IEEE/CVF Conference on Computer Vision and Pattern Recognition (CVPR), Seattle, WA, USA, 14–19 June 2020; pp. 11920–11929.
53. Wu, Y.; Lim, J.; Yang, M.-H. Online object tracking: A benchmark. In Proceedings of the IEEE Conference on Computer Vision and Pattern Recognition (CVPR), Portland, OR, USA, 23–28 June 2013; pp. 2411–2418.
54. Wu, Y.; Lim, J.; Yang, M.-H. Object tracking benchmark. *IEEE Trans. Pattern Anal. Mach. Intell.* **2015**, *37*, 1834–1848. [CrossRef] [PubMed]
55. Li, S.; Yeung, D. Visual object tracking for unmanned aerial vehicles: A benchmark and new motion models. In Proceedings of the AAAI Conference on Artificial Intelligence, San Francisco, CA, USA, 4–9 February 2017; pp. 4140–4146.
56. Mueller, M.; Smith, N.; Ghanem, B. A benchmark and simulator for UAV tracking. In Proceedings of the European Conference on Computer Vision, Amsterdam, The Netherlands, 8–16 October 2016; pp. 445–461.
57. Du, D.; Qi, Y.; Yu, H.; Yang, Y.; Duan, K.; Li, G.; Zhang, W.; Huang, Q.; Tian, Q. The unmanned aerial vehicle benchmark: object detection and tracking. In Proceedings of the ECCV, Munich, Germany, 8–14 September 2018; pp. 370–386.
58. Ou, W.; You, X.; Tao, D.; Zhang, P.; Tang, Y.; Zhu, Z. Robust face recognition via occlusion dictionary learning. *Pattern Recognit.* **2014**, *47*, 1559–1572. [CrossRef]
59. Ou, W.; Luan, X.; Gou, J.; Zhou, Q.; Xiao, W.; Xiong, X.; Zeng, W. Robust discriminative nonnegative dictionary learning for occluded face recognition. *Pattern Recognit. Lett.* **2018**, *107*, 41–49. [CrossRef]
60. Sharma, S.; Kumar, V. Voxel-based 3d occlusion-invariant face recognition using game theory and simulated annealing. *Multimed. Tools Appl.* **2020**, *79*, 26517–26547. [CrossRef]
61. Zhu, H.; Qiao, Y.; Xu, G.; Deng, L.; Yu, Y.-F. Dspnet: A lightweight dilated convolution neural networks for spectral deconvolution with selfpaced learning. *IEEE Trans. Ind. Inform.* **2020**, *16*, 7392–7401. [CrossRef]

mathematics

Article

A RUL Prediction Method of Small Sample Equipment Based on DCNN-BiLSTM and Domain Adaptation

Wenbai Chen [1,*], Weizhao Chen [1], Huixiang Liu [1], Yiqun Wang [1], Chunli Bi [2] and Yu Gu [3,4,5]

1 School of Automation, Beijing Information Science and Technology University, Beijing 100101, China; chenwz312@163.com (W.C.); liuhx@bistu.edu.cn (H.L.); wangyiqun@bistu.edu.cn (Y.W.)
2 China Academy of Information and Communications Technology, Beijing 100191, China; bichunli@caict.ac.cn
3 Guangdong Province Key Laboratory of Petrochemical Equipment Fault Diagnosis, Guangdong University of Petrochemical Technology, Maoming 525000, China; guyufrankfurt@163.com
4 College of Information Science and Technology, Beijing University of Chemical Technology, Beijing 100029, China
5 Department of Chemistry, Institute of Inorganic and Analytical Chemistry, Goethe-University, Max-von-Laue-Str. 9, 60438 Frankfurt, Germany
* Correspondence: chenwb@bistu.edu.cn

Abstract: To solve the problem of low accuracy of remaining useful life (RUL) prediction caused by insufficient sample data of equipment under complex operating conditions, an RUL prediction method of small sample equipment based on a deep convolutional neural network—bidirectional long short-term memory network (DCNN-BiLSTM) and domain adaptation is proposed. Firstly, in order to extract the common features of the equipment under the condition of sufficient samples, a network model that combines the deep convolutional neural network (DCNN) and the bidirectional long short-term memory network (BiLSTM) was used to train the source domain and target domain data simultaneously. The Maximum Mean Discrepancy (MMD) was used to constrain the distribution difference and achieve adaptive matching and feature alignment between the target domain samples and the source domain samples. After obtaining the pre-trained model, fine-tuning was used to transfer the network structure and parameters of the pre-trained model to the target domain for training, perform network optimization and finally obtain an RUL prediction model that was more suitable for the target domain data. The method was validated on a simulation dataset of commercial modular aero-propulsion provided by NASA, and the experimental results show that the method improves the prediction accuracy and generalization ability of equipment RUL under cross-working conditions and small sample conditions.

Keywords: DCNN-BiLSTM; domain adaptation; MMD; fine-tuning; C-MAPSS; cross-working; small sample

Citation: Chen, W.; Chen, W.; Liu, H.; Wang, Y.; Bi, C.; Gu, Y. A RUL Prediction Method of Small Sample Equipment Based on DCNN-BiLSTM and Domain Adaptation. *Mathematics* **2022**, *10*, 1022. https://doi.org/10.3390/math10071022

Academic Editors: Jianping Gou, Weihua Ou, Shaoning Zeng and Lan Du

Received: 16 February 2022
Accepted: 19 March 2022
Published: 23 March 2022

1. Introduction

As one of the key technologies of Prognosis and Health Management (PHM), RUL prediction has become an important research content. RUL refers to the length of continuous working time of equipment components or systems from the current moment to the moment when a specific function cannot be performed [1]. Accurate RUL prediction plays a crucial role in guaranteeing system reliability and preventing system failures [2].

At present, the widely studied equipment RUL prediction methods can be divided into physical model-based methods and data-driven methods [3]. Due to the complex structure of some systems, the diverse failure modes, and the uncertainty of operating conditions, it is difficult to establish a physical failure model [4]. Data-driven methods without prior knowledge and complex physical modeling process [5] have become a research hotspot in recent years. Among them, deep learning has attracted much attention due to its powerful nonlinear mapping ability and high-dimensional feature extraction ability [6]. Babu et al. [7]

first tried to use the Convolutional Neural Network (CNN) to apply it to the RUL prediction of aero-engines. This model can automatically extract multi-dimensional sensor features and obtain better results than the shallow regression model. Zheng et al. [8] proposed a prediction model based on a Long Short-Term Memory (LSTM) network, which can extract the features of time series, is suitable for RUL prediction of most equipment.

The premise of data-driven methods is that the training and test data come from the same operating conditions. As a new machine learning method, transfer learning relaxes the premise that training samples and test samples must obey the same data distribution. The knowledge learned from the source domain is applied to different but related target domains to solve the problem of only a small number of labeled sample data in the target domain. Transfer learning improves the generalization ability of the machine learning model to a certain extent [9]. When the feature space and data distribution between the source domain and target domain samples are quite different, how to use the transfer learning strategy to solve the small sample problem becomes the focus of research.

Domain adaptation is an important research direction in transfer learning, which is used to solve the problem of transfer learning when the feature space and category space of two domains are consistent but the feature distribution is inconsistent. Domain adaptation methods have been used in the field of RUL prediction of equipment. Fu et al. [10] proposed a domain adaptation SAE-LSTM model, which adopted MMD to reduce the data distribution difference in RUL prediction. Li et al. [11] first proposed a multi-core MMD-based convolutional neural network model. Ragab [12] proposed a Contrastive Adversarial Domain Adaptation (CADA) method to learn similar features between different domains and improve the RUL prediction accuracy and noise immunity. Miao [13] proposed a Deep Domain Adaptative Network (DDAN) to solve the problem of cross-domain feature distribution shift under different operating conditions and failure modes. Costa et al. [14] proposed a domain adaptation method for RUL prediction under cross-working conditions based on LSTM and Domain Adversarial Neural Network (DANN). In order to solve the problem of low RUL prediction accuracy caused by small sample data sets, Lv et al. [15] proposed a Sequence Adaptation Adversarial Network (SAAN) to expand the dataset.

Traditional deep learning relies heavily on labeled data. Therefore, in view of the problem that small-sample equipment status data under different working conditions affect the RUL prediction accuracy, this paper proposes a small-sample equipment RUL prediction method based on DCNN-BiLSTM and domain adaptation. The model includes a pre-training stage, a parameter-transfer stage, and an RUL predicting stage. The pre-training and MMD constraints are used to reduce the distribution differences of sample data under different working conditions and learn the common characteristics of the source domain samples and the target domain samples after domain adaptation. Then transfer the trained model to the target domain for training fine-tune the pre-trained model to obtain an RUL prediction model more suitable for the target domain task. Finally, the Commercial Modular Aero-Propulsion System Simulation (C-MAPSS) dataset provided by NASA was used to verify the effectiveness of the method proposed in this paper.

2. Related Work

2.1. CNN Convolution Model

The CNN has powerful parameter learning and feature extraction capabilities and can be used to process multi-dimensional matrix data. In practical engineering applications, each device has multiple sensors to detect the operating status of the device, and the collected data also contains a lot of information. In order to extract deeper features, this paper used a DCNN, which consists of multiple layers of CNN.

Since the degradation data of the equipment is the time series data collected by the sensor, in this study, the input data is a two-dimensional vector, the length represents the number of features collected by the sensor, and the width represents the time series of each feature. After the two-dimensional data is processed by time window, the size of each sample obtained is represented as (N_w, m), where N_w represents the size of the time window and m represents the number of features. Each convolutional layer performs convolution operations on the input data along the time series direction through convolution kernels of different sizes, which can extract different features between the data, and finally combine the generated local feature maps as the input of the BiLSTM.

2.2. BiLSTM Network Model

The LSTM model is used to process sequence data. Compared with the Recurrent Neural Network (RNN), LSTM is mainly used to solve the problems of gradient disappearance and gradient explosion in the training process of long sequence data. The LSTM model consists of an input layer, a hidden layer, and an output layer, with three gating units and memory units, and the historical information is affected by the input gate, forgetting gate, and output gate, respectively [16]. The dependencies between long and short periods of time series can be better learned.

As shown in Figure 1, i_t, o_t, f_t represent the input gate, output gate, and forget gate, respectively. The forget gate decides whether to retain the previous cell state information C_{t-1}; the input gate updates the long-term memory of the cell state; the output gate is the output of the current LSTM; $\widetilde{C}_t$ represents the current temporary memory unit; x_t represents the time series of moments t; h_{t-1} represents the output value of the previous moment; h_t represents the output value of the current moment. Then the calculation formula of each threshold state in the forward propagation process of LSTM is as follows:

$$\widetilde{C}_t = \tanh(W_{xc}x_t + W_{hc}h_{t-1} + b_c) \tag{1}$$

$$C_t = f_t C_{t-1} + i_t\widetilde{C}_t \tag{2}$$

$$i_t = \sigma(W_{xi}x_t + W_{hi}h_{t-1} + W_{ci}c_{t-1} + b_i) \tag{3}$$

$$f_t = \sigma\left(W_{xf}x_t + W_{hf}h_{t-1} + W_{cf}c_{t-1} + b_f\right) \tag{4}$$

$$o_t = \sigma(W_{xo}x_t + W_{ho}h_{t-1} + W_{co}c_{t-1} + b_o) \tag{5}$$

$$h_t = o_t \cdot \tanh(c_t) \tag{6}$$

where σ represents the sigmoid activation function, tanh is the hyperbolic tangent activation function, W_{xc}, W_{hc}, W_{xi}, W_{hi}, W_{ci}, W_{xf}, W_{hf}, W_{cf}, W_{xo}, W_{ho}, W_{co}, b_c, b_i, b_f, and b_o represent the weights and bias terms of each respective gate. LSTM contains many neurons, and the neurons exchange information with each other to extract time-dependent features of the data.

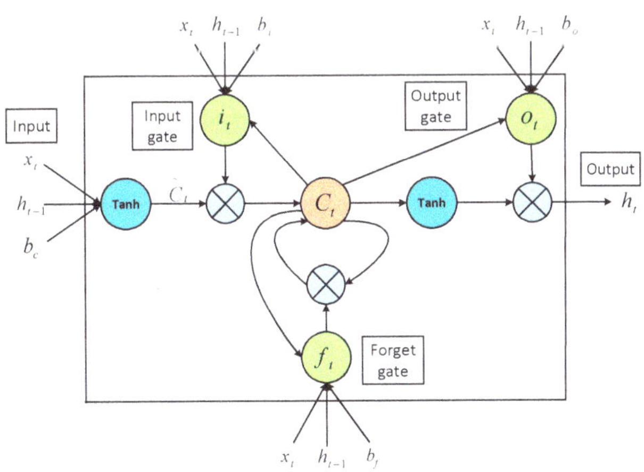

Figure 1. LSTM structure diagram.

Bi-directional LSTM (BiLSTM) contains two LSTM network layers in opposite directions, namely the forward propagation layer and the backward propagation layer, which connect the input layer and the output layer at the same time, perform time-sequence and reverse-order calculations, respectively, and obtain the output of the forward and backward hidden layer at each moment in turn. Finally, the final output is obtained by combining the corresponding output results of the forward layer and the backward layer at each moment. The BiLSTM structure diagram is shown in Figure 2. The specific calculation formula is as follows:

$$h_t = f(w_1 x_t + w_2 h_{t-1}) \tag{7}$$

$$h_t{}' = f(w_3 x_t + w_5 h_{t-1}{}') \tag{8}$$

$$o_t = g(w_4 x_4 + w_6 h_t{}') \tag{9}$$

where h_t and h_t' are the outputs of the forward propagation layer and the backward propagation layer at time t, respectively. w_1 and w_3 are the weight matrices from the input layer to the forward and backward propagation layers, respectively. w_2 and w_5 are the weight matrices from the forward and backward propagation layers to the self-propagation layer, respectively. w_4 and w_6 are the weight matrices from the forward and backward propagation layers to the output layer, respectively. o_t is the output values of the final output gate. g are the functions for splicing the forward and backward propagation results.

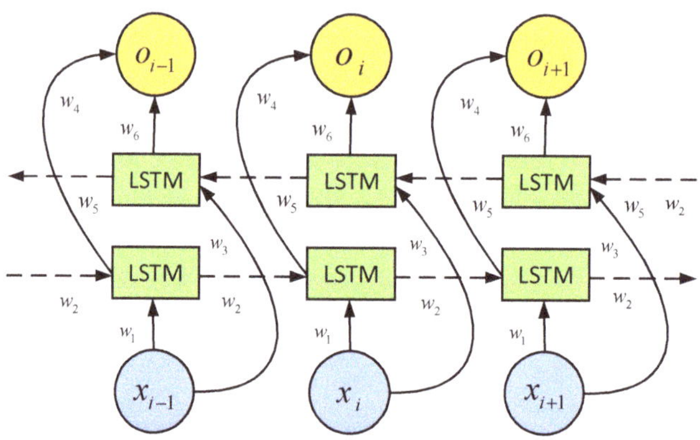

Figure 2. BiLSTM structure diagram.

3. Proposed Method

3.1. RUL Prediction Model Based on DCNN-BiLSTM

The multi-dimensional sensor data obtained through time window processing is used as the input of the DCNN-BiLSTM fusion model, and the structure of the fusion model is shown in Figure 3. DCNN and BiLSTM process the input data, where DCNN consists of four layers of CNN and activation functions. Each layer of CNN performs low-level feature extraction by setting convolution kernels of different sizes, and then input to two layers of BiLSTM to extract time-series features, and finally two layers of fully connected layers. The BiLSTM network can comprehensively consider the historical information and future information at each moment and make full use of the information of the previous and subsequent moments to make the feature extraction process more comprehensive, improve the prediction accuracy of the time series model, and reduce the risk of overfitting. The output of the first fully connected layer is used as the measurement value of MMD. The second layer is the final prediction layer, and the output represents the RUL value of the device.

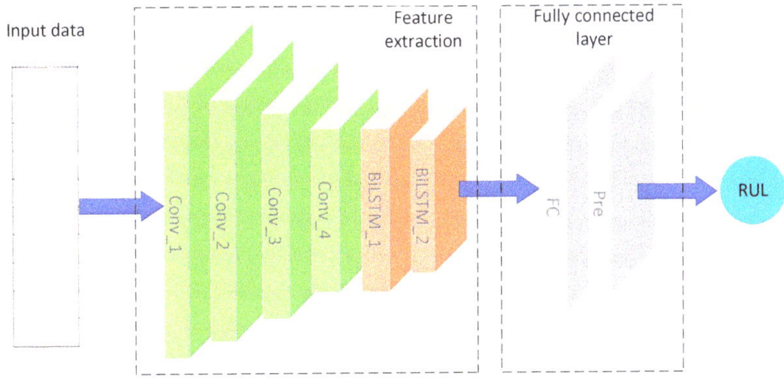

Figure 3. DCNN-BiLSTM structure diagram.

3.2. Domain Adaptation Method Based on MMD

Domain adaptation is a method of transfer learning. Domain adaptation is a machine learning algorithm that targets the distribution difference between source and target domains. A wide variety of domain adaptation methods aim to apply knowledge learned from the source domain to the target domain in the absence or few labels of the target domain by learning domain-invariant features of the source and target domains.

The MMD is the most widely used loss function in transfer learning, especially domain adaptation, and is mainly used to measure the distance between two different but similar distributions. Compared to other metrics, MMD can estimate nonparametric distances between various distributions and avoid the computation of intermediate process quantities. MMD maps the source and target domains to a Reproducing kernel Hilbert space (RKHS) and then calculates the distribution distance between the two domains. MMD is defined as:

$$MMD(X, Y) = \left\| \frac{1}{n_s} \sum_{i=1}^{n_s} \varphi(x_i) - \frac{1}{n_t} \sum_{j=1}^{n_t} \varphi(y_j) \right\|_{\mathcal{H}}^2 \tag{10}$$

where $\mathcal{H}$ represents the RHKS space, n_s and n_t represents the number of samples in the source domain and the target domain, respectively, $\varphi(x) : X \to \mathcal{H}$ represents the mapping function from the original feature space to the RKHS, and then uses the kernel method to calculate the inner product to avoid high-dimensional complex operations, usually using a Gaussian kernel function, which represents for:

$$K(\mu, \nu) = e^{\frac{-\|\mu-\nu\|^2}{\sigma}} \tag{11}$$

where μ and ν represent different samples and σ is the width parameter of the function, which controls the radial range of the function.

In the case where there is a difference in the distribution between the source domain data and the target domain data, the MMD is added to the loss function to optimize the target. Therefore, the loss function of the pre-trained network model is defined as:

$$Loss = MSE\_loss + \lambda MMD\_loss \tag{12}$$

where MSE_loss is the mean square loss function and λ represents the balance function, $\lambda > 0$.

The transfer learning in this paper is based on the method of domain adaptation. During the pre-training process, the source domain and target domain datasets are trained at the same time. The output value of the first fully connected layer of the DCNN-BiLSTM network model is used as the sample space for calculating the distribution distance between the two domainsm, and finally, the pre-training model after domain adaptation is obtained. The training process is shown in Figure 4.

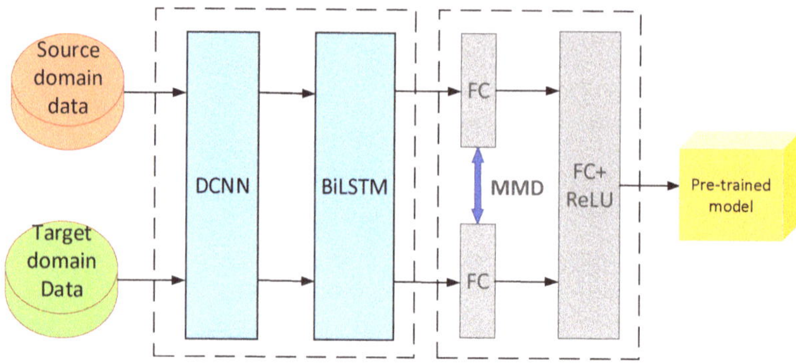

Figure 4. The pre-training framework based on domain adaptation.

3.3. Fine-Tune the Target Model

In order to shorten the training time of the target model, make the target model more adaptable to different operating conditions and environments, and improve the generalization ability. In this section, the Adam optimizer is used to fine-tune the pre-trained model. The flowchart of fine-tuning is shown in Figure 5. First, initialize the target model with the weights and parameters of the pre-trained model, then freeze the parameters of the feature extraction layers, including 4-layer CNN and 2-layer BiLSTM, and only update the parameters of the task-specific layer, i.e., the two-layer fully connected layer. Furthermore, to prevent overfitting, different learning rates are set for the two fully connected layers. Finally, a prediction model that is more suitable for the target domain task and has strong generalization ability is obtained by training.

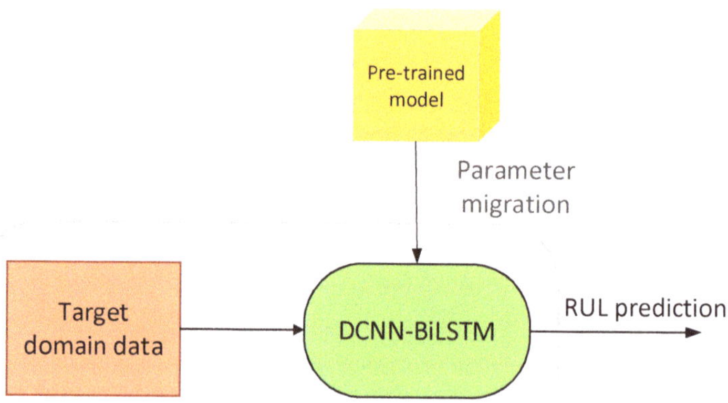

Figure 5. The flowchart of fine-tuning.

4. Experimental Results and Analysis

4.1. Dataset Description

The method in this paper was evaluated using the turbofan engine degradation data of the Commercial Modular Aero-Propulsion System Simulation (C-MAPSS) dataset provided by NASA. The detailed information of the dataset is presented in Table 1.This dataset consists of four different sub-datasets with different operational conditions and fault modes. Each sub-dataset contains time-series information collected by 21 sensors and 3 measurements of operational conditions. The training set and the test set have different numbers of degraded engines, each with a different degree of initial wear, and after the number of cycles increases, the engine slowly ages until it fails to work. The training set records the degradation process of the entire life cycle of the engine, while the test set only includes a certain moment before failure. The task is to predict the remaining useful life (RUL) of the engine units in the test set.

Table 1. Information of the C-MAPSS dataset.

Subdataset	FD001	FD002	FD003	FD004
Training set engine unit	100	260	100	249
Test set engine unit	100	259	100	248
Training set sample size	17,731	48,558	21,220	56,815
Test set sample size	100	259	100	248
Maximum life cycle	362	378	512	128
Operational conditions	1	6	1	6
Fault modes	1	1	2	2

Seven sensor values were observed to remain unchanged within the FD001 subset. In order to save computing resources, meaningless data is eliminated, and 14 sensors were obtained as 2, 3, 4, 7, 8, 9, 11, 12, 13, 14, 15, 17, 20, and 21.

4.2. Data Processing

The original data is composed of data detected by multiple sensors. Different data sets have different sequence lengths, and the data dimensions are high and have different dimensions. Therefore, the min-max normalization method is used to unify the data into the range [−1,1]. Each measurement $x_{i,j}$ is min-max normalized and can be expressed as [17]:

$$\widetilde{x}_{i,j} = \frac{2\left(x_{i,j} - x^{j}_{min}\right)}{\left(x^{j}_{max} - x^{j}_{min}\right)} - 1 \tag{13}$$

where $\widetilde{x}_{i,j}$ represents the normalized data, x^{j}_{min} and x^{j}_{max} represents the minimum and maximum values of the data monitored by the jth sensor in one operating cycle, respectively.

In order to obtain more useful temporal information from the input data, the normalized data is subjected to time windowing. For continuous time-series data, a sliding time window is used to define data labels, and the size of the input model sequence is determined by the size of the time window.

The window of size N_w slides along the time series, and each time step slides l will feedback the data to the slider, which is used as the input of the prediction model, so the input size of the network is $N_w \times m$. To get more samples and reduce the risk of overfitting, the sliding time step is set to 1.

When the engine is running under normal conditions, taking the remaining operating cycle period as RUL, then we assume that RUL decreases linearly, using a piecewise linear function, choose 125 as the initial life period [18], and apply it to the training set and test set.

4.3. Selection of Evaluation Indicators

To verify the effectiveness of the method in this paper, two functions were used as evaluation metrics, namely the Root Mean Square Error (RMSE) function and the Score function [19]. The RMSE function formula is:

$$RMSE = \sqrt{\frac{1}{N}\sum_{i=1}^{N}(\hat{y}_i - y_i)} \quad (14)$$

The formula for the Score function is:

$$Score = \begin{cases} \sum_{i=1}^{N}(e^{-\frac{\hat{y}_i - y_i}{13}} - 1), \hat{y}_i - y_i < 0 \\ \sum_{i=1}^{N}(e^{\frac{\hat{y}_i - y_i}{10}} - 1), \hat{y}_i - y_i \geq 0 \end{cases} \quad (15)$$

where $\hat{y}_i$ and y_i represent the predicted value and the actual value of RUL, respectively.

RMSE reflects the degree of fit between the predicted life and the actual life, and the size of the Score measures the rationality of life prediction. The lower the values of RMSE and Score, the better the predictive ability of the model.

4.4. Experimental Configuration and Parameters

All experiments in this paper are performed on a processor configured with 16 GB memory (RAM), NVIDIA GeForce TITAN XP graphics card, and Intel(R) Xeon(R) CPU E5-2620 v4 @ 2.10GHz processor. The network model proposed in this paper is based on Python3.6 and the PyTorch deep learning framework. In the experiments in this paper, considering the influence of the sample size on the prediction accuracy and the influence of different operational conditions and fault modes, in order to improve the generalization ability of the RUL prediction model, according to the size of the data, we use FD002 and FD004 with the sufficient sample size in C-MAPPS as source domain datasets, and FD001 and FD003 datasets in C-MAPPS with insufficient sample size as target domains. We evaluate the performance of transfer learning in RUL prediction of the target domain and investigate how different working conditions and the number of samples of the source and target domain datasets affect the performance of the final prediction model. Therefore, set the experimental tasks as shown in Table 2.

Table 2. Transfer learning experiment tasks.

Source Domain	Target Domain	Operational Conditions	Fault Mode
FD002	FD001	6→1	1→1
	FD003	6→1	1→2
FD004	FD001	6→1	2→1
	FD003	6→1	2→2

4.5. Model Prediction Results and Analysis

In order to compare the effectiveness of the transfer learning method proposed in this paper, the results of the method were compared with the experiments without transfer, as shown in Table 3. Source-Only refers to directly testing the target domain with the pre-trained model, Target-Only refers to training and testing only on the target domain.

Table 3. Compare transfer learning with no transfer.

Methods	FD002→FD001		FD002→FD003		FD004→FD001		FD004→FD003	
	RMSE	Score	RMSE	Score	RMSE	Score	RMSE	Score
Source-Only	84.63	5,355,207.6	51.39	362,392.1	41.45	18,345.5	42.65	14,591.2
Target-Only	15.84	534.13	14.66	281.12	17.28	473.87	16.32	349.55
TL	14.36	371.86	13.66	243.22	16.35	432.37	14.79	296.34

As can be seen from Table 3, the transfer learning algorithm proposed in this paper greatly improves the accuracy of the prediction model. Due to the influence of the difference in the distribution of the data set, the pre-training model of Source-Only was directly used for testing, and the effect was very bad. On the basis of the traditional Target-Only prediction method, the pre-training model after domain adaptation was loaded, and then the model was optimized in the target domain, and the prediction accuracy was improved. Take FD002→FD003 as an example, the RMSE increased by at least 6.82%, and the score function value increased by at least 13.48%.

In the pre-training stage, the MMD item of the tuning process not only affected the prediction accuracy of the data set but also affected the matching degree of the conditional distribution. Therefore, the coefficient λ of MMD_loss of the loss function had a greater impact on the adaptive effect. Taking FD002→FD001 as an example, when -1 was used as the median value, a large number of comparative experiments were carried out by increasing or decreasing order of magnitude. As shown in Figure 6, the horizontal axis is the value size, and the vertical axis is the two evaluation indicators values of RMSE and Score. It can be seen that when $\lambda = 0.001$, both RMSE and Score achieve the minimum value, so the coefficient value λ of MMD_loss in this experiment was 0.001.

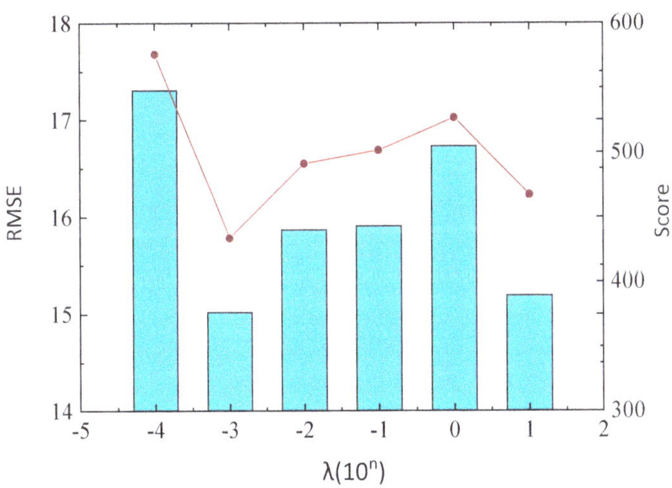

Figure 6. The impact of different λ values on the prediction results.

In order to compare the prediction effect of the DCNN-BiLSTM model based on transfer learning on the small sample data set, Figure 7 shows the prediction results of all the engine units on the test set sorted from small to large according to the RUL value of the four tasks of experiments. The horizontal axis represents the test engine unit, and the vertical axis represents the RUL. It can be seen from Figure 7 that the DCNN model could effectively extract the detailed features and similar features of the engine degradation, even if it is difficult to predict at the beginning of the operation. The value was also closer to the set value of 125. As the running period increases, BiLSTM could effectively obtain the relationship between the time series before and after. Combining the functions of fusion model and domain adaptation, it can be seen from Figure 7 that its prediction trend was stable and could better fit the real degradation curve. Therefore, the transfer learning model proposed in this paper shows a good prediction effect.

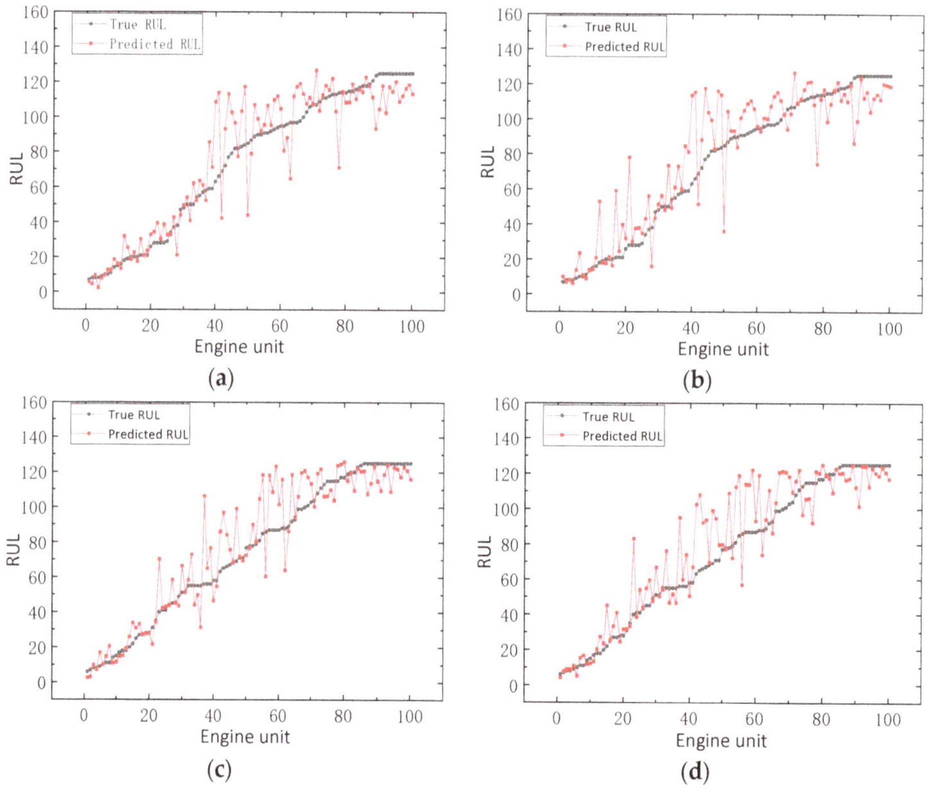

Figure 7. RUL prediction results of four tasks of experiments. (**a**) FD001 Engine Prediction Results (FD002→FD001). (**b**) FD001 Engine Prediction Results (FD004→FD001). (**c**) FD003 Engine Prediction Results (FD002→FD003). (**d**) FD003 Engine Prediction Results (FD004→FD003).

Taking FD002→FD001 as an example, the error and relative error of all engines in FD001 are used to intuitively show the accuracy of RUL prediction with the method in this paper. The results are shown in Figure 8. It can be seen from Figure 8a that when the engine starts to run, the RUL value is relatively large, and the prediction error is relatively large. When the engine runs for a long time or is about to fail, the degradation information is more obvious, and the prediction performance is significantly enhanced. Under a limited sample, it is difficult to accurately predict the equipment life of one set of different working conditions with the sensor data of another set of working conditions. The method in this paper improves this problem to a certain level so that the relative error generally remains at [−25%, 25%] as the Figure 8b.

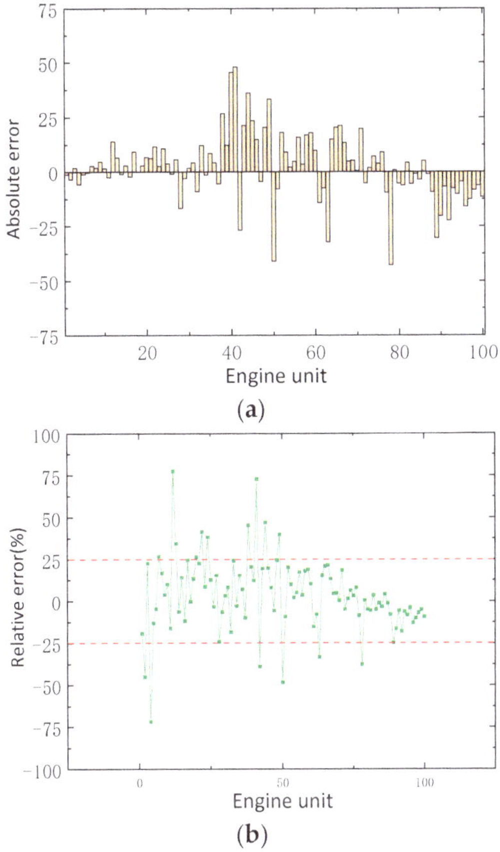

Figure 8. Error curve of RUL prediction results in task FD002→FD001. (**a**) Absolute error. (**b**)Relative error.

In order to verify the effectiveness of the DCNN-BiLSTM, the five state-of-the-art network models are used to compare the hybrid network DCNN-BiLSTM; the RUL prediction results are shown in Table 4. It can be observed that the DCNN-BiLSTM model performed significantly better than SVM, MLP, CNN, LSTM, and CNN-LSTM in datasets FD001 and FD003. The DCNN-BiLSTM adopts a multi-layer convolutional network structure and a bidirectional long and short-term memory network, which can extract spatial and temporal features in detail, strengthen the feature extraction ability, and effectively improve the prediction accuracy.

Table 4. The results of the hybrid network model in this paper are compared with other network models on the C-MAPSS dataset.

Methods	FD001		FD003	
	Score	RMSE	Score	RMSE
SVM [20]	7730.33	40.72	22,541.58	46.32
MLP [20]	560.59	16.78	479.85	18.47
CNN [7]	1290	18.45	1600	19.82
LSTM [8]	338	16.14	852	16.18
CNN-LSTM [21]	303	16.13	1420	17.12
DCNN-BiLSTM	532.16	15.98	365.41	15.63

To further verify the effectiveness and superiority of the proposed method in this paper, this method is compared with the advanced methods in recent years, and the comparison results with CORAL, WDGRL, DDC, ADDA, and RULDDA methods are shown in Table 5.

Table 5. The results of the methods in this paper are compared with other methods on the C-MAPSS dataset.

Methods	FD002→FD001		FD002→FD003		FD004→FD001		FD004→FD003	
	Score	RMSE	Score	RMSE	Score	RMSE	Score	RMSE
CORAL [22]	3590	24.43	23,071	42.66	154,842	51.44	6919	30.44
WDGRL [23]	157,672	15.24	19,053	41.45	45,394	42.01	77,977	18.18
DDC [24]	640	46.96	62,823	39.87	162,100	41.55	1623	44.47
ADDA [25]	689	19.73	11,029	37.22	43,794	37.81	1117	23.59
RULDDA [14]	2430	23.91	12,756	47.26	13,377	32.37	1679	23.31
DCNN-BiLSTM (TL)	371.86	14.36	243.22	13.66	432.37	16.35	296.34	14.79

From Table 5, we can see the proposed DCNN-BiLSTM (TL) method obtained substantially improved RMSE and Score prediction accuracy on all tasks. More specifically, RMSE and Score indicators on four tasks had reduced 5.77%, 63.26%, 49.49%, 18.65%, and 41.89%, 97.79%, 96.76%, and 73.47%, respectively, compared with the best result in the state-of-the-art methods. In addition, it can be observed that knowledge transfer between simple and complex datasets is challenging due to the large domain shift. For example, FD002→FD003 and FD004→FD001 are the transfer learning tasks of simple and complex datasets, and our proposed method obtained the greatest improvement and successfully aligned the two distant domains. The results show that the proposed transfer learning method could reduce the impact of operational conditions and fault modes on the RUL prediction accuracy of the target domain and effectively transfer the knowledge of the source domain with a large sample size, which is equivalent to data augmentation effectively for the target domain with small sample sizes. It improves the performance of the RUL prediction model. This is of great significance for equipment RUL prediction with small sample sizes in complex environments. Therefore, the proposed method is very promising in solving the small sample problem in the field of RUL prediction.

5. Conclusions

In the traditional data-driven RUL prediction method, the state detection data of the training set and the test set are required to have the same or similar distribution. However, due to different operational conditions, fault modes, and some force majeure factors in the actual working environment, it is generally difficult to obtain data sets that satisfy the same data distribution. In order to solve the problem that it is difficult to collect equipment operational data in some specific environments and the RUL prediction accuracy of equipment is not high, and the generalization ability is weak under different working conditions, this paper proposes a transfer learning-based RUL prediction method for small-sample equipment.

The method in this paper uses the DCNN-BiLSTM model to simultaneously train the source and target domain data and uses MMD to constrain the distribution difference between the two domains so as to realize the adaptation matching and feature alignment of the target domain samples and the source domain samples. The deep features are extracted to obtain a pre-trained model. Then, the network structure and parameters of the pre-trained model are transferred to the target domain for training by a fine-tuned transfer learning strategy, and the network is optimized. Finally, an RUL prediction model that is more suitable for the target domain data is obtained. When used on the C-MAPSS dataset, compared with other state-of-the-art methods, it verifies the effectiveness of the method proposed in this paper for predicting the RUL of aero-engines. For the subsets FD002 and FD004 with complex operating conditions and sufficient sample data, the transfer learning method is used to solve the subsets FD001 and FD003 with single operating conditions and small data samples, and the effect is significantly improved.

In future research, more experiments will be conducted on different degradation datasets to demonstrate the reliability and generality of the proposed model. Furthermore, domain adaptation methods are applied to make unsupervised predictions on incomplete data of target domains with missing labels. Although the experiments in this paper have obtained good experimental results, it is still necessary to further optimize the network structure and parameters to improve the performance of the RUL model.

Author Contributions: Conceptualization, W.C. (Weizhao Chen) and W.C. (Wenbai Chen); methodology, W.C. (Weizhao Chen); validation, H.L. and Y.W.; formal analysis, H.L. and Y.W.; investigation, W.C. (Weizhao Chen) and W.C. (Wenbai Chen); resources, C.B. and Y.G.; writing—original draft preparation, W.C. (Weizhao Chen); writing—review and editing, W.C. (Weizhao Chen); supervision, W.C. (Wenbai Chen); project administration, W.C. (Wenbai Chen); funding acquisition, W.C. (Wenbai Chen), C.B. and Y.G. All authors have read and agreed to the published version of the manuscript.

Funding: This research was funded by The Major Project of Scientific and Technological Innovation 2030 (2021ZD0113603), The Qin Xin Talents Cultivation Program, Beijing Information Science and Technology University (QXTCP A202102), and The General Project of Beijing Municipal Education Commission Scientific Research Program (KM202011232023).

Institutional Review Board Statement: Not applicable.

Informed Consent Statement: Not applicable.

Data Availability Statement: The data of this paper came from the NASA Prognostics Center of Excellence, and the data acquisition website was: https://ti.arc.nasa.gov/tech/dash/groups/pcoe/prognostic-data-repository/#turbofan, accessed on 10 February 2022.

Conflicts of Interest: The authors declare no conflict of interest.

References

1. Hao, J.; Hu, Y.; Cui, N.; Han, F.; Xu, C. Research on GRU-BP for life prediction of key components in digital workshop. *J. Chin. Comput. Syst.* **2020**, *41*, 637–642.
2. Yurek, O.E.; Birant, D. Remaining useful life estimation for predictive maintenance using feature engineering. In Proceedings of the 2019 Innovations in Intelligent Systems and Applications Conference (ASYU), Izmir, Turkey, 31 October–2 November 2019; IEEE: Piscataway, NJ, USA; pp. 1–5.
3. Ahmadzadeh, F.; Lundberg, J. Remaining useful life estimation. *Int. J. Syst. Assur. Eng. Manag.* **2014**, *5*, 461–474. [CrossRef]
4. El-Thalji, I.; Jantunen, E. A summary of fault modelling and predictive health monitoring of rolling element bearings. *Mech. Syst. Signal Processing* **2015**, *60*, 252–272. [CrossRef]
5. Qin, S.J. Survey on data-driven industrial process monitoring and diagnosis. *Annu. Rev. Control.* **2012**, *36*, 220–234. [CrossRef]
6. Gou, J.; Yu, B.; Maybank, S.J.; Tao, D. Knowledge distillation: A survey. *Int. J. Comput. Vis.* **2021**, *129*, 1789–1819. [CrossRef]
7. Babu, G.S.; Zhao, P.; Li, X.L. Deep convolutional neural network based regression approach for estimation of remaining useful life. In *International Conference on Database Systems for Advanced Applications*; Springer: Cham, Switzerland, 2016; pp. 214–228.
8. Zheng, S.; Ristovski, K.; Farahat, A.; Gupta, C. Long short-term memory network for remaining useful life estimation. In Proceedings of the 2017 IEEE International Conference on Prognostics and Health Management (ICPHM), Dallas, TX, USA, 19–21 June 2017; IEEE: Piscataway, NJ, USA; pp. 88–95.
9. Zhuang, F.Z.; Luo, P.; He, Q.; Shi, Z. Survey on transfer learning research. *J. Softw.* **2015**, *26*, 26–39.
10. Fu, B.; Wu, Z.; Guo, J. Remaining Useful Life Prediction under Multiple Operation Conditions Based on Domain Adaptive Sparse Auto-Encoder. In Proceedings of the 2020 IEEE International Conference on Prognostics and Health Management (ICPHM), Detroit, MI, USA, 8–10 June 2020; IEEE: Piscataway, NJ, USA; pp. 1–8.
11. Li, X.; Zhang, W.; Ding, Q.; Sun, J.Q. Multi-layer domain adaptation method for rolling bearing fault diagnosis. *Signal Processing* **2019**, *157*, 180–197. [CrossRef]
12. Ragab, M.; Chen, Z.; Wu, M.; Foo, C.S.; Kwoh, C.K.; Yan, R.; Li, X. Contrastive adversarial domain adaptation for machine remaining useful life prediction. *IEEE Trans. Ind. Inform.* **2020**, *17*, 5239–5249. [CrossRef]
13. Miao, M.; Yu, J. A Deep Domain Adaptative Network for Remaining Useful Life Prediction of Machines under Different Working Conditions and Fault Modes. *IEEE Trans. Instrum. Meas.* **2021**, *70*, 1–14. [CrossRef]

14. da Costa, P.R.D.O.; Akçay, A.; Zhang, Y.; Kaymak, U. Remaining useful lifetime prediction via deep domain adaptation. *Reliab. Eng. Syst. Saf.* **2020**, *195*, 106682. [CrossRef]
15. Lv, H.; Chen, J.; Pan, T. Sequence Adaptation Adversarial Network for Remaining Useful Life Prediction Using Small Data Set. In Proceedings of the 2020 IEEE 18th International Conference on Industrial Informatics (INDIN), Warwick, UK, 20–23 July 2020; IEEE: Piscataway, NJ, USA; Volume 1, pp. 115–118.
16. Yao, K.; Cohn, T.; Vylomova, K.; Duh, K.; Dyer, C. Depth-gated LSTM. *arXiv* **2015**, arXiv:1508.03790.
17. Chen, W.; Liu, H.; Chen, Q.; Wu, P. A Prediction Method for the RUL of Equipment for Missing Data. *Complexity* **2021**, *2021*, 2122655.
18. Listou Ellefsen, A.; Bjørlykhaug, E.; Æsøy, V.; Ushakov, S.; Zhang, H. Remaining usefullife predictions for turbofan engine degradation using semi-supervised deep archi-tecture. *Reliab. Eng. Syst. Saf.* **2019**, *183*, 240–251. [CrossRef]
19. Zhang, A.; Wang, H.; Li, S.; Cui, Y.; Liu, Z.; Yang, G.; Hu, J. Transfer learning with deep recurrent neural networks for remaining useful life estimation. *Appl. Sci.* **2018**, *8*, 2416. [CrossRef]
20. Zhang, C.; Lim, P.; Qin, A.K.; Tan, K.C. Multiobjective deep belief networks ensemble for remaining useful life estimation in prognostics. *IEEE Trans. Neural Netw. Learn. Syst.* **2016**, *28*, 2306–2318. [CrossRef] [PubMed]
21. Kong, Z.; Cui, Y.; Xia, Z.; Lv, H. Convolution and long short-term memory hybrid deep neural networks for remaining useful life prognostics. *Appl. Sci.* **2019**, *9*, 4156. [CrossRef]
22. Sun, B.; Feng, J.; Saenko, K. Correlation alignment for unsuperviseddomain adaptation. In *Domain Adaptation in Computer Vision Applications*; Springer: Cham, Switzerland, 2017; pp. 153–171.
23. Shen, J.; Qu, Y.; Zhang, W.; Yu, Y. Wasserstein distance guided representation learning for domain adaptation. In Proceedings of the Association Advancement Artificial Intelligence (AAAI), New Orleans, LA, USA, 2–7 February 2018; pp. 4058–4065.
24. Tzeng, E.; Hoffman, J.; Zhang, N.; Saenko, K.; Darrell, T. Deep domainconfusion: Maximizing for domain invariance. *arXiv* **2014**, arXiv:1412.3474.
25. Tzeng, E.; Hoffman, J.; Saenko, K.; Darrell, T. Adversarial discrim-inative domain adaptation. In Proceedings of the IEEE Conference on Computer Vision and Pattern Recognition, Honolulu, HI, USA, 21–26 July 2017; pp. 7167–7176.

mathematics

MDPI

Article

Blind Image Deblurring via a Novel Sparse Channel Prior

Dayi Yang [1,2*], Xiaojun Wu [1,2,*] and Hefeng Yin [1,2]

1 School of Artificial Intelligence and Computer Science, Jiangnan University, Wuxi 214122, China; yin_hefeng@jiangnan.edu.cn
2 Jiangsu Provincial Engineering Laboratory of Pattern Recognition and Computational Intelligence, Jiangnan University, Wuxi 214122, China
* Correspondence: 7151905005@vip.jiangnan.edu.cn (D.Y.); wu_xiaojun@jiangnan.edu.cn (X.W.)

Abstract: Blind image deblurring (BID) is a long-standing challenging problem in low-level image processing. To achieve visually pleasing results, it is of utmost importance to select good image priors. In this work, we develop the ratio of the dark channel prior (DCP) to the bright channel prior (BCP) as an image prior for solving the BID problem. Specifically, the above two channel priors obtained from RGB images are used to construct an innovative sparse channel prior at first, and then the learned prior is incorporated into the BID tasks. The proposed sparse channel prior enhances the sparsity of the DCP. At the same time, it also shows the inverse relationship between the DCP and BCP. We employ the auxiliary variable technique to integrate the proposed sparse prior information into the iterative restoration procedure. Extensive experiments on real and synthetic blurry sets show that the proposed algorithm is efficient and competitive compared with the state-of-the-art methods and that the proposed sparse channel prior for blind deblurring is effective.

Keywords: blind image deblurring; image prior; sparse channel; sparsity

MSC: 68U10

Citation: Yang, D.; Wu, X.; Yin, H. Blind Image Deblurring via a Novel Sparse Channel Prior. *Mathematics* **2022**, *10*, 1238. https://doi.org/10.3390/math10081238

Academic Editors: Jianping Gou, Weihua Ou, Shaoning Zeng and Lan Du

Received: 25 February 2022
Accepted: 6 April 2022
Published: 9 April 2022

1. Introduction

The goal of blind image deblurring is to restore a sharp image and a blur kernel from the input degraded image. The degradation types include motion blur, noise, out-of-focus and camera shake. Assuming that the blur is uniform and spatially invariant, the mathematical formulation of the blurring process can be modeled as

$$b = l * k + n \tag{1}$$

where b is the blurry input, k is the blur kernel and n is the additive noise. The $*$ denotes the convolution operator. This problem is highly ill-posed because both the latent sharp image l and blur kernel k are unknown. In order to make this problem well-posed, most existing methods utilize the statistics of natural images to estimate the blur kernel. For example, a heavy-tailed distribution [1], patch recurrence prior [2], nuclear norm [3,4], low-rank prior [5], sparse prior [6], multiscale latent prior [7] or additional information of a specific image [8–10] have been used to estimate a better kernel.

Strong sparsity of image intensity and gradient has been widely used in low-level computer vision processing problems. It also has mature applications in the field of image deblurring [6,11–13], such as the L_1/L_2 [14] norm, the reweighted L_1 norm [15], the L_0 norm prior [16–19] and the sparse prior–local maximum gradient (LMG) [20]. For favoring clear images over blurry ones, the edge selection method [21–23] is embedded in the blind deconvolution framework. However, strong edges are not always available in many cases. The channel prior was introduced by He et al. for image defogging in Ref. [24]. Then, Pan et al. [18] enforced the sparsity of the dark channel by the L_0 norm for kernel estimation. Unfortunately, this prior does not work well on images with large noise and large numbers of pixels. To solve this problem, Yan et al. [19] proposed an extreme channel prior (ECP) which utilizes both the dark channel and bright channel for estimating the blur kernel.

In this paper, a novel sparse channel prior is proposed for blind image deblurring. Inspired by [18,19,24], we take the advantages of the DCP and BCP to construct a confrontation constraint D/B. We prove its characteristic from a mathematical perspective and explore how these properties can be used to estimate the blur kernel. In the proposed algorithm, the optimization of the proposed prior is a challenging problem. We use the idea of auxiliary variables and the alternating minimization method to decompose the problem into independent subproblems optimised by the alternating direction minimization (ADM) method. The main contributions of this work can be stated as follows:

- A new D/B prior is presented for kernel estimation, which fully explores the relationship between the DCP and BCP. We also verify the effectiveness of D/B.
- We develop an effective optimization strategy for kernel estimation based on the idea of auxiliary variables and the alternating direction minimization (ADM) method.
- Experiments on four databases show that the proposed method is competitive compared with the state-of-the-art blind deblurring algorithms.

The rest of this paper is organized as follows. Section 2 introduces the related work. The proposed D/B is detailed in Section 3. Our blind deblurring model and optimization strategy are presented in Section 4. Section 5 shows the experimental results. Further discussion of our proposed deblurring algorithm is given in Section 6. Section 7 summarizes this paper.

2. Related Work

Blind image deblurring algorithms have made great progress due to the use of the proper kernel estimation model. In this part, we introduce the methods related to our work in an appropriate context.

The success of many blind image deblurring algorithms is based on the use of the statistical characteristics of the image intensity and gradient. Krishnan et al. [14] presented the L_1/L_2 norm based on the sparsity of image intensity. The L_1/L_2 norm is a normalized version of L_1, which enhances the sparsity of L_1. Levin et al. [1] observed the heavy-tailed distribution of image intensities and introduced a maximum posteriori (MAP) framework. Shan et al. [25] introduced a probability model to fit the sparse gradient distribution of a natural image. Pan et al. [16] developed a method in which both intensity and gradient are regularized by the L_0 norm for text image deblurring. These methods are limited by the modeling of more complex image structures and contexts.

Another group of blind image deblurring methods [22,23] employs a significant edge detection step for kernel estimation. Specifically, Cho et al. [21] predicted sharp edges by the bilateral and shock filters. Joshi et al. [26] detected image contours by locating the subpixels' extrema. These methods cannot capture the sparse kernel and structures, which makes the restored image blurry and noisy sometimes. To solve these problems, researchers have proposed many better models to estimate the blur kernel. Xu et al. [27] presented a two-phase kernel estimation algorithm, which separates kernel initialization from the iterative support detection (ISD)-based kernel refinement step, giving an efficient estimation process and maintaining many small structures. Zoran and Weiss [28] proposed the expected patch log likelihood (EPLL) method, which imposes a prior on the patches of the final image. However, this will iteratively restore the degradation. Vardan et al. [29] exploited the multiscale prior to further improve the EPLL and reduce the error to that of the global modeling. Bai et al. [7] developed a multiscale latent structures (MSLS) prior. Based on the MSLS prior, their deblurring algorithm consists of two stages: sharp image estimation in the coarse scales and a refinement process in the finest scale. For the patch-based methods, global modeling is a difficult problem.

With the rapid development of the deep learning method, remarkable results have been achieved in the field of blind image deblurring [30–34]. For example, convolutional neural networsk (CNN) [35], Wasserste generative adversarial networks (GAN) [36], deep hierarchical multipatch networks (DMPHN) [37], ConvLSTM [38] and scale-recurrent networks (SRN) [39] are all designed for image deblurring. Zheng et al. [40] presented an edge heuristic multiscale GAN, which utilizes the edge's information to conduct the deblurring process in a coarse-to-fine manner for nonuniform blur. Liang et al. [41] learned novel neural network structures from RAW images and achieved superb performance. Chang et al. [42] proposed a long–short-exposure fusion network (LSFNet) for low-light image restoration by using the pairs of long- and short-exposure images. The success of deep-learning-based methods mainly relies on the consistency between training and test data, which limits the generalization ability of these methods.

Recently, the classical dark channel prior (DCP) has been proved effective for image deblurring. The DCP was introduced by He et al. [24] for image defogging. It is based on the observation that there is at least one color channel that has very low and close-to-zero pixel values on outdoor haze-free nonsky image patches. Pan et al. [18] further found that most elements of the dark channel are zero for nature images and then enhanced the sparsity of dark channel for image deblurring. Inspired by the DCP, the bright channel prior (BCP) is proposed. That is, in most of nature patches, at least one color channel has very high pixel values. Yan et al. [19] used the simple addition of the DCP and BCP to form an extreme channel prior (ECP) for a blind image deblurring algorithm. However, the relationship between the BCP and DCP is not fully explored in the ECP.

3. Proposed Sparse Channel Prior

To explain that the proposed sparse channel vary after blurring, we model the blurring process as described in [43]. For an image I, consider the noise is small enough to be neglected. We have:

$$b(x) = \sum_{z \in \Psi(x)} I\left(x + \left[\frac{m}{2}\right] - z\right) k(z) \tag{2}$$

where x and m denote the coordinates of the pixel and the size of the blur kernel k, respectively. $\Psi(x)$ represents an image patch centered at x, $\sum_{z \in \Psi(x)} k(z) = 1$ and $k(z) \geq 0$. $[\cdot]$ is a rounding operator.

Inspired by the two channels (dark and bright channels) and the statistics of images, we observe that when the dark channel is more different from the bright channel of one image patch, the edges are more salient, which is helpful to estimate an accurate blur kernel. To formally describe this observation, the proposed sparse channel prior is defined by:

$$\begin{aligned} R(x) = & \min_{y \in \Psi(x)} \left(\min_{c \in (r,g,b)} (I^c(y)) \right) \\ & / \left(\max_{y \in \Psi(x)} \left(\max_{c \in (r,g,b)} (I^c(y)) \right) + \epsilon \right) \\ = & D(x) / (B(x) + \epsilon) \end{aligned} \tag{3}$$

where x and y denote the coordinates of the pixel, ϵ is a non-negative constant and $\Psi(x)$ represents an image patch centered at x. I^c is the c-th color channel of image I. As described in Equation (3), $B(x) = \max_{y \in \Psi(x)} \left(\max_{c \in (r,g,b)} (I^c(y)) \right)$ represents the BCP and $D(x) = \min_{y \in \Psi(x)} \left(\min_{c \in (r,g,b)} (I^c(y)) \right)$ represents the DCP. Dark channels are obtained by two minimization operations: $\min_{c \in (r,g,b)}$ and $\min_{y \in \Psi(x)}$. The bright channel is obtained by two maximization operations: $\max_{c \in (r,g,b)}$ and $\max_{y \in \Psi(x)}$. In the implementations of the DCP and BCP, if I is a gray image, then only the latter operation is performed. A small value of $R(x)$ implies there are salient edges in the image patch. On the contrary, a large $R(x)$ implies that there are fine structures in an image patch. The reason is that when the edge is salient, the pixel values are more different between the two sides of edges. It means that the minimum value is more different from the maximum value of the image patch. Conversely, when the difference between the DCP and BCP is not that large, the image edge is unclear, and the value of $R(x)$ is large. Therefore, it is natural to think that if the

DCP is equal to or slightly smaller than the BCP, small edges can be accurately removed by minimizing Equation (3).

Consider a natural image that was blurred by a blur kernel. Blur reduces the maximum pixel value and increases the minimum pixel value of one patch. In other words, the DCP of one patch will increase and the BCP will decrease. Let $R(b)$ and $R(l)$ denote the proposed sparse channel of the blurred and clear image, respectively, when the $l(x) = \max_{y\in\Psi(x)} l(y) = \min_{y\in\Psi(x)} l(y)$, $R(b)(x) \geq R(l)(x)$. To further apply this proposition to the definition of the proposed sparse channel, we have:

$$\begin{aligned}
R(b)(x) &= \frac{\min_{y\in\Psi(x)}\left(\min_{c\in(r,g,b)}(b^c(y))\right)}{\max_{y\in\Psi(x)}\left(\max_{c\in(r,g,b)}(b^c(y))\right)+\epsilon} \\
&= \frac{\min_{y\in\Psi(x)} b(y)}{\max_{y\in\Psi(x)} b(y) + \epsilon} \\
&= \frac{\min_{y\in\Psi(x)} \sum_{z\in\Phi(x)} l(y+[\frac{m}{2}]-z)k(z)}{\max_{y\in\Psi(x)} \sum_{z\in\Phi(x)} l(y+[\frac{m}{2}]-z)k(z)+\epsilon} \\
&\geq \frac{\sum_{z\in\Phi(x)} \min_{y\in\Psi(x)} l(y+[\frac{m}{2}]-z)k(z)}{\sum_{z\in\Phi(x)} \max_{y\in\Psi(x)} l(y+[\frac{m}{2}]-z)k(z)+\epsilon} \\
&\geq \frac{\sum_{z\in\Phi(x)} \min_{\widehat{y}\in\widehat{\Psi}(x)} l(\widehat{y}+[\frac{m}{2}]-z)k(z)}{\sum_{z\in\Phi(x)} \max_{\widehat{y}\in\widehat{\Psi}(x)} l(\widehat{y}+[\frac{m}{2}]-z)k(z)+\epsilon} \\
&= \frac{\min_{\widehat{y}\in\widehat{\Psi}(x)} l(\widehat{y})}{\max_{\widehat{y}\in\widehat{\Psi}(x)} l(\widehat{y}) + \epsilon} \\
&= R(l)(x)
\end{aligned} \tag{4}$$

Let $\widehat{m}$ and S_Ψ denote the size of $\widehat{\Psi}(x)$ and $\Psi(x)$, respectively. Then we have $\widehat{m} = S_\Psi + m$. Equation (4) shows that $R(x)$ of the image patch centered at x after blurring is no less than the value of the original image patch centered at x.

Equation (4) proves $R(l)(x) \leq R(b)(x)$. This means that after blurring, the difference between the DCP and the BCP is smaller than that of the corresponding patch in a sharp image. In other words, $R(x)$ always favors the sharp image. We further validate our analysis on the dataset [44]. Figure 1a–c show the histogram of the average number of dark channel pixels, bright channel pixels and D/B channel pixels, respectively. As can be observed, a large portion of the pixels in the dark channels and bright channels possess very small or large values, and our D/B channel pixels possess smaller values than those of the DCP and BCP. As shown in Figure 1, the proposed sparse channels of clear images have significantly more zero elements than those of blurred images. Thus, the sparsity of the proposed channel is a natural metric to distinguish clear images from blurred images. This observation motivates us to introduce a new regularization term to enforce sparsity of the proposed channels in latent images.

Proposed Sparse Channel as an Image Prior

Equation (4) shows that after blurring, the difference between the DCP and BCP is smaller than that of the corresponding patch in a sharp image. Therefore, in order to generate sharp and reliable salient edges, we propose a novel sparse channel prior which combines the D/B and L_0 norm:

$$P(x) = \frac{\|D(x)\|_0}{\|B(x)\|_0 + \epsilon} \tag{5}$$

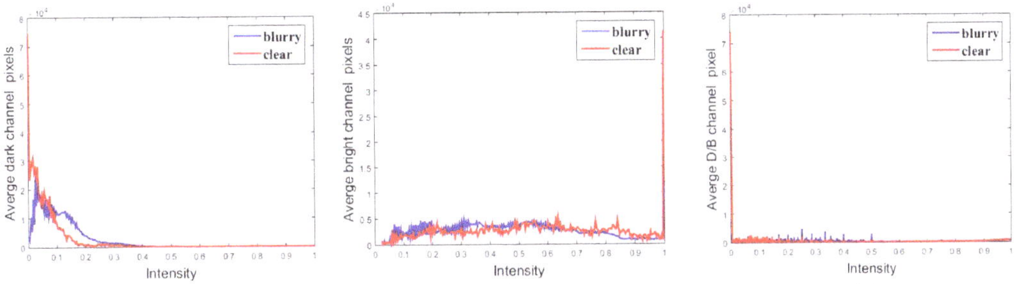

(a) (b) (c)

Figure 1. The statistics of the DCP, the BCP and our proposed D/B prior: (**a–c**) average channel pixels distribution of bright, dark and our D/B, respectively.

We define $P(x)$ as a D/B prior, and the L_0 norm is used for sparsity. Let $\Psi(x)$ denote one patch of the image I. If there exist some pixels $x \in \Psi(x)$ such that $I(x) = 0$, we have

$$P(b)(x) \geq P(l)(x) \tag{6}$$

where $P(b)(x)$ and $P(l)(x)$ denote the D/B prior of the blurred and clear image, respectively. This property directly follows from Equation (4). In the framework of MAP, by minimizing the sparse prior $P(x)$, we obtain a result that favors a sharp image. This property is also validated using dataset [44]. As shown in Figure 1c, the average number of D/B channels in clear images has significantly more zero elements than that of blurred ones.

4. Proposed Blind Deblurring Model

Based on the proposed D/B prior, we construct the blind deblurring model under the maximum a posteriori (MAP) framework.

$$\text{argmin}_{l,k}||l \otimes k - b||_2^2 + \mu P(l) + \vartheta||\nabla l||_0 + \gamma||k||_2^2 \tag{7}$$

where $P(l)$ is our proposed prior, ∇ denotes the gradient operation and μ, ϑ and γ are non-negative weights. The data-fitting term of our model ensures that the latent sharp image is consistent with the observed image. $||\nabla l||_0$ is the L_0 norm of the image gradient, which is used to suppress ringing and artifacts. Finally, we use the L_2 norm to increase the sparsity of the blur kernel.

4.1. Optimization

In this part, we adopt the ADM method to obtain the solution to the objective function. By using the idea of alternating optimization, we can obtain two independent subproblems about l and k, respectively:

$$\text{argmin}_l||l \otimes k - b||_2^2 + \mu\frac{||D(l)||_0}{||B(l)||_0 + \epsilon} + \vartheta||\nabla l||_0 \tag{8}$$

and

$$\text{argmin}_k||l \otimes k - b||_2^2 + \gamma||k||_2^2 \tag{9}$$

Equation (9) is a classical least squares problem with respect to k. By introducing the auxiliary variable g, which is related to ∇l, Equation (8) can be written as follows:

$$\text{argmin}_{l,g}||l \otimes k - b||_2^2 + \lambda||\nabla l - g||_2^2 + \mu\frac{||D(l)||_0}{||B(l)||_0 + \epsilon} + \vartheta||g||_0 \tag{10}$$

Equation (10) can be decomposed into:

$$\text{argmin}_l \|l \otimes k - b\|_2^2 + \lambda \|\nabla l - g\|_2^2 + \mu \frac{\|D(l)\|_0}{\|B(l)\|_0 + \epsilon} \tag{11}$$

and

$$\text{argmin}_g \lambda \|\nabla l - g\|_2^2 + \vartheta \|g\|_0 \tag{12}$$

Equation (12) is an L_0 norm minimization problem for g.

4.2. Estimating Intermediate Image l

For the k-th iteration, we consider $B(l)$ estimated in the $(k-1)$-th iteration as a constant. Denoting

$$w_k = \mu / (\|B(l)\|_0 + \epsilon) \tag{13}$$

Equation (11) can be rewritten as follows:

$$\text{argmin}_l \|l \otimes k - b\|_2^2 + \lambda \|\nabla l - g\|_2^2 + w_k \|D(l)\|_0 \tag{14}$$

By introducing an auxiliary variable, p, which is related to $D(l)$, Equation (14) can be reformulated as follows:

$$\text{argmin}_{l,p} \|l \otimes k - b\|_2^2 + \xi \|D(l) - p\|_2^2 + \lambda \|\nabla l - g\|_2^2 + w_k \|p\|_0 \tag{15}$$

Using the idea of alternating optimization, we can obtain two independent subproblems to solve for l and p, respectively:

$$\text{argmin}_l \|l \otimes k - b\|_2^2 + \xi \|D(l) - p\|_2^2 + \lambda \|\nabla l - g\|_2^2 \tag{16}$$

and

$$\text{argmin}_p \xi \|D(l) - p\|_2^2 + w_k \|p\|_0 \tag{17}$$

Equation (16) contains all quadratic terms, and we can obtain its solution by the least squares method. In each iteration, the FFT (Fast Fourier Transform) is used to accelerate the computation process. Its closed-form solution is given as follows:

$$l = \mathcal{F}^{-1}\left(\frac{\overline{\mathcal{F}(k)}\mathcal{F}(b) + \xi \mathcal{F}(p) + \lambda \mathcal{F}_g}{\overline{\mathcal{F}(k)}\mathcal{F}(k) + \lambda \overline{\mathcal{F}(\nabla)}\mathcal{F}(\nabla) + \xi} \right) \tag{18}$$

where $\mathcal{F}_g = \left(\overline{\mathcal{F}(\nabla_v)}\mathcal{F}(g_v) + \overline{\mathcal{F}(\nabla_\text{h})}\mathcal{F}(g_\text{h}) \right)$ and $\mathcal{F}(\cdot)$ and $\mathcal{F}^{-1}(\cdot)$ are the Fast Fourier Transform (FFT) and its inverse, respectively. $\overline{\mathcal{F}(\cdot)}$ denotes the complex conjugate operator of FFT and ∇_v and ∇_h are gradients in the vertical and horizontal directions, respectively.

4.3. Estimating p and g

Equations (12) and (17) are minimization problems of the L_0 norm. Due to the difficulty of solving the L_0 norm minimization problem, we adopt the method described in Ref. [13]. As a result, the solution of Equation (17) can be expressed as:

$$p = \begin{cases} D(l), & D(l) \geq \frac{w_k}{\xi} \\ 0, & \text{otherwise} \end{cases} \tag{19}$$

Given l, the solution of Equation (12) can be expressed as:

$$g = \begin{cases} \nabla l, & |\nabla l|^2 \geq \frac{\vartheta}{\lambda} \\ 0, & \text{otherwise} \end{cases} \tag{20}$$

4.4. Estimating Blur Kernel k

Since the updating of the blur kernel is an independent subproblem, we estimate k in the gradient space. Specifically, we obtain the solution to the blur kernel by minimizing the following problem though the known intermediate image l:

$$\min_k ||\nabla l \otimes k - \nabla y||_2^2 + \gamma ||k||_2^2 \tag{21}$$

where ∇ denotes the gradient operation. Note that we use Equation (21) to estimate the blur kernel instead of Equation (9), which helps to suppress ringing artifacts and eliminate noise. The closed-form solution to Equation (21) is obtained by FFT.

$$k = \mathcal{F}^{-1}\left(\frac{\overline{\mathcal{F}(\nabla l)}\mathcal{F}(\nabla y)}{\overline{\mathcal{F}(\nabla l)}\mathcal{F}(\nabla l) + \gamma} \right) \tag{22}$$

The coarse-to-fine strategy is used in the process of blur kernel estimation, which is similar to that used in [26,45]. In the process of solving the problem, it is very important to restrict the small values of the blur kernel by thresholding at fine scale, which enhances the robustness of the algorithm to noise.

4.5. Estimating Latent Sharp Image

Although the latent sharp images can be estimated from Equation (18), this formulation is less effective for fine-texture details. For the purpose of suppressing ringing and artifacts, we fine-tune the final restored image. With the estimated blur kernel and blur input image y, we can use the nonblind deconvolution method to obtain the final latent sharp image l_{latent}. Algorithm 1 summarizes the main steps of the final latent sharp image restoration method. Firstly, we estimate the restored image l_h by the method in Ref. [46] using the hyper-Laplacian prior. Then we restore image l_r according to the method in Ref. [47] using the total variation prior. Finally, the latent sharp image l_{latent} is calculated by the average of the two restored images, i.e., $l_{latent} = (l_h + l_r)/2$. The main steps of our proposed algorithm are summarized as Algorithm 2.

Algorithm 1 Final latent sharp image restoration.

Input: Blurry image b and estimated kernel k.

1: Estimate latent image l_h by using the method described in [46] with Laplacian prior;
2: Estimate latent image l_r by using the method described in [47] with total variation prior;

3: Restore the final sharp image l_{latent}:
$l_{latent} = (l_h + l_r)/2$.

Output: Sharp latent image l_{latent}.

Algorithm 2 The proposed blind deblurring algorithm.

Input: Blurry image y;

1: Initialize the intermediate image l and blur kernel k;
2: Estimate blur kernel k from b;
3: Alternately calculate l and k by the manner of coarse-to-fine levels:
4:     Estimate intermediate image l by Equation (18);
5:     Estimate blur kernel k by Equation (22);
6: Interpolate solution to finer level as initialization;
7: Calculate the latent sharp image according to Algorithm 1.

Output: Sharp latent image l_{latent}.

We first initialize the intermediate image l and blur kernel k according to the blurry input. Then we alternately update l and k. In order to avoid falling into a local minimum, our algorithm is executed in a coarse-to-fine manner. The results of the coarse layer are up-sampled with the bilinear interpolation method as the initialization of the next fine layer. Finally, a latent sharp image is obtained by Algorithm 1 with the estimated blur kernel.

5. Results

We examine our method and compare it with the state-of-the-art BID methods on different image datasets, including a synthetic image dataset and real-world blurred images. We then evaluate the quality of deblurring models by different metrics, including the peak signal-to-noise ratio (PSNR, unit: dB), which is a measure of image quality, and cumulative error ratio (CER). The higher the CER value, the better the model.

In all the experiments, the parameter settings of our model are as follows: $\mu = \vartheta = 0.003$, $\gamma = 2$ and the size of image patch to compute the D/B channel is set to be 35. The maximum iteration is empirically set to 5 as a trade-off between accuracy and speed.

5.1. Synthetic Image Deblurring

We first test our method on the synthetic image dataset [44] for quantitative evaluations. This dataset includes 4 ground truth images and 12 different kernels. We compare our results with the state-of-the-art methods [11,14,18,19,21,27,48]. Our algorithm performs well with other methods on this benchmark dataset. Additionally, we present a challenging example in Figure 2. We record the largest PSNR calculated by comparing each restored result with 199 ground truth images captured along the camera shake trajectory in Figure 3. Since the proposed method considers not only BCP and DCP information but also the relationship between them, the PSNR values of the restored images achieved by our method are higher than those of the state-of-the-art algorithms [11,14,18,19,25,45,48–50].

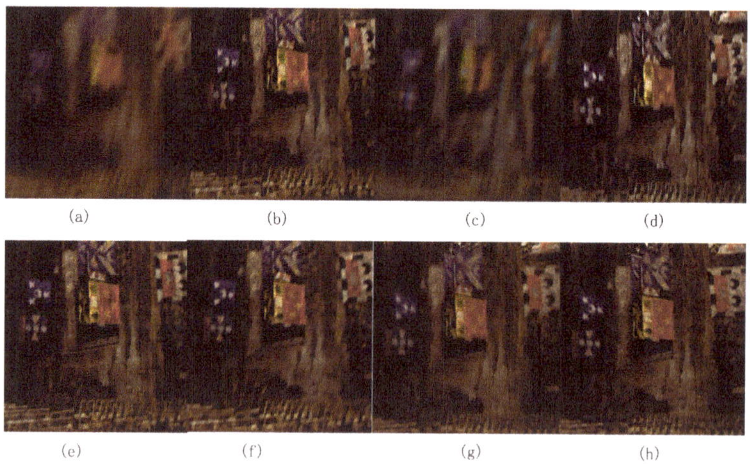

Figure 2. Visual comparison of the results using one challenging image from dataset [44]. The image (**a**) is blurry input; (**b–h**) are deblurring results of Ref. [21], Ref. [27], Ref. [14], Ref. [48], Ref. [18], Ref. [19] and our proposed method, respectively.

We also test our algorithm against the competing methods [6,14,18,19,21,48,51,52] on another benchmark dataset [12], which includes four ground truth images and eight different kernels. One example is shown in Figure 4 with a visual result comparison against the state-of-the-art methods [18,19]. Although the image restored by Pan et al. [18] performs well against other approaches, the generated image still contains significant fake textures and blur regions in Figure 4b. The algorithm proposed by Yan et al. [19] considers both the DCP and BCP, but the generated result still has unclear edges, as Figure 4c shows. However, our method generates a sharp image with fine textures, as shown in Figure 4d. We can observe that the result is more visually pleasing than that of others. The main reason is that the enhanced edges in local patches help to remove the small textures and fine details.

Figure 5a plots the cumulative error ratios of our method and the other competing methods. Note that our D/B-based method outperforms state-of-the-art algorithms by 100% under error ratio 2. All the experimental results consistently show that our method is competitive on this dataset.

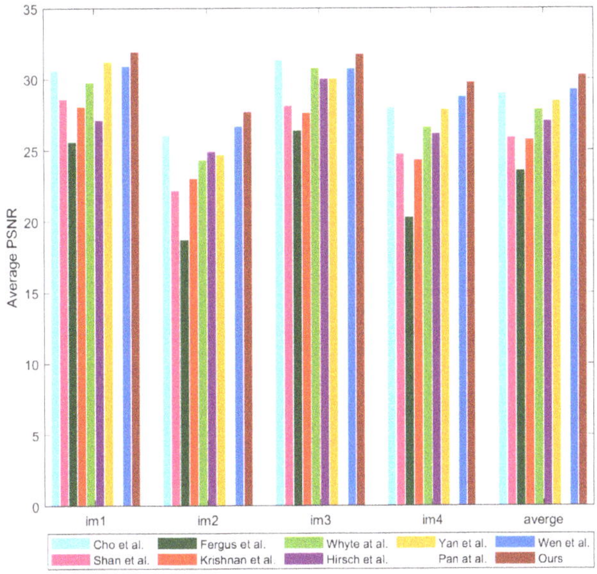

Figure 3. Quantitative evaluations on benchmark dataset [44]. Our method performs competitively against the state-of-the-art deblurring approaches.

Figure 4. A comparison of our method with state-of-the-art methods. The images (**a–d**) are blurry input, result of Pan et al. [18], result of Yan et al. [19] and our result, respectively. The PSNR values of (**b–d**) are 30.19, 30.33 and 32.15, respectively.

We further carry out experiments of our method against the state-of-the-art approaches [16,19] on text images from the dataset [16]. This dataset consists of 15 images and eight different kernels ranging in size from 13 × 13 to 27 × 27. Figure 6 visually shows that our method performs well on a challenging blurry image in comparison with [19] and the method designed for text images [16]. As shown in the figure, the DCP and ECP also help the blind deblurring of text images. Our deblurred result in Figure 6d utilizing the proposed D/B generates sharper edges and clearer text compared to other results [16,19]. Another text example is shown in Figure 7. Note that the text becomes extremely sharper after the deblurring process, which demonstrates that our proposed L_0 norm based on the D/B is helpful for kernel estimation and image deblurring. In particular, sharp text images contain more salient edges in local patches, which drives our D/B to perform well. Table 1 presents the average PSNR values of the deblurred results on the text image dataset [16] compared with the state-of-the-art methods. Our method achieves the maximum PSNR value.

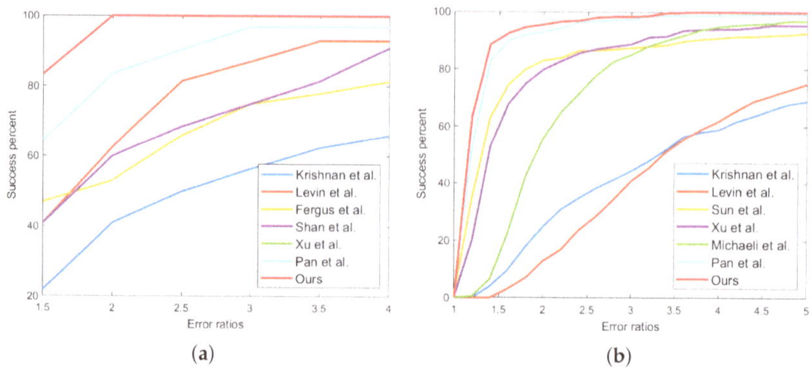

Figure 5. Quantitative results of our method on two benchmark datasets [12,22]: (**a**) error ratios comparison between our approach and the other methods on the benchmark dataset [12]; (**b**) quantitative evaluations on the benchmark dataset [22].

Figure 6. A comparison of our method with state-of-the-art methods. The images (**a**–**d**) are blurry input, result of Pan et al. [16], result of Yan et al. [19] and our result, respectively.

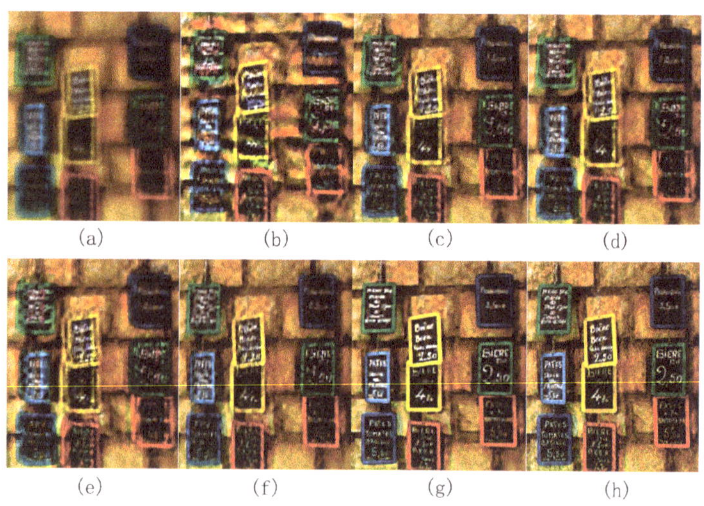

Figure 7. Visual comparison of the results using one challenging image: (**a**) blurry image; (**b**–**h**) deblurring results generated by Ref. [14], Ref. [6], Ref. [52], Ref. [48], Ref. [19], Ref. [18] and our method, respectively. The recovered image by the proposed algorithm is visually more pleasing.

Table 1. PSNR values of state-of-the-art text image deblurring methods.

Method	Cho et al. [21]	Xu et al. [13]	Levin et al. [1]	Pan et al. [16]	Ours
PSNR	23.80	26.21	24.90	27.94	28.23

5.2. Real Image Delurring

In this part, we test our method on real-world blurred images against the recent state-of-the-art blind single image deblurring methods [11,14,18,19,21,48]. We analyze the deblurring results qualitatively as the blur kernels and ground truth images are unknown. Figure 8 shows one challenging real-world blurred image. The recovered images generated by the proposed algorithm are sharper and clearer than those generated by [11,14,18,19,21,48]. As shown in Figure 8, the blurry image contains large and small edges and textures, which causes trouble for deblurring with the methods designed for natural images. Pan et al. [18] exploited the dark channel and achieved encouraging results. However, the deblurred image still contains visually blurry artifacts. In contrast, by further utilizing the edge information in local patches, our method generates sharper and clearer image details compared with other methods as shown in Figure 8. As a second example, we present deblurring results on a challenging image in Figure 9. Note that our deblurred image has clear background and sharp edges against other results.

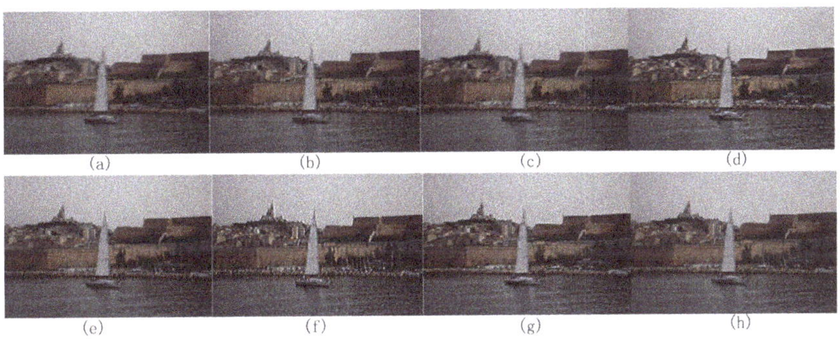

Figure 8. Visual comparison of the results using one challenging image. (**a**) is blurry input and (**b–h**) are generated by [11,14,18,19,21,48] and our proposed method, respectively.

Figure 9. An example of real-world image results. The images (**a–e**) are blurry input, result of Krishnan et al. [14], result of Pan et al. [18], result of Yan et al. [19] and our result, respectively

5.3. The Effectiveness of Proposed Sparse Channel Prior

In this subsection, experiments are conducted to verify the performance of the proposed D/B for blind image deblurring. As mentioned above, the proposed D/B regularization term considers the contrast and salient edges' information in local patches. To demonstrate the effectiveness of the proposed prior, we compare the proposed method with the DCP-based method [18] and the ECP-based method [19] in image deblurring. Figure 10 shows the changes of the DCP, the BCP and the proposed sparse channel prior in each phase of the image. Initially, the contrast and clarity of the DCP, the BCP and the proposed sparse channel prior of the proceeding blurred images are very low, while the contrast of the middle layer is significantly improved and the final restored images have a higher contrast and sharper contour. At this time, the ringing and artifacts in the images are greatly reduced. Note in each stage, the proposed sparse channel prior has a clearer outline than the DCP and BCP. Compared with the literature [18], the proposed method estimates the blur kernels better with less artifacts. Figure 11 shows the quantitative evaluations on the benchmark dataset [12] by the ECP and our method with and without the proposed D/B. Note that the PSNR (Figure 11a) of the proposed D/B-based method is higher than that of the ECP and our method without D/B. Moreover, our method with the proposed D/B prior performs more favorably in terms of error ratio (Figure 11b) than without the D/B regularization, which further demonstrates the effectiveness of the proposed D/B-based methods. The proposed D/B-based algorithm generates the results with PSNR values higher than the other two methods.

Figure 10. Visual comparison of the intermediate results generated during iteration. (**a–c**) are intermediate results generated during iteration using the DCP, ECP and our sparse channel prior, respectively.

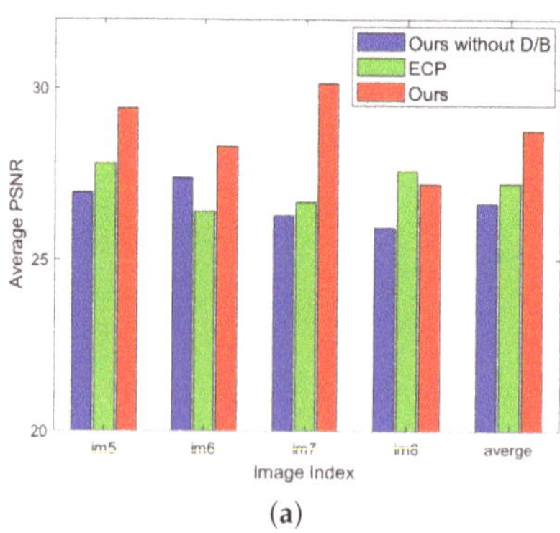

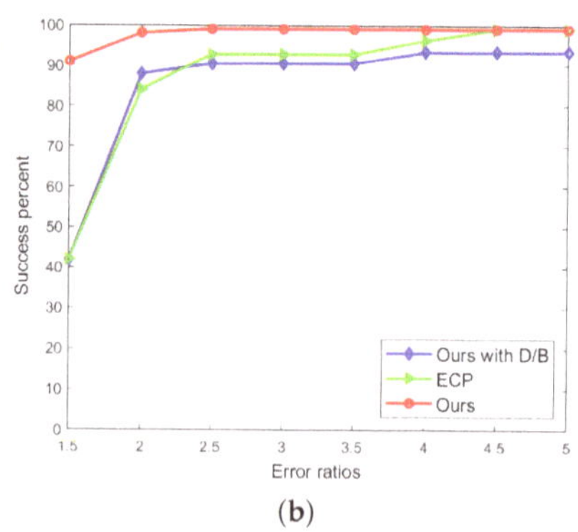

Figure 11. Quantitative results of our method on benchmark dataset [12]: (**a**) quantitative evaluations on the benchmark dataset by [12] and our method with and without D/B; (**b**) error comparison between our approach and the other methods.

In addition, our method has a higher success rate on the dataset [22], as shown in Figure 5b. All the results consistently demonstrate that the proposed sparse channel prior improves the deblurring performance.

6. Discussion

6.1. Comparison with Other Related Methods

In this part, we will discuss some methods most related to the algorithm in this paper. The dark channel prior was used by Pan et al. [18] for blind image deblurring. They enhanced the sparsity of the DCP and achieved good results on low-light images. Yan et al. [19] used the ECP to solve the problem that the DCP has less effect on sky images. However, the ECP is a simple addition of the DCP and BCP, and the relationship between them has not been deeply studied.

Figure 10 shows the intermediate images of three different methods (Refs. [18,19] and ours). Although the intermediate results become clearer and sharper as iterations increase, the images (Figure 10c) generated by our method have sharper edges and clearer contents than those of Refs. [18] (Figure 10a) and [19] (Figure 10b). Figure 12 shows the results generated by these three methods on some challenging images, including real blurred and low-light images. Our results have fewer blurred areas and ringings, which look more pleasant. Table 2 shows the error ratio of two related approaches [18,19] on dataset [22], and the proposed method fails on one image in which the error ratio value is larger than 4.

(a) (b) (c) (d)

Figure 12. Deblurring results on some challenging examples. (**a**) Blurry inputs. (**b**–**d**) Deblurring results generated by Ref. [18], Ref. [19] and our method, respectively.

In order to analyze the three methods in more detail, we show the different maps of the DCP, the BCP and our D/B in Figure 13. Although the dark channel, bright channel and our D/B map of the recovered image all have improvement with respect to that of the corresponding blurry image, our D/B map improves more than the dark channel and bright channel. Moreover, our D/B map is clearer (higher contrast and sharper edges) than the dark channel and bright channel in both the blurry image and recovered image. All have improvement with respect to that of the corresponding blurry image.

Table 2. Quality evaluation of competitive methods on dataset [22] in terms of error ratio.

Error Ratio	≤2	≤3	≤4
Pan et al. [18]	594/640	627/640	633/640
Yan et al. [19]	596/640	636/640	638/640
Ours	623/640	639/640	639/640

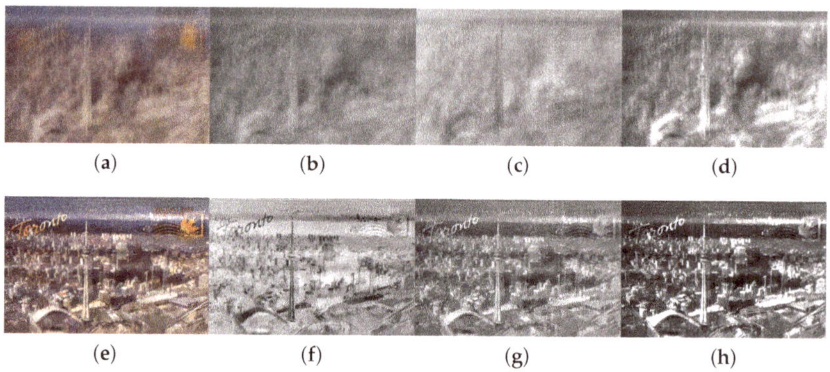

Figure 13. Visual comparison of different maps. (**a**) is blurry image. (**b–d**) are dark channel, bright channel and our D/B map of (**a**), respectively. (**e**) is recovered image. (**f**,**g**) are dark channel, bright channel and our D/B map of (**h**), respectively.

6.2. Convergence Analysis

Blind deconvolution is a highly ill-posed problem and we introduce a new spare prior to make the problem produce feasible results in this paper. The optimization scheme of our model is challenging, and with the idea of auxiliary variables and the alternating direction minimization (ADM) method, one may question the convergence. Thus, we show the traces of the objective function (computed from Equation (8)) and kernel similarity [53] on dataset [12] with respect to iterations in Figure 14. Figure 14a shows our method converges after less than 30 iterations, and Figure 14b shows the kernel similarity [53] becomes higher with more iterations. Overall, our method converges well after less than 30 iterations.

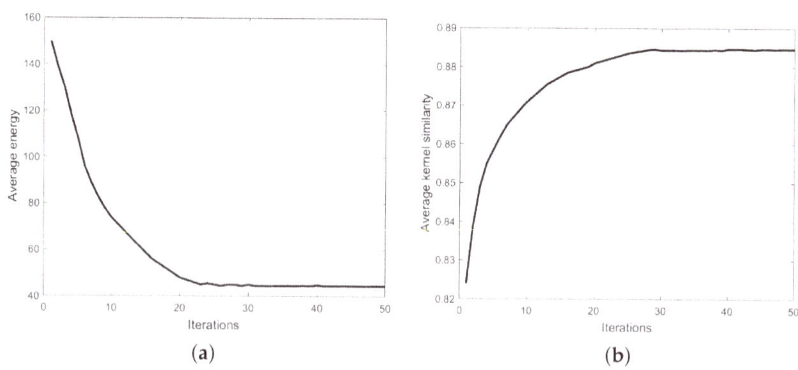

Figure 14. Convergence analysis of the proposed algorithm. (**a**) Energy value computed from Equation (8). (**b**) Average kernel similarity [53] becomes higher with more iterations.

6.3. Running Time

We simply explain the computational complexity through the running time of the algorithms. We select several competing algorithms closely related to this paper to run on the same database as this algorithm. All experiments were carried out under the same computer. The running time on different sizes of images is summarized in Table 3. As can be seen from the table, our algorithm is faster than [19] and slower than [14].

Table 3. Running time (s) of competing approaches.

Image Size	Krishnan et al. [14]	Pan et al. [18]	Yan et al. [19]	Ours
255 × 255	4.80	111.51	306.56	115.04
600 × 600	21.82	563.33	1250.12	571.57
800 × 800	95.62	1150.17	2331.02	1202.51

7. Conclusions

In this paper, a novel, simple yet efficient image prior D/B for blind image deblurring is proposed, which builds on the DCP and BCP. An extensive investigation on natural images shows that the DCP behaves inversely to the BCP, and a large difference between the DCP and BCP preserves salient edges. For blind image deblurring, salient edges are helpful to estimate the blur kernel. In order to utilize the advantages of the DCP and BCP and further exploit the edge information in a local patch, we propose the D/B prior for image deblurring. The D/B prior preserves the main edges and eliminates the fine textures of intermediate latent images. Meanwhile, it retains the advantages of the DCP and BCP. The feasibility and effectiveness of using the D/B prior to estimate the blur kernel are discussed. The experimental results show that our algorithm is competitive with the state-of-the-art algorithms. In addition, experiments with our proposed prior show that it can significantly improve the performance of the deblurring algorithm.

Author Contributions: Conceptualization, D.Y. and X.W.; methodology, D.Y.; software, D.Y.; validation, D.Y., H.Y. and X.W.; formal analysis, D.Y.; investigation, D.Y., H.Y. and X.W.; resources, D.Y.; data curation, D.Y.; writing—original draft preparation, D.Y.; writing—review and editing, D.Y., H.Y. and X.W.; visualization, D.Y. and H.Y.; supervision, D.Y. and X.W.; project administration, X.W.; funding acquisition, X.W. All authors have read and agreed to the published version of the manuscript.

Funding: The research was funded by the National Natural Science Foundation of China (Grant No.62020106012, U1836218) and the 111 Project of Ministry of Education of China (Grant No. B12018).

Institutional Review Board Statement: Not applicable.

Informed Consent Statement: Not applicable.

Data Availability Statement: The data presented in this study are available on request from the corresponding author.

Conflicts of Interest: The authors declare no conflict of interest.

References

1. Levin, A.; Weiss, Y.; Durand, F.; Freeman, W.T. Efficient marginal likelihood optimization in blind deconvolution. In Proceedings of the CVPR 2011, Colorado Springs, CO, USA, 20–25 June 2011; pp. 2657–2664.
2. Michaeli, T.; Irani, M. Blind deblurring using internal patch recurrence. In *European Conference on Computer Vision*; Springer: Cham, Switzerland, 2014; pp. 783–798.
3. Gu, S.; Zhang, L.; Zuo, W.; Feng, X. Weighted Nuclear Norm Minimization with Application to Image Denoising. In Proceedings of the 2014 IEEE Conference on Computer Vision and Pattern Recognition, Columbus, OH, USA, 23–28 June 2014; pp. 2862–2869. [CrossRef]
4. Yair, N.; Michaeli, T. Multi-scale weighted nuclear norm image restoration. In Proceedings of the IEEE Conference on Computer Vision and Pattern Recognition, Salt Lake City, UT, USA, 18–22 June 2018; pp. 3165–3174.

5. Ren, W.; Cao, X.; Pan, J.; Guo, X.; Zuo, W.; Yang, M.H. Image deblurring via enhanced low-rank prior. *IEEE Trans. Image Process.* **2016**, *25*, 3426–3437. [CrossRef] [PubMed]
6. Xu, L.; Zheng, S.; Jia, J. Unnatural l0 sparse representation for natural image deblurring. In Proceedings of the IEEE Conference on Computer Vision and Pattern Recognition, Portland, OR, USA, 23–28 June 2013; pp. 1107–1114.
7. Bai, Y.; Jia, H.; Jiang, M.; Liu, X.; Xie, X.; Gao, W. Single Image Blind Deblurring Using Multi-Scale Latent Structure Prior. *IEEE Trans. Circuits Syst. Video Technol.* **2019**, *30*, 2033–2045. [CrossRef]
8. Han, Y.; Kan, J. Blind color-image deblurring based on color image gradients. *Signal Process.* **2019**, *155*, 14–24. [CrossRef]
9. Cao, X.; Ren, W.; Zuo, W.; Guo, X.; Foroosh, H. Scene text deblurring using text-specific multiscale dictionaries. *IEEE Trans. Image Process.* **2015**, *24*, 1302–1314. [PubMed]
10. Varghese, N.; Mohan Mahesh M.R.; Rajagopalan, A.N. Fast Motion-Deblurring of IR Images. *IEEE Signal Process. Lett.* **2022**, *29*, 459–463. doi: [CrossRef]
11. Fergus, R.; Singh, B.; Hertzmann, A.; Roweis, S.T.; Freeman, W.T. Removing camera shake from a single photograph. In *ACM Transactions on Graphics (TOG)*; ACM: New York, NY, USA, 2006; Volume 25, pp. 787–794.
12. Levin, A.; Weiss, Y.; Durand, F.; Freeman, W.T. Understanding and evaluating blind deconvolution algorithms. In Proceedings of the 2009 IEEE Conference on Computer Vision and Pattern Recognition, Miami, FL, USA, 20–25 June 2009; pp. 1964–1971.
13. Xu, L.; Lu, C.; Xu, Y.; Jia, J. Image smoothing via L 0 gradient minimization. In *ACM Transactions on Graphics (TOG)*; ACM: New York, NY, USA, 2011; Volume 30, p. 174.
14. Krishnan, D.; Tay, T.; Fergus, R. Blind deconvolution using a normalized sparsity measure. In Proceedings of the CVPR 2011, Colorado Springs, CO, USA, 20–25 June 2011; pp. 233–240.
15. Yang, D.Y.; Wu, X.J.; Yin, H.F. Blind image deblurring via enhanced sparse prior. *J. Electron. Imaging* **2021**, *30*, 023031. [CrossRef]
16. Pan, J.; Hu, Z.; Su, Z.; Yang, M.H. *l*_0-regularized intensity and gradient prior for deblurring text images and beyond. *IEEE Trans. Pattern Anal. Mach. Intell.* **2016**, *39*, 342–355. [CrossRef] [PubMed]
17. Liu, R.W.; Yin, W.; Xiong, S.; Peng, S. Lo-Regularized Hybrid Gradient Sparsity Priors for Robust Single-Image Blind Deblurring. In Proceedings of the 2018 IEEE International Conference on Acoustics, Speech and Signal Processing, Calgary, AB, Canada, 15–20 April 2018; pp. 1348–1352.
18. Pan, J.; Sun, D.; Pfister, H.; Yang, M. Deblurring Images via Dark Channel Prior. *IEEE Trans. Pattern Anal. Mach. Intell.* **2018**, *40*, 2315–2328. [CrossRef] [PubMed]
19. Yan, Y.; Ren, W.; Guo, Y.; Wang, R.; Cao, X. Image deblurring via extreme channels prior. In Proceedings of the 2017 IEEE Conference on Computer Vision and Pattern Recognition, Honolulu, HI, USA, 21–26 July 2017; pp. 4003–4011.
20. Chen, L.; Fang, F.; Wang, T.; Zhang, G. Blind Image Deblurring with Local Maximum Gradient Prior. In Proceedings of the 2019 IEEE/CVF Conference on Computer Vision and Pattern Recognition (CVPR), Long Beach, CA, USA, 15–20 June 2019.
21. Cho, S.; Lee, S. Fast motion deblurring. *ACM Trans. Graph. (TOG)* **2009**, *28*, 145. [CrossRef]
22. Sun, L.; Cho, S.; Wang, J.; Hays, J. Edge-based blur kernel estimation using patch priors. In Proceedings of the IEEE International Conference on Computational Photography (ICCP), Cambridge, MA, USA, 19–21 April 2013; pp. 1–8.
23. Zhou, Y.; Komodakis, N. A map-estimation framework for blind deblurring using high-level edge priors. In *European Conference on Computer Vision*; Springer: Cham, Switzerland, 2014; pp. 142–157.
24. He, K.; Sun, J.; Tang, X. Single image haze removal using dark channel prior. *IEEE Trans. Pattern Anal. Mach. Intell.* **2010**, *33*, 2341–2353. [PubMed]
25. Shan, Q.; Jia, J.; Agarwala, A. High-quality motion deblurring from a single image. *ACM Trans. Graph. (TOG)* **2008**, *27*, 73. [CrossRef]
26. Joshi, N.; Szeliski, R.; Kriegman, D.J. PSF estimation using sharp edge prediction. In Proceedings of the 2008 IEEE Conference on Computer Vision and Pattern Recognition, Anchorage, AK, USA, 23–28 June 2008; pp. 1–8.
27. Xu, L.; Jia, J. Two-phase kernel estimation for robust motion deblurring. In *European Conference on Computer Vision*; Springer: Berlin/Heidelberg, Germany, 2010; pp. 157–170.
28. Zoran, D.; Weiss, Y. From learning models of natural image patches to whole image restoration. In Proceedings of the 2011 International Conference on Computer Vision, Barcelona, Spain, 6–13 November 2011; pp. 479–486. [CrossRef]
29. Papyan, V.; Elad, M. Multi-Scale Patch-Based Image Restoration. *IEEE Trans. Image Process.* **2016**, *25*, 249–261. [CrossRef] [PubMed]
30. Sun, J.; Cao, W.; Xu, Z.; Ponce, J. Learning a convolutional neural network for non-uniform motion blur removal. In Proceedings of the 2015 IEEE Conference on Computer Vision and Pattern Recognition (CVPR), Boston, MA, USA, 7–12 June 2015; pp. 769–777. [CrossRef]
31. Ren, D.; Zuo, W.; Zhang, D.; Xu, J.; Zhang, L. Partial Deconvolution With Inaccurate Blur Kernel. *IEEE Trans. Image Process.* **2018**, *27*, 511–524. [CrossRef]
32. Nah, S.; Kim, T.H.; Lee, K.M. Deep Multi-scale Convolutional Neural Network for Dynamic Scene Deblurring. In Proceedings of the 2017 IEEE Conference on Computer Vision and Pattern Recognition (CVPR), Honolulu, HI, USA, 21–26 June 2017.
33. Su, S.; Delbracio, M.; Wang, J.; Sapiro, G.; Heidrich, W.; Wang, O. Deep Video Deblurring for Hand-Held Cameras. In Proceedings of the 2017 IEEE Conference on Computer Vision and Pattern Recognition (CVPR), Honolulu, HI, USA, 21–26 June 2017; pp. 237–246. [CrossRef]

34. Gong, D.; Yang, J.; Liu, L.; Zhang, Y.; Reid, I.; Shen, C.; Van Den Hengel, A.; Shi, Q. From Motion Blur to Motion Flow: A Deep Learning Solution for Removing Heterogeneous Motion Blur. In Proceedings of the 2017 IEEE Conference on Computer Vision and Pattern Recognition (CVPR), Honolulu, HI, USA, 21–26 June 2017; pp. 3806–3815. [CrossRef]
35. Li, L.; Pan, J.; Lai, W.; Gao, C.; Sang, N.; Yang, M. Learning a Discriminative Prior for Blind Image Deblurring. In Proceedings of the 2018 IEEE/CVF Conference on Computer Vision and Pattern Recognition, Salt Lake City, UT, USA, 18–23 June 2018; pp. 6616–6625. [CrossRef]
36. Kupyn, O.; Budzan, V.; Mykhailych, M.; Mishkin, D.; Matas, J. DeblurGAN: Blind Motion Deblurring Using Conditional Adversarial Networks. In Proceedings of the 2018 IEEE Conference on Computer Vision and Pattern Recognition, Salt Lake City, UT, USA, 18–23 June 2018; pp. 8183–8192.
37. Zhang, H.; Dai, Y.; Li, H.; Koniusz, P. Deep Stacked Hierarchical Multi-Patch Network for Image Deblurring. In Proceedings of the 2019 IEEE/CVF Conference on Computer Vision and Pattern Recognition (CVPR), Long Beach, CA, USA, 15–20 June 2019; pp. 5971–5979. [CrossRef]
38. Shi, X.; Chen, Z.; Wang, H.; Yeung, D.Y.; Wong, W.K.; Woo, W.C. Convolutional LSTM Network: A Machine Learning Approach for Precipitation Nowcasting. In *Advances in Neural Information Processing Systems*; MIT Press: Cambridge, MA, USA, 2015; pp. 802–810.
39. Tao, X.; Gao, H.; Shen, X.; Wang, J.; Jia, J. Scale-Recurrent Network for Deep Image Deblurring. In Proceedings of the 2018 IEEE/CVF Conference on Computer Vision and Pattern Recognition, Salt Lake City, UT, USA, 18–23 June 2018; pp. 8174–8182. [CrossRef]
40. Zheng, S.; Zhu, Z.; Cheng, J.; Guo, Y.; Zhao, Y. Edge Heuristic GAN for Non-Uniform Blind Deblurring. *IEEE Signal Process. Lett.* **2019**, *26*, 1546–1550. [CrossRef]
41. Liang, C.H.; Chen, Y.A.; Liu, Y.C.; Hsu, W.H. Raw Image Deblurring. *IEEE Trans. Multimed.* **2022**, *24*, 61–72. [CrossRef]
42. Chang, M.; Feng, H.; Xu, Z.; Li, Q. Low-Light Image Restoration With Short- and Long-Exposure Raw Pairs. *IEEE Trans. Multimed.* **2022**, *24*, 702–714. [CrossRef]
43. Pan, J.; Sun, D.; Pfister, H.; Yang, M.H. Blind image deblurring using dark channel prior. In Proceedings of the IEEE Conference on Computer Vision and Pattern Recognition, Las Vegas, NV, USA, 27–30 June 2016; pp. 1628–1636.
44. Köhler, R.; Hirsch, M.; Mohler, B.; Schölkopf, B.; Harmeling, S. Recording and playback of camera shake: Benchmarking blind deconvolution with a real-world database. In *European Conference on Computer Vision*; Springer: Berlin/Heidelberg, Germany, 2012; pp. 27–40.
45. Hirsch, M.; Schuler, C.J.; Harmeling, S.; Schölkopf, B. Fast removal of non-uniform camera shake. In Proceedings of the 2011 International Conference on Computer Vision, Barcelona, Spain, 6–13 November 2011; pp. 463–470.
46. Krishnan, D.; Fergus, R. Fast image deconvolution using hyper-Laplacian priors. In Proceedings of the 22nd International Conference on Neural Information Processing Systems (NIPS'09), Vancouver British, BC, Canada, 7–10 December 2009; Curran Associates Inc.: Red Hook, NY, USA, 2009; pp. 1033–1041.
47. Chan, S.H.; Khoshabeh, R.; Gibson, K.B.; Gill, P.E.; Nguyen, T.Q. An augmented Lagrangian method for total variation video restoration. *IEEE Trans. Image Process.* **2011**, *20*, 3097–3111. [CrossRef] [PubMed]
48. Wen, F.; Ying, R.; Liu, Y.; Liu, P.; Truong, T.K. A Simple Local Minimal Intensity Prior and An Improved Algorithm for Blind Image Deblurring. *IEEE Trans. Circuits Syst. Video Technol.* **2020**, *31*, 2923–2937. [CrossRef]
49. Cho, T.S.; Paris, S.; Horn, B.K.; Freeman, W.T. Blur kernel estimation using the radon transform. In Proceedings of the CVPR 2011, Colorado Springs, CO, USA, 20–25 June 2011; pp. 241–248.
50. Whyte, O.; Sivic, J.; Zisserman, A.; Ponce, J. Non-uniform deblurring for shaken images. *Int. J. Comput. Vis.* **2012**, *98*, 168–186. [CrossRef]
51. Dong, J.; Pan, J.; Su, Z.; Yang, M.H. Blind image deblurring with outlier handling. In Proceedings of the IEEE International Conference on Computer Vision, Venice, Italy, 22–29 October 2017; pp. 2478–2486.
52. Pan, L.; Hartley, R.; Liu, M.; Dai, Y. Phase-Only Image Based Kernel Estimation for Single Image Blind Deblurring. In Proceedings of the 2019 IEEE/CVF Conference on Computer Vision and Pattern Recognition (CVPR), Long Beach, CA, USA, 15–20 June 2019; pp. 6027–6036. [CrossRef]
53. Hu, Z.; Yang, M.H. Good Regions to Deblur. In *European Conference on Computer Vision*; Springer: Berlin/Heidelberg, Germany, 2012; pp. 59–72. [CrossRef]

mathematics

MDPI

Article

Geometric Metric Learning for Multi-Output Learning

Huiping Gao and Zhongchen Ma *

The School of Computer Science & Communications Engineering, Jiangsu University, Zhenjiang 212013, China; huiping.gao@nuaa.edu.cn
* Correspondence: 555mzc@163.com

Abstract: Due to its wide applications, multi-output learning that predicts multiple output values for a single input at the same time is becoming more and more attractive. As one of the most popular frameworks for dealing with multi-output learning, the performance of the k-nearest neighbor (kNN) algorithm mainly depends on the metric used to compute the distance between different instances. In this paper, we propose a novel cost-weighted geometric mean metric learning method for multi-output learning. Specifically, this method learns a geometric mean metric which can make the distance between the input embedding and its correct output be smaller than the distance between the input embedding and the outputs of its nearest neighbors. The learned geometric mean metric can discover output dependencies and move the instances with different outputs far away in the embedding space. In addition, our objective function has a closed solution, and thus the calculation speed is very fast. Compared with state-of-the-art methods, it is easier to explain and also has a faster calculation speed. Experiments conducted on two multi-output learning tasks (i.e., multi-label classification and multi-objective regression) have confirmed that our method provides better results than state-of-the-art methods.

Keywords: multi-output; kNN; metric learning; cost-weighted; geometric mean metric

MSC: 68T10

Citation: Gao, H.; Ma, Z. Geometric Metric Learning for Multi-Output Learning. *Mathematics* **2022**, *10*, 1632. https://doi.org/10.3390/math10101632

Academic Editor: Daniel Gómez Gonzalez

Received: 13 March 2022
Accepted: 5 May 2022
Published: 11 May 2022

1. Introduction

In real-world applications, many machine-learning problems, e.g., multi-label learning and multi-target regression, involving diverse prediction can be classified as multi-output learning. Multi-output learning is an emerging machine-learning paradigm that aims to predict multiple output values of a given input at the same time [1]. For example, text documents or semantic scenes can be assigned to multiple topics; one sensor can output different environmental coefficients; a gene can have multiple biological functions; a patient may suffer from multiple diseases, and so on.

Let there be a multi-output training set $\mathcal{D} = \{\mathbf{x}_j, \mathbf{y}_j | 1 \leq j \leq n\}$, where n is the number of instances, $\mathbf{x}_j \in \mathcal{X}$ and $\mathbf{y}_j \in \mathcal{Y}$ are the feature vector and the output vector for the j-th instance, respectively, and $\mathcal{X} \in \mathbb{R}^p$ denote the p-dimensional input space and $\mathcal{Y} \in \mathbb{R}^c$ denote the output space with c output variables. Multi-output learning aims to learn a mapping function $h : \mathcal{X} \to \mathcal{Y}$ from $\mathcal{D}$ to assign an instance with a proper output vector. Compared with the traditional single-output learning, multi-output learning has a multivariate nature and its output values have diverse data types; thus it subsumes many learning problems in many real-world applications. For example, binary output values $\mathbf{y}_j \in \{0,1\}^c$ can refer to a multi-label classification problem [2] and real-valued outputs $\mathbf{y}_j \in \mathbb{R}^c$ to a multi-target regression problem [3].

As one of the the most popular frameworks for solving multi-output problems, it has been proven that the k nearest neighbor (kNN) algorithm's prediction performance can be significantly improved by learning a proper distance metric. For example, by imposing the constraint that two nearby instances from different classes will be pushed further apart with a large margin, Gou et al. [4,5] show that the prediction performance of kNN can be greatly improved. For handling multi-label learing, Zhang et al. [6] proposed a novel maximum margin output coding (MMOC) method based on structural SVMs [7,8]. It learns a distance metric such that the instances with different multiple outputs will be moved far away. Unfortunately, the training and testing of MMOC are time-consuming, which involves both solving a box-constrained quadratic programming (QP) problem for each training sample and a QP problem on $\{0,1\}^c$ space, respectively. Even if approximate inference is used to solve this QP problem, it is still computationally expensive. Inspired by kNN and MMOC, Liu et al. [9] proposed a large margin metric learning paradigm (LMMO) for multi-output tasks with only k nearest neighbor constraints, reducing the training computationally complexity from $\mathcal{O}(nc^3 + npc^2 + n^4)$ of MMOC to $\mathcal{O}(c^3 + knpc^2)$ for each iteration, and the testing computationally complexity from $\mathcal{O}(c^3)$ of MMOC to $\mathcal{O}(cn + pc)$, thus significantly breaking the bottleneck of MMOC. Nevertheless, as the state-of-the-art metric learning method for multi-output learning, the LMMO algorithm adopts the accelerated proximal gradient (APG) method to train LMMO, but cannot directly obtain the optimal metric with a closed-form solution. To achieve an ε-solution, the number of iterations needed by APG update is at least $\mathcal{O}(\frac{1}{\sqrt{\varepsilon}})$. In order to obtain the metric with good performance, more iterations of APG are needed to obtain the more accurate solution.

Therefore, it is non-trivial to develop a gradient-free metric learning algorithm for a multi-output task. To achieve this goal, this paper presents a novel geometric mean metric learning method for multi-output tasks, which learns a cost-weighted metric such that the instances with very different multiple outputs will be moved far away. Our formulation also possesses several attractive properties: closed-form solution, ease of interpretability, and computational speed several orders of magnitude faster than the state-of-the-art method.

Our contributions are as follows. (1) We propose a novel geometric mean metric learning method for multi-output tasks, which possesses several attractive properties: closed-form solution, ease of interpretability, and computational speed several orders of magnitude faster than the state-of-the-art method. (2) Experiments conducted on two multi-output learning tasks have confirmed that our method provides better results than the state-of-the-art methods.

This paper is organized as follows. Section 2 gives related work. Section 3 presents our geometric mean metric learning method for multi-output tasks. The performance of our proposed method for MLC and MTR is evaluated in Section 4. Section 5 concludes the work.

2. Related Work

2.1. Multi-Output Learning

Multi-output learning is an important machine-learning paradigm, which subsumes many learning problems in many practical applications. This paper focuses on the following two most popular multi-output learning tasks, namely multi-label classification and multi-objective regression.

Multi-label Classification aims to predict multiple different labels of a single sample. It has become an attractive emerging field and can be used in many practical applications, such as document classification [10], image retrieval [11], and image annotation [12]. In the past few years, many multi-label classification algorithms have been proposed. According to [2], these methods can be roughly divided into two categories: problem transformation and algorithm adaptation. By transforming popular learning techniques, algorithm adaptation methods try to directly deal with multi-label learning problems. ML-kNN [13], ML-DT [14], and Rank-SVM [15] are the typical methods. By converting the original problem into other well-established learning problems, the problem transformation methods try to use off-the-shelf techniques to solve the problem. Binary relevance [16], random k-labelsets [17], calibrated label ranking [18] and classifier chains [19] are the representive methods.

Multi-target Regression aims to predict the values of multiple continuous target variables for a set of predictor variables. Similar to multi-label learning methods, multi-objective regression methods can also be roughly divided into two categories: algorithm adaptation and problem transformation [20]. Compared with the existing problem transformation methods, the algorithm adaptive methods usually generate a single multi-output model, which is easier to interpret and can be extended to a larger output space. On the other hand, by adopting suitable basic learners, the problem transformation methods can easily adapt to the the problem at hand, and it is found that it is generally better than the algorithm adaptive method in terms of accuracy [21].

2.2. Metric Learning

Given a set of a pair of similar/dissimilar points, metric learning aims to learn the distance metric to keep similar/dissimilar points close/away in the embedding space. The distance metric retains the distance relationship between the training data [22]. The previous works [23–25] show that designing appropriate metrics can significantly improve the kNN classification accuracy of single-output learning tasks and multi-output learning tasks.

Metric learning methods can be roughly divided into global distance metric learning and local distance metric learning. Global distance metric learning learns appropriate metrics to keep all data points in the same class close, while pulling instances of different classes away. The most representative methods are found in [26,27]. The second type of methods tries to learn the distance metric that satisfies the local pairwise constraints, which is particularly useful for the kNN classifier. The most representative methods are found in [9,28]. However, these methods usually use gradient-based optimization methods to obtain appropriate metrics. On the contrary, we proposed a novel cost-weighted geometric mean metric learning method for multi-output tasks. It learns a cost-weighted metric with a gradient-free optimization method. This makes the learned metric more accurate and the training procedure more efficient.

3. The Proposed Method

3.1. Background

Suppose we are given a multi-output training set with n instances, i.e., $\mathcal{D} = \{\mathbf{x}_j, \mathbf{y}_j | 1 \leq j \leq n\}$, where $\mathbf{x}_j \in \mathcal{X}$ and $\mathbf{y}_j \in \mathcal{Y}$ are the feature vector and the output vector for the j-th instance, respectively. Multi-output learning aims to learn a function $h : \mathcal{X} \to \mathcal{Y}$ from $\mathcal{D}$ to predict the corresponding output vector of an instance.

To address this problem, a linear regression model simply learns the matrix $\mathbf{W}$ according to the following formulation:

$$\min_{\mathbf{W} \in \mathbb{R}^{p \times c}} \frac{1}{2} \|\mathbf{X}\mathbf{W} - \mathbf{Y}\|_F^2, \tag{1}$$

where $\|\cdot\|_F$ is the Frobenius norm, $\mathbf{X} \in \mathbb{R}^{n \times p}$ is the input matrix and $\mathbf{Y} \in \mathbb{R}^{n \times c}$ is the output matrix. However, due to a lack of modeling correlations of output space, this method usually yields low performance.

LMMO [9] learns a large margin metric to model correlations of output space. It forces the distance between input $\mathbf{W}^T\mathbf{x}_i$ and its corresponding output $\mathbf{y}_i$ to be smaller than the distance between $\mathbf{W}^T\mathbf{x}_i$ and the output $\mathbf{y}$ of the nearest neighbors of $\mathbf{x}_i$ with at least a margin, which is measured by $\Delta(\mathbf{y}_i, \mathbf{y})$, the difference between $\mathbf{y}_i$ and $\mathbf{y}$. The large margin metric learning formulation is formulated as follows:

$$\begin{aligned} &\min\nolimits_{\mathbf{Q} \in S_c^+, \{\xi_i \geq 0\}_{i=1}^n} \tfrac{1}{2}\operatorname{trace}(\mathbf{Q}) + \tfrac{C}{n}\textstyle\sum_{i=1}^n \xi_i^2 \\ &\quad \text{s.t. } \phi_{\mathbf{x}_i,\mathbf{y}_i}^T \mathbf{Q} \phi_{\mathbf{x}_i,\mathbf{y}_i} + \Delta(\mathbf{y}_i, \mathbf{y}) - \xi_i \\ &\quad \leq \phi_{\mathbf{x}_i,\mathbf{y}}^T \mathbf{Q} \phi_{\mathbf{x}_i,\mathbf{y}}, \forall \mathbf{y} \in Nei(i), \forall i \end{aligned}, \tag{2}$$

where S_c^+ represents a $c \times c$ symmetric positive semidefinite matrix, $\phi_{\mathbf{x}_i,\mathbf{y}_i} = \mathbf{W}^T\mathbf{x}_i - \mathbf{y}_i$, ξ_i is the slack variable, C is a positive constant that controls the trade-off between the square loss function and the regularizer and $Nei(i)$ is the output set of k nearest neighbors of input instance $\mathbf{x}_i$. The constraints in Equation (2) guarantee that the distance between $\mathbf{W}^T\mathbf{x}_i$ and its correct output $\mathbf{y}_i$ stays closer, but it enlarges the distance between $\mathbf{W}^T\mathbf{x}_i$ and any other output in the metric space.

However, as the state-of-the-art metric learning method for multi-output learning, the LMMO algorithm cannot directly obtain the optimal metric with a closed-form solution. To achieve an ε-solution, the number of iterations needed is at least $\mathcal{O}(\frac{1}{\sqrt{\varepsilon}})$. Thus, it is worth studying to further improve the computing efficiency of metric learning in multi-output learning.

3.2. Proposed Formulation

It is non-trivial to further obtain a closed-formed solution for LMMO. Inspired by GMML [29], we propose a novel metric learning method with a closed-form solution for multi-output learning, namely, geometric metric learning for cost-weighted multi-output learning (GCMoL), as follows:

$$\min_{\mathbf{Q}\in S_c^+} \sum_{i=1}^{n} \left(\phi_{\mathbf{x}_i,\mathbf{y}_i}^T \mathbf{Q} \phi_{\mathbf{x}_i,\mathbf{y}_i} + \sum_{\forall \mathbf{y}\in Nei(i)} \Delta(\mathbf{y}_i,\mathbf{y}) \phi_{\mathbf{x}_i,\mathbf{y}}^T \mathbf{Q}^{-1} \phi_{\mathbf{x}_i,\mathbf{y}} \right), \tag{3}$$

where S_c^+ represents a $c \times c$ symmetric positive semidefinite matrix, $\phi_{\mathbf{x}_i,\mathbf{y}_i} = \mathbf{W}^T\mathbf{x}_i - \mathbf{y}_i$ and $Nei(i)$ is the output set of k nearest neighbors of input instance $\mathbf{x}_i$, and $\Delta(\cdot)$ represents the cost functions of interest.

Compared with LMMO, in Equation (2), we have transformed several independent inequality constraints into a very uniform formulation. According to Lemma 1, the distance between input $\mathbf{W}^T\mathbf{x}_i$ and its correct output $\mathbf{y}_i$ increases monotonically in $\mathbf{G}$, whereas the distance between $\mathbf{W}^T\mathbf{x}_i$ and the output $\mathbf{y}$ of the nearest neighbors of $\mathbf{x}_i$ decreases monotonically in $\mathbf{G}$. By optimizing the object function in Equation (3), the distance between input $\mathbf{W}^T\mathbf{x}_i$ and its correct output $\mathbf{y}_i$ is naturally smaller than the distance between $\mathbf{W}^T\mathbf{x}_i$ and the output $\mathbf{y}$ of the nearest neighbors of $\mathbf{x}_i$.

For GCMoL, Equation (3), it is cost-weighted of the distance between $\mathbf{W}^T\mathbf{x}_i$ and the output $\mathbf{y}$ of the nearest neighbors of $\mathbf{x}_i$. Thus, by using the loss function $\Delta(\cdot)$ the metric $\mathbf{G}$ can be learned in the cost-sensitive way. For simplicity, the loss functions $\Delta(\cdot) = \|\cdot\|_1$ is always used to measure the distance between different outputs for multi-label learning and mutli-target regression.

Lemma 1. *Let* $\mathbf{A}$, $\mathbf{B}$ *be (strictly) positive definite matrices such that* $\mathbf{A} \succ \mathbf{B}$. *Then,* $\mathbf{A}^{-1} \prec \mathbf{B}^{-1}$.

In the following, we further simplify the objective function in Equation (3). Let us define the following two matrices:

$$\mathbf{S} := \sum_{i=1}^{n} \phi_{\mathbf{x}_i,\mathbf{y}_i} \phi_{\mathbf{x}_i,\mathbf{y}_i}^T \tag{4}$$

$$\mathbf{D} := \sum_{i=1}^{n} \sum_{\forall \mathbf{y}\in Nei(i)} \Delta(\mathbf{y}_i, y) \phi_{\mathbf{x}_i,\mathbf{y}} \phi_{\mathbf{x}_i,\mathbf{y}}^T. \tag{5}$$

Then, the objective function in Equation (3) can be reformulated as

$$\min_{\mathbf{G}} tr(\mathbf{GS}) + tr(\mathbf{G}^{-1}\mathbf{D}). \tag{6}$$

The minimization problem (6) is both strictly convex and strictly geodesically convex (Theorem 3 of [29]), which is similar to problem (13) of [29]. It has a global optimal solution and a closed form solution as shown below:

$$\mathbf{G} = \mathbf{S}^{-1}_{\sharp_{1/2}}\mathbf{D} = \mathbf{S}^{-1/2}\left(\mathbf{S}^{1/2}\mathbf{D}\mathbf{S}^{1/2}\right)^{1/2}\mathbf{S}^{-1/2}. \tag{7}$$

Clearly, solution of (6) is the geometric mean between $\mathbf{S}^{-1}$ and $\mathbf{D}$. But the matrix $\mathbf{S}$ might sometimes be non-invertible or near-singular in practice. To address this issue, a regularizing term, which can be used to incorporate prior knowledge about the distance function, is added to the objective function,

$$\min_{\mathbf{G}\succ\mathbf{0}} \quad \lambda D_{\text{sld}}(\mathbf{G}, \mathbf{G}_0) + \text{tr}(\mathbf{G}\mathbf{S}) + \text{tr}\left(\mathbf{G}^{-1}\mathbf{D}\right), \tag{8}$$

where $\mathbf{G}_0$ is the "prior" and $D_{sld}(\mathbf{G}, \mathbf{G}_0)$ is the symmetrized LogDet divergence, which is equal to

$$D_{\text{sld}}(\mathbf{G}, \mathbf{G}_0) := \text{tr}\left(\mathbf{G}\mathbf{G}_0^{-1}\right) + \text{tr}\left(\mathbf{G}^{-1}\mathbf{G}_0\right) - 2c. \tag{9}$$

The minimization problem in (8) also has a closed-form solution,

$$\mathbf{G}_{\text{reg}} = \left(\mathbf{S} + \lambda\mathbf{G}_0^{-1}\right)^{-1}\sharp_{\frac{1}{2}}(\mathbf{D} + \lambda\mathbf{G}_0). \tag{10}$$

From Equation (10), we can see that the solution is given by the midpoint of the geodesic joining $\mathbf{S} + \lambda\mathbf{G}_0^{-1}$ and $\mathbf{D} + \lambda\mathbf{G}_0$. From a geodesic viewpoint, assigning different weights to the matrices is also pivotal for the solution of (3). Therefore, we introduce a nonlinear cost guided by Riemannian geometry of the SPD manifold and obtain a weighted version of (3) below:

$$\min_{\mathbf{G}\succ 0} h_t(\mathbf{G}) := (1-t)\delta_R^2\left(\mathbf{G}, \mathbf{S}^{-1}\right) + t\delta_R^2(\mathbf{G}, \mathbf{D}), \tag{11}$$

where t is a parameter that determines the balance between the cost terms of $\delta_R^2(\mathbf{G}, \mathbf{S}^{-1})$ and $\delta_R^2(\mathbf{G}, \mathbf{D})$. Moreover, δ_R denotes the Riemannian distance

$$\delta_R(\mathbf{X}, \mathbf{Y}) := \left\|\log\left(\mathbf{Y}^{-1/2}\mathbf{X}\mathbf{Y}^{-1/2}\right)\right\|_{\text{F}} \quad \text{for } \mathbf{X}, \mathbf{Y} \succ 0 \tag{12}$$

on SPD matrices.

The problem outlined in (11) is geodesically covex and its unique solution is the weighted geometric mean

$$\mathbf{G} = \mathbf{S}^{-1}\sharp_t\mathbf{D}. \tag{13}$$

Similar to the regularized solution to problem (8), the solution to the regularized form of problem (11) is given by

$$\mathbf{G}_{\text{reg}} = \left(\mathbf{S} + \lambda\mathbf{G}_0^{-1}\right)^{-1}_{\sharp_t}(\mathbf{D} + \lambda\mathbf{G}_0), \tag{14}$$

for $t \in [0, 1]$. In the case where $t = 1/2$, it is equal to (10). Many approaches, e.g., Cholesky–Schur and scaled Newton methods, can be used for fast computation of Riemannian geodesics of SPD matrices. In this paper, we use the Cholesky–Schur method to implement the computation of Riemannian geodesics. The summary of our GCMoL algorithm for multi-output learning is presented in Algorithm 1.

Algorithm 1: GCMoL.

Require: Input: Training dataset matrix $\mathbf{X} \in \mathbb{R}^{n\times p}$ and its corresponding output set $\mathbf{Y} \in \mathbb{R}^{n\times c}$, the number of nearest neighbors k, the loss function $\Delta(\cdot)$, step length of geodesic t, regularization parameter λ and prior knowledge $\mathbf{G}_0$.
Ensure: Output: Regression matrix $\mathbf{W}$ and the learned metric $\mathbf{G}$.
1. Set $\mathbf{W} := \arg\min_{\mathbf{W}\in\mathbb{R}^{p\times c}} \frac{1}{2}\|\mathbf{XW}-\mathbf{Y}\|_F^2$.
2.Search the output set of k nearest neighbors of each input instance, namely $Nei(i), \forall i$.
3. Compute $\mathbf{S} = \sum_{i=1}^{n} \phi_{\mathbf{x}_i,\mathbf{y}_i}\phi_{\mathbf{x}_i,\mathbf{y}_i}^T$.
4. Compute $\mathbf{D} := \sum_{i=1}^{n} \sum_{\forall \mathbf{y}\in Nei(i)} \Delta(\mathbf{y}_i,\mathbf{y})\phi_{\mathbf{x}_i,\mathbf{y}}\phi_{\mathbf{x}_i,\mathbf{y}}^T$.
5. Compute $\mathbf{G} = \left(\mathbf{S}+\lambda\mathbf{G}_0^{-1}\right)^{-1}_{\sharp_t}(\mathbf{D}+\lambda\mathbf{G}_0)$.

3.3. Prediction

In the metric space, our metric learning formulation can make the input $\mathbf{W}^T\mathbf{x}_i$ and its correct output $\mathbf{y}_i$ as close as possible. For a new test instance $\mathbf{x}$, we can obtain its output by a decoding method. In general, the decoding process requires solving the QP problem on a combinatorial space [6], which is computationally expensive. In this paper, we follow the same prediction method as in [9]. Specifically, we find k nearest neighbors for a new testing input instance $\mathbf{x}$ in our learned metric space, where the distance between $\mathbf{x}$ and $\mathbf{x}_i$ can be computed as $(\mathbf{W}^T\mathbf{x}-\mathbf{W}^T\mathbf{x}_i)^T)\mathbf{G}(\mathbf{W}^T\mathbf{x}-\mathbf{W}^T\mathbf{x}_i)$. Then, we conduct voting based on weighted nearest neighbors for the prediction. In particular, for multi-label classification problems, we set 0.5 as the threshold.

3.4. Complexity Analysis

In this subsection, we compare the training and testing time complexity of different methods.

3.4.1. Training Time

The training of MMOC involves an exponential number of constraints and solving a box-constrained QP problem for each training instance. The authors therefore use the over-generating technique with the cutting plane method and CVX (http://cvxr.com/cvx/, accessed on 8 March 2022) to solve these problems, respectively. Because MMOC is optimized based on the gradient method, it is assumed that this method iterates η times at least to get the desired performance. From Liu et al. [9], the training time complexity of MMOC is at least $\mathcal{O}(nc^3+npc^2+n^4)$ for each iteration. Therefore, the total training time complexity of MMOC is at least $\mathcal{O}(\eta nc^3+\eta npc^2+\eta n^4)$. The training time of LMMO is dominated by the APG algorithm. To achieve an ε-solution, the number of iterations needed by the APG update is $\mathcal{O}(\frac{1}{\sqrt{\varepsilon}})$. According to Liu et al. [30] , the time complexity for each iteration is $\mathcal{O}(c^3+knpc^2)$. Therefore, the total training time complexity of LMMO is at least $\mathcal{O}(\frac{1}{\sqrt{\varepsilon}}c^3+\frac{1}{\sqrt{\varepsilon}}knpc^2)$. The training time of our method (GCMoL) is dominated by the computation of Riemannian geodesics for SPD matrices. Many approaches, e.g., Cholesky–Schur and scaled Newton methods, can be used for fast computation of Riemannian geodesics of SPD matrices. Following [29], we use the Cholesky–Schur method to implement the computation of Riemannian geodesics. So, the time complexity of GCMoL is $\mathcal{O}(c^3+knpc^2)$.

3.4.2. Testing Time

We analyze the testing time for each testing instance. Because the test time of MMOC involves solving a QP problem on the $\{0,1\}^c$ space, which is essentially a combinatorial optimization problem, it is very intractable. To address this problem, MMOC uses a mean-field approximation to iteratively obtain approximate solutions. The time complexity of each iteration of the average approximate field is $\mathcal{O}(c^2)$. If it iterates many times until convergence, its time complexity is at least $\mathcal{O}(c^3)$. Both LMMO and our method (GCMoL) use the same prediction method and therefore have the same prediction time complexity, i.e., $\mathcal{O}(nc + pc)$.

4. Experiments

In this section, we extensively compared the proposed GCMoL method with related approaches on real-world multi-label classification and multi-target regression datasets. All the methods compared are implemented in MatLab. All experiments are conducted on a desktop with a 3.2 GHZ Intel CPU and 32 GB main memory running on a Windows platform.

4.1. Experimental Setup

(1) Datasets: We conduct experiments on five benchmark multi-label datasets (http://mulan.sourceforge.net/, accessed on 9 March 2022), including emotions, scene, cal500 and genbase, and four benchmark multi-target regression datasets (http://mulan.sourceforge.net/, accessed on 9 March 2022), including edm, enb, jura, and scpf. We summarize the dataset details in the Table 1, where $|S|$ represents the number of examples, $dim(S)$ represents the number of features, $L(S)$ represents the number of class labels, and $Card(S)$ represents the average number of labels per example, $Dom(S)$ represents the feature type of the dataset S, and Cat represents the type of task category.

Table 1. Characteristics of datasets.

$Cat(S)$	**Dataset**	$\|S\|$	$dim(S)$	$L(S)$	$Card(S)$
MLC	emotions	593	72	6	1.869
	scene	2407	294	6	1.074
	cal500	502	68	174	26.044
	genbase	662	1186	27	1.252
MTR	edm	154	16	2	-
	enb	768	8	2	-
	jura	359	15	3	-
	scpf	1137	23	3	-

(2) Evaluation Metrics: To testify to the performance, we focus on two evaluation metrics, i.e., Micro-F1 and Macro-F1, for multi-label classification datasets, and one evaluation metric, i.e., aRMAE, for multi-target regression datasets. For Micro-F1 and Macro-F1, the larger the values the better the performance. Their concrete metric definitions are defined in [2]. For aRMAE, the smaller the values the better the performance. It is defined as:

$$aRMAE(\mathbf{h}, \mathbf{D}) = \frac{1}{m} \sum_{j=1}^{m} \frac{\sum_{(\mathbf{x},\mathbf{y}) \in D} |\hat{y}_j - y_j|}{\sum_{(\mathbf{x},\mathbf{y}) \in D} |\bar{Y}_j - y_j|}, \tag{15}$$

where $\bar{Y}_j$ is the mean value of Y_j over dataset $\mathbf{D}$ and $\hat{y}_j$ is the prediction of $\mathbf{h}$ for Y_j. Intuitively, aRMAE measures how much better ($aRMAE < 1$) or worse ($aRMAE > 1$) the prediction model is compared to a naive baseline that always predicts the mean value of each target.

(3) Comparing Methods: We compare our proposed method GCMoL with the following state-of-the-art multi-output learning methods.

- BR [16] is the most intuitive solution to multi-label learning. It works by decomposing the multi-label learning task into multiple independent binary learning tasks, so it is a problem transformation method. In order to be fair in the experiment, we use the kNN model as the base classifier and set $k = 10$.
- ML-kNN [13] is also a problem transformation method, which learns a classifier for each label by combining kNN and Bayesian inference. According to [13] , we still use $k = 10$ in our experiments, which usually yields the best performance.

- LMMO [9] is a recently proposed large-margin metric learning method for multi-output tasks. It projects both input and output into the same embedding space, and then learns a distance metric to keep instances with the same output close and instances with very different outputs farther away. Its formulation is presented in Equation (2) and can only be used for multi-label learning task. Parameter λ is selected from $\{10^{-5}, 10^{-4}, \cdots, 10^{4}, 10^{5}\}$.

The hyper-parameters in compared methods are selected via 10-fold cross-validation on the training set. The parameter λ is selected from $\{10^{-5}, 10^{-4}, \cdots, 10^{4}, 10^{5}\}$, and t is selected from $\{0.2, 0.5, 0.7\}$. We adopt $k = 10$, which yields the best performance.

4.2. Experimental Results

Detailed experimental results are reported in Table 2, where the performance rank on each dataset is also shown in the parentheses. Moreover, to show whether GCMoL achieves statistically superior performance against compared approaches, we employ a Nemenyi test (at 0.05 significance level) whose statistical test results are summarized in Figure 1. The performances between two methods will be significantly different if their average ranks differ by at least one critical difference $CD = q_\alpha \sqrt{k(k+1)/6N}$. For the Nemenyi test, $q_\alpha =$ at significance level $\alpha = 0.05$, and thus $CD = 1.2075 (k = 4, N = 12)$. In Figure 1, the connected algorithms indicate that their average rank difference is within one CD. Any unconnected pair of algorithms is considered to have a significant difference in performance.

Table 2. Experimental results for multi-output learning. The best ones are in bold.

Task	Criteria	Dataset	Method			
			BR	MLkNN	LMMO	GCMoL
MLC	Micro-F1	emotions	0.4905	0.4918	0.6753	**0.6774**
		genbase	0.9607	0.9505	0.9697	**0.9791**
		yeast	0.6330	**0.6392**	0.5600	0.6376
		CAL500	0.3131	0.3185	0.3339	**0.3709**
	Macro-F1	emotions	0.4170	0.3811	0.6563	**0.6634**
		genbase	0.5683	0.5321	0.5877	**0.6258**
		yeast	0.3892	0.3697	0.3748	**0.4056**
		CAL500	0.0738	0.0534	0.0689	**0.1049**
MTR	aRMAE	edm	0.9335	-	0.9010	**0.8591**
		enb	0.2230	-	0.2488	**0.1538**
		jura	0.6030	-	0.7158	**0.5704**
		wq	**0.8628**	-	0.9933	0.8713

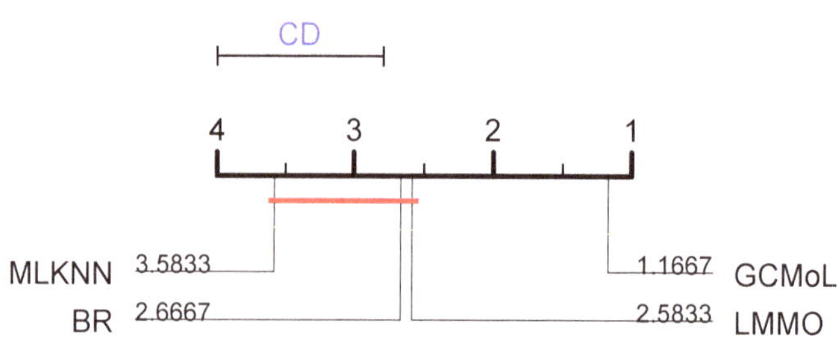

Figure 1. Comparison of GCMoL against other comparing algorithms with the Nemenyi test.

Based on the reported experimental results, the following observations can be made: (1) Regarding Micro-F1 of the MLC task, GCMoL is basically better than other methods and only slightly inferior to MLkNN on the yeast dataset. (2) Regrading Macro-F1 of the MLC task, GCMoL is always better than other methods. (3) Regarding aRMAE of the MTR task, GCMoL is also basically better than other methods and only slightly inferior to BR on the wq dataset. (4) According to the Nemenyi test results, MLKNN, LMMO, and BR perform not significantly differently from each other, but GCMoL performs significantly better than other methods, which verifies the effectiveness of our method.

4.3. Analysis

4.3.1. Hyper-Parameter Sensitivity Analysis

There are two hyper-parameters, i.e., λ and t, in our proposed method. To give their sensitivity analysis, we conduct experiments on CAL500 and edm datasets. The experimental results of GCMoL with different values of λ and t are depicted in Figure 2a–f. From the experimental results, we note that the performance of GCMoL is relatively insensitive to the value of λ and t.

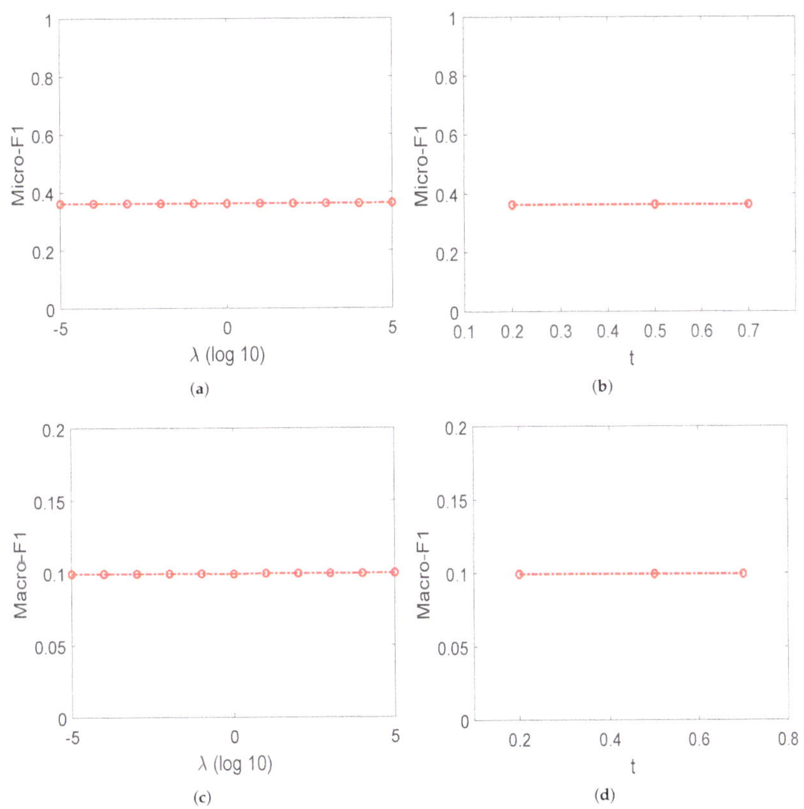

Figure 2. *Cont.*

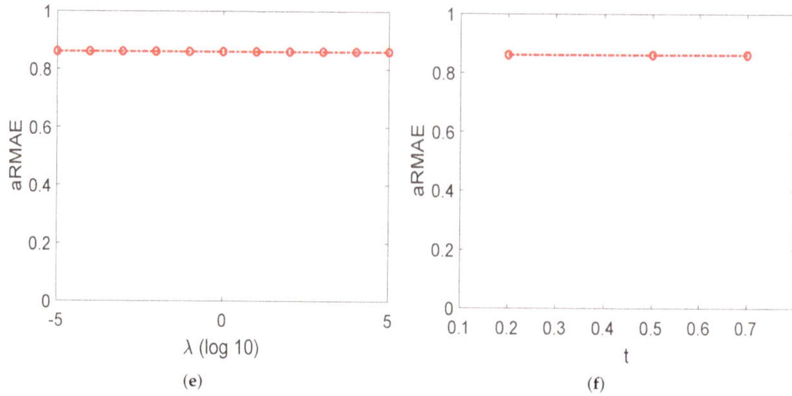

Figure 2. Sensitivity analysis about GCMoL with different λ and t. (**a**) Micro-F1 scores of different λ on CAL500 dataset. (**b**) Micro-F1 scores of different t on CAL500 dataset. (**c**) Macro-F1 scores of different λ on CAL500 dataset. (**d**) Macro-F1 scores of different t on CAL500 dataset. (**e**) aRMAE of different λ on edm dataset. (**f**) aRMAE of different t on edm dataset.

4.3.2. Time-Comsuming Analysis

To further compare the time consumption of different methods, Figure 3 reports the single training time of 10-fold cross validation of our method and baseline approaches in terms of CAL500 dataset. The results illustrate that BR, MLkNN, and GCMoL complete the training in 3 s, but LMMO lasts more than 240 s. Our method is almost 100 times faster than LMMO. In Section 3.4, the results of theoretical analysis for the time complexity show that our method runs slower than BR and MLkNN, but faster than LMMO. The experimental results also confirmed this conclusion.

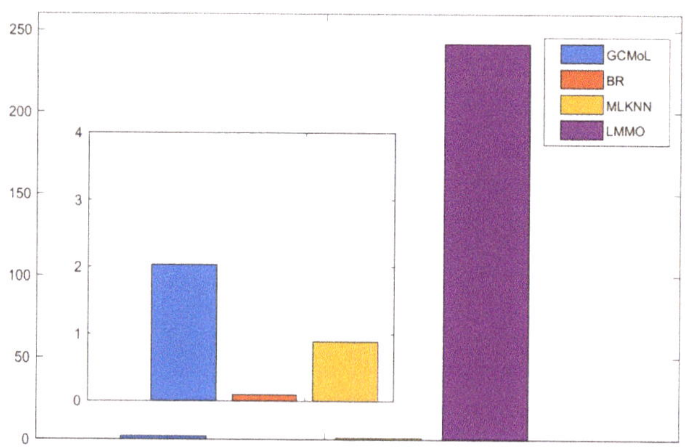

Figure 3. Running time results of different methods on the CAL500 dataset.

5. Conclusions

We proposed a novel cost-weighted geometric mean metric learning method for multi-output tasks in this paper. Our method can model output dependency by the learned geometric mean metric, which can make the instances with very different outputs far away. It also admits a closed-form solution and computational speed several orders of magnitude faster than the state-of-the-art LMMO method. Experiments show that our method outperforms the state-of-the-art methods on multi-output learning tasks.

There are several directions worth exploring further in our future work. First, we will try to design a novel robust geometric metric learning method to generalize our technique to weakly supervised multi-output learning task. In weakly supervised multi-output learning tasks, missing or noisy supervision information may bring great challenges to metric learning. Secondly, we will try to design new weakly supervised contrastive learning methods to effectively apply self-supervised learning techniques to a multi-output learning task.

Author Contributions: Methodology, H.G.; Writing—review & editing, Z.M. All authors have read and agreed to the published version of the manuscript.

Funding: This work is supported by the National Natural Science Foundation of China (No. 62006098) and the China Postdoctoral Science Foundation (No. 2020M681515).

Conflicts of Interest: The authors declare no conflict of interest.

References

1. Xu, D.; Shi, Y.; Tsang, I.W.; Ong, Y.S.; Gong, C.; Shen, X. Survey on Multi-Output Learning. *IEEE Trans. Neural Netw. Learn. Syst.* **2019**, *31*, 2409–2429. [CrossRef]
2. Zhang, M.L.; Zhou, Z.H. A review on multi-label learning algorithms. *IEEE Trans. Knowl. Data Eng.* **2013**, *26*, 1819–1837. [CrossRef]
3. Borchani, H.; Varando, G.; Bielza, C.; Larrañaga, P. A survey on multi-output regression. *Wiley Interdiscip. Rev. Data Min. Knowl. Discov.* **2015**, *5*, 216–233. [CrossRef]
4. Gou, J.; Qiu, W.; Yi, Z.; Shen, X.; Zhan, Y.; Ou, W. Locality constrained representation-based K-nearest neighbor classification. *Knowl.-Based Syst.* **2019**, *167*, 38–52. [CrossRef]
5. Gou, J.; Sun, L.; Du, L.; Ma, H.; Xiong, T.; Ou, W.; Zhan, Y. A representation coefficient-based k-nearest centroid neighbor classifier. *Expert Syst. Appl.* **2022**, *194*, 116529. [CrossRef]
6. Zhang, Y.; Schneider, J. Maximum margin output coding. In Proceedings of the 29th International Coference on International Conference on Machine Learning, Edinburgh, UK, 26 June–1 July 2012; pp. 379–386.
7. Tsochantaridis, I.; Joachims, T.; Hofmann, T.; Altun, Y. Large margin methods for structured and interdependent output variables. *J. Mach. Learn. Res.* **2005**, *6*, 1453–1484.
8. BakIr, G.; Hofmann, T.; Schölkopf, B.; Smola, A.J.; Taskar, B.; Vishwanathan, S. *Generalization Bounds and Consistency for Structured Labeling*; MIT Press: Cambridge, MA, USA, 2007.
9. Liu, W.; Xu, D.; Tsang, I.W.; Zhang, W. Metric learning for multi-output tasks. *IEEE Trans. Pattern Anal. Mach. Intell.* **2018**, *41*, 408–422. [CrossRef] [PubMed]
10. Rubin, T.N.; Chambers, A.; Smyth, P.; Steyvers, M. Statistical topic models for multi-label document classification. *Mach. Learn.* **2012**, *88*, 157–208. [CrossRef]
11. Verma, Y.; Jawahar, C. Image annotation by propagating labels from semantic neighbourhoods. *Int. J. Comput. Vis.* **2017**, *121*, 126–148. [CrossRef]
12. Nguyen, C.T.; Zhan, D.C.; Zhou, Z.H. Multi-modal image annotation with multi-instance multi-label LDA. In Proceedings of the Twenty-Third International Joint Conference on Artificial Intelligence, Beijing, China, 3–9 August 2013.
13. Zhang, M.L.; Zhou, Z.H. ML-KNN: A lazy learning approach to multi-label learning. *Pattern Recognit.* **2007**, *40*, 2038–2048. [CrossRef]
14. Clare, A.; King, R.D. Knowledge discovery in multi label phenotype data. In Proceedings of the European Conference on Principles of Data Mining and Knowledge Discovery, Freiburg, Germany, 3–5 September 2001; Springer: Berlin/Heidelberg, Germany, 2001; pp. 42–53.
15. Elisseeff, A.; Weston, J. A kernel method for multi-labelled classification. In *Advances in Neural Information Processing Systems*; Springer: Berlin/Heidelberg, Germany, 2002; pp. 681–687.
16. Boutell, M.R.; Luo, J.; Shen, X.; Brown, C.M. Learning multi-label scene classification. *Pattern Recognit.* **2004**, *37*, 1757–1771. [CrossRef]
17. Tsoumakas, G.; Vlahavas, I. Random k-labelsets: An ensemble method for multilabel classification. In Proceedings of the European Conference on Machine Learning, Warsaw, Poland, 17–21 September 2007; Springer: Berlin/Heidelberg, Germany, 2007; pp. 406–417.
18. Fürnkranz, J.; Hüllermeier, E.; Mencía, E.L.; Brinker, K. Multilabel classification via calibrated label ranking. *Mach. Learn.* **2008**, *73*, 133–153. [CrossRef]
19. Read, J.; Pfahringer, B.; Holmes, G.; Frank, E. Classifier chains for multi-label classification. *Mach. Learn.* **2011**, *85*, 333. [CrossRef]
20. Spyromitros-Xioufis, E.; Sechidis, K.; Vlahavas, I. Multi-target regression via output space quantization. *arXiv* **2020**, arXiv:2003.09896.
21. Spyromitros-Xioufis, E.; Tsoumakas, G.; Groves, W.; Vlahavas, I. Multi-target regression via input space expansion: Treating targets as inputs. *Mach. Learn.* **2016**, *104*, 55–98. [CrossRef]
22. Yang, L.; Jin, R. Distance metric learning: A comprehensive survey. *Mich. State Univ.* **2006**, *2*, 4.

23. He, X.; King, O.; Ma, W.Y.; Li, M.; Zhang, H.J. Learning a semantic space from user's relevance feedback for image retrieval. *IEEE Trans. Circuits Syst. Video Technol.* **2003**, *13*, 39–48.
24. He, X.; Ma, W.Y.; Zhang, H.J. Learning an image manifold for retrieval. In Proceedings of the 12th Annual ACM International Conference on Multimedia, New York, NY, USA, 10–16 October 2004; pp. 17–23.
25. He, J.; Li, M.; Zhang, H.J.; Tong, H.; Zhang, C. Manifold-ranking based image retrieval. In Proceedings of the 12th Annual ACM International Conference on Multimedia, New York, NY, USA, 10–16 October 2004; pp. 9–16.
26. Weinberger, K.Q.; Saul, L.K. Distance metric learning for large margin nearest neighbor classification. *J. Mach. Learn. Res.* **2009**, *10*, 207–244.
27. Xing, E.P.; Jordan, M.I.; Russell, S.J.; Ng, A.Y. Distance metric learning with application to clustering with side-information. In *Advances in Neural Information Processing Systems*; Springer: Berlin/Heidelberg, Germany, 2003; pp. 521–528.
28. Peng, J.; Heisterkamp, D.R.; Dai, H. Adaptive kernel metric nearest neighbor classification. In Proceedings of the 2002 International Conference on Pattern Recognition, Quebec City, QC, Canada, 11–15 August 2002; Volume 3, pp. 33–36.
29. Zadeh, P.; Hosseini, R.; Sra, S. Geometric mean metric learning. In Proceedings of the International Conference on Machine Learning, New York, NY, USA, 19–24 June 2016; pp. 2464–2471.
30. Liu, W.; Tsang, I.W. Large margin metric learning for multi-label prediction. In Proceedings of the Twenty-Ninth AAAI Conference on Artificial Intelligence, Austin, TX, USA, 25–30 January 2015.

mathematics

Article

Decoupling Induction and Multi-Order Attention Drop-Out Gating Based Joint Motion Deblurring and Image Super-Resolution

Yuezhong Chu, Xuefeng Zhang and Heng Liu *

School of Computer Science and Technology, Anhui University of Technology, Ma'anshan 243002, China; yzchu@ahut.edu.cn (Y.C.); zxf_06@ahut.edu.cn (X.Z.)
* Correspondence: hengliu@ahut.edu.cn

Abstract: Resolution decrease and motion blur are two typical image degradation processes that are usually addressed by deep networks, specifically convolutional neural networks (CNNs). However, since real images are usually obtained through multiple degradations, the vast majority of current CNN methods that employ a single degradation process inevitably need to be improved to account for multiple degradation effects. In this work, motivated by degradation decoupling and multiple-order attention drop-out gating, we propose a joint deep recovery model to efficiently address motion blur and resolution reduction simultaneously. Our degradation decoupling style improves the continence and the efficiency of model construction and training. Moreover, the proposed multi-order attention mechanism comprehensively and hierarchically extracts multiple attention features and fuses them properly by drop-out gating. The proposed approach is evaluated using diverse benchmark datasets including natural and synthetic images. The experimental results show that our proposed method can efficiently complete joint motion blur and image super-resolution (SR).

Keywords: motion deblurring; image super-resolution; multi-order attention; gated learning; decoupling

MSC: 37M99

Citation: Chu, Y.; Zhang, X.; Liu, H. Decoupling Induction and Multi-Order Attention Drop-Out Gating Based Joint Motion Deblurring and Image Super-Resolution. *Mathematics* **2022**, *10*, 1837. https://doi.org/10.3390/math10111837

Academic Editors: Jianping Gou, Weihua Ou, Shaoning Zeng, Lan Du and Catalin Stoean

Received: 11 March 2022
Accepted: 24 May 2022
Published: 26 May 2022

1. Introduction

Motion blur and resolution decrease are the two dominant forms of image quality degradation. The former is caused by the relative motion between the camera and the object, while the latter is generally originated by down-sampling. The inverse processes of these degradation forms are individual motion deblurring and image SR—recovering clear images from blurred ones or reconstructing high-resolution (HR) images from low resolution (LR) ones, respectively, which are the practical main means to deal with image quality degradation.

Assuming the original sharp image is x, and the blurred image is y; if ignoring the effect of the non-linear camera response function (CRF), theoretically the motion blur degradation may be represented as:

$$y = (x * h) + n, \qquad (1)$$

where h represents the motion blur kernel, $*$ denotes the convolution operation and n usually indicates the random noise. According to Equation (1), obviously, the inverse motion deblurring process is a typical ill-conditioned problem because for one clear image there are possibly many blur images corresponding to it.

Actually, there are two different implementation methods for motion deblurring, namely, blind deblurring or the non-blind method. The usual non-blind method acquires the clear image x based on the estimated blur kernel and the observation y. However, the major difference in blind deblurring is that no kernel estimation is required. Due to the end-to-end mapping and the powerful approximation properties, CNNs are particularly well suited for blind motion deblurring. For example, some recent CNN-based works [1,2] are presented for blind deblurring duties.

Compared with motion blur degradation, in the process of resolution degeneration, in addition to the low pass blur filter $\boldsymbol{k}$ and the noise $\boldsymbol{n}$, there is another degradation down-sampling operator at work. For an HR image $\boldsymbol{x}$, a typical resolution degradation model to acquire the corresponding LR image $\boldsymbol{y}$ is formulated as:

$$\mathbf{y} = (\mathbf{x} * \boldsymbol{k}) \downarrow_{\mathbf{s}} + \mathbf{n}\cdot \tag{2}$$

where $\boldsymbol{k}$ denotes a low pass blur filter, $*$ denotes the convolution operation, $\downarrow_s$ indicates a $s\times$ down-sampling (decimating) operation, and $\boldsymbol{n}$ represents the noise. Obviously, the inverse problem of Equation (2)—image SR—is also a typical ill-posed one as there is usually a non-unique solution.

Motion blur degradation is superficially seen to be a simpler problem than resolution degeneration due to there being no down-sampling operation. However, motion blur is most likely to be non-linear or non-uniform, which is usually more complex than resolution degradation (the blur kernel is generally linear and uniform). This makes it a difficult challenge to directly estimate the blur kernel used for non-blind deblurring.

In recent years, deep learning-based networks, especially CNN-based methods, have been the mainstream of image SR and motion deblurring research, such as [3–5]. Although CNN-based image SR and deblurring methods have reported fairly good results, CNN-based image restoration is far from simple when the resolution and motion blur are reduced simultaneously. In this case, either image SR or motion deblurring does not work well due to degraded convolution or the blur kernels not being equivalent, and the two degradation processes are not complementary with each other when they occur simultaneously.

Recently, there have been some CNN works [6–8] that have addressed simultaneous image SR and motion deblurring. All of these methods explicitly or implicitly adopt a global or local feature coupling structure—a deblurring part and an SR part are involved or intervene with each other, to recover the resolution and the motion details at the same time. Actually, these recovery methods only construct different comprehensive CNN mapping networks from the degraded images to the corresponding sharp and high-resolution ones, but do not fully utilize the characteristics of motion deblurring and image SR to achieve decoupling. Therefore, even if the results of these methods are good, they lack an explanation and have low efficiency.

On the other hand, typical deep image recovery models always use the residual connection to convey features. However, due to a lack of ability to mine the feature information across different layers, some complex residual variants are proposed, such as DRRN [9] and RDN [10], etc. Among them, RDN (Residual Dense Network) is representative, which uses not only local dense residual learning but also global residual learning, to extract and adaptively fuse the local and global features from all the observed layers. Since RDN makes full use of multiple hierarchical features, it is very beneficial to construct an image restoration model. In addition to the work on feature learning across different layers, recent attention mechanism-based methods, for example, RCAN [11] and SAN [12], select and enhance useful and important channel feature maps of the same layer through weighting for image or video restoration. In fact, these channel feature attention methods utilize the first- or second-order statistics of the channel maps of certain layers to calculate the dependence of channel features, and then select and weigh the important features. However, single first- or second-order feature statistics cannot make full use of the relationship between different channel feature maps.

In order to overcome the limitations of coupling recovery and single-order attention feature weighting, in this work, we first analyze the compound multiple degradation model of motion blur and resolution reduction and discuss the maximum likelihood (ML) solution of the degradation model. Then, based on the analysis, we discuss decoupling induction multi-task learning and the CNN model construction method for multiple degradation image restoration. In addition, we obtain the first-order and second-order attention features of the decoupled structures for motion deblurring and SR, respectively, and obtain the third-order attention features by combining local series and parallel features. On this basis, for the sake of improving the feature redundancy and generalization ability of multi-order attention fusion, we utilize the drop-out gating integration method, which enhances the robustness and stability of the proposed multi-order attention mechanism.

An example result of the proposed method to deal with compound degeneration (motion blur as well as 4× down-sampling) is shown in Figure 1, where the comparisons to those results of RCAN [11] and SCGAN [6] are also demonstrated. The dominant contributions of the work are summed up as follows:

- We propose a novel joint motion deblurring and image SR model based on decoupling induction and multi-order attention drop-out gating. The proposed method can overcome the limitation of the single type degeneration assumption to achieve joint recovery with the aid of decoupling induction multi-task learning.
- We propose the use of decoupling dual-branch multi-order attention features for clear HR image reconstruction and select the drop-out gating learning method to enhance the robustness and the generalization of features' fusion.
- We validate and compare the presented model, not only with the publicly available and widely used natural image datasets, but also with synthetic images completely different from the training images. We show that, through decoupling induction and multi-order attention drop-out gating learning, our method can produce visual results of a quality that competes with the most advanced motion deblurring and image SR methods for LR and blurred images.

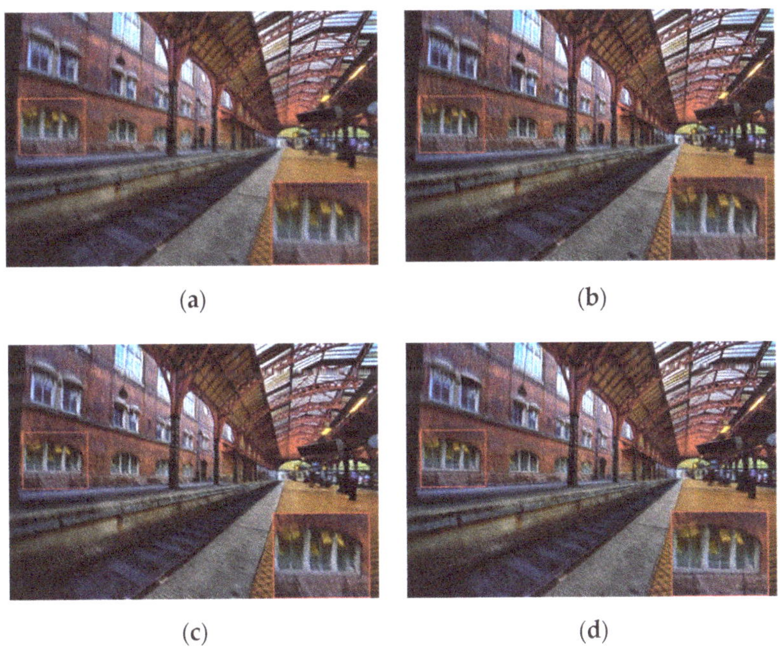

Figure 1. An example result of the presented decoupling induction and multi-order attention gating model for joint deblurring and 4× super-resolution. The details in the recovered image of our proposed method (**d**) are much clearer than those of RCAN [11] (**b**) and SCGAN [6] (**c**); the LR and blurred image is shown (**a**).

2. Related Work

2.1. Joint Image Deblur and SR

Compared with the traditional image SR methods, the first CNN-based image SR method, SRCNN [3,4], proposed by Dong et al., can generate more accurate HR details owing to powerful non-linear mapping. To extend three convolutional layers of SRCNN to a deeper level, Kim et al. [13] presented a true deep image SR model called VDSR via residual connection [14]. Recently, Liu et al. [15] also proposed a multi-scale deep encoder–decoder network called MSDEPC to super resolve LR images with the edge maps' prior information. In addition, Ledig et al. [16] proposed the application of a generative adversarial network (GAN) [17] for image SR, called SRGAN. SRGAN takes the perceptual loss and the adversarial loss to supervise the reconstruction of super-resolved images and can obtain more realistic SR results.

CNNs also play an effective role in motion deblurring. Xu et al. [18] and Sun et al. [1] developed some CNN-based methods to recover blurred images based on blur kernel estimation. Besides these non-blind deep methods, some deep blind deblurring methods [2,5] are also proposed. Nah et al. [2] applied a multiple scales CNN to recover clear images directly. Motivated by the work, Tao et al. [5] designed a simple structure motion deblurring network characterized by scale recursion. Moreover, inspired by the work of image translation [19], Ramakrishnan et al. [20] first applied GAN for motion deblurring. Then, Kupyn et al. [21] proposed DeblurGAN for blind motion deblurring, which utilizes the WGAN [22] with a gradient penalty to avoid the mode collapse issue in the classical GAN. Subsequently, Kupyn et al. [23] presented a new and very efficient GAN-based model for single image motion deblurring, named DeblurGAN-v2, which is based on a relativistic conditional GAN with a double-scale discriminator. Furthermore, for meteorological prediction application, Manzo et al. [24] adopted a pretrained deep network-based architecture for clouds' image description and classification. Recently, in order to address the problem that blurred images suffer from other degradation such as down-scaling and compression, Xu et al. [25] proposed the enhanced deep pyramid network (EDPN) model for blurry image restoration, by fully exploiting the self-scale and cross-scale similarities.

Few works can use CNNs for simultaneous motion deblurring and SISR. Xu et al. [6] solve the problem of super-resolving blurred facial images by SCGAN. However, their method is restricted to facial images, and it is not easy to obtain a good performance in real scenarios. Zhang et al. [7] proposed using a deep encoder–decoder model to perform joint motion deblurring and image SR. Zhang et al. [8] once again proposed a gated fusion method for concurrent motion deblurring and image SR. Recently, Liang et al. [26] utilized the dual supervised network to address this issue. However, they did not achieve satisfactory results. In addition, for plug-and-play image SR, Zhang et al. [27] proposed a new blind SR framework to achieve the processing of arbitrary blur kernels. In addition, Zhang et al. [28] proposed a dual supervised learning strategy to fully exploit the representation capacity of their deep model, which imposes constraints between LR and HR images.

2.2. Attention

In addition to feature transfer by residual connection, the attention mechanism is another widely used method for feature preservation and enhancement used in many image SR models [11,12,29,30]. Zhang et al. presented the RCAN [11] (residual channel attention network) model that utilizes channel attention with residual blocks to adjust the task adaptability of channel features and to strengthen their expression ability. Since RCAN only uses the first-order statistical information of channel features, Dai et al. [12] presented the so-called SAN (second-order attention network) model, which replaces the global average pooling with the global covariance pooling (second-order statistics) to obtain a better effect of channel features' selection and enhancement. Very recently, Niu et al. [31] designed a novel pixel-guided dual-branch attention network (PDAN) to jointly restore image details and the spatial scale.

In addition, Wang et al. [29] proposed the extraction and fusion of temporal and spatial attention features for video restoration. Furthermore, Fu et al. [30] introduced a dual attention network—containing one spatial branch and one channel branch for scene segmentation, which can adaptively extract and integrate the local and non-local features of spatial and channel attention.

3. Methodology

3.1. Multiple Degradation Decoupling Induction

For motion deblurring and image SR, we used the following equations to describe the corresponding degradation models, which are used to generate the LR and blur images for training.

$$y = \left(\sum_{i=1}^{N} x_i\right)/N + n \tag{3}$$

$$y = (x \downarrow_s) + n, \tag{4}$$

where Equation (3) represents one typical motion degradation of a certain image sequence-averaging blur and Equation (4) denotes the process of image resolution reduction. Here, x_i and y in Equation (3) represent a sharp image of one clear HR image sequence (the image number of the sequence is N) and the corresponding blur image, respectively; and x and y in Equation (4) are the HR image and the corresponding LR image, respectively. N in the equation denotes the additional noise (normally it is Gaussian white noise). $\downarrow_s$ is $s\times$ the down-sampling operator (can be bicubic sub-sampling).

Based on Equations (3) and (4), the motion blur and the resolution reduction compound degeneration may be formulated as

$$y = \left(\left(\sum_{i=1}^{N} x_i\right)/N\right) \downarrow s + n \tag{5}$$

Obviously, averaging N frame images lead to blurring degradation and the subsequent down-sampling operation also reduces the resolution of the generated blur image.

Theoretically, if the frame averaging blur kernel and the spatial down-sampling kernel are denoted as h and k, respectively, Equation (5) can be generalized as the following:

$$y = (x * h) * k + n, y = (x * S) + n \tag{6}$$

Here the kernel convolution $h * k$ is defined as a new kernel S. This equation means the comprehensive function of multi-degradation basically equals one blur operation. Moreover, according to Equation (6), the residual r between the sharp HR image x and the degraded observation y is easily calculated. Assuming the image data obey the Gaussian distribution, a solution of maximum likelihood estimation (MLE) for Equation (6) can be obtained by $\widetilde{x} = y + r$. Naturally, if the residual r is looked upon as the high-frequency details of x, the observation y becomes its approximation component. Here, if assuming the details r can be decoupled into the deblurring details r_{db} and the SR details r_{sr} that is $r = r_{db} + r_{sr}$, the MLE solution is further expressed as

$$\widetilde{x} = y + r_{db} + r_{sr} \tag{7}$$

According to Equation (7), if we can obtain the deblurring and the SR details individually through deep decoupling induction learning, then the original clear and HR image can be recovered. Moreover, although changing the sequence between motion blur and resolution reduction will lead to the multiple degraded models being different from Equation (5), the MLE solution with decoupling details (Equation (7)) remains the same. This indicates that our proposed decoupling induction method is robust to different sequences of multiple degenerated images.

3.2. Multi-Order Attention Gating

The decoupled deblurring features and SR features were then exploited to calculate the first-order channel attention (FOCA) and the second-order channel attention (SOCA), respectively. Meanwhile, their SOCAs were concatenated to calculate the FOCA again, which acquires the so-called third-order channel attention (TOCA). Then, all the acquired multiple order attentions were fused with multi-routes gating. Closing a route means that the corresponding feature attention is blocked and cannot be used for subsequent reconstruction. In fact, we used the drop-out mechanism—a probability of 0.5 was used to turn off some feature attentions randomly. The above processes are called multi-order attention drop-out gating. We used a similar method to calculate the FOCA and the SOCA, as explored in RCAN [11] and SAN [12]. Based on the principles of the SOCA and FOCA, we give the mathematical description of the third-order channel attention (TOCA) and multi-order attention drop-out gating learning in the following.

Given the deblurring feature maps x_{db} and the SR feature maps x_{sr}, assume they are with C feature channels and size $H \times W$. Note that the channel size of x_{db} and x_{sr} does not need to be equal and in the following we just take x_{db} as an example. We reshape the feature map x_{db} to a matrix X with the size $H \times W$; each element of which is C dimension. Here, if we treat the feature elements as samples, then the covariance matrix may be calculated and decomposed by the eigenvalue decomposition (EIG) as:

$$\sum X\bar{I}X^T = U\Lambda U^T \tag{8}$$

where $\bar{I} = \frac{1}{s}\left(I - \frac{1}{s}\mathbf{1}\right)$, $s = H \times W$, and I and $\mathbf{1}$ are the identity matrix and the all-ones matrix, respectively. In addition, U is an orthogonal matrix and $\Lambda = diag(\lambda_1, \ldots, \lambda_C)$ is a diagonal matrix with eigenvalues in decreasing order. Then, the normalized covariance matrix can be acquired as $\hat{Y} = \sum^{\alpha} = U\Lambda^{\alpha}U^T$; α is a positive real number. Obviously, the normalized covariance contains the correlations of channel-wise features. Let $\hat{Y} = y_1, \ldots, y_C$; the c-th channel-wise statistics z_c can be obtained by global pooling $\hat{Y}$ as:

$$z_c = \frac{1}{C}\sum_{i=1}^{C} y_c(i) \tag{9}$$

Based on the equation, the feature weighting coefficient can be obtained through a simple sigmoid gating function [32] as:

$$\omega_c = f(W_U\delta(W_D z_c)) \tag{10}$$

where W_D and W_U are usually the convolution layers to adjust the number of feature channels to C/r and C, respectively. $f(\cdot)$ and $\delta(\cdot)$ are individually the sigmoid functions and RELU function. Thus, for deblurring feature x_{db} the second-order channel attention (SOCA) weighting is represented as:

$$\overline{x}_{db} = \omega_c \cdot x_{db,c} \tag{11}$$

Based on the equation, the SOCA weighting for image SR features x_{sr}, can be similarly described as $\overline{x}_{sr} = \omega_c \cdot x_{sr,c}$. Then, $\overline{x}_{db,c}$ and $\overline{x}_{sr,c}$ are concatenated and passed through the FOCA to obtain the final TOCA. Let $x_{cat} = concat(\overline{x}_{db}, \overline{x}_{sr}) = [x_{cat,1}, \ldots, x_{cat,2C}]$; we calculate the global average pooling along each channel dimension and then transform the statistics with channel scaling convolution layers and proper activation functions to obtain the FOCA weighting, which can be described as:

$$z_{toa,c} = \frac{1}{H \times W} = \sum_{i=1}^{H}\sum_{j=1}^{W} concat(\overline{x}_{db}, \overline{x}_{sr})_c(i,j), \tag{12}$$

$$S_{toa,c} = f(W_S\delta(W_I z_{toa,c})) \tag{13}$$

where $x_{cat,c}(i,j)$ is the value at the position (i,j) of the c-th concatenated SOCA features x_{cat}, and W_S and W_I are the channel up-scaling and down-scaling convolution layers, similar to W_U and W_D in Equation (10). Finally, the third-order channel attention (TOCA) weighting can be denoted as:

$$\hat{x}_{toa,c} = S_{toa,c} \cdot x_{ccat} \tag{14}$$

If the FOCA of the deblurring features and SR features are denoted as $\dot{x}_{db}$ and $\dot{x}_{sr}$, respectively, then all the multi-order attention features, $\dot{x}_{db}$, $\overline{x}_{db}$, $\dot{x}_{sr}$, $\overline{x}_{sr}$, and $\hat{x}_{toa}$, are sent to one five-routes gate for fusion. The gate works with the drop-out mechanism. Let the j-th route switch be a random variable r_j and obey the Bernoulli distribution with the parameter p (which is set to 0.5 in our practice)—that is $r_j \sim \boldsymbol{Bernoulli(p)}$—and then, all the attention that can pass through will be fused by concatenation as:

$$\widetilde{x} = \boldsymbol{concat}(r_1\dot{x}_{db}, r_2\overline{x}_{db}, r_3\dot{x}_{sr}, r_4\overline{x}_{sr}, r_5\hat{x}_{toa}) \tag{15}$$

3.3. Network Architecture

Based on Equation (7), we can design two CNN branches to learn the deblurring details r_{db} and the SR details r_{sr} separately. This step is called decoupling induction learning. Moreover, we can individually calculate their multiple orders attention features, and utilize the drop-out gating method to fuse them. Here the step is named multi-order attention drop-out gating. The fused attention features concatenated with the LR and blur input images are then sent to the subsequent reconstruction module to obtain the final SR result.

The overall architecture of the proposed model is illustrated in Figure 2. Our model contains four dominant modules: the first one is the deblurring features extraction module, which can be used to predict the sharp LR image; the second one is the SR features extraction module, which can be utilized to obtain the super-resolved blur images; the third is the proposed multi-order attention drop-out gating module, which calculates different order attentions and fuses them with the drop-out gating mechanism; and the fourth one is the reconstruction module to recover the final clear and SR result. In the figure, the four modules mentioned are indicated by dashed boxes of different colors.

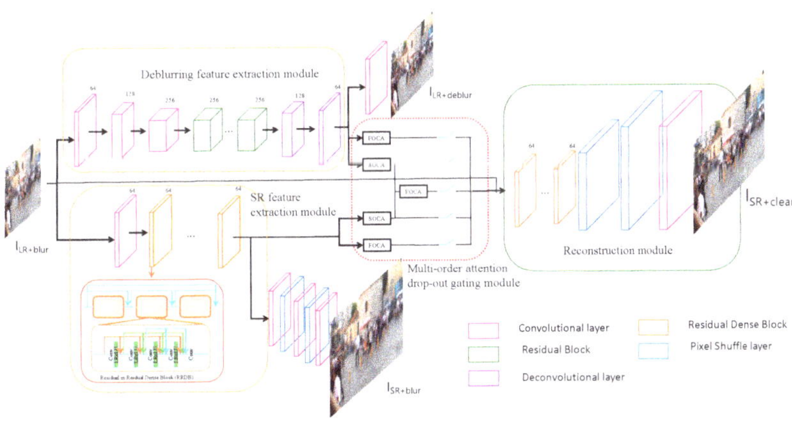

Figure 2. The overall architecture of the proposed model. Our model mainly contains four modules—deblurring feature extraction, SR feature extraction, multi-order attention drop-out gating, and reconstruction. An LR and blur input image is first passed through the separate SR and deblurring branches to obtain the decoupled features; then, they go through a multi-order attention drop-out gating fusion, before being reconstructed to output a super-resolved and clear image.

3.3.1. Deblurring Feature Extraction

This module aims to acquire the decoupled deblurring features, and henceforth, sharp LR images from blurry LR images $I_{LR+blur}$. Inspired by [21], we adopted a residual encoder–decoder structure in this module. The encoder part is composed of several convolution layers which reduce the size of feature maps to a quarter of the input image size. We then added nine residual blocks between the encoder and decoder to refine the deblurring features. Then, the decoder exploits two deconvolutional upscaling layers to raise the resolution of the deblurring feature maps. Additionally, based on the deblurring features, we can use another two convolution operations to obtain a deblur LR image $I_{LR+deblur}$ (see Figure 2).

Here, we denote the output deblurring features of the decoder as x_{db}, which were later sent to the multi-order attention gating module. All the used activation layers are the leaky rectified linear units (LeakyReLU), and we used IN (instance normalization) operations in the residual blocks instead of the BN (batch normalization) ones, because the BN layer may reduce the flexibility of the network and undermine the scale information by normalizing the features and increasing computation. The mapping relationship learned from this module between the input $I_{LR+blur}$ and the output x_{db} can be described as:

$$x_{db} = H_{\uparrow 2}(H_{\uparrow 1}(RB(H_{\downarrow 2}(H_{\downarrow 1}(H_c(I_{LR+blur}))))))\tag{16}$$

where $H_{\downarrow 2}$ and $H_{\downarrow 1}$ are the down-scaling convolution layers of an encoder, $H_{\uparrow 1}$ and $H_{\downarrow 1}$ are the deconvolution layers of a decoder, RB represents the nine residual blocks, and H_c is the first convolution layer acting on the input $I_{LR+blur}$. The activation and normalization operations are included in the layers by default.

3.3.2. SR Feature Extraction

The purpose of this module is to obtain decoupled SR image details. We utilized eight residual dense blocks [10] (each block contains five convolution operations with four LeakyReLU layers; see Figure 2 for reference) and one convolution layer to construct the deep structure to extract the high-frequency spatial detail features. From this, the super-resolved blur image $I_{LR+blur}$ can also be acquired through two consecutive pixel shuffle layers and several convolution layers. To maintain the spatial information, neither the pooling layer nor stride operation is used in the module. At the same time, no normalization operations are applied. If denoting the extracted SR features as x_{sr}, then the mapping relationship learned from the module between the input $I_{LR+blur}$ and the output x_{sr} can be described as:

$$x_{sr} = RDB_8(H_c(I_{LR+blur}))\tag{17}$$

where RDB_8 represents the eight consecutive residual dense blocks.

3.3.3. Multi-Order Attention Drop-Out Gating

This module summarizes the multiple orders attention of the learned deblurring features x_{db} and the SR features x_{sr} to obtain high-frequency image recovering details. x_{db} and x_{sr} are the inputs of the module and their first-order, second-order, and common third-order feature attention maps are calculated, respectively. Then, all these attention features are concatenated and sent to the drop-out layer to obtain the final feature maps $\tilde{x}$. The mapping relationship of this module and its processing details can be referred to in the previous Section 3.3.2 and Figure 2.

3.3.4. Reconstruction Module

In this module, the gated attention features $\tilde{x}$ and the blur LR image are sent into 16 residual dense blocks [10] and the result is further fed to two-pixel shuffle layers to improve the spatial resolution to $4\times$. After that, two convolution layers are used to acquire the final SR and clear image $I_{SR+clear}$. Since most operations of our model are performed in the LR low dimension functional space, the computation cost both in training and in the testing stages is quite low. The mapping relationship of the module is described as:

$$I_{SR+clear} = H_{2c}(P_2(P_1(RDB_{16}(concat(\tilde{x}, I_{LR+blur}))))) \quad (18)$$

where RDB_{16} is the 16 consecutive residual dense blocks, P_1 and P_2 are the two-pixel shuffle layers, and H_{2c} represents two convolution operations.

3.4. Loss Functions

Our proposed model has three outputs: the LR deblurring image I_{LR+db}, the SR blur image $I_{SR+blur}$, and the clear SR image $I_{SR+clear}$. Then, the total loss of our model contains three parts: the LR but clear image loss, the HR but blur image loss, and the final HR and clear image loss. In our case, we usually calculate the difference between a certain output and its expectation with the ℓ_1 norm and treat it as the loss. The three losses of our model can be described as:

$$\ell_1 = \sum_{i=1}^{N} \|y_{HR+clear,i} - I_{SR+clear,i}\|_1 \quad (19)$$

$$\ell_2 = \sum_{i=1}^{N} \|y_{LR+clear,i} - I_{LR+db,i}\|_1 \quad (20)$$

$$\ell_3 = \sum_{i=1}^{N} \|y_{HR+blur,i} - I_{SR+blur,i}\|_1 \quad (21)$$

where $y_{HR+clear,i}$, $y_{LR+clear,i}$, and $y_{HR+blur,i}$ are the expectations of the three outputs, respectively. N is the number of training samples. Thus, the total loss is the sum of the above three losses:

$$L = \ell_1 + \alpha \ell_2 + (1 - \alpha)\, \ell_3 \quad (22)$$

where α is the loss balance factor, which is set to be 0.5 in our experiments.

In addition, sometimes in order to generate a more realistic image, we also consider introducing an SSIM [33] measure into the loss ℓ_1. At this time, the loss ℓ_1 can be modified as:

$$\ell_1 = \sum_{i=1}^{N} (\beta SSIM\left(y_{HR+clear,i}, I_{SR+clear,i}\right) + (1 - \beta)\|y_{HR+clear,i} - I_{SR+clear,i}\|_2 \quad (23)$$

where the β is used to balance these two terms, which is set to 0.84.

4. Experimental Results

4.1. Datasets and Training Details

Many experiments and performance comparisons are performed on the well-known public blur datasets: the GOPRO dataset [2] and the dataset developed by Lai et al. [34]. Originated from some natural video sequences, the GOPRO [2] dataset contains 2103 high-resolution training pairs (the sharp image and the blurry image) and 1111 test images. The size of every image in the dataset is 1280 × 720. The motion-blurred image is obtained by averaging several neighboring frame images and the LR image can be acquired by bicubic down-sampling on the corresponding HR image. In contrast to GOPRO, the dataset of Lai et al. [34] is composed of many man-made generated blur images, in which each degenerated image is the convolution result of the sharp image with a blur kernel. Here, the size of the degraded kernel may range from 21 × 21 to 75 × 75. Note that Lai et al.'s dataset [34] contains both uniform and non-uniform blurred images. The main characteristics of the two datasets are summarized in Table 1.

The training of the proposed model can be divided into two steps. In the first step, the model is trained by supervision with the LR blurry patches $I_{LR+blur}$, the sharp LR patches $I_{LR+clear}$, and the clear HR patches $I_{HR+clear}$. During training, the loss of our model (Equation (22)) is minimized. In the second step, the trained model is finetuned by using Equation (23) to replace the original ℓ_1 in Equation (22). The training procedure is implemented by the SGD solver from Pytorch [35] and the learning rate decreases from 0.01 to 0.00001 and the decay is set to be 0.5. In addition, the moment of the used solver is 0.9 and the batch size of the training samples is 12. It takes about two days to train the proposed model if using an Nvidia Titan GTX1080ti GPU.

Table 1. Basic dataset characteristics of GOPRO [2] and Lai et al. [34].

Dataset	Lai et al. [34]	GOPRO [2]
Synthetic/Real	Synthetic and Real	Real
Blur type	Uniform and Non-uniform	Uniform
Ground-truth images	125	3214
Blurred images	300	3214
Depth variation	Yes	No

4.2. Experiments and Comparisons

Based on numerous LR and blurry input images on different test datasets, we performed lots of joint image deblurring and SR experiments and made comparisons with some recent SOTA (state-of-the-art) image SR models [10–12], the deblurring method [5], and the multiple degradations recovery approaches [6–8,36]. We also compared the combination method of the SR algorithm [10] and the deblurring method [5]. For fair play, all the comparisons were made by using the public codes provided by these methods. For those ones which cannot be publicly acquired (such as ED-DSRN [7]), we used our dataset to retrain the original networks. The comparisons with these related methods using the datasets of GOPRO [2] and Lai et al. [34], in terms of the PSNR, the SSIM, the model parameters, and the test time, are demonstrated in Tables 2 and 3. The visual results of these methods are also compared in Figures 3–5.

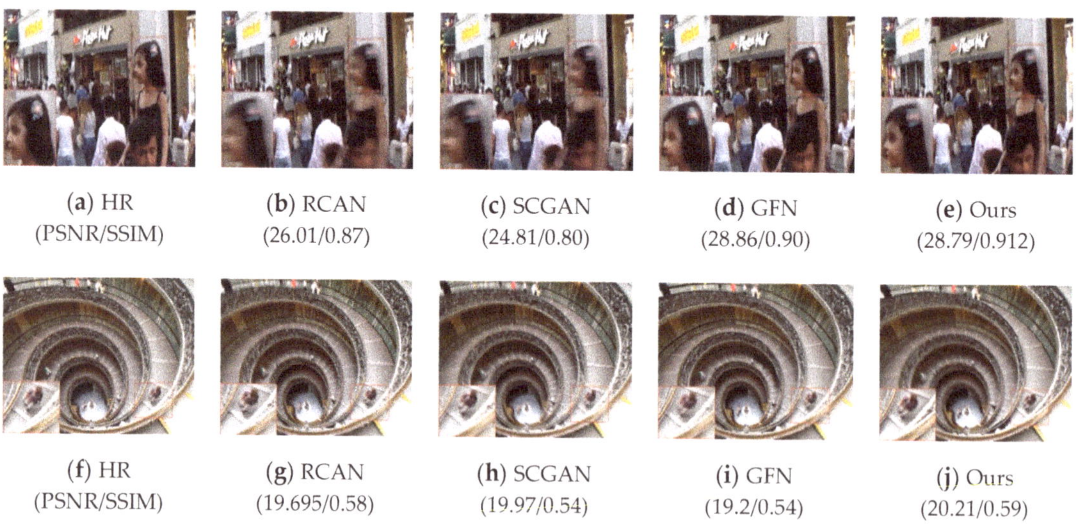

(**a**) HR (PSNR/SSIM) (**b**) RCAN (26.01/0.87) (**c**) SCGAN (24.81/0.80) (**d**) GFN (28.86/0.90) (**e**) Ours (28.79/0.912)

(**f**) HR (PSNR/SSIM) (**g**) RCAN (19.695/0.58) (**h**) SCGAN (19.97/0.54) (**i**) GFN (19.2/0.54) (**j**) Ours (20.21/0.59)

Figure 3. The details in the deblurred and super-resolved (4×) images generated by the presented decoupled induction and multi-attention drop-out gating model on GOPRO [2] and Lai et al. [34]; using our method, the image details are clearer than the ones acquired from RCAN [11], SCGAN [6], and GFN [8].

Table 2. The comparisons with SOTA methods of the quantitative performance on GOPRO dataset [2]. Best results are marked in bold.

Measures	RDN [10]	SRN [5]	SCG-AN [6]	RCAN [11]	RDN [10] + SRN [5]	ED-DSRN [7]	Zhang et al. [33]	GFN [8]	Our Proposed
PSNR	24.370	25.829	22.791	25.328	26.211	26.331	25.80	27.81	**27.82**
SSIM	0.739	0.782	0.783	0.804	0.792	0.810	0.768	0.83	**0.848**
Parameters	178 M	28.8 M	15 M	**1.5 M**	305 M	25 M	7 M	11 M	27 M
Training/Inference time	1.0 day/2.8 s	3 days/0.4 s	1.5 days/0.68 s	1.5 day/0.55 s	3.8 days/4 s	1.5 days/0.22 s	2 days/1.3 s	**2 days/0.07 s**	2 day/0.33 s

Table 3. The comparisons with SOTA methods of the quantitative performance on Lai et al. dataset [34]. Best results are marked in bold.

Measures	RDN [10]	SRN [5]	SCG-AN [6]	RCAN [11]	RDN [10] + SRN [5]	ED-DSRN [7]	Zhang et al. [33]	GFN [8]	Our Proposed
PSNR	17.780	17.444	18.572	17.729	18.861	18.791	19.003	19.12	**19.17**
SSIM	0.416	0.408	0.460	0.471	0.423	0.473	0.466	0.574	**0.59**
Inference time	2.3 s	0.3 s	0.50 s	0.9 s	2.2 s	**0.20 s**	1.1 s	0.42 s	0.5 s

(**a**) HR (PSNR/SSIM) (**b**) RCAN (27.874/0.821) (**c**) SCGAN (24.61/0.727) (**d**) GFN (30.271/0.869) (**e**) Ours (30.316/0.872)

(**f**) HR (PSNR/SSIM) (**g**) RCAN (26.948/0.881) (**h**) SCGAN (23.10/0.786) (**i**) GFN (31.904/0.931) (**j**) Ours (31.886/0.935)

Figure 4. More visual comparison of our model with other methods on GOPRO [2].

(**a**) HR (PSNR/SSIM) (**b**) RCAN (24.555/0.72) (**c**) SCGAN (24.39/0.67) (**d**) GFN (25.297/0.713) (**e**) Ours (25.279/0.731)

(**f**) HR (PSNR/SSIM) (**g**) RCAN (21.446/0.61) (**h**) SCGAN (21.295/0.56) (**i**) GFN (21.358/0.578) (**j**) Ours (21.78/0.61)

Figure 5. More visual comparison of our model with other methods on Lai et al. [34].

According to Tables 2 and 3, it is clear that in most cases our model achieves the best multi-degradation recovery effects, and only in certain special scenarios, it is slightly inferior to GFN [8] (see Figure 3d,e), which seems to be the best joint image SR and the deblurring algorithm available at present. In Figure 3d,e and Figure 4, although the PSNR is slightly lower, the image we recovered looks better than the image generated by GFN [8]. Such contradictions may stem from the fact that the calculation of PSNR or SSIM only requires the neighborhood operations of certain image pixels and cannot reflect the true perception of human vision. In light of the quantitative metrics in Tables 2 and 3, it is easy to see that, compared to the other methods, even under multiple different blurs and LR datasets, the proposed method can achieve the best or the second best PSNR and SSIM performance.

According to Figure 5, we can easily see that on the Lai et al. [34] dataset, our approach shows a significant improvement. Although adjustments have been made to RCAN by fine-tuning the dataset, it still cannot compete with our trained network (see Figure 5b,g). It is clear that Figure 5b,g contains less texture detail than Figure 5e,j. This performance gap is mainly due to the lack of an encoder–decoder structure, which is a key architecture when designing a blind deblurring network. Although the performance of the retrained SCGAN is better than its pre-trained model, because of its small model capacity, this method cannot handle complex non-uniform blurs well.

In general, compared with other methods, especially GFN, the superiority of our method lies in (1) our two branches (super-resolution and motion deblurring), which are fully disentangled, whereas GFN's are not; and (2) we use multi-order attention to obtain the attention features of the two branches at different orders separately, and perform gated fusion through the drop-out mechanism, whereas GFN computes the correlation of different branches for fusion. Due to the simpler structure, the GFN method has fewer parameters and a faster computation speed than our approach. However, in practical applications, assuming no particular requirements for machine memory or computing speed, our method can be used in preference if the scene is rich in significant textures and the objects have multi-scale variations. Benefiting from joint attention learning, our method produces clearer and higher resolution images with good perceptual quality.

5. Ablation Study

For the sake of dissecting the role of the key components of the proposed decoupling induction and multi-order attention gating model, several variants were developed and tested: (1) deblurring alone, (2) SR alone, (3) without TOCA, and (4) no drop-out gating. These variants were trained with almost the same hyper-parameters as our original model. For the variants of deblurring alone and SR alone, the FOCA and SOCA features were concatenated and pushed to the reconstruction module. For the variant without TOCA, there were only four attention routes ($\dot{x}_{db}, \overline{x}_{db}, \dot{x}_{sr}, \overline{x}_{sr}$) for drop-out gating. The final variant used direct concatenating to replace drop-out gating. The results are shown in Table 4.

Table 4. Ablation study on GOPRO [2] dataset. The best results are indicated in bold.

Methods	GOPRO [2]	
	PSNR	**SSIM**
Deblurring alone	26.97	0.815
SR alone	25.84	0.791
Without TOCA	27.51	0.833
No drop-out gating	27.20	0.827
Ours	**27.82**	**0.848**

From Table 4, it is clear that without drop-out gating, the performance of the proposed approach is much suppressed. At the same time, the high-order attention TOCA really can help to improve the reconstruction effects. In addition, it seems that the deblurring branch contributes more than the SR forking in multiple degradation decoupling reconstruction. Thus, we can conclude that the proposed mechanism of multi-order attention and drop-out gating is very effective for joint deblurring and super-resolution.

6. Conclusions

In this work, we proposed an effective end-to-end deep model which can deal with multiple degeneration problems for concurrent motion deblurring and image SR. Inspired by the idea of decoupled learning and multi-order attention features selection, our model firstly manages to construct the discrete network structures of motion deblurring and image SR respectively, and then realizes selective features' enhancement and fusion through multi-order attention drop-out gating. Many experimental results and comparisons to other SOTA methods were carried out to demonstrate the superior performance of our method in compound degradation recovery and generalization power.

Future work will focus on two aspects. The first one is to investigate why the deblurring branch matters more than SR forking in the proposed multiple degradation reconstruction approaches. Secondly, based on blur and resolution reduction, if more degeneration action (such as noise interference) is also introduced, a way to obtain a good image recovery effect will be investigated.

Author Contributions: Conceptualization, Y.C. and H.L.; methodology, Y.C. and H.L.; software, Y.C. and X.Z.; writing—original draft preparation, Y.C.; writing—review and editing, H.L.; visualization, X.Z.; funding acquisition, H.L. All authors have read and agreed to the published version of the manuscript.

Funding: This research was funded by the National Natural Science Foundation of China, grant No. 61971004, the Natural Science Foundation of Anhui Province, grant No. 2008085MF190, the Key Project of Natural Science of Anhui Provincial Department of Education, grant No. KJ2019A0083 and KJ2021A1289, and the Open Project Fund of the Key Laboratory of Computational Intelligence and Signal Processing of the Ministry of Education (Anhui University), grant No. 2020A002.

Data Availability Statement: The links to the public datasets used in the paper are as follows: GOPRO dataset: https://github.com/SeungjunNah/DeepDeblur_release (accessed on 1 December 2021), Lai's dataset [34]: http://vllab.ucmerced.edu/wlai24/cvpr16_deblur_study/ (accessed on 1 December 2021).

Conflicts of Interest: The authors declare no conflict of interest.

References

1. Sun, J.; Cao, W.; Xu, Z.; Ponce, J. Learning a convolutional neural network for non-uniform motion blur removal. In Proceedings of the IEEE Conference on Computer Vision and Pattern Recognition, Boston, MA, USA, 7–12 June 2015; pp. 769–777. [CrossRef]
2. Nah, S.; Kim, T.H.; Lee, K.M. Deep multi-scale convolutional neural network for dynamic scene deblurring. In Proceedings of the IEEE Conference on Computer Vision and Pattern Recognition, Hawaii, HI, USA, 21–26 July 2017; pp. 3883–3891. [CrossRef]
3. Dong, C.; Loy, C.C.; He, K.; Tang, X. Learning a deep convolutional network for image super-resolution. In Proceedings of the European Conference on Computer Vision, Zurich, Switzerland, 6–12 September 2014; pp. 184–199. [CrossRef]
4. Xi, S.; Wei, J.; Zhang, W. Pixel-Guided Dual-Branch Attention Network for Joint Image Deblurring and Super-Resolution. In Proceedings of the 2021 IEEE/CVF Conference on Computer Vision and Pattern Recognition Workshops (CVPRW), Nashville, TN, USA, 19–25 June 2021; pp. 532–540. [CrossRef]
5. Tao, X.; Gao, H.; Shen, X.; Wang, J.; Jia, J. Scale-recurrent network for deep image deblurring. In Proceedings of the IEEE Conference on Computer Vision and Pattern Recognition (CVPR), Salt Lake City, UT, USA, 18–23 June 2018; pp. 8174–8182. [CrossRef]
6. Xu, X.; Sun, D.; Pan, J.; Zhang, Y.; Pfister, H.; Yang, M.-H. Learning to super-resolve blurry face and text images. In Proceedings of the IEEE Conference on Computer Vision and Pattern Recognition, Hawaii, HI, USA, 21–26 July 2017; pp. 251–260. [CrossRef]
7. Zhang, X.; Wang, F.; Dong, H.; Guo, Y. A deep encoder-decoder networks for joint deblurring and super-resolution. In Proceedings of the 2018 IEEE International Conference on Acoustics, Speech and Signal Processing (ICASSP), Alberta, AB, Canada, 15–20 April 2018; pp. 1448–1452. [CrossRef]
8. Zhang, X.; Dong, H.; Hu, Z.; Hu, Z.; Lai, W.-S.; Wang, F.; Yang, M.-H. Gated fusion network for joint image deblurring and super-resolution. In *British Machine Vision Conference (BMVC)*; Springer: London, UK, 2018. [CrossRef]

9. Ying, T.; Jian, Y.; Liu, X. Image super-resolution via deep recursive residual network. In Proceedings of the IEEE Conference on Computer Vision and Pattern Recognition, Hawaii, HI, USA, 21–26 July 2017; pp. 3147–3155. [CrossRef]
10. Zhang, Y.; Tian, Y.; Kong, Y.; Zhong, B.; Fu, Y. Residual dense network for image super-resolution. In Proceedings of the IEEE conference on computer vision and pattern recognition, Salt Lake City, UT, USA, 18–23 June 2018; pp. 2472–2481. [CrossRef]
11. Zhang, Y.; Li, K.; Li, K.; Wang, L.; Zhong, B.; Fu, Y. Image super-resolution using very deep residual channel attention networks. In Proceedings of the European Conference on Computer Vision (ECCV), Munich, Germany, 8–14 August 2018; pp. 286–301. [CrossRef]
12. Dai, T.; Cai, J.; Zhang, Y.; Xia, S.-T.; Zhang, L. Second-order attention network for single image super-resolution. In Proceedings of the IEEE Conference on Computer Vision and Pattern Recognition, Long Beach, NY, USA, 15–20 June 2019; pp. 11065–11074. [CrossRef]
13. Kim, J.; Lee, J.K.; Lee, K.M. Accurate image super-resolution using very deep convolutional networks. In Proceedings of the IEEE Conference on Computer Vision and Pattern Recognition, Las Vegas, NV, USA, 27–30 June 2016; pp. 1646–1654. [CrossRef]
14. He, K.; Zhang, X.; Ren, S.; Sun, J. Deep residual learning for image recognition. In Proceedings of the IEEE Conference on Computer Vision and Pattern Recognition, Las Vegas, NV, USA, 27–30 June 2016; pp. 770–778. [CrossRef]
15. Liu, H.; Fu, Z.; Han, J.; Shao, L.; Hou, S.; Chu, Y. Single image super resolution using multi-scale deep encoder-decoder with phase congruency edge map guidance. *Inf. Sci.* **2019**, *473*, 44–58. [CrossRef]
16. Ledig, C.; Theis, L.; Huszar, F.; Caballero, J.; Cunningham, A.; Acosta, A.; Aitken, A.; Tejani, A.; Totz, J.; Wang, Z.; et al. Photo-realistic single image super-resolution using a generative adversarial network. In Proceedings of the IEEE Conference on Computer Vision and Pattern Recognition, Honolulu, HI, USA, 21–26 July 2017; pp. 4681–4690. [CrossRef]
17. Goodfellow, I.; Pouget-Abadie, J.; Mirza, M.; Xu, B.; Farley, W.D.; Ozair, S.; Courville, A.; Bengio, Y. Generative adversarial nets. *Adv. Neural Inf. Process. Syst.* **2014**, *27*, 2672–2680.
18. Xu, L.; Ren, J.S.; Liu, C.; Jia, J. Deep convolutional neural network for image deconvolution. In *Advances in Neural Information Processing Systems*; Cornel University: Ithaca, NY, USA, 2014; pp. 1790–1798, Available online: http://citeseerx.ist.psu.edu/viewdoc/download?doi=10.1.1.709.7888&rep=rep1&type=pdf (accessed on 1 November 2021).
19. Isola, P.; Zhu, J.-Y.; Zhou, T.; Efros, A.A. Image-to-image translation with conditional adversarial networks. In Proceedings of the IEEE Conference on Computer Vision and Pattern Recognition, Hawaii, HI, USA, 21–26 July 2017; pp. 1125–1134. [CrossRef]
20. Ramakrishnan, S.; Pachori, S.; Gangopadhyay, A.; Raman, S. Deep generative filter for motion deblurring. In Proceedings of the IEEE International Conference on Computer Vision, Honolulu, HI, USA, 21–26 July 2017; pp. 2993–3000. [CrossRef]
21. Kupyn, O.; Budzan, V.; Mykhailych, M.; Mishkin, D.; Matas, J. DeblurGAN: Blind motion deblurring using conditional adversarial networks. In Proceedings of the IEEE Conference on Computer Vision and Pattern Recognition, Salt Lake City, UT, USA, 18–23 June 2018; pp. 8183–8192. [CrossRef]
22. Arjovsky, M.; Chintala, S.; Bottou, L. Wasserstein Gan. *arXiv* **2017**. Available online: https://arxiv.org/abs/1701.07875 (accessed on 1 November 2021).
23. Kupyn, O.; Martyniuk, T.; Wu, J.; Wang, Z. DeblurGAN-v2: Deblurring (Orders-of-Magnitude) Faster and Better. In Proceedings of the IEEE/CVF International Conference on Computer Vision (ICCV), Seoul, Korea, 27 October–2 November 2019; pp. 8878–8887. [CrossRef]
24. Manzo, M.; Pellino, S. Voting in transfer learning system for ground-based cloud classification. In *Machine Learning and Knowledge Extraction*; Cornel University: Ithaca, NY, USA, 2021; Volume 3, pp. 542–553. [CrossRef]
25. Xu, R.; Xiao, Z.; Huang, J.; Zhang, Y.; Xiong, Z. EDPN: Enhanced deep pyramid network for blurry image restoration. In Proceedings of the IEEE/CVF Conference on Computer Vision and Pattern Recognition (CVPR), Nashville, TN, USA, 19–25 June 2021; pp. 414–423. [CrossRef]
26. Liang, Z.; Zhang, D.; Shao, J. Jointly solving deblurring and super-resolution problems with dual supervised network. In Proceedings of the 2019 IEEE International Conference on Multimedia and Expo (ICME), Shanghai, China, 8–12 July 2019; pp. 790–795. [CrossRef]
27. Zhang, K.; Zuo, W.; Zhang, L. Deep plug-and-play super-resolution for arbitrary blur kernels. In Proceedings of the IEEE/CVF Conference on Computer Vision and Pattern Recognition (CVPR), Long Beach, CA, USA, 15–20 June 2019; pp. 1671–1681. [CrossRef]
28. Zhang, D.; Liang, Z.; Shao, J. Joint image deblurring and super-resolution with attention dual supervised network. *Neurocomputing* **2020**, *412*, 187–196. [CrossRef]
29. Wang, X.; Chan, K.C.; Yu, K.; Dong, C.; Loy, C.C. Edvr: Video restoration with enhanced deformable convolutional networks. In Proceedings of the IEEE Conference on Computer Vision and Pattern Recognition Workshops, Long Beach, CA, USA, 16–17 June 2019; pp. 1954–1963.
30. Fu, J.; Liu, J.; Tian, H.; Li, Y.; Bao, Y.; Fang, Z.; Lu, H. Dual attention network for scene segmentation. In Proceedings of the IEEE Conference on Computer Vision and Pattern Recognition, Long Beach, CA, USA, 18–20 June 2019; pp. 3146–3154. [CrossRef]
31. Niu, W.; Zhang, K.; Luo, W.; Zhong, Y. Blind motion deblurring super-resolution: When dynamic spatio-temporal learning meets static image understanding. *IEEE Trans. Image Process.* **2021**, *30*, 7101–7111. [CrossRef] [PubMed]
32. Hu, J.; Shen, L.; Sun, G. Squeeze-and-excitation networks. In Proceedings of the IEEE Conference on Computer Vision and Pattern Recognition, Salt Lake City, UT, USA, 18–23 June 2018; pp. 7132–7141.

33. Wang, Z.; Bovik, A.C.; Sheikh, H.R.; Simoncelli, E.P. Image quality assessment: From error visibility to structural similarity. *IEEE Trans. Image Process.* **2004**, *13*, 600–612. [CrossRef] [PubMed]
34. Lai, W.-S.; Huang, J.-B.; Hu, Z.; Ahuja, N.; Yang, M.-H. A comparative study for single image blind deblurring. In Proceedings of the IEEE Conference on Computer Vision and Pattern Recognition, Las Vegas, NV, USA, 27–30 June 2016; pp. 1701–1709. [CrossRef]
35. Paszke, A.; Gross, S.; Massa, F.; Lerer, A.; Bradbury, J.; Chanan, G.; Killeen, T.; Lin, Z.; Gimelshein, N.; Antiga, L.; et al. Pytorch: An imperative style, high-performance deep learning library. *Adv. Neural Inf. Process. Syst.* **2019**, *32*, 8024–8035.
36. Zhang, K.; Zuo, W.; Zhang, L. Learning a single convolutional super resolution network for multiple degradations. In Proceedings of the IEEE Conference on Computer Vision and Pattern Recognition, Salt Lake City, UT, USA, 18–23 June 2018; pp. 3262–3271. [CrossRef]

mathematics

MDPI

Article

Face Recognition via Compact Second-Order Image Gradient Orientations

He-Feng Yin [1,2,*], Xiao-Jun Wu [1,2,*], Cong Hu [1,2] and Xiaoning Song [1,2]

1 School of Artificial Intelligence and Computer Science, Jiangnan University, Wuxi 214122, China; conghu@jiangnan.edu.cn (C.H.); x.song@jiangnan.edu.cn (X.S.)
2 Jiangsu Provincial Engineering Laboratory of Pattern Recognition and Computational Intelligence, Jiangnan University, Wuxi 214122, China
* Correspondence: yin_hefeng@jiangnan.edu.cn (H.-F.Y.); wu_xiaojun@jiangnan.edu.cn (X.-J.W.)

Abstract: Conventional subspace learning approaches based on image gradient orientations only employ first-order gradient information, which may ignore second-order or higher-order gradient information. Moreover, recent researches on the human vision system (HVS) have uncovered that the neural image is a landscape or a surface whose geometric properties can be captured through second-order gradient information. The second-order image gradient orientations (SOIGO) can mitigate the adverse effect of noise in face images. To reduce the redundancy of SOIGO, we propose compact SOIGO (CSOIGO) by applying linear complex principal component analysis (PCA) in SOIGO. To be more specific, the SOIGO of training data are firstly obtained. Then, linear complex PCA is applied to obtain features of reduced dimensionality. Combined with collaborative-representation-based classification (CRC) algorithm, the classification performance of CSOIGO is further enhanced. CSOIGO is evaluated under real-world disguise, synthesized occlusion, and mixed variations. Under the real disguise scenario, CSOIGO makes 2.67% and 1.09% improvement regarding accuracy when one and two neutral face images per subject are used as training samples, respectively. For the mixed variations, CSOIGO achieves a 0.86% improvement in terms of accuracy. These results indicate that the proposed method is superior to its competing approaches with few training samples, and even outperforms some prevailing deep-neural-network-based approaches.

Keywords: face recognition; second-order gradient; image gradient orientations; collaborative-representation-based classification

MSC: 68T10

Citation: Yin, H.-F.; Wu, X.-J.; Hu, C.; Song, X. Face Recognition via Compact Second-Order Image Gradient Orientations. *Mathematics* **2022**, *10*, 2587. https://doi.org/10.3390math10152587

Academic Editors: Jianping Gou, Weihua Ou, Shaoning Zeng and Lan Du

Received: 9 June 2022
Accepted: 22 July 2022
Published: 25 July 2022

Publisher's Note: MDPI stays neutral with regard to jurisdictional claims in published maps and institutional affiliations.

1. Introduction

As one of the most active research topics, face recognition (FR) has aroused great attention in the domain of pattern recognition and computer vision. Considerable progress has been made during the past decades and many successful methods have been proposed. Nevertheless, complicated variations in face images (e.g., occlusion, illumination, and expression) bring a great challenge for FR systems. To increase the robustness to occlusion, researchers have developed a variety of approaches. Sparse representation-based classification (SRC) [1] was developed for FR and shows robustness to occlusion and corruption in the test images when combined with the block partition technique. Naseem et al. [2] proposed a modular linear regression classification (Modular LRC) approach with a distance-based evidence fusion (DEF) algorithm to tackle the problem of contiguous occlusion. Dividing an image into different blocks is an effective way for feature extraction. Adjabi et al. [3] developed the multiblock color-binarized statistical image features (MB-C-BSIF) method for single-sample face recognition. Abdulhussain et al. [4] presented a method for fast calculation of features of overlapping image blocks. To further enhance the performance of SRC, Li et al. [5] proposed a sparsity augmented weighted CRC approach for image recognition. Dong et al. [6] designed a low-rank Laplacian-uniform mixed (LR-LUM) model, which characterizes complex errors as a combination of continuous structured noises and random noises. Yang et al. [7] presented nuclear norm-based matrix regression (NMR), which employs two dimensional image-matrix-based error model rather than the one-dimensional pixel-based error model. The representation vector in NMR is imposed by the ℓ_2 norm, to make use of the discriminative property of sparsity, Chen et al. [8] proposed a sparse regularized NMR (SR-NMR) by replacing the ℓ_2 norm constraint on the representation vector with the ℓ_1 norm. However, the above approaches need uncorrupted training images. When providing corrupted training data, their performance will be deteriorated. To tackle the situation that both the training and test data are corrupted, low-rank matrix recovery (LRMR) can be applied. Chen et al. [9] proposed a discriminative low-rank representation (DLRR) method, which introduces the structural incoherence into the framework of low-rank representation (LRR) [10]. Gao et al. [11] proposed to learn robust and discriminative low-rank representation (RDLRR) by introducing low-rank constraint to simultaneously model the representation and each error term. Hu et al. [12] presented a robust FR method, which employs dual nuclear norm low-rank representation and a self-representation induced classifier. Yang et al. [13] developed a sparse low-rank component-based representation (SLCR) method for FR with low-quality images. Recently, Yang et al. [14] extended SLCR and proposed a FR technique named sparse individual low-rank component representation (SILR) for IoT-based systems. Inspired by LRR and deep learning techniques, Xia et al. [15] developed an embedded conformal deep low-rank autoencoder (ECLAE) neural network architecture for matrix recovery.

Recently, image gradient orientation (IGO) has attracted much attention due to its impressive results in occluded FR. Wu et al. [16] presented a gradient direction-based hierarchical adaptive sparse and low-rank (GD-HASLR) model, which performs in the image gradient direction domain rather than the image intensity domain. Li et al. [17] incorporated IGO into robust error coding and proposed an IGO-embedded structural error coding (IGO-SEC) model for FR with occlusion. Apart from the above two works, Zhang et al. [18] designed Gradientfaces for FR under varying illumination conditions. In essence, Gradientfaces is the IGO. Tzimiropoulos et al. [19] introduced the notion of subspace learning from IGO and developed approaches such as IGO-PCA and IGO-LDA. Vu [20] proposed a face representation approach called patterns of orientation difference (POD), which explores the relations of both gradient orientations and magnitudes. Zheng et al. [21] presented an online image alignment method via subspace learning from IGO. Qian et al. [22] presented a method called ID-NMR, in which the local gradient distribution is exploited to decompose the image into several gradient images. Wu et al. [23] proposed a new feature descriptor called the histogram of maximum gradient and edge orientation (HGEO) for the purpose of multispectral image matching.

The above IGO-based approaches only take the first-order gradient information into account, thus neglecting the second-order or higher-order gradient information. Latest researches on human vision have discovered that the neural image is a landscape or a surface whose geometric properties can be described by local curvatures of differential geometry through second-order gradient information [24,25]. Based on the second-order gradient, Huang et al. [24] presented a new local image descriptor called histograms of second-order gradient (HSOG). Li et al. [26] proposed a patterned fabric defect detection method based on the second-order, orientation-aware descriptor. Zhang et al. [27] designed a blind image quality assessment (IQA) method based on multiorder gradient statistics. Bastian et al. [28] developed a pedestrian detector utilizing both the first-order and the second-order gradient information in the image. Nevertheless, the above second-order-gradient-based approaches do not involve a dimensionality reduction technique, which results in redundant information. To alleviate this problem, we introduce PCA into the framework of SOIGO to extract more compact features. Moreover, we employ CRC as the final classifier due to its effectiveness and efficiency. Experimental results show that our proposed method (CSOIGO) is robust to real disguise, synthesized occlusion, and mixed variations and is superior to some popular deep-neural-network-based approaches.

Our main contributions are outlined as follows:

1. We find that SOIGO is more robust to variations in face images compared with the first-order IGO. After extracting the SOIGO features of training samples, linear complex PCA is applied to reduce the redundancy of SOIGO.
2. The classic CRC algorithm is utilized to predict the identity of test samples, and it can further enhance the classification performance of CSOIGO.
3. Experiments on different scenarios demonstrate the efficacy and robustness of CSOIGO compared with other approaches.

The remainder of this paper is arranged as follows. Section 2 reviews some related work. In Section 3, we present our proposed approach. Section 4 conducts several experiments to demonstrate the efficacy of our proposed method. Finally, conclusions are drawn in Section 5.

2. Related Work

2.1. IGO-PCA

Given a set of images $\{\mathbf{Z}_i\}$ $(i = 1, 2, \ldots, N)$, where N denotes the number of training images and $\mathbf{Z}_i \in \mathbb{R}^{m \times n}$. Suppose that $\mathbf{I}(x, y)$ is the image intensities at pixel coordinates (x, y) of sample $\mathbf{Z}_i$, the horizontal and vertical gradient can be obtained by the following formulations:

$$\begin{aligned} \mathbf{G}_{i,x} &= h_x * \mathbf{I}(x, y) \\ \mathbf{G}_{i,y} &= h_y * \mathbf{I}(x, y), \end{aligned} \tag{1}$$

where $*$ expresses convolution, and h_x and h_y are filters employed to approximate the ideal differentiation operator along the image horizontal and vertical directions, respectively [29]. Image gradient contains edge information and is used to characterize the structure of an image. In [30], gradient feature map is extracted from the input image and exploited as a structural prior to guide the process of image reconstruction. However, the image data mostly distribute discretely in real-world scenarios; so, we usually use differences to compute the gradients, i.e., achieving the gradients through the difference between adjacent pixels' gray values. Thus, horizontal and vertical gradients can be reformulated as

$$\begin{aligned} \mathbf{G}_{i,x} &= \mathbf{I}(x+1, y) - \mathbf{I}(x, y) \\ \mathbf{G}_{i,y} &= \mathbf{I}(x, y+1) - \mathbf{I}(x, y). \end{aligned} \tag{2}$$

Then, the gradient orientation of the pixel location (x, y) is

$$\Phi_i(x, y) = \arctan \frac{\mathbf{G}_{i,y}}{\mathbf{G}_{i,x}}, i = 1, 2, \ldots, N. \tag{3}$$

For each image $\mathbf{Z}_i$ whose size is $m \times n$, we can obtain a corresponding gradient orientation matrix $\Phi_i \in [0, 2\pi)^{m \times n}$. Then, we can obtain the corresponding sample vectors by converting 2D images Φ_i into 1D vectors ϕ_i. Referring to [19], we also define the mapping from $[0, 2\pi)^K (K = m \times n)$ onto a subset of complex sphere with radius $\sqrt{K}$,

$$\boldsymbol{t}_i(\phi_i) = e^{j\phi_i}, \tag{4}$$

where $e^{j\phi_i} = [e^{j\phi_1}, e^{j\phi_2}, \ldots, e^{j\phi_K}]^T$ and $e^{j\theta}$ is Euler form, i.e., $e^{j\theta} = \cos\theta + j\sin\theta$. Then, we can apply complex linear PCA to the transformed $\boldsymbol{t}_i$—that is, we seek for a set of $d < K$ orthonormal bases $\mathbf{U} = [\mathbf{u}_1, \mathbf{u}_2, \ldots, \mathbf{u}_d] \in \mathbb{C}^{K \times d}$ by solving the following problem:

$$\epsilon(\mathbf{U}) = \left\| \mathbf{X} - \mathbf{U}\mathbf{U}^H \mathbf{X} \right\|_F^2, \tag{5}$$

where $\mathbf{X} = [\boldsymbol{t}_1, \boldsymbol{t}_2, ..., \boldsymbol{t}_N] \in \mathbb{C}^{K \times N}$, $\mathbf{U}^H$ is the conjugate transpose of $\mathbf{U}$, and $||.||_F$ denotes the Frobenius norm. Equation (5) can be reformulated as

$$\mathbf{U}_o = \arg\max_{\mathbf{U}} tr(\mathbf{U}^H \mathbf{X}\mathbf{X}^H \mathbf{U}), \text{ s.t. } \mathbf{U}^H \mathbf{U} = \mathbf{I}. \tag{6}$$

The solution is given by the d eigenvectors of $\mathbf{X}\mathbf{X}^H$ corresponding to the d largest eigenvalues. Then, the d-dimensional embedding $\mathbf{Y} \in \mathbb{C}^{d \times N}$ of $\mathbf{X}$ is produced by $\mathbf{Y} = \mathbf{U}^H \mathbf{X}$.

2.2. Collaborative-Representation-Based Classification

During the past few years, the representation-based classification method (RBCM) has attracted lots of attention in the community of pattern recognition. The pioneering work is SRC [1]. In SRC, the ℓ_1 norm constraint is employed to attain the sparse coefficient of test data. Zhang et al. [31] argued that it is the collaborative representation mechanism rather than the ℓ_1 norm constraint that makes SRC successful for FR. Therefore, they developed the CRC method, which replaces the ℓ_1 norm constraint with the ℓ_2 norm. Afterwards, many improved methods were proposed to further boost the classification performance of CRC. Gou et al. [32] developed a class-specific mean vector-based weighted competitive and collaborative representation (CMWCCR) method, which fully employs the discrimination information in different ways. Motivated by the idea of linear representation, Gou et al. [33] proposed a representation coefficient-based k-nearest centroid neighbor (RCKNCN) method. Recently, Gou et al. [34] presented a hierarchical graph augmented deep collaborative dictionary learning (HGDCDL) model, which applies collaborative representation to the deepest-level representation learning. For simplicity, in this paper, we employ the original CRC as the classifier, and the objective function of CRC is formulated as follows:

$$\min_{\boldsymbol{\alpha}} \left\{ ||\boldsymbol{y} - \mathbf{D}\boldsymbol{\alpha}||_2^2 + \lambda ||\boldsymbol{\alpha}||_2^2 \right\}, \tag{7}$$

where $\boldsymbol{y}$ is the test sample, $\mathbf{D}$ is the dictionary that contains all the training data from C classes, and λ is a balancing parameter. Equation (7) has the following closed-form solution,

$$\boldsymbol{\alpha} = (\mathbf{D}^T \mathbf{D} + \lambda \mathbf{I})^{-1} \mathbf{D}^T \boldsymbol{y}. \tag{8}$$

In the classification stage, apart from the class-specific reconstruction error $||\boldsymbol{y} - \mathbf{D}_j \boldsymbol{\alpha}_j||_2$, $j = 1, 2, \ldots, C$, where $\boldsymbol{\alpha}_j$ is the coefficient vector corresponding to the jth class, Zhang et al. [31] found that $||\boldsymbol{\alpha}_j||_2$ also contains some discriminative information for classification. Thus, they presented the following regularized residuals for classification,

$$\text{identity}(\boldsymbol{y}) = \arg\min_j \frac{||\boldsymbol{y} - \mathbf{D}_j \boldsymbol{\alpha}_j||_2}{||\boldsymbol{\alpha}_j||_2}. \tag{9}$$

3. Proposed Method

Previous studies revealed that gradient information at different orders characterize different structural features of natural scenes. The first-order gradient information is related to the slope and elasticity of a surface, while the second-order gradient delivers the curvature-related geometric properties. Figure 1 depicts two images and their corresponding landscapes plotted as surfaces; one can see that these landscapes contain a variety of local shapes, such as cliffs, ridges, summits, valleys, and basins. Inspired by the above results, we propose a new FR method that exploits the SOIGO. The second-order gradient is obtained based on the first-order gradient information defined in Equation (2),

$$\begin{aligned} \mathbf{G}_{i,x}^2 &= \mathbf{G}_{i,x}(x+1, y) - \mathbf{G}_{i,x}(x, y) \\ \mathbf{G}_{i,y}^2 &= \mathbf{G}_{i,y}(x, y+1) - \mathbf{G}_{i,y}(x, y), \end{aligned} \tag{10}$$

where $\mathbf{G}^2_{i,x}$ and $\mathbf{G}^2_{i,y}$ are the second-order gradient along the horizontal and vertical directions, respectively. Therefore, the SOIGO is computed as follows:

$$\Phi^2_i(x,y) = \arctan\frac{\mathbf{G}^2_{i,y}}{\mathbf{G}^2_{i,x}}. \tag{11}$$

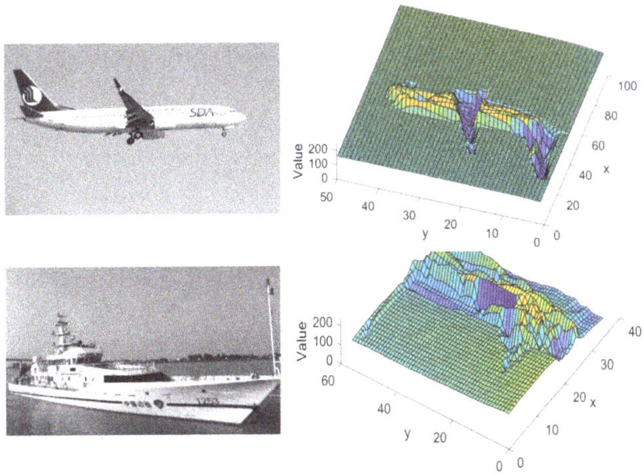

Figure 1. Original images (**left part**) and their surface plots (**right part**).

Figure 2 presents an original face image and its gradient orientations of the first and second orders; one can see that, compared with the first-order IGO, the SOIGO significantly depresses the noise in the orientation domain. Moreover, the SOIGO contains more fine information than the first-order IGO, e.g., areas around the eyes, nose, and mouth.

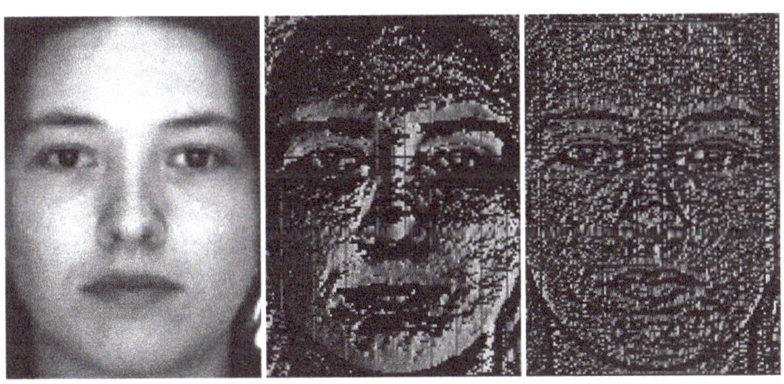

Figure 2. Original face image and its gradient orientations of the first and second orders, respectively.

To further illustrate the effectiveness of using the SOIGO, we visualize the original data, the first-order IGO, and the SOIGO on the AR database by employing the t-SNE algorithm [35] in Figure 3. These data are selected from the first ten subjects on the AR database; for each person, seven nonoccluded face images in Session 1 are used. Then, these images are occluded by a square baboon image with a percentage of 30%. For detailed experimental settings, please refer to Section 4.3. As can be seen from Figure 3, though the first-order IGO looks better compared with the original data, clusters of different classes are mixed together. In Figure 3c, the cluster of the same class is more compact than that of Figure 3b, which is beneficial for subsequent classification.

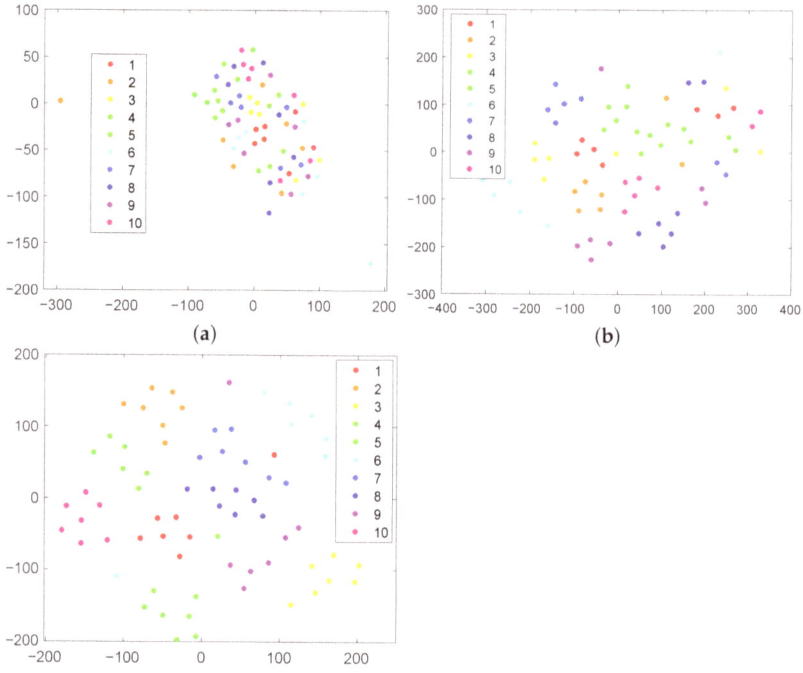

Figure 3. t-SNE visualization of (**a**) original data, (**b**) the first-order IGO with the mapping defined in Equation (4), and (**c**) the SOIGO with the mapping defined in Equation (4); each color represents a class. For better visualization, please refer to the electronic version of this paper.

The procedures of obtaining the projection matrix $\mathbf{U}$ is the same as in IGO-PCA. Then, for a test image $\mathbf{Z}_t$, we first compute its SOIGO and obtain $\boldsymbol{t}$ after the mapping defined by Equation (4). Embeddings of training and test images are derived as follows:

$$\mathbf{Y} = \mathbf{U}^H\mathbf{X},\ z = \mathbf{U}^H\boldsymbol{t}, \tag{12}$$

where $\mathbf{Y} \in \mathbb{C}^{d\times N}$ and $z \in \mathbb{C}^{d\times 1}$. To make the embeddings of training and test images suitable for CRC, we employ both the real and imaginary parts of $\mathbf{Y}$ and z as the input of CRC; let

$$\mathbf{D} = \begin{bmatrix} \text{real}(\mathbf{Y}) \\ \text{imag}(\mathbf{Y}) \end{bmatrix},\ y = \begin{bmatrix} \text{real}(z) \\ \text{imag}(z), \end{bmatrix} \tag{13}$$

where real$(\cdot)$ and imag$(\cdot)$ are the real part and imaginary part of complex number, respectively. Then, we compute the representation coefficient vector of y over $\mathbf{D}$; this is followed by checking which class results in the least regularized residual. The pipeline of our proposed CSOIGO is illustrated in Figure 4, and the complete process of CSOIGO is outlined in Algorithm 1.

When assessing the performance of an algorithm, we should take its computational complexity into account. The major consumption of CSOIGO lies in the linear complex PCA and CRC, and they both involve the operation of matrix. It takes $\mathcal{O}(K^2N)$ to compute the covariance matrix and $\mathcal{O}(K^3)$ for eigen-decomposition in the process of PCA, where $K = m \times n$ and N denote the dimensionality and total number of training images. From Equation (8), one can see that CRC contains matrix multiplication and matrix inversion, and it takes $\mathcal{O}(N^2d)$ to compute $\mathbf{D}^T\mathbf{D}$ and $\mathcal{O}(N^3)$ for the inverse operation of matrix, where d is the reduced dimensionality. Suppose there are p test samples, CRC takes

$\mathcal{O}(N^2d + N^3 + Ndp)$ to completely classify them. Therefore, the total computational complexity of CSOIGO is $\mathcal{O}(K^2N + K^3 + N^2d + N^3 + Ndp)$.

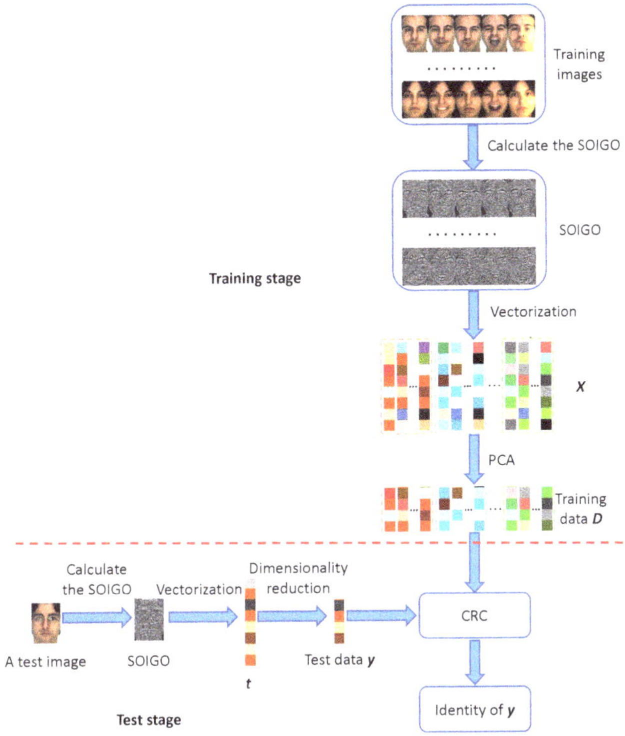

Figure 4. The pipeline of our proposed CSOIGO.

Algorithm 1 CSOIGO

Input: A set of N training images $\{\mathbf{Z}_i\}(i = 1, 2, \ldots, N)$ from C classes, test image $\mathbf{Z}_t$, the number of principal components d, and the regularization parameter λ for CRC.

1. Obtain the SOIGO Φ_i^2 of training images and convert it to 1D vector ϕ_i^2.
2. Compute $\mathbf{t}_i(\phi_i^2) = e^{j\phi_i^2}$; all the SOIGO of training images form the matrix $\mathbf{X} = [\mathbf{t}_1, \mathbf{t}_2, \ldots, \mathbf{t}_N]$.
3. Obtain the projection matrix $\mathbf{U}$ via Equation (6).
4. For the test image $\mathbf{Z}_t$, obtain its SOIGO Φ_t^2 and convert it to 1D vector ϕ_t^2; then, compute $\boldsymbol{t} = e^{j\phi_t^2}$.
5. Obtain the embeddings of training and test images via Equation (12).
6. Obtain $\mathbf{D}$ and $\boldsymbol{y}$ by Equation (13).
7. Code $\boldsymbol{y}$ over $\mathbf{D}$ by Equation (8).
8. Compute the regularized residuals $r_j = \frac{\|\boldsymbol{y} - \mathbf{D}_j\boldsymbol{\alpha}_j\|_2}{\|\boldsymbol{\alpha}_j\|_2}, j = 1, 2, \ldots, C$.

Output: identity$(\mathbf{Z}_t) = \arg\min_j r_j$.

4. Experimental Results and Analysis

In this section, experiments are conducted under different scenarios to validate the effectiveness of the proposed method. For reproduction, the source code of CSOIGO is available at https://github.com/yinhefeng/SOIGO.

4.1. Recognition with Real Disguise

The AR database contains over 4000 images of 126 subjects. For each individual, 26 images are taken in two separate sessions. There are 13 images for each session, in which three images with sunglasses, another three with scarves, and the remaining seven have different illumination and expression changes; the 13 images of one subject from Session 1 are shown in Figure 5. Each image is 165 × 120 pixels. For fair comparison, we use the same subset as in [16], which consists of 50 men and 50 women, and all images are resized to 42 × 30 pixels. The neutral face image of each subject is used as training data, and the sunglasses/scarf occluded images in each session for testing. The proposed method is compared with other state-of-the-art approaches, including HQPAMI [36], NR [37], ProCRC [38], F-LR-IRNNLS [39], EGSNR [40], LDMR [41], and GD-HASLR [16]. To better illustrate the superiority of CSOIGO, we also present the results of IGO-PCA-NNC [19], IGO-PCA-CRC, and SOIGO-PCA-NNC. Table 1 summarizes the experimental results; one can see that CSOIGO achieves the highest recognition accuracy under all cases except for the sunglasses scenario of session 1. Since the test images are partially occluded by sunglasses or scarf, HQPAMI, NR, ProCRC, and LDMR seem not very robust to contiguous occlusion. Due to the preprocessing step that separates outlier pixels and corruptions from the training samples, the overall classification accuracy of F-LR-IRNNLS is higher than that of EGSNR. IGO-PCA-CRC ranks second over all methods and achieves 5.66% higher accuracy than IGO-PCA-NNC, which validates the efficacy of CRC when coping with IGO features. GD-HASLR has competitive performance with SOIGO-PCA-NNC. However, the overall accuracy gain of CSOIGO over GD-HASLR and IGO-PCA-CRC is 4.5% and 2.67%, respectively. The above experimental results indicate that our proposed CSOIGO is robust to real disguise even when a single training sample per person is available.

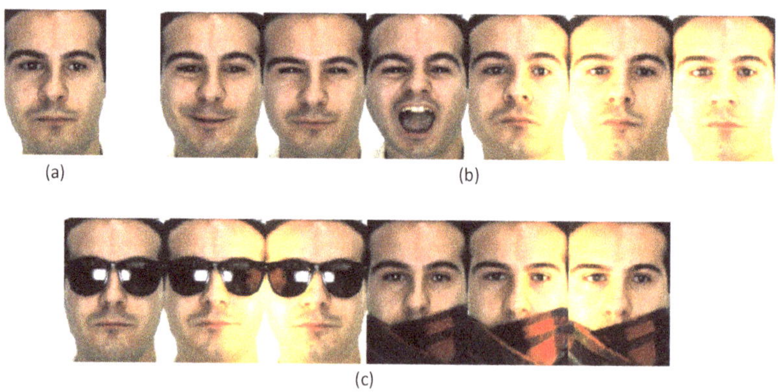

Figure 5. Some example face images from the AR database: (**a**) the neutral image of a subject from Session 1; (**b**) face images with illumination and expression variations; (**c**) images occluded by sunglasses/scarf.

Next, we utilize two neutral face images per subject from Sessions 1 and 2 for training, and the test sets are identical with the first experiment. The results are reported in Table 2. As can be seen from Table 2, CSOIGO yields the best overall recognition accuracy and outperforms GD-HASLR by 2.92%. Again, IGO-PCA-CRC ranks second in all methods. SOIGO-PCA-NNC outperforms IGO-PCA-NNC, and CSOIGO achieves higher accuracy than IGO-PCA-CRC, which indicates that SOIGO is more robust to occlusion than IGO.

Table 1. Recognition accuracy (%) of competing approaches on a subset of the AR database (test samples contain sunglasses occlusion or scarf occlusion) when only one neutral face image per subject from Session 1 is used as training sample. The dimension that leads to the best result for IGO- and SOIGO-based approaches is given in parentheses.

Methods	Sunglasses		Scarf		Overall
	Session 1	Session 2	Session 1	Session 2	
HQPAMI [36]	56.67	38.00	38.00	22.33	38.75
NR [37]	28.33	16.67	29.67	17.33	23.00
ProCRC [38]	53.07	31.00	18.67	7.33	27.52
F-LR-IRNNLS [39]	88.67	60.33	67.00	49.67	66.42
EGSNR [40]	84.00	54.00	70.33	48.33	64.16
LDMR [41]	68.33	45.67	59.67	34.00	51.92
GD-HASLR [16]	92.00	66.67	82.67	58.67	75.00
IGO-PCA-NNC [19]	89.00 (99)	69.00 (99)	73.33 (97)	53.33 (96)	71.17
IGO-PCA-CRC	**93.00 (85)**	74.33 (92)	81.67 (88)	58.33 (95)	76.83
SOIGO-PCA-NNC	88.67 (92)	73.33 (96)	80.33 (99)	61.00 (88)	75.83
CSOIGO	92.67 (89)	**76.67 (93)**	**83.33 (75)**	**65.33 (99)**	**79.50**

Bold values indicate the best recognition accuracy.

Table 2. Recognition accuracy (%) of competing approaches on a subset of the AR database (test samples contain sunglasses occlusion or scarf occlusion) when two neutral face images (from Sessions 1 and 2) per subject are used as training samples, the dimension that leads to the best result for IGO- and SOIGO-based approaches is given in parentheses.

Methods	Sunglasses		Scarf		Overall
	Session 1	Session 2	Session 1	Session 2	
HQPAMI [36]	61.33	59.33	44.67	48.00	53.33
NR [37]	34.00	33.33	33.00	35.67	34.00
ProCRC [38]	53.00	54.67	18.00	17.67	35.84
F-LR-IRNNLS [39]	90.33	87.67	78.67	76.00	83.17
EGSNR [40]	88.00	89.33	80.00	73.00	82.58
LDMR [41]	71.00	63.67	64.00	61.00	64.92
GD-HASLR [16]	93.00	93.33	82.67	84.00	88.25
IGO-PCA-NNC [19]	93.00 (182)	91.67 (191)	78.00 (199)	74.00 (193)	84.17
IGO-PCA-CRC	96.00 (128)	95.33 (116)	85.00 (190)	84.00 (160)	90.08
SOIGO-PCA-NNC	96.33 (187)	92.67 (197)	**86.33 (166)**	83.67 (189)	89.75
CSOIGO	**97.33 (144)**	**95.67 (124)**	86.00 (119)	**85.67 (198)**	**91.17**

Bold values indicate the best recognition accuracy.

4.2. Comparison with CNN-Based Approaches

In this subsection, we compare our proposed method with prevailing deep-learning-based approaches. The first one is VGGFace [42], which is based on the VGGNet [43] and has 16 convolutional layers, five max-pooling layers, three fully-connected layers, and a final linear layer with softmax layer. In our experiments, we employ FC6 and FC7 for feature extraction. The second one is Lightened CNN [44], which has a low computational complexity. Lightened CNN consists of two different models, i.e., Model A and Model B. Model A is based on the AlexNet [45], which contains four convolution layers using the max feature map (MFM) activation functions, four max-pooling layers, two fully-connected layers, and a linear layer with softmax activation in the output. Model B is based on the Network in Network model [46] and consists of five convolution layers using the MFM activation functions, four convolutional layers for dimensionality reduction, five max-pooling layers, two fully-connected layers, and a linear layer with softmax activation in the output. For Lightened CNN, FC1 is used for feature extraction. All the features extracted by VGGFace and Lightened CNN are classified using the nearest neighbor classifier with cosine distance. When training VGGFace, the size of input image is 224×224, and the preprocessing operation involves subtracting the mean RGB value, computed on the training set, from each pixel. The batch size, number of epochs, and optimizer are 256, 74, and *sgdm*, respectively. The learning rate is initially set to 1×10^{-2} and then decreased by a factor of 10. For training Lightened CNN, the size of input image is 144×144, and the input image is cropped into 128×128 and mirrored. The batch size, number of epochs, and optimizer are 20, 150, and *rmsprop*, respectively. The learning rate is set to 1×10^{-3} initially and reduced to 5×10^{-5} gradually.

As in Section 4.1, the first experiment is one neutral face of each subject for training on the AR database, and the experimental results are summarized in Table 3. Table 4 lists the results when two neutral faces are used for training. From Tables 3 and 4, we can see that VGGFace performs better in the scarf scenario than in the sunglasses scenario. This indicates that VGGFace has difficulty tackling the upper face occlusion, and this phenomenon is also observed in [47]. Moreover, when using more training samples, the performance of VGGFace does not improve. Hence, to increase robustness to upper face occlusion, VGGFace may need much more training data. By comparison, our proposed CSOIGO can achieve better results even with few training samples. In practical applications, training data may be insufficient. In this situation, CSOIGO is more appropriate to realize robust face recognition than VGGFace.

Table 3. Comparison with CNN-based approaches on a subset of the AR database (test samples contain sunglasses occlusion or scarf occlusion) when only one neutral face image per subject from Session 1 is used as training samples. The dimension that leads to the best result for IGO- and SOIGO-based approaches is given in parentheses.

Methods	Sunglasses		Scarf		Overall
	Session 1	Session 2	Session 1	Session 2	
VGGFace FC6 [42]	54.00	45.00	**91.67**	**88.00**	69.67
VGGFace FC7 [42]	45.67	40.00	88.67	84.00	64.59
Lightened CNN (A) [44]	67.33	56.00	87.00	82.33	73.17
Lightened CNN (B) [44]	36.33	31.33	80.67	73.67	55.50
GD-HASLR [16]	92.00	66.67	82.67	58.67	75.00
IGO-PCA-NNC [19]	89.00 (99)	69.00 (99)	73.33 (97)	53.33 (96)	71.17
IGO-PCA-CRC	**93.00 (85)**	74.33 (92)	81.67 (88)	58.33 (95)	76.83
SOIGO-PCA-NNC	88.67 (92)	73.33 (96)	80.33 (99)	61.00 (88)	75.83
CSOIGO	92.67 (89)	**76.67 (93)**	83.33 (75)	65.33 (99)	**79.50**

Bold values indicate the best recognition accuracy.

Table 4. Comparison with CNN-based approaches on a subset of the AR database (test samples contain sunglasses occlusion or scarf occlusion) when two neutral face images (from Sessions 1 and 2) per subject are used as training samples. The dimension that leads to the best result for IGO- and SOIGO-based approaches is given in parentheses.

Methods	Sunglasses		Scarf		Overall
	Session 1	Session 2	Session 1	Session 2	
VGGFace FC6 [42]	44.67	51.00	**91.67**	**93.33**	70.17
VGGFace FC7 [42]	41.67	44.67	88.67	89.33	66.08
Lightened CNN (A) [44]	64.67	58.33	86.67	85.33	73.75
Lightened CNN (B) [44]	38.67	38.00	81.67	79.33	59.42
GD-HASLR [16]	93.00	93.33	82.67	84.00	88.25
IGO-PCA-NNC [19]	93.00 (182)	91.67 (191)	78.00 (199)	74.00 (193)	84.17
IGO-PCA-CRC	96.00 (128)	95.33 (116)	85.00 (190)	84.00 (160)	90.08
SOIGO-PCA-NNC	96.33 (187)	92.67 (197)	86.33 (166)	83.67 (189)	89.75
CSOIGO	**97.33 (144)**	**95.67 (124)**	86.00 (119)	85.67 (198)	**91.17**

Bold values indicate the best recognition accuracy.

Similar to the results of VGGFace, Lightened CNN performs worse in the sunglasses scenario than in the scarf scenario. Additionally, Model A outperforms Model B, and Model

A also achieves higher accuracy than VGGFace. However, whether one or two neutral face images per subject are used for training, our proposed CSOIGO achieves the best overall recognition accuracy.

4.3. Random Block Occlusion

Here, we conduct other experiments using synthesized occluded face data as testing data. For each subject, seven nonoccluded face images in the AR dataset in Session 1 are used for training and the other seven nonoccluded images in Session 2 for testing, the image size is 42 × 30 pixels. Block occlusion is tested by placing the square baboon image on each test image. The location of the occlusion is randomly chosen and is unknown during training. We consider different sizes of the object such that the face is covered with the occluded object from 30% to 50% of its area; some occluded face images are shown in Figure 6. The above experimental results indicate that GD-HASLR is superior to other competing approaches; therefore, in this subsection and the following subsection, we report the result of GD-HASLR for comparison. Recognition results for different levels of occlusion are shown in Table 5. One can see that CSOIGO outperforms GD-HASLR by a large margin, and the performance gain is significant with the increasing percentage of occlusion. Moreover, SOIGO-PCA-NNC outperforms IGO-PCA-NNC and CSOIGO performs better than IGO-PCA-CRC, which demonstrates that SOIGO is more robust than IGO when dealing with artificial occlusion.

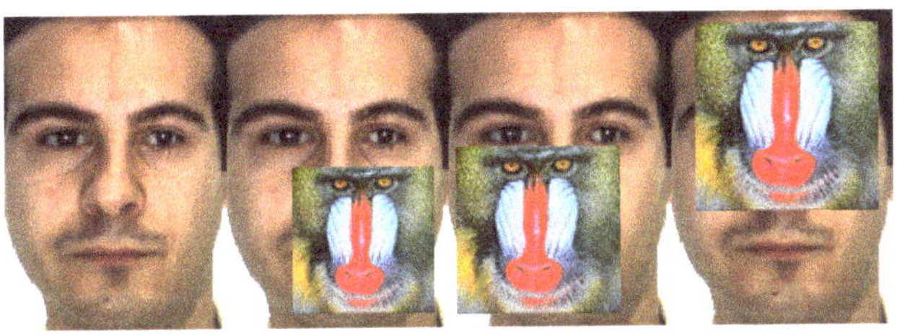

Figure 6. Original face image and its occluded images with different occlusion percentages; from the second to the last, the percentage is 30%, 40%, and 50%, respectively.

Table 5. Recognition accuracy (%) of competing methods under different percentages of occlusion on a subset of the AR database (original training and test samples have no sunglasses occlusion or scarf occlusion). The dimension that leads to the best result for IGO- and SOIGO-based approaches is given in parentheses.

Occlusion Percentage	30%	40%	50%
GD-HASLR [16]	81.29	71.14	56.14
IGO-PCA-NNC [19]	86.14 (588)	80.57 (606)	66.29 (321)
IGO-PCA-CRC	89.14 (205)	80.14 (185)	71.29 (569)
SOIGO-PCA-NNC	88.86 (458)	84.57 (575)	73.29 (693)
CSOIGO	**93.57 (423)**	**87.00 (533)**	**76.57 (698)**

Bold values indicate the best recognition accuracy.

To vividly show the performance of IGO- and SOIGO-based approaches under different numbers of features, in Figure 7 we plot the recognition accuracy against the number of features when the percentage of occlusion is 30%. We can clearly see that with the increasing number of features, CSOIGO consistently outperforms the other three competing approaches.

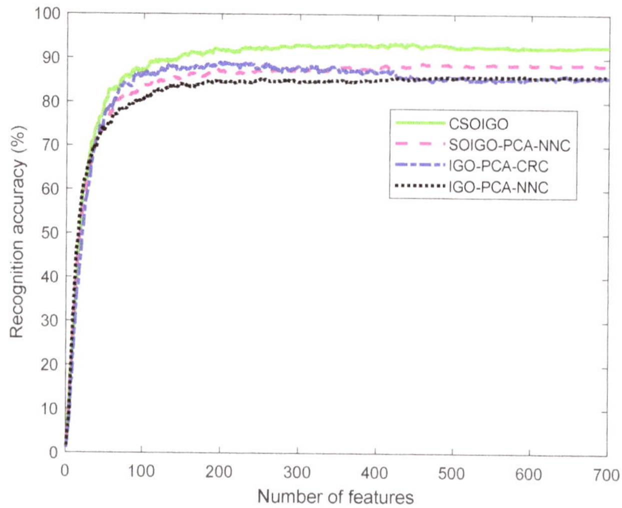

Figure 7. Recognition accuracy versus different numbers of features when the percentage of occlusion is 30%.

4.4. Recognition with Mixed Variations

In this subsection, we evaluate our proposed CSOIGO and other compared approaches under the mixed variations. As shown in Figure 5a,b, the first seven images per subject in Session 1 have variations of expression and illumination; thus, seven nonoccluded images from Session 1 of the AR database are selected for training and another seven undisguised images from Session 2 are used for testing. Recognition accuracy and testing time of compared methods are shown in Table 6. It should be noted that the testing time refers to the time that classifies all the test samples. All experiments are performed on a laptop with Windows 10, an Intel Core i9-8950HK CPU at 2.90 GHz, and 32.00 GB RAM. The implementation software is MATLAB R2022a. From Table 6, we can see that CSOIGO has the best classification performance. Specifically, it makes 1.86% and 0.86% improvement in terms of accuracy over GD-HASLR and IGO-PCA-CRC, respectively. Due to the complex optimization process, GD-HASLR consumes much more time than the other approaches. The testing time is almost the same for both IGO-PCA-NNC and SOIGO-PCA-NNC. NNC is a simple and efficient classifier, while CRC involves the computations of coefficient vector and classwise residual. As a result, CSOIGO takes a little longer than SOIGO-PCA-NNC. However, CSOIGO is much faster than GD-HASLR.

Table 6. Recognition accuracy (%) and testing time (s) of compared approaches with mixed variations on a subset of the AR database (training and test samples have expression and illumination changes). The dimension that leads to the best result for IGO- and SOIGO-based approaches is given in parentheses.

Methods	Accuracy (%)	Testing Time (s)
GD-HASLR [16]	96.71	414.29
IGO-PCA-NNC [19]	93.14 (478)	0.50
IGO-PCA-CRC	97.71 (100)	1.92
SOIGO-PCA-NNC	94.71 (371)	0.45
CSOIGO	**98.57 (171)**	2.43

Bold values indicate the best recognition accuracy.

As in the previous subsection, we show the recognition accuracy against the number of features in Figure 8. It can be seen that as the number of features increases, the recognition accuracies of IGO-PCA-NNC, SOIGO-PCA-NNC, and CSOIGO also increase. The recognition accuracy of IGO-PCA-CRC firstly increases, then decreases to some extent, and then it increases again. When the number of features exceeds 108, CSOIGO always achieves higher accuracy than its competing methods. This again demonstrates that CSOIGO is robust to mixed variations in face images.

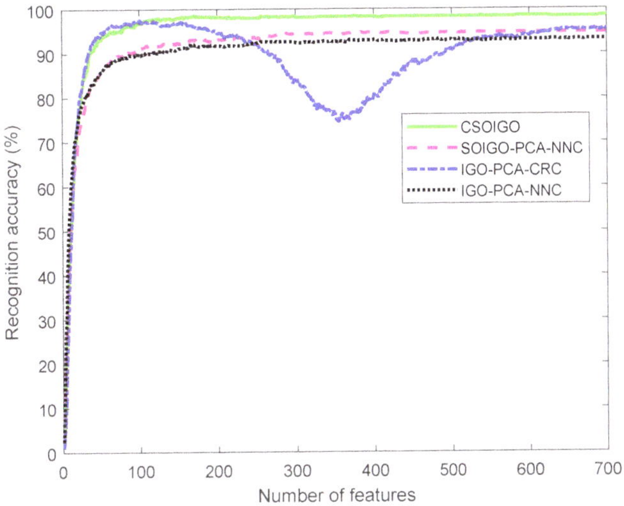

Figure 8. Recognition accuracy versus different number of features under mixed variations.

5. Conclusions

In this paper, we present a new method for occluded face recognition, namely, CSOIGO, by exploiting the second-order gradient information. SOIGO is robust to real disguise, synthesized occlusion, and mixed variations. By employing CRC as the final classifier, our proposed method achieves impressive results in various scenarios and even outperforms some deep-neural-network-based approaches. Taking the real disguise experiment as an example, when one and two neutral face images per subject are used as training samples, CSOIGO attains an overall accuracy of 79.50% and 91.17%, respectively. Therefore, our proposed CSOIGO is superior to its competing approaches.

The limitation of CSOIGO is that it needs registered images for training and testing, i.e., when classifying face images with pose changes, its recognition performance will be degraded. Consequently, CSOIGO can be applied to applications of access control, automatic teller machines, or other security facilities. In these circumstances, we can obtain controlled training images in advance and the test images will be collected under similar scenarios. However, if registered face images cannot be collected during either the training or test stage, one can employ image registration methods to remedy the above limitation to some extent.

In future work, we will introduce SOIGO into other popular subspace learning approaches, e.g., linear discriminant analysis (LDA), to extract more discriminative features. Moreover, other variants of CRC will also be investigated to further enhance the performance of recognition.

Author Contributions: Conceptualization, H.-F.Y.; methodology, H.-F.Y. and X.-J.W.; software, H.-F.Y.; validation, H.-F.Y., X.-J.W., C.H. and X.S.; formal analysis, H.-F.Y. and X.-J.W.; investigation, H.-F.Y. and X.-J.W.; resources, H.-F.Y.; data curation, H.-F.Y., X.-J.W. and X.S.; writing—original draft preparation, H.-F.Y.; writing—review and editing, X.-J.W., C.H. and X.S.; visualization, H.-F.Y.; supervision, X.-J.W.; project administration, X.-J.W. and X.S.; funding acquisition, X.-J.W., C.H. and X.S. All authors have read and agreed to the published version of the manuscript.

Funding: This research was funded in part by the National Natural Science Foundation of China (Grant 62020106012, Grant U1836218, Grant 61902153, Grant 61876072, Grant 62006097, Grant 61672265), in part by the Fundamental Research Funds for the Central Universities (Grant JUSRP121104), in part by the Major Project of National Social Science Foundation of China (Grant 21&ZD166), in part by the Natural Science Foundation of Jiangsu Province (Grant BK20200593), and in part by the 111 Project of Ministry of Education of China (Grant B12018).

Institutional Review Board Statement: Not applicable.

Informed Consent Statement: Not applicable.

Data Availability Statement: The data presented in this study are available on request from the corresponding author.

Conflicts of Interest: The authors declare no conflict of interest.

References

1. Wright, J.; Yang, A.Y.; Ganesh, A.; Sastry, S.S.; Ma, Y. Robust face recognition via sparse representation. *IEEE Trans. Pattern Anal. Mach. Intell.* **2009**, *31*, 210–227. [CrossRef] [PubMed]
2. Naseem, I.; Togneri, R.; Bennamoun, M. Linear regression for face recognition. *IEEE Trans. Pattern Anal. Mach. Intell.* **2010**, *32*, 2106–2112. [CrossRef] [PubMed]
3. Adjabi, I.; Ouahabi, A.; Benzaoui, A.; Jacques, S. Multi-block color-binarized statistical images for single-sample face recognition. *Sensors* **2021**, *21*, 728. [CrossRef] [PubMed]
4. Abdulhussain, S.H.; Mahmmod, B.M.; Flusser, J.; AL-Utaibi, K.A.; Sait, S.M. Fast Overlapping Block Processing Algorithm for Feature Extraction. *Symmetry* **2022**, *14*, 715. [CrossRef]
5. Li, Z.Q.; Sun, J.; Wu, X.J.; Yin, H. Sparsity augmented weighted collaborative representation for image classification. *J. Electron. Imaging* **2019**, *28*, 053032. [CrossRef]
6. Dong, J.; Zheng, H.; Lian, L. Low-rank laplacian-uniform mixed model for robust face recognition. In Proceedings of the IEEE/CVF Conference on Computer Vision and Pattern Recognition, Long Beach, CA, USA, 15–20 June 2019; pp. 11897–11906.
7. Yang, J.; Luo, L.; Qian, J.; Tai, Y.; Zhang, F.; Xu, Y. Nuclear norm based matrix regression with applications to face recognition with occlusion and illumination changes. *IEEE Trans. Pattern Anal. Mach. Intell.* **2017**, *39*, 156–171. [CrossRef]
8. Chen, Z.; Wu, X.J.; Kittler, J. A sparse regularized nuclear norm based matrix regression for face recognition with contiguous occlusion. *Pattern Recognit. Lett.* **2019**, *125*, 494–499. [CrossRef]
9. Chen, J.; Yi, Z. Sparse representation for face recognition by discriminative low-rank matrix recovery. *J. Vis. Commun. Image Represent.* **2014**, *25*, 763–773. [CrossRef]
10. Liu, G.; Lin, Z.; Yan, S.; Sun, J.; Yu, Y.; Ma, Y. Robust recovery of subspace structures by low-rank representation. *IEEE Trans. Pattern Anal. Mach. Intell.* **2012**, *35*, 171–184. [CrossRef]
11. Gao, G.; Yang, J.; Jing, X.Y.; Shen, F.; Yang, W.; Yue, D. Learning robust and discriminative low-rank representations for face recognition with occlusion. *Pattern Recognit.* **2017**, *66*, 129–143. [CrossRef]
12. Hu, Z.; Gao, G.; Gao, H.; Wu, S.; Zhu, D.; Yue, D. Robust Face Recognition Via Dual Nuclear Norm Low-rank Representation and Self-representation Induced Classifier. In Proceedings of the 2018 5th IEEE International Conference on Cloud Computing and Intelligence Systems (CCIS), Nanjing, China, 23–25 November 2018; pp. 920–924.
13. Yang, S.; Zhang, L.; He, L.; Wen, Y. Sparse low-rank component-based representation for face recognition with low-quality images. *IEEE Trans. Inf. Forensics Secur.* **2018**, *14*, 251–261. [CrossRef]
14. Yang, S.; Wen, Y.; He, L.; Zhou, M.; Abusorrah, A. Sparse Individual Low-Rank Component Representation for Face Recognition in the IoT-Based System. *IEEE Internet Things J.* **2021**, *8*, 17320–17332. [CrossRef]
15. Xia, H.; Feng, G.; Cai, J.X.; Tang, X.; Chi, H. Embedded conformal deep low-rank auto-encoder network for matrix recovery. *Pattern Recognit. Lett.* **2020**, *132*, 38–45. [CrossRef]
16. Wu, C.Y.; Ding, J.J. Occluded face recognition using low-rank regression with generalized gradient direction. *Pattern Recognit.* **2018**, *80*, 256–268. [CrossRef]
17. Li, X.X.; Hao, P.; He, L.; Feng, Y. Image gradient orientations embedded structural error coding for face recognition with occlusion. *J. Ambient. Intell. Humaniz. Comput.* **2020**, *11*, 2349–2367. [CrossRef]
18. Zhang, T.; Tang, Y.Y.; Fang, B.; Shang, Z.; Liu, X. Face recognition under varying illumination using gradientfaces. *IEEE Trans. Image Process.* **2009**, *18*, 2599–2606. [CrossRef]
19. Tzimiropoulos, G.; Zafeiriou, S.; Pantic, M. Subspace learning from image gradient orientations. *IEEE Trans. Pattern Anal. Mach. Intell.* **2012**, *34*, 2454–2466. [CrossRef]
20. Vu, N.S. Exploring patterns of gradient orientations and magnitudes for face recognition. *IEEE Trans. Inf. Forensics Secur.* **2012**, *8*, 295–304. [CrossRef]
21. Zheng, Q.; Wang, Y.; Heng, P.A. Online Subspace Learning from Gradient Orientations for Robust Image Alignment. *IEEE Trans. Image Process.* **2019**, *28*, 3383–3394. [CrossRef]

22. Qian, J.; Yang, J.; Xu, Y.; Xie, J.; Lai, Z.; Zhang, B. Image decomposition based matrix regression with applications to robust face recognition. *Pattern Recognit.* **2020**, *102*, 107204. [CrossRef]
23. Wu, Q.; Zhu, S. Multispectral Image Matching Method Based on Histogram of Maximum Gradient and Edge Orientation. *IEEE Geosci. Remote. Sens. Lett.* **2022**, *19*, 1–5. [CrossRef]
24. Huang, D.; Zhu, C.; Wang, Y.; Chen, L. HSOG: a novel local image descriptor based on histograms of the second-order gradients. *IEEE Trans. Image Process.* **2014**, *23*, 4680–4695. [CrossRef]
25. Morgan, M.J. Features and the primal sketch. *Vis. Res.* **2011**, *51*, 738–753. [CrossRef]
26. Li, C.; Gao, G.; Liu, Z.; Huang, D.; Xi, J. Defect detection for patterned fabric images based on GHOG and low-rank decomposition. *IEEE Access* **2019**, *7*, 83962–83973. [CrossRef]
27. Zhang, Y.; Bai, X.; Yan, J.; Xiao, Y.; Chatwin, C.R.; Young, R.; Birch, P. No-reference image quality assessment based on multi-order gradients statistics. *J. Imaging Sci. Technol.* **2020**, *64*, 10505-1. [CrossRef]
28. Bastian, B.T.; Jiji, C. Pedestrian detection using first-and second-order aggregate channel features. *Int. J. Multimed. Inf. Retr.* **2019**, *8*, 127–133. [CrossRef]
29. Abdulhussain, S.H.; Ramli, A.R.; Hussain, A.J.; Mahmmod, B.M.; Jassim, W.A. Orthogonal polynomial embedded image kernel. In Proceedings of the International Conference on Information and Communication Technology, Nanning, China, 11–13 January 2019; pp. 215–221.
30. Chen, J.; Huang, D.; Zhu, X.; Chen, F. Gradient-Guided and Multi-Scale Feature Network for Image Super-Resolution. *Appl. Sci.* **2022**, *12*, 2935. [CrossRef]
31. Zhang, L.; Yang, M.; Feng, X. Sparse representation or collaborative representation: Which helps face recognition? In Proceedings of the 2011 International Conference on Computer Vision, Barcelona, Spain, 6–11 November 2011; pp. 471–478.
32. Gou, J.; He, X.; Lu, J.; Ma, H.; Ou, W.; Yuan, Y. A class-specific mean vector-based weighted competitive and collaborative representation method for classification. *Neural Netw.* **2022**, *150*, 12–27. [CrossRef] [PubMed]
33. Gou, J.; Sun, L.; Du, L.; Ma, H.; Xiong, T.; Ou, W.; Zhan, Y. A representation coefficient-based k-nearest centroid neighbor classifier. *Expert Syst. Appl.* **2022**, *194*, 116529. [CrossRef]
34. Gou, J.; Yuan, X.; Du, L.; Xia, S.; Yi, Z. Hierarchical Graph Augmented Deep Collaborative Dictionary Learning for Classification. *IEEE Trans. Intell. Transp. Syst.* **2022**. [CrossRef]
35. Maaten, L.v.d.; Hinton, G. Visualizing data using t-SNE. *J. Mach. Learn. Res.* **2008**, *9*, 2579–2605.
36. He, R.; Zheng, W.S.; Tan, T.; Sun, Z. Half-quadratic-based iterative minimization for robust sparse representation. *IEEE Trans. Pattern Anal. Mach. Intell.* **2013**, *36*, 261–275.
37. Qian, J.; Luo, L.; Yang, J.; Zhang, F.; Lin, Z. Robust nuclear norm regularized regression for face recognition with occlusion. *Pattern Recognit.* **2015**, *48*, 3145–3159. [CrossRef]
38. Cai, S.; Zhang, L.; Zuo, W.; Feng, X. A probabilistic collaborative representation based approach for pattern classification. In Proceedings of the IEEE Conference on Computer Vision and Pattern Recognition, Las Vegas, NV, USA, 27–30 June 2016; pp. 2950–2959.
39. Iliadis, M.; Wang, H.; Molina, R.; Katsaggelos, A.K. Robust and low-rank representation for fast face identification with occlusions. *IEEE Trans. Image Process.* **2017**, *26*, 2203–2218. [CrossRef]
40. Zhang, C.; Li, H.; Chen, C.; Qian, Y.; Zhou, X. Enhanced group sparse regularized nonconvex regression for face recognition. *IEEE Trans. Pattern Anal. Mach. Intell.* **2022**, *44*, 2438–2452. [CrossRef]
41. Zhang, C.; Li, H.; Qian, Y.; Chen, C.; Zhou, X. Locality-constrained discriminative matrix regression for robust face identification. *IEEE Trans. Neural Netw. Learn. Syst.* **2022**, *33*, 1254–1268. [CrossRef]
42. Parkhi, O.M.; Vedaldi, A.; Zisserman, A.; et al. Deep face recognition. In Proceedings of the British Machine Vision Conference, Swansea, UK, 7–11 September 2015.
43. Simonyan, K.; Zisserman, A. Very deep convolutional networks for large-scale image recognition. *arXiv* **2014**, arXiv:1409.1556.
44. Wu, X.; He, R.; Sun, Z. A lightened cnn for deep face representation. *arXiv* **2015**, arXiv:1511.02683.
45. Krizhevsky, A.; Sutskever, I.; Hinton, G.E. Imagenet classification with deep convolutional neural networks. In Proceedings of the Advances in Neural Information Processing Systems, Lake Tahoe, NV, USA, 3–6 December 2012; pp. 1097–1105.
46. Lin, M.; Chen, Q.; Yan, S. Network in network. *arXiv* **2013**, arXiv:1312.4400.
47. Mehdipour Ghazi, M.; Kemal Ekenel, H. A comprehensive analysis of deep learning based representation for face recognition. In Proceedings of the IEEE Conference on Computer Vision and Pattern Recognition Workshops, Las Vegas, NV, USA, 27–30 June 2016; pp. 34–41.

mathematics

Article

Theme-Aware Semi-Supervised Image Aesthetic Quality Assessment

Xiaodan Zhang [1,†], Xun Zhang [1,†], Yuan Xiao [1] and Gang Liu [2,*]

[1] Science and Technology of Information Institute, Northwest University, Xi'an 710127, China; xiaodanzhang@nwu.edu.cn (X.Z.); zhangxun@stumail.nwu.edu.cn (X.Z.); 202133583@stumail.nwu.edu.cn (Y.X.)
[2] Xi'an Institute of Optics and Precision Mechanics, Chinese Academy of Sciences, Xi'an 710119, China
* Correspondence: liugang@opt.cn
† These authors contributed equally to this work.

Abstract: Image aesthetic quality assessment (IAQA) has aroused considerable interest in recent years and is widely used in various applications, such as image retrieval, album management, chat robot and social media. However, existing methods need an excessive amount of labeled data to train the model. Collecting the enormous quantity of human scored training data is not always feasible due to a number of factors, such as the expensiveness of the labeling process and the difficulty in correctly classifying data. Previous studies have evaluated the aesthetic of a photo based only on image features, but have ignored the criterion bias associated with the themes. In this work, we present a new theme-aware semi-supervised image quality assessment method to address these difficulties. Specifically, the proposed method consists of two steps: a representation learning step and a label propagation step. In the representation learning step, we propose a robust theme-aware attention network (TAAN) to cope with the theme criterion bias problem. In the label propagation step, we use preliminary trained TAAN by step one to extract features and utilize the label propagation with a cumulative confidence (LPCC) algorithm to assign pseudo-labels to the unlabeled data. This enables use of both labeled and unlabeled data to train the TAAN model. To the best of our knowledge, this is the first time that a semi-supervised learning method to address image aesthetic assessment problems has been studied. We evaluate our approach on three benchmark datasets and show that it can achieve almost the same performance as a fully supervised learning method for a small number of samples. Furthermore, we show that our semi-supervised approach is robust to using varying quantities of labeled data.

Keywords: image aesthetic assessment; semi-supervised learning; label propagation; deep learning; computer vision

MSC: 68T07

Citation: Zhang, X.; Zhang, X.; Xiao, Y.; Liu, G. Theme-Aware Semi-Supervised Image Aesthetic Quality Assessment. *Mathematics* **2022**, *10*, 2609. https://doi.org/10.3390/math10152609

Academic Editors: Jianping Gou, Weihua Ou, Shaoning Zeng and Lan Du

Received: 20 June 2022
Accepted: 22 July 2022
Published: 26 July 2022

1. Introduction

With the vigorous development of mobile Internet, images have become an indispensable part of our life. In the face of vast amounts of data, relying solely on human beings for the aesthetic analysis of images is not able to meet our needs, so the design of automatic aesthetic assessment algorithms has aroused considerable interest in the research community.

With respect to the various methods available for generating features, existing image aesthetic quality assessment methods can be broadly divided into two categories. The first category includes shallow modeling methods which use hand-crafted features to infer image aesthetic quality [1–3]. These methods use global, local and general features to represent aesthetic attributes. Among them, the Fisher vector (FC) [3] is used to construct aesthetic attributes and predict aesthetic quality. However, The representation ability of hand-crafted features is limited. The second category includes deep-learning-based methods. Because of the outstanding capabilities in efficient feature learning, convolutional neural networks (CNNs) have been used to infer composition information and learn new aesthetic representations (see, for example, [4–6]). Since the high-level features constructed by convolutional neural networks can better express the aesthetic quality, the performance of convolutional neural networks is better than that of traditional hand-crafted feature methods. Earlier attempts to develop CNNs [4–11] were able to help computers learn how to automatically evaluate an image. However, there are two major flaws in existing deep learning-based methods: Firstly, existing deep-learning-based methods require a large number of labeled datasets to train the network. However, collecting the enormity of human scored training data is not always feasible since manual annotation of aesthetic quality is a time-consuming, expensive and error-prone task. Thus, it is crucial to develop a method that only uses a small quantity of training data to reduce the reliance on manual annotation. Second, most previous research has only focused on the aesthetic features of the images but has ignored the criterion bias associated with their themes. Photographers shoot different scenes with different shooting methods. The scenes shot by each shooting method can be regarded as having a specific theme, but different shooting methods have different standards for the assessment of aesthetic quality. Thus, different themes use different evaluation criteria. For example, a highly blurred image may obtain a significant high score under the theme "Motion Blur" because blurring is regarded as a good feature'; however, it will obtain a low aesthetic score under the theme "Landscape", since blurring is considered to be a drawback for landscape images. Thus, it is appropriate to take the themes into account when aesthetic decisions are made.

Therefore, we propose a theme-aware semi-supervised image aesthetic quality assessment to solve the above-mentioned problems. To deal with the first problem, we employ a deep-learning-based label propagation method which is based on the assumption of making predictions on the entire dataset and using these to generate pseudo-labels for the unlabeled data. To handle the noise label problem in the process of label propagation, we also propose a cumulative confidence algorithm which can apply different weights to different unlabeled data. For data similar to previous prediction results, we apply a higher confidence weight; for dissimilar data, we apply a lower confidence weight. For the second problem, we propose a theme-aware attention network that considers the theme of an image when an aesthetic decision is made. This network consists of three components: an image feature extractor (backbone), a self-attention-based theme encoder and a residual connection module. The proposed network not only aims to extract visual features more effectively, but also leverages the theme power of tag and challenges to make aesthetic predictions more accurate.

The contributions of this paper are as follows:

- We are the first to tackle the image aesthetic quality assessment task via a semi-supervised learning method. We propose a label propagation with cumulative confidence algorithm (LPCC) to infer the pseudo-labels for unlabeled data. The proposed method greatly reduces reliance on human annotation.
- We design a theme-aware attention network to combine theme information with visual features to predict aesthetic quality. The proposed network can alleviate the criterion bias of the human aesthetic quality assessment process.
- We conduct extensive experiments to demonstrate the superiority of our proposed theme-aware semi-supervised method. Experimental results obtained show that our method can achieve almost the same performance as fully supervised learning.

The remainder of this paper is organized as follows: Section 2 summarizes related work. Section 3 introduces the methodology of the proposed theme aware semi-supervised approach. Section 4 quantitatively analyses the effectiveness of the proposed method and compares it with state-of-the-art results. Finally, Section 5 contains a summary and plans for future work.

2. Related Work

2.1. Image Aesthetics Quality Assessment

Image aesthetic quality assessment is a branch of image quality assessment (IQA) [12–14]. A broad collection of methods has been proposed in the last few years. Earlier image aesthetic assessment methods rely on handcrafted features to extract the aesthetic attributes of images [1,2]. These hand-crafted features include global features, such as saturation, brightness and hue, local features, such as contrast, and general features, such as SIFT and the Fisher vector [3]. With the advent of deep convolutional neural networks, deep CNNs have been deployed in image aesthetic quality assessment and have proved to be effective. For instance, Lu et al. [4] proposed a double-column DNN architecture, the RAPID-Net, which extracts global features from the whole image and local features from a randomly cropped patch. To capture more high-resolution fine-grained details, Lu et al. [5] proposed a deep multi-patch aggregation network, the DMA-Net. The DMA-Net extracts aesthetic features from a bag of randomly cropped patches, and uses statistics and sorting network layers to aggregate these multiple patches. Later, researchers found that processing images in the data augmentation stage entails loss of the original information of the image, which will affect the performance of the network. Thus, Mai et al. [6] added an adaptive spatial pooling layer onto the regular convolution to handle images with original sizes. In a similar vein, Ma et al. [15] proposed the non-random selection of multiple patches to extract image features according to the significance of the image without any transformation. Jia et al. [10] combined padding with ROI pooling to handle the arbitrary sizes of batch inputs.

Since previous work has focused only on the aesthetic features of images and ignored image content, some researchers have resorted to the use of semantic information to enhance the accuracy of aesthetic prediction. For example, Kao et al. [9] proposed the use of semantic labels to guide aesthetic assessment. Kong et al. [16] regularized the complicated photo aesthetics rating problem by applying joint learning of meaningful photographic attributes and image content information. However, these methods still cannot cope with the theme criterion bias problem. Using the method of [16], photographic attributes cannot solve the problem of theme criterion bias well. Firstly, the same image can belong to multiple aesthetic attributes, so we cannot uniquely determine the theme of the image through photographic attributes. Secondly, photographic attributes focus on different perspectives to evaluate an image, such as light, color, DOF, etc., rather than the theme. In the method of Kao et al. [9], although semantic labels can guide the aesthetic assessment, the semantic information is used simply as ground truth labels, which cannot fully interact with images. In this paper, we take the tag and challenge themes into account. To fully utilize them, we encode the theme information and combine it with the extracted visual features via an attention mechanism. Experiments undertaken demonstrated the effectiveness of the proposed module.

2.2. Semi-Supervised Learning

Supervised learning methods need to use labeled data to build models. However, labeling training data in the real world may be expensive or time-consuming. A semi-supervised learning (SSL) model can allow the model to integrate part or all of the unlabeled data in its supervised learning to solve this inherent bottleneck. The goal is to maximize the learning performance of the model through information revealed by both limited labeled images and sufficient unlabeled images. The study of semi-supervised learning (SSL) has a long history with various models being proposed. For example, Zhang et al. [17] proposed a simple learning principle, MixUp, to reduce memory and sensitivity to antagonistic examples of large deep neural networks. Berthelot et al. [18] unified the mainstream methods of semi-supervised learning and proposed MixMatch that guesses low-entropy labels for unlabeled examples and uses MixUp to mix labeled and unlabeled data. Laine et al. [19] introduced self-ensembling, in which the output of the network in different periods of training is used to form a consistent prediction of unknown tags. However, since the target changes only once in each epoch, temporal ensembling becomes very clumsy when learning huge datasets. To overcome this problem, Tarvainen et al. [20] proposed Mean Teacher, a method that defines the weight of the teacher model parameters obtained in each round as an exponential moving average. Iscen et al. [21] proposed a label propagation method based on transductive learning, which can assign pseudo-labels to unlabeled data using a k-nearest neighbor graph. Although based on this method, our proposed method represents an improvement in terms of cumulative confidence. The experimental results demonstrate that our improved method can solve the problems caused by label noise.

Although SSL has been evaluated for various tasks, few investigations have considered its application to an image aesthetic prediction task. Image aesthetic prediction is highly subjective and complex. Annotating aesthetic labels is a time-consuming and error-prone task. To reduce reliance on manual annotation, it is crucial to develop the SSL method to leverage dependencies on labeled data. Therefore, in this paper, we propose a theme-aware semi-supervised method which exhibits equivalent performance to that of a fully supervised method.

3. Methodology

In this section, we first describe preliminary details and the overall architecture of our method. Then, we introduce each module in detail.

3.1. Preliminaries

In semi-supervised image aesthetic assessment prediction, a dataset can be expressed as $X := (x_1, \ldots, x_l, x_{l+1}, \ldots, x_n)$. The dataset contains l labeled examples and $u = n - l$ unlabeled examples. The labeled examples x_i for $i \in L := (1, \ldots, l)$, denoted by X_L, are labeled according to $Y_L := (y_1, \ldots, y_l)$ with $y_i \in C$, where $C := (1, \ldots, c)$ is a discrete label set for c classes. The remaining unlabeled examples are denoted as $X_U = x_{l+1}, \ldots, x_n$. The goal in semi-supervised learning (SSL) is to use all examples X and labels Y_L to train a classifier that maps previously unseen samples to class labels.

In supervised learning, the network is trained by minimizing the following supervised loss term:

$$L_s(X_L, Y_L; \theta) := \sum_{i=1}^{l} loss(f_\theta(x_i), y_i), \tag{1}$$

where θ is the parameters of the network and f_θ is the forward function of the network.

The supervised loss applies only to labeled data in X_L. The loss function in classification is cross-entropy (CE) loss under standard conditions, which is given by

$$loss(p, y) := \sum_{i=1}^{l} (-y_i \log p_i), \tag{2}$$

where y is the label and p is the predict logits.

In semi-supervised learning, pseudo-labeling is the process of using the labeled data trained model to assign labels for unlabeled data. The additional pseudo-label loss term is defined as follows:

$$L_p(X_U, Y_U; \theta) := \sum_{i=l+1}^{n} loss(f_\theta(x_i), y_i), \tag{3}$$

where $Y_U := (y_{l+1}, \ldots, y_n)$ denote the collection of pseudo-labels for X_U, and the *loss* can be any supervised loss function, such as cross-entropy.

3.2. Overall Architecture

An overview of our proposed framework is illustrated in Figure 1. Our training is divided into two steps: a representation learning step and a label propagation step. These two steps are iteratively trained. In the representation learning step, we train the theme-aware attention network in a fully supervised fashion on the l labeled examples. The theme-aware attention network generates two outputs: an embedding output $\hat{f}_v$ and a category prediction output. In the label propagation stage, we construct a k-nearest neighbor graph through the embedding output $\hat{f}_v$ and perform label propagation on the training set. The known labels Y_L are propagated from X_L to X_U, creating pseudo-labels Y_U. Then, we estimate confidence scores reflecting the uncertainty of each unlabeled example. The confidence scores are then used as loss weights during the representation learning stage. Finally, we inject the obtained labels into the representation learning step. By iteratively applying the label propagation and representation learning steps, our model builds a good underlying representation and trains an accurate classifier for the image aesthetic prediction task.

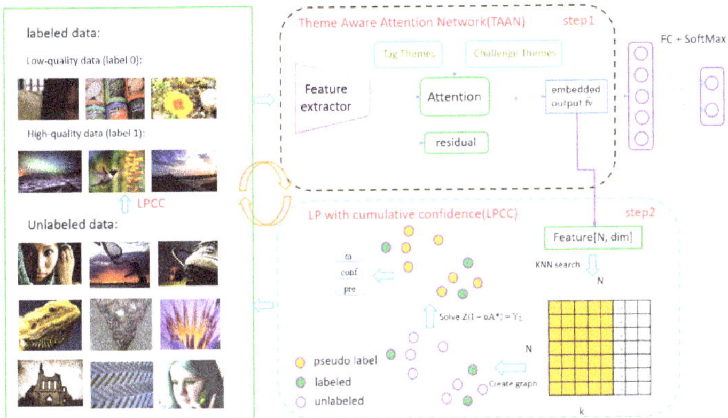

Figure 1. Overall architecture of our theme-aware semi-supervised image aesthetic quality assessment. First, in step one, we train our theme-aware attention network (TAAN) using a small amount of labeled data in a supervised fashion. In step 2, we use a label propagation with cumulative confidence algorithm (LPCC) to transduct the pseudo-labels for unlabeled data. We extract the features of the entire training set and compute a k-nearest neighbor graph. Then we propagate labels by transductive learning and train the theme-aware attention network (TAAN) on the entire training set. These two steps are iteratively trained. When testing, we send the input image directly into the trained TAAN model to obtain the predicted aesthetic quality. More detailed illustrations of label propagation with cumulative confidence algorithm (LPCC) can be found in Algorithm 1.

3.3. *Theme-Aware Attention Network*

In recent years, the attention mechanism has been shown to be effective in capturing important information from raw features in either linguistic or visual representations [22]. In contrast to the above approaches, we propose theme-aware attention to jointly exploit attention mechanisms to encode the theme features. Inspired by the success of self-attention, the proposed theme-aware attention module can capture the complex interactions between the theme features and different spatial locations in the input image.

The pipeline of our proposed theme-aware attention network (TAAN) is shown in Figure 2, which consists of the following three parts: an image feature extractor (backbone), a self-attention-based theme encoder and a residual connection module. Given the image, the image feature extractor firstly extracts high level features. Then these features are sent into the self-attention-based theme encoder. Finally, the visual features and the theme-based features are combined via a residual connection module.

Algorithm 1 Label propagation with cumulative confidence.

procedure LPCC(X, Y_L)
  $\theta \leftarrow$ initialize randomly
for epoch $\in [1, \dots, T_1]$ **do** ▷ step 1
  $J \leftarrow CrossEntropy(f_\theta(X_L), Y_L)$
  $\theta \leftarrow \theta - \eta \bigtriangledown J / \bigtriangledown \theta$
  end for
for epoch $\in [1, \dots, T_1]$ **do** ▷ step 2
  $F \leftarrow f_\theta(X)$ ▷ extract features
  $D, I \leftarrow search(F, k)$ ▷ knn search for the graph
  $A \leftarrow compress(D, I)$ ▷ create the adjacency matrix of the graph
  $A \leftarrow A + A^T$ ▷ symmetric affinity
  $A^* \leftarrow D^{-1/2} A D^{-1/2}$ ▷ normalize the graph
  $Z \leftarrow Z(I - \alpha A^*) = Y_L$ ▷ solve the equation
  $Y_U \leftarrow argmax(normalize(Z))$ ▷ get pseudo-label
  $\omega \leftarrow 1 - (Entropy(Z)/log(c))$ ▷ get entropy weight
  $conf \leftarrow similarity(Y_U, pre)$ ▷ cumulative confidence weight
  $pre \leftarrow epoch * pre + Y_U)/(epoch + 1)$ ▷ update cumulative info
  $J \leftarrow CrossEntropy(f_\theta(X_L), Y_L) \times \omega \times conf$
  $\theta \leftarrow \theta - \eta \bigtriangledown J / \bigtriangledown \theta$
  end for
end procedure

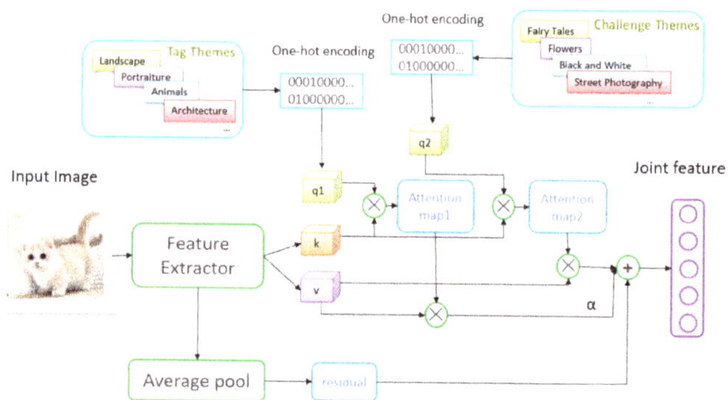

Figure 2. Details of our theme-aware attention network (TAAN). The TAAN consists of an image feature extractor (backbone), a self-attention-based theme encoder and a residual connection module.

The image feature extractor is a residual network with 18 layers, as described in [23], pretrained on ImageNet [24]. Images in the AVA dataset not only have semantic tag information (such as Macro, Animals and Portraiture), but also have challenge information (such as Fairy Tales, Flowers, Black and White, Street Photography). The tag information and challenge information both encode the theme information. Thus, we turn the tag information and challenge information into one-hot codes, and then process the one-hot codes with a fully connected layer to extract the theme features. Given the extracted visual feature f_v and theme features f_{theme}, the self-attention-based theme encoder first produces a set of query, key and value pairs by linear transformations as $q_1 = W_q f_{tag}$, $k = W_k f_v$, $q_2 = W_{q2} f_{challenge}$, $v = W_v f_v$, where W_q, W_{q2}, W_k, W_v are part of the model parameters to be learned. Then the tag-theme-based attention and the challenge-theme-based attention are computed as follows:

$$\begin{aligned} \alpha_{tag} &= Softmax(q_1^T k) \\ \alpha_{challenge} &= Softmax(q_2^T k), \end{aligned} \tag{4}$$

where α_{tag} and $\alpha_{challenge}$ denote the tag-theme-based attention and the challenge-theme-based attention, respectively. Then the final theme-attentive features $\hat{v}$ are computed as follows:

$$\hat{v} = \alpha_{tag} \times v + \alpha_{challenge} \times v \tag{5}$$

We then combine the theme-attentive features with visual features via a residual connection. This allows the insertion of the proposed module into any backbone network without disrupting its initial behavior. The operations can be defined as follows:

$$\hat{f_v} = \hat{v} + f_v \tag{6}$$

where $\hat{v}$ is the theme-attentive features, f_v is the extracted visual feature, and $\hat{f_v}$ denotes theme-attentive features with residual features.

3.4. Label Propagation with Cumulative Confidence Algorithm

The label propagation algorithm is an iterative process for semi-supervised learning. More specifically, we first construct a nearest neighbor graph and perform label propagation on the whole training set. Then, we calculate an entropy weight reflecting the uncertainty of label propagation for each unlabeled example. Inspired by [25], we believe that the results obtained from early propagation should also be considered as a constraint, so we propose a cumulative confidence weight to improve the traditional label propagation [21]. Finally, we inject the obtained pseudo-labels into the network training process. This method is described in detail below; the process of the proposed approach is demonstrated in Algorithm 1.

K-nearest neighbor search for the graph. Given an image feature matrix $\hat{f_v}$ with dimensions (n, dim), we first calculate the similarity between every two points (the Euclidean distance or cosine similarity can be used).

Create the adjacency matrix of the graph. For the first k nearest neighbors of each point, the similarity is the weight of the edge, and the weight of the edge after more than k is set to 0. A sparse affinity matrix $A \in \mathbb{R}_{n\times n}$ is constructed as follows:

$$a_{ij} = \begin{cases} [f_{v_i}^T f_{v_j}]^\gamma, & if \quad i \neq j \wedge f_{v_i} \in KNN(f_{v_j}); \\ 0, & otherwise. \end{cases} \tag{7}$$

where KNN denotes the set of the first k nearest neighbors in X, and γ is a parameter following work on a manifold-based search [26]. So far, we obtain the adjacency matrix A.

Normalize the graph. Since the full affinity matrix is not tractable, it may lead to the following problems: node a is the k-nearest neighbor of node b, but node b is not the k-nearest neighbor of node a, so we symmetrize it and turn it into a real undirected graph. The operation is defined in Equation (8). Then we use regularization of the Laplace matrix for the adjacency matrix A to build its symmetrically normalized counterpart A^*, which is defined in Equation (9);

$$A = A + A^T, \tag{8}$$

$$A^* = D^{-1/2} A D^{-1/2}, \tag{9}$$

where A is the adjacency matrix, D is the degree matrix of A, which is defined as $D := diag(A1_n)$, where 1_n is the all-ones n-vector , and A^* is the normalized adjacency matrix.

Diffusion for transductive learning [27]. The label matrix $Y(nc)$ is defined with elements:

$$Y_{ij} = \begin{cases} 1, & if \quad i \in L \wedge y_i = j; \\ 0, & otherwise. \end{cases} \tag{10}$$

where L represents the index of labeled data. This means that the rows of the label matrix Y corresponding to the labeled examples are one-hot encoded labels. The remaining elements are zero. The diffusion process is equivalent to the solution of linear equations:

$$(I - \alpha A^*)Z = Y \tag{11}$$

where α is the adjustable parameter and I is the identity matrix. Because matrix $(I - \alpha A^*)$ is positive-definite, we can use the conjugate gradient (CG) method to solve the linear system. This solution is known to be faster than the iterative solution. Finally, we infer the pseudo-labels:

$$Z^* = normalize((I - \alpha A^*)^{-1}Y) \tag{12}$$

$$Y_U = argmax(Z^*) \tag{13}$$

where Z^* is the row-wise normalized counterpart of Z and Y_U are the predicted pseudo-labels.

Entropy weight. We need to evaluate the reliability of the predicted pseudo-labels. Firstly, we consider the credibility of a single round. The prediction matrix Z we obtained has a probability prediction value for the category to which each sample point belongs. For points with small entropy, we think it is more credible, while for points with large entropy, we think it is less credible, so our weight is calculated by the following:

$$\omega = 1 - \frac{H(Z^*)}{\log c} \tag{14}$$

where Z^* is the row-wise normalized counterpart of Z and c is the number of classes, so $\log(c)$ is the maximum possible entropy.

Cumulative confidence weight. To improve the fault tolerance and reliability of label propagation, we propose a second weight, the cumulative confidence weight F_{conf}. We maintain an array F_{pre} to record the average value of the previous prediction. F_{pre} reflects the reliability of the prediction (higher F_{pre} means higher reliability). F_{conf} denotes the similarity between F_{pre} and the pseudo-labels in each epoch; it can be directly multiplied with the previous entropy weight. We have also designed three similarity functions and can manually select the appropriate one to deploy to the final architecture. F_{conf} is calculated by the following equation:

$$F_{conf} = similarity(Y_U, F_{pre}) \tag{15}$$

$$F_{pre} = \frac{epoch \times F_{pre} + Y_U}{epoch + 1} \tag{16}$$

where Y_U denote the pseudo-labels of unlabeled data. So, the final loss with weight is calculated by the following formula:

$$L_p(X_U, Y_U; \theta) := \sum_{i=l+1}^{n} loss(f_\theta(x_i), y_i) \times \omega_i \times F^i_{conf}. \tag{17}$$

where X_U denote the image features of unlabeled data, Y_U denote the pseudo-labels of unlabeled data, ω_i denote the entropy weights in index i and F^i_{conf} denote the cumulative confidence weights in i.

4. Experiments

4.1. Datasets

AVA. Aesthetic Visual Analysis (AVA) [28] is a large-scale database for image aesthetics quality assessment. The images of this dataset are crawled from www.DPChanllenge.com (accessed on 5 May 2022). It contains more than 255,000 images. The aesthetic assessment is scored by 78 to 549 individuals, and the scores given by the voters are from 1 to 10. The AVA dataset provides 66 kinds of semantic tags and 1409 kinds of style tags. Each image in the AVA dataset has 0 to 2 semantic tags and belongs to one specific challenge theme. We follow the official dataset partition as in [28], randomly selecting 235,508 images as the training set, and 20,000 images as the testing set.

Photo.net. The Photo.net dataset [1] contains about 20,278 images. Unlike the AVA dataset, it contains only aesthetic labels. The aesthetic assessment is scored by at least 10 individuals, and the scores given by the voters are from 1 to 7. For some images, only the mean score and standard deviation are given and voting information is lost. Since the website has been updated several times, there are only 17,253 images that can be downloaded. The Photo.net dataset contains no theme information. Thus, similar to previous work [10], we only use Photo.net as a test set.

CUHK. CUHK [2] is a small-scale dataset that can clearly distinguish high-quality and low-quality images. We only use photos that have a clear consensus on their quality. The images of this dataset are also crawled from www.DPChanllenge.com (accessed on 5 May 2022). About 3000 images (half of the photos) were used for testing. For the same reason as the Photo.net dataset, we only use the test dataset of CUHK to evaluate our model.

4.2. Implementation Details

We implemented our method using the PyTorch framework. We used the Adam optimizer with $\beta1 = 0.9$ and $\beta2 = 0.999$, and the learning rate was 1×10^{-5}. Our GPU uses GeForce RTX 3080Ti.

Networks. We used many backbone networks in our experiment. For VGG, ResNet and DenseNet, we used the implementation provided in the Torchvision project [29]. For Swin-T, we used the implementation provided in https://github.com/WZMIAOMIAO/deep-learning-for-image-processing (accessed on 5 May 2022). In our experiment, the input image size was [3, 224, 224]. When we used ResNet18, ResNet34 or VGG16, the output feature dim was 512; when we used ResNet50, ResNet101 or ResNet152, the output feature dim was 2048; when we used Swin-T, the output feature dim was 768. Then we used the flattened feature as our image feature vector.

Hyper-parameters. We trained 10 epochs for step one (i.e., the representation learning step) and 20 epochs for step two (i.e., the label propagation step). Step two uses the embedding output $\hat{f}_v$ of step one to infer the pseudo-labels. For step one, the mini-batch size is a certain number which is determined by the depth of the network backbone (usually 32 or 64). For step two, the mini-batch size needs to use two steam samplers: the labeled data sampler and the unlabeled sampler. The unlabeled data sampler guarantees that all unlabeled data will be traversed, while the labeled data sampler constantly iterates over the labeled data. The total mini-batch size $B = B_l + B_u$. B_l is the labeled mini-batch size and Bu is the unlabeled mini-batch size. The value of B_l is usually half that of B. In our TAAN network, we set the scale factor $\alpha = 1$. In our LPCC algorithm, the diffusion parameters were set as follows: the value of γ was set to 3, k was set to 50 and the CG iteration was set to 20.

4.3. Ablation Studies

Effectiveness of the theme-aware attention network. The proposed method employs themes as privileged information to improve the performance. To evaluate the performance of our proposed theme-aware attention network, we compared the proposed module with the following models:

- ResNet18: ResNet18 means baseline ResNet18 network. In this model, we did not add theme information.
- ResNet18 + Theme: In this baseline, the theme information is directly added to the ResNet18 network.
- ResNet18 + TAAN: ResNet18 + TAAN denotes the proposed theme aware attention network.

The comparison results are shown in Table 1. To prove the effectiveness of the proposed module, we tested it both in a full supervised condition and in a semi-supervised condition. From the Table, we make the following observations. First, the proposed

ResNet18 + TAAN had the best performance. For example, ResNet18 + TAAN achieved 76.6% in full supervised method, while the other two models achieved 76.28% and 76.32%, respectively. Similar results were also found for the semi-supervised learning method. Second, compared to ResNet18, ResNet18 + Theme achieved better performance, using both the fully supervised method and the semi-supervised method, which demonstrates the effectiveness of the theme information. Third, ResNet18 + TAAN performed better than ResNet18 + Theme, which demonstrates the superiority of the attention mechanism. This is because the attention mechanism makes the visual features and theme features fully interact with each other.

Table 1. Accuracy (%) of different modules. For the semi-supervised method, the value is the accuracy of step 2 ($\delta = 1$).

Modules	Fully Supervised	Semi-Supervised (Labeled Rate: 0.05)
ResNet18	76.28	76.02
ResNet18 + Theme	76.32	76.10
ResNet18 + TAAN	76.60	76.23

Effectiveness of cumulative confidence weight. We propose a cumulative confidence weight to estimate the fault tolerance and reliability of the samples. We tested three different similarity estimation methods for the cumulative confidence weight, i.e., the linear function, the square function and the sigmoid function. We first define distance

$$d = Y_u - F_{pre} \tag{18}$$

where Y_U are the pseudo-labels of all the data items, F_{pre} is the average value of the previous prediction, and d means the distance between the current predicted pseudo-label Y_U and the average previous prediction value F_{pre}. The linear function is defined as follows:

$$similarity_{linear} = 1 - d \tag{19}$$

The square function is defined as follows:

$$similarity_{square} = 1 - d^2 \tag{20}$$

The sigmoid function is defined as follows:

$$similarity_{sigmoid} = 1 - \frac{1}{e^{(0.5-d)\times\lambda}} \tag{21}$$

where λ controls the slope of the sigmoid function. To separate the predicted values into two categories, we use $\lambda = 10$ as our final method. Table 2 illustrates the comparison results. The base-line model in Table 2 did not include a cumulative confidence weight. From the table, we can draw the following conclusions. First, adding a cumulative confidence weight can result in better performance. For example, the performance of the base-line model was 75.01%; by adding a cumulative confidence weight (using the linear similarity function for the cumulative confidence weight) the model was able to achieve at least 75.96%. Second, it can be seen that using the square similarity function resulted in slightly better performance than for the other two similarity functions. Thus, in this paper, we use the square function as the similarity function for the cumulative confidence weight.

Table 2. Accuracy (%) of different similarity strategies in the cumulative confidence algorithm ($\delta = 1$).

LP Strategies	Semi-Supervised (Labeled Rate: 0.05)
base-line model	75.01
linear similarity function	75.96
square similarity function	76.09
sigmoid similarity function	76.03

4.4. Experiments on Different Label Rates

To evaluate how good the proposed model is at using unlabeled images, we trained our model under different labeling rates. As can be seen from Table 3, with the 90% label missing (i.e., the labeling rate was 10%), step one achieved 73.86% accuracy. However, with the help of unlabeled images, in step two, our model improved the accuracy to 76.12%. This demonstrates that the proposed method consistently benefits from additional unlabelled images. Similar results were also found for other labeling rates, such as 5% and 2%. Figure 3 shows the t-SNE visualization of the embedded output $\hat{f}_v$ under different labeling rates. Purple dots represent unlabeled images, yellow dots represent labeled low-quality images and green dots represent labeled high-quality images. From the figure, we can easily make the following two observations: First, our method can cluster unlabeled data (purple) with labeled data under these three labeling rates. Thus we can easily deploy our LPCC algorithm. Second, our method has a robust discrimination effect for data under different labeling rates.

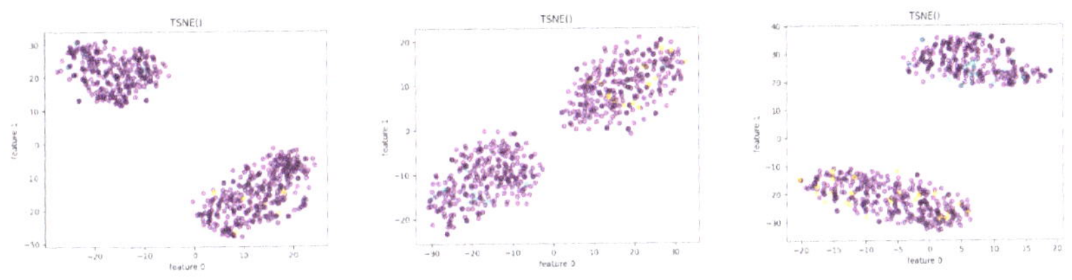

Figure 3. Visualization of the features of labeling rate 0.02 (**left**), 0.05 (**middle**) and 0.1 (**right**) on the test set by TSNE. Purple dots represent unlabeled images, yellow dots represent labeled low-quality images and green dots represent labeled high-quality images.

Table 3. Accuracy (%) of experiments on different labeled rates.

labeling Rates	Step 1	Step 2 (Best)
1.0 (Fully supervised)	76.31	-
10%	73.86	**76.12**
5%	72.75	**76.09**
2%	71.67	**74.18**

4.5. Extension to Different Backbones

Our model can use a variety of different feature extractors. Therefore, we used different pre-training models as our backbones. We chose VGG16, ResNet18 [23], ResNet34, ResNet50, ResNet101, DenseNet121 [30] and Swin Transformer-T [31] to experiment on the label rate of 0.05 with the AVA dataset. All networks were pretrained on ImageNet [24]. The performance of different CNN feature extractors is given in Table 4.

Table 4. Accuracy (%) on different backbones. For the semi-supervised method, the value is the accuracy of step 2.

Architecture Backbones	Semi-Supervised
VGG16	75.73
ResNet18	76.09
ResNet34	75.82
ResNet50	76.16
ResNet101	76.63
Densenet121	76.45
Swin-T	**76.82**

It can be seen that with increase in the complexity of the model, the accuracy increases. Figure 4 illustrates the embedded features $\hat{f}_v$ with different backbones. We can also clearly see that the discrimination of features extracted with a better backbone framework is significantly higher.

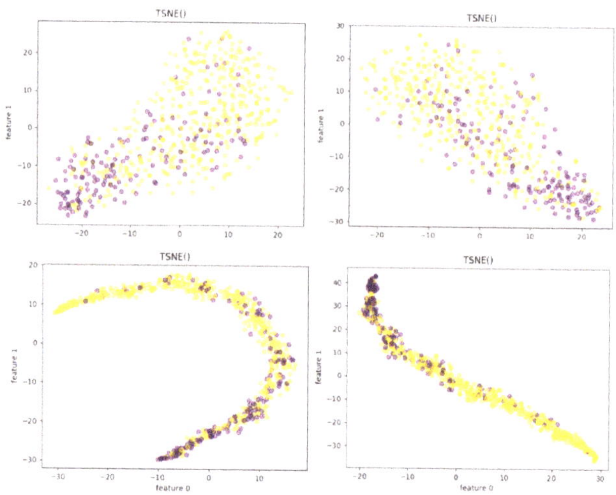

Figure 4. Visualization of the fc-features of ResNet18 (**top left**), ResNet34 (**top right**), ResNet50 (**bottom left**) and ResNet101 (**bottom right**) on the test set by TSNE. Purple dots represent low-quality images and yellow dots represent high-quality images.

4.6. Performance Evaluation

To demonstrate the effectiveness of our method, we performed a comparative evaluation with existing approaches on the AVA dataset. It should be noted that the existing methods are based on the assumption of full supervision, while our method is a semi-supervised method. We selected some mainstream methods for comparison. During the comparative study, it was found that the source codes of [4–6,9] were unavailable and the experimental details were not mentioned. As a result, it might be infeasible to implement them precisely. Thus the experimental data were taken from their paper. For those methods that published the code, such as [7,32,33], we used the same dataset (5% labeling rates) to evaluate their models and to obtain the corresponding experimental data provided in Table 5.

Table 5. Comparison with state-of-the-art methods on AVA dataset.

Method	Accuracy (%)
RAPID	73.70
DMA-Net	75.42
MNA-CNN	76.10
MTCNN#1	75.90
Enhanced MTCNN	76.04
NIMA	74.87 (5% labeling rates)
MPA	70.52 (5% labeling rates)
MUSIQ	73.46 (5% labeling rates)
Our Semi-supervised (ResNet18)	**76.09** (5% labeling rates)
Our Semi-supervised (Swin-T)	**76.82** (5% labeling rates)

The methods we compared were as follows:

- **RAPID:** The authors of [4] proposed a method called RAPID, which consists of two columns of neural networks, representing global and local inputs, respectively.
- **DMA-Net:** The deep multi-patch aggregation network (DMA-Net) [5] is an improvement on RAPID. It is a multi-shared column CNN with four convolution layers and three fully connected layers.
- **MNA-CNN:** The MNA-CNN [6] is a neural network with multiple subnets sharing the same input image. Its output is combined with the average operator to obtain the overall aesthetic prediction of the picture.
- **MTCNN#1:** The MTCNN was proposed by [9] and predicts both aesthetic quality and tag labels. **Enhanced MTCNN:** The Enhanced MTCNN is an improved framework for MTCNN which adds extra aesthetic details supervised in the first two layers in MTCNN #1 and provides two convolutional layers and two fully-connected layers which are learned for two tasks (aesthetic quality and tag labels).
- **NIMA:** NIMA [7] formulates the aesthetic prediction task as a label distribution prediction problem, which is different from the above aesthetic prediction task. EMD loss is used to deal with the aesthetic distribution for the first time, and achieved good results. The code of NIMA is available at https://github.com/truskovskiyk/nima.pytorch (accessed on 20 May 2022).
- **MPA:** MPA [32] uses an attention-based mechanism to dynamically adjust the weight of each patch. It assigns larger weights to patches on which the current model has made incorrect predictions during the training process and aggregates the prediction results of multiple patches during the test. The code of MPA is available at https://github.com/Openning07/MPADA (accessed on 20 May 2022).
- **MUSIQ:** MUSIQ [33] uses a multi-scale image quality transformer to process original resolution images with different sizes and aspect ratios. The code of MUSIQ is available at https://github.com/anse3832/MUSIQ (accessed on 20 May 2022).

The experimental results are illustrated in Table 5. From the table, we can make the following two observations: First, the semi-supervised accuracy can reach, or even exceed, that of some fully supervised models. For example, MTCNN [9] achieved 75.9% accuracy, while our method achieved 76.82% accuracy with only 5% labeling rates. Second, our semi-supervised accuracy can exceed the current model when using the same labeling rate. For example, MPA [32] and NIMA [7] achieved 70.52% and 74.87% accuracy, respectively, while our method achieved 76.82% accuracy with only 5% labeling rates. The reason for the difference is clear: the lack of data leads to the degradation of the other models' performance, while our proposed model can improve performance by using a large quantity of unlabeled data.

4.7. Experimental Results on Photo.net and CUHK Dataset

Tables 6 and 7 show the comparison results for the Photo.net and CUHK datasets, respectively. As stated earlier, the Photo.net and CUHK datasets are both small datasets and have no theme information. Thus, we used the AVA dataset to train the model, and tested on the Photo.net and CUHK datasets. We used the published Pytorch code of NIMA [7] and MUSIQ [33] to implement 5% labeling rates for the Photo.net and CUHK datasets; these are compared with our method in Tables 6 and 7. From Tables 6 and 7, we can see that our proposed method outperformed previously used methods by using a large quantity of unlabeled data. This also demonstrates that our proposed model produces good generalization performance for different datasets.

Table 6. Comparison with state-of-the-art methods on the Photo.net dataset.

Method	Accuracy (%)
MTCNN#1	65.20
NIMA	67.63 (5% labeling rates)
MUSIQ	68.84 (5% labeling rates)
Our Semi-supervised (ResNet18)	**73.10** (5% labeling rates)

Table 7. Comparison with state-of-the-art methods on CUHK dataset.

Method	Accuracy (%)
NIMA	75.12 (5% labeling rates)
MUSIQ	77.85 (5% labeling rates)
Our Semi-supervised(ResNet18)	**78.25** (5% labeling rates)

4.8. Discussion of Experiment on Labeled Data Sensitivity

To explore whether the proposed method is sensitive to the labeled data, we randomly divided the labeled data under labeling rate 5% into five groups: split 1, 2, 3, 4 and 5. We used these groups of labeled data to train our model and record the best accuracy. The experimental results are shown in Table 8. Evidently, no matter which split we used, the accuracy did not fluctuate significantly. Therefore, we hold that our model is insensitive to the selection of labeled data.

Table 8. Experiment on sensitivity analysis. Split 1, 2, 3, 4 and 5 are random labeled data splits under labeling rate 5%. The best accuracy (%) of each split is recorded.

Split 1	Split 2	Split 3	Split 4	Split 5
76.09	75.92	75.96	76.02	75.97

4.9. Computational Complexity

4.9.1. Theoretical Analysis

Our training was divided into two steps. In the first step, we trained our theme-aware attention network (TAAN) using small quantities of labeled data in a supervised fashion. In the second step, we used the label propagation with cumulative confidence algorithm (LPCC) to transduct the pseudo-labels for unlabeled data. These two steps were iteratively trained. Since label propagation tends to be viewed as entailing considerable complexity, we mainly analyzed the computational complexity of label propagation theoretically.

The computational complexity of traditional label propagation is mainly composed of KNN search and creation of the graph. Suppose the data scale is n, if no optimization measures are taken, the computational complexity of the KNN search is $O(n \times n)$. This is because the KNN search needs to traverse n features to find the k most similar vectors. The floating-point operation required by a vector point multiplication is proportional to the vector dimension. Suppose the vector dimension is m, the computational complexity of the KNN search is

$$FLOPs = n \times n \times m \tag{22}$$

Considering the computational cost is quite high, we use the inverted file system (IVF) and product quantification (PQ) in the Faiss library to reduce the computational complexity of label propagation.

Using the inverted file system(IFS) to optimize the KNN search: we index the entire dataset and cluster it into several subspaces. When we query a vector, we first calculate the subspace of query vector, and then search in the corresponding subspace. Suppose that the average size of our subspace is $\frac{1}{s}$ of the original space size, the computational complexity of the KNN search can be reduced to:

$$FLOPs = \frac{n \times n \times m}{s} \tag{23}$$

Using product quantification(PQ) to further optimize the KNN search: the details of the product quantification are illustrated in Figure 5. As can be seen from Figure 5, we assume that the vector dimension m is 128 (our whole dataset is $n \times 128$). We split each vector into four sub-vectors with 32 dimensions and group the n sub-vectors (in four columns) into 256 classes, respectively. The sub-vectors of each data item are represented by four class centers (such as $[12, 45, 240, 48]$); thus, each vector can be saved in four bytes (int type). We need to calculate the distance table in advance. Building the distance table requires $4 \times 256 \times 32$ floating-point operations, which are independent of n. Once the distance table is built, our distance query calculation (needing $n \times 4$ times) is a table lookup operation, which takes much less time than performing floating-point multiplication calculations, so we also need to divide by a constant c to derive the computational complexity. The final computational complexity can be reduced to:

$$FLOPs = \frac{n \times 4 + 4 \times 256 \times 32}{s \times c} \tag{24}$$

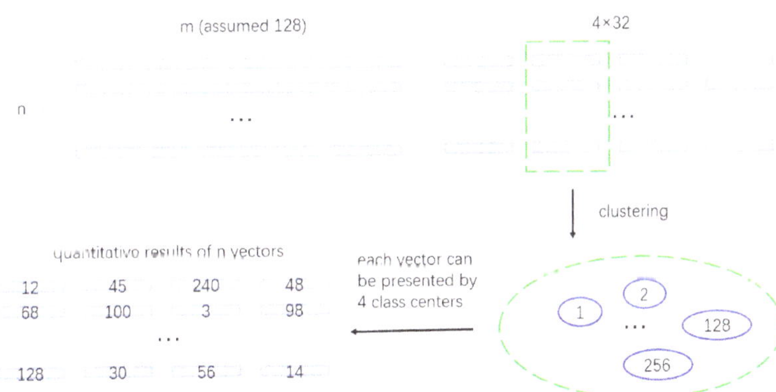

Figure 5. Details of Product Quantification.

When n is particularly large (large-scale data), $4 \times 256 \times 32$ can be ignored. When s is set to 10, c is set to 5, and m is 512, the IFS + PQ algorithm can be 6400 times faster than using a violent search method. To verify the reliability of the theoretical analysis, we tested one epoch running time for our whole AVA dataset. The running times for each step of our method are reported in Table 9. It can be seen clearly from the table that the time required for label propagation is negligible compared with the time in training.

Table 9. The one epoch running time in each step of our method are reported in the table. When training, we used the whole training set of the AVA dataset. When inferring, we used the whole testing set of the AVA dataset. Step 1 DNN means deep neural network pass of step 1. Step 2 LP means label propagation of step 2. The items explain in more detail what is done at each step. FP means forward pass and BP means back propagation.

Training & Inferring	Steps	Items	Running Time (s)
Training	Step 1 DNN	FP + BP	580.86 s
	Step 1 DNN	Extract $\hat{f}_v$ (FP)	345.02 s
	Step 2 LP	Label propagation	2.2063 s
Inferring	Step 1 DNN	FP	74.56 s

4.9.2. Inference Computational Cost Comparison

We analyzed the time consumption to compare the computational complexity of different methods. Thus, we only compared the computational complexity with methods that published the code, such as NIMA, MPA and MUSIQ. Table 10 shows the computational complexity results. The timings of an image forward pass are reported in the table. Our inference Pytorch implementation and TensorFlow implementation were tested on an Intel i7-11700H @ 2.5 GHz with 32 GB memory and 8 cores, and NVIDIA 3080Ti GPU. From the table, we can see that our method has similar running time to NIMA and MPA when using the same ResNet18 backbone.

Table 10. Comparison of image forward pass running time for different methods (ResNet18 backbone).

Method	Running Time (s)
NIMA	0.345 s
MPA	0.362 s
MUSIQ	0.410 s
Our Semi-supervised (ResNet18)	0.351 s

5. Conclusions and Discussion

In this paper, we propose a theme-aware semi-supervised architecture for image aesthetic quality assessment with the aim of reducing the dependence on image label annotation and making full use of a large number of unlabeled images on the network. For the noise label problem encountered in the process of label propagation, we propose a cumulative confidence algorithm by improving the traditional label propagation algorithm. We applied it to our image aesthetic quality assessment task, and achieved satisfactory results. We also found that our theme-aware architecture can solve the problem of theme sensitivity in image aesthetic quality assessment. The experimental results show that our method is robust to different label rates, different labeled data selection and different datasets.

Although our method achieves promising results, several issues need to be considered in our future research. First, we will continue to focus on how to use EMD loss for the label propagation algorithm to improve the accuracy of semi-supervised learning. Second, to make good use of the collaborative attention between images and other information, such as user comments, we will start from a multi-modality position to seek better solutions. We will also explore new semi-supervised algorithms, such as curriculum learning, to improve the existing label propagation algorithms.

Author Contributions: Investigation, G.L.; Methodology, X.Z. (Xiaodan Zhang) and X.Z. (Xun Zhang); Resources, G.L.; Software, X.Z. (Xun Zhang) and Y.X.; Validation, G.L.; Writing—original draft, X.Z. (Xiaodan Zhang); Writing—review & editing, X.Z. (Xiaodan Zhang). All authors have read and agreed to the published version of the manuscript.

Funding: This work was supported in part by the National Natural Science Foundation of China under Grant No. 62001385,62002290, in part by the Key RD Program of Shaanxi under Grant 2021ZDLGY15-03, and in part by the Project funded by China Postdoctoral Science Foundation (Grant No. 2021MD703883).

Institutional Review Board Statement: Not applicable.

Informed Consent Statement: Not applicable.

Data Availability Statement: The data presented in this study are available in [1,2,28].

Conflicts of Interest: The authors declare that they have no known competing financial interests or personal relationships that could have appeared to influence the work reported in this paper.

References

1. Datta, R.; Joshi, D.; Li, J.; Wang, J.Z. Studying aesthetics in photographic images using a computational approach. In *European Conference on Computer Vision*; Springer: Berlin/Heidelberg, Germany, 2006; pp. 288–301.
2. Ke, Y.; Tang, X.; Jing, F. The design of high-level features for photo quality assessment. In Proceedings of the 2006 IEEE Computer Society Conference on Computer Vision and Pattern Recognition (CVPR'06), New York, NY, USA, 17–22 June 2006; Volume 1, pp. 419–426.
3. Marchesotti, L.; Perronnin, F.; Larlus, D.; Csurka, G. Assessing the aesthetic quality of photographs using generic image descriptors. In Proceedings of the 2011 International Conference on Computer Vision, Washington, DC, USA, 6–13 November 2011; pp. 1784–1791.
4. Lu, X.; Lin, Z.; Jin, H.; Yang, J.; Wang, J.Z. Rating image aesthetics using deep learning. *IEEE Trans. Multimed.* **2015**, *17*, 2021–2034. [CrossRef]
5. Lu, X.; Lin, Z.; Shen, X.; Mech, R.; Wang, J.Z. Deep multi-patch aggregation network for image style, aesthetics, and quality estimation. In Proceedings of the IEEE International Conference on Computer Vision, Washington, DC, USA, 7–13 December 2015; pp. 990–998.
6. Mai, L.; Jin, H.; Liu, F. Composition-preserving deep photo aesthetics assessment. In Proceedings of the IEEE Conference on Computer Vision and Pattern Recognition, Las Vegas, NV, USA, 27–30 June 2016; pp. 497–506.
7. Talebi, H.; Milanfar, P. NIMA: Neural image assessment. *IEEE Trans. Image Process.* **2018**, *27*, 3998–4011. [CrossRef] [PubMed]
8. Hosu, V.; Goldlucke, B.; Saupe, D. Effective aesthetics prediction with multi-level spatially pooled features. In Proceedings of the IEEE/CVF Conference on Computer Vision and Pattern Recognition, Long Beach, CA, USA, 15–20 June 2019; pp. 9375–9383.
9. Kao, Y.; He, R.; Huang, K. Deep aesthetic quality assessment with semantic information. *IEEE Trans. Image Process.* **2017**, *26*, 1482–1495. [CrossRef] [PubMed]
10. Jia, G.; Li, P.; He, R. Theme aware aesthetic distribution prediction with full resolution photos. *arXiv* **2019**, arXiv:1908.01308.
11. Miao, H.; Zhang, Y.; Wang, D.; Feng, S. Multi-Output Learning Based on Multimodal GCN and Co-Attention for Image Aesthetics and Emotion Analysis. *Mathematics* **2021**, *9*, 1437. [CrossRef]
12. Li, L.; Lin, W.; Wang, X.; Yang, G.; Bahrami, K.; Kot, A.C. No-reference image blur assessment based on discrete orthogonal moments. *IEEE Trans. Cybern.* **2015**, *46*, 39–50. [CrossRef] [PubMed]
13. Gao, X.; Lu, W.; Tao, D.; Li, X. Image quality assessment based on multiscale geometric analysis. *IEEE Trans. Image Process.* **2009**, *18*, 1409–1423. [PubMed]
14. Zhang, W.; Ma, K.; Yan, J.; Deng, D.; Wang, Z. Blind image quality assessment using a deep bilinear convolutional neural network. *IEEE Trans. Circuits Syst. Video Technol.* **2018**, *30*, 36–47. [CrossRef]
15. Ma, S.; Liu, J.; Wen Chen, C. A-lamp: Adaptive layout-aware multi-patch deep convolutional neural network for photo aesthetic assessment. In Proceedings of the IEEE Conference on Computer Vision and Pattern Recognition, Honolulu, HI, USA, 21–26 July 2017; pp. 4535–4544.
16. Kong, S.; Shen, X.; Lin, Z.; Mech, R.; Fowlkes, C. Photo aesthetics ranking network with attributes and content adaptation. In *European Conference on Computer Vision*; Springer: Berlin/Heidelberg, Germany, 2016; pp. 662–679.
17. Zhang, H.; Cisse, M.; Dauphin, Y.N.; Lopez-Paz, D. mixup: Beyond empirical risk minimization. *arXiv* **2017**, arXiv:1710.09412.
18. Berthelot, D.; Carlini, N.; Goodfellow, I.; Papernot, N.; Oliver, A.; Raffel, C. Mixmatch: A holistic approach to semi-supervised learning. *arXiv* **2019**, arXiv:1905.02249.
19. Laine, S.; Aila, T. Temporal ensembling for semi-supervised learning. *arXiv* **2016**, arXiv:1610.02242.
20. Tarvainen, A.; Valpola, H. Mean teachers are better role models: Weight-averaged consistency targets improve semi-supervised deep learning results. *arXiv* **2017**, arXiv:1703.01780.
21. Iscen, A.; Tolias, G.; Avrithis, Y.; Chum, O. Label propagation for deep semi-supervised learning. In Proceedings of the IEEE/CVF Conference on Computer Vision and Pattern Recognition, Long Beach, CA, USA, 15–20 June 2019; pp. 5070–5079.
22. Vaswani, A.; Shazeer, N.; Parmar, N.; Uszkoreit, J.; Jones, L.; Gomez, A.N.; Kaiser, Ł.; Polosukhin, I. Attention is all you need. In Proceedings of the Annual Conference on Advances in Neural Information Processing Systems, Long Beach, CA, USA, 4–9 December 2017; pp. 5998–6008.

23. He, K.; Zhang, X.; Ren, S.; Sun, J. Deep residual learning for image recognition. In Proceedings of the IEEE Conference on Computer Vision and Pattern Recognition, Las Vegas, CA, USA, 27–30 June 2016; pp. 770–778.
24. Russakovsky, O.; Deng, J.; Su, H.; Krause, J.; Satheesh, S.; Ma, S.; Huang, Z.; Karpathy, A.; Khosla, A.; Bernstein, M.; et al. Imagenet large scale visual recognition challenge. *Int. J. Comput. Vis.* **2015**, *115*, 211–252. [CrossRef]
25. Liu, S.; Niles-Weed, J.; Razavian, N.; Fernandez-Granda, C. Early-learning regularization prevents memorization of noisy labels. *arXiv* **2020**, arXiv:2007.00151.
26. Iscen, A.; Tolias, G.; Avrithis, Y.; Furon, T.; Chum, O. Efficient diffusion on region manifolds: Recovering small objects with compact cnn representations. In Proceedings of the IEEE Conference on Computer Vision and Pattern Recognition, Honolulu, HI, USA, 21–26 July 2017; pp. 2077–2086.
27. Zhou, D.; Bousquet, O.; Lal, T.N.; Weston, J.; Schölkopf, B. Learning with local and global consistency. In Proceedings of the Advances in Neural Information Processing Systems, London, UK, 6–14 December 2004; pp. 321–328.
28. Murray, N.; Marchesotti, L.; Perronnin, F. AVA: A large-scale database for aesthetic visual analysis. In Proceedings of the 2012 IEEE Conference on Computer Vision and Pattern Recognition, Providence, RI, USA,16–21 June 2012; pp. 2408–2415.
29. Marcel, S.; Rodriguez, Y. Torchvision the machine-vision package of torch. In Proceedings of the 18th ACM international conference on Multimedia, Firenze, Italy, 25–29 October 2010; pp. 1485–1488.
30. Huang, G.; Liu, Z.; Van Der Maaten, L.; Weinberger, K.Q. Densely connected convolutional networks. In Proceedings of the IEEE Conference on Computer Vision and Pattern Recognition, Honolulu, HI, USA, 21–26 July 2017; pp. 4700–4708.
31. Liu, Z.; Lin, Y.; Cao, Y.; Hu, H.; Wei, Y.; Zhang, Z.; Lin, S.; Guo, B. Swin transformer: Hierarchical vision transformer using shifted windows. *arXiv* **2021**, arXiv:2103.14030.
32. Sheng, K.; Dong, W.; Ma, C.; Mei, X.; Huang, F.; Hu, B.G. Attention-based multi-patch aggregation for image aesthetic assessment. In Proceedings of the 26th ACM international conference on Multimedia, Seoul, Korea, 22–26 October 2018; pp. 879–886.
33. Ke, J.; Wang, Q.; Wang, Y.; Milanfar, P.; Yang, F. Musiq: Multi-scale image quality transformer. In Proceedings of the IEEE/CVF International Conference on Computer Vision, Montreal, QC, Canada, 10–17 October 2021; pp. 5148–5157.

mathematics

MDPI

Article

An Improved Soft-YOLOX for Garbage Quantity Identification

Junran Lin, Cuimei Yang, Yi Lu, Yuxing Cai, Hanjie Zhan and Zhen Zhang *

School of Computer Science and Engineering, Huizhou University, Huizhou 516007, China; hzurang@gmail.com (J.L.); meikoyoung@gmail.com (C.Y.); ly97264833@gmail.com (Y.L.); hzucyx@gmail.com (Y.C.); 1914080902532@stu.hzu.edu.cn or zhanhanjie123@gmail.com (H.Z.)
* Correspondence: zzsjbme@sjtu.edu.cn; Tel.: +86-182-1726-7715

Abstract: Urban waterlogging is mainly caused by garbage clogging the sewer manhole covers. If the amount of garbage at a sewer manhole cover can be detected, together with an early warning signal when the amount is large enough, it will be of great significance in preventing urban waterlogging from occurring. Based on the YOLOX algorithm, this paper accomplishes identifying manhole covers and garbage and building a flood control system that can automatically recognize and monitor the accumulation of garbage. This system can also display the statistical results and send early warning information. During garbage identification, it can lead to inaccurate counting and a missed detection if the garbage is occluded. To reduce the occurrence of missed detections as much as possible and improve the performance of detection models, Soft-YOLOX, a method using a new detection model for counting, was used as it can prevent the occurrence of missed detections by reducing the scores of adjacent detection frames reasonably. The Soft-YOLOX improves the accuracy of garbage counting. Compared with the traditional YOLOX, the mAP value of Soft-YOLOX for garbage identification increased from 89.72% to 91.89%.

Keywords: garbage quantity identification; YOLOX; NMS; Soft-NMS

MSC: 68T45

Citation: Lin, J.; Yang, C.; Lu, Y.; Cai, Y.; Zhan, H.; Zhang, Z. An Improved Soft-YOLOX for Garbage Quantity Identification. *Mathematics* **2022**, *10*, 2650. https://doi.org/10.3390/math10152650

Academic Editors: Jianping Gou, Weihua Ou, Shaoning Zeng and Lan Du

Received: 20 June 2022
Accepted: 25 July 2022
Published: 28 July 2022

1. Introduction

With the development of science and technology competing with the gradual improvement of urban construction levels, image recognition is increasingly being applied to urban informatization and digital construction. Among the recognition methods, the YOLOX detection framework is particularly famous. It is widely used in urban object detection [1], pedestrian detection [2], and other environments due to its advantage of fast response and high precision.

Modern cities are divided into regions and assigned sanitation workers for garbage cleaning using a grid management method [3] to improve the efficiency of urban management and sanitation. Workers only need to conduct regular inspections and cleanings of the place they are responsible for to ensure basic hygiene everywhere in the city. However, the regionalization management level is still insufficient. The fixed personnel allocation method cannot adjust the number of people according to the dynamic change in the amount of garbage in each area. There is a situation where the garbage accumulates in some areas, but there are insufficient sanitation workers there. However, sanitation workers in other places have few things to do. Relying on regular inspections by sanitation workers cannot keep up with the real-time changes in the amount of garbage. If the sanitation workers do not clean in time, accumulation of garbage will happen. Over time, garbage accumulation has become a hidden danger of flood disasters. The work of dealing with urban floods has remained a tricky problem for a long time.

With the help of target detection technology and the support of the urban public surveillance system, real-time monitoring is prevailing in the maintenance of various areas, roads, and sewer manholes. The monitoring capability of an urban flood control system highly depends on the in-time identification of a garbage's type and quantity and the collection of data. An efficient urban flood control system can help sanitation workers check and clean up the underlying danger areas such as sewer manhole covers. Committed to the goals of improving the city's ability to prevent floods and waterlogging while reducing the work intensity of sanitation workers, a method based on the YOLOX detection framework was designed to reflect the garbage accumulation in the flood control area. The working mechanisms of analyzing the monitoring images and identifying the type and quantity of garbage on the manhole cover have improved the efficiency and ability of urban sanitation cleaning, flood controlling, and waterlogging prevention. If the garbage is occluded by other garbage during detection, it causes inaccurate counting and missed detection. A well-designed detection scheme is sufficient to solve such problems. To further improve the detection accuracy, reduce the missed detection rate, and give early warning signals more precisely, our team proposed a new detection method, Soft-YOLOX, to solve the problems above.

2. Related Work

Garbage counting is a basic application scenario in target detection [4], and many machine learning methods have been proposed in this field to solve target detection and counting problems. Traditional machine learning cases include multi-vehicle counting algorithms based on the Haar feature principle [5], SVM based on HOG [6] and LBP [7] features, and others. These traditional machine learning target detection algorithms mainly rely on manual feature extraction. First, the features are extracted from the image, then a classifier is built to classify, and finally, the wanted target is obtained. However, most of these traditional target detection algorithms do not have high accuracy and good generalization ability.

With the continuous development of artificial intelligence, deep learning technology in image recognition [8] has been relatively mature [9]. For example, great achievements have been made in the fields of face recognition [10], medical image recognition [11], remote sensing image classification [12], ImageNet classification and recognition, traffic recognition, and character recognition. Deep learning can extract image features and achieve the function of image classification [13] and recognition after a large-scale training. Therefore, deep learning is a very effective and universal technology in the field of target detection. Currently, target detection algorithms using deep learning methods are mainly divided into three categories, and the difference is whether there is a region proposal in the algorithm. The first category is multi-stage algorithms, such as R-CNN [14] and SPPNet [15]. The second is two-stage algorithms such as Fast R-CNN [16], Faster R-CNN [17], Mask R-CNN [18], and Light-Head R-CNN [19]. The third is single-stage algorithms, including YOLOV1 [20], YOLOV2 [21], YOLOV3 [22], SSD [23], Retina U-Net [24], CenterNet [25], FSAF [26], FCOS [27], YOLOV4 [28], and YOLOX [29]. The detection performance of the multi-stage algorithm and the two-stage algorithm is outstanding, but the detection rate in practical applications is not as good as that of the single-stage algorithm. Although the single-stage algorithm has a fast recognition speed, the accuracy rate is not high, and there are still cases of missed detection when the target to be detected is occluded. Therefore, our goal is to improve the YOLOX model and devise a solution that can address the above problems.

In traditional YOLOX, non-maximum suppression (NMS) sets the score of adjacent detection frames (the number of adjacent detection frames containing similar targets is greater than or equal to 2) to 0, resulting in the final output missing some of the target objects. This mechanism leads to missed detection that reduces detection accuracy [30]. The Soft-NMS algorithm attenuates the scores of the above types of adjacent detection frames, rather than directly reducing their scores to 0. As long as the final score of the adjacent detection frame is greater than a certain threshold, the final output detection frame meets the expected result. The improved YOLOX is called Soft-YOLOX (using Soft-NMS instead of NMS in YOLOX). After Soft-NMS processing, the mAP value of YOLOX was 91.89%, which is 2.17% higher than that of the Original-NMS method. In the real-time detection case, the FPS reached 15.46. To further ensure the effectiveness of the improvement, we also used Soft-YOLOX to compare with other target detection algorithms, such as YOLOV4, Fast R-CNN, SSD, YOLOV5, etc. It can be seen from the mAP value in the comparison that Soft-YOLOX has greater detection performance and a lower missed detection rate. We make the following contributions:

1. We reveal why the traditional YOLOX model easily misses the target when the target is occluded, resulting in missed detection;
2. By improving YOLOX, we propose a new detection scheme (Soft-YOLOX). Experiments on the datasets show that the improved Soft-YOLOX can detect objects more accurately;
3. We compare Soft-YOLOX with other previous object detection algorithms, showing that Soft-YOLOX has better performance and is more favorable for deployment in real applications.

3. Methods

3.1. YOLOX and NMS Algorithms

The most significant thing in the YOLOX target detection algorithm is the YOLOX-CSPDarknet53 network structure. Figure 1 shows the network structure of YOLOX-CSPDarknet53. We split the YOLOX-CSPDarknet53 network structure into four parts: input, backbone network, neck, and prediction.

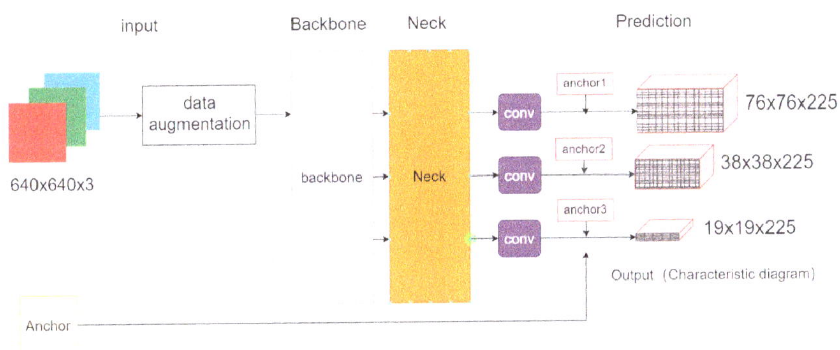

Figure 1. YOLOX-CSPDarknet53 network structure diagram.

1. Input: YOLOX adopts two data enhancement methods, Mosaic [31] and Mixup [32]. In the realization process of this system, we only used the Mosaic data enhancement. Mosaic achieves data enhancement by using four images to be randomly scaled, cropped, and spliced, further improving the detection effect of small targets;
2. Backbone network: YOLOX uses the CSPDarknet53 network, which has 53 layers in total of convolutional networks. The last of these is a fully connected layer. What is used in the CSPDarknet53 is the residual network, Residual, which consists of two parts. One is mainly a 1×1 and 3×3 convolution, and another is the non-processed residual side part;
3. Neck: In the neck is a construction of the FPN feature pyramid for enhanced feature extraction. The FPN can fuse feature layers of different shapes, which can help improve the performance of the model and the detection ability of small targets;
4. Prediction:
    a. The decoupled head is used in YOLOX. Compared with the previous target detection algorithm of the YOLO series, the decoupling head of YOLOX consists of two parts which are implemented separately and integrated at the final prediction;

b. The anchor-free detector does not use a priori box;
c. The SimOTA strategy, which can dynamically match positive samples to objects of different sizes, is adopted.

The original YOLOX model uses NMS to filter out the detection frames with the highest scores in a certain area belonging to the same category. However, only considering the detection frame and its IOU (Intersection over Union) in the calculation process, the elimination mechanism of NMS is very rigid, which easily leads to missed detection. Figure 2 shows the missed detection of a target object.

Figure 2. The situation of missed detection using NMS.

As can be seen from Figure 2, the sample is wrong. There are three leaves and a box on the drain cover. After NMS processing, there are cases of missed detection, such as the one leaf that is not detected in the figure. Obviously, the predicted results are not in line with the reality and cannot meet our expectation.

The critical step of accurate counting is meant to detect the targets successfully. When the target objects are blocked by each other, it is easy to cause missed detection. Therefore, we used Soft-NMS instead of the NMS method in the original YOLOX model as an improvement to solve this problem.

3.2. Principle of Soft-NMS Algorithm

First of all, from a mathematical point of view, the following principles explain the mechanism of NMS removing redundant frames:

$$\mathrm{score_i} = \begin{cases} 0, \mathrm{IOU(M, b_i)} \geq \text{threshold of IOU} \\ \mathrm{score_i}, \mathrm{IOU(M, b_i)} < \text{threshold of IOU} \end{cases} \tag{1}$$

The $\mathrm{score_i}$ is the score of the current detection frame. After multiple tests on the dataset of this experiment, we found that the best threshold for IOU is 0.5.

During the experiment, we further found that when the detection frame with a higher IOU is adjacent to the detection frame with the highest score in all current detection frames,

NMS reduces the score of this frame to 0, and then deletes it from the candidate frame set. Like the case in Figure 2, it is likely to cause missed detection. Soft-NMS can solve this problem very well, and its mechanism for removing redundant frames is as follows:

$$\text{score}_i = \text{score}_i\, e^{-\frac{\text{IOU}(M,b_i)^2}{\theta}} \quad (2)$$

It means that when Soft-NMS encounters a detection frame with a high IOU adjacent to the detection frame with the highest score, it does not directly set the score of the frame to 0. Compared with NMS, Soft-NMS adopts a penalty mechanism, which assigns the multiplication of the score of the current detection frame and the weight function as a penalty score and assigns it to the current detection frame. We used the Gaussian function as the weight function (θ is the parameter of the weight function; after many times of debugging, we defined the value of theta and set it to 0.1 according to the reference [30]):

$$e^{-\frac{\text{IOU}(M,b_i)^2}{\theta}} \quad (3)$$

The larger the overlapped area of the detection frame with the highest score, the smaller the score this detection frame obtains. Lastly, only those detection frames with scores greater than or equal to 0.5 were left in the frame set, which is the candidate. Thus, Soft-NMS can remove redundant detection frames to reduce the rate of missed detection with effect. The flow chart that describes the Soft-NMS method is shown in Figure 3.

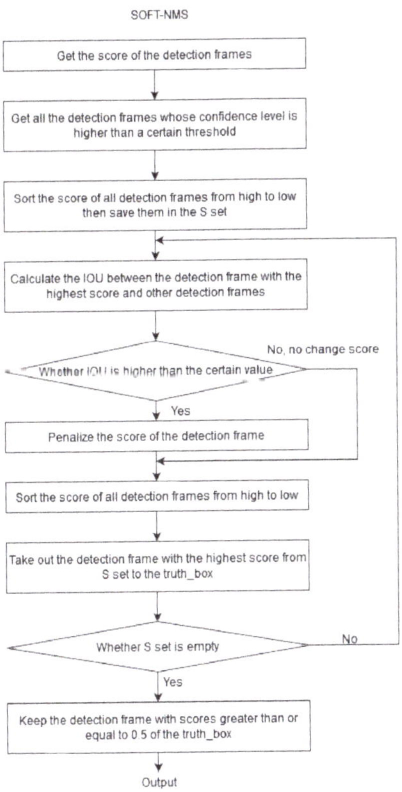

Figure 3. Flowchart of Soft-NMS.

The main idea of the Soft-NMS is as follows. At first, find all detection frames with a confidence higher than a threshold set manually from an image (no target object in the detection frame if below). Then, process the detection frames belonging to the same class. Finally, put all these detection frames into an established set S.

1. Sort all the detection frames in the set S according to their scores from high to low. The higher the score is, the higher the probability that the detection frame belongs to the category. Then, select the detection frame F with the highest score from the ordered set S;
2. Traverse each detection frame in set S, and then calculate the IOU of each detection frame and F. The Soft-NMS uses the weight function to calculate the weighted score of the current detection frame, and further assigns the weighted score to the currently traversed detection frame. The larger the overlapped area between the detection frame and F, the more serious the score attenuation. Finally, save F into the truth_box;
3. Go back to step 1 until the set S is empty. Finally, in truth_box, select detection frames with a score greater than or equal to 0.5 as the output of the target object.

After using the Soft-NMS method to process Figure 2, the detection result can be seen in Figure 4.

Figure 4. No missed detection after using Soft-NMS.

As can be seen from Figure 4, the correct sample was obtained. There are three leaves and a box on the drain cover. After Soft-NMS processing, the missed detection in Figure 2 disappeared. All objects in the image can be detected correctly. Obviously, the predicted results are in accordance with the reality and can meet our expectations.

3.3. System Framework

Figure 5 shows the application hierarchy of the system built on the problems studied in this paper.

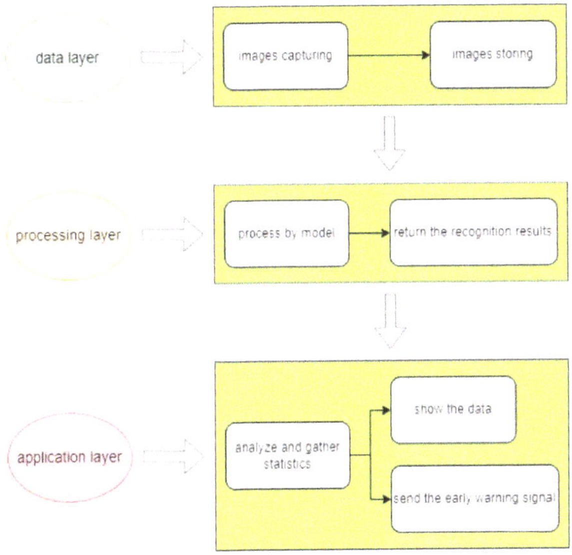

Figure 5. Flowchart of the application deployed by YOLOX.

1. Data layer: The area of sewer manhole covers is photographed and collected by road surveillance cameras. The camera is responsible for collecting image data, storing the image data in the system, and transmitting the image to the model in real time;
2. Processing layer: The recognition layer is the image processing layer of the system. It identifies manhole covers and garbage on them by the trained network model and returns the identification results to the system;
3. Application layer: The system makes real-time statistics and analysis according to the identification results of the model. Apart from this, the system also displays the results. If the amount of the garbage on the cover reaches the threshold, the system sends a corresponding early warning signal to the relevant staff.

4. Experimental Datasets and Evaluation Metrics

The datasets in this paper came from a research group that used a camera to simulate a road surveillance camera in a specific road scene, acquiring the situation of garbage near the sewer manhole covers at different periods and under various weather conditions at a roughly fixed angle. The advantage of doing this is that the trained model can make predictions for different scenarios and has better adaptability. Each video obtained ranged from more than ten seconds to several minutes, and the resolution of all videos was 1365×1024. Lastly, videos were split into frames, which were divided into two parts. Both parts contain the above datasets from different periods and under various circumstances. One of the parts was used as training sets and validating sets for training and validation of convolutional networks. The other part was used as a test for the trained model.

The annotation of the dataset was in the Pascal VOC format, and the size of each image was 1365×1024. For the YOLOX model, the input image was 640×640, thus all images could be preprocessed. There were 1800 images in the processed dataset with different types of garbage, drainage covers, and road information under different periods, weather, and road sections. To strengthen the effectiveness of the data in training, the research team also framed the data at different frame rates to reduce the workload of labeling and improve the learning efficiency of the model. Finally, we divided the dataset into the training set, verification set, and test set in the ratio of 7:2:1.

In the model evaluating the works of this paper, we had Precision, Recall, and mAP values as the evaluation indexes to evaluate the model [33]. The calculation of Precision and Recall values are expressed by Formula (4) and Formula (5), respectively.

$$\text{Precision} = \frac{\text{TP}}{\text{TP} + \text{FP}} \tag{4}$$

$$\text{Recall} = \frac{\text{TP}}{\text{TP} + \text{FN}} \tag{5}$$

In the above two equations, TP means the prediction result is correctly classified as a positive sample, FP means the result is incorrectly classified as a positive sample, and FN means the result is incorrectly classified as a negative sample.

The dataset used in the evaluation includes the environment of daytime and rainy days, but excludes nighttime. In Figure 6, the mAP values processed by NMS and Soft-NMS can be seen.

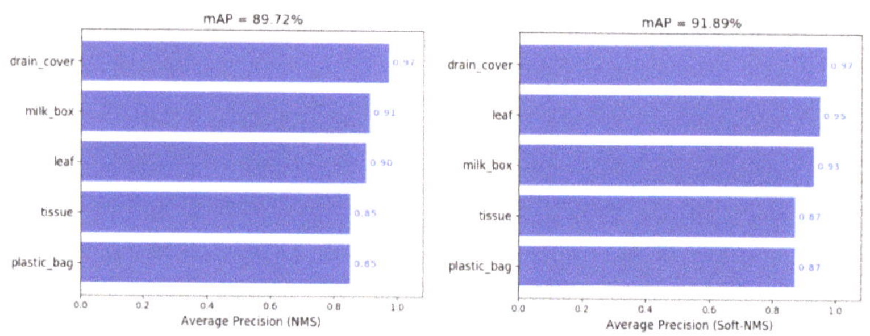

Figure 6. The mAP values processed by NMS and Soft-NMS.

AP refers to the combination of Precision and Recall; Precision shows the prediction ability of the hit target passing the threshold in all prediction results, whereas Recall shows the ability to cover the real target in the test set. By combining the two, we can better evaluate our model. The mAP is the average of the average accuracy of each category, that is, the average AP of each category. The higher the mAP, the better the prediction ability of the model.

5. Results

5.1. Principle of Soft-NMS Algorithm

For YOLOX and Soft-YOLOX, the same prediction parameters and datasets were used to verify the effectiveness of the improvement we made. The difference is that YOLOX uses NMS, whereas Soft-YOLOX uses Soft-NMS. In the verification process, the detection effect and performance of the model are reflected by the evaluation metrics.

The mAP value of the YOLOX model processed by NMS is 89.72%, Precision is 91.54%, and Recall is 89.53%. The prediction results of the Soft-YOLOX model processed by Soft-NMS are improved, in which the mAP value is 91.89%, Precision is 92.93%, and Recall is 88.42%. The comparison results between the YOLOX model before and after improvement are shown in Table 1.

Table 1. The comparison results.

Model	mAP/%	Precision/%	Recall/%
Original YOLOX	89.72	91.54	89.53
Soft YOLOX	91.89	92.93	88.42

Since Recall and Precision cannot comprehensively evaluate the effect of the algorithm, the mAP index was selected for analysis. As can be seen from the results in Table 1, the mAP value and Precision value are higher than those of the original model, whereas Recall is lower. Soft-NMS removes redundant detection frames through the penalty mechanism of the weight function, thus reducing the missed detection rate. We found that the improvement of Soft-NMS was effective from the results.

5.2. Comparison with State-of-the-Art Methods

The experiments included the following comparison methods: Fast R-CNN [16], target detection algorithm based on YOLOV4 (abbreviated as YOLOV4 [34]), SSD [23], and target detection algorithm based on YOLOV5 (abbreviated as YOLOV5 [35]). All methods used the same evaluation index. It is not difficult to see that the Soft-YOLOX model improved performance compared with other algorithms. The detection results of each method on our dataset are shown in Table 2.

Table 2. Experimental results of different algorithms.

Model	mAP/%
YOLOV4	88.54
Fast R-CNN	89.34
SSD	85.52
YOLOV5	89.72
Soft YOLOX	91.89

5.3. Actual Application of the System

The left side of Figure 7 shows that the system can detect the specific types and quantities of garbage in a complex garbage environment, which is convenient and allows for the system to further send early warning signals. The right side of Figure 7 shows the real-time prediction results of the system on rainy days, in which the graphics card model used for reasoning was the RTX 1060 Ti, and the FPS (frames per second) was 15.46. The above results effectively demonstrate the feasibility of the project, and support our team in carrying out further research and development.

Figure 7. The application of the system.

Currently, there are many cases about embedded deployment in YOLO series of algorithms, such as Fast YOLO [36], Efficient YOLO [37], YOLO nano [38], and so on. The YOLOX algorithm in this paper can be implemented by exporting the ONNX model for embedded deployment, or by pruning and quantization to build the lightweight model of YOLO to, finally, achieve embedded deployment.

6. Conclusions

Compared with other target detection models, the new detection model and counting method of Soft-YOLOX proposed in this paper has better detection performance and robustness, and a lower missed detection rate. Garbage can be identified and counted accurately in the case of occlusion, which effectively avoids the phenomenon of missed detection.

With the help of public surveillance cameras on urban roads, the system collects real-time images of sanitary conditions in the areas with urban sewer manhole covers. After identifying, analyzing, and processing data by the Soft-YOLOX model, the client is shown the returned results. With future development of urban public facilities, the number of urban surveillance cameras and the area covered by cameras will continue to increase. A large amount of available image data can improve the accuracy of the model and the availability of the system. The enhancement of identification accuracy and processing capacity will also effectively help urban sanitation construction and improve urban sanitation levels [39].

This paper proposed a new detection model called Soft-YOLOX based on YOLOX. By using Soft-NMS, the number of garbage can be accurately counted and the performance close to the actual application requirements obtained. The original YOLOX model is based on the NMS algorithm to remove redundant detection frames, whereas the YOLOX model proposed in this paper penalizes the score of detection frames based on the Soft-NMS algorithm. After comparative analysis, Soft-YOLOX had higher accuracy and lower missed detection in garbage detection applications. The mAP value of Soft-YOLOX was 91.89%, which is 2.17% higher than the YOLOX model. Therefore, Soft-YOLOX is more suitable for accumulated garbage quantity detection.

Author Contributions: Conceptualization, Z.Z. and J.L.; data curation, Y.L. and J.L.; validation, J.L., Y.L. and C.Y.; formal analysis, J.L., C.Y., Y.L., H.Z., Y.C. and Z.Z; funding acquisition, Z.Z. and J.L.; investigation, J.L.; supervision, Z.Z. All authors have read and agreed to the published version of the manuscript.

Funding: This research was funded by [the Young Innovative Talents Project of colleges and universities in Guangdong Province] grant number [2021KQNCX092]; [Doctoral program of Huizhou University] grant number [2020JB028]; [Outstanding Youth Cultivation Project of Huizhou University] grant number [HZU202009]; [Innovation Training Program for Chinese College Students] grant number [S202110577044]; [Special Funds for the Cultivation of Guangdong College Students' Scientific and Technological Innovation. ("Climbing Program" Special Funds)] grant number [No. pdjh2022b0494].

Institutional Review Board Statement: Not applicable.

Informed Consent Statement: Not applicable.

Data Availability Statement: The dataset used in this paper is made by our team members, and some parts of the dataset can be found at the following link: [https://github.com/Hzurang/Dataset]. (accessed on 1 July 2022).

Conflicts of Interest: The authors declare no conflict of interest.

References

1. Jin, H.; Wu, Y.; Xu, G.; Wu, Z. Research on an Urban Low-Altitude Target Detection Method Based on Image Classification. *Electronics* **2022**, *11*, 657. [CrossRef]
2. Li, F.; Li, X.; Liu, Q.; Li, Z. Occlusion Handling and Multi-scale Pedestrian Detection Based on Deep Learning: A Review. *IEEE Access* **2022**, *10*, 19937–19957. [CrossRef]

3. Chen, Y.; Zhou, H.; Zhang, H.; Du, G.; Zhou, J. Urban flood risk warning under rapid urbanization. *Environ. Res.* **2015**, *139*, 3–10. [CrossRef] [PubMed]
4. Mikami, K.; Chen, Y.; Nakazawa, J. Deepcounter: Using deep learning to count garbage bags. In Proceedings of the 2018 IEEE 24th International Conference on Embedded and Real-Time Computing Systems and Applications (RTCSA), Hokkaido, Japan, 28–31 August 2018; pp. 1–10.
5. Wei, Y.; Tian, Q.; Guo, J.; Huang, W.; Cao, J. Multi-vehicle detection algorithm through combining Harr and HOG features. *Math. Comput. Simul.* **2019**, *155*, 130–145. [CrossRef]
6. Tan, G.X.; Sun, C.M.; Wang, J.H. Design of video vehicle detection system based on HOG features and SVM. *J. Guangxi Univ. Sci. Technol.* **2021**, *32*, 19–23.
7. Zhai, J.; Zhou, X.; Wang, C. A moving target detection algorithm based on combination of GMM and LBP texture pattern. In Proceedings of the 2016 IEEE Chinese Guidance, Navigation and Control Conference (CGNCC), Nanjing, China, 12–14 August 2016; pp. 1057–1060.
8. Pak, M.; Kim, S. A review of deep learning in image recognition. In Proceedings of the 2017 4th International Conference on Computer Applications and Information Processing Technology (CAIPT), Bali, Indonesia, 8–10 August 2017; pp. 1–3.
9. Gou, J.; Yuan, X.; Du, L.; Xia, S.; Yi, Z. Hierarchical Graph Augmented Deep Collaborative Dictionary Learning for Classification. In Proceedings of the IEEE Transactions on Intelligent Transportation Systems, Macau, China, 8–12 October 2022.
10. Li, L.; Mu, X.; Li, S.; Peng, H. A review of face recognition technology. *IEEE Access* **2020**, *8*, 139110–139120. [CrossRef]
11. Shen, D.; Wu, G.; Suk, H.I. Deep learning in medical image analysis. *Annu. Rev. Biomed. Eng.* **2017**, *19*, 221–248. [CrossRef] [PubMed]
12. Zhang, L.; Xia, G.-S.; Wu, T.; Lin, L.; Tai, X.-C. Deep learning for remote sensing image understanding. *J. Sens.* **2016**, *2016*, 7954154. [CrossRef]
13. Gou, J.; Sun, L.; Du, L.; Ma, H.; Xiong, T.; Ou, W.; Zhan, Y. A representation coefficient-based k-nearest centroid neighbor classifier. *Expert Syst. Appl.* **2022**, *194*, 116529. [CrossRef]
14. Chen, C.; Liu, M.Y.; Tuzel, O. *R-CNN for Small Object Detection. Asian Conference on Computer Vision*; Springer: Cham, Switzerland, 2016; pp. 214–230.
15. He, K.; Zhang, X.; Ren, S.; Sun, J. Spatial pyramid pooling in deep convolutional networks for visual recognition. *IEEE Trans. Pattern Anal. Mach. Intell.* **2015**, *37*, 1904–1916. [CrossRef] [PubMed]
16. Li, J.; Liang, X.; Shen, S.; Xu, T.; Feng, J.; Yan, S. Scale-aware fast R-CNN for pedestrian detection. *IEEE Trans. Multimed.* **2017**, *20*, 985–996. [CrossRef]
17. Ren, S.; He, K.; Girshick, R.; Sun, J. Faster R-CNN: Towards real-time object detection with region proposal networks. *IEEE Trans. Pattern Anal. Mach. Intell.* **2016**, *39*, 1137–1149. [CrossRef] [PubMed]
18. He, K.; Gkioxari, G.; Dollár, P. Mask r-cnn. In Proceedings of the IEEE International Conference on Computer Vision, Venice, Italy, 22–29 October 2017; pp. 2961–2969.
19. Li, Z.; Peng, C.; Yu, G. Light-head r-cnn: In defense of two-stage object detector. *arXiv* **2017**, arXiv:1711.07264.
20. Redmon, J.; Divvala, S.; Girshick, R. You only look once: Unified, real-time object detection. In Proceedings of the IEEE Conference on Computer Vision and Pattern Recognition, Las Vegas, NV, USA, 26 June–1 July 2016; pp. 779–788.
21. Redmon, J.; Farhadi, A. YOLO9000: Better, faster, stronger. In Proceedings of the IEEE Conference on Computer Vision and Pattern Recognition, Honolulu, HI, USA, 21–26 July 2017; pp. 7263–7271.
22. Redmon, J.; Farhadi, A. Yolov3: An incremental improvement. *arXiv* **2018**, arXiv:1804.02767.
23. Liu, W.; Anguelov, D.; Erhan, D. *Ssd: Single Shot Multibox Detector. European Conference on Computer Vision*; Springer: Cham, Switzerland, 2016; pp. 21–37.
24. Jaeger, P.F.; Kohl, S.A.A.; Bickelhaupt, S.; Isensee, F.; Kuder, T.A.; Schlemmer, H.-P.; Maier-Hein, K.H. Retina U-Net: Embarrassingly simple exploitation of segmentation supervision for medical object detection. In Proceedings of the Machine Learning for Health Workshop, PMLR, Vancouver, BC, Canada, 13 December 2019; pp. 171–183.
25. Duan, K.; Bai, S.; Xie, L. Centernet: Keypoint triplets for object detection. In Proceedings of the IEEE/CVF International Conference on Computer Vision, Seoul, Korea, 27 October–2 November 2019; pp. 6569–6578.
26. Zhu, C.; He, Y.; Savvides, M. Feature selective anchor-free module for single-shot object detection. In Proceedings of the IEEE/CVF Conference on Computer Vision and Pattern Recognition, Long Beach, CA, USA, 16–17 June 2019; pp. 840–849.
27. Tian, Z.; Shen, C.; Chen, H. Fcos: Fully convolutional one-stage object detection. In Proceedings of the IEEE/CVF International Conference on Computer Vision, Seoul, Korea, 27 October–2 November 2019; pp. 9627–9636.
28. Bochkovskiy, A.; Wang, C.Y.; Liao, H.Y.M. Yolov4: Optimal speed and accuracy of object detection. *arXiv* **2020**, arXiv:2004.10934.
29. Ge, Z.; Liu, S.; Wang, F. Yolox: Exceeding yolo series in 2021. *arXiv* **2021**, arXiv:2107.08430.
30. Bodla, N.; Singh, B.; Chellappa, R.; Davis, L.S. Soft-NMS—Improving object detection with one line of code. In Proceedings of the IEEE International Conference on Computer Vision, Venice, Italy, 22–29 October 2017; pp. 5561–5569.
31. Zeng, G.; Yu, W.; Wang, R. Research on Mosaic Image Data Enhancement for Overlapping Ship Targets. *arXiv* **2021**, arXiv:2105.05090.
32. Fu, Y.; Wang, H.; Xu, K. Mixup based privacy preserving mixed collaboration learning. In Proceedings of the 2019 IEEE International Conference on Service-Oriented System Engineering (SOSE), San Francisco, CA, USA, 4–9 April 2019; pp. 275–2755.

33. Zhang, M.; Wang, C.; Yang, J. Research on Engineering Vehicle Target Detection in Aerial Photography Environment based on YOLOX. In Proceedings of the 2021 14th International Symposium on Computational Intelligence and Design (ISCID), Hangzhou, China, 11–12 December 2021; pp. 254–256.
34. Zhang, Z.; Xia, S.; Cai, Y. A Soft-YoloV4 for High-Performance Head Detection and Counting. *Mathematics* **2021**, *9*, 3096. [CrossRef]
35. Zhou, F.; Zhao, H.; Nie, Z. Safety helmet detection based on YOLOv5. In Proceedings of the 2021 IEEE International Conference on Power Electronics, Computer Applications (ICPECA), Shenyang, China, 22–24 January 2021; pp. 6–11.
36. Shaifee, M.J.; Chywl, B.; Li, F.; Wong, A. Fast YOLO: A fast you only look once system for real-time embedded object detection in video. *arXiv* **2017**, arXiv:1709.05943. [CrossRef]
37. Wang, Z.; Zhang, J.; Zhao, Z. Efficient yolo: A lightweight model for embedded deep learning object detection. In Proceedings of the 2020 IEEE International Conference on Multimedia & Expo Workshops (ICMEW), London, UK, 6–10 July 2020; pp. 1–6.
38. Wong, A.; Famuori, M.; Shafiee, M.J. Yolo nano: A highly compact you only look once convolutional neural network for object detection. In Proceedings of the 2019 Fifth Workshop on Energy Efficient Machine Learning and Cognitive Computing-NeurIPS Edition (EMC2-NIPS), Vancouver, BC, Canada, 13 December 2019; pp. 22–25.
39. Wang, Y.; Zhang, X. Autonomous garbage detection for intelligent urban management. MATEC Web of Conferences. *EDP Sci.* **2018**, *232*, 01056.

mathematics

Article

Stability of Switched Systems with Time-Varying Delays under State-Dependent Switching

Chao Liu *,† and Xiaoyang Liu †

School of Computer Science and Engineering, Chongqing University of Technology, Chongqing 400054, China; lxy3103@cqut.edu.cn
* Correspondence: 20140058@cqut.edu.cn or xiuwenzheng2000@163.com
† These authors contributed equally to this work.

Abstract: This paper studies the stability of linear switched systems with time-varying delays and all unstable subsystems. According to the largest region function strategy, the state-dependent switching rule is designed. By bringing in integral inequality and multiple Lyapunov-Krasovskii functionals, the stability results of delayed switched systems with or without sliding motions under the designed state-dependent switching rule are derived for different assumptions on time delay. Several numerical examples are employed to show the effectiveness and superiority of the proposed results.

Keywords: stability; switched system; state-dependent switching; time delay

MSC: 93D20; 93C10

Citation: Liu, C.; Liu, X. Stability of Switched Systems with Time-Varying Delays under State-Dependent Switching. *Mathematics* **2022**, *10*, 2722. https://doi.org/10.3390/math10152722

Academic Editors: Jianping Gou, Weihua Ou, Shaoning Zeng, Lan Du and Asier Ibeas

Received: 22 June 2022
Accepted: 27 July 2022
Published: 1 August 2022

1. Introduction

The dynamics of switched systems are affected by both subsystems and switching rules. For example, Decarlo R A has indicated that some appropriate switching rules can make switched systems unstable (or asymptotically stable) even if all subsystems are asymptotically stable (or unstable) [1]. Therefore, we must concentrate on both subsystems and switching rules to derive the stability results. In recent years, the stability issue of switched systems with unstable subsystems has been extensively investigated. For instance, in [2–7] the researchers have derived some stability results for switched systems with both stable and unstable subsystems. The main strategy of some literature is to ensure that the dwell time of stable subsystems is sufficiently large to compensate for the state divergence caused by unstable subsystems and switching behaviors. Obviously, if there is no stable subsystem to absorb the state divergence, these results proposed in [2–7] are disabled.

Because of the absence of stable subsystems, the stability analysis of switched systems with all unstable subsystems is more complicated. How to design appropriate switching rules to stabilize switched systems with all unstable subsystems has become an interesting and challenging problem. Ordinarily, switching rules can be designed by two strategies: time-dependent switching and state-dependent switching. The main idea of the first one is to use the stabilization of switching behaviors to stabilize switched systems and the designed switching rules usually have both upper and lower bounds. In [8–12], the time-dependent switching rules are designed to stabilize switched systems with or without time delay by using discretized Lyapunov function approach or bound maximum average dwell time. The time-dependent switching strategy requires that switching behaviors have a good characteristic of stabilization. Therefore, when all switching behaviors do not contain stabilization characteristics, the time-dependent switching strategy is invalid.

In many instances, time-dependent switching rules that can stabilize switched systems are hard to design or even non-existent, which signifies that the state-dependent switching strategy becomes the unique way to stabilize switched systems. Up to now, the state-dependent switching rules can be designed by two methods. The first one is based on the regional partition of state space. Its basic idea can be summarized as follows: (a) divide the state space into different switching regions; (b) determine the index of activated subsystems for each switching region; (c) derive the stability conditions for switched systems under the designed switching rule. Under the assumption that there exists a Hurwitz convex combination of system matrices, the state-dependent switching rules have been designed via the regional partition of state space and some significant stability results have been deduced by common Lyapunov function (functional) in [13–19]. Remarkably, this assumption is a severe prerequisite. In order to relax this assumption, by employing some free matrices, a more flexible Hurwitz convex combination is presented in [20]. In [21] the regional partition of state space is implemented directly by the negative definite of the time-derivative of common Lyapunov functional. To ensure the strict completeness of regional partition, one additional condition is introduced. Based on newly introduced symmetric matrices, Pettersson S has defined switching rules via the largest region function strategy and established the stability results by multiple Lyapunov functionals [22,23]. Some restrictions are also employed to guarantee the decrease of Lyapunov functional when switching events occur. However, the largest region function strategy has not been generalized to switched systems with time delay. The second one is that the switching rules are defined in terms of the set-valued function. One typical state-dependent switching rule is given by $\sigma(t) = \arg\min\{x^T(t)P_1x(t), \cdots, x^T(t)P_mx(t)\}$, where P_i is a symmetric positive determined matrix, m is number of subsystems. In [24–27], the authors have designed the switching rules by the set-valued function and given the stability conditions with the Lyapunov-Metzler inequalities. Although there are numerous results for state-dependent switching, it is noteworthy that this issue still needs to be further studied. Designing new state-dependent switching rules and getting lower conservative stability results is still our research motivation.

Up to now, the literatures on the stability of delayed switched systems with state-dependent switching rules include [15–21,27]. However, the assumption that there exists a Hurwitz convex combination of system matrices is serious, which affects the effectiveness of stability results presented in [15–20]. The additional condition on strict completeness of regional partition makes it difficult to get appropriate switching regions [21]. Additionally, the results presented in [27] are only available for switched systems with constant delay. Therefore, the stability of switched systems with time-varying delays under state-dependent switching rules still deserves further attention. The main objective of this paper is to derive some new stability results for this problem. Based on the largest region function strategy, we design a state-dependent switching rule. By using integral inequality and the Leibniz-Newton formula, novel asymptotic stability results under different assumptions on time delay are presented in the form of bilinear matrix inequalities (BMIs). The effectiveness of the proposed results is shown via several numerical examples.

Notations: matrix $A > 0(<0)$ yields that A is symmetric positive(negative) matrix, R^n denotes the $n-$dimension Euclidean space, $arg \max S$ is defined as the index of maximum element of order set S.

2. Preliminaries

This paper considers the following switched systems with time-varying delay

$$\begin{cases} \dot{x}(t) = A_{\sigma(x(t))}x(t) + B_{\sigma(x(t))}x(t-d(t)), t > 0, \\ x(s) = \phi(s), s \in [-d, 0], \end{cases} \tag{1}$$

where $x(t) \in R^n$ is the state vector, $\sigma(x(t)) \in M = \{1, 2, \cdots, m\}$ is the switching rule, $A_p, B_p \in R^{n\times n}$, $p \in M$, are known matrices, $d(t)$ is the time-varying delay, $\phi(s)$ is a piecewise continuous function. If $\sigma(t) = p$, we say that the p-th subsystem $\dot{x}(t) = A_px(t) + B_px(t-d(t))$ is activated.

Remark 1. *$\sigma(x(t))$ is a state-dependent switching rule which is generated by switching device [13]. Similar to [13–23], in this paper we also assume that there is no delay produced in switching device.*

That is to say, the switching rule $\sigma(x(t))$ is one dependent on the current state but irrelevant to the delayed state.

We would like to design a state-dependent switching rule $\sigma(t)$ such that switched system (1) is globally asymptotically stable. We employ the state-dependent switching strategy introduced in [22,23], which is based on the appropriate choice of symmetric matrices Q_p, $p \in M$. Define the following regions

$$\Omega_p = \Big\{x \in R^n | x^T Q_p x \geq 0\Big\}, p \in M,$$
$$\Omega_{pq} = \Big\{x \in R^n | x^T Q_q x = x^T Q_p x \geq 0\Big\}, p, q \in M, p \neq q.$$

We hope that the p-th subsystem is activated if $x(t) \in \Omega_p$ and switching events occur at the region Ω_{pq}. The following properties should be satisfied to ensure that the switched system (1) is well-defined [22],

(a) Covering property: $\bigcup_{p \in M} \Omega_p = R^n$,
(b) Switching property: $\Omega_{pq} \subseteq \Omega_p \bigcap \Omega_q$.

The covering property points out that there is at least one activated subsystem on an arbitrary region of the state space. The switching property implies that the switch from subsystem p to q occurs only if regions Ω_p and Ω_q are adjacent. According to [22,23], the covering property is satisfied, if there exists $\theta_p > 0$, $p \in M$, such that for any $x \in R^n$,

$$\sum_{p \in M} \theta_p x^T Q_p x \geq 0. \tag{2}$$

The switching rule can be defined as the following largest region function strategy [22,23]

$$\sigma(x(t)) = arg \max \Big\{x^T(t) Q_1 x(t), \cdots, x^T(t) Q_m x(t)\Big\}. \tag{3}$$

As can be seen from [22] we know that if (2) is true and the switching rule (3) is used, the switching property is also satisfied.

The main purpose of this work is to get the stability results under one of the following assumptions.

Assumption 1. *The time delay and its time-derivative are bounded. Namely, there exist nonnegative constants $d, \bar{d}$ and constant $\tilde{d}$ such that*

$$0 \leq d(t) \leq d, \tilde{d} \leq \dot{d}(t) \leq \bar{d}. \tag{4}$$

Assumption 2. *The time delay is bounded. Namely, there exists a nonnegative constant d such that*

$$0 \leq d(t) \leq d. \tag{5}$$

The following lemma is the core of this research.

Lemma 1 ([28]). *If matrix $M > 0$ and function $x : [a, b] \to R^n$ is differentiable, then the following inequality is satisfied*

$$(b-a) \int_a^b \dot{x}^T(s) M \dot{x}(s) ds \geq \beta^T diag(M, 3M, 5M) \beta,$$

where $\beta = (\beta_1^T, \beta_2^T, \beta_3^T)^T$, $\beta_1 = x(b) - x(a)$, $\beta_2 = x(b) + x(a) - \frac{2}{b-a} \int_a^b x(s) ds$, $\beta_3 = x(b) - x(a) + \frac{6}{b-a} \int_a^b x(s) ds - \frac{12}{(b-a)^2} \int_a^b \int_\theta^b x(s) ds d\theta$.

3. Main Results

This section presents the stability criteria for the switched system (1) under the state-dependent switching rule (3). Owing to the Leibniz-Newton formula, we have the following equation

$$x(t) - x(t - d(t)) = \int_{t-d(t)}^{t} \dot{x}(s)ds. \tag{6}$$

Some notations are given as follows

$$\begin{aligned} v_1 =& \frac{2}{d - d(t)} \int_{t-d(t)}^{t} x(s)ds, v_2 = \frac{12}{(d-d(t))^2} \int_{t-d(t)}^{t} \int_{\theta}^{t} x(s)dsd\theta, \\ \eta(t) =& \Big(x^T(t), x^T(t-d(t)), x^T(t-d), \dot{x}^T(t-d(t)), \dot{x}^T(t-d), v_1^T, v_2^T\Big)^T. \end{aligned}$$

Theorem 1. *Under Assumption 1, assume that for any $p \in M$, there exist $n \times n$ matrices $P_p > 0$, $R_i > 0, S_i > 0, U > 0$, $(i = 1,2)$, $Q_p = Q_p^T$, positive constants μ_p, θ_p, constants $\eta_{p,q}$, $q \in M$, $q \neq p$, such that*

$$\begin{pmatrix} \Lambda_l^p + \mu_p e_1^T Q_p e_1 & \sqrt{d} e_1^T P_p B_p \\ \sqrt{d} B_p^T P_p e_1 & -U \end{pmatrix} < 0, l = 1,2, \tag{7}$$

$$P_p = P_q + \eta_{p,q}(Q_q - Q_p), q \in M, q \neq p, \tag{8}$$

$$\sum_{j \in M} \theta_j Q_j \geq 0, \tag{9}$$

where

$$\begin{aligned} \Lambda_1^p =& \Phi_1^p + \Phi_2 + \Phi_3^p + \Phi_4^p + (1-\bar{d})(\Psi_2 + \Psi_3) - \frac{1}{d}\Xi_4, \Lambda_2^p = \Phi_1^p + \Phi_2 + \Phi_3^p + \Phi_4^p + \\ & (1-\tilde{d})(\Psi_2 + \Psi_3) - \frac{1}{d}\Xi_4, \Phi_1^p = e_1^T\Big((A_p + B_p)^T P_p + P_p(A_p + B_p)\Big)e_1, \\ \Phi_2 =& e_1^T R_1 e_1 - e_3^T R_2 e_3, \Phi_3^p = (A_p e_1 + B_p e_2)^T S_1 (A_p e_1 + B_p e_2) - e_5^T S_2 e_5, \\ \Phi_4^p =& d(A_p e_1 + B_p e_2)^T U (A_p e_1 + B_p e_2), \Psi_2 = e_2^T(R_2 - R_1)e_2, \Psi_3 = e_4^T(S_2 - S_1)e_4, \\ \Xi_4 =& (e_2 - e_3)^T U (e_2 - e_3) + 3(e_2 + e_3 - e_6)^T U (e_2 + e_3 - e_6) + 5(e_2 - e_3 + 3e_6 - e_7)^T U \times \\ & (e_2 - e_3 + 3e_6 - e_7), e_i = \Big(0_{n\times(i-1)n}, I, 0_{n\times(7-i)n}\Big), i = 1, 2, \cdots, 7. \end{aligned}$$

Then, the switched system (1) is globally asymptotically stable under the state-dependent switching rule (3), if there is no sliding motion or there exist sliding motions on the switching surface Ω_{pq} with $\eta_{p,q} > 0$.

Proof. Condition (9) implies that (2) is true, which indicates that the covering property holds. Therefore, under the switching rule (3), the switched system (1) is well-defined.

Now we prove that the switched system (1) is globally asymptotically stable. Similar to [29,30], for each subsystem p, we choose the Lyapunov-Krasovskii functional as follows

$$V_p(t) = V_{p1}(t) + \sum_{i=2}^{4} V_i(t), \tag{10}$$

where

$$V_{p1}(t) = x^T(t)P_p x(t), V_2(t) = \int_{t-d(t)}^{t} x^T(s)R_1 x(s)ds + \int_{t-d}^{t-d(t)} x^T(s)R_2 x(s)ds,$$

$$V_3(t) = \int_{t-d(t)}^{t} \dot{x}(s)S_1\dot{x}(s)ds + \int_{t-d}^{t-d(t)} \dot{x}^T(s)S_2\dot{x}(s)ds, V_4(t) = \int_{-d}^{0}\int_{t+\theta}^{t} \dot{x}(s)U\dot{x}(s)dsd\theta.$$

In each region Ω_p, the time derivate of $V_{p1}(t)$, $V_i(t)$, $i = 2,3,4$, along the trajectory of the subsystem p are given as follows

$$\begin{aligned}
&\dot{V}_{p1}(t)\\
=&x^T(t)\Big((A_p+B_p)^TP_p+P_p(A_p+B_p)\Big)x(t)-\int_{t-d(t)}^{t}\Big(\dot{x}^T(s)B_p^TP_px(t)+x^T(t)P_pB_p\dot{x}(s)\Big)ds\\
\leq&x^T(t)\Big((A_p+B_p)^TP_p+P_p(A_p+B_p)+d(t)P_pB_pU^{-1}B_p^TP_p\Big)x(t)+\int_{t-d(t)}^{t}\dot{x}^T(s)U\dot{x}(s)ds \qquad (11)\\
=&\eta^T(t)\Big(\Phi_1^p+d(t)\Theta_1^p\Big)\eta^T(t)+\int_{t-d(t)}^{t}\dot{x}^T(s)U\dot{x}(s)ds.
\end{aligned}$$

$$\begin{aligned}
\dot{V}_2(t)=&x^T(t)R_1x(t)+(1-\dot{d}(t))x^T(t-d(t))(R_2-R_1)x(t-d(t))-x^T(t-d)R_2x(t-d)\\
=&\eta^T(t)(\Phi_2+(1-\dot{d}(t))\Psi_2)\eta(t). \qquad (12)
\end{aligned}$$

$$\begin{aligned}
&\dot{V}_3(t)\\
=&\dot{x}^T(t)S_1\dot{x}(t)-\dot{x}^T(t-d)S_2\dot{x}(t-d)+(1-\dot{d}(t))\dot{x}^T(t-d(t))(S_2-S_1)\dot{x}(t-d(t))\\
=&(A_px(t)+B_px(t-d(t)))^TS_1(A_px(t)+B_px(t-d(t)))-\dot{x}^T(t-d)S_2\dot{x}(t-d) \qquad (13)\\
&+(1-\dot{d}(t))\dot{x}^T(t-d(t))(S_2-S_1)\dot{x}(t-d(t))\\
=&\eta^T(t)\Big(\Phi_3^p+(1-\dot{d}(t))\Psi_3\Big)\eta(t).
\end{aligned}$$

$$\begin{aligned}
&\dot{V}_4(t)\\
=&d\dot{x}^TU\dot{x}(t)-\int_{t-d(t)}^{t}\dot{x}^T(s)U\dot{x}(s)ds-\int_{t-d}^{t-d(t)}\dot{x}^T(s)U\dot{x}(s)ds\\
=&d(A_px(t)+B_px(t-d(t)))^TU(A_px(t)+B_px(t-d(t)))-\int_{t-d(t)}^{t}\dot{x}^T(s)U\dot{x}(s)ds \qquad (14)\\
&-\int_{t-d}^{t-d(t)}\dot{x}^T(s)U\dot{x}(s)ds.
\end{aligned}$$

where $\Theta_1^p = e_1^TP_pB_pU^{-1}B_p^TP_pe_1$. Under Lemma 1, one can obtain

$$(d-d(t))\int_{t-d}^{t-d(t)}\dot{x}^T(s)U\dot{x}(s)ds \geq \xi_1^TU\xi_1+3\xi_2^TU\xi_2+5\xi_3^TU\xi_3=\eta^T(t)\Xi_4\eta(t),$$

where $\xi_1 = x(t-d(t)) - x(t-d)$, $\xi_2 = x(t-d(t)) + x(t-d) - v_1$, $\xi_3 = x(t-d(t)) - x(t-d) + 3v_1 - v_2$. Above inequality implies that (14) can be continued as

$$\dot{V}_4(t) \leq \eta^T(t)\Big(\Phi_4^\sigma - \frac{1}{d-d(t)}\Xi_1\Big)\eta(t) - \int_{t-d}^{t-d(t)}\dot{x}^T(s)U\dot{x}(s)ds \qquad (15)$$

Then, it follows from (10)–(13), (15) that

$$\begin{aligned}
&\dot{V}_p(t)\\
\leq&\eta^T(t)\Big(\phi_1^p+\phi_2+\phi_3^p+\phi_4^p+d(t)\Theta_1^p+(1-\dot{d}(t))(\Psi_2+\Psi_3)-\frac{1}{d-d(t)}\Xi_4\Big)\eta(t) \qquad (16)\\
=&\frac{1}{d-d(t)}\eta^T(t)\Big((d-d(t))\Big(\phi_1^p+\phi_2+\phi_3^p+\phi_4^p+d(t)\Theta_1^p+(1-\dot{d}(t))(\Psi_2+\Psi_3)\Big)-\Xi_4\Big).
\end{aligned}$$

Due to Schur complements [31], Condition (7) indicates that

$$\Lambda_l^p + d\Theta_1^p + \mu_p e_1^T Q_p e_1 < 0, l = 1, 2. \tag{17}$$

Namely,

$$\begin{cases} \phi_1^p + \phi_2 + \phi_3^p + \phi_4^p + (1-\bar{d})(\Psi_2 + \Psi_3) + d\Theta_1^p + \mu_p e_1^T Q_p e_1 - \frac{1}{d}\Xi_4 < 0, \\ \phi_1^p + \phi_2 + \phi_3^p + \phi_4^p + (1-\tilde{d})(\Psi_2 + \Psi_3) + d\Theta_1^p + \mu_p e_1^T Q_p e_1 - \frac{1}{d}\Xi_4 < 0. \end{cases} \tag{18}$$

The above inequalities declare that

$$\phi_1^p + \phi_2 + \phi_3^p + \phi_4^p + (1-\dot{d}(t))(\Psi_2 + \Psi_3) + d\Theta_1^p + \mu_p e_1^T Q_p e_1 - \frac{1}{d}\Xi_4 < 0. \tag{19}$$

Due to $0 \le d(t) \le d$ and $\Theta_1^p > 0$, it is clear from (19) that

$$d\Big(\phi_1^p + \phi_2 + \phi_3^p + \phi_4^p + (1-\dot{d}(t))(\Psi_2 + \Psi_3) + d(t)\Theta_1^p + \mu_p e_1^T Q_p e_1\Big) - \Xi_4 < 0. \tag{20}$$

Noting that $0 \le d - d(t) \le d$ and $\Xi > 0$, (20) shows that

$$(d - d(t))\Big(\phi_1^p + \phi_2 + \phi_3^p + \phi_4^p + (1-\dot{d}(t))(\Psi_2 + \Psi_3) + d(t)\Theta_1^p + \mu_p e_1^T Q_p e_1\Big) - \Xi_4 < 0. \tag{21}$$

Based on (16) and (21), one can derive that

$$\dot{V}_p(t) < -\mu_p \eta^T(t) Q_p \eta(t) \le 0, \tag{22}$$

where the fact $x^T(t)Q_\sigma x(t) \ge 0$ is used.

Note that for arbitrary $x \in \Omega_{pq}$, $x^T Q_p x = x^T Q_q x$. Then, due to Condition (8) we can derive that $V_p(t) = V_q(t)$ if $x(t) \in \Omega_{pq}$. Therefore, when the trajectory $x(t)$ traverses from Ω_p to Ω_q, the Lyapunov functional $V_\sigma(t)$ is not increasing. In particular, if the sliding motion does not occur, the Lyapunov functional $V_\sigma(t)$ will be approximate to zero and shows that the switched system (1) is globally asymptotically stable.

Now we consider the case of sliding motions. Assume that the sliding motions occur along the switching surface Ω_{pq} at the boundary of regions Ω_p and Ω_q. According to Filippov's definition [32], we get

$$\begin{aligned} \dot{x}(t) =& \alpha(A_p x(t) + B_p x(t - d(t))) + \tilde{\alpha}(A_q x(t) + B_q x(t - d(t)) \\ =& \alpha\Big((A_p + B_p)x(t) - B_p \int_{t-d(t)}^{t} \dot{x}(s)ds\Big) + \tilde{\alpha}\Big((A_q + B_q)x(t) - B_q \int_{t-d(t)}^{t} \dot{x}(s)ds\Big), \end{aligned} \tag{23}$$

where $\alpha \in (0, 1)$,$\tilde{\alpha} = 1 - \alpha$. Under the analysis of sliding motions [33], the sliding motions on the surface Ω_{pq} state that

$$\begin{aligned} x^T\Big((A_p + B_p)^T Q_{pq} + Q_{pq}(A_p + B_p)\Big)x(t) - x^T(t) Q_{pq} B_p \int_{t-d(t)}^{t} \dot{x}(s)ds \\ - \int_{t-d(t)}^{t} \dot{x}^T(s) ds B_p^T Q_{pq} x(t) < 0, \end{aligned} \tag{24}$$

and

$$x^T\Big((A_q+B_q)^T Q_{pq}+Q_{pq}(A_q+B_q)\Big)x(t)-x^T(t)Q_{pq}B_q\int_{t-d(t)}^{t}\dot{x}(s)ds$$
$$-\int_{t-d(t)}^{t}\dot{x}^T(s)dsB_q^T Q_{pq}x(t)>0 \tag{25}$$

hold, where $Q_{pq}=Q_p-Q_q$. Let $P_{qp}=P_q-P_p$. Owing to Condition (8) and $\eta_{p,q}>0$, we obtain

$$x^T\Big((A_p+B_p)^T P_{qp}+(P_q-P_p)(A_p+B_p)\Big)x(t)-x^T(t)P_{qp}B_p\int_{t-d(t)}^{t}\dot{x}(s)ds$$
$$-\int_{t-d(t)}^{t}\dot{x}^T(s)dsB_p^T P_{qp}x(t)<0, \tag{26}$$

$$x^T\Big((A_q+B_q)^T P_{qp}+(P_q-P_p)(A_q+B_q)\Big)x(t)-x^T(t)P_{qp}B_q\int_{t-d(t)}^{t}\dot{x}(s)ds$$
$$-\int_{t-d(t)}^{t}\dot{x}^T(s)dsB_q^T P_{qp}x(t)>0, \tag{27}$$

which are equivalent to

$$\begin{aligned}
&x^T(t)\Big((A_p+B_p)^T P_q+P_q(A_p+B_p)\Big)x(t)-x^T(t)P_qB_p\int_{t-d(t)}^{t}\dot{x}(s)ds\\
&-\int_{t-d(t)}^{t}\dot{x}^T(s)dsB_p^T P_q x(t)\\
<&x^T(t)\Big((A_p+B_p)^T P_p+P_p(A_p+B_p)\Big)x(t)-x^T(t)P_pB_p\int_{t-d(t)}^{t}\dot{x}(s)ds\\
&-\int_{t-d(t)}^{t}\dot{x}^T(s)dsB_p^T P_p x(t),
\end{aligned}\tag{28}$$

$$\begin{aligned}
&x^T(t)\Big((A_q+B_q)^T P_p+P_p(A_q+B_q)\Big)x(t)-x^T(t)P_pB_q\int_{t-d(t)}^{t}\dot{x}(s)ds\\
&-\int_{t-d(t)}^{t}\dot{x}^T(s)dsB_q^T P_p x(t)\\
<&x^T(t)\Big((A_q+B_q)^T P_q+P_q(A_q+B_q)\Big)x(t)-x^T(t)P_qB_q\int_{t-d(t)}^{t}\dot{x}(s)ds\\
&-\int_{t-d(t)}^{t}\dot{x}^T(s)dsB_q^T P_q x(t).
\end{aligned}\tag{29}$$

Note that the switching signal is not unique on sliding surface Ω_{pq}. If $\sigma(t)=p$, one can derive

$$\begin{aligned}
&\dot{V}_{p1}(t)\\
=&\alpha x^T(t)\Big((A_p+B_p)^T P_p+P_p(A_p+B_p)\Big)x(t)-\alpha x^T(t)P_pB_p\int_{t-d(t)}^{t}\dot{x}(s)ds\\
&-\alpha\int_{t-d(t)}^{t}\dot{x}^T(s)dsB_p^T P_p x(t)+\tilde{\alpha}x^T(t)\Big((A_q+B_q)^T P_p+P_p(A_q+B_q)\Big)x(t)\\
&-\tilde{\alpha}\left(x^T(t)P_pB_q\int_{t-d(t)}^{t}\dot{x}(s)ds+\int_{t-d(t)}^{t}\dot{x}^T(s)dsB_q^T P_p x(t)\right)\\
\le&\alpha x^T(t)\Big((A_p+B_p)^T P_p+P_p(A_p+B_p)\Big)x(t)-\alpha x^T(t)P_pB_p\int_{t-d(t)}^{t}\dot{x}(s)ds
\end{aligned}\tag{30}$$

$$
\begin{aligned}
& - \alpha \int_{t-d(t)}^{t} \dot{x}^T(s) ds B_p^T P_p x(t) \\
& + \tilde{\alpha} x^T(t) \Big((A_q + B_q)^T P_q + P_q (A_q + B_q) \Big) x(t) - \tilde{\alpha} \Big(x^T(t) P_q B_q \int_{t-d(t)}^{t} \dot{x}(s) ds \\
& + \int_{t-d(t)}^{t} \dot{x}^T(s) ds B_q^T P_q x(t) \Big) \\
\leq & \alpha \eta^T(t) e_1^T \Big(\Phi_1^p + d(t) \Theta_1^p \Big) e_1 \eta(t) + \tilde{\alpha} \eta^T(t) e_1^T \Big(\Phi_1^q + d(t) \Theta_1^q \Big) e_1 \eta(t) + \int_{t-d(t)}^{t} \dot{x}^T(s) U \dot{x}(s) ds.
\end{aligned}
$$

Under (7), (10)–(13), (21) and (30), it is easy to deduce that

$$
\dot{V}_p(t) < -\eta^T(t) \Big(\alpha e_1^T Q_p e_1 + \tilde{\alpha} e_1^T Q_q e_1 \Big) \eta(t) \leq 0.
$$

Similarly, when $\sigma(t) = q$, we can also obtain

$$
\begin{aligned}
\dot{V}_{q1}(t) \leq & \alpha \eta^T(t) e_1^T \Big(\Phi_1^p + d(t) \Theta_1^p \Big) e_1 \eta(t) + \tilde{\alpha} \eta^T(t) e_1^T \Big(\Phi_1^q + d(t) \Theta_1^q \Big) e_1 \eta(t) \\
& + \int_{t-d(t)}^{t} \dot{x}^T(s) U \dot{x}(s) ds,
\end{aligned}
$$

which further yields $\dot{V}_q(t) < 0$. Therefore, the Lyapunov-Krasovskii functional $V_\sigma(t)$ is decreasing when the sliding motions occur on switching surface Ω_{pq}. According to (22) one can deduce that the switched system (1) under the switching rule (3) is also globally asymptotically stable if the sliding motions occur on switching surfaces Ω_{pq} with $\eta_{p,q} > 0$. □

Remark 2. *According to the Proof of Theorem 1, one can see that the chosen Lyapunov functional is function of $x(t)$ and $\dot{x}(t)$. Similar Lyapunov functionals have been employed to establish the stability results for delayed systems [29,30]. This is because such Lyapunov functionals can fully utilize the features of systems. Most noteworthy, the proposed Lyapunov functional can be viewed as a special case of that presented in [29,30].*

Remark 3. *Condition (7) ensures that the time derivate of Lyapunov functional along the trajectory of switched systems is less than zero for each region Ω_p. Condition (8) guarantees that the Lyapunov functional is not increasing when the switching event occurs in the absence of sliding motion. When sliding motions occur, Conditions (7) and (8) can warrant that the time derivate of Lyapunov functional along the trajectory is less than zero when the trajectory slides on the surfaces Ω_{pq}. Condition (9) ensures that the switched system is well-defined.*

Remark 4. *In [15–19], the researchers have also studied the stability of delayed switched systems under state-dependent switchings. However, these results assume that there exists a Hurwitz linear convex combination of $A_p + B_p$(or A_p). Generally speaking, this assumption is rigorous and may not be satisfied in some cases. Obviously, in Theorem 1 we have removed this restriction, which yields that our results are more flexible. Moreover, in the proof of Theorem 1 new inequality (Lemma 1) is employed, which states that Theorem 1 is less conservative.*

Remark 5. *When there exist infinite switching events in an arbitrary time interval, we call it Zeno-behaviors. The switching rule (3) cannot avoid Zeno-behaviors. However, Theorem 1 can also ensure stability when Zeno-behaviors occur. The reasons can be listed as follows: (a) If the switching event does not occur, it is obvious that the time derivate of Lyapunov functional along the trajectory is less than zero. (b) If the switching event occurs, there are two cases. The first one is that the sliding motion does not occur. Obviously, for this case, the Lyapunov functional is not increasing. The second one is that the sliding motions occur. For this case, we have that the time derivate of Lyapunov functional along the trajectory is still less than zero. Although Zeno-behaviors* *may lead to the accumulation of switches in finite time, the Lyapunov functional along the trajectory is always gradually decreasing.*

By restricting $R_1 = R_2 = R$ and $S_1 = S_2 = S$, one can obtain the stability results under Assumption 2.

Theorem 2. *Under Assumption 2, assume that for any $p \in M$, there exist $n \times n$ matrices $P_p > 0$, $R > 0, S > 0, U > 0$, $Q_p = Q_p^T$, positive constants μ_p, θ_p, constants $\eta_{p,q}$, $q \in M$, $q \neq p$, such that Conditions (8) and (9) and*

$$\begin{pmatrix} \Lambda^p + \mu_p e_1^T Q_p e_1 & \sqrt{d} e_1^T P_p B_p \\ \sqrt{d} B_p^T P_p e_1 & -U \end{pmatrix} < 0, \tag{31}$$

where $\Lambda^p = \Lambda_1^p$ with $R_1 = R_2 = R$ and $S_1 = S_2 = S$. Then, the switched system (1) is globally asymptotically stable under the state-dependent switching rule (3), if there is no sliding motion or there exist sliding motions on the switching surface Ω_{pq} with $\eta_{p,q} > 0$.

Due to the existence of the product of unknown scalars and matrices, the conditions in Theorems 1 and 2 are BMIs. Therefore, the standard semi-positive definite programming methods cannot work. One can adopt two strategies to get a feasible solution. The first one is to utilize directly BMI solvers (such as PENBMI) to obtain these undetermined scalars and matrices. The second one, which is similar to [22], is to grid up the unknown scalars μ_p, θ_p and $\eta_{p,q}$. While these parameters are fixed, the BMIs in Theorems 1 and 2 degenerate into ordinary linear matrix inequalities, which can be solved by standard solvers such as lmilab and mosek.

When the switched system (1) is composed of two subsystems, one can set $Q_1 = -Q_2 = Q = Q^T$, $\eta_{1,2} = \eta_{2,1} = \eta$, $P_2 = P$, $P_1 = P - 2\eta Q$, constants $\theta_1 = \theta_2 = 1$. Then, Conditions (8) and (9) are always satisfied. The following corollaries can be derived readily from Theorems 1 and 2.

Corollary 1. *When $M = \{1, 2\}$, under Assumption 1, assume that there exist $n \times n$ matrices $P > 0$, $R_i > 0, S_i > 0, U > 0$, $(i = 1, 2)$, $Q = Q^T$, positive constants μ_1, μ_2, constant η, such that*

$$\begin{pmatrix} \Lambda_l^{1*} + \mu_1 e_1^T Q e_1 & \sqrt{d} e_1^T (P - 2\eta Q) B_1 \\ \sqrt{d} B_1^T (P - 2\eta Q) e_1 & -U \end{pmatrix} < 0, \tag{32}$$

$$\begin{pmatrix} \Lambda_l^{2*} - \mu_2 e_1^T Q e_1 & \sqrt{d} e_1^T P B_2 \\ \sqrt{d} B_2^T P e_1 & -U \end{pmatrix} < 0, l = 1, 2, \tag{33}$$

where

$$\begin{aligned}
\Lambda_1^{1*} =& \Phi_1^{1*} + \Phi_2 + \Phi_3^1 + \Phi_4^1 + (1 - \tilde{d})(\Psi_2 + \Psi_3) - \frac{1}{d}\Xi_4, \\
\Lambda_1^{2*} =& \Phi_1^{2*} + \Phi_2 + \Phi_3^2 + \Phi_4^2 + (1 - \tilde{d})(\Psi_2 + \Psi_3) - \frac{1}{d}\Xi_4, \\
\Lambda_2^{1*} =& \Phi_1^{1*} + \Phi_2 + \Phi_3^1 + \Phi_4^1 + (1 - \tilde{d})(\Psi_2 + \Psi_3) - \frac{1}{d}\Xi_4, \\
\Lambda_2^{2*} =& \Phi_1^{2*} + \Phi_2 + \Phi_3^2 + \Phi_4^2 + (1 - \tilde{d})(\Psi_2 + \Psi_3) - \frac{1}{d}\Xi_4, \\
\Phi_1^{1*} =& e_1^T \Big((A_1 + B_1)^T (P - 2\eta Q) + (P - 2\eta Q)\,(A_1 + B_1) \big) e_1, \\
\Phi_1^{2*} =& e_1^T \Big((A_2 + B_2)^T P + P (A_2 + B_2) \Big) e_1,
\end{aligned}$$

and the other notations are in agreement with the ones presented in Theorem 1. Then, the switched system (1) is globally asymptotically stable under the state-dependent switching rule (3) if there is no sliding motion or there exist sliding motions on switching surfaces with $\eta > 0$.

Corollary 2. *When $M = \{1,2\}$, under Assumption 2, assume that there exist $n \times n$ matrices $P > 0, R > 0, S > 0, U > 0$, $Q = Q^T$, positive constants μ_1, μ_2, constant η, such that*

$$\begin{pmatrix} \bar{\Lambda}^{1*} + \mu_1 e_1^T Q e_1 & \sqrt{d} e_1^T (P - 2\eta Q) B_1 \\ \sqrt{d} B_1^T (P - 2\eta Q) e_1 & -U \end{pmatrix} < 0, \tag{34}$$

$$\begin{pmatrix} \bar{\Lambda}^{2*} - \mu_2 e_1^T Q e_1 & \sqrt{d} e_1^T P B_2 \\ \sqrt{d} B_2^T P e_1 & -U \end{pmatrix} < 0, \tag{35}$$

where $\bar{\Lambda}^{1*} = \Lambda_1^{1*}$, $\bar{\Lambda}^{2*} = \Lambda_1^{2*}$ with $R_1 = R_2 = R$ and $S_1 = S_2 = S$. Then, the switched system (1) is globally asymptotically stable under the state-dependent switching rule (3), if there is no sliding motion or there exist sliding motions on switching surfaces with $\eta > 0$.

4. Numerical Simulations

In this section, several numerical examples are employed to illustrate the validity of the proposed results.

Example 1. *Consider the switched system (1) with $M = \{1,2\}$ and*

$$A_1 = \begin{pmatrix} 0.8 & -4 \\ 0 & 0.8 \end{pmatrix}, B_1 = \begin{pmatrix} 0.2 & -1 \\ 0 & 0.2 \end{pmatrix}, A_2 = \begin{pmatrix} 0.8 & 0 \\ 4 & 0.9 \end{pmatrix}, B_2 = \begin{pmatrix} 0.2 & 0 \\ 1 & 0.1 \end{pmatrix}.$$

By choosing $\mu_1 = \mu_2 = 1$, $\eta = -0.7$ and letting $\bar{d} = -\tilde{d} = \delta$, according to Corollaries 1 and 2, we can obtain the upper bound d for different δ, which is given in Table 1 (in order to avoid zero solution, the matrix inequalities $P, R_i, S_i, U > aI$ with $a = 10^{-7}$ are employed to replace $P, R_i, S_i, U > 0$, $i = 1,2$). For numerical simulation, we choose $d(t) = 0.1 + 0.1\sin(10t)$, which shows $d = 0.2$ and $\bar{d} = -\tilde{d} = 1$. By solving the matrix inequalities in Corollary 1, we get

$$Q_1 = -Q_2 = Q = \begin{pmatrix} -0.2567 & 0.1996 \\ 0.1996 & 0.2565 \end{pmatrix}, P_1 = P - 2\eta Q = \begin{pmatrix} 0.0935 & 0.1402 \\ 0.1402 & 4516 \end{pmatrix},$$
$$P_2 = P = \begin{pmatrix} 0.4528 & -0.1393 \\ -0.1393 & 0.0925 \end{pmatrix}.$$

The stable dynamics and convergent time response curves with $\phi(s) = (-1,2)^T$, $s = [-0.2, 0]$, are plotted in Figure 1. The corresponding switching rule (3) is also shown in the sub-figure of Figure 1. Numerical simulations indicate that there is no sliding motion.

Now we give some comparisons with the existing results for this example to validate the superiority of our results.

(a) *Note that for any $\alpha \in [0,1]$, the eigenvalues of $\alpha(A_1 + B_1) + (1-\alpha)(A_2 + B_2)$ are $1 \pm 5i\sqrt{\alpha(1-\alpha)}$, which yields that there is no Hurwitz linear convex combination of $A_1 + B_1$ and $A_2 + B_2$. Therefore, the stability results proposed in [15–17,19] are not available for this example. Additionally, the eigenvalues of $\alpha A_1 + (1-\alpha)A_2$ are $0.85 + 0.05\alpha \pm 0.5\sqrt{64.01\alpha^2 - 63.98\alpha - 0.01}$, $\alpha \in [0,1]$, which indicates that there is no Hurwitz linear convex combination of matrices A_1 and A_2. This shows that the stability results in [18] are also invalid for this example.*

(b) *The results derived in [20,21] are also applicable for the switched system (1). For comparison, by restricting $d = 0.01$ we solve the stability conditions in ([20] Corollary 2) and ([21] Theorem 3.1) for $\bar{d} = 0, 0.1, 0.2, 0.5, 0.8$ and 1, respectively. Unfortunately, there is no feasible solution, which demonstrates that the results in [20,21] are not flexible for this example.*

(c) *For the case of constant time delay, by solving the matrix inequalities in ([27] Theorem 5), one can get the upper bound $d = 0.2455$, which is also less than $d = 0.2489$. Therefore, the restriction on the time delay of our results is weaker than that proposed in ([27] Theorem 5).*

Table 1. The upper bound d of time delay for different $\bar{d} = -\tilde{d} = \delta$.

0	0.1	0.2	0.5	0.8	1	δ is Unknown
0.2489	0.2445	0.2417	0.2411	0.2411	0.2411	0.2411

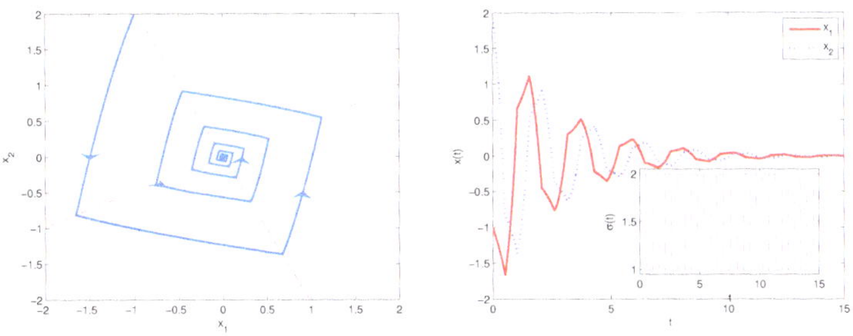

Figure 1. The stable dynamics (**Left**) and convergent response curves (**Right**) of the system in Example 1 with $d(t) = 0.1 + 0.1\sin(10t)$.

Example 2. *Consider the switched system (1) wiht $M = \{1,2\}$, $d(t) = 0.01 + 0.01\sin(50t)$, and*

$$A_1 = \begin{pmatrix} 0 & 1 \\ 2 & -8 \end{pmatrix}, B_1 = \begin{pmatrix} 0 & 0 \\ 0 & -1 \end{pmatrix}, A_2 = \begin{pmatrix} 0 & 0.5 \\ -2 & 1 \end{pmatrix}, B_2 = \begin{pmatrix} 0 & 0.5 \\ 0 & 1 \end{pmatrix}.$$

It is easy to derive that $d = 0.02$, $\bar{d} = -\tilde{d} = 0.5$. By choosing $\eta = 0.01$, $\mu_1 = \mu_2 = 1$, according to Corollary 1, we get the following feasible solution

$$Q_1 = -Q_2 = Q = \begin{pmatrix} -0.02252 & 0.0251 \\ 0.0251 & 0.0287 \end{pmatrix}, P_1 = P - 2\eta Q = \begin{pmatrix} 0.0202 & 0.1940 \\ 0.0055 & 0.0028 \end{pmatrix},$$
$$P_2 = P = \begin{pmatrix} 0.0198 & 0.0060 \\ 0.0060 & 0.0034 \end{pmatrix}.$$

The sliding dynamics and stable responce curves are shown in Figure 2. Numerical simulations indicate that there are sliding motions, which can make the trajectory approach the origin along the switching surfaces.

If we choose $\eta = -1$, $\mu_1 = \mu_2 = 1$, by solving the matrix inequalities in Corollary 1, we obtain

$$Q_1 = -Q_2 = Q = \begin{pmatrix} 0.0127 & -0.0964 \\ -0.0964 & 0.4049 \end{pmatrix}, P_1 = P - 2\eta Q = \begin{pmatrix} 0.0397 & -0.1802 \\ -0.1802 & 0.8545 \end{pmatrix},$$
$$P_2 = P = \begin{pmatrix} 0.0143 & 0.0125 \\ 0.0125 & 0.0446 \end{pmatrix}.$$

Numerical simulations show that there are unstable sliding motions for this case (see Figure 3), which is due to $\eta_{1,2} = \eta_{2,1} = \eta < 0$. This demonstrates that $\eta_{p,q} > 0$ is essential for the stability of the switched system (1) when sliding motions occur.

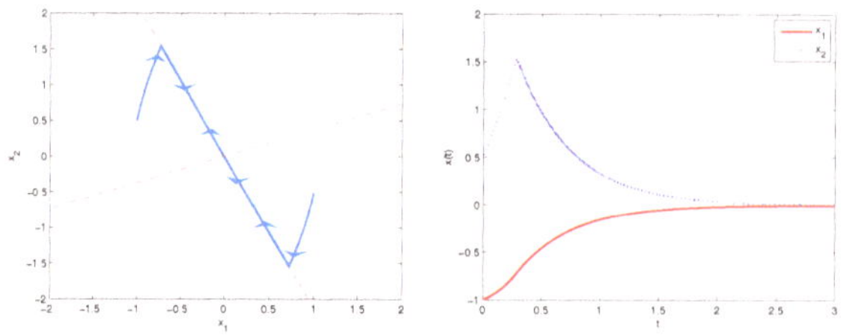

Figure 2. The stable dynamics (**Left**) and convergent response curves (**Right**) of the system in Example 2.

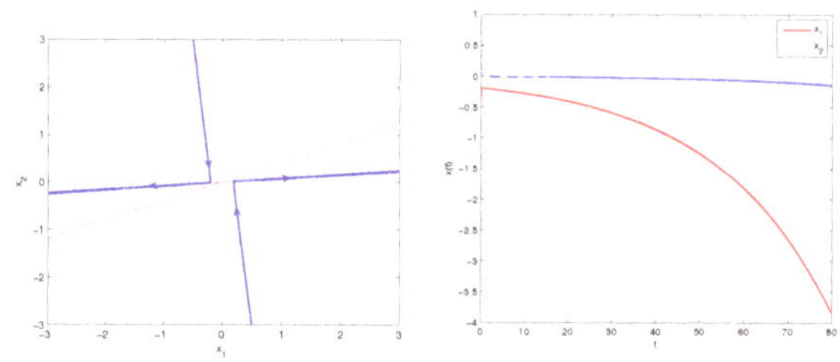

Figure 3. The unstable dynamics (**Left**) and unstable response curves (**Right**) of the system in Example 2.

5. Conclusions

This paper has investigated the stability of delayed switched systems with all unstable subsystems. Under the designed state-dependent switching rule, some stability results for different assumptions on time delay are derived via integral inequality and multiple Lyapunov-Krasovskii functionals. Numerical simulations demonstrate that the proposed results are more effective and less conservative than that presented in [15–21,27].

The main deficiency of this paper is that the condition that determines whether sliding motions occur is not employed. As a matter of fact, similar to [21,22], we have derived some conditions to verify the existence or non-existence of sliding motions. Unfortunately, if we introduce these conditions to the stability results, it is difficult to get a feasible solution. In desperation, we adopt the way which is used in [34,35]. Namely, the condition to determine whether sliding motions occur is not given and the existence or non-existence of sliding motions is revealed via numerical simulation. We hope some more feasible conditions on sliding motions can be deduced in the future.

Author Contributions: Investigation, C.L.; Writing—original draft, X.L. All authors have read and agreed to the published version of the manuscript.

Funding: This research was funded by the Research Foundation of the Natural Foundation of Chongqing City, Grant Nomber: cstc2019jcyj-msxmX0492.

Conflicts of Interest: The authors declare no conflict of interest.

References

1. Decarlo, R.A.; Branicky, M.S. Pettersson, S.; Lennartson, B. Perspectives and results on the stability and stabilizability of hybrid systems. *Proc. IEEE* **2000**, *10*, 1069–1082. [CrossRef]
2. Zhai, G.; Hu, B.; Yasuda, K.; Michel, A.N. Stability analysis of switched systems with stable and unstable subsystems: An average dwell time approach. *Int. J. Syst. Sci.* **2001**, *32*, 1055–1061. [CrossRef]
3. Xiang, Z.; Xiang, W. Stability analysis of switched systems under dynamical dwell time control approach. *Int. J. Syst. Sci.* **2009**, *40*, 347–355. [CrossRef]
4. Xiang, W.; Xiao, J.; Iqbal, M.N. Asymptotic stability, l_2 gain, boundness analysis, and control synthesis for switched systems: A switching frequency approach. *Int. J. Adapt. Control Signal Process.* **2012**, *26*, 350–373. [CrossRef]

5. Zhai, G.; Hu, B.; Yasuda, K.; Michel, A.N. Disturbance attenuation properties of time-controlled switched systems. *J. Frankl. Inst.* **2001**, *338*, 765–779. [CrossRef]
6. Zhang, L.; Gao, H. Asynchronously switched control of switched linear systems with average dwell time. *Automatica* **2010**, *46*, 953–938. [CrossRef]
7. Liu, C.; Yang, Z.; Sun, D.; Liu, X.; Liu, W. Stability of switched neural networks with time-varying delays. *Neural Comput. Appl.* **2018**, *30*, 2229–2244. [CrossRef]
8. Xiang, W.; Xiao, J. Stabilization of switched continuous-time systems with all modes unstable via dwell time switching. *Automatica* **2014**, *50*, 940–945. [CrossRef]
9. Qi, J.; Li, C.; Huang, T.; Zhang, W. Exponential stability of switched time-varying delayed neural networks with all modes being unstable. *Neural Process. Lett.* **2016**, *43*, 553–565. [CrossRef]
10. Wang, Q.; Sun, H.; Zong, G. Stability analysis of switched delay systems with all subsystems unstable. *Int. J. Control Autom. Syst.* **2016**, *14*, 1262–1269. [CrossRef]
11. Luo, S.; Deng, F.; Chen, W. Unified dwell time-based stability and stabilization criteria for switched linear stochastic systems and their application to intermittent control. *Int. J. Robust Nonlinear Control.* **2017**, *28*, 2014–2030. [CrossRef]
12. Mao, X.; Zhu, H.; Chen, W.; Zhang, H. New results on stability of switched continuous-time systems with all subsystems unstable. *ISA Trans.* **2019**, *87*, 28–33. [CrossRef] [PubMed]
13. Sun, Z.; Ge, S.S. *Switched Linear System-Control and Design*; Springer: London, UK, 2005.
14. Liberzon, D. *Switching in Systems and Control*; Birkhuser: Boston, MA, USA, 2003.
15. Kim, S.; Campbell, S.A.; Liu, X. Stability of a class of linear switching systems with time delay. *IEEE Trans. Circuits Syst. I Regul. Pap.* **2006**, *53*, 384–393.
16. Sun, X.; Wang, W.; Liu, G.; Zhao, J. Stability analysis for linear switched systems with time-varying delay. *IEEE Trans. Syst. Man Cybern. Part Cybern.* **2008**, *238*, 528–533.
17. Li, Z.; Xu, Y.; Fei, Z.; Agarwal, R. Exponential stability analysis and stabilization of switched delay systems. *J. Frankl. Inst.* **2015**, *352*, 4980–5002. [CrossRef]
18. Lian, J.; Zhang, K.; Feng, Z. Stability analysis for switched Hopfield neural networks with time delay. *Optim. Control. Appl. Methods* **2012**, *33*, 433–444. [CrossRef]
19. Liu, C.; Yang, Z.; Liu, X.; Huang, X. Stability of delayed switched systems with state-dependent switching. *IEEE/CAA J. Autom. Sin.* **2020**, *7*, 872–881. [CrossRef]
20. Lien, C.; Yu, K.; Chung, Y. Switching signal design for global exponential stability of uncertain switched nonlinear systems with time-varying delay. *Nonlinear Anal. Hybrid Syst.* **2011**, *5*, 10–19. [CrossRef]
21. Phat, V.N.; Botmart, T.; Niamsup, P. Switching design for exponential stability of a class of nonlinear hybrid time-delay systems. *Nonlinear Anal. Hybrid Syst.* **2009**, *3*, 1–10. [CrossRef]
22. Pettersson, S. Synthesis of switched linear systems. In Proceedings of the 42nd IEEE Conference on Decision and Control, Maui, HI, USA, 9–12 December 2003.
23. Pettersson, S. Controller design of switched linear systems. In Proceedings of the 2004 American Control Conference, Boston, MA, USA, 30 June–2 July 2004.
24. Geromel, J.C.; Colaneri, P. Stability and stabilization of continuous-time switched linear systems. *SIAM J. Control. Optim.* **2006**, *45*, 915–1930. [CrossRef]
25. Allerhand, L.I.; Shaked, U. Robust state-dependent switching of linear systems with dwell time. *IEEE Trans. Autom. Control.* **2013**, *58*, 994–1001. [CrossRef]
26. Souza, M.; Fioravanti, A.R.; Corless, M.; Shorten, R.N. Switching controller design with dwell-times and sampling. *IEEE Trans. Autom. Control* **2017**, *62*, 5837–5843. [CrossRef]
27. Galbusera, L.; Bolzern, P. H_∞ control of time-delay switched linear systems by state-dependent switching. *IFAC Proc. Vol.* **2010**, *43*, 218–223. [CrossRef]
28. Park, P.G.; Lee, W.I.; Lee, S.Y. Auxiliary function-based integral inequalities for quadratic functions and their applications to time-delay systems. *J. Frankl. Inst.* **2015**, *352*, 1378–1396. [CrossRef]
29. Lee, T.H.; Park, J.H.; Xu, S. Relaxed conditions for stability of time-varying delay systems. *Automatica* **2017**, *53*, 11–15. [CrossRef]
30. Park, M.J.; Kwon, O.M.; Ryu, J.H. Advanced stability criteria for linear systems with time-varying delays. *J. Frankl. Inst.* **2017**, *355*, 520–543. [CrossRef]
31. Boyd. S.; Ghaoui, L.E.; Feron, E.; Boyd, S.P. *Linear Matrix Inequalities in System and Control Theory*; Society for Industrial and Applied Mathematics: Philadelphia, PA, USA, 1994.
32. Filippov, A.F. *Differential Equations with Discontinuous Right-Hand Sides*; Kluwer Academic Press: Dordrecht, The Netherlands, 1988.
33. Pettersson, S. Synthesis of switched linear systems handling sliding motions. In Proceedings of the 2005 IEEE International Symposium on Intelligent Control, Limassol, Cyprus, 27–29 June 2005.
34. Lu, L.; Lin, Z. Design of switched linear systems in the presence of actuator saturation. *IEEE Trans. Autom. Control* **2008**, *53*, 1536–1542. [CrossRef]
35. Lu, L.; Lin, Z.; Fang, H. L_2 gain analysis for a class of switched systems. *Automatica* **2009**, *45*, 965–972. [CrossRef]

Σ mathematics

MDPI

Article

A Novel Multi-Source Domain Adaptation Method with Dempster–Shafer Evidence Theory for Cross-Domain Classification

Min Huang * **and Chang Zhang** *

School of Software Engineering, South China University of Technology (SCUT), Guangzhou 510006, China
* Correspondence: minh@scut.edu.cn (M.H.); sezchang_2020@mail.scut.edu.cn (C.Z.)

Abstract: In this era of big data, Multi-source Domain Adaptation (MDA) becomes more and more popular and is employed to make full use of available source data collected from several different, but related domains. Although multiple source domains provide much information, the processing of domain shifts becomes more challenging, especially in learning a common domain-invariant representation for all domains. Moreover, it is counter-intuitive to treat multiple source domains equally as most existing MDA algorithms do. Therefore, the domain-specific distribution for each source–target domain pair is aligned, respectively. Nevertheless, it is hard to combine adaptation outputs from different domain-specific classifiers effectively, because of ambiguity on the category boundary. Subjective Logic (SL) is introduced to measure the uncertainty (credibility) of each domain-specific classifier, so that MDA could be bridged with DST. Due to the advantage of information fusion, Dempster–Shafer evidence Theory (DST) is utilized to reduce the category boundary ambiguity and output reasonable decisions by combining adaptation outputs based on uncertainty. Finally, extensive comparative experiments on three popular benchmark datasets for cross-domain image classification are conducted to evaluate the performance of the proposed method via various aspects.

Keywords: multi-source domain adaptation; Dempster–Shafer evidence theory; cross-domain classification

MSC: 68T07

Citation: Huang, M.; Zhang, C. A Novel Multi-Source Domain Adaptation Method with Dempster–Shafer Evidence Theory for Cross-Domain Classification. *Mathematics* **2022**, *10*, 2797. https://doi.org/10.3390/math10152797

Academic Editors: Jianping Gou, Weihua Ou, Shaoning Zeng and Lan Du

Received: 23 June 2022
Accepted: 4 August 2022
Published: 6 August 2022

1. Introduction

Recently, Deep Learning (DL) has made remarkable advances in various fields [1–7], especially in classification [8–10]. Despite excellent results, the success of deep methods highly relies on: (1) large-scale labeled data for supervised learning and (2) the training and test data meeting the requirement of being Independently Identically Distributed (IID). However, annotation is time-consuming and unaffordable in practice. If a model is trained on a dataset (known as the source domain), but tested on another non-IID dataset (known as the target domain), domain shifts occur and tend to severely degrade the performance of the learned model [11,12]. Therefore, it is necessary to develop models that are trained on the given labeled datasets, but that can generalize well to a non-IID unlabeled dataset.

Domain Adaptation (DA) aims to learn a discriminative model by reducing domain shifts between training and test distributions [13]. DA transfers the given labeled source domain knowledge to tackle the task to the different, but related target domain by learning domain-invariant representation between domains. Most approaches focus on Single-source Domain Adaptation (SDA), where the labeled data from only one single source domain are considered. Many achievements have emerged in this decade [14–18]. For example, DDC [14] adds an adaptation layer to the pre-trained AlexNet model to confuse the feature representation between the single source domain and the target domain. DSAN [16] proposes a novel fine-grained metric function to align the distribution of the single source domain and the target domain. Most of them learn to map the data from both domains into a common feature space to learn domain-invariant representations by minimizing domain distribution discrepancy, so that the source classifier could then be directly applied to target instances.

However, in practice, it is very likely to obtain multiple available source domains, while SDA is not up to employing those source data adequately. Hence, more challenging, Multi-source Domain Adaptation (MDA) is developed to utilize labeled data from multiple source domains with different distributions and has attracted extensive attention these days [19–21]. The most straightforward way is to combine all source domains into one single source domain and, then, directly apply SDA methods to align distributions. Due to the dataset expansion, the methods might improve the performance. However, the improvements might not be sufficient; the more accurate ways are supposed to explore to make full use of source domains.

With the spurt of progress in DL and SDA today, MDA has been gradually developed. However, there are two typical issues with most techniques [22–28]. (1) Firstly, it is more challenging to learn a common domain-invariant representation for all domains in MDA, because the damages of domain shifts cannot be eliminated even in SDA. Thereby, MDA is processed by aligning the domain-specific distribution for each source–target domain pair. (2) Secondly, multiple source domains are treated as equivalents. However, the benefits of each source domain to the target domain tasks are diverse in reality. The final output should be closer to the adaptation output of the source–target domain pairs with higher credibility. Some studies [29,30] add extra neural network components to measure the credibility (i.e., transferability). In this research study, we employed Subjective Logic (SL) [31] to obtain the uncertainty of every source domain without any addition of the neural network. Regarding source–target domain pairs as witnesses with different credibility (uncertainty), we introduced Dempster–Shafer evidence Theory (DST) to combine all domain-specific adaptation outputs.

As an uncertainty reasoning method, DST can effectively and reliably deal with uncertainty. It relies on Basic Probability Assignment Functions (BPAFs) to measure the initial degree of belief in the occurrence of an event, which is similar to the concept of the "probability" of a random event in probability theory. To generate BPAFs, DST is bridged with MDA and DL by subjective logic.

Our contributions are summarized as follows:

- A novel multi-source domain adaptation method with Dempster–Shafer evidence theory is proposed. We provide an effective cross-domain classification solution without any addition of the neural network.
- There are few studies combining multi-source domain adaptation and Dempster–Shafer evidence theory as of yet. We explored this kind of research early. In our work, DST is employed to fuse all domain-specific adaptation results and output the final credible results.
- The effectiveness of our cross-domain classification method is verified by conducting comprehensive experiments on three well-known benchmarks. The experimental results prove that the proposed method has better performance than other compared approaches.

The rest of this paper is organized as follows. Section 2 reviews the related work. In Section 3, the preliminaries are given. Section 4 describes the proposed method in detail. A series of experiments is reported in Section 5 and discussed in Section 6. Finally, Section 7 summarizes this research study.

2. Related Work

2.1. Single-Source Domain Adaptation

Single-source Domain Adaptation (SDA) is bound up with multi-source domain adaptation. SDA aims to generalize a model learned from a labeled source domain to a related unlabeled target domain with a different data distribution by reducing the domain shift. SDA can be roughly divided into three categories according to different alignment strategies. (1) Discrepancy-based approaches utilize different metric schemas to explicitly measure the distance between the source and target domains and diminish the domain shift. Commonly used discrepancy metrics for domain adaptation include Maximum Mean Discrepancy (MMD) [32–34], moment matching [35,36], Kullback–Leibler (KL) divergence [37], correlation alignment [38,39], and mixture distance [40]. (2) Adversarial-based approaches align different data distributions by confusing a well-trained discriminator (domain classifier). Many methods [41–46] are based on Generative Adversarial Networks (GANs), which align different data distributions by implicitly learning the metric function (i.e., domain discriminator) between the source and target domains. (3) Reconstruction-based approaches assume that reconstructing the target domain from a latent representation by using the source task model can help learn domain-invariant representations. The reconstruction is usually obtained via an auto-decoder [47–49] or a GAN discriminator [50–52].

In our work, the first kind of approach was chosen and the most widely used discrepancy MMD was employed to align the distributions.

2.2. Multi-Source Domain Adaptation

In practice, available source data often come from several different, but related domains. Multi-source Domain Adaptation (MDA) is developed to make full use of these data. However, multiple source domain data provide much information, but challenge the processing of domain shifts. (1) Based on the assumption that the target domain distribution can be approximated by mixing the source domain distribution [53,54], some MDA methods focus on the weighted combination of source domains. For example, Sun and Shi [22] designed a method to weight the source domain classifiers based on the Bayesian learning principle. Xu et al. [23] proposed a voting method for multiple classifiers, which is based on the output of domain discriminators. (2) In addition, some methods are devised to map all source domains and the target domain to a unified feature space. For instance, MDAN [24] aligns the distribution of source domains with the target domain through multiple domain discriminators. M^3SDA [25] employs moment matching to align the source–target and source-source domains in a common feature space. HoMM [26] exploits the high-order statistics for domain alignment in a reproducing kernel Hilbert space. (3) Some other methods are based on reconstruction [27,28], which reconstruct multiple source domains into an intermediate single source domain and then directly carry out SDA.

Sadly, the damages of domain shifts cannot be eliminated in SDA. It is more difficult to learn a common domain-invariant representation for all domains in MDA. Following MFSAN [55], the domain-specific distribution and classifier alignment architecture for cross-domain classification has proceeded. However, MFSAN treats every source domain equally. This is counter-intuitive because different source domains help the target task differently. Thus, regarding source–target domain pairs as witnesses with different credibility (uncertainty), DST is employed to combine all domain-specific adaptation results. Specifically, the uncertainty is captured, and BPAFs are generated by using subjective logic.

2.3. Dempster–Shafer Evidence Theory

Dempster–Shafer evidence Theory (DST) was first introduced in the 1960s. Based on the investigation of statistical problems, Arthur P. Dempster introduced the concept of upper and lower probabilities and their combining rules [56]. Then, the form of probability that does not satisfy additivity was defined for the first time [57]. Later, Glenn Shafer reinterpreted the upper and lower probabilities based on the belief function and developed the theory into a general framework for modeling epistemic uncertainty [58]. DST allows beliefs from different sources to be fused with various operators to obtain new beliefs considering all available evidence [59]. Currently, generating the belief function through DL has proven to be successful and efficient [60]. These unique characteristics make DST particularly suitable for information fusion [61,62]. Similar to information fusion, the idea of our MDA method is to combine evidence from multiple sources.

3. Preliminaries

3.1. Unsupervised Multi-Source Domain Adaptation

In this research study, the unsupervised MDA problem is investigated. Let $\mathcal{D}_s = \{\mathcal{D}_{si}\}_{i=1}^{N}$ denote a collection of N available datasets of source domains, and each labeled source dataset $\mathcal{D}_{si} = \{(\mathbf{X}_{si}^{(j)}, y_{si}^{(j)})\}_{j=1}^{n_{si}}$ with n_{si} samples is sufficient to train a source domain distribution model. Meanwhile, a target dataset $\mathcal{D}_t = \{\mathbf{X}_t^{(j)}\}_{j=1}^{n_t}$ with n_t samples drawn from the target domain $\mathcal{D}_t$ has no labels to support training a reasonable distribution model. With given $\mathcal{D}_s \cup \mathcal{D}_t$, the general goal of this problem is to train a cross-domain classifier $f_\theta(x)$, which has a low target risk $\epsilon_t = \mathbb{E}_{x \in \mathcal{D}_t}[f_\theta(x) \neq y_t]$.

The domain-specific distribution and classifier alignment architecture in MFSAN [55] has proceeded to cross-domain classification. Thus, the domain adaptation model involves the source domain task loss $\mathcal{L}_s$, the domain adaptation loss $\mathcal{L}_d$, and the classifier constraint loss $\mathcal{L}_r$. As shown in (1), λ and γ are trade-off parameters.

$$\mathcal{L} = \mathcal{L}_s + \lambda \mathcal{L}_d + \gamma \mathcal{L}_r \tag{1}$$

3.2. Maximum Mean Discrepancy

Maximum mean discrepancy, inspired by the two-sample test in statistics [63,64], is the most widely used discrepancy to align the distributions in domain adaptation. In general, MMD is interpreted as the maximum value (upper bound) of the expectation difference between two distributions mapped by any function f in a predefined function field $\mathcal{F}$, which is an arbitrary vector in the unit sphere (i.e., $\|f\| < 1$) of the reproducing Hilbert space:

$$\text{MMD}[\mathcal{F}, p, q] := \sup_{f \in \mathcal{F}} \left(\mathbf{E}_p[f(x)] - \mathbf{E}_q[f(y)] \right) \tag{2}$$

In practice, an estimate of the MMD compares the square distance between the empirical kernel mean embeddings as (3). $\mathcal{H}$ is the Reproducing Kernel Hilbert Space (RKHS) endowed with a characteristic kernel k. k means $k(\mathbf{x}^s, \mathbf{x}^t) = \langle \phi(\mathbf{x}^s), \phi(\mathbf{x}^t) \rangle$, where $\langle \cdot, \cdot \rangle$ represents the inner product of vectors and $\phi(\cdot)$ denotes some feature map to map the original samples to the RKHS $\mathcal{H}$.

$$\text{MMD}^2[\mathcal{F}, X_s, X_t] = \left\| \frac{1}{n_s} \sum_{\mathbf{x}_i \in \mathcal{D}_s} \phi(\mathbf{x}_i) - \frac{1}{n_t} \sum_{\mathbf{x}_j \in \mathcal{D}_t} \phi(\mathbf{x}_j) \right\|_{\mathcal{H}}^2 \tag{3}$$

3.3. Basic Concepts of DST

The Basic Probability Assignment Function (BPAF) is the fundamental unit of DST, which expresses the initial degree of belief in the proposition. Let Θ be a frame of discernment, which specifies the proposition range. The function $m : 2^\Theta \to [0,1]$ becomes the BPAF when it satisfies (4). If $m(A) > 0$, $m(A)$ is also called the belief mass, and A is named the focal element.

$$\begin{cases} m(\emptyset) = 0 \\ \sum_{A \subseteq \Theta} m(A) = 1 \end{cases} \tag{4}$$

Dempster's rule $\oplus$ is at the core of DST, as it provides algorithmic rules for combining two pieces of evidence, as shown in (5). Besides, Dempster's rule is invoked $N-1$ times to combine N sets of evidence.

$$m_1(X) \oplus m_2(X) = \begin{cases} 0, X = \emptyset \\ \frac{1}{1-K} \sum_{A_i \cap B_j = X} m_1(A_i) m_2(B_j), X \neq \emptyset \end{cases} \tag{5}$$

The definition of conflict factor K, shown in (6), reflects the degree of conflict between m_1 and m_2, whereby $1/(1-K)$ represents the normalization factor. Obviously, Dempster's rule tries to fuse shared parts from different sources and ignores conflicting beliefs.

$$K = \sum_{A_i \cap B_j = \varnothing} m_1(A_i) m_2(B_j) \tag{6}$$

3.4. Dirichlet Distribution

The Dirichlet distribution is involved in SL, which bridges DL, MDA, and DST. In the context of multi-class classification, SL converts the outputs (from DL and MDA) of the neural networks into the concentration parameter of the Dirichlet distribution and associates it with the belief masses (for DST). Accordingly, DST could combine multi-source evidence after BPAFs are obtained and output the final decision.

If the probability density function of multivariate continuous random variable $\theta = \{\theta_1, \theta_2, \ldots, \theta_k\}$ is (7):

$$p(\theta \mid \alpha) = \frac{\Gamma\left(\sum_{i=1}^{k} \alpha_i\right)}{\prod_{i=1}^{k} \Gamma(\alpha_i)} \prod_{i=1}^{k} \theta_i^{\alpha_i - 1} \tag{7}$$

where $\sum_{i=1}^{k} \theta_i = 1, \quad \theta_i \geq 0, \quad \alpha_i > 0, \quad i = 1, 2, \ldots, k$, and $\Gamma(\cdot)$ is the Gamma function. Then, the random variable θ is said to obey the Dirichlet distribution with concentration parameter α and denoted as $\theta \sim Dir(\alpha)$.

Dirichlet distribution θ exists on the $(k-1)$-dimensional simplex, as shown in Figure 1.

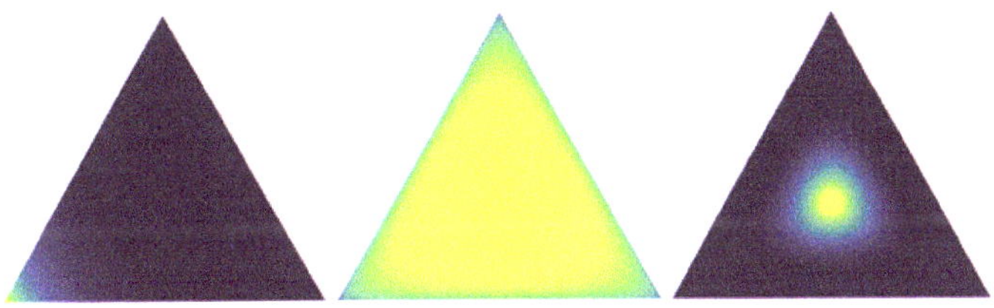

(a) (b) (c)

Figure 1. Visualization of Dirichlet distribution, where $\theta = \{\theta_1, \theta_2, \theta_3\}$ and $\theta_1, \theta_2, \theta_3 \geq 0$, $\theta_1 + \theta_2 + \theta_3 = 1$. **(a)** $\alpha = (10, 1, 1)$; **(b)** $\alpha = (1.001, 1.001, 1.001)$; **(c)** $\alpha = (10, 10, 10)$. Bright yellow represents high probability, and dark blue represents low probability. In the multi-classification problem, each vertex is regarded as a category.

The most important property of the Dirichlet distribution is that it is the conjugate prior to the multinomial distribution. If θ follows the Dirichlet distribution, its prior probability distribution is $p(\theta|\alpha) = Dir(\theta|\alpha)$ and posterior probability distribution is $p(\theta|D, \alpha) = Dir(\theta|\alpha + n)$, where D is the given simplex and $n = (n_1, n_2, \ldots, n_k)$ is the observation count of the multinomial distribution. The concentration parameters $\alpha = \{\alpha_1, \alpha_2, \ldots, \alpha_k\}$ of the Dirichlet distribution as a priori distribution are also called the hyperparameters of the posterior distribution. Hence, it is convenient to obtain the posterior distribution from the prior distribution.

4. Research Methodology

Following the two-stage alignment framework in MFSAN [55], a novel Multi-source domain Adaptation Network with Dempster–Shafer evidence theory (MAN-DS) for cross-domain classification is proposed. MAN-DS aims to train a model based on multi-source domain labeled samples and adapts to classify target instances with different distributions. As shown in Figure 2, the MAN-DS framework consists of four key components, i.e., common feature extractor, domain-specific feature extractor, domain-specific classifier, and Dempster's combination. Different source domains are extracted into different feature spaces, and then, the distribution alignment of each pair of source and target domains and the output alignment of every source classifier are imposed. Domain-specific adaptation outputs are combined by Dempster's rule in the end. Besides, the *softmax* layer of the classifier is replaced with an activation layer (e.g., ReLU).

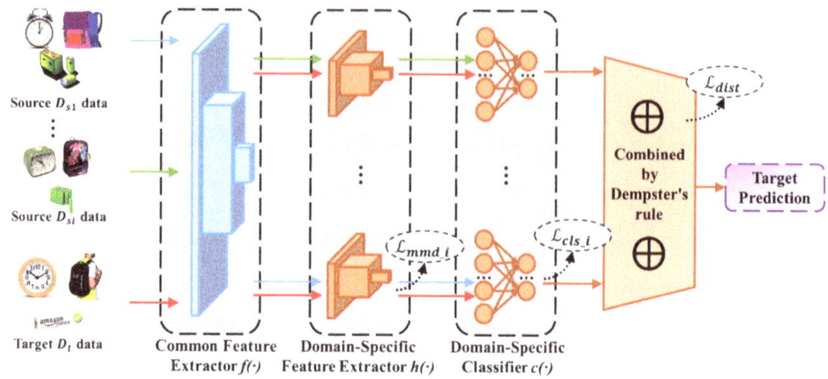

Figure 2. The overall structure of MAN-DS.

4.1. Common Feature Extractor

The damages of domain shifts cannot be eliminated in SDA, so it is more difficult to learn a common domain-invariant representation for all domains in MDA. To address this problem, the easiest way is to train multiple networks to map each source–target domain pair into a specific feature space. However, this would take too much time and space. Thus, the feature extractor is divided into two parts. The first part extracts common features, and the second part extracts domain-specific features (see the next section). In the first part, a common convolutional neural subnetwork $f(\cdot)$ is used to automatically map samples in all domains from the original feature space into a common feature space.

4.2. Domain-Specific Feature Extractor

Now, we come to the second part where domain-specific features are extracted by different extractors. For each pair of source and target domains, a specific subnetwork $h_i(\cdot)$ aims to map $f(\mathbf{x}_{si})$ and $f(\mathbf{x}_t)$ into the same domain-specific feature space. The objective of domain adaptation is to find a domain-invariant representation between domains. In other words, an $h_i(\cdot)$ is desired, which makes the distribution discrepancy between $h_i(f(\mathbf{x}_{si}))$ and $h_i(f(\mathbf{x}_t))$ as small as possible. There are many explicit or implicit methods to achieve this goal. Here, the most widely used MMD is employed to reduce the distribution discrepancy between domains. The MMD loss is reformulated as:

$$\mathcal{L}_{mmd} = \frac{1}{N}\sum_{i=1}^{N} \text{MMD}^2[\mathcal{F}, h_i(f(X_s i)), h_i(f(X_t))] \tag{8}$$

4.3. Domain-Specific Classifier

Traditionally, a series of *softmax* classifiers $c_i(\cdot)$ is employed to classify the source domain samples after extracting domain-specific invariant features, respectively. However, the use of the exponent in the *softmax* function leads to the probability of the predicted category being inflated. It was replaced with an activation function (e.g., RELU) to ensure that the network outputs non-negative values in this research study. The multi-classification problem is a multinomial distribution fitting problem. As the conjugate prior, the Dirichlet distribution is convenient to obtain the posterior distribution from the prior distribution.

Subjective logic [31] defines a theoretical framework for obtaining the probabilities of different classes and the overall uncertainty of the multi-classification problem based on the *evidence* collected from the data. SL provides an additional mass function, which allows the model to distinguish between a lack of evidence. In our model, SL provides the degree of overall uncertainty of each source, which is important for final decisions to some extent.

For the K-classification problem, the nonnegative-activated output $e = (e_1, e_2, \ldots, e_k)$ of the last fully connected layer of the classifier refers to *evidence* and is closely related to the concentration parameters $\alpha = (\alpha_1, \alpha_2, \ldots, \alpha + k)$ of the Dirichlet distribution, as shown in the following:

$$\alpha_k = e_k + 1, \quad k = 1, 2, \ldots, K \tag{9}$$

With subjective logic, for each pair of the source–target domain, the probability $b_k^{(i)}$ for the kth category and the overall uncertainty $u^{(i)}$ are calculated by:

$$\begin{aligned} b_k^{(i)} &= \frac{e_k^{(i)}}{S^{(i)}} = \frac{\alpha_k^{(i)} - 1}{S^{(i)}} \\ u^{(i)} &= \frac{K}{S^{(i)}} \end{aligned} \tag{10}$$

where $S^{(i)} = \sum_{k=1}^{K}(e_k^{(i)} + 1) = \sum_{k=1}^{K}(\alpha_k^{(i)})$ is the Dirichlet strength. Obviously, $u^{(i)} + \sum_{k=1}^{K} b_k^{(i)} = 1$. Correspondingly, the less total evidence observed, the greater the total uncertainty is. The mean of the corresponding Dirichlet distribution $\hat{\boldsymbol{P}}_{si}$ for the probability $\hat{p}_i^{(k)}$ is computed as $\hat{p}_i^{(k)} = \frac{\alpha_i^{(i)}}{S^{(i)}}$.

In addition, Figure 3 demonstrates the process of the outputs of multiple domain-specific classifiers in detail. The evidence of each source is obtained using neural networks (Step ①). According to subjective logic [31] , the obtained evidence parameterizes the Dirichlet distribution (Step ②) to induce the classification probability and uncertainty (Step ③). The classification probability and overall uncertainty are inferred by combining the belief masses of multiple sources based on Dempster's rule (Step ④). Dempster's combining is discussed in Section 4.4.

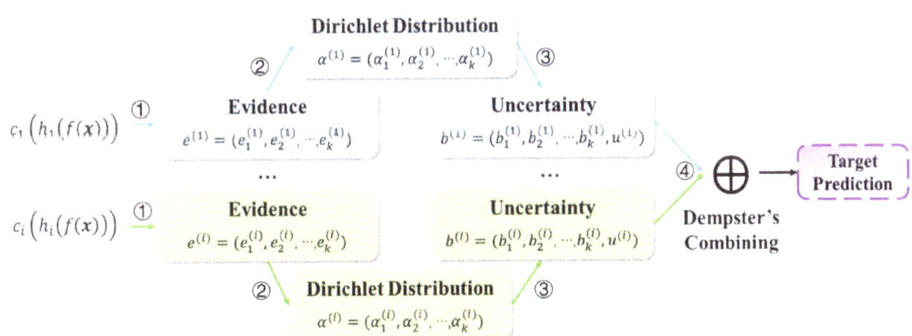

Figure 3. The process of combining the outputs of multiple domain-specific classifiers.

Source domain task loss $\mathcal{L}_{cls}$ is calculated here. To adapt to the Dirichlet distribution [65], the cross-entropy function is formulated as (11).

$$\begin{aligned} \mathcal{L}_{ace}\left(\boldsymbol{\alpha}^{(i)}\right) &= \int \left[\sum_{k=1}^{K} -y_{ij}\log\left(p_{jk}\right)\right] \frac{1}{B\left(\boldsymbol{\alpha}_j\right)} \prod_{k=1}^{K} p_{jk}^{\alpha_{jk}^{(i)}-1} d\mathbf{p}_j \\ &= \sum_{k=1}^{K} y_{jk}\left(\psi\left(S^{(i)}\right) - \psi\left(\alpha_{jk}^{(i)}\right)\right) \end{aligned} \tag{11}$$

where $\psi(\cdot)$ is the digamma function, the parameter $\boldsymbol{\alpha}_i$ of the Dirichlet distribution and forming the multinomial opinions $D(\boldsymbol{p}_i\ \boldsymbol{\alpha}_i)$, where $\boldsymbol{p}_i$ is the category assignment probabilities on a simplex, and p_{jk} is the predicted probability of the j_{th} sample for category k.

The above loss function ensures that more evidence is generated for the correct label of each sample than for other classes, but there is no guarantee that less evidence is generated for the incorrect label. That is, in MAN-DS, the expected evidence of incorrect labels shrinks to 0 [66]. To this end, the following KL divergence term is introduced:

$$\begin{aligned} KL\left[D(\mathbf{p}_j \mid \tilde{\boldsymbol{\alpha}}_j) \| D(\mathbf{p}_j \mid \mathbf{1})\right] = \log\left(\frac{\Gamma\left(\sum_{k=1}^{K}\tilde{\alpha}_{jk}\right)}{\Gamma(K)\prod_{k=1}^{K}\Gamma\left(\tilde{\alpha}_{jk}\right)}\right) \\ +\sum_{k=1}^{K}\left(\tilde{\alpha}_{jk}-1\right)\left[\psi\left(\tilde{\alpha}_{jk}\right)-\psi\left(\sum_{r=1}^{K}\tilde{\alpha}_{jr}\right)\right] \end{aligned} \tag{12}$$

Therefore, given parameter $\boldsymbol{\alpha}_j$ of the Dirichlet distribution for each sample j, the loss is:

$$\mathcal{L}\left(\boldsymbol{\alpha}^{(i)}\right) = \sum_{j=1}^{n_{si}} \mathcal{L}(\boldsymbol{\alpha}_j) = \sum_{j=1}^{n_{si}} \left\{\mathcal{L}_{ace}(\boldsymbol{\alpha}_j) + \rho KL\left[D(\mathbf{p}_j \mid \tilde{\boldsymbol{\alpha}}_j) \| D(\mathbf{p}_j \mid \mathbf{1})\right]\right\} \tag{13}$$

where $\rho > 0$ is a balance factor. In practice, ρ increases slowly from zero to 1 to avoid paying too much attention to the KL divergence term in the early stage of learning.

That is, the classification loss is formulated as:

$$\mathcal{L}_{cls} = \sum_{i}^{N} \mathcal{L}\left(\boldsymbol{\alpha}^{(i)}\right) \tag{14}$$

4.4. Dempster's Combination

With subjective logic, there is an FoD $\Theta = \{1, 2, \ldots, K\}$ and $K+1$ focal elements $\{\{1\}, \{2\}, \ldots, \{K\}, \Theta\}$ with belief mass $\{b_1, b_2, \ldots, b_k, u\}$ in every source–target domain pair. To fuse these adaptation outputs from N sources, only call Dempster's rule (defined in (5)) $N-1$ times as:

$$m_{\oplus}(b_k) = m_1(b_k) \oplus m_2(b_k) \oplus, \ldots, \oplus m_{N-1}(b_k) \tag{15}$$

In addition, the prediction results of multiple classifiers for the same target sample should be consistent. Dempster's combination could help to avoid ambiguity and large uncertainty on the category boundary, which is demonstrated in Figure 4.

Moreover, the Manhattan distance is used to measure the difference among the classifiers to achieve this goal, as well. Denote $e^{(i)} = e_1^{(i)}, e_2^{(i)}, \ldots, e_k^{(i)}, e^{(i)} = \alpha^{(i)} - 1 = b^{(i)} S^{(i)}$ as the final output of the ith source–target domain pair. The loss-of-label Manhattan distance is formulated as:

$$\mathcal{L}_{dist} = \frac{1}{N} \sum_{i}^{N} |e^{(i)} - m_{\oplus}(e)| \tag{16}$$

4.5. Objective Function and Algorithm

The overall objective function of the proposed model is formulated as (17).

$$\underset{f,h,c}{\arg\min}(\mathcal{L}_{cls} + \gamma \mathcal{L}_{mmd} + \lambda \mathcal{L}_{disc}) \tag{17}$$

In detail, $\mathcal{L}_{cls}$ is minimized to accomplish the source domain task; $\mathcal{L}_{mmd}$ is minimized to reduce the domain shifts between each source domain and the target domain; $\mathcal{L}_{disc}$ is a consistent regular term and minimized to constrain the outputs of domain-specific classifiers. In addition, γ and λ are trade-off parameters; refer to (1).

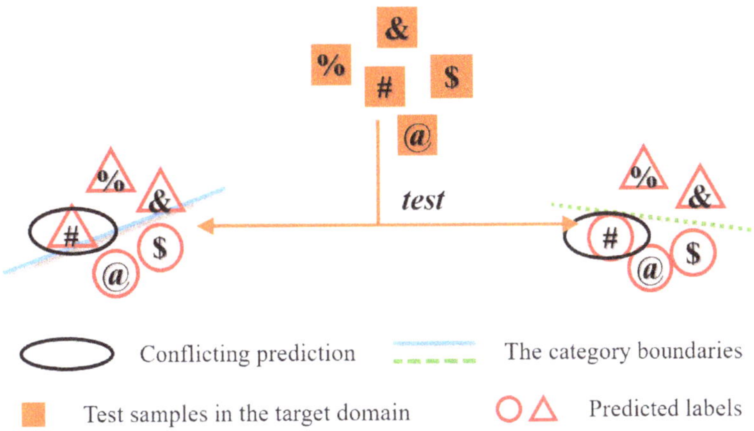

Figure 4. The demonstration the prediction conflict of domain-specific classifiers.

The algorithm of MAN-DS is summarized in Algorithm 1, and it can be trained by the standard back-propagation.

Algorithm 1 The algorithm of the proposed method

Input: source domain data $\{\mathcal{D}_{si}\}_{i=1}^{N}$, target domain data $\mathcal{D}_t$, the number of training iterations T, and batch size M;
Output: model parameters;
1: Initialize the parameters of $f(\cdot)$, $g(\cdot)$, $h_i(\cdot)$, $c_i(\cdot)$;
2: **for** $t = 1, \ldots, T$ **do**
3: Randomly sample a batch of $\{(\boldsymbol{x}_{si}^{(j)}, y_{si}^{(j)})\}_{j=1}^{M}$ from $\mathcal{D}_{si}$, respectively;
4: Randomly sample a batch of $\{\boldsymbol{x}_t^{(j)}\}_{j=1}^{M}$ from $\mathcal{D}_t$;
5: Extract common features $f(\boldsymbol{x}_{si}^{(j)})$ and $f(\boldsymbol{x}_t^{(j)})$;
6: Extract domain-specific features $h_i(f(\boldsymbol{x}_{si}^{(j)}))$ and $h_i(f(\boldsymbol{x}_t^{(j)}))$;
7: Compute $\mathcal{L}_{mmd}$ with $h_i(f(\boldsymbol{x}_{si}^{(j)}))$ and $h_i(f(\boldsymbol{x}_t^{(j)}))$ by (8);
8: Obtain $c_i(h_i(f(\boldsymbol{x}_{si}^{(j)})))$ for classification and compute $\mathcal{L}_{cls}$ by (14);
9: Obtain $c_i(h_i(f(\boldsymbol{x}_t^{(j)})))$, and combine them by (5)
10: Compute $\mathcal{L}_{dist}$ by (16);
11: Update parameters by (17).
12: **end for**

---

5. Experiment

The effectiveness of our cross-domain classification method was verified by conducting comprehensive experiments on three well-known benchmarks: **ImageCLEF-DA**, **Office-31**, and **Office-Home**.

5.1. Data Preparation

ImageCLEF-DA [67] is a benchmark dataset for the ImageCLEF 2014 domain adaptation challenge, which is organized by selecting the 12 common categories shared by the following three public datasets, each considered as a domain: Caltech-256(**C**), ImageNet ILSVRC 2012(**I**), and Pascal VOC 2012 (**P**). There are 50 images in each category and 600 images in each domain. All domain combinations were used, and three transfer tasks were built: **C**, **I** → **P**; **C**,**P** → **I**; **I**,**P** → **C**.

Office-31 [68] is a benchmark for domain adaptation, comprising 4110 images in 31 classes collected from three distinct domains: Amazon (**A**), which contains images downloaded from amazon.com, Webcam (**W**), and DSLR (**D**), which contains images taken by a web camera and digital SLR camera with different photographic settings. The images in each domain are unbalanced. To enable unbiased evaluation, all methods were evaluated on all three transfer tasks: **A, W → D; A,W → D; W,D → A**.

Office-Home [69] consists of 15,588 images, larger than Office-31 and ImageCLEF-DA. It consists of images from 4 different domains: Artistic images (**A**), Clip Art (**C**), Product images (**P**), and Real-World images (**R**). For each domain, the dataset contains images of 65 object categories collected in the office and home settings. All domain combinations were used, and four transfer tasks were built:: **A, P, R → C; A, P, C → R; A, R, C → P; P, R, C → A**.

5.2. Compared Method

There is a small amount of MDA work based on a domain-specific distribution and classifier alignment architecture. To verify the effectiveness of our MDSAN model, the Multiple Feature Spaces Adaptation Network (MFSAN) [55] was introduced as the multi-source baseline. In addition, the proposed method was compared with ResNet [70], Deep Domain Confusion (DDC) [14], the Deep Adaptation Network (DAN) [71], Deep CORAL (DCORAL) [72], and Reverse Gradient (RevGrad) [73].

There are several comparative standards for different purposes. (1) **Source combine**: all source domains are combined into a traditional single-source vs. target setting; (2) **Single best**: the best single source transfer results among the multiple candidate source domains with SDA methods; (3) **Multi-source**: the results of MDA methods. The first standard is to verify whether multiple source domains are beneficial for the target task or whether the simple combination of source domains will lead to negative transfer. In addition, the second standard evaluates whether the best SDA method could be further improved by introducing other source domains. The third standard demonstrates the effectiveness of the proposed approach.

Furthermore, ablation experiments were performed to verify the effectiveness of DST for adaptation outputs' fusion. This variant is denoted as V_1, which simply averages the outputs in the end. In addition, variant V_2 does not consider $\mathcal{L}_{mmd}$, and variant V_3 ignores $\mathcal{L}_{dist}$.

5.3. Implementation Details

All methods were implemented based on the PyTorch framework and deployed and testified on the same device. For a fair comparison, the same data pre-processing routines and model architecture were utilized in all experiments. The pre-trained ResNet50 [70] was employed as the common feature extractor, where the fine-tuning strategy was used to save time. For all domain-specific feature extractors, the same structure $(conv(1 \times 1), conv(3 \times 3), conv(1 \times 1))$ was utilized. At the end of the neural network, the channels were reduced to 256, like DDC [14]. According to subjective logic, the $softmax$ layer was replaced with $softplus$ to activate the outputs and avoid negative values. The optimization method was mini-batch stochastic gradient descent with a momentum of 0.9. The learning rate was gradually decreased by $\eta_p = \frac{\eta_0}{(1+\alpha)^{\beta}}$, where p is the training progress linearly changing from 0 to 1, and $\eta_0 = 0.01, \alpha = 10, \beta = 0.75$. This would optimize to promote convergence and low error on the source domain. As for the hyperparameters, $\gamma = \rho = 100\lambda$ was simply set. They were changed from 0 to 1 by a progressive schedule $\gamma_p = \frac{2}{\exp(-\theta p)} - 1, (\theta = 10)$, instead of fixing them throughout the experiments.

5.4. Experimental Results

MAN-DS was compared with the above-mentioned methods on three datasets, and the average results of five repeated experiments are reported in Tables 1–3, respectively. The maximum accuracy in a transfer task is marked in bold.

Table 1. Performance comparison of classification accuracy (%) on Office-31 dataset.

Standards	Method	A,W→D	A,D→W	W,D→A	Average
Single Best	ResNet	99.33	96.50	61.87	85.90
	DDC	99.33	95.80	67.33	87.49
	DAN	99.43	97.61	66.70	87.91
	DCORAL	99.53	98.20	65.20	87.64
	RevGrad	99.27	96.67	68.53	88.16
Source Combine	DAN	99.57	97.50	67.73	88.27
	DCORAL	99.33	98.00	67.83	88.39
	RevGrad	99.73	97.67	67.77	88.39
Multi-Source	MFSAN	99.33	98.67	71.50	89.83
	V_1	99.79	98.50	67.02	88.44
	V_2	99.73	98.74	66.02	88.16
	V_3	99.79	98.86	73.87	90.84
	MAN-DS	**100.00**	**99.12**	**74.16**	**91.09**

Table 2. Performance comparison of classification accuracy (%) on Image-CLEF dataset.

Standards	Method	C,P→I	I,P→C	I,C→P	Average
Single Best	ResNet	74.83	91.53	83.90	83.42
	DDC	74.37	91.33	85.33	83.68
	DAN	75.10	93.33	86.13	84.85
	DCORAL	76.67	93.43	88.33	86.14
	RevGrad	75.07	94.00	87.07	85.38
Source Combine	DAN	77.67	93.00	91.70	87.46
	DCORAL	77.73	93.20	91.33	87.42
	RevGrad	78.00	93.03	91.87	87.63
Multi-Source	MFSAN	79.17	94.50	**93.33**	89.00
	V_1	77.67	95.50	92.83	88.67
	V_2	77.16	93.50	91.33	87.33
	V_3	**79.56**	94.50	91.87	88.40
	MAN-DS	79.00	**95.67**	93.17	**89.28**

Table 3. Performance comparison of classification accuracy (%) on Office-Home dataset.

Standards	Method	C,P,R→A	A,P,R→C	A,C,R→P	A,C,P→R	Average
Single Best	ResNet	65.28	48.54	77.56	74.55	66.48
	DDC	64.13	50.22	78.42	75.00	66.94
	DAN	69.07	56.46	79.63	74.65	69.95
	DCORAL	66.56	55.15	81.38	76.32	69.85
	RevGrad	67.58	55.88	80.32	75.86	69.91
Source Combine	DAN	69.07	59.40	78.41	82.50	72.35
	DCORAL	68.24	57.62	79.67	83.24	72.19
	RevGrad	67.88	57.22	79.52	82.74	71.84
Multi-Source	MFSAN	72.86	62.34	80.32	81.86	74.35
	V_1	74.32	62.12	82.31	83.13	75.47
	V_2	72.86	62.34	80.32	81.86	74.35
	V_3	74.12	63.56	82.52	82.74	75.74
	MAN-DS	**74.50**	**64.44**	**82.56**	**83.29**	**76.20**

6. Discussion

6.1. Result Observations

From these experimental results, insightful observations are given:

- The results of Source combine were better than Single best, which shows that the knowledge of the multi-source domain is useful to the target task. That is, the multi-source domains have transferability. Combining sources into a single source is helpful in most domain adaptation methods. The performance improvement might be attributed to the data enrichment.
- MAN-DS outperformed all compared methods on most transfer tasks in all three datasets, especially in the Office-Home dataset. The results indicate that it is beneficial to learn the domain-invariant representation and align the distribution in each pair of the source and target domain with considering domain-specific category boundaries. Besides, DST alleviates the ambiguity and uncertainty of the prediction and promotes classification accuracy successfully.
- Comparing MAN-DS with the variant V_1, the only difference is that the proposed method employs DST to fuse the adaptation outputs, while V_1 averages them simply. Although DST was applied in $\mathcal{L}_{dist}$ to align domain-specific boundaries, the proposed method still has an improvement over V_1. Thus, DST is excellent to tackle the ambiguity and uncertainty of the prediction.
- Comparing MAN-DS with the variant V_2, the only difference is that V_2 does not consider $\mathcal{L}_{mmd}$. The experimental results show that MMD helps domain adaptation very little. Meanwhile, the proposed $\mathcal{L}_{dist}$ and Dempster's combination rule could also help to align the distribution to some extent.
- Comparing MAN-DS with the variant V_3, the only difference is that V_3 ignores $\mathcal{L}_{dist}$. There is little difference in the experimental results, which indicates that DST is powerful to handle the prediction conflicts on the category boundaries.

6.2. Ablation Experiment

Ablation experiments were implemented by conducting V_1, V_2, and V_3, as shown in Tables 1–3. The encouraging results show that every component of MAN-DS is positive to improve performance.

To further verify the effectiveness of the DST fusion strategy, supplementary experiments were carried out where S_i is the $i$sth domain-specific classifier, as reported in Table 4. The maximum accuracy in a transfer task is marked in bold.

Table 4. Classification accuracy (%) with and without DST fusion strategy on Office-Home dataset.

Method	C,P,R→A	A,P,R→C	A,C,R→P	A,C,P→R
S_1	72.56	59.48	80.33	80.59
S_2	65.58	61.54	75.54	75.78
S_3	71.39	60.56	79.87	82.36
DST	**74.50**	**64.44**	**82.56**	**83.29**

6.3. Feature Visualization

Feature visualization is demonstrated in Figure 5. The category boundaries of the domain-specific classifier on the task **D,W→A** learned by MAN-DS and MFSAN are visualized by using t-SNE embeddings. It is clear that MAN-DS is more effective in dealing with prediction conflicts, in which DST is effective.

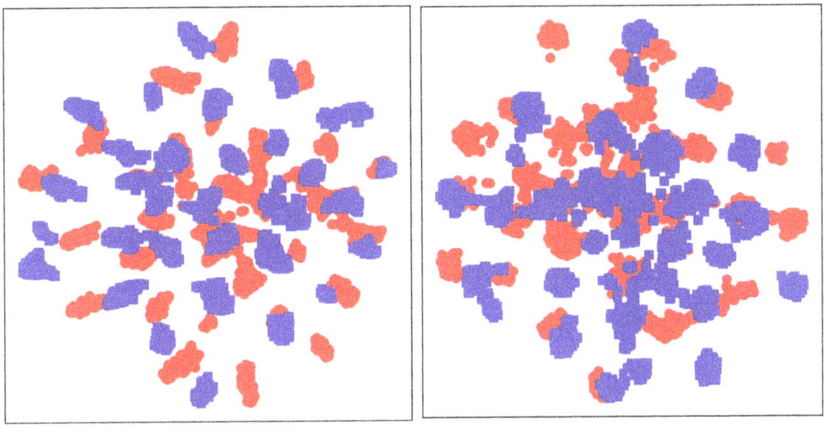

(**a**) MAN-DS (**b**) MFSAN

Figure 5. Domain-specific classifier feature visualization.

6.4. Parameter Sensitivity

Parameter sensitivity was tested by sampling the trade-off parameter (where $\gamma = \rho = 100\lambda$ for simplicity) values in $\{0.01, 0.02, 0.05, 0.1, 0.2, 0.5, 1, 2\}$. To study the parameters' sensitivity, the experiments were implemented on task **D**,**W**→**A** and **A**,**C**→**R**, and the results are shown in Figure 6. As observed, the accuracy increases with the increase of γ and reaches a peak at $\gamma = 1$, then decreases. The proposed method MAN-DS can keep a relatively stable result in the range of $(0.1, 2)$ of γ, which is higher than the baseline. Generally, MAN-DS is not sensitive to changes in the parameters in a certain range. Hence, setting γ to $(0.1, 2)$ is recommended to achieve better performance. In the reported experiment, the parameters $\{\gamma, \rho, \lambda\}$ were set to $\{1, 1, 0.01\}$, respectively.

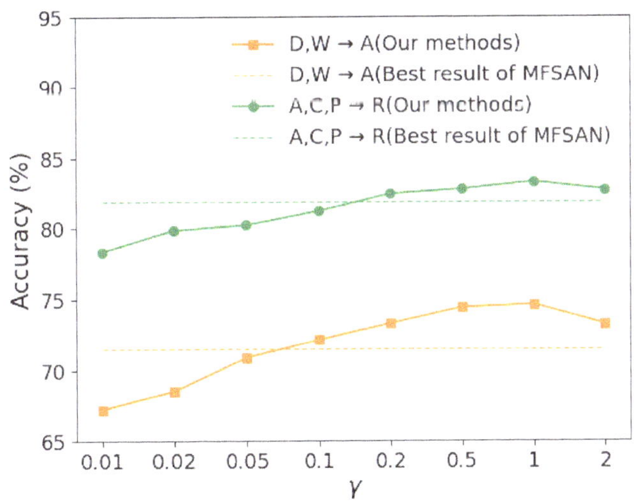

Figure 6. Accuracy with respect to $\gamma = \rho = 100\lambda$.

6.5. Computational Complexity

The FLoating point OPerations (FLOPs) were used to measure the operation times of forward propagation in neural network; the smaller the FLOPs, the faster the computation speed is. In addition, the smaller the number of PARAMeters (PARAMs) in the neural network, the smaller the size of the model is. Table 5 shows the FLOPs and PARAMs of MAN-DS, MFSAN, and ResNet50. Compared with ResNet50, the small increase of computational complexity mainly comes from the component of domain-specific feature extractors and classifiers. Compared with the baseline MFSAN, MAN-DS improves the accuracy without increasing the computational complexity.

Table 5. FLOPs and PARAMs.

Method	FLOPs	PARAMs
MAN-DS	4.23 G	25.88 M
MFSAN	4.23 G	25.88 M
ResNet50	4.12 G	25.56 M

Moreover, Dempster's combination does not increase the computational complexity of the algorithm. For the K-classification task, MAN-DS always obtains $K+1$ instead of 2^K focal elements, which is $\{1, 2, \ldots, K, \Theta\}$. That is, the computational complexity caused by Dempster's combination is not $O(2^n)$, but $O(n)$.

7. Conclusions

The core of MDA is making full use of available source data collected from several different, but related domains. However, it becomes difficult and challenging due to the multiple domain shifts. Following the domain-specific alignment architecture, this study proposed a novel multi-source domain adaptation network combing Dempster–Shafer evidence theory for cross-domain image classification to reduce multiple domain shifts and enhance transfer accuracy. In addition, SL and the Dirichlet distribution were employed to bridge MDA with DST.

To evaluate the effectiveness of the proposed method, three popular benchmark datasets were used and ten transfer tasks were devised to train and validate MAN-DS. Extensive experiments demonstrated that MAN-DS outperforms its competitors in cross-domain image classification. The insightful conclusions are as follows:

- MAN-DS achieved good accuracy in all ten transfer tasks of three datasets. On the Office-Home dataset, MAN-DS even improved the average adaptation accuracy to 76.20%, which is about 2% higher than the best baseline.
- Feature visualization shows that MAN-DS could alleviate boundary conflicts to some extent, due to effective DST.
- MAN-DS is not sensitive to changes in parameters in a certain range $\gamma \in (0.1, 2)$, generally.
- MAN-DS improved accuracy without increasing computational complexity. Compared with the baseline MFSAN, the FLOPs and PARAMs of MAN-DS were 4.23 G and 25.88 M, which are close to the 4.12 G and 25.56 M of ResNet. Especially, MAN-DS reduced the computational overhead of the outputs' combination from $O(2^n)$ to $O(n)$.
- Ablation experiments indicated that every component of MAN-DS is positive to improve performance.
- The encouraging results show that SL could effectively bridge MDA with DST.
- This research study empirically demonstrates DST could reduce the category boundary ambiguity, so as to mitigate the negative impact of multiple domain shifts.

In this research study, the original and unimproved Dempster's rule was used. In the future, the combination rules will be optimized based on the improved information entropy method to take more evidence information into account. Besides, more effective MDA and DST bridging methods will be investigated.

Author Contributions: Conceptualization, M.H. and C.Z.; methodology, M.H. and C.Z.; software, C.Z.; validation, M.H.; formal analysis, M.H.; investigation, M.H. and C.Z.; resources, M.H.; data curation, M.H.; writing—original draft preparation, C.Z.; writing—review and editing, M.H. and C.Z.; visualization, C.Z.; supervision, M.H.; project administration, M.H.; funding acquisition, M.H. All authors have read and agreed to the published version of the manuscript.

Funding: The work described in this paper was partially funded by two Natural Science Foundation of Guangdong Province Projects of Grant Number 2021A1515011496 and Grant Number 2022A1515011370.

Institutional Review Board Statement: Not applicable.

Informed Consent Statement: Not applicable.

Data Availability Statement: Not applicable.

Acknowledgments: The authors would like to thank the Editor and the Reviewers for their valuable comments and suggestions.

Conflicts of Interest: The authors declare no conflict of interest.

Abbreviations

The following abbreviations are used in this manuscript:

DA	Domain Adaptation
SDA	Single-source Domain Adaptation
MDA	Multi-source Domain Adaptation
SL	Subjective Logic
DL	Deep Learning
DST	Dempster–Shafer evidence Theory
BPAF	Basic Probability Assignment Function
MMD	Maximum Mean Discrepancy
FLOPs	FLoating point OPerations
PARAMs	PARAMeters

References

1. Dai, Z.; Cai, B.; Lin, Y.; Chen, J. Up-detr: Unsupervised pre-training for object detection with transformers. In Proceedings of the IEEE/CVF Conference on Computer Vision and Pattern Recognition, Nashville, TN, USA, 20–25 June 2021; pp. 1601–1610. [CrossRef]
2. Xu, J.; Zhou, H.; Gan, C.; Zheng, Z.; Li, L. Vocabulary learning via optimal transport for neural machine translation. In Proceedings of the 59th Annual Meeting of the Association for Computational Linguistics and the 11th International Joint Conference on Natural Language Processing, Virtual, 1–6 August, 2021; Volume 1, pp. 7361–7373. [CrossRef]
3. Zhou, H.; Zhang, S.; Peng, J.; Zhang, S.; Li, J.; Xiong, H.; Zhang, W. Informer: Beyond efficient transformer for long sequence time-series forecasting. In Proceedings of the Thirty-Fifth AAAI Conference on Artificial Intelligence, Virtual, 2–9 Februarys 2021.
4. Huang, M.; Cheng, C.; De Luca, G. Remote Sensing Data Detection Based on Multiscale Fusion and Attention Mechanism. *Mob. Inf. Syst.* **2021**, 2021, 6466051. [CrossRef]
5. Yu, Y.; Rashidi, M.; Samali, B.; Mohammadi, M.; Nguyen, T.N.; Zhou, X. Crack detection of concrete structures using deep convolutional neural networks optimized by enhanced chicken swarm algorithm. *Struct. Health Monit.* **2022**. [CrossRef]
6. Lyu, Z.; Yu, Y.; Samali, B.; Rashidi, M.; Mohammadi, M.; Nguyen, T.N.; Nguyen, A. Back-Propagation Neural Network Optimized by K-Fold Cross-Validation for Prediction of Torsional Strength of Reinforced Concrete Beam. *Materials* **2022**, *15*, 1477. [CrossRef]
7. Liu, J.; Mohammadi, M.; Zhan, Y.; Zheng, P.; Rashidi, M.; Mehrabi, P. Utilizing Artificial Intelligence to Predict the Superplasticizer Demand of Self-Consolidating Concrete Incorporating Pumice, Slag, and Fly Ash Powders. *Materials* **2021**, *14*, 6792. [CrossRef]
8. Gou, J.; He, X.; Lu, J.; Ma, H.; Ou, W.; Yuan, Y. A Class-Specific Mean Vector-Based Weighted Competitive and Collaborative Representation Method for Classification. *Neural Netw.* **2022**, *150*, 12–27. [CrossRef]
9. Gou, J.; Yuan, X.; Du, L.; Xia, S.; Yi, Z. Hierarchical Graph Augmented Deep Collaborative Dictionary Learning for Classification. *IEEE Trans. Intell. Transp. Syst.* **2022**. [CrossRef]
10. Gou, J.; Qiu, W.; Yi, Z.; Xu, Y.; Mao, Q.; Zhan, Y. A Local Mean Representation-Based K-Nearest Neighbor Classifier. *ACM Trans. Intell. Syst. Technol.* **2019**, *10*, 1–25. [CrossRef]
11. Pan, S.J.; Yang, Q. A Survey on Transfer Learning. *IEEE Trans. Knowl. Data Eng.* **2010**, *22*, 1345–1359. [CrossRef]
12. Gou, J.; Yu, B.; Maybank, S.J.; Tao, D. Knowledge distillation: A survey. *Int. J. Comput. Vis.* **2021**, *129*, 1789–1819. [CrossRef]
13. Zhuang, F.; Qi, Z.; Duan, K.; Xi, D.; Zhu, Y.; Zhu, H.; Xiong, H.; He, Q. A Comprehensive Survey on Transfer Learning. *Proc. IEEE* **2021**, *109*, 43–76. [CrossRef]

14. Tzeng, E.; Hoffman, J.; Zhang, N.; Saenko, K.; Darrell, T. Deep Domain Confusion: Maximizing for Domain Invariance. *arXiv* **2014**, arXiv:1412.3474.
15. Chen, S.; Harandi, M.; Jin, X.; Yang, X. Domain Adaptation by Joint Distribution Invariant Projections. *IEEE Trans. Image Process.* **2020**, *29*, 8264–8277. [CrossRef]
16. Zhu, Y.; Zhuang, F.; Wang, J.; Ke, G.; Chen, J.; Bian, J.; Xiong, H.; He, Q. Deep Subdomain Adaptation Network for Image Classification. *IEEE Trans. Neural Netw. Learn. Syst.* **2021**, *32*, 1713–1722. [CrossRef]
17. Qiu, Z.; Zhang, Y.; Lin, H.; Niu, S.; Liu, Y.; Du, Q.; Tan, M. Source-free Domain Adaptation via Avatar Prototype Generation and Adaptation. In Proceedings of the 30th International Joint Conference on Artificial Intelligence, Virtual, 19–26 August 2021. [CrossRef]
18. Chen, S.; Hong, Z.; Harandi, M.; Yang, X. Domain Neural Adaptation. *IEEE Trans. Neural Netw. Learn. Syst.* **2022**, 1–12. [CrossRef]
19. Liu, J.; Li, J.; Lu, K. Coupled local–global adaptation for multi-source transfer learning. *Neurocomputing* **2018**, *275*, 247–254. [CrossRef]
20. Yin, Y.; Yang, Z.; Hu, H.; Wu, X. Universal multi-Source domain adaptation for image classification. *Pattern Recognit.* **2022**, *121*, 108238. [CrossRef]
21. Renchunzi, X.; Pratama, M. Automatic online multi-source domain adaptation. *Inf. Sci.* **2022**, *582*, 480–494. [CrossRef]
22. Sun, S.L.; Shi, H.L. Bayesian multi-source domain adaptation. In Proceedings of the 2013 International Conference on Machine Learning and Cybernetics, Tianjin, China, 14–17 July 2013; Volume 1, pp. 24–28. [CrossRef]
23. Chen, Z.; Wei, P.; Zhuang, J.; Li, G.; Lin, L. Deep CockTail Networks A Universal Framework for Visual Multi-source Domain Adaptation. *Int. J. Comput. Vis.* **2021**, *129*, 2328–2351. [CrossRef]
24. Zhao, H.; Zhang, S.; Wu, G.; Costeira, J.A.P.; Moura, J.M.F.; Gordon, G.J. Adversarial multiple source domain adaptation. In Proceedings of the 32nd International Conference on Neural Information Processing Systems, Red Hook, NY, USA, 3–8 December 2018; Curran Associates Inc.: Red Hook, NY, USA, 2018; p. 8568–8579.
25. Peng, X.; Bai, Q.; Xia, X.; Huang, Z.; Saenko, K.; Wang, B. Moment matching for multi-source domain adaptation. In Proceedings of the 2019 IEEE/CVF International Conference on Computer Vision (ICCV 2019), Seoul, Korea, 28–27 Octomber 2019; IEEE Computer Soc.: Los Alamitos, CA, USA, 2019; pp. 1406–1415. [CrossRef]
26. Chen, C.; Fu, Z.; Chen, Z.; Jin, S.; Cheng, Z.; Jin, X.; Hua, X.S. HoMM: Higher-Order Moment Matching for Unsupervised Domain Adaptation. *Proc. AAAI Conf. Artif. Intell.* **2020**, *34*, 3422–3429. [CrossRef]
27. Lin, C.; Zhao, S.; Meng, L.; Chua, T.S. Multi-Source Domain Adaptation for Visual Sentiment Classification. *Proc. AAAI Conf. Artif. Intell.* **2020**, *34*, 2661–2668. [CrossRef]
28. Fernandes Montesuma, E.; Mboula, F. Wasserstein barycenter for multi-source domain adaptation. In Proceedings of the 2021 IEEE/CVF Conference on Computer Vision and Pattern Recognition, Nashville, TN, USA, 20–25 June 2021; pp. 16780–16788. [CrossRef]
29. Zuo, Y.; Yao, H.; Xu, C. Attention-Based Multi-Source Domain Adaptation. *IEEE Trans. Image Process.* **2021**, *30*, 3793–3803. [CrossRef]
30. Zhang, D.; Ye, M.; Liu, Y.; Xiong, L.; Zhou, L. Multi-source unsupervised domain adaptation for object detection. *Inf. Fusion* **2022**, *78*, 138–148. [CrossRef]
31. Jøsang, A. *Subjective Logic: A Formalism for Reasoning Under Uncertainty*; Springer: Berlin/Heidelberg, Germany, 2016; Volume 3.
32. Chen, Y.; Song, S.; Li, S.; Wu, C. A Graph Embedding Framework for Maximum Mean Discrepancy-Based Domain Adaptation Algorithms. *IEEE Trans. Image Process.* **2020**, *29*, 199–213. [CrossRef]
33. Yan, H.; Li, Z.; Wang, Q.; Li, P.; Xu, Y.; Zuo, W. Weighted and Class-Specific Maximum Mean Discrepancy for Unsupervised Domain Adaptation. *IEEE Trans. Multimed.* **2020**, *22*, 2420–2433. [CrossRef]
34. Liu, W.; Li, J.; Liu, B.; Guan, W.; Zhou, Y.; Xu, C. Unified Cross-domain Classification via Geometric and Statistical Adaptations. *Pattern Recognit.* **2021**, *110*. [CrossRef]
35. Zhen, Z.; Wang, M.; Yan, H.; Nehorai, A. Aligning infinite-dimensional covariance matrices in reproducing Kernel Hilbert spaces for domain adaptation. In Proceedings of the 2018 IEEE/CVF Conference on Computer Vision and Pattern Recognition, Salt Lake City, UT, USA, 18–23 June 2018.
36. Han, C.; Lei, Y.; Xie, Y.; Zhou, D.; Gong, M. Learning smooth representations with generalized softmax for unsupervised domain adaptation. *Inf. Sci.* **2021**, *544*, 415–426. [CrossRef]
37. Li, J.; Luo, P.; Lin, F.; Chen, B. Conversational model adaptation via KL divergence regularization. In Proceedings of the Thirty-second AAAI Conference on Artificial Intelligence, New Orleans, LA, USA, 2–7 February 2018; pp. 5213–5219.
38. Sun, B.; Kate, S. *Deep CORAL: Correlation Alignment for Deep Domain Adaptation*; Springer International Publishing: Berlin/Heidelberg, Germany, 2016.
39. Chen, C.; Jiang, B.; Cheng, Z.; Jin, X. Joint Domain Matching and Classification for cross-domain adaptation via ELM. *Neurocomputing* **2019**, *349*, 314–325. [CrossRef]
40. Han Guo, Ramakanth Pasunuru, M.B. Multi-source domain adaptation for text classification via distanceNet-bandits. *Proc. AAAI Conf. Artif. Intell.* **2020**, *34*, 7830–7838.
41. Ganin, Y.; Ustinova, E.; Ajakan, H.; Germain, P.; Larochelle, H.; Laviolette, F.; Marchand, M.; Lempitsky, V. Domain-adversarial training of neural networks. *J. Mach. Learn. Res.* **2016**, *17*, 2096–2030.

42. Tzeng, E.; Hoffman, J.; Saenko, K.; Darrell, T. Adversarial discriminative domain adaptation. In Proceedings of the IEEE Conference on Computer Vision and Pattern Recognition, New York, NY, USA, 15–17 June 2017; pp. 2962–2971. [CrossRef]
43. Yu, C.; Wang, J.; Chen, Y.; Huang, M. Transfer learning with dynamic adversarial adaptation network. In Proceedigns of the 2019 IEEE International Conference on Data Mining (ICDM), Beijing, China, 8–14 November 2019; pp. 778–786.
44. Feng, C.; He, Z.; Wang, J.; Lin, Q.; Zhu, Z.; Lu, J.; Xie, S. Domain adaptation with SBADA-GAN and Mean Teacher. *Neurocomputing* **2020**, *396*, 577–586. [CrossRef]
45. Chen, W.; Hu, H. Generative attention adversarial classification network for unsupervised domain adaptation. *Pattern Recognit.* **2020**, *107*. [CrossRef]
46. Kang, Q.; Yao, S.; Zhou, M.; Zhang, K.; Abusorrah, A. Effective Visual Domain Adaptation via Generative Adversarial Distribution Matching. *IEEE Trans. Neural Netw. Learn. Syst.* **2021**, *32*, 3919–3929. [CrossRef]
47. Ghifary, M.; Kleijn, W.B.; Zhang, M.; Balduzzi, D.; Li, W. Deep reconstruction-classification networks for unsupervised domain adaptation. In *Computer Vision—ECCV 2016, PT IV*; Leibe, B., Matas, J., Sebe, N., Welling, M., Eds.; Lecture Notes in Computer Science; Springer, Cham, 2016; Volume 9908, pp. 597–613. [CrossRef]
48. Jiang, B.; Chen, C.; Jin, X. Unsupervised domain adaptation with target reconstruction and label confusion in the common subspace. *Neural Comput. Appl.* **2020**, *32*, 4743–4756. [CrossRef]
49. Wang, S.; Zhang, L.; Zuo, W.; Zhang, B. Class-Specific Reconstruction Transfer Learning for Visual Recognition Across Domains. *IEEE Trans. Image Process.* **2020**, *29*, 2424–2438. [CrossRef]
50. Zhu, J.Y.; Park, T.; Isola, P.; Efros, A.A. Unpaired Image-to-Image Translation using Cycle-Consistent Adversarial Networks. In Proceedings of the IEEE International Conference on Computer Vision, Venice, Italy, 22–29 October 2017; pp. 2242–2251. [CrossRef]
51. Yi, Z.; Zhang, H.; Tan, P.; Gong, M. DualGAN: Unsupervised Dual Learning for Image-to-Image Translation. In Proceedings of theIEEE International Conference on Computer Vision, Venice, Italy, 22–29 October 2017; pp. 2868–2876. [CrossRef]
52. Kim, T.; Cha, M.; Kim, H.; Lee, J.K.; Kim, J. Learning to discover cross-domain relations with generative adversarial networks. In Proceedings of the International Conference on Machine Learning, Sydney, Australia, 6–11 August 2017; Volume 70.
53. Blitzer, J.; Crammer, K.; Kulesza, A.; Pereira, F.; Wortman, J. Learning bounds for domain adaptation. In Proceedings of the 20th International Conference on Neural Information Processing Systems, Daegu, Korea, 3–7 November 2007; Curran Associates Inc.: Red Hook, NY, USA, 2007; pp. 129–136.
54. Ben-David, S.; Blitzer, J.; Crammer, K.; Kulesza, A.; Vaughan, P.J.W. A theory of learning from different domains. *Mach. Learn.* **2010**, *79*, 151–175 [CrossRef]
55. Zhu, Y.; Zhuang, F.; Wang, D. Aligning Domain-Specific Distribution and Classifier for Cross-Domain Classification from Multiple Sources. *Proc. AAAI Conf. Artif. Intell.* **2019**, *33*, 5989–5996. [CrossRef]
56. Dempster, A.P. Upper and lower probabilities generated by a random closed interval. *Ann. Math. Stat.* **1967**, *39*, 957–966. [CrossRef]
57. Dempster, A.P. A generalization of Bayesian inference. *J. R. Stat. Soc. Ser.* **1968**, *30*, 205–232. [CrossRef]
58. Shafer, G. A mathematical theory of evidence. In *A Mathematical Theory of Evidence*; Princeton University Press: Princeton, NJ, USA, 1976.
59. Jøsang, A.; Hankin, R. Interpretation and fusion of hyper opinions in subjective logic. In Proceedings of the 2012 15th International Conference on Information Fusion, Chicago, IL, USA, 5–8 July 2012; pp. 1225–1232.
60. Tong, Z.; Xu, P.; Denœux, T. An evidential classifier based on Dempster–Shafer theory and deep learning. *Neurocomputing* **2021**, *450*, 275–293. [CrossRef]
61. Huang, M.; Liu, Z. Research on mechanical fault prediction method based on multifeature fusion of vibration sensing data. *Sensors* **2019**, *20*, 6. [CrossRef]
62. Huang, M.; Liu, Z.; Tao, Y. Mechanical fault diagnosis and prediction in IoT based on multi-source sensing data fusion. *Simul. Model. Pract. Theory* **2020**, *102*, 101981. doi: 10.1016/j.simpat.2019.101981. [CrossRef]
63. Gretton, A.; Borgwardt, K.M.; Rasch, M.J.; Schoelkopf, B.; Smola, A. A Kernel Two-Sample Test. *J. Mach. Learn. Res.* **2012**, *13*, 723–773.
64. Gretton, A.; Sriperumbudur, B.; Sejdinovic, D.; Strathmann, H.; Kenji, F. Optimal kernel choice for large-scale two-sample tests. *Adv. Neural Inf. Process. Syst.* **2012**, *25*, 1205–1213.
65. Sensoy, M.; Kaplan, L.; Kandemir, M. Evidential deep learning to quantify classification uncertainty. *Adv. Neural Inf. Process. Syst.* **2018**, *31*, 3179–3189
66. Han, Z.; Zhang, C.; Fu, H.; Zhou, J.T. Trusted Multi-View Classification with Dynamic Evidential Fusion. *IEEE Trans. Pattern Anal. Mach. Intell.* **2022**. [CrossRef]
67. CLEF. ImageCLEF-DA. Available online: https://www.imageclef.org/2014/adaptation (accessed 24 May 2022).
68. Saenko, K.; Kulis, B.; Fritz, M.; Darrell, T. Adapting visual category models to new domains. In European Conference on Computer Vision, Heraklion, Greece, 5–11 September 2010; Springer: Berlin/Heidelberg, Germany, 1225–1232. 2010; pp. 213–226.
69. Venkateswara, H.; Eusebio, J.; Chakraborty, S.; Panchanathan, S. Deep hashing network for unsupervised domain adaptation. In Proceedings of the IEEE Conference on Computer Vision and Pattern Recognition, Honolulu, HI, USA, 21–26 July 2017; pp. 5018–5027.

70. He, K.; Zhang, X.; Ren, S.; Sun, J. Deep residual learning for image Recognition. In Proceedings of the 2016 IEEE Conference on Computer Vision and Pattern Recognition (CVPR), Las Vegas, NV, USA, 27–30 June 2016; pp. 770–778. 1225–1232. [CrossRef]
71. Long, M.; Cao, Y.; Cao, Z.; Wang, J.; Jordan, M.I. Transferable Representation Learning with Deep Adaptation Networks. *IEEE Trans. Pattern Anal. Mach. Intell.* **2019**, *41*, 3071–3085. [CrossRef]
72. Sun, B.; Saenko, K. Deep CORAL: Correlation alignment for deep domain adaptation. In *Computer Vision—ECCV 2016 Workshops*; Hua, G., Jégou, H., Eds.; Springer International Publishing: Cham, Switzerland, 2016; pp. 443–450. [CrossRef]
73. Ganin, Y.; Lempitsky, V. Unsupervised Domain Adaptation by Backpropagation. *arXiv* **2014**, arXiv:1409.7495v2 .

mathematics

MDPI

Article

An Improved Matting-SfM Algorithm for 3D Reconstruction of Self-Rotating Objects

Zinuo Li †, Zhen Zhang *,†, Shenghong Luo, Yuxing Cai and Shuna Guo

School of Computer Science and Engineering, Huizhou University, Huizhou 516007, China
* Correspondence: zzsjbme@sjtu.edu.cn; Tel.: +86-182-1726-7715
† These authors contributed equally to this work.

Abstract: The 3D reconstruction experiment can be performed accurately in most cases based on the structure from motion (SfM) algorithm with the combination of the multi-view stereo (MVS) framework through a video recorded around the object. However, we need to artificially hold the camera and stabilize the recording process as much as possible to obtain better accuracy. To eliminate the inaccurate recording caused by shaking during the recording process, we tried to fix the camera on a camera stand and placed the object on a motorized turntable to record. However, in this case, the background did not change when the camera position was kept still, and the large number of feature points from the background were not useful for 3D reconstruction, resulting in the failure of reconstructing the targeted object. To solve this problem, we performed video segmentation based on background matting to segment the object from the background, so that the original background would not affect the 3D reconstruction experiment. By intercepting the frames in the video, which eliminates the background as the input of the 3D reconstruction system, we could obtain an accurate 3D reconstruction result of an object that could not be reconstructed originally when the PSNR and SSIM increased to 11.51 and 0.26, respectively. It was proved that this algorithm can be applied to the display of online merchandise, providing an easy way for merchants to obtain an accurate model.

Keywords: 3D reconstruction; multi-view stereo; structure from motion; background matting

MSC: 68T45

Citation: Li, Z.; Zhang, Z.; Luo, S.; Cai, Y.; Guo, S. An Improved Matting-SfM Algorithm for 3D Reconstruction of Self-Rotating Objects. *Mathematics* **2022**, *10*, 2892. https://doi.org/10.3390/math10162892

Academic Editor: Jakub Nalepa

Received: 26 June 2022
Accepted: 11 August 2022
Published: 12 August 2022

1. Introduction

3D reconstruction refers to the establishment of mathematical models of three-dimensional objects that are suitable for computers to process, which is the foundation for processing, manipulating, and analyzing their properties in a computer environment and the key technology for establishing a virtual reality expressing the objective world in a computer. 3D reconstruction is generally vision-based, and is a way to obtain a 3D model of the target object by collecting images from a camera and obtaining 3D coordinates according to the triangulation principle [1]. 3D reconstruction plays a very significant role in object recognition, scenery understanding, 3D modeling and animation, industrial control, etc. [2]. The development of deep learning in recent years has also brought a new impact and convenience to 3D reconstruction [3].

Applications of 3D reconstruction have appeared in many fields such as the real-time reconstruction of nearby scenes in robot navigation and mobile robots [4], the research on tumors in the medical field [5], and the reconstruction of artifacts in tourist attractions [6]. During the development of computer vision, techniques to study the direction of 3D reconstruction have become more and more mature, and many methods have been proposed for this direction, but some problems still remain inevitable. For example, 3D reconstruction can be an issue for weak texture regions and highlight regions. Both of the problems are caused by the regions having a lot of similar RGB information, which leads to failures in feature extraction and feature point matching. Another example is that in some scenarios, a constant background or a too complex background can also have a significant impact on the 3D reconstruction.

When we sell products online, we often choose to record an introductory video about our products and then upload the video with the details of the item online. In this case, users are able to look at the pictures or watch the pre-recorded video by the merchants, but cannot freely view the appearance and details of the product, so there are limitations to this approach. In this paper, we wished to apply the SfM algorithm to the field of commodity reconstruction to provide multiple views for customers. Hence, we considered a fixed camera instead of a moving one to remove any artificial influence such as shaking to improve the accuracy of the results obtained from SfM. For many online merchants, it may be more convenient for them to put an object on an auto turntable since they may not know how to take pictures appropriately. If the background has not changed and only the object is rotating, we call it a "self-rotating" state, since it is the same as the rotation of the Earth. Most of the feature points will come from the outside of the object instead of the object itself, which are not useful at all for 3D reconstruction. This kind of problem will also lead to a poorly reconstructed model. When using the SfM algorithm provided by OpenMVG [7] in performing SIFT (scale-invariant feature transform) feature extraction [8] and feature point matching, we found that such an algorithm was very flawed in the case where the object is in a self-rotating state while the background does not change.

From the issues above, it can be concluded that the background has a bad influence on the accuracy of 3D reconstruction, so we proposed a Matting-SfM algorithm in this paper, in which we eliminated the background of the targeted object. This method removed the influence of the background on the SfM and thus helped us obtain a good result in the end.

In summary, the conventional SfM algorithm is not able to reconstruct an accurate result of an object that is in a self-rotating state. In response to such a problem, we propose the Matting-SfM method, which has made the following contributions:

1. We reveal the reason why conventional SfM cannot reconstruct self-rotating objects.
2. We propose a new algorithm called Matting-SfM, and compare the results of the two algorithms (Matting-SfM and the SfM) after the MVS reconstruction. It was proven that Matting-SfM algorithm possessed more accurate results and solved the problem that the self-rotating objects could not be reconstructed.

The rest of this paper is organized as follows. Section 2 introduces the existing 3D reconstruction techniques. Section 3 presents our methods. The illustration of our experimental materials is provided in Section 4. Our experimental results are provided in Section 5, and the conclusions is presented in the last section.

2. Related Work

At present, the major 3D reconstruction methods generally include visual geometric 3D reconstruction and deep learning reconstruction. In visual geometry 3D reconstruction, there are some classical open source projects such as Colmap [9], OpenMVG [10], VisualSfM [11], etc. On the other hand, there are also some deep learning methods for 3D reconstruction such as PatchMatchNet [12], MVSNet [13], R-MVSNet [14], PointMVSNet [15], Cascade series [16], etc. All of these methods can be used with a MVS framework such as OpenMVS [17], CMVS [18], PMVS [19], etc. to obtain a good reconstruction result. Moreover, further developments such as real-time reconstruction [20] or the applications in embedded devices and hardware [21,22] are also very impressive.

Several 3D reconstruction algorithms are currently being widely used. In terms of computing camera poses, there are two representative examples. One is based on RGB-D (e.g., BundleFusion [23]), which requires a camera with depth information and has more accuracy, but it also causes a device limitation. The other is RGB-based such as SfM (structure from motion) [24] or SLAM [25], which does not require the camera to have depth information, but the depth should be calculated during the computing process. These methods can be applied to the MVS system after obtaining the camera poses and a surface-optimized model with mapping will be obtained. In classical visual geometric reconstructions, the SfM algorithm has been widely used, and thanks to the achievements of people nowadays, we obtained a global SfM with high efficiency optimization [26]. Zhu et al. used a hybrid global and incremental SfM algorithm [27], and the following year, they pushed the global SfM to a scale of millions of input images, larger than any previous work [28]. Chen et al. proposed a tree-structured SfM algorithm [29], which greatly improved the efficiency compared to the traditional SfM algorithm and also handled the outliers more reliably, making the SfM algorithm more efficient and fault-tolerant.

Although the previous algorithm produced these exciting results, there is currently none that can specifically handle the 3D reconstruction of self-rotating objects well. In order to solve such a problem, we used the ResNet [30] to solve the defect of the algorithm, which cannot reconstruct the rotating objects. We propose a Matting-SfM algorithm, in which we segmented the targeted object based on Background Matting v2 [31], using it to eliminate the background completely. It largely removes the influence of the background on SfM. The experiment proved that the Matting-SfM algorithm showed a great improvement over the traditional SfM algorithm in the case of rotating objects and the background remains unchanged, thus laying a good foundation for subsequent MVS reconstruction.

3. Methods

3.1. Video Segmentation and Background Replacement

Conventionally, the matting approach contains some of the classical algorithms, among which the Canny algorithm [32] suits our task most. The problem is, for some complex backgrounds, the results of the traditional algorithm are not always satisfying (Figure 1). In Figure 1, the left background such as the areas marked in red boxes are not useful and the object in the yellow box is the only area of interest. That is, the traditional algorithm cannot eliminate the background totally.

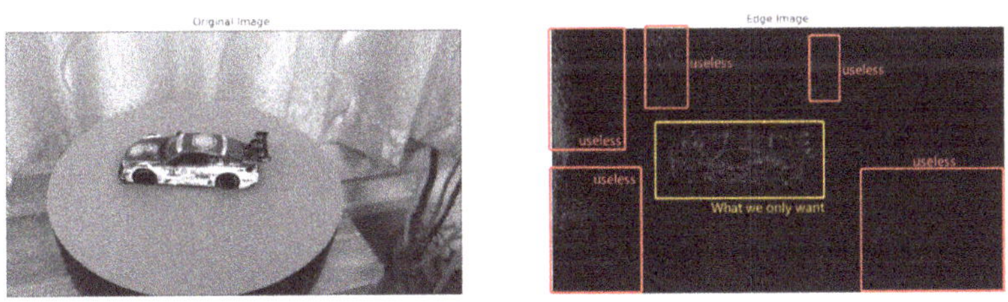

Figure 1. The matting result of the Canny algorithm.

To solve this problem, in this paper, foreground segmentation and background replacement of objects were performed based on Background Matting v2 (BGMv2 for shortcut). We needed to provide a video or an image dataset of the object with the background and a background image without the object. The more accurately the background is aligned with the original video, the better (Figure 2).

We trained a new model by ourselves based on the approach of Lin's team [31], which was more suitable for our task to perform 3D reconstruction. The network was ResNet 50, the epoch was set to 30 with a batch size of 16. We first trained the base network and the refinement network was trained after it. Our two datasets comprised VideoMatte240 K and a dataset made by ourselves. VideoMatte240 K contained 484 pairs of high-resolution Alpha matte and foreground video clips extracted from green screen stock footage, constituting 240,709 unique frames. The self-made dataset contained 1000 pictures of different objects such as toys and models. The Alpha matte α and foreground F were extracted by Photoshop manually.

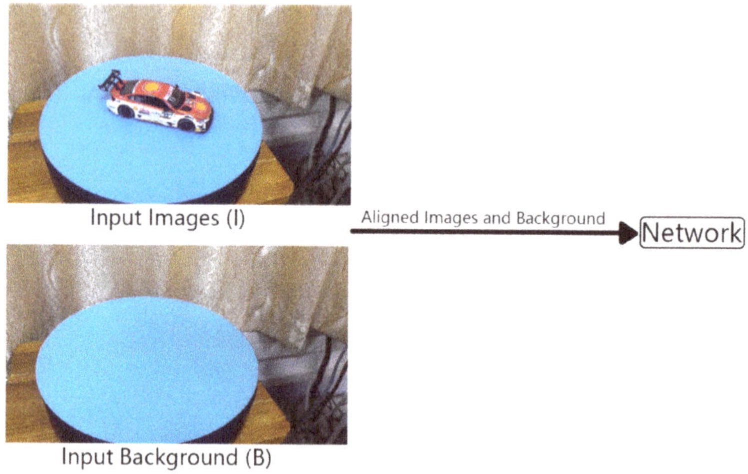

Figure 2. The input video (I) and background image (B).

First, the original video or image I and the background image B were linked to a size of $6 * H_C * W_C$, where the H represents the Height of the image, W represents the Width of the image. Then, the image will be downsampled with multiplier C to generate an input of size x $6 * H_C * W_C$, which is fed to the basenet. The input and output results of the two networks can be briefly represented as follows (Figure 3). The model ends up with five results: Alpha, Foreground, ...Error Map, Refine, and Composite. For us, Composite was the result that we needed to focus on, which is the core input of our 3D reconstruction system.

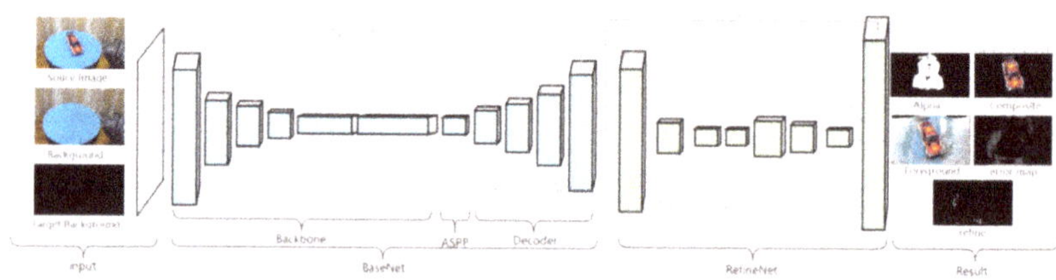

Figure 3. The two network structures of BGMv2 and the input and output results.

The architecture of the basenet is based on DeepLabV3 [33] and DeepLabV3+ [34], where basenet consists of the backbone and ASPP module [35] along with a decoder module. The above generated images of size $6 * H_C * W_C$ are input to the backbone for feature extraction. Behind the backbone, the atrous spatial pyramid pooling (ASPP) module is connected, which is a model that combines null convolution [33] with spatial pyramid pooling (SPP) [36]. The decoder is connected behind the ASPP and stitches together the previous output and the extracted special features of the backbone through skip connection and performs bilinear upsampling, and then extracts the coarse result that consists of four parts: Coarse Alpha α_C; Foreground Residual F_C^R; Error Map E_c; Hidden H_c. The subscript C indicates the downsampling multiplier and the R refers to the word residual. We set the downsampling multiplier to 4, which means that the four coarse results generated by basenet were 1/16 of the original image.

Unlike basenet, operations are not performed on the original map in refinenet, but on the patches with the K highest prediction errors extracted from the feature map with the help of Error Map E_C. Since the multiplier C in the previous step was set to 4, the input E_C obtained in refinenet is 1/16 of the original image, so each pixel within E_C corresponds to a patch of 4 * 4 size of the original image. Refinenet connects the four coarse results output from basenet with the processed image I and background map B as feature maps, selects patches in the feature maps by E_C, and then performs two 3 * 3 convolutions to output 4 * 4 patches. The next step performs upsampling to output 8 * 8 patches, connects this patch with the corresponding 8 * 8 patches in the original map, performs two 3 * 3 convolutions again, and finally obtains 4 * 4 Alpha outputs and Error Map patches. Finally, the coarse Alpha and coarse Error Map are upsampled until the original size, and then the patches are replaced with the 4 * 4 Alpha and Error Map patches obtained by refinenet.

Using the black background as the final composite image background, given as image I, background map B using the obtained Alpha mask map α and foreground map F, the new image I' can be synthesized by replacing the B with B' as follows (1):

$$I' = \alpha F + (1 - \alpha)B' \tag{1}$$

While the above I and background map B were provided by us, B' was set to a black background since we wanted to remove the background. Alpha mask and foreground F were predicted by the network structure of BGMv2 as follows. After performing the processing of the two networks, the final output foreground residual F^R can be expressed in Equation (2):

$$F^R = F - I \tag{2}$$

F can then be obtained by feeding F^R into image I in Equation (3), and by combining Equations (2) and (3), we can obtain a more detailed foreground image F:

$$F = \max\left(\min\left(F^R + I, 1\right), 0\right) \tag{3}$$

The L_1 loss is employed over the entire Alpha matte and its (Sobel) gradient to learn with respect to the ground truth, α is the ground truth of α obtained by manual processing:

$$L_\alpha = \|\alpha - \alpha^*\|_1 + \|\nabla\alpha - \nabla\alpha^*\|_1 \tag{4}$$

Using Equation (3), we can calculate the foreground layer using the predicted foreground residual F^R. We only calculated the L_1 loss on pixels when $\alpha > 0$, where $\alpha > 0$ is a Boolean expression, and F^* is the ground truth of F obtained by manual processing:

$$L_F = \|(\alpha^* > 0) * (F - F^*)\|_1 \tag{5}$$

The ground truth error map is defined as in Equation (6) for the refinement region selection. Next, we determined the loss by computing the mean squared error between the expected error map and the actual error map E, where E^* is the ground truth error map defined by [28]:

$$E^* = |\alpha - \alpha^*| \tag{6}$$

$$L_E = \|E - E^*\|_2 \tag{7}$$

According to the above formulas, the base network *(αc, FcR, Ec, Hc) = Gbase (Ic, Bc)* operates at $1/c$ of the original image resolution and the loss function is used as:

$$L_{base} = L_{\alpha_C} + L_{F_C} + L_{E_C} \tag{8}$$

The same as refinenet *(α, F, R) = Grefine (αc, FcR, Ec, Hc, I, B)*, the loss function of it is used as Equation (9):

$$L_{refine} = L_\alpha + L_F \tag{9}$$

3.2. Reconstructing Sparse Point Cloud

In visual geometric 3D reconstruction, there are two methods of the SfM algorithm: incremental SfM and global SfM. In this paper, we used incremental SfM for reconstruction, so the Global SfM was not included. Before the steps of 3D reconstruction, we had to conduct some pre-processing steps such as SIFT feature extraction [8], AC-RANSAC [37] for linear fitting, etc. The main steps of pre-processing can be described as follows (Figure 4).

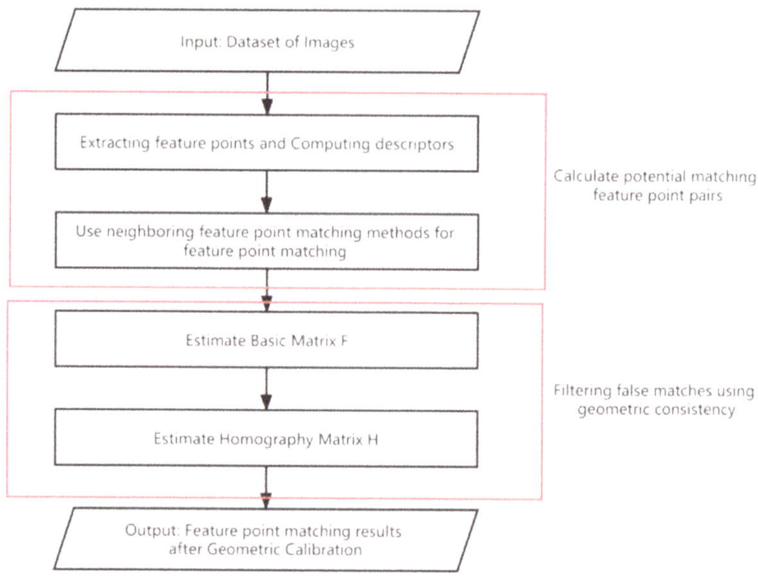

Figure 4. The pre-processing process.

In order to find the connection between p and p′, we used the AC-RANSAC algorithm provided by OpenMVG to calculate the Basic Matrix in Equation (10), and the parameters in the formula can be referred to in Figure 5.

$$F = K'^{-T}[T_X]RK^{-1} \tag{10}$$

where F is the basic matrix, and K and K' are the internal parameter matrix of the two cameras. l and l' are the rays of p and p', I and I' are two different planes. O_1 and O_2 two diferent views. R and T are the rotation and translation matrix in 3D coordinates, and $[T_X]R$ is referred to as the essential matrix in Equation (11):

$$E = T \times R = [T_X]R \tag{11}$$

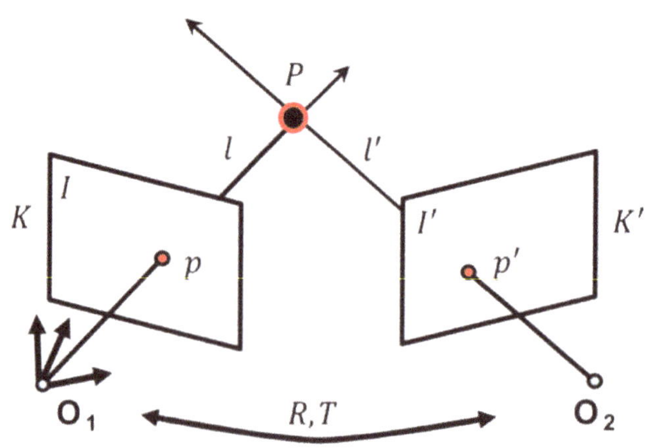

Figure 5. The parameter in the basic matrix.

In the pre-processing stage, we also need to obtain the homography matrix (Figure 6). It is known that the internal parameter matrix K of the first camera, the internal parameter matrix K' of the second camera, the position of the second camera with respect to the first camera is $\left(R, \vec{t}\right)$, $\vec{t}$ is a vector, $\vec{n}$ is the unit normal vector of the plane π in the coordinate system of the first camera, and d is the distance from the coordinate origin to the plane π (7). P, p and p' are three corresponding points in different planes. Through the parameters above, we can gain the homography matrix in (12). Once the basic matrix and homography matrix are obtained, we can use these two matrices to the following triangulation calculation, which is a very important step of the SfM.

$$H = K'\left(R + \vec{t} \times \vec{n}_d^{\,T}\right) \quad (12)$$

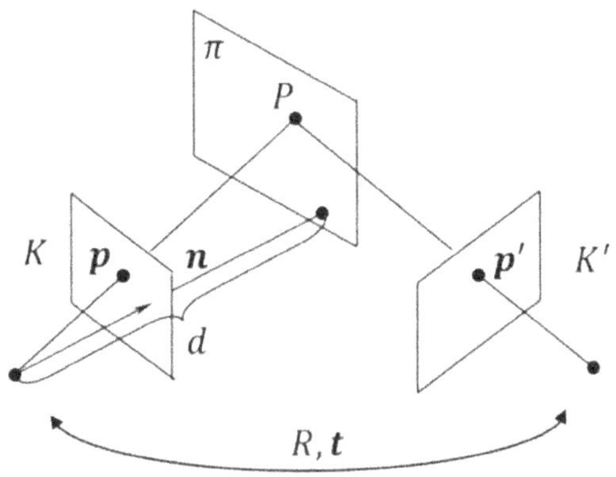

Figure 6. The parameter in the homography matrix.

In the pre-processing stage, we could see a certain problem that the same background feature points could be observed in every image with the same background; instead, the feature points of the reconstructed object showed less matching compared to the background. We used OpenMVG as an example and the SfM algorithm provided by OpenMVG for reconstruction, which has the following approximate steps (Figure 7).

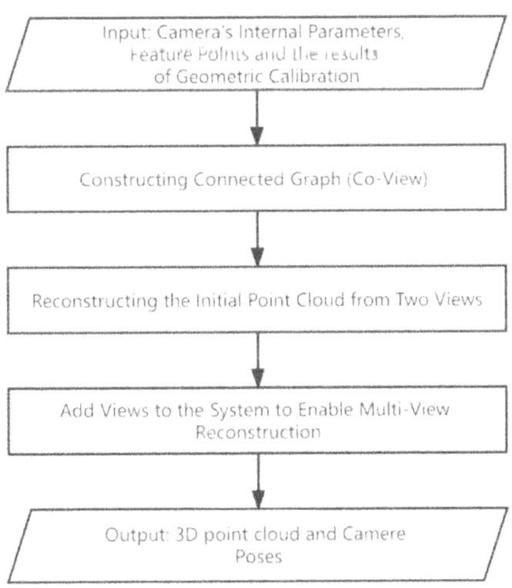

Figure 7. The steps of the SfM provided by OpenMVG for 3D reconstruction.

In the step of 'Reconstructing the Initial Point Cloud from Two Views' (see Figure 7), we needed to select an edge from the connected graph obtained from the previous step. In this step, the relationship between the edges should be satisfied that when all points correspond to point triangulation, the median angle between the camera and the ray on the 2D image cannot be greater than 60°, but not less than 3°. For a dataset with a large number of feature points that come from the background, the ray pinch angle is basically constant, which is the reason why no feature points meet the requirement. In the 2D image, it looks like there is a certain angle (see Figure 8) between these two pairs of points, but the corresponding 3D points of these two pairs are completely unchanged after triangulation and do not satisfy the case where the median of the ray angle is greater than 3° when the corresponding points are triangulated, so such pairs of points will not be selected. All of the features extracted from the dataset and their matches are shown in Figures 9 and 10. Although there were indeed a large number of matches in Figure 9, most of them were not useful at all because they came from the background.

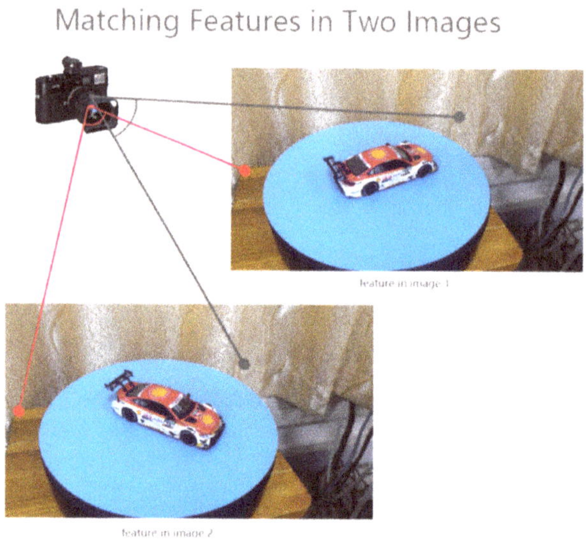

Figure 8. The angle of the ray at the triangulation point.

Figure 9. The features extracted from the image.

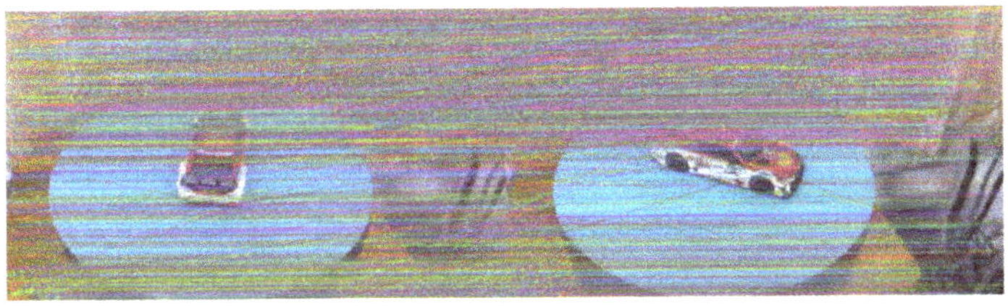

Figure 10. The useless matches between two images.

The dataset of the Composite result after segmentation was input (Figure 2). It is easy to extract feature points from such a dataset; for the SIFT feature extractor, a large amount of the same black RGB information in the background cannot be extracted as features, so most of the feature points will come from the object that needs to be reconstructed and a sparse point cloud will be gained step-by-step (Figure 11).

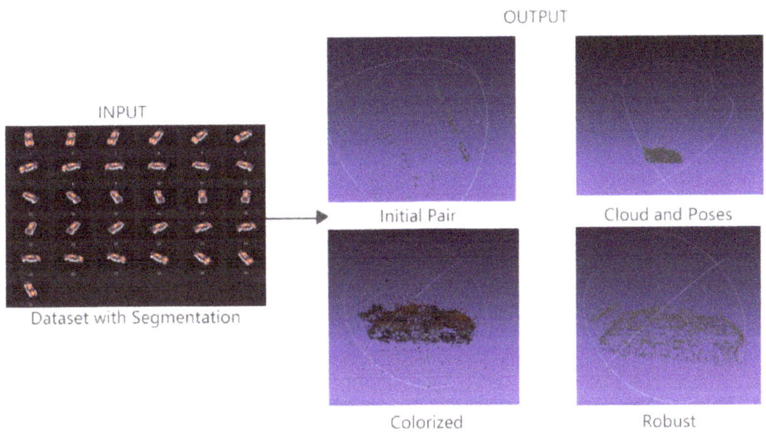

Figure 11. The sparse point cloud obtained from the SfM.

3.3. Densifying the Sparse Point Cloud by MVS

After obtaining the sparse point cloud and camera poses in the previous step, for a better observation, these results were used as the input to MVS to densify the sparse point cloud. For all of the sparse point clouds in this paper, OpenMVS [16] was used to finish that task except for VisualSfM. Note that OpenMVS does not support VisualSfM anymore since 2 years ago, so we were only able to use CMVS-PMVS [18,19] to densify the sparse point cloud, but there will not be too much difference. The inputs to the whole MVS system are the image dataset and the camera poses, which need to be processed with domain frame selection [38] as well as the global best domain frame selection [39] in the initial stage of data preparation. In the DensifyPointCloud step, the semi-global matching (SGM) [40] is used to compute the depth of the image and input the computed depth map into MVS to obtain the dense point cloud, which is more complete and tighter than the sparse point cloud.

In this way, the sparse point cloud is made more tighter and easy to observe, which means that we have an intuitive way to compare the results obtained by different methods. The output can be clearly seen in Figure 12 and the difference between the sparse point cloud and dense point cloud can be well observed in Figure 13.

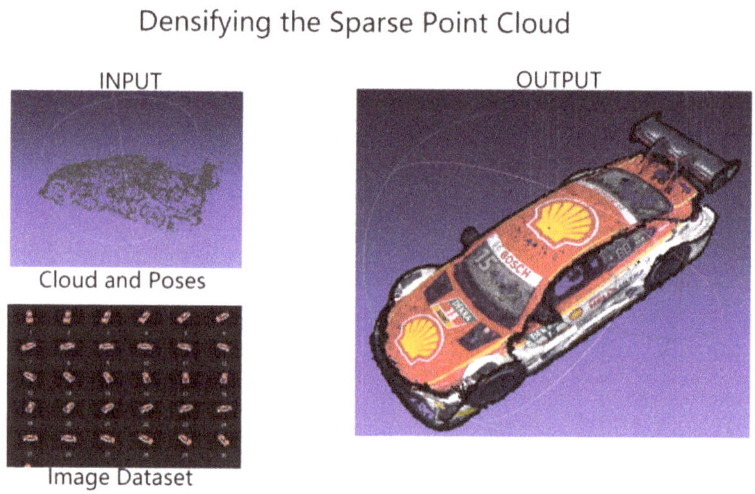

Figure 12. The output of densifying the sparse point cloud by MVS.

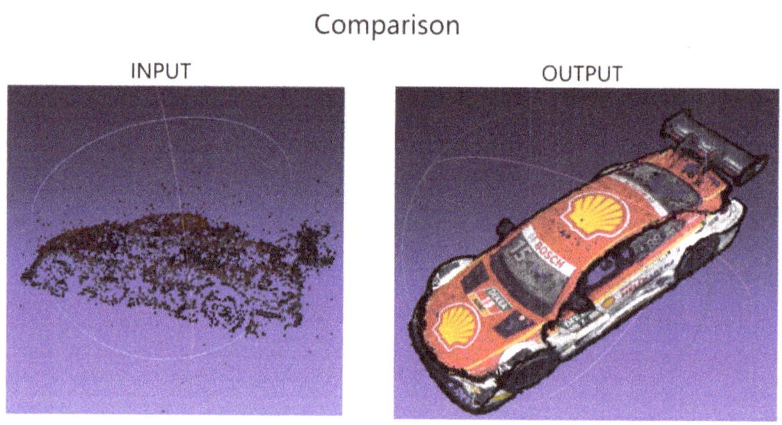

Figure 13. The comparison between the sparse and dense point cloud.

4. Experiment Materials and Evaluation Indices

For the experimental part, the dataset organization is shown in Figure 14, and more details will be introduced as follows. A single image was selected to see the details, and for better observation, some of the total were chosen to show the continuous images in the dataset. Four representative experiments were selected in this paper. These experiments were all conducted in a well-lit environment, and the resolution and frame rate of the three videos were all 4 k/60 Hz. Thirty frames of each of these three videos were used as the three groups of the dataset that were input to Colmap, VisualSfM, and OpenMVG. Since we wanted to place more emphasis on the influence of the background, a single typical car model was chosen to test our algorithm. Our final purpose was to gain a very accurate object without any residue of the background since merchants may not know how to eliminate the residual 3D points in the point cloud. All of the experiments focused on the influence of the background.

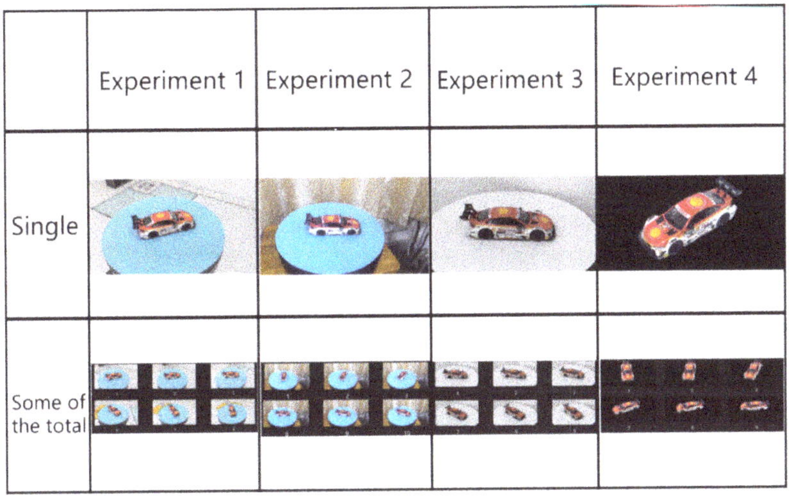

Figure 14. The dataset organization.

The first experiment was to verify the performance of the traditional reconstruction method by putting the object on the turntable and recording a video using a camera to shoot around the targeted object. The targeted object of the video was a car model, and there were a large number of feature points on the object that could be provided to the algorithm for computation. The left side of Figure 15 shows one of the images in the object's image dataset obtained from the video, and the right side shows a general overview of the 30 image dataset of the object.

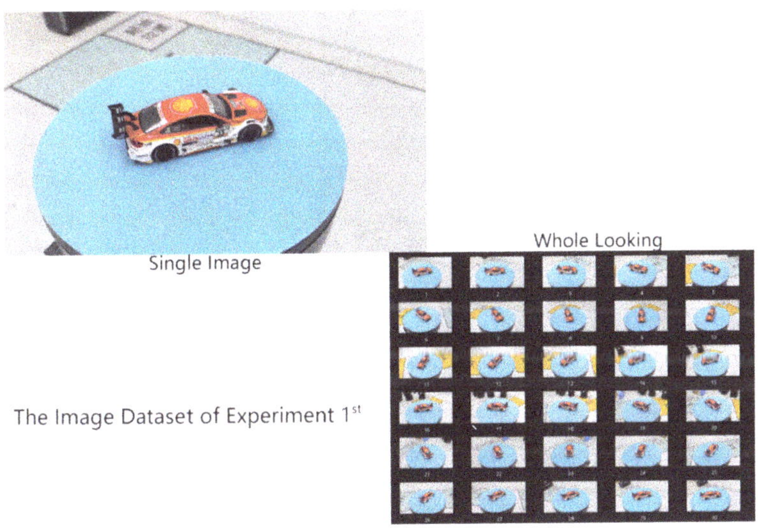

Figure 15. The image dataset used in experiment 1.

The second experiment was to investigate whether the traditional algorithm could use the dataset of a self-rotating object for 3D reconstruction. The object of the video was the same car model, and we put the car on a motorized turntable and fixed the camera on a camera mount. In this experiment, the background was complicated. The left side of

Figure 16 shows one of the images in the object's image dataset obtained from the video, and the right side shows a whole look of the 30 image dataset.

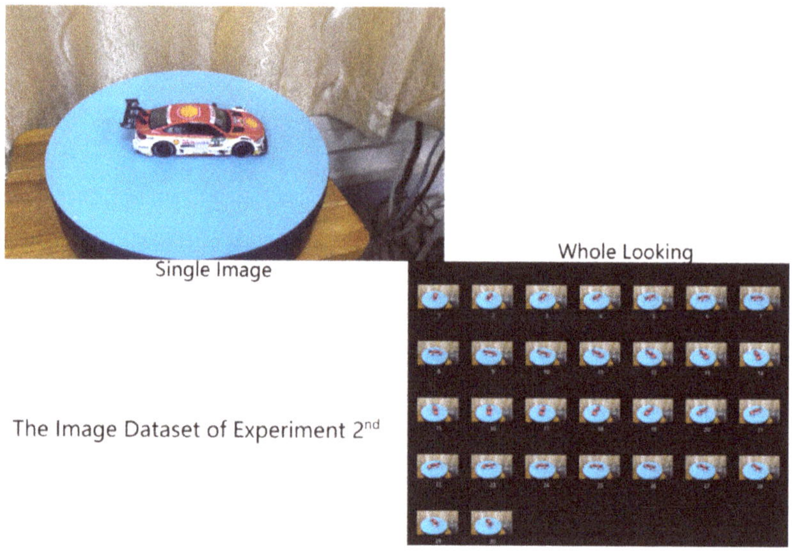

Figure 16. The image dataset used in experiment 2.

Next, to eliminate the impact of the background, we tried to artificially remove the background of the dataset, making it as simple as possible. Therefore, we proceeded with the third experiment. A smooth and white background was chosen to obtain the dataset. The same as in the above figures, on the left side of Figure 17 is one of the images of the object's image dataset from the video, and on the right side is an overview of the 37 image dataset of the object.

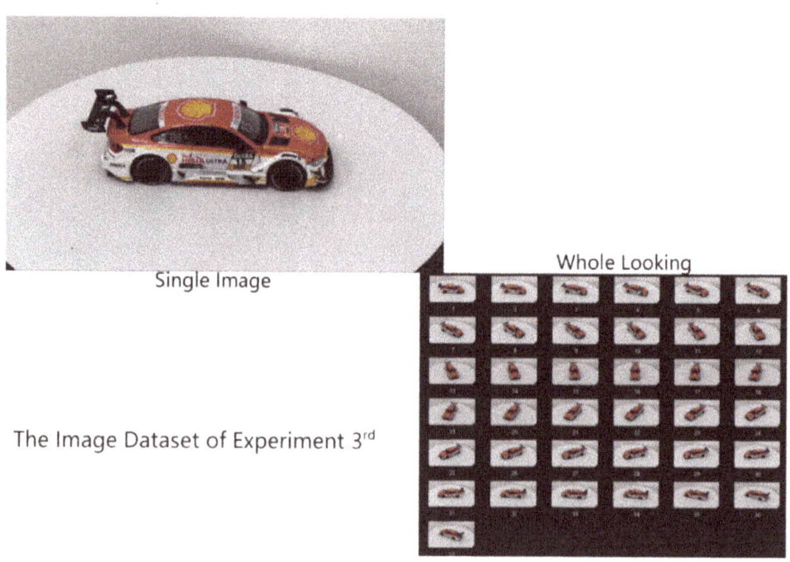

Figure 17. The image dataset used in experiment 3.

The fourth experiment was to explore the performance and accuracy of the Matting-SfM algorithm. The background of the second dataset was replaced with a black background without feature points, which means that the original background eliminated the background totally. Figure 18 shows the intermediate products of the Matting-SfM, that is, the dataset after segmentation.

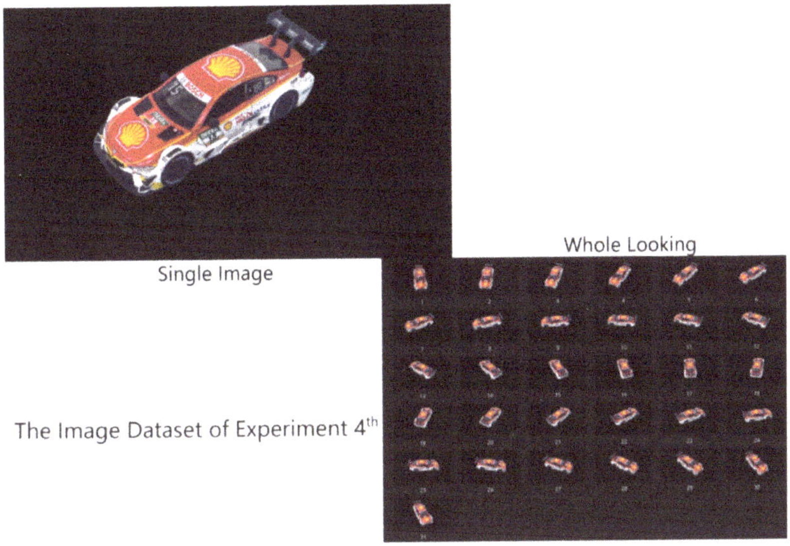

Figure 18. The image dataset used in experiment 4.

When it came to the evaluation, we choose three methods: hist similarity; peak signal to noise ratio (PSNR); and the structural similarity index (SSIM). All of these were used to evaluate the similarity between the original image and the models.

For the hist similarity, the histogram data of the source image and the image to be filtered were collected, and the collected image histograms were normalized, then we directly performed a correlation comparison provided by OpenCV.

For the PSNR, given a clean image I and noisy image K of size $m * n$, the formulas used were:

$$\mathrm{MSE} = \frac{1}{\mathrm{mn}} \sum_{i=0}^{m-1} \sum_{j=0}^{n-1} [I(i,j) - K(i,j)]^2 \tag{13}$$

$$\mathrm{PNSR} = 10 \times \log_{10}\left(\frac{\mathrm{MAX}_I^2}{\mathrm{MSE}}\right) \tag{14}$$

where the MSE is the mean square error; $\mathrm{MAX}_I{}^2$ refers to the maximum possible pixel value for the images.

For SSIM, given two images X and Y, the formulas are as follows. The $L(X,Y)$, $C(X,Y)$ and $S(X,Y)$ refer to the luminance, contrast, and structure of two images, respectively:

$$L(X,Y) = \frac{2u_X u_Y + C_1}{u_{X^2} + u_{Y^2} + C_1} \tag{15}$$

$$C(X,Y) = \frac{2\sigma_X \sigma_Y + C_2}{\sigma_{X^2} + \sigma_{Y^2} + C_2} \tag{16}$$

$$S(X,Y) = \frac{\sigma_{X_Y} + C_3}{\sigma_X \sigma_Y + C_3} \tag{17}$$

where u_X, u_Y represent the mean of image X and Y; σ_X and σ_Y represent the standard deviation of image X and Y; σ_{X2} and σ_{Y2} represent the variance of image X and Y; σ_{XY} represents the covariance of image X and Y; C_1, C_2, and C_3 are constants to avoid the denominator being 0 and maintain stability. Usually $C_1 = (K_1 * L)\hat{}2$, $C_2 = (K_2 * L)\hat{}2$, $C_3 = C_2/2$, and generally $K_1 = 0.01$, $K_2 = 0.03$, $L = 255$.

Finally SSIM can be expressed as:

$$\text{SSIM}(X,Y) = L(X,Y) * C(X,Y) * S(X,Y) \tag{18}$$

5. Results

For all of the experiments, the SfM system was set to a high quality mode to ensure that all of the SfM systems were run in the same way, but in some cases, the high quality mode still did not go well.

The first experiment was to explore the performance of the traditional SfM algorithm. The experiment results proved that the traditional SfM algorithm worked well when the camera recorded around the object (the object was kept still and the background changed, see Figure 12). In the first experiment, the models were indeed obtained, but the background influenced the accuracy (see the blue edges around the model in Figure 19) of the model, making it look coarse and rough. Furthermore, the shaking of the video will also have an impact on the result, so we must make a lot of effort to stabilize the camera in our hands.

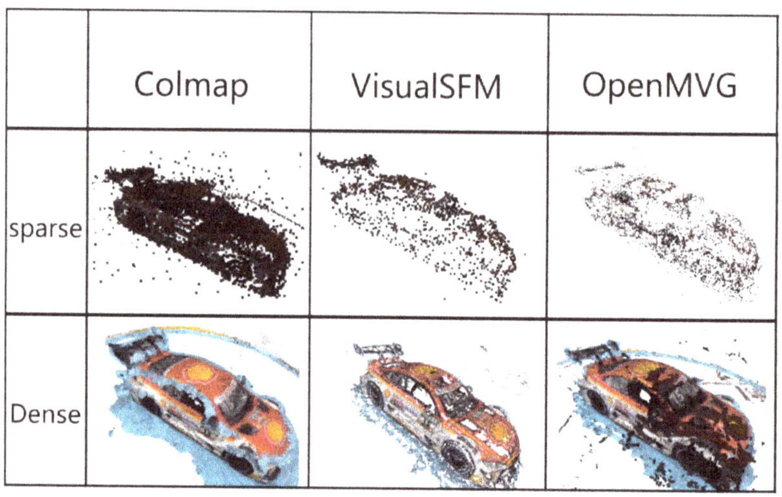

Figure 19. The results of experiment 1.

In order to solve the problem raised in experiment 1, we proceeded with experiment 2. The recording method of fixing the camera position and making the targeted object rotate was used. This way avoided the bad impact of human factors on the reconstruction. However, for this dataset, we could not obtain any results at all, and all of the methods failed when reconstructing the second dataset (Figure 20).

It is deduced that this phenomenon was due to the unchanged background, so next, the third dataset was used for testing. Although we tried to simplify the background, the background still had a certain impact on the accuracy of the result (Figure 21). In this case, the results were obtained but they were still not satisfactory, so the influence of background still existed. Moreover, a result could not be gained even in the high quality mode for OpenMVG, as we only obtained a defective result from it.

	Colmap	VisualSFM	OpenMVG
sparse	FAILED	FAILED	FAILED
Dense	FAILED	FAILED	FAILED

Figure 20. The results of experiment 2.

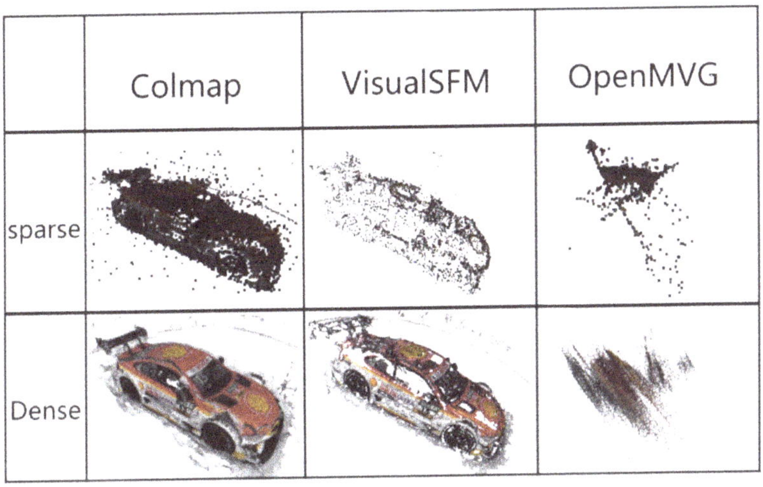

Figure 21. The results of experiment 3.

After several experiments, it was obvious that the effect of the background of the datasets was always bad for the traditional SfM algorithm, so we introduced our method of Matting-SfM. In experiment 4, Matting-SfM was used to process the second dataset by simply providing a background image (Figure 2) and totally eliminated the background (Figure 22).

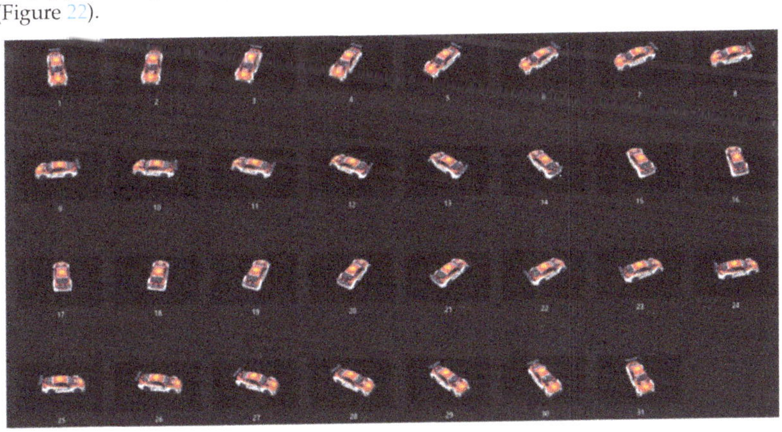

Figure 22. The dataset after segmentation.

The second dataset was put directly into our Matting-SfM algorithm, and after processing, it produced an intermedia dataset (Figure 22). In this experiment, we removed the effect caused by the background. Finally, we performed the whole procedure of 3D reconstruction, where it can be seen that a 3D model with high accuracy and detailed texture was reconstructed (Figure 23).

Figure 23. The final reconstruction of Matting-SfM after segmentation.

For all of the datasets above-mentioned, except for the first one, we used the same method to process the dataset, and finally, the comparisons are listed in Table 1. Note that Table 1 only includes the third dataset because Colmap, VisualSfM, and OpenMVG did not obtain any results from the second dataset; since Matting-SfM is an algorithm that focuses on the self-rotating object, the first dataset was not included.

Table 1. A comparison of all of the datasets using the mathematical method.

Methods	Hist Similarity (%)	PNSR	SSIM
Colmap	99.85%	10.95	0.25
VisualSfM	99.80%	10.79	0.21
OpenMVG	99.50%	9.55	0.14
Matting-SfM	99.90%	11.51	0.26

The experiments used three methods to evaluate the results, all of which were used to evaluate the similarity between the original image and the models. To ensure the accuracy of the results, all models were set to the same direction and the screenshot was compared to the original image. We compared all of the same angles with the datasets and calculated the mean values of the three methods. For the parameters above, the higher the parameters, the more similar the model to the original image.

What should be emphasized is that the parameters are only a digital way to evaluate the results, and the mathematical method is not always the best way to distinguish the differences between images as they may produce some misunderstandings and the models actually look more different than the display of numbers. Therefore, we have to use a visible way to evaluate the results, as shown in Figure 24. Through the mathematical methods and visible ways, we can clearly distinguish the results of four approaches, where Matting-SfM obtained more accurate results than the others.

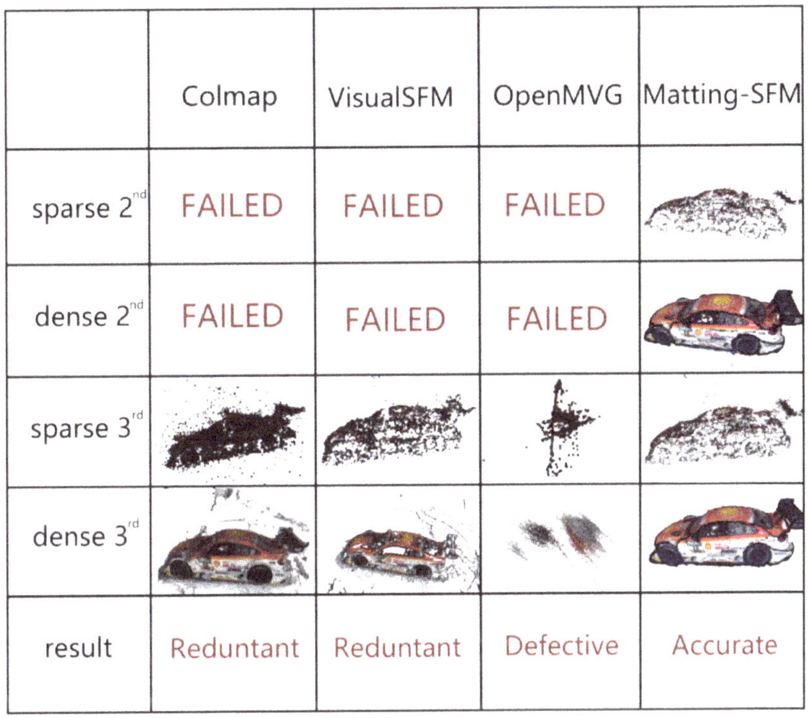

Figure 24. A comparison of all of the datasets using the visible method.

In addition, the performance of Matting-SfM was tested on other objects (Figure 25). Three objects were selected, the first one being a money jar, the second one being a dog doll, and the last was a very small accessory. Note that the background of the three datasets was chosen to be as complex as possible. It can be seen that the first two objects were reconstructed well through Matting-SfM, however, it did not work well on the conventional SfM. Furthermore, due to the tiny size and the complex background of the last object, the conventional SfM did not produce any results, while for Matting-SfM, the object was indeed reconstructed, but the quality leaves some small room to be improved.

It can be concluded that Matting-SfM can work properly with fixed camera position and self-rotating object and it can reconstruct a good result. Matting-SfM solves the problem of not being able to reconstruct self-rotating objects with unchanging background. Experiments have shown that our results are greatly improved after applying the Matting-SfM algorithm. The result shows that the Matting-SfM algorithm is able to reconstruct the object under rotation normally, which solves the problem that the traditional SfM algorithm cannot reconstruct the object under a self-rotating state.

Figure 25. More objects used to test the performance of Matting-SfM.

6. Conclusions

In this paper, we proposed a Matting-SfM algorithm to solve the problem of reconstruction failure under the condition of a self-rotating object and maintain a high accuracy. Since the SfM algorithm has certain requirements on the stability and lighting of the camera, we selected an indoor environment. We fixed the camera using a camera support and placed the object on a motorized turntable to make the object rotate for shooting. This approach not only ensured the stability to achieve high precision reconstruction, but also avoided the negative impact of artificial recording.

At present, we have embedded the algorithm in our system and have deployed it on the server. By uploading the format of mp4 videos and the background image, the algorithm in the server will eliminate the background using deep learning methods, then output the video with the background in black after segmenting the object. The video is processed by intercepting key frames and outputting them as an image dataset, and the output dataset will be automatically reconstructed after the processing is completed. Finally, the system downloads the results (GLTF Files and PNG Texture Image) to the computer, so we can simply view the result through the website constructed by Web OpenGL.

Although this algorithm solves the problem that self-rotating objects with unchanging background cannot be reconstructed, there is still no way to match the feature points well for some objects with not enough feature points, or regions with highlights and weak textures such as the back of the car in Figure 22. We can see that the depth information was wrong when calculating, leading to a dent in the back of the model. For some excessively detailed and skeletonized areas, a background that is very aligned with the original video needs to be provided, otherwise it will output less accurate results. Sine we cared more about accuracy than real-time, in the future, we will try to solve the problem of highlights and weakly textured areas with a deep learning approach, replacing such areas with valid RGB information from a deep learning method in a better way. In this way, feature extraction, feature point matching, and texture mapping will not be affected badly. Furthermore, it is a good way to improve feature extraction by replacing the CNN (convolutional neural network) [41–45] with a traditional algorithm such as SIFT as it may perform better.

Author Contributions: Conceptualization, Z.Z. and Z.L.; Data curation, Z.Z. and Z.L.; Formal analysis, Z.Z., Z.L., Y.C., S.L. and S.G.; Funding acquisition, Z.Z. and Z.L.; Investigation, S.L.; Supervision, Z.Z. All authors have read and agreed to the published version of the manuscript.

Funding: This research was funded by the Young Innovative Talents Project of Colleges and Universities in Guangdong Province (grant number 2021KQNCX092); the Doctoral program of Huizhou University (grant number 2020JB028); Outstanding Youth Cultivation Project of Huizhou University (grant number HZU202009); The Science and Technology Program of Guangzhou (grant number NO.202201020625).

Institutional Review Board Statement: Not applicable.

Informed Consent Statement: Not applicable.

Data Availability Statement: The VideoMatte240K dataset was used in this study, and the dataset can be found here. [https://grail.cs.washington.edu/projects/background-matting-v2/#/datasets, accessed on 16 January 2022].

Conflicts of Interest: The authors declare no conflict of interest.

References

1. Han, R.; Yan, H.; Ma, L. Research on 3D Reconstruction methods Based on Binocular Structured Light Vision. *J. Phys. Conf. Ser.* **2021**, *1744*, 032002. [CrossRef]
2. Han, X.F.; Laga, H.; Bennamoun, M. Image-based 3D object reconstruction: State-of-the-art and trends in the deep learning era. *IEEE Trans. Pattern Anal. Mach. Intell.* **2019**, *43*, 1578–1604. [CrossRef] [PubMed]
3. Fahim, G.; Amin, K.; Zarif, S. Single-View 3D reconstruction: A Survey of deep learning methods. *Comput. Graph.* **2021**, *94*, 164–190. [CrossRef]
4. Li, G.; Hou, J.; Chen, Z.; Yu, L.; Fei, S. Real-time 3D reconstruction system using multi-task feature extraction network and surfel. *Opt. Eng.* **2021**, *60*, 083104. [CrossRef]
5. Campos, T.J.F.L.; Filho, F.E.d.V.; Rocha, M.F.H. Assessment of the complexity of renal tumors by nephrometry (RENAL score) with CT and MRI images versus 3D reconstruction model images. *Int. Braz. J. Urol.* **2021**, *47*, 896–901. [CrossRef]
6. Kadi, H.; Anouche, K. Knowledge-based parametric modeling for heritage interpretation and 3D reconstruction. *Digit. Appl. Archaeol. Cult. Herit.* **2020**, *19*, e00160. [CrossRef]
7. Moulon, P.; Monasse, P.; Marlet, R. Adaptive structure from motion with a contrario model estimation. In *Asian Conference on Computer Vision*; Springer: Berlin/Heidelberg, Germany, 2012; pp. 257–270.
8. Lowe, D.G. Object recognition from local scale-invariant features. In Proceedings of the Seventh IEEE International Conference on Computer Vision, Kerkyra, Greece, 20–27 September 1999; Volume 2, pp. 1150–1157.
9. Schönberger, J.L.; Price, T.; Sattler, T.; Frahm, J.M.; Pollefeys, M. A vote-and-verify strategy for fast spatial verification in image retrieval. In *Asian Conference on Computer Vision*; Springer: Cham, Switzerland, 2016; pp. 321–337.
10. Pierre, M.; Pascal, M.; Romuald, P.; Renaud, M. OpenMVG: Open multiple view geometry. In *International Workshop on Reproducible Research in Pattern Recognition*; Springer: Cham, Switzerland, 2016; Volume 10214, pp. 60–74.
11. Wu, C. Towards linear-time incremental structure from motion. In Proceedings of the 3DV-Conference, International Conference on IEEE Computer Society, Seattle, WA, USA, 29 June–1 July 2013; pp. 127–134.
12. Wang, F.; Galliani, S.; Vogel, C.; Speciale, P.; Pollefeys, M. Patchmatchnet: Learned multi-view patchmatch stereo. In Proceedings of the IEEE/CVF Conference on Computer Vision and Pattern Recognition, Nashville, TN, USA, 20–25 June 2021; pp. 14194–14203.
13. Yao, Y.; Luo, Z.; Li, S.; Quan, L. Mvsnet: Depth inference for unstructured multi-view stereo. In Proceedings of the European Conference on Computer Vision, Munich, Germany, 8–14 September 2018; pp. 767–783.
14. Yao, Y.; Luo, Z.; Li, S.; Shen, T.; Fang, T.; Quan, L. Recurrent MVSnet for high-resolution multi-view stereo depth inference. In Proceedings of the IEEE/CVF Conference on Computer Vision and Pattern Recognition, Long Beach, CA, USA, 15–20 June 2019; pp. 5525–5534.
15. Chen, R.; Han, S.; Xu, J.; Su, H. Point-based multi-view stereo network. In Proceedings of the IEEE/CVF International Conference on Computer Vision, Seoul, Korea, 27 October–2 November 2019; pp. 1538–1547.
16. Cai, Z.; Vasconcelos, N. Cascade r-CNN: Delving into high quality object detection. In Proceedings of the IEEE Conference on Computer Vision and Pattern Recognition, Salt Lake City, UT, USA, 18–23 June 2018; pp. 6154–6162.
17. Cernea, D. OpenMVS: Multi-View Stereo Reconstruction Library. 2020. Volume 5, p. 7. Available online: https://cdcseacave.github.io/openMVS (accessed on 27 October 2021).
18. Furukawa, Y.; Curless, B.; Seitz, S.M.; Szeliskiet, R. Towards internet-scale multi-view stereo. In Proceedings of the 2010 IEEE Computer Society Conference on Computer Vision and Pattern Recognition, San Francisco, CA, USA, 13–18 June 2010; pp. 1434–1441.
19. Furukawa, Y.; Ponce, J. Accurate, dense, and robust multiview stereopsis. *IEEE Trans. Pattern Anal. Mach. Intell.* **2009**, *32*, 1362–1376. [CrossRef] [PubMed]

20. Sun, J.; Xie, Y.; Chen, L.; Zhou, X.; Bao, H. NeuralRecon: Real-time coherent 3D reconstruction from monocular video. In Proceedings of the IEEE/CVF Conference on Computer Vision and Pattern Recognition, Nashville, TN, USA, 20–25 June 2021; pp. 15598–15607.
21. Kim, J.; Chung, D.; Kim, Y.; Kim, H. Deep learning-based 3D reconstruction of scaffolds using a robot dog. *Autom. Constr.* **2022**, *134*, 104092. [CrossRef]
22. Chen, J.; Kira, Z.; Cho, Y.K. Deep Learning Approach to Point Cloud Scene Understanding for Automated Scan to 3D Reconstruction. *J. Comput. Civ. Eng.* **2019**, *33*, 04019027. [CrossRef]
23. Dai, A.; Nießner, M.; Zollhöfer, M.; Izadi, S.; Theobalt, C. Bundlefusion: Real-time globally consistent 3D reconstruction using on-the-fly surface reintegration. *ACM Trans. Graph.* **2017**, *36*, 76a. [CrossRef]
24. Schonberger, J.L.; Frahm, J.M. Structure-from-motion revisited. In Proceedings of the IEEE Conference on Computer Vision and Pattern Recognition, Las Vegas, NV, USA, 27–30 June 2016; pp. 4104–4113.
25. Campos, C.; Elvira, R.; Rodriguez, J.J.G.; Montiel, J.M.M.; Tardos, J.D. ORB-SLAM3: An Accurate Open-Source Library for Visual, Visual–Inertial, and Multimap SLAM. *IEEE Trans. Robot.* **2021**, *37*, 1874–1890. [CrossRef]
26. Barath, D.; Mishkin, D.; Eichhardt, I.; Shipachev, I.; Matas, J. Efficient initial pose-graph generation for global SfM. In Proceedings of the IEEE/CVF Conference on Computer Vision and Pattern Recognition, Nashville, TN, USA, 20–25 June 2021; pp. 14546–14555.
27. Zhu, S.; Shen, T.; Zhou, L.; Zhang, R.; Wang, J.; Fang, T.; Quan, L. Parallel structure from motion from local increment to global averaging. *arXiv* **2017**, arXiv:1702.08601.
28. Zhu, S.; Zhang, R.; Zhou, L.; Shen, T.; Fang, T.; Tan, P.; Quan, L. Very large-scale global SfM by distributed motion averaging. In Proceedings of the IEEE Conference on Computer Vision and Pattern Recognition, Salt Lake City, UT, USA, 18–23 June 2018; pp. 4568–4577.
29. Chen, Y.; Chan, A.B.; Lin, Z.; Suzuki, K.; Wang, G. Efficient tree-structured SfM by RANSAC generalized Procrustes analysis. *Comput. Vis. Image Underst.* **2017**, *157*, 179–189. [CrossRef]
30. He, K.; Zhang, X.; Ren, S.; Sun, J. Deep residual learning for image recognition. In Proceedings of the IEEE Conference on Computer Vision and Pattern Recognition, Las Vegas, NV, USA, 27–30 June 2016; pp. 770–778.
31. Lin, S.; Ryabtsev, A.; Sengupta, S.; Cureless, B.L.; Seitz, S.M.; Kemelmacher-Shlizerman, I. Real-time high-resolution background matting. In Proceedings of the IEEE/CVF Conference on Computer Vision and Pattern Recognition, Nashville, TN, USA, 20–25 June 2021; pp. 8762–8771.
32. Canny, J. A computational approach to edge detection. *IEEE Trans. Pattern Anal. Mach. Intell.* **1986**, *PAMI-8*, 679–698. [CrossRef]
33. Florian, L.C.; Adam, S.H. Rethinking atrous convolution for semantic image segmentation. *arXiv* **2017**, arXiv:1706.05587v3.
34. Chen, L.C.; Zhu, Y.; Papandreou, G.; Schroff, F.; Adam, H. Encoder-decoder with atrous separable convolution for semantic image segmentation. In Proceedings of the European Conference on Computer Vision, Munich, Germany, 8–14 September 2018; pp. 801–818.
35. Yu, F.; Koltun, V. Multi-scale context aggregation by dilated convolutions. *arXiv* **2015**, arXiv:1511.07122.
36. He, K.; Zhang, X.; Ren, S.; Sun, J. Spatial Pyramid Pooling in Deep Convolutional Networks for Visual Recognition. *IEEE Trans. Pattern Anal. Mach. Intell.* **2015**, *37*, 1904–1916. [CrossRef]
37. Moisan, L.; Moulon, P.; Monasse, P. Automatic Homographic Registration of a Pair of Images, with A Contrario Elimination of Outliers. *Image Process. Line* **2012**, *2*, 56–73. [CrossRef]
38. Goesele, M.; Snavely, N.; Curless, B.; Hoppe, H.; Seitz, S.M. Multi-view stereo for community photo collections. In Proceedings of the 2007 IEEE 11th International Conference on Computer Vision, Rio de Janeiro, Brazil, 14–21 October 2007; pp. 1–8.
39. Kolmogorov, V. Convergent tree-reweighted message passing for energy minimization. *IEEE Trans. Pattern Anal. Mach. Intell.* **2006**, *28*, 1568–1583. [CrossRef] [PubMed]
40. Hirschmuller, H. Stereo processing by semi-global matching and mutual information. *IEEE Trans. Pattern Anal. Mach. Intell.* **2007**, *30*, 328–341. [CrossRef]
41. Hao, Y.; Wang, N.; Li, J.; Gao, X. HSME: Hypersphere manifold embedding for visible thermal person re-identification. In Proceedings of the AAAI Conference on Artificial Intelligence, Honolulu, HI, USA, 27 January–1 February 2019; Volume 33, pp. 8385–8392.
42. Liu, H.; Cheng, J.; Wang, W.; Su, Y.; Bai, H. Enhancing the discriminative feature learning for visible-thermal cross-modality person re-identification. *Neurocomputing* **2020**, *398*, 11–19. [CrossRef]
43. Shin, H.C.; Roth, H.R.; Gao, M.; Lu, L.; Xu, Z.; Nogues, I.; Yao, J.; Mollura, D.; Summers, R.M. Deep convolutional neural networks for computer-aided detection: CNN architectures, dataset characteristics and transfer learning. *IEEE Trans. Med. Imaging* **2016**, *35*, 1285–1298. [CrossRef] [PubMed]
44. Kim, D.H.; Mackinnon, T. Artificial intelligence in fracture detection: Transfer learning from deep convolutional neural networks. *Clin. Radiol.* **2018**, *73*, 439–445. [CrossRef] [PubMed]
45. Lin, J.W.; Li, H. HPILN: A feature learning framework for cross-modality person re-identification. *arXiv* **2019**, arXiv:1906.03142.

mathematics

MDPI

Article

Enhancing the Transferability of Adversarial Examples with Feature Transformation

Hao-Qi Xu [1,2], Cong Hu [1,2,*] and He-Feng Yin [1,2]

1 School of Artificial Intelligence and Computer Science, Jiangnan University, Wuxi 214122, China
2 Jiangsu Provincial Engineering Laboratory of Pattern Recognition and Computational Intelligence, Jiangnan University, Wuxi 214122, China
* Correspondence: conghu@jiangnan.edu.cn

Abstract: The transferability of adversarial examples allows the attacker to fool deep neural networks (DNNs) without knowing any information about the target models. The current input transformation-based method generates adversarial examples by transforming the image in the input space, which implicitly integrates a set of models by concatenating image transformation into the trained model. However, the input transformation-based methods ignore the manifold embedding and hardly extract intrinsic information from high-dimensional data. To this end, we propose a novel feature transformation-based method (FTM), which conducts feature transformation in the feature space. FTM can improve the robustness of adversarial example by transforming the features of data. Combining with FTM, the intrinsic features of adversarial examples are extracted to generate transferable adversarial examples. The experimental results on two benchmark datasets show that FTM could effectively improve the attack success rate (ASR) of the state-of-the-art (SOTA) methods. FTM improves the attack success rate of the Scale-Invariant Method on Inception_v3 from 62.6% to 75.1% on ImageNet, which is a large margin of 12.5%.

Keywords: adversarial example; feature transformation; black-box attack; ensemble attack; deep neural network

MSC: 68T10

Citation: Xu, H.-Q.; Hu, C.; Yin, H.-F. Enhancing the Transferability of Adversarial Examples with Feature Transformation. *Mathematics* **2022**, *10*, 2976. https://doi.org/10.3390/math10162976

Academic Editors: Jianping Gou, Weihua Ou, Shaoning Zeng and Lan Du

Received: 26 July 2022
Accepted: 17 August 2022
Published: 18 August 2022

1. Introduction

DNNs have been shown to perform well in many fields, for example, image classification [1–3], human recognition [4], image segmentation [5], image fusion [6], visual object tracking [7,8], super-resolution [9], etc [10]. The ultimate goal of these studies is to make DNN-based applications more practicable and efficient. However, the existence of adversarial examples presents a concern for security of many applications, such as autonomous driving [11], face recognition [12–14], etc.

Adversarial examples [15], generated by adding indistinguishable perturbations to the raw images, can lead the DNNs to make completely different predictions. They can even take effect for completely unknown models, which is called the transferability of adversarial examples. In addition to this, there are several studies on universal adversarial perturbations [16,17], which are able to take effect on any image. Some studies are devoted to the application of adversarial examples to real-world scenarios, such as face recognition, autonomous driving, etc. [18–22]. Studying both adversarial attack and defense [23–26] is of significance, not only in revealing the vulnerability of DNNs, but also in improving the robustness of DNNs.

Many white-box attack methods have been proposed, such as Fast Gradient Sign Method (FGSM) [27], Basic Iterative Method (BIM) [28], etc. However, it is difficult for an attacker to obtain the structure and other parameters of the target model in the real-world situation. Therefore, various approaches have emerged to enhance the transferability of adversarial examples for black-box attack. Ensemble Attack [29] is an effective method to enhance the transferability of adversarial examples. Lin et al. [30] proposed Scale-Invariant Method (SIM), which utilizes input transformation to obtain a new model. A set of models can be obtained by using different transformations several times. With this approach, they can perform an ensemble attack with only one trained model, which is an implicit ensemble attack. Input transformation-based methods are successfully used for an adversarial attack, such as Diverse Input Method (DIM) [31], Translation-Invariant Method (TIM) [32], Admix Attack Method (Admix) [33], etc. However, these methods ignore the manifold structure of adversarial examples and few works focus on feature transformation. To this end, this work proposes a feature transformation-based method (FTM) to improve the transferability of adversarial examples. Compared with the input transformation, our approach transforms the intrinsic features of data instead of the input images. FTM is an implicit ensemble attack that can simultaneously attack multiple models that extract different features. It can improve the robustness of the adversarial example at the feature level. This work proposes several feature transformation strategies. FTM could effectively improve the performance of the SOTA adversarial attacks. Our contributions can be summarized as follows.

- This work proposes a novel feature transformation-based method (FTM) for enhancing the transferability of adversarial examples.
- We propose several feature transformation strategies and comprehensively analyze the hyper-parameters of them.
- The experimental results on two benchmark datasets show that FTM could effectively improve the attack success rate of the SOTA methods.

The structure of the paper is organized as follows. Section 2 introduces related work. Section 3 details the proposed FTM. Section 4 shows the experimental results. Section 5 gives a summary of this work.

2. Related Work

2.1. Adversarial Example and Transferability

It is firstly pointed out by Szegedy et al. [15] that DNNs are vulnerable to adversarial examples, which are generated by adding imperceptible noises to raw images.

Let x be a clean image, $y = f(x;\theta)$ be the output label predicted by the model with parameters θ, and $||\cdots||_p$ denotes the p-norm. The adversarial example is an image x^{adv} whose output label $f(x^{adv},\theta) \neq f(x,\theta)$, and the L_p norm of the adversarial perturbation $x^{adv} - x$ is smaller than a threshold ϵ as $||x^{adv} - x|| \leq \epsilon$. $p = \infty$ is used to limit the distortion. Many methods are proposed to improve the attack success rate (ASR) of adversarial examples. These methods can be divided into two branches: advanced gradient calculation and input transformations.

2.2. Advanced Gradient Calculation

This branch exploits better gradient calculation algorithms to enhance the performance of adversarial examples in both white-box settings and black-box settings.

Fast Gradient Sign Method (FGSM): Szegedy et al. [27] make the point that linear behavior in high-dimensional spaces is sufficient to cause adversarial examples. According to this point, they propose the FGSM, which generates an adversarial example x^{adv} by maximizing the loss function $J(x^{adv}, y;\theta)$ with a one-step update:

$$x^{adv} = x + \epsilon \cdot sign(\nabla_x J(x, y, \theta)) \tag{1}$$

where $J(x, y : \theta)$ denotes the loss function of classifier $f(x : \theta)$, $\nabla_x J(x, y, \theta)$ is the gradient of loss function with regard to x and $sign(\cdot)$ is the sign function to make the perturbation meet the L_p norm bound.

Basic Iterative Method (BIM): Kurakin et al. [28] extend FGSM to an iterative version by iteratively applying gradient updates multiple times with a small step size α. BIM can be expressed as:

$$x_{t+1}^{adv} = Clip_x^{\epsilon}\{x_t^{adv} + \alpha \cdot sign(\nabla_x J(x, y, \theta))\} \tag{2}$$

where $x_0 = x$ and $Cilp_x^{\epsilon}(\cdot)$ restricts generated adversarial examples to be within the ϵ-ball of x.

Momentum Iterative Fast Gradient Sign Method (MI-FGSM): To reduce the variation in update direction and avoid local minima, Dong et al. [34] introduce momentum into the BIM. The update procedure is formulated as follows:

$$g_{t+1} = \mu \cdot g_t + \frac{\nabla_x J(x, y, \theta)}{||\nabla_x J(x, y, \theta)||_1} \tag{3}$$

$$x_{t+1}^{adv} = Clip_x^{\epsilon}\{x_t^{adv} + \alpha \cdot sign(g_{t+1})\} \tag{4}$$

where g_t gathers the gradient of the first t iterations with a decay factor μ.

Nesterov Iterative Fast Gradient Sign Method (NI-FGSM): NI-FGSM [30] adopts Nesterov's accelerated gradient to improve the transferability of MI-FGSM. This method replaces x_t^{adv} in Equation (4) with x_{nest}, while x_{nest} can be formulated as follows:

$$x_{nest} = x_t^{adv} + \alpha \cdot \mu \cdot g_t \tag{5}$$

2.3. Input Transformations

Various input transformation-based methods, such as DIM, TIM, SIM, and Admix, are proposed to generate transferable adversarial examples.

Diverse Input Method (DIM): Inspired by the facts that data augmentation is effective to prevent networks from overfitting, Xie et al. [31] apply random resizing and random padding to the inputs to improve the transferability of adversarial examples.

Translation-Invariant Method (TIM): Dong et al. [32] propose to replace the gradient on the original image with the average value of multiple translated images for the update. Inspired by the translation-invariant property, they approximate this process by convolving the gradient with a predefined kernel matrix to avoid introducing much more computations.

Scale-Invariant Method (SIM): Lin et al. [30] discover the scale-invariant property of deep learning models and introduce the definition of loss-preserving transformation and model augmentation. Accordingly, they present SIM that calculates the average gradient on the scaled copies of the original image for the update.

Admix Attack Method (Admix): Admix is proposed by [33] to enhance the transferability of the adversarial examples. It integrates gradient information of different categories of images for the update. Specifically, Admix randomly selects a number of different categories of images and then admix the sampled image with a minor weight to the original input image. It calculates the gradient on the mixed image for update.

2.4. Adversarial Defense

In addition to adversarial attacks, many works on adversarial defense have been proposed to improve the robustness of the classifiers. The current defense methods can be divided into two categories.

One category aims to improve the robustness of the classifier itself, such as adversarial training [27,35]. It adds adversarial examples to the training set during the training of the model, making it immune to the adversarial examples. This is a popular and effective defense method and has many great following works [36,37]. However, its effectiveness is largely limited by the method of generation of the added adversarial examples.

Another category of defense methods reduces the impact of adversarial perturbations by modifying the input images, such as adding noises and compressing the images [38,39]. Xie et al. [40] propose to perform randomized resizing and padding to inputs at inference time, which is the top-1 defense solution in the NIPS competition. Nips-r3 fuse multiple adversarial trained models and perform several input transformations at inference time. These methods require no additional training computational overhead and are effective against various attack approaches.

3. Our Approach

A DNN model could be formulated as $f(x) = \text{lin}(\text{con}(x))$, where $\text{con}(\cdot)$ and $\text{lin}(\cdot)$ denote the convolutional part and the fully connected part, respectively. $\boldsymbol{p} = \text{con}(x)$ denotes the feature extracted by the convolutional part.

To obtain an ensemble of models that extract different features, we propose the feature transformation denoted as $\text{FT}(\cdot)$. Through introducing feature transformation, we can obtain a new model $f'(x) = \text{lin}(p') = \text{lin}(\text{FT}(\text{con}(x)))$ extracting different features from the original model during every iteration. FTM optimizes the adversarial perturbations over several different transformed features:

$$\underset{x^{adv}}{\arg\min} \ \frac{1}{m}\sum_{i=0}^{m} \text{J}(\text{lin}(\text{FT}_\text{i}(\text{con}(x^{adv}))), y_{true}), \tag{6}$$

$$s.t., \ \|x^{adv} - x\|_\infty \le \epsilon, \tag{7}$$

where m denotes the number of iterations and $\text{FT}(\cdot)$ denotes the feature transformation. Thus, FTM is an implicit ensemble attack that simultaneously attacks m models. The illustration of the FTM is shown in Figure 1.

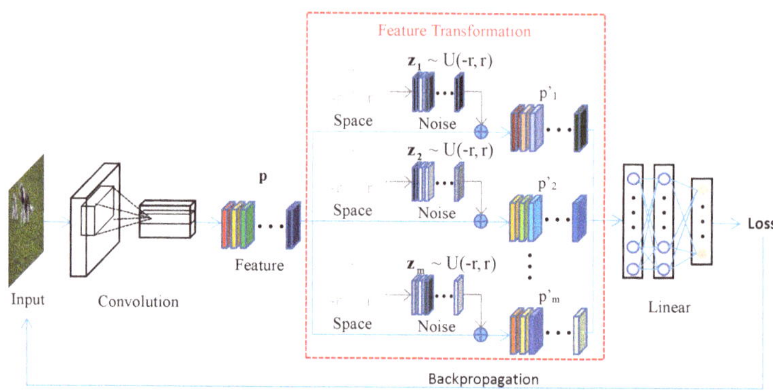

Figure 1. Illustration of the proposed FTM. The feature transformation shown in the illustration is the Strategy I. The random noise vectors z_i sampled from the uniform distribution are added to the feature $\boldsymbol{p}$. The average loss of the transformed features is calculated to update the input image.

In this paper, we consider five strategies of feature transformation as follows:

Strategy I: Fixed threshold random noise: Add a random vector z sampled from the uniform distribution $\mathcal{U}(-r, r)$:

$$\text{FT}(p) = \boldsymbol{p} + z \tag{8}$$

Strategy II: Mean-based threshold random noise: z is a random vector sampled from the uniform distribution $\mathcal{U}(-r, r)$ and $\overline{p}$ is the mean value of feature $\boldsymbol{p}$. Adding $\overline{p} \cdot z$ to feature p:

$$\text{FT}(p) = \boldsymbol{p} + \overline{p} \cdot z \tag{9}$$

Strategy III: Feature overall scaled: Multiply the features $\boldsymbol{p}$ by a random number k sampled from the uniform distribution $\mathcal{U}(-r,r)$:

$$\mathrm{FT}(p) = k \cdot \boldsymbol{p} \tag{10}$$

Strategy IV: Each value of feature scaled separately: Multiply feature $\boldsymbol{p}$ by a random vector $\boldsymbol{z}$ sampled from the uniform distribution $\mathcal{U}(-r,r)$:

$$\mathrm{FT}(p) = \boldsymbol{z} \cdot \boldsymbol{p} \tag{11}$$

Strategy V: Offset mean random noise: Add a random vector $\boldsymbol{z}$ sampled from the uniform distribution $\mathcal{U}(-r+s, r+s)$ to feature $\boldsymbol{p}$:

$$\mathrm{FT}(p) = \boldsymbol{p} + \boldsymbol{z} \tag{12}$$

The feature transformation should also be an accuracy-preserving transformation. We define the accuracy-preserving feature transformation as follows:

Definition 1 (Acc-preserving Feature Transformation)**.** *Given a test set X and a classifier* $f(x) = \mathrm{lin}(\mathrm{con}(x))$, $Acc(\mathrm{lin}(\mathrm{con}(x)), X)$ *denotes the accuracy of model* $f(x)$ *on data set X. If there exists an feature transformation* $\mathrm{FT}(\cdot)$ *that satisfies* $Acc(\mathrm{lin}(\mathrm{con}(x)), X) \approx Acc(\mathrm{lin}(\mathrm{FT}(\mathrm{con}(x))), X)$, *we say* $\mathrm{FT}(\cdot)$ *is an accuracy-preserving feature transformation.*

We experimentally study the acc-preserving feature transformation strategies in Section 4.1.2. We determine the magnitude r of uniform distribution to ensure that our feature transformations are accuracy-preserving transformations. The algorithm of the FTM attack is summarized in Algorithm 1.

Algorithm 1 Algorithm of FTM.

Input: Original image x, true label y^{true}, a classifier $f = \mathrm{lin}(\mathrm{con}(x))$, loss function J, feature transformation $\mathrm{FT}(\cdot)$
Hyper-parameters: Perturbation size ϵ, maximum iterations T, number of iterations of feature transformation m
Output: Adversarial example x_{adv}
1: perturbation size in each iteration: $\alpha = \epsilon / T$
2: **while** $0 \leq t < T - 1$.
3: **if** $k = 0$.
4: $x_0 = x$.
5: **end if**
6: $g = 0$
7: **while** $0 \leq i < m - 1$
8: feature:$\boldsymbol{p} = \mathrm{con}(x)$
9: transformed feature: $\boldsymbol{p}' = \mathrm{FT}(\boldsymbol{p})$
10: Get the gradients by $\nabla_x J(\mathrm{lin}(\boldsymbol{p}'), y^{true})$
11: Update $g = g + \nabla_x J(\mathrm{lin}(\boldsymbol{p}'), y^{true})$
12: **end while**
13: Get average gradients as $\overline{g} = \frac{1}{m} \cdot g$
14: Update $x_{i+1}^{adv} = \mathrm{Clip}_x^{\epsilon}\{x_i^{adv} + \alpha \cdot \mathrm{sign}(\overline{g})\}$
15: **end while**
16: return $x^{adv} = x_T^{adv}$

4. Experimental Results

4.1. Experiment on ImageNet

4.1.1. Experimental Setup

Dataset. We perform experiments on ImageNet, which is the most common and challenging image classification dataset. 1000 images from the ImageNet [41] are selected as our test set. The 1000 benign images belong to 1000 different categories and can be correctly classified by the tested models.

Networks. This work selects four mainstream models, including Inception_v3 (Inc_v3) [42], Inception_v4 (Inc_v4), Inception-Resnet_v2 (IncRes_v2) [43], and Xception(Xcep) [44].

Attack setting. We follow the setting in Lin et al. [30] with the maximum perturbation as $\epsilon = 16$, number of iteration $T = 16$, and step size $\alpha = 1.6$, which is a difficult and challenging attack setting. We adopt the decay factor $\mu = 1.0$ for MI-FGSM. The transformation probability is set to 0.5 for DIM. The number of scale copies is set to $m = 5$ for SIM. We set $m_1 = 5$, and randomly sample $m_2 = 3$ images with $\eta = 0.2$ for Admix. The hyper-parameter settings of these attack methods are all consistent with the original papers.

4.1.2. Accuracy-Preserving Transformation

To investigate accuracy-preserving transformations, we test the accuracy of the models integrated with the five strategies on the ImageNet dataset. We keep the magnitude r of uniform distribution in the range of $[0, 10]$.

The magnitude of uniform distribution is an important hyper-parameter of FTM. A larger magnitude will increase the diversity of the implicit ensemble models and thus improve the transferability of the adversarial examples. However, too large a magnitude will make the model invalid and thus lose the ability to guide the generation of AE. As shown in Figure 2, the accuracy curves are smooth and stable for strategies I, II, and V when the magnitude is in the range of $[0, 4]$. They drop significantly after the magnitude exceeds 4. Moreover, the accuracies for strategy III and IV are extremely low when the magnitude is close to 0. They turn to remain stable after the magnitude exceeds 4. It can be seen that the feature transformation strategy with scaled operation is more sensitive to small magnitude, e.g., strategies III and IV. The feature transformation strategy of adding noise is more sensitive to a large magnitude, e.g., strategies I, II, and V. Based on the experimental results, the magnitude of uniform distribution is set to 4 in the following experiment to ensure that the feature transformations are accuracy-preserving transformations.

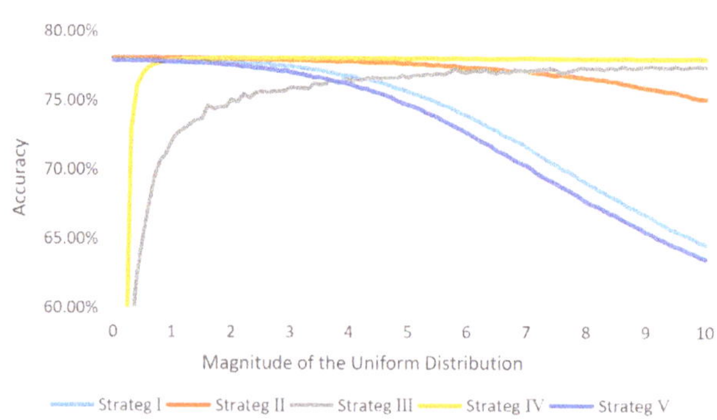

Figure 2. The average classification accuracy of Inc_v3, Inc_v4, IncRes_v2, and Xcep integrated with five different feature transformation strategies on ImageNet. The horizontal coordinate is the magnitude of uniform distribution and the vertical coordinate is the accuracy of the model.

4.1.3. Feature Transformation Strategies

In this section, we show the experimental results of the proposed FTM with five feature transformation strategies. We set $m = 1$ and generate adversarial examples on the Inc_v3 by FT-FGSM, FT-MI-FGSM, and FT-SIM. The ASRs against the other three black-box models are presented in Table 1.

Table 1. The black-box ASRs (%) of FT-FGSM, FT-MI-FGSM, and FT-SIM with five strategies on ImageNet. The adversarial examples are generated on Inc_v3. The highest ASRs are shown in bold.

Method	Strategy	Inc_v3	Inc_v4	IncRes_v2	Xcep
FT-FGSM	I	-	36.1	33.5	35.3
	II	-	37.3	33.7	35.1
	III	-	37.0	**35.9**	**37.5**
	IV	-	37.5	32.0	34.7
	V	-	**37.7**	33.4	34.4
FT-MI-FGSM	I	-	55.1	52.5	**59.8**
	II	-	53.0	50.4	54.4
	III	-	54.9	51.6	57.8
	IV	-	53.4	50.8	56.5
	V	-	**57.0**	**53.3**	59.2
FT-SIM	I	-	**43.0**	41.3	42.9
	II	-	38.5	34.9	39.3
	III	-	42.9	**42.6**	**44.0**
	IV	-	42.2	42.4	43.5
	V	-	41.1	41.9	42.6

When combined with FT-FGSM, Strategy III achieves the best overall attack performance, reaching 35.9% and 37.5% when attacking IncRes_v2 and Xcep, respectively. When attacking with FT-MI-FGSM, Strategy V attains the best overall attack performance, reaching 57% and 53.3% when attacking Inv_v4 and IncRes_v2, respectively. When FT-SIM is used to attack IncRes_v2 and Xcep, Strategy III achieves the ASRs of 35.9% and 37.5%, which outperforms the other strategies. It can be seen that the overall performance of Strategy III is better and it performs better in the experiments combined with SIM, which is an input transformation-based method. Thus, we adopt Strategy III in the following experiments.

4.1.4. Attack with Input Transformations

We test the ASRs of MI-FGSM, SIM, DIM, and Admix, respectively. Then we combine these methods with FTM as FT-MI-FGSM, FT-SIM, FT-DIM, and FT-Admix. Some adversarial examples are shown in Figure 3. We adopt Strategy III, set $m = 1$, set the magnitude of uniform distribution $r = 4$, and then use the generated adversarial examples to attack the four models. We compare the black-box ASRs of FT-MI-FGSM, FT-SIM, FT-DIM, and FT-Admix with MI-FGSM, SIM, DIM, and Admix in Tables 2–5. In the tables, the first columns are the local models, and the first rows are the target models. The values in the tables are the attack success rates (ASRs) on the target models using the adversarial examples generated from the local models. The higher ASRs are bolded.

When combined with MI-FGSM, the ASRs is increased by up to 9.4%, from 55% to 64.4% when attacking Xcep with Inc_v4. When FT-SIM is used to attack IncV3 with IncRes_v2, the ASR is improved from 62.6% to 75.1%, which outperforms the SIM by 12.5%. The adversarial examples generated by FT-DIM achieved about 55% ASR against all models. When FT-Admix is used to attack IncV3 with Xecp, the ASR reaches 72.2%.

According to the reported experimental results, it can be observed that FTM could improve the ASRs of adversarial examples generated by the SOTA black-box attack methods. It is confirmed that feature transformation can improve the transferability and robustness of adversarial examples.

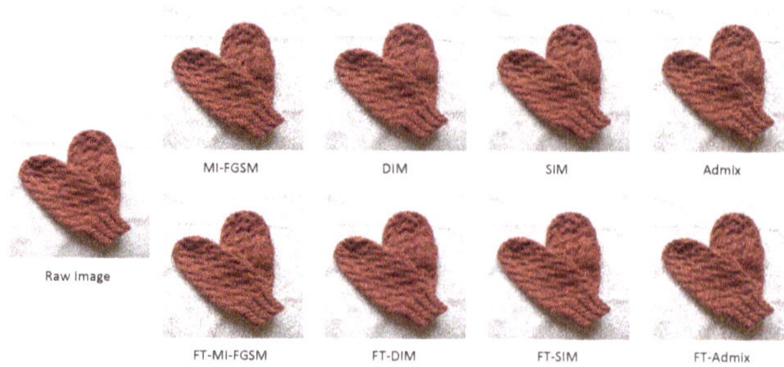

Figure 3. Adversarial examples generated by MI-FGSM, DIM, SIM, Admix, the proposed FT-MI-FGSM, FT-DIM, FT-SIM, and FT-Admix on the Inc_v3.

Table 2. The black-box ASRs of MI-FGSM and FT-MI-FGSM on ImageNet. The first column is the local model, and the first row is the target model. The values in the table are the ASRs (%) on the target models using the adversarial examples generated with the local models. The higher ASRs are shown in bold.

Local Model	Attack Method	Inc_v3	Inc_v4	IncRes_v2	Xcep
Inc_v3	MI-FGSM	-	51.3	49.6	53.0
	FT-MI-FGSM	-	**54.9**	**51.6**	**57.8**
Inc_v4	MI-FGSM	56.0	-	48.5	55.0
	FT-MI-FGSM	**58.9**	-	**53.1**	**64.4**
IncRes_v2	MI-FGSM	56.2	51.8	-	55.9
	FT-MI-FGSM	**64.1**	**57.4**	-	**63.0**
Xcep	MI-FGSM	51.4	50.8	45.3	-
	FT-MI-FGSM	**54.4**	**55.0**	**48.7**	-

Table 3. The black-box ASRs of SIM and FT-SIM on ImageNet. The first column is the local model, and the first row is the target model. The values in the table are the ASRs (%) on the target models using the adversarial examples generated with the local models. The higher ASRs are shown in bold.

Local Model	Attack Method	Inc_v3	Inc_v4	IncRes_v2	Xcep
Inc_v3	SIM	-	37.4	34.7	37.0
	FT-SIM	-	**42.9**	**42.6**	**44.0**
Inc_v4	SIM	64.0	-	51.9	59.7
	FT-SIM	**71.0**	-	**59.0**	**64.9**
IncRes_v2	SIM	62.6	52.8	-	55.2
	FT-SIM	**75.1**	**63.4**	-	**65.2**
Xcep	SIM	57.9	54.3	50.0	-
	FT-SIM	**63.4**	**58.9**	**53.0**	-

Table 4. The black-box ASRs of DIM and FT-DIM on ImageNet. The first column is the local model, and the first row is the target model. The values in the table are the ASRs (%) on the target models using the adversarial examples generated with the local models. The higher ASRs are shown in bold.

Local Model	Attack Method	Inc_v3	Inc_v4	IncRes_v2	Xcep
Inc_v3	DIM	-	59.5	55.3	56.3
	FT-DIM	-	**61.8**	**58.3**	**60.4**
Inc_v4	DIM	59.0	-	52.0	61.7
	FT-DIM	**63.4**	-	**56.5**	**66.6**
IncRes_v2	DIM	58.6	57.7	-	60.7
	FT-DIM	**67.2**	**66.8**	-	**66.5**
Xcep	DIM	57.3	64.3	55.6	-
	FT-DIM	**61.8**	**69.1**	**58.2**	-

Table 5. The black-box ASRs of Admix and FT-Admix on ImageNet. The first column is the local model, and the first row is the target model. The values in the table are the ASRs (%) on the target models using the adversarial examples generated with the local models. The higher ASRs are shown in bold.

Local Model	Attack Method	Inc_v3	Inc_v4	IncRes_v2	Xcep
Inc_v3	Admix	-	52.8	49.1	56.2
	FT-Admix	-	**57.3**	**54.4**	**60.0**
Inc_v4	Admix	70.8	-	61.1	67.2
	FT-Admix	**72.2**	-	**64.0**	**68.3**
IncRes_v2	Admix	64.1	57.4	-	60.5
	FT-Admix	**66.0**	**58.7**	-	**60.4**
Xcep	Admix	70.4	64.3	60.0	-
	FT-Admix	**72.2**	**65.2**	**61.6**	-

4.1.5. Attack against Defense Method

In this section, we quantify the effectiveness of FTM against several defense methods, including random resizing and padding (RandP) [40], JPEG compression (JPEG) [39], randomized smoothing (RS) [38], and the rank-3 submission in the NIPS-2017 (NIPS-r3). RandP is the top-1 submission in the NIPS competition, which mitigates the effect of adversarial perturbations by randomized resizing and padding. JPEG is a defensive compression framework, which could rectify adversarial examples without reducing classification accuracy on benign data. RS constructs a "smoothed" classifier from an arbitrary base classifier, which is more adversarially robust. NIPS-r3 fuses multiple adversarial trained models and performs several input transformation at inference time.

We choose SIM as the comparison method and generate adversarial examples with Inc_v3. The average ASRs on Inc_v4, IncRes_v2, and Xcep are shown in Table 6. The ASRs are improved by a large margin of 9.5% on average. It validates that the adversarial examples generated by FTM are more robust to fool models with defense mechanisms.

Table 6. The black-box ASRs of SIM and FT-SIM on ImageNet against four defense methods. The adversarial examples are generated with Inc_v3. The values in the table are the average ASRs (%) on the Inc_v4, IncRes_v2, and Xcep. The higher ASRs are shown in bold.

Attack Method	RandP	JPEG	RS	Nips-r3
SIM	30.3	32.7	25.2	31.6
FT-SIM	**38.5**	**41.0**	**37.8**	**39.5**

4.1.6. Parameter Analysis

In this section, we perform additional analysis for the difference among different numbers of iterations m. The adversarial examples are generated by FT-DIM on Inc_v3. The number of iterations of feature transformation ranges from 1 to 9.

As shown in Figure 4, the average black-box ASR increases from 59.2% for 1 iteration to 62.7% for 3 iterations. As the number of iterations increases to 9, the success rate of the attack increases to 65.3%. It validates that the ASR of FTM increases as the number of iterations of feature transformation increases. The sensitivity of the attack success rate gradually decreases as the number of iterations increases. Since a higher number of iterations results in a larger computational overhead, the trade-off between effectiveness and overhead needs to be made according to the specific scenario.

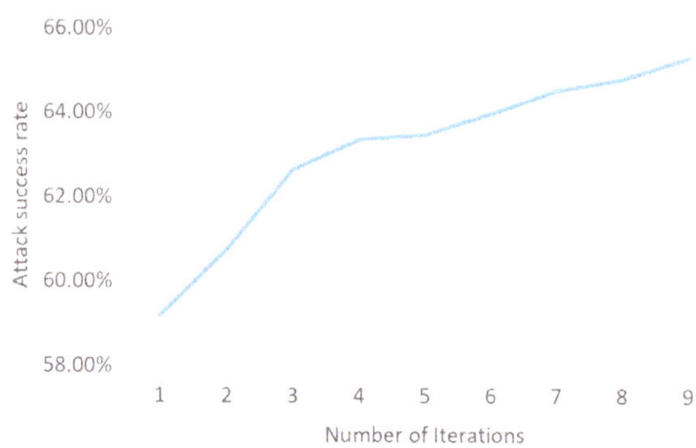

Figure 4. The black-box ASRs of FT-DIM attack with different number of iterations on ImageNet. The adversarial examples are generated on Inc_v3 and the ASRs are the average ASRs on Inc_v4, IncRes_v2, and Xcep.

4.2. *Experiment on Cifar10*

Cifar10

To further demonstrate the effectiveness of our approach, we also conducted experiments on the Cifar10 [45] dataset. Cifar10 has 60,000 color images with 32×32 pixels and is divided into 10 categories. We select 1000 images belonging to the 10 categories from the test set, which are correctly classified by all the experimental models. We compare the effects of the FTM with the MI-FGSM, SIM and Admix using the ResNet [46] family of models. The maximum perturbation $\epsilon = 4$, number of attack iterations $T = 4$, and the step size $\alpha = 1$.

The experimental results for FT-MI-FGSM, FT-SIM, and FT-Admix are shown in Tables 7–9. The first columns are the local models and the first rows are the target models. It can be seen that our method improves the ASRs across all experiments. FT-MI-FGSM achieves 83.8% ASR, when attacking Res152 with Res50. FT-SIM improves the ASR of SIM from 66.6% to 73.9%, when attacking Res101 with Res152. FT-Admix boosts the ASR of Admix attack from 43.1% to 55.1%, when attacking Res101 with Res152.

The experimental results on Cifar10 validate that FTM is effective not only on large image dataset, but also on small image dataset. Moreover, FTM can significantly improve the transferability and robustness of the adversarial examples generated by the SOTA black-box attack methods.

Table 7. The black-box ASRs of MIM (MI-FGSM) and FT-MIM (FT-MI-FGSM) on Cifar10. The first column is the local model, and the first row is the target model. The values in the table are the ASRs (%) on the target models using the adversarial examples generated with the local models. The higher ASRs are shown in bold.

Local Model	Attack Method	Res18	Res34	Res50	Res101	Res152
Res18	MIM	-	78.3	68.7	67.3	71.1
	FT-MIM	-	**78.8**	**69.2**	**70.5**	**73.4**
Res34	MIM	78.7	-	70.0	69.5	72.3
	FT-MIM	**79.8**	-	**72.9**	**71.2**	**74.1**
Res50	MIM	76.5	76.8	-	80.2	82.5
	FT-MIM	**77.8**	**78.1**	-	**82.4**	**83.8**
Res101	MIM	71.4	71.7	76.9	-	80.5
	FT-MIM	**74.2**	**73.2**	**79.3**	-	**82.6**
Res152	MIM	75.2	73.4	76.8	81.0	-
	FT-MIM	**76.8**	**74.9**	**78.7**	**82.0**	-

Table 8. The black-box ASRs of SIM and FT-SIM on Cifar10. The first column is the local model, and the first row is the target model. The values in the table are the ASRs (%) on the target models using the adversarial examples generated with the local models. The higher ASRs are shown in bold.

Local Model	Attack Method	Res18	Res34	Res50	Res101	Res152
Res18	SIM	-	73.0	60.1	59.5	62.3
	FT-SIM	-	**73.9**	**62.2**	**62.9**	**66.0**
Res34	SIM	74.9	-	60.2	60.9	63.3
	FT-SIM	**76.2**	-	**61.5**	**62.8**	**63.4**
Res50	SIM	68.0	69.3	-	70.6	71.9
	FT-SIM	**72.2**	**68.2**	-	**73.9**	**76.0**
Res101	SIM	69.2	67.7	71.0	-	73.9
	FT-SIM	**71.5**	**69.9**	**71.9**	-	**75.9**
Res152	SIM	65.6	62.3	63.8	66.6	-
	FT-SIM	**69.5**	**67.9**	**70.4**	**73.9**	-

Table 9. The black-box ASRs of Admix and FT-Admix on Cifar10. The first column is the local model, and the first row is the target model. The values in the table are the ASRs (%) on the target models using the adversarial examples generated with the local models. The higher ASRs are shown in bold.

Local Model	Attack Method	Res18	Res34	Res50	Res101	Res152
Res18	Admix	-	49.0	41.9	42.5	45.0
	FT-Admix	-	**56.4**	**47.3**	**50.4**	**51.9**
Res34	Admix	52.5	-	42.7	46.5	46.0
	FT-Admix	**58.5**	-	**47.5**	**50.1**	**50.4**
Res50	Admix	48.6	43.9	-	44.9	47.4
	FT-Admix	**56.1**	**50.7**	-	**53.9**	**54.4**
Res101	Admix	48.2	44.6	44.6	-	49.3
	FT-Admix	**54.0**	**50.5**	**50.8**	-	**57.7**
Res152	Admix	45.3	40.6	39.5	43.1	-
	FT-Admix	**55.0**	**51.6**	**50.2**	**55.1**	-

5. Conclusions

We propose a novel feature transformation-based method (FTM), which effectively improves the transferability of adversarial examples. Five feature transformation strategies are proposed and the hyper-parameters of them are comprehensively analyzed. The experimental results on two benchmark datasets show that FTM can improve the transferability of the adversarial example significantly. It improves the ASRs of the SOTA methods by up to 12.5% on ImageNet. Our method can be combined with not only any gradient-based attack methods but also any neural networks that can extract features. However, the tuning of hyper-parameters is difficult, because different models and feature transformation strategies require a large number of experiments to choose the magnitude of uniform distribution. In the future, we will explore more feature transformation strategies to improve the transferability of adversarial examples while reducing the difficulty of tuning hyper-parameters.

Author Contributions: Conceptualization, H.-Q.X. and C.H.; methodology, H.-Q.X., C.H. and H.-F.Y.; software, H.-Q.X.; data curation, H.-Q.X.; resources, C.H.; writing—original draft preparation, H.-Q.X., C.H. and H.-F.Y.; project administration, C.H.; funding acquisition, C.H. All authors have read and agreed to the published version of the manuscript.

Funding: This research was funded in part by the National Natural Science Foundation of China (Grant No. 62006097), in part by the Natural Science Foundation of Jiangsu Province (Grant No. BK20200593), in part by the China Postdoctoral Science Foundation (Grant No. 2021M701456), and in part by the Fundamental Research Funds for the Central Universities (Grant No. JUSRP121074).

Institutional Review Board Statement: Not applicable.

Informed Consent Statement: Not applicable.

Data Availability Statement: The ImageNet and Cifar10 datasets were analyzed in this study. The ImageNet dataset can be found at https://image-net.org/ (accessed on 10 July 2022). Cifar10 dataset can be found at https://www.cs.toronto.edu/~kriz/cifar.html (accessed on 10 July 2022).

Conflicts of Interest: The authors declare no conflict of interest.

References

1. Gou, J.; Yuan, X.; Du, L.; Xia, S.; Yi, Z. Hierarchical Graph Augmented Deep Collaborative Dictionary Learning for Classification. *IEEE Trans. Intell. Transp. Syst.* **2022**. [CrossRef]
2. Gou, J.; Sun, L.; Du, L.; Ma, H.; Xiong, T.; Ou, W.; Zhan, Y. A representation coefficient-based k-nearest centroid neighbor classifier. *Expert Syst. Appl.* **2022**, *194*, 116529. [CrossRef]
3. Gou, J.; He, X.; Lu, J.; Ma, H.; Ou, W.; Yuan, Y. A class-specific mean vector-based weighted competitive and collaborative representation method for classification. *Neural Netw.* **2022**, *150*, 12–27. [CrossRef] [PubMed]
4. Koo, J.H.; Cho, S.W.; Baek, N.R.; Lee, Y.W.; Park, K.R. A Survey on Face and Body Based Human Recognition Robust to Image Blurring and Low Illumination. *Mathematics* **2022**, *10*, 1522. [CrossRef]
5. Wang, T.; Ji, Z.; Yang, J.; Sun, Q.; Fu, P. Global Manifold Learning for Interactive Image Segmentation. *IEEE Trans. Multimed.* **2021**, *23*, 3239–3249. [CrossRef]
6. Cheng, C.; Wu, X.J.; Xu, T.; Chen, G. UNIFusion: A Lightweight Unified Image Fusion Network. *IEEE Trans. Instrum. Meas.* **2021**, *70*, 1–14. [CrossRef]
7. Liu, Q.; Fan, J.; Song, H.; Chen, W.; Zhang, K. Visual Tracking via Nonlocal Similarity Learning. *IEEE Trans. Circuits Syst. Video Technol.* **2018**, *28*, 2826–2835. [CrossRef]
8. Zhu, X.F.; Wu, X.J.; Xu, T.; Feng, Z.H.; Kittler, J. Complementary Discriminative Correlation Filters Based on Collaborative Representation for Visual Object Tracking. *IEEE Trans. Circuits Syst. Video Technol.* **2021**, *31*, 557–568. [CrossRef]
9. Ma, C.; Rao, Y.; Lu, J.; Zhou, J. Structure-Preserving Image Super-Resolution. *IEEE Trans. Pattern Anal. Mach. Intell.* **2021**. [CrossRef]
10. Gou, J.; Yu, B.; Maybank, S.J.; Tao, D. Knowledge distillation: A survey. *Int. J. Comput. Vis.* **2021**, *129*, 1789–1819. [CrossRef]
11. Su, Y.; Zhang, Y.; Lu, T.; Yang, J.; Kong, H. Vanishing Point Constrained Lane Detection With a Stereo Camera. *IEEE Trans. Intell. Transp. Syst.* **2018**, *19*, 2739–2744. [CrossRef]
12. Chen, Z.; Wu, X.J.; Yin, H.F.; Kittler, J. Robust Low-Rank Recovery with a Distance-Measure Structure for Face Recognition. In Proceedings of the PRICAI 2018: Trends in Artificial Intelligence, Nanjing, China, 28–31 August 2018; Geng, X., Kang, B.H., Eds.; Springer International Publishing: Cham, Switzerland, 2018; pp. 464–472.
13. Kortli, Y.; Jridi, M.; Al Falou, A.; Atri, M. Face Recognition Systems: A Survey. *Sensors* **2020**, *20*, 342. [CrossRef]

14. Adjabi, I.; Ouahabi, A.; Benzaoui, A.; Taleb-Ahmed, A. Past, Present, and Future of Face Recognition: A Review. *Electronics* **2020**, *9*, 1188. [CrossRef]
15. Szegedy, C.; Zaremba, W.; Sutskever, I.; Bruna, J.; Erhan, D.; Goodfellow, I.; Fergus, R. Intriguing properties of neural networks. *arXiv* **2013**, arXiv:1312.6199.
16. Li, J.; Ji, R.; Liu, H.; Hong, X.; Gao, Y.; Tian, Q. Universal Perturbation Attack Against Image Retrieval. In Proceedings of the 2019 IEEE/CVF International Conference on Computer Vision (ICCV), Seoul, Korea, 27–28 October 2019; pp. 4898–4907. [CrossRef]
17. Liu, H.; Ji, R.; Li, J.; Zhang, B.; Gao, Y.; Wu, Y.; Huang, F. Universal Adversarial Perturbation via Prior Driven Uncertainty Approximation. In Proceedings of the 2019 IEEE/CVF International Conference on Computer Vision (ICCV), Seoul, Korea, 27–28 October 2019; pp. 2941–2949. [CrossRef]
18. Li, H.; Zhou, S.; Yuan, W.; Li, J.; Leung, H. Adversarial-Example Attacks Toward Android Malware Detection System. *IEEE Syst. J.* **2020**, *14*, 653–656. [CrossRef]
19. Kwon, H.; Kim, Y.; Yoon, H.; Choi, D. Fooling a Neural Network in Military Environments: Random Untargeted Adversarial Example. In Proceedings of the MILCOM 2018—2018 IEEE Military Communications Conference (MILCOM), Los Angeles, CA, USA, 29–31 October 2018; pp. 456–461. [CrossRef]
20. Zhu, Z.A.; Lu, Y.Z.; Chiang, C.K. Generating Adversarial Examples By Makeup Attacks on Face Recognition. In Proceedings of the 2019 IEEE International Conference on Image Processing (ICIP), Taipei, Taiwan, 22–25 September 2019; pp. 2516–2520. [CrossRef]
21. Wang, K.; Li, F.; Chen, C.M.; Hassan, M.M.; Long, J.; Kumar, N. Interpreting Adversarial Examples and Robustness for Deep Learning-Based Auto-Driving Systems. *IEEE Trans. Intell. Transp. Syst.* **2021**. [CrossRef]
22. Rana, K.; Madaan, R. Evaluating Effectiveness of Adversarial Examples on State of Art License Plate Recognition Models. In Proceedings of the 2020 IEEE International Conference on Intelligence and Security Informatics (ISI), Arlington, VA, USA, 9–10 November 2020; pp. 1–3. [CrossRef]
23. Hu, C.; Wu, X.J.; Li, Z.Y. Generating adversarial examples with elastic-net regularized boundary equilibrium generative adversarial network. *Pattern Recognit. Lett.* **2020**, *140*, 281–287. [CrossRef]
24. Li, Z.; Feng, C.; Wu, M.; Yu, H.; Zheng, J.; Zhu, F. Adversarial robustness via attention transfer. *Pattern Recognit. Lett.* **2021**, *146*, 172–178. [CrossRef]
25. Agarwal, A.; Vatsa, M.; Singh, R.; Ratha, N. Cognitive data augmentation for adversarial defense via pixel masking. *Pattern Recognit. Lett.* **2021**, *146*, 244–251. [CrossRef]
26. Massoli, F.V.; Falchi, F.; Amato, G. Cross-resolution face recognition adversarial attacks. *Pattern Recognit. Lett.* **2020**, *140*, 222–229. [CrossRef]
27. Goodfellow, I.J.; Shlens, J.; Szegedy, C. Explaining and Harnessing Adversarial Examples. *arXiv* **2014**, arXiv:1412.6572.
28. Kurakin, A.; Goodfellow, I.; Bengio, S. Adversarial examples in the physical world. In Proceedings of the International Conference on Learning Representations Workshop, Toulon, France, 24–26 April 2017; pp. 1–14. [CrossRef]
29. Liu, Y.; Chen, X.; Liu, C.; Song, D. Delving into transferable adversarial examples and black-box attacks. In Proceedings of the International Conference on Learning Representations, Toulon, France, 24–26 April 2017; pp. 1–24.
30. Lin, J.; Song, C.; He, K.; Wang, L.; Hopcroft, J.E. Nesterov Accelerated Gradient and Scale Invariance for Adversarial Attacks. In Proceedings of the International Conference on Learning Representations, Addis Ababa, Ethiopia, 26–30 April 2020; pp. 1–12.
31. Xie, C.; Zhang, Z.; Zhou, Y.; Bai, S.; Wang, J.; Ren, Z.; Yuille, A.L. Improving Transferability of Adversarial Examples With Input Diversity. In Proceedings of the IEEE/CVF Conference on Computer Vision and Pattern Recognition (CVPR), Long Beach, CA, USA, 15–20 June 2019; pp. 2725–2734. [CrossRef]
32. Dong, Y.; Pang, T.; Su, H.; Zhu, J. Evading Defenses to Transferable Adversarial Examples by Translation-Invariant Attacks. In Proceedings of the IEEE/CVF Conference on Computer Vision and Pattern Recognition (CVPR), Long Beach, CA, USA, 15–20 June 2019; pp. 4312–4321.
33. Wang, X.; He, X.; Wang, J.; He, K. Admix: Enhancing the Transferability of Adversarial Attacks. In Proceedings of the IEEE/CVF International Conference on Computer Vision (ICCV), Montreal, BC, Canada, 11–17 October 2021; pp. 16158–16167.
34. Dong, Y.; Liao, F.; Pang, T.; Su, H.; Zhu, J.; Hu, X.; Li, J. Boosting Adversarial Attacks with Momentum. In Proceedings of the 2018 IEEE/CVF Conference on Computer Vision and Pattern Recognition, Salt Lake City, UT, USA, 18–22 June 2018; pp. 9185–9193. [CrossRef]
35. Kurakin, A.; Goodfellow, I.; Bengio, S. Adversarial Machine Learning at Scale. In Proceedings of the International Conference on Learning Representations, Toulon, France, 24–26 April 2017; pp. 1–17.
36. Madry, A.; Makelov, A.; Schmidt, L.; Tsipras, D.; Vladu, A. Towards Deep Learning Models Resistant to Adversarial Attacks. In Proceedings of the International Conference on Learning Representations, Vancouver, BC, Canada, 30 April–3 May 2018; pp. 1–28.
37. Tramèr, F.; Kurakin, A.; Papernot, N.; Goodfellow, I.; Boneh, D.; Mcdaniel, P. Ensemble Adversarial Training: Attacks and Defenses. In Proceedings of the International Conference on Learning Representations, Vancouver, BC, Canada, 30 April–3 May 2018; pp. 1–22.
38. Cohen, J.M.; Rosenfeld, E.; Kolter, J.Z. Certified Adversarial Robustness via Randomized Smoothing. In Proceedings of the International Conference on Machine Learning, Long Beach, CA, USA, 9–15 June 2019; pp. 1–36.
39. Guo, C.; Rana, M.; Cisse, M.; van der Maaten, L. Countering Adversarial Images using Input Transformations. In Proceedings of the International Conference on Learning Representations, Vancouver, BC, Canada, 30 April–3 May 2018; pp. 1–12.

40. Xie, C.; Wang, J.; Zhang, Z.; Ren, Z.; Yuille, A. Mitigating Adversarial Effects Through Randomization. In Proceedings of the International Conference on Learning Representations, Toulon, France, 24–26 April 2017; pp. 1–16.
41. Russakovsky, O.; Deng, J.; Su, H.; Krause, J.; Satheesh, S.; Ma, S.; Huang, Z.; Karpathy, A.; Khosla, A.; Bernstein, M.; et al. Imagenet large scale visual recognition challenge. *Int. J. Comput. Vis.* **2015**, *115*, 211–252. [CrossRef]
42. Szegedy, C.; Vanhoucke, V.; Ioffe, S.; Shlens, J.; Wojna, Z. Rethinking the Inception Architecture for Computer Vision. In Proceedings of the IEEE Conference on Computer Vision and Pattern Recognition (CVPR), Los Alamitos, CA, USA, 27–30 June 2016; pp. 2818–2826. [CrossRef]
43. Szegedy, C.; Ioffe, S.; Vanhoucke, V.; Alemi, A.A. Inception-v4, Inception-ResNet and the Impact of Residual Connections on Learning. In Proceedings of the Thirty-First AAAI Conference on Artificial Intelligence, San Francisco, CA, USA, 4–9 February 2017; pp. 4278–4284.
44. Chollet, F. Xception: Deep Learning with Depthwise Separable Convolutions. In Proceedings of the 2017 IEEE Conference on Computer Vision and Pattern Recognition (CVPR), Honolulu, HI, USA, 21–27 July 2017; pp. 1800–1807. [CrossRef]
45. Krizhevsky, A. *Learning Multiple Layers of Features from Tiny Images*; University of Toronto: Toronto, ON, USA, 2009; pp. 1–60.
46. He, K.; Zhang, X.; Ren, S.; Sun, J. Deep residual learning for image recognition. In Proceedings of the IEEE Conference on Computer Vision and Pattern Recognition, Las Vegas, NV, USA, 27–30 June 2016; pp. 770–778.

mathematics

MDPI

Article

Extension Design Pattern of Requirement Analysis for Complex Mechanical Products Scheme Design

Tichun Wang *, Hao Li and Xianwei Wang

College of Mechanical and Electrical Engineering, Nanjing University of Aeronautics and Astronautics, Nanjing 210016, China
* Correspondence: wangtichun2010@nuaa.edu.cn

Abstract: Due to the configuration process of a complex product scheme, a design structure often has the characteristics of multi-level, multi-attribute, creativity, and complexity; in order to improve the efficiency and quality of product scheme design, it has important research value to reasonably organize, reason, and reuse design knowledge. In this paper, the extension modeling problem under the extension design mode of complex product scheme is studied, the multitype design knowledge element modeling expression model of complex product scheme design is given, and the extension process model and the implication process model of requirement analysis of complex product scheme design is established. A new demand element weight assignment method based on extension distance is proposed to obtain accurate demand analysis index weight from the perspective of combined qualitative and quantitative analysis. On the basis of constructing the extension correlation degree of demand primitives, this paper puts forward the implementation method of the extension design pattern for the demand analysis of a complex product scheme design and gives the specific implementation algorithm. Finally, an example of product design is given to illustrate the method, and the results show the effectiveness and operability of the method.

Keywords: intelligent design; data analysis; models and algorithms; extension theory; scheme design

MSC: 68T20

Citation: Wang, T.; Li, H.; Wang, X. Extension Design Pattern of Requirement Analysis for Complex Mechanical Products Scheme Design. *Mathematics* **2022**, *10*, 3132. https://doi.org/10.3390/math10173132

Academic Editor: Bo-Hao Chen

Received: 5 July 2022
Accepted: 12 August 2022
Published: 1 September 2022

1. Introduction

The product scheme design of the aerospace industry or power generation equipment industry is creative, skilled labor based on the combination of some theories and a large amount of practical experience; its design process is a multi-level multi-attribute creative and complex configuration process, the interaction of various design factors generate design constraints and design conflicts in the design process [1–4], so accurately describing analyzing and transforming the customers' requirements is very important for the smooth development of the product. Requirement analysis is not only considering the customer's requirement information but also considering the information of the entire life cycle of the product, that is, the design's feasibility, manufacturability, reliability, maintainability, energy, and environmental protection; they are the design goals of the various activities in the product development process to make requirements analysis better guide the subsequent design. Because of that, scheme design cannot, in isolation, describe the requirement model from the customer's point of view; it should consider the entire life cycle of the product and strive to make the requirement model, and not only output necessary design requirements but also be conducive to the mapping between product's function and structure, and lay the foundation for product design automation [5–7].

Currently, many scholars analyze and discuss the customer's requirements from different perspectives and give its corresponding method of requirement analysis [8–11], but it usually has some problems, such as the formalization of requirement description is not enough or the information of product requirements lack objectivity [12–14]. Extenics, which is founded by Chinese scholar Professor Cai Wen, is an emerging discipline; it uses a formal model to study the possibility of object extension, and its pioneering and innovative rules and methods use formal implementation to search the rules of contradiction issues from qualitative and quantitative angles [15–17]. Extenics, which depends on basic element theory and extension mathematics, formalize the process of solving problems to establish the corresponding mathematical model and, on the basis of it, develops a new calculation method and technology that is more intelligent and formally resolves the issue of deep knowledge's storage representation and processing in the knowledge base [18,19], to promote knowledge in knowledge engineering more formal, deeper, and more fundamental. At present, extenics has some successful applications in the field of product design [15,20–23], but the study of systematically applying extenics in requirement analysis of complex mechanical products is rare, and it is still in its infancy. Axiomatic design is a new conceptual product design theory proposed by Suh of MIT in the early 1990s. Its purpose is to establish a scientific basis for complex product design and improve design activities in product development by providing designers with thinking methods and tools based on logic and rationality [24–27]. Different from the research method of discrete products [28,29], the research method of this paper is the extension intelligent design method, which aims to study and analyze the extension and implication of design problems in the process of requirement analysis of complex product scheme design. The formal modeling problem of design knowledge is solved by establishing a knowledge model, the extension reasoning problem of requirement analysis is solved by establishing a requirement analysis process model, and the extension design mode of requirement analysis is established to realize the extension requirement analysis of complex product scheme design.

Therefore, on the basis of integrating extension design and axiomatic design, and the relevant design methods and the concept of optimal solution [30–33]. This paper studies the extension process model and implication process model of requirement analysis in complex product concept design. Due to the problem of multi-attribute and multi-parameter requirement analysis, we put forward an allocation model of requirement basic element weight based on extensible distance, calculated the extensible relational degree of requirement basic element from the angle of a combination of qualitative and quantitative, and constructed the framework of extension design pattern of requirement analysis for complex mechanical product scheme design. In this paper, we will give the specific process with examples. Firstly, the extension modeling for the extension design pattern of concept design is given in Section 2. Then, the extension design pattern of requirement analysis of conceptual design is described in Section 3. Then, an extension design pattern of requirement analysis for complex mechanical products scheme design is provided in Section 4. Finally, the discussions and acknowledgments are given in Sections 5 and 6, respectively.

2. Extension Modeling for Extension Design Pattern of Concept Design

Due to dealing with the various complex design reasoning problems in product concept design, it needs to solve the issue of deep knowledge's storage representation and processing in the process of concept design reasoning. For this, extenics introduces basic element theory into product concept design; it takes a basic element as the logic cell of extensible design, and it gathers the represented design object's quality, quantity, action, and relation into an ordered triple $J = (\Gamma, c, v)$ which is constituted of the design object Γ, object's characteristics c and the value v of characteristics. Formal modeling describes the information action and relation in the design process and puts forward a new methodology system for people to know the world and solve contradictions in the real world.

2.1. The Basic Element Modeling of Multitype Design Knowledge

On the basis of the semantic segmentation method multitype, design information in the conceptual design process is analyzed and arranged to form the minimum complete independent units of design information that can represent the design characteristics.

Due to the manifestations of different units, we can establish the corresponding design knowledge units; formal and modeling describe it by basic element. In this paper, the design information in the conceptual design is divided into static design information, behavioral design information, and relational design information.

When modeling the static design information, we can describe it by the matter element model $\boldsymbol{J}(\boldsymbol{R})$, which belongs to basic element theory. If the design object has characteristics, then its matter element model $\boldsymbol{J}(\boldsymbol{R})$ is as below:

$$\boldsymbol{J}(\boldsymbol{R}) = \begin{bmatrix} \Gamma(N) & C(N)_1 & [V(C)_1, W(C)_1] \\ & C(N)_2 & [V(C)_2, W(C)_2] \\ & \vdots & \vdots \\ & C(N)_n & [V(C)_n, W(C)_n] \end{bmatrix} \tag{1}$$

Among it, $\Gamma(N)$ describes the name of the object, $V(C)$ is the value of design characteristic, $W(C)$ is the weight of design characteristic, $V(C)$ and $W(C)$ have many forms such as the value of precise point, interval value with Fuzzy Information, subordinate function, the qualitative semantic description, and so on. Thus, in order to express more general, assuming $V = \left[v^L, v^R\right]$, $W = \left[w^L, w^R\right]$, both of them are interval values with Fuzzy Information, then Formula (1) can be expressed as follows:

$$\boldsymbol{J}(\boldsymbol{R}) = \begin{bmatrix} \Gamma(N) & C(N)_1 & \left(\left[v(C)_1^L, v(C)_1^R\right], \left[w(C)_1^L, w(C)_1^R\right]\right) \\ & C(N)_2 & \left(\left[v(C)_2^L, v(C)_2^R\right], \left[w(C)_2^L, w(C)_2^R\right]\right) \\ & \vdots & \vdots \\ & C(N)_n & \left(\left[v(C)_n^L, v(C)_n^R\right], \left[w(C)_n^L, w(C)_n^R\right]\right) \end{bmatrix} \tag{2}$$

When modeling the behavioral design information, we can describe it by the affair element model $\boldsymbol{J}(\boldsymbol{I})$, which belongs to basic element theory. If the design object has m characteristics, then its affair element model $\boldsymbol{J}(\boldsymbol{I})$ is as below:

$$\boldsymbol{J}(\boldsymbol{I}) = \begin{bmatrix} \Gamma(D) & B(D)_1 & \left(U(B)_1, \left[w(B)_1^L, w(B)_1^R\right]\right) \\ & B(D)_2 & \left(U(B)_2, \left[w(B)_2^L, w(B)_2^R\right]\right) \\ & \vdots & \vdots \\ & B(D)_m & \left(U(B)_m, \left[w(B)_m^L, w(B)_m^R\right]\right) \end{bmatrix} \tag{3}$$

Among it, $\Gamma(D)$ is the name of design behavior, $B(D)$ is the operating characteristic of design behavior, and $W(B)$ is the weight of operating characteristic.

When modeling the relational design information, we can take the relational element model $\boldsymbol{J}(\boldsymbol{Q})$ to describe the configuration relationship, logical relationship, implication relationship, comparative relationship, and assembly relationship in the design process; if the design constraints relationship has characteristics, then its relational element model $\boldsymbol{J}(\boldsymbol{Q})$ is as below:

$$\boldsymbol{J}(\boldsymbol{Q}) = \begin{bmatrix} \Gamma(S) & A(S)_1 & \left(G(A)_1, \left[w(A)_1^L, w(A)_1^R\right]\right) \\ & A(S)_2 & \left(G(A)_2, \left[w(A)_2^L, w(A)_2^R\right]\right) \\ & \vdots & \vdots \\ & A(S)_k & \left(G(A)_k, \left[w(A)_k^L, w(A)_k^R\right]\right) \end{bmatrix} \tag{4}$$

Among it, $\Gamma(S)$ is the name of the design constraints relationship, $A(S)$ is the relational characteristic of the design constraints relationship, and $W(A)$ is the weight of the relational characteristic.

In the process of complex product conceptual design, the design knowledge often has mixing characteristics; that is, the combination of static design information, behavioral design information, and relational design information; for this, we describe it by the compound element model $\boldsymbol{J}(\boldsymbol{F})$, which belongs to basic element theory. Through the function of conjunction Θ to represent the multilayer semantic and more abundant design information, which is the frequently used conjunction, Θ is conjunction "∧" and/or conjunction "∨" and forms the corresponding and compound element or compound element and/or compound element, thus forming the overall design information of scheme design. The compound element model $\boldsymbol{J}(\boldsymbol{F})$ can be expressed as follow:

$$\boldsymbol{J}(\boldsymbol{F}) = \begin{bmatrix} \Gamma(F) & (\Theta)\Gamma(\boldsymbol{J}(\boldsymbol{R}_i)) & (V(\boldsymbol{J}(\boldsymbol{R}_i)), W(\boldsymbol{J}(\boldsymbol{R}_i))) \\ & (\Theta)\Gamma(\boldsymbol{J}(\boldsymbol{I}_j)) & (V(\boldsymbol{J}(\boldsymbol{I}_j)), W(\boldsymbol{J}(\boldsymbol{I}_j))) \\ & (\Theta)\Gamma(\boldsymbol{J}(\boldsymbol{Q}_s)) & (V(\boldsymbol{J}(\boldsymbol{Q}_s)), W(\boldsymbol{J}(\boldsymbol{Q}_s))) \end{bmatrix} \tag{5}$$

Among it, i, j, s separately represent the number of matter element, affair element, and relational element.

It should be emphasized that when taking the above models as representing design knowledge, it only expresses a state of the design attributes and does not express the degree of importance; the weight will not have to be contained in the above models.

2.2. Construction of Extension Set of Basic Element

In the process of product design, the customer's requirements can be divided into two components of common requirements and personalized requirements. Common requirements are the customer's knowledge and requirements for the product convergence; for this part of the design, we generally use the existing classical structure model or variant structure of the existing structure model to accomplish the conceptual product design. Personalized requirements are the customer's special knowledge and requirements for the product, and conceptual product design is often required by attaining innovation or extension on the structure or function of the existing product. Thus, in order to meet the customer's requirements comprehensively, the design process has the characteristics of dynamics, diversity, relevance, and level; the existing dominant design information may not be able to fully meet the design requirements; for this, it needs to mine design knowledge and form a set of design knowledge to improve the innovation ability of conceptual design.

According to the basic element theory of extenics, we know that the basic element has properties of implication and extension; through extension transformation, we can obtain more abundant tacit knowledge and obtain the corresponding extension set; this provides a means of support for the smooth implementation of the conceptual product design.

(1) Implication and the set of the basic element. For basic element J_1 and J_2, if J_1 exists, then J_2 must exist, we call it J_1 contains J_2, recording it as $@J_1 \Rightarrow @J_2$, among it, @represents identification of existing. Because basic elements can be complex by conjunction Θ, the implication of basic element can be represented by $@J_i\Theta@J_j \Rightarrow @J_s\Theta@J_t$, among it, i, j, s, t all represent the number of basic elements. Form the implication set of basic elements by basic elements, which is obtained by implication. The implication of basic elements can transmit and transform, so we can carry out the reasoning of the conceptual design process by the implication.

(2) Extensibility and basic element extension set. The extensibility of basic elements contains three aspects: divergence, expansion, and relevance. In the design field, through carrying out extension transformation of basic element characteristics and the value of characteristics, on the one hand, it can create the ways and approaches for design objects to outward divergence and expand, and acquire the extension design knowledge in the design field, on the other hand, it can build relationships between design objects, and acquire the relational design knowledge in the design field. We can acquire an extension set of the basic element $S(J)_T$ by extension transformation.

$$\begin{aligned} S(J)_T = \Big\{(J, \Phi, \Psi)\Big| J \in T_{\Omega(J)}\Omega(J),\ \Phi = K(J) = k(X), \\ \Psi = T_K K(T_J J) = T_k k(X^*),\ X = c(J), X^* = c^*(T_J J)\Big\} \end{aligned} \tag{6}$$

Among it, T_Ω, T_K, and T_J separately represent design object J's extension transformation of the domain, correlation function, basic element characteristics, and its value. c is the evaluation characteristic of J; its value is $X = c(J)$; c^* is the evaluation characteristic of J that is acquired by extension transformation T_J, its value is $X^* = c^*(T_J J)$; $\Phi = k(X)$ is the correlation function of evaluation characteristic, $\Psi = T_k k(X^*)$ is correlation function of evaluation characteristic that is acquired by extension transformation T_J.

By Equation (6), the objects in the existing basic element set can be subject to extension transformation in many ways, such as domain, correlation function, basic element feature, and eigenvalue, so as to obtain more extensive design knowledge in the design field and related design knowledge among the design fields, thus providing support for subsequent extension reasoning.

3. The Extension Design Pattern of Requirement Analysis of Conceptual

For the conceptual design of complex products, the customer's requirements generally have the characteristics of abstraction, ambiguity, variability, diversity levels, and relevance; this often troubles designers in obtaining a correct understanding of the customer's design purpose, and it affects the design quality and design efficiency of products. Thus, on the basis of extension theory, analyze the customer's requirements, transform the design requirement into an objective expression of formal and modeling product requirement information, clearly reflect the level relationship and relational characteristics of customer's requirements, make the requirements information transform into technology requirements information effectively to guide products conceptual design, on the basis of these, to make the requirement analysis of products conceptual design more reasonable comprehensive and standard.

3.1. The Extension Process Model of Requirement Analysis

Due to the requirement analysis of products can acquire the initial design scheme of products conceptual design, the model of requirement analysis will directly affect the subsequent product's whole process of design, manufacturing, use, and maintenance; it can be seen that requirement analysis is an important part in the process of product design. Thus, for requirement analysis of complex product conceptual design, we cannot, in isolation, describe the requirement model from the customer's requirements and should carry out requirement transformation from the angle of the product life cycle; this process involves the whole product life cycle information, such as the design feasibility, manufacturability, assembly, maintainability, reliability. Strive to make the requirement model useful for the relevance and mapping of customer domain, functional domains, structural domain, and process domain in conceptual product design, and then provides a theoretical foundation and practical means and methods for the automation of complex product design.

On the basis of basic element theory, we can build a basic element model for every requirements information in requirements analysis, separately build the matter-type requirement basic element model $J(R)_C$, behavior-type requirement basic element model $J(I)_C$, relation-type requirement basic element model $J(Q)_C$ and compound -type requirement basic element model $J(F)_C$. Matter-type requirement basic element model $J(R)_C$ describes characteristics requirements, functional requirements, structural requirements, environmental requirements, performance requirements, and other aspects of static properties and design information. Behavior-type requirement basic element model $J(I)_C$ describes design behavior-type information related to requirement analysis in the product design process, such as solving problems, judgment knowledge, process planning, and reasoning. Relation-type requirement basic element model $J(Q)_C$ describes the various constraints or dependent information between requirement characteristics in the product design process, such as configuration relationship, comparative relationship, and logical relationship. The compound-type requirement basic element model $J(F)_C$ is the combination of the various requirement basic elements. On the basis of the above basic element models, we can acquire the set of requirement basic element $S(J)_{CT}$ and the corresponding knowledge database of various requirement basic elements. Based on the extension theory, the demand information is analyzed, evaluated, and transformed to form the subsequent product design information, which can better support the rapid design of complex products. The extension process model of requirement analysis in complex product conceptual design is shown in Figure 1.

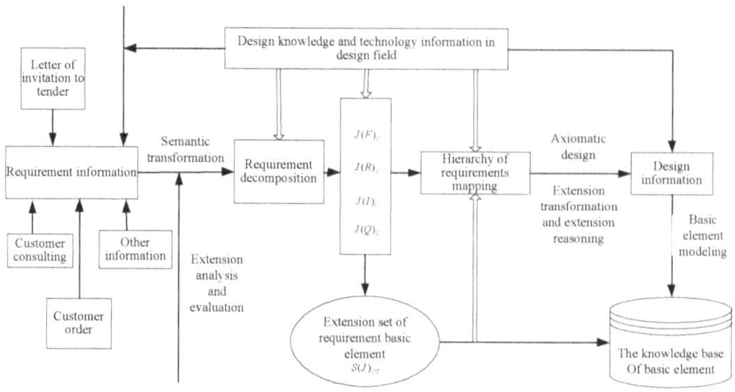

Figure 1. The extension process model of requirement analysis of complex product conceptual design.

It can be seen that after obtaining the corresponding demand information based on the relevant design requirements, the demand information can be decomposed based on semantic transformation and combined with extension analysis and evaluation methods, and then the primitive modeling can be carried out to form the extension set of demand primitives Extension reasoning and extension transformation are used to map the requirements hierarchically, so as to obtain the design information that meets the design requirements. After the primitive modeling, it is stored in the primitive knowledge base.

3.2. *The Implication Process Model of Requirement Analysis*

In the extension process model of the requirement of complex product conceptual design, after semantic transforming requirement information, extension analyzing, and evaluating it, we can acquire the minimum, complete, independent design information unit in the representation design process, and after modeling it, we can acquire its corresponding requirement basic element. By requirement analysis process of product design, we know that customer requirements in the field of product design can generally be divided into common customer requirements and individual customer requirements; common customer requirements are the converging understanding and requirements of the customers for the product in the design field, individual customer requirements are some special understanding and requirements based on common customer requirements.

Because the representation of common customer requirements is common design information in the design field, obviously, in order to provide improved support for the rapid design of the product, it needs effectively reuse this part of the common design information, which is a common requirement basic element. Because the basic elements have the property of implication, the experts in the design field use the method of analysis and evaluation or the method of data mining to acquire the implication relationship in the extension set of requirement analysis, and due to the implication relationship, in new product design, it only needs to match the condition items of implication, then we can reuse the result items of implication relationship, thus to effectively reuse existing design results, short the design cycle and improve the design efficiency. The implication process model of requirement analysis that is oriented toward the rapid design of the product is expressed as follows:

$$\begin{cases} \forall(J_{Cm},J_{Cn})J_{Cm} \in \Omega \wedge J_{Cn} \in \Omega \wedge (J_{Cm}\Theta J_{Cn}) \in \Omega \wedge ((J_{Cm}\Theta J_{Cn}) \Rightarrow (J_s\Theta J_t)) \in \Omega, \quad m \neq n \\ if \quad @J_{C0i} \in \Omega \wedge @J_{C0j} \in \Omega \wedge @\left(J_{C0i}\Theta J_{C0j}\right) \in \Omega, \quad i \neq j \\ \exists\left(\left(J_{C0i}\Theta J_{C0j}\right)\Xi(J_{Cm}\Theta J_{Cn})\right) \wedge K\left(\left(J_{C0i}\Theta J_{C0j}\right)\Xi(J_{Cm}\Theta J_{Cn})\right) \geq K_0(\Omega) \\ then \quad \left(J_{C0i}\Theta J_{C0j}\right) \in S(J_{Cm}\Theta J_{Cn})_{CT} \end{cases} \tag{7}$$

Among it, J_{Cm} and J_{Cn} represent the existing requirement basic elements, J_s and J_t represent the basic elements of design result in extension set, J_{C0i} and J_{C0j} represent basic requirement elements in the process of requirement analysis, Ω represents discourse domain of design, Ξ represents matching identification of basic element model, $K((J_{C0i}\Theta J_{C0j})\Xi(J_{Cm}\Theta J_{Cn}))$ represents the matching degree of basic element model, $K_0(\Omega)$ represents the allowable matching threshold in discourse domain.

From the above implication process model of requirement analysis, it can be seen that when the match degree between the requirement basic element or its compound element and the existing requirement basic element or its compound element meets the given match threshold, the design results contained in the existing requirement basic element or its compound element can apply into product scheme design as an effective reusable object. In the extension multiplexing method of fast configuration conceptual design, the basic element matching algorithm based on extension theory is described.

3.3. The Weight Distribution Model of Requirement Basic Element Based on Extension Distance

The extension process model of requirement analysis based on complex product conceptual design can achieve the decomposition and mapping of the design requirements, but because requirement information in requirement analysis of conceptual product design has characteristics of fuzziness and relevance, the weight of requirement characteristics and design parameters is usually not easy to be determined. For this, this paper puts forwards a new method of weight allocation based on extension distance compared with the existing weight allocation method; the weight allocation method based on extension distance is an analysis method combined qualitative and quantitative, and it can preferably solve the problems that evaluation indicators are difficult to quantify and statistical in requirement analysis, and can exclude the impact of human factors, make the result of weight allocation more scientific, more objective and more accurate.

Assuming after decomposing the requirement, it has P requirement basic elements; According to the design requirement, it needs to invite Z experts in the design field; On the basis of importance degree of costumer's requirement, separate ratio scale of requirement basic element into 0~9, form the ratio scale interval $u_{ij} = [u^l_{ij}, u^r_{ij}]$; that is, j the expert evaluates the requirement basic element J_i, among it $0 \leq u^l_{ij} \leq 9$, $0 \leq u^r_{ij} \leq 9$, $u^l_{ij} \leq u^r_{ij}$. Thus acquire the ratio scale interval sequence of requirement basic element J_i that is expressed by $U(J_i) = ([u^l_{i1}, u^r_{i1}], [u^l_{i2}, u^r_{i2}], \cdots, [u^l_{iZ}, u^r_{iZ}])$. Build ideal ratio scale interval sequence of basic requirement element $U(J_0) = ([u^l_{01}, u^r_{01}], [u^l_{02}, u^r_{02}], \cdots, [u^l_{0Z}, u^r_{0Z}])$ based on P requirement basic elements' ratio scale interval sequence, and meets $[u^l_{0j}, u^r_{0j}] = \left[\max\limits_{1 \leq i \leq p} u^l_{ij}, \max\limits_{1 \leq i \leq p} u^r_{ij}\right]$.

Then construct the extension relational coefficient ρ_{ij} that is $U(J_i)$ and $U(J_0)$ concerning j the scale value based on extension distance:

$$\begin{aligned} \rho_{ij} = \rho\left(\left[u^l_{ij}, u^r_{ij}\right], \left[u^l_{0j}, u^r_{0j}\right]\right) &= \frac{\rho\left(u^l_{ij}, \left[u^l_{0j}, u^r_{0j}\right]\right) + \rho\left(u^r_{ij}, \left[u^l_{0j}, u^r_{0j}\right]\right)}{2} \\ &= \frac{\left(\left|u^l_{ij} - \frac{u^l_{0j}+u^r_{0j}}{2}\right| - \frac{1}{2}\left(u^r_{0j} - u^l_{0j}\right)\right) + \left(\left|u^r_{ij} - \frac{u^l_{0j}+u^r_{0j}}{2}\right| - \frac{1}{2}\left(u^r_{0j} - u^l_{0j}\right)\right)}{2} \end{aligned} \tag{8}$$

Then the extension degree λ_i between $U(J_i)$ and $U(J_0)$ is:

$$\lambda_i = \frac{1}{Z}\sum_{j=1}^{Z}(9 - \rho_{ij}) \tag{9}$$

Then the relatively of requirement is expressed by:

$$w_{Ui} = \lambda_i / \sum_{i=1}^{P} \lambda_i \tag{10}$$

Thus, obtaining the sequence of the weight of basic requirement element $w_U = [w_{U1}, w_{U2}, \cdots, w_{UP}]^T$, and meet $\sum_{i=1}^{P} w_{Ui} = 1$.

The weight distribution of basic elements of design parameters obtained by mapping requirements analysis takes each basic element of demand as the standard, that is, the scale interval of each basic element of demand as the ideal scale interval, and the extension correlation coefficient is calculated. Assuming it has $\boldsymbol{Q}$ design parameters and basic elements, it needs to invite $\boldsymbol{Z}$ experts in the design field. On the basis of the importance degree of costumer's requirement, a separate ratio scale of requirement basic element into 0~9 acquire design parameter basic element $\boldsymbol{J}_k$'s ratio scale interval sequence $V(\boldsymbol{J}_k) = (lbracku^l_{k1}, u^r_{k1}], [u^l_{k2}, u^r_{k2}], \cdots, [u^l_{kZ}, u^r_{kZ}]), k = 1, 2, \cdots, P$. By using the above similarly processing process, take the requirement basic element $\boldsymbol{J}_i$ as the evaluation standard, then the extension relational degree λ_{ik} between design parameter basic element $\boldsymbol{J}_k$ and requirement basic element $\boldsymbol{J}_i$ can be expressed by:

$$\begin{aligned}\lambda_{ik} &= \tfrac{1}{Z}\sum_{j=1}^{Z}\rho\left(\left[v^l_{kj}, v^r_{kj}\right], \left[u^l_{ij}, u^r_{ij}\right]\right) = \tfrac{1}{Z}\sum_{j=1}^{Z}\left(9 - \frac{\rho\left(v^l_{kj}, \left[u^l_{ij}, u^r_{ij}\right]\right) + \rho\left(v^r_{kj}, \left[u^l_{ij}, u^r_{ij}\right]\right)}{2}\right) \\ &= \tfrac{1}{Z}\sum_{j=1}^{Z}\left(9\text{-}\frac{\left(\left|v^l_{kj} - \frac{u^l_{ij}+u^r_{ij}}{2}\right| - \frac{1}{2}\left(u^r_{ij} - u^l_{ij}\right)\right) + \left(\left|v^r_{kj} - \frac{u^l_{ij}+u^r_{ij}}{2}\right| - \frac{1}{2}\left(u^r_{ij} - u^l_{ij}\right)\right)}{2}\right)\end{aligned} \tag{11}$$

On the basis of it, we can acquire an extension relational degree matrix A_J between Q design parameter basic elements and P requirement basic elements:

$$A_J = \begin{bmatrix} \lambda_{11} & \lambda_{12} & \cdots & \lambda_{1Q} \\ \lambda_{21} & \lambda_{22} & \cdots & \lambda_{2Q} \\ \vdots & \vdots & \vdots & \vdots \\ \lambda_{P1} & \lambda_{P2} & \cdots & \lambda_{PQ} \end{bmatrix}_{P\times Q} \tag{12}$$

The design parameter basic element weighting extension relational degree sequence w_V based on requirement basic element weight sequence is:

$$w_V = w_U^T * A_J = [w_1, w_2, \ldots, w_P]_{1\times P} * \begin{bmatrix} \lambda_{11} & \lambda_{12} & \cdots & \lambda_{1Q} \\ \lambda_{21} & \lambda_{22} & \cdots & \lambda_{2Q} \\ \vdots & \vdots & \vdots & \vdots \\ \lambda_{P1} & \lambda_{P2} & \cdots & \lambda_{PQ} \end{bmatrix}_{P\times Q} \tag{13}$$

Then absolutely weight w_{Vk} of design parameter basic element $\boldsymbol{J}_k$ is:

$$w_{Vk} = \sum_{i=1}^{P}(w_{Ui} * \lambda_{ik}), 1 \le i \le P \tag{14}$$

Then absolutely weight w^*_{Vk} of design parameter basic element $\boldsymbol{J}_k$ is:

$$w^*_{Vk} = w_{Vk} / \sum_{k=1}^{Q} w_{Vk} \tag{15}$$

From these, acquire design parameter basic element weight sequence $w_V = \left[w_{V1}^*, w_{V2}^*, \cdots, w_{VQ}^*\right]^T$, and meets $\sum_{k=1}^{Q} w_{Vk} = 1$.

3.4. The Implementation of Extension Design Pattern of Requirement Analysis

The final result of product conceptual design requirements analysis can effectively map the design parameters of subsequent products, including functional design parameters, structural design parameters, and process design parameters. The essence of extension design for requirement analysis of conceptual product design effectively transformed the basic requirement element into a design parameter basic element and formed an extensible design frame. Based on extension theory and axiomatic design, the traditional QFD is improved, and a demand analysis extension design mode that transforms customer requirements into design parameters is proposed. Compared with traditional quality function deployment QFD [34,35], the extension design pattern of requirement analysis is not just formulate the product planning or improve the product structure; it also uses the improved quality function deployment QFD to acquire design information that guides and runs through the product lifecycle. Figure 2 gives the frame of implementation of the extension design pattern of requirement analysis.

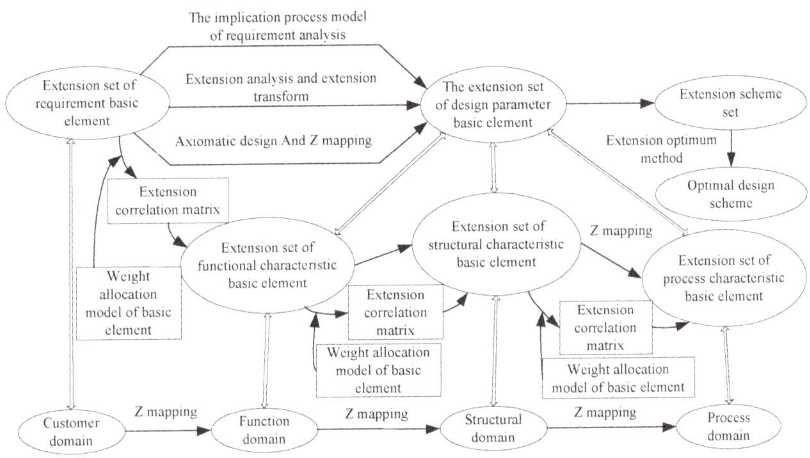

Figure 2. The extension design pattern of requirement analysis of conceptual product design.

It can be seen from Figure 2 that the extension design mode of product scheme design requirement analysis divides the process of product scheme design requirement analysis into customer domain, function domain, structure domain, process domain, etc. The extension set of the basic requirement element corresponds to the extension modeling of the customer domain. The extension set of the design parameter basic element includes the extension set of the functional characteristic basic element, the extension set of the structural characteristic basic element, and the extension set of the process characteristic basic element. The extension set of the functional characteristic basic element corresponds to the extension modeling of the functional domain, the extension set of the structural characteristic basic element corresponds to the extension modeling of the structural domain, and the extension set of process characteristic basic element corresponds to the extension modeling of the process domain. Based on axiomatic design theory, adjacent design domains have corresponding mapping relations, which can be realized by z-mapping. Similarly, the corresponding basic element extension sets of adjacent design domains also have corresponding z-mapping and corresponding extension incidence matrix. By using the demand analysis implication process model, extension analysis and extension transformation, and the z-mapping of axiomatic design, the extension set of the design parameter basic element and extension scheme set is generated, and the optimal design scheme is obtained based on the extension optimization method. The extension optimization method will be discussed in detail in the subsequent papers. It needs to be explained here that the effective construction of the extension set of the design parameter basic element is acquired by the combination of Z mapping in the design field, the implication process model of requirement analysis, and the method of extension analysis and transformation. Specifically, by Z mapping in the design field based on axiomatic design, design parameters commonly have the structural characteristics of the level association. However, using compound elements can formally and, with modeling, describe the design parameters which have the structural characteristics of the level association so that the product extension design can be implemented smoothly.

In summary, the implementation steps of the extension design pattern of requirement analysis for conceptual product design can be expressed as follow:

Step1: Acquire requirement information in the design field, decompose the requirement, build the unit of requirement information, and build the model of the basic requirement element.

Step 2: Construct the extension set of the basic requirement element, and build the implication process model of the basic requirement element.

Step 3: On the basis of axiomatic design, hierarchical Z-mapping requirement basic element in customer domain into design parameter basic element in function domain, structural domain, and process domain, transform the design parameters combined with the implication process model of requirement basic element and its relational extension transformation method and acquire its relational extension set of design parameter basic element.

Step 4: Construct a weight allocation model of the basic requirement element, and build an extension correlation matrix in different design fields.

Step 5: On the basis of the basic element knowledge base, rule base, and case base that is constructed in the design field, they match the design parameter basic element to acquire the set of conceptual design schemes.

4. Application Example

This paper takes a selection scheme of large-scale hydropower turbines as an example to describe the implementation of extension design patterns for complex products. Due to the different areas of local geology, topography, water quality, current, and the environment have a big difference, so the design requirement of hydroelectric power stations in the different regions has characteristics of diversity and dynamic; it needs a variety of types of turbines to meet the corresponding design requirements. However, because the large turbine design theory is imperfect, the internal fluid motion of the turbine is complex, and the production model of turbine design has characteristics of a single piece, small-batch, and large sets; these make the large turbine design process have characteristics that are multi-level, multi-attribute, multi-constrained and multi-objective, and the implementation of the design scheme becomes very cumbersome. Therefore, based on the extension design mode of complex products, this paper conducts an extension analysis of design requirements for a large turbine selection scheme, determines the design domain of turbine products, and obtains the basic design parameters of a large turbine selection scheme in the design domain.

It is known that a large-scale hydropower's geographical environment is a multi-mountainous region; its terrain is relatively steep, the water's silt content is high, the water flow is relatively large, and the head is relatively high. Table 1 gives the design requirement parameters of a hydropower station.

Table 1. The Design and Exploitation Requirement Parameters of a Hydropower Station.

Requirement Item	The Value of Requirement	Requirement Item	The Value of Requirement
Average annual flow	≥235.0 m^3/s	Design flow	≥307.0 m^3/s
Maximum head	126.0 m	Minimum head	86.0 m
Design head	112.0 m	Rated power	≥300.0 MW
Maximum power	≥306.0 MW	Rated speed	125.0 r/min
Runaway rotation rate	≤260.0 r/min	Prototype efficiency	≥93.5%
Amount of leakage	≤0.1 m^3/s	Control mode	Automatic control
Operational stability	Long-term stability	Energy consumption property	Low
Environmental protection property	Less pollution	Noise property	Low
Structure type	Compact	Runner weight	Light

To make a selection design of the turbine, you must first determine the direction of the design of the turbine, that is, determine the structure type of turbine based on the actual situation of hydropower, such as geology, topography, water quality, and water flow. According to the experience in the field of design, we know that large turbine structure type contains Francis, axial, oblique flow, tubular, and pelton, and each type of turbine applies to different conditions; it is generally determined by the head, power, load changes, sediment concentration, flow, etc. By analyzing the hydropower station's requirement information, we know that the hydropower station has a high head, medium-power, medium load changes, high sediment concentration, and large water flow, so it is suitable to use a Francis turbine. By experts' analysis, discussion, and evaluation, the hydropower design requirement information is broken down into common requirement information and individual requirement information; the specific content is shown in Table 2.

Table 2. The Decomposition of Design Requirement Information.

<table>
<tr><th>Design Direction</th><th>The Category of Requirement Information</th><th colspan="2">Requirement Characteristic</th></tr>
<tr><td rowspan="12">Francis turbine</td><td rowspan="2">Common requirement</td><td colspan="2">Head</td></tr>
<tr><td colspan="2">Output</td></tr>
<tr><td rowspan="3">Information</td><td colspan="2">Efficiency</td></tr>
<tr><td colspan="2">Cavitation property</td></tr>
<tr><td colspan="2">Runaway property</td></tr>
<tr><td rowspan="7">Individual requirement information</td><td rowspan="2">Operation controllability</td><td>Automatic control</td></tr>
<tr><td>Simple, safe</td></tr>
<tr><td rowspan="3">Environmental protection and energy saving property</td><td>Low energy consumption</td></tr>
<tr><td>Low pollution</td></tr>
<tr><td>Low noise</td></tr>
<tr><td rowspan="2">Structure type and weight</td><td>Compact</td></tr>
<tr><td>Light</td></tr>
</table>

For common requirement information, new product design parameters can be obtained based on common design requirements templates in the design field; For individual requirement information, due to the diversity of information change, there are no corresponding templates to be chosen, and we need to take an approach that is same as common design requirements templates to the analysis, that is transformation and mapping among the customer domain, functional domains, structure domain and process domain based on the axiomatic design theory to obtain the corresponding product design parameters.

Figure 3 shows the framework of the Francis turbine's common design requirements information template based on axiomatic design theory and extension theory.

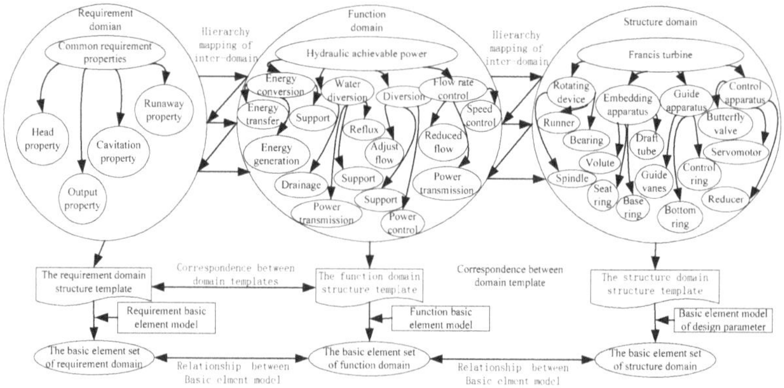

Figure 3. The framework of the Francis turbine's common design requirements information template.

It can be seen from Figure 3 that the common design requirement information template for the hydraulic turbine includes three parts: the requirement domain, the functional domain, and the structural domain. For different design domains, the corresponding design domain structural template and the corresponding basic element set can be generated; that is, the requirement domain corresponds to the requirement domain structural template and the requirement domain basic element set, and the functional domain corresponds to the functional domain structural template and the functional domain basic element set. The structure domain corresponds to the structure template of the structure domain and the basic element set of the structure domain. Based on the axiomatic design theory, it can be seen that the structure template of the demand domain, the structure template of the function domain, and the structure template of the structure domain have the same mapping relationship. Similarly, there is the same mapping relationship between the demand domain basic element set, the functional domain basic element set, and the structure domain basic element set.

Quick configuration of the selection of the turbine design is to determine the turbine's critical flow path model such as runner, volute, draft tube, the guide vane, and so on. In shunt turbine general design requirements information as you can see, in the framework of the template, volute, guide tube, and turbine guide vane wheel are key design components in turbine products secondary components devices, thus determine key flow turbine model can obtain the key design parameters of the turbine design, be able to support the smooth implementation of subsequent turbine design. To this end, in the framework of the common Francis turbine design requirements template, we use the extension process model of requirement analysis to model the design requirement information and two object-type basic elements to describe design requirement items in Table 1, which are fundamental design parameter requirement basic element $J(\boldsymbol{R})_{C0\text{-}D}$ and auxiliary design parameter requirement basic element $J(\boldsymbol{R})_{C0\text{-}P}$. The fundamental design parameter requirement basic element $J(\boldsymbol{R})_{C0\text{-}D}$ is used to design the runner model and volute, draft tube, the guide vane flow path model, and the auxiliary design parameter requirement basic element $J(\boldsymbol{R})_{C0\text{-}P}$ is used to assist and guide selection design of the turbine.

$$
J(R)_{C0\text{-}D} = \begin{bmatrix}
\text{Basic design requirements} & \text{Maximum head } H_{\max}\ (\text{m}) & 126.0 \\
 & \text{Rated head } H_0\ (\text{m}) & 112.0 \\
 & \text{Minimum head } H_{\min}\ (\text{m}) & 86.0 \\
 & \text{Design flow } Q_d\ (\text{m}^3/\text{s}) & \geq 307.0 \\
 & \text{Average flow } Q_v\ (\text{m}^3/\text{s}) & \geq 235.0 \\
 & \text{Rated power } P_r\ (\text{MW}) & \geq 300.0 \\
 & \text{Maximum power } P_{\max}\ (\text{MW}) & \geq 306.0 \\
 & \text{Rated rotation rate } n_r\ (\text{r/min}) & 125.0 \\
 & \text{Runaway rotation rate } n_R\ (\text{r/min}) & \leq 260.0 \\
 & \text{Amount of leakage } q\ (\text{m}^3/\text{s}) & \leq 0.1 \\
 & \text{Efficiency } \eta & \geq 93.3\%
\end{bmatrix}
$$

$$
J(R)_{C0\text{-}P} = \begin{bmatrix}
\text{Auxiliary design requirement} & \text{Control mode} & \text{Automation} \\
 & \text{Operational stability} & \text{Long-term} \\
 & \text{Energy consumptionproperty} & \text{Low} \\
 & \text{Environmental protection property} & \text{Less pollution} \\
 & \text{Noise property} & \text{Low} \\
 & \text{Structure type} & \text{Compact} \\
 & \text{Wheelweight} & \text{Light}
\end{bmatrix}
$$

After modeling the design information, it can build the corresponding extension set of basic elements and the basic element knowledge base. Therefore, according to the fundamental design parameter requirement, basic element $J(\boldsymbol{R})_{C0\text{-}D}$'s head to retrieve basic element knowledge base and acquire runner model which meets head range requirements, the matched runner, basic element models, in basic element knowledge base are as below:

$$
J_{Turb\text{-}Runner01} = \begin{bmatrix}
D257 & \text{Maximum head } H_{\max}\ (\text{m}) & 109.5 \\
 & \text{Rated head } H_0\ (\text{m}) & 101.1 \\
 & \text{Minimum head } H_{\min}\ (\text{m}) & 62.1 \\
 & \text{Rated power } P_r\ (\text{MW}) & 102.0 \\
 & \text{Maximum power } P_{\max}\ (\text{MW}) & 114.3 \\
 & \text{Efficiency } \eta & 93.53
\end{bmatrix}
$$

$$
J_{Turb\text{-}Runner02} = \begin{bmatrix}
A630 & \text{Maximum head } H_{\max}\ (\text{m}) & 143.0 \\
 & \text{Rated head } H_0\ (\text{m}) & 119.9 \\
 & \text{Minimum head } H_{\min}\ (\text{m}) & 83.0 \\
 & \text{Rated power } P_r\ (\text{MW}) & 310.0 \\
 & \text{Maximum power } P_{\max}\ (\text{MW}) & 340.0 \\
 & \text{Efficiency } \eta & 93.20
\end{bmatrix}
$$

$$
J_{Turb\text{-}Runner03} = \begin{bmatrix}
D203 & \text{Maximum head } H_{\max}\ (\text{m}) & 135.6 \\
 & \text{Rated head } H_0\ (\text{m}) & 130.5 \\
 & \text{Minimum head } H_{\min}\ (\text{m}) & 114.5 \\
 & \text{Rated power } P_r\ (\text{MW}) & 408.2 \\
 & \text{Maximum power } P_{\max}\ (\text{MW}) & 408.8 \\
 & \text{Efficiency } \eta & 92.57
\end{bmatrix}
$$

$$
J_{Turb\text{-}Runner04} = \begin{bmatrix}
A364 & \text{Maximum head } H_{\max}\ (\text{m}) & 121.5 \\
 & \text{Rated head } H_0\ (\text{m}) & 106.7 \\
 & \text{Minimum head } H_{\min}\ (\text{m}) & 80.7 \\
 & \text{Rated power } P_r\ (\text{MW}) & 310.0 \\
 & \text{Maximum power } P_{\max}\ (\text{MW}) & 330.0 \\
 & \text{Efficiency } \eta & 94.00
\end{bmatrix}
$$

According to the experience in the selection of the turbine design, we know that when it meets head range requirements, the power and efficiency are the main basis for selecting the runner model. It can be seen that in matched runner basic element models, $J_{Turb\text{-}Runner01}$ cannot meet the power design requirement, $J_{Turb\text{-}Runner03}$ cannot meet the efficiency design requirement. Although $J_{Turb\text{-}Runner02}$ and $J_{Turb\text{-}Runner04}$ both can meet the power design requirement and efficiency design requirement when rated power and maximum power are close, $J_{Turb\text{-}Runner04}$ has higher efficiency, so $J_{Turb\text{-}Runner04}$ is the best runner matching object in the basic element knowledge base.

Take basic element model $J_{Turb\text{-}Runner04}$'s name as the condition item for the extension process model of requirement analysis, use the classic frequent pattern tree algorithm (FP_growth), set condition item $A364$ as the root node of frequent pattern tree, carry out frequent pattern mining among runner models and volute, draft tube, guide vane's flow path models in basic element knowledge base and rule base. If the acquired frequent pattern meets the requirements of the support and confidence, then we can acquire a strong implication relationship between runner model and volute, draft tube, guide vane's flow path models, that is $J_{Turb\text{-}Runner04}|A364 \Rightarrow J_{WK\text{-}94}|A364$, $J_{Turb\text{-}Runner04}|A364 \Rightarrow J_{DY\text{-}43}|A364$, $J_{Turb\text{-}Runner04}|A364 \Rightarrow J_{WSG\text{-}51}|A364$. According to the extension implication relationship, and on the basis of volute $J_{WK\text{-}94}|A364$, draft tube $A364 \Rightarrow J_{WSG\text{-}51}$ and guide vane $J_{DY\text{-}43}|A364$, we can carry out selection design of volute, draft tube, guide vane's flow path which is associated to target runner.

At the same time, although $J_{Turb\text{-}Runner04}$ is the best runner matching object in the basic element knowledge base, $J_{Turb\text{-}Runner04}$'s property parameters are not fully compliant with design requirements; for this, it needs to carry out an extension transform for the value of characteristics of $J_{Turb\text{-}Runner04}$, that is use expertise of turbine to analyze and optimize the value of characteristics of $J_{Turb\text{-}Runner04}$, acquire reasonable nominal diameter of runner, rotational rate and flow path combination which meet force requirement and have high efficiency, and then to determine the other design parameters of target runner. On the basis of the description in the paper, combined with knowledge in the turbine design field, and according to the comprehensive characteristic curve of the existing turbine runner, we can first take the maximum head, design head, and head range as the characteristics of extension transform, take the force and efficiency as constraints of extension transform, to carry out multi-level reasoning analysis for runner $J_{Turb\text{-}Runner04}$, find design parameter combination of matched runner's unit speed and unit flow in the comprehensive characteristic curve of the turbine runner. If the design parameter combination meets the design requirements, then take it as an extension reuse object; If the design parameter combination cannot meet the design requirements, it needs to take unit speed and unit flow as characteristics of extension transform to carry out the next level extension transformation, and so forth, ultimately acquire runner basic element model that meets requirements:

$$J_{Turb\text{-}TA364\text{-}1} = \begin{bmatrix} \text{Runner } TA364\text{-}1 & \text{Nominal diameter } D_1 \text{ (m)} & 5.50 \\ & \text{Maximum height } H_1 \text{ (m)} & 2.92 \\ & \text{Design flow } Q_d \text{ (m}^3\text{/s)} & 307.00 \\ & \text{Rated rotation rate } n_r \text{ (r/min)} & 125.00 \\ & \text{Runaway rotation rate } n_R \text{ (r/min)} & \leq 260.0 \\ & \text{Efficiency } \eta \text{ (\%)} & 94.30 \\ & \text{Reliability } \Gamma \text{ (\%)} & 95.00 \end{bmatrix}$$

$$J_{Turb\text{-}TA364\text{-}2} = \begin{bmatrix} \text{Runner } TA364\text{-}2 & \text{Nominal diameter } D_1 \ (m) & 5.775 \\ & \text{Maximum height } H_1 \text{ (m)} & 3.202 \\ & \text{Design flow } Q_d \text{ (m}^3\text{/s)} & 301.20 \\ & \text{Rated rotation rate } n_r \text{ (r/min)} & 136.40 \\ & \text{Runaway rotation rate } n_R \text{ (r/min)} & \leq 260.0 \\ & \text{Efficiency } \eta \text{ (\%)} & 95.03 \\ & \text{Reliability } \Gamma \text{ (\%)} & 92.00 \end{bmatrix}$$

$$J_{Turb\text{-}TA364\text{-}3} = \begin{bmatrix} \text{Runner } TA364\text{-}3 & \text{Nominal diameter } D_1 \text{ (m)} & 5.50 \\ & \text{Maximum height } H_1 \text{ (m)} & 3.217 \\ & \text{Design flow } Q_d \text{ (m}^3\text{/s)} & 348.00 \\ & \text{Rated rotation rate } n_r \text{ (r/min)} & 125.00 \\ & \text{Runaway rotation rate } n_R \text{ (r/min)} & \leq 250.0 \\ & \text{Efficiency } \eta \text{ (\%)} & 93.50 \\ & \text{Reliability } \Gamma \text{ (\%)} & 93.00 \end{bmatrix}$$

$$J_{Turb\text{-}TA364\text{-}4} = \begin{bmatrix} \text{Runner } TA364\text{-}4 & \text{Nominal diameter } D_1 \text{ (m)} & 5.734 \\ & \text{Maximum height } H_1 \text{ (m)} & 3.337 \\ & \text{Design flow } Q_d \text{ (m}^3\text{/s)} & 326.00 \\ & \text{Rated rotation rate } n_r \text{ (r/min)} & 136.40 \\ & \text{Runaway rotation rate } n_R \text{ (r/min)} & \leq 270.0 \\ & \text{Efficiency } \eta \text{ (\%)} & 94.00 \\ & \text{Reliability } \Gamma \text{ (\%)} & 93.00 \end{bmatrix}$$

Take efficiency and reliability as the main evaluation characteristics in the extension design of runner selection, and take the compact of structure type (that is, the diameter and height dimensions), runaway rotation rate, rated rotation rate, and rated flow as referenced evaluation characteristics, it can be seen that $J_{Turb\text{-}TA364\text{-}1}$ is the best runner object of extension transform, that is:

$$J_{Turb\text{-}best} = J_{Turb\text{-}TA364\text{-}1} = \begin{bmatrix} \text{Runner } TA364\text{-}1 & \text{Nominal diameter } D_1\ (\text{m}) & 5.50 \\ & \text{Maximum height } H_1\ (\text{m}) & 2.92 \\ & \text{Design flow } Q_d\ (\text{m}^3/\text{s}) & 307.00 \\ & \text{Rated rotation rate } n_r\ (\text{r/min}) & 125.00 \\ & \text{Runaway rotation rate } n_R\ (\text{r/min}) & \leq 260.0 \\ & \text{Efficiency } \eta\ (\%) & 94.30 \\ & \text{Reliability } \Gamma\ (\%) & 95.00 \end{bmatrix}$$

Because there is an extension implication relationship between runner $J_{Turb\text{-}Runner04}$ and volute $J_{WK\text{-}94} \mid A364$, draft tube $J_{WSG\text{-}51} \mid A364$, guide vane $J_{DY\text{-}43} \mid A364$, when carrying out extension transform for runner $J_{Turb\text{-}Runner04}$'s characteristic value, the volute $J_{WK\text{-}94} \mid A364$, draft tube $J_{WSG\text{-}51} \mid A364$ and guide vane $J_{DY\text{-}43} \mid A364$'s design requirement parameters would change. According to the comprehensive characteristic curve of the turbine runner, we can acquire the corresponding design requirement interval. Table 3 gives the design requirement parameters of the partial flow path model.

Table 3. The Design Requirement Parameters of Partial Flow Path Model.

The Name of Characteristic	The Value of Characteristic	The Name of Characteristic	The Value of Characteristic
The diameter of volute inlet side	6.200–7.800 (m)	The pitch circle diameter of guide vane	5.300–6.650 (m)
The thickness of the volute inlet side	35.000–65.000 (mm)	The height of the guide vane	1.000–1.560 (m)
The thickness of the end of volute	18.500–26.000 (mm)	The relative height of the guide vane	0.200–0.275
The weight of volute	140.000–180.000 (T)	The weight of the guide vane	1.650–2.820 (T)
The thickness of draft tube lining	15.000–18.500 (mm)	The weight of draft tube lining	15.700–21.100 (T)

For this, it needs to carry out volute, draft tube, and guide vane's extension configuration design and extension adaptive design based on the new design requirement parameters, and then complete the scheme design of large turbine selection. If carrying out extension configuration design and extension adaptive design, it needs to carry out weight allocation for every characteristic. Because extension configuration design is mainly too fast and extensible to match the design objects based on existing design instances or design results, so the influence of common requirement characteristics for the weight of every characteristic parameter is most prominent; for this, this paper takes common requirement characteristics as evaluation standards of the design characteristic parameters weight allocation. On the basis of the description in the paper, take common requirement characteristics of the head, output, efficiency, cavitation property, and runaway property as requirement basic element items, and take volute, draft tube, and guide vane as design parameter basic element items, invite six experts in the turbine design field to grade requirement basic element items and design parameter basic element items by ratio scale interval [1–9], the specific values are shown in Tables 4 and 5.

Table 4. The Scoring Results of Requirement Basic Element Items.

The Requirement Basic Element Item	The Scoring Result
head	([7.0, 8.0], [7.5, 8.0], [7.0, 8.0], [8.0, 8.5], [8.0, 9.0], [7.5, 8.0])
Output	([9.0, 9.0], [9.0, 9.0], [9.0, 9.0], [9.0, 9.0], [9.0, 9.0], [9.0, 9.0])
Efficiency	([7.5, 8.0], [8.0, 8.5], [8.0, 8.5], [7.5, 8.0], [7.5, 8.5], [8.0, 9.0])
Cavitation property	([6.0, 7.0], [6.5, 7.5], [6.0, 6.5], [7.0, 7.5], [7.5, 8.0], [7.0, 8.0])
Runaway property	([7.5, 8.0], [7.5, 8.0], [8.0, 9.0], [8.0, 8.5], [7.5, 8.0], [7.5, 8.0])

Table 5. The Scoring Results of Design Parameter Items.

The Design Parameter Item	The Scoring Result
Volute	([7.5, 8.0], [8.0, 8.5], [8.0, 8.5], [8.0, 8.5], [7.5, 8.0], [7.5, 8.0])
Draft tube	([7.5, 8.0], [8.0, 8.5], [7.0, 7.5], [8.0, 8.5], [7.0, 7.5], [7.5, 8.0])
Guide vane	([8.0, 8.5], [8.5, 9, 0], [8.0, 8.5], [8.0, 8.5], [8.5, 9.0], [8.5, 9.0])

Build requirement basic elements' ideal ratio scale interval sequence $U(0)$ = ([9, 9], [9, 9], [9, 9], [9, 9], [9, 9], [9, 9],), based on the Formula (7) build extension correlation coefficient matrix ρ between the requirement basic element items and requirement basic elements' ideal ratio scale interval sequence $U(0)$:

$$\rho = \begin{bmatrix} 7.500 & 7.750 & 7.500 & 8.250 & 8.500 & 7.750 \\ 9.000 & 9.000 & 9.000 & 9.000 & 9.000 & 9.000 \\ 7.750 & 8.250 & 8.250 & 7.750 & 8.000 & 8.500 \\ 6.500 & 7.000 & 6.250 & 7.250 & 7.750 & 7.500 \\ 7.750 & 7.750 & 8.500 & 8.250 & 7.750 & 7.750 \end{bmatrix}$$

Build extension correlation sequence λ between the requirement basic element items and requirement basic elements' ideal ratio scale interval sequence $U(0)$ based on Formula (8):

$$\lambda = [7.875,\ 9.000,\ 8.083,\ 7.042,\ 7.958]^T$$

Acquire the weight sequence of requirement basic element items based on Formula (9):

$$w_U = [0.197,\ 0.226,\ 0.202,\ 0.176,\ 0.199]^T$$

For design parameters items, separately select requirement basic element items as ideal ratio scale interval sequence, acquire extension correlation degree matrix A_J between design parameters and requirement basic element items based on Formulas (10) and (11):

$$A_J = \begin{bmatrix} 8.917 & 8.917 & 8.708 \\ 8.000 & 7.750 & 8.500 \\ 8.958 & 8.792 & 8.875 \\ 8.375 & 8.500 & 7.917 \\ 9.000 & 8.792 & 8.625 \end{bmatrix}$$

We can acquire the design parameters' weight sequence $w_V = [0.364, 0.321, 0.333]^T$ based on Formulas (12)–(14). By weight sequence, it can be seen that the weights of the various design parameters are consistent with turbine design because volute, draft tube, and guide vane are all the core components of each functional unit, so when carrying out fast configuration design, the weight of them is little difference; At the same time, due to the volute as diversion components, we should lead water into hydraulic components by minimum hydraulic losses and ensure water flow uniform, then it is conducive to the guiding apparatus that the guide vanes carry out flow regulation and draining parts that are draft tube carry out reflow processes, so the weight of volute is slightly higher.

In addition, as the volute, draft tube, and guide vane's design requirement parameters are all the key control parameters, so volute, draft tube, and guide vane's respective design attributes have the same weight; that is, the volute's respective design attributes weights are $w_{V\text{-}WK} = 0.250$, draft tube's respective design attributes weights are $w_{V\text{-}WSG} = 0.500$, guide vane's respective design attributes weights are $w_{V\text{-}DY} = 0.250$.

5. Discussion

From the above theoretical discussion and application cases, it can be seen that the method proposed in this paper has a strong theoretical foundation. From the topological knowledge modeling, extension analysis, implication analysis, demand analysis index weight acquisition, and extension pattern generation in demand analysis, an extension demand analysis method system for complex product scheme design is formed, which has good engineering applicability.

By establishing the basic element model of complex product scheme design requirement information and the corresponding extension set of requirement basic elements, this method can formally represent various deep-seated design requirement information. This method establishes the extension process model of complex product scheme design requirement analysis and the implication process model of requirement analysis. Based on the inherent implication and relevance of design requirement information, the rapid transformation and hybrid reasoning of design requirements are carried out, which makes the mapping of complex product scheme design requirements more intuitive and effective. Moreover, this method gives a basic demand element weight distribution model based on extension distance, which can obtain accurate demand analysis weight from the combination of qualitative and quantitative perspectives and can take into account the influence of design constraints and design characteristics on the design demand attribute weight. At the same time, based on the extension correlation degree of basic demand elements, this paper establishes the implementation framework and algorithm of the extension design pattern for the demand analysis of complex product scheme design, which comprehensively reflects the design requirements and design intent of the scheme and provides support for the smooth implementation of complex product design. The application of the example also verifies the effectiveness and feasibility of the algorithm.

In addition, the application of knowledge extension reuse technology in complex product scheme design not only makes product design standardized and systematic but also expands the application field of expert systems, provides a theoretical basis for computer-aided product conceptual design, and plays an important role in the smooth implementation of complex product design scheme development.

6. Conclusions

In view of the multi-level, multi-attribute, and creative product structure configuration process of complex products, this paper studies and analyzes the extension design mode of complex product scheme design demand analysis with the characteristics of abstraction, fuzziness, variability, diversity, hierarchy, and relevance. The specific results and conclusions are as follows: (1) The basic element model of the demand information of complex product scheme design and the corresponding extension set of the basic demand element are established to realize the formal modeling of the demand analysis and design information of the product scheme design. (2) The extension process model and the implication process model of demand analysis for complex product scheme design are established, which provides support for generating more abundant knowledge of demand analysis. (3) The weight distribution model of the basic demand element based on extension distance is established, which provides support for improving the reasoning ability of product demand analysis. (4) The framework and algorithm of the extension design pattern for the requirement analysis of complex product scheme design are proposed, and the extension requirement analysis of complex product scheme design is realized. On the basis of obtaining the results of extension requirement analysis, how to effectively carry out extension knowledge reasoning and extension knowledge reuse of complex product scheme design will have important research significance, which will provide important support for rapid configuration design of complex products.

Author Contributions: Conceptualization, T.W.; Data curation, T.W.; Formal analysis, T.W., H.L. and X.W.; Funding acquisition, T.W.; Methodology, T.W.; Validation, H.L. and X.W.; Writing—original draft, T.W.; Writing—review & editing, T.W. All authors have read and agreed to the published version of the manuscript.

Funding: This research was funded by Natural Science Foundation of Jiangsu Province of China (No. BK20221481), the National Natural Science Foundation of China (No. 51775272, No. 51005114).

Institutional Review Board Statement: Not applicable.

Informed Consent Statement: Not applicable.

Data Availability Statement: The labeled dataset used to support the findings of this study are available from the corresponding author upon request.

Conflicts of Interest: The authors declare no conflict of interest.

References

1. Yi, Y.; Yan, Y.; Liu, X.; Ni, Z.; Feng, J.; Liu, J. Digital twin-based smart assembly process design and application framework for complex products and its case study. *J. Manuf. Syst.* **2021**, *58*, 94–107. [CrossRef]
2. Delaram, J.; Houshamand, M.; Ashtiani, F.; Valilai, O.F. A utility-based matching mechanism for stable and optimal resource allocation in cloud manufacturing platforms using deferred acceptance algorithm. *J. Manuf. Syst.* **2021**, *60*, 569–584. [CrossRef]
3. Zhang, L.; Zhou, L.; Ren, L.; Laili, Y. Modeling and simulation in intelligent manufacturing. *Comput. Ind.* **2019**, *112*, 103123. [CrossRef]
4. Tao, Y.; Meng, K.; Lou, P.; Peng, X.; Qian, X. Joint decision-making on automated disassembly system scheme selection and recovery route assignment using multi-objective meta-heuristic algorithm. *Int. J. Prod. Res.* **2019**, *57*, 124–142. [CrossRef]
5. Liu, F.; Zhang, Y.; Zheng, C.; Qin, X.; Eynard, B. Survey of Configuration Design Approaches: A Focus on Design of Complex Industrial Manufacturing Systems. *Procedia CIRP* **2019**, *81*, 340–345. [CrossRef]
6. Shabestari, S.S.; Bender, B.; Neumann, M.; Song, Y. Decision support for Design Conflicts: A model-based method to analyze the interactions between technical requirements and product characteristics. *Procedia Manuf.* **2020**, *52*, 203–208. [CrossRef]
7. Xiuli, G.E.N.G.; Shidong, X.U.; Chunming, Y.E. Optimal design method of product function requirements considering quantitative KANO analysis. *Comput. Integr. Manuf. Syst.* **2016**, *22*, 1645–1653.
8. Lee, C.; Chen, C.; Lee, Y. Customer requirement-driven design method and computer-aided design system for supporting service innovation conceptualization handling. *Adv. Eng. Inform.* **2020**, *45*, 101117. [CrossRef]
9. Silva, J.M.; Silva, J.R. A new hierarchical approach to requirement analysis of problems in automated planning. *Eng. Appl. Artif. Intell.* **2019**, *81*, 373–386. [CrossRef]
10. Geng, X.; Ye, C. Importance weights determination of based on feature selection customer requirements technique. *Comput. Integr. Manuf. Syst.* **2014**, *20*, 1751–1757.
11. Li, Y.; Chen, H.; Zhao, Z. An integrated identification approach of agile engineering characteristics considering sensitive customer requirements. *CIRP J. Manuf. Sci. Technol.* **2021**, *35*, 13–24. [CrossRef]
12. Zhang, J.; Qiao, L.; Rao, P.; Wulan, M. Product Requirement Information Modeling for the Life Cycle of the Port Hoisting Equipment. *Procedia CIRP* **2016**, *56*, 79–83. [CrossRef]
13. Wei, W.; Liu, A.; Lu, S.C.-Y.; Wuest, T. Product Requirement Modeling and Optimization Method Based on Product Configuration Design. *Procedia CIRP* **2015**, *36*, 1–5. [CrossRef]
14. Dong, C.; Yang, Y.; Chen, Q.; Wu, Z. A complex network-based response method for changes in customer requirements for design processes of complex mechanical products. *Expert Syst. Appl.* **2022**, *19*, 117124. [CrossRef]
15. Wang, T.; Wang, J. A fault diagnosis model based on weighted extension neural network for turbo-generator sets on small samples with noise. *Chin. J. Aeronaut.* **2020**, *33*, 2757–2769. [CrossRef]
16. Ma, L.; Chen, H.; Yan, H.; Li, W.; Zhang, J.; Zhang, W. Post evaluation of distributed energy generation combining the attribute hierarchical model and matter-element extension theory. *J. Clean. Prod.* **2018**, *184*, 503–510. [CrossRef]
17. Zhou, Y.; Shi, J.; Wu, L. Application of Extension Theory in Emotion Management. *Procedia Comput. Sci.* **2017**, *122*, 502–509. [CrossRef]
18. Ren, J. Technology selection for ballast water treatment by multi-stakeholders: A multi-attribute decision analysis approach based on the combined weights and extension theory. *Chemosphere* **2018**, *191*, 747–760. [CrossRef]
19. Tao, W.; Qingying, H.; Dongsheng, W.; Adeyeye, K.; Peng, Y. Extension Theory for the Reconstruction of Traditional Villages: Case example in Dawa Village. *Procedia Comput. Sci.* **2019**, *162*, 191–198. [CrossRef]

20. Wang, W.; Wang, H.; Zhang, B.; Wang, S.; Xing, W. Coal and gas outburst prediction model based on extension theory and its application. *Process Saf. Environ. Prot.* **2021**, *154*, 329–337. [CrossRef]
21. Zhang, X.; Yue, J. Measurement Model and its Application of Enterprise Innovation Capability Based on Matter Element Extension Theory. *Procedia Eng.* **2017**, *174*, 275–280. [CrossRef]
22. Wang, J.; Guo, H.; Chen, J. Research on Extension Innovation Model in the Creation Process of Service Design. *Procedia Comput. Sci.* **2022**, *199*, 992–999. [CrossRef]
23. Du, Y.; Zheng, Y.; Wu, G.; Tang, Y. Decision-making method of heavy-duty machine tool remanufacturing based on AHP-entropy weight and extension theory. *J. Clean. Prod.* **2020**, *252*, 119607. [CrossRef]
24. Kulak, O.; Cebi, S.; Kahraman, C. Applications of axiomatic design principles: A literature review. *Expert Syst. Appl.* **2010**, *37*, 6705–6717. [CrossRef]
25. Houshmand, M.; Jamshidnezhad, B. An extended model of design process of lean production systems by means of process variables. *Robot. Comput.-Integr. Manuf.* **2006**, *22*, 1–16. [CrossRef]
26. Delaram, J.; Valilai, O.F. An architectural view to computer integrated manufacturing systems based on Axiomatic Design Theory. *Comput. Ind.* **2018**, *100*, 96–114. [CrossRef]
27. Fan, L.X.; Cai, M.Y.; Lin, Y.; Zhang, W.J. Axiomatic design theory: Further notes and its guideline to applications. *Int. J. Mater. Prod. Technol.* **2015**, *51*, 359–374. [CrossRef]
28. Liu, F.; Niu, B.; Xing, M.; Wu, L.; Feng, Y. Optimal cross-trained worker assignment for a hybrid seru production system to minimize makespan and workload imbalance. *Comput. Ind. Eng.* **2021**, *160*, 107552. [CrossRef]
29. Fan, X.; Weng, J. Tabu-search-based order seat planning for engineer-to-order manufacturing. *Asian J. Manag. Sci. Appl.* **2020**, *5*, 160–180. [CrossRef]
30. Cross, N. *Engineering Design Methods: Strategies for Product Design*; John Wiley & Sons: Hoboken, NJ, USA, 2008.
31. Daalhuizen, J.; Cash, P. Method content theory: Towards a new understanding of methods in design. *Des. Stud.* **2021**, *75*, 101018. [CrossRef]
32. Harding, J.E.; Shepherd, P. Meta-Parametric Design. *Des. Stud.* **2017**, *52*, 73–95. [CrossRef]
33. Osiński, P.; Deptuła, A.; Partyka, M.A. Discrete optimization of a gear pump after tooth root undercutting by means of multi—Valued logic trees. *Arch. Civ. Mech. Eng.* **2013**, *13*, 422–431. [CrossRef]
34. Yang, W.; Cao, G.; Peng, Q.; Sun, Y. Effective radical innovations using integrated QFD and TRIZ. *Comput. Ind. Eng.* **2021**, *162*, 107716. [CrossRef]
35. Rampal, A.; Mehra, A.; Singh, R.; Yadav, A.; Nath, K.; Chauhan, A.S. Kano and QFD analyses for autonomous electric car: Design for enhancing customer contentment. *Mater. Today Proc.* **2022**, *62*, 1481–1488. [CrossRef]

mathematics

MDPI

Article

Research on Adversarial Domain Adaptation Method and Its Application in Power Load Forecasting

Min Huang * and Jinghan Yin

Department of Software Engineering, South China University of Technology (SCUT), Guangzhou 510006, China
* Correspondence: minh@scut.edu.cn

Abstract: Domain adaptation has been used to transfer the knowledge from the source domain to the target domain where training data is insufficient in the target domain; thus, it can overcome the data shortage problem of power load forecasting effectively. Inspired by Generative Adversarial Networks (GANs), adversarial domain adaptation transfers knowledge in adversarial learning. Existing adversarial domain adaptation faces the problems of adversarial disequilibrium and a lack of transferability quantification, which will eventually decrease the prediction accuracy. To address this issue, a novel adversarial domain adaptation method is proposed. Firstly, by analyzing the causes of the adversarial disequilibrium, an initial state fusion strategy is proposed to improve the reliability of the domain discriminator, thus maintaining the adversarial equilibrium. Secondly, domain similarity is calculated to quantify the transferability of source domain samples based on information entropy; through weighting in the process of domain alignment, the knowledge is transferred selectively and the negative transfer is suppressed. Finally, the Building Data Genome Project 2 (BDGP2) dataset is used to validate the proposed method. The experimental results demonstrate that the proposed method can alleviate the problem of adversarial disequilibrium and reasonably quantify the transferability to improve the accuracy of power load forecasting.

Keywords: domain adaptation; adversarial learning; adversarial equilibrium; transferability quantification; power load forecasting

MSC: 68T07

Citation: Huang, M.; Yin, J. Research on Adversarial Domain Adaptation Method and Its Application in Power Load Forecasting. *Mathematics* **2022**, *10*, 3223. https://doi.org/10.3390/math10183223

Academic Editors: Jianping Gou, Weihua Ou, Shaoning Zeng and Lan Du

Received: 22 June 2022
Accepted: 31 August 2022
Published: 6 September 2022

1. Introduction

Power load forecasting aims to predict the power load in the power system in the future by mining the characteristics of users' power consumption behavior hidden in historical records, weather, dates, and other data. According to the forecast time, power load forecasting can be divided into long-term, medium-term, and short-term. Short-term power load forecasting refers to prediction of the power load value several hours or days in the future, which is an important basis for realizing the rapid response of the power system to changes in power load.

Recently, machine learning has accomplished extraordinary triumphs in the avenue of computer vision [1], semantic segmentation [2], regression prediction [3], natural language processing [4], etc. However, two problems of traditional machine learning are gradually exposed: Firstly, traditional machine learning requires a large amount of labeled data, and the cost of collecting and labeling data is expensive; thus, it is difficult to be applied in fields that lack the data required for training models. Secondly, an important condition for traditional machine learning being effective is that test and train data obey the assumption of independent and identical distributions (IIDs); however, the condition of IID is usually not satisfied in the real world, resulting in a decrease in the accuracy and generalization capabilities. Correspondingly, due to the strong personalization of power consumption behavior, there are differences in the distribution of power load data of different users. Due to the difficulty in collecting historical data, there is a lack of labeled data for training. The above factors hinder the application of traditional machine learning methods in short-term power load forecasting.

Domain adaptation has received extensive attention as one of the effective methods to overcome the difficulties of few-shot learning [5–7]. Domain adaptation aims to transfer knowledge from related labeled data by reducing the distribution difference between the source domain and the target domain. Domain adaptation reduces the number of labeled samples required to achieve the target task and does not strictly require the data to satisfy the condition of IID.

The key aim of the domain adaptation method is to align the feature distribution of the source domain and target domain data. The process of aligning the feature distribution is also called domain alignment. Domain adaptation methods can be divided into three types roughly according to different alignment strategies: discrepancy-based, adversarial-based, and reconstruction-based.

Discrepancy-based methods use different metric schemas to measure the distance between the source domain and the target domain; it aligns the distribution by reducing the difference metric schemas. The method adds different distance loss functions to the artificial neural network. The most widely used metric schemas include Maximum Mean Discrepancy (MMD) [8–10], KL (Kullback–Leibler) divergence [11], JS (Jensen–Shannon) divergence [12], Wasserstein distance [13–15], CORAL (CORrelation ALignment) [16,17], etc.

Adversarial-based methods [18–25] are inspired by GANs and use artificial neural network modules instead of metric schemas to measure the distance. The key components of the adversarial domain adaptation model include a feature extractor and a domain discriminator. The feature extractor extracts the domain-invariant features of the source and target domains to confuse the domain discriminator; at the same time, the domain discriminator distinguishes a sample from the source domain or the target domain, and the strategy of maximizing and minimizing the domain discrimination loss is used to form a confrontation between the two and to implement domain alignment during the adversarial training.

Reconstruction-based methods [26–29] aim to reconstruct all domain data under the premise of preserving domain-specific features to better help learn domain-invariant features. The encoder–decoder is a typical implementation of reconstruction-based methods, the shared encoder encodes the input data as hidden features and learns domain-invariant features, and the decoder reconstructs the hidden features and preserves domain-specific features.

Domain adaptation methods realize the cross-domain transfer and reuse of knowledge, and so many researchers use it to overcome the problem of data shortage in power load forecasting: Ref. [30] proposes a general framework for adversarial domain adaptation methods on time series prediction problems; Ref. [31] introduces a contrastive evaluation module to protect the task-specific features of the target domain in domain alignment; Ref. [32] builds adversarial feature capture networks to achieve reliable energy prediction. Ref. [33] proposes an electricity load forecasting algorithm through bidirectional generative adversarial networks and validates it on user data with different behavior patterns; the flexibility and accuracy of the algorithm are improved. Ref. [34] proposes to construct a time-independent model by maximizing the segmentation of time series differences to suppress the unstable prediction accuracy caused by the time distribution shift. The above studies focus on solving the problem that traditional machine learning relies on a large amount of labeled data and cannot learn knowledge from non-IID data. However, the methods do not consider the problem of lack of transferability quantification, and the adversarial-based methods [30,33] do not consider the problem of adversarial disequilibrium. Both of the above two problems will lead to the decline of the accuracy of the domain adaptation method and the robustness of the model. Therefore, this paper focuses on analyzing and researching these two problems and their solutions.

The main contributions of this paper include:

- This paper proposes a novel adversarial domain adaptation method, which alleviates the adversarial disequilibrium problem through the initial state fusion strategy and quantifies transferability by calculating domain similarity based on information entropy.
- The proposed method is used for power load forecasting, which improves the accuracy of power load forecasting with a small amount of data.
- This paper compares and analyzes the proposed method with a variety of baselines. The results show that the proposed method can effectively maintain the adversarial equilibrium and reasonably quantify the transferability.

The rest of this paper is organized as follows: Section 2 analyzes two problems and summarizes the current solutions; Section 3 details the framework of the proposed method; Section 4 shows the experimental content and the analysis of the results; Section 5 concludes this article.

2. Related Work

This section briefly summarizes the current solutions for the adversarial disequilibrium and the approaches to design metrics of transferability.

2.1. Adversarial Disequilibrium Problem

For adversarial-based methods, the domain discriminator distinguishes whether they originate from the source domain or the target domain according to the features generated by the feature extractor; the domain discriminant results make a key impact on the parameter update of the model. However, the feature extractor easily wins the competition when it only retains shallow feature representation and discards the deep feature representation, which leads to the fact that the domain discriminator cannot accurately reflect the distance in distribution. The methods for solving the adversarial disequilibrium problem can be divided into two categories according to different enhancement strategies.

One way to address this problem is to combine the different metrics, which means the metric is introduced in adversarial training, and the training goal is to confuse the discriminator and reduce the metric. When adversarial disequilibrium occurs and the domain discriminator fails, the model can continue to optimize parameters according to the metric, so the method can effectively improve the training stability. Difference metrics have been maturely applied, but they are suitable for different scenarios due to differences in measurement dimensions, time overhead, gradient information, etc. Therefore, an effective selection from numerous metrics becomes the key to the feasibility of the method. Ref. [35] adopts Maximum Density Divergence (MDD) to minimize inter-domain distance and maximize intra-domain density, and embeds MDD into an adversarial-based domain adaptation framework to overcome the adversarial disequilibrium problem. Ref. [36] combines Multi-Kernel Maximum Mean Discrepancy (MK-MMD) reduces the fluctuation of the training process and maintains the adversarial equilibrium; Ref. [37] integrates MK-MMD in the partial adversarial domain adaptive network to deal with the adversarial disequilibrium problem.

Domain discriminator augmentation increases the domain information contained in the input features of the domain discriminator. From the view of the adversarial game, the method adds information to the domain discriminator for avoiding it being in a weak position in the confrontation. The stronger the domain discriminator, the better it can guide the feature extractor to learn domain-invariant features in adversarial. Ref. [38] proposes a conditional adversarial domain adaptation method, which supplements category information in the input features of the domain discriminator, and uses a multi-linear mapping method to describe the joint representation of feature information and category information. Ref. [39] combines features and labels to help model learning discriminative features, and proposed the principle of entropy minimization to set reliable pseudo-labels for the target domain. Ref. [40] proposed to normalize the conditional information so that it has the same norm as the feature, expand the conditional output norm, and improve the conditional strategy based on the prototype. Ref. [41] proposes that the sample adversarial domain adaptively converts the noncentral sample distribution to the central sample distribution to improve the classification degree of feature distribution, and indirectly adds category information to the input of the feature extractor through clustering methods.

2.2. Lack of Transferability Quantification Problem

Domain adaptation learns domain-invariant features by reducing the distribution distance between the source domain and the target domain and then transferring knowledge from the source domain to the target domain. However, not all source domain knowledge can promote the achievement of the target task. Traditional domain adaptation methods lack the contribution differentiation of source domain knowledge. Useless information and noise in the source domain will hinder the model from achieving the target task, which will eventually lead to the degradation of method performance and the occurrence of negative transfer. The similarity-based quantification of transferability is currently an effective method for alleviating this problem.

The similarity-based transferability quantification method is based on the assumption that the higher the similarity is, the higher the transferability is, and the contribution of the source domain to the target task is distinguished according to the domain similarity, and the knowledge that is conducive to achieving the target task is selectively transferred. The key to this method is how to quantify domain similarity. Ref. [42] proposes an attention mechanism to quantify domain similarity, enhance semantic information with high transferability between domains and within domains, and improve the generalization ability and robustness of the algorithm. Ref. [43] proposes a weighted moment distance to quantify domain similarity, enhance the impact of high domain similarity data on the transfer process. Ref. [44] fuses batch spectral penalty in an adversarial-based domain adaptive network to suppress the phenomenon of forced alignment of low-transfer features, and enhance method transferability and discriminating ability.

3. Proposed Method

This section mainly introduces the novel method: Section 3.1 proposes an initial state fusion strategy to maintain the adversarial equilibrium, Section 3.2 designs a selective transfer method based on information entropy, and Section 3.3 details the architecture of models.

3.1. Adversarial Equilibrium Strategy Based on Initial State Fusion

The key of the domain discriminator augmentation is to supply domain structure information to the features, thereby improving the reliability of the domain discrimination and avoiding adversarial disequilibrium; therefore, the information introduced in the features has a crucial impact on the effectiveness of the method.

The initial state refers to the original data without feature extraction and distribution alignment, which has the most complete domain structure information, and the statistical features of the source domain and target domain data are highly distinguishable. These characteristics meet the requirements of the information for implementing domain discriminator augmentation. Therefore, this paper proposes to fuse the initial state in the input features of the domain discriminator. The reliability of the domain discrimination results is improved by supplementing the domain structure information of the input features. It avoids the domain discriminator being weak in the adversarial training and finally realizes the domain discriminator to reflect the distance of distribution implicitly and more accurately.

Due to the large dimensional difference between the intermediate features and the initial state, conventional feature fusion operations such as concat and add are easy to fail. We propose a strategy of splitting features first and then fusing them. Critical steps are shown in Figure 1. Firstly, the domain features (yellow in Figure 1) of the data are extracted using the feature extractor. Secondly, the domain features are split into several subfeatures with dimensions equivalent to the initial state (pink in Figure 1), and subfeatures gradually dot the product with the initial state; the dot product is given by

$$a \bullet b = \sum_{i=1}^{n} a_i b_i = a_1 b_1 + a_2 b_2 + \cdots + a_n b_n \quad (1)$$

where a and b represent the subfeature and the initial state, respectively, and a_i and b_i represent the i-th element.

Each subfeature will perform the operation of (1) with the initial state; new feature elements are merged to form the fused feature (red in Figure 1). Finally, the fused feature is input into the domain discriminator for domain discrimination.

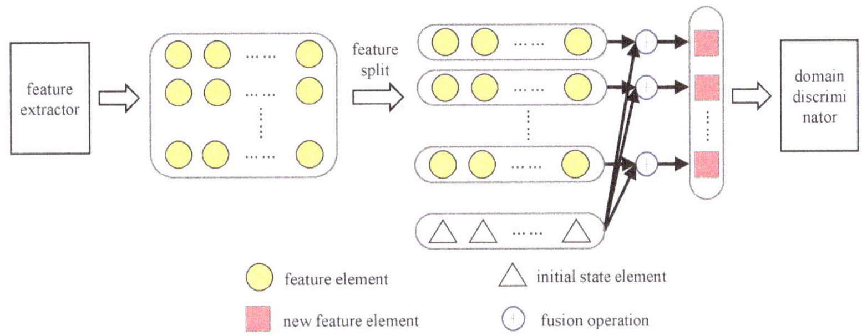

Figure 1. Initial state fusion strategy.

3.2. *Transferability Quantification Based on Information Entropy*

The quantification of transferability is based on the premise that domain similarity and transferability are positively correlated. In the adversarial domain adaptation method, the information entropy of domain discrimination can objectively reflect domain similarity. Therefore, we propose a transferability quantification method based on information entropy, which realizes the transfer source domain samples selectively and inhibits the occurrence of negative migration to a certain extent.

In information theory, information entropy is used to measure the information content of an event. The smaller the probability of an event, the greater the amount of information it contains, and the information entropy also increases. $p(x_i)$ is used to represent the probability density of event $x_i \in X, i = 1, 2, \ldots, n$, and the information entropy of event X is calculated by

$$H(X) = -\sum_{x_i \in X} p(x_i) ln p(x_i) \quad (2)$$

The domain discrimination is the basis for the adversarial domain adaptation method to reflect the degree of feature distribution alignment. The essence of domain discrimination is a two-class prediction task of the sample belonging to the source domain or the target domain. When the output layer of the domain discriminator is activated by the Softmax function, the output after activation is two predicted values whose sum equals 1, denoted as $[p_s, p_t]$, which respectively represent the probability that the domain discriminator thinks the sample belongs to the source domain or the target domain. The Softmax activation is calculated by

$$S_i = \frac{e^i}{\sum_{j=1}^{n} e^j} \quad (3)$$

The information entropy of the domain prediction value is used to reflect the domain similarity. The closer the outputs p_s and p_t of the domain discriminator are, the more successfully the features of the source domain sample confuse the domain discriminator, making it impossible to make accurate domain discrimination. Furthermore, the high domain similarity means that the information entropy of the domain prediction value is maximized, and the source domain samples that generate this feature should be given a higher weight during the transfer process. The weight is calculated by

$$\omega_i = exp[-p_s ln(p_s) - p_t ln(p_t)] - 1 \tag{4}$$

where the exponential is the information entropy of p_s and p_t.

We propose to quantify transferability based on information entropy to tackle the problem of the lack of transferability quantification method, by weighting the source domain samples according to the quantification results to transfer knowledge selectively. The process of transferability quantification is shown in Figure 2. Firstly, the features of samples are extracted. Samples with high domain similarity are shown as having more domain-invariant features in the feature space, and the feature distribution of the source domain and target domain has a high degree of coincidence. Then, make the domain discrimination; the smaller the difference between the p_s and p_t output by the domain discriminator, the higher the similarity that the samples have, and the richer the transferable knowledge that is contained. At this time, the information entropy of the domain discrimination increases. Finally, calculate the weights; samples with higher transferability cause a greater impact on the transfer.

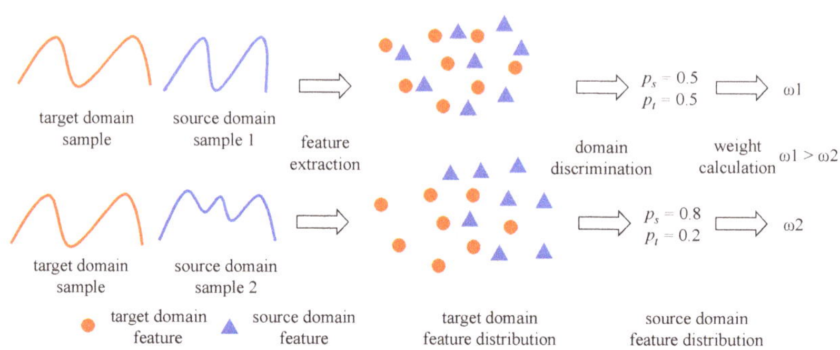

Figure 2. Transferability quantification process.

3.3. *A Novel Adversarial Domain Adaptation Method*

3.3.1. Model Structure

The one-dimensional convolutional neural network and Bidirectional Long Short Term Memory Networks (1DCNN-BiLSTM) has both the efficient feature extraction ability of 1DCNN and the advantages of BiLSTM in describing the dependencies of a time series [45,46]. We use 1DCNN to build a feature extractor and BiLSTM to build a predictor; the model structure is shown in Figure 3. The model consists of three basic modules, a feature extractor, predictor, and domain discriminator. In addition, the initial state fusion module (the light blue module in Figure 3) is added before the domain discriminator, and the transferability quantification module (light green module in Figure 3) is added after the domain discriminator.

The model hyperparameters are shown in Table 1. The column hyperparameter are the properties required to build the model, followed by the corresponding values. The first line indicates that the feature extractor has three layers of 1DCNN. The values in the brackets in the second row represent the respective kernel size of the aforementioned three layers. The source domain and target domain data are convolved with 1DCNN to generate domain-invariant features. Dropout [47] is used in the BiLSTM layer of the predictor to randomly suppress neurons to avoid model overfitting. The features are fused with the initial state, and domain discriminant results are used to calculate the total loss.

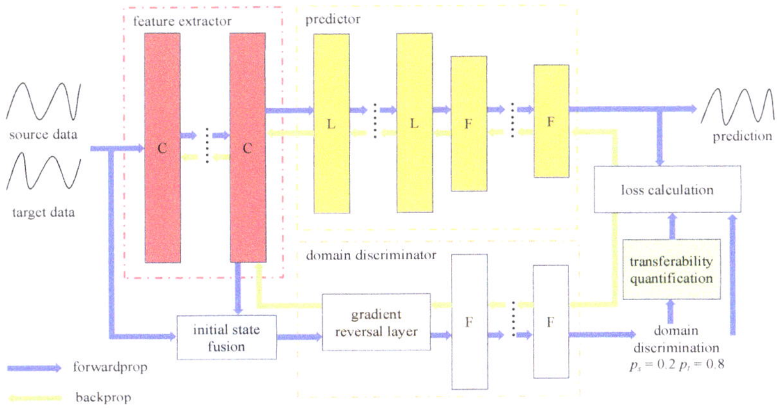

Figure 3. Model structure. C represents 1DCNN, L represents BiLSTM, F represents fully connected layer.

Table 1. Model Hyperparameters.

Module	Hyperparameter	Value
feature extractor	Layer of 1DCNN	3
	Size of the convolving kernel by each layer of convolution	(3, 3, 3)
	The number of channels produced by each layer of convolution	(64, 64, 64)
domain discriminator	Layer of Dense	2
	Size of each output sample by each layer of Dense	(32, 2)
predictor	Layer of BiLSTM	2
	The number of features in the hidden state by each layer of BiLSTM	(64, 64)
	Dropout probability	0.5
	Layer of Dense	2
	Size of each output sample by each layer of Dense	(32, 1)

The domain discriminant loss is composed of the cross-entropy between the domain discriminantion and the real domain label, which is calculated by

$$Loss_{dcls} = \frac{1}{n_s}\sum_{i=1}^{n_s} L_{ce}(d_s^i, y_s^{di}) + \frac{1}{n_t}\sum_{i=1}^{n_t} L_{ce}(d_t^i, y_t^{dt}) \tag{5}$$

The prediction loss consists of two parts: the weighted source domain prediction loss and the target domain prediction loss, which is calculated by

$$Loss_{pred} = \frac{1}{n_s}\sum_{i=1}^{n_s} \omega_i (y_s^i - y_s^{pi})^2 + \frac{1}{n_t}\sum_{i=1}^{n_t} (y_t^i - y_t^{pi})^2 \tag{6}$$

The total loss of the model is composed of the domain discrimination loss and the prediction loss, which is calculated by

$$Loss = Loss_{dcls} + Loss_{pred} \tag{7}$$

where subscript s indicates that the variable belongs to the source domain, subscript t indicates that the variable belongs to the target domain, n is the number of samples in the domain; d^i is the domain label, y^{di} is the predicted domain label, y^i is the true value, y^{pi} is the prediction, ω_i is the weight, and L_{ce} is the cross-entropy loss function.

3.3.2. The Critical Steps of the Algorithm

The algorithm flow is shown in Figure 4. The critical steps of each epoch during training include:

1. Feature extraction; the feature extractor performs feature extraction and distribution alignment on the source domain and target domain data to generate domain-invariant features.
2. Initial state fusion; the domain-invariant features are split into sub-features, and the sub-features are gradually fused with the initial state to generate fused features.
3. Prediction and domain discrimination; the input domain-invariant features into the predictor and output predicted values, and input the fused features into the domain discriminator and output domain discriminant values.
4. Transferability quantification; measure the domain similarity according to the domain discriminant value and calculate the weight of the source domain samples.
5. Loss calculation; calculate the prediction loss and the domain discrimination loss separately, then obtain the total loss.
6. Model parameter optimization; the gradient information is calculated based on the loss value, and the model parameters are updated through the preset optimizer.

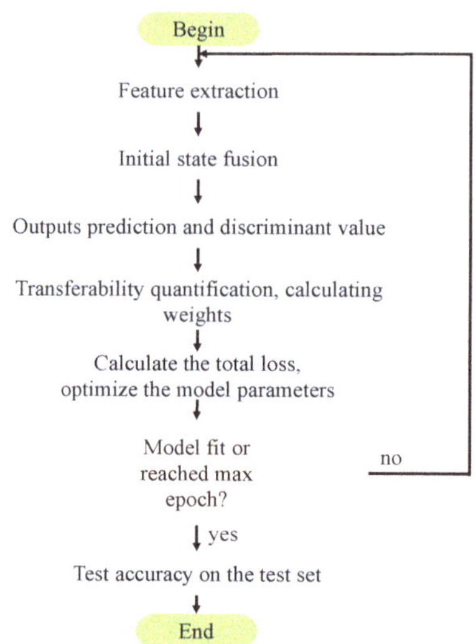

Figure 4. Algorithm flow chart.

4. Experimental Setup and Results

In this section, we extensively evaluate our approach and compare it with state-of-the-art domain adaptation methods. We also provide a detailed analysis of the proposed framework, demonstrating empirically the effect of our contributions.

4.1. Datasets

We evaluate the proposed approach to the BDGP2 dataset [48]. The time range is from 2016 to 2017. The sampling interval is 1 h. The sampling value includes power load, heating, cooling water, steam, and other meter data; in addition, this data set integrates outdoor temperature, humidity, cloud cover, and other climatic factors that can affect power consumption.

Four residential buildings are selected for analysis, namely Bear_lodging_Evan (domain A), Robin_lodging_Renea (domain B), Rat_lodging_Ardell (domain C), and Fox_lodging_Angla (domain D); the load has a periodic characteristic with the user's living habits, which is shown in Figure 5. We use the Augmented Dickey Fuller (ADF) to test that the time series is stationary. The p value is 0.00000218, and the absence of missing values is also the important reason for selecting the mentioned building's data. The variables of the inputs are shown in Table 2.

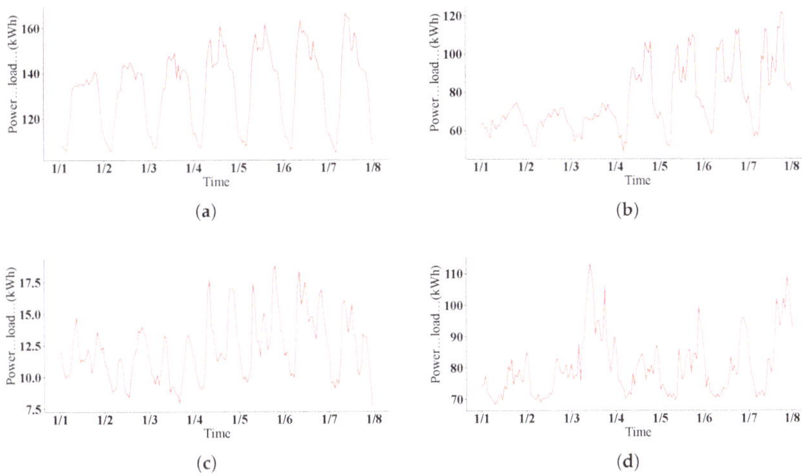

Figure 5. Power load for the four buildings. (a) Building A; (b) building B; (c) building C; (d) building D.

Table 2. The Dataset Variables of Model Inputs.

Variables	Units	Definition
TimeStamp	-	Date and time in the local timezone
Load	kWh	The sum of the electric power used over a certain time
AirTemperature	°C	The temperature of the air in degrees Celsius
DewTemperature	°C	The temperature to which a given parcel of air must be cooled at constant pressure and water vapor content for saturation to occur
SeaLevelPressure	hPa	The air pressure is relative to the mean sea level
WindSpeed	m/s	The rate of horizontal travel of air past a fixed point

The experiment adopts single-step time series forecasting, the input are the variables in Table 2 of the first 24 h in each sliding window, and the true value is the load of the next hour. To verify the effectiveness and accuracy of the proposed method, we construct 12 transfer tasks for each method, and each task is denoted as S→T, which means the S is the source domain and the T is the target domain. When a building is selected as the source domain, we use all the samples of the building as the source domain data train set. When another building is selected as the target domain, we use 10% of the building's samples as the target domain train set and 20% of the samples as the target domain test set; the remaining 70% of the samples are not used. We use samples from two different buildings to create the condition of non-IID by retaining only a few samples of the target building to simulate the lack of data in the target domain.

4.2. Implementation Details

The experiments in this paper are all implemented under the same framework; the programming language is Python3.7.11, the deep learning framework is Pytorch1.10.1, the CUDA11.3, the CUDNN8.2, and the operating system is Windows 10. The CPU is Intel i5-11400H, the base frequency is 2.7 GHz, the memory is 16 G, the GPU is RTX3050Ti, and the GPU memory is 4 G.

The experiment in this paper adopts the same train setting; the optimizer is Adam, the max epoch is 50, and the batch size is 32, the initial parameters are generated by Pytorch-1.10.1 defaulted, and the learning rate can be calculated as

$$LR = \frac{0.01}{(1 + 10 * p)^{0.75}} \tag{8}$$

where LR is the learning rate of the current epoch, and p is the ratio of the current epoch round to the max epochs.

4.3. Results

The objective indicators for the experimental evaluation of prediction accuracy are Root Mean Square Error (RMSE), Mean Absolute Error (MAE), and Mean Absolute Percentage Error (MAPE).

RMSE is sensitive to outliers, and when it is small, it can be considered that the method outputs less predictable values with great deviations. MAE describes the absolute error between the prediction value and the true value, which is the most intuitive. MAPE converts the error value into an error rate, which can evaluate the method performance without considering the order of magnitude of the data.

$$\text{RMSE} = \sqrt{\frac{1}{n}\sum_{i=0}^{n}(y_i - y_{pi})^2} \tag{9}$$

$$\text{MAE} = \frac{1}{n}\sum_{i=0}^{n}|y_i - y_{pi}| \tag{10}$$

$$\text{MAPE} = \frac{100\%}{n}\sum_{i=0}^{n}\left|\frac{y_i - y_{pi}}{y_i}\right| \tag{11}$$

where n is the number of test samples, y_i is the true value, and y_{pi} is the prediction.

The proposed method was compared with FineTune (FT) [49], Wasserstein Distance Guided Representation Learning (WDGRL) [50], Deep Adaptation Networks (DAN) [51], Domain Adversarial Neural Networks–Long Short Term Memory Networks (DANN-LSTM) [52], and Deep CORAL (DCORAL) [53].

FT is the lightest and most widely used method for knowledge transfer. DAN and DCORAL use MMD and CORAL to measure the distance between domains, respectively, which are widely used in discrepancy-based methods. The proposed method, WDGRL, and DANN-LSTM are based on adversarial; however, the difference is our consideration, and attempts to alleviate the adversarial disequilibrium problem. The performances of RMSE, MAE, and MAPE are shown in Tables 3–5. The last row represents the average performance of each method in different tasks, and the best performance of each task is highlighted in bold.

The prediction error of the proposed method is smaller than other methods in most of the adaptation tasks. The proposed method reduces RMSE by 1.53, MAE by 1.29, and MAPE by 1.53%. The reduction in RMSE proves that the method predicts fewer outliers and has a better stability. MAE is used to measure the absolute error, and MAPE is used to measure the error rate. The reduction in the two factors proves that the proposed method can improve the generalization ability of the model and the prediction accuracy effectively.

Table 3. RMSE Performance. The best performance of each task is highlighted in bold.

Task	FT	WDGRL	DAN	DANN-LSTM	DCORAL	Ours
B→A	25.13	15.55	13.71	13.68	14.55	**11.73**
C→A	27.84	14.83	15.30	13.69	16.57	**12.64**
D→A	22.98	13.40	17.78	13.27	15.47	**12.65**
A→B	13.04	10.69	12.49	11.52	10.19	**9.41**
C→B	14.45	9.43	11.30	9.02	9.27	**8.32**
D→B	16.34	11.84	13.65	14.89	10.14	**9.30**
A→C	3.13	2.96	2.68	2.54	2.53	**2.45**
B→C	3.31	4.07	3.10	**2.75**	3.74	2.90
D→C	2.64	3.46	2.66	2.44	2.24	**2.17**
A→D	14.93	13.73	10.96	11.86	11.24	**10.91**
B→D	18.47	16.09	11.09	11.31	**9.66**	10.19
C→D	17.43	13.96	13.85	13.98	10.69	**9.41**
Average	14.97	10.83	10.71	10.08	9.69	**8.51**

Table 4. MAE Performance. The best performance of each task is highlighted in bold.

Task	FT	WDGRL	DAN	DANN-LSTM	DCORAL	Ours
B→A	21.32	12.50	10.53	10.26	11.71	**9.10**
C→A	23.39	11.80	11.66	10.20	13.73	**9.77**
D→A	18.95	10.40	14.45	10.77	13.09	**9.57**
A→B	10.25	7.45	9.78	9.21	7.63	**6.32**
C→B	11.54	6.58	8.58	6.29	6.59	**5.57**
D→B	13.88	9.06	10.24	11.22	8.00	**6.71**
A→C	2.55	2.30	2.17	2.01	2.09	**1.87**
B→C	2.57	3.40	2.53	**2.17**	2.79	2.21
D→C	2.12	2.78	2.10	2.03	1.86	**1.72**
A→D	11.71	10.85	**8.39**	9.52	8.92	8.52
B→D	14.74	12.47	8.66	8.49	**7.23**	7.81
C→D	13.72	10.83	11.10	10.92	7.98	**6.94**
Average	12.23	8.37	8.35	7.76	7.63	**6.34**

Table 5. MAPE Performance. The best performance of each task is highlighted in bold.

Task	FT	WDGRL	DAN	DANN-LSTM	DCORAL	Ours
B→A	12.22	7.12	5.88	5.65	6.56	**5.29**
C→A	13.84	6.76	6.10	5.67	7.96	**5.55**
D→A	12.31	5.91	8.78	6.67	8.73	**5.33**
A→B	11.87	8.33	11.33	10.72	8.96	**6.98**
C→B	13.83	7.41	9.45	7.07	7.28	**6.08**
D→B	16.88	10.06	10.72	13.31	9.73	**7.78**
A→C	16.47	13.91	15.25	14.09	14.05	**11.57**
B→C	15.65	22.12	17.38	13.98	14.57	**12.83**
D→C	13.87	17.63	13.63	15.94	13.54	**11.89**
A→D	11.64	10.53	**8.25**	9.45	8.58	8.32
B→D	14.20	11.36	8.74	8.41	**6.80**	7.45
C→D	14.11	10.32	11.23	11.02	7.31	**6.60**
Average	13.91	10.95	10.56	10.17	9.50	**7.97**

In the domain adaptation tasks of the same target domain but different source domains, such as B→A, C→A, and D→A, the prediction error fluctuation of the method due to the change of the source domain is the slightest, which proves the transferability quantification based on information entropy success selectively transfers the knowledge in the source domain and mitigates negative effects where the low-correlation samples in the source domain lead to negative transfer.

The difference between the proposed method and other adversarial domain adaptation methods (DANN-LSTM and WDGRL) is the addition of the initial state fusion module to maintain the adversarial equilibrium. The proposed method has advantages in multiple tasks, and reduces RMSE by 1.57, MAE by 1.42, and MAPE by 2.2%; the adversarial equilibrium strategy based on initial state fusion effectively alleviates the adversarial disequilibrium problem. Domain structure information is supplemented in the intermediate features, which increases the reliability of domain discrimination. The domain discriminator supervises the feature extractor to achieve feature distribution alignment more effectively, thereby improving prediction accuracy.

The power load forecasting curves of the proposed method for one week from 0:00 on 14 March 2016, to 0:00 on 21 March 2016, are shown in Figure 6. The fitting degree between the prediction and the true value is high. The proposed method improves the load prediction accuracy effectively. However, the prediction error of the method for local peaks and valleys in the four fields is relatively large, and the power load mutation in field C is the most frequent, which means the user's personalized behavior is the most significant; thus, the prediction error of peaks is the largest, indicating that the prediction is easily affected by user personalized behavior. The transfer is not precise enough. Therefore, it is necessary to enhance the method's ability to learn domain-specific features, achieve more detailed selective transfer, suppress the occurrence of negative transfer more effectively, and further improve the prediction accuracy.

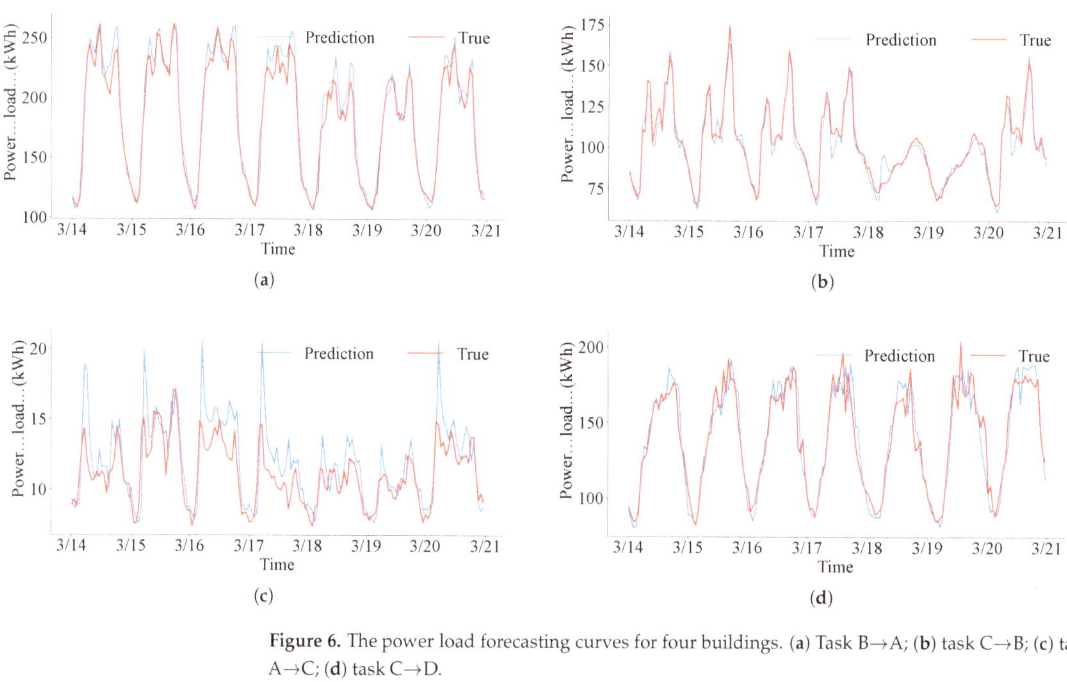

Figure 6. The power load forecasting curves for four buildings. (**a**) Task B→A; (**b**) task C→B; (**c**) task A→C; (**d**) task C→D.

Feature visualization is an important tool to measure the alignment degree of feature distribution. T-SNE [54] is widely used to visualize the high-dimensional data distribution in domain adaptation. The feature visualization results are shown in Figure 7. Red points correspond to the source domain, while blue ones correspond to the target domain. The more similar the source and target domain features are, the more effective the method is. In the proposed method, the source domain and target domain features have the smallest deviation, and the overlap between the two has a large proportion. Upon further analysis, it can be found that the features extracted and aligned by the proposed method are clustered, and the boundaries of each cluster are sharper than the baseline method. Clusters represent the features that the method extracts from different aspects, it indicates that the initial state fusion strategy improves the domain discrimination ability of the domain discriminator, further supervising the feature extraction to extract domain-invariant features effectively during the adversarial training. There are few features that the proposed method fails to align relative to the baseline method, indicating that the proposed method effectively suppresses the low-correlation information in the source domain, and retains information that can be transferred to the target effectively.

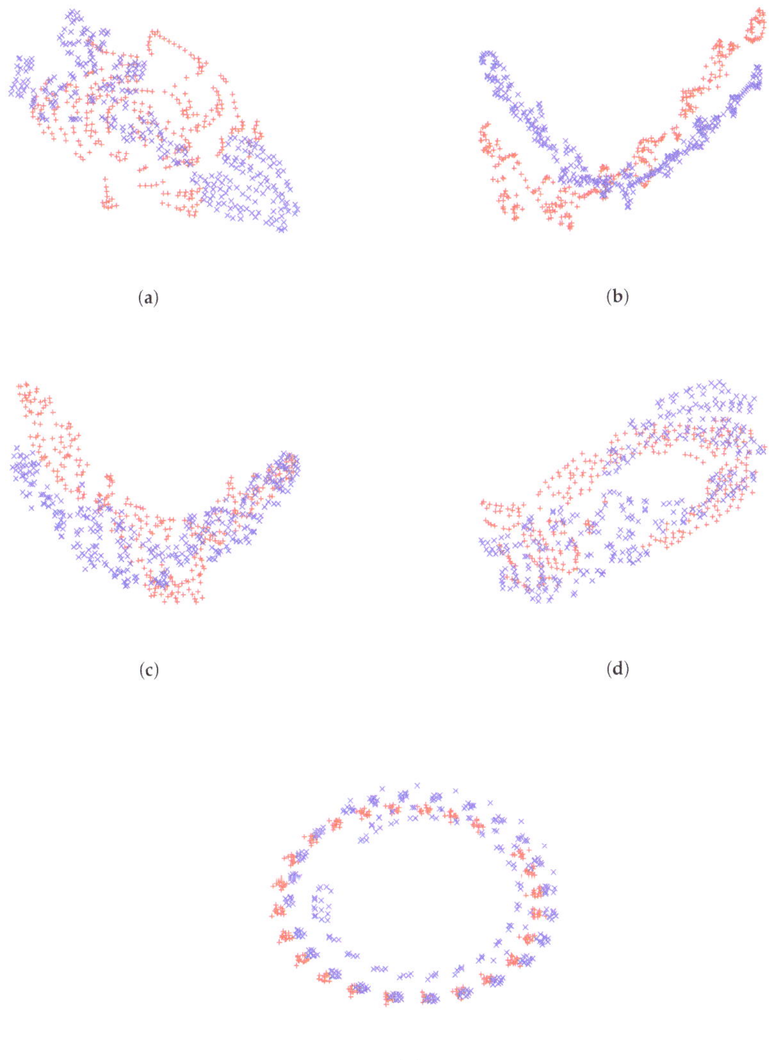

(a) (b) (c) (d) (e)

Figure 7. Feature visualization for different methods. Red points correspond to the source domain, while blue ones correspond to the target domain. (**a**) WDGRL; (**b**) DAN; (**c**) DANN-LSTM; (**d**) DCORAL; (**e**) Ours.

5. Conclusions

This paper focuses on the adversarial domain adaptation method and its application in power load forecasting. Domain adaptation alleviates the problem where traditional machine learning methods are limited by the amount of labeled data and the condition of IID; this has a strong significance for promoting intelligent power load forecasting systems. The adversarial domain adaptation method faces the problems of adversarial disequilibrium and a lack of transferability quantitation. This paper proposes corresponding solutions to the above two problems and conducts sufficient experimental verifications. The experimental results in the BDGP2 dataset prove that the proposed method gains a high power load prediction accuracy. This paper provides a research reference for solving the problems of adversarial disequilibrium and a lack of transferability quantitation, and provides an application reference for implementing power load forecasting based on the adversarial domain adaptation method. Furthermore, due to the strong personalization of users' electricity consumption behavior, the method does not perform well in the local peaks and valleys. Therefore, it is necessary to enhance the ability of the method to learn domain-specific features to achieve more refined selective transfer. Our future work will explore how to suppress the negative transfer better, and improve the prediction accuracy more effectively.

Author Contributions: Conceptualization, M.H. and J.Y.; methodology, M.H. and J.Y.; software, J.Y.; validation, M.H. and J.Y.; writing—original draft preparation, J.Y.; writing—review and editing, M.H.; funding acquisition, M.H. All authors have read and agreed to the published version of the manuscript.

Funding: This research was funded by two Guangdong Natural Science Foundation Projects (Grant No. 2021A1515011496 and Grant No. 2022A1515011370).

Institutional Review Board Statement: Not applicable.

Informed Consent Statement: Not applicable.

Data Availability Statement: Not applicable.

Conflicts of Interest: The authors declare no conflict of interest.

Abbreviations

The following abbreviations are used in this manuscript:

GANs	Generative Adversarial Networks
BDGP2	Building Data Genome Project 2
IID	Independent and Identical Distributions
MMD	Maximum Mean Discrepancy
MK-MMD	Multi-Kernel Maximum Mean Discrepancy
KL	Kullback–Leibler
JS	Jensen–Shannon
CORAL	CORrelation ALignment
1DCNN	One-dimensional convolutional neural network
BiLSTM	Bidirectional Long Short Term Memory networks
ADF	Augmented Dickey Fuller
RMSE	Root Mean Square Error
MAE	Mean Absolute Error
MAPE	Mean Absolute Percentage Error
FT	FineTune
WDGRL	Wasserstein Distance Guided Representation Learning
DAN	Deep Adaptation Networks
DANN-LSTM	Domain Adversarial Neural Networks-Long Short Term Memory Networks
DCORAL	Deep CORAL

References

1. Douklias, A.; Karagiannidis, L.; Misichroni, F.; Amditis, A. Design and Implementation of a UAV-Based Airborne Computing Platform for Computer Vision and Machine Learning Applications. *Sensors* **2022**, *22*, 2049. [CrossRef] [PubMed]
2. Tabata, K.; Hashimoto, M.; Takahashi, H.; Wang, Z.; Nagaoka, N.; Hara, T.; Kamioka, H. A Morphometric Analysis of the Osteocyte Canaliculus Using Applied Automatic Semantic Segmentation by Machine Learning. *J. Bone Miner. Metab.* **2022**, *40*, 571–580. [CrossRef] [PubMed]
3. Yang, J.; Zhao, J.; Song, J.; Wu, J.; Zhao, C.; Leng, H. A Hybrid Method Using HAVOK Analysis and Machine Learning for Predicting Chaotic Time Series. *Entropy* **2022**, *24*, 408. [CrossRef] [PubMed]
4. Shankar, V.; Parsana, S. An Overview and Empirical Comparison of Natural Language Processing (NLP) Models and an Introduction to and Empirical Application of Autoencoder Models in Marketing. *J. Acad. Mark. Sci.* **2022**. [CrossRef]
5. Zhao, S.; Yue, X.; Zhang, S.; Li, B.; Zhao, H.; Wu, B.; Krishna, R.; Gonzalez, J.E.; Sangiovanni-Vincentelli, A.L.; Seshia, S.A.; et al. A Review of Single-Source Deep Unsupervised Visual Domain Adaptation. *IEEE Trans. Neural Netw. Learn. Syst.* **2022**, *33*, 473–493. [CrossRef]
6. Zhuang, F.; Qi, Z.; Duan, K.; Xi, D.; Zhu, Y.; Zhu, H.; Xiong, H.; He, Q. A Comprehensive Survey on Transfer Learning. *Proc. IEEE* **2021**, *109*, 43–76. [CrossRef]
7. Wilson, G.; Cook, D.J. A Survey of Unsupervised Deep Domain Adaptation. *ACM Trans. Intell. Syst. Technol.* **2020**, *11*, 51. [CrossRef]
8. Yan, H.; Li, Z.; Wang, Q.; Li, P.; Xu, Y.; Zuo, W. Weighted and Class-Specific Maximum Mean Discrepancy for Unsupervised Domain Adaptation. *IEEE Trans. Multimed.* **2020**, *22*, 2420–2433. [CrossRef]
9. Chen, Y.; Song, S.; Li, S.; Wu, C. A Graph Embedding Framework for Maximum Mean Discrepancy-Based Domain Adaptation Algorithms. *IEEE Trans. Image Process.* **2020**, *29*, 199–213. [CrossRef]
10. Wang, W.; Li, H.; Ding, Z.; Nie, F.; Chen, J.; Dong, X.; Wang, Z. Rethinking Maximum Mean Discrepancy for Visual Domain Adaptation. *IEEE Trans. Neural Netw. Learn. Syst.* **2021**, 1–14. [CrossRef]
11. Tóth, L.; Gosztolya, G. Adaptation of DNN Acoustic Models Using KL-Divergence Regularization and Multi-Task Training. In *Speech and Computer*; Ronzhin, A., Potapova, R., Németh, G., Eds.; Springer International Publishing: Cham, Switzerland, 2016; Volume 9811, pp. 108–115. [CrossRef]
12. Jiang, J.; Wang, X.; Long, M.; Wang, J. Resource Efficient Domain Adaptation. In Proceedings of the 28th ACM International Conference on Multimedia, Seattle, WA, USA, 12–16 October 2020; pp. 2220–2228. [CrossRef]
13. Zhu, Z.; Wang, L.; Peng, G.; Li, S. WDA: An Improved Wasserstein Distance-Based Transfer Learning Fault Diagnosis Method. *Sensors* **2021**, *21*, 4394. [CrossRef]
14. Lee, C.Y.; Batra, T.; Baig, M.H.; Ulbricht, D. Sliced Wasserstein Discrepancy for Unsupervised Domain Adaptation. In Proceedings of the 2019 IEEE/CVF Conference on Computer Vision and Pattern Recognition (CVPR), Long Beach, CA, USA, 15–20 June 2019; pp. 10277–10287. [CrossRef]
15. Cheng, C.; Zhou, B.; Ma, G.; Wu, D.; Yuan, Y. Wasserstein Distance Based Deep Adversarial Transfer Learning for Intelligent Fault Diagnosis. *arXiv* **2019**, arXiv:1903.06753.
16. Chen, C.; Chen, Z.; Jiang, B.; Jin, X. Joint Domain Alignment and Discriminative Feature Learning for Unsupervised Deep Domain Adaptation. *arXiv* **2018**, arXiv:1808.09347.
17. Rahman, M.M.; Fookes, C.; Baktashmotlagh, M.; Sridharan, S. On Minimum Discrepancy Estimation for Deep Domain Adaptation. *arXiv* **2019**, arXiv:1901.00282.
18. Tang, H.; Jia, K. Discriminative Adversarial Domain Adaptation. *arXiv* **2019**, arXiv:1911.12036.
19. Zhang, Y.; Tang, H.; Jia, K.; Tan, M. Domain-Symmetric Networks for Adversarial Domain Adaptation. In Proceedings of the 2019 IEEE/CVF Conference on Computer Vision and Pattern Recognition (CVPR), Long Beach, CA, USA, 15–20 June 2019; pp. 5026–5035. [CrossRef]
20. Jing, T.; Ding, Z. Adversarial Dual Distinct Classifiers for Unsupervised Domain Adaptation. *arXiv* **2020**, arXiv:2008.11878.
21. Akkaya, I.B.; Altinel, F.; Halici, U. Self-Training Guided Adversarial Domain Adaptation For Thermal Imagery. In Proceedings of the 2021 IEEE/CVF Conference on Computer Vision and Pattern Recognition Workshops (CVPRW), Nashville, TN, USA, 19–25 June 2021; pp. 4317–4326. [CrossRef]
22. Zhang, Y.; Ye, H.; Davison, B.D. Adversarial Reinforcement Learning for Unsupervised Domain Adaptation. In Proceedings of the 2021 IEEE Winter Conference on Applications of Computer Vision (WACV), Waikoloa, HI, USA, 3–8 January 2021; pp. 635–644. [CrossRef]
23. Zhang, Y.; Davison, B.D. Adversarial Regression Learning for Bone Age Estimation. *arXiv* **2021**, arXiv:2103.0614.
24. Ganin, Y.; Ustinova, E.; Ajakan, H.; Germain, P.; Larochelle, H.; Laviolette, F.; Marchand, M.; Lempitsky, V. Domain-Adversarial Training of Neural Networks. *arXiv* **2015**, arXiv:1505.07818.
25. Ma, A.; Li, J.; Lu, K.; Zhu, L.; Shen, H.T. Adversarial Entropy Optimization for Unsupervised Domain Adaptation. *IEEE Trans. Neural Netw. Learn. Syst.* **2021**, 1–12. [CrossRef]
26. Wu, H.; Zhu, H.; Yan, Y.; Wu, J.; Zhang, Y.; Ng, M.K. Heterogeneous Domain Adaptation by Information Capturing and Distribution Matching. *IEEE Trans. Image Process.* **2021**, *30*, 6364–6376. [CrossRef]
27. Deng, W.; Zhao, L.; Kuang, G.; Hu, D.; Pietikainen, M.; Liu, L. Deep Ladder-Suppression Network for Unsupervised Domain Adaptation. *IEEE Trans. Cybern.* **2021**, 1–15. [CrossRef] [PubMed]

28. Jiang, B.; Chen, C.; Jin, X. Unsupervised Domain Adaptation with Target Reconstruction and Label Confusion in the Common Subspace. *Neural Comput. Appl.* **2020**, *32*, 4743–4756. [CrossRef]
29. Wang, S.; Zhang, L.; Zuo, W.; Zhang, B. Class-Specific Reconstruction Transfer Learning for Visual Recognition Across Domains. *IEEE Trans. Image Process.* **2020**, *29*, 2424–2438. [CrossRef]
30. Ragab, M.; Chen, Z.; Wu, M.; Kwoh, C.K.; Li, X. Adversarial Transfer Learning for Machine Remaining Useful Life Prediction. In Proceedings of the 2020 IEEE International Conference on Prognostics and Health Management (ICPHM), Detroit, MI, USA, 8–10 June 2020; pp. 1–7. [CrossRef]
31. Ragab, M.; Chen, Z.; Wu, M.; Foo, C.S.; Kwoh, C.K.; Yan, R.; Li, X. Contrastive Adversarial Domain Adaptation for Machine Remaining Useful Life Prediction. *IEEE Trans. Ind. Inform.* **2021**, *17*, 5239–5249. [CrossRef]
32. Du, Y.; Wang, J.; Feng, W.; Pan, S.; Qin, T.; Xu, R.; Wang, C. AdaRNN: Adaptive Learning and Forecasting of Time Series. *arXiv* **2021**, arXiv:2108.04443.
33. Zhou, D.; Ma, S.; Hao, J.; Han, D.; Huang, D.; Yan, S.; Li, T. An Electricity Load Forecasting Model for Integrated Energy System Based on BiGAN and Transfer Learning. *Energy Rep.* **2020**, *6*, 3446–3461. [CrossRef]
34. Du, L.; Zhang, L.; Wang, X. Generative Adversarial Framework-Based One-day-ahead Forecasting Method of Photovoltaic Power Output. *IET Gener. Transm. Distrib.* **2020**, *14*, 4234–4245. [CrossRef]
35. Li, J.; Chen, E.; Ding, Z.; Zhu, L.; Lu, K.; Shen, H.T. Maximum Density Divergence for Domain Adaptation. *IEEE Trans. Pattern Anal. Mach. Intell.* **2021**, *43*, 3918–3930. [CrossRef]
36. Yang, J.; Zou, H.; Zhou, Y.; Xie, L. Robust Adversarial Discriminative Domain Adaptation for Real-World Cross-Domain Visual Recognition. *Neurocomputing* **2021**, *433*, 28–36. [CrossRef]
37. Wu, L.; Li, C.; Chen, Q.; Li, B. Deep Adversarial Domain Adaptation Network. *Int. J. Adv. Robot. Syst.* **2020**, *17*, 172988142096464. [CrossRef]
38. Long, M.; Cao, Z.; Wang, J.; Jordan, M.I. Conditional Adversarial Domain Adaptation. *arXiv* **2018**, arXiv:1705.10667.
39. Zhao, P.; Zang, W.; Liu, B.; Kang, Z.; Bai, K.; Huang, K.; Xu, Z. Domain Adaptation with Feature and Label Adversarial Networks. *Neurocomputing* **2021**, *439*, 294–301. [CrossRef]
40. Hu, D.; Liang, J.; Hou, Q.; Yan, H.; Chen, Y. Adversarial Domain Adaptation with Prototype-Based Normalized Output Conditioner. *IEEE Trans. Image Process.* **2021**, *30*, 9359–9371. [CrossRef] [PubMed]
41. Fan, C.; Liu, P.; Xiao, T.; Zhao, W.; Tang, X. Domain Adaptation Based on Domain-Invariant and Class-Distinguishable Feature Learning Using Multiple Adversarial Networks. *Neurocomputing* **2020**, *411*, 178–192. [CrossRef]
42. Wang, Y.; Zhang, Z.; Hao, W.; Song, C. Attention Guided Multiple Source and Target Domain Adaptation. *IEEE Trans. Image Process.* **2021**, *30*, 892–906. [CrossRef]
43. Zuo, Y.; Yao, H.; Xu, C. Attention-Based Multi-Source Domain Adaptation. *IEEE Trans. Image Process.* **2021**, *30*, 3793–3803. [CrossRef]
44. Zhang, C.; Zhao, Q.; Wang, Y. Transferable Attention Networks for Adversarial Domain Adaptation. *Inf. Sci.* **2020**, *539*, 422–433. [CrossRef]
45. Bazi, R.; Benkedjouh, T.; Habbouche, H.; Rechak, S.; Zerhouni, N. A Hybrid CNN-BiLSTM Approach-Based Variational Mode Decomposition for Tool Wear Monitoring. *Int. J. Adv. Manuf. Technol.* **2022**, *119*, 3803–3817. [CrossRef]
46. Gupta, B.; Prakasam, P.; Velmurugan, T. Integrated BERT Embeddings, BiLSTM-BiGRU and 1-D CNN Model for Binary Sentiment Classification Analysis of Movie Reviews. *Multimed. Tools Appl.* **2022**, *81*, 33067–33086. [CrossRef]
47. Srivastava, N.; Hinton, G.; Krizhevsky, A.; Sutskever, I.; Salakhutdinov, R. Dropout: A Simple Way to Prevent Neural Networks from Overfitting. *J. Mach. Learn. Res.* **2014**, *15*, 1929–1958.
48. Miller, C.; Kathirgamanathan, A.; Picchetti, B.; Arjunan, P.; Park, J.Y.; Nagy, Z.; Raftery, P.; Hobson, B.W.; Shi, Z.; Meggers, F. The Building Data Genome Project 2, Energy Meter Data from the ASHRAE Great Energy Predictor III Competition. *Sci. Data* **2020**, *7*, 368. [CrossRef] [PubMed]
49. Tian, Y.; Sehovac, L.; Grolinger, K. Similarity-Based Chained Transfer Learning for Energy Forecasting With Big Data. *IEEE Access* **2019**, *7*, 139895–139908. [CrossRef]
50. Shen, J.; Qu, Y.; Zhang, W.; Yu, Y. Wasserstein Distance Guided Representation Learning for Domain Adaptation. *arXiv* **2018**, arXiv:1707.01217.
51. Long, M.; Cao, Y.; Wang, J.; Jordan, M.I. Learning Transferable Features with Deep Adaptation Networks. *arXiv* **2015**, arXiv:1502.02791.
52. Xi, F.A.; Gg, A.; Gl, B.; Liang, C.A.; Wl, A.; Pei, P.A. A Hybrid Deep Transfer Learning Strategy for Short Term Cross-Building Energy Prediction. *Energy* **2020**, *215*, 119208.
53. Sun, B.; Saenko, K. Deep CORAL: Correlation Alignment for Deep Domain Adaptation. *arXiv* **2016**, arXiv:1607.01719.
54. Laurens, V.D.M.; Hinton, G. Visualizing Data Using T-SNE. *J. Mach. Learn. Res.* **2008**, *9*, 2579–2605.

mathematics

Article

Deep Reinforcement Learning-Based RMSA Policy Distillation for Elastic Optical Networks

Bixia Tang [1], Yue-Cai Huang [2,*], Yun Xue [1,2] and Weixing Zhou [1,2]

[1] School of Physics and Telecommunication Engineering, South China Normal University, Guangzhou 510006, China
[2] School of Electronics and Information Engineering, South China Normal University, Foshan 528200, China
* Correspondence: huangyuecai@scnu.edu.cn

Abstract: The reinforcement learning-based routing, modulation, and spectrum assignment has been regarded as an emerging paradigm for resource allocation in the elastic optical networks. One limitation is that the learning process is highly dependent on the training environment, such as the traffic pattern or the optical network topology. Therefore, re-training is required in case of network topology or traffic pattern variations, which consumes a great amount of computation power and time. To ease the requirement of re-training, we propose a policy distillation scheme, which distills knowledge from a well-trained teacher model and then transfers the knowledge to the to-be-trained student model, so that the training of the latter can be accelerated. Specifically, the teacher model is trained for one training environment (e.g., the topology and traffic pattern) and the student model is for another training environment. The simulation results indicate that our proposed method can effectively speed up the training process of the student model, and it even leads to a lower blocking probability, compared with the case that the student model is trained without knowledge distillation.

Keywords: routing, modulation and spectrum assignment; elastic optical networks; deep reinforcement learning; knowledge distillation

MSC: 68T07

Citation: Tang, B.; Huang, Y.-C.; Xue, Y.; Zhou, W. Deep Reinforcement Learning-Based RMSA Policy Distillation for Elastic Optical Networks. *Mathematics* **2022**, *10*, 3293. https://doi.org/10.3390/math10183293

Academic Editors: Jianping Gou, Weihua Ou, Shaoning Zeng and Lan Du

Received: 14 August 2022
Accepted: 8 September 2022
Published: 11 September 2022

1. Introduction

Accompanied with the rapid development of the Internet technology, services such as audio and video conferencing, webcasting, and cloud computing have become popular. The growing demand of these services leads to an exponential increase in data traffic and poses great challenges to the bearing communication networks [1]. Elastic optical networks (EONs) have been regarded to be a promising candidate for the next-generation optical communications [2,3]. In EONs, the spectrum is divided into narrow frequency slots, and traffic requests can be served by different numbers of frequency slots according to their data rate requirements and the quality of the connection. This flex-grid scheme greatly increases the network resource allocation flexibility compared to the traditional wavelength-division multiplexing (WDM)-based networks [4]. Meanwhile, it also brings difficulties for the network resource management.

The routing, modulation, and spectrum assignment (RMSA) [5] is a key problem for the EONs resource management. Due to the complexity, the RMSA problem is generally divided into two sub-problems: the routing and spectrum assignment [6], each of them tackled by heuristic solutions [7–10]. For the routing sub-problem, representative approaches include fixed routing, fixed alternative routing [11,12], and adaptive routing [4]. For the spectrum assignment sub-problem, there are the first-fit [13] and random-fit schemes and other methods. However, these rule-based heuristics, mostly relying on researchers' cognition, cannot comprehensively capture the effect of the complex network conditions.

To overcome the above limitation, deep reinforcement learning (DRL) has recently been introduced to the RMSA problem [14–19], where the RMSA policies are parameterized by deep neural networks and the RMSA policies are improved through interactions with the optical network environment. Many of them have achieved a better performance than heuristic methods. However, the learned policies of these DRL-based approaches are highly related to the training environment, such as the traffic patterns and the network topologies. However, in a practical network, the traffic patterns and the network topologies are very likely to be changed. For example, the traffic volume from commercial and residential areas varies from working hours to off-duty hours. Meanwhile, the network topology becomes different in the case of a network failure or disasters. Once the environment is changed, the effectiveness of the learned RMSA policies deteriorates significantly [20]. Therefore, re-training is required and consumes a lot of computing power and time. To ease the requirement of re-training, Chen et al. [20] investigated the transfer learning (TL) between different network topologies. They first trained and obtained a model from source tasks, and then copied the parameters of the trained model as the starting point when training the target task. The limitation is that the target task needs to use the same neural network architecture with the source task. Moreover, the effect of traffic variation has not yet been investigated.

In this paper, we extend our previously published conference paper [19] and apply policy distillation [21] to the RMSA problem, combining knowledge distillation [22] with reinforcement learning (RL). First, a teacher model is trained for one task with a specific traffic pattern and network topology. Then, the well-trained policy of a teacher model is distilled, and the knowledge is transferred to a student model with a different traffic pattern and network topology, to assist the training of the student model. A major difference between our work and the transfer learning in [20] is that the student model (target) and the teacher model (source) can be different. This allows knowledge transfer in a broader context. We have applied the proposed design in three different application scenarios, which consider different traffic patterns and different topologies. The simulation results demonstrate that policy distillation can accelerate the training speed of the student model and improve its performance.

The rest of this paper is organized as follows. Section 2 surveys the related work. In Section 3, we briefly introduce some basics of RL. In Section 4, we introduce the proposed policy distillation architecture, including the problem formulation and the training of the teacher model and the student model. Then, we present the simulation results in Section 5. Lastly, we conclude the paper in Section 6.

2. Related Work

2.1. Deep Reinforcement Learning in RMSA of EONs

In recent years, research has emerged by exploiting DRL to solve the routing and spectrum assignment problem in the optical networks. Chen et al. [23] proposed a DRL framework, namely DeepRMSA, for the optical network management and resource allocation. The DeepRMSA uses the deep Q-learning algorithm for the training. Because the input-state representation has a significant impact on the performance, a series of work has explored different state representations. Chen et al. [14] defined a list of features of the candidate paths. Yan et al. [24] introduced the concept of a multi-modal optical network by considering the topology modality and routing modality to represent different features of the optical network and uses the actor–critic (AC) algorithm for the training. Suárez-Varela et al. [25] captured the key relationships between the links in the input-state representation, making the DRL agents easier and faster to learn. The same team then [26] introduced the Graph Neural Networks to further capture the network-state features. Xu et al. [18] introduced a link–path relationship matrix to capture the path information of the elastic optical networks.

There are some other works exploring various aspects by applying DRL in the optical network management. Huang et al. [15] proposed a DRL-based self-learning routing scheme for the WDM-based networks. It allows the agent to continuously improve its performance by self-comparison. Koch et al. [27] adopted the RL algorithm for parameter optimization in EONs. In addition, a cost-efficient routing, modulation, wavelength, and port assignment algorithm based on DRL was developed in [28]. Moreover, Li et al. [29] investigated collaborative DRL agents for multi-domain provisioning in multi-area optical networks.

2.2. Transfer Learning in EONs

Transfer learning in EONs has recently attracted research interest. Yao et al. [30] proposed a TL-based resource optimization strategy for predicting the spectrum defragmentation time in space-division multiplexing EONs. Liu et al. [31] applied a TL approach to implement a scalable quality-of-transmission estimation in EONs. To our knowledge, the most relevant work of this paper is [20], where the authors propose a knowledge transfer design that alleviates scalability issues by transferring knowledge between RMSA agents with different tasks through a modular DRL agent structure. As mentioned in Section 1, its limitation is that the target task needs to use the same neural network architecture with the source task. In our previously published conference paper [19], we propose a knowledge distillation scheme based on DRL to achieve RMSA policy scalability in EONs. This paper extends [19] in three aspects: (1) the authors of [19] only consider different traffic patterns, while this paper considers different traffic patterns and topologies; (2) the training algorithm is updated to the most advanced asynchronous advantage actor–critic (A3C); and (3) many more simulation results are provided to verify our proposal.

3. Preliminaries

As this work is based on RL, we first explain some basics about RL for the facility of the readers.

3.1. Reinforcement Learning

Reinforcement learning is an important branch of machine learning. Many RL tasks can be modeled as Markov decision processes (MDP), expressed as tuples $\{S, A, R, P\}$. S is the state space of the environment; A is the action space of the agent; R is the reward function; and P represents the state transition probabilities. In the RL framework, the agent interacts with the environment. Specifically, given a state $s_t \in S$, the agent performs an action $a_t \in A$ according to a *policy*, and then the environment emits a reward r_t and changes its state from s_t to a new state s_{t+1} according to the state transition probabilities P. In this process, the agent influences the environment by taking the actions, and the environment feeds back reward r_t to the agent, which will guide the agent to choose better actions. The goal of the agent is to improve its action policy by optimizing the cumulative future reward.

3.2. Asynchronous Advantage Actor–Critic

The RL agent needs to be trained by some training algorithm. In this work, we use the A3C algorithm [32] for the training. It is the asynchronous multi-threaded version of the AC algorithm [33]. The AC algorithm uses a policy network (also called actor) to select the action and a value network (also called critic) to evaluate actions. The actor updates its policy (i.e., action selection probability) according to the critic. Through the agent–environment interaction, the critic improves its evaluation accuracy, and the actor improves its policy gradually.

A3C makes the AC algorithm much easier and faster to converge. It adopts a multi-threaded method, where each thread has an independent actor–critic pair interacting with a copy of the environment. Each thread collects the exploration experience from its environment copy and then regularly updates a shared global actor–critic pair. By doing this, the algorithm converges faster.

4. Policy Distillation Design with EONs

4.1. Elastic Optical Networks

In the EONs, the RMSA problem is to establish corresponding end-to-end paths and allocate appropriate frequency slots (FSs) for different traffic requests according to their data rate requirements. Furthermore, RMSA [6] algorithm must satisfy the spectrum contiguity constraint and spectrum continuity constraint. The topology of the EONs can be denoted by a graph $G(V, E)$, where V and E represent the set of nodes and links, respectively. When a traffic request, denoted by $TR(v_s, v_d, b)$, arrives, RMSA is needed from the source node $v_s \in V$ to the target node $v_d \in V$ with the required bandwidth b. The routing algorithm first calculates all possible paths from the source to the destination, then selects one path P_{v_s,v_d} from the K-shortest paths. Corresponding number of FS n required on the selected path P_{v_s,v_d} can be calculated by Equation (1) and Table 1.

$$n = \lceil b/(W \cdot m(P_{v_s,v_d})) \rceil + 1 \tag{1}$$

W denotes the spectrum width of each FS; $m(P_{v_s,v_d}) \in [1, 2, 3, 4]$ corresponds to the modulation format selected according to the physical length of P_{v_s,v_d} [34]; and one FS is used for the guard band. Then, n allocated FSs must be contiguous (spectrum contiguity constraint), and each link along the demand path P_{v_s,v_d} must be assigned the same n contiguous FSs (spectrum continuity constraint).

Table 1. Transmission reach for different modulation formats [35].

$m(P_{v_s,v_d})$	Modulation Format	Transmission Reach
1	BPSK	5000 km
2	QPSK	2500 km
3	8-QAM	1250 km
4	16-QAM	625 km

4.2. Policy Distillation Scheme

We propose to integrate policy distillation into the RMSA problems of the optical networks. The whole architecture is shown in Figure 1. Two models, namely the teacher model and the student model, are trained for different tasks. First, a teacher model is trained for one task with specific traffic pattern and network topology. Then, the well-trained policy of the teacher model is distilled, and the knowledge is transferred to a student model with a different traffic pattern and network topology, to assist the training of the student model. There are three steps in the training process:

- Step 1: Train the teacher model. It is trained by interacting with the teacher environment.
- Step 2: Distill the knowledge from the teacher model and transfer the knowledge to the student model. The training data of the student model are generated by calling the well-trained teacher model obtained in Step 1, and then the student model is trained by fitting these data.
- Step 3: Train the student model by itself. After the training in Step 2, the student model will be further updated by interacting with student environment and no longer rely on the knowledge distilled from the teacher model.

The RMSA policy for the student task is learned by the student model via Steps 2 and 3. Step 2 distills the knowledge from the well-trained policy network of the teacher model and transfers the knowledge to the student model to assist its training.

4.3. State, Action, and Reward

The optical network RMSA problem can be modeled as an MDP and solved in an RL-based framework. In the RL framework, three essential elements are the state, the action, and the reward. We consider the state only when there is a new traffic request. The state s_t is a $1 \times 5K$ vector containing spectrum utilization information on the K-shortest candidate paths of the traffic request [14]. For each candidate path, we considered five elements of spectrum utilization as follows:

- Starting index of the first available FS-block;
- Size of the first available FS-block;
- Number of required FSs;
- Average size of the available FS-block;
- Total number of available FSs.

In addition, the action of the RMSA problem is to choose one path from the K-candidate paths and allocate spectrum on the selected path based on the first-fit strategy. Therefore, action $a_t \in \{1, 2, \cdots, K\}$. The reward r_t is defined to be 1 when the traffic request is accepted, and -1 otherwise.

4.4. Teacher Model

According to Step 1 in Figure 1, a teacher model is first trained, which is illustrated in more detail in Step 1 of Figure 2. We use DRL to train the teacher model and obtain the RMSA policy to optimize the EONs resource management. The A3C algorithm is adopted for the training, where multiple local actor–critic pairs are trained by interacting with the copies of the environment in parallel, and then periodically update the global actor–critic pair. The actor and critic are parameterized by two neural networks: the policy network $\pi(a_t|s_t;\theta_{p,\mathbb{T}})$ and the value network $V(s_t;\theta_{v,\mathbb{T}})$. The policy network $\pi(a_t|s_t;\theta_{p,\mathbb{T}})$ is used to generate the policy of RMSA, which is represented by a probability distribution. The value network $V(s_t;\theta_{v,\mathbb{T}})$ is used to obtain the value of s_t and evaluate the RMSA policy. $\mathbb{T}$ denotes the teacher model. $\theta_{p,\mathbb{T}}$ and $\theta_{v,\mathbb{T}}$ are the parameters of the policy and the value network, respectively. The global parameters maintained by the A3C algorithm are represented as $\theta^*_{p,\mathbb{T}}$ and $\theta^*_{v,\mathbb{T}}$.

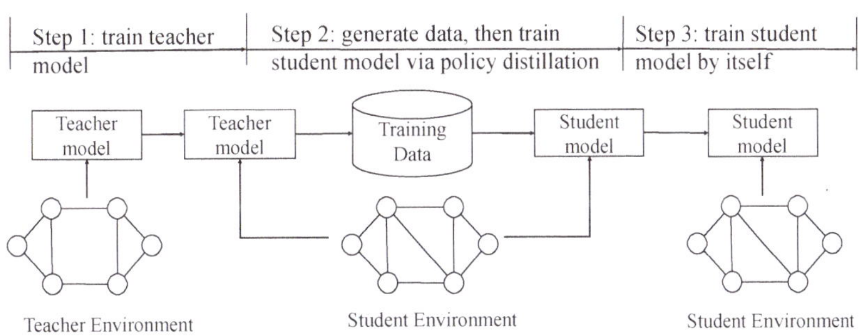

Figure 1. Overview of the policy distillation design with EONs.

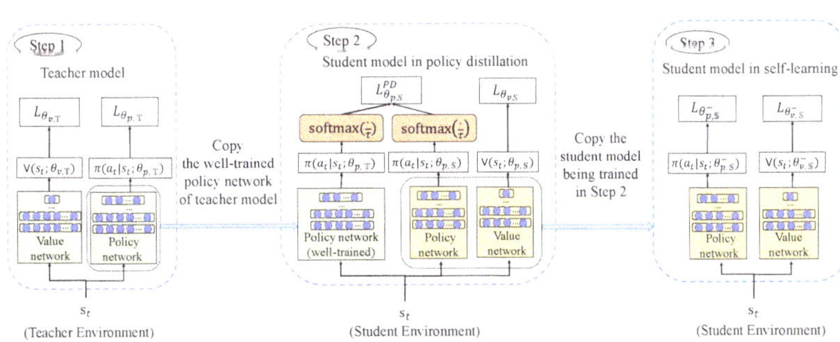

Figure 2. Detailed illustration of policy distillation design with EONs.

The details of training process for the teacher model are given in Algorithm 1. First, we initialize the experience buffer D to empty and set the initial exploration rate ε to 1. In line 3, each actor–critic pair thread parameters are firstly updated by the global parameters. Notice that for a general DRL task that can be modeled as a Markov decision process $\{S, A, R, P\}$ mentioned in Section 3, the state transition from s_t to s_{t+1} follows a probability distribution P. However, for the RMSA task in this paper, as the state space is extremely large, state transitions are difficult to be modeled. Therefore, the RMSA task here belongs to the model-free MDP and can only be optimized through samples. In lines 6–10, during the sampling, we first input the $1 \times 5K$-dimensional state s_t into the policy and value networks. Then, the policy network outputs a $1 \times K$-dimensional probability distribution $\pi(a_t|s_t; \theta_{p,\mathbb{T}})$, where each probability ranges from 0 to 1, and the summation of the output K probabilities is 1. The value network outputs a value $V(s_t; \theta_{v,\mathbb{T}})$, which is a real number. Finally, we store the sample $(s_t, a_t, r_t, V(s_t; \theta_{v,\mathbb{T}}))$ generated by the interaction of the agent and the environment in an experience buffer D. When the size of experience buffer reaches $2N - 1$, we perform training based on the first N samples (lines 13–19). For each sample at time t, the advantage function is calculated in line 15. To obtain the advantage function, we first make cumulative the discounted reward for this sample (we only consider an episode consisting of N consecutive samples after this sample and ignore the discounted reward after N samples) by,

$$Q_\pi(s_t, a_t; \theta_{p,\mathbb{T}}) = \sum_{i=0}^{N-1} \gamma^i r_{t+i}, t \in \{t_0, t_0 + N - 1\}, \tag{2}$$

where γ is the discount factor, $0 < \gamma < 1$. Then, the advantage of each action taken can be obtained by,

$$A(s_t, a_t; \theta_{p,\mathbb{T}}, \theta_{v,\mathbb{T}}) = Q_\pi(s_t, a_t; \theta_{p,\mathbb{T}}) - V(s_t; \theta_{v,\mathbb{T}}). \tag{3}$$

Equation (3) indicates how much better the actual selected action is than the average.

Note that an episode is defined to consist of N consecutive samples, where N is equal to batch size. This way, all samples needed to calculate the advantage function can be found in the experience buffer [14].

Then, the objective function of policy network $L_{\theta_{p,\mathbb{T}}}$ and the loss function of value network $L_{\theta_{v,\mathbb{T}}}$ can be used to calculate the gradient of the policy and the value network, and then the global parameters $\theta^*_{p,\mathbb{T}}$ and $\theta^*_{v,\mathbb{T}}$ can be updated according to the gradient (line 18). $L_{\theta_{p,\mathbb{T}}}$ and $L_{\theta_{v,\mathbb{T}}}$ can be expressed as follows:

$$\begin{aligned} L_{\theta_{p,\mathbb{T}}} = &- \sum_{t=t_0}^{t_0+N-1} A(s_t, a_t; \theta_{p,\mathbb{T}}, \theta_{v,\mathbb{T}}) \log \pi(a_t|s_t; \theta_{p,\mathbb{T}}) \\ &- \alpha \sum_{t=t_0}^{t_0+N-1} \sum_{a_t \in \{1,2,\cdots,K\}} \pi(a_t|s; \theta_{p,\mathbb{T}}) \log \pi(a_t|s; \theta_{p,\mathbb{T}}), \end{aligned} \tag{4}$$

$$L_{\theta_{v,\mathbb{T}}} = \sum_{t=t_0}^{t_0+N-1} A(s_t, a_t; \theta_{p,\mathbb{T}}, \theta_{v,\mathbb{T}})^2. \tag{5}$$

To increase the diversity of the actions, the second term of $L_{\theta_{p,\mathbb{T}}}$ introduces the policy entropy to improve the agent's ability to explore the environment, and α controls the strength of the entropy regularization term. β and η are the learning rates.

The stopping criterion is that the model has converged. Specifically, we trace the changing of the average blocking probabilities. If the difference between consecutive average blocking probabilities is smaller than a pre-defined threshold, we regard the model to be converged and therefore criterion is satisfied. Through the above steps with Algorithm 1, we train a teacher model that can improve its RMSA policy under a certain task.

Algorithm 1 Training algorithm of the teacher model.

```
Initialize: experience buffer D = ϕ, ε = 1.
while not stopping criterion do
    Initialize each thread-specific policy network and value network:
    θ_{p,T} ← θ*_{p,T}, θ_{v,T} ← θ*_{v,T}.
    while |D| < 2N − 1 do
        #SAMPLING
        Upon the TR(v_s, v_d, b) arriving, obtain the state s_t.
        Obtain π(a_t|s_t; θ_{p,T}) and V(s_t; θ_{v,T}) by the policy and the value network.
        With probability ε select an action a_t according to π(a_t|s_t; θ_{p,T}), otherwise a_t =
        argmax_a{π(a_t|s_t, θ_{p,T})}.
        Obtain reward r_t.
        Store sample (s_t, a_t, r_t, V(s_t; θ_{v,T})) in D.
    end while
    #TRAINING
    For the first N samples (t ∈ {t_0, t_0 + N − 1}) in the experience buffer D.
    for t ∈ {t_0, t_0 + N − 1} do
        Calculate A(s_t, a_t; θ_{p,T}, θ_{v,T}) by Equation (3).
    end for
    Calculate L_{θ_{p,T}} and L_{θ_{v,T}} by Equations (4) and (5).
    Obtain the policy network and value network gradients dθ_{p,T} and dθ_{v,T} with L_{θ_{p,T}}
    and L_{θ_{v,T}}.
    Global parameters θ*_{p,T} and θ*_{v,T} can be updated by:
    θ*_{p,T} ← θ*_{p,T} − β dθ_{v,T} and θ*_{v,T} ← θ*_{v,T} − η dθ_{v,T}.
    Delete the first N samples in D and set ε = max{ε − ε_0, ε_min}.
end while
```

4.5. Student Model

Due to the similarities between tasks, we try to use the well-trained teacher model to "teach" the student model to learn the optimal RMSA policy for student tasks, as shown in Step 2 of Figure 1. This process is described in more detail in Step 2 of Figure 2. In this way, the student model adjusts its training according to the experience knowledge of the teacher model, in order to expect faster training speed or better performance.

Distillation is a method to transfer experience knowledge from a teacher model $\mathbb{T}$ to a student model $\mathbb{S}$. To transfer the knowledge, a straightforward method is to minimize the distance between the output of the student model and the teacher model. Because the action probability distribution of the output of policy network reflects the learned RMSA policy, we use cross-entropy to fit the output of the two models' policy networks. In order to transfer more knowledge, the teacher model can utilize a relaxed (higher-temperature) softmax than the one used during training [21]. Choose a temperature τ, the outputs of the teacher model's and the student model's policy network are processed by softmax functions to obtain the distributions: $q_\tau(s_t, \theta_{p,\mathbb{T}})$ and $q_\tau(s_t, \theta_{p,\mathbb{S}})$,

$$q_\tau(s_t, \theta_{p,\mathbb{T}}) = \text{softmax}(\frac{\pi(a_t|s_t;\theta_{p,\mathbb{T}})}{\tau}), \tag{6}$$

$$q_\tau(s_t, \theta_{p,\mathbb{S}}) = \text{softmax}(\frac{\pi(a_t|s_t;\theta_{p,\mathbb{S}})}{\tau}). \tag{7}$$

The softmax$(\cdot)$ is defined by:

$$\text{softmax}(i) = \frac{e^i}{\sum_j e^j}. \tag{8}$$

Algorithm 2 describes in detail the training process of the student model. The sampling part is same as the teacher model. When the training conditions are met, we first calculate the cumulative discounted reward for each sample (we only consider the first N samples and ignore the discounted reward after N samples) by:

$$Q_\pi(s_t, a_t; \theta_{p,\mathbb{S}}) = \sum_{i=0}^{N-1} \gamma^i r_{t+i}, t \in \{t_0, t_0 + N - 1\} \tag{9}$$

The advantage of each action can be calculated by:

$$A(s_t, a_t; \theta_{p,\mathbb{S}}, \theta_{v,\mathbb{S}}) = Q_\pi(s_t, a_t; \theta_{p,\mathbb{S}}) - V(s_t; \theta_{v,\mathbb{S}}). \tag{10}$$

Let $H(\cdot,\cdot)$ be the cross-entropy function. Then, the similarity between the student model's and the teacher model's policy network can be increased by minimizing the objective function given below:

$$L^{PD}_{\theta_{p,\mathbb{S}}} = \sum_{t=t_0}^{t_0+N-1} H(q_\tau(s_t, \theta_{p,\mathbb{T}}), q_\tau(s_t, \theta_{p,\mathbb{S}})). \tag{11}$$

During the distillation stage, although the value network did not directly obtain the experience knowledge from the teacher model by cross-entropy fitting, the output of the student model's policy network trained via policy distillation affected the generation of the samples, which indirectly affects the training of the value network.

The loss function $L_{\theta_{v,\mathbb{S}}}$ of the student model's value network during distillation is given by:

$$L_{\theta_{v,\mathbb{S}}} = \sum_{t=t_0}^{t_0+N-1} A(s_t, a_t; \theta_{p,\mathbb{S}}, \theta_{v,\mathbb{S}})^2. \tag{12}$$

By optimizing the objective and the loss function above, we can transfer knowledge from the teacher model to the student model.

When the student model is initialized, its DRL agents start from tabula rasa, which means that they have no professional knowledge about the optical network environment of the task, and therefore, they need to learn the optimal RMSA policy by exploring the state and action space for a long time. Therefore, we transfer the knowledge of the teacher model to the poorly performing student model through distillation to reduce ineffective exploration of the student model.

However, although the teacher model is well-trained for the teacher tasks, in the process of policy distillation, its policy has limitations guiding the training of the student model for the student tasks. Therefore, we conduct the policy distillation for the beginning M $TR(s, d, b)$ requests, and then let the student model learn by itself as shown in Step 3 of Figure 2. The objective function and loss function of the first M traffic requests are given by Equations (11) and (12), and the afterward is given by:

$$\begin{aligned} L_{\theta^-_{p,\mathbb{S}}} = &- \sum_{t=t_0}^{t_0+N-1} A(s_t, a_t; \theta^-_{p,\mathbb{S}}, \theta^-_{v,\mathbb{S}}) \log \pi(a_t|s_t; \theta^-_{p,\mathbb{S}}) \\ &- \alpha \sum_{t=t_0}^{t_0+N-1} \sum_{a_t \in \{1,2,\cdots,K\}} \pi(a_t|s; \theta^-_{p,\mathbb{S}}) \log \pi(a_t|s_t; \theta^-_{p,\mathbb{S}}), \end{aligned} \tag{13}$$

$$L_{\theta^-_{v,\mathbb{S}}} = \sum_{t=t_0}^{t_0+N-1} A(s_t, a_t; \theta^-_{p,\mathbb{S}}, \theta^-_{v,\mathbb{S}})^2. \tag{14}$$

where $\theta^-_{p,\mathbb{S}}$ and $\theta^-_{v,\mathbb{S}}$ are the parameters of the policy and the value network of the student model during self-learning, respectively.

Algorithm 2 Training algorithm of student model.

```
Initialize: experience buffer D = ϕ, ε = 1.
while not stopping criterion do
    Initialize each thread-specific policy network and critic network by:
    θ_{p,S} ← θ*_{p,S}, θ_{v,S} ← θ*_{v,S}.
    while |D| < 2D − 1 do
        #SAMPLING
        Upon the TR(v_s, v_d, b) arriving, obtain the state s_t.
        Obtain π(a_t|s_t; θ_{p,S}) and V(s_t; θ_{v,S}) by the policy and the value network.
        With probability ε select an action a_t according to π(a_t|s_t; θ_{p,S}), otherwise a_t =
        argmax_a{π(a_t|s_t; θ_{p,S})}.
        Obtain reward r_t and store sample (s_t, a_t, r_t, V(s_t; θ_{v,S})) in D.
    end while
    #TRAINING
    if before M requests then
        #DISTILLATION
        For the first N samples (t ∈ {t_0, t_0 + N − 1}) in the experience buffer D.
        for t ∈ {t_0, t_0 + N − 1} do
            Calculate A(s_t, a_t; θ_{p,S}, θ_{v,S}) by Equation (10).
        end for
        Obtaining training samples {(s_t^j, q_T(s_t^j, θ_{p,T}))}_{j=1}^N.
        Calculate L^{PD}_{θ_{p,S}} by Equation (11) and L_{θ_{v,S}} by Equation (12).
        Obtain the policy network and value network gradients dθ_{p,S} and dθ_{v,S} with L^{PD}_{θ_{p,S}},
        L_{θ_{v,S}}.
        Global parameters θ*_{p,S} and θ*_{v,S} can be updated by:
        θ*_{p,S} ← θ*_{p,S} − βdθ_{v,S} and θ*_{v,S} ← θ*_{v,S} − ηdθ_{v,S}.
        Delete the first N samples in D and set ε = max{ε - ε_0, ε_min}.
    else
        #SELF-LEARNING
        θ^{−,*}_{p,S} = θ*_{p,S}, θ^{−,*}_{v,S} = θ*_{v,S}.
        For the first N samples (t ∈ {t_0, t_0 + N − 1}) in the experience buffer D.
        for t ∈ {t_0, t_0 + N − 1} do
            Calculate A(s_t, a_t; θ^−_{p,S}, θ^−_{v,S}) by Equation (10).
        end for
        Calculate L_{θ^−_{p,S}} and L_{θ^−_{v,S}} by Equations (13) and (14).
        Obtain the policy network and value network gradients dθ^−_{p,S} and dθ^−_{v,S} with L_{θ^−_{p,S}}
        and L_{θ^−_{v,S}}.
        Global parameters θ^{−,*}_{p,S} and θ^{−,*}_{v,S} can be updated by:
        θ^{−,*}_{p,S} ← θ^{−,*}_{p,S} − βdθ^−_{v,S} and θ^{−,*}_{v,S} ← θ^{−,*}_{v,S} − ηdθ^−_{v,S}.
        Delete the first N samples in D and set ε = max{ε - ε_0, ε_min}.
    end if
end while
```

5. Performance Evaluation

In this section, we introduce the simulation results of the proposed policy distillation design with the EONs. We applied the proposed method to three different scenarios: (1) policy distillation between different traffic patterns, (2) policy distillation between different topologies, and (3) policy distillation between different traffic patterns and topologies.

5.1. Parameter Settings

The common parameters used in the simulations are explained in below. For the simulations in Sections 5.2–5.5, these common parameters are used unless otherwise specified. Moreover, for convenience, the symbols of these key common parameters and their corresponding meanings and values are listed in Table 2.

Table 2. Key parameters and their corresponding meaning and values.

	Notation	Meaning	Value
DRL Environment (i.e., EONs)		Number of frequency slots per link	100
	B	Bandwidth requirement	$[25, 100]$ Gb/s
	K	Number of candidate paths	5
		Bandwidth of a spectrum slot	12.5 GHz
DRL agent	L	Number of hidden layers (teacher model/student model)	8/5
	H	Number of neurons for each hidden layer (teacher model/student model)	256/128
DRL training	γ	Discount rate	0.95
	β/η	Learning rate	1×10^{-5}
	α	Entropy regularization coefficient	0.01
	N	Mini-batch size	200
	M	Number of traffic requests for distillation	100,000
	τ	Temperature	5
	ε_{min}	Final explore rate	0.05

All the topologies used in the simulations are shown in Figure 3, where the weight of each edge of the topology represents the physical length of each link, and they will be used to calculate the FSs in Equation (1). We set the capacity of each fiber link to be 100 FSs. The traffic requests are generated according to independent Poisson processes. In order to ensure that the blocking probabilities of different topologies can fall within a reasonable range, we set a different traffic load for all the different topologies. The traffic patterns and the load for different simulation scenarios will be described in detail later. In addition, the bandwidth requirement of each traffic request is evenly distributed within $[25, 100]$ Gb/s. The number of the shortest paths K is set to be 5, which means the DRL agent is to select a path from 5 candidate paths.

In terms of the neural network architecture, for the teacher model, the policy and value networks both have five hidden layers, with 256 neurons per layer. For the student model, the policy and value networks both have five hidden layers, with 128 neurons per layer. ReLU is used as the activation function for the hidden layers. We set the discount factor γ, the learning rate β and η, the coefficient of the entropy regularization term α, and the temperature of distillation τ to be 0.95, 1×10^{-5}, 1×10^{-5}, 0.01, and 5, respectively. In addition, the number of traffic requests for distillation M is 100,000. During the training, the mini-batch gradient descent algorithm and the Adam optimizer are used, with the mini-batch size N to be 200. The exploration rate ε is set to be 1 at the beginning and gradually decays by ε_0 (set to be 10^{-5}) units during each training process until it reaches ε_{min}, which is 0.05.

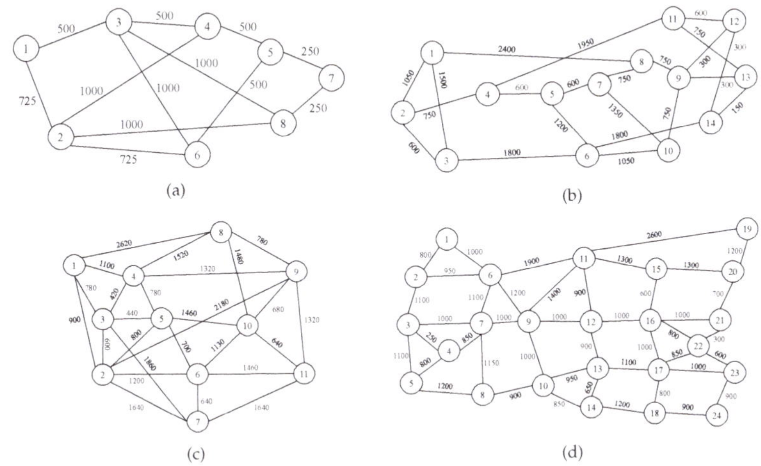

Figure 3. Optical network topologies: (**a**) 8-node, (**b**) 14-node NSFNET, (**c**) 11-node COST 239, and (**d**) 24-node US Backbone.

5.2. Policy Distillation for Different Traffic Patterns

We first evaluate the performance of our proposed scheme for different traffic patterns and the same network topology. In this subsection, both the teacher and the student models are trained over the same network topology: the 14-node NSFNET. The traffic patterns are different. We set the model trained under a uniformly distributed traffic pattern as the teacher model and the model applied for the non-uniformly distributed traffic patterns as the student models.

The traffic pattern is denoted by an $N \times N$ matrix TP, where N(=14) denotes the number of nodes of the NSFNET. The element TP_{ij} represents the traffic load ratio from node i to node j, where $TP_{ij} = 0$ when $i = j$. If TP_{ij} are the same for all i-j pairs ($i \neq j$), the traffic pattern is uniformly distributed. Otherwise, it is non-uniformly distributed. For the student model, we designed three different non-uniform traffic patterns, namely pattern A, pattern B, and pattern C, as shown in Figure 4a,c,e. They correspond to the following three settings:

- Pattern A: non-uniform; $TP_{ij} = TP_{ji}, \forall i,j$; $TP_{ij} \neq 0, \forall i \neq j$.
- Pattern B: non-uniform; $TP_{ij} = TP_{ji}, \forall i,j$; exist $TP_{ij} = 0$ when $i \neq j$.
- Pattern C: non-uniform; exist $TP_{ij} \neq TP_{ji}$; exist $TP_{ij} = 0$ when $i \neq j$.

For the uniform traffic patterns, the arrival rate is 12 arrivals per time unit and the average service time is 16 time units, while for the non-uniform traffic pattern, the arrival rate is 16 arrivals per time unit and the average service time is 25 time units. Table 3 records the traffic loads for all the traffic patterns in Section 5.2.

Figure 4b,d,f show the evolution of the simulation results as the number of requests increase, with the blocking probability calculated every 1000 $TR(v_s, v_d, b)$ requests. The blue lines represent the blocking probabilities of the agents learning from scratch without policy distillation ("w/o PD"), while the red lines represent the blocking probabilities of the agents that learn with the policy distilled from the teacher model which is trained with the uniform traffic pattern ("PD-14-Node-uniform"). The green lines represent the blocking probabilities of the baseline algorithm: the K-shortest-path routing and first-fit spectrum allocation (KSP-FF) [36]. The "KSP-FF" in Figure 4b,d,f are the results of applying the KSP-FF algorithm to pattern A, pattern B, and pattern C of the 14-node NSFNET topology, respectively. We can see that, by policy distillation ("PD-14-Node-uniform"), the agent converges faster and achieves lower blocking probabilities, compared to the cases without policy distillation ("w/o PD"). Specifically, the blocking probability reductions are 10%,

10.7%, and 3.6% with pattern A, pattern B, and pattern C, respectively. These results imply that the policy distillation does well in traffic pattern variation tasks.

$$\begin{bmatrix} 0 & 2 & 1 & 1 & 1 & 4 & 1 & 1 & 2 & 1 & 1 & 1 & 1 & 1 \\ 2 & 0 & 2 & 1 & 8 & 2 & 1 & 5 & 3 & 5 & 1 & 5 & 1 & 4 \\ 1 & 2 & 0 & 2 & 3 & 2 & 11 & 20 & 5 & 2 & 1 & 1 & 1 & 2 \\ 1 & 1 & 2 & 0 & 1 & 1 & 2 & 1 & 2 & 2 & 1 & 2 & 1 & 2 \\ 1 & 8 & 3 & 1 & 0 & 3 & 3 & 7 & 3 & 3 & 1 & 5 & 2 & 5 \\ 4 & 2 & 2 & 1 & 3 & 0 & 2 & 1 & 2 & 2 & 1 & 1 & 1 & 2 \\ 1 & 1 & 11 & 2 & 3 & 2 & 0 & 9 & 4 & 20 & 1 & 8 & 1 & 4 \\ 1 & 5 & 20 & 1 & 7 & 1 & 9 & 0 & 27 & 7 & 2 & 3 & 2 & 4 \\ 2 & 3 & 5 & 2 & 3 & 2 & 4 & 27 & 0 & 75 & 2 & 9 & 3 & 1 \\ 1 & 5 & 2 & 2 & 3 & 2 & 20 & 7 & 75 & 0 & 1 & 1 & 2 & 1 \\ 1 & 1 & 1 & 1 & 1 & 1 & 1 & 2 & 2 & 1 & 0 & 2 & 1 & 61 \\ 1 & 5 & 1 & 2 & 5 & 1 & 8 & 3 & 9 & 1 & 2 & 0 & 1 & 81 \\ 1 & 1 & 1 & 1 & 2 & 1 & 1 & 2 & 3 & 2 & 1 & 1 & 0 & 2 \\ 1 & 4 & 2 & 2 & 5 & 2 & 4 & 4 & 1 & 1 & 61 & 81 & 2 & 0 \end{bmatrix}$$

(a) pattern A

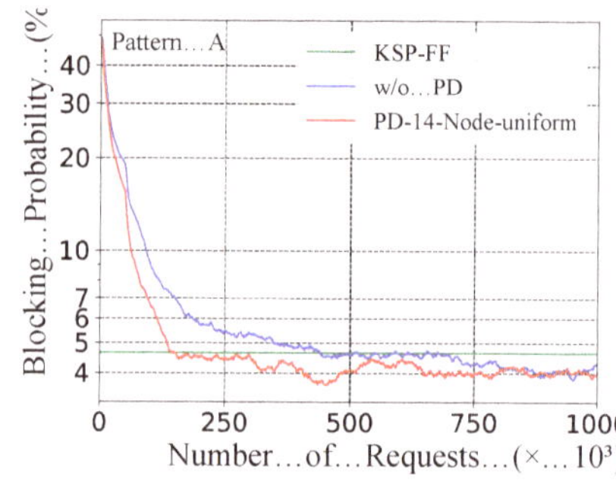

(b)

$$\begin{bmatrix} 0 & 2 & 1 & 1 & 1 & 4 & 0 & 1 & 2 & 1 & 0 & 1 & 1 & 1 \\ 2 & 0 & 2 & 0 & 8 & 2 & 1 & 5 & 3 & 5 & 1 & 5 & 1 & 0 \\ 1 & 2 & 0 & 2 & 3 & 2 & 0 & 20 & 0 & 2 & 0 & 1 & 1 & 2 \\ 1 & 0 & 2 & 0 & 1 & 1 & 2 & 1 & 2 & 0 & 1 & 2 & 1 & 2 \\ 1 & 8 & 3 & 1 & 0 & 3 & 0 & 7 & 3 & 3 & 1 & 0 & 0 & 5 \\ 4 & 2 & 2 & 1 & 3 & 0 & 2 & 1 & 2 & 2 & 1 & 1 & 1 & 0 \\ 0 & 1 & 0 & 2 & 0 & 2 & 0 & 9 & 0 & 20 & 0 & 8 & 0 & 4 \\ 1 & 5 & 20 & 1 & 7 & 1 & 9 & 0 & 27 & 0 & 2 & 0 & 2 & 4 \\ 2 & 3 & 0 & 2 & 3 & 2 & 0 & 27 & 0 & 75 & 2 & 9 & 3 & 0 \\ 1 & 5 & 2 & 0 & 3 & 2 & 20 & 0 & 75 & 0 & 1 & 1 & 2 & 1 \\ 0 & 1 & 0 & 1 & 1 & 1 & 0 & 2 & 2 & 1 & 0 & 2 & 1 & 61 \\ 1 & 5 & 1 & 2 & 0 & 1 & 8 & 0 & 9 & 1 & 2 & 0 & 1 & 8 \\ 1 & 1 & 1 & 1 & 0 & 1 & 0 & 2 & 3 & 2 & 1 & 1 & 0 & 2 \\ 1 & 0 & 2 & 2 & 5 & 0 & 4 & 4 & 0 & 1 & 61 & 8 & 2 & 0 \end{bmatrix}$$

(c) pattern B

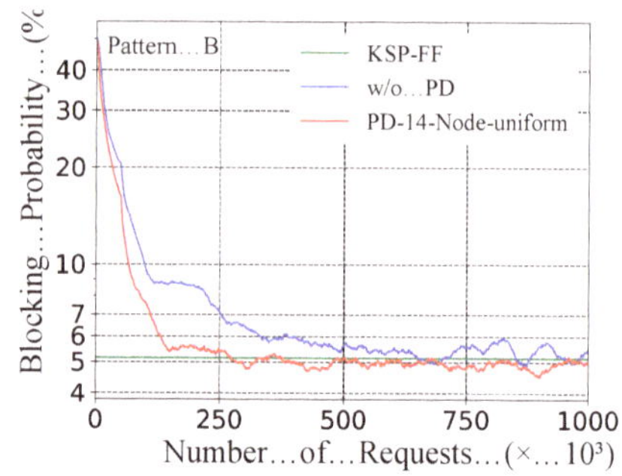

(d)

$$\begin{bmatrix} 0 & 9 & 1 & 10 & 1 & 4 & 0 & 1 & 2 & 1 & 0 & 1 & 9 & 1 \\ 2 & 0 & 2 & 0 & 8 & 2 & 1 & 5 & 3 & 5 & 1 & 5 & 1 & 0 \\ 1 & 2 & 0 & 2 & 3 & 2 & 0 & 20 & 0 & 2 & 12 & 1 & 1 & 2 \\ 11 & 0 & 2 & 0 & 1 & 1 & 2 & 1 & 2 & 0 & 1 & 2 & 7 & 2 \\ 1 & 8 & 3 & 1 & 0 & 7 & 0 & 7 & 2 & 3 & 1 & 0 & 0 & 5 \\ 4 & 2 & 3 & 1 & 3 & 0 & 2 & 1 & 2 & 2 & 1 & 1 & 1 & 0 \\ 0 & 1 & 0 & 2 & 0 & 2 & 0 & 9 & 0 & 18 & 0 & 9 & 0 & 4 \\ 6 & 5 & 20 & 1 & 7 & 1 & 9 & 0 & 27 & 0 & 2 & 0 & 2 & 4 \\ 2 & 3 & 24 & 2 & 3 & 2 & 0 & 25 & 0 & 75 & 2 & 9 & 3 & 8 \\ 1 & 15 & 2 & 0 & 3 & 2 & 20 & 0 & 60 & 0 & 1 & 1 & 2 & 1 \\ 0 & 1 & 0 & 11 & 1 & 1 & 0 & 2 & 2 & 1 & 0 & 2 & 1 & 61 \\ 1 & 5 & 1 & 2 & 0 & 1 & 8 & 0 & 9 & 1 & 2 & 0 & 1 & 8 \\ 1 & 4 & 1 & 1 & 6 & 1 & 6 & 5 & 13 & 21 & 1 & 1 & 0 & 2 \\ 1 & 0 & 2 & 2 & 5 & 0 & 4 & 6 & 0 & 1 & 61 & 8 & 2 & 0 \end{bmatrix}$$

(e) pattern C

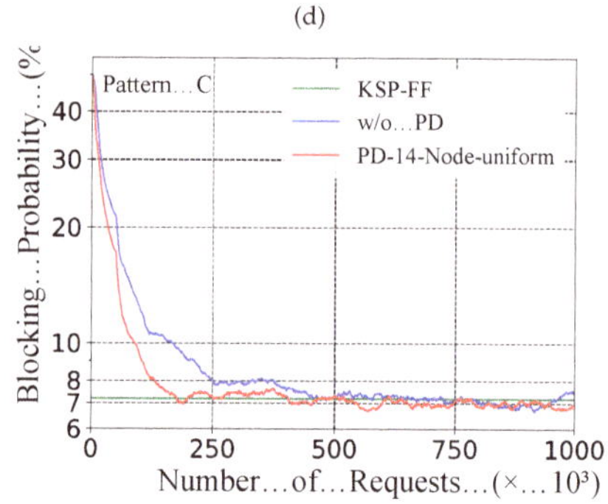

(f)

Figure 4. (**a**,**c**,**e**): The non-uniform traffic patterns for the student models. (**b**,**d**,**f**): Blocking probabilities under different traffic patterns ((**b**) pattern A, (**d**) pattern B, and (**f**) pattern C) for student model with policy distillation, student model without policy distillation, and the baseline KSP-FF algorithm.

Table 3. Traffic loads for all traffic patterns in Section 5.2.

	Topology	Traffic Pattern	Load
Teacher model	14-node NSFNET	uniform	0.75
Student model	14-node NSFNET	pattern A	0.64
	14-node NSFNET	pattern B	0.64
	14-node NSFNET	pattern C	0.64

5.3. Policy Distillation for Different Topologies

We have also conducted simulations for different topologies to evaluate the performance of the policy distillation scheme. In this case, we train two teacher models in the 8-node topology and the 14-node NSFNET topology, while the other two topologies (the 11-node COST 239 topology and the 24-node US Backbone topology) are used for training the student models. The traffic patterns for all the teacher and student models are the same in terms of distributions: uniform. For the 8-node, 11-node COST239, 14-node NSFNET, and 24-node US Backbone topology, the arrival rate is 14, 16, 12, and 12 arrivals per time unit, and the average service time is 25, 25, 16, and 14 time units, respectively. Table 4 records the traffic loads for all the traffic patterns in Section 5.3.

Table 4. Traffic loads for all traffic patterns in Section 5.3.

	Topology	Traffic Pattern	Load
Teacher model	8-node	uniform	0.56
	14-node NSFNET	uniform	0.75
Student model	11-node COST 239	uniform	0.64
	24-node US Backbone	uniform	0.86

Figure 5a,b show the evolution of the blocking probability by the student models trained in different topologies. We denote the agents that learn with the policy distilled from the teacher models for the 8-node and 14-node NSFNET as "PD-Eight-Node" and "PD-14-Node", respectively. The KSP-FF algorithm is adopted as the baseline, it is applied to the training environment of the uniform distribution 11-node COST239 and 24-node US Backbone topology, respectively, and the results of the "KSP-FF" in Figure 5a,b are obtained. We can observe from Figure 5a that, for the student model trained in the 11-node COST239 topological environment, the cases with policy distillation ("PD-Eight-Node" and "PD-14-Node") reach the performance level of "KSP-FF" faster than the case without the policy distillation ("w/o PD"). Specifically, the blocking performance of the "PD-Eight-Node" and "PD-14-Node" matches that of the "KSP-FF" after about 150,000 and 244,000 traffic requests, but the "w/o PD" consistently performs worse than the "KSP-FF" before 1,000,000 traffic requests.

Similar results are observed in Figure 5b when the student model is trained in the 24-node US Backbone topological environment. Moreover, it can be seen from Figure 5a,b that the cases with the policy distillation ("PD-Eight-Node" and "PD-14-Node") have lower blocking probabilities after convergence compared with the case without the policy distillation ("w/o PD"). These results show that when the topology changes, policy distillation can assist the policy learning in the new environment. Figure 5c,d show the complementary cumulative distribution function (CCDF) with a blocking reduction compared to the "KSP-FF" from different schemes after training with 750,000 traffic requests. For the COST 239 topology, the "PD-Eight-Node" and "PD-14-Node" outperform the "KSP-FF" for around 54% and 52% cases, respectively, while the "w/o PD" only outperforms the "KSP-FF" for around 33% of the cases. For the US Backbone topology, the "PD-Eight-Node" and "PD-14-Node" outperform the "KSP-FF" for around 55.8% and 46.3% of the cases, respectively, while the "w/o PD" outperforms the "KSP-FF" for around 29.5% of the cases. This indicates the effectiveness of policy distillation.

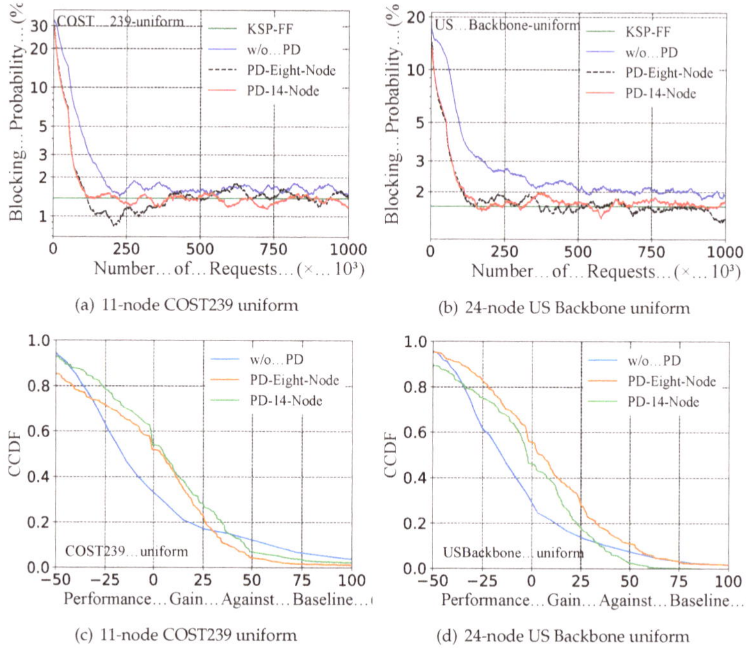

Figure 5. (**a**,**b**): Blocking probability in training with different topologies, and (**c**,**d**): complementary cumulative distribution function (CCDF) with blocking reduction compared to KSP-FF algorithm after training with 750,000 traffic requests.

5.4. Policy Distillation for Different Traffic Patterns and Topologies

In this subsection, we change both the traffic patterns and the network topologies for the policy distillation. Similar with Section 5.3, two teacher models are trained under the 8-node topology and the 14-node NSFNET topology, while the student models are applied for the 11-node COST 239 topology and the 24-node US Backbone topology. Besides that, the teacher models are trained under uniform traffic patterns, while the student models are trained under a non-uniform traffic pattern. We have conducted four sets of simulations, denoted as Simulation T-1 to T-4. Detailed simulation settings of the student models are shown in Table 5, and the traffic loads of all the traffic patterns in Section 5.4 are shown in Table 6.

The simulation results are shown in Figure 6a–d. First, we can see that compared with the case without policy distillation ("w/o PD"), taking policy distillation from an eight-node-topology-and-uniform-traffic-pattern teacher ("PD-Eight-Node") and an NSFNET-topology-and-uniform-traffic-pattern teacher ("PD-14-Node") can effectively accelerate the training of student models and obtain lower blocking probabilities for all simulations. Specifically, the "PD-Eight-Node" achieves blocking reductions of 8.3%, 11.9%, 7.8%, and 9.8% for simulations T-1∼T-4, respectively. For the "PD-14-Node", the blocking probability reductions are 7.5%, 11%, 3.9%, and 2.4% for simulations T-1∼T-4, respectively. Meanwhile, Table 7 records the time (approximately) spent by different schemes when the blocking performance reaches the level of the "KSP-FF" in Simulation T-1∼Simulation T-4. In this section, the "KSP-FF" in Figure 6a–d are the results of applying the KSP-FF algorithm to the training environment of Simulation T-1∼Simulation T-4, respectively. We can notice that the "PD-Eight-Node" and "PD-14-Node" learn faster. In Simulation T-1∼Simulation T-4, when the blocking performance reaches that of the KSP-FF, the training time of the "PD-Eight-Node" is reduced by 31.4%, 14%, 57%, and 60.3% compared with that of the "w/o PD", respectively. A similar trend can be seen between the "PD-14-Node" and "w/o PD".

Table 5. Simulation settings for the student models in Section 4.4.

		Student Model
Simulation T-1	Topology	11-node COST239
	Traffic pattern	pattern D (non-uniform; $TP_{ij} = TP_{ji}, \forall i, j$; $TP_{ij} \neq 0, \forall i \neq j$)
Simulation T-2	Topology	11-node COST239
	Traffic pattern	pattern E (non-uniform; $TP_{ij} = TP_{ji}, \forall i, j$; exist $TP_{ij} = 0$ when $i \neq j$)
Simulation T-3	Topology	24-node US Backbone
	Traffic pattern	pattern F (non-uniform; $TP_{ij} = TP_{ji}, \forall i, j$; $TP_{ij} \neq 0, \forall i \neq j$)
Simulation T-4	Topology	24-node US Backbone
	Traffic pattern	pattern G (non-uniform; $TP_{ij} = TP_{ji}, \forall i, j$; exist $TP_{ij} = 0$ when $i \neq j$)

Table 6. Traffic loads for all traffic patterns in Section 5.4.

	Topology	Traffic Pattern	Load
Teacher model	8-node	uniform	0.56
	14-node NSFNET	uniform	0.75
Student model	11-node COST 239	pattern D	0.64
	11-node COST 239	pattern E	0.64
	24-node US Backbone	pattern F	0.86
	24-node US Backbone	pattern G	0.86

Table 7. Training duration when performance reaches KSP-FF (in seconds).

	"PD-Eight-Node"	"PD-14-Node"	"w/o PD"
Simulation T-1	1963	1956	2863
Simulation T-2	1939	1895	2258
Simulation T-3	3131	2868	7277
Simulation T-4	3743	3373	9427

For all of the above simulations, we only use the KSP-FF heuristic algorithm as the baseline. As can be seen from the experimental figures, some DRL-based approaches can only achieve a comparable performance with the KSP-FF. For such results, we believe that the performance of the DRL-based approaches is limited by the design of the reward. In this regard, our work [37] has investigated the reward design, and the results are significantly better than the KSP-FF in terms of the blocking probability. However, the focus of this paper is not on the reward design. We pay more attention to the performance comparison before and after the introduction of knowledge distillation. From the above simulations, it can be seen that the blocking performance can be improved by integrating the knowledge distillation method.

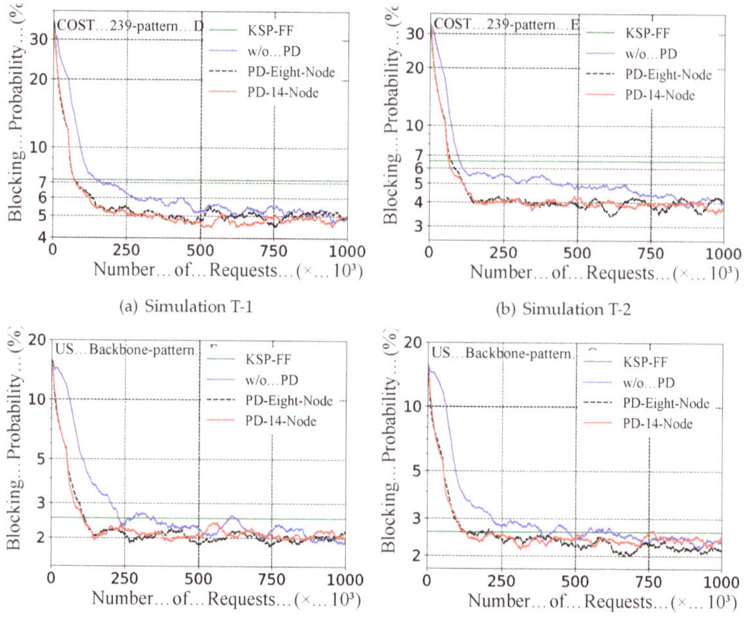

(a) Simulation T-1

(b) Simulation T-2

(c) Simulation T-3

(d) Simulation T-4

Figure 6. Blocking probability of different topologies with different non-uniform traffic patterns.

5.5. Policy Distillation with Different Neural Network Size of the Teacher Model

We have also investigated the effect of the size of the teacher model's neural network on the performance of the proposed policy distillation design. Specifically, we design three different neural network settings for the teacher model: (1) three hidden layers with 64 neurons per layer (3 × 64) , (2) five hidden layers with 128 neurons per layer (5 × 128), and (3) eight hidden layers with 258 neurons per layer (8 × 256). The teacher model is trained under the uniform traffic pattern over the 14-node NSFNET, and the student models are trained under the uniform traffic pattern over the COST239 topology. The arrival rate and average service time are the same as in Section 5.2. The results of the blocking probability are shown in Figure 7.

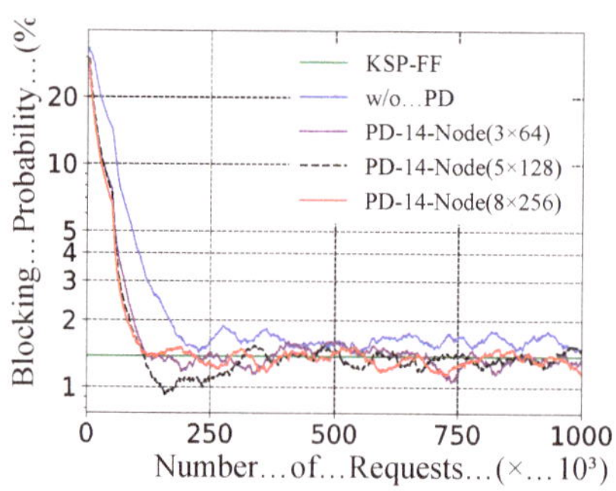

Figure 7. Blocking probability in training with different size of teacher model's neural network.

The result shows that teacher models with different neural network sizes (PD-14-Node (3 × 64), PD-14-Node (5 × 128), and PD-14-Node (8 × 256)) can carry out policy distillation to the student models. This shows that the proposed policy distillation scheme is not limited by the size of the teacher models' neural network. When the neural network architecture of the teacher model and the student model are different, policy learning with policy distillation can also be carried out. This allows knowledge transfer in a broader context.

6. Conclusions

This paper proposes a deep reinforcement learning-based RMSA policy distillation design for the elastic optical networks. It allows the knowledge transfer from a well-trained teacher model under one training environment to a student model under a different environment, so that the training of the latter is accelerated with a better final performance. One highlight is that the student model and the teacher model can be different in terms of the neural network architecture. This allows the knowledge transfer in a broader context. Our method is verified by the simulations of the policy distillation over different traffic patterns and network topologies.

One limitation of our proposal is that the input dimension of the teacher model and the student model must be the same. Recall that the input represents the state of the elastic optical network; the above limitation poses constraints on the state representation. How to break this limitation can be considered for future work. Meanwhile, the performance of the learned RMSA policy in real optical networks should be studied experimentally in future work.

Author Contributions: B.T.: Conceptualization, Methodology, Software, Writing—original draft. Y.-C.H.: Conceptualization, Validation, Writing—review & editing. Y.X.: Conceptualization, Writing—review. W.Z.: Supervision, Writing—review. All authors have read and agreed to the published version of the manuscript.

Funding: This research was funded by the National Natural Science Foundation of China (62006084), the Basic and Applied Basic Research Foundation of Guangdong Province (2020A1515111110), and the Guangdong Science and Technology Department (2016A010101020, 2016A010101021, and 2016A010101022).

Institutional Review Board Statement: Not applicable.

Informed Consent Statement: Not applicable.

Data Availability Statement: Not applicable.

Acknowledgments: The authors would like to express their sincere thanks to the Editors and Referees for their enthusiastic guidance and help.

Conflicts of Interest: The authors declare no conflict of interest.

References

1. Cisco Visual Networking Index: Forecast and Trends, 2017–2022. Available online: https://www.cisco.com/c/en_in/index.html (accessed on 1 November 2018).
2. Jinno, M.; Takara, H.; Kozicki, B.; Tsukishima, Y.; Sone, Y.; Matsuoka, S. Spectrum-efficient and scalable elastic optical path network: architecture, benefits, and enabling technologies. *IEEE Commun. Mag.* **2009**, *47*, 66–73. [CrossRef]
3. Gerstel, O.; Jinno, M.; Lord, A.; Yoo, S.B. Elastic optical networking: A new dawn for the optical layer? *IEEE Commun. Mag.* **2012**, *50*, s12–s20. [CrossRef]
4. Zang, H.; Jue, J.P.; Mukherjee, B. A review of routing and wavelength assignment approaches for wavelength-routed optical WDM networks. *Opt. Netw. Mag.* **2000**, *1*, 47–60.
5. Dinarte, H.A.; Correia, B.V.; Chaves, D.A.; Almeida, R.C. Routing and spectrum assignment: A metaheuristic for hybrid ordering selection in elastic optical networks. *Comput. Netw.* **2021**, *197*, 108287. [CrossRef]
6. Zhang, G.; De Leenheer, M.; Morea, A.; Mukherjee, B. A survey on OFDM-based elastic core optical networking. *IEEE Commun. Surv. Tutor.* **2012**, *15*, 65–87. [CrossRef]
7. Halder, J.; Acharya, T.; Chatterjee, M.; Bhattacharya, U. E-S-RSM-RSA: A novel energy and spectrum efficient regenerator aware multipath based survivable RSA in offline EON. *IEEE Trans. Green Commun. Netw.* **2021**, *5*, 1451–1466. [CrossRef]
8. Halder, J.; Acharya, T.; Bhattacharya, U. On crosstalk aware energy and spectrum efficient survivable RSCA scheme in offline SDM-EON *J. Netw. Syst. Manag.* **2022**, *30*, 6. [CrossRef]
9. Jia, W.B.; Xu, Z.Q.; Ding, Z.; Wang, K. An efficient routing and spectrum assignment algorithm using prediction for elastic optical networks. In Proceedings of the 2016 International Conference on Information System and Artificial Intelligence (ISAI), Hong Kong, China, 24–26 June 2016; pp. 89–93.

10. Cavalcante, M.; Pereira, H.; Chaves, D.; Almeida, R. Optimizing the cost function of power series routing algorithm for transparent elastic optical networks. *Opt. Switch. Netw.* **2018**, *29*, 57–64. [CrossRef]
11. Harai, H.; Murata, M.; Miyahara, H. Performance of alternate routing methods in all-optical switching networks. In Proceedings of the International Conference on Computer Communications (INFOCOM), Hong Kong, China, 24–26 June 1997; Volume 2, pp. 516–524.
12. Ramamurthy, R.; Mukherjee, B. Fixed-alternate routing and wavelength conversion in wavelength-routed optical networks. *IEEE/ACM Trans. Netw.* **2002**, *10*, 351–367. [CrossRef]
13. Rosa, A.; Cavdar, C.; Carvalho, S.; Costa, J.; Wosinska, L. Spectrum allocation policy modeling for elastic optical networks. In *High Capacity Optical Networks and Emerging/Enabling Technologies (HONET)*; IEEE: Piscataway, NJ, USA; New York, NY, USA, 2012 ; pp. 242–246.
14. Chen, X.; Li, B.; Proietti, R.; Lu, H.; Zhu, Z.; Yoo, S.B. DeepRMSA: A deep reinforcement learning framework for routing, modulation and spectrum assignment in elastic optical networks. *J. Light. Technol.* **2019**, *37*, 4155–4163. [CrossRef]
15. Huang, Y.C.; Zhang, J.; Yu, S. Self-learning routing for optical networks. In *Lecture Notes in Computer Science* ; Springer: Berlin/Heidelberg, Germany, 2020. pp. 467–478.
16. Zhao, Z.; Zhao, Y.; Li, Y.; Wang, F.; Li, X.; Han, D.; Zhang, J. Service restoration in multi-modal optical transport networks with reinforcement learning. *Opt. Express* **2021**, *29*, 3825–3840. [CrossRef] [PubMed]
17. Zhao, Y.; Yan, B.; Liu, D.; He, Y.; Wang, D.; Zhang, J. SOON: Self-optimizing optical networks with machine learning. *Opt. Express* **2018**, *26*, 28713–28726. [CrossRef]
18. Xu, L.; Huang, Y.C.; Xue, Y.; Hu, X. Spectrum continuity and contiguity aware state representation for deep reinforcement learning-based routing of EONs. In Proceedings of the IEEE Optoelectronics Global Conference (OGC), Shenzhen, China, 15–18 September 2021; pp. 73–76.
19. Tang, B.; Chen, J.; Huang, Y.C.; Xue, Y.; Zhou, W. Optical network routing by deep reinforcement learning and knowledge distillation. In Proceedings of the Asia Communications and Photonics Conference (ACP), Shanghai, China, 24–27 October 2021; pp. 1–3.
20. Chen, X.; Proietti, R.; Liu, C.Y.; Yoo, S.B. A multi-task-learning-based transfer deep reinforcement learning design for autonomic optical networks. *IEEE J. Sel. Areas Commun.* **2021**, *39*, 2878–2889. [CrossRef]
21. Rusu, A.A.; Colmenarejo, S.G.; Gulcehre, C.; Desjardins, G.; Kirkpatrick, J.; Pascanu, R.; Mnih, V.; Kavukcuoglu, K.; Hadsell, R. Policy distillation. In Proceedings of the International Conference on Learning Representations (ICLR), San Juan, Puerto Rico, 2–4 May 2016.
22. Gou, J.; Yu, B.; Maybank, S.; Tao, D. Knowledge distillation: a survey. *Int. J. Comput. Vision.* **2021**, *129*, 1789–1819. [CrossRef]
23. Chen, X.; Guo, J.; Zhu, Z.; Proietti, R.; Castro, A.; Yoo, S.B. Deep-RMSA: A deep-reinforcement-learning routing, modulation and spectrum assignment agent for elastic optical networks. In Proceedings of the Optical Fiber Communications Conference and Exposition (OFC), San Diego, CA, USA, 11–15 March 2018; pp. 1–3.
24. Yan, B.; Zhao, Y.; Li, Y.; Yu, X.; Zhang, J.; Wang, Y.; Yan, L.; Rahman, S. Actor-critic-based resource allocation for multi-modal optical networks. In Proceedings of the IEEE Globecom Workshops (GC Wkshps), Abu Dhabi, United Arab Emirates, 9–13 December 2018; pp. 1–6.
25. Suárez-Varela, J.; Mestres, A.; Yu, J.; Kuang, L.; Feng, H.; Cabellos-Aparicio, A.; Barlet-Ros, P. Routing in optical transport networks with deep reinforcement learning. *J. Opt. Commun. Netw.* **2019**, *11*, 547–558. [CrossRef]
26. Pujol-Perich, D.; Suárez-Varela, J.; Ferriol, M.; Xiao, S.; Wu, B.; Cabellos-Aparicio, A.; Barlet-Ros, P. IGNNITION: Bridging the gap between graph neural networks and networking systems. *IEEE Netw.* **2021**, *35*, 171–177. [CrossRef]
27. Koch, R.; Kühl, S.; Morais, R.M.; Spinnler, B.; Schairer, W.; Sommernkorn-Krombholz, B.; Pachnicke, S. Reinforcement learning for generalized parameter optimization in elastic optical networks. *J. Light. Technol.* **2022**, *40*, 567–574. [CrossRef]
28. Zhao, Z.; Zhao, Y.; Ma, H.; Li, Y.; Rahman, S.; Han, D.; Zhang, H.; Zhang, J. Cost-efficient routing, modulation, wavelength and port assignment using reinforcement learning in optical transport networks. *Opt. Fiber Technol.* **2021**, *64*, 102571. [CrossRef]
29. Li, B.; Zhu, Z. DeepCoop: Leveraging cooperative DRL agents to achieve scalable network automation for multi-domain SD-EONs. In Proceedings of the Optical Fiber Communication Conference (OFC), San Diego, CA, USA, 8–12 March 2020; p. Th2A-29.
30. Yao, Q.; Yang, H.; Yu, A.; Zhang, J. Transductive transfer learning-based spectrum optimization for resource reservation in seven-core elastic optical networks. *J. Light. Technol.* **2019**, *37*, 4164–4172. [CrossRef]
31. Liu, C.Y.; Chen, X.; Proietti, R.; Yoo, S.B. Evol-TL: Evolutionary transfer learning for QoT estimation in multi-domain networks. In Proceedings of the Optical Fiber Communications Conference and Exhibition (OFC), San Diego, CA, USA, 8–12 March 2020; pp. 1–3.
32. Mnih, V.; Badia, A.P.; Mirza, M.; Graves, A.; Lillicrap, T.; Harley, T.; Silver, D.; Kavukcuoglu, K. Asynchronous methods for deep reinforcement learning. In Proceedings of the International Conference on Machine Learning (ICML), New York, NY, USA, 19–24 June 2016; pp. 1928–1937.
33. Konda, V.R.; Tsitsiklis, J.N. Actor-critic algorithms. In Proceedings of the Advances in Neural Information Processing Systems (NeurIPS), Denver, CO, USA, 2000; pp. 1008–1014.

34. Kozicki, B.; Takara, H.; Sone, Y.; Watanabe, A.; Jinno, M. Distance-adaptive spectrum allocation in elastic optical path network (SLICE) with bit per symbol adjustment. In Proceedings of the Optical Fiber Communications Conference and Exhibition (OFC), 8–12 March 2020, San Diego, CA, USA, 2010; pp. 1–3.
35. Zhu, Z.; Lu, W.; Zhang, L.; Ansari, N. Dynamic service provisioning in elastic optical networks with hybrid single-/multi-path routing. *J. Lightw. Technol.* **2012**, *31*, 15–22. [CrossRef]
36. Jinno, M.; Kozicki, B.; Takara, H.; Watanabe, A.; Sone, Y.; Tanaka, T.; Hirano, A. Distance-adaptive spectrum resource allocation in spectrum-sliced elastic optical path network. *IEEE Commun. Mag.* **2010**, *48*, 138–145. [CrossRef]
37. Tang, B.; Huang, Y.-C.; Xue, Y.; Zhou, W. Heuristic reward design for deep reinforcement learning-based routing, modulation and spectrum assignment of elastic optical networks. *IEEE Commun. Lett.* **2022**. [CrossRef]

mathematics

MDPI

Article

Syntactically Enhanced Dependency-POS Weighted Graph Convolutional Network for Aspect-Based Sentiment Analysis

Jinjie Yang [1], Anan Dai [1], Yun Xue [1], Biqing Zeng [2] and Xuejie Liu [1,*]

[1] School of Electronics and Information Engineering, South China Normal University, Foshan 528225, China
[2] School of Software, South China Normal University, Foshan 528225, China
* Correspondence: xuejie.liu@m.scnu.edu.cn

Abstract: Aspect-based sentiment analysis (ABSA) is a fine-grained task of sentiment analysis that presents great benefits to real-word applications. Recently, the methods utilizing graph neural networks over dependency trees are popular, but most of them merely considered if there exist dependencies between words, ignoring the types of these dependencies, which carry important information, as dependencies with different types have different effects. In addition, they neglected the correlations between dependency types and part-of-speech (POS) labels, which are helpful for utilizing dependency imformation. To address such limitations and the deficiency of insufficient syntactic and semantic feature mining, we propose a novel model containing three modules, which aims to leverage dependency trees more reasonably by distinguishing different dependencies and extracting beneficial syntactic and semantic features to further enhance model performance. To enrich word embeddings, we design a syntactic feature encoder (SynFE). In particular, we design Dependency-POS Weighted Graph Convolutional Network (DPGCN) to weight different dependencies by a graph attention mechanism we proposed. Additionally, to capture aspect-oriented semantic information, we design a semantic feature extractor (SemFE). Extensive experiments on five popular benchmark databases validate that our model can better employ dependency information and effectively extract favorable syntactic and semantic features to achieve new state-of-the-art performance.

Keywords: aspect-based sentiment analysis; graph neural networks; dependency trees; dependency types; graph attention mechanism; syntactic; semantic

MSC: 18C50

Citation: Yang, J.; Dai, A.; Xue, Y.; Zeng, B.; Liu, X. Syntactically Enhanced Dependency-POS Weighted Graph Convolutional Network for Aspect-Based Sentiment Analysis. *Mathematics* **2022**, *10*, 3353. https://doi.org/10.3390/math10183353

Academic Editors: Jianping Gou, Weihua Ou, Shaoning Zeng and Lan Du

Received: 2 August 2022
Accepted: 13 September 2022
Published: 15 September 2022

1. Introduction

Aspect-based sentiment analysis (ABSA) is a popular topic in natural language processing with the purpose of identifying the sentiment polarities (i.e., positive, neutral and negative) toward the specific aspects in given sentences. Take this review *"The **food** in this restaurant is delicious but the **service** is terrible"* as an example. For aspect *"food"*, the polarity is positive, while it is negative for aspect *"service"*. An ABSA model aims to infer the sentiment polarities of the given aspects accurately on the fine-grained level.

The key to solving the ABSA task is to find the relations between aspects and corresponding opinion words properly. Early works combined recurrent neueal networks (RNNs) and the attention mechanism [1–5] to capture semantic information related to aspects and generate aspect-specific sentence representation. However, these methods are vulnerable to noises introduced by unrelated words. They also ignored the syntactic dependency information in the sentences, which makes it difficult for them to link aspects and corresponding opinion words due to the long position distance between them. Most recent works [6–10] applied graph-based networks such as graph convolutional networks (GCNs) and graph attention networks (GATs) over dependency trees to explicitly exploit syntactic dependency information, which achieved better performance. However, the drawback of these methods is that all dependencies are treated equally without weighting them according to their types. Linguistically, the dependencies with different types have dividual significance, with some dependencies among words providing benefits to the ABSA task, while others introduce noises that hurt model performance. As shown in Figure 1, the aspect *"food"* has dependencies with two other words *"the"* and *"delicious"*. Obviously, *"delicious"* as the opinion word is more important for sentiment analysis of aspect *"food"*, while *"the"* does not show explicit information. Thus, the dependency type *"nsubj"* means that *"food"* is a nominal subject of *"delicious"* and should be assigned more attention weight than *"det"* only meaning that *"The"* is a determiner of *"food"*. It can be seen that modeling dependency types properly is necessary for advancing the ABSA task. Meanwhile, the previous GCN-based models omitted the correlations between dependency types and POS labels. For example, with comprehensive investigation from the datasets, we find that the important dependency type *"nsubj"* is frequently connected with noun labels and verb labels such as *"JJ"*, *"NN"*, *"NNS"*, etc. Normally, there are many words in a sentence, but a few words are valuable for sentiment analysis of the aspect. After the investigation, we conclude that the POS of opinion words is typically an adjective or verb due to words with these POS usually carrying clear sentiment information. So, incorporating dependency information and POS information is a potential way for upgrading the ABSA task.

To tackle the above limitations and improve model performance, we propose a novel model including three effective modules: SynFE, DPGCN and SemFE. Particularly, the main module DPGCN incorporates dependency information and POS information to weight different dependencies. SynFE and SemFE supplement syntactic and semantic features for aspects to further improve model performance.

Our contributions are summarized as follows:

- We propose to weight dependencies with different types in dependency trees according to their contribution to ABSA task by capturing the correlations between dependency types and POS labels.
- We propose DPGCN to weight different dependencies with a graph attention mechanism which incorporates dependency information and POS information. SynFE and SemFE are developed to extract more feature information for elevating model performance.
- We conduct extensive experiments on five benchmark datasets, and the results prove the effectiveness of our model.

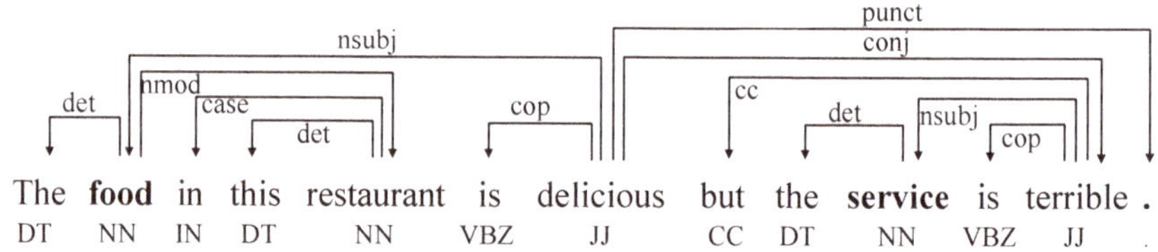

Figure 1. An example sentence with its dependency tree and POS labels.

2. Related Work

With the booming development of deep learning, relevant models were applied to this task. Many early attention-based neural network models [1–5] achieved promising performance, which aroused great concern. Ref. [1] proposed an attention-based LSTM which focuses on the key part of sentences to obtain contextual representations. Refs. [2,3] introduced a memory network with an attention mechanism to extract sentiment information related to aspects. Ref. [4] utilized a multi-grained attention mechanism to capture word-level interactions between aspects and contexts. Ref. [5] exploited the Attention over Attention network to learn aspect representations and sentence representations together. In addition, pre-trained language model BERT [11] has achieved remarkable performance in a number of NLP tasks, including ABSA. Ref. [12] transformed the ABSA task into sentence–aspect pair classification and achieved excellent performance by fine-tuning the BERT model.

Early works lost sight of the usefulness of syntactic knowledge to the ABSA task. To explicitly exploit syntactic dependency information, ref. [13] proposed an attention model with syntactic dependency information to obtain attention weights, and ref. [14] introduced syntactic relative distance to reduce the negative effects of words that are weakly related to aspects. Graph Convolutional Network (GCN) [15] had achieved surprising performance in many NLP tasks, including ABSA. Applying a GCN-based model over dependency trees became a new trend, which developed several outstanding models. Refs. [6,7] applied GCN over dependency trees to capture the syntactic dependency information for aspects. Ref. [8] noticed the word co-occurrence information, building a hierarchical syntactic graph and lexical graph for graph convolution. Ref. [16] proposed a relational graph attention network (R-GAT) to encode the new dependency trees for sentiment analysis. Ref. [17] designed DualGCN including SynGCN and SemGCN to extract syntactic and semantic information for aspects, respectively.

3. Method

In this section, we elaborate the details of our proposed model. The overall structure of our model is shown in Figure 2, and the details of SynFE and DPGCN are depicted in Figure 3.

Our model mainly consists of three modules: (1) **SynFE**, which encodes the dependency information and POS information of the sentences to enrich word-level vector representations; (2) **DPGCN**, which captures the correlations between dependency types and POS labels to weight dependencies with different types; and (3) **SemFE**, which extracts semantic features from the overall sentence to supplement sentiment features for aspect representations. Each component will be presented in detail and analyzed for their contribution.

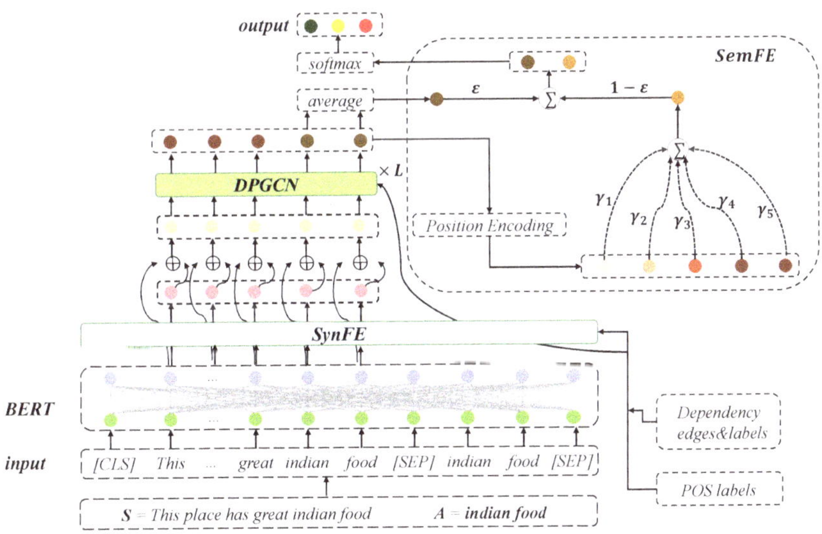

Figure 2. The overall structure of our proposed model.

3.1. Problem Definition (ABSA)

Given an n-word review sentence $S = \{w_1, w_2, \cdots, w_{a+1}, \cdots, w_{a+m}, \cdots, w_n\}$ with an m-word aspect $A = \{w_{a+1}, \cdots, w_{a+m}\}$ in it, ABSA aims at identifying the sentiment polarity (i.e., positive, neutral or negative) of the given aspect in a sentence. If there is more than one m-word aspect in a sentence, our model processes the sentence several times, i.e., outputting the sentiment polarity of one aspect once.

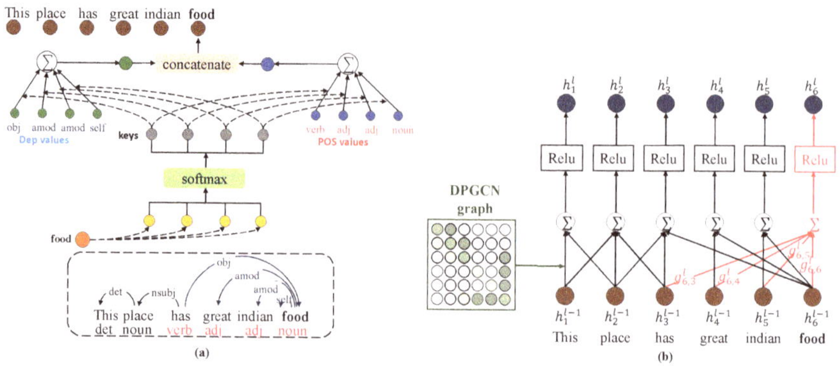

Figure 3. The details of (**a**) SynFE and (**b**) DPGCN.

3.2. Initial Embedding Module

The pre-trained language model BERT has the ability to provide word embeddnings with rich feature information; thus, we construct a sentence–aspect pair (S, A) as the input of BERT to initialize aspect-aware word vectors with the input form: *"[CLS] sentence [SEP] aspect [SEP]"*, where 'CLS' is a symbol token for encoding overall sentence-level representation, and 'SEP' is a separator for separating sentence and aspect. The calculations in BERT are as follows:

$$\{h^{CLS}, H^S, H^A\} = BERT(\{CLS, S, SEP, A, SEP\}) \tag{1}$$

where $h^{CLS} \in \mathbb{R}^{d_a}$ is the overall sentence-level representation, $H^S = \{h_1, h_2, \cdots, h_n\} \in \mathbb{R}^{n \times d_a}$ are the word-level representations of the sentence, where n is the number of words in one sentence and d_a is the dimension of each word vector, and $H^A = \{h_{a+i}, \cdots, h_{a+m}\} \in \mathbb{R}^{m \times d_a}$ are the aspect representations. We only adopt H^S, which contain aspect representations and contextual representations of the sentence.

3.3. Syntactic Feature Encoder (SynFE)

The quality of textual representations is critical to all NLP tasks. To enrich the features for word representations of aspects and contexts, we encode syntactic information (i.e., dependency information and POS information) and fuse them into word representations.

According to the structures of dependency trees, we construct a key–value network to learn syntax-aware representations. In detail, our module obtains dependency trees of the given sentences from an off-the-shelf NLP toolkit (i.e., StanfordCoreNLP). We map dependencies to key sets K, and dependency types and POS labels are mapped to dependency value sets V^D and POS value set V^P. As illustrated in Figure 1, each word has dependencies with other words. For w_i (i.e., the i-th word in the sentence), we map the dependencies related to it and corresponding dependency types to a key set $K_i = \{k_{i,1}, k_{i,2}, \cdots, k_{i,n}\}$ in K and a value set $V_i^D = \{v_{i,1}^d, v_{i,2}^d, \cdots, v_{i,n}^d\} \in \mathbb{R}^{n \times d_b}$ in V^D, respectively. Each element in K_i represents the weight for corresponding dependency; $K_{i,j} = 0$ if there is no dependency between w_i and w_j. For V_i^D, the element is the embedding vector for the corresponding dependency type. For example, $v_{i,j}^d \in \mathbb{R}^{d_b}$ in V_i^D represents a d_b-dimensional embedding vector for the dependency type between w_i and w_j. In particular, the type is denoted as *"none"* if there is no dependency between two words, while it is *"self"* between one word and itself. $V^P = \{v_1^p, v_2^p, \cdots, v_n^p\} \in \mathbb{R}^{n \times d_c}$ represent the embedding vectors of POS labels for words in the sentence. The embedding vectors in V^D and V^P are randomly initialized and trainable, but the weights in K are calculated by:

$$k_{i,j} = \frac{a_{i,j} * exp(h_i h_j^T)}{\sum_{k=1}^{n} a_{i,k} * exp(h_i h_k^T)} \tag{2}$$

where T denotes vector transpose, $a_{i,j} = 1$ if a dependency exists between w_i and w_j, and it is 0 otherwise, $*$ is element-wise multiplication, and $h_i \in \mathbb{R}^{d_a}$ and $h_j \in \mathbb{R}^{d_a}$ are the word representations of w_i and w_j from BERT. The syntactic feature representations for words are learnt by:

$$o_i^d = \sum_{j=1}^{n} k_{i,j} * v_{i,j}^d, \quad o_i^p = \sum_{j=1}^{n} k_{i,j} * v_j^p \tag{3}$$

where $v_{i,j}^d \in \mathbb{R}^{d_b}$ and $v_j^p \in \mathbb{R}^{d_c}$ are the embedding vectors for the dependency type between w_i and w_j and the POS label of w_j, and $o_i^d \in \mathbb{R}^{d_b}$ and $o_i^p \in \mathbb{R}^{d_c}$ are the dependency representation and POS representation for w_i that provide beneficial syntactic features for word representation. Afterward, we incorporate them into the word representations from BERT by:

$$x_i = h_i \oplus o_i^d \oplus o_i^p \tag{4}$$

where x_i refers to the output of the key-value network for w_i, and $\oplus$ denotes vector concatenation. $X = \{x_1, x_2, \cdots, x_n\} \in \mathbb{R}^{n \times (d_a + d_b + d_c)}$ are updated word representations with syntactic features output by the key-value network.

3.4. Dependency-POS Weighted Graph Convolutional Network (DPGCN)

An adjacency matrix $A = \{a_{i,j}\}_{n \times n}$ is used to represent the structure of a dependency tree in a traditional GCN-based model, A is a 0-1 matrix where $a_{i,j} = 1$ if there exists a dependency between w_i and w_j, and $a_{i,j} = 0$ otherwise. In order to make better use of syntactic dependency information, we propose a graph attention mechanism to construct DPGCN graph $G = \{g_{i,j}\}_{n \times n}$ by combining dependency types and POS labels, where $g_{i,j} \in [0,1]$ while $a_{i,j} = \{0,1\}$. First, $t_{i,j}$ is denoted as the dependency type between w_i and w_j, and there is a trainable embedding vector $\alpha_{i,j} \in \mathbb{R}^{2*d_a}$ for each type $t_{i,j}$. Then, to alleviate noises introduced from POS, the POS labels of all words are divided into five categories (i.e., Nouns, Verbs, Adjectives, Adverbs and Others), where there is a POS mapping matrix $w^p \in \mathbb{R}^{d_a \times d_a}$ corresponding to each POS category. DPGCN is an L-layer GCN-based module; each layer exists to a corresponding DPGCN graph $G^l = \{g_{i,j}^l\}_{n \times n}$, and all $g_{i,j}^l$ are calculated by:

$$r_{i,j}^l = Relu(\alpha_{i,j}^T [h_i^{l-1} w_i^p \oplus h_j^{l-1} w_j^p]) \tag{5}$$

$$g_{i,j}^l = softmax(r_{i,j}^l) = \frac{a_{i,j} * exp(r_{i,j}^l)}{\sum_{k=1}^{n} a_{i,k} * exp(r_{i,k}^l)} \tag{6}$$

where $a_{i,j} \in A$, $h_i^{l-1} \in \mathbb{R}^{d_a}$ and $h_j^{l-1} \in \mathbb{R}^{d_a}$ are hidden state representations for w_i and w_j output by the (L − 1)-th layer of DPGCN, l stands for the L-th DPGCN layer, and $g_{i,j}^l$ denotes the dependency weight between w_i and w_j at the L-th layer.

Based on DPGCN graph G^l, DPGCN learns refined word representations (i.e., both aspect representations and contextual representations). First, $X = \{x_1, x_2, \cdots, x_n\} \in \mathbb{R}^{n \times (d_a + d_b + d_c)}$ from SynFE are fed into a feedforward network to obtain 768-dimensional hidden state representations $H^0 = \{h_1^0, h_2^0, \cdots, h_n^0\} \in \mathbb{R}^{n \times d_a}$ as the input of DPGCN by:

$$H^0 = H^S W^S + b^S \tag{7}$$

where $W^S \in \mathbb{R}^{(d_a+d_b+d_c)\times d_a}$ and $b^S \in \mathbb{R}^{d_a}$ are trainable weight matrix and bias. Then, all layers of DPGCN proceed convolution as follows:

$$h_i^l = \sigma(\sum_{j=1}^{n} g_{i,j}^l * (h_j^{l-1} W^l + b^l)) \tag{8}$$

$$H^l = \sigma(G^l (H^{l-1} W^l + b^l)) \tag{9}$$

where $W^l \in \mathbb{R}^{d_a \times d_a}$ and $b^l \in \mathbb{R}^{d_a}$ are the trainable weight matrix and bias in the L-th layer, σ is the Relu activation function, and $H^l = \{h_1^l, h_2^l, \cdots, h_n^l\} \in \mathbb{R}^{n \times d_a}$ output by DPGCN represents the refined word representations for aspect and contexts. DPGCN learns high-quality word representations in the way of more reasonably leveraging dependency trees.

3.5. Semantic Feature Extractor (SemFE)

To retrieve more sentiment features from the overall sentence for sentiment classification, we extract semantic features related to aspect upon contexts to generate aspect-oriented sentence representation.

Position Encoding: In terms of the common sense of linguistics, contexts close to aspect generally have greater influences on the sentiment expression of aspect, so position weights are defined as follows:

$$d_t = \begin{cases} 1, & dis = 0, \\ 1 - \frac{dis}{n}, & 1 \le dis \le d, \quad 1 \le t \le n \\ 0, & dis > d, \end{cases} \tag{10}$$

where dis denotes the distance from contexts to aspect; it is aspect itself when dis = 0, and we mask the word representations when $dis > d$ to avoid introducing noises. Take this simple sentence "*The served food is delicious*" as an example; the position weights are set to $d_t = [0.8, 1, 1, 0.8, 0]$ when the aspect is "*served food*" and $d = 1$. The position-encoded word representations P are obtained by:

$$p_t = d_t * h_t^l, \quad 1 \le t \le n \tag{11}$$

$$P = p_t(1 \le t \le n) = \{p_1, p_2, \cdots, p_n\} \tag{12}$$

where $h_t^l \in \mathbb{R}^{d_a}$ is a word representation for w_t from DPGCN. The final aspect-oriented sentence representation s containing abundant semantic information is generated by:

$$\delta_t = \sum_{i=1}^{m} h_{a+i}^l p_t^T, \quad \gamma_t = \frac{exp(\delta_t)}{\sum_{i=1}^{n} exp(\delta_i)} \tag{13}$$

$$s = \sum_{i=1}^{n} \gamma_t * p_t \tag{14}$$

where $h_{a+i}^l \in \mathbb{R}^{d_a}$ is the aspect representation from DPGCN for the i-th aspect word, and m and n are the length of the aspect and sentence, respectively.

3.6. Model Training

We obtain the final aspect representation $h_a \in \mathbb{R}^{d_a}$ and incorporate it and aspect-oriented sentence representation $s \in \mathbb{R}^{d_a}$ to obtain final representation $z \in \mathbb{R}^{d_a}$ by:

$$h_a = \frac{1}{m} * \sum_{i=1}^{m} h_{a+i}^l \tag{15}$$

$$z = \varepsilon * h_a + (1 - \varepsilon) * s \tag{16}$$

where $\varepsilon \in (0,1)$ is a trainable coefficient.The final representation z is passed through a fully connected layer and a softmax activation function to obtain the probability distribution of sentiment polarity, and the label of highest probability is chosen as the sentiment polarity of the specific aspect by:

$$u = softmax(zw_u + b_u) \tag{17}$$

where u is the probability distribution, and $w_u \in \mathbb{R}^{d_a \times 3}$ and $b_u \in \mathbb{R}^3$ are the trainable weight matrix and bias.

The model is trained by using the standard stochastic gradient descent to minimize the cross-entropy loss of sentiment classification. The loss function is formulated as:

$$L(\theta) = -\sum_{i}^{N} u_i log\dot{u}_i + \lambda||\theta|| \tag{18}$$

where N is the number of training samples, u_i is the prediction for the sentiment polarity of aspect, $\dot{u}_i$ is the target label, θ represents all trainable parameters, and λ is the L2 regularization coefficient.

4. Experiments

4.1. Datasets

For the experiments, five benchmark datasets are adopted for the ABSA task to evaluate our model, including the Twitter dataset constructed by [18] and another four datasets ($Lap14, Res14, Res15, Res16$) all from the SemEval tasks [19–21], which are user reviews related to computers and restaurants. The samples in these datasets contain a given sentence, a specific aspect and the sentiment polarity (i.e., positive, neutral or negative) toward the aspect. The information of these five datasets is shown in Table 1.

Table 1. The statistics of datasets.

Datasets	Positive		Negative		Neutral	
	Train	Test	Train	Test	Train	Test
Twitter	1561	173	1560	173	3127	346
Lap14	994	341	870	128	464	169
Res14	2164	728	807	196	637	196
Res15	912	326	256	182	36	34
Res16	1240	469	439	117	69	30

4.2. Experimental Settings

In our experiments, the syntactic dependency trees and POS labels of the given sentences are constructed via using StanfordCoreNLP toolkit (https://stanfordnlp.github.io/CoreNLP/, accessed on 1 August 2022). The given sentences are encoded by pre-trained model BERT (we obtain the BERT model from (https://github.com/huggingface/pytorch-pretrained-BERT, accessed on 1 August 2022) to obtain 768-dimensional initialized word-embedding vectors for each word. In addition, the dimensions of dependency-embedding vectors and POS-embedding vectors are set to 100 and 50, respectively. For the parameter settings, BERT is initialized with pre-trained parameters, while other trainable parameters are initialized by Xavier [22]. The loss function of the model training is the cross-entropy function, and the Adam optimizer is adopted. For key hyper-parameter settings, the batch size is 16, the learning rate is 1×10^{-5}, the L2 regularization coefficient λ is 0.001, and the dropout rate is 0.1. Our model is evaluated by both accuracy and macro-averaged F1 score.

4.3. Baselines

To verify the effectiveness of our model, many comparative state-of-art models are adopted and briefly described as follows:

IAN [23] proposes an interactive attention network based on LSTM and attention mechanism to generate representations for aspects and sentences.

MGAN [4] designs a novel multi-grained attention network model to capture interactions between the aspects and contexts.

ASGCN [6] first proposes leveraging GCN over dependency trees to learn aspect-specific representations for the ABSA task.

CDT [7] utilizes GCN over dependency trees to extract syntactic information for aspect representations.

BIGCN [8] constructs a syntactic graph and lexical graph for GCN to leverage word co-occurrence information and syntactic information.

BERT [11] is the vanilla BERT, which adopts "[CLS] sentence [SEP] aspect [SEP]" as input and uses the representation of [CLS] for predictions.

TD [24] implements a target-dependent BERT-based model with positioned output at the target terms and an optional sentence for the ABSA task.

R-GAT [16] employs a relational graph attention network to exploit syntactic structure information.

DGEDT [25] considers the flat representations and graph-based representations jointly to alleviate the noise and instability of dependency trees.

LCFS [14] models contextual and syntactical features for the ABSA task.

TGCN [26] encodes dependency types and integrates the representations from all GCN layers to learn aspect representations.

DualGCN [17] designs SynGCN and SemGCN to learn aspect representations by considering syntax structures and semantic correlations simultaneously.

4.4. Results and Analysis

Comparisons of all model performance are presented in Table 2. It can be seen that the results on the four SemEval task datasets ($Lap14$, $Res14$, $Res15$, $Res16$) outperform the previous models, but the performance on the Twitter dataset is lower than DualGCN and DGEDT due to the comments on the Twitter being informal and inclined to colloquial, which are insensitive to syntactic information. The comparisons show that our model surpasses many state-of-art GCN-based models, indicating that our model can better utilize syntactic dependency information, and extracting sufficient syntactic and semantic features for sentiment analysis is helpful for model performance.

Compared with the attention-based models IAN and MGAN, our model avoids the noises introduced by the ordinary attention mechanism. Compared with the GCN-based models utilizing dependency information, such as ASGCN, CDT, R-GAT, TGCN, DualGCN and so on, our model combines dependency types and POS labels to weight dependencies with different types according to their contribution to the ABSA task, which better exploits syntactic dependency information.

Table 2. The results of comparisons.

Model	Twitter		Lap14		Rest14		Rest15		Rest16	
	Acc	F1	Acc	F1	Acc	F1	Acc	F1	Acc	F1
IAN	72.50	70.81	72.05	67.38	79.26	70.09	78.54	52.65	84.74	55.21
MGAN	72.54	70.81	75.39	72.47	81.25	71.94	79.36	57.26	87.06	62.29
ASGCN ≀	72.15	70.40	75.55	71.05	80.77	72.02	79.89	61.89	88.99	67.48
CDT ≀	73.29	72.02	75.63	72.01	83.10	73.01	79.42	61.68	86.24	67.62
BIGCN ≀	74.16	73.35	74.59	71.84	81.97	73.48	81.16	64.79	88.96	70.84
BERT	73.27	71.52	77.59	73.28	84.11	76.68	83.48	66.18	90.10	74.16
TD †≀	76.69	74.28	78.87	74.38	85.10	78.35	–	–	–	–
R-GAT †≀	76.15	74.88	78.21	74.07	86.60	81.35	–	–	–	–
DGEDT †≀	**77.9**	75.4	79.8	75.6	86.3	80.0	84.0	71.0	91.9	79.0
LCFS †≀	–	–	80.52	77.13	86.71	80.31	–	–	–	–
TGCN †≀	76.45	75.25	80.88	77.03	86.16	79.95	85.26	71.69	92.32	77.29
DualGCN †≀	77.40	**76.02**	81.80	78.10	87.13	81.16	–	–	–	–
Ours †≀	76.88	75.01	**82.13**	**78.86**	**87.23**	**81.38**	**85.61**	**73.03**	**92.69**	**80.25**

Models using BERT are marked by "†" and models using GCN and dependency information are maked by "≀".

4.5. Ablation Study

To explore the significance of each module, we conduct a series of ablation experiments, where the results are shown in Table 3. The findings are listed as follows:

(1) The results decrease after removing the SynFE module, which indicates that the SynFE module can effectively encode the syntactic information in the sentences to enrich textual features. (2) If DPGCN removes dependency information (D) or POS information (P) separately, the results slightly reduce, but they strongly reduce when removing both simultaneously. It shows that DPGCN weighting dependencies with different types has a great impact on model performance; both (D) and (P) contribute to it. (3) For the SemFE module, similarly, the results demonstrate that position encoding helps to avoid introducing noises, and aspect-oriented sentence representation has the ability to supplement semantic features for a better performance. Overall, each component makes a contribution to the model performance.

Table 3. The results of ablation study.

Models	Twitter		Lap14		Rest14		Rest15		Rest16	
	Acc	F1	Acc	F1	Acc	F1	Acc	F1	Acc	F1
-SynFE	76.01	74.02	81.03	77.76	86.79	80.07	85.06	71.88	92.05	77.65
DPGCN -dep	76.16	74.54	80.56	77.12	86.16	79.11	84.87	70.24	91.88	77.98
DPGCN -POS	76.45	74.75	81.19	77.52	86.60	78.82	85.24	72.22	92.21	78.85
DPGCN -both	75.87	73.57	80.25	76.13	85.62	78.21	84.69	69.92	91.56	76.02
SemFE -PE	76.45	74.82	81.50	77.92	86.96	80.48	85.42	71.95	92.37	78.76
-SemFE	76.01	74.30	80.88	77.36	86.16	79.57	85.24	71.42	92.05	76.61
ours	**76.88**	**75.01**	**82.13**	**78.86**	**87.23**	**81.38**	**85.61**	**73.03**	**92.69**	**80.25**

- indicates the removal of a part of the model. -pos: remove w^p. -dep: replace $\alpha_{i,j}$ with α. -both: replace DPGCN with GCN.

4.6. Case Study

For the purpose of illustrating the effectiveness of our model, we randomly select sample data from the test set to launch a case analysis.

4.6.1. Weights Visualization

As can be seen in Figure 4a, for the aspect *"food"*, linguistically, the opinion word *"delicious"* leads to the sentiment polarity of *"food"*; our model has learnt to assign higher weight to dependency type *"nsubj"* between *"food"* and *"delicious"*. The dependency type *"conj"* between *"delicious"* and *"terrible"* may cause a negative effect for aspect *"food"*; our model reduces the dependency weight for *"conj"* denoting the relation between two elements connected by a coordinating conjunction. In addition, other secondary dependencies are assigned lower weights. In Figure 4b, under the guidance of DPGCN, aspect *"food"* has higher semantic-based attention weight with opinion word *"delicious"*.

Similarly, as seen in Figure 4c,d, vital dependencies are assigned higher weights; thus, aspect *"service"* aggregates feature information from important contexts which account for *"service"* having higher semantic-based attention weights with them. Specially, our model notices the semantic reversal information that *"but"* with dependency type *"cc"* standing for a coordination relation expresses.

4.6.2. Probability Distribution Visualization

As shown in Figure 5, the SemFE module increases the probabilities of the true sentiment polarities for aspects *"food"* and *"service"*. Due to pre-trained model BERT being pretrained on large amounts of textual datasets, it can provide text embeddings containing rich semantic features. Thus, *"delicious"* is encoded with positive sentiment features and negative sentiment features for *"terrible"*. SemFE generating aspect-oriented sentence representation s is able to supplement corresponding sentiment features for aspects. For aspect *"food"*, the context words *"service"* and *"terrible"* carrying negative sentiment features are masked by position encoding, and the positive sentiment features from *"delicious"* are incorporated into s, which makes our model predict the sentiment polarity of *"food"* more accurately. Similarly, for *"service"*, although it is disturbed by *"delicious"*, *"service"* has higher semantic weight with *"terrible"*, and the s also can provide correct sentiment features for *"service"*.

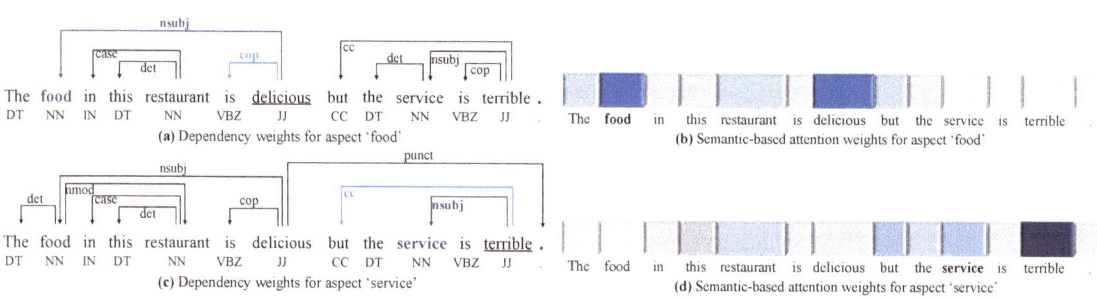

Figure 4. Visualization results of weights (darker color denotes higher weight).

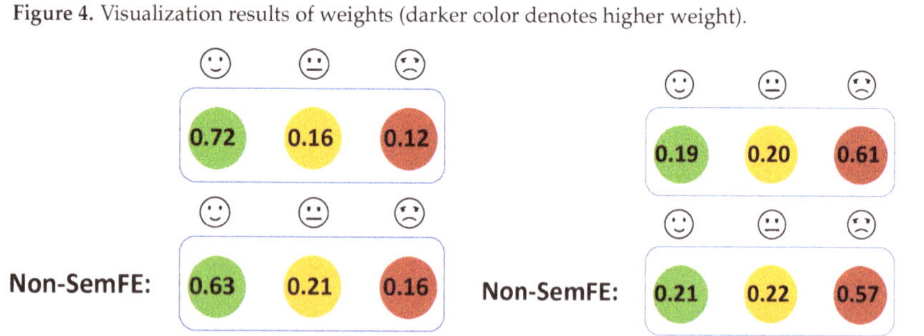

(a) Probability distribution of aspect 'food' **(b)** Probability distribution of aspect 'service'

Figure 5. Visualization results of probability distributions.

4.7. Impacts of DPGCN Layer Number

An appropriate layer number L for DPGCN is also beneficial to model performance, so the impacts of different L values are explored, and the results are shown in Figure 6.

It shows that the accuracy and F1 score on all datasets are highest when $L = 2$, and we will analyze this phenomenon. As described in Figure 7a, aspect "*place*" has different syntactic distances with contexts; through one DPGCN layer, each word node aggregates feature information from neighbor word nodes (i.e., SD = 1), so aspect "*place*" only captures feature information from contexts that SD = 1 with it when $L = 1$. Obviously, "*good*" misleads the sentiment analysis for "*place*"; a two-layer DPGCN makes "*place*" capture vital sentiment features from $SD = 2$ context word "*not*". However, if $L = 3$ or more, it will introduce irrelevant feature information such as "*Thai*" and "*wonderful*", which carry positive sentiment features.

As described in Figure 7b, when $L = 3$, aspect "*place*" has high semantic weights (from SemFE) on itself and "*good*" through the 1st DPGCN layer. Through the 2nd DPGCN layer, the semantic weight on "*good*" decreases and increases on "*not*". After through the 3rd DPGCN layer, the distribution of semantic weights on contexts is decentralized, so aspect "*place*" is difficult to focus on vital information, and much irrelevant information is introduced.

In conclusion, our model is unable to capture sufficient contextual feature information for aspects when $L = 1$, but it may introduce much more irrelevant information for aspects that damage model performance when $L = 3$ or more. $L = 2$ is favorable for our model.

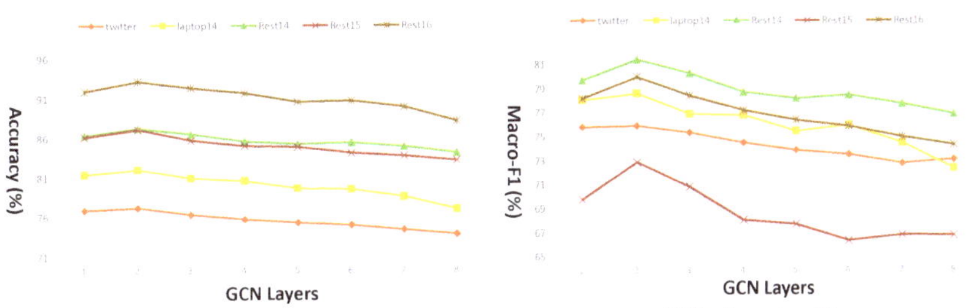

(a) The impacts on accuracy **(b)** The impacts on F1 score

Figure 6. Impacts of the layer number *L*.

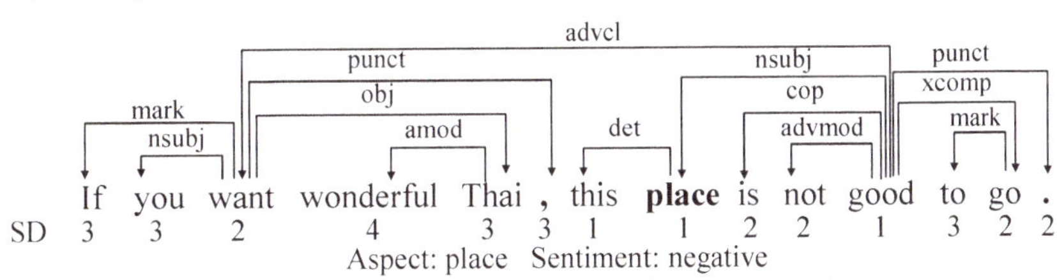

(a) Syntactic distances of contexts with aspect 'place'

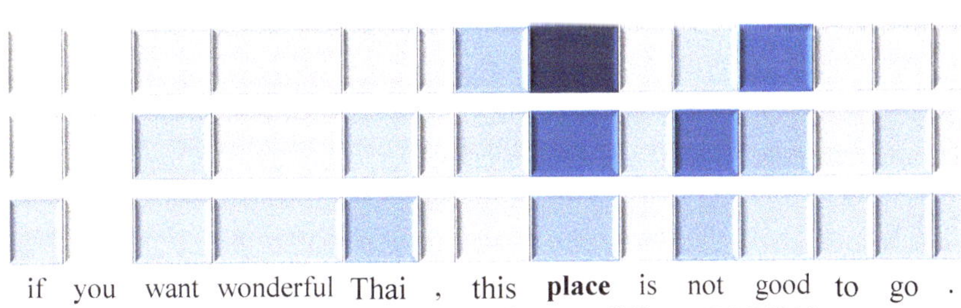

(b) Semantic weights for aspect 'place' on different DPGCN layers

Figure 7. Syntactic distances and semantic weights for aspect 'place'.

5. Conclusions

In this paper, we propose a novel model containing three effective modules (i.e., SynFE, DPGCN and SemFE) for the ABSA task. To address the limitations upon utilizing the syntactic dependency information of previous works, we propose to weight dependencies with different types according to their contribution to the ABSA task, and the DPGCN module is designed to combine dependency information and POS information to more reasonably and comprehensively leveraged syntactic dependency information. To further improve the model performance, SynFE is designed to encode syntax-aware features to enrich word representations, and SemFE is designed to extract aspect-oriented semantic information that supplements sentiment features for sentiment classification.

Extensive experiments are conducted on five benchmark datasets to demonstrate the validity of our model, and the results show that our model achieves new state-of-the-art performance. Compared to other outstanding models, our model achieves a higher accuracy and F1 score. The ablation experiments show that each module in our model contributes to the model performance, and the case study demonstrates that DPGCN has learnt to assign appropriate weights to dependency types, which overcome the shortcomings of the previous model on utilizing dependency trees. In addition, we have analyzed how SemFE is auxiliary for sentiment prediction and explored the effects of the number of DPGCN layers on the model performance.

Author Contributions: Conceptualization, J.Y. and Y.X.; methodology, J.Y.; formal analysis, J.Y. and A.D.; writing—original draft preparation, J.Y.; writing—review and editing, X.L. and B.Z.; supervision, Y.X. and B.Z.; funding acquisition, X.L. All authors have read and agreed to the published version of the manuscript.

Funding: This work was funded by the Science and Technology Plan Project of Guangzhou under Grant Nos. 202102080258 and 202102020902.

Institutional Review Board Statement: Not applicable.

Informed Consent Statement: Not applicable.

Data Availability Statement: Not applicable.

Conflicts of Interest: The authors declare no conflict of interest.

References

1. Wang, Y.; Huang, M.; Zhu, X.; Zhao, L. Attention-based LSTM for aspect-level sentiment classification. In Proceedings of the 2016 Conference on Empirical Methods in Natural Language Processing, Austin, TX, USA, 1–5 November 2016; pp. 606–615.
2. Tang, D.; Qin, B.; Liu, T. Aspect level sentiment classification with deep memory network. *arXiv* **2016**, arXiv:1605.08900.
3. Chen, P.; Sun, Z.; Bing, L.; Yang, W. Recurrent attention network on memory for aspect sentiment analysis. In Proceedings of the 2017 Conference on Empirical Methods in Natural Language Processing, Copenhagen, Denmark, 7–11 September 2017; pp. 452–461.
4. Fan, F.; Feng, Y.; Zhao, D. Multi-grained attention network for aspect-level sentiment classification. In Proceedings of the 2018 Conference on Empirical Methods in Natural Language Processing, Brussels, Belgium, 31 October–4 November 2018; pp. 3433–3442.
5. Huang, B.; Ou, Y.; Carley, K.M. Aspect level sentiment classification with attention-over-attention neural networks. In Proceedings of the International Conference on Social Computing, Behavioral-Cultural Modeling and Prediction and Behavior Representation in Modeling and Simulation, Washington, DC, USA, 10–13 July 2018; Springer: Berlin/Heidelberg, Germany, 2018; pp. 197–206.
6. Zhang, C.; Li, Q.; Song, D. Aspect-based sentiment classification with aspect-specific graph convolutional networks. *arXiv* **2019**, arXiv:1909.03477.
7. Sun, K.; Zhang, R.; Mensah, S.; Mao, Y.; Liu, X. Aspect-level sentiment analysis via convolution over dependency tree. In Proceedings of the 2019 Conference on Empirical Methods in Natural Language Processing and the 9th International Joint Conference on Natural Language Processing (EMNLP-IJCNLP), Hong Kong, China, 3–7 November 2019; pp. 5679–5688.
8. Zhang, M.; Qian, T. Convolution over hierarchical syntactic and lexical graphs for aspect level sentiment analysis. In Proceedings of the 2020 Conference on Empirical Methods in Natural Language Processing (EMNLP), Online, 16–20 November 2020; pp. 3540–3549.
9. Chen, C.; Teng, Z.; Zhang, Y. Inducing target-specific latent structures for aspect sentiment classification. In Proceedings of the 2020 Conference on Empirical Methods in Natural Language Processing (EMNLP), Online, 16–20 November 2020; pp. 5596–5607.

10. Liang, B.; Yin, R.; Gui, L.; Du, J.; Xu, R. Jointly learning aspect-focused and inter-aspect relations with graph convolutional networks for aspect sentiment analysis. In Proceedings of the 28th International Conference on Computational Linguistics, Barcelona, Spain, 8–13 December 2020; pp. 150–161.
11. Devlin, J.; Chang, M.W.; Lee, K.; Toutanova, K. Bert: Pre-training of deep bidirectional transformers for language understanding. *arXiv* **2018**, arXiv:1810.04805.
12. Sun, C.; Huang, L.; Qiu, X. Utilizing BERT for aspect-based sentiment analysis via constructing auxiliary sentence. *arXiv* **2019**, arXiv:1903.09588.
13. Nguyen, H.T.; Le Nguyen, M. Effective attention networks for aspect-level sentiment classification. In Proceedings of the 2018 10th International Conference on Knowledge and Systems Engineering (KSE), Ho Chi Minh City, Vietnam, 1–3 November 2018; pp. 25–30.
14. Phan, M.H.; Ogunbona, P.O. Modelling context and syntactical features for aspect-based sentiment analysis. In Proceedings of the 58th Annual Meeting of the Association for Computational Linguistics, Online, 5–10 July 2020; pp. 3211–3220.
15. Kipf, T.N.; Welling, M. Semi-supervised classification with graph convolutional networks. *arXiv* **2016**, arXiv:1609.02907.
16. Wang, K.; Shen, W.; Yang, Y.; Quan, X.; Wang, R. Relational graph attention network for aspect-based sentiment analysis. *arXiv* **2020**, arXiv:2004.12362.
17. Li, R.; Chen, H.; Feng, F.; Ma, Z.; Wang, X.; Hovy, E. Dual graph convolutional networks for aspect-based sentiment analysis. In *Proceedings of the 59th Annual Meeting of the Association for Computational Linguistics and the 11th International Joint Conference on Natural Language Processing*; Volume 1: Long Papers; Association for Computational Linguistics: Stroudsburg, PA, USA, 2021; pp. 6319–6329.
18. Dong, L.; Wei, F.; Tan, C.; Tang, D.; Zhou, M.; Xu, K. Adaptive Recursive Neural Network for Target-dependent Twitter Sentiment Classification. In Proceedings of the ACL, Baltimore, MD, USA, 22–27 June 2014; pp. 49–54.
19. Pontiki, M.; Papageorgiou, H.; Galanis, D.; Androutsopoulos, I.; Pavlopoulos, J.; Manandhar, S. SemEval-2014 Task 4: Aspect Based Sentiment Analysis. *SemEval* **2014**, *2014*, 27.
20. Pontiki, M.; Galanis, D.; Papageorgiou, H.; Manandhar, S.; Androutsopoulos, I. Semeval-2015 task 12: Aspect based sentiment analysis. In Proceedings of the 9th International Workshop on Semantic Evaluation (SemEval 2015), Denver, CO, USA, 4–5 June 2015; pp. 486–495.
21. Pontiki, M.; Galanis, D.; Papageorgiou, H.; Androutsopoulos, I.; Manandhar, S.; Al-Smadi, M.; Al-Ayyoub, M.; Zhao, Y.; Qin, B.; De Clercq, O.; et al. Semeval-2016 task 5: Aspect based sentiment analysis. In Proceedings of the International Workshop on Semantic Evaluation, San Diego, CA, USA, 16–17 June 2016; pp. 19–30.
22. Glorot, X.; Bengio, Y. Understanding the difficulty of training deep feedforward neural networks. In Proceedings of the Thirteenth International Conference on Artificial Intelligence and Statistics, JMLR Workshop and Conference Proceedings, Sardinia, Italy 13–15 May 2010; pp. 249–256.
23. Ma, D.; Li, S.; Zhang, X.; Wang, H. Interactive attention networks for aspect-level sentiment classification. *arXiv* **2017**, arXiv:1709.00893.
24. Gao, Z.; Feng, A.; Song, X.; Wu, X. Target-dependent sentiment classification with BERT. *IEEE Access* **2019**, *7*, 154290–154299. [CrossRef]
25. Tang, H.; Ji, D.; Li, C. Dependency graph enhanced dual-transformer structure for aspect-based sentiment classification. In Proceedings of the Proceedings of the 58th Annual Meeting of the Association for Computational Linguistics, Online, 5–10 July 2020; pp. 6578–6588.
26. Tian, Y.; Chen, G.; Song, Y. Aspect-based Sentiment Analysis with Type-aware Graph Convolutional Networks and Layer Ensemble. In Proceedings of the 2021 Conference of the North American Chapter of the Association for Computational Linguistics: Human Language Technologies, Online, 6–11 June 2021; pp. 2910–2922.

mathematics

MDPI

Article

Joint Semantic Intelligent Detection of Vehicle Color under Rainy Conditions

Mingdi Hu [1,*,†], Yi Wu [1], Jiulun Fan [1] and Bingyi Jing [2,*,†]

1 School of Communications and Information Engineering, Xi'an University of Posts and Telecommunications, Xi'an 710121, China
2 Department of Statistics & Data Science, Southern University of Science and Technology, Shenzhen 518055, China
* Correspondence: humingdi2005@xupt.edu.cn (M.H.); jingby@sustech.edu.cn (B.J.)
† These authors contributed equally to this work.

Abstract: Color is an important feature of vehicles, and it plays a key role in intelligent traffic management and criminal investigation. Existing algorithms for vehicle color recognition are typically trained on data under good weather conditions and have poor robustness for outdoor visual tasks. Fine vehicle color recognition under rainy conditions is still a challenging problem. In this paper, an algorithm for jointly deraining and recognizing vehicle color, (*JADAR*), is proposed, where three layers of *UNet* are embedded into *RetinaNet*-50 to obtain joint semantic fusion information. More precisely, the *UNet* subnet is used for deraining, and the feature maps of the recovered clean image and the extracted feature maps of the input image are cascaded into the Feature Pyramid Net (*FPN*) module to achieve joint semantic learning. The joint feature maps are then fed into the class and box subnets to classify and locate objects. The *Rain Vehicle Color*-24 dataset is used to train the *JADAR* for vehicle color recognition under rainy conditions, and extensive experiments are conducted. Since the deraining and detecting modules share the feature extraction layers, our algorithm maintains the test time of *RetinaNet*-50 while improving its robustness. Testing on self-built and public real datasets, the mean average precision (mAP) of vehicle color recognition reaches 72.07%, which beats both sate-of-the-art algorithms for vehicle color recognition and popular target detection algorithms.

Keywords: vehicle color recognition; low–high level joint task; object detection; joint semantic learning; deep neural network; rainy image recovery

MSC: 54H30; 68U10; 94A08

Citation: Hu, M.; Wu, Y.; Fan, J.; Jing, B. Joint Semantic Intelligent Detection of Vehicle Color under Rainy Conditions. *Mathematics* **2022**, *10*, 3512. https://doi.org/10.3390/math10193512

Academic Editors: Jianping Gou, Weihua Ou, Shaoning Zeng and Lan Du

Received: 9 August 2022
Accepted: 20 September 2022
Published: 26 September 2022

1. Introduction

Vehicle information recognition has been applied in the field of intelligent traffic management and criminal investigation. License plate, model, and vehicle color comprise the main vehicle information. Although license plate recognition is a commonly used vehicle information recognition technology [1], it also faces many challenges in criminal investigation and for intelligent traffic law enforcement, as license plates can be easily obscured (partially or fully) or faked/duplicated by criminals. As it can still be identified despite partial occlusion or viewpoint changes, vehicle color recognition is widely applied in video surveillance [2], vehicle detection [3], vehicle tracking [4], automatic driving [5,6], criminal investigation [7], etc. All the above-mentioned tasks inevitably encounter adverse weather conditions, especially rain. This, in turn, adversely affects the performance of object recognition/retrieval, because rain can significantly reduce the contrast of the scene and reduces visibility, compromising image quality. Many scholars have conducted research on how to improve the performance of object detection under rainy conditions.

Vehicle color recognition methods are typically classified as traditional model-driven [8–11] or data-driven deep learning [12–18]. Traditional methods usually use handcrafted feature descriptors to extract visual features and train a classifier to recognize vehicle color. For example, Chen et al. [8] select the region of interest (ROI) of the vehicle to recognize its dominant color and than train a linear support vector machine to classify it. Jeong et al. [9] adopt *AdaBoost* to classify an *HSV* histogram of the vehicle's homogeneity patches into seven color categories.

Deep neural networks have been employed to learn effective feature representations from raw pixels, which has proven to be more powerful than traditional methods. To be more specific, these deep learning methods fall into two groups: general object detection algorithms [19–24] applied to vehicle color recognition [16–18] and algorithms specially designed for color recognition. All these algorithms are trained on datasets with 7–24 colors [8–10,18] obtained under normal weather conditions. Of course, there exists some research to address object recognition under rainy conditions; basically, these proposed methods adopt two-stage instead of end-to-end procedures, which inevitably increases the running time of the entire task.

On the other hand, a number of scholars have paid attention to joint processing of low-level and high-level tasks. Generally, they improve the robustness of object detection [25–28] by embedding domain adaptation, image restoration, style transfer, or other modules into the object detection framework, or by a few-shot transfer learning mechanism [29–32]. These methods have explored the robustness of performance for downstream tasks in many harsh environments except under rainy weather conditions, which motivated our work in the present paper.

In this paper, a Joint Algorithm for Deraining And Recognition (*JADAR*) is proposed for fine recognition of vehicle color under rainy conditions. The network architecture is shown in Figure 1. To be more specific, we embed the three-layer decoder of *UNet*-3 into the last three layers of the feature extraction submodule of *RetinaNet*-50. The main contributions are as follows:

1. *JADAR* contains far fewer parameters than previous two-stage methods since its subnets, *UNET* and *RetinaNet* share the same feature extracting layers. This is of high practical value as the size of outdoor mobile equipment can be substantially reduced.
2. In *JADAR*, the multi-scale fusion information obtained by cascading feature maps of original rainy images and recovered images are fed into the subsequent class-box subnet. In so doing, multi-scale information across domains is crucially beneficial for fine vehicle color recognition.
3. The joint processing of low-level and high-level tasks can be mutually beneficial. Embedding the image restoration module can help improve the performance of subsequent high-level tasks under severe weather; conversely, the performance of subsequent high-level tasks as evaluation metrics can, in turn, fine-tune the image restoration algorithms.
4. Comprehensive experiments show that our proposed methods outperform basic detection networks and two-stage network and transfer learning methods for the task of color recognition under rainy conditions. Further, our training and testing times are shortened.

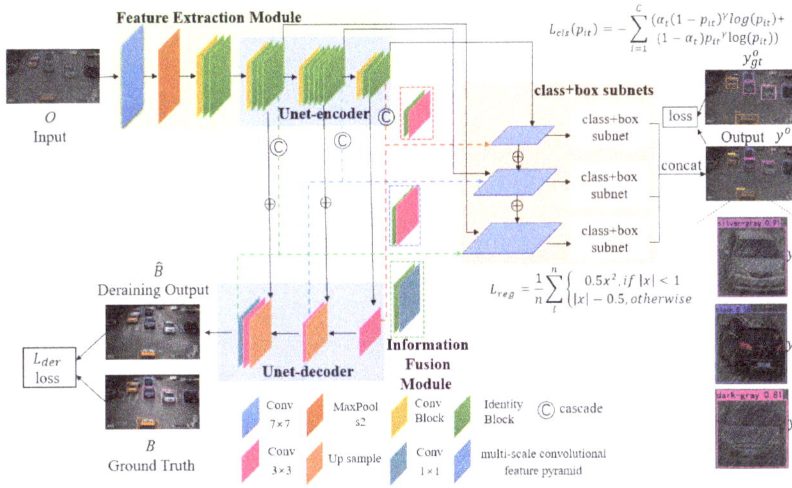

Figure 1. Framework overview for our $JADAR$; detailed explanations are in the text.

Next, related work is introduced in Section 2. $JADAR$ is constructed in Section 3. Section 4 shows that our method is superior to the state-of-the-art quantitatively and qualitatively. Section 5 concludes the main content.

2. Related Work

There exists some research on vehicle color recognition under normal weather and object detection under adverse weather conditions, which is reviewed below.

2.1. Vehicle Color Recognition under Normal Weather Conditions

Vehicle color recognition methods generally fall into traditional model-based methods [8–11] and data-based deep learning methods [12–18]. Regarding traditional model-based methods, Chen et al. [8] train a linear support vector machine classifier on the region of interest ROI in vehicle images based on eight color types; Jeong et al. [9] adopt the multi-class AdaBoost algorithm to classify the color of front-of-vehicle images into seven types; Dule et al. [11] train three classifiers (KNN, ANN, and SVM) for two ROIs (smooth hood section and semi-front of vehicle).

Data-based methods have been receiving increasing attention for vehicle color recognition. Hu et al. [12] were the first to apply a convolutional neural network (CNN) with a spatial pyramid strategy to boost the accuracy of vehicle color recognition. Zhang et al. [15] proposed a lightweight CNN for vehicle color recognition. Fu et al. [16] designed $MCFF$-CNN (Multiscale Comprehensive Feature Fusion Convolutional Neural Network) to recognize eight vehicle colors. Hu et al. [18] proposed vehicle color recognition based on a Smooth Modulation Neural Network with Multi-Scale Feature Fusion ($SMNN$-$MSFF$).

It is worth mentioning that there has been no research on vehicle color detection under bad weather conditions, which is the focus of this paper.

2.2. Object Detection under Adverse Weather Conditions

Bad weather includes rain, snow, haze, etc. The quality of outdoor images or videos collected in these weathers is severely degraded, so target-detection models trained on high-quality images have difficulty handling bad weather. This challenge has been investigated by many scholars with many solutions provided, such as embedding a domain-adaptation module [25–28,31,33,34] into the object detection backbone, such as $YOLO$, $Faster\ RCNN$, $RetinaNet$, etc., two-stages methods consisting of preprocessing and object detection [35–40], or using a few-shot transfer learning mechanism [29–32].

For example, Chen et al. [33] embedded two domain adaptation modules into *Faster RCNN* to reduce the domain discrepancy on image level and instance level. Sindagi et al. [31] proposed an unsupervised domain-adapting method to improve generalization of object detection under hazy and rainy conditions. Style transfer is considered in [27], in which the authors construct a cross-domain representation learning method including domain diversification and a multi-domain invariant. Huang et al. [41] combine dual subnet frameworks for object detection under foggy conditions.

Except for the two-stage methods, the above-mentioned methods do not pay special attention to the rainy conditions. However, two-stage methods such as [35–39,42] do pay attention to image deraining instead of object detection. in other words, the joint tasks of deraining and object detection are not taken seriously. Motivated by the above considerations, we propose *JADAR* for joint semantic intelligent detection of vehicle color in rainy scenes.

3. *JADAR* Algorithm

3.1. Fusion Network Design

In this paper, a Joint Algorithm for Deraining And Recognition (JADAR) is designed for vehicle color recognition in inclement weather conditions; it is based on *RetinaNet*-50, as shown in Figure 1. In Figure 1, O is the rainy image input, B is the corresponding clean background image, $\widehat{B}$ and y^o, respectively, are the outputs of the deraining and detecting results. To see results clearly, we zoom in on the recognition results of each car in picture $y_i^o(i = 1, 2, 3)$; y_1^o is the enlarged result of the first car in the picture—the recognition color is silver-gray with a confidence level of 0.91; y_2^o is the enlarged result of the second car in the picture—the recognition color is black with a confidence level of 0.58; y_3^o is the enlarged result of the third car in the picture—the recognition color is dark gray with a confidence level of 0.81. The green/blue/purple/orange boxes represent the feature extraction module/*UNet-3*/ information fusion module/*class+bbox subnets*, respectively. L_{reg} is the regression loss using the smooth *L1* loss. L_{cls} is the classification loss using the focal loss. The loss function for deraining is *MSE* loss. *JADAR* is trained by the weighted sum of these three losses (see Equation (7)).

The *JADAR* framework is designed by embedding the three-layer decoder of *UNet-3* [43] into the last three sub-blocks of the feature extraction module, as illustrated by the green-tinted box in Figure 1. The whole framework consists of four main modules: image feature extraction module, deraining module, information fusion module, and $class + box$ subnets. The rain removal and feature extraction modules share three layers, avoiding extra computational burden. In fact, Section 4.5 shows that *JADAR* has the same testing time as *RetinaNet*-50. The last three feature maps and the corresponding recovered feature maps are cascaded together and then fed into their respective $class + box$ subnets, which can learn multi-scale joint semantic representations to improve object detection accuracy under rainy conditions. The feature fusion sub-module setting is illustrated in Figure 2.

The overall object function is back-propagated to train the deraining module and to improve rainy image deraining performance recursively. The object detection backbone network uses three-scale $class + box$ subnets to leverage multi-scale fusion color feature maps to classify 24 car color types and locate the bounding-box.

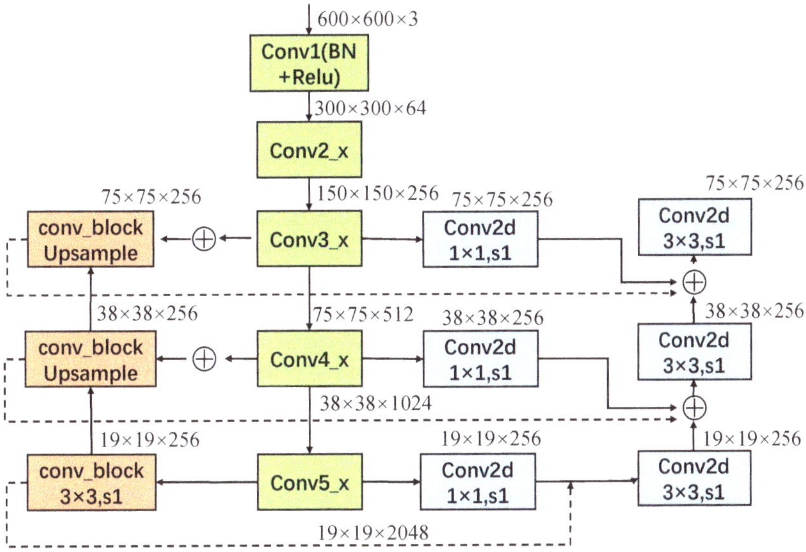

Figure 2. Architecture and weights of the proposed network in detail.

3.2. Model Formulation and Model Optimization

Let the physical mechanism of rainy image corruption be

$$x = y + z \tag{1}$$

where x, y, z denote rainy image O, recovered clean background image B, and rain layer R, respectively. To tackle the problem of supervised vehicle object detection by color in inclement weather conditions, a joint network is proposed to learn joint semantic representation from an input rainy image x. Let y denote the corresponding label of rainy image x.

As demonstrated by the green box in Figure 1, the last three feature maps $f_1(x)$, $f_2(x)$, $f_3(x)$ are taken from the feature extraction sub-blocks of *RetinaNet*. Then, $f_1(x)$ is fed into the corresponding last layer of the decoder of *UNet*-3, and $g_1(x)$ is output. Next, $g_1(x)$ and $f_2(x)$ are cascaded into the penultimate layer *UNet*-3, and $g_2(x)$ is output; then $g_2(x)$ and $f_3(x)$ are cascaded into the last decoder layer of *UNet*-3, and $g_3(x)$ is output. The output of the deraining module $\hat{y}$ is denoted by $g_3(x)$. Thus, the mean square error (*MSE* loss) is used as deraining object function L_{der} as follows:

$$L_{der} = \frac{1}{n}\sum_{i=1}^{n} \|(\hat{y} - y)\|^2 \tag{2}$$

where n is the number of rainy images. Finally, $f_1(x)$ and $g_1(x)$, $f_2(x)$ and $g_2(x)$, and $f_3(x)$ and $g_3(x)$ are cascaded and input into differently scaled *class* + *box* subnets, where joint semantic information is fused, 24 vehicle colors are classified, and box-bounded regressions are achieved; the last cascading output image is denoted y^0.

The classification loss function is

$$L_{cls}(p_{it}) = -\sum_{i=1}^{C}(\alpha_t(1 - p_{it})^{\gamma}\log(p_{it}) + (1 - \alpha_t)(p_{it})^{\gamma}\log(p_{it})) \tag{3}$$

where α_t is a balancing factor to balance the uneven proportion of positive and negative examples of every vehicle color category, $C = 24$ denotes the number of all vehicle color categories, $\gamma \geq 0$ is a tunable focusing parameter (we take $\gamma = 2.0$ in Section 4 following [24]),

t is equal to 0 or 1, which denotes the positive or negative sample, $p_{i1} \in [0,1]$ denotes the prediction probability of the positive sample of the i-th vehicle color class, and $1-p_{i1}$ indicates the prediction probability of negative examples of every vehicle color category $i \in \{1,2,\cdots,24\}$; i.e.,

$$p_{it} = \begin{cases} rc1p_i & \text{if} \quad t=1 \\ 1-p_i & \text{if} \quad otherwise \end{cases}. \tag{4}$$

The loss function of the box bounding regression is

$$L_{reg} = \frac{1}{n}\sum_{i=1}^{n} L_{reg}(i), \tag{5}$$

with

$$L_{reg}(i) = \begin{cases} 0.5a^2 & \text{if} \quad |a|<1 \\ |a|-0.5 & \text{if} \quad otherwise \end{cases}, \tag{6}$$

where $a = t_i - t_i^*$, and $t_i = \{t_x, t_y, t_w, t_h\}, t_i^* = \{t_x^*, t_y^*, t_w^*, t_h^*\}$. Here (x,y) denotes the center coordinates of the bounding box, w/h denotes the width / height, and $t_i(t_i^*)$ represents the offset of the prediction box (the ground truth box).

Now, $L_{reg}(i)$ represents the regression loss for the i-th image, and L_{reg} represents the total regression loss for all images. The total loss function is then given by

$$L_{tol} = L_{cls}(p_{it}) + L_{reg} + \lambda L_{der}, \tag{7}$$

where $\lambda \in [0,1]$ is a hyperparameter controlling the strength of the image deraining module's adjustment to the rainy weather target detection performance. In this context, for $\lambda = 0.5$, mAP of the proposed network detection is optimal from many ablation experiments. See Section 4.3 for details.

4. Experiments

4.1. Experimental Setup

Implementation Details. *JADAR* is trained end-to-end on the *Rain Vehicle Color*-24 image set using the *Adam* optimizer [44] to simultaneously learn image deraining, color classification, and object localization on the *PyTorch* platform. All experiments are implemented on the *AutoDL* platform with a *Tesla* P40. The hyper-parameters α and γ of the classification loss function L_{cls} are set to 0.25 and 2, respectively. We divide *Rain Vehicle Color*-24 into a training set, a validation set and a testing set at a ratio of 8:1:1. The batch size is 4, the epoch is 100, and the confidence threshold is 0.5. The learning rate is 10^{-4} for the first 50 epochs, 10^{-5} for the next 30 epochs, and 10^{-6} for the last 20 epochs.

Evaluation Metric. Generally, object detection uses *IoU* (Intersection over Union) [21], *Precision* (accuracy) [45], *Recall* [45], *AP* (Average Precision) [18], *mAP* (mean Average Precision) [41], or other evaluation metrics; these concepts are well-known, so we list the formulas in brief:

$$IoU = \frac{A \cap B}{A \cup B} \tag{8}$$

where A/B denotes GT (bounding box of the object) / the prediction bounding box.

Mathematical definitions of *Precision* and *Recall* are as follows:

$$precision = \frac{TP}{TP+FP} \tag{9}$$

$$recall = \frac{TP}{TP+FN} \tag{10}$$

where TP is true positives (correctly predicted as positive), FP is false positives (incorrectly predicted as positive), and FN is false negatives (failed to predict a positive).

AP is calculated by

$$AP = \int_0^1 p(r)dr \tag{11}$$

where p is *Precision*, and r is *Recall*.

The mAP (mean Average Precision) is the average of AP, so mAP is calculated by

$$mAP = \frac{\sum_1^N AP}{N} \tag{12}$$

where N is the number of categories.

4.2. Datasets

4.2.1. Synthetic Dataset *Rain Vehicle Color*-24

Few datasets are available for vehicle color recognition under rainy weather conditions. All our experiments are conducted on enhanced *Rain Vehicle Color*-24 [46], from which some examples are illustrated in Figure 3.

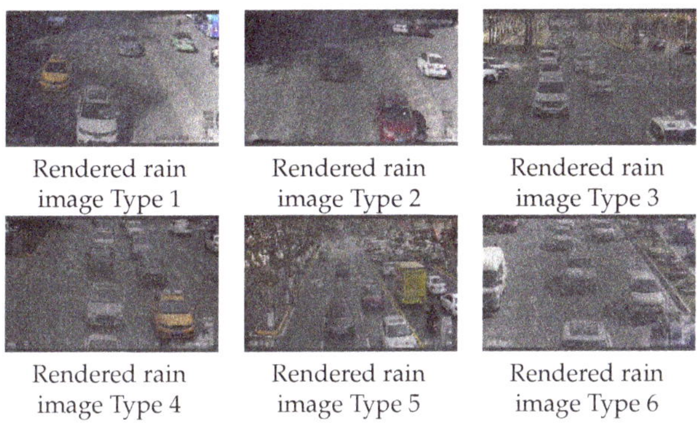

Figure 3. Examples from *Rain Vehicle Color*-24.

4.2.2. Real Rain Vehicle Datasets: *RID* and *RIS*

Li et al. collected two real rainy image vehicle datasets, *RID* and *RIS* [38], for testing object detection. *RID* is rainy images collected from in-vehicle cameras while driving on rainy days, and *RIS* is surveillance rainy images collected from network traffic surveillance cameras during rainy weather conditions. The two datasets differ in many aspects: rainfall type, image quality, target size and angle, etc. They represent real-world application scenarios where deraining may be required. *RID* includes 2495 images, and its rainy image effect is closest to "raindrops" on the camera lens. *RIS* includes 2048 images, and its rainy image effect is closest to "rain and fog" (many cameras have fog condensation when it rains, and lower resolutions also cause more fog effects) [47]. Due to the highly complex scenes of these two rainy image datasets, it is a challenging dataset, and we choose these two datasets for testing to better illustrate the effectiveness of our proposed algorithm. Examples of these two datasets are given in Figure 4.

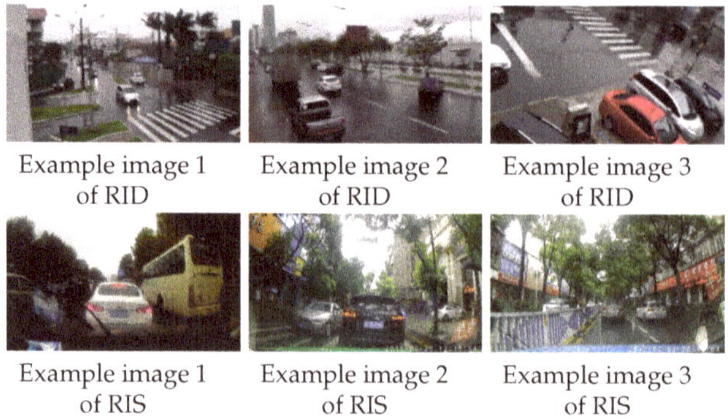

Figure 4. Examples of RID and RIS images [38].

4.3. Ablation Study

To determine the optimal design of our proposed framework, we train four combinations on the *Rain Vehicle Color*-24 dataset: *RetinaNet*, *JADAR*1, *JADAR*2, and *JADAR*. All these models are trained and tested on *Rain Vehicle Color*-24 using different loss functions: $\lambda = 0, 0.1, 1.0$, and 0.5, respectively. Figure 5 shows that the testing *mAP* values of the *JADAR*1, *JADAR*2, and *JADAR* models are 2.92%, −3.99%, and 4.3% higher, respectively, than the *RetinaNet* model, which clarifies that joint semantic feature extraction is beneficial to improve vehicle color recognition performance under rainy weather conditions. Referring to Table 1, when the hyper-parameter λ is 0.1, the rain removal module provides a weak assisting effect on vehicle color recognition under rainy weather conditions. When λ is 1.0, it plays the opposite effect. When λ is 0.5, *JADAR* performs best; so we choose this value in our method.

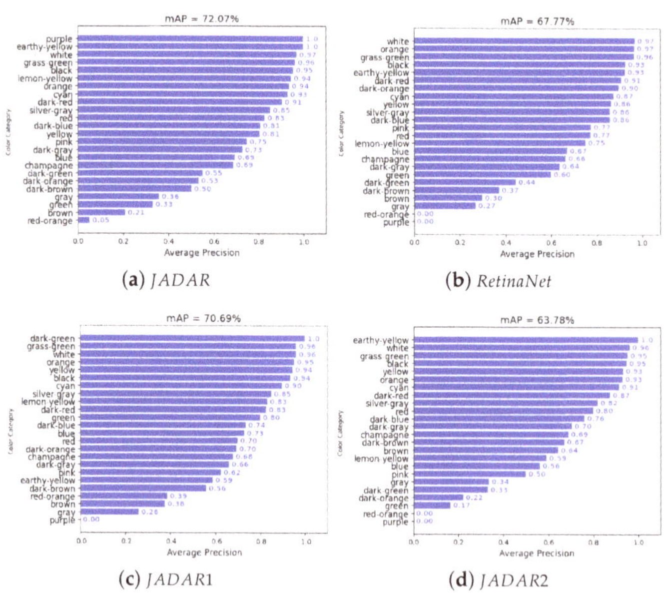

(**a**) *JADAR* (**b**) *RetinaNet* (**c**) *JADAR*1 (**d**) *JADAR*2

Figure 5. *AP*s of different models on the Rain Vehicle Color-24 test set. The x-axis represents the average precision, and the y-axis represents the color categories (24 categories in total).

Table 1. The mAPs using different values for the loss function coefficient λ of the deraining module in *JADAR* on the *RVC*-24 test set.

λ	Model	mAP
0.1	*JADAR*1	70.69%
0.5	*JADAR*	72.07%
1.0	*JADAR*2	63.78%

4.4. Experiments and Analysis

4.4.1. Results on Synthetic Datasets

In this section, our proposed algorithm, the vehicle color recognition method, the target detection method, the two-stage method combining rain removal with target detection, and the transfer learning method are compared.

To discuss vehicle color recognition performance, *JADAR* and *SMNN-MSFF* [18] are compared. Both are trained on *Rain Vehicle Color*-24 training subset and tested on its test subset. The quantitative results are shown in the second column of Table 2. These quantitative results confirm that the *mAP* of our method reaches 72.07%, which is 23.49% higher than *SMNN-MSFF*. The qualitative results are shown in Figure 6. *JADAR* outperforms *SMNN-MSFF* under rainy conditions; for example, there are five vehicles recognized by *JADAR*, while three vehicles are recognized by *SMNN-MSFF*. A white vehicle is recognized by *JADAR* with a confidence score of 0.79, while *SMNN-MSFF* recognizes it with a confidence score of 0.62.

To compare object detection performance, *JADAR*, *RetinaNet* [24], *Faster RCNN* [19], *SSD* [20], and *YOLO V3* [21] are compared qualitatively and evaluated by *mAP* quantitatively. In our experiments, the loss function and settings (i.e., scale, anchor or default box, backbone network, classifier, etc.) of each compared method remains unchanged from the original work. Furthermore, all methods are trained on the *Rain Vehicle Color*-24 dataset and tested on its test set. The qualitative results of *JADAR*, *Faster RCNN*, *YOLO V3*, *SSD*, and *RetinaNet* for vehicle color recognition in rain are shown in Figures 7 and 8. As can be seen from the figures, our proposed *JADAR* outperforms other models for fine vehicle color recognition. The quantitative results show that the proposed *JADAR* is 11.42%, 22.19%, 5.74%, and 4.3% better than *Faster RCNN*, *YOLO V3*, *SSD* and *RetinaNet*, respectively, from Table 2.

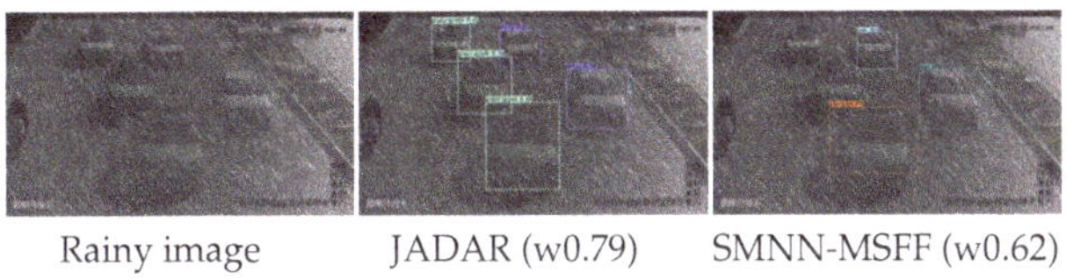

Figure 6. Test results of *JADAR* and *SMNN-MSFF* on the Rain Vehicle Color-24 test set. Each subtitle gives object detection method with the corresponding confidence value in parentheses.

To compare recognition performances of different joint methods, three state-of-the-art rain removal methods, i.e., *LPNet* [35], *PReNet* [48], and *RCDNet* [49]), are chosen to first derain the images, and then *RetinaNet* is leveraged to recognize vehicle colors. These methods are denoted *LR*, *PR*, and *RR*. Figures 9 and 10 give qualitative comparisons of our *JADAR* and three two-stage methods for vehicle color recognition under rainy weather conditions. *JADAR* performs better than other models. From Table 3, our *JADAR* is 15.56%, 20.37%, and 2.06% higher than *LR*, *PR*, and *RR*, respectively.

To compare with transfer learning methods, two domain-adaptation methods, *Dafaster* [33] and *ATF* [50], are compared with *JADAR*. Here, the *VC*-24 is the source domain, and *Rain Vehicle Color*-24 is the target domain; they are leveraged to train the above algorithms. From the 5-th and 6-th columns of Table 3, our method is 25.95% and 9.14% better than *Da-faster* and *ATF*, respectively. The qualitative results in Figures 9 and 10 show that JADAR identifies more vehicles with higher confidence than the other two methods.

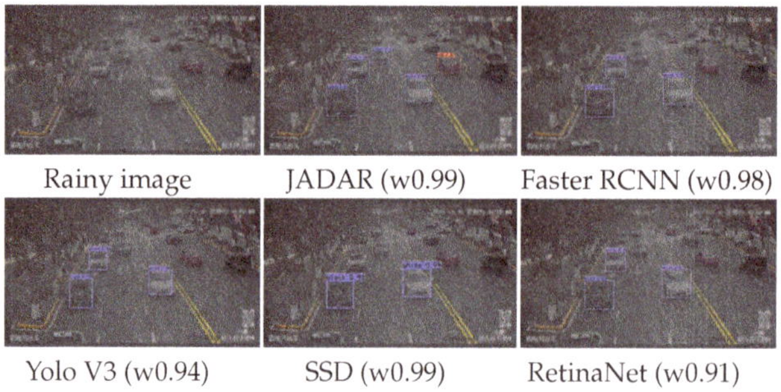

Figure 7. Example 1 of test results of JADAR and object detection methods on the Rain Vehicle Color-24 test set.

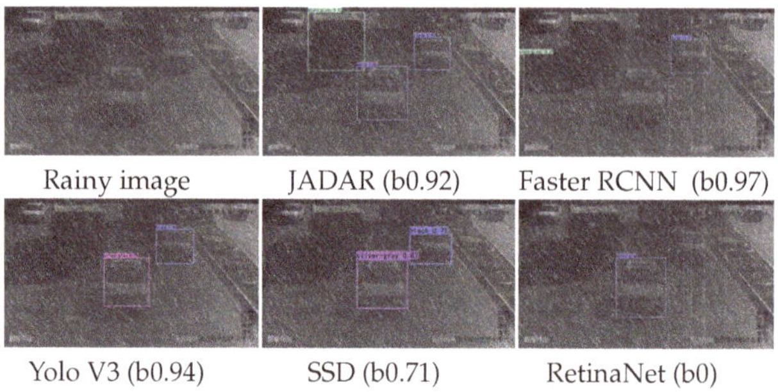

Figure 8. Example 2 of test results of JADAR and object detection methods and domain adaptation methods on the Rain Vehicle Color-24 test set.

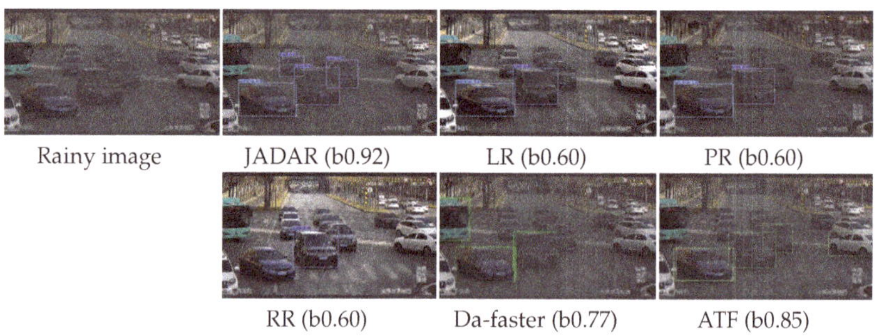

Figure 9. Example 1 of test results of JADAR and two-stage methods on the Rain Vehicle Color-24 test set.

Table 2. Comparison of recognition accuracy of 24 colors for different network classifications: SM, SMNN-MSFF; FR, Faster RCNN; Yolo, Yolo V3; RN, RetinaNet.

Category (R, G, B)	SM	FR	Yolo	SSD	RN	JADAR
white (255, 255, 255)	0.60	0.96	0.95	0.95	0.97	0.97
black (0, 0, 0)	0.69	0.69	0.92	0.93	0.93	0.95
orange (237, 145, 33)	0.77	0.90	0.93	0.95	0.97	0.94
silver-gray (128, 138, 135)	0.31	0.81	0.86	0.86	0.86	0.85
grass-green (0, 255, 0)	0.82	0.93	0.95	0.96	0.96	0.96
dark-gray (128, 128, 105)	0.43	0.69	0.63	0.67	0.64	0.73
dark-red (156, 102, 31)	0.48	0.79	0.75	0.88	0.91	0.91
gray (192, 192, 192)	0.31	0.41	0.15	0.31	0.27	0.36
red (255, 0, 0)	0.44	0.56	0.60	0.76	0.77	0.83
cyan (0, 255, 255)	0.62	0.82	0.81	0.87	0.87	0.93
champagne (255, 227, 132)	0.28	0.74	0.58	0.73	0.66	0.69
dark-blue (25, 25, 112)	0.52	0.79	0.77	0.75	0.86	0.81
blue (0, 0, 255)	0.56	0.69	0.55	0.69	0.67	0.69
dark-brown (94, 38, 18)	0.35	0.18	0.40	0.47	0.37	0.50
brown (128, 128, 42)	0.35	0.10	0.22	0.34	0.30	0.21
yellow (255, 255, 0)	0.35	0.83	0.74	0.92	0.86	0.81
lemon-yellow (255, 215, 0)	0.57	0.99	0.73	0.75	0.75	0.94
dark-orange (210, 105, 30)	0.32	0.28	0.44	0.47	0.90	0.53
dark-green (48, 128, 20)	0.59	0.18	0.00	0.34	0.44	0.55
red-orange (255, 97, 0)	0.38	0.07	0.00	0.52	0.00	0.05
earthy-yellow (184, 134, 11)	0.68	0.45	0.00	0.28	0.93	1.00
green (0, 255, 0)	0.18	0.85	0.00	0.97	0.60	0.33
pink (255, 192, 203)	0.84	0.54	0.00	0.52	0.77	0.75
purple (160, 32, 240)	0.22	0.03	0.00	0.06	0.00	1.00
mAP	48.58%	60.65%	49.88%	66.33%	67.77%	72.07%

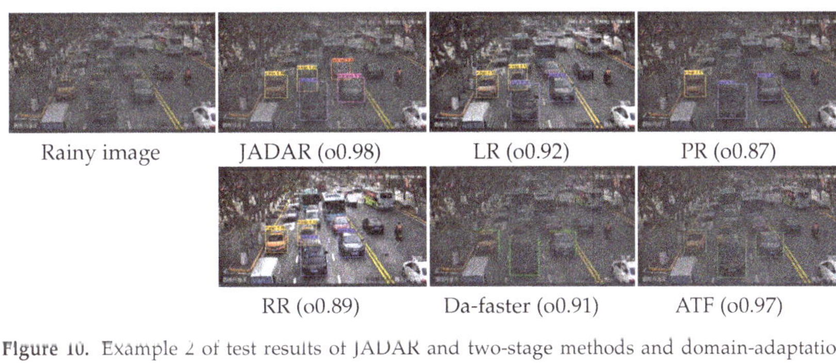

Figure 10. Example 2 of test results of JADAR and two-stage methods and domain-adaptation methods on the Rain Vehicle Color-24 test set.

Table 3. Comparison of recognition accuracy of 24 colors for different network classifications.

Category (R, G, B)	LR	PR	RR	Da-Faster	ATF	JADAR
white (255, 255, 255)	0.88	0.86	0.95	0.74	0.93	0.97
black (0, 0, 0)	0.75	0.75	0.92	0.61	0.87	0.95
orange (237, 145, 33)	0.91	0.92	0.96	0.73	0.90	0.94
silver-gray (128, 138, 135)	0.71	0.66	0.82	0.63	0.63	0.85
grass-green (0, 255, 0)	0.84	0.88	0.95	0.73	0.92	0.96
dark-gray (128, 128, 105)	0.55	0.44	0.73	0.38	0.65	0.73
dark-red (156, 102, 31)	0.67	0.75	0.87	0.54	0.66	0.91
gray (192, 192, 192)	0.27	0.20	0.37	0.19	0.27	0.36
red (255, 0, 0)	0.74	0.70	0.87	0.46	0.63	0.83
cyan (0, 255, 255)	0.81	0.78	0.92	0.75	0.93	0.93
champagne (255, 227, 132)	0.42	0.43	0.62	0.18	0.67	0.69
dark-blue (25, 25, 112)	0.58	0.30	0.67	0.16	0.89	0.81
blue (0, 0, 255)	0.33	0.48	0.53	0.44	0.92	0.69
dark-brown (94, 38, 18)	0.44	0.32	0.56	0.37	0.75	0.50
brown (128, 128, 42)	0.33	0.25	0.45	0.06	0.00	0.21
yellow (255, 255, 0)	0.79	0.77	0.89	0.39	1.00	0.81
lemon-yellow(255, 215, 0)	0.77	0.78	0.97	0.06	0.00	0.94
dark-orange (210, 105, 30)	0.56	0.18	0.90	1.00	0.00	0.53
dark-green (48, 128, 20)	0.65	0.50	0.95	0.22	0.07	0.55
red-orange (255, 97, 0)	0.00	0.00	0.00	0.39	1.00	0.05
earthy-yellow (184, 134, 11)	0.05	0.67	0.25	0.01	0.40	1.00
green (0, 255, 0)	0.06	0.13	0.00	1.00	1.00	0.33
pink (255, 192, 203)	0.44	0.67	0.67	0.92	0.93	0.75
purple (160, 32,240)	1.00	0.00	1.00	0.00	0.00	1.00
mAP	56.51%	51.70%	70.01%	46.12%	62.93%	72.07%

4.4.2. Results on Real Datasets

We train *JADAR*, *RetinaNet*, *Faster RCNN*, *SSD*, *YOLO V3*, *LR*, *PR*, *RR*, *Da-faster*, and *ATF* on *Rain Vehicle Color*-24 and test them on real rainy image vehicle datasets, *RID* and *RIS*. The test results are shown in Figures 11–14. As can be seen from these figures, the test results of *JADAR* on the real datasets, *RID* and *RIS*, are generally better than those of other methods. As can be seen from Figure 11, the *JADAR* and *SSD* algorithms can correctly identify the two cars in the picture; *Yolo V3* can also identify the two cars in the picture, but the black color is mistakenly identified as silver-gray; while the other three algorithms can hardly identify any vehicles in the picture. Referring to Figure 12, because the recognition effects of *Faster RCNN* and *SSD* are better than others', we find a limitation of *JADAR* in recognizing small targets. Referring to Figure 13, all algorithms can identify the color of the vehicle in the image but with different confidence values; specifically, *ATF* has the highest confidence value for blue vehicle, with 0.98. However, Figure 14 shows that only *JADAR* and *ATF* can identify a certain white vehicle.

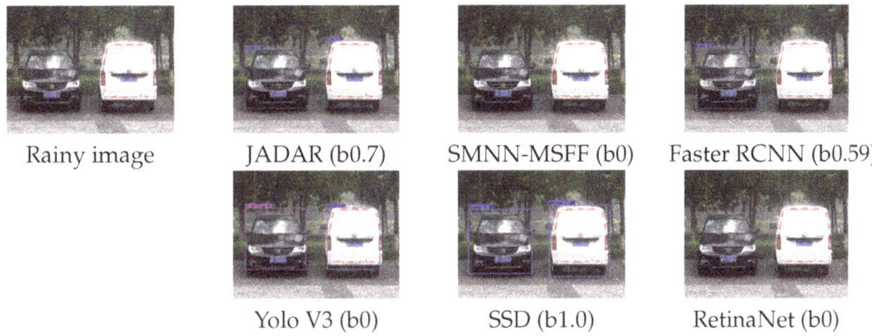

Figure 11. Test results of JADAR and color recognition and object detection methods on the RID.

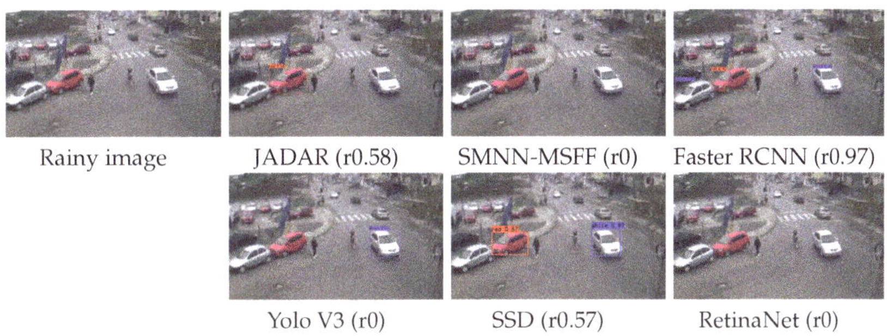

Figure 12. Test results of JADAR and color recognition and object detection methods on the RIS.

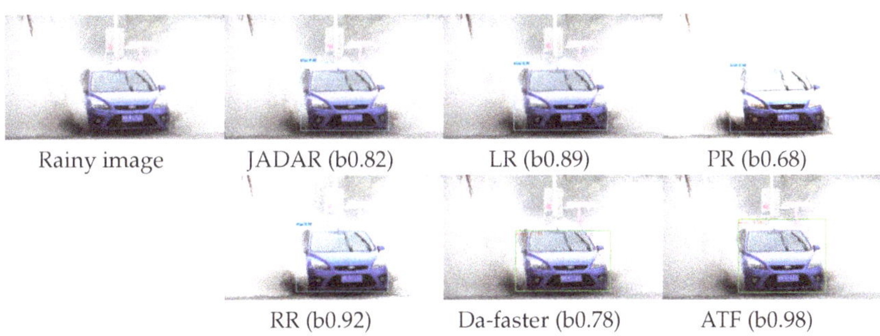

Figure 13. Test results of JADAR and two-stage and domain-adaptation methods on the RID.

Figure 14. Test results of *JADAR* and two-stage and domain-adaptation methods on the *RIS*.

4.5. Inference Time

In order to compare the test time of all methods, all network models are tested on a testing subset with an input of 1920 × 1080 images. The test times are shown in Table 4. JADAR takes 1.7 s per image on a single Tesla P40 GPU, which is the same as for *RetinaNet*, but JADAR is 21.8, 1.1, 4.4, 0.8, and 0.9 seconds faster than *LR*, *PR* and *RR*, *Da-faster*, and *ATF*, respectively. Therefore, although *JADAR* has one more decoder module than *RetinaNet*, it still maintains its original high detection speed.

Table 4. Comparison of different network recognition speeds (GPU).

Algorithm	RN	LR	PR	RR	Da-Faster	ATF	JADAR
Speed (s)	1.7	23.5	2.8	6.1	2.5	2.6	1.7

5. Conclusions

In this paper, we study vehicle color recognition under rainy conditions and propose a joint semantics learning method *JADAR*, which is designed by embedding *UNet*-3 into *RetinaNet*. The *UNet* module achieves rainy image removal and restores the clean background image. The recovered background image and the rainy image are input together into the $class + bbox$ sub-module of *RetinaNet* network to accurately extract the joint semantic of the vehicle color features maps. *JADAR* outperforms other methods under rainy as well as normal conditions for fine vehicle color recognition. Extensive experimental results show that the mAP of the proposed method reaches 72.07% in identifying 24 colors under rainy conditions. Because our algorithm is trained on synthetic datasets, its generalization is not guaranteed. In the future, semi-supervised or few-shot learning is planned to further improve the generalization and realizability of the algorithm. As a further research topic, one can consider fusing overlap functions and fuzzy (rough) sets (see [51–55]) to develop the method of this paper.

Author Contributions: Writing—original draft preparation, M.H.; Experiments and editing, Y.W.; review, J.F., writing—review, B.J. All authors have read and agreed to the published version of the manuscript.

Funding: This study was funded by the National Natural Science Foundation of China (no. 62071378), the Shaanxi Province International Science and Technology Cooperation Program (no. 2022KW-04), and the Xi'an Science and Technology Plan Project (no. 21XJZZ0072).

Data Availability Statement: The data that support the findings of this study are openly available at humingdi2005@github.com.

Conflicts of Interest: The authors declare that they have no conflict of interest.

References

1. Tang, J.; Zeng, J. Spatiotemporal gated graph attention network for urban traffic flow prediction based on license plate recognition data. *Comput.-Aided Civ. Infrastruct. Eng.* **2022**, *37*, 3–23. [CrossRef]
2. Rajavel, R.; Ravichandran, S.K.; Harimoorthy, K.; Nagappan, P.; Gobichettipalayam, K.R. IoT-based smart healthcare video surveillance system using edge computing. *J. Ambient. Intell. Humaniz. Comput.* **2022**, *13*, 3195–3207. [CrossRef]
3. Wang, Z.; Zhan, J.; Duan, C.; Guan, X.; Lu, P. A review of vehicle detection techniques for intelligent vehicles. *IEEE Trans. Neural Netw. Learn. Syst.* **2022**, *23*, 1–21. [CrossRef]
4. Wang, J.; Gao, J.; Zhao, S.; Zhu, R.; Jiang, Z. From Model to Algorithms: Distributed Magnetic Sensor System for Vehicle Tracking. *IEEE Trans. Ind. Inform.* **2022**, *33*, 1. [CrossRef]
5. Lee, S.; Park, S.H. Concept drift modeling for robust autonomous vehicle control systems in time-varying traffic environments. *Expert Syst. Appl.* **2022**, *190*, 116–206. [CrossRef]
6. Khan, M.A.; Sayed, H.E.; Malik, S.; Zia, T.; Khan, J. Level-5 Autonomous Driving—Are We There Yet? A Review of Research Literature. *ACM Comput. Surv.* **2022**, *55*, 1–38. [CrossRef]
7. Custers, B. AI in Criminal Law: An Overview of AI Applications in Substantive and Procedural Criminal Law. In *Law and Artificial Intelligence*; Asser Press: The Hague, The Netherlands, 2022; pp. 205–223.

8. Chen, P.; Bai, X.; Liu, W. Vehicle color recognition on urban road by feature context. *IEEE Trans. Intell. Transp. Syst.* **2014**, *15*, 2340–2346. [CrossRef]
9. Jeong, Y.; Park, K.H.; Park, D. Homogeneity patch search method for voting-based efficient vehicle color classification using front-of-vehicle image. *Multimed. Tools Appl.* **2019**, *78*, 28633–28648. [CrossRef]
10. Tilakaratna, D.S.; Watchareeruetai, U.; Siddhichai, S.; Natcharapinchai, N. Image analysis algorithms for vehicle color recognition. In Proceedings of the 2017 International Electrical Engineering Congress, Pattaya, Thailand, 8–10 March 2017; pp. 1–4.
11. Dule, E.; Gokmen, M.; Beratoglu, M.S. A convenient feature vector construction for vehicle color recognition. In Proceedings of the 11th WSEAS International Conference on Nural Networks and 11th WSEAS International Conference on Evolutionary Computing and 11th WSEAS International Conference on Fuzzy Systems, Iasi Romania, 13–15 June 2010; pp. 250–255.
12. Hu, C.; Bai, X.; Qi, L.; Chen, P.; Xue, G. Vehicle color recognition with spatial pyramid deep learning. *IEEE Trans. Intell. Transp. Syst.* **2015**, *16*, 2925–2934. [CrossRef]
13. Rachmadi, R.F.; Purnama, I.K. Vehicle color recognition using convolutional neural network. In Proceedings of the IEEE International Conference on Computer Vision and Pattern Recognition, Boston, MA, USA, 7–10 June 2015.
14. Zhuo, L.; Zhang, Q.; Li, J.; Zhang, J.; Li, X. High-accuracy vehicle color recognition using hierarchical fine-tuning strategy for urban surveillance videos. *J. Electron. Imaging* **2018**, *27*, 1–9. [CrossRef]
15. Zhang, Q.; Zhuo, L.; Li, J.; Zhang, J.; Zhang, H. Vehicle color recognition using Multiple-Layer Feature Representations of lightweight convolutional neural network. *Signal Process.* **2018**, *147*, 146–153. [CrossRef]
16. Fu, H.; Ma, H.; Wang, G.; Zhang, X.; Zhang, Y. Mcff-cnn: Multiscale comprehensive feature fusion convolutional neural network for vehicle color recognition based on residual learning. *Neurocomputing* **2020**, *395*, 178–187. [CrossRef]
17. Nafzi, M.; Brauckmann, M.; Glasmachers, T. Vehicle shape and color classification using convolutional neural network. In Proceedings of the IEEE International Conference on Computer Vision and Pattern Recognition, Long Beach, CA, USA, 16–21 June 2019.
18. Hu, M.; Bai, L.; Li, Y.; Zhao, S.R.; Chen, E.H. Vehicle Color Recognition Based on Smooth Modulation Neural Network with Multi-Scale Feature Fusion. *arXiv* **2021**, arXiv:2107.09944.
19. Ren, S.; He, K.; Girshick, R.; Sun, J. Faster r-cnn: Towards real-time object detection with region proposal networks. *IEEE Trans. Pattern Anal. Mach. Intell.* **2017**, *39*, 1137–1149. [CrossRef]
20. Liu, W.; Anguelov, D.; Erhan, D.; Szegedy, C.; Reed, S. Ssd: Single shot multi-box detector. In Proceedings of the European Conference on Computer Vision, Amsterdam, The Netherlands, 8–16 October 2016; pp. 21–37.
21. Redmon, J.; Divvala, S.; Girshick, R.; Farhadi, A. You only look once: Unified, real-time object detection. In Proceedings of the 2016 IEEE Conference on Computer Vision and Pattern Recognition, Las Vegas, NV, USA, 27–30 June 2016; pp. 779–788.
22. Bochkovskiy, A.; Wang, C.Y.; Liao, H.Y. Yolov4: Optimal speed and accuracy of object detection. In Proceedings of the 2020 IEEE Conference on Computer Vision and Pattern Recognition, Seattle, WA, USA, 13–19 June 2020.
23. Tan, M.; Pang, R.; Le, Q.V. Efficientdet: Scalable and efficient object detection. In Proceedings of the 2020 IEEE Conference on Computer Vision and Pattern Recognition, Seattle, WA, USA, 13–19 June 2020; pp. 10781–10790.
24. Lin, T.Y.; Goyal, P.; Girshick, R.; He, K.; Dollár, P. Focal loss for dense object detection. In Proceedings of the 2017 IEEE Conference on Computer Vision and Pattern Recognition, Honolulu, HI, USA, 21–26 July 2017; pp. 2980–2988.
25. Xu, M.; Wang, H.; Ni, B.; Tian, Q.; Zhang, W. Cross-domain detection via graph-induced prototype alignment. In Proceedings of the IEEE/CVF Conference on Computer Vision and Pattern Recognition, Seattle, WA, USA, 13–19 June 2020; pp. 12355–12364.
26. Zhang, Y.; Wang, Z.; Mao, Y. Rpn prototype alignment for domain adaptive object detector. In Proceedings of the IEEE/CVF Conference on Computer Vision and Pattern Recognition, Nashville, TN, USA, 20–25 June 2021; pp. 12425–12434.
27. Kim, T.; Jeong, M.; Kim, S.; Choi, S.; Kim, C. Diversify and match: A domain adaptive representation learning paradigm for object detection. In Proceedings of the IEEE/CVF Conference on Computer Vision and Pattern Recognition, Long Beach, CA, USA, 15–20 June 2019; pp. 12456–12465.
28. Dong, H.; Pan, J.; Xiang, L.; Hu, Z.; Zhang, X.; Wang, F.; Yang, M.H. Multi scale boosted dehazing network with dense feature fusion. In Proceedings of the IEEE/CVF Conference on Computer Vision and Pattern Recognition, Seattle, WA, USA, 13–19 June 2020; pp. 2157–2167.
29. Xu, C.D.; Zhao, X.R.; Jin, X.; Wei, X.S. Exploring categorical regularization for domain adaptive object detection. In Proceedings of the IEEE/CVF Conference on Computer Vision and Pattern Recognition, Seattle, WA, USA, 13–19 June 2020; pp. 11724–11733.
30. Vs, V.; Gupta, V.; Oza, P.; Sindagi, V.A.; Patel, V.M. Mega-cda: Memory guided attention for category-aware unsupervised domain adaptive object detection. In Proceedings of the IEEE/CVF Conference on Computer Vision and Pattern Recognition, Nashville, TN, USA, 20–25 June 2021; pp. 4516–4526.
31. Sindagi, V.A.; Oza, P.; Yasarla, R.; Patel, V.M. Prior-based domain adaptive object detection for hazy and rainy conditions. In Proceedings of the European Conference on Computer Vision, Glasgow, UK, 23–28 August 2020; Springer: Berlin/Heidelberg, Germany, 2020; pp. 763–780.
32. Wang, T.; Zhang, X.; Yuan, L.; Feng, J. Few-shot adaptive faster r-cnn. In Proceedings of the IEEE/CVF Conference on Computer Vision and Pattern Recognition, Long Beach, CA, USA, 15–20 June 2019; pp. 7173–7182.
33. Chen, Y.; Li, W.; Sakaridis, C.; Dai, D.; Van, G.L. Domain adaptive faster rcnn for object detection in the wild. In Proceedings of the European Conference on Computer Vision, Munich, Germany, 8–14 September 2018; pp. 3339–3348.

34. Liu, W.; Ren, G.; Yu, R.; Guo, S.; Zhu, J. Image-adaptive yolo for object detection in adverse weather conditions. In Proceedings of the AAAI Conference on Artificial Intelligence, Arlington, VA, USA, 17–19 November 2022; pp. 1792–1800.
35. Fu, X.; Liang, B.; Huang, Y.; Ding, X.; Paisley, J. Lightweight pyramid networks for image deraining. *IEEE Trans. Neural Netw. Learn. Syst.* **2019**, *31*, 1794–1807. [CrossRef]
36. Fan, Z.; Wu, H.; Fu, X.; Hunag, Y.; Ding, X. Residual-guide feature fusion network for single image deraining. *arXiv* **2018**, arXiv:1804.07493.
37. Jiang, K.; Wang, Z.; Yi, P.; Chen, C.; Huang, B. Multi-scale progressive fusion network for single image deraining. In Proceedings of the IEEE/CVF Conference on Computer Vision and Pattern Recognition, Seattle, WA, USA, 13–19 June 2020; pp. 8346–8355.
38. Li, S.Y.; Araujo, I.B.; Ren, W.Q.; Wang, Z.Y.; Tokuda, E.K. Single image deraining: A comprehensive benchmark analysis. In Proceedings of the 2019 IEEE/CVF Conference on Computer Vision and Pattern Recognition, Long Beach, CA, USA, 15–20 June 2019; pp. 3833–3842.
39. Tremblay, M.; Halder, S.S.; De Charette, R.; Lalonde, J.F. Rain rendering for evaluating and improving robustness to bad weather. *Int. J. Comput. Vis.* **2021**, *129*, 341–360. [CrossRef]
40. Zhang, H.; Sindagi, V.; Patel, V.M. Image de-raining using a conditional generative adversarial network. *IEEE Trans. Circuits Syst. Video Technol.* **2020**, *30*, 3943–3956. [CrossRef]
41. Huang, S.C.; Le, T.H.; Jaw, D.W. DSNet: Joint semantic learning for object detection in inclement weather conditions. *IEEE Trans. Pattern Anal. Mach. Intell.* **2020**, *43*, 2623–2633. [CrossRef]
42. Hu, M.; Yang, J.; Lin, N.; Liu, Y.; Fan, J. Lightweight single image deraining algorithm incorporating visual saliency. *IET Image Process.* **2022**, *16*, 3190–3200. [CrossRef]
43. Ronneberger, O.; Fischer, P.; Brox, T. U-net: Convolutional networks for biomedical image segmentation. In Proceedings of the International Conference on Medical Image Computing and Computer-Assisted Intervention, Munich, Germany, 5–9 October 2015; Springer: Cham, Switzerland, 2015; pp. 234–241.
44. Kingma, D.P.; Ba, J. Adam: A method for stochastic optimization. *arXiv* **2014**, arXiv:1412.6980.
45. Jose, H.; Vadivukarasi, T.; Devakumar, J. Extraction of protein interaction data: A comparative analysis of methods in use. *EURASIP J. Bioinform. Syst. Biol.* **2007**, *43*, 53096. [CrossRef] [PubMed]
46. Hu, M.; Wang, C.; Yang, J.; Wu, Y.; Fan, J.; Jing, B. Rain Rendering and Construction of Rain Vehicle Color-24 Dataset. *Mathematics* **2022**, *10*, 3210. [CrossRef]
47. Hu, M.; Wu, Y.; Song, Y.; Yang, J.B.; Zhang, R.F. The integrated evaluation and review of single image rain removal based datasets and deep methods. *J. Image Graph.* **2022**, *27*, 1359–1391.
48. Ren, D.; Zuo, W.; Hu, Q.; Zhu, P.; Meng, D.Y. Progressive image deraining networks: a better and simpler baseline. In Proceedings of the 2019 IEEE/CVF Conference on Computer Vision and Pattern Recognition, Long Beach, CA, USA, 15–20 June 2019; pp. 3937–3946.
49. Wang, H.; Xie, Q.; Zhao, Q.; Meng, D.Y. A model-driven deep neural network for single image rain removal. In Proceedings of the 2020 IEEE/CVF Conference on Computer Vision and Pattern Recognition, Seattle, WA, USA, 14–19 June 2020; pp. 3100–3109.
50. He, Z.; Zhang, L. Domain adaptive object detection via asymmetric tri-way faster-rcnn. In Proceedings of the European Conference on Computer Vision, Glasgow, UK, 23–28 August 2020; Springer: Cham, Switzerland, 2020; pp. 309–324.
51. Liang, R.; Zhang, X. Interval-valued pseudo overlap functions and application. *Axioms* **2022**, *11*, 216. [CrossRef]
52. Wang, J.; Zhang, X. A novel multi-criteria decision-making method based on rough sets and fuzzy measures. *Axioms* **2022**, *11*, 275. [CrossRef]
53. Zhang, X.; Wang, J.; Zhan, J.; Dai, J. Fuzzy measures and Choquet integrals based on fuzzy covering rough sets. *IEEE Trans. Fuzzy Syst.* **2021**, *30*, 2360–2374. [CrossRef]
54. Sheng, N.; Zhang, X. Regular partial residuated lattices and their filters. *Mathematics* **2022**, *10*, 2429. [CrossRef]
55. Wang, J.; Zhang, X.; Hu, Q. Three-way fuzzy sets and their applications (II). *Axioms* **2022**, *under review of the second version.*

mathematics

MDPI

Article

Resolving Cross-Site Scripting Attacks through Fusion Verification and Machine Learning

Jiazhong Lu †, Zhitan Wei †, Zhi Qin, Yan Chang and Shibin Zhang *

School of Cybersecurity, Chengdu University of Information Technology, Chengdu 610225, China
* Correspondence: cuitzsb@cuit.edu.cn
† These authors contributed equally to this work as co-first authors.

Abstract: The frequent variations of XSS (cross-site scripting) payloads make static and dynamic analysis difficult to detect effectively. In this paper, we proposed a fusion verification method that combines traffic detection with XSS payload detection, using machine learning to detect XSS attacks. In addition, we also proposed seven new payload features to improve detection efficiency. In order to verify the effectiveness of our method, we simulated and tested 20 public CVE (Common Vulnerabilities and Exposures) XSS attacks. The experimental results show that our proposed method has better accuracy than the single traffic detection model. Among them, the recall rate increased by an average of 48%, the F1 score increased by an average of 27.94%, the accuracy rate increased by 9.29%, and the accuracy rate increased by 3.81%. Moreover, the seven new features proposed in this paper account for 34.12% of the total contribution rate of the classifier.

Keywords: XSS attack; traffic detection; payloads; fusion verification

MSC: 68T09

Citation: Lu, J.; Wei, Z.; Qin, Z.; Chang, Y.; Zhang, S. Resolving Cross-Site Scripting Attacks through Fusion Verification and Machine Learning. *Mathematics* **2022**, *10*, 3787. https://doi.org/10.3390/math10203787

Academic Editors: Jianping Gou, Weihua Ou, Shaoning Zeng and Lan Du

Received: 9 September 2022
Accepted: 8 October 2022
Published: 14 October 2022

1. Introduction

XSS (cross-site scripting) attacks have caused enormous damage to economics and individual privacy [1]. Moreover, XSS attacks have been adjusted from the seventh to the third most common in the newly released 2021 version of OWASP (Open Web Application Security Project) Top 10 [2].

Normally, there are three types of XSS attack, namely reflected XSS attack, stored XSS attack, and DOM-based XSS attack. These three attack types usually use the GET or POST methods of the HTTP protocol to inject malicious code at the URL or POST Body. Reflected XSS usually injects malicious code into the URL, which can only be triggered in the current browser and does not store malicious code permanently. The malicious code of stored XSS is injected into the server-side database through vulnerabilities, which can cause long-term information leakage and other hazards. In fact, we can think of DOM-based XSS as a special kind of reflected XSS. Its malicious code can only be triggered in the current browser when it runs the script on the client side for front-end page rendering.

In general, there are two popular methods to defend against XSS attack: static analysis and dynamic analysis. Static analysis finds vulnerabilities by scanning the source code to analyze information such as lexical, grammar, control flow, data flow, and other information. It is in the development and coding phase of the program that requires developers to master a lot of security-related knowledge. Dynamic analysis inputs test data during program execution and analyze the output information to determine whether there are loopholes. However, this method relies on the completeness of the test data.

In the face of frequent variations in XSS payloads, it is hard for traditional XSS detection to have a pleasing result. There are some factors that have a significant impact on the results. For example, traditional XSS detection requires a large number of manual participation and the integrity of the attack vector.

Recently, machine learning techniques have been widely used in XSS attack detection and achieved good results. However, most of the detection approaches based on machine learning only focus on one of the traffic or XSS payloads. On the one hand, traffic detection has certain timeliness, but it is difficult to accurately detect and identify XSS attacks. On the other hand, XSS payload detection has a certain degree of accuracy, but it lacks timeliness. Another reason for this may be that there is currently no public dataset that includes both normal traffic and XSS attack traffic (the only type of attack in the attack traffic is XSS).

As a result, a lot of XSS detection methods cannot meet the dual requirements of timeliness and accuracy in real environments, and the pros and cons of a single model will directly affect the performance of the entire detection model. This leads to the problem of low accuracy and a high false negative rate for a single model.

The primary contribution of this paper is to propose a fusion verification method that combines traffic detection and XSS payload detection. Previously, both traffic detection and XSS payload detection have been separately applied to XSS detection. However, to the best of our knowledge, fusion verification methods combining the two methods have not been reported in the literature for detecting XSS attacks. The main contributions of this paper are:

- Combine traffic detection and XSS payload detection for XSS attack detection through fusion verification
- Propose seven new payload detection features through feature extraction based on XSS attack methods
- Obtain datasets of normal traffic and XSS attack traffic by simulating public CVE

2. Related Work

For the study of XSS attack detection, network security researchers have successively put forward some effective detection methods and preventive measures.

In terms of static analysis, Medeiros et al. [3] proposed a cross-site scripting vulnerability detection method combining static source code analysis and data mining in 2015. The accuracy of XSS vulnerability detection and the effect of fixing code as improved by this method, but the disadvantage was false positives. Choi et al. [4] proposed an HXD (Hybrid XSS Detection) system. The system used both static string analysis and dynamic browser rendering with a black-box detection approach. Experimental results showed that HXD had a low false positive rate. Mohammadiet al. [5] detected XSS vulnerabilities through an automatic unit testing method. They preferred to automatically construct an XSS vulnerability unit test from each web page; the test input pair framework was then automatically generated using a grammar-based attack generator, which was then evaluated. The proposed method reduced the error rate of XSS vulnerabilities. In 2019, YAN et al. [6] proposed a PHP code vulnerability detection method based on sensitive path and taint analysis. The method first converted the background code of the web application into the intermediate representation of the code, such as the abstract syntax tree, then found the slot (dangerous function), then determined the sensitive path through the slot, and finally performed taint analysis on this path to determine whether the vulnerability exists. However, the disadvantages of static analysis were obvious, it relied on a lot of manual work by human experts with knowledge of both programming and security domains, and the source code was usually not open-source.

In terms of dynamic analysis, Parameshwaran et al. [7] designed a DOM-based XSS test platform, which was based on taint analysis in 2015. The platform included a vulnerability generator and a detection engine. Experiments showed that the method had an excellent effect on detecting DOM-based XSS attacks. Wang et al. [8] proposed a TT-XSS framework to detect DOM-based XSS using dynamic taint analysis. The application dynamically analyzed the collected URLs that were then sent to the taint tracking analysis module, the obtained taint trajectories were sent to the automatic vulnerability verification module, and the verification module was completed by generating attack vectors from taint trajectories. In 2021, Khalaf et al. [9] proposed an algorithm that allowed attack detection and prevention using an input validation mechanism. This approach supported web security testing by providing an easy-to-use and accurate vulnerability prediction model and validation method, which had the advantage of having a very low false positive rate. However, this method relied on the completeness of the testing dataset. If the testing dataset was not perfect or faced deformation attacks, it would produce a high false negative rate. In addition, this is a common problem for all dynamic analyses.

In recent years, zero-day attacks and deformation attacks are common, and it is difficult for traditional static analysis and dynamic analysis to play an effective role in XSS detection. Therefore, a large number of scholars have introduced machine learning technology for XSS detection and achieved good results. Zuhair et al. [10] also extracted features from Web pages and URLs but made a mixed feature subset division, combined with phishing attacks, and finally used the SVM algorithm for training and testing. Rathore et al. [11] proposed a machine learning method based on URLs, web pages, and SNSs to detect XSS attacks in 2017, extracted twenty-five XSS attack features, and used ten classifiers for detection. To achieve better performance, Hosseini et al. [12] proposed a model for detecting malicious crawler behavior using machine learning techniques and tested and compared several machine learning algorithms, such as Bayesian networks, SVM, and decision trees. Finally, in this experiment, it was found that the SVM-based model had higher detection accuracy for malicious crawlers and extracting effective features could improve the detection accuracy. In 2021, Hu et al. [13] designed and implemented an XSS attack detection model for web applications. This model added the verification code recognition function to solve the problem of submitting data to the server just by entering the verification code; this model had a low false positive rate. Malviya et al. [14] developed a web browser for machine learning classification to mitigate XSS attacks. Experimental results showed that the proposed method outperforms other proposed methods in classification accuracy, recall, precision, and F1-score. Mokbal et al. [15] proposed a novel XSS attack detection framework based on the ensemble learning technique for web applications, which used the XG boost (Extreme Gradient Boosting) algorithm and the extreme parameter optimization method. The proposed framework passed multiple tests on the testing dataset, and the accuracy could reach 99.59%. Soltani et al. [16] proposed a framework for a DID (Deep Intrusion Detection) system. The authors deployed and evaluated offline IDS (Intrusion Detection System) following this framework. Experiments showed that the evaluation indicators, such as the precision rate and recall rate, of this method, reached 0.992 and 0.998, respectively. In addition, the shortage of high-quality data has always been a key problem in machine learning. Multi-fidelity classification algorithms [17–19] solve this type of problem by incorporating information from other sources that can be obtained at a low cost while maintaining good correlation. In this regard, it can also be applied to the XSS attack detection model in the future to improve the generalization ability of the model.

Our previous work [20] can detect XSS attacks more accurately by using machine learning to jointly detect traffic and logs and at the same time, trace the process of XSS attacks in the entire network, but it needs to collect a large number of network device logs for analysis.

To sum up, the current XSS attack detection approaches still have the following problems:

- XSS remains one of the most serious and common types of attacks. Therefore, a more effective detection method is needed to defend against XSS attacks.
- The pros and cons of a single model of the existing detection methods will directly affect the effectiveness of the entire detection model.
- Existing detection methods have a high false negative rate in the face of the frequent variations in XSS payloads, which needs to be reduced.
- There is currently no public dataset that includes both normal traffic and XSS attack traffic (the only type of attack in the attack traffic is XSS).

Therefore, this paper focuses on developing a fusion verification method. We obtain a real-world experimental dataset by simulating XSS vulnerabilities in CVE (Common Vulnerabilities and Exposures) and capturing network traffic on the web server side. Then we combined traffic detection with XSS payload detection to form a fusion verification method to defend against XSS attacks. Moreover, this method combines the timeliness advantages of traffic detection and the accuracy advantages of payload detection. We expect that this method can improve the performance of detection models and solve the problems that existing solutions have that make it difficult to meet actual needs.

3. Proposed Methodology

Figure 1 shows the overall framework for detecting the XSS proposed in this paper. First, the original dataset of the experiment is obtained by reproducing the CVE vulnerability. Then we use the rdpcap function of the Scapy library in Python to read the pcap file of the original dataset and summarize the data according to the upstream and downstream of the two-way communication. In addition, it is divided into two detection modules, one is traffic detection and the other is XSS payload detection. We extract the traffic dataset and the payload dataset separately through different modules. The two modules perform preprocessing and feature extraction, respectively, to form a data format that can be recognized by machine learning input. Next, the two modules separately perform preprocessing and feature extraction to form a recognizable data format for machine learning input and send it to the classifier for detection. Due to the particularity of the traffic itself, we found that each flow in the pcap packet corresponds to multiple payloads at the same time, and each result of the traffic detection module may correspond to the results of multiple payload detection modules. Therefore, we can combine the results of the two modules by matching the source port feature (src_port) common to both detection modules. Finally, the final detection result is obtained through the fusion verification of the two detection models so as to improve the detection performance of the entire model.

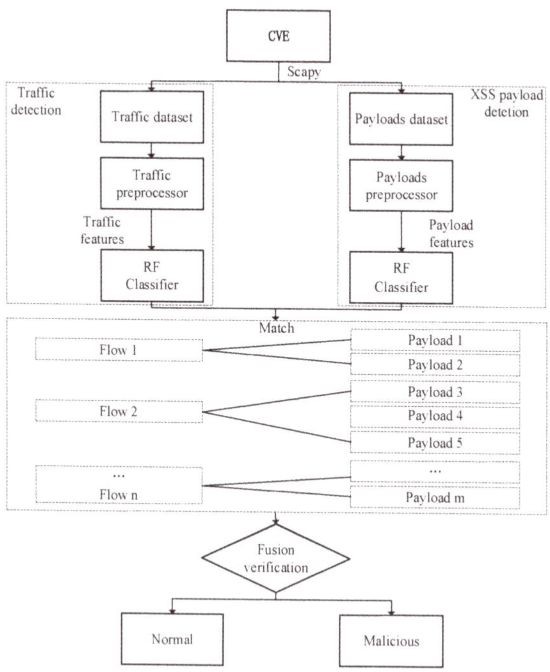

Figure 1. The framework of the proposed method.

3.1. *CVE Vulnerability Set*

This paper targets the widely used content management system—WordPress [21] (43.0% of websites worldwide use WordPress). From NVD [22] (National Vulnerability

Database), we have selected 10 recent XSS vulnerabilities for both reflected XSS and stored XSS. The specific CVE list is shown in Table 1. Then, the original dataset is formed by simulating locally and using WireShark [23] to capture the traffic packets of the reproduced process, and the dataset format is pcap packet.

Table 1. CVE list.

XSS Type	Vulnerability Number
Reflected XSS	CVE-2021-25067, CVE-2021-24234, CVE-2021-24180, CVE-2021-24225, CVE-2021-24436, CVE-2021-24437, CVE-2021-24452, CVE-2021-25041, CVE-2021-25047, CVE-2021-25065
Stored XSS	CVE-2021-25046, CVE-2021-24988, CVE-2021-24315, CVE-2021-24528, CVE-2021-24658, CVE-2021-24518, CVE-2021-24505, CVE-2021-24504, CVE-2022-1915, CVE-2022-1896

3.2. *Traffic Features Extraction*

After detection and analysis, it is found that the XSS attack traffic is different from the normal traffic. Since XSS attack traffic not only needs to load normal web pages but also needs to load malicious js files or external malicious links, resulting in extra network resources and system resources. Thus, the packets of XSS attack traffic are generally larger.

A total of 1947 flows have been extracted for analysis in this paper. Two types of features have been used for learning: traffic-related features and time-related features, which help the classifier to distinguish between normal traffic and XSS attack traffic. Moreover, the traffic-related features include the five-tuple features of the communication process (due to the particularity of the format of the IP address itself, the source IP address and the destination IP address are omitted), as shown in Table 2. This experiment has used enough traffic to reflect the real network environment and real traffic features.

Table 2. Traffic features and descriptions.

Feature Type	Feature Name	Descriptions
Traffic-related features	proto	Transfer protocol number
	src_port	Source port
	dst_port	Destination port
	up_pkts	Total number of upstream packets
	dw_pkts	Total number of downlink packets
	up_pl_bytes	Total uplink load
	dw_pl_bytes	Total downlink load
	up_min_plsize	Upstream minimum payload
	dw_min_plsize	Downlink minimum payload
	up_avg_plsize	Upstream load average
	dw_avg_plsize	Downstream load average
	up_max_plsize	Upstream maximum payload
	dw_max_plsize	Downlink maximum payload
	up_stdev_plsize	Upstream load variance
	dw_stdev_plsize	Downlink load variance
Time-related features	duration	Stream duration
	up_avg_ipt	Average time interval of upstream packets
	dw_avg_ipt	Average time interval of downlink packets
	up_min_ipt	Uplink minimum time interval
	dw_min_ipt	Downlink minimum time interval
	up_max_ipt	Uplink maximum time interval
	dw_max_ipt	Downlink maximum time interval
	up_stdev_ipt	Upstream time interval variance
	dw_stdev_ipt	Downlink time interval variance

3.3. Payload Features Extraction

In this section, after an in-depth study of XSS attack methods and causes, we have summarized three representative attack methods from the attackers' point of view. Then we extracted seven attribute features of the payloads according to the summarized attack methods.

3.3.1. XSS Attack Methods

(1) Script: Script injection can be divided into static script injection and dynamic script injection. Static script injection usually constructs malicious code within <script></script> tags to trigger scripts. Dynamic script injection refers to triggering the browser to introduce external malicious links through the src attribute of the script tag.
(2) JavaScript pseudo-protocol: XSS attack using JavaScript pseudo-protocol is also a common injection method. The JavaScript pseudo-protocol treats the segment after the code "javascript:" as a JavaScript script and executes it.
(3) Inline events: JavaScript interacts with HTML through DOM events. The HTML DOM allows JavaScript to react to HTML events and execute JavaScript when events occur. XSS attack can use DOM events to bind malicious code. Most DOM events have names starting with "on", and most HTML tags can use the on-event to trigger script code. Table 3 shows some on-events.

Table 3. Some on-events and descriptions.

Attribute	Descriptions
onerror	Run the script when an error occurs
onload	Run the script when the document loads
onfocus	Run script when window gets focus
onclick	Run a script when the mouse is clicked
onmouseover	Run a script when the mouse pointer moves over an element

Table 4 shows examples of three XSS attack methods:

Table 4. XSS attack examples.

Methods	Examples
Script	<script>alert(123);</script>
JavaScript pseudo-protocol	<iframe src="javascript:alert('xss')">
Inline events	<img src=# onerror="alert(document.cookie)">

3.3.2. Attribute Features

Usually, experienced attackers will change the encoding or capitalization of malicious code to carry out deformation attacks. Therefore, this paper has preprocessed the extracted sentences to convert them into original sentences. The preprocessing includes lowercase conversion, URL decoding, HTML decoding, JavaScript decoding, ASCII decoding, Unicode decoding, and URL decoding twice. Values are then extracted from the processed dataset to fit the features proposed in this paper.

Through extensive research on XSS attack methods and analysis of their lexical features, we have found that text characters commonly found in malicious code are often combined with certain fixed symbols. Therefore, matching the combined form can reduce the detection of false positive rate compared to just matching text characters. The following seven attribute features are summarized:

(1) HTML_Tags

HTML tags in XSS attacks typically appear more frequently than text loads in normal traffic. In HTML tags, the label starts with a left angle bracket. For example, <script, <iframe, and <img in Table 5 appear in the form of left angle brackets plus script, iframe, and img characters. Therefore, the combination of the left angle bracket and the label character is classified into a class of features.

Table 5. Seven new attribute features.

Features	Examples
HTML_Tags	<script, <img, <body, etc.
JavaScript	javascript:
On_Event	onerror=, onmouseover=, onload=, etc.
Function_Body	alert(, confirm(, eval(, etc.
Document_Object	document.cookie, etc.
Third_Party_Links	src=, href=, http:, https:, //
Delimiter	space,/, +

(2) JavaScript

The JavaScript pseudo-protocol is usually combined with HTML tags to form malicious code, such as <iframe src="javascript:alert('xss')">, where the code feature that will always appear is "javascript:".

(3) On_Event

HTML5 allows browsers to trigger scripts through various events. For example, in the malicious code "<img src=#onerror="alert(document.cookie)">", the attacker deliberately sets the src attribute of the img tag to be wrong and then uses the onerror event (run the script when an error occurs) to trigger the malicious script. Therefore, the alert function is triggered here, causing the cookie to be leaked. The features of the event attribute are the form of the on-event followed by an equal sign, such as "onerror=".

(4) Function_Body

Attackers can use some "dangerous functions" in JavaScript to steal sensitive information. For example, the "alert()" function is often used to pop up a dialog box. If an attacker combines it with the document object, the purpose of stealing cookies can be achieved. The code feature of the JavaScript function body is "alert()", which is obviously different from ordinary characters.

(5) Document_Object

The document object is the root node of the HTML document. An attacker can use the "document.write" property to write JavaScript code to the document or use "document.cookie" to return all cookies associated with the current document. Its code feature is "document."

(6) Third_Party_Links

In order to better conceal cross-site scripting attacks, experienced attackers will build an XSS attack server to receive and store the stolen sensitive information. As a result, there will be third-party links in the attack traffic, which are mostly characterized by a combination of src or href and third-party links.

(7) Delimiter

Delimiters, such as spaces, are unavoidably used within HTML tags due to the grammatical nature of HTML. Therefore, attackers must use delimiters to construct attack statements when exploiting cross-site scripting vulnerabilities. "space", "/", and"+" are known to be used as delimiters for malicious code.

In this paper, we have added 7 new features to the 30 features extracted by Zhou and Wang (2019) [1], totaling 37 attribute features of the XSS payloads. Table 5 shows the seven new attribute features added in this paper:

3.4. Fusion Verification

Both the traffic detection module and the XSS payload detection module can present the malicious or normal status of the current stream or payload in binary form. In this paper, we have adopted the fusion verification method. If either of the two detection modules declares that the current detection sample is malicious, it is considered to be malicious. In addition, if both of them declare that it is normal, it is considered to be normal.

In this paper, Boolean variables F_v and P_v are used to represent the detection results of the traffic detection module and the detection results of the XSS payload detection module, respectively. The Boolean variable R_s is used to represent the final result of fusion verification, and its calculation formula is as follows:

$$Rs = Fv \vee Pv \tag{1}$$

It is easy to know from Formula (1) that there are four cases in total. In these four cases, the final result is normal only when the traffic detection determines that it is normal and the payload detection determines that it is normal. In other cases, the result is judged to be malicious.

3.5. Random Forest

The research of a large number of scholars shows that the ensemble method has good performance in classification performance and robustness in the face of overfitting. Therefore, these kinds of algorithms are very popular in the field of machine learning. In this paper, the random forest algorithm has been used as the classification technique of the experiment. Random forest is an ensemble algorithm based on decision tree, which not only has good scalability but is also easy to use. The principle of random forest is to build a strong model with better generalization performance and less overfitting by separately averaging multiple decision trees affected by large variance.

In this paper, the random forest algorithm has been used as the classifier. The random forest algorithm does not need to worry about the choice of hyperparameter values, and pruning it is usually not necessary because of its strong resistance to noise from a single decision tree. In this experiment, we have taken the size of the training dataset as the size, n, of the bootstrap samples in order to obtain a better bias-variance tradeoff. We set the number of features, d, in each split to a value less than the total number of features in the training dataset. We have used the random forest classifier already implemented by scikit-learn with relatively reasonable parameter settings. The default value is d $= \sqrt{m}$, where m represents the total number of features in the training dataset. Additionally, we have chosen entropy as the criterion used for splitting nodes. We have set the value of the n_estimators parameter of the number of decision trees to 100. Because when the n_estimators parameter reaches 100, the accuracy of the model no longer increases. We have set the number of parallel computations, n_jobs, to 10 to use the multi-core computer parallel computing model.

4. Experiments and Discussions

4.1. Experimental Dataset

This paper has formed a traffic dataset containing normal traffic and XSS attack traffic by simulating the CVE. This dataset is called "CVE traffic". "CVE traffic" contains 1747 normal traffic and 200 XSS attack traffic. Then we used Scapy's rdpcap function to extract the XSS payload dataset, referred to as "CVE payloads". It contains 10083 normal records and 231 XSS payloads.

XSS payloads [24] have been collected from GitHub and used as a training dataset with a total of 151,658 records, including 135,507 normal records and 16,151 XSS payloads. The testing dataset has been extracted from the traffic dataset above through the rdpcap function of the Scapy library.

The specific information on the experimental datasets is shown in Table 6

Table 6. Experimental dataset.

Datasets	Normal	XSS
CVE traffic	1747	200
CVE payloads	10,083	231
XSS payloads [24]	135,507	16,151

4.2. Experimental Results

This experiment uses twenty-fold cross-validations to assess the performance of the model. In this method, 19 of the 20 CVE traffic datasets are used as training datasets, and the remaining one is used as the test dataset. Additionally, each of the 20 subsets is only used once as a test dataset. The cross-validation process has been repeated 20 times, and the average of the twenty results for each CVE are taken as the result of this experiment. Then, we used the fusion verification method mentioned in Section 3.4 of this paper to take the average of 20 results for each CVE traffic detection result and XSS payload detection result as the final result of our method.

This experiment aimed to solve a typical binary classification problem. As shown in Table 7, we use a confusion matrix to represent the results.

Table 7. Confusion matrix.

	Actual XSS	Actual Normal
Predicted XSS	TP	FP
Predicted Normal	FN	TN

The confusion matrix is divided into four categories. TP (True Positive) means the number of correctly classified as attack samples, and FP (False Positive) means the number of normal samples classified as attack samples. In addition, TN (True Negative) means the number of correctly classified as normal samples, and FN (False Negative) means the number of attack samples classified as normal samples. This paper evaluates the accuracy, precision, recall, and F1 score of the experimental results. The calculation formulae are as follows:

$$Accuracy = \frac{TP + TN}{TP + TN + FP + FN} \tag{2}$$

$$Precision = \frac{TP}{TP + FP} \tag{3}$$

$$Recall = \frac{TP}{TP + FN} \tag{4}$$

$$F1 = \frac{2 \times Precision \times Recall}{Precision + Recall} \tag{5}$$

The experimental results are shown in Figure 2.

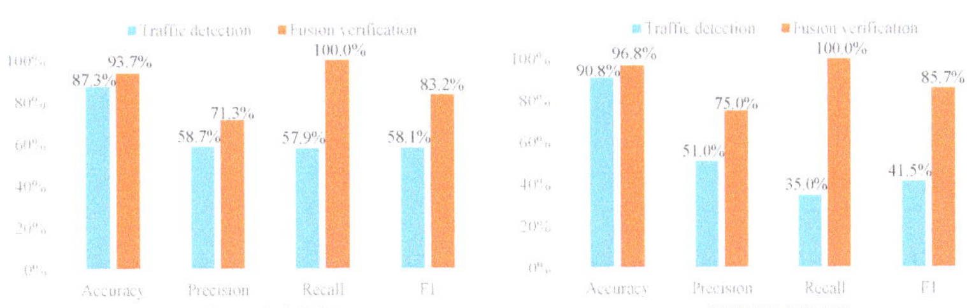

(a) (b)

Figure 2. *Cont.*

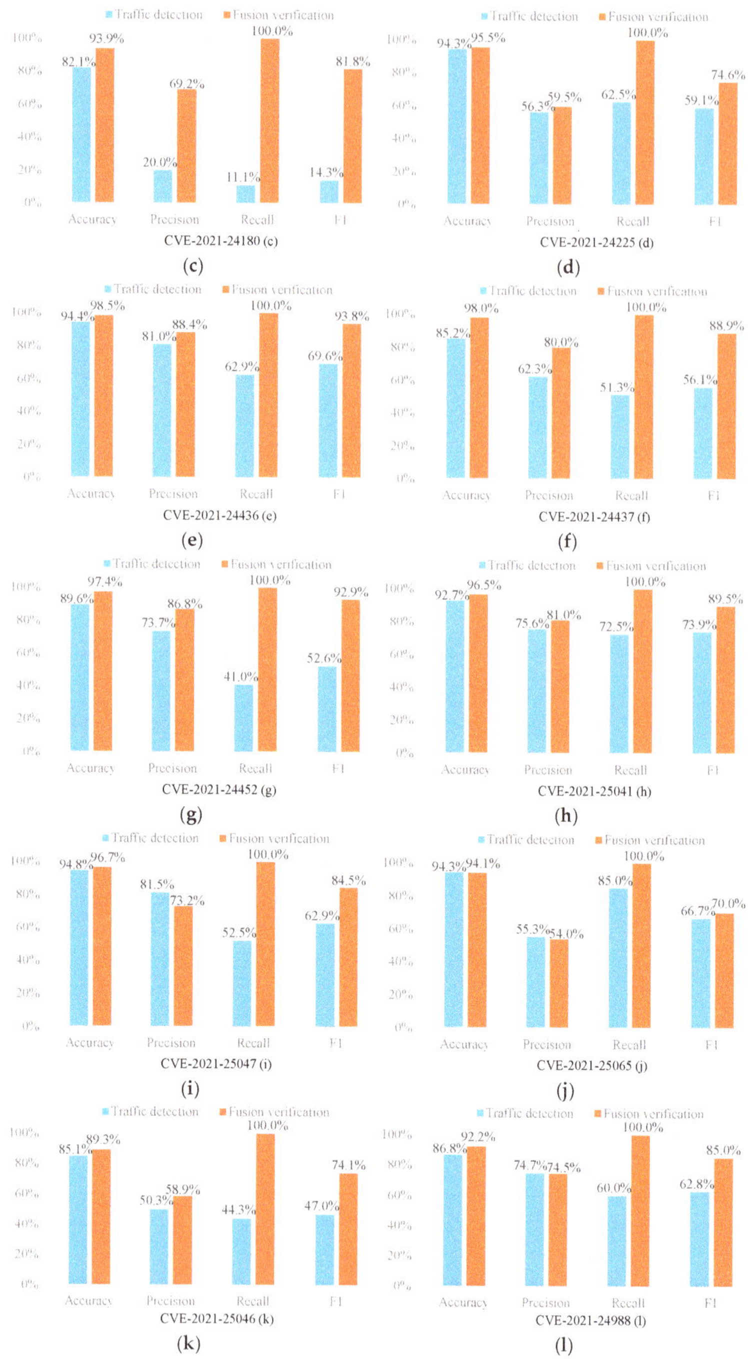

Figure 2. *Cont.*

Figure 2. Experimental results (**a**–**t**).

As can be seen from Figure 2, in 17 out of 20 CVE experiments, the recall of our fusion verification method can reach an astonishing 100%. We can know from Figure 3 that under such a high recall rate, our accuracy is an average of 94.9%, which also remains at a high level. Therefore, the fusion verification method can effectively defend against XSS attacks. In addition, as shown in Figure 3, the average accuracy, precision, recall, and F1 score of this method are significantly improved compared to the single traffic detection model. Among them, the average improvement in the recall rate is as high as 48%, the average increase in F1 score is as high as 27.94%, the average increase in precision is 9.29%, and the average increase in accuracy rate is 3.81%. The results show that our proposed fusion verification model outperforms the single traffic detection model. However, the number of experimental samples in the load detection process is relatively small. Therefore, the performance of a few fusion validation models is slightly lower than that of a single detection model. In this regard, we consider using multi-fidelity classification algorithms in future research and experiments to solve the problem caused by fewer training samples.

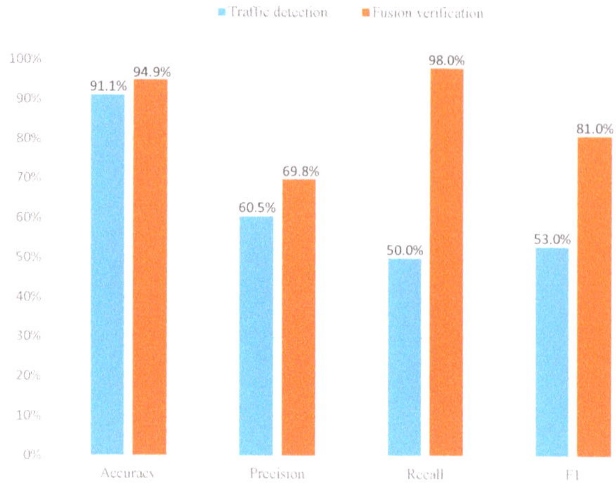

Figure 3. Average performance comparison.

In addition, taking XSS payloads [24] as the dataset, with a ratio of 7:3 between the training set and test set, random forest is used to evaluate the importance of 37 features of the payload detection link used in this paper. Among them, there are 30 features whose contribution rate is larger than 0.01%, as shown in Figure 4. The first is the feature "Function_Body" proposed in this paper, whose contribution rate is as high as 23.95%. Moreover, the total contribution rate of the seven features in this paper is as high as 34.12%. This means that it is feasible to extract detection features by summarizing XSS attack methods in this paper, and it has better generalization and can detect variations in attacks more effectively.

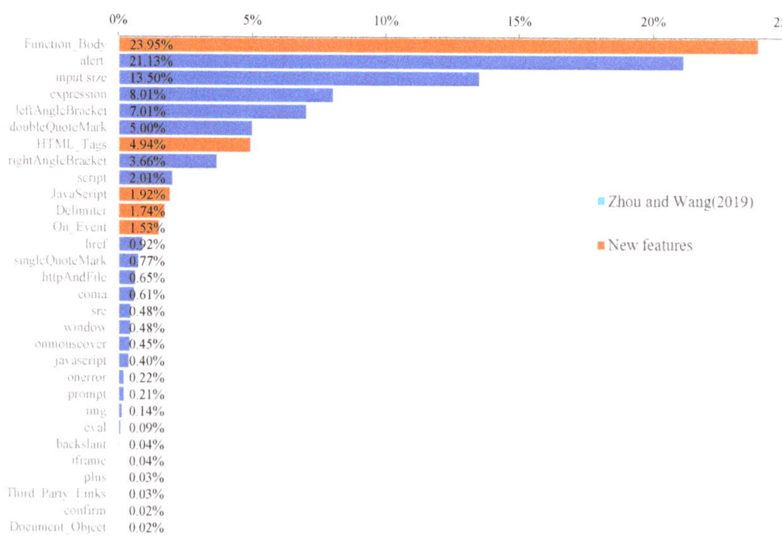

Figure 4. Assess the importance of the features of Zhou and Wang (2019) [1] and the newly proposed features in this paper.

5. Conclusions

We propose a fusion verification method that combines traffic detection with XSS payload detection to effectively detect XSS attacks. The results show that the method proposed in this paper has significant advantages for reducing the false negative rate of the model. Under the premise of uniform sample distribution, there will be almost no false negatives. Therefore, the fusion verification method can effectively defend against XSS attacks. Moreover, compared with the traditional single-flow detection model, the average recall rate of this method, F1 score, precision, and accuracy rate is increased by 48%, 27.94%, 9.29%, and 3.81%, respectively. Further, the seven new features of the XSS payloads proposed in this paper account for 34.12% of the total contribution rate of the 37 features.

However, the method proposed in this paper has certain limitations. The cost of keeping the false negative rate low is that the false positive rate of the entire model will increase. In the follow-up research, we will try to solve the existing problem.

Author Contributions: Data curation, Z.Q.; Resources, Y.C.; Software, Z.W.; Writing—original draft, S.Z.; Writing—review & editing, J.L. All authors have read and agreed to the published version of the manuscript.

Funding: This work was supported by the National Natural Science Foundation of China (Grant No. 62102049). Secondly, thanks to the Key Research and Development Project of Sichuan Province (No. 2022YFS0571, No. 2021YFSY0012, No. 2020YFG0307).

Institutional Review Board Statement: Not applicable.

Informed Consent Statement: Not applicable.

Data Availability Statement: Not applicable.

Conflicts of Interest: The authors declare that they have no known competing financial interests or personal relationships that could appear to influence the work reported in this paper.

References

1. Zhou, Y.; Wang, P. An ensemble learning approach for XSS attack detection with domain knowledge and threat intelligence. *Comput. Secur.* **2019**, *82*, 261–269. [CrossRef]
2. Open Web Application Security Project. OWASP Top Ten. Available online: https://owasp.org/www-project-top-ten/ (accessed on 25 September 2022).
3. Medeiros, I.; Neves, N.; Correia, M. Detecting and removing web application vulnerabilities with static analysis and data mining. *IEEE Trans. Reliab.* **2015**, *65*, 54–69. [CrossRef]
4. Choi, H.; Hong, S.; Cho, S.; Kim, Y.-G. HXD: Hybrid XSS detection by using a headless browser. In Proceedings of the 2017 4th International Conference on Computer Applications and Information Processing Technology (CAIPT), Kuta Bali, Indonesia, 8–10 August 2017; pp. 1–4.
5. Mohammadi, M.; Chu, B.-T.; Lipford, H.R. Automated detecting and repair of cross-site scripting vulnerabilities. *arXiv* **2018**, arXiv:1804.01862.
6. Yan, X.-X.; Wang, Q.-X.; Ma, H.-T. Path sensitive static analysis of taint style vulnerabilities in PHP code. In Proceedings of the 2017 IEEE 17th International Conference on Communication Technology (ICCT), Chengdu, China, 27–30 October 2017; pp. 1382–1386.
7. Parameshwaran, I.; Budianto, E.; Shinde, S.; Dang, H.; Sadhu, A.; Saxena, P. DexterJS: Robust testing platform for DOM-based XSS vulnerabilities. In Proceedings of the 2015 10th Joint Meeting on Foundations of Software Engineering, Bergamo, Italy, 30 August–4 September 2015; pp. 946–949.
8. Wang, R.; Xu, G.; Zeng, X.; Li, X.; Feng, Z. TT-XSS: A novel taint tracking based dynamic detection framework for DOM Cross-Site Scripting. *J. Parallel Distrib. Comput.* **2018**, *118*, 100–106. [CrossRef]
9. Khalaf, O.I.; Sokiyna, M.; Alotaibi, Y.; Alsufyani, A.; Alghamdi, S. Web attack detection using the input validation method: Dpda theory. *Comput. Mater. Contin.* **2021**, *68*, 3167–3184.
10. Zuhair, H.; Selamat, A.; Salleh, M. Selection of Robust Feature Subsets for Phish Webpage Prediction Using Maximum Relevance and Minimum Redundancy Criterion. *J. Theor. Appl. Inf. Technol.* **2015**, *81*, 188–205.
11. Rathore, S.; Sharma, P.K.; Park, J.H. XSSClassifier: An efficient XSS attack detection approach based on machine learning classifier on SNSs. *J. Inf. Process. Syst.* **2017**, *13*, 1014–1028. [CrossRef]
12. Hosseini, N.; Fakhar, F.; Kiani, B.; Eslami, S. Enhancing the security of patients' portals and websites by detecting malicious web crawlers using machine learning techniques. *Int. J. Med. Inform.* **2019**, *132*, 103976. [CrossRef] [PubMed]

13. Hu, L.; Chang, J.; Chen, Z.; Hou, B. Web application vulnerability detection method based on machine learning. *J. Phys. Conf. Ser.* **2021**, *1827*, 012061. [CrossRef]
14. Malviya, V.K.; Rai, S.; Gupta, A. Development of web browser prototype with embedded classification capability for mitigating Cross-Site Scripting attacks. *Appl. Soft Comput.* **2021**, *102*, 106873. [CrossRef]
15. Mokbal, F.M.M.; Dan, W.; Xiaoxi, W.; Wenbin, Z.; Lihua, F. XGBXSS: An extreme gradient boosting detection framework for cross-site scripting attacks based on hybrid feature selection approach and parameters optimization. *J. Inf. Secur. Appl.* **2021**, *58*, 102813. [CrossRef]
16. Soltani, M.; Siavoshani, M.J.; Jahangir, A.H. A content-based deep intrusion detection system. *Int. J. Inf. Secur.* **2022**, *21*, 547–562. [CrossRef]
17. Pawar, S.; San, O.; Vedula, P.; Rasheed, A.; Kvamsdal, T. Multi-fidelity information fusion with concatenated neural networks. *Sci. Rep.* **2022**, *12*, 5900. [CrossRef]
18. Yang, C.-H.; Pokuri, B.S.S.; Lee, X.Y.; Balakrishnan, S.; Hegde, C.; Sarkar, S.; Ganapathysubramanian, B. Multi-fidelity machine learning models for structure–property mapping of organic electronics. *Comput. Mater. Sci.* **2022**, *213*, 111599. [CrossRef]
19. Guo, M.; Manzoni, A.; Amendt, M.; Conti, P.; Hesthaven, J.S. Multi-fidelity regression using artificial neural networks: Efficient approximation of parameter-dependent output quantities. *Comput. Methods Appl. Mech. Eng.* **2022**, *389*, 114378. [CrossRef]
20. Lu, J.; Lv, F.; Zhuo, Z.; Zhang, X.; Liu, X.; Hu, T.; Deng, W. Integrating traffics with network device logs for anomaly detection. *Secur. Commun. Netw.* **2019**, *2019*, 5695021. [CrossRef]
21. W3Techs. Usage Statistics of Content Management Systems. Available online: https://w3techs.com/technologies/overview/content_management (accessed on 25 September 2022).
22. National Institute of Standards and Technology. National Vulnerability Database. Available online: https://nvd.nist.gov/ (accessed on 25 September 2022).
23. Wireshark. Available online: https://www.wireshark.org/ (accessed on 25 September 2022).
24. duoergun0729. XSS Payloads. Available online: https://github.com/duoergun0729/1book/tree/master/data (accessed on 25 September 2022).

mathematics

Article

Tensor Affinity Learning for Hyperorder Graph Matching

Zhongyang Wang, Yahong Wu and Feng Liu *

School of Communications and Information Engineering, Nanjing University of Posts and Telecommunications, Nanjing 210003, China
* Correspondence: liuf@njupt.edu.cn

Abstract: Hypergraph matching has been attractive in the application of computer vision in recent years. The interference of external factors, such as squeezing, pulling, occlusion, and noise, results in the same target displaying different image characteristics under different influencing factors. After extracting the image feature point description, the traditional method directly measures the feature description using distance measurement methods such as Euclidean distance, cosine distance, and Manhattan distance, which lack a sufficient generalization ability and negatively impact the accuracy and effectiveness of matching. This paper proposes a metric-learning-based hypergraph matching (MLGM) approach that employs metric learning to express the similarity relationship between high-order image descriptors and learns a new metric function based on scene requirements and target characteristics. The experimental results show that our proposed method performs better than state-of-the-art algorithms on both synthetic and natural images.

Keywords: hypergraph matching; similarity metric; information-theoretic metric learning

MSC: 68T20

Citation: Wang, Z.; Wu, Y.; Liu, F. Tensor Affinity Learning for Hyperorder Graph Matching. *Mathematics* **2022**, *10*, 3806. https://doi.org/10.3390/math10203806

Academic Editor: Catalin Stoean

Received: 17 July 2022
Accepted: 12 October 2022
Published: 15 October 2022

1. Introduction

Graph matching has been applied in a variety of fields, including biological applications [1], remote sensing image recognition [2], and image retrieval [3]. The key to graph matching is to find correspondences between image visual features using particular algorithms. Graph matching is typically viewed as a quadratic assignment problem (QAP) [4], and since the quadratic objective function is also non-convex, obtaining the global optimal value is challenging [5]. Various approximation algorithms have been developed to settle them under relatively relaxed conditions. Ref. [6] proposed a matching approach based on linear programming. In [7], semidefinite programming was used to solve such a problem, and [8] adopted a similar strategy. However, these algorithms are locally optimal in the discrete domain, and discretization can cause extra errors. There are other methods based on tree search that focus on the suboptimality; for instance, Sanfeliu improved the previous method by considering the joint probability of points and edges in [9]. In [10], it is shown that random walk-based models greatly enhance the graph topological features. A. Robles-Kelly [11] introduced a novel algorithm based on the relationship between the adjacent matrix of the two graphs and their stationary distribution.

Matching-based techniques have been adopted in a variety of study fields. Early classification based on sparse representation (SRC) [12] is not satisfactory in the treatment of occlusion. With the development of multiview non-negative matrix factorization (NMF) methods [13], the local geometry is preserved while global representation under a global alignment strategy is obtained. However, these methods are still affected by various noises and cannot highlight the target characteristics. In [14], Ou et al. proposed a method that used adaptively estimated occlusion information and robustly selected features to improve the performance of facial recognition. The K-nearest neighbor (KNN) is also a non-parametric classifier that is widely used in pattern recognition. However, the performance of KNN-based classification is severely affected by the sensitivity of the neighbourhood size, especially when the sample size is small and there are outliers. Refs. [15,16] improve this problem by weighting and averaging, and have a robust and effective classification performance.

In recent years, high-order graph matching algorithms have put a large amount of attention on the better fusion of structural similarities in order to improve the matching accuracy. Zass and Shashua [17] proposed a probabilistic setting-based hypergraph matching approach that uses an iterative successive projection process to find the global optimal solution. Lee et al. [18] expanded the reweighted random walk approach to hypergraph matching and probabilistically reinterpreted the idea of random walk on hypergraphs. However, these matching algorithms employ Euclidean distance to generate an affinity matrix, and each feature attribute is regarded as being independent from the others. Traditional methods lack a specific metric for feature description, their performance on different types of data is highly variable, and their overall accuracy is low. In this paper, we present an improved hypergraph matching algorithm on the basis of the metric learning theory. By learning the training dataset, it obtains a Mahalanobis matrix that is used to consummate the affinity formulation. Since the Mahalanobis distance is a measure considering the correlation between feature descriptions as well as scaling relations, the assignment matrix obtained by this method would be closer to the ground truth; in fact, experiments show that our algorithm can improve the accuracy of their matching results. The main contributions of this manuscript are described as follows:

- A novel approach for graph matching based on metric learning is proposed, in which, the correlation of different features is well considered so that it can perform better.
- An information-theoretic metric learning (ITML) method was applied to solve the learning task under high-order graph matching.
- The metric learning algorithm is proved by parallel computation, which greatly reduces the communication demands.
- Compared with other state-of-the-art algorithms in experiments on test datasets, our proposed method can obtain more accurate results in an efficient way.

The rest of this article is structured as follows. Section 2 begins with an overview of graph-matching-related work. Section 3 presents the proposed model as well as the generic formula for graph matching. Section 4 develops the MLGM approach for optimizing the suggested graph matching model. Section 5 evaluates and analyzes the experimental results of the proposed method on synthetic and natural picture benchmarks. The final section is the conclusion.

2. Related Works

In the last few years, spectral methods have developed into one of the most representative algorithms in graph matching. The eigenvalues of a matrix do not change when its rows and columns are shuffled; thus, we can utilize this fact to find the adjacency matrix that has the same eigenvalues between similar pictures. Earlier, the spectral method was applied to perform feature matching [19]. Ref. [20] introduced a method incorporating the grey level information around the feature points to improve the matching accuracy. Leordeanu et al. [8] proposed a matching algorithm by building an affinity matrix of the feature points that considered the effect of different weight functions in point matching. In another direction, the grouping method can also improve the effectiveness of matching. Egozi et al. [21] proposed a probabilistic interpretation of spectral matching schemes and developed a unique probabilistic matching (PM) scheme that outperforms earlier methods. Feature matching carried out by means of alternating the embedding and matching of the adjacency spectrum was introduced in [22], and, in [23], a relaxation scheme with matching constraints was proposed. Duchenne et al. [9] proposed a class algorithm that uses a tensor to represent similarities between higher-order features, and the graph can be matched after rank-one decomposition of the similarity tensor. This algorithm extends the spectral method to the hypergraph, and it has been further improved through research [24]. The adjacency spectrum optimization of undirected weighted graphs [25] and the approximation of the proximal matrix spectrum of undirected weighted graphs [26] have been developed in recent years, and results have been gained in image processing applications.

The graph edit distance (GED), which represents the matching link between nodes and edges in two graphs, was utilized to solve graph matching. For example, Ref. [27] proposed a self-organizing mapping algorithm to learn the distance, which makes the distance between similar images smaller, and this method was improved in [28]. Serratosa proposed a method based on an adaptive learning paradigm, which was improved in [29]. Andreas Fischer and Kaspar Riesen presented an algorithm [30] combining Hausdorff matching with greedy allocation to improve the quadratic time approximation of GED.

Metric learning has been widely used in face recognition [31,32], image retrieval [33], re-recognition [34], and other fields. For traditional metric methods such as Euclidean distance, it is challenging to capture the structure of diverse data sets. In order to increase the performance of classification models, it is important to learn a specific measure for various data sets, which is the objective of metric learning. The algorithm for metric learning based on the Mahalanobis distance is still the primary focus of metric learning research at the present time. Bohne et al. [35] proposed dividing the data and learning a metric for each cluster, and Wang et al. [36] suggested learning a set of basis metrics and a set of weights for each sample.

3. Problem Statement

As a mathematical expression of a relationship, a graph model [37] is composed of a node set and edge set. Finding the corresponding relationship between two graphs is the objective of graph matching. Generally, it seeks the relationship between nodes in graphs, and the specific node may be a pixel, a graph area, or a feature point. In the study of the graph matching and hypergraph matching algorithm, in order to express the relationship between graph features more comprehensively, the structure information of graph model is used to represent the problem in graph matching. Figure 1 depicts a graph matching example diagram.

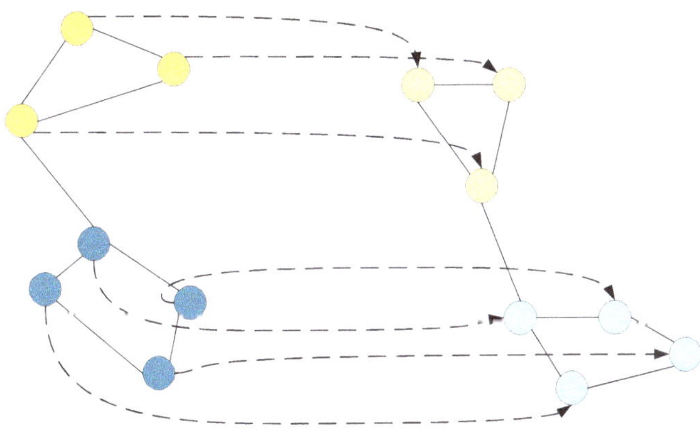

Figure 1. Graph matching schematic diagram.

We now consider two sets of feature points $P = \{p_1, p_2 \dots, p_m\}$ and $Q = \{q_1, q_2 \dots, q_n\}$, which are extracted from graphs A and B, respectively. The number of points obtained in each graph is m and n, which can be the same or different. In the high-order graph matching algorithm [9], what is different from the previous methods is that it matches a tuple of points instead of one to one or pair to pair, and k is used here to represent the number of points in each tuple. High-order graph matching has a good robustness under unfavorable conditions such as noise deformation and the rotation of external points [38], but it requires more space and time complexity. The third order can reflect the invariance of the similarity transformation in the field of computer vision, and, as the smallest higher-order topology, it can measure the subtle differences between high-order graphs. For convenience, only third-order graph matching is discussed in this paper, and it is straightforward to generalize to higher-order potentials.

The matching problem of the two graphs is to compute an optimal assignment relationship between points. Mathematically, this is the equivalent of finding an $m \times n$ assignment matrix X. If the feature point p_i in P matches q_j in Q, then the corresponding $X_{i,j}$ is equal to 1; otherwise, it is 0. In this paper, we assumed that each feature point in P can match zero or more feature points in Q, but each point in Q can match only one point in P. As a result, the set of assignment matrix X can be denoted as $\mathcal{X}$.

$$\mathcal{X} = \left\{ X \mid X \in \{0,1\}^{m \times n}, \forall i, \sum_{j=1}^{n} X_{i,j} = 1 \right\} \tag{1}$$

where $i \in [1, m]$.

The universal second-order graph matching model can be used to solve X as

$$\max_{X} Score(X) = \sum_{i_1,i_2,j_1,j_2} M_{i_1,i_2,j_1,j_2} X_{i_1,j_1} X_{i_2,j_2} \tag{2}$$

where M is an affinity tensor and represents the affinity relationship between point pairs (i_1, j_1) and (i_2, j_2). $Score(X)$ is the sum of the affinity values of all of the matched tuples; the higher the value corresponds to, the more precise the matching result. Establishing the affinity tensor M for two graphs A and B requires taking into account the similarity between pairs of nodes and pairs of edges.

$$M_{i_1,i_2,j_1,j_2} = \exp(-\gamma \| f_{i_1 j_1} - f_{i_2 j_2} \|) \tag{3}$$

f is the feature of each tuple, which is represented by Euclidean distance between points in second-order graph matching, and γ is the parameter [9].

However, the second-order graph matching model can only express paired relations, which are not resistant to scale changes and difficult to express higher-order feature information. Considering the high-order relation of feature points, we describe the similarity between feature point sets based on the relation between point tuples. Given two point sets P and Q, the affinity tensor can be expressed as

$$M_{i_1,i_2,j_1,j_2,k_1,k_2} = \exp\left(-\xi \left\| f_{i_1,j_1,k_1} - f_{i_2,j_2,k_2} \right\|^2\right) \tag{4}$$

where i_1, j_1, k_1 represent the point tuples in point set P of graph A, i_2, j_2, k_2 represent the three potential point tuples to be matched in point set Q of graph B, ξ is a constant that controls the distribution of the intimacy tensor value, and f_{i_1,j_1,k_1} and f_{i_2,j_2,k_2} represent the vectors constructed from the feature information of point tuples in point set P and Q, respectively. There are numerous ways to represent feature information; for ease of calculation, we use the sine value of the inner angle of the triangle formed by point tuples.

Similar to model (2), the high-order graph matching model can be formulated as

$$\max_{X} Score(X) = \sum_{i_1,i_2,j_1,j_2,k_1,k_2} M_{i_1,i_2,j_1,j_2,k_1,k_2} X_{i_1,i_2} X_{j_1,j_2} X_{k_1,k_2} \tag{5}$$

In (5), only when point tuples (i_1, j_1, k_1) match (i_2, j_2, k_2) separately does $X_{i1,i2} X_{j1,j2} X_{k1,k2}$ equal 1. This is an optimal solution problem; by finding the assignment matrix corresponding to the maximum value of $Score(X)$, the matching relation between tuples can be obtained. We can also write (5) as (6) by using the notation of tensor–vector multiplication:

$$\max_{\tilde{X}} Score(\tilde{X}) = \tilde{M} \otimes_3 \tilde{X} \otimes_2 \tilde{X} \otimes_1 \tilde{X} \tag{6}$$

where $\tilde{X}$ represents the vector created by combining the X columns, $\tilde{M}$ stands for the symmetric matrix produced by tensor expansion, and I, J, and K are the three dimensions of tensor M.

In the traditional affinity measure, Function (4), each feature is considered to be of the same importance. However, because these features may have different correlations with sample categories, their weights need to be reconsidered. In other words, a suitable distance or similarity measure based on the feature space of the sample should be used to measure the difference in the sample. Due to its two characteristics, decoupling and dimensionality independence, Mahalanobis distance [39] is an excellent measurement function for image processing and computer vision. In this paper, we used the Mahalanobis distance function to measure the affinity of feature vectors and create the appropriate metric learning model.

4. Tensor Affinity Learning for Hyperorder Graph Matching

4.1. A Short Introduction to Metric Learning

The study of metric learning has significant theoretical implications. Metric learning is concerned with developing an accurate function model for an input feature vector and obtaining an accurate similarity measure by learning the model's parameters. It can enhance the performance of the classifier by generating similarity relationships with high accuracy [40]. However, how to accurately measure the similarity of samples affected by different external factors is overlooked. The simple normalization method is used to preprocess data samples in classical learning algorithms, and then Euclidean distance is used to measure similarity. These normalization and measurement methods are crude, and the resulting classifier's performance is easily influenced by noise and interference.

Euclidean distance is a representative distance metric function, defined as

$$d(x_1, x_2) = \sqrt{(x_1 - x_2)^T (x_1 - x_2)} \tag{7}$$

where x_1, x_2 are paired sets of samples. Although Euclidean distance is simple to understand, it has several flaws. It treats the differences between the feature vectors of the sample as the same, which is incompatible with the application requirements of high-order graph matching. Another limitation of Euclidean distance is that it cannot handle data coupling relationships. When calculating the similarity of point tuples, for example, it is necessary to consider how points and edges are related to each other via the global structure formed.

To improve the deficiencies of traditional distance measurement, the (squared) Mahalanobis distance was used to measure similarity in this paper, which is defined as

$$d_M(x_1, x_2) = (x_1 - x_2)^T W (x_1 - x_2) \tag{8}$$

W represents the Mahalanobis matrix [39], which is a positive semidefinite symmetric matrix. The purpose of the metric learning process is to obtain a positive semidefinite symmetric matrix W for a given training dataset, which is used to establish the similarity measurement between the features of the samples. In other words, it aims to make the metric distance of similar features closer, and dissimilar features are estranged from each other.

4.2. The Establishment of Training Constraints

For graph supervised learning, the assignment matrix represents the correspondence between the points of two graphs. In hypergraph matching, it is easy to obtain the matching relation of tuples according to the relationship between points represented by the assignment matrix.

To consider the correlation of feature vectors in hypergraph matching and find the Mahalanobis matrix, we used the binary tuple constraint [41] to represent the similarity relation of training samples.

$$\{(x_i, x_j), w_{ij}\} \tag{9}$$

where w_{ij} refers to whether the two training samples x_i and x_j are similar. If w_{ij} equals 1, indicating that (x_i, x_j) belongs to the set of similar samples, the given pair of samples should be close to each other under the learned distance metric function. Similarly, when (x_i, x_j) belongs to a dissimilar pairs set, w_{ij} equals -1, indicating that a given pair of samples should be far apart under the learned distance metric function. For a training dataset, w_{ij} can be easily obtained according to the assignment matrix. Each tuple is stored as a feature vector; in order to reduce the distance between similar pairs and increase the distance between dissimilar pairs in metric learning, we further constrain similar pairs set S and dissimilar pairs set D by establishing thresholds.

$$\begin{aligned} S &= \{(f_i, f_j) : d_M(f_i, f_j) \leq g\} \\ D &= \{(f_i, f_j) : d_M(f_i, f_j) \geq h\} \end{aligned} \tag{10}$$

where g and h are constants, and (f_i, f_j) represents the pair of feature vectors.

4.3. Metric Learning Algorithm

Given a set of distance constraints as described in (10), our aim is to learn a positive-definite matrix W that parameterizes the corresponding Mahalanobis distance. In order to improve the computational efficiency, an information-theoretic metric learning approach (ITML) [42] is introduced. It uses a natural information theoretic approach to handle constraints on the distance function while minimizing the relative entropy between two multivariate Gaussians. There is a straightforward bijection between the set of Mahalanobis distances and the set of equalmean multivariate Gaussian distributions, and the multivariate Gaussian that corresponds to a Mahalanobis distance parameterized by W can be stated as follows:

$$p(x; W) = \frac{1}{z} \exp(\frac{1}{2} d_M(x, \mu)) \tag{11}$$

where μ is the mean value and z is the normalization factor. The relative entropy between corresponding multivariate Gaussians is used to measure the distance between two Mahalanobis distance functions parameterized by W_0 and W:

$$KL(p(x; W_0) || p(x; W)) = \int p(x; W_0) \log \frac{p(x; W_0)}{p(x; W)} dx \tag{12}$$

$KL(\cdot)$ stands for relative entropy, which is known as Kullback–Leibler divergence [43]. We use it to represent the difference between two probability distributions. Given a similar pair set S and a dissimilar pair set D, the distance measurement learning problem can be transformed into:

$$\begin{aligned} &\min_{W \geq 0} KL(p(x; W_0) || p(x; W)) \\ &s.t. \\ &d_M(f_i, f_j) \leq g, (f_i, f_j) \in S \\ &d_M(f_i, f_j) \geq h, (f_i, f_j) \in D \end{aligned} \tag{13}$$

where g and h are constants.

It has been demonstrated that the Mahalanobis distance between mean vectors and the LogDet divergence between covariance matrices can be combined convexly to express the differential relative entropy between two multivariate Gaussians [44]. To solve this optimization function, the Logdet distance $D_{ld}(\cdot)$ for measuring the difference of the matrix was introduced to calculate:

$$\begin{aligned} KL(p(x; W_0) || p(x; W)) &= \frac{1}{2} D_{ld}(W_0^{-1}, W^{-1}) \\ D_{ld}(W, W_0) &= tr(W W_0^{-1}) - \log\det(W W_0^{-1}) - d \end{aligned} \tag{14}$$

where d is the number of rows in W.

To facilitate the solution in the wider feasible region, the ITML algorithm introduces the relaxation variable ξ, initializes it into ξ_0, and further rewrites (14) as follows:

$$\begin{aligned} &\min_{W\geq 0,\xi} (D_{ld}(W,W_0)+\rho D_{ld}(diag\{\xi\},diag\{\xi_0\})) \\ &s.t. \\ &tr(W(f_i-f_j)(f_i-f_j)^T)\leq \xi_{i,j},(f_i-f_j)\in S \\ &tr(W(f_i-f_j)(f_i-f_j)^T)\geq \xi_{i,j},(f_i-f_j)\in D \end{aligned} \tag{15}$$

ρ is the equilibrium parameter. According to the principle of Logdet distance optimization in [45], the iterative formula of optimization can be obtained:

$$W_{t+1} = W_t + \beta W_t(f_i - f_j)(f_i - f_j)^T W_t \tag{16}$$

where W_t is the metric matrix calculated by the t-th iteration, β is the mapping parameter, and f_i and f_j are the constraint pairs.

4.4. Parallel Learning Algorithm

It is not feasible to apply the ITML method for distance measurement learning with high-dimensional training data. The complexity of the ITML algorithm has a direct correlation with the square of the data dimension, which leads to high heterogeneity in processing high-dimensional data. Furthermore, the ITML method learns a full rank metric matrix that scales quadratically with the number of input data dimensions, imposing a significant computing overhead on the learning process.

Typically, actual high-dimensional datasets are contaminated with noise or contain redundant information, so the algorithm cannot learn an effective measurement matrix. Therefore, when the dimensions of training samples are large enough, the measurement matrix obtained through ITML algorithm learning cannot effectively suppress the noise and also has disadvantages, such as a low solving efficiency and vulnerability to inadequate training data. To address the above challenges, we improved the metric learning algorithm through parallel computing.

The following proposes a parallel computing process. We may reconstruct the Mahalanobis matrix W as $W = I + \sum_i \alpha_i z_i z_i^T$ using the principle in [46] that every positive semidefinite matrix can be decomposed into linear combinations of rank-one matrices, where $z_i \in \mathbb{R}^d$. It is clear that $W_t(f_i - f_j)$ is d-dimensional, and $W_t(f_i - f_j)(f_i - f_j)^T W_t^T$ is a rank-one matrix. We can concretize the expression for W by adding the Bregman projections [47] of all pairs of constraints:

$$W_{t+1} = I + \sum_{i=1}^{C} \beta_i(t) z_i(t) z_i(t)^T \tag{17}$$

I represents the identity matrix of d dimensions, C is the number of constraint pairs that represent the mapping parameters, β denotes the learning rate, and $z_i(t) = W_t c_i$ and $c_i = f_j - f_k$ correspond to constraint pair (f_j, f_k). In the algorithm framework, only z is saved instead of W_t, preventing the issue where W tends to grow as d gets larger. Therefore, the iteration is changed into the update formula of z:

$$z_k(t+1) = W_{t+1} c_k = (I + \sum_{i=1}^{C} \beta_i(t) z_i(t) z_i(t)^T) c_k \tag{18}$$

According to the original algorithm, $\beta_i(t)$ should be the upper or lower bound constraint of the measured distance function. The key step in updating is to calculate the actual distance. Equation (19) can be used to express the real distance of the k-th constraint c_k when combined with Equation (17):

$$\begin{aligned} p_k(t) &= c_k^T W_t c_k \\ &= c_k^T \left(I + \sum_{i=1}^{C} \beta_i(t) z_i(t) z_i^T(t) \right) c_k \\ &= c_k^T c_k + \sum_{i=1}^{C} \beta_i(t) c_k^T z_i(t) z_i^T(t) c_k \end{aligned} \tag{19}$$

Due to the decomposable nature of W, the task of updating z and p is assigned to C work units (worker), which reflects the concept of parallel execution. In our framework, worker k needs to receive all z values generated by previous iterations from other workers and then carry out the next iteration update. Each worker only needs to send the vector z and receive $(c-1)z$ instead of the entire metric matrix. Therefore, the transfer amount of each step is reduced from $O(d^2)$ to $O(d)$. When d exceeds the number of constraints C, the transfer requirements will be significantly reduced, which greatly reduces the computational complexity.

We define affinity Ω in terms of the Mahalanobis distance instead of (4), which can better account for the correlation between tuples through learning the training set.

$$\begin{aligned} &\Omega_{i_1,i_2,j_1,j_2,k_1,k_2} = \exp\left(-\frac{(f_1 - f_2)^T W (f_1 - f_2)}{\gamma}\right) \\ &f_1 = (i_1, j_1, k_1) \\ &f_2 = (i_2, j_2, k_2) \end{aligned} \tag{20}$$

Then, M is defined as the following:

$$\begin{aligned} &M_{i_1,i_2,j_1,j_2,k_1,k_2} = \Omega_{i_1,i_2,j_1,j_2,k_1,k_2}, if ||f_1 - f_2|| \leq \sigma \\ &otherwise\ 0 \end{aligned} \tag{21}$$

The value of parameter σ corresponds to the degree of triplets deformation; a larger value of σ reduces the sensitivity of matching. The resulting algorithm is given as Algorithm 1.

Algorithm 1 Parallel Metric Learning

Input: S: similar data; D: dissimilar data; u, l: distance thresholds: γ: slack parameter
Output: W: Mahalanobis matrix

$W = I, C = |S| + |D|$
for constraint $(x_p, x_q)_k, k \in \{1, 2, \ldots, C\}$ **do**
  $\lambda_k \leftarrow 0$
  $d_k \leftarrow u$ for $(x_p, x_q)_k \in S$ otherwise $d_k \leftarrow l$
  $c_k \leftarrow (x_p - x_q)_k, z_k \leftarrow c_k$
end for
while β does not converge **do**
  for all worker $k \in \{1, 2, \ldots, C\}$ **do in parallel**
    $zk = ck + \sum_{i=1}^{C} \beta_i z_i z_i^T c_k$
    $p \leftarrow c_k^T z_k$
    if $(x_p, x_q)_k \in S$ **then**
      $\alpha \leftarrow \min\left(\lambda_k, \frac{1}{2}(\frac{1}{p} - \frac{\gamma}{d_k})\right)$
      $\beta \leftarrow \frac{\alpha}{1 - \alpha p}$
      $d_k \leftarrow \frac{\gamma d_k}{\gamma + \alpha d_k}$
    else
      $\alpha \leftarrow \min\left(\lambda_k, \frac{1}{2}(\frac{\gamma}{d_k} - \frac{1}{p})\right)$
      $\beta \leftarrow \frac{-\alpha}{1 - \alpha p}$
      $d_k \leftarrow \frac{\gamma d_k}{\gamma - \alpha d_k}$
    end if
    $\lambda_k \leftarrow \lambda_k - \alpha$
    $z_k \leftarrow \left(I + \sum_{i=1}^{C} \beta_i z_i z_i^T\right) c_k$
    send z_k to other workers
  end for
end while
$W = I + \sum_{i=1}^{C} \beta_i z_i z_i^T$

5. Experiments

In the following, we compare our method to advanced hyper-graph matching algorithms using benchmark data sets in which the original information for a specific sample graph is the feature point set. In order to express conveniently, the proposed method was represented by MLGM. We used the following advanced methods to compare with MLGM: spectral matching (SM) [8], max-pooling matching (MPM) [22] and IPFP [29], probabilistic graph matching (HGM) [17], tensor matching (TM) [9], reweighted random walk hypergraph matching (RRWHM) [18], block coordinate ascent graph matching (BCAGM) [23], and alternating direction graph matching (ADGM) [48]. We introduced noise and distortion to several datasets to distinguish our method's performance from that of other approaches. We compared the results to other algorithms in terms of accuracy and matching score. Accuracy was determined as the ratio between the number of accurate matches and the total amount of points and score was determined by Equation (6). The parameter settings for all of the state-of-art algorithms were identical to those suggested in their respective articles.

In our method, the dimension of the feature vector for each tuple of points was set to 3. We used Equation (21) to compute the affinity tensor M, and γ was set as in [9]. In the calculation process, we simply randomly selected $N \times m$ triplets from the graph model, where N is a user-defined parameter (this paper was set to 50). For the best empirical performance, only K nearest tuples matching for each triplet in the target image were selected, where K was set to 300 in this paper.

5.1. Synthetic Dataset

In this section, we introduce the popular benchmark datasets Blessing and Fish [49] in our experiment, which are reliable in evaluating graph matching algorithms.

In Figures 2 and 3, we show examples of the existing synthetic database (the Chinese character "blessing" and a tropical fish). The model shape is shown in the first column, in which, the images of Blessing and Fish are composed of 105 and 98 points, respectively. In order to validate the robustness of the proposed algorithm under noise, deformation, outliers, and rotation conditions, we conducted four sets of experiments. Column b contains examples of noisy targets produced by the addition of Gaussian random noise. Column c contains examples of deformed targets created by applying nonrigid deformation to model points. Column d contains examples of targets with outliers created by combining random points with a normal distribution of unit variance and moderate degrees of rotation. Column e contains examples of targets with large rotations and moderate Gaussian noise. We then experimented with each group of graphs and evaluated the robustness of these methods. The results are shown in Figures 4–7.

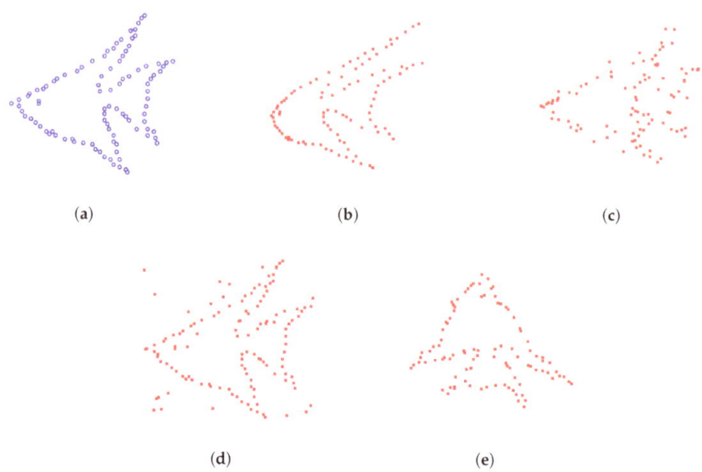

Figure 2. (**a**) shows model fish point sets, and (**b–e**) show point sets added with deformation, noise, outliers, and rotation, respectively.

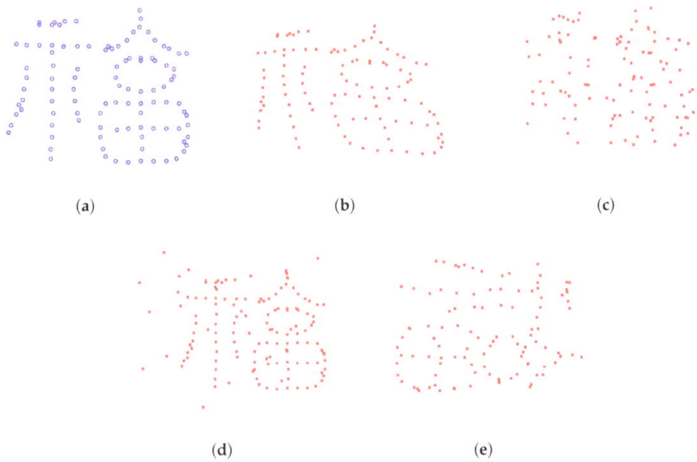

Figure 3. (**a**) shows model blessing point sets, and (**b–e**) show point sets added with deformation, noise, outliers, and rotation, respectively.

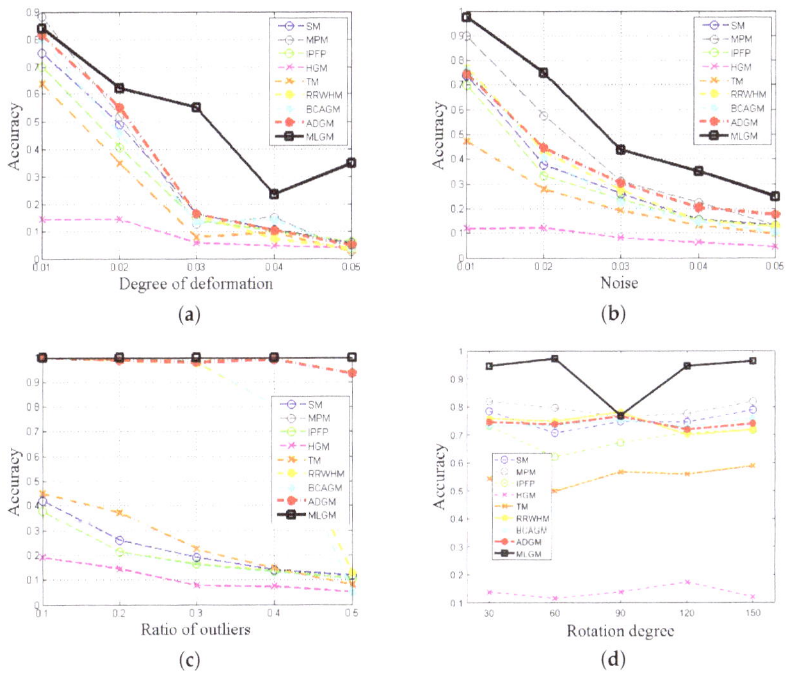

Figure 4. Accuracy comparison on the Fish dataset. (**a**) Accuracy with different degree of deformation. (**b**) Accuracy with different noise level. (**c**) Accuracy with different number of outliers. (**d**) Accuracy with different rotation angle.

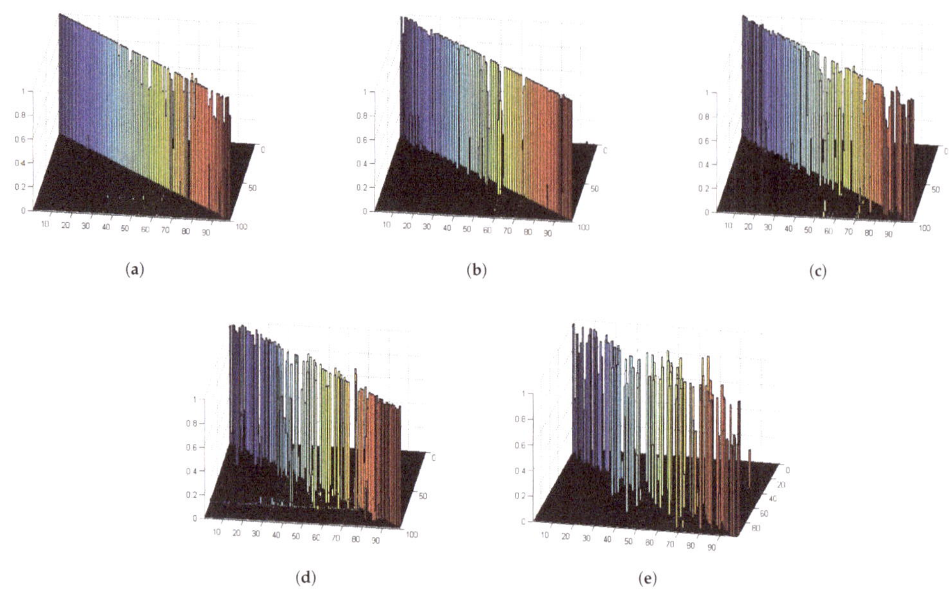

Figure 5. The assignment matrix obtained by MLGM from matching results on the Fish dataset with different degree of deformation (**a**–**e**).

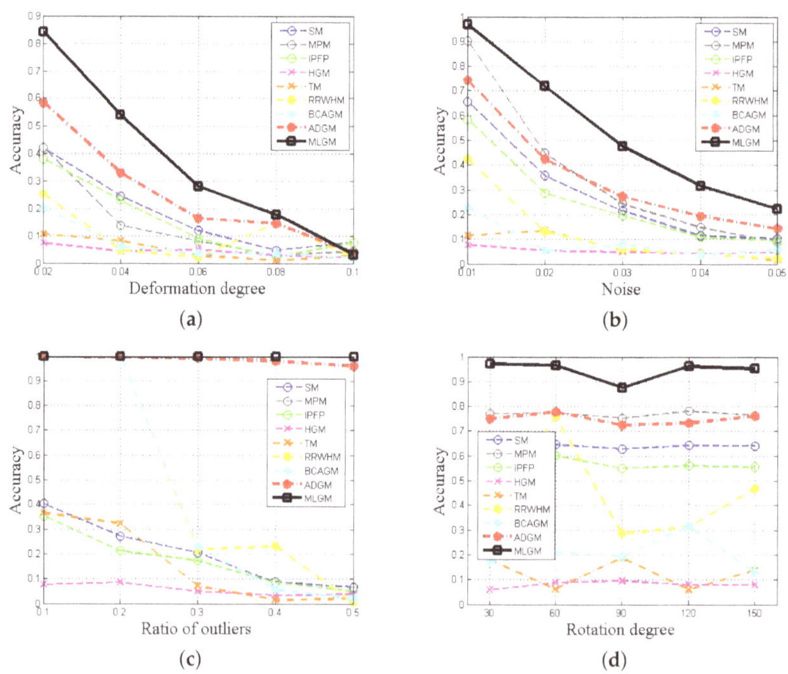

Figure 6. Accuracy comparison on the Blessing dataset. (**a**) Accuracy with different degree of deformation. (**b**) Accuracy with different noise level. (**c**) Accuracy with different number of outliers. (**d**) Accuracy with different rotation angle.

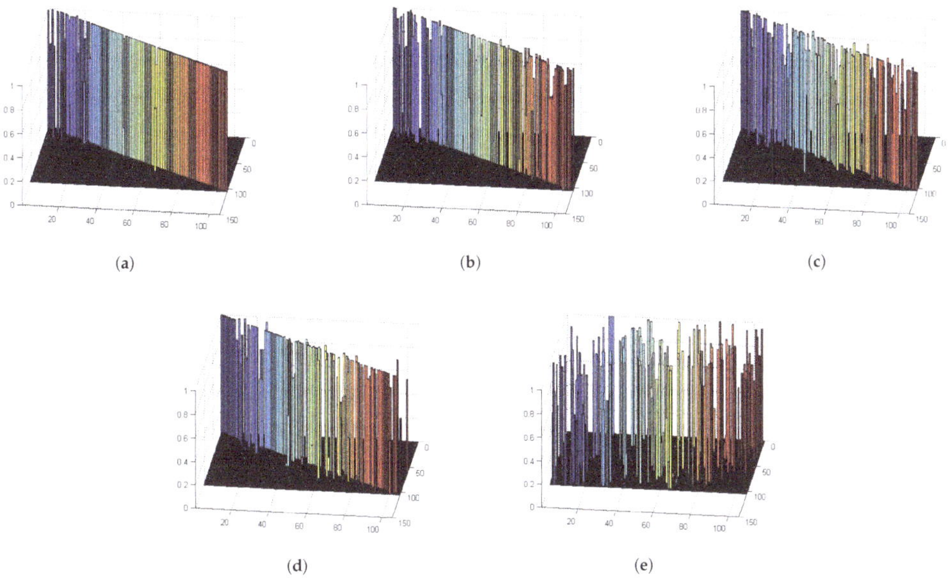

Figure 7. The assignment matrix obtained by MLGM from matching results on the Blessing dataset with different degree of deformation (a–e).

In the case of deformation disposal, the degree of deformation was set from 0.02 to 0.1; as it increases, the matching accuracy of all algorithms decreases correspondingly. For each graph pair, we fixed the points of an image and used algorithms to find the corresponding points in the other image. Each experimental result is the average of a multigroup parallel experiment to ensure the reliability of the test. The results show that the ITML method has an obvious advantage in this situation. For the noise condition experiments, the target points were obtained by adding Gaussian random noise from $\sigma = 0.01$ to $\sigma = 0.05$; we can see from Figures 4 and 6 that the methods using high-order graph matching can achieve a higher accuracy because the internal information of the image topology is applied to the feature description. For these groups of experiments on synthetic database, our algorithm can obtain more accurate matching results. In particular, our method can achieve 100% accuracy for datasets with outliers. Graphs in Figures 8 and 9 also display the matching scores under varying experimental conditions. In the case of increased interference, the matching score remains steady at a higher level, demonstrating that the affinity metric of the feature in our method is totally invariant to massive affine deformations and strong Gaussian noise. With the addition of rotation, the results of images show that the rotation angle has little effect on the matching results, but when the rotation angle reaches 90 degrees, the accuracy obtained by our method has a slight decline at this point. We believe that this is mainly because the 90-degree rotation has a degree of influence on the algorithm that focuses on correlation. The experiments show that, after the metric learning of the dataset, the results of matching can be improved.

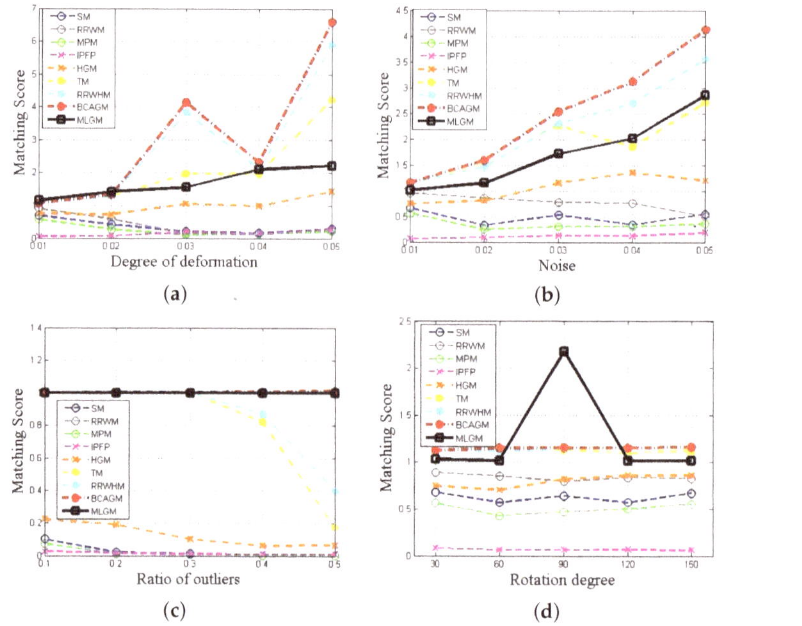

Figure 8. Matching score comparison on the Fish dataset. (**a**) Matching score with different degree of deformation. (**b**) Matching score with different noise level. (**c**) Matching score with different number of outliers. (**d**) Matching score with different rotation angle.

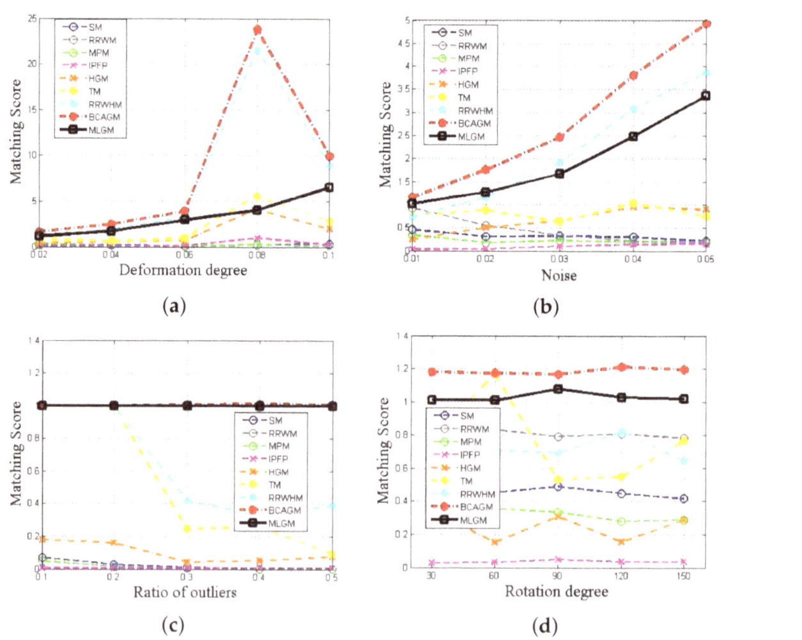

Figure 9. Matching score comparison on the Blessing dataset. (**a**) Matching score with different degree of deformation. (**b**) Matching score with different noise level. (**c**) Matching score with different number of outliers. (**d**) Matching score with different rotation angle.

5.2. Face Dataset and Duck Dataset

In this section, we compare the performance of our method to other methods on the Face dataset and Duck dataset, which are the sub-datasets from Caltech-256 [50]. These datasets contain images from specific classes: 109 face images, and 50 duck images. The ground truth is known for each graph pair. We chose 70 pairs of faces at random from the data set for testing, manually picked 10 feature points from each picture, and chose 20 photographs from each class at random as the training dataset for metric learning. The baseline was varied from 10 to 80 frames, and we tested all algorithms and obtained the average of the results. The accuracy and matching scores were obtained by averaging experiments of 10 frames to 80 frames. To make it more intuitive, we show several examples of matching results in Figures 10 and 11. It can be seen that our algorithm performes better. Figures 12 and 13 show that the MLGM method achieves the largest score value, and obtains more accurate matching results than other test methods. It also demonstrates that the compared approaches are easily affected by noise and distortion. The MLGM method can obtain a better matching result for the entire dataset.

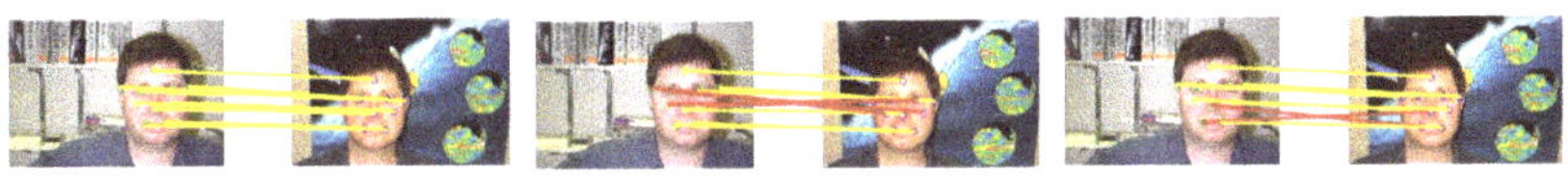

(**a**) (MLGM-SM-MPM)

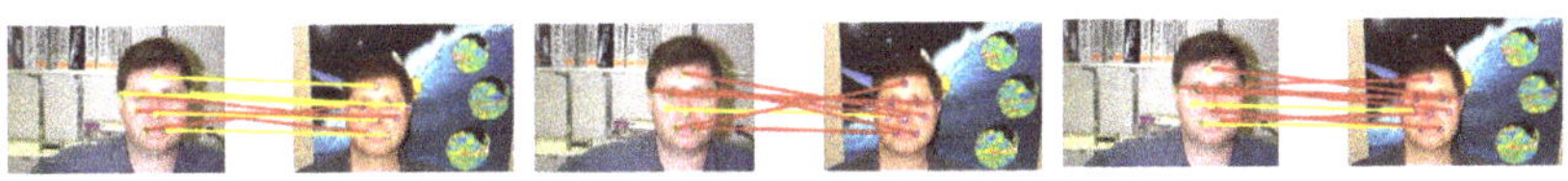

(**b**) (IPFP-HGM-TM)

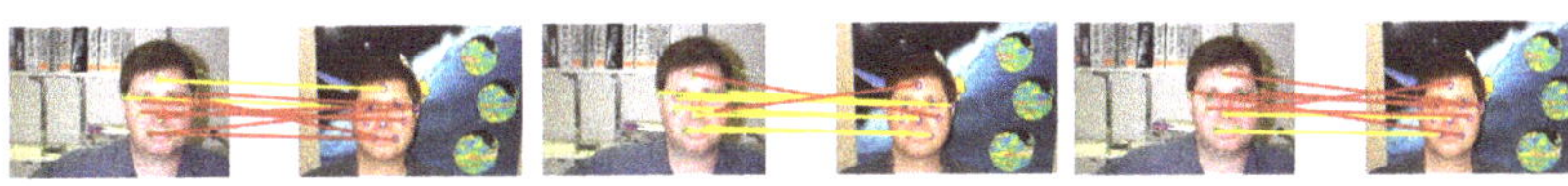

(**c**) (RRWHM-BCAGM-ADGM)

Figure 10. Example results of experiments on the Face dataset, in which red and yellow lines denote correct and incorrect matching results.

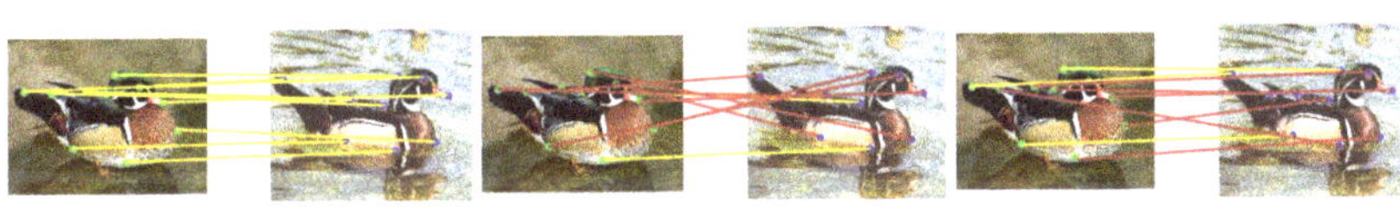

(**a**) (MLGM-SM-MPM)

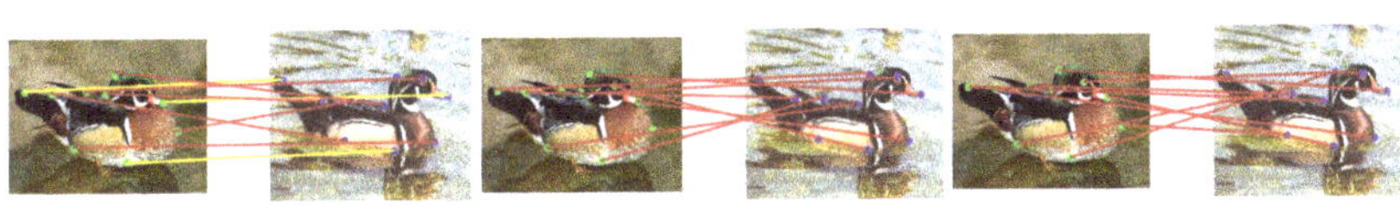

(**b**) (IPFP-HGM-TM)

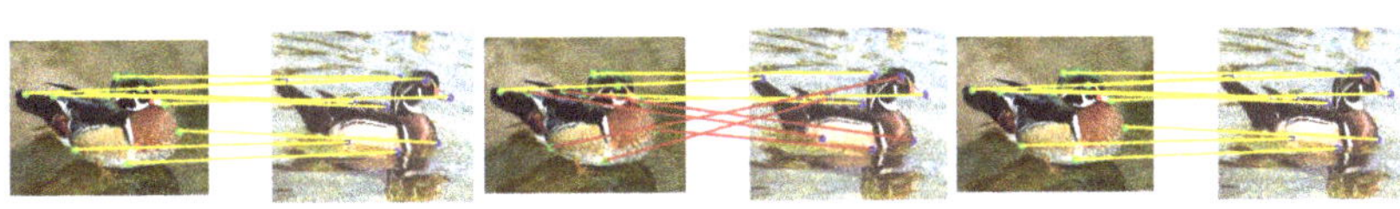

(**c**) (RRWHM-BCAGM-ADGM)

Figure 11. Example results of experiments on the Duck dataset.

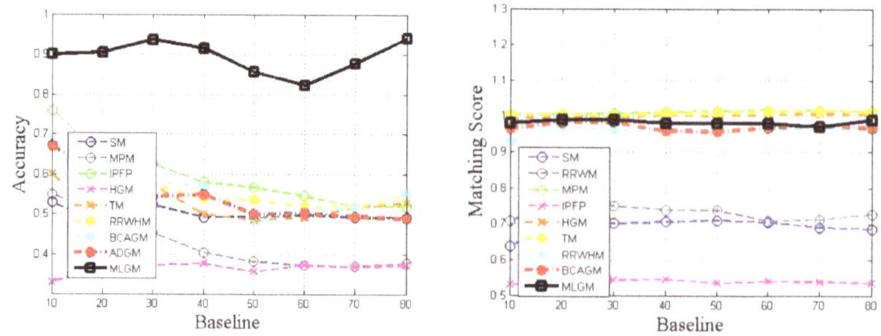

(**a**) (**b**)

Figure 12. Trend chart of matching accuracy and score of the Face dataset. (**a**) Accuracy of the Face dataset. (**b**) Matching score of the Face dataset.

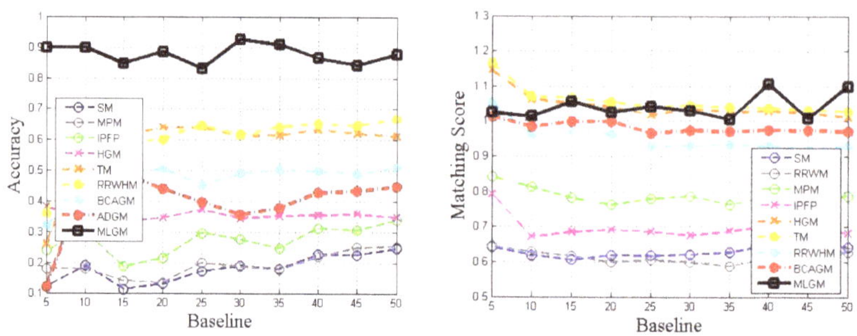

(**a**) (**b**)

Figure 13. Trend chart of matching accuracy and score of the Duck dataset. (**a**) Accuracy of the Duck dataset. (**b**) Matching score of the Duck dataset.

6. Conclusions

In this paper, we proposed a tensor graph matching model based on metric learning that uses Mahalanobis distance as the affinity measure function and makes full use of the distribution information and geometric information of hypergraphs. To solve the proposed model, a parallel distance metric learning approach was used, which can learn appropriate metrics from high-dimensional data without using low-rank approximation. The experimental results of testing on several databases, such as the synthetic datasets of Blessing, Fish, and Face datasets, and the Duck dataset, indicated that the suggested method performs better than the existing ones. In the future, we may consider combining this strategy with deep learning.

Author Contributions: Methodology, Z.W. and Y.W.; Project administration, F.L.; Supervision, F.L.; Writing—original draft, Z.W.; Writing—review & editing, Y.W. All authors have read and agreed to the published version of the manuscript.

Funding: This work is supported by the National Natural Science Foundation of China under Grant No. 62072256, the Natural Science Foundation of Nanjing University of Posts and Telecommunications (Grant No. NY221057 and NY220003) and the Postgraduate Research & Practice Innovation Program of Jiangsu Province, China (Grant No. SJCX19_0248).

Data Availability Statement: Not applicable.

Conflicts of Interest: The authors declare no conflict of interest.

References

1. Tian, Y.; Mceachin, R.C.; Santos, C.; States, D.J.; Patel, J.M. SAGA: A subgraph matching tool for biological graphs. *Bioinformatics* **2007**, *23*, 232–239. [CrossRef] [PubMed]
2. Chaudhuri, B.; Demir, B.; Chaudhuri, S.; Bruzzone, L. Multilabel remote sensing image retrieval using a semisupervised graph-theoretic method. *IEEE Trans. Geosci. Remote. Sens.* **2017**, *56*, 1144–1158. [CrossRef]
3. Yang, X.; Latecki, L.J. Affinity learning on a tensor product graph with applications to shape and image Retrieval. In Proceedings of the CVPR 2011, Colorado Springs, CO, USA, 20–25 June 2011; pp. 2369–2376.
4. Lawler, E.L. The quadratic assignment problem. *Manag. Sci.* **1963**, *9*, 586–599. [CrossRef]
5. Gold, S.; Rangarajan, A. A graduated assignment algorithm for graph matching. *IEEE Trans. Pattern Anal. Mach. Intell.* **1996**, *18*, 377–388. [CrossRef]
6. Almohamad, H.; Duffuaa, S. A linear programming approach for the weighted graph matching problem. *IEEE Trans. Pattern Anal. Mach. Intell.* **1993**, *15*, 522–525. [CrossRef]
7. Torr, P.H. Solving markov random fields using semi definite programming. In Proceedings of the International Workshop on Artificial Intelligence and Statistics PMLR, Key West, FL, USA, 3–6 January 2003; pp. 292–299.
8. Leordeanu, M.; Hebert, M. *A Spectral Technique for Correspondence Problems Using Pairwise Constraints*; The Robotics Institute, Carnegie Mellon University: Pittsburgh, PA, USA, 2005; pp. 1482–1489.
9. Duchenne, O.; Bach, F.; Kweon, I.S.; Ponce, J. A tensor-based algorithm for high-order graph matching. *IEEE Trans. Pattern Anal. Mach. Intell.* **2011**, *33*, 2383–2395. [CrossRef]
10. Medasani, S.; Krishnapuram, R.; Choi, Y. Graph matching by relaxation of fuzzy assignments. *IEEE Trans. Fuzzy Syst.* **2001**, *9*, 173–182. [CrossRef]
11. Nocedal, J.; Wright, S. *Numerical Optimization*; Springer: Berlin/Heidelberg, Germany, 2006.
12. Ou, W.; You, X.; Tao, D.; Zhang, P.; Tang, Y.; Zhu, Z. Robust face recognition via occlusion dictionary learning. *Pattern Recognit.* **2014**, *47*, 1559–1572. [CrossRef]
13. Ou, W.; Yu, S.; Li, G.; Lu, J.; Zhang, K.; Xie, G. Multi-view non-negative matrix factorization by patch alignment framework with view consistency. *Neurocomputing* **2016**, *204*, 116–124. [CrossRef]
14. Ou, W.; Luan, X.; Gou, J.; Zhou, Q.; Xiao, W.; Xiong, X.; Zeng, W. Robust discriminative nonnegative dictionary learning for occluded face recognition. *Pattern Recognit. Lett.* **2018**, *107*, 41–49. [CrossRef]
15. Gou, J.; Qiu, W.; Yi, Z.; Shen, X.; Zhan, Y.; Ou, W. Locality constrained representation-based K-nearest neighbor classification. *Knowl. Based Syst.* **2019**, *167*, 38–52. [CrossRef]
16. Gou, J.; Ma, H.; Ou, W.; Zeng, S.; Rao, Y.; Yang, H. A generalized mean distance-based k-nearest neighbor classifier. *Expert Syst. Appl.* **2019**, *115*, 356–372. [CrossRef]
17. Zass, R.; Shashua, A. Probabilistic graph and hypergraph matching. In Proceedings of the 2008 IEEE Conference on Computer Vision and Pattern Recognition, Anchorage, AK, USA, 23–28 June 2008; pp. 1–8.
18. Lee, J.; Cho, M.; Lee, K.M. Hyper-graph matching via reweighted random walks. In Proceedings of the CVPR 2011, Colorado Springs, CO, USA, 20–25 June 2011; pp. 1633–1640.
19. Byrd, R.H.; Lu, P.; Nocedal, J.; Zhu, C. A limited memory algorithm for bound constrained optimization. *SIAM J. Sci. Comput.* **1995**, *16*, 1190–1208. [CrossRef]
20. Ni, Q.; Yuan, Y.x. A subspace limited memory quasi-Newton algorithm for large-scale nonlinear bound constrained optimization. *Math. Comput.* **1997**, *66*, 1509–1520. [CrossRef]
21. Egozi, A.; Keller, Y.; Guterman, H. A probabilistic approach to spectral graph matching. *IEEE Trans. Pattern Anal. Mach. Intell.* **2012**, *35*, 18–27. [CrossRef]
22. Cho, M.; Sun, J.; Duchenne, O.; Ponce, J. Finding matches in a haystack: A max-pooling strategy for graph matching in the presence of outliers. In Proceedings of the IEEE Conference on Computer Vision and Pattern Recognition, Columbus, OH, USA, 23–28 June 2014; pp. 2083–2090.
23. Nguyen, Q.; Gautier, A.; Hein, M. A flexible tensor block coordinate ascent scheme for hypergraph matching. In Proceedings of the IEEE Conference on Computer Vision and Pattern Recognition, Boston, MA, USA, 7–12 June 2015; pp. 5270–5278.
24. Jiang, B.; Tang, J.; Ding, C.; Luo, B. A local sparse model for matching problem. In Proceedings of the Twenty-Ninth AAAI Conference on Artificial Intelligence, Austin, TX, USA, 25–30 January 2015.
25. Gillis, D.B.; Bowles, J.H. Hyperspectral image segmentation using spatial-spectral graphs. In Proceedings of the Algorithms and Technologies for Multispectral, Hyperspectral, and Ultraspectral Imagery XVIII. SPIE, Baltimore, MD, USA, 23–27 April 2012; Volume 8390, pp. 527–537.
26. Meng, D.; Fazel, M.; Mesbahi, M. Proximal alternating direction method of multipliers for distributed optimization on weighted graphs. In Proceedings of the 2015 54th IEEE Conference on Decision and Control (CDC), Osaka, Japan, 15–18 December 2015; pp. 1396–1401.
27. Liu, Z.Y.; Qiao, H.; Yang, X.; Hoi, S.C. Graph matching by simplified convex-concave relaxation procedure. *Int. J. Comput. Vis.* **2014**, *109*, 169–186. [CrossRef]
28. Chertok, M.; Keller, Y. Efficient high order matching. *IEEE Trans. Pattern Anal. Mach. Intell.* **2010**, *32*, 2205–2215. [CrossRef]
29. Leordeanu, M.; Hebert, M.; Sukthankar, R. An integer projected fixed point method for graph matching and map inference. *Adv. Neural Inf. Process. Syst.* **2009**, 1114–1122.

30. Cho, M.; Lee, J.; Lee, K.M. Reweighted random walks for graph matching. In Proceedings of the European Conference on Computer Vision, Heraklion, Crete, Greece, 5–11 September 2010; pp. 492–505.
31. Xu, Y.; Wu, L.; Jian, M.; Zheng, W.S.; Ma, Y.; Wang, Z. Identity-constrained noise modeling with metric learning for face anti-spoofing. *Neurocomputing* **2021**, *434*, 149–164. [CrossRef]
32. Yu, J.; Hu, C.H.; Jing, X.Y.; Feng, Y.J. Deep metric learning with dynamic margin hard sampling loss for face verification. *Signal Image Video Process.* **2020**, *14*, 791–798. [CrossRef]
33. Cao, R.; Zhang, Q.; Zhu, J.; Li, Q.; Li, Q.; Liu, B.; Qiu, G. Enhancing remote sensing image retrieval using a triplet deep metric learning network. *Int. J. Remote Sens.* **2020**, *41*, 740–751. [CrossRef]
34. Jin, Y.; Li, C.; Li, Y.; Peng, P.; Giannopoulos, G.A. Model latent views with multi-center metric learning for vehicle re-identification. *IEEE Trans. Intell. Transp. Syst.* **2021**, *22*, 1919–1931. [CrossRef]
35. Bohné, J.; Ying, Y.; Gentric, S.; Pontil, M. Large margin local metric learning. In Proceedings of the European Conference on Computer Vision, Zurich, Switzerland, 6–12 September 2014; pp. 679–694.
36. Wang, J.; Kalousis, A.; Woznica, A. Parametric local metric learning for nearest neighbor classification. *Adv. Neural Inf. Process. Syst.* **2012**, *25*, 1601–1609.
37. Kilgour, D.M.; Hipel, K.W.; Fang, L. The graph model for conflicts. *Automatica* **1987**, *23*, 41–55. [CrossRef]
38. Zhu, H.; Cui, C.; Deng, L.; Cheung, R.C.; Yan, H. Elastic net constraint-based tensor model for high-order graph matching. *IEEE Trans. Cybern.* **2019**, *51*, 4062–4074. [CrossRef]
39. De Maesschalck, R.; Jouan-Rimbaud, D.; Massart, D.L. The mahalanobis distance. *Chemom. Intell. Lab. Syst.* **2000**, *50*, 1–18. [CrossRef]
40. Wang, X.; Han, X.; Huang, W.; Dong, D.; Scott, M.R. Multi-similarity loss with general pair weighting for deep metric learning. In Proceedings of the IEEE/CVF Conference on Computer Vision and Pattern Recognition, Long Beach, CA, USA, 15–20 June 2019; pp. 5022–5030.
41. Xing, E.; Jordan, M.; Russell, S.J.; Ng, A. Distance metric learning with application to clustering with side-information. *Adv. Neural Inf. Process. Syst.* **2002**, *15*.
42. Davis, J.V.; Kulis, B.; Jain, P.; Sra, S.; Dhillon, I.S. Information-theoretic metric learning. In Proceedings of the 24th International Conference on Machine Learning, New York, NY, USA, 20–24 June 2007; pp. 209–216.
43. Kullback, S.; Leibler, R.A. On information and sufficiency. *Ann. Math. Stat.* **1951**, *22*, 79–86. [CrossRef]
44. Davis, J.; Dhillon, I. Differential entropic clustering of multivariate gaussians. *Adv. Neural Inf. Process. Syst.* **2006**, *19*.
45. Kulis, B.; Sustik, M.A.; Dhillon, I.S. Low-Rank Kernel Learning with Bregman Matrix Divergences. *J. Mach. Learn. Res.* **2009**, *10*.
46. Shen, C.; Kim, J.; Wang, L.; Van Den Hengel, A. Positive semidefinite metric learning using boosting-like algorithms. *J. Mach. Learn. Researc* **2012**, *13*, 1007–1036.
47. Bregman, L.M. The relaxation method of finding the common point of convex sets and its application to the solution of problems in convex programming. *USSR Comput. Math. Math. Phys.* **1967**, *7*, 200–217. [CrossRef]
48. Lê-Huu, D.K.; Paragios, N. Alternating direction graph matching. In Proceedings of the 2017 IEEE Conference on Computer Vision and Pattern Recognition (CVPR), Honolulu, HI, USA, 21–26 July 2017; pp. 4914–4922.
49. Chui, H.; Rangarajan, A. A new point matching algorithm for non-rigid registration. *Comput. Vis. Image Underst.* **2003**, *89*, 114–141. [CrossRef]
50. Griffin, G.; Holub, A.; Perona, P. *Caltech-256 Object Category Dataset*; Technical Report 7694; Caltech: Pasadena, CA, USA, 2007.

mathematics

Article

Plug-and-Play-Based Algorithm for Mixed Noise Removal with the Logarithm Norm Approximation Model

Jinhua Liu [1,*], Jiayun Wu [1], Mulian Xu [1] and Yuanyuan Huang [2]

1 School of Mathematics and Computer Science, Shangrao Normal University, Shangrao 334001, China
2 Department of Network Engineering, Chengdu University of Information Technology, Chengdu 610225, China
* Correspondence: 314103@sru.edu.cn

Abstract: During imaging and transmission, images are easily affected by several factors, including sensors, camera motion, and transmission channels. In practice, images are commonly corrupted by a mixture of Gaussian and impulse noises, further complicating the denoising problem. Therefore, in this work, we propose a novel mixed noise removal model that combines a deterministic low-rankness prior and an implicit regularization scheme. In the optimization model, we apply the matrix logarithm norm approximation model to characterize the global low-rankness of the original image. We further adopt the plug-and-play (PnP) scheme to formulate an implicit regularizer by plugging an image denoiser, which is used to preserve image details. The above two building blocks are complementary to each other. The mixed noise removal algorithm is thus established. Within the framework of the PnP scheme, we address the proposed optimization model via the alternating directional method of multipliers (ADMM). Finally, we perform extensive experiments to demonstrate the effectiveness of the proposed algorithm. Correspondingly, the simulation results show that our algorithm can recover the global structure and detailed information of images well and achieves superior performance over competing methods in terms of quantitative evaluation and visual inspection.

Keywords: mixed noise removal; matrix nuclear norm; logarithm norm; ADMM; plug-and-play

MSC: 68U10

Citation: Liu, J.; Wu, J.; Xu, M.; Huang, Y. Plug-and-Play-Based Algorithm for Mixed Noise Removal with the Logarithm Norm Approximation Model. *Mathematics* **2022**, *10*, 3810. https://doi.org/10.3390/math10203810

Academic Editor: Radu Tudor Ionescu

Received: 2 September 2022
Accepted: 12 October 2022
Published: 15 October 2022

Publisher's Note: MDPI stays neutral with regard to jurisdictional claims in published maps and institutional affiliations.

1. Introduction

Image denoising has been widely used in many applications, such as hyperspectral imaging (HSI) [1], scene recognition [2], and image restoration [3]. However, due to imaging conditions, natural images inevitably suffer from various kinds of noises, e.g., Gaussian, random, salt-and-pepper (S&P), and stripe noises, which critically influence subsequent applications. In particular, many images are contaminated by mixed noise, including Gaussian noise plus random noise or Gaussian noise plus stripe noise. Therefore, restoring a clean image from its corrupted version is the central issue in image denoising. From a mathematical perspective, the denoising problem is morbid and irreversible. Hence, to some extent, the prior knowledge of the image is of great importance.

In the past decade, scholars have proposed numerous image denoising models, such as bivariate probability [4], Gaussian–Hermite distribution [5], total variation [6], autoregressive [7], Block-Matching 3D (BM3D) [8], and sparse representation-based image modeling [9–11]. Among these models, the image sparse representation model has been extensively studied and applied. It transforms a natural image into a linear combination of a group of base or dictionary atoms and makes the transformed image coefficient sparse and compressible. Finally, only a few coefficients are unequal to 0. A few examples of this model are the common cosine, wavelet, and Fourier base methods. However, this image denoising method can only address white Gaussian noise. In actual applications, images are often affected by many types of noise, such as Gaussian, S&P, or random noises. The traditional denoising method cannot easily remove impulse noises, because it maintains impulse noise points at edges [12,13].

In general, two types of typical impulse noises exist, i.e., S&P and random noises. Conventional methods use two approaches to remove the mixture of Gaussian–impulse noises. The first is the detection-based noise removal method, and the second is the modeling-based method. The detection-based denoising method has been discussed in existing research [14–17]. This method first detects the locations of damaged image pixels, then handles the mixed noise. In fact, the accuracy of the detection of the damaged pixels is very important for removing mixed noise. Generally, detection-based methods are effective in removing impulse noise. However, their fidelity terms do not take Gaussian noise into account. Therefore, they cannot remove Gaussian noise effectively.

The second method treats impulse noise as a sparse signal and constructs a statistical distribution model on the basis of the impulse noise. A previously reported method [18] adopts Laplacian scale mixture (LSM) modeling to characterize impulse noise and estimates the hidden variables and impulse noise jointly from the noisy image. This method utilizes a nonlocal low-rank regularizer to regularize the denoising model. Liu et al. [19] proposed a mixed noise removal algorithm using weighted dictionary learning. Although this method can handle mixed noise, its training process is time-consuming. Jiang et al. [20] developed an image denoising method by combining weighted encoding and nonlocal self-similarity. This method can remove Gaussian and impulse noises jointly. However, its denoising performance relies on the design of the diagonal weight matrix.

Recently, low-rank matrix recovery has attracted considerable attention in the field of image restoration [4,21–24]. The fundamental problem of this process is how to find and use the low-dimensional structures of images. In contrast to the traditional mixed noise denoising method, low-rank matrix recovery can handle different noise types without any noisy prior information. Therefore, many researchers have applied the low-rank matrix restoration model to reconstruct images. Zhang et al. [25] proposed a denoising method for hyperspectral images based on a low-rank matrix recovery model. Subsequently, a noise-adjustable low-rank matrix approximation model was applied to hyperspectral image denoising [26]. However, in the above two methods [25,26], the upper bound of the rank of a given matrix must be set. Nuclear norm was introduced to design the rank approximation function in [27] for hyperspectral image denoising to solve the above issue. This nuclear norm-based rank approximation function is mainly characterized by its treatment of each singular value as equal. However, this approach ignores the fact that the contribution of each nonzero singular value is different. As a result, some nonconvex low-rank-based approaches are exploited for hyperspectral image restoration [28,29]. In addition, the total variation-regularized low-rank restoration method has been developed to remove mixed noise from HSI images [30,31]. In recent years, deep learning-based approaches to image denoising have been extensively studied. Instead of mathematical model construction, learning-based methods directly learn a mapping function from a noisy image to a clean image. These methods include convolutional neural network-based CT denoising [32], autonomous illumination systems [33], and deep plug-and-play (PnP) image restoration [34]. Additionally, some low-rank tensor-based HSI restoration algorithms have been proposed. These algorithms include weighted group sparsity-regularized low-rank tensor decomposition (LRTDGS) [35] and fibered rank constrained tensor restoration PnP [36].

In this work, inspired by PnP-based [34,36–39] and low-rank based [40,41] methods, we propose a mixed noise removal algorithm by applying the PnP regularization-based logarithm norm approximation (LNAM) model. First, the LNAM is used to characterize the global low-rankness of the original image. Second, the PnP regularization method is adopted to preserve the image detail information. Finally, the experimental results obtained through simulations on test images are used to confirm the effectiveness of the proposed denoising method. The contributions of the proposed method can be summarized as follows:

First, instead of utilizing the matrix-based low-rank approximation function, we introduce a logarithm norm-based smooth rank function and propose the LNAM. Compared with the nuclear norm-based low-rank function, the proposed model could more effectively exploit the global low-rank structure of HSI and provides a tighter approximation.

Second, the low-rankness prior is known to usually face limitations in preserving the local details of images. Therefore, the PnP framework is incorporated into the LNAM model to break through this limitation. Furthermore, we introduce a classic BM3D denoiser [8] that extensively exploits the nonlocal self-similarity prior of images.

Third, several simple subproblems are solved by decomposing the original problem by using the framework of the alternating direction multiplier method (ADMM) to address the LNAM optimization problem effectively.

The remainder of this article is organized as follows: Section 2 introduces the related works using mixed noise denoising models on hyperspectral images. As described in Section 3, the LNAM model is proposed and solved with the ADMM-based optimization algorithm. Section 4 presents the experimental results of the test images and a discussion on the effect of several parameters on the proposed algorithm. Finally, we conclude this paper in Section 5.

2. Background of the Low-Rank-Based Hyperspectral Image Denoising Method

Mixed noise removal techniques based on low-rank matrix recovery are mainly inspired by the robust principal component analysis (RPCA) [42]. The main concept of RPCA is that it aims to find the underlying low-dimensional subspace structure of high-dimensional signals from the corrupted observation. The RPCA model can be expressed as

$$\begin{aligned} &\min_{X,S} rank(\boldsymbol{X}) + \lambda \|\boldsymbol{S}\|_0 \\ &s.t. \boldsymbol{Y} = \boldsymbol{X} + \boldsymbol{S} \end{aligned} , \tag{1}$$

where λ denotes the regularization parameter; $\boldsymbol{Y}$ represents the corrupted observational data; $\boldsymbol{X}$ and $\boldsymbol{S}$ are denoted the unknown low-rank matrix and the sparse matrix, respectively; and $\|\cdot\|_0$ represents the ℓ_0-norm, which attempts to promote sparsity. Although the RPCA model can be utilized to remove the sparse noise, however, it cannot work well when the hyperspectral image is polluted by mixed noise, e.g., Gaussian noise plus sparse noise. Therefore, an improved model has been proposed by considering the Gaussian noise $\boldsymbol{E}$ in the following:

$$\begin{aligned} &\min_{X,S,E} rank(\boldsymbol{X}) + \lambda \|\boldsymbol{S}\|_0 + \tfrac{\eta}{2} \|\boldsymbol{E}\|_F^2 \\ &s.t.\ \boldsymbol{Y} = \boldsymbol{X} + \boldsymbol{S} + \boldsymbol{E} \end{aligned} , \tag{2}$$

where λ, η are both the regularization parameters. Problems (1) and (2) are NP-hard problems. One common approach is replacing the rank function with the nuclear norm, and correspondingly, the ℓ_0-norm is replaced with the ℓ_1-norm [43].

$$\begin{aligned} &\min_{X,S,E} \|\boldsymbol{X}\|_* + \lambda \|\boldsymbol{S}\|_1 + \tfrac{\eta}{2} \|\boldsymbol{E}\|_F^2 \\ &s.t.\ \boldsymbol{Y} = \boldsymbol{X} + \boldsymbol{S} + \boldsymbol{E} \end{aligned} , \tag{3}$$

The low-rank matrix approximation model has been widely used in most hyperspectral image denoising applications. However, this model suffers from the following aspects: First, all nonzero singular values are known to have the same contribution to the rank function. In fact, different singular values have different contributions. Large singular values would be penalized more heavily than small ones by using the nuclear norm approach. This situation easily leads to the overshrinking of the rank. Second, the rank function may be impractical. Third, low-rank matrix approximation approaches require numerous iterations. This requirement results in low computational efficiency.

Recently, the nonconvex relaxation approach has been utilized to approximate the nuclear norm [44]. In particular, a well-known method named the weighted Schatten p-norm model was introduced [45] for hyperspectral image denoising. This method is represented as

$$\begin{aligned} &\min_{X,S} C\|X\|^p_{w,S_p} + \lambda\|S\|_1 \\ &s.t.\ Y = X + S + E,\ \|E\|_F \leq \xi \end{aligned}, \tag{4}$$

where C denotes the weights for the low-rank constraint, λ represents the regularization constraint parameter, and ξ denotes the noise level. In $\|X\|^p_{w,S_p} = \sum_i w_i \sigma_i^p(X)$, w_i represents the ith non-negative weighted value, and σ_i is the ith singular value of matrix X. $\|E\|_F$ denotes the Frobenius-norm of matrix E.

This weighted Schatten p-norm model can effectively remove noise. However, it is sensitive to the initial parameters, such as the noise level and the weights. Furthermore, the model is difficult to adapt for the removal of mixed noise. Therefore, inspired by the idea presented in a previous work [40,41], in this work, we use the matrix LNAM to eliminate mixed noise from images.

3. Proposed Mixed Denoising Algorithm

As mentioned above, hyperspectral images are often contaminated by mixed noise, and a strong structural correlation exists among the image blocks. This situation prompted us to apply the rank function-based method. In this work, we propose a PnP-based LNAM for mixed noise removal from hyperspectral images. Next, we adopt the ADMM optimization algorithm to solve the proposed mixed noise removal model within the PnP framework and develop the corresponding hyperspectral image denoising algorithm.

3.1. PnP-Based LNAM Model

Given that various noises in natural images are independent, we propose the mixed noise removal model based on a logarithm norm-based rank approximation as follows:

$$\begin{aligned} &\min_{X,S} \|X\|_L + \lambda\|S\|_1 + \rho\phi(X) \\ &s.t.\ \|Y - X - S\|_F^2 \leq \zeta \end{aligned}, \tag{5}$$

where λ, ρ are the regularization parameters, Y is the corrupted image, and S denotes the sparse noise. $\zeta > 0$. $\|X\|_L$ represents the logarithmic norm-based low-rank function. The subscript "L" is the first letter of the logarithm, which can be expressed as

$$\|X\|_L = \sum_{i=1}^{\min\{m_1,m_2\}} \log(\sigma_i^p(X) + \delta), \tag{6}$$

where X denotes a clear image with the size of $m_1 \times m_2$, and $\sigma_i(X)$ represents the ith singular value of X. $0 < p \leq 1$, and $\delta > 0$ denotes a constant that is used to avoid dividing the result by 0.

In model (5), $\phi(X)$ denotes an implicit regularizer exploiting certain priors of natural images, which can be selected from many famous denoisers, such as the BM3D denoiser [8], DnCNN denoiser [46] and FFDNET [47]. In this work, the BM3D denoiser is selected as the embedded regularization module. In summary, $\|X\|_L$ characterize the global information of the original image, i.e., low-rankness. Additionally, the image details can be persevered by plugging the regularization module $\phi(X)$ into the PnP framework. To preserve the global structure and detailed information of the image, the two above complementary modules are used in our work.

Compared with the nuclear norm function, the logarithmic norm-based low-rank function can obtain a superior sparseness on real images. In reference to a previous work [48], we suppose that a constant M is the boundary of feasible set X, such that $\|X\| = |x| \leq M$, and the convex envelop of rank(x) is $\frac{1}{M}\|X\|_* = \frac{1}{M}|x|_1$. The logarithmic function is clearly closer to rank(x) than the convex envelope when the positive constant $\delta \to 0$. Therefore, the logarithmic function can achieve stronger sparsity than the nuclear norm.

3.2. Optimization Method

We introduce an auxiliary variable $\boldsymbol{L}$ to address the PnP-based logarithmic norm approximation model (7). Correspondingly, model (7) can be represented as

$$\begin{array}{l} \min\limits_{X,S} \|\boldsymbol{X}\|_L + \lambda\|\boldsymbol{S}\|_1 + \rho\phi(\boldsymbol{L}) \\ s.t.\ \|\boldsymbol{Y}-\boldsymbol{X}-\boldsymbol{S}\|_F^2 \le \zeta\,;\,\boldsymbol{X}=\boldsymbol{L} \end{array}, \tag{7}$$

Furthermore, the augmented Lagrangian function of (7) is constructed as

$$\begin{array}{l} \ell(\boldsymbol{X},\boldsymbol{L},\boldsymbol{S},\Lambda_1,\Lambda_2,\lambda,\rho,\beta_1,\beta_2) = \|\boldsymbol{X}\|_L + \lambda\|\boldsymbol{S}\|_1 \\ \quad +\langle \boldsymbol{\Lambda}_1, \boldsymbol{Y}-\boldsymbol{X}-\boldsymbol{S}\rangle + \frac{\beta_1}{2}\|\boldsymbol{Y}-\boldsymbol{X}-\boldsymbol{S}\|_F^2 + \rho\phi(\boldsymbol{L}) + \langle \boldsymbol{\Lambda}_2, \boldsymbol{X}-\boldsymbol{L}\rangle + \frac{\beta_2}{2}\|\boldsymbol{X}-\boldsymbol{L}\|_F^2 \end{array}, \tag{8}$$

where $\boldsymbol{\Lambda}_1, \boldsymbol{\Lambda}_2$ denote the Lagrangian multipliers, and β_1, β_2 represent the penalty parameters. Within the framework of ADMM, we minimize the augmented Lagrangian function (8) by using an alternating strategy, i.e., at the (k + 1)th step. We thus update the solution by fixing some variables and solving the remaining ones. Finally, the proposed mixed noise removal method can be divided into the following three subproblems and summarized in Algorithm 1.

(1) X-Subproblem

Given $\boldsymbol{S}^k$ and $\boldsymbol{L}^k$, we update $\boldsymbol{X}^k$ as

$$\begin{aligned} \boldsymbol{X}^{k+1} &= \underset{X}{\operatorname{argmin}}\Big\{ \|\boldsymbol{X}\|_L + \Big\langle \boldsymbol{\Lambda}_1, \boldsymbol{Y}-\boldsymbol{X}-\boldsymbol{S}^k \Big\rangle + \tfrac{\beta_1}{2}\|\boldsymbol{Y}-\boldsymbol{X}-\boldsymbol{S}^k\|_F^2 \\ &\quad + \Big\langle \boldsymbol{\Lambda}_2, \boldsymbol{X}-\boldsymbol{L}^k \Big\rangle + \tfrac{\beta_2}{2}\|\boldsymbol{X}-\boldsymbol{L}^k\|_F^2 \Big\} \\ &= \underset{X}{\operatorname{argmin}}\Big\{ \|\boldsymbol{X}\|_L + \tfrac{\beta_1}{2}\|\boldsymbol{X}-(\boldsymbol{Y}-\boldsymbol{S}^k+\tfrac{\boldsymbol{\Lambda}_1}{\beta_1})\|_F^2 + \tfrac{\beta_2}{2}\|\boldsymbol{X}-\boldsymbol{L}^k+\tfrac{\boldsymbol{\Lambda}_2}{\beta_2}\|_F^2 \Big\} \\ &= \underset{X}{\operatorname{argmin}}\Big\{ \|\boldsymbol{X}\|_L + \tfrac{\beta_1+\beta_2}{2}\|\boldsymbol{X} - \tfrac{\beta_1\boldsymbol{A}+\beta_2\boldsymbol{B}}{\beta_1+\beta_2}\|_F^2 \Big\} \end{aligned}, \tag{9}$$

where $\boldsymbol{A} = \boldsymbol{Y} - \boldsymbol{S}^k + \frac{\boldsymbol{\Lambda}_1}{\beta_1}$, $\boldsymbol{B} = \boldsymbol{L}^k - \frac{\boldsymbol{\Lambda}_2}{\beta_2}$. We introduce the following theorem to obtain the solution to (9).

Theorem 1 (Logarithmic Singular Value Thresholding [40]). *Let $G \in R^{m_1\times m_2}$ be a given matrix, and the SVD of G is $G = \boldsymbol{U}_G \sum_G \boldsymbol{V}_G^T$, where $\sum_G$ is the diagonal matrix whose diagonal elements are the singular values. For any $\alpha > 0$,the closed-form solution of the following problem:*

$$\min_X \alpha\|\boldsymbol{X}\|_L + \frac{1}{2}\|\boldsymbol{X}-\boldsymbol{G}\|_F^2, \tag{10}$$

is given by $\boldsymbol{X} = \boldsymbol{U}_G \mathrm{T}_{\alpha,\xi}(\sum_G)\boldsymbol{V}_G^T$, where $\mathrm{T}_{\alpha,\xi}(\cdot)$ represents the logarithmic singular value thresholding function, which can be expressed as

$$\mathrm{T}_{\alpha,\xi}(x) = \begin{cases} 0, \Delta \le 0 \\ \underset{y\in\{0,\,(x-\xi+\sqrt{\Delta})/2\}}{\operatorname{argmin}} \varphi(y), \Delta > 0 \end{cases}, \tag{11}$$

where $\Delta = (x-\xi)^2 - 4(\alpha - x\xi)$ and $\varphi(y) = \alpha\log(y+\xi) + (y-x)^2/2$.

(2) L-Subproblem

Given $\boldsymbol{X}^k$ and $\boldsymbol{S}^k$, we update $\boldsymbol{L}^k$ as

$$L^{k+1} = \underset{L}{\operatorname{argmin}} \rho\phi\left(L^k\right) + \frac{\beta_2}{2}\|X^{k+1} - L + \frac{\Lambda_2}{\beta_2}\|_F^2. \tag{12}$$

Let $\hat{\sigma}^2 = \frac{\rho}{\beta_2}$. Equation (12) can be represented as

$$prox_\phi\left(L^{k+1}\right) = \underset{L}{\operatorname{argmin}} \phi(L) + \frac{1}{2\hat{\sigma}^2}\|X^{k+1} - L + \frac{\Lambda_2}{\beta_2}\|_F^2, \tag{13}$$

where $prox_\phi(\cdot)$ denotes the proximal operator of regularization, which is replaced by the embedded denoiser. It is known that BM3D [8] and FFDNET [47] are both famous image denoisers. The main advantage of the BM3D denoiser is that it can be applied to characterize the piecewise smoothness and the nonlocal self-similarity of images in a 3D transform domain. Recently, deep learning-based image denoisers have shown promising performance. However, the deep learning-based method needs a massive amount of training data, and these datasets are difficult to obtain. Therefore, the BM3D denoiser [8] is selected as a module within the PnP framework. By plugging in the BM3D denoiser, the solution can be expressed as

$$L^{k+1} = BM3D\left(X^{k+1} + \frac{\Lambda_2}{\beta_2}, \hat{\sigma}\right). \tag{14}$$

(3) S-Subproblem

Given X^{k+1} and L^{k+1}, we update S^k as

$$\begin{aligned} S^{k+1} &= \underset{S}{\operatorname{argmin}}\left\{\lambda\|S\|_1 + \left\langle \Lambda_1, Y - X^{k+1} - S\right\rangle + \tfrac{\beta_1}{2}\|Y - X^{k+1} - S\|_F^2\right\} \\ &= \underset{S}{\operatorname{argmin}}\left\{\lambda\|S\|_1 + \tfrac{\beta_1}{2}\|Y - X^{k+1} - S + \tfrac{\Lambda_1}{\beta_1}\|_F^2\right\} \end{aligned} \tag{15}$$

We apply the soft thresholding operator $soft(\cdot)$ to obtain the solution to the subproblem of (15). The operator is defined as $soft_\tau(x) = \max(|x| - \tau, 0)\operatorname{sgn}(x)$, where x denotes the variable, and τ represents a parameter. Accordingly, the solution of (15) can be represented as

$$S^{k+1} = soft_{\frac{\lambda}{\beta_1}}\left(Y - X^{k+1} + \frac{\Lambda_1}{\beta_1}\right). \tag{16}$$

(4) Update Multipliers

The Lagrangian multipliers are updated as follows:

$$\begin{cases} \Lambda_1 = \Lambda_1 + \beta_1(Y - X^{k+1} - S^{k+1}) \\ \Lambda_2 = \Lambda_2 + \beta_2(X^{k+1} - L^{k+1}) \end{cases}. \tag{17}$$

Algorithm 1. ADMM for Solving the PnP-Based LNAM Model.

Input: The noisy image Y, parameter λ, ρ, stopping criteria ε.

Initialization: $t = 0$, let X, L, S, and Lagrangian multiplies Λ_1,Λ_2 be zeros matrices, penalty parameter $\beta_1 = 1.1$; $\beta_2 = 1.2$.
Step 1: Calculate X via (9).
Step 2: Calculate L via (14).
Step 3: Calculate S via (16).
Step 4: Update the multiplies Λ_1, Λ_2 via (17).
Step 5: Check convergence criteria: $\frac{\|X^{t+1} - X^t\|_F}{\|X^t\|_F} \leq \varepsilon$.
Step 6: If the convergence criteria are not met, set $t = t + 1$ and go to **Step 1**.
Output: The restored HSI X.

4. Experimental Results

Simulated and real HSI image sets are selected to evaluate the performance of the proposed method. Meanwhile, we conduct comparison experiments on these HSI datasets with other mixed noise removal algorithms, including the modified BM3D method [8], low-rank matrix recovery (LRMR) [25], low-rank global total variation (LRGTV) [31], and a weighted group sparsity-regularized low-rank tensor decomposition (LRTDGS) method [35]. In all experiments, each band of the HSI data is normalized into [0, 1], and the parameters of the methods for comparison are based on the suggested values in the original article. Moreover, the modified BM3D method proposed in [8] is used to remove the Gaussian noise. Before denoising, the sparse noise is detected and removed through adaptive median filtering. Then, BM3D can remove the Gaussian noise. Hence, the modified BM3D method is called A-BM3D.

All the algorithm simulation environments used MATLAB R2018 and a 64-bit Windows 10 operating system with 2.6 GB CPU and 16 GB memory. The configuration of the experimental environmental parameters is summarized in Table 1.

Table 1. Experimental environmental configuration.

Name	Configuration
Simulated images and size	Sumi-Indian (145 × 145 × 224), Pavia (200 × 200 × 80)
Real HSI image and size	Urban (307 × 307 × 210)
Performance Evaluation	PSNR (dB), SSIM [49]
Experimental platform	Windows 10, MATLAB R2018b, 16GB Memory

4.1. Simulated Data Experiment

In this study, the ground truth of the Simu–Indian data [50] and the Pavia City Center data [51] are adopted to generate the synthetic data for our experiments. The sizes of the Simu–Indian and the Pavia data are 145 × 145 × 224 and 200 × 200 × 80, respectively. In addition, we normalize each band of the HSI data into [0, 1] and consider the synthetic HSI data as the clean data. The mean of the peak signal-to-noise ratio (MPSNR) and the mean of structural similarity (MSSIM) over all the bands are utilized to assess the performances of different mixed noise removal algorithms. For the generation of a noisy image, Gaussian and S&P noises are added into all the bands of the clean HSI data, as in the following two cases:

Case 1: In this case, the noise intensity is equal in all bands. First, we add the Gaussian noise with a zero mean into all bands with the noise standard variances G = 0.025, 0.05, 0.075, and 0.10. Second, we add S&P noise into all bands with the noise proportions S&P = 0.05, 0.10, 0.15, and 0.20.

Case 2: In contrast to that in Case 1, the noise intensity in different bands differs in Case 2. We add different zero-mean Gaussian noises into each band. In contrast to that in Case 1, the Gaussian noise variance is randomly selected from 0.02 to 0.10. Then, different percentages of S&P noise, which are randomly selected from [0.10, 0.20], are added into each band. In addition, five selected bands of the Simu–Indian data and 10 selected bands of the Pavia City Center data are corrupted with 10 and 15 stripes, respectively.

Tables 2 and 3 report the comparison results of different denoising methods for the Simu–Indian and Pavia datasets in the above two cases. MPSNR and MSSIM are used to evaluate the performances of different denoising algorithms. These two tables show that, on the whole, the proposed algorithm provides satisfactory PSNR and SSIM values in most cases when compared with other methods. This situation confirms the advantages of the proposed algorithm in mixed noise denoising. For the Simu–Indian data, the performance of the proposed algorithm is close to that of the LRTDGS algorithm when the mixed noise intensity is low. For the Pavia data, the quality results of the LRGTV method are the best likely, because the LRGTV algorithm processes all the patches together and uses the spatial–spectral total variation regularization method to recover the whole 3D HSI. The restoration effect of the LRMR algorithm is relatively unsatisfactory when the Gaussian noise is strong. Although the A-BM3D algorithm adopts the adaptive filter to remove S&P noise, its denoising effect is not ideal when the density of the S&P noise is high. Table 3 shows that, surprisingly, the LRTDGS algorithm performs poorly on the Pavia data.

Table 2. Quantitative evaluation of the different methods on the Simu–Indian dataset.

Case	Noise Level	Evaluation Index	A-BM3D	LRMR	LRGTV	LRTDGS	Proposed
Case 1	G = 0.025, S&P = 0.05	MPSNR (dB)	32.7384	43.8913	48.3861	47.7429	47.8694
		MSSIM	0.9603	0.9917	0.9966	0.9986	0.9928
	G = 0.05, S&P = 0.10	MPSNR (dB)	31.3988	39.4308	43.8277	44.1583	43.9426
		MSSIM	0.9459	0.9756	0.9873	0.9950	0.9907
	G = 0.075, S&P = 0.15	MPSNR (dB)	29.5997	36.2251	40.2178	41.4578	40.3526
		MSSIM	0.9121	0.9492	0.9701	0.9962	0.9821
	G = 0.10, S&P = 0.20	MPSNR (dB)	27.2071	33.6607	37.2842	39.0910	37.6930
		MSSIM	0.8156	0.9122	0.9448	0.9912	0.9810
Case 2		MPSNR (dB)	25.0932	31.2765	34.9218	36.2435	35.1372
		MSSIM	0.7126	0.9094	0.9343	0.9447	0.9351

Table 3. Quantitative evaluation of the different methods on the Pavia dataset.

Case	Noise Level	Evaluation Index	A-BM3D	LRMR	LRGTV	LRTDGS	Proposed
Case 1	G = 0.025, S&P = 0.05	MPSNR (dB)	29.1858	40.8327	43.1464	31.7501	42.4572
		MSSIM	0.8255	0.9871	0.9916	0.9049	0.9689
	G = 0.05, S&P = 0.10	MPSNR (dB)	28.4427	36.3285	38.3019	30.3034	37.6853
		MSSIM	0.8002	0.9663	0.9756	0.8690	0.9314
	G = 0.075, S&P = 0.15	MPSNR (dB)	27.4632	33.2836	34.9636	29.1936	33.7557
		MSSIM	0.7656	0.9370	0.9512	0.8352	0.8888
	G = 0.10, S&P = 0.20	MPSNR (dB)	26.1708	31.1647	32.3247	28.1507	31.6958
		MSSIM	0.7142	0.9026	0.9208	0.7980	0.8402
Case 2		MPSNR (dB)	24.7539	30.3447	31.5693	27.1295	30.9436
		MSSIM	0.6820	0.9083	0.9205	0.7356	0.9347

Figures 1 and 2 provide a visual representation of the performances of different methods based on their restoration results for the Simu–Indian dataset. In Figure 1, the zero-mean Gaussian noise standard variance is 0.10, and the S&P noise intensity is 0.10. Meanwhile, in Figure 2, we set the Gaussian intensity to be the same as that in Figure 1, but the noise intensity of S&P is 0.20. Furthermore, the same subregion of each subfigure is marked with red boxes and enlarged. Figures 1 and 2 show that all the compared algorithms can remove mixed noise to some extent. The image tends to be blurry after the A-BM3D method is used. Although the two LRMR algorithms can remove noise and preserve spectral information, they cannot remove the Gaussian noise completely. LRGTV, by taking advantage of the whole 3D structure and spatial–spectral total variation regularization, can obtain satisfactory denoising results. However, it fails to recover the local details well. The performance of the proposed method is close to that of the LRTDGS algorithm mainly because we use the logarithm norm and PnP prior to describe the global structure and nonlocal similarity of the HSI image.

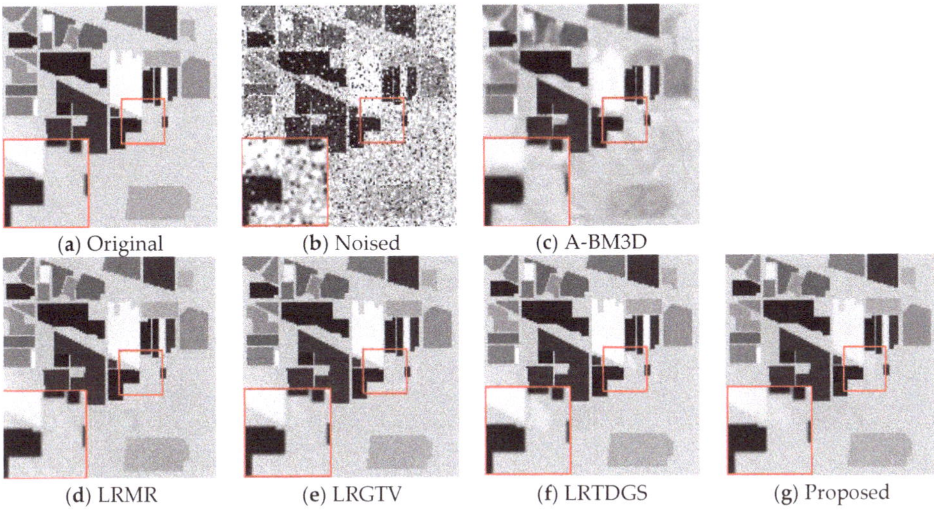

Figure 1. Restored results of band 35 on Simu–Indian. From top to bottom: the results under a subcase (the standard deviation of zero-mean Gaussian noise is G = 0.10, and the noise proportion of S&P noise is S = 0.10).

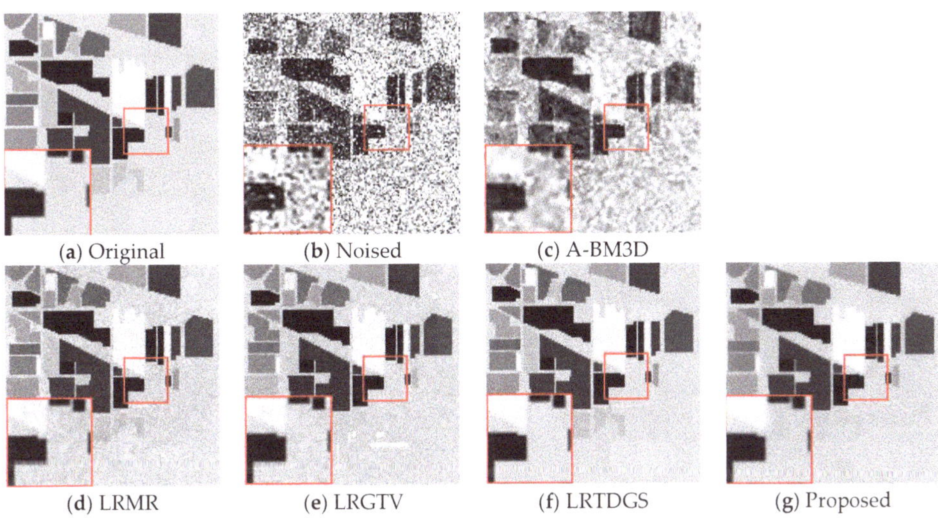

Figure 2. Restored results of band 57 on Simu–Indian. From top to bottom: the results under a subcase (the standard deviation of zero-mean Gaussian noise is G = 0.10, and the noise proportion of S&P noise is S = 0.20).

The visual results of the different denoising methods for the Pavia dataset are presented in Figures 3 and 4. The noise intensity in these figures is the same as that in Figures 1 and 2. Figures 3 and 4 show that the denoising performance of the proposed method is satisfactory. However, Figure 4 illustrates that LRGTV is the best algorithm, mainly because it employs the global structure and the spectral information in the low-rank constraint. Compared with the LRGTV method, the proposed method is more sensitive to S&P noise when the noise level is strong. We will address this issue in our future work.

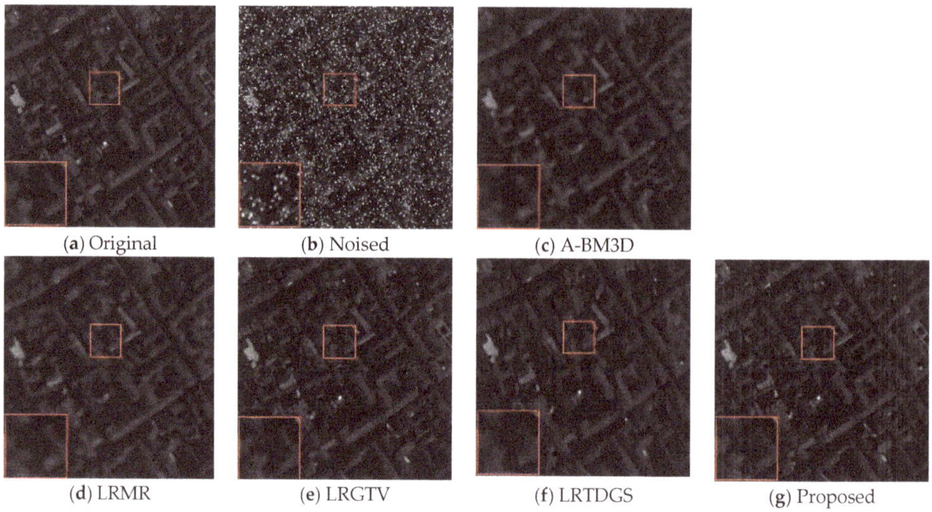

Figure 3. Restored results of band 35 on Pavia. From top to bottom: the results under a subcase (the standard deviation of zero-mean Gaussian noise is G = 0.10, and the noise proportion of S&P noise is S = 0.10).

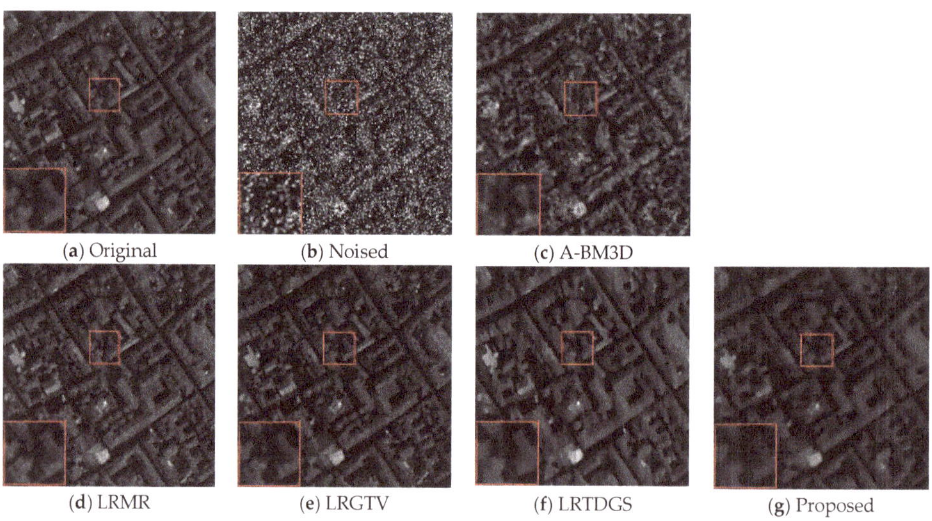

Figure 4. Restored results of band 57 on Pavia. From top to bottom: the results under a subcase (the standard deviation of zero-mean Gaussian noise is G = 0.10, and the noise proportion of S&P noise is S = 0.20).

Figures 5–8 provide the PSNR and SSIM values of each band for the Simu–Indian and Pavia datasets, respectively. As shown in Figures 5 and 6, the proposed algorithm presents satisfactory PSNR and SSIM values for almost all bands in the Simu–Indian dataset, indicating that the proposed algorithm outperforms the algorithms for comparison in mixed noise removal. As mentioned above, and as illustrated in Figures 7 and 8, LRGTV achieves the best PSNR and SSIM values for each band in the Pavia dataset. However, the performance of the proposed method is relatively weak. The main reason for this result is not yet clear and will be addressed in our next work.

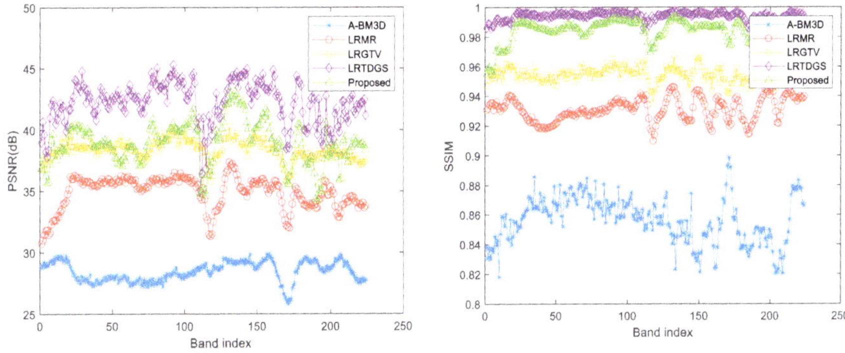

(**a**) PSNR (**b**) SSIM

Figure 5. PSNR and SSIM values of restored results by different methods on Simu–Indian data (G = 0.10, S = 0.10).

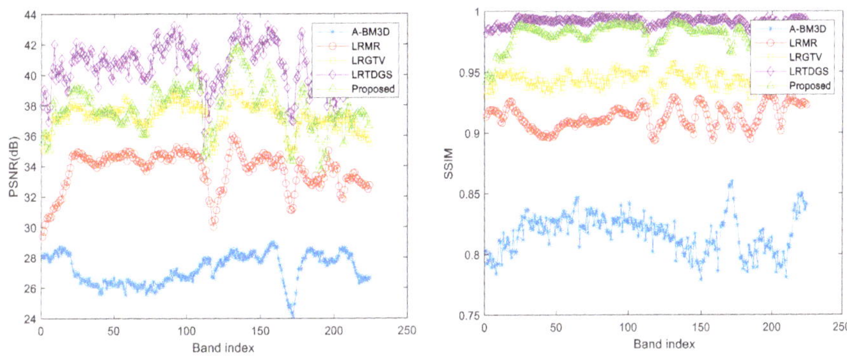

(**a**) PSNR (**b**) SSIM

Figure 6. PSNR and SSIM values of restored results by different methods on Simu–Indian data (G = 0.10, S = 0.20).

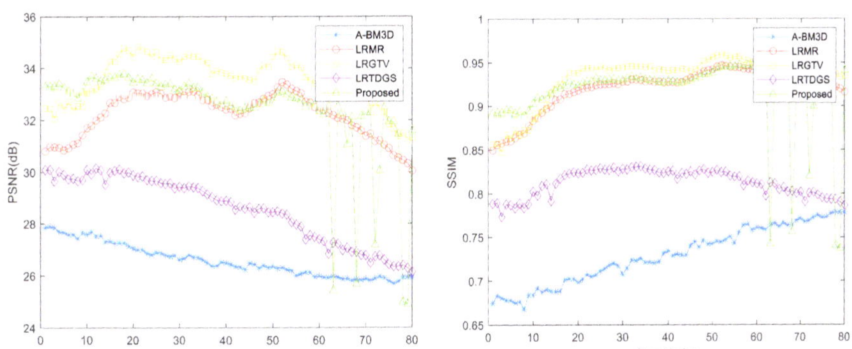

(**a**) PSNR (**b**) SSIM

Figure 7. PSNR and SSIM values of restored results by different methods on Pavia data (G = 0.10, S = 0.10).

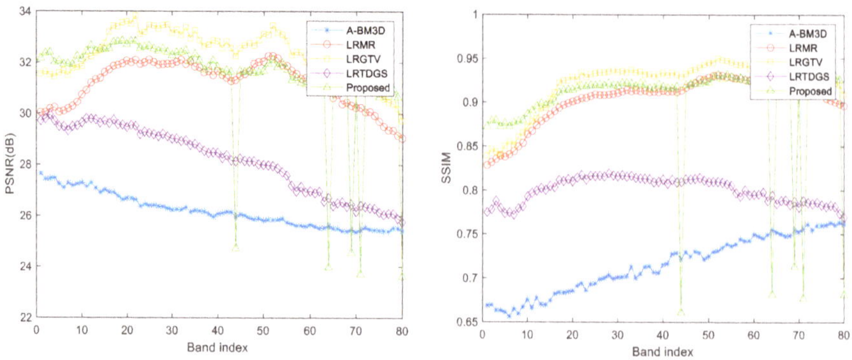

(**a**) PSNR (**b**) SSIM

Figure 8. PSNR and SSIM values of restored results by different methods on Pavia data. (G = 0.10, S = 0.20).

4.2. *Real Experiments*

Only the Hyper-spectral Digital Imagery Collection Experiment urban dataset, which can be downloaded online [52], is utilized in this experiment and described in this paper due to space limitations. The size of the urban image is 307 × 307 × 210. Figure 9 shows the real-world urban data.

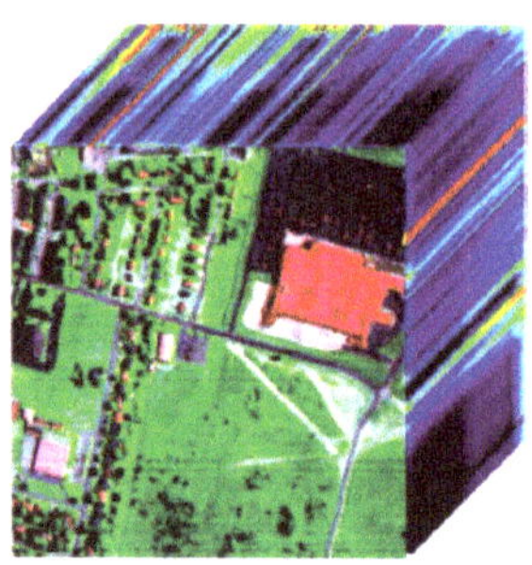

Figure 9. Real-world urban data.

Figures 10 and 11 present bands 83 and 205 of the restored images. As shown in Figure 10, the restoration result of A-BM3D is oversmoothed, causing the local details to become distorted. Most other methods, such as LRMR and LRGTV, can effectively remove noise from the urban image. Overall, the results show that the proposed algorithm performs satisfactorily. However, when the band is in the range of [199, 210], the stripes are considered to be the low-rank part, which is assumed to be the clean data, in the low-rank decomposition. Although we use PnP-based regularization to mine the spatial information of the real urban image, the proposed method cannot completely remove the stripes in Figure 11. Therefore, we will explore and address the reason for this problem in our future work.

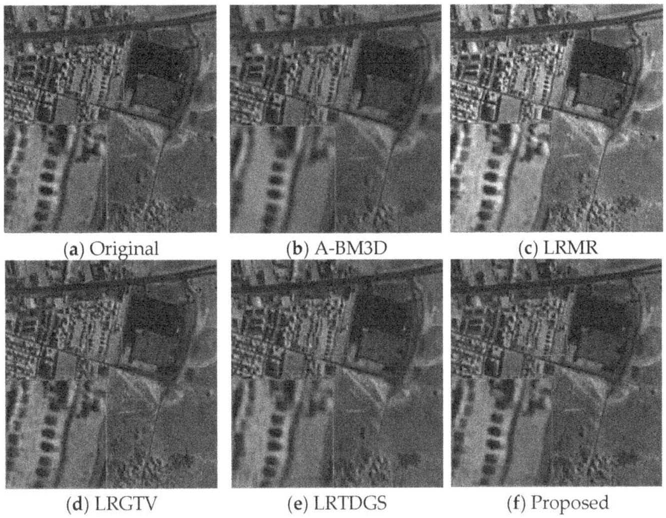

Figure 10. Restoration results on HYDICE urban image set: slight noise band.

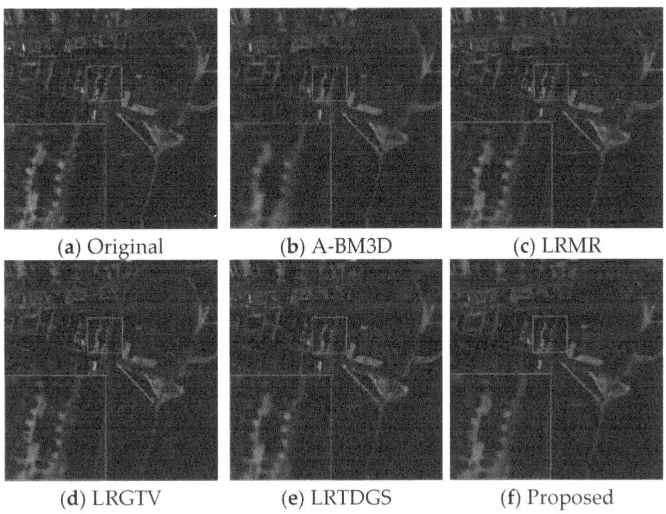

Figure 11. Restoration results on HYDICE urban image set: moderate noise band.

Figure 12 shows the vertical mean profiles of band 205 before and after restoration. Concretely, it illustrates the spectral curves at one spatial location of the restored results by different algorithms. In this figure, the horizontal axis represents the band index, and the vertical axis represents the mean digital number value of each column. Rapid fluctuations are observed in the curve given the presence of mixed noise. After restoration, the fluctuations are more or less suppressed. Here, the proposed method appears to perform satisfactorily in accordance with the visual results presented in Figure 11. In summary, the above observations in Figure 12 prove that the proposed algorithm achieves satisfied results on mixed noise removal and fine details preservation. The reason why our method performs well is that it utilizes the logarithm norm-based rank function to exploit the global information and PnP regularization module to preserve the details of the image. Furthermore, the small singular values can be eliminated by using the logarithm-norm rank function. It helps to reconstruct the global structure information. However, the elimination of small singular values results in the loss of image details. This can be restored by using the BM3D regularization method.

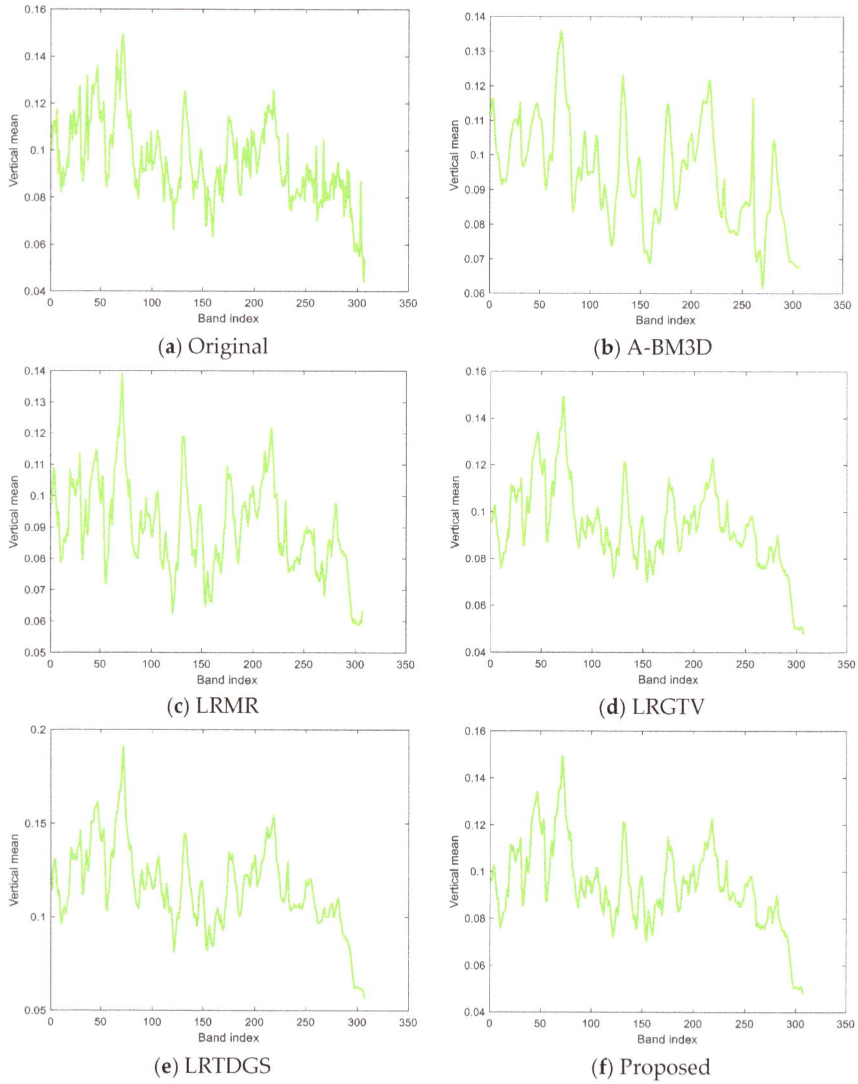

Figure 12. The vertical mean profiles of band 205 on a real urban image.

4.3. *Performance Analysis*

Generally speaking, HSI mixed noise removal is a highly ill-posed problem. In this work, we introduce a PnP prior to make the problem produce feasible results. The non-convex optimization of the proposed model is challenging, and with the idea of auxiliary variables and the ADMM scheme, one problem that has been noted is convergence.

Therefore, we show the traces of the quality index PSNR with respect to the iterations in Figure 13 to further verify the stability of the proposed algorithm. Figure 13 provides the curve of PSNR vs. iteration number for the Simu–Indian and Pavia datasets.

The Gaussian and S&P noise intensities are set as 0.10 and 0.20, respectively. Figure 13 shows that, when the iteration number exceeds 60, the PSNR value tends to be stable. Therefore, the effectiveness of the proposed algorithm is further demonstrated by these experimental results.

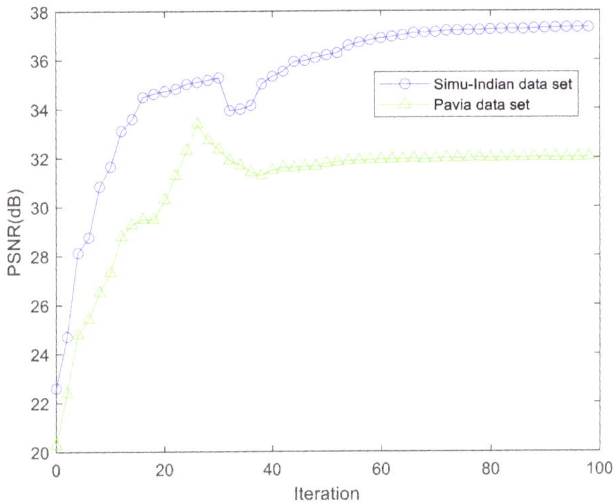

Figure 13. PSNR values with respect to the iterations for different datasets.

Finally, we provide the computational time of the different methods in Table 4. Note that all the results are implemented in MATLAB R2018. The Gaussian and S&P noise intensities are also set as 0.10 and 0.20, respectively. As shown in Table 4, most of the denoising methods have high computational efficiency. A-BM3D has the shortest running time. However, the proposed algorithm has relatively low computational efficiency, mainly because we use the PnP-based BM3D module to restore the HSI image, which is highly time-consuming. Concretely, this is mainly because the whole HSI image has been divided into image patches, and each image patch is restored by using the BM3D module separately.

Table 4. Computational times of different methods (unit: s).

HSI Image	A-BM3D	LRMR	LRGTV	LRTDGS	Proposed
Simu-Indian	0.0906	62.9295	119.9487	74.8305	961.2586
Pavia	0.1807	54.4320	92.1933	49.3622	723.0967
Urban	0.5035	292.0146	507.7214	254.9293	1669.3409

5. Conclusions

We propose a logarithm norm nonconvex approximation-based HSI algorithm for mixed noise removal. Specifically, the logarithm norm-based nonconvex low-rank is used to characterize the global spatial–spectral correlation among all hyperspectral image bands, and PnP-based regularization is introduced to further exploit the local detailed information of HSI. Then, we develop the ADMM optimization scheme to address the proposed model. Finally, through simulations, real experiments, and discussion, we demonstrate quantitatively and qualitatively that the proposed algorithm achieves satisfactory performance, because the logarithm norm-based low-rank can help restore the global information of the target hyperspectral image, while the embedded BM3D denoiser helps preserve the image details and remove the image structure noise. Our future work will include investigating a novel mixed noise removal algorithm by applying other technologies, such as LSM modeling, deep convolution neural network, attention mechanism, and transformer frameworks.

Author Contributions: J.L. conceived the idea, designed the experiments, and wrote the paper; J.W. and M.X. helped to analyze the experimental data; and Y.H. helped to review this manuscript. All authors have read and agreed to the published version of the manuscript.

Funding: This research was funded by the Science and Technology Research Program of Shangrao (No. 2021J005). This work was also supported by the Natural Science Foundation of Sichuan (No. 2022NSFSC0557).

Data Availability Statement: From this study, the ground truth of the Simu–Indian data can be downloaded online at https://engineering.purdue.edu/~biehl/MultiSpec/hyperspectral.html (accessed on 12 March 2022) [50], and the Pavia City center data used in our work can be downloaded from http://www.ehu.eus/ccwintco/index.php?title=Hyperspectral_Remote_Sensing_Scenes (accessed on 19 March 2022) [51]. The Hyper-spectral Digital Imagery Collection Experiment (HYDICE) urban dataset can be downloaded online from [52].

Conflicts of Interest: The authors declare no conflict of interest.

References

1. Zhao, X.-L.; Wang, F.; Huang, T.; Ng, M.K.; Plemmons, R. Deblurring and sparse unmixing for hyperspectral images. *IEEE Trans. Geosci. Remote Sens.* **2013**, *51*, 4045–4058. [CrossRef]
2. Ma, Y.; Lei, Y.; Wang, T. A natural scene recognition learning based on label correlation. *IEEE Trans. Emerg. Top. Comput. Intell.* **2022**, *6*, 150–158. [CrossRef]
3. Zha, Z.; Wen, B.; Yuan, X.; Zhou, T.; Zhou, J.; Zhu, C. Triply complementary priors for image restoration. *IEEE Trans. Image Process.* **2021**, *30*, 5819–5834. [CrossRef] [PubMed]
4. Dong, W.; Shi, G.; Li, X. Nonlocal image restoration with bilateral variance estimation: A low-rank approach. *IEEE Trans. Image Process.* **2013**, *22*, 700–711. [CrossRef]
5. Rahman, S.; Ahmad, M.O.; Swamy, M.N. Bayesian wavelet-based image denoising using the Gaussian-hermite expansion. *IEEE Trans. Image Process.* **2008**, *17*, 1755–1771. [CrossRef] [PubMed]
6. Oliveira, J.; Bioucas, J.M.; Figueiredo, M. Adaptive total variation image deblurring: A majorization-minimization approach. *Signal Process.* **2009**, *89*, 1683–1693. [CrossRef]
7. Zhang, X.; Wu, X. Image interpolation by 2-D autoregressive modeling and soft-decision estimation. *IEEE Trans. Image Process.* **2008**, *17*, 887–896. [CrossRef] [PubMed]
8. Dabov, K.; Foi, A.; Katkovnik, V.; Egiazarian, K. Image denoising by sparse 3-D transform-domain collaborative filtering. *IEEE Trans. Image Process.* **2007**, *16*, 2080–2095. [CrossRef]
9. Aharon, M.; Elad, M.; Bruckstein, A. K-SVD: An algorithm for designing overcomplete dictionaries for sparse representation. *IEEE Trans. Signal Process.* **2006**, *54*, 4311–4322. [CrossRef]
10. Wu, W.; Jia, Y.; Li, P.; Zhang, J.; Yuan, J. Manifold kernel sparse representation of symmetric positive-definite matrices and its applications. *IEEE Trans. Image Process.* **2015**, *24*, 3729–3741. [CrossRef]
11. Dong, W.; Fu, F.; Shi, G.; Cao, X.; Wu, J.; Li, G.; Li, X. Hyperspectral image super-resolution via non-negative structured sparse representation. *IEEE Trans. Image Process.* **2016**, *25*, 2337–2351. [CrossRef] [PubMed]
12. Hwang, H.; Haddad, R.A. Adaptive median filters: New algorithm and results. *IEEE Trans. Image Process.* **1995**, *4*, 499–502. [CrossRef] [PubMed]
13. Nikolova, M. A variational approach to remove outliers and impulse noise. *J. Math. Imaging Vis.* **2004**, *20*, 99–120. [CrossRef]
14. Cai, J.; Chan, R.; Nikolova, M. Two-phase approach for deblurring images corrupted by impulse plus Gaussian noise. *Inverse Probl. Imaging* **2008**, *2*, 187–204. [CrossRef]
15. Xiao, Y.; Zeng, T.; Yu, J.; Ng, M. Restoration of images corrupted by mixed Gaussian-impulse noise via L1-L0 minimization. *Pattern Recogn.* **2011**, *44*, 1708–1720. [CrossRef]
16. Xiong, B.; Yin, Z.P. A universal denoising framework with a new impulse detector and nonlocal means. *IEEE Trans. Image Process.* **2012**, *21*, 1663–1675. [CrossRef]
17. Liu, L.; Chen, C.; Zhou, Y.; You, X. A new weighted mean filter with a two-phase detector for removing impulse noise. *Infor. Sci.* **2015**, *315*, 1–16. [CrossRef]
18. Huang, T.; Dong, W.; Xie, X.; Shi, G.; Bai, X. Mixed noise removal via Laplacian scale mixture modeling and local low-rank approximation. *IEEE Trans. Image Process.* **2017**, *26*, 3171–3186. [CrossRef]
19. Liu, J.; Tai, X.; Huang, H.; Huan, Z. A weighted dictionary learning model for denoising images corrupted by mixed noise. *IEEE Trans. Image Process.* **2013**, *22*, 1108–1120. [CrossRef]
20. Jiang, J.; Zhang, L.; Yang, J. Mixed noise removal by weighted encoding with sparse nonlocal regularization. *IEEE Trans. Image Process.* **2014**, *23*, 2651–2662. [CrossRef]
21. Xie, Y.; Gu, S.; Liu, Y.; Zuo, W.; Zhang, W.; Zhang, L. Weighted schatten p-norm minimization for image denoising and background subtraction. *IEEE Trans. Image Process.* **2016**, *25*, 4842–4857. [CrossRef]

22. Zhou, P.; Lu, C.; Feng, J.; Lin, C.; Yan, S. Tensor low-rank representation for data recovery and clustering. *IEEE Trans. Pattern Anal. Mach. Intell.* **2021**, *43*, 1718–1732. [CrossRef]
23. Chen, Y.; Huang, T.; He, W.; Yokoya, N.; Zhao, X.-L. Hyperspectral image compressive sensing reconstruction using subspace-based nonlocal tensor ring decomposition. *IEEE Trans. Image Process.* **2020**, *29*, 6813–6828. [CrossRef]
24. Zha, Z.; Wen, B.; Yuan, X.; Zhou, J.; Zhu, C. Image restoration via reconciliation of group sparsity and low-rank models. *IEEE Trans. Image Process.* **2021**, *30*, 5223–5238. [CrossRef]
25. Zhang, H.; He, W.; Zhang, L.; Shen, H.; Yuan, Q. Hyperspectral image restoration using low-rank matrix recovery. *IEEE Trans. Geosci. Remote Sens.* **2014**, *52*, 4729–4743. [CrossRef]
26. He, W.; Zhang, H.; Zhang, L.; Shen, H. Hyperspectral image denoising via noise-adjusted iterative low-rank matrix approximation. *IEEE J. Sel. Top. Appl. Earth Obs. Remote Sens.* **2015**, *8*, 3050–3061. [CrossRef]
27. Song, H.; Wang, G.; Zhang, K. Hyperspectral image denoising via low-rank matrix recovery. *Remote Sens. Lett.* **2014**, *5*, 872–881. [CrossRef]
28. Chen, Y.; Guo, Y.; Wang, Y.; Wang, D.; Peng, C.; He, G. Denoising of hyperspectral images using nonconvex low rank matrix approximation. *IEEE Trans. Geosci. Remote Sens.* **2017**, *55*, 5366–5380. [CrossRef]
29. Ye, H.; Li, H.; Yang, B.; Cao, F.; Tang, Y. A novel rank approximation method for mixture noise removal of hyperspectral images. *IEEE Trans. Geosci. Remote Sens.* **2019**, *57*, 4457–4469. [CrossRef]
30. He, W.; Zhang, H.; Zhang, L.; Shen, H. Total-variation-regularized low-rank matrix factorization for hyperspectral image restoration. *IEEE Trans. Geosci. Remote Sens.* **2016**, *54*, 178–188. [CrossRef]
31. He, W.; Zhang, H.; Shen, H.; Zhang, L. Hyperspectral image denoising using local low-rank matrix recovery and global spatial–spectral total variation. *IEEE J. Sel. Top. Appl. Earth Obs. Remote Sens.* **2018**, *11*, 713–727. [CrossRef]
32. Kim, B.; Divel, S.; Pelc, N.; Baek, J. A methodology to train a convolutional neural network-based low-dose CT denoiser with an accurate image domain noise insertion technique. *IEEE Access* **2022**, *10*, 86395–86407. [CrossRef]
33. Leontaris, L.; Dimitriou, N.; Ioannidis, D.; Votis, K.; Tzovaras, D.; Papageorgiou, E. An autonomous illumination system for vehicle documentation based on deep reinforcement learning. *IEEE Access* **2021**, *9*, 75336–75348. [CrossRef]
34. Zhang, K.; Li, Y.; Zuo, W.; Zhang, L.; Gool, L.; Timofte, R. Plug-and-play image restoration with deep denoiser prior. *IEEE Trans. Pattern Anal. Mach. Intell.* **2021**, *44*, 6360–6376. [CrossRef] [PubMed]
35. Chen, Y.; He, W.; Yokoya, N.; Huang, T. Hyperspectral image restoration using weighted group sparsity-regularized low-rank tensor decomposition. *IEEE Trans. Cybernetics* **2020**, *50*, 3556–3570. [CrossRef]
36. Liu, Y.; Zhao, X.-L.; Zheng, Y.; Ma, T.; Zhang, H. Hyperspectral image restoration by tensor fibered rank constrained optimization and plug-and-play regularization. *IEEE Trans. Geosci. Remote Sens.* **2022**, *60*, 5500717. [CrossRef]
37. Venkatakrishnan, S.; Bouman, C.; Wohlberg, B. Plug-and-play priors for model based reconstruction. In Proceedings of the IEEE Global Conference on Signal and Information Processing, Austin, TX, USA, 3–5 December 2013; pp. 945–948.
38. Chan, S.H.; Wang, X.; Elgendy, O. Plug-and-play ADMM for image restoration: Fixed-point convergence and applications. *IEEE Trans. Comput. Imaging* **2017**, *3*, 84–98. [CrossRef]
39. Zhao, X.-L.; Xu, W.; Jiang, T.; Wang, Y.; Ng, M.K. Deep plug-and-play prior for low-rank tensor completion. *Neurocomputing* **2020**, *400*, 137–149. [CrossRef]
40. Chen, L.; Jiang, X.; Liu, X.; Zhou, Z. Robust low-rank tensor recovery via nonconvex singular value minimization. *IEEE Trans. Image Process.* **2020**, *29*, 9044–9059. [CrossRef]
41. Chen, L.; Jiang, X.; Liu, X.; Zhou, Z. Logarithmic norm regularized low-rank factorization for matrix and tensor completion. *IEEE Trans. Image Process.* **2021**, *30*, 3434–3449. [CrossRef]
42. Wright, J.; Ganesh, A.; Rao, S.; Peng, Y.; Ma, Y. Robust principalcomponent analysis: Exact recovery of corrupted low-rank matrices via convex optimization. In Proceedings of the Neural Information Processing Systems, Vancouver, BC, Canada, 7–10 December 2009; pp. 2080–2088.
43. Zhou, Z.; Li, X.; Wright, J.; Candes, E.; Ma, Y. Stable principal component pursuit. In Proceedings of the IEEE international symposium on information theory, Austin, TX, USA, 13–18 June 2010; pp. 1518–1522.
44. Cao, F.; Chen, J.; Ye, H.; Zhao, J.; Zhou, Z. Recovering low-rank and sparse matrix based on the truncated nuclear norm. *Neural Netw.* **2017**, *85*, 10–20. [CrossRef] [PubMed]
45. Xie, Y.; Qu, Y.; Tao, D.; Wu, W.; Yuan, Q.; Zhang, W. Hyperspectral image restoration via iteratively regularized weighted schatten p-norm minimization. *IEEE Trans. Geosci. Remote Sens.* **2016**, *54*, 4642–4659. [CrossRef]
46. Zhang, K.; Zuo, W.; Chen, Y.; Meng, D.; Zhang, L. Beyond a Gaussian denoiser: Residual learning of deep CNN for image denoising. *IEEE Trans. Image Process.* **2017**, *26*, 3142–3155. [CrossRef] [PubMed]
47. Zhang, K.; Zuo, W.; Zhang, L. FFDNet: Toward a fast and flexible solution for CNN-based image denoising. *IEEE Trans. Image Process.* **2018**, *27*, 4608–4622. [CrossRef] [PubMed]
48. Fazel, M. Matrix Rank Minimization With Applications. Ph.D. Dissertation, Stanford University, Stanford, CA, USA, 2002.
49. Wang, Z.; Bovik, A.C.; Sheikh, H.R.; Simoncelli, E.P. Image quality assessment: From error visibility to structural similarity. *IEEE Trans. Image Process.* **2004**, *13*, 600–612. [CrossRef] [PubMed]
50. Available online: https://engineering.purdue.edu/~biehl/MultiSpec/hyperspectral.html (accessed on 12 March 2022).

51. Available online: http://www.ehu.eus/ccwintco/index.php?title=Hyperspectral_Remote_Sensing_Scenes (accessed on 19 March 2022).
52. Available online: http://www.tec.army.mil/hypercube (accessed on 20 April 2022).

mathematics

MDPI

Article

A KGE Based Knowledge Enhancing Method for Aspect-Level Sentiment Classification

Haibo Yu [1,2], Guojun Lu [1], Qianhua Cai [2,*] and Yun Xue [2]

1 School of Physics and Telecommunication Engineering, South China Normal University, Guangzhou 510006, China
2 School of Electronics and Information Engineering, South China Normal University, Foshan 528225, China
* Correspondence: caiqianhua@m.scnu.edu.cn

Abstract: ALSC (Aspect-level Sentiment Classification) is a fine-grained task in the field of NLP (Natural Language Processing) which aims to identify the sentiment toward a given aspect. In addition to exploiting the sentence semantics and syntax, current ALSC methods focus on introducing external knowledge as a supplementary to the sentence information. However, the integration of the three categories of information is still challenging. In this paper, a novel method is devised to effectively combine sufficient semantic and syntactic information as well as use of external knowledge. The proposed model contains a sentence encoder, a semantic learning module, a syntax learning module, a knowledge enhancement module, an information fusion module and a sentiment classifier. The semantic information and syntactic information are respectively extracted via a self-attention network and a graphical convolutional network. Specifically, the KGE (Knowledge Graph Embedding) is employed to enhance the feature representation of the aspect. Then, the attention-based gate mechanism is taken to fuse three types of information. We evaluated the proposed model on three benchmark datasets and the experimental results establish strong evidence of high accuracy.

Keywords: aspect-level sentiment classification; external knowledge; KGE; GCN

MSC: 18C50

Citation: Yu, H.; Lu, G.; Cai Q.; Xue Y. A KGE Based Knowledge Enhancing Method for Aspect-Level Sentiment Classification. *Mathematics* **2022**, *10*, 3908. https://doi.org/10.3390/math10203908

Academic Editors: Jianping Gou, Weihua Ou, Shaoning Zeng and Lan Du

Received: 21 September 2022
Accepted: 17 October 2022
Published: 21 October 2022

1. Introduction

The aspect-level sentiment classification, as a fine grained sentiment analysis task, is widely considered as a main focus in the field of natural language processing. In ALSC tasks, the sentiment polarity of a given aspect in a given text is classified as either positive, neutral or negative [1]. As an example, in the sentence 'the ambience was nice, but service wasn't so great', the sentiment of the two discussed aspects, 'ambience' and 'service', are predicted as positive and negative, respectively. In practice, ALSC has become an effective approach to identify opinions and preferences towards products, stock and anything in the world.

Currently, most methods involving ALSC are performed using the following steps: sentence encoding, syntax dependency tree constructing, syntactic information capturing via graph convolution network (GCN) [2], semantic information extracting based on attention mechanism, information fusion and sentiment classification. So much is the effectiveness of attention networks in attentive weights distribution, a number of studies show their superiority in ALSC tasks [3–5]. Notwithstanding, for a long distance between aspect and its dependency-words, more weight may be assigned to irrelevant words. On this occasion, the establishment of the relation between aspect and its opinion words is thus proposed, which exploits the sentence syntax dependency tree [6]. Figure 1 shows the syntax dependency tree of a given sentence. One can easily see that the syntactical-related words to the aspect, such as 'nice' and 'great', have impressive effects on sentiment polarity prediction. In spite of the significance of syntax structure, the ALSC for informal grammar styles (e.g., colloquial comments, slang language, etc.) remains challenging. In these cases, the connection between aspect and opinion words can be confusing. Thereby, the extracted syntax can even become noise, which results in the misunderstanding of the sentiment.

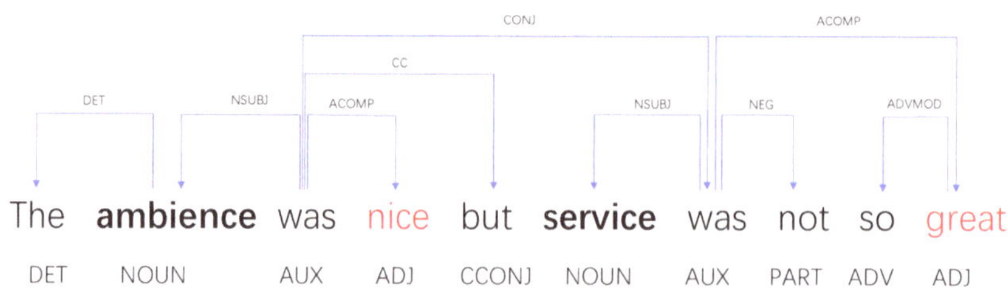

Figure 1. Syntax dependency tree.

Encouragingly, according to recent publications, external knowledge is also employed to enhance the information of aspect for ALSC [7]. Generally, the exploiting of external knowledge is carried out by searching the information related to the given aspect. That is, the aspect is taken as the central node of the knowledge graph, based on which the subgraphs are built up using its neighbor nodes. In such a manner, the selection of the neighboring nodes is highlighted. The distinctiveness of the external knowledge is mainly restricted by the selection method. Further, for the searched knowledge of substantial distinction, the selected nodes must be revised to a large extent. Moreover, when dealing with the knowledge graph, most of the previous methods used graph neural networks such as the graph convolutional network to search the knowledge graph nodes, which is inefficient.

In Consideration of the aforementioned issues, we propose a method that integrates the sentence semantics and syntax as well as the external knowledge toward the aspect. In order to fully extract the sentence information, the semantic relation between aspect and its contexts is built. Likewise, the connection of opinion words to the aspect is set up. With respect to external knowledge, the knowledge graph embedding (KGE) [8] is employed to obtained the knowledge embeddings of the aspect which makes it more efficient to deal with the knowldege graph. In addition, a fusion module is devised to incorporate the relevant external information and the sentence information for sentiment classification. The contributions of this paper are threefold and summarized as follows:

- The external knowledge is effectively applied to enhance the aspect information, which is also supplementary to the sentence information.
- An information fusion approach is dedicatedly designed to integrate different types of information for ALSC.
- Comparing with the state-of-the-art methods, experimental results on three benchmark datasets corroborate the competitiveness of the proposed methods.

The rest of this paper is organized as follows: we review the recent studies on ALSC methods and the KGE applications in Section 2. Section 3 presents the proposed model in detail. In Section 4, experiments are carried out to investigate the working performance of our model. Finally, concluding remarks of this work are given in Section 5.

2. Related Work

2.1. Aspect-Level Sentiment Classification

Early deep-learning based ALSC methods generally concentrate on extracting the contextual semantics by using the integration of a RNN (Recurrent Neural Network) and attention mechanism [9]. In terms of multiple aspects, the sentiment polarity determination via only semantic information becomes insufficient. In addition to the semantic-based models, the exploiting of sentence syntax is one such approach as well. The relation between an aspect and its opinion words can be conveyed by a syntax dependency tree. Because of the graph structure of dependency trees, graph neural networks [10] are employed to cope with the syntactic information. Distinctively, the graph convolutional network is most pronounced for processing graph structured data in a variety of tasks. In terms of ALSC, GCN-based models are capable of not just aggregating and delivering information among neighboring nodes, but also of extracting features and syntactic information of the graph. Zhao [11] takes a GCN to model the sentiment dependencies between aspect words, and thereby captures the sentiment relationships of multiple aspects in a sentence. Zhang [12] characterizes the sentence using a syntax dependency tree, and extracts syntactic information via the GCN. Furthermore, aiming to distinguish the importance of each node in the graph, the attention mechanism is integrated into GCN-based methods. To comprehensively understand the relation between aspect and its opinion words, Tian [13] exploits the attention mechanism to assign the attention weight to each word syntactically connected with the aspect word, based on which the syntactic information can be precisely extracted by GCN. By constructing an aspect-centered syntax dependency tree, Wang [14] focuses on identifying each node using a graph attention, and thus aggregating information from neighboring nodes.

2.2. Semantics and Syntax

Since both semantics and syntax have their own advantages and disadvantages, some recent research solves ALSC by combining these two pieces of information together. Zhang et al. [15] propose an aspect-aware attention mechanism combined with self-attention to obtain the attention score matrices of a sentence, which can not only learn the aspect-related semantic correlations, but also learn the global semantics of a sentence. Bie et al. [16] propose an end-to-end ABSA model, which fuses the syntactic structure information and the lexical semantic information, to address the limitation that existing end-to-end methods do not fully exploit the textual information. Zhang et al. [17] also analyze sentences both syntactically and semantically, and they propose a simple and effective fusion mechanism to make the integration of aspect information and context information more adequate. Some researchers also utilize GCN to capture the neighbor's information [18–20]. However, this research generally ignores that the sentence may not be well formed, and that slang language and informal writing can be found in most user-generated content. As a result, more information is required to help in these situations.

2.3. Knowledge Graph

A knowledge graph involves a great number of entities and their relationship types. The application of a knowledge graph is carried out in a variety of domains, such as education [21], medicine [22], cybersecurity [23], etc. More recent work validates the significance of the knowledge graph in natural language processing [24]. As such, the utilization of the knowledge graph is currently a main focus in NLP tasks. This also gives rise to new opportunities for its use in ALSC. Zhou [25] has devised a GCN-based method that combines syntactic information and external knowledge. Liang [26] introduced knowledge from the SenticNet knowledge base, thus enhancing the information about aspectual word sentiment in this context. However, these approaches generally ignore the inefficiency of the GCN-based method when dealing with the knowledge graph.

Knowledge graph embedding (KGE) is a creative and practical method for introducing the knowledge graph. Theoretically, KGE aims to represent both complex and sparse entity relationship types with low-dimensional and continuous embeddings, which facilitates the computation of introduced knowledge. KGE is currently a widely-used approach in question answering [27], semantic retrieval [28] and recommendation systems [29]. Early KGE methods, such as TransE [30], and TransH [31], consider the "relationship" as the interpretation between head and tail entities. Furthermore, advances in deep-neural networks have optimized the working performance of KGE. The state-of-the-art KGE methods, such as ConvE [32] and CapsE [33], are developed based on capsule neural networks, which obtain the feature and calculate the credibility of a triplet through convolutional layers.

3. Methodology

Figure 2 shows the architecture of the proposed model. There are five main components, namely the sentence encoder, semantic learning module, syntax learning module, knowledge enhancement module, information fusion module and sentiment classifier. More details of each component are presented as follows.

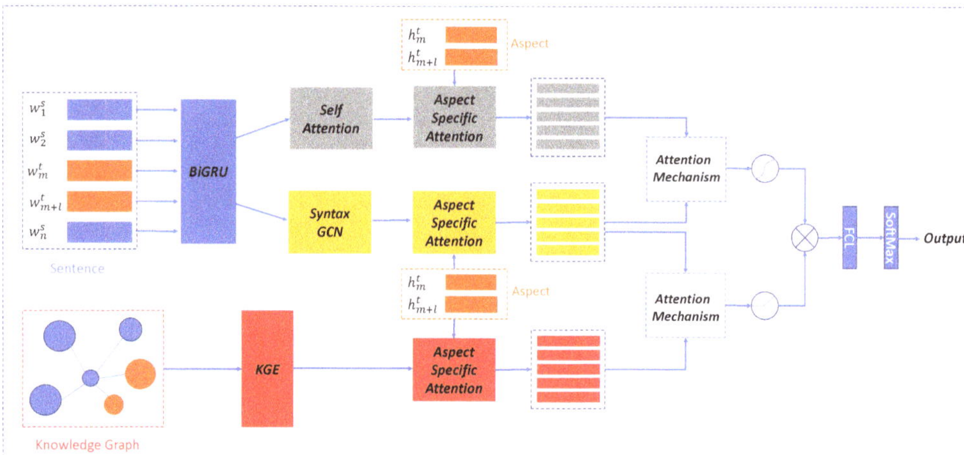

Figure 2. Model architecture.

3.1. Sentence Encoder

Let $x = \left\{w^s_1, w^s_2, \ldots, w^t_m, \ldots, w^t_{m+l}, \ldots, w^s_n\right\}$ be an n-word sentence containing the aspect. Each word is mapped into a low-dimensional vector by looking up in a pretrained word embedding matrix. We can thus obtain the sentence embedding.

Then, the hidden state of the given sentence is extracted via Bidirectional-Gate Recurrent Unit (Bi-GRU) which outperforms other methods in extracting the long-term information of a sentence. As a result, we use Bi-GRU to encode the sentence for further processing. The forward and backward hidden states of the sentence are delivered as $\overrightarrow{H}^{GRU} = \left\{\overrightarrow{h}^s_1, \overrightarrow{h}^s_2, \ldots, \overrightarrow{h}^t_m, \ldots, \overrightarrow{h}^t_{m+l}, \overrightarrow{h}^s_n\right\}$ and $\overleftarrow{H}^{GRU} = \left\{\overleftarrow{h}^s_1, \overleftarrow{h}^s_2, \ldots, \overleftarrow{h}^t_m, \ldots, \overleftarrow{h}^t_{m+l}, \ldots, \overleftarrow{h}^s_n\right\}$, respectively. The sentence representation is the concatenation of $\overrightarrow{H}^{GRU}$ and $\overleftarrow{H}^{GRU}$, i.e.,

$$H^{GRU} = \left[\overrightarrow{H}^{GRU}, \overleftarrow{H}^{GRU}\right] \tag{1}$$

3.2. Semantic Learning Module

The semantic learning module is mainly developed to establish the semantic relation between aspect and its context. With the input sentence representation, in order to corcapture the semantic relation between aspect and its context, we proposed two attention mechanisms. The self-attention mechanism is first performed to obtain the contextual dependency of the given sentence. Subsequently, the aspect-specific attention mechanism is carried out to determine the relation between the aspect and context. Concretely, the attention weights of each context word is computed:

$$SelfAtt = \frac{\left(H^{GRU}W^k\right)\left(H^{GRU}W^q\right)^T}{\sqrt{d_k}} \tag{2}$$

where W^k and W^q are trainable parameter matrices and d_k is the dimension of input vector.

Based on the attention weight, the hidden state in relation to the aspect can be derived, which is:

$$H^{se} = Att\left(H^{SelfAtt}, H^a\right) \tag{3}$$

where $H^{SelfAtt}$ represents the outcome of the self-attention network and H^a is the hidden state of the aspect word output from Bi-GRU. We take H^{se} as the semantic representation for further processing.

3.3. Syntax Learning Module

Syntax can be seen as a supplement of semantics and it has shown to be helpful in sentiment classification. So, to fully extract sentence information, syntactic information is necessary. With respect to the syntactic information, the syntax dependency tree of the given sentence is built in advance. In the syntax learning module, the syntax dependency tree is transformed to the graph $G_{sy} = \left(H^{GRU}, A^{sy}\right)$ to facilitate processing. Notably, H^{GRU} is the feature matrix derived from Bi-GRU, while A^{sy} is the adjacency matrix of the syntax dependency tree.

We employ GCN to extract the syntactic information of the sentence, which can be written as:

$$H^{sy(l+1)} = GCN\left(H^{sy(l)}, \widetilde{A}^{sy}, W^{sy(l+1)}\right) \tag{4}$$

$$GCN\left(H^l, \widetilde{A}, W^{(l+1)}\right) = ReLU\left(H^l\widetilde{A}W^{(l+1)}\right) \tag{5}$$

with

$$\widetilde{A}^{sy} = \widetilde{D}^{-\frac{1}{2}}\left(A^{sy} + I^f\right)\widetilde{D}^{-\frac{1}{2}} \tag{6}$$

where $H^{sy(l+1)}$ stands for the output of the l-th layer in the GCN. The initial $H^{sy(0)}$ is the output from Bi-GRU. $\widetilde{A}^{sy}$ represents the adjacency matrix with self-circulation. $W^{sy(l+1)}$ is the learnable-parameter-matrix of the l-th layer.

With the convolution of each layer, the information of every single node is aggregated from its neighboring node, based on which the node information can be updated during the iterative computation of the GCN. Thus, the syntax representation is the output of the GCN after the last iteration.

3.4. Knowledge Enhancement Module

For the purpose of the aspect feature, supplementary, external knowledge is leveraged to enhance the information of the aspect. Specifically, we use Freebase [34] as an external knowledge base, which contains a large number of words together with various semantic relations.

For a word beyond comprehension, one can search for known information involved with this word for better understanding. In such a manner, the external knowledge can be applied to complement information related to the aspect during learning.

In most user-generated content, informal writing, such as errors in spelling and grammar and slang language, can be found. On this occasion, the exploiting of external knowledge makes a contribution to the determination of sentiment polarity. For instance, the sentence 'check out these songs! Especially that amazing rock one' contains an aspect word 'songs'. Syntactically, there is no explicit opinion word in direct relation to the aspect 'songs' for sentiment classification. For this reason, external knowledge can be introduced, based on which the relation between 'songs' and 'rock' is set up. That is, the word 'rock' indicates a type of song, which is a subordinate of 'songs'. Seeing that the opinion word toward 'rock' is 'amazing', the sentiment polarity is identified as positive. In this way, the sentiment polarity of the aspect 'songs' is similar to that of 'rock'.

In the knowledge enhancement module, we introduce the knowledge graph and take KGE to tackle the external knowledge from Freebase. Notably, most state-of-the-art methods employ GCN to encode the external knowledge. Whereas, a certain amount of external knowledge bases contain heterogeneous graphs, which is challenging for the GCN to deal with. In our model, the external knowledge is mapped into a continuous vector space using KGE, which is more efficient. The enhancement of aspect is conducted by computing the weights between aspect words and the knowledge embeddings.

On this occasion, we select DistMult [35] as the KGE of the proposed model. Every single entity within the knowledge graph base is delivered as:

$$y_e = f(Wx_e) \tag{7}$$

where f stands for either a linear or nonlinear function. W is the parameter matrix. x_e is a vector that represents an entity. Notably, the relationship representation is typically obtained from the score function. DistMult takes the basic bilinear score function as:

$$g_r^b(y_{e1}, y_{e2}) = y_{e1}^T M_r y_{e2} \tag{8}$$

where the relation matrix M_r is a diagonal matrix whilst y_{e1} and y_{e2} are the vector representations of entities x_{e1} and x_{e2}, respectively. The aspect-based knowledge embedding H^{kg} can be obtained by computing the attentive weight between the aspect and its knowledge embedding:

$$H^{kg} = Att(DistMult(x_e), H^a) \tag{9}$$

3.5. Information Fusion Module

Since we have gained different kinds of information including syntactic information, semantic information and external knowledge information, how to effectively combine these three kinds of information is of vital importance. The information fusion module is devised to make full use of the syntactic information, the semantic information and the external information. Both the syntax and the semantics can be considered as sentence information while the external knowledge is the supplementary. During information fusion, each type of information has to be controlled within a certain extent to prevent the introduction of noise. Therefore, we shall compute the attention weights of syntactic information toward the other two types of information. The attention weight between H^{sy} and H^{se} is expressed as:

$$Att(H^{sy}, H^{se}) = \sum_{i=1}^{N} \alpha_{(i)} \cdot H_{(i)}^{sy} \tag{10}$$

$$\alpha_{(i)} = \frac{\exp\left(\sum_{i=1}^{N} H_{(i)}^{sy^T} H_{(i)}^{se}\right)}{\sum_{j=1}^{N} \exp\left(\sum_{i=1}^{N} H_{(i)}^{sy} H_{(i)}^{se}\right)} \tag{11}$$

Likewise, the attention weight of H^{sy} and H^{kg} is:

$$Att\left(H^{sy}, H^{kg}\right) = \sum_{i=1}^{N} \alpha_{(i)} \cdot H_{(i)}^{kg} \tag{12}$$

Then, two gating units are established to filter the noise from the input information, which are:

$$H_i^L = tanh\left[Att\left(H_i^{sy}, H_i^{se}\right) \cdot W_s + b_s\right] \tag{13}$$

$$H_i^K = ReLU\left[Att\left(H_i^{sy}, H_i^{kg}\right) \cdot W_k + b_k\right] \tag{14}$$

where W_k, W_s, b_k and b_s are trainable parameters of the proposed model. The aspect-related sentence representation is computed using cross product operation:

$$H = H^L \times H^K \tag{15}$$

3.6. Sentiment Classifier

The sentence representation H is sent to the sentiment classifier for sentiment polarity classification. A fully connected layer is developed to obtain the score for each sentiment polarity. The final sentiment probability distribution of the aspect is determined using a SoftMax classifier, which is written as:

$$\widetilde{H} = \mathrm{Re}\,LU\left(W_1^T H + b_1\right) \tag{16}$$

$$\widetilde{y} = softmax(\widetilde{H}) \tag{17}$$

where W_1^T and b_1 are trainable parameters, and $\widetilde{y}$ is the predicted sentiment polarity.

The training of the proposed is conducted using the cross entropy and regularization as the loss function, i.e.

$$L = -\sum_i \sum_{j=1}^{N} y_i^j \log \widetilde{y}_i^j \tag{18}$$

where i represents the i-th sample while j represents the j-th sentiment polarity. N is the number of sentiment polarities. y is the real distribution of sentiment and $\widetilde{y}$ is the predicted one.

4. Experiment

4.1. Dataset

In this experiment, three publicly available benchmark datasets are used for working performance evaluation, which are Laptop14 and Restaurant14 from SemEval2014 [36] and Twitter [37]. All the samples in the experiment are labeled as three different polarities, i.e., positive, neutral and negative. Each sample is a review sentence with the tagged aspect within it. Details of each dataset are exhibited in Table 1.

Table 1. Statistics of datasets.

Dataset	Positive		Negative		Neutral	
	Train	Test	Train	Test	Train	Test
Restaurant	2164	728	805	196	633	196
Laptop	987	341	866	128	466	169
Twitter	1560	173	1560	173	3127	346

4.2. Implementation Details

The initialization of sentence embeddings is conducted using both Glove [38] and Bert [39]. The batch sizes of Restaurant14, Laptop14 and Twitter are 32, 64 and 32, respectively. The learning rates of the Glove-based model and BERT-based model are separately set to 1e-3 and 2e-5. In addition, the Adam optimizer is adopted during model training.

4.3. Baseline Methods

Aiming to corroborate the working performance of the proposed model, seven state-of-the-art methods are taken for comparison.

Syntax- and semantic-based methods:

- BiGCN [40]: Two graphs, i.e., a global lexical graph and a concept hierarchy graph, are constructed. A bi-level interactive GCN is established to deal with these graphs.
- R-GAT: An aspect-oriented dependency tree is constructed, which is encoded by a relational graph attention network.

- AFGCN [41]: An aspect fusion graph is constructed based on the syntax dependency tree, which captures the aspect-related context words.
- InterGCN [42]: To capture the relation between multiple aspect words, an inter-aspect GCN is devised on the foundation of the AFGCN.

KG-based methods:

- SK-GCN: A two-GCN-based model that deals with the syntax dependency tree and knowledge graph, respectively.
- Sentic GCN: The external knowledge from SenticNet is introduced to the GCN, which enhances the sentiment dependency between aspects and their contexts.

4.4. Experiment Results

Table 2 shows the experiment results on all datasets. As presented in Table 2, the proposed model outperforms the-state-of-the-art methods on the datasets Restaurant14 and Twitter. Notably, there is a considerable gap between our model and the baselines. The minimum accuracy gaps of the Glove-based model and Bert-based model are 3.57% (versus SK-GCN) and 3.15% (versus RGAT+BERT), which are significant. The main reason is that the introduction of external knowledge from Freebase provides a large amount of semantic information and relationships. With the enhancement of external information toward the aspect, the sentiment classification performance can be optimized. With respect to Laptop14, the working performance of the Sentic-GCN model is slightly better than the proposed method. One possible explanation for this is that the syntactic structure plays a more important role in the sentiment determination in sentences from Laptop14. The utilization of SenticNet [43] brings information to the adjacency matrices. In this way, the syntactic information can be extracted via graph convolution. Moreover, the pre-training of Bert further provides an improvement to the ALSC results. Since the proposed model is capable of integrating the sentence semantics, the sentence syntax and the external knowledge, we can thus expect better sentiment classification results with information supplementary on each other.

Table 2. Experimental results.

Models	Restaurant		Laptop		Twitter	
	Acc	F1	Acc	F1	Acc	F1
BiGCN	81.96	73.53	74.61	71.19	74.13	72.64
AFGCN	81.70	73.43	76.80	72.88	-	-
InterGCN	82.23	72.81	77.12	72.87	-	-
RGAT	83.30	76.08	77.74	73.91	73.12	72.40
SK-GCN	81.53	72.90	77.62	73.84	71.97	70.22
Sentic-GCN	84.03	75.38	**77.90**	**74.71**	-	-
Ours	**84.23**	**76.12**	77.81	73.47	**77.70**	**76.27**
BERT only	84.11	76.66	77.90	73.30	73.27	71.52
AFGCN+BERT	86.16	79.34	80.88	77.24	-	-
RGAT+BERT	86.61	80.99	78.53	74.06	75.72	74.60
InterGCN+BERT	86.43	80.75	82.29	78.9	-	-
Ours+BERT	**86.93**	**81.05**	**82.41**	**79.32**	**78.87**	**77.97**

4.5. Impact of GCN Layer Number

An GCN is a key component in the syntax learning module for syntactic information encoding. On this occasion, we tend to explore the optimal GCN layer number for ALSC. The number of GCN is set to 1, 2, 3, 4 and 5, respectively. According to Table 3, the GCN layer number of 2 obtains the best result in all evaluation settings. Comprehensively, the configuration of the GCN determines the amount of contextual information that is aggregated toward the aspect. It is clear that a one-layer GCN fails to capture sufficient syntactic information from the sentence. When the GCN layer number ranges from 3 to 5, the working performance of our model declines with the increasing number of layers. As such, there are two main considerations. Firstly, the connected context words increase in line with the increment of layer number, based on which the syntactic noise is introduced. Secondly, after multi-layer graph convolution, the nodes become less distinguishable whilst the node representation vectors tend to be consistent, which results in the over-smoothing problem of multi-layer GCN.

Table 3. ALSC accuracy in line with GCN layer numbers.

Num of GCN Layers	Restaurant	Laptop	Twitter
1	83.68	76.94	77.13
2	**84.23**	**77.81**	**77.70**
3	83.12	76.55	76.81
4	82.83	75.98	76.44
5	82.35	75.50	75.93

4.6. Impact of KGE

We employ four distinguishing KGE methods and investigate their effectiveness in external knowledge enhancement. Table 4 exhibits the ALSC results of the Glove-based model of different KGEs.

Table 4. ALSC results of different KGE methods.

KGE Methods	Restaurant	Laptop	Twitter
TransE	82.37	77.13	75.89
TransR	82.65	77.44	75.80
TransH	82.80	77.63	76.12
DistMult	**84.23**	**77.81**	**77.70**

TransE, TransR and TransH have minor accuracy compared with DistMult. The reason for this is that these three translation models determine the word relationship by using head and tail entities, rather than semantic information. By contrast, DistMult uses bilinear methods, which are capable of computing the semantic credibility of entities and relationships within vector space. That is, the introduction of semantic information results in the incorporating of external knowledge, and thus a better sentiment classification accuracy.

4.7. Run Time and Parametric Amount

To further evaluate the efficacy of the proposed model, the run time for training and testing, as well as the size of the parametric quantities of different methods are compared, see Table 5. Both SK-GCN and our model take advantage of the knowledge graph. Our model has a better performance in not only run time, but also the parameter amount. In this way, our model shows its superiority over the GCN-based method in dealing with knowledge graphs. On the other hand, the run time of BiGCN and the proposed model is comparable, but the test accuracy of our model is far better than RGAT and BiGCN, which indicates a higher working efficiency.

Table 5. Results of run time and the parameter amount of different methods.

Method	Training Speed (secs.)	Params (M)
BiGCN	6.88	1.9
RGAT	4.22	3.9
SK-GCN	8.92	8.5
Ours	7.43	7.8

4.8. Case Study

The visualization of attention weights distribution of a given sentence is presented in Figure 3. Words in the darker color are of greater weight, and vice versa. The former is processed by integration of the semantic learning module and syntax learning module, while the latter incorporates the external knowledge as well. According to Figure 3, more attention is given to the words that are close to the aspect by using only sentence-related information. One can easily see that the opinion word 'love' to aspect 'drinks' obtains a higher attentive weight, which is the same with 'great' to 'food'. However, for the aspect 'lychee martini', few syntactic- or semantic-related words are identified via the semantic learning module and syntax learning module. The introduction of external knowledge facilitates the sentiment word determination of 'lychee martini', which contributes to the sentiment classification.

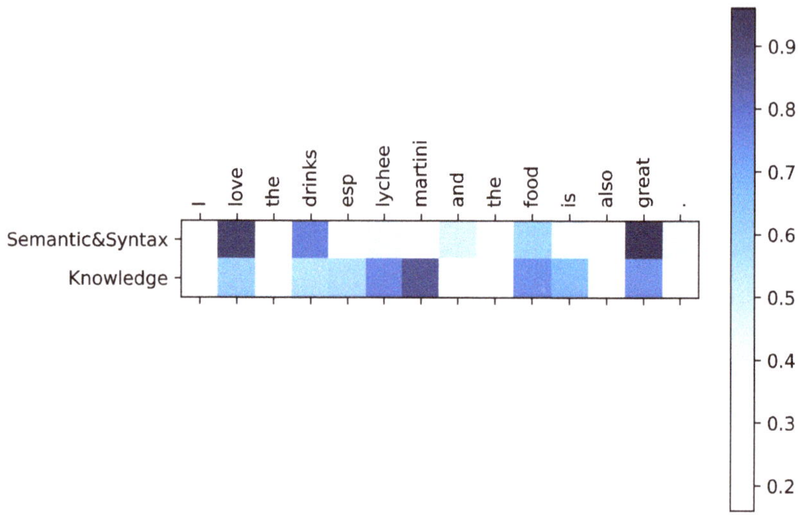

Figure 3. Attention weights to aspects 'drinks', 'lychee martini' and 'food'.

5. Conclusions

In this work, we propose a model that integrates semantics, syntax and external knowledge on the task of ALSC. Aiming to sufficiently incorporate the external information into aspect words, we employ the KGE and aspect-specific attention mechanism to enhance the aspect features. Further, a semantic-learning module and a syntactic-learning module are devised to extract the sentence information. In addition, an information fusion module is established to integrate three types of information for sentiment classification. Experiments are carried out on three benchmark datasets. Our model is the best-performing method compared with the baselines.

Further work will focus on more details of the knowledge graph processing. The loss of graph structural information is still a question that in suspense.

Author Contributions: Conceptualization, H.Y. and Y.X.; methodology, H.Y.; formal analysis, H.Y. and G.L.; writing—original draft preparation, H.Y.; writing—review and editing, Q.C.; supervision, Y.X. and Q.C.; funding acquisition, Q.C. All authors have read and agreed to the published version of the manuscript.

Funding: This work was funded by the Characteristic Innovation Projects of Guangdong Colleges and Universities (Nos. 2018KTSCX049), the Science and Technology Plan Project of Guangzhou under Grant Nos. 202102080258 and 201903010013.

Institutional Review Board Statement: Not applicable.

Informed Consent Statement: Not applicable.

Data Availability Statement: Not applicable.

Conflicts of Interest: The authors declare no conflict of interest.

References

1. Zhou, J.; Huang, J.X.; Chen, Q.; Hu, Q.V.; Wang, T.; He, L. Deep learning for aspect-level sentiment classification: Survey, vision, and challenges. *IEEE Access* **2019**, *7*, 78454–78483. [CrossRef]
2. Kipf, T.N.; Welling, M. Semi-supervised classification with graph convolutional networks. *arXiv* **2016**, arXiv:1609.02907.
3. Wang, Y.; Huang, M.; Zhu, X.; Zhao, L. Attention-based LSTM for aspect-level sentiment classification. In Proceedings of the 2016 Conference on Empirical Methods in Natural Language Processing, Austin, TX, USA, 1–5 November 2016.
4. Yang, M.; Tu, W.; Wang, J.; Xu, F.; Chen, X. Attention based LSTM for target dependent sentiment classification. In Proceedings of the AAAI Conference on Artificial Intelligence, San Francisco, CA, USA, 4–9 February 2017; Volume 31.
5. Zhou, X.; Wan, X.; Xiao, J. Attention-based LSTM network for cross-lingual sentiment classification. In Proceedings of the 2016 Conference on Empirical Methods in Natural Language Processing, Austin, TX, USA, 1–5 November 2016.
6. Nakagawa, T.; Inui, K.; Kurohashi, S. Dependency tree-based sentiment classification using CRFs with hidden variables. In Proceedings of the Human Language Technologies: The 2010 Annual Conference of the North American Chapter of the Association for Computational Linguistics, Los Angeles, CA, USA, 2–4 June 2010.
7. Wu, S.; Xu, Y.; Wu, F.; Yuan, Z.; Huang, Y.; Li, X. Aspect-based sentiment analysis via fusing multiple sources of textual knowledge. *Knowl.-Based Syst.* **2019**, *183*, 104868. [CrossRef]
8. Wang, Q.; Mao, Z.; Wang, B.; Guo, L. Knowledge Graph Embedding: A Survey of Approaches and Applications. *IEEE Trans. Knowl. Data Eng.* **2017**, *29*, 2724–2743. [CrossRef]
9. Medhat, W.; Hassan, A.; Korashy, H. Sentiment analysis algorithms and applications: A survey. *Ain Shams Eng. J.* **2014**, *5*, 1093–1113. [CrossRef]
10. Wu, Z.; Pan, S.; Chen, F.; Long, G.; Zhang, C. A comprehensive survey on graph neural networks. *IEEE Trans. Neural Networks Learn. Syst.* **2020**, *32*, 4–24. [CrossRef] [PubMed]
11. Zhao, P.; Hou, L.; Wu, O. Modeling sentiment dependencies with graph convolutional networks for aspect-level sentiment classification. *Knowl.-Based Syst.* **2020**, *193*, 105443. [CrossRef]
12. Zhang, C.; Li, Q.; Song, D. Aspect-based Sentiment Classification with Aspect-specific Graph Convolutional Networks. In Proceedings of the 2019 Conference on Empirical Methods in Natural Language Processing and the 9th International Joint Conference on Natural Language Processing (EMNLP-IJCNLP), Hong Kong, China, 3–7 November 2019.
13. Tian, Y.; Chen, G.; Song, Y. Aspect-based sentiment analysis with type-aware graph convolutional networks and layer ensemble. In Proceedings of the 2021 Conference of the North American Chapter of the Association for Computational Linguistics: Human Language Technologies, Online, 6–11 June 2021.
14. Wang, K.; Shen, W.; Yang, Y.; Quan, X.; Wang, R. Relational Graph Attention Network for Aspect-based Sentiment Analysis. In Proceedings of the 58th Annual Meeting of the Association for Computational Linguistics, Online, 5–10 July 2020.
15. Zhang, Z.; Zhou, Z.; Wang, Y. SSEGCN: Syntactic and Semantic Enhanced Graph Convolutional Network for Aspect-based Sentiment Analysis. In Proceedings of the 2022 Conference of the North American Chapter of the Association for Computational Linguistics: Human Language Technologies, Seattle, WA, USA, 10–15 July 2022; pp. 4916–4925.
16. Bie, Y.; Yang, Y.; Zhang, Y. Fusing Syntactic Structure Information and Lexical Semantic Information for End-to-End Aspect-Based Sentiment Analysis. *Tsinghua Sci. Technol.* **2022**, *28*, 230–243. [CrossRef]
17. Zhang, D.; Zhu, Z.; Kang, S.; Zhang, G.; Liu, P. Syntactic and semantic analysis network for aspect-level sentiment classification. *Appl. Intell.* **2021**, *51*, 6136–6147. [CrossRef]
18. Wu, H.; Zhang, Z.; Shi, S.; Wu, Q.; Song, H. Phrase dependency relational graph attention network for Aspect-based Sentiment Analysis. *Knowl.-Based Syst.* **2022**, *236*, 107736. [CrossRef]
19. Phan, H.T.; Nguyen, N.T.; Hwang, D. Convolutional attention neural network over graph structures for improving the performance of aspect-level sentiment analysis. *Inf. Sci.* **2022**, *589*, 416–439. [CrossRef]
20. He, J.; Wumaier, A.; Kadeer, Z.; Sun, W.; Xin, X.; Zheng, L. A Local and Global Context Focus Multilingual Learning Model for Aspect-Based Sentiment Analysis. *IEEE Access* **2022**, *10*, 84135–84146. [CrossRef]

21. Chen, P.; Lu, Y.; Zheng, V.W.; Chen, X.; Yang, B. KnowEdu: A System to Construct Knowledge Graph for Education. *IEEE Access* **2018**, *6*, 31553–31563. [CrossRef]
22. Rotmensch, M.; Halpern, Y.; Tlimat, A.; Horng, S.; Sontag, D. Learning a Health Knowledge Graph from Electronic Medical Records. *Sci. Rep.* **2017**, *7*, 5994. [CrossRef] [PubMed]
23. Jia, Y.; Qi, Y.; Shang, H.; Jiang, R.; Li, A. A Practical Approach to Constructing a Knowledge Graph for Cybersecurity. *Engineering* **2018**, *4*, 53–60. [CrossRef]
24. Chen, X.; Jia, S.; Xiang, Y. A review: Knowledge reasoning over knowledge graph. *Expert Syst. Appl.* **2020**, *141*, 112948. [CrossRef]
25. Zhou, J.; Huang, J.X.; Hu, Q.V.; He, L. SK-GCN: Modeling Syntax and Knowledge via Graph Convolutional Network for aspect-level sentiment classification. *Knowl.-Based Syst.* **2020**, *205*, 106292. [CrossRef]
26. Liang, B.; Su, H.; Gui, L.; Cambria, E.; Xu, R. Aspect-based sentiment analysis via affective knowledge enhanced graph convolutional networks. *Knowl.-Based Syst.* **2022**, *235*, 107643. [CrossRef]
27. Huang, X.; Zhang, J.; Li, D.; Li, P. Knowledge graph embedding based question answering. In Proceedings of the Twelfth ACM International Conference on Web Search and Data Mining, Melbourne, VIC, Australia, 11–15 February 2019.
28. Gerritse, E.J.; Hasibi, F.; Vries, A.P. Graph-embedding empowered entity retrieval. In *European Conference on Information Retrieval*; Springer: Cham, Switzerland, 2020.
29. Sun, Z.; Yang, J.; Zhang, J.; Bozzon, A.; Huang, L.K. Recurrent knowledge graph embedding for effective recommendation. In Proceedings of the 12th ACM Conference on Recommender Systems, New York, NY, USA, 2 October 2018.
30. Bordes, A.; Weston, J.; Collobert, R.; Bengio, Y. Learning structured embeddings of knowledge bases. In Proceedings of the Twenty-Fifth AAAI Conference on Artificial Intelligence, San Francisco, CA, USA, 7–8 August 2011.
31. Wang, Z.; Zhang, J.; Feng, J.; Chen, Z. Knowledge graph embedding by translating on hyperplanes. In Proceedings of the AAAI Conference on Artificial Intelligence, Québec City, QC, Canada, 27–31 July 2014; Volume 28.
32. Dettmers, T.; Minervini, P.; Stenetorp, P. Convolutional 2d knowledge graph embeddings. In Proceedings of the AAAI Conference on Artificial Intelligence, New Orleans, LA, USA, 2–7 February 2018; Volume 32.
33. Vu, T.; Nguyen, T.D.; Nguyen, D.Q. A capsule network-based embedding model for knowledge graph completion and search personalization. In Proceedings of the 2019 Conference of the North American Chapter of the Association for Computational Linguistics: Human Language Technologies, Minneapolis, MN, USA, 2–7 June 2019; Volume 1.
34. Bollacker, K.; Evans, C.; Paritosh, P.; Sturge, T. Freebase: A collaboratively created graph database for structuring human knowledge. In Proceedings of the 2008 ACM SIGMOD International Conference on Management of Data, Vancouver, BC, Canada, 10–12 June 2008.
35. Yang, B.; Yih, W.; He, X.; Gao, J.; Deng, L. Embedding Entities and Relations for Learning and Inference in Knowledge Bases. In Proceedings of the International Conference on Learning Representations (ICLR) 2015, San Diego, CA, USA, 7–9 May 2015.
36. Pontiki, M.; Galanis, D.; Papageorgiou, H. SemEval-2014 Task 4: Aspect Based Sentiment Analysis. *SemEval* **2014**, *2014*, 27.
37. Dong, L.; Wei, F.; Tan, C.; Tang, D.; Zhou, M. Adaptive recursive neural network for target-dependent twitter sentiment classification. In Proceedings of the 52nd Annual Meeting of the Association for Computational Linguistics (Volume 2: Short Papers), Baltimore, MD, USA, 22–27 June 2014.
38. Pennington, J.; Socher, R.; Manning, C.D. Glove: Global vectors for word representation. In Proceedings of the 2014 Conference on Empirical Methods in Natural Language Processing (EMNLP), Doha, Qatar, 25–29 October 2014.
39. Kenton, J.; Chang, D.M.-W.; Toutanova, L.K. BERT: Pre-training of Deep Bidirectional Transformers for Language Understanding. In Proceedings of the NAACL-HLT, Minneapolis, MN, USA, 2–7 June 2019.
40. Chen, Z.; Ma, T.; Jin, Z.; Song, Y.; Wang, Y. BiGCN: A bi-directional low-pass filtering graph neural network. *arXiv* **2021**, arXiv:2101.05519.
41. Zhang, F.; Zhang, Y.; Hou, S.; Chen, F.; Lu, M. Aspect Fusion Graph Convolutional Networks for Aspect-Based Sentiment Analysis. In *China Conference on Information Retrieval*; Springer: Cham, Switzerland, 2021.
42. Liang, B.; Yin, R.; Gui, L.; Du, J.; Xu, R. Jointly learning aspect-focused and inter-aspect relations with graph convolutional networks for aspect sentiment analysis. In Proceedings of the 28th International Conference on Computational Linguistics, Barcelona, Spain, 8–13 December 2020.
43. Cambria, E.; Speer, R.; Havasi, C.; Hussain, A. Senticnet: A publicly available semantic resource for opinion mining. In Proceedings of the 2010 AAAI Fall Symposium Series, Arlington, VA, USA, 11–13 November 2010.

mathematics

MDPI

Article

Pairwise Constraints Multidimensional Scaling for Discriminative Feature Learning

Linghao Zhang [1], Bo Pang [1], Haitao Tang [2,3], Hongjun Wang [2,3,*], Chongshou Li [2,3] and Zhipeng Luo [2,3]

1 State Gid Sichuan Electric Power Research Institute, Power Internet of Things Key Laboratory of Sichuan Province, Chengdu 610094, China
2 School of Computing and Artificial Intelligence, Southwest Jiaotong University, Chengdu 611731, China
3 Manufacturing Industry Chains Collaboration and Information Support Technology Key Laboratory of Sichuan Province, Chengdu 611731, China
* Correspondence: wanghongjun@swjtu.edu.cn

Abstract: As an important data analysis method in the field of machine learning and data mining, feature learning has a wide range of applications in various industries. The traditional multidimensional scaling (MDS) maintains the topology of data points in the low-dimensional embeddings obtained during feature learning, but ignores the discriminative nature between classes of low-dimensional embedded data. Thus, the discriminative multidimensional scaling based on pairwise constraints for feature learning (pcDMDS) model is proposed in this paper. The model enhances the discriminativeness from two aspects. The first aspect is to increase the compactness of the new data representation in the same cluster through fuzzy *k*-means. The second aspect is to obtain more extended pairwise constraint information between samples. In the whole feature learning process, the model considers both the topology of samples in the original space and the cluster structure in the new space. It also incorporates the extended pairwise constraint information in the samples, which further improves the model's ability to obtain discriminative features. Finally, the experimental results on twelve datasets show that pcDMDS performs 10.31% and 8.31% higher than PMDS model in terms of accuracy and purity.

Keywords: discriminative feature learning; multidimensional scaling; fuzzy *k*-means; pairwise constraint propagation; iterative majorization algorithm

MSC: 62P25

Citation: Zhang, L.; Pang, B.; Tang, H.; Wang, H.; Li, C.; Luo, Z. Pairwise Constraints Multidimensional Scaling for Discriminative Feature Learning. *Mathematics* **2022**, *10*, 4059. https://doi.org/10.3390/math10214059

Academic Editor: Jianping Gou

Received: 17 September 2022
Accepted: 24 October 2022
Published: 1 November 2022

1. Introduction

The high-dimensional nature of large amounts of image data, text data, and video data is inevitable in today's big data era. Although image data and text data are simple and intuitive for humans, for machine learning models, there is a dimensional disaster. Because the direct use of raw data will not only increase the processing time of subsequent machine learning models, but may also reduce the performance of classification models and clustering models due to the influence of information such as redundancy and noise in the data. Based on this, how to obtain a more discriminative feature from the raw data has also become a research objective for many scholars.

In feature learning, supervised, semi-supervised and unsupervised feature learning methods are classified by whether or not the annotation information of the data is used in the learning process. The classical methods for unsupervised feature learning, semi-supervised feature learning and unsupervised feature learning are principal component analysis (PCA) [1], semi-supervised dimensionality deduction (SSDR) [2] and linear discriminant analysis (LDA) [3], respectively. PCA, SSDR and LDA are all linear feature learning methods, which have the advantage of fast computation and the ability to quickly compute the data representation of a new sample through the projection matrix when a new sample arrives. In contrast, nonlinear feature learning based on stream learning allows the low-dimensional data representation to preserve the local topology of the original data as much as possible, such as locally linear embedding (LLE) [4], multidimensional scaling (MDS) [5] and laplacian eigenmaps (LE) [6], etc. Nonlinear feature learning can discover the potential flow structure inside the data well, but face the problem of new samples [7], so there are also a number of algorithms that maintain the local topology as much as possible in the projection process. For example, locality preserving projection (LPP) [8] and neighborhood preserving embedding [9] are projection matrices added to LE and LLE, respectively.

Feature learning has important research significance because of its many applications, such as data visualization [10], information retrieval [11], and clustering [12]. The MDS, as a commonly used streaming learning method, considers the distance information between samples in the feature learning process, but ignores the discriminative nature between data categories. Based on this, a discriminative multidimensional scaling based on pairwise constraints for feature learning (pcDMDS) is proposed in this paper in order to obtain more discriminative features.

The main contributions of this paper are shown below.

- A feature learning algorithm named pcDMDS is proposed, and its corresponding target formula is designed. The target formula reflects the topological and discriminative nature of learning, and the cluster structure is discovered while learning the low-dimensional data representation. It makes the low-dimensional data representation of the same cluster closer.
- The objective function is approximated using an iterative optimization method, and the corresponding algorithm is designed according to the inference process.
- Comparative experiments are conducted using public datasets and evaluation criteria, and the results show that the low-dimensional embeddings obtained by the algorithm are more discriminative.

The remainder of this paper is organized as follows. In Section 2, existing works that related to this paper is reviewed. In Section 3, some preliminaries about our work are introduced. In Section 4, the details of the proposed model, including objective function and inference are illustrated. Experiments and results are described in Section 5. Finally, conclusions are drawn in Section 6.

2. Related Work

As a feature learning method that maintains the non-similarity of samples (generally distance), the MDS is widely used because of its simplicity and efficiency. Feature learning based on MDS can be divided into two categories [13], one is metric multidimensional scaling (MMDS) and the other one is non-metric multidimensional scaling (NMDS). In MMDS, the learned low-dimensional data representation is to preserve the distance of the original data as much as possible. But in NMDS, the low-dimensional data representation is to maintain the relationship of distance of the original data. Since the model proposed in this paper is a MDS of metrics, the MDS of metrics is described in detail below, and MDS generally refers to MMDS.

Different MDS methods have been proposed successively. The most classical MDS is to give the distance between samples and then find a suitable low-dimensional embedding. This method belongs to a nonlinear feature learning method, so that the sample distance between the low-dimensional embedding points keeps the distance corresponding to the original sample as much as possible, and its disadvantage is that it faces the problem of new samples. Webb [14] introduced a set of basis functions for feature mapping, and then achieved dimensionality reduction through a projection matrix. At the same time, the new data representation keeps the Euclidean distance of the original samples as much as possible, and an iterative update method was proposed to optimize the projection matrix. As an important manifold learning method, isometric feature mapping [15] uses the geodesic distance between samples to represent the dissimilarity between samples, and finally uses classical MDS to get low-dimensional embedding of data. Bronstein et al. [16] proposed a generalized multidimensional scaling (GMDS), which uses a non-euclidean distance to represent the non-similarity of samples, and applied GMDS to 3D face matching. In order to enhance the discriminativeness of the features learned by MDS, Biswas [17] not only considered that the low-dimensional embedding points should keep the distance between the original images, but also considered that the distance between the low-dimensional embedding points corresponding to the same face should be as small as possible.

Clustering, as an unsupervised machine learning method, is widely used in many fields [18–20], and its purpose is to divide data into different clusters or subsets by some criteria. In order to efficiently discover potential cluster structures in data, different scholars have proposed different clustering algorithms, such as k-means (KM) algorithm [21], affinity propagation (AP) algorithm [22], and density peak (DP) algorithm [23]. With the proposal and refinement of fuzzy set theory, fuzzy clustering was proposed [24]. Unlike hard clustering such as k-means, soft clustering algorithms such as fuzzy clustering can not only discover the cluster structure among data efficiently, but also give the degree of affiliation between samples and class clusters, which can discover the overlapping class cluster structure well.

Fuzzy k-means was proposed by Bezdek et al. [24], which adopted the idea of fuzzy sets. They believe that there is a degree of attribution between a sample and a cluster ranging from 0 to 1. To improve the clustering performance of fuzzy k-means, Wang et al. [25] proposed a fuzzy k-means model based on the Euclidean distance with weights by considering the feature weights while calculating the distance. The traditional FKM fails when the input sample point information is not known and only the non-similarity information of sample points is available. Therefore, Hathaway et al. [26] proposed a non-euclidean relational fuzzy clustering, which can complete the fuzzy clustering under the condition of only given the dissimilarity between sample points. In order to adopt the clustering algorithm to noisy data, Nie et al. [27] combined fuzzy k-means with principal component analysis so that fuzzy k-means can be performed in the low-dimensional subspace obtained by principal component analysis. To obtain the potential cluster structure of the data on multi-view data, Zhu et al. [28] proposed an adaptive weighted multi-view clustering method. This method can not only automatically discover the importance, dispersion and other information of each view from multi-view data, but also synthesize the common information of each view to accomplish the clustering task.

Paired constraint information is widely used in feature learning to enhance the discriminant of the learned features because of its ability to provide similar relationships between samples. Zhang et al. [2] proposed a semi-supervised dimensionality reduction method based on paired constraint information, whose idea is to obtain new sample points by transforming the matrix so that the points with must-connect constraints are close together after the transformation, while the points with do-not-connect constraints are far away after the transformation. Du et al. [29] applied constraint transferring to dimensionality reduction and proposed a new semi supervised feature learning method. The method first requires a pairwise constraint matrix with only 1, 0 and -1 values initially, where 1 means constraints must be connected, -1 means constraints do not connected and 0 means the constraint information is unknown. Then the constraint transferring algorithm is used to extend the constraint information to other samples. Then it constructs a new weight matrix using the extended constraint matrix, and finally uses the LPP algorithm for the new data representation.

3. Preliminaries

3.1. Multidimensional Scaling

The classical MDS is a nonlinear feature learning method. Its characteristic is that when only the dissimilarity between any two points is given, the corresponding new data representation can be directly obtained so that the Euclidean distance between samples is as equal to the given dissimilarity as possible, but it faces the problem of new samples.

Webb [14] proposed the projective MDS (PMDS), so that the new data representation can be obtained from the original data representation by projection transformation. In this paper, a PMDS-based feature learning method is proposed and its principles are described in detail below.

Given the original data matrix $X = [x_1, \ldots, x_N] \in \mathbb{R}^{n \times N}$, where n and N denote the dimensionality and the number of the original samples, respectively. The learned low-dimensional data representation $Y = [y_1, \ldots, y_N] \in \mathbb{R}^{l \times N}$, where l denotes the dimensionality of the low-dimensional data representation. The loss function of MDS, a feature learning method that maintains the sample distance, is [30]:

$$O_{mds}(Y) = 1/2 \sum_{i=1}^{N} \sum_{j=1}^{N} s_{ij} \left(d_{ij} - \hat{d}_{ij} \right)^2. \tag{1}$$

d_{ij} denotes the distance between the original data points x_i and x_j, and $\hat{d}_{ij}$ denotes the distance between the corresponding low-dimensional data representation y_i and y_j. And $S = [s_{ij}] \in \mathbb{R}^{N \times N}$ is a non-negative symmetric weight matrix, with larger s_{ij} indicating a greater desire for $\hat{d}_{ij}$ to be close to d_{ij}, and the literature [6] gives two ways of constructing the weights.

- Heat kernel weighting: $s_{ij} = \exp\left(-\|x_i - x_j\|_2^2 / t\right)$ if x_i is a near neighbor to x_j or x_j is a near neighbor to x_i, otherwise $s_j = 0$, where t is a real number.
- 0–1 weights: $s_{ij} = 1$ if x_i is a near neighbor to x_j or x_j is a near neighbor to x_i, otherwise $s_{ij} = 0$.

The MDS in Equation (1) is a nonlinear feature learning method that obtains a direct low-dimensional data representation Y. If new data arrives, its corresponding low-dimensional data representation cannot be obtained directly, that is, the so-called new sample problem. Webb incorporated the projection matrix into the MDS by means of pre-given radial basis functions to achieve nonlinear transformations, and proposed the PMDS, whose objective formulation is [14]:

$$\begin{aligned} O_{pmds}(W) &= \sum_{i=1}^{N} \sum_{j=1}^{N} s_{ij} \left(d_{ij} - \hat{d}_{ij} \right)^2 \\ &= \sum_{i=1}^{N} \sum_{j=1}^{N} s_{ij} \left(d_{ij} - \left\| W^{\mathrm{T}} (x_i - x_j) \right\|_2 \right)^2. \end{aligned} \tag{2}$$

$\| \cdot \|_2$ denotes the two-parametric number of vectors and $W \in \mathbb{R}^{n \times d}$ denotes the projection matrix, and it can be seen that Y is directly projected from X.

3.2. Fuzzy k-Means Clustering

Fuzzy clustering can give the degree of affiliation of samples with clusters, and the objective formula for fuzzy k-means is:

$$\begin{aligned} O_{fkm}(U, V) &= \sum_{k=1}^{C} \sum_{i=1}^{N} u_{ik}^m \|x_i - v_k\|_2^2, \\ \text{s.t.} &\sum_{k=1}^{C} u_{ik} = 1, \forall i = 1, 2, \ldots, N, u_{ik} \geq 0, \forall i = 1, \ldots, N, \forall k = 1, \ldots, C. \end{aligned} \tag{3}$$

$U = [u_{ik}] \in \mathbb{R}^{N \times C}$ is the affiliation matrix, u_{ik} denotes the affiliation of x_i with cluster C_k, and $m \geqslant 1$ denotes the fuzzy index weights.

3.3. Pairwise Constraint Transmission

Given a sample $X = [x_1, \ldots, x_N] \in \mathbb{R}^{n \times N}$, and the pairwise constraint matrix $P = [p_{ij}] \in \mathbb{R}^{N \times N}$. $p_{ij} = 1$ if there is a must-connect constraint between samples x_i and x_j, $p_{ij} = -1$ if there is a do-not-connect constraint between samples x_i and x_j, and $p_{ij} = 0$, if the constraint between x_i and x_j is unknown.

The constraint-passing algorithm is to extend the constraint matrix P to obtain more pairwise constraint information. The result matrix is $F = [f_{ij}] \in \mathbb{R}^{N \times N}$, and F has the following properties:

- f_{ij} takes the value in the range of $[-1, 1]$, and the larger the absolute value, the higher the confidence of the constraint information.
- $f_{ij} > 0$ means that the constraint between x_i and x_j is must-connect.
- $f_{ij} < 0$ means that the constraint between x_i and x_j is do-not-connect.
- $f_{ij} = 0$ means that the constraint information is unknown.

4. Proposed Method

4.1. Discriminative Multidimensional Scaling Based on Pairwise Constraints for Feature Learning

The overall process of model pcDMDS is shown in Figure 1, which shows that after obtaining some of the pairwise constraint information through data X, more constraint information is first extended by the constraint transferring algorithm. For the extended constraint information, its value is $[-1, 1]$. If the value is greater than 0, it indicates a must-connect constraint, while if it is less than 0, it indicates a do-not-connect constraint. And the larger the absolute value, the higher the confidence level of the constraint. After obtaining the extended pairwise constraint information, for each iteration of the model, we hope to maintain the topology of the samples on the one hand. On the other hand, we hope to find the cluster structure within the samples and make the data representations of the samples in the same cluster close to their cluster centers. Furthermore, we hope to make the data representations of the samples with the must-connect constraints close to each other and the data representations of the samples with the do-not-connect constraints far from each other through pairwise constraints. After several iterations, the model can reach a balance between these three aspects. Thus, it further improves the discriminative properties of the learned features. After the model converges or reaches the maximum number of iterations, the new data representation is obtained by transforming the matrix.

Following this idea, the loss function can be described as the minimum of $\mathcal{O}_{pcdmds}(W, U, V)$. Moreover,

$$
\begin{aligned}
\mathcal{O}_{pcdmds}(W,U,V) = & \sum_{i=1}^{N}\sum_{j=1}^{N} s_{ij}\left(d_{ij} - \left\|W^T(x_i - x_j)\right\|_2\right)^2 \\
& + \beta \sum_{i=1}^{N}\sum_{k=1}^{c} u_{ik}{}^{m}\left\|W^T x_i - v_k\right\|_2^2 \\
& + \lambda\left(\frac{1}{2N_{ML}}\sum_{(i,j)\in ML}\phi_{ij}\left\|W^T(x_i - x_j)\right\|_2^2 \right. \\
& \left. - \frac{1}{2N_{CL}}\sum_{(i,j)\in CL}\phi_{ij}\left\|W^T(x_i - x_j)\right\|_2^2\right) \\
= & \mathcal{O}_1(W) + \beta\mathcal{O}_2(W,U,V) + \lambda O_{pcloss}(W), \\
& \text{s. } t. \sum_{k=1}^{c} u_{ik} = 1, \quad i = 1,2,\ldots,N, \\
& u_{ik} \geq 0, \quad i = 1,\ldots,N, \quad k = 1,\ldots,C.
\end{aligned}
\tag{4}
$$

In Equation (4), ML denotes the set of the indexes of the sample pairs with must-connect constraints and CL denotes the set of the indexes of the sample pairs with do-not-connect constraints. N_{ML} denotes the number of sample pairs with must-connect constraints, and ML is the size of the set. Similarly, N_{CL} denotes the number of sample pairs with do-not-connect constraints, and CL is the size of the set. $\Phi = [\phi_{ij}]$ denotes the confidence of the pairwise constraint between samples x_i and x_j, which takes the values [0, 1], and a larger value indicates a higher confidence of the pairwise constraint and a symmetric matrix.

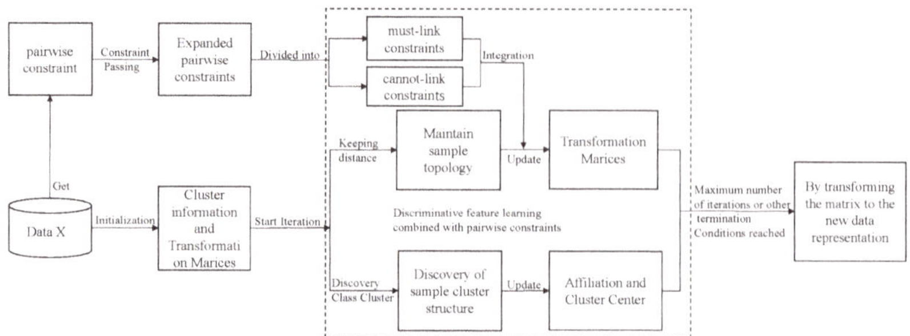

Figure 1. The overall process of discriminative multidimensional scalar learning based on pairwise constraints.

From Equation (4), it can be seen that the objective formulation of the pcDMDS model can be divided into three parts. It can be seen that the pcDMDS model is a balance among these three terms.

i. The first part is used to make the Euclidean distance $\hat{d}_{ij}$ between any samples x_i and the new data representation corresponding to x_j keeps the Euclidean distance d_{ij}in the original space as much as possible, which reflects the feature learning process in which the new data representation keeps the topology in the original data representation.
ii. The second part is used to automatically discover the cluster structure in the samples and make the data representation in the same cluster close to its cluster center in the new data representation, increasing the compactness of the new data representation in the same cluster, and reflecting the unsupervised way to enhance the discriminative nature of the learned data representation and adjust its weight by the parameter β.
iii. The third term is the loss term of the pairwise constraint, which aims to make the data representation of sample points with the must-connect constraint close and the data representation of sample points with the do-not-connect constraint. The third term is the pairwise constraint loss term, which aims to make the data representations of sample points with the must-connect constraint close and those of sample points with the do-not-connect constraint far away, thus further enhancing the model's ability to learn discriminative features and controlling its weights by the parameter λ.

To simplify Equation (4) for subsequent optimization, note the matrix $\Psi = [\psi_{ij}] \in \mathbb{R}^{N \times N}$, whose elements are defined as:

$$\psi_{ij} = \begin{cases} \frac{1}{N_{\mathrm{ML}}}\phi_{ij} & (i,j) \in \mathrm{ML}, \\ -\frac{1}{N_{\mathrm{CL}}}\phi_{ij} & (i,j) \in \mathrm{CL}, \\ 0 & \text{otherwise}. \end{cases} \quad (5)$$

Since $\Phi = \Phi^{\top}$, it follows that $\Psi = \Psi^T$. Then Equation (4) can be rewritten as:

$$\begin{aligned} O_{pcdmds}(W, U, V) = & \sum_{i=1}^{N}\sum_{j=1}^{N} s_{ij}\left(d_{ij} - \left\|W^{\mathrm{T}}(x_i - x_j)\right\|_2\right)^2 \\ & + \beta \sum_{i=1}^{N}\sum_{k=1}^{C} u_{ik}{}^{m}\left\|W^{\mathrm{T}}x_i - v_k\right\|_2^2 \\ & + \frac{\lambda}{2}\sum_{i=1}^{N}\sum_{j=1}^{N} \psi_{ij}\left\|W^{\mathrm{T}}(x_i - x_j)\right\|_2^2, \\ & \text{s.t.} \sum_{k=1}^{C} u_{ik} = 1, i = 1, 2, \ldots, N, \\ & u_{ik} \geq 0, i = 1, \ldots, N, k = 1, \ldots, C. \end{aligned} \tag{6}$$

4.2. The Inference of Discriminative Multidimensional Scaling Based on Pairwise Constraints for Feature Learning

For the objective Equation (6), the parameters to be solved are the transformation matrix W, the samples and cluster affiliation matrix U, and the cluster center matrix V. Since the closed-form solutions of Equation (6) with respect to W, U, and V cannot be obtained directly, an iterative optimization approach is used for solving the problem.

(1) Fix U and V, and update W. At this point the target equation in Equation (6) is a function of W only and can be expressed as:

$$L_1(W) = \mathcal{O}_1(W) + \beta\mathcal{O}_2(W) + \lambda\mathcal{O}_{\text{pcloss}}(W), \tag{7}$$

to facilitate the solution, first rewrite $O_{pcloss}(W)$:

$$\begin{aligned} O_{\text{pcloss}}(W) &= \frac{1}{2}\operatorname{Tr}\left(YD_{\Psi}Y^{\mathrm{T}}\right) - \operatorname{Tr}\left(Y\Psi Y^{\mathrm{T}}\right) + \frac{1}{2}\operatorname{Tr}\left(YD_{\Psi^{\mathrm{T}}}Y^{\mathrm{T}}\right) \\ &= \operatorname{Tr}\left(Y(D_{\Psi} - \Psi)Y^{\mathrm{T}}\right) \\ &= \operatorname{Tr}\left(YL_{\Psi}Y^{\mathrm{T}}\right) \\ &= \operatorname{Tr}\left(W^{\mathrm{T}}XL_{\Psi}X^{\mathrm{T}}W\right). \end{aligned} \tag{8}$$

Since $\|A\|_2^2 = \operatorname{Tr}(AA^{\mathrm{T}}) = \operatorname{Tr}(A^{\mathrm{T}}A)$, $\operatorname{Tr}(\cdot)$ denotes the trace of the matrix, a simplification of the second term $O_2(W)$ in Equation (7) gives:

$$\mathcal{O}_2(W) = \operatorname{Tr}(W^TXD_{\tilde{U}}X^TW) - 2\operatorname{Tr}\left(W^TX\tilde{U}V^T\right) + \operatorname{Tr}(VD_{\tilde{U}^T}V^T). \tag{9}$$

$\tilde{U} = \left[u_{ik}^{m}\right] \in \mathbb{R}^{N\times C}$, $D_{\tilde{U}}$ and $D_{\tilde{U}^{\mathrm{T}}}$ are all diagonal arrays,

$$D_{\tilde{v}} = \begin{bmatrix} (D_{\tilde{v}})_{11} & & \\ & \ddots & \\ & & (D_{\tilde{U}})_{NN} \end{bmatrix}, \quad D_{\tilde{U}^{\mathrm{T}}} = \begin{bmatrix} (D_{\tilde{U}^{\mathrm{T}}})_{11} & & \\ & \ddots & \\ & & (D_{\tilde{U}^{\mathrm{T}}})_{CC} \end{bmatrix}. \tag{10}$$

The objective function in Equation (8) can be optimized using the IMA [5,14,17] algorithm, the constructed auxiliary function is $\sigma_{pcdnds}(W, Z)$, which is defined as:

$$\begin{aligned}\sigma_{pcdmds}(W, Z) = &\operatorname{Tr}\left(W^{\mathrm{T}} A W\right) + \sum_{i=1}^{N} \sum_{j=1}^{N} s_{ij} d_{ij}^2 - 2 \operatorname{Tr}\left(Z^{\mathrm{T}} \mathrm{D}(Z) W\right) \\ &+ \beta\left(\operatorname{Tr}\left(W^{\mathrm{T}} X D_{\tilde{U}} X^{\mathrm{T}} W\right) - 2 \operatorname{Tr}\left(W^{\mathrm{T}} X \tilde{U} V^{\mathrm{T}}\right) + \operatorname{Tr}\left(V D_{\tilde{U}^{\mathrm{T}}} V^{\mathrm{T}}\right)\right) \\ &+ \lambda \operatorname{Tr}\left(W^{\mathrm{T}} X L_{\Psi} X^{\mathrm{T}} W\right).\end{aligned} \tag{11}$$

A in Equation (11) is defined as:

$$A = \sum_{i=1}^{N} \sum_{j=1}^{N} s_{ij} (x_i - x_j) (x_i - x_j)^{\mathrm{T}}. \tag{12}$$

The definition of $D(Z)$ in Equation (11) is:

$$\begin{aligned}&\mathrm{D}(Z) = \textstyle\sum_{i=1}^{N} \sum_{j=1}^{N} c_{ij}(Z) (x_i - x_j) (x_i - x_j)^{\mathrm{T}}, \\ &c_{ij}(Z) = \begin{cases} s_{ij} d_{ij} / \hat{d}_{ij}(Z) & \hat{d}_{ij}(Z) > 0, \\ 0 & \hat{d}_{ij}(Z) = 0. \end{cases}\end{aligned} \tag{13}$$

In Equation (13), $\hat{d}_{ij}(Z) = \left\|Z^{\mathrm{T}}(x_i - x_j)\right\|_2$.

Calculate the gradient of W with respect to Equation (11) and set the gradient to be 0, then we have the update equation of W:

$$W = \left(A + \beta X D_{\tilde{U}} X^{\mathrm{T}} + \lambda X L_{\Psi} X^{\mathrm{T}}\right)^{-1} \left(\mathrm{D}(Z) Z + \beta X \tilde{U} V^{\mathrm{T}}\right). \tag{14}$$

(2) Fix the matrices W and V, and solve for U. At this point, the first and third terms in Equation (6) are constant terms, and the optimization of Equation (6) is equivalent to the optimization of:

$$\begin{aligned}\mathrm{L}_2(\mathbf{U}) &= \sum_{i=1}^{N} \sum_{k=1}^{C} u_{ik}^m \|y_i - v_k\|_2^2 \\ &= \sum_{i=1}^{N} \sum_{k=1}^{C} u_{ik'}^m d^2(y_i, v_k), \\ &\text{s.t.} \sum_{k=1}^{C} u_{ik} = 1, i = 1, 2, \ldots, N, \\ &u_{ik} \geq 0, i = 1, \ldots, N, k = 1, \ldots, C.\end{aligned} \tag{15}$$

Using the Lagrangian multiplier method [31]:

$$\mathrm{L}_\lambda(U) = \sum_{i=1}^{N} \sum_{k=1}^{C} u_{ik}^m d^2(y_i, v_k) + \lambda\left(\sum_{k=1}^{C} u_{ik} - 1\right). \tag{16}$$

By:

$$\begin{aligned}&\frac{\partial \mathrm{L}_\lambda(U)}{\partial u_{ik}} = m(u_{ik})^{m-1} d^2(y_i, v_k) - \lambda = 0, \\ &\frac{\partial \mathrm{L}_\lambda(U)}{\partial \lambda} = \textstyle\sum_{k=1}^{C} u_{ik} - 1 = 0,\end{aligned} \tag{17}$$

solve the update equation for u_{ik} as:

$$u_{i\hbar} = \frac{1}{\sum_{j=1}^{c}\left(\frac{1}{d(y_i,v_j)}\right)^{\frac{2}{m-1}}}\left(\frac{1}{d(y_i,v_k)}\right)^{\frac{2}{m-1}} = \frac{1}{\sum_{j=1}^{c}\left(\frac{d(y_i,v_k)}{d(y_i,v_j)}\right)^{\frac{2}{m-1}}}. \tag{18}$$

The iterative update of the U matrix is given by:

$$u_{ik} = \begin{cases} 1/\sum_{j=1}^{c}\left(\frac{d(y_i,v_k)}{d(y_i,v_j)}\right)^{\frac{2}{m-1}} & \mathrm{I}_i = \varnothing, \\ \frac{1}{|\mathrm{I}_i|} & \mathrm{I}_i \neq \varnothing, k \in \mathrm{I}_i, \\ 0 & \mathrm{I}_i \neq \varnothing, k \notin \mathrm{I}_i. \end{cases} \tag{19}$$

$\mathrm{I}_i = \{r \in \mathbb{N}_{\leq C} \mid y_i = v_r\}$, $\mathbb{N}_{\leq C}$ denotes the set of positive integers less than or equal to C, and $|\mathrm{I}_i|$ denotes the number of elements in the set I_i. It means that when there exists a sample point y_i that happens to be the cluster center of multiple clusters, y_i has equal affiliation with these clusters, both being $1/|I_i|$.

(3) Fix W and U, and update V. Similar to step (2):

$$\begin{aligned} \mathrm{L}_3(V) &= \sum_{i=1}^{N}\sum_{k=1}^{C} u_{ik}^{m}\left\|W^{\mathrm{T}}x_i - v_k\right\|_2^2 \\ &= \sum_{i=1}^{N}\sum_{k=1}^{C} u_{ik}^{m}\,\mathrm{Tr}\left(y_i y_i^{\mathrm{T}} - y_i v_k^{\mathrm{T}} - v_k y_i^{\mathrm{T}} + v_k v_k^{\mathrm{T}}\right). \end{aligned} \tag{20}$$

Calculate the partial derivative with respect to vk for Equation (20):

$$\frac{\partial \mathrm{L}_3(V)}{\partial v_k} = \sum_{i=1}^{N} u_{ik}^{m}(-y_i - y_i + 2v_k) = \sum_{i=1}^{N} u_{ik}^{m}(2v_k - 2y_i). \tag{21}$$

According to Equations (20) and (21), the iterative update of V can be derived as:

$$v_k = \sum_{i=1}^{N} u_{ik}^{m} y_i / \sum_{i=1}^{N} u_{ik}^{m}. \tag{22}$$

4.3. *Algorithm*

4.3.1. Algorithm Description

It can be seen from Algorithm 1 that the algorithm flow of pcDMDS is mainly divided into two processes. The first process is mainly to expand pairwise constraint information through constraint transferring. The second process is to update it iteratively according to the update formulas of W, U and V, and output the transformation matrix after the iteration is completed. Specifically, for the first process, the pairwise constraint matrix P is first constructed according to the set of sample pairwise constraints. Then the extended pairwise constraint information F is obtained through the constraint transfer algorithm, and F is post-processed and assigned to Ψ. Then the distance matrices D, S and A are calculated respectively, and then the W, V and U matrices are initialized. The second process starts the iteration process, updating W, U and V in turn, and stops iteration when W and U are stable or reach the maximum number of iterations. Finally, the transformation matrix W is returned.

Algorithm 1: pcDMDS feature learning algorithm

Input: X: data matrix; C: number of clusters; l: dimensionality of the low-dimensional data representation; m: fuzzy index weight; β: discriminative weight; λ: pairwise constraint loss weight; ML: set of must-connect constraints; CL: set of do-not-connect constraints; α: constraint transferring parameter; $\eth$: stopping condition; T: maximum number of iterations

Output: W: Projection matrix;

```
Construct the pairwise constraint matrix P from ML and CL;
Call the E^2CP constraint transferring algorithm to obtain the constraint
  transferring result F;
The maximum value of the absolute value of each element of the F matrix divided
  by the absolute value in the F matrix;
Assignment Ψ = F ;
Constructing the distance matrix D from the data matrix X;
Construct the distance weight matrix S;
Calculate A = 2X(D_S − S)X^T ;
Initialize the matrices W and V as random numbers obeying a uniform
  distribution of [−1,1];
Initialize the elements of the matrix [−1,1]U to 1/C;
for 1: T do
    W' ← W, U' ← U, Z ← W;
    Calculate Ũ = [u_ik^m] , and use Equation (10) to calculate D_ũ ;
    Use Equation (13) to calculate D(Z);
    Update W using Equation (14);
    Computation of the low-dimensional data representation Y = W^T X ;
    Update the matrix U using Equation (19);
    Update the matrix V using Equation (22);
    if |W' − W| ≤ o and |U' − U| ≤ o then
        return W
    end
end
return W
```

4.3.2. Study on Computational Complexity

The time complexity of the model is discussed. According to the algorithm flow in Algorithm 1, pcDMDS needs to call the constraint passing algorithm of the E^2CP with a time complexity of $O(N^3)$. The time complexity of the matrix $D(Z)$ is $O(n^2N + nN^2)$. The symmetric matrix of size $D(Z)$ and its Moore-Penrose inverse can be obtained by singular value decomposition, and since the time complexity of singular value decomposition is $O(n^3)$ [32], the time complexity of updating W once is $O(n^2N + nN^2 + n^3)$ according to Equation (14). According to Equation (19), the time complexity of updating the matrix U once is $O(NC^2l)$. From Equation (22), it is known that the time complexity of updating the cluster center matrix V once is $O(NCl)$. Considering that the updates of matrices W, U and V are performed sequentially, and the time complexity of the three updates and the time complexity of constraint passing are combined, it is known that the time complexity of the pcDMDS algorithm is $O(N^3 = T(nN^2 + nn^2N + n^3 + NC^2l))$, where T is the maximum number of iterations.

Then, the space complexity of the model is discussed. The input data matrix X has size of Nn. The space complexity of P, F, D and S are $O(N^2)$. The space complexity of A is $O(Nn + N^2 + n^2)$. W, V and U has the size of nl, lC and NC, respectively. During the iteration, the space complexity of $\tilde{U}$ and $D_{\tilde{U}}$ are $O(NC)$ and $O(N)$. The space complexity of $D(Z)$ is $O(Nl)$. The space complexity of W is $O(n^2 + nN + N^2 + nl + NC + Cl)$. The space complexity of Y is $O(lN + ln + nN)$. Therefore, the total space complexity is $O(Nn + N^2 + n^2 + nl + lC + NC + Nl)$.

4.3.3. Visualization

Figure 2 shows the visualization results of the wine dataset with 178 samples, 3 categories, and the number of attributes of each sample is 13. It can be seen from the visualization results in Figure 2a that the boundaries of different categories in the 2D data representation are fuzzy and unclear, that is, the discriminability between different categories has not been improved, and since the MDS method maintains the distance between samples, the samples in the same category are not more compact. In order to more intuitively show that pcDMDS can learn more discriminative features, the visualization result graph of pcDMDS is shown in Figure 2b. By comparing Figure 2a,b, it can be found that compared with MDS, pcDMDS has a more compact sample distribution in the same category in the new data representation, and the boundaries between different categories are clearer, which makes the learning features more discriminative.

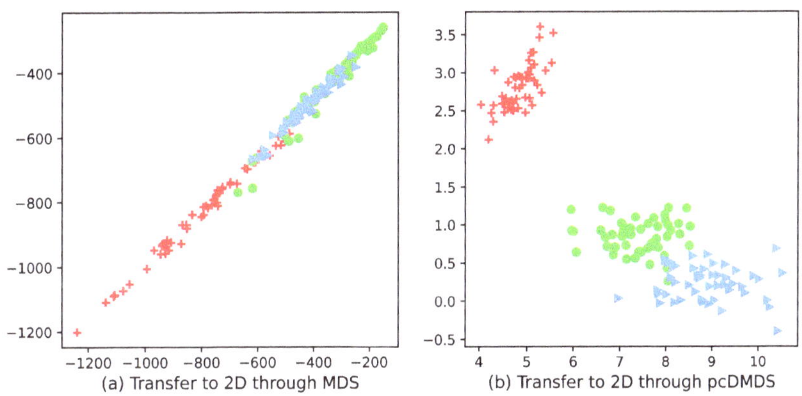

Figure 2. Visualization of wine dataset after dimensionality reduction using MDS and pcDMDS.

5. Experiments

5.1. Datasets

The datasets used for the experiments on the discriminative multidimensional scalar feature learning algorithm based on pairwise constraints are from 12 publicly available datasets in the MSRA- MM [33] database. Table 1 describes the details of the 12 datasets used.

Table 1. Datasets.

No.	Dataset	Samples	Features	Categories
D1	amber	880	892	3
D2	arrow	834	892	3
D3	balloon	830	892	3
D4	bicycle	844	892	3
D5	birthdaycake	932	892	3
D6	boomerang	910	892	3
D7	border	840	892	3

Table 1. *Cont.*

No.	Dataset	Samples	Features	Categories
D8	bow	834	892	3
D9	brain	891	892	3
D10	cactus	919	892	3
D11	vistawallpaper	799	899	3
D12	weapon	858	899	3

5.2. Experimental Setting

The pairwise constraint loss terms in pcDMDS are controlled by the parameter λ to control their weights. The pairwise constraint information in the experiment is obtained directly from the ten percent label information, and then the constraint transferring algorithm obtains the extended constraint information as the final pairwise constraint information. For the pcDMDS algorithm, the parameter λ is set to 0.8, and the parameter α in the constraint transferring algorithm is set to 0.1. In order to reduce the differences in the experimental results, all feature learning algorithms are run 10 times in the experiments, and then the average of the 10 times is taken as the final result.

The experiments of pcDMDS algorithm are to evaluate the ability of pcDMDS to learn discriminative features. The experiments are designed in such a way that multiple clustering experiments are performed on the low-dimensional data representation obtained from the original data, the low-dimensional data representation obtained from the PMDS algorithm and the data representation obtained from pcDMDS, respectively. If the data representation is more discriminative, the clustering algorithm performs better. The selected clustering algorithms include KM, AP and DP.

5.3. Evaluation Metric

Since features with discriminative properties tend to improve the performance of subsequent machine learning tasks, the discriminative properties of the learned features can be evaluated by evaluating the performance of subsequent machine learning tasks. The subsequent machine learning tasks include clustering tasks and classification tasks, so the performance of the learned features is evaluated by using the evaluation metrics of clustering and classification.

5.3.1. Accuracy

Accuracy, a common metric for clustering, measures the degree of difference between the sample cluster results given by a clustering model and the true labels of the samples. The calculation of clustering accuracy and classification accuracy is slightly different. For clustering, the accuracy is computed as [34].

$$Acc = \frac{1}{N}\sum_{i=1}^{N}\delta(l_i, map(r_i)). \tag{23}$$

N denotes the number of sample points, and $map(\cdot)$ is a function that maps the cluster index to the category label. l_i and r_i denote the category label and the cluster index of sample point x_i, respectively. $\delta(a,b)$ is a function whose value is 1 when $a = b$. Otherwise, it is 0. For the classification task, r_i denotes the classifier's predicted category label, at this time $map(\cdot)$ can be considered as a constant mapping. The output value is equal to the input value.

5.3.2. Purity

Purity is a common metric used to measure the performance of clustering algorithms and is defined as [35]:

$$\text{Purity} = \frac{1}{N}\sum_{k=1}^{C}\max_{1\leq r\leq q} n_k^r. \tag{24}$$

N denotes the number of sample points, C denotes the number of clusters, k denotes the cluster index, and q is the number of classes. In general, q is equal to C. n_k^r denotes the number of samples with class label r in the k cluster.

5.3.3. Friedman Test

Friedman statistic is a statistical method for non-parametric testing to evaluate the overall difference in performance of a set of algorithms on different datasets. Friedman statistic requires first getting the ranking of each algorithm's performance on the same dataset, with the best performing algorithm ranked as 1, the next best algorithm ranked as 2, and so on to get the rankings of all algorithms, and if there is the same performance, the average ranking value is taken. The ranking value of an algorithm is also called rank value. Specifically, the Friedman statistic is defined as [36]:

$$X_2^F = \frac{12a}{b(b+1)}\left[\sum_{j=1}^{b} R_j^2 - \frac{b(b+1)^2}{4}\right]. \tag{25}$$

The a denotes the number of datasets, b denotes the number of algorithms, $R_j = \frac{1}{a}\sum_{i=1}^{a} r_{ji}$, r_{ji} denotes the rank value of the j-th algorithm on the i-th dataset, and it can be seen that R_j denotes the average rank value of the j-th algorithm on all datasets, X_F^2 obeys the chi-square distribution with degrees of freedom $b-1$.

Iman and Davenport improved the deficiencies of the Friedman statistic X_F^2 by proposing a better statistic defined as [37]:

$$F_F = \frac{(a-1)X_F^2}{a(b-1) - X_F^2}. \tag{26}$$

F_F is the F distribution with degrees of freedom $b-1$ and $(b-1)(a-1)$. The p-value is obtained by looking up the table, and the significance of the differences between all algorithms is evaluated based on the p-value.

5.4. Results

Tables 2 and 3 give the accuracy and purity results obtained by clustering the 12 data sets by KM, AP and DP under three different data representations, respectively. Specifically, in Table 2, columns KM, AP and DP are the clustering accuracies of the three algorithms on the original data representation. PMDS-KM, PMDS-AP and PMDS-DP are the clustering accuracies of the three clustering algorithms on the low-dimensional data representation obtained by the PMDS algorithm. pcDMDS-KM, pcDMDS-AP and pcDMDS-DP are the clustering accuracies of the three clustering algorithms on the low-dimensional data representation obtained by the pcDMDS algorithm. The Avg column is the mean of columns KM, AP and DP. Column PMDS-Avg is the mean value of columns PMDS-KM, PMDS-AP and PMDS-DP. Similarly, column pcDMDS-Avg is the mean value of columns pcDMDS-KM, pcDMDS-AP and pcDMDS-DP. The meaning of the table headers in Table 3 is similar to that in Table 2, except that the data in the table are purity rather than accuracy, which is not repeated here.

From Table 2, it can be seen that 10 of the models with the highest accuracy in these 12 datasets are on the data representation learned by pcDMDS features (bolded data in the table), and 2 are on the original data representation, which indicates that pcDMDS can improve the discriminatory performance of the data representation. Moreover, for the same clustering algorithm, the performance exhibited on the data representation obtained by the pcDMDS algorithm is overwhelmingly better than the original data representation and the PMDS data representation. In addition, in terms of the average accuracy, the 12 highest average accuracies are in the feature representation of the pcDMDS algorithm, and the average accuracy of the data representation obtained by the pcDMDS algorithm is 10.31% and 7.41% higher than that of the PMDS and the original space, respectively. This also reflects that the data representation obtained after the DMDS feature learning algorithm can improve the performance of the subsequent machine learning compared with the PMDS and the original data representation.

Table 2. Accuracy of clustering with different data representations.

NO.	KM	AP	DP	PMDS -KM	PMDS -AP	PMDS -DP	pcDMDS -KM	pcDMDS -AP	pcDMDS -DP	Avg	PMDS -Avg	pcDMDS -Avg
01	0.5352	0.6761	0.5318	0.3693	0.4227	0.3897	**0.7306**	0.6568	0.6568	0.5810	0.3939	**0.6814**
02	0.5131	0.5011	0.5059	0.5203	0.4340	0.4964	0.5287	**0.5647**	0.5287	0.5067	0.4836	**0.5407**
03	0.4204	**0.5710**	0.4289	0.4096	0.4867	0.4012	0.5204	0.5204	0.5204	0.4734	0.4325	**0.5204**
04	0.4324	0.5426	0.4099	0.4170	0.5521	0.4206	**0.5687**	0.5177	0.5177	0.4616	0.4632	**0.5347**
05	0.4860	0.5954	0.4452	0.5246	0.5557	0.5815	**0.6952**	0.5633	0.5633	0.5088	0.5539	**0.6073**
06	0.4505	0.4428	0.4857	0.4142	0.4560	0.5098	**0.5593**	0.5538	0.4945	0.4596	0.4600	**0.5359**
07	0.5047	0.4440	0.4428	0.5238	0.4416	0.4059	0.5202	0.5535	0.5202	0.4638	0.4571	**0.5313**
08	0.3860	0.4376	0.4208	0.3764	0.4460	0.4328	**0.5227**	0.5215	0.5215	0.4184	0.4184	**0.5219**
09	0.3883	0.4406	0.4938	0.3860	0.3827	0.4107	0.3928	**0.5824**	0.5409	0.4409	0.3931	**0.5054**
10	0.4374	**0.6702**	0.5799	0.4744	0.5005	0.4124	0.5179	0.6659	0.5201	0.5625	0.4624	**0.5680**
11	0.4705	0.3904	0.4881	0.4605	0.4881	0.4242	0.5519	**0.6020**	0.4267	0.4496	0.4576	**0.5269**
12	0.4055	0.3613	0.4230	0.4032	0.3846	0.4090	**0.5384**	**0.5384**	**0.5384**	0.3966	0.3989	**0.5384**

Table 3. Purity of clustering with different data representations.

NO.	KM	AP	DP	PMDS -KM	PMDS -AP	PMDS -DP	pcDMDS -KM	pcDMDS -AP	pcDMDS -DP	Avg	PMDS -Avg	pcDMDS -Avg
01	0.6818	0.6909	0.5806	0.5715	0.5715	0.5715	**0.7693**	**0.7693**	**0.7693**	0.6511	0.5715	**0.7693**
02	0.5515	0.5023	0.5239	0.5563	0.4988	0.5143	**0.5839**	0.5647	**0.5839**	0.5259	0.5231	**0.5775**
03	0.5759	0.5759	0.5759	0.5759	0.5771	0.5759	**0.6337**	**0.6337**	**0.6337**	0.5759	0.5763	**0.6337**
04	0.5450	0.5473	0.5450	0.5462	0.5521	0.5450	**0.5746**	0.5616	0.5616	0.5457	0.5478	**0.5659**
05	0.6738	0.6083	0.5965	0.6652	0.6040	0.6330	**0.7178**	**0.7178**	**0.7178**	0.6262	0.6341	**0.7178**
06	0.5362	0.5362	0.5362	0.5362	0.5362	0.5373	**0.5736**	0.5582	0.5725	0.5362	0.5366	**0.5681**
07	0.5642	0.4452	0.4476	0.5595	0.4452	0.4476	**0.5821**	**0.5821**	**0.5821**	0.4856	0.4841	**0.5821**
08	0.4652	0.4700	0.4652	0.4652	0.4700	0.4652	**0.5227**	0.5215	0.5215	0.4668	0.4668	**0.5219**
09	0.5476	0.5476	0.5566	0.5476	0.5476	0.5555	0.5476	**0.5824**	0.5656	0.5506	0.5502	**0.5652**
10	0.6637	0.6735	0.6637	0.6637	0.6637	0.6637	**0.6855**	0.6670	0.6659	0.6669	0.6637	**0.6728**
11	0.6445	0.6320	0.6320	0.6382	0.6408	0.6320	**0.6996**	0.6495	0.6320	0.6361	0.6370	**0.6604**
12	0.4860	0.4860	0.4860	0.4860	0.4860	0.4860	**0.5384**	**0.5384**	**0.5384**	0.4860	0.4860	**0.5384**

The overall performance of the model is then evaluated based on the Friedman statistic. Based on the last three columns of Table 2, the ranking values for the performance of different data representations in each dataset can be first derived. The average ranking values of 2.4583, 2.5416 and 1 for Avg, PMDS-Avg and pcDMDS-Avg on the 12 datasets can be calculated, respectively. Since there are 12 datasets with three types of averages, F_F obeys a degree of freedom of $3-1=2$ and $(12-1)(3-1)=22$ for the F distribution. From the $F(2,22)$ distribution, the p-value can be calculated as 2.2082×10^{-7}, so the original hypothesis is rejected at a high significance level, and the comprehensive evaluation of the pcDMDS algorithm outperforms the PMDS algorithm. The data representation obtained by the pcDMDS algorithm is more discriminative than the data representation obtained by PMDS and the original data representation.

Table 3 lists the purity of the clustering results on the different data representations. It can be seen that the 12 highest purity are on the data representation of pcDMDS. Overall, the clustering performance on pcDMDS is better than PMDS and raw space. Also, the average purity of the data representation obtained by the pcDMDS algorithm is 8.31% and 9.18% higher than that of the PMDS and the original space, respectively.

Similarly, the Friedman statistic is used to evaluate the overall performance of the model. According to the last three columns of Table 3, the average ranking values of Avg, PMDS-Avg and pcDMDS-Avg can be obtained as 2.5, 2.5 and 1, respectively. The Friedman statistic can be calculated as $X_F^2 = 13.0833$, and then the Iman-Davenport as $F_F = 13.1832$. The p-value can be calculated from the $F(2,22)$ distribution as 1.7245×10^4, so the original hypothesis is rejected at a higher significance level, and the combined evaluation of pcDMDS algorithm is better than PMDS and the original space.

In terms of accuracy and purity, it can be seen that the data representation obtained by pcDMDS has a better performance for subsequent clustering algorithms than the original data representation and the data representation obtained by PMDS, which can learn more discriminative features. For big datasets, pcDMDS can enhance the discriminativeness by considering both the topology of samples in the original space and the cluster structure in the new space, and also incorporating the extended pairwise constraint information in the samples.

6. Conclusions

In this paper, a feature learning algorithm named pcDMDS is proposed and the discriminability is enhanced in two aspects. Firstly, the ability to automatically discover clusters in samples by fuzzy *k*-means, so that new data representations corresponding to samples in the same cluster are close to the cluster center during feature learning. Then the pairwise constraint information between more samples, noted as extended pairwise constraint information, is obtained by a constraint transferring algorithm based on the pairwise constraint information between a given part of samples. In the whole process of feature learning, the ability of the original model to obtain discriminative features is further improved. Because pcDMDS not only considers the topological structure of the sample in the original space and the cluster structure in the new space, but also incorporates the extended pairwise constraint information in the sample. However, the effect of different values of parameter λ on the clustering performance of pcDMDS was analyzed in pcDMDS, but the values are fixed, so the effect of β and λ can be considered jointly in the future. Plus, the model does not use incremental learning, and it can be put into research in the future work.

Author Contributions: Conceptualization, L.Z., B.P., H.T. and H.W.; methodology, L.Z., B.P. and H.T.; software, L.Z., B.P., H.T. and H.W.; validation, C.L., Z.L. and H.T.; formal analysis, L.Z.; investigation, Z.L.; resources, B.P., H.T., H.W. and C.L.; data curation, L.Z.; writing—original draft, L.Z., B.P., H.T., H.W. and C.L.; writing—review and editing, L.Z., B.P., H.T., H.W., C.L. and Z.L.; visualization, L.Z., B.P. and H.W.; supervision, H.W. and C.L.; project administration, Z.L. All authors have read and agreed to the published version of the manuscript.

Funding: This research work was supported by Science and Technology Project of State Grid Sichuan Electric Power Company (52199722000Y), and by the National Natural Science Foundation of China under Grant Nos (62276216, 62202395).

Data Availability Statement: Data are freely available from MSRA.

Conflicts of Interest: The authors declare no conflict of interest.

References

1. Wold, S.; Esbensen, K.; Geladi, P. Principal component analysis. *Chemom. Intell. Lab. Syst.* **1987**, *2*, 37–52. [CrossRef]
2. Zhang, D.; Zhou, Z.H.; Chen, S. Semi-supervised dimensionality reduction. In Proceedings of the 2007 SIAM International Conference on Data Mining, Minneapolis, MI, USA, 26–28 April 2007; SIAM: Philadelphia, PA, USA, 2007; pp. 629–634.
3. Martinez, A.M.; Kak, A.C. Pca versus lda. *IEEE Trans. Pattern Anal. Mach. Intell.* **2001**, *23*, 228–233. [CrossRef]
4. Roweis, S.T.; Saul, L.K. Nonlinear dimensionality reduction by locally linear embedding. *Science* **2000**, *290*, 2323–2326. [CrossRef] [PubMed]
5. Borg, I.; Groenen, P.J. *Modern Multidimensional Scaling: Theory and Applications*; Springer Science & Business Media: Berlin/Heidelberg, Germany, 2005.
6. Belkin, M.; Niyogi, P. Laplacian eigenmaps for dimensionality reduction and data representation. *Neural Comput.* **2003**, *15*, 1373–1396. [CrossRef]
7. Bengio, Y.; Paiement, J.F.; Vincent, P.; Delalleau, O.; Roux, N.; Ouimet, M. Out-of-sample extensions for lle, isomap, mds, eigenmaps, and spectral clustering. *Adv. Neural Inf. Process. Syst.* **2003**, *16*, 177–184.
8. He, X.; Niyogi, P. Locality preserving projections. *Adv. Neural Inf. Process. Syst.* **2003**, *16*, 153–160.
9. He, X.; Cai, D.; Yan, S.; Zhang, H.J. Neighborhood preserving embedding. In Proceedings of the Tenth IEEE International Conference on Computer Vision (ICCV'05), Volume 1, Beijing, China, 17–21 October 2005; IEEE: Piscataway, NJ, USA, 2005; Volume 2, pp. 1208–1213.
10. Tsai, F.S. Dimensionality reduction techniques for blog visualization. *Expert Syst. Appl.* **2011**, *38*, 2766–2773. [CrossRef]

11. Ingram, S.; Munzner, T. Dimensionality reduction for documents with nearest neighbor queries. *Neurocomputing* **2015**, *150*, 557–569. [CrossRef]
12. Xu, J.; Han, J.; Nie, F. Discriminatively embedded k-means for multi-view clustering. In Proceedings of the IEEE Conference on Computer Vision and Pattern Recognition, Las Vegas, NV, USA, 27–30 June 2016; pp. 5356–5364.
13. Saeed, N.; Nam, H.; Haq, M.I.U.; Muhammad Saqib, D.B. A survey on multidimensional scaling. *ACM Comput. Surv. (CSUR)* **2018**, *51*, 1–25. [CrossRef]
14. Webb, A.R. Multidimensional scaling by iterative majorization using radial basis functions. *Pattern Recognit.* **1995**, *28*, 753–759. [CrossRef]
15. Tenenbaum, J.B.; Silva, V.d.; Langford, J.C. A global geometric framework for nonlinear dimensionality reduction. *Science* **2000**, *290*, 2319–2323. [CrossRef] [PubMed]
16. Bronstein, A.M.; Bronstein, M.M.; Kimmel, R. Generalized multidimensional scaling: A framework for isometry-invariant partial surface matching. *Proc. Natl. Acad. Sci. USA* **2006**, *103*, 1168–1172. [CrossRef] [PubMed]
17. Biswas, S.; Bowyer, K.W.; Flynn, P.J. Multidimensional scaling for matching low-resolution face images. *IEEE Trans. Pattern Anal. Mach. Intell.* **2011**, *34*, 2019–2030. [CrossRef] [PubMed]
18. Janani, R.; Vijayarani, S. Text document clustering using spectral clustering algorithm with particle swarm optimization. *Expert Syst. Appl.* **2019**, *134*, 192–200. [CrossRef]
19. McDowell, I.C.; Manandhar, D.; Vockley, C.M.; Schmid, A.K.; Reddy, T.E.; Engelhardt, B.E. Clustering gene expression time series data using an infinite Gaussian process mixture model. *PLoS Comput. Biol.* **2018**, *14*, e1005896. [CrossRef]
20. Alashwal, H.; El Halaby, M.; Crouse, J.J.; Abdalla, A.; Moustafa, A.A. The application of unsupervised clustering methods to Alzheimer's disease. *Front. Comput. Neurosci.* **2019**, *13*, 31. [CrossRef]
21. Likas, A.; Vlassis, N.; Verbeek, J.J. The global k-means clustering algorithm. *Pattern Recognit.* **2003**, *36*, 451–461. [CrossRef]
22. Frey, B.J.; Dueck, D. Clustering by passing messages between data points. *Science* **2007**, *315*, 972–976. [CrossRef]
23. Rodriguez, A.; Laio, A. Clustering by fast search and find of density peaks. *Science* **2014**, *344*, 1492–1496. [CrossRef]
24. Bezdek, J.C.; Ehrlich, R.; Full, W. FCM: The fuzzy c-means clustering algorithm. *Comput. Geosci.* **1984**, *10*, 191–203. [CrossRef]
25. Wang, X.; Wang, Y.; Wang, L. Improving fuzzy c-means clustering based on feature-weight learning. *Pattern Recognit. Lett.* **2004**, *25*, 1123–1132. [CrossRef]
26. Hathaway, R.J.; Bezdek, J.C. NERF c-means: Non-Euclidean relational fuzzy clustering. *Pattern Recognit.* **1994**, *27*, 429–437. [CrossRef]
27. Nie, F.; Zhao, X.; Wang, R.; Li, X.; Li, Z. Fuzzy K-means clustering with discriminative embedding. *IEEE Trans. Knowl. Data Eng.* **2020**, *34*, 1221–1230. [CrossRef]
28. Zhu, X.; Zhang, S.; Zhu, Y.; Zheng, W.; Yang, Y. Self-weighted multi-view fuzzy clustering. *ACM Trans. Knowl. Discov. Data (TKDD)* **2020**, *14*, 1–17. [CrossRef]
29. Du, W.; Lv, M.; Hou, Q.; Jing, L. Semisupervised dimension reduction based on pairwise constraint propagation for hyperspectral images. *IEEE Geosci. Remote. Sens. Lett.* **2016**, *13*, 1880–1884. [CrossRef]
30. De Leeuw, J. Convergence of the majorization method for multidimensional scaling. *J. Classif.* **1988**, *5*, 163–180. [CrossRef]
31. Huang, H.C.; Chuang, Y.Y.; Chen, C.S. Multiple kernel fuzzy clustering. *IEEE Trans. Fuzzy Syst.* **2011**, *20*, 120–134. [CrossRef]
32. Golub, G.H.; Van Loan, C.F. *Matrix Computations*; JHU Press: Baltimore, MD, USA, 2013.
33. Li, H.; Wang, M.; Hua, X.S. Msra-mm 2.0: A large-scale web multimedia dataset. In Proceedings of the 2009 IEEE International Conference on Data Mining Workshops, Miami, FL, USA, 6 December 2009; pp. 164–169.
34. Hou, C.; Nie, F.; Yi, D.; Tao, D. Discriminative embedded clustering: A framework for grouping high-dimensional data. *IEEE Trans. Neural Netw. Learn. Syst.* **2014**, *26*, 1287–1299.
35. Yang, Z.; Oja, E. Linear and nonlinear projective nonnegative matrix factorization. *IEEE Trans. Neural Netw.* **2010**, *21*, 734–749. [CrossRef]
36. García, S.; Fernández, A.; Luengo, J.; Herrera, F. Advanced nonparametric tests for multiple comparisons in the design of experiments in computational intelligence and data mining: Experimental analysis of power. *Inf. Sci.* **2010**, *180*, 2044–2064. [CrossRef]
37. Iman, R.L.; Davenport, J.M. Approximations of the critical region of the fbietkan statistic. *Commun. Stat.-Theory Methods* **1980**, *9*, 571–595. [CrossRef]

mathematics

MDPI

Article

Triplet Contrastive Learning for Aspect Level Sentiment Classification

Haoliang Xiong [1,†], Zehao Yan [1,†], Hongya Zhao [2], Zhenhua Huang [3] and Yun Xue [1,*]

1 School of Electronics and Information Engineering, South China Normal University, Foshan 528225, China; xionghl@m.scnu.edu.cn (H.X.); yzh_scnu@m.scnu.edu.cn (Z.Y.)
2 Industrial Center, Shenzhen Polytechnic, Shenzhen 518055, China; hy.zhao@szpt.edu.cn
3 School of Computer Science, South China Normal University, Guangzhou 510631, China; huangzhenhua@m.scnu.edu.cn
* Correspondence: xueyun@m.scnu.edu.cn
† These authors contributed equally to this work.

Abstract: The domain of Aspect Level Sentiment Classification, in which the sentiment toward a given aspect is analyzed, attracts much attention in NLP. Recently, the state-of-the-art Aspect Level Sentiment Classification methods are devised by using the Graph Convolutional Networks to deal with both the semantics and the syntax of the sentence. Generally, the parsing of syntactic structure inevitably incorporates irrelevant information toward the aspect. Besides, the syntactic and semantic alignment and uniformity that contribute to the sentiment delivery is currently neglected during processing. In this work, a **Triplet Contrastive Learning Network** is developed to coordinate the syntactic information and the semantic information. To start with, the aspect-oriented sub-tree is constructed to replace the syntactic adjacency matrix. Further, a sentence-level contrastive learning scheme is proposed to highlight the features of sentiment words. Based on The Triple Contrastive Learning, the syntactic information and the semantic information are thoroughly interacted and coordinated whilst the global semantics and syntax can be exploited. Extensive experiments are performed on three benchmark datasets and achieve accuracies (BERT-based) of 87.40, 82.80, 77.55 on Rest14, Lap14, and Twitter datasets, which demonstrate that our approach achieves state-of-the-art results in Aspect Level Sentiment Classification task.

Keywords: Aspect Level Sentiment Classification; Contrasitve Learning; Graph Convolutional Networks

MSC: 18C50

Citation: Xiong, H.; Yan, Z.; Zhao, H.; Huang, Z.; Xue, Y. Triplet Contrastive Learning for Aspect Level Sentiment Classification. *Mathematics* **2022**, *10*, 4099. https://doi.org/10.3390/math10214099

Academic Editors: Jianping Gou, Weihua Ou, Shaoning Zeng and Lan Du

Received: 7 October 2022
Accepted: 1 November 2022
Published: 3 November 2022

1. Introduction

Aspect Level Sentiment Classification (ALSC) is a fundamental subtask of fine-grained sentiment analysis, which currently receives a great deal of attention [1]. The main focus of ALSC is to identify the sentiment polarity (e.g., positive, neutral or negative) of aspects explicitly given in sentences. For example, in the sentence "*The price is reasonable although the service is poor*" (Figure 1), the sentiment toward aspects *price* and *service* is positive and negative, respectively.

Advances of deep neural networks bring paradigm shift to various tasks of NLP and the ALSC is no different [2–4]. The attention-based network is a most common approach that exploits the semantic information to capture the sentiment words of the given aspect. In Figure 1, more attentive weights can be assigned to the sentiment words *reasonable* and *poor* via attention mechanism. However, the use of semantic feature alone can result in the misunderstanding of contextual words, especially for sentences of complex syntax structure. More recently, the application of Graph Convolutional Networks (GCN) in ALSC is both creative and practical [5]. For one thing, the encoding of syntactic information using GCN mitigates the deficiencies of long-distance dependencies among words [6,7]. For another, not just the syntax, but also the semantic information can be processed by GCN, which gives rise to opportunities to the integration of semantic features. As such, the state-of-the-art approaches work on developing multi-channel GCNs to deal with multiple information [8,9].

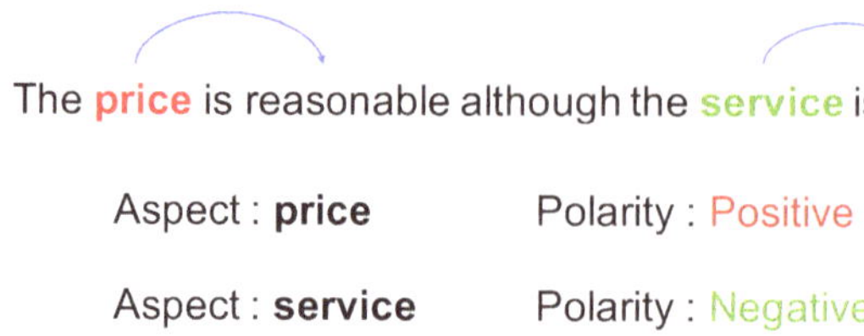

Figure 1. An example of ALSC.

Despite the progress of GCN-based method in ALSC, two main limitations are observed. **On the one hand**, most syntactic parsing is performed on the whole sentence without considering the importance of key phrases (e.g., aspect words, opinion words and etc.) to sentiment determination. In such a manner, redundant information or even noise can be incorporated during feature extraction. **On the other hand**, current methods set the semantic information and syntactic information in two individual spaces for feature extraction and fuse their features in a elementary way. But the alignment and uniformity of these two categories of features are ignored [10].

Inspired by the methods reported by [8,11], a **Triplet Contrastive Learning Network (TCL)** for ALSC is proposed to address the aforementioned issues. For the exploiting of syntactic information, we start with reconstructing the syntax dependency tree by setting the aspect as the root according to [12] (Figure 2). The dependencies between aspect word and other words are explicitly established, which contributes to the capturing of opinions words to the aspect and restricting the introduction of redundant information. As presented in [13], the key phrase plays a pivot role in delivering the essence of texts. To further filter the noise and highlight the key information, a contrastive learning scheme is proposed to magnify the significance of sentiment-related words. In ALSC tasks, the key phrases are either nouns, verbs, adjectives, or adverbs of degree [14]. With the application of masking mechanism, both positive and negative examples are generated and fed into the contrastive learning module to enhance the impacts of key phrases and distill the syntactic features.

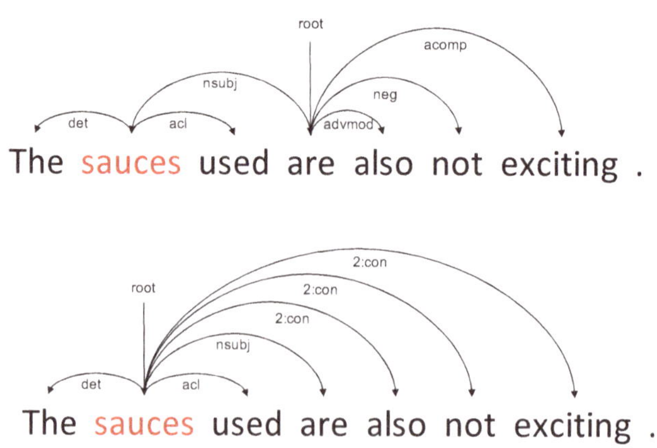

Figure 2. Reconstruction of aspect-oriented syntax dependency tree.

With respect to the integration of sentence syntax and semantics, recent publications reveal that they are distinct and related [8,15]. Likewise, the features from both space, conveying sentiment toward the aspect, also have a similar relationship between each other. For this reason, the alignment of both features can facilitate the information integration. Concretely, the features, within either syntactic or semantic space, expressing the same sentiment polarity can be aligned while those expressing different sentiment polarities can be separated. With this, the interaction between syntactic information and semantic information is carried out, based on which a dual-contrastive learning scheme is devised. For each data within the mini-batch, the features of the same sentiment polarity are getting closer based on dual-contrastive learning, and vice versa. In this way, features of both categories are thoroughly interacted and aligned. We can thus leverage feature integration to improve the ALSC performance.

The contributions of this paper are as follows:

- The syntactic adjacency matrix of the dual-channel graph convolutional neural network is replaced with an aspect-oriented tree structure, which helps the model to better capture the information of opinion words related to aspect words.
- A syntactic contrastive learning scheme is designed to encourage the model to focus on keywords that are helpful for sentiment polarity classification, and to better learn features related to aspect words.
- Constructing the dual contrastive learning module can make the semantic features and syntactic features of sentences more fully interact and align.
- Experiments show that our method outperforms baseline models on three benchmark datasets.

This work is organized as follows. Section 2 gives an overview of relevant work of ALSC and contrastive learning. Section 3 describes the TCL model in details. In Section 4, the experiment is depicted, as well as the presentation of result analysis. Concluding remarks are given in Section 5.

2. Related Work

2.1. Aspect Level Sentiment Classification

Sentiment classification tasks mainly focus on capturing the sentiment information from the given text [16,17]. ALSC aims to classify the sentiment polarity of a specific aspect from given texts. Within ALSC, a more detailed analysis about the sentiment associated with the aspect is performed by using the textual information. Early research focuses on employing CNN- and RNN-based method, together with the integration of attention mechanisms or knowledge distillation [18,19], to obtain aspect-related information. As such, the utilization of attention mechanism to precisely capture the aspect-aware contextual information becomes a main topic [2,3]. In recent years, GCN-based models rise to prominence in a variety of NLP tasks, which is capable of alleviating the defects of attention networks. On the task of ALSC, Ref. [6] first apply GCN to tackle the syntax dependency and resolve the long-term multi-word dependencies. Later work aims to establish the syntax structure and extract aspect-related features [7]. Ref. [12] re-shape the syntax dependency tree into an aspect-oriented sub-tree, in order to determine the connection between aspects and its opinion words. Ref. [20], fuse the syntax dependency types into GCN, based on which to highlight the syntax corresponds to sentiment classification. So far, there is an ongoing trend to combine the sentence syntax and semantics [8,9,21]. Most approaches tend to separately construct adjacency matrix for syntactic and semantic information, generate corresponding feature representations, and concatenate the representations for sentiment classification.

2.2. Contrastive Learning

A fundamental focus of contrastive learning is the learning of alignment and uniformity of given data [10]. Comprehensively, alignment is taken to indicate the similarity among positive examples while uniformity refers to informative-distribution of features, so that negative examples are isolated from positive ones. In practical use, both alignment and the uniformity are used as indexes to optimize the feature learning. That is, the capturing intra-class similarities and inter-class differences can benefit the performance in downstream tasks.

Recently, a number of studies apply contrastive learning to NLP tasks and achieve satisfying results [22–24]. Ref. [22] devise a simple contrastive sentence embedding framework, which can produce superior sentence embeddings on semantic textual similarity tasks. For the aspect words absent from the training set, Ref. [25] take contrastive learning to capture aspect-invariant and aspect-dependent features to distinguish the roles of valuable sentiment features. Ref. [11] propose a novel contrastive-learning-based approach that simultaneously learns the features of input samples and the parameters of classifiers in the same space on the task of text classification.

3. Proposed Method

Figure 3 shows the framework of the TCL Network. Let $X = \{x_1, x_2, \ldots, x_a, \ldots, x_{a+l_a}, \ldots, x_N\}$ be a N-word sentence with aspect $A = \{x_a, \ldots, x_{a+l_a}\}$ in it where a represents the starting index of A and l_a is the length of A. We feed the sentence into GloVe [26] or BERT [27] encoder for sentence embedding establishment. For GloVe-based model, each word is mapped into a low-dimensional vector by looking up in a pretrained word embedding matrix $E \in \mathbb{R}^{|V| \times d_E}$ where $|V|$ is the lexicon size and d_E is the dimension of word vector. The sentence embedding is given as $x = \{e_1, e_2, \ldots, e_N\}$. The hidden states of the sentence are extracted via Bi-LSTM. The contextual feature vector is $H = \{h_1, h_2, \ldots, h_N\}$ with $H \in \mathbb{R}^{N \times 2d}$ and d representing the hidden layer dimension. In addition, the sequence $[CLS]X[SEP]A[SEP]$ can also sent to BERT encoder to obtain the contextual feature vector H. Subsequently, H is taken as the input of both semantic-learning GCN module and syntactic-aware GCN module. A multi-layer Biaffine unit is proposed to integrate the semantic features and syntactic features. To further align the features from both space, the dual contrastive learning scheme is carried out. More details of each component are presented as follows.

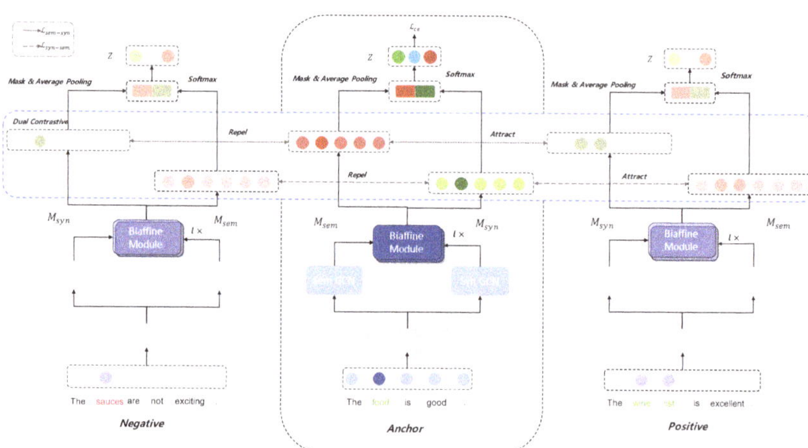

Figure 3. The overall architecture of our Triplet Contrastive Learning Network.

3.1. *Syntactic-Aware GCN Module*

The architecture of syntactic-aware module is exhibited in Figure 4. As pointed out in the Introduction, the syntactic-aware GCN in our model tends to precisely capture the aspect-related context words and remove the redundant information. According to [12], a relational graph attention network is devised. Specifically, we construct an aspect-oriented dependency tree to replace the adjacency matrix of classical syntax dependency tree. Then, the attention mechanism is applied to the reshape sub-tree to capture the aspect-specific contextual features. Moreover, to resolve the long-dependencies among words, we set four categories of words as the key phrases that contributes to sentiment delivery, i.e., nouns, verbs, adjectives, and adverbs of degree. As such, the contrastive learning is performed to enhance the features of key phrases and effectively capture the word feature of long dependency.

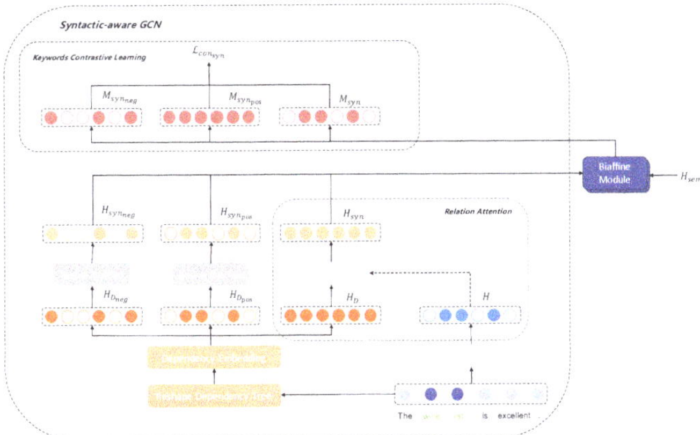

Figure 4. Architecture of syntactic-aware GCN module

3.1.1. Relational Graph Attention Module

At this stage, the aspect A is taken as the central word to construct the aspect-oriented dependency tree; see Algorithm 1 For words syntactically related to the central word of one hop, the corresponding dependency types are established. Through iteration, for words syntactically related to the central word of n hops$(n \geq 2)$, the dependency types are characterized by $(con : n)$. If the aspect contains multiple words, these words are considered as a whole. In such a manner, we shall thus obtain the re-constructed dependency tree as $D = \{dep_1, dep_1, \ldots, dep_N\}$ and map it into embedding space to generate the dependency representation $H_D = \{h_{D_1}, h_{D_2}, \ldots, h_{D_N}\}$. Notably, the randomly initialized dependency embedding $E_D \in \mathbb{R}^{|V_d| \times d_D}$ is employed with $|V_d|$ standing for the number of dependency types. For $H_D \in \mathbb{R}^{N \times d_D}$, we have d_D representing the dimension of dependency type embeddings.

The relational attention between aspect and the dependency type representation is computed. Specifically, the syntactic dependency of context toward the aspect is incorporated within H_D. Thus, the attentive weight between H_D and H is calculated using a simplified inner product operation, which is:

$$att = f\left(\frac{(W_D H_D + b_D) \times (W_h H + b_h)^T}{\sqrt{d_m}}\right) \tag{1}$$

where $W_D \in \mathbb{R}^{d_D \times d_m}$ and $W_h \in \mathbb{R}^{2d \times d_m}$ are linear layer weights; b_D and b_h are bias terms; $f(\cdot)$ stands for the softmax activation function; and d_m is the hidden layer dimension of the attention module.

Then, the syntactic representation is given as:

$$H_{syn} = att * H \tag{2}$$

Algorithm 1 Aspect-Oriented Dependency Tree

Input: sentence $X = \{x_1, x_2, \ldots, x_N\}$, aspect$A = \{x_a, \ldots, x_{a+l_a}\}$, dependency tree T, and dependency relations R.
Output: aspect-oriented dependency $\tilde{T}$.

Construct the aspect root $\tilde{R}$ for $\tilde{T}$
for a to $a + l_a$ **do**
  for $j = 1$ to n **do**
    if $x_j \notin A$ and $x_j \xrightarrow{R_{ja}} x_a$ **then**
      $x_j \xrightarrow{R_{ja}} \tilde{R}$
    else if $x_j \notin A$ and $x_j \xleftarrow{R_{ja}} x_a$ **then**
      $x_j \xleftarrow{R_{ja}} \tilde{R}$
    else
      n = distance(a, j)
      $x_j \xrightarrow{n:con} \tilde{R}$
    end if
  end for
end for
return $\tilde{T}$

3.1.2. Syntactic Contrastive Learning Scheme

The effectiveness of key phrases (i.e., nouns, verbs, adjectives or adverbs of degree) is highlighted by using based on a sentence-level key phrases contrastive learning module. To be specific, a mask operation, based on the POS information of phrases in the sentence, is performed. Only if the position mask 1 assigned to key phrase and mask 0 to others, can this representation defined as a positive example, i.e., $M_{pos} \in \mathbb{R}^N$. Conversely, a negative example indicates a key phrase with a position mask 0 while other words with a mask 1, i.e., $M_{neg} \in \mathbb{R}^N$.

The dependency type can be integrated into both positive and negative examples. We shall thus compute the positive example dependency type representation and the positive example dependency type representation as:

$$H_{D_{pos}} = H_D * M_{pos} \tag{3}$$

$$H_{D_{neg}} = H_D * M_{neg} \tag{4}$$

Similar to Equation (1), the attention weights of $H_{D_{pos}}$ and $H_{D_{neg}}$ toward the context representation are available, as presented in Equations (5) and (6). Thus, the syntactic representation of both positive examples and negative examples can be obtained (Equations (7) and (8)):

$$att_{pos} = f\left(\frac{\left(W_{D_{pos}} H_{D_{pos}} + b_{D_{pos}}\right) \times \left(W_{h_{pos}} H + b_{h_{pos}}\right)^T}{\sqrt{d_m}}\right) \tag{5}$$

$$att_{neg} = f\left(\frac{\left(W_{D_{neg}} H_{D_{neg}} + b_{D_{neg}}\right) \times \left(W_{h_{neg}} H + b_{h_{neg}}\right)^T}{\sqrt{d_m}}\right) \tag{6}$$

$$H_{syn_{pos}} = att_{pos} * H \tag{7}$$

$$H_{syn_{neg}} = att_{neg} * H \tag{8}$$

For every sentence, we have its syntactic representation H_{syn}, the syntactic representation with key phrases $H_{syn_{pos}}$ and syntactic representation without key phrases $H_{syn_{neg}}$. Each of these syntactic representations is fed into a shared-weight biaffine unit to fuse with the semantic representation in following section. The final syntactic representations, with the integration of semantic information, are presented as M_{syn} (derived from Equation (13)), $M_{syn_{pos}}$ and $M_{syn_{neg}}$, respectively.

Aiming to focus more on the key phrases, the contrastive learning scheme is carried out with the loss function set as:

$$\mathcal{L}_{con_{syn}} = -\frac{1}{B}\sum_{j=1}^{B}\frac{1}{N}\sum_{i=1}^{N}\log\frac{e^{\text{sim}(M^{i}_{syn_{pos}},M^{i}_{syn})/\tau_1}}{\sum_{t=1}^{N}\left(e^{\text{sim}\left(M^{t}_{syn_{pos}},M^{i}_{syn}\right)/\tau_1}+e^{\text{sim}(M^{t}_{syn_{neg}},M^{i}_{syn})/\tau_1}\right)} \tag{9}$$

where τ_1 is the temperature coefficient, B is the batch size and N is sentence length mentioned above.

Distinguishing from the current contrastive learning approaches, in addition to the positive example $M^{i}_{syn_{pos}}$, the other examples, containing $N-1$ key-phrases-related syntactic representations $M^{t}_{syn_{pos}}(t \neq i)$ and N syntactic representations without key phrases $M_{syn_{neg}}$, are all considered as negative examples. In other words, the negative examples of each word in the sentence is $2N-1$.

3.2. Semantic-Learning GCN Module

The sentence semantics is also encoded via GCN to enhance the modelling of sentiment information. Seeing that the self-attention mechanism is capable of extracting the semantic relevance of other words and the given word, we use self-attention network to construct a semantic adjacency matrix $A^{\text{sem}} \in \mathbb{R}^{N\times N}$:

$$A^{\text{sem}} = f\left(\frac{QW^{q}\times\left(KW^{k}\right)^{T}}{\sqrt{d}}\right) \tag{10}$$

where both Q and K equal the context representation H, W^{q} and W^{k} are trainable weighting parameters and d is the hidden layer size of attention network.

The semantic representation is derived from graph convolution, which is:

$$H_{sem} = \sigma(A^{sem}WH + b) \tag{11}$$

where $\sigma(\cdot)$ stands for the linear activation function, such as ReLU function.

3.3. Biaffine Unit

The interaction of semantic information and syntactic information is conducted via multi-layer mutual Biaffine transformation. In Equation (12), H_{syn} and H_{sem} are first multiplied to obtain a syntactic-related matrix containing the semantic information. Then, the syntactic-related matrix is mapped via Softmax and multiplied by the original semantic information to obtain the final syntactic feature representation with semantic information integrated. Via multi-layers of Biaffine unit, the semantic features can be fused to the syntactic representation for sentiment polarity classification. So is Equation (13).

$$H^{(l)}_{\text{syn}} = f\left(H^{(l-1)}_{\text{syn}}W^{(l-1)}_{1}\left(H^{(l-1)}_{\text{sem}}\right)^{T}\right)H^{(l-1)}_{\text{sem}} \tag{12}$$

$$H^{(l)}_{sem} = f\left(H^{(l-1)}_{sem}W^{(l-1)}_{2}\left(H^{(l-1)}_{syn}\right)^{T}\right)H^{(l-1)}_{syn} \tag{13}$$

where $l(l=1,2,\ldots)$ stands for the layer number of the biaffine unit; both $W_1 \in \mathbb{R}^{2d\times 2d}$ and $W_2 \in \mathbb{R}^{2d\times 2d}$ are learnable parameters. Specifically, we take $H^{(0)}_{sem}$ and $H^{(0)}_{sem}$ to represent $H_{sem} \in \mathbb{R}^{N\times 2d}$ and $H_{syn} \in \mathbb{R}^{N\times 2d}$, which are the inputs of biaffine unit.

With the mutual Biaffine transformation, we thus obtain the final semantic representation with fused syntactic features $H^{(l)}_{sem}$ which also presented as M_{sem} and the final syntactic representation with fused semantic features $H_{syn}^{(l)}$ which also presented as M_{syn}. The average pooling is performed on the outcomes in relation to the aspect.

$$M_{sem}^{A} = \text{avgpool}\left(M_{\text{sem}_a}, \ldots, M_{\text{sem}_{a+la}}\right) \tag{14}$$

$$M_{syn}^{A} = \text{avgpool}\left(M_{syn_a}, \ldots, M_{syn_{a+la}}\right) \tag{15}$$

Then, both the semantic representation and the syntactic representation of the aspect are concatenated and sent to the linear classifier to determine the sentiment polarity of the given aspect:

$$Z = f\left(W\left[M_{sem}^{A}; M_{syn}^{A}\right] + b\right) \tag{16}$$

where $[;]$ stands for the vector concatenation, W and b are learnable parameters in the linear layer.

3.4. Dual Contrastive Learning Scheme

In the proposed model, the main purpose of the dual contrastive learning is to comprehensively align the features of both syntactic space and semantic space. The global syntactic features and semantic features can thus be captured. Notably, the output of the biaffine unit (i.e., M_{syn} and M_{sem} are taken as the input of the dual contrastive learning module. For each input X_i, the sequence with the same sentiment polarity within the same batch is considered as the positive example $\mathcal{P}$, otherwise as negative example $\mathcal{N}$. The loss function of the dual contrastive learning is presented as:

$$\mathcal{L}_{syn-sem} = -\frac{1}{B}\sum_{i=1}^{B}\frac{1}{|\mathcal{P}|}\sum_{j\in\mathcal{P}}\log\frac{e^{\text{sim}(M_{syn_i}, M_{sem_j})/\tau_2}}{\sum_{t=1}^{B} e^{\text{sim}(M_{syn_i}, M_{sem_t})/\tau_2}} \tag{17}$$

$$\mathcal{L}_{sem-syn} = -\frac{1}{B}\sum_{i=1}^{B}\frac{1}{|\mathcal{P}|}\sum_{j\in\mathcal{P}}\log\frac{e^{\text{sim}(M_{sem_i}, M_{syn_j})/\tau_3}}{\sum_{t=1}^{B} e^{\text{sim}(M_{sem_i}, M_{syn_t})/\tau_3}} \tag{18}$$

where τ_2 and τ_3 are the temperature coefficients of contrastive loss.

3.5. Loss Function

The loss function for model training is expressed:

$$\begin{aligned}\mathcal{L} = \mathcal{L}_{CE} + \alpha\mathcal{L}_o + \beta\left(\mathcal{L}_{syn-sem} + \mathcal{L}_{sem-syn}\right) \\ + \gamma\mathcal{L}_{con_{syn}} + \lambda||\Theta||\end{aligned} \tag{19}$$

with

$$\mathcal{L}_o = ||A^{sem}A^{\text{sem}\,T} - I||_F \tag{20}$$

where α, β and γ are hyperparameters; L_{CE} represents the cross-entropy loss for sentiment polarity classification; Θ denotes the training parameter set; λ represents the coefficient of L2 regularization. Inspired by [8], for each word in the sentence, its attention distribution on every other word is distinguishing. In other words, the overlap of attentive weights has to be minimized especially for the application of semantic graph adjacency matrix. Therefore, an additional orthogonal regularized loss function L_o is thereby introduced. The parameter I in Equation (20) is an identity matrix and the subscript F stands for the Frobenius norm.

Since the contrastive learning loss results are derived from various weighting parameters, the back propagation can be applied to optimize these parameters during the loss function optimizing.

4. Experiments

4.1. Datasets and Settings

Datasets: We evaluate the working performance of TCL network on three benchmark datasets, which are Rest14 and Lap14 from SemEval 2014 Task4 [28] and Twitter [29]. Each sample in these datasets is either a product review or tweet sentence, which contains explicit aspect words and the corresponding sentiment polarities. Each aspect from the product reviews or tweets in our experiments is labeled as positive, neutral or negative. Details of each dataset are exhibited in Table 1.

Experimental Settings: For GloVe-based model, we initialize the word embeddings with 300-dimensional vectors pretrained by Glove [26]. The dimension of the dependent syntactic embeddings is set to 30. The hidden layer dimension of BiLSTM is 50. All the weights in the model are initialized by Xavier uniform distribution. The layer number of biaffine unit is set as 2. For the contrastive learning scheme, the temperature coefficient determines how much attention the contrastive learning loss assign to the outlier negative samples. The larger the temperature coefficient is, the greater the tolerance to negative samples, and vice versa. In the syntactic contrastive learning module, it is desirable that more attention is given to key phrases with a certain tolerance to other words. Therefore, τ_1 of the syntactic contrastive learning is 1 while τ_2 and τ_3 of the dual contrastive learning is set to 0.1. In addition, he Adam optimizer is adopted with a learning rate of 2×10^{-3}. The batch size ranges from 16 to 64. The L2 regularization coefficient λ is set to 1×10^{-4}. Notably, the values of α, β and γ vary in line with the datasets, which are 0.1, 0.5 and 0.5 for Rest14, 0.5, 0.7 and 0.8 for Lap14 and 0.2, 0.2 and 0.7 for Twitter.

Table 1. Statistics of datasets.

Dataset		#Pos.	#Neu.	#Neg.	Total
Rest14	Train	2164	637	807	3608
	Test	728	196	196	1120
Lap14	Train	994	464	870	2328
	Test	341	169	128	638
Twitter	Train	1561	3127	1560	6248
	Test	173	346	173	692

4.2. Baselines

In order to validate the effectiveness of the proposed model in ALSC, we take 10 state-of-the-art methods for comparison:

1. **ASGCN** [6] The syntactical features are obtained using GCN via syntax dependency tree while the aspect-specific attention is applied to extract the features related to aspects.
2. **CDT** [30] The Bi-LSTM is taken to learn the sentence representations and the GCN encodes the syntactic information and capture the aspect-related syntactic features.
3. **RGAT** [12] The aspect-oriented dependency tree is constructed, based on which the relation graph attention network is developed to learn the dependencies between aspect and other words.
4. **BiGCN** [31] A global lexical graph and a concept hierarchy graph are constructed, which aims to integrate word pair co-occurrence and syntactic dependencies.
5. **DualGCN** [8] A dual-channel GCN method is proposed to extract both syntactic and semantic information, and then fuse the two categories of information .
6. **BERT-SPC** [27] The sentence-aspect pair is sent to BERT model with its token [CLS] used for sentiment classification.
7. **T-GCN** [20] A multilayer type-aware GCN is established to learn the relationship among words.
8. **BERT4GCN** [32] The intermediate layers of BERT is employed to augment GCN for ALSC.

9. **DR-BERT** [33] The Dynamic Re-weighting Adapter is proposed to encourage model to better understand aspect-aware sentiment through

4.3. Experimental Results and Analysis

We take two metrics, accuracy and Macro-F1, to evaluate the working performance of the proposed model. The experimental results of 13 different methods are presented in Table 2. Comparing with the state-of-the-arts, the TCL network is the best performing method in most datasets. There is a considerable performance gap between the proposed model and the baselines. According to Table 2, one can easily see that models using BERT-based embeddings have a better performance than those of GloVe-based embeddings. Indeed, the employment of GCN substantially contributes to the encoding of sentence syntax and semantics. With respect to our model, the effectively use of syntactic information highlights the contextual words related to the aspect. As a result, more attentive weights are given to words that contribute to the sentiment delivery. In comparison with the single-channel GCN (i.e., [6,12,30]), the dual-channel GCN methods (i.e., [8]), which deal with both the syntactic information and the semantic information, shows their superiorities in ALSC tasks. In this way, our model not just integrates different types of features, but also exploits the global information to further optimize the sentiment classification results.

Table 2. Experimental results. Bold numbers represent the best results among methods of the same type.

Models	Rest14		Lap14		Twitter	
	Accuracy	Macro-F1	Accuracy	Macro-F1	Accuracy	Macro-F1
ASGCN [6]	80.77	72.02	75.55	71.05	72.15	70.40
CDT [30]	82.30	74.02	77.19	72.99	74.66	73.66
RGAT [12]	83.30	76.08	77.42	73.76	75.57	73.82
BiGCN [31]	81.97	73.48	74.59	71.84	74.16	73.35
DualGCN [8]	**84.27**	**78.08**	78.48	74.74	75.92	74.29
Our TCL	**84.27**	77.04	**79.27**	**76.05**	**76.81**	**75.53**
BERT-SPCBERT-SPC [27]	86.15	80.29	81.01	76.69	75.18	74.01
RGAT+BERT [12]	86.60	81.35	78.21	74.07	76.15	74.88
T-GCN [20]	86.16	77.11	77.49	73.01	74.73	73.76
DualGCN+BERT [8]	87.13	81.16	**81.80**	78.10	77.40	76.02
BERT4GCN [32]	84.75	77.11	77.49	73.01	74.73	73.36
DR-BERT [33]	**87.72**	**82.31**	81.45	78.16	77.24	76.10
Our TCL+BERT	87.40	82.12	**81.80**	**78.96**	**77.55**	**76.57**

However, the TCL network fails to overperform DR-BERT on the Rest14. A possible explanation is that the samples of distinguishing sentiment occupy significantly different proportion in the Rest14 dataset, which affects performance of contrastive learning scheme as the generation of positive and negative samples is obtained by random sampling.

4.4. Ablation Study

An ablation study is carried out on three datasets to investigate the importance of the contrastive learning losses; see Table 3. The dual contrastive learning scheme concerns the syntactic-based semantic learning loss function $\mathcal{L}_{sem-syn}$ and the semantic-based syntactic learning loss function $\mathcal{L}_{syn-sem}$. The results show that the ablating of both loss functions leads to the most significant drop. The main reason is that the employment of global features within the minibatch does benefit the sentiment delivery. We see that the contribution of $\mathcal{L}_{sem-syn}$ is slightly higher than that of $\mathcal{L}_{syn-sem}$, which indicates the effectiveness of semantic alignment. By contrast, the contribution of $\mathcal{L}_{con_{syn}}$ in the syntactic learning module is relatively small, but its removal still results in an average decrease of 1.2% in accuracy.

Table 3. Ablation study results. Bold numbers represent the best results.

Models	Rest14		Lap14		Twitter	
	Accuracy	Macro-F1	Accuracy	Macro-F1	Accuracy	Macro-F1
TCL $w/o\ \mathcal{L}_{syn-sem}$	82.31	74.14	77.69	74.11	75.18	73.59
TCL $w/o\ \mathcal{L}_{sem-syn}$	82.30	74.73	78.01	74.72	75.33	74.01
TCL $w/o\ \mathcal{L}_{syn-sem}\&\mathcal{L}_{sem-syn}$	81.94	74.17	77.53	74.57	74.00	72.76
TCL $w/o\ \mathcal{L}_{con_{syn}}$	83.02	74.96	78.32	74.75	75.48	74.27
TCL	**84.27**	**77.04**	**79.27**	**76.05**	**76.81**	**75.53**

4.5. Case Study

Four examples of ALSC tasks are conducted and presented in Figure 5. The aspect words in green, blue, and red represent the positive, neutral, and negative sentiment polarities, respectively. The first case is a sentence of simple syntax and semantics. All the three models are capable of identifying the sentiment as negative. Sentence 2 contains multiple aspects. The ASGCN fails to determine the sentiment of aspect '*disc drive*', because '*disc drive*' is syntactically close to the word negative word '*not*'. Similarly, in sentence 3, the aspect '*apple OS*' has a long distance dependency with its opinion word, which results in the misunderstanding of the sentiment using ASGCN. By contrast, the DualGCN, which integrates both syntactic and semantic information, can classify the sentiment toward aspect '*apple OS*' correctly. In the last sentence, despite the complexity in both the syntax and semantics, the TCL network is capable of identifying the sentiment polarities of all aspects. The application of triplet contrastive learning effectively obtains alignment between semantic and syntactic features, indicating its efficacy in ALSC of complex sentences.

Sentence	ASGCN	DualGCN	Our TCL
but the mountain lion is just too slow .	(✓)	(✓)	(✓)
the latest version does not have a disc drive .	(✓, ✗)	(✓, ✓)	(✓, ✓)
Works well, and I am extremely happy to be back to an apple OS .	(✓, ✗)	(✓, ✓)	(✓, ✓)
the power plug has to be connected to the power adaptor to charge the battery but won't stay connected .	(✓, ✗, ✗)	(✓, ✗, ✗)	(✓, ✓, ✓)

Figure 5. Case study. ALSC results of TCL, ASGCN and DualGCN on testing examples, along with their predictions and correspondingly, golden labels. The marker ✓ and ✗ indicate the correct classification and incorrect classification, respectively

4.6. Visualization

4.6.1. Comparison of Syntactic and Semantic Vectors

The distribution of semantic and syntactic representations aims to verify the effectiveness of the dual contrastive learning scheme. Figure 6 shows the visualization of semantic and syntactic outputs of the dual contrastive learning module using t-SNE algorithm [34]. To facilitate the comparison, we only take the data with positive and negative sentiment polarities for visualization. Apparently, both the basic TCL network and TCL without dual contrastive learning can distinguish one type of representations. Notably, the proposed model without dual contrastive learning fails to resolve the two types of vectors with the same sentiment polarity, such as the distribution of red dots, which indicates the importance of alignment between the semantic and syntactic spaces. Moreover, there are large amount of overlapping for vectors with different sentiment polarities. The uniformity of syntax and semantics is absent. In comparison, the TCL network considers both the alignment and the uniformity of features. With the application of dual contrastive learning scheme, not only the distribution of the same-polarity-representations is more concentrated, but also the overlapping within different-polarities-representations are reduced to a large extent.

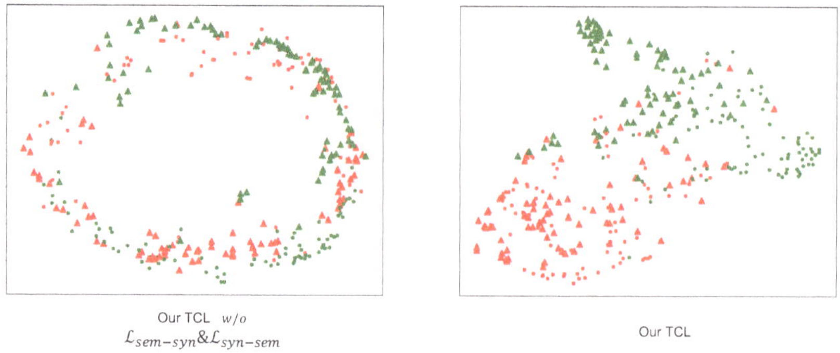

Figure 6. Visualization of semantic and syntactic vectors. Triangle dots represent syntactic vectors; round dots represent semantic vectors; dots in red represent positive samples; dots in green represent negative samples.

4.6.2. Sentiment Classification Visualization

Similarly, the visualization of triplet contrastive learning is also performed; see Figure 7. For the ASGCN that merely exploits the syntactic features, the neural samples can be distinguished from those of other two sentiment polarities. Whereas, the classification between positive and negative samples is challenging, with large amount of misunderstanding of the sentiment. Since DualGCN tackles both syntactic and semantic information, the samples of three sentiment polarities can be better discriminated. The distribution of neural samples is still not that distinctive, especially comparing with the negative samples. By contrast, our model shows its dominance in sentiment classification. It is clearly that a more concentrated distribution of samples with the same sentiment is accessible. Due to the introduction of triple contrastive learning, a better performance of feature learning and sentiment classification can be expected.

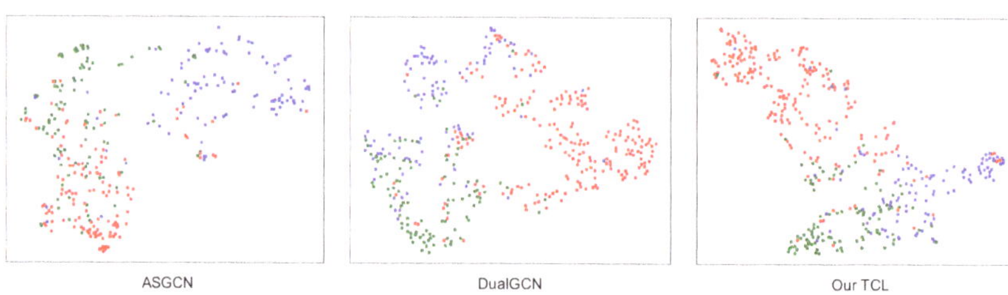

Figure 7. Visualization of sentiment classification results. The dots in green, red and blue respectively represent the positive, neural and negative samples.

5. Conclusions

In this work, a TCL network is developed to deal with the ALSC tasks, which not just exploits the global information, but also obtains the alignment of semantics and syntax. To start with, an aspect-oriented dependency tree is constructed by reshaping the syntactic adjacency matrix. Then, the sentence-level contrastive learning is applied to highlight the effectiveness of key phrases toward sentiment delivery. Two GCNs are employed to respectively encode the syntactic and semantic information. A dual contrastive learning scheme is proposed to align the features from both syntactic and semantic spaces. Experiments are carried out on three benchmark datasets. Our method produces results considerably better than the state-of-the-art methods on the task of ALSC.

Author Contributions: Conceptualization, H.X. and Y.X.; methodology, H.X.; formal analysis, H.X. and Z.Y.; writing—original draft preparation, H.X. and Z.Y.; writing—review and editing, Y.X. and H.Z.; supervision, Y.X., Z.H. and H.Z.; funding acquisition H.Z. and Z.H. All authors have read and agreed to the published version of the manuscript.

Funding: This work was supported by the Characteristic Innovation Projects of Guangdong Colleges and Universities (Nos. 2018KTSCX049), the Science and Technology Plan Project of Guangzhou under Grant Nos. 202102080258 and 201903010013.

Institutional Review Board Statement: Not applicable.

Informed Consent Statement: Not applicable.

Data Availability Statement: Not applicable.

Conflicts of Interest: The authors declare no conflict of interest.

References

1. Tang, D.; Qin, B.; Feng, X.; Liu, T. Effective LSTMs for target-dependent sentiment classification. *arXiv* **2015**, arXiv:1512.01100.
2. Ma, D.; Li, S.; Zhang, X.; Wang, H. Interactive attention networks for aspect-level sentiment classification. *arXiv* **2017**, arXiv:1709.00893.
3. Chen, P.; Sun, Z.; Bing, L.; Yang, W. Recurrent attention network on memory for aspect sentiment analysis. In Proceedings of the 2017 Conference on Empirical Methods in Natural Language Processing, Copenhagen, Denmark, 7–11 September 2017; pp. 452–461.
4. Xu, G.; Zhang, Z.; Zhang, T.; Yu, S.; Meng, Y.; Chen, S. Aspect-level sentiment classification based on attention-BiLSTM model and transfer learning. *Knowl.-Based Syst.* **2022**, *245*, 108586. [CrossRef]
5. Kipf, T.N.; Welling, M. Semi-supervised classification with graph convolutional networks. *arXiv* **2016**, arXiv:1609.02907.
6. Zhang, C.; Li, Q.; Song, D. Aspect-based sentiment classification with aspect-specific graph convolutional networks. *arXiv* **2019**, arXiv:1909.03477.
7. Xu, K.; Zhao, H.; Liu, T. Aspect-specific heterogeneous graph convolutional network for aspect-based sentiment classification. *IEEE Access* **2020**, *8*, 139346–139355. [CrossRef]
8. Li, R.; Chen, H.; Feng, F.; Ma, Z.; Wang, X.; Hovy, E. Dual graph convolutional networks for aspect-based sentiment analysis. In Proceedings of the 59th Annual Meeting of the Association for Computational Linguistics and the 11th International Joint Conference on Natural Language Processing (Volume 1: Long Papers), Bangkok, Thailand, 1–6 August 2021; pp. 6319–6329.
9. Pang, S.; Xue, Y.; Yan, Z.; Huang, W.; Feng, J. Dynamic and multi-channel graph convolutional networks for aspect-based sentiment analysis. In Proceedings of the Findings of the Association for Computational Linguistics: ACL-IJCNLP 2021, Online, 1–6 August 2021; pp. 2627–2636.
10. Wang, T.; Isola, P. Understanding contrastive representation learning through alignment and uniformity on the hypersphere. In Proceedings of the International Conference on Machine Learning. PMLR, Virtual, 13–18 July 2020; pp. 9929–9939.
11. Chen, Q.; Zhang, R.; Zheng, Y.; Mao, Y. Dual Contrastive Learning: Text Classification via Label-Aware Data Augmentation. *arXiv* **2022**, arXiv:2201.08702.
12. Wang, K.; Shen, W.; Yang, Y.; Quan, X.; Wang, R. Relational graph attention network for aspect-based sentiment analysis. *arXiv* **2020**, arXiv:2004.12362.
13. Hu, J.; Li, Z.; Chen, Z.; Li, Z.; Wan, X.; Chang, T.H. Graph Enhanced Contrastive Learning for Radiology Findings Summarization. *arXiv* **2022**, arXiv:2204.00203.
14. Karamibekr, M.; Ghorbani, A.A. Sentiment analysis of social issues. In Proceedings of the 2012 international conference on social informatics, Alexandria, VA, USA, 14–16 December 2012; IEEE: Piscataway, NJ, USA, 2012; pp. 215–221.
15. Pylkkänen, L. The neural basis of combinatory syntax and semantics. *Science* **2019**, *366*, 62–66. [CrossRef]
16. Shahi, T.; Sitaula, C.; Paudel, N. A Hybrid Feature Extraction Method for Nepali COVID-19-Related Tweets Classification. *Comput. Intell. Neurosci.* **2022**, *2022*, 5681574. [PubMed]
17. Sitaula, C.; Basnet, A.; Mainali, A.; Shahi, T.B. Deep learning-based methods for sentiment analysis on Nepali covid-19-related tweets. *Comput. Intell. Neurosci.* **2021**, *2021*, 2158184. [CrossRef] [PubMed]
18. Gou, J.; Yu, B.; Maybank, S.J.; Tao, D. Knowledge distillation: A survey. *Int. J. Comput. Vis.* **2021**, *129*, 1789–1819. [CrossRef]
19. Yang, M.; Jiang, Q.; Shen, Y.; Wu, Q.; Zhao, Z.; Zhou, W. Hierarchical human-like strategy for aspect-level sentiment classification with sentiment linguistic knowledge and reinforcement learning. *Neural Netw.* **2019**, *117*, 240–248. [CrossRef]
20. Tian, Y.; Chen, G.; Song, Y. Aspect-based sentiment analysis with type-aware graph convolutional networks and layer ensemble. In Proceedings of the 2021 Conference of the North American Chapter of the Association for Computational Linguistics: Human Language Technologies, Online, 6–11 June 2021; pp. 2910–2922.
21. Yan, Z.; Pang, S.; Xue, Y. Semantic Enhanced Dual-Channel Graph Communication Network for Aspect-Based Sentiment Analysis. In Proceedings of the CCF International Conference on Natural Language Processing and Chinese Computing, Guilin, China, 24–25 September 2021; Springer: Berlin/Heidelberg, Germany, 2021; pp. 531–543.

22. Gao, T.; Yao, X.; Chen, D. Simcse: Simple contrastive learning of sentence embeddings. *arXiv* **2021**, arXiv:2104.08821.
23. Xu, P.; Chen, X.; Ma, X.; Huang, Z.; Xiang, B. Contrastive Document Representation Learning with Graph Attention Networks. *arXiv* **2021**, arXiv:2110.10778.
24. Li, Z.; Xu, B.; Zhu, C.; Zhao, T. CLMLF: A Contrastive Learning and Multi-Layer Fusion Method for Multimodal Sentiment Detection. *arXiv* **2022**, arXiv:2204.05515.
25. Liang, B.; Luo, W.; Li, X.; Gui, L.; Yang, M.; Yu, X.; Xu, R. Enhancing aspect-based sentiment analysis with supervised contrastive learning. In Proceedings of the 30th ACM International Conference on Information & Knowledge Management, Online, 1–5 November 2021; pp. 3242–3247.
26. Pennington, J.; Socher, R.; Manning, C. GloVe: Global Vectors for Word Representation. In Proceedings of the 2014 Conference on Empirical Methods in Natural Language Processing (EMNLP), Doha, Qatar, 25–29 October 2014; Association for Computational Linguistics: Doha, Qatar, 2014; pp. 1532–1543. [CrossRef]
27. Devlin, J.; Chang, M.W.; Lee, K.; Toutanova, K. Bert: Pre-training of deep bidirectional transformers for language understanding. *arXiv* **2018**, arXiv:1810.04805.
28. Pontiki, M.; Galanis, D.; Pavlopoulos, J.; Papageorgiou, H.; Androutsopoulos, I.; Manandhar, S. SemEval-2014 Task 4: Aspect Based Sentiment Analysis. In Proceedings of the 8th International Workshop on Semantic Evaluation (SemEval 2014), Dublin, Ireland, 23–24 August 2014; Association for Computational Linguistics: Dublin, Ireland, 2014; pp. 27–35. [CrossRef]
29. Dong, L.; Wei, F.; Tan, C.; Tang, D.; Zhou, M.; Xu, K. Adaptive Recursive Neural Network for Target-dependent Twitter Sentiment Classification. In Proceedings of the 52nd Annual Meeting of the Association for Computational Linguistics (Volume 2: Short Papers), Baltimore, MD, USA, 22–27 June 2014; Association for Computational Linguistics: Baltimore, MD, USA, 2014; pp. 49–54. [CrossRef]
30. Sun, K.; Zhang, R.; Mensah, S.; Mao, Y.; Liu, X. Aspect-level sentiment analysis via convolution over dependency tree. In Proceedings of the 2019 Conference on Empirical Methods in Natural Language Processing and the 9th International Joint Conference on Natural Language Processing (EMNLP-IJCNLP), Hong Kong, China, 3–7 November 2019; pp. 5679–5688.
31. Zhang, M.; Qian, T. Convolution over hierarchical syntactic and lexical graphs for aspect level sentiment analysis. In Proceedings of the 2020 Conference on Empirical Methods in Natural Language Processing (EMNLP), Punta Cana, Dominican Republic, 8–12 November 2020; pp. 3540–3549.
32. Xiao, Z.; Wu, J.; Chen, Q.; Deng, C. BERT4GCN: Using BERT Intermediate Layers to Augment GCN for Aspect-based Sentiment Classification. *arXiv* **2021**, arXiv:2110.00171.
33. Zhang, K.; Zhang, K.; Zhang, M.; Zhao, H.; Liu, Q.; Wu, W.; Chen, E. Incorporating Dynamic Semantics into Pre-Trained Language Model for Aspect-based Sentiment Analysis. *arXiv* **2022**, arXiv:2203.16369.
34. Van der Maaten, L.; Hinton, G. Visualizing data using t-SNE. *J. Mach. Learn. Res.* **2008**, *9*, 2579–2605.

mathematics

MDPI

Article

Knowledge-Enhanced Dual-Channel GCN for Aspect-Based Sentiment Analysis

Zhengxuan Zhang [1], Zhihao Ma [2], Shaohua Cai [3,*], Jiehai Chen [1] and Yun Xue [1]

[1] School of Electronics and Information Engineering, South China Normal University, Foshan 528225, China
[2] Wechat Open Platform Department, Tencent, Guangzhou 510220, China
[3] Center for Faculty Development, South China Normal University, Guangzhou 510631, China
* Correspondence: caishaohua@m.scnu.edu.cn

Abstract: As a subtask of sentiment analysis, aspect-based sentiment analysis (ABSA) refers to identifying the sentiment polarity of the given aspect. The state-of-the-art ABSA models are developed by using the graph neural networks to deal with the semantics and the syntax of the sentence. These methods are challenged by two issues. For one thing, the semantic-based graph convolution networks fail to capture the relation between aspect and its opinion word. For another, minor attention is assigned to the aspect word within graph convolution, resulting in the introduction of contextual noise. In this work, we propose a knowledge-enhanced dual-channel graph convolutional network. On the task of ABSA, a semantic-based graph convolutional netwok (GCN) and a syntactic-based GCN are established. With respect to semantic learning, the sentence semantics are enhanced by using commonsense knowledge. The multi-head attention mechanism is taken to construct the semantic graph and filter the noise, which facilitates the information aggregation of the aspect and the opinion words. For syntactic information processing, the syntax dependency tree is pruned to remove the irrelevant words, based on which more attention weights are given to the aspect words. Experiments are carried out on four benchmark datasets to evaluate the working performance of the proposed model. Our model significantly outperforms the baseline models and verifies its effectiveness in ABSA tasks.

Keywords: aspect-based sentiment analysis; graph convolutional networks; commonsense knowledge graph

MSC: 18C50

Citation: Zhang, Z.; Ma, Z.; Cai, S.; Chen, J.; Xue, Y. Knowledge-Enhanced Dual-Channel GCN for Aspect-Based Sentiment Analysis. *Mathematics* **2022**, *10*, 4273. https://doi.org/10.3390/math10224273

Academic Editors: Jianping Gou, Weihua Ou, Shaoning Zeng and Lan Du

Received: 13 October 2022
Accepted: 11 November 2022
Published: 15 November 2022

1. Introduction

Aspect-based sentiment analysis (ABSA) is a sentiment classification task that aims to identify the sentiment of given aspects [1]. Within ABSA, the sentiment of each aspect is classified according to a predefined set of sentiment polarities, i.e., positive, neutral or negative [2]. In recent years, ABSA yields very fine-grained sentiment information, which is useful for applications in a variety of domains [3].

In the context of advancing deep neural networks, state-of-the-art ABSA methods report high accuracy and strong robustness on benchmark datasets. During the progressing stage in ABSA tasks, efforts are generally made in two directions: one is to enhance significant information from the given text and the other is to filter the irrelevant information and its impact. A major step toward the comprehension of semantic information is the integration of attention mechanism with deep neural networks [4–6]. More attentive weights are assigned to aspect-related words, based on which to classify the sentiment polarity. Nevertheless, it can be challenging to capture syntax dependencies between the aspect and its contexts for attention-based models. More recently, research on graph neural networks (GNNs) has given rise to dealing with the syntactic information from dependency trees, a manner in which to prevent the syntactically irrelevant contextual noise [7–9]. The widespread GNNs, such as graph convolutional networks (GCNs) and graph attention networks (GATs), are capable of encoding both the semantics and the syntax. This has been an ongoing trend to incorporate syntactic information and semantic information into GNN-based models [10–12].

In spite of the collaborative exploiting of syntax and semantics, two main limitations can be observed :

(1) For one thing, GNNs are generally used for tackling global syntactic information, while the mask operation is lastly performed to conceal the context words. Thereby, the sentiment of the aspect is determined. In practical application, the contextual noise can be introduced, which results in minor importance given to the aspect words.

(2) For another, the semantic-based GNNs are typically built up based on attention weights. With respect to the delicate relationship between aspects and opinion words, more attention is assigned to other words instead of the sentiment words. This can further confuse the sentiment aggregation. As presented in Figure 1, in the sentence *'Meal is very expensive for what you get'*, the aspect *'meal'* and its opinion word *'expensive'* are semantically insensitive.

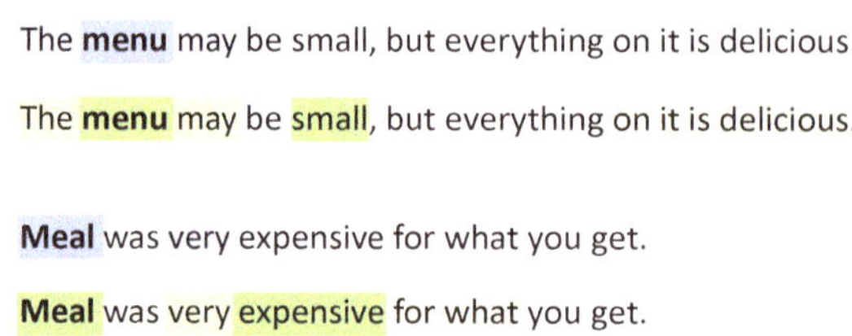

Figure 1. Attention weights towards aspects. Words in black bold are aspects; words with a blue background are predicted attention weights; words with a green background represent desirable attention distribution. A word in the darker color indicates a greater weight and vice versa.

On the task of ABSA, this work focuses on establishing a Knowledge-Enhanced Dual-Channel Graph Convolutional Network (KDGCN). Two GCN-based modules, referred to as syntax-based GCN and semantic-based GCN, are developed to separately deal with the syntax structure and the semantic information. On the one hand, the syntactical dependency tree of the sentence is pruned to remove the connections of minor relevance to the aspect. Hence, the aspect-oriented syntactic information is sent to the syntax-based GCN. Besides, the position information and the attention mechanisms are taken to highlight the importance of the aspect. On the other hand, the external knowledge is introduced to enhance the semantic-based GCN. The word sentiment vectors, together with the supplementary of the aspect, are obtained (derived) by using SenticNet (i.e., a commonsense knowledge base); see Figure 2. A multi-headed attention mechanism is carried out to re-assign the attentive weights among words. The sentiment of the opinion words can thus be aggregated to the aspect via the knowledge-enhanced semantic-based GCN.

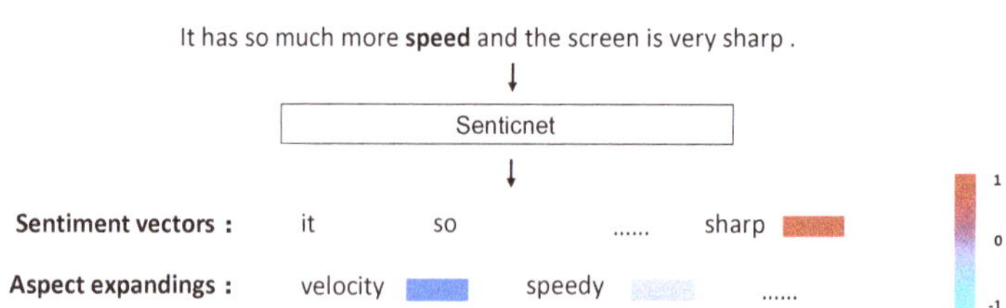

Figure 2. Sentiment vectors and aspect supplementary based on SenticNet. The different colors and shades represent the emotional polarity score of the word in SenticNet, where −1 is negative and 1 is positive.

Notably, a certain number of studies leverage the commonsense knowledge to enhance the sentiment expression and classify the sentiment polarity of the aspect [13,14]. Theoretically, the commonsense knowledge is involved with the background materials of the entities under discussion. The commonsense knowledge is preserved in the commonsense bases, such as ConceptNet [15], SenticNet [16] and WordNet [17], and recalled for processing. In most cases, the integration of semantic-related commonsense knowledge can generate noise from external information. Our model aims to exploit the sentence-related external knowledge, not just the sentiment information of each word, but also the relative knowledge of the aspect. In such a manner, the input of semantic-based GCN is distilled. Accordingly, the more-related information is preserved with the noise removed. The contributions of this paper are threefold and summarized as follows:

- Considering the deficiencies of the current ABSA methods, a dual-channel GCN based model is proposed, which processes both the syntax structure and the semantic information.
- The external knowledge is incorporated to enhance the semantics of the sentence, while the multi-head attention mechanism is taken to further filter the noise.
- Experiments on a variety of datasets indicate the effectiveness of the proposed method. Our model produces results considerably better than the baselines.

The paper is mainly divided into six sections. In the Introduction, we summarize the content of the article in general and propose our solutions for the challenge of the current ABSA task; in the Section 2, we will summarize the research related to our work; in the Section 3, we will introduce our proposed model and each module in detail; in the Section 4, we will conduct experiments on four public datasets and design ablation experiments; in the Section 5, we will further analyze the general situation of the model and the experimental results; in the Section 6, we summarize the full text.

2. Related Work

2.1. Aspect-Based Sentiment Analysis

As pointed out in the introduction, ABSA is a fine-grained sentiment classification task. Rather than assigning an overall sentiment polarity to a sentence or a document, ABSA aims at precisely determining the sentiment of a certain aspect. Early methods usually rely on manual features when predicting, which cannnot model the dependency relationship between the aspect and its context [18–20].

In recent years, advances in deep-learning algorithms significantly improved the working performance of ABSA, while a more detailed analysis of the textual information has risen [21,22]. The integrating of an attention mechanism into deep neural networks highlights the contribution of opinion words towards the aspects. [4–6,23–25] The relationship between aspect and its opinion words are reliably modeled in attention-based networks. Wang et al. [4] proposed an attention-long short-term memory (LSTM) method to obtain more related information about a given aspect. Chen et al. [5] devised a hierarchical multi-attention model to address the long-range dependency between aspect and the opinion words. Whereas the attention mechanisms fails to cope with sentence syntax, by contrast, the employment of GCN takes advantages of the syntactic dependencies of the aspect and the opinion words. To be specific, an adjacency matrix is formed based on the syntactic dependent tree, which is further modeled to aggregate the sentiment information to the aspect by GCN [7,8]. Wang et al. [9] eliminated the noise from irrelevant contexts by constructing an aspect-oriented syntactic dependency tree, and then encoded the syntax relation by GNN. More recently, modules of multi-channel-GCNs have been carried out to resolve the syntax and semantics of the given sentence, which effectively optimizes the results of ABSA.

2.2. *Graph Convolutional Networks*

As a classical variant of GNN, GCN was originally proposed by Kipf et al. [26] in 2017. So far, GCN has shown its superiority in diversified NLP tasks, such as text classification [27,28], relation extraction [29,30], knowledge distillation [31] and machine translation [32].

Most studies [7,8] take GCNs to capture the syntactic information of a sentence where the nodes represent the words and the edges indicate the dependencies, which can induce representation vectors of nodes based on their neighborhoods' features. Likewise, the semantic relation within the sentence can also be obtained using GCN. In [10,11], the semantic graph was constructed with edges standing for the attention weights. Therefore, both semantic features and syntactic features can be extracted via GCN-based modules.

Considering a graph as structured data, the multilayers of GCN are responsible for information delivery. As such, every single node within the graph can learn the global information. Let $G = (V, E)$, where $V = \{v_i, v_2, \ldots, v_n\}$ is a set of $N = |V|$ nodes and E is the set of edges, and it represents an $n-$node graph with an adjacency matrix of $A \in \mathbb{R}^{k \times k}$. In a graph, let $v_i \in V$ to denote a node and $e_{ij} = (v_i, v_j) \in E$ to denote an edge between v_i and v_j.

GCN can only capture information about neighbors with a layer. However, information about more neighborhoods can be integrated when multilayers of GCN are stacked. We define h_i^l as the output of node i on the $l-th$ layer and h_i^0 as the initial state of node i. The graph convolution of node i can be written as:

$$h_i^l = \sigma(\sum_{j=1}^{k} A_{ij} W^l h_j^{l-1} + b^l) \tag{1}$$

where W^l is the weight of linear transformation, b^l is the bias and σ is a nonlinear function such as $Relu$.

2.3. *Commonsense Knowledge*

The commonsense knowledge for NLP is typically obtained through large-scale corpus training and saved in commonsense bases. The commonsense is taken as prior knowledge for the pre-training of knowledge-enhanced approaches. SenticNet [16] is one such commonsense knowledge base, which contains 100*k* concepts related to sentiment expression. (e.g., mood, polarity, semantics and so on). Additionally, these affective properties provide concept-level representation and semantic connections to the words.

To facilitate access to corresponding knowledge, SenticNet provides an application programming interface. A series of sentiment scores of the word and its related concepts can be obtained from the interface (as shown in Figure 2), which can expand the semantics of the sentence.

The application of SenticNet into ABSA shows its distinctiveness in sentiment representation learning [13,33]. Ma et al. [13] utilized the commonsense from SenticNet to generate essays more closely surrounding the semantics of the input topics. Zhou et al. [14] enlarged the sentence semantics using SenticNet 5, and then jointly modeled the syntactic dependency trees and commonsense graph. Regardless of additional key information, the filter of the noise during the external knowledge introducing remains unsettled.

3. Methodology

The architecture of KDGCN is presented in Figure 3. Our model consists of five key components, i.e., a sentence encoder, a knowledge enhancement module, a semantic learning module, a syntax aware module and a sentiment classifier. Firstly, each word of the sentence is encoded as a vector by the sentence encoder. At the same time, the sentence is input into the knowledge enhancement module, and the sentiment vector of each word and the expanding words of aspect are obtained from SenticNet; secondly, the hidden state vector of the sentence is sent into a semantic learning module and a syntax aware module, respectively, to obtain the syntactic and semantic representation. Finally, we can obtain the sentiment polarity of the aspect from the sentiment classifier.

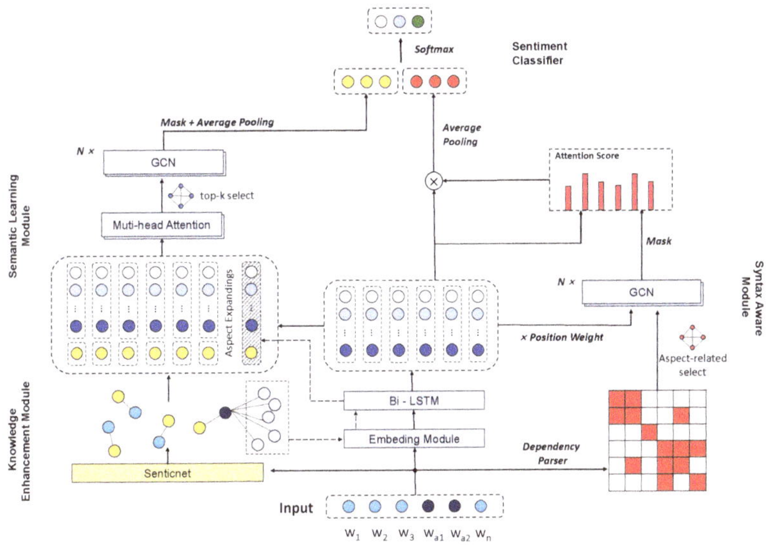

Figure 3. Overall architecture of the proposed Knowledge-Enhanced Dual-Channel Graph Convolutional Network.

3.1. Sentence Encoder

Glove embedding. For a sentence $c = \{w_1, w_2, \ldots, w_n\}$ with the aspects $a = \{w_{a1}, w_{a2}, \ldots, w_{an}\}$, we take the pre-trained embedding matrix $E \in \mathbb{R}^{|V| \times d_e}$ to map each word into a low-dimensional vector, where $|V|$ represents the lexicon size and d_e is the dimension of the word vector [34].

BERT embedding. BERT [35] is a commonly used sentence encoder in recent years. Each sentence is pre-processed by adding *[CLS]* at the beginning and *[SEP]* at the end, respectively, to obtain $c' = \{w_0, w_1, \ldots, w_{n+1}\}$, where w_0 and w_{n+1} denote the two special tokens inserted. Then, c' is fed into BERT to obtain the textual feature representation $X = \{x_0, x_1, \ldots, x_{n+1}\}$, where $x_i \in \mathbb{R}^{d_{bert}}$.

A Bidirectional LSTM (Bi-LSTM) is employed for sentence encoding. The given sentence embedding is sent to Bi-LSTM to generate the hidden state vector $H^{LSTM} = \{h_1, h_2, \ldots, h_n\}$. Specifically, the vector $H^{LSTM} \in \mathbb{R}^{2d_h}$ is the hidden state at a time step and is the hidden state vector dimension of LSTM.

3.2. Knowledge Enhancement Module

Word sentiment enhancement: For the given sentence c, the sentiment vector of each word can be obtained based on the commonsense from SenticNet. A 23-dimensional sentiment vector $H^{LSTM} \in \mathbb{R}^{23}$ hat represents the sentence that is derived. Besides, for the words that do not appear in SenticNet, the zero-vector is used instead. Then, H^{LSTM} and H^{sen} are fused to obtain the sentence representation, which is:

$$H^c = [H^{LSTM}; H^{sen}] \tag{2}$$

with $H^c \in \mathbb{R}^{2d_h+23}$.

Aspect knowledge enhancement: In terms of the aspects a, the relative words of each word within a is collected from SenticNet, i.e., $\{w_{ex1}, w_{ex2}, \ldots, w_{exn}\}$. For the purpose of word supplementary, the first five words in relation to the aspect are used. All the relative words are also mapped to word embeddings and encoded with the Bi-LSTM encoder.

$$H^{ex} = [H_{ex}^{LSTM}; H_{ex}^{sen}] \tag{3}$$

where H_{ex}^{LSTM} stands for the hidden state vector of Bi-LSTM, and H_{ex}^{sen} is the corresponding sentiment vector. The aspect expanding vector is denoted as $H^{ex} \in \mathbb{R}^{2d_h+23}$.

Notably, since the word co-occurrence in the corpus has an impact on the word embedding of glove, to prevent the noise fusion, the aspect relative words are not pre-trained by glove. We take a $\langle unk \rangle$ for relative words that are absent from the given texts. Similarly, the absent-words of SenticNet are taken in place of zero.

3.3. Semantic Learning Module

Motivated by [10], most short sentences are of confused syntactic structure. That is, the rigid extraction of syntactic information can lead to the misinterpretation of the sentiment information. For this reason, a semantic learning module based on GCN is proposed to capture the semantic information among words. Both the enhanced sentiment vector and the aspect expanding vector are sent to the semantic learning module, which aims to further enrich the semantic information.

Node construction: Each word w_i from the sentence, together with each aspect relative word w_{exi}, is taken as a node. All nodes constitute a node set V.

Edge construction: The edge indicates the relationship between word nodes. Concretely, two semantic-related nodes are connected with an edge and vice versa. To capture the semantic relation of each word, we employ $K - heads$ multi-head self-attention mechanism to compute the attention weight, i.e.,

$$A_{ttn} = \frac{(H_{se}W_{se,k})(H_{se}W_{se,q})^T}{\sqrt{d_{head}}} \tag{4}$$

where

$$H_{se}^{(0)} = H^c \tag{5}$$

$$d_{head} = \frac{d_{lstm}}{k} \tag{6}$$

where $H_{se}^{(0)} \in \mathbb{R}^{2d_h+23}$ is the commonsense-enhanced hidden layer output; K is the head number of multi-head attention mechanism; $W_{se,k}$ and $W_{se,q} \in \mathbb{R}^{(2d_h+23)\times d_{head}}$ are trainable matrices. Subsequently, based on the top-k selecting approach, the largest k values of each dimension are selected and set to 1, while others are set to 0. Hence, the adjacency matrix A_{se} is obtained; see Equation (7). Corresponding to the edge construction principle, the adjacency matrix with value 1 denotes the semantic relevance between nodes. Notably, the A_{se} remains symmetric with the application of the top-k selector.

$$A_{se} = topk \sum_{i=0}^{k} A_{ttn} \tag{7}$$

Thereby, a graph $G_{sem} = (A_{se}, H^c)$ that concerns the node representations and the adjacency matrix is constructed. The graph is fed into the N-layer GCN to obtain the hidden layer state H_{se} :

$$H_{se}^{(l+1)} = GCN(A_{se}, H_{se}^{(l)}, W_{se}^{(l)}) \tag{8}$$

where $H_{se}^{(l)} \in \mathbb{R}^{(2d_h+23)\times d_{gcn}}$ stands for the parametric matrix of GCN. The mask operation is conducted on non-aspect words, following with the average pooling to compute semantic hidden layer output h_{se}, which is written as:

$$mask = \begin{cases} 0 & 1 \leq t < \tau+1, \tau+m < t < n \\ 1 & \tau+1 \leq t \leq \tau+m \end{cases} \tag{9}$$

$$h_{se} = f(mask(H_{se})) \tag{10}$$

where $\tau + 1 \leq t \leq \tau + m$ indicates the aspect index and $f(\cdot)$ is the average pooling function.

3.4. Syntax Aware Module

The syntax aware module is devised by modifying the method proposed by Zhang et al. [7]. The sentence syntax is characterized by the syntax dependency tree. Note that not all context words are syntactically related to the aspect—an aspect-related selection approach is taken to reshape the syntax dependency tree. Only if a context word reaches the aspect within n hops can the dependency edge between nodes be kept. We can thus revise the adjacency matrix A_0 to A_{sy}. In this way, the revised graph is written as $G_{sy} = (A_{sy}, H^{LSTM})$, where H^{LSTM} is the current node representation. Before sending G_{sy} to GCN, the position-aware transformation is performed [7]:

$$q_i = \begin{cases} 1 - \frac{\tau+1-i}{n} & 1 \leq i \leq i+1 \\ 0 & \tau+1 \leq i \leq \tau+m \\ 1 - \frac{\tau+1-i}{n} & \tau+m < i \leq n \end{cases} \tag{11}$$

with

$$\mathcal{F}(h_i) = q_i h_i \tag{12}$$

where $q_i \in \mathbb{R}$ the position weight of the i-th token and $\mathcal{F}(\cdot)$ is the function for position weight assignment. The syntactic information is learned by using graph convolution. The syntactic hidden layer output is expressed as:

$$H_{sy}^{(l)} = \mathcal{F}(H_{sy}^{(l-1)}) \tag{13}$$

$$H_{sy}^{(l+1)} = GCN(A_{sy}, H_{sy}^{(l)}, W_{sy}^{(l)}) \tag{14}$$

$$H_{sy}^{(0)} = \mathcal{F}(H^{LSTM}) \tag{15}$$

where $H^{(l)} \in \mathbb{R}^{2d_h \times d_{gcn}}$ is a trainable parametric matrix. Similar to the semantic-based GCN, the syntactic hidden state representation W_{sy} is revised via masking (Equation (16)). The

$$H^t = mask(H_{sy}) \tag{16}$$

where $H^t = \{h_1^t, h_2^t, \ldots, h_j^t\}$. The outcome hidden layer state from Equation (16) concentrates more on the aspect words. In addition, to further detect the significant semantic feature concealed within the syntax structure, the attention weight of each context word is assigned. The dot product of h_i^t and h_i are obtained to denote the syntactic representation, i.e.,

$$h_{sy} = \sum_{j=1}^{n} a_j h_j^t \tag{17}$$

$$a_j = \frac{exp(\beta_j)}{\sum_{i=1}^{n} exp(\beta_j)} \tag{18}$$

$$\beta_t = \sum_{i=1}^{n} h_j^t h_i = \sum_{i=\tau+1}^{\tau+m} h_j^t h_i \tag{19}$$

3.5. Sentiment Classifier

Both the semantic representation and the syntactic representation are so far computed. We shall thus concatenate h_se and h_sy to obtain the final representation h_a (Equation (20)). The sentiment polarity of the given aspect is classified by sending h_a to the Softmax classifier, which is:

$$H_a = [H_{se}; H_{sy}] \tag{20}$$

$$y = softmax(h_a) \tag{21}$$

3.6. Model Training

The training process is performed by using the categorical cross entropy and L_2 regularization as the loss function:

$$Loss = -\sum_i \sum_j y_i^j log(p_i^j) \tag{22}$$

where i is the index of the ABSA sample and j is the corresponding sentiment polarity.

4. Experiment

In this section, we designed the main experiment and attention visualization to verify the effectiveness of our model on the ABSA task. Specifically, we first introduce the benchmark datasets used in our experiment, and then briefly introduce the details of the experiment and the selected baseline. Then, we carried out the main experiment and analyzed the experimental results. In addition, in order to explore the contribution of each module to the model, we designed ablation experiments and analyzed the mechanism of knowledge enhancement in attention visualization.

4.1. Dataset

To verify the working performance of the proposed model, experiments were carried out on four publicly available benchmark datasets, i.e., Rest14 and Lap14 from SemEval 2014 [36], Rest15 from SemEval 2015 [37] and Rest16 from SemEval 2016 [1], containing reviews of restaurant and laptop domains.

Every single sentence from the datasets contains at least one aspect. The sentiment polarity of each aspect is given as well, including: positive, negative and neutral. For example, in the sentence *"Great food but the service was dreamful!"*, there are two aspect terms, *'food'* and *'service'*, and their sentiment polarity are positive and negative, respectively. The details of each dataset are presented in Table 1.

Table 1. Statistics of datasets.

Dataset	Positive		Neutral		Negative	
	Train	**Test**	**Train**	**Test**	**Train**	**Test**
Rest14	2164	728	637	196	807	196
Lap14	994	341	464	169	870	128
Rest15	1178	439	1c50	35	382	328
Rest16	1620	597	88	38	709	190

4.2. Implementation Details

The best test result of each method was taken for evaluation. For the proposed model, the initialization of word embeddings was conducted using Glove [38] and uncased BERT [35], respectively. The pretrained Glove provides a 300-dimensional word vector, with a learning rate of 0.001 and a batch size of 64. Moreover, the dimension of Bert-based word embeddings was 768, with a learning rate of 0.00002 and a batch size of 32. The head number of multi-head attention network was set to 1. The value of top-k selection was 2. Besides, the Adam optimizer was employed. The L_2 regularization weight was 0.0001. The value of dropout was determined within the interval of [0.4, 0.6] using grid searching. With respect to the GCN in our model, the number of layers and the dimension of hidden layers ranged within [1,4] and [100, 200], respectively, which were also selected via grid searching.

4.3. Baseline

For the purpose of validating the effectiveness of our model, twelve state-of-the-art methods were taken for comparison, which are presented as follows:

- **CDT** [8]: GCN is taken to deal with the syntax dependency tree, which aims to learn the sentence syntactic information. Specifically, it exploits a GCN to model the structure of a sentence through its dependency tree, where node (word) embeddings of the tree are initialized by means of a Bi-LSTM network.
- **ASGCN** [7]: On the task of ABSA, GCN is applied to learn the aspect-specific representation for the first time. Specifically, it starts with a LSTM layer to encode the sentence, and a multi-layered graph convolution structure is implemented on top of the LSTM output to obtain aspect-specific features.
- **SK-GCN** [14]: A syntax-based GCN and a knowledge-based GCN are designed to model the syntax dependency tree and knowledge graph, respectively. Specifically, it obtains the sentiment information from the SenticNet to enrich the representation of a sentence toward a given aspect.
- **R-GAT** [4]: It reshapes and prunes an ordinary dependency parse tree to obtain an aspect-oriented dependency tree structure rooted at a target aspect. Then, a relational graph attention network (R-GAT) is introduced to encode the new tree structure for sentiment prediction.
- **DualGCN** [5]: Considering the complementarity of syntax structures and semantic correlations, a dual graph convolutional network is proposed to tackle both the syntactic information and semantic information.
- **DMGCN** [11]: A multi-channel GCN-based method is developed to exploit not only the syntax and the semantics, but also the correlated information from the generated graph.
- **BERT** [35]: The basic BERT model is established based on a bidirectional transformer. With the concatenation of sentence and the corresponding aspect, BERT can be applied to ABSA.
- **SK-GCN+BERT** [14], **R-GAT+BERT** [9],**DualGCN+BERT** [10], **DMGCN+BERT** [11] : The pre-trained BERT is integrated with SK-GCN, R-GAT, DualGCN and DMGCN, respectively, where BERT is used for sentence encoding.
- **TGCN+BERT** [39]: The dependency type is identified with type-aware graph convolutional networks, while the relation is distinguished with attention mechanism. The pre-trained BERT is used for sentence encoding.

4.4. Experimental Results

Experimental results on all datasets are exhibited in Table 2. In this experiment, we took accuracy and macro-F1 as the method evaluation metrics. Comparing with the baseline models, **KDGCN** generally obtained the best and most consistent results in all evaluation settings. However, our model with the Bert encoder was less competitive than **DMGCN+BERT** on the dataset of Rest14. A possible explanation is that the pre-trained Bert contains a wealth of semantic information. The semantic enhancement via SenticNet is not that distinctive. With respect to the Glove-based word embeddings, the performance of **KDGCN** was 0.93% and 2.89% higher than **DMGCN** in accuracy and Macro-F1, respectively.

Comprehensively, current GCN-based models focus on encoding either the syntactic information (e.g., **ASGCN**, **CDT**, **R-GAT** and **TGCN+BERT**) or the semantic-integrated syntactic information (e.g., **DualGCN** and **DMGCN**). The performance of these methods largely depends on their fitting capabilities. By contrast, the proposed model adopted the aspect-related selection approach to prune the edges of the syntax dependency tree, based on which the unrelated information to the aspect was eliminated. On the other hand, the commonsense knowledge was introduced to enhance the semantic information and the sentiment of the aspect. In this way, the results of ABSA can be improved.

Furthermore, **SK-GCN** also uses the external knowledge derived from SenticNet to construct the syntax-based GCN and semantic-based GCN. In comparison with **SKGCN**, our model performs significantly better on all datasets. Clearly, **KDGCN** is capable of exploiting the commonsense knowledge in ABSA tasks. As such, it is rational to expect the integration of external knowledge into the given sentence and thus improved sentiment classification results.

Table 2. Experimental results on four public datasets. The results of **R-GAT** and **R-GAT+BERT** are retrieved from [40], and others are retrieved from the original papers.

Models	**Rest14**		**Lap14**		**Rest15**		**Rest16**	
	Accuracy	**Macro-F1**	**Accuracy**	**Macro-F1**	**Accuracy**	**Macro-F1**	**Accuracy**	**Macro-F1**
CDT [8]	74.66	73.66	77.19	72.99	-	-	85.58	69.93
ASGCN [7]	80.77	72.02	75.55	71.05	79.89	61.89	88.99	67.48
SK-GCN [14]	80.36	70.43	73.20	69.18	80.12	60.70	85.17	68.08
R-GAT [9]	83.30	76.08	77.42	73.76	80.83	64.17	88.92	70.89
DualGCN [10]	84.27	78.08	78.48	74.74	-	-	-	-
DMGCN [11]	83.98	75.59	78.48	74.90	-	-	-	-
Our KDGCN	**84.91**	**78.48**	**79.00**	**75.03**	**82.10**	**67.13**	**90.74**	**73.46**
BERT [35]	85.62	78.28	77.58	72.38	83.48	66.18	90.10	74.16
SK-GCN+BERT [14]	83.48	75.19	79.00	75.57	83.20	66.78	87.19	72.02
R-GAT+BERT [9]	86.60	81.35	78.21	74.07	83.22	69.73	89.71	76.62
DualGCN+BERT [10]	87.13	81.16	81.80	78.10	-	-	-	-
DMGCN+BERT [11]	**87.66**	**82.79**	80.22	77.28	-	-	-	-
TGCN+BERT [39]	86.16	79.95	80.88	77.03	85.26	71.69	92.32	77.29
Our KDGCN+BERT	87.23	81.69	**82.60**	**79.55**	**85.98**	**72.40**	**93.66**	**82.49**

4.5. Ablation Study

An ablation study was conducted to quantitively investigate the importance of different modules in the proposed model. The results of the ablation study are given in Table 3 and Figure 4. We took the basic KDGCN as the baseline and ablated the knowledge enhancement module, semantic learning module, syntax aware module and the aspect-related select procedure. According to Table 3, the most important component for the proposed model is the syntax aware module. The accuracy drop on four datasets were 6.78%, 6.12%, 4.61% and 3.08%, which are significant. Obviously, the use of syntactic information plays a pivotal role in ABSA. Moreover, the contributions of the semantic learning module and the knowledge enhancement module are comparable. The integration of commonsense knowledge into the semantic learning process gives an improvement of the sentiment classification performance. Lastly, withdrawal of the aspect-related selection also caused a minor decrease of the working performance.

Table 3. Results of the ablation study.

Model	**Rest14**		**Lap14**		**Rest15**		**Rest16**	
	Accuracy	**Macro-F1**	**Accuracy**	**Macro-F1**	**Accuracy**	**Macro-F1**	**Accuracy**	**Macro-F1**
KDGCN *w/o* aspect-related select	84.11	77.02	76.96	73.14	80.10	66.48	89.61	70.94
KDGCN *w/o* syntax aware module	78.13	68.34	72.88	68.13	77.49	52.19	87.66	66.74
KDGCN *w/o* knowleage enhancement	83.13	76.01	76.49	72.38	81.55	58.71	89.61	72.01
KDGCN *w/o* semantic learning module	83.22	75.35	76.33	73.27	79.89	60.87	89.28	71.96
KDGCN	**84.91**	**78.48**	**79.00**	**75.03**	**82.10**	**67.13**	**90.74**	**73.46**

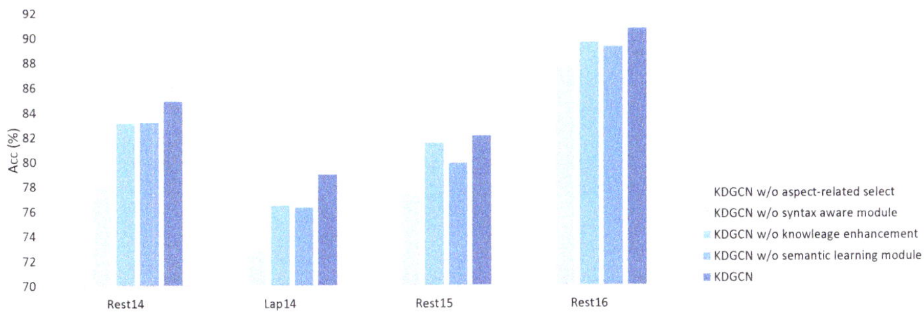

Figure 4. Results of the ablation study. Different columns show the performance of different models on different datasets.

4.6. Attention Visualization

To investigate the effectiveness of the knowledge enhancement, we visualized the attention matrix. In our model, the semantics enhancement is carried out by using the commonsense from SenticNet. The connection between the aspect and its opinion word is established and enhanced. The syntax-based GCN also removes the irrelevant information by encoding the syntax dependency tree. Cases are presented to demonstrate the attention weight distribution. In the first line of Figure 5 , the attentive weights are assigned based on a basic multi-head attention mechanism. One can easily see that the minor attention was given to the opinion word **'excellent'** of the aspect **'food'**. Likewise, the attention weight of **'food'** toward **'excellent'** was also weakened. With the integration of commonsense knowledge, the relationships of both **'food'** and **'excellent'** to the context word **'meal'** were established. That is, the **'food-meal'** edge and the **'excellent-meal'** edge can be constructed by using a top-k selection. As a result, the sentiment information of **'excellent'** can be aggregated on the aspect word **'food'** with the encoding of GCN. Besides, the syntactic-based GCN, which deals with the syntactic relation among words, also facilitates the determination of aspect sentiment polarity.

Similarly, from the two figures in the second line, we can see that the aspect word **'waiter'** established a direct connection with the opinion word **'helpful'** after knowledge enhancement. Additionally, from the two figures in the last line, the aspect word **'sauce'** and the opinion word **'flavorful'** are connected through the path **'sauce-dough-flavorful'** after knowledge enhancement, so that the sentiment polarity of the aspect words can be better predicted after the subsequent network structure.

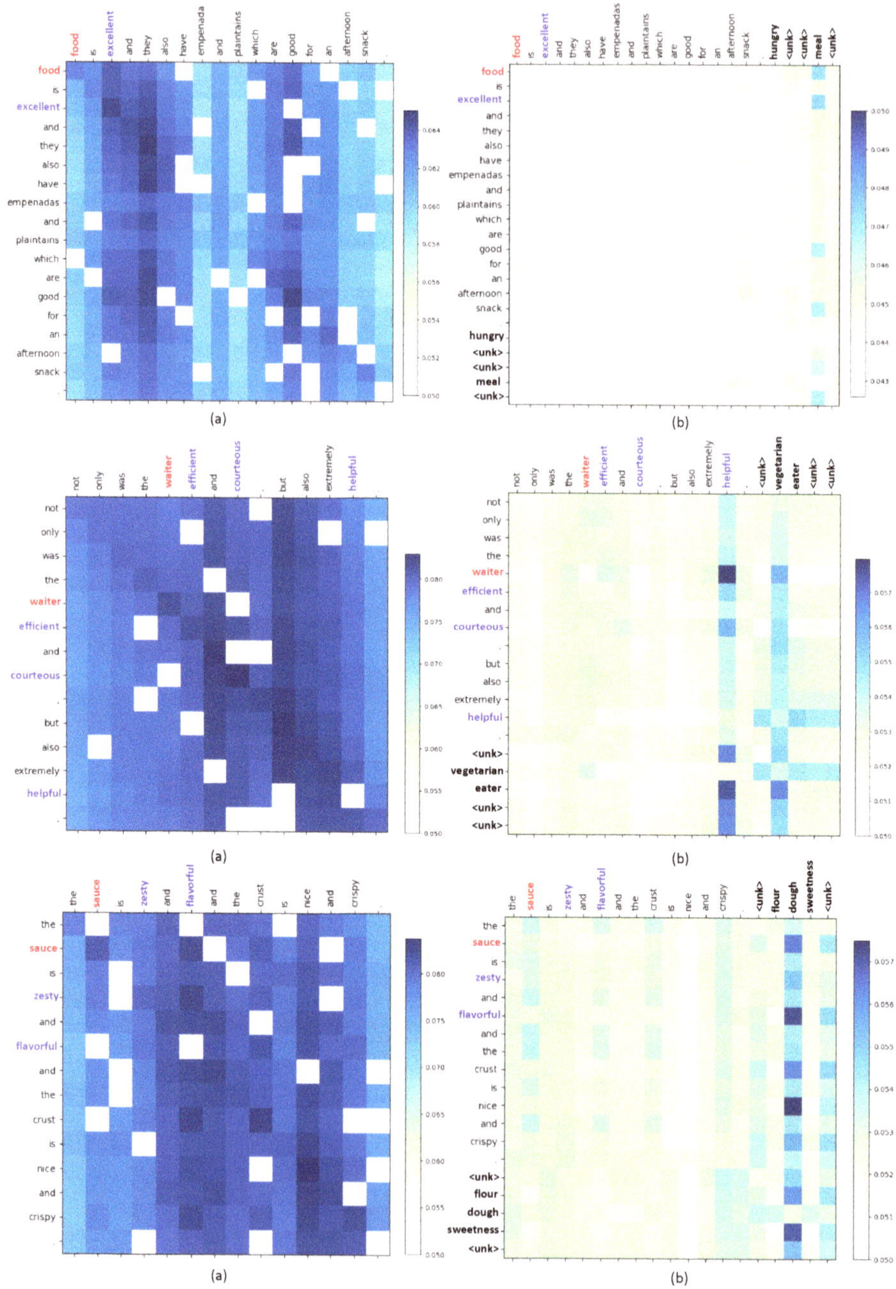

Figure 5. An illustration on knowledge-enhancement. (**a**) Basic attention matrix of the sentence. (**b**) Knowledge-enhanced attention matrix of the sentence. The red words are aspect words, the blue words are opinion words and the black bold words are aspect-expansion words.

5. Discussion

Through a series of experiments, we can see that our KDGCN performs well on the ABSA task. Specifically, in the main experiment part (Section 4.4), the accuracy and F1-score of our model on the four datasets are generally higher than baselines, especially compared with SK-GCN [14], which also uses SenticNet for knowledge enhancement; our improvement was 2–5%. In the ablation study, we removed the semantic learning module, the syntax aware module and so on, which proves that semantics and syntax are both important for ABSA tasks. In addition, after removing the knowledge enhancement module, the model performance also decreased significantly on the four datasets, indicating that our knowledge enhancement facilitates ABSA tasks.

Moreover, we also found the limitations of our model. Take DMGCN [11] and the use of the glove encoder as an example—KDGCN's improvement on Lap14 was not as big as that on rest14 (0.52% and 0.93%, respectively). This may be because most of the Lap14 datasets are proper nouns (such as *Windows 7* and *Microsoft*), and they do not have obvious emotional clues. Different from it, most of the words in Rest14 are daily words, so the sentiment information is rich and can be further enhanced through SenticNet. In order to obtain more semantic information and deeper connections, large-scale knowledge graphs can be introduced into the ABSA task in future work.

6. Conclusions

In this work, we propose a knowledge-enhanced dual-channel graph convolutional network to deal with the ABSA tasks. A semantic-based GCN and a syntactic-based GCN are devised to encode both the sentence semantics and the syntax. On the one hand, the external commonsense knowledge is introduced to enhance the semantics, based on which more attention is assigned to the aspect and its relevant words. On the other hand, the syntactic-based GCN processing on the syntax dependency tree further filters the low-dependency words. We demonstrate the effectiveness of our method on four benchmark datasets, obtaining state-of-the-art results on both accuracy and macro-F1. Comparing with the baseline models, the proposed method is the best alternative that produces results considerably better than the widely-applied approaches in ABSA. In the ablation experiment, we tested the contribution of each module to the model and verified that our innovation is effective. In addition, we also carried out a case analysis to further intuitively demonstrate the role of knowledge enhancement in promoting our task.

However, SenticNet is a small-scale knowledge base with shallow and limited semantics, which limits the performance of the model. Therefore, future work can consider exploring the use of a larger scale knowledge graph (such as Wikipedia) to enhance the knowledge of ABSA tasks, which can provide more clues to predict the sentiment polarity of the aspect.

Author Contributions: Conceptualization, Z.Z. and Y.X.; methodology, Z.Z.; formal analysis, Z.Z. and Z.M.; writing—original draft preparation, Z.Z.; writing—review and editing, S.C., J.C. and Y.X.; supervision, S.C. and Y.X.; funding acquisition, S.C. All authors have read and agreed to the published version of the manuscript.

Funding: This work was supported by the Characteristic Innovation Projects of Guangdong Colleges and Universities (Nos. 2018KTSCX049), the Science and Technology Plan Project of Guangzhou under Grant Nos. 202102080258 and 201903010013.

Institutional Review Board Statement: Not applicable.

Informed Consent Statement: Not applicable.

Data Availability Statement: Not applicable.

Conflicts of Interest: The authors declare no conflict of interest.

References

1. Pontiki, M.; Galanis, D.; Papageorgiou, H.; Androutsopoulos, I.; Manandhar, S.; Al-Smadi, M.; Al-Ayyoub, M.; Zhao, Y.; Qin, B.; De Clercq, O.; et al. Semeval-2016 task 5: Aspect based sentiment analysis. In Proceedings of the 10th International Workshop on Semantic Evaluation, San Diego, CA, USA, 16–17 June 2016.
2. Li, H.; Xue, Y.; Zhao, H.; Hu, X.; Peng, S. Co-attention networks for aspect-level sentiment analysis. In Proceedings of the CCF International Conference on Natural Language Processing and Chinese Computing, Guilin, China, 24–25 September 2019; Springer: Cham, Switzerland, 2019.
3. Schouten, K.; Frasincar, F. Survey on aspect-level sentiment analysis. *IEEE Trans. Knowl. Data Eng.* **2015**, *28*, 813–830. [CrossRef]
4. Wang, Y.; Huang, M.; Zhu, X.; Zhao, L. Attention-based LSTM for aspect-level sentiment classification. In Proceedings of the 2016 Conference on Empirical Methods in Natural Language Processing, Austin, TX, USA, 1–5 November 2016.
5. Chen, P.; Sun, Z.; Bing, L.; Yang, W. Recurrent attention network on memory for aspect sentiment analysis. In Proceedings of the 2017 Conference on Empirical Methods in Natural Language Processing, Copenhagen, Denmark, 9–11 September 2017.
6. Fan, F.; Feng, Y.; Zhao, D. Multi-grained attention network for aspect-level sentiment classification. Proceedings of the 2018 Conference on Empirical Methods in Natural Language Processing, Brussels, Belgium, 31 October–4 November 2018.
7. Zhang, C.; Li, Q.; Song, D. Aspect-based sentiment classification with aspect-specific graph convolutional networks. In Proceedings of the 2019 Conference on Empirical Methods in Natural Language Processing and the 9th International Joint Conference on Natural Language Processing (EMNLP-IJCNLP), Hong Kong, China, 3–7 November 2019; pp. 4567–4577.
8. Sun, K.; Zhang, R.; Mensah, S.; Mao, Y.; Liu, X. Aspect-level sentiment analysis via convolution over dependency tree. In Proceedings of the 2019 Conference on Empirical Methods in Natural Language Processing and the 9th International Joint Conference on Natural Language Processing (EMNLP-IJCNLP), Hong Kong, China, 3–7 November 2019; pp. 5679–5688
9. Wang, K.; Shen, W.; Yang, Y.; Quan, X.; Wang, R. Relational graph attention network for aspect-based sentiment analysis. In Proceedings of the 58th Annual Meeting of the Association for Computational Linguistics, online, 5–10 July 2020; pp. 3229–3238.
10. Li, R.; Chen, H.; Feng, F.; Ma, Z.; Wang, X.; Hovy, E. Dual graph convolutional networks for aspect-based sentiment analysis. In Proceedings of the 59th Annual Meeting of the Association for Computational Linguistics and the 11th International Joint Conference on Natural Language Processing (Volume 1: Long Papers), Virtual Event, 1–6 August 2021.
11. Pang, S.; Xue, Y.; Yan, Z.; Huang, W.; Feng, J. Dynamic and multi-channel graph convolutional networks for aspect-based sentiment analysis. In *Findings of the Association for Computational Linguistics: ACL-IJCNLP 2021*, Virtual, 1–6 August 2021.
12. Dai, A.; Hu, X.; Nie, J.; Chen, J. Learning from word semantics to sentence syntax by graph convolutional networks for aspect-based sentiment analysis. *Int. J. Data Sci. Anal.* **2022**, *14*, 17–26. [CrossRef]
13. Yang, P.; Li, L.; Luo, F.; Liu, T.; Sun, X. Enhancing topic-to-essay generation with external commonsense knowledge. In Proceedings of the 57th Annual Meeting of the Association for Computational Linguistics, Florence, Italy 28 July–2 August 2019; pp. 2002–2012.
14. Zhou, J.; Huang, J.X.; Hu, Q.V.; He, L. Sk-gcn: Modeling syntax and knowledge via graph convolutional network for aspect-level sentiment classification. *Knowl.-Based Syst.* **2020**, *205*, 106292. [CrossRef]
15. Speer, R.; Chin, J.; Havasi, C. Conceptnet 5.5: An open multilingual graph ofgeneral knowledge. In Proceedings of the AAAI, San Francisco, CA, USA, 4–9 February 2017.
16. Cambria, E.; Poria, S.; Hazarika, D.; Kwok, K. SenticNet 5: Discovering conceptual primitives for sentiment analysis by means of context embeddings. In Proceedings of the AAAI, Edmonton, AB, Canada, 13–17 November 2018.
17. Miller, G.A. WordNet: A lexical database for English. *Commun. ACM* **1995**, *38*, 39–41. [CrossRef]
18. Jiang, L.; Yu, M.; Zhou, M.; Liu, X.; Zhao, T. Target-dependent twitter sentiment classification. In Proceedings of the 49th Annual Meeting of the Association for Computational Linguistics: Human Language Technologies, Portland, ON, USA, 19–24 June 2011.
19. Kiritchenko, S.; Zhu, X.; Cherry, C.; Mohammad, S. NRC-Canada-2014: Detecting aspects and sentiment in customer reviews. In Proceedings of the 8th International Workshop on Semantic Evaluation (SemEval 2014), Dublin, Ireland, 23–24 August 2014.
20. Ding, X.; Zhang, Y.; Liu, T.; Duan, J. Deep learning for event-driven stock prediction. In Proceedings of the Twenty-Fourth International Joint Conference on Artificial Intelligence, Buenos Aires, Argentina, 25–31 July 2015.
21. Tang, D.; Qin, B.; Feng, X.; Liu, T. Effective LSTMs for target-dependent sentiment classification. In Proceedings of the COLING 2016, the 26th International Conference on Computational Linguistics: Technical Papers, Osaka, Japan, 11–16 December 2016; pp. 3298–3307.
22. Majumder, N.; Poria, S.; Gelbukh, A.; Akhtar, M.S.; Cambria, E.; Ekbal, A. IARM:Inter-aspect relation modeling with memory networks in aspect-based sentiment analysis. In Proceedings of the 2018 Conference on Empirical Methods in Natural Language Processing, Brussels, Belgium, 31 October–4 November 2018; pp. 3402–3411.
23. Tang, D.; Qin, B.; Liu, T. Aspect level sentiment classification with deep memory network. *arXiv* **2016**, arXiv:1605.08900.
24. Ma, D.; Li, S.; Zhang, X.; Wang, H. Interactive attention networks for aspect-level sentiment classification. *arXiv* **2017**, arXiv:1709.00893.
25. Huang, B.; Ou, Y.; Carley, K.M. Aspect level sentiment classification with attention-over-attention neural networks. In Proceedings of the International Conference on Social Computing, Behavioral-Cultural Modeling and Prediction and Behavior Representation in Modeling and Simulation, Stockholm, Sweden, 10–15 July 2018; Springer: Cham, Switzerland, 2018.
26. Kipf, T.N.; Welling, M. Semi-supervised classification with graph convolutional networks. In Proceedings of the ICLR, Toulon, France, 24–26 April 2017.

27. Yao, L.; Mao, C.; Luo, Y. Graph convolutional networks for text classification. In Proceedings of the AAAI Conference on Artificial Intelligence, Honolulu, HI, USA, 27 January–1 February 2019; Volume 33, pp. 7370–7377.
28. Huang, L.; Ma, D.; Li, S.; Zhang, X.; Wang, H. Text level graph neural network for text classification. In Proceedings of the 2019 Conference on Empirical Methods in Natural Language Processing and the 9th International Joint Conference on Natural Language Processing (EMNLP-IJCNLP), Hong Kong, China, 3–7 November 2019; pp. 3444–3450.
29. Zhang, Y.; Qi, P.; Manning, C.D. Graph convolution over pruned dependency trees improves relation extraction. In Proceedings of the 2018 Conference on Empirical Methods in Natural Language Processing, Brussels, Belgium, 31 October–4 November 2018; pp. 2205–2215.
30. Sun, K.; Zhang, R.; Mao, Y.; Mensah, S.; Liu, X. Relation extraction with convolutional network over learnable syntax-transport graph. In Proceedings of the AAAI Conference on Artificial Intelligence, New York, NY, USA, 7–12 February 2020; Volume 34.
31. Gou, J.; Yu, B.; Maybank, S.J.; Tao, D. Knowledge distillation: A survey. *Int. J. Comput. Vis.* **2021**, *129*, 1789–1819. [CrossRef]
32. Bastings, J.; Titov, I.; Aziz, W.; Marcheggiani, D.; Sima'an, K. Graph convolutional encoders for syntax-aware neural machine translation. In Proceedings of the EMNLP, Copenhagen, Denmark, 9–11 September 2017; pp. 1957–1967.
33. Li, Y.; Pan, Q.; Yang, T.; Wang, S.; Tang, J.; Cambria, E. Learning word representations for sentiment analysis. *Cogn. Comput.* **2017**, *9*, 843–851. [CrossRef]
34. Bengio, Y.; Ducharme, R.; Vincent, P.; Jauvin, C. A neural probabilistic language model. *J. Mach. Learn. Res.* **2003**, *3*, 1137–1155.
35. Devlin, J.; Chang, M.W.; Lee, K.; Toutanova, K. BERT: Pre-training of deep bidirectional transformers for language understanding. In Proceedings of the 2019 Conference of the North American Chapter of the Association for Computational Linguistics: Human Language Technologies, Volume 1 (Long and Short Papers), Minneapolis, MI, USA, 2–7 June 2019; pp. 4171–4186.
36. Suresh, M. Semeval-2014 task 4: Aspect based sentiment analysis. In Proceedings of the 8th International Workshop on Semantic Evaluation (SemEval 2014), Dublin, Ireland, 23–24 August 2014.
37. Pontiki, M.; Galanis, D.; Papageorgiou, H.; Man, har, S.; Androutsopoulos, I. Semeval-2015 task 12: Aspect based sentiment analysis. In Proceedings of the 9th International Workshop on Semantic Evaluation (SemEval 2015), Denver, CL, USA, 4–5 June 2015.
38. Pennington, J.; Socher, R.; Manning, C.D. Glove: Global vectors for word representation. In Proceedings of the 2014 Conferenceon Empirical Methods in Natural Language Processing (EMNLP), Doha, Qatar, 25–29 October 2014; pp. 1532–1543.
39. Tian, Y.; Chen, G.; Song, Y. Aspect-based sentiment analysis with type-aware graph convolutional networks and layer ensemble. In Proceedings of the 2021 Conference of the North American Chapter of the Association for Computational Linguistics: Human Language Technologies, Mexico City , Mexico, 6–11 June 2021.
40. Liang, B.; Su, H.; Gui, L.; Cambria, E.; Xu, R. Aspect-based sentiment analysis via affective knowledge enhanced graph convolutional networks. *Knowl.-Based Syst.* **2022**, *235*, 107643. [CrossRef]

mathematics

MDPI

Article

Deep Learning-Based Cyber–Physical Feature Fusion for Anomaly Detection in Industrial Control Systems

Yan Du [1], Yuanyuan Huang [1,*], Guogen Wan [1] and Peilin He [2]

1 Department of Network Engineering, Chengdu University of Information Technology, Chengdu 610225, China
2 Department of Informatics and Networked Systems, University of Pittsburgh, Pittsburgh, PA 15260, USA
* Correspondence: iyyhuang@hotmail.com

Abstract: In this paper, we propose an unsupervised anomaly detection method based on the Autoencoder with Long Short-Term Memory (LSTM-Autoencoder) network and Generative Adversarial Network (GAN) to detect anomalies in industrial control system (ICS) using cyber–physical fusion features. This method improves the recall of anomaly detection and overcomes the challenges of unbalanced datasets and insufficient labeled samples in ICS. As a first step, additional network features are extracted and fused with physical features to create a cyber–physical dataset. Following this, the model is trained using normal data to ensure that it can properly reconstruct the normal data. In the testing phase, samples with unknown labels are used as inputs to the model. The model will output an anomaly score for each sample, and whether a sample is anomalous depends on whether the anomaly score exceeds the threshold. Whether using supervised or unsupervised algorithms, experimentation has shown that (1) cyber–physical fusion features can significantly improve the performance of anomaly detection algorithms; (2) the proposed method outperforms several other unsupervised anomaly detection methods in terms of accuracy, recall, and F1 score; (3) the proposed method can detect the majority of anomalous events with a low false negative rate.

Keywords: deep learning; anomaly detection; cyber–physical; industrial control systems

MSC: 68T09

Citation: Du, Y.; Huang, Y.; Wan, G.; He, P. Deep Learning-Based Cyber–Physical Feature Fusion for Anomaly Detection in Industrial Control Systems. *Mathematics* **2022**, *10*, 4373. https://doi.org/10.3390/math10224373

Academic Editor: Jonathan Blackledge

Received: 23 October 2022
Accepted: 18 November 2022
Published: 20 November 2022

1. Introduction

In recent years, cyberattacks have caused significant damage to industrial production and national infrastructure [1]; the Stuxnet virus swept the global industry in 2010 and was able to carry out targeted attacks on infrastructure, with Iran suffering the most severe effects [2]. In 2015, a malicious program called BlackEnergy affected multiple substations in the Ukrainian power sector [3]. Many Ukrainian government agencies and companies were attacked by the ransomware NotPetya in 2017, which ultimately caused havoc worldwide [4]. A serious disaster can also result from the failure of hardware or software within an ICS as well as threats from the Internet. Globally, ICS security incidents occur frequently.

In order to secure ICS, anomaly detection is a promising approach [5]. It is usually physical faults or network attacks that cause anomalous events to occur in ICS. Sensors, actuators, pipelines, and other industrial equipment may malfunction due to physical faults. A network attack refers to an attack on a communication channel, host, or process control system, such as a man-in-the-middle attack (MITM), a denial of service (DoS), or a scanning attack. The purpose of industrial sensors is to collect status information (referred to in this paper as physical information) about the various industrial equipment in the system and to reflect the physical processes that take place within it. Physical faults have an impact on the physical operation of the system, but not on its network traffic. This results in physical faults not being detected by anomaly detection methods based solely on network traffic. The physical processes of a system may not necessarily be affected by some network attacks. Consequently, algorithms that detect anomalies based solely on physical information are not able to detect these attacks. The use of anomaly detection algorithms that are based solely on physical information cannot detect network attacks in a timely manner, since most network attacks against ICS do not immediately cause the system to enter an abnormal state. Our conclusion is that taking into account both network traffic information and physical information is an effective way to improve the detection performance for anomaly detection algorithms that are used in industrial control systems [6], which has tended to be ignored in past studies.

In the past decade, artificial intelligence (AI) has been rapidly developed and applied in various fields [7–10]. A number of AI-based approaches have emerged in ICS security, which can be categorized as supervised and unsupervised algorithms as a result of the success of AI in traditional IT security [11]. In the past, many anomaly detection algorithms based on supervised algorithms have been proposed. Although the industrial Internet continues to develop, attacks from the Internet are emerging in new ways, and supervised algorithms have a limited ability to detect unknown attacks, making them increasingly unsuitable for ICS security. As ICS datasets have significant imbalances and abnormal data are much smaller than normal data, coupled with a lack of sufficient labeled samples, supervised algorithms are no longer suitable for application in ICS security problems. The limitations of supervised learning can be overcome by unsupervised algorithms such as One-Class SVM (OCSVM) [12] and isolation forests [13].

Autoencoder is an unsupervised algorithm that contains an encoder and a decoder [14]. The input X is mapped by the encoder to the latent variable Z, and subsequently Z is mapped by the decoder to the reconstruction R. The deviation between the input X and the reconstruction R is called reconstruction error. For autoencoder-based anomaly detection, the reconstruction error is used to calculate an anomaly score. Detecting anomalies can be accomplished using autoencoders trained using only normal data. When training a model, it is assumed that the model will only learn how to reconstruct for normal samples. During the testing phase, the model may not be able to reconstruct the anomaly sample well, so the anomaly sample will produce a higher reconstruction error compared to the reconstruction error of the normal sample. In some cases, small anomalies can lead to small reconstruction errors, making it difficult to detect small anomalies. Generative adversarial networks (GANs) may be used to identify small anomalies and amplify reconstruction errors [15]. Autoencoders and GANs are both unsupervised artificial neural networks, with the difference being that GANs include an adversarial game mechanism [16]. The goal of training the generator is to generate data that are as realistic as possible and thus fool the discriminator (i.e., maximizing the likelihood that the discriminator will be incorrect). As well as a generator, the GAN contains a discriminator. When training a discriminator, the objective is to minimize its own error probability, i.e., to be able to distinguish with high accuracy whether the data are real or generated. Due to the time series nature of ICS data, individual samples cannot be considered independently. Compared with ordinary autoencoders, LSTM-based autoencoders [17] have more powerful capability in reconstructing time series data.

In light of the above issues, the main contributions of this paper include the following:

- Based on the latest public ICS dataset, a method for extracting system network features is designed for ICS, and the original physical features are fused with additionally extracted network features to create a cyber–physical dataset with fusion features.
- A model is proposed for unsupervised anomaly detection for ICS based on LSTM-Autoencoder and GAN, which is evaluated using the cyber–physical dataset. In terms of precision, recall, and F1-score, the model outperforms several other methods.
- Both supervised and unsupervised algorithms are used to investigate the effects of additional extracted network features on anomaly detection results. As a result of the experiments performed in this paper, it has been found that the features extracted

from the network can significantly improve the performance of the anomaly detection algorithm.

Acquiring data from industrial sensors is an inherent function of ICS, and ICS network traffic data can be collected by listening to communication channels. It is feasible to collect both network data and physical data, and then extract the cyber–physical fusion features. The massive amount of data generated during the normal operation of the ICS is sufficient to train the unsupervised model. Without significantly changing the components of the ICS, the models need to be trained only once to detect anomalies, including various novel attack methods. It is undeniable that the components of an ICS are fixed for a long time, and the network topology is not easily changed. Therefore, the unsupervised anomaly detection model using the cyber–physical fusion features proposed in this paper can help industrial control systems cope with various cyber and physical threats, attacks, and challenges in a cost-effective and profitable manner.

In the remainder of this paper, the following sections are presented: Section 2 discusses related work in the area of anomaly detection of ICS; Section 3 describes the dataset used in this paper; Section 4 describes the method proposed in this paper; Section 5 describes the experimental setup and presents the experimental results and analysis; and Section 6 concludes with our future plans.

2. Related Work

It is necessary to detect anomalies in ICS in order to ensure its security. Studies conducted in the past can be categorized according to their use of physical information or network traffic, depending on the features selected.

(1) Studies using physical information. Industrial sensors collect physical data such as water level, temperature, and humidity. Ahmed et al. [18] use the hardware characteristics of the sensor and the physical characteristics of the process to create a unique fingerprint for each sensor. In normal operation, noise-based fingerprints are created and can be used to detect attacks by comparing the differences between the noise pattern and the fingerprint pattern. According to Lin et al. [19], timed automata can be used to learn the laws that govern the change of sensor value. Furthermore, sensor and actuator dependencies are analyzed using a Bayesian network. The method is capable of detecting anomalies and locating the abnormal sensor or actuator. Industrial sensor data can be analyzed based on their time and frequency characteristics. In their study, Nguyen et al. [20] developed a method for detecting outliers in time-frequency data using continuous wavelet transforms. The authors of Zhao et al. [21] proposed a correlation-based method for detecting anomalies using sensor data and the correlations between them. Compared with only using sensor data, their method achieved higher accuracy.

(2) Studies using network traffic. Since ICS networks are more stable than IT networks, abnormal network traffic usually indicates that the system is being attacked. Network traffic-based anomaly detection methods can be further divided into packet based detection, flow-based detection, and session-based detection [22]. To detect abnormal behavior in ICS, Song et al. [23] extracted the behavioral sequence data from Modbus traffic to model the system's normal behavior, and compared the actual behavioral data with the model's predictions. Lee et al. [24] proposed AE-CGAN (autoencoder-conditional GAN) to oversample rare classes on the basis of the GAN model. It is able to achieve more accurate performance metrics in the case of significant imbalance between normal and abnormal traffic. Benaddi et al. [25] used Distributional Reinforcement Learning (DRL) and GAN to help distributional RL-based IDS enhance the detection of minority network attacks and improve the efficiency and robustness of anomaly detection systems in the Industrial Internet of Things (IIoT). By extracting the temporal characteristics of the original traffic in the SCADA system, Kalech et al. [26] proposed a method for detecting network anomalies based on temporal pattern recognition. In order to detect abnormal behavior, Hidden Markov models and artificial

neural networks are used. A multi-level anomaly detection scheme combining LSTMs and Bloom filters was proposed by Feng et al. [27] in order to detect malicious traffic in SCADA datasets. An algorithm for detecting anomalous traffic was proposed by Zhang et al. [28]. A grayscale image was created by converting the ICS traffic feature values into grayscale images, and then the model was trained with the resulting grayscale images, which improved the accuracy of anomaly detection.

According to another perspective, past research can also be divided into supervised and unsupervised research. The use of supervised machine learning has been demonstrated in some studies [29,30] as a means of detecting anomalous events or attacks. In spite of good results, the system was only able to detect known attacks and not unknown or zero-day attacks. ICS datasets are also often imbalanced, i.e., the anomalous samples are much smaller than the normal samples, which limits the performance of the supervised algorithm. Unsupervised or semi-supervised algorithms have been used in other studies to overcome the limitations of supervised algorithms. According to Kravchik et al. [31], their algorithm was able to detect 31 out of 36 network attacks using a one-dimensional CNN-based semi-supervised algorithm. Chang et al. [32] reported that an anomaly detection framework based on k-means and convolutional autoencoders achieved an F1-score of 0.9373 for water storage tank datasets. An autoencoder-based anomaly detection model was proposed by Audibert et al. [33], which used the reconstruction error as the loss function during the training phase and as the anomaly score during the testing phase. An anomaly is determined when the sample's anomaly score exceeds a predetermined threshold. Using an adaptive update strategy based on WGAN-GP, Lu et al. [34] proposed an improved generative adversarial network that produces fake anomaly samples, improving the accuracy of anomaly detection. Li et al.'s [35] GAN-based semi-supervised method, MAD-GAN, utilizes both LSTMs as generators and discriminators to capture the temporal correlation between time series distributions and potential interactions between variables, and it can detect anomalies effectively.

Anomaly detection algorithms are designed based on the selection of appropriate features. In order to detect anomalies in ICS, it is not enough to rely solely on physical information, but it is also necessary to consider network information. However, there are some limitations to the above methods due to the dataset. It was found that the datasets they selected had the following problems: (1) the dataset was not acquired in an ICS environment; (2) the dataset was nonpublic; (3) the dataset was outdated; and (4) the dataset was either restricted to physical process data or to network traffic. The authors in [36] compared the classification performance achieved by the algorithm when only using network features with that achieved by the algorithm when using physical network features, demonstrating that the fusion of physical and network information contributes to improved classification accuracy. The experiment was conducted on four supervised machine learning algorithms, but unsupervised algorithms were not considered.

Due to the above deficiencies, the following improvements have been made in this paper.

- In terms of the dataset, the latest ICS public dataset WDT [37] is utilized, which provides data on physical processes and their corresponding network traffic.
- When extracting features, we take into account the physical information and network traffic of ICS.
- Both supervised and unsupervised algorithms are used in the evaluation of performance to determine whether cyber–physical features contribute to the improvement of anomaly detection.
- An unsupervised anomaly detection model based on LSTM-Autoencoder and GAN is proposed, which solves the problem of low recall in past anomaly detection models, and is suitable for the ICS field that does not have sufficient labeled samples.

3. Dataset Description

During the normal operation of the Water Distribution Testbed as well as in the event of network attacks or physical faults, the dataset used in this study was compiled from four acquisitions. In Table 1, each acquisition is represented as a sub-dataset. During the first acquisition, eight network attacks or physical failures were conducted, resulting in eight scenarios. In a similar manner, the second and third acquisitions yielded thirteen and seven scenarios, respectively. As of the time of the fourth acquisition, the system was functioning normally, without any network attacks or physical faults. In total, physical faults included two water leaks and six sensors and pumps breakdowns, and network attacks included eight man-in-the-middle (MITM) attacks, five denial of service (DoS) attacks, and seven scanning attacks. Figure 1 shows the number and proportion of samples divided into normal and malicious for each acquisition.

Table 1. Data acquisition and description.

Acquisitions	Description (Scenario Number: 1.1–1.8, 2.1–2.13, 3.1–3.7)
First (Attack 1)	phy_att_1.csv, attack_1.pcap 5 MITM attack scenarios. (1.1, 1.3, 1.5, 1.7, 1.8) 3 physical fault scenarios. (1.2, 1.4, 1.6)
Second (Attack 2)	phy_att_2.csv, attack_2.pcap 7 scan attack scenarios. (2.1, 2.2, 2.3, 2.4, 2.7, 2.9, 2.11) 3 Dos attack scenarios. (2.5, 2.10, 2.13) 2 physical fault scenarios. (2.6, 2.8) 1 MITM attack scenarios. (2.12)
Third (Attack 3)	phy_att_3.csv, attack_3.pcap 3 physical fault scenarios. (3.1, 3.3, 3.4) 2 Dos attack scenarios. (3.2, 3.5) 2 MITM attack scenarios. (3.6, 3.7)
Fourth (Normal)	phy_normal.csv, normal.pcap No attack.

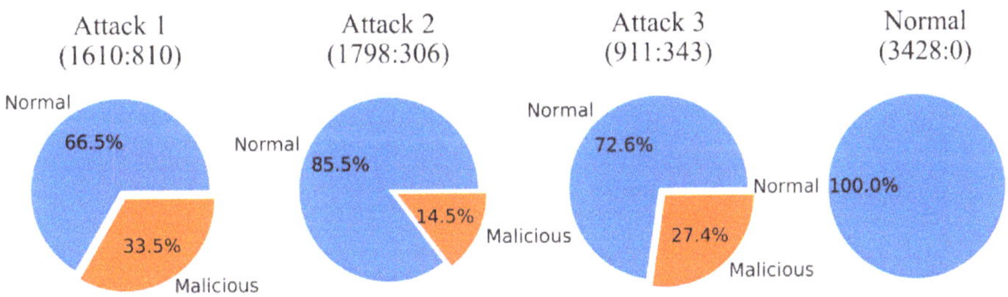

Figure 1. Number and proportion of samples divided into normal and malicious.

This dataset provides both the physical process data and the corresponding raw network traffic. The physical process data describe the information for the 40 physical statuses of the system in every second, such as whether the pump is turned on and the pressure sensor value of the water tank. In addition, the dataset also provides some network features extracted from raw network traffic data, such as the IP and MAC addresses of packets. For more detailed information on this dataset, please refer to [37].

4. Methodology

Firstly, we describe how to extract additional network features and fuse them with the original physical features. Then we formulate the problem, and finally we describe our proposed anomaly detection model in more detail.

4.1. Extraction and Fusion of Additional Network Features

The physical information collected by industrial sensors alone is not capable of detecting abnormal behavior in time owing to the widespread adoption of traditional information technology in ICS, and the damage caused by cyberattacks has a hysteresis. It is therefore important to take into account both physical information and network traffic when extracting features for anomaly detection.

The original physical process datasets have a sampling interval of one second, while the number of samples collected per second in the original network datasets is over 1000. By re-extracting the network features from the original network traffic according to the specifics of the ICS network, we can fuse the physical and network features together and summarize the situation every second. To enhance the performance of anomaly detection, 22 additional features were extracted from the original dataset. In Table 2, you will find a list of the new features that have been added.

Table 2. Additional extracted features.

No.	Features	Description
1	pkt_num	Number of all types of packets
2	icmp_pkt_num	Number of ICMP packets
3	arp_pkt_num	Number of ARP packets
4	tcp_pkt_num	Number of TCP packets
5	mb_q_num	Number of MODBUS request packets
6	mb_r_num	Number of MODBUS response packets
7	avg_pkt_size	Average packet byte size
8	avg_payload_size	Average packet payload byte size
9	mb_q_avg	Average MODBUS request packet payload byte size
10	mb_r_avg	Average MODBUS response packet payload byte size
11	illegal_mac	Illegal MAC address appears
12	illegal_ip	Illegal IP address appears
13	fc1_pkt_num	Number of Modbus packets with function code 1
14	fc3_pkt_num	Number of Modbus packets with function code 3
15	fc5_pkt_num	Number of Modbus packets with function code 5
16	fc6_pkt_num	Number of Modbus packets with function code 6
17	fin_flag_num	Number of packets with FIN in the TCP flag
18	syn_flag_num	Number of packets with SYN in the TCP flag
19	rst_flag_num	Number of packets with RST in the TCP flag
20	psh_flag_num	Number of packets with PSH in the TCP flag
21	ack_flag_num	Number of packets with ACK in the TCP flag
22	stage	Stage of the current moment in a process cycle

In addition, a feature named stage is added, which describes the stage of the current moment in the process cycle, and its value range is (0,1]. Taking the fourth acquisition as an example, there are a total of 3423 sampling points, including 12 complete process cycles. As shown in Figure 2, in each process cycle, the water level of Tank_1 gradually increases from 0 to the maximum value, and then gradually decreases to 0 and maintains for a period of time. Correspondingly, the value of stage is gradually increased from 0 to 1 and maintained for a period of time.

The architecture of additional feature extraction and fusion is shown in Figure 3. For each row (sample) in the original physical dataset, its sampling time is time t (e.g., 09/04/2021 11:30:55). All packets with time t are aggregated from the network traffic corresponding to this physical dataset, and the features described in Table 2 are extracted from those packets. Subsequently, the newly extracted features are fused with the original physical features to form a cyber–physical dataset. Some incomplete data were deleted, which were mainly concentrated in the first and last part of the dataset. The reason for the incomplete data is that when the original physical dataset is acquired, the corresponding original network dataset has not yet been acquired or the acquisition has been completed. The information of the finally formed cyber–physical dataset is shown in Table 3.

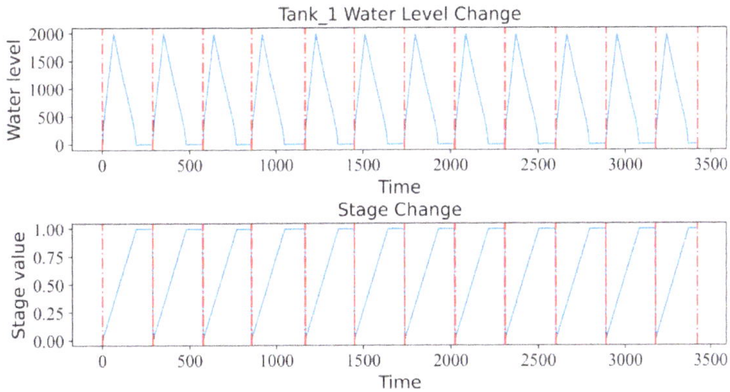

Figure 2. Changes of stage value and Tank_1 water level during process cycle.

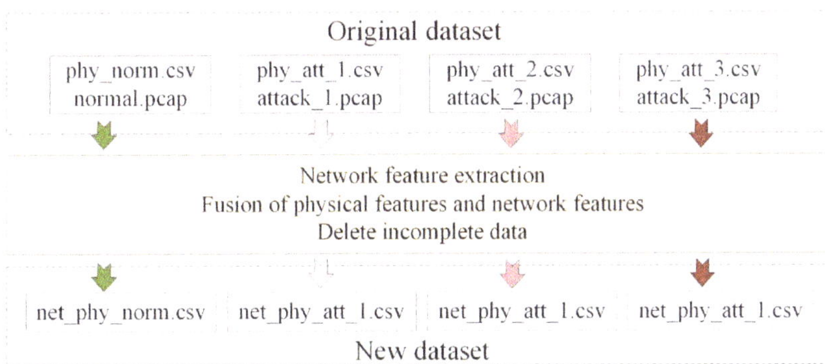

Figure 3. Additional network feature extraction and fusion architecture.

Table 3. Cyber–physical dataset after feature fusion.

Dataset	Number of Samples and Features
net_phy_att_1.csv	(2409, 62)
net_phy_att_2.csv	(2092, 62)
net_phy_att_3.csv	(1248, 62)
net_phy_norm.csv	(3421, 62)
Total samples	9170

4.2. Problem Formulation

In this paper, a dataset with sample number T is considered a multivariate time series TS of length T. x_t is a vector consisting of all physical features and network features at time t, and the number of features is m.

$$TS = \{x_1, x_2, \ldots, x_T\}(x_t \in \mathbb{R}^m, 1 \leq t \leq T) \tag{1}$$

In order to make better use of the correlation between observations at the current moment and previous observations, a time window W_t is defined. For each observation, its correlation with the previous K observations is considered. Therefore, the original time series TS can be transformed into a time window series W.

$$W = \{W_1, W_2, \ldots, W_T\}(W_t = \{x_{t-K+1}, \ldots, x_{t-1}, x_t\} \in \mathbb{R}^{K*m}, 1 \leq t \leq T) \tag{2}$$

Use the time window series W as the input to the model instead of the raw time series TS. Before conversion to a time window series, each observation x_t in the TS was normalized by

$$TS^j = \left\{x_1^j, x_2^j, \ldots, x_T^j\right\} \left(x_t^j = \frac{x_t^j - \min(TS^j)}{\varepsilon + max(TS^j) - min(TS^j)}, 1 \le j \le m, 1 \le t \le T\right) \quad (3)$$

where ε is a very small number in order to prevent zero-division.

4.3. Proposed Model

The proposed model consists of three modules: an encoder network LE using LSTM, and two decoder networks LD_1 and LD_2 using LSTM. As can be seen from Figure 4, these three modules constitute two LSTM-Autoencoders LAE_1 and LAE_2 that share the encoder network. The hyperparameters of the model are shown in Table 4. The training of the model consists of two phases.

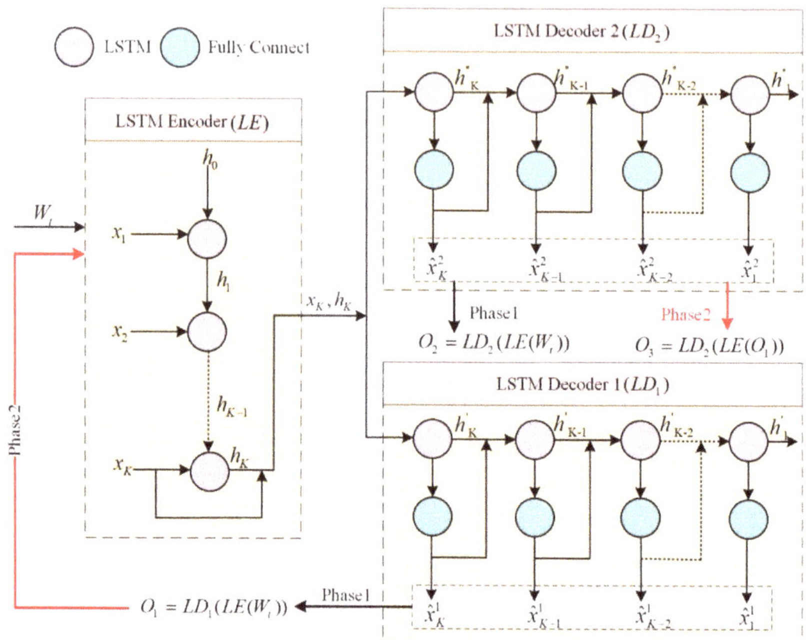

Figure 4. Proposed model architecture. The proposed model consists of three modules: an encoder network LE, and two decoder networks LD_1 and LD_2.

Table 4. Model hyperparameters.

Module	Hyperparameter	Value
LSTM encoder	Layer of LSTM	1
	Input size and hidden size for each layer of LSTM	(62, 128)
	Dropout	0.2
LSTM decoder1 and LSTM decoder2	Layer of LSTM	1
	Input size and hidden size for each layer of LSTM	(62, 128)
	Dropout	0.2
	Layer of Dense	1
	Size of each layer of the Dense	(128, 62)

4.3.1. Phase 1—Input Reconstruction

The goal of this phase is to train LAE_1 and LAE_2 to reconstruct the input. LSTM-Autoencoder can reconstruct each time window $W_t = \{x_1, \ldots, x_{K-1}, x_K\}$. The time window W_t is used as the input of the model, and the encoder network LE will output the hidden variable $h_K \in \mathbb{R}^n$ (n is the number of cells in the LSTM hidden layer). Then, the two decoder networks will output the reconstructions of W_t (O_1 and O_2) according to h_K and x_K in reverse order, where x_K is the last of W_t. Use L2-norm to define the reconstruction loss for each decoder:

$$O_1 = LAE_1(W_t), O_2 = LAE_2(W_t) \tag{4}$$

$$Loss1 = ||W_t - O_1||_2, Loss2 = ||W_t - O_2||_2 \tag{5}$$

4.3.2. Phase 2—Adversarial Training

In the second phase, LAE_1 and LAE_2 are trained adversarially. Put reconstruction O_1 as input to LAE_2 again and output reconstruction O_3. The purpose of training LAE_2 is to hope that it can distinguish whether O_3 is the real data or a reconstruction of the output of LAE_1. Conversely, LAE_1 is trained to fool LAE_2, that is, making LAE_2 unable to judge whether O_3 is the real data. The training objective is:

$$O_3 = LAE_2(LAE_1(W_t)) \tag{6}$$

$$\underset{LAE_1}{min} \; \underset{LAE_2}{max} ||W_t - O_3||_2 \tag{7}$$

Therefore, the goal of LAE_1 is to minimize the distance between O_3 and W_t, and the goal of LAE_2 is to maximize this distance, and the loss is defined as follows:

$$Loss1 = +||W_t - O_3||_2, Loss2 = -||W_t - O_3||_2 \tag{8}$$

Then, the evolutionary loss function is used to combine the losses of the two phases as the total loss for each LAE.

$$Loss1 = \frac{1}{n}||W_t - O_1||_2 + (1 - \frac{1}{n})||W_t - O_3||_2 \tag{9}$$

$$Loss2 = \frac{1}{n}||W_t - O_2||_2 - (1 - \frac{1}{n})||W_t - O_3||_2 \tag{10}$$

where n denotes the number of training iterations. The training process of the model can be seen in Figure 5a. Now define the anomaly score:

$$AnomalyScore = \frac{1}{2}||W_t - O_1||_2 + \frac{1}{2}||W_t - O_3||_2 \tag{11}$$

After the training is completed, the model is used to calculate the anomaly scores for each time window in the normal dataset, and then a threshold is determined based on the distribution of the anomaly scores. During the testing phase, shown in Figure 5b, for each unseen time window, the trained model will output its anomaly score. When the anomaly score of a time window is higher than the threshold, the model judges it as an anomaly.

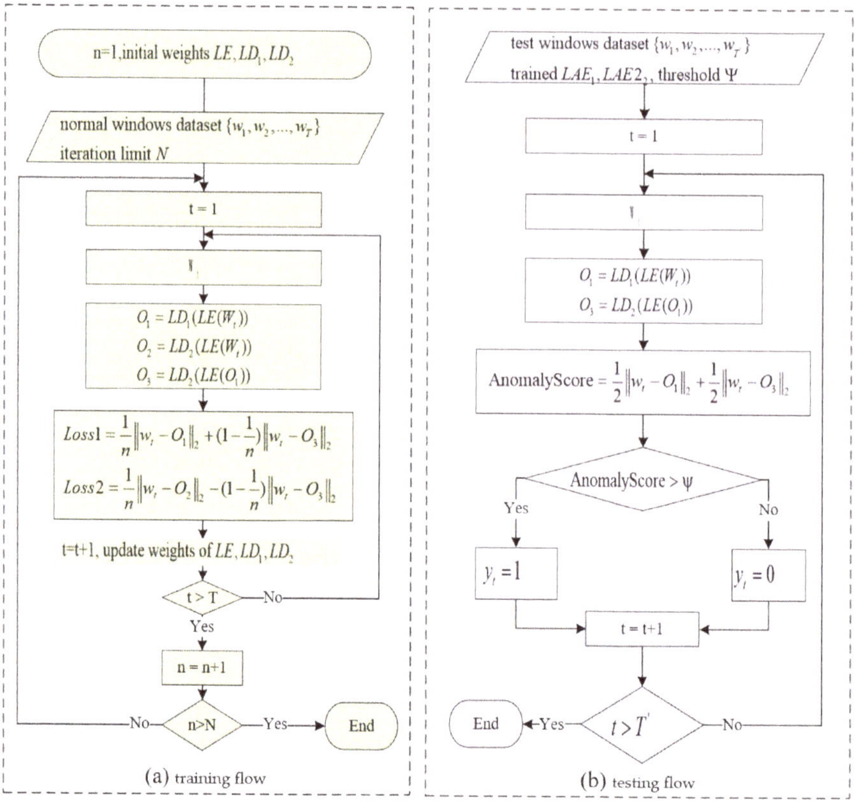

Figure 5. Proposed model training and testing flow chart. (**a**) Training flow chart; (**b**) testing flow chart.

5. Experiments and Results Analysis

5.1. Experiment Environment and Metrics

The experiments were performed using the following hardware and software platforms: Intel(R) Core (TM) i5-12400 CPU, Windows 10 Professional (64 bits), NVIDIA GeForce GTX 1650 Super, NVIDIA CUDA 11.1, Python 3.7.13, Pytorch 1.8.2, Python Scikit-learn library 1.0.2.

The proposed model is evaluated using recall, precision, F1-score, and accuracy. *TP*, *TN*, *FP*, and *FN* represent true positive, true negative, false positive, and false negative, respectively.

$$Recall = \frac{TP}{TP + FN} \tag{12}$$

$$Precision = \frac{TP}{TP + FP} \tag{13}$$

$$F1 - score = 2 \times \frac{Recall \times Precision}{Recall + Precision} \tag{14}$$

$$Accuracy = \frac{TP + TN}{TP + FP + FN + TN} \tag{15}$$

5.2. Dataset

The dataset needs to be divided differently for supervised and unsupervised algorithms.

5.2.1. Dataset for Supervised Algorithms

In this paper, the datasets are organized chronologically, with each cyberattack or physical fault lasting for a period of time, corresponding to multiple consecutive samples. When the dataset is shuffled and then divided, some samples from an abnormal event will be placed in the training set, and the remainder will be placed in the testing set. As a result, the model is able to achieve a higher accuracy on the testing set, but this is an illusion [36]. As a result, all samples will be either divided into training sets or testing sets, depending on the scenario. Divide 85% of the normal data into the training set and the rest into the testing set. For the anomaly scenarios, scenario 1.1–1.6, 2.1–2.7, 3.1–3.3 are divided into the training set and the rest are divided into the testing set. Use min–max to normalize the data, and the information of the dataset is shown in Table 5.

Table 5. Dataset information for supervised algorithms.

Label	Training Set	Testing Set
Normal	5848	1864
Physical fault	426	385
MITM	358	126
DoS	67	89
Scan	5	2
Total	6704	2466

5.2.2. Dataset for Unsupervised Algorithms

The fourth acquisition (no anomalies) is used as the training set to train the model. The other three acquisitions (with anomalies) were used as testing sets to evaluate the model.

5.3. Experiments of Using Supervised Algorithms

Three supervised machine learning algorithms were used for training and testing: random forest (RF), support vector machine (SVM), and naïve Bayes (NB). Use *RandomForestClassifier*, *SVC*, and *GaussianNB* in the Python Scikit-learn library to implement the above algorithm, and the hyperparameters for all of the above algorithms are generated by Python Scikit-learn library 1.0.2 defaulted.

The experimental results are shown in Table 6. All three algorithms achieve poor performance when only using physical features. The best performance is achieved by RF, but its F1 score is only 0.28. When using cyber–physical features, the performance achieved by all three algorithms is greatly improved, with F1 scores exceeding 0.87. The results show that the additionally extracted network features can significantly improve the anomaly detection performance of the supervised algorithm.

Table 6. Performance of three supervised machine learning algorithms.

Algorithm	Physical Features				Cyber–Physical Features			
	F1	P	R	A	F1	P	R	A
RF	0.257	0.754	0.155	0.777	0.907	1.000	0.831	0.958
SVM	0.126	0.764	0.068	0.763	0.895	1.000	0.809	0.953
NB	0.196	0.276	0.151	0.690	0.878	0.982	0.795	0.945

5.4. Experiments of Unsupervised Algorithms

5.4.1. Performance of the Proposed Model

Consider two situations, one using only physical features and another using cyber–physical features. Table 7 shows the performance achieved by the proposed model in the above two situations. In addition, the anomaly scores of the three test sets obtained by the model in the above two situations are shown in Figures 6 and 7, respectively. Cyberattacks and physical faults are marked in red and blue, respectively, in the figure.

Table 7. Performance of the proposed model.

Acquisition	Physical Features				Cyber–Physical Features			
	F1	P	R	A	F1	P	R	A
Attack 1	0.574	0.574	0.574	0.657	0.827	0.827	0.826	0.860
Attack 2	0.292	0.293	0.292	0.730	0.646	0.646	0.645	0.865
Attack 3	0.029	0.143	0.016	0.667	0.692	0.957	0.542	0.851
Sum	0.425	0.479	0.382	0.686	**0.758**	**0.800**	**0.720**	**0.860**

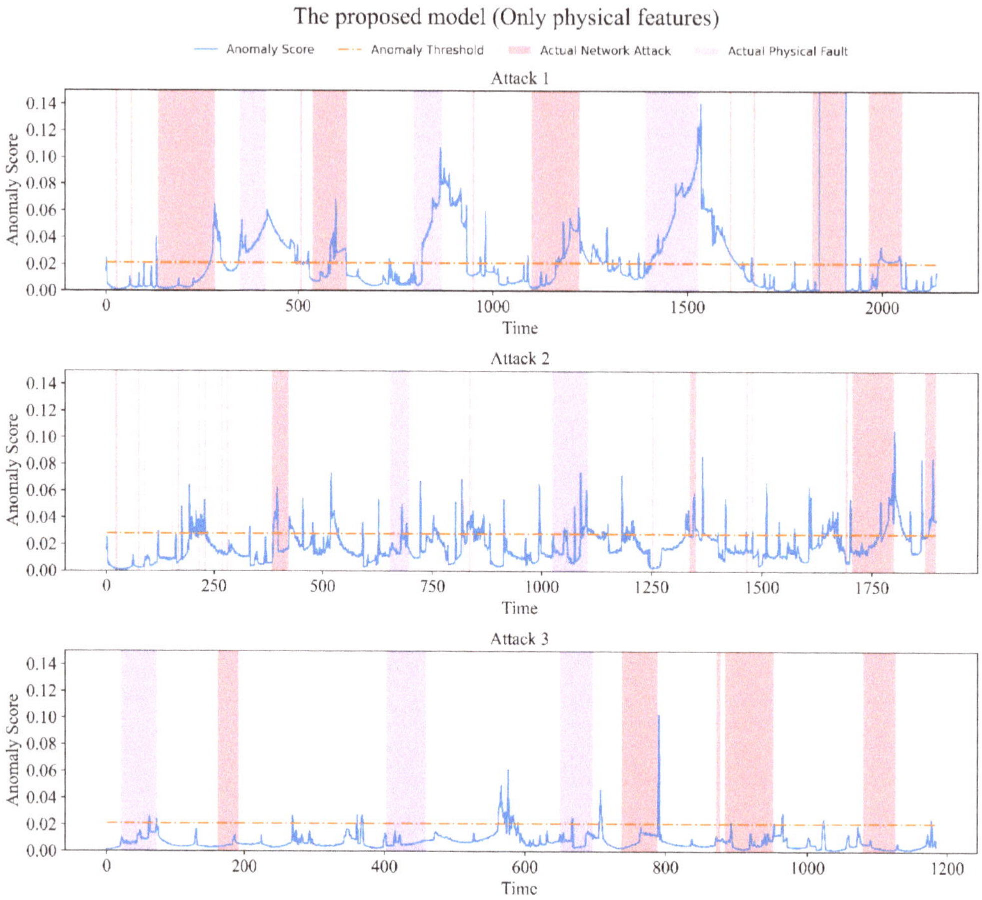

Figure 6. Anomaly scores for the proposed model (using only physical features).

When using only physical features, the model performed poorly on all test sets. Conversely, when combining additionally extracted network features, the performance is greatly improved on each test set. We believe that the reason for the poor results obtained by physical features alone is that there are some network attacks that do not affect the physical state of the system too much, so the model fails to detect these network attacks. For the network attack scenario, the anomaly score given by the model for anomalous time points is significantly higher than that for non-anomalous time points, indicating that the model can easily detect network attack events. For physical fault scenarios, the anomaly scores given to anomalous time points are not very significant, but are sufficient to detect most physical fault events.

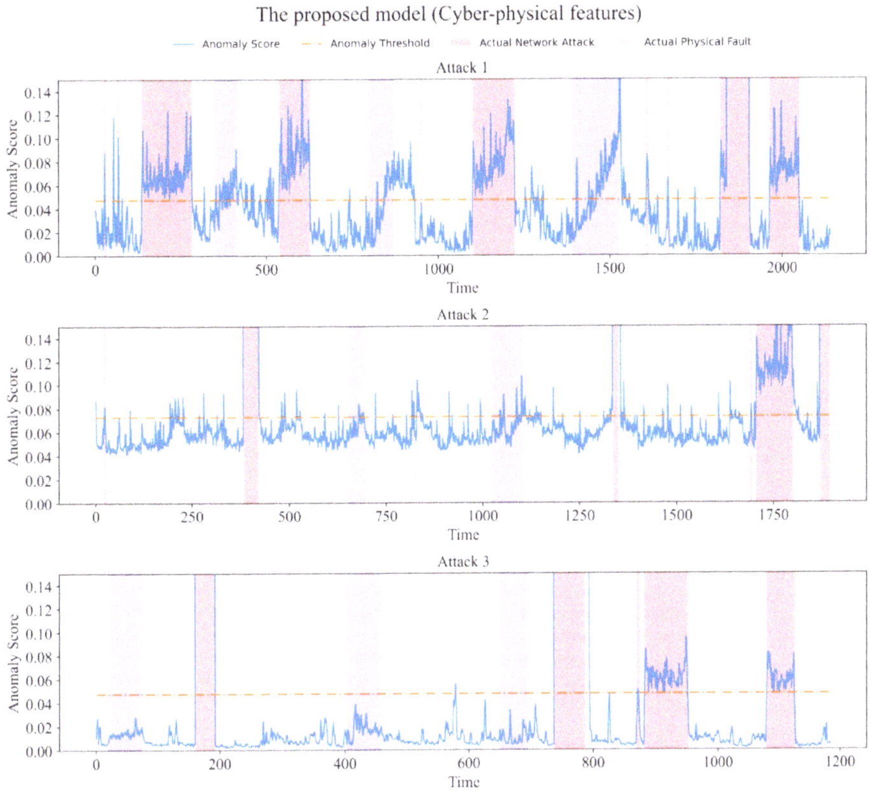

Figure 7. Anomaly scores for the proposed model (using cyber–physical features).

Due to the continuous increase in the degree of impact of an attack or fault on the system, it may not cause immediate damage to the system at the beginning, resulting in false negatives. Furthermore, it may still take some time for the attacked system to return to normal after the attack has ended, which may result in false positives. An example would be Scenario 1.6, which simulates the rise of the water level in Tank 3 as a result of a leak in the pipeline. A graph of the water level in Tank 3 over time is shown in Figure 8a. Figure 8b shows the corresponding anomaly scores, as well as the time period during which the fault occurred (scenario 1.6). While the water level rose initially, it was consistent with the normal rise in the tank's level. In this period, the anomaly score does not exceed the threshold, and the model considers it to be a normal period. Persistent faults cause the water level to exceed the normal level and continue to rise. As a result, the anomaly score for this period gradually increases and exceeds the threshold. Upon the resolution of the fault, the water level begins to decline, which is reflected in the anomaly score as well. Nevertheless, the water level remains above the normal level for a period of time after the faults have been resolved, so the anomaly score remains above the threshold, and the model still considers the system to be abnormal.

Figure 9a shows the changes of the water levels of Tank 1 and Tank 5 over time, and Figure 9b shows the corresponding anomaly scores. The time periods of the three fault scenarios are marked by red, green, and blue, respectively. Scenario 3.1 simulates a fault that pauses the transfer of water from Tank 1 to Tank 5. Scenario 3.3 simulates a fault by closing the Tank 5 outlet valve, thus achieving a slowdown in the flow of water from Tank 5. Scenario 3.4 simulates a fault that suspends the transfer of water from the reservoir to Tank 1. None of the above three faults caused the water level to exceed the normal level, so none of the anomaly scores exceeded the threshold and the model considered the system to be in a normal state.

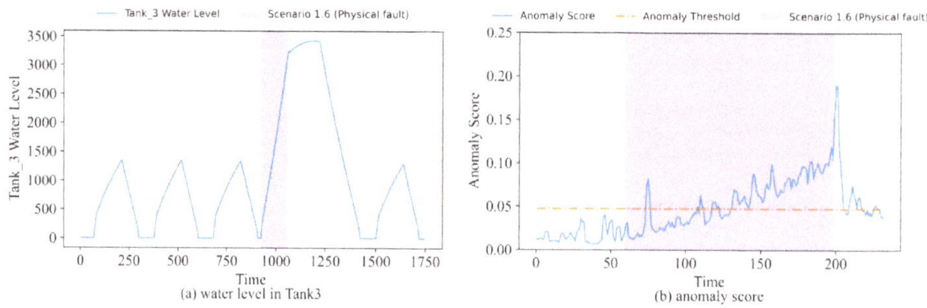

Figure 8. Scenario 1.6. (**a**) Water level in Tank 3; (**b**) anomaly score.

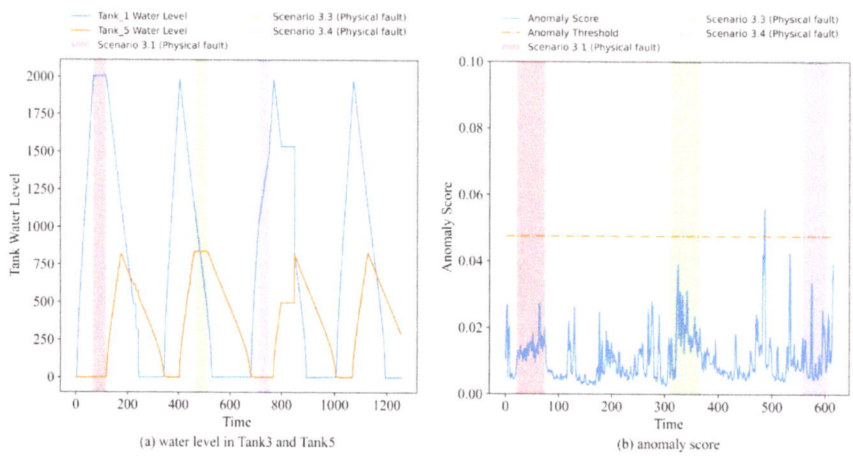

Figure 9. Scenario 3.1, 3.3, 3.4. (**a**) Water level in Tank 3 and Tank 5; (**b**) anomaly score.

5.4.2. Comparison with Other Unsupervised Algorithms

This section compares the performance of OCSVM [12], Isolation Forest (iForest) [13], USAD [33], and the proposed model. This paper implements USAD based on the author's GitHub repository. Both One-Class SVM and Isolation Forest are provided by the Python Scikit-learn library and use default parameters.

As can be seen in Table 8, the proposed model outperforms several other algorithms. OCSVM and iForest achieved a high recall rate, but too many false positives resulted in a low F1 score. Compared with the first two algorithms, the F1 score of USAD has been greatly improved, but the recall rate is lower. Low recall means that there are more false negatives, meaning that the model does not effectively detect anomalies, which is fatal for anomaly detection systems. As shown in Figure 10, USAD is able to detect most network attacks, but it is almost incapable of detecting physical faults. In contrast, the proposed model can detect most physical faults. The experimental results show that for the ICS anomaly detection task, the model proposed in this paper can achieve better performance.

Table 8. Performance comparison of the proposed model with other methods.

Methods	F1	P	R	A
OC-SVM	0.489	0.324	0.999	0.364
iForest	0.484	0.341	0.834	0.458
USAD	0.622	0.632	0.613	0.774
Proposed model	0.758	0.800	0.720	0.860

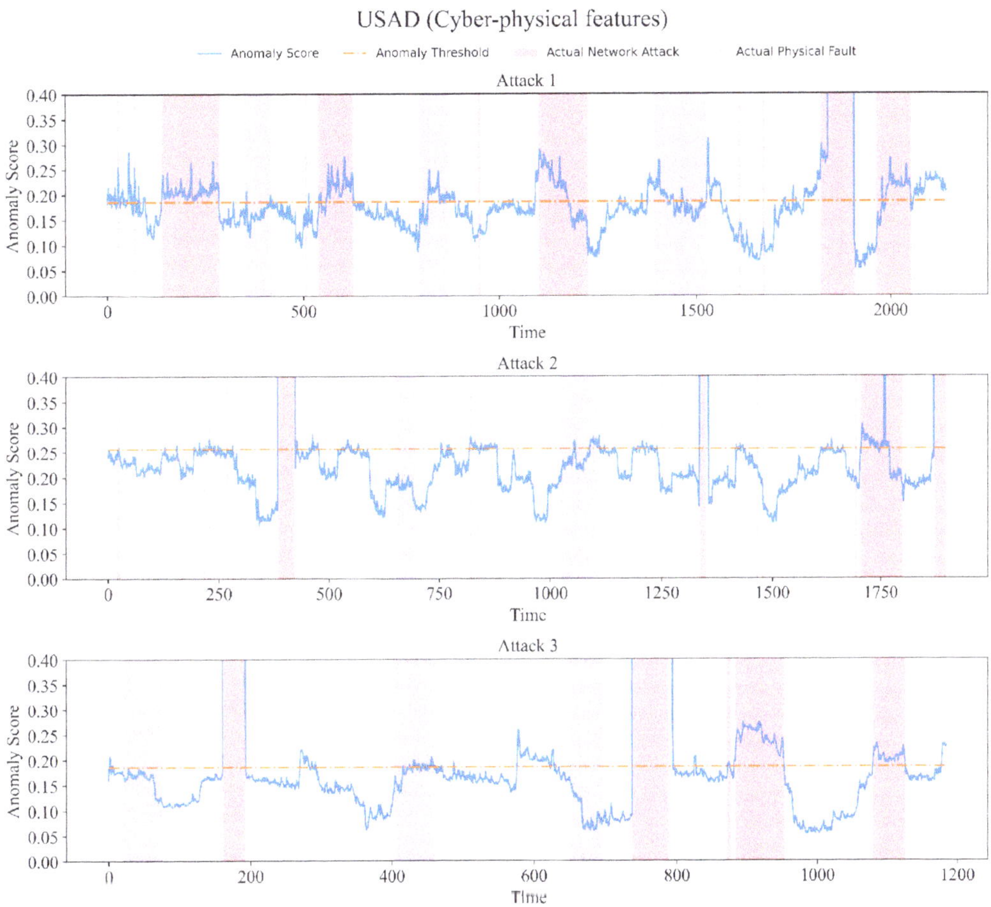

Figure 10. Anomaly scores for USAD (using network and physical features).

5.5. Ablation Experiments

The LSTM autoencoder in the proposed model is replaced by the standard autoencoder, BiLSTM autoencoder, and GRU autoencoder, and their hyperparameters are shown in Table 9. We removed the adversarial training phase from the proposed model, which is hereafter referred to as the proposed model with no adversarial training. The same training settings were set for the above models: the batch size is 32, the window size is 3, the optimizer is Adam, the learning rate is 0.001, the max epoch is 100, and the initial parameters are generated by Pytorch-1.8.2 defaulted.

Table 9. Three autoencoder hyperparameters.

Category		Hyperparameter	Value
Standard autoencoder	Encoder	Layer of Dense	2
		Size of the Dense (W means window size)	(62 × W, 128) (128, 64)
		Dropout, Activation function	0.1, ReLu
	Decoder	Layer of Dense	2
		Size of the Dense (W means window size)	(64, 128) (128, 62 × W)
		Dropout, Activation function	0.1, ReLu
BiLSTM autoencoder	Encoder	Layer of BiLSTM	1
		Input size and hidden size for each layer of BiLSTM	(62, 128)
		Dropout	0.2
	Decoder	Layer of BiLSTM	1
		Input size and hidden size for each layer of BiLSTM	(62, 128)
		Dropout	0.2
		Layer of Dense	1
		Size of each layer of the Dense	(128, 62)
GRU autoencoder	Encoder	Layer of GRU	1
		Input size and hidden size for each layer of GRU	(62, 128)
		Dropout	0.2
	Decoder	Layer of GRU	1
		Input size and hidden size for each layer of GRU	(62, 128)
		Dropout	0.2
		Layer of Dense	1
		Size of each layer of the Dense	(128, 62)

5.6. Discussion

As shown in Table 6, with the addition of network features, the accuracies of RF, SVM, and NB improved from 0.777, 0.763, and 0.690 to 0.958, 0.953, and 0.945, respectively, and the F1 score, precision, recall, and accuracies of the proposed model improved from 0.425, 0.479, 0.382, and 0.686 to 0.758, 0.800, 0.720, and 0.860, respectively. This is due to the existence of some network attacks, such as scanning attacks, which only generate some anomalous network traffic data, but do not have a substantial impact on the physical conduct of the system. Therefore, the fusion of network traffic data and physical sensor data definitely helps to improve the anomaly detection capability.

Compared with other unsupervised algorithms, the unsupervised anomaly detection model proposed in this paper has better performance. As shown in Table 8, the USAD model achieves a recall of only 0.613 when using cyber–physical fusion features, while the proposed model can improve the recall to 0.720, with a performance improvement of about 17.5%. As can be seen from Figures 7 and 10, the USAD model gives anomaly scores for normal and abnormal data that are not very different in general, which means that it does not reconstruct normal data perfectly and therefore cannot clearly distinguish between normal and abnormal samples. In contrast, the proposed model gives a large difference in the abnormal scores for normal and abnormal data, which indicates that the model can detect abnormalities well.

Table 10 depicts the performance of the standard autoencoder, BiLSTM autoencoder, GRU autoencoder, the proposed model (LSTM autoencoder), and the proposed model with no adversarial training, and Figure 11 shows the time they need to consume for one training. It can be seen that the standard autoencoder achieves the fastest training speed as well as the highest recall rate, but its precision and F1 scores are the lowest. This means that the model identifies numerous normal data as abnormal. The BiLSTM autoencoder took more time to train, but the improvement in performance was marginal. The time cost of training the GRU autoencoder is slightly lower than the time cost of training the proposed model, but the performance of the GRU autoencoder is much worse than the proposed model. It achieves a recall of 0.618, while the proposed model achieves a recall of 0.72, which we believe is worth the small time cost to obtain such a significant improvement. As shown in Figure 12, the model is able to reduce the loss earlier and with smaller loss values when adversarial training is performed. Furthermore, when adversarial training is removed, the recall decreases from 0.72 to 0.652, which is sufficient to demonstrate that adversarial training based on generative adversarial networks is indeed able to identify small anomalies by amplifying the reconstruction error.

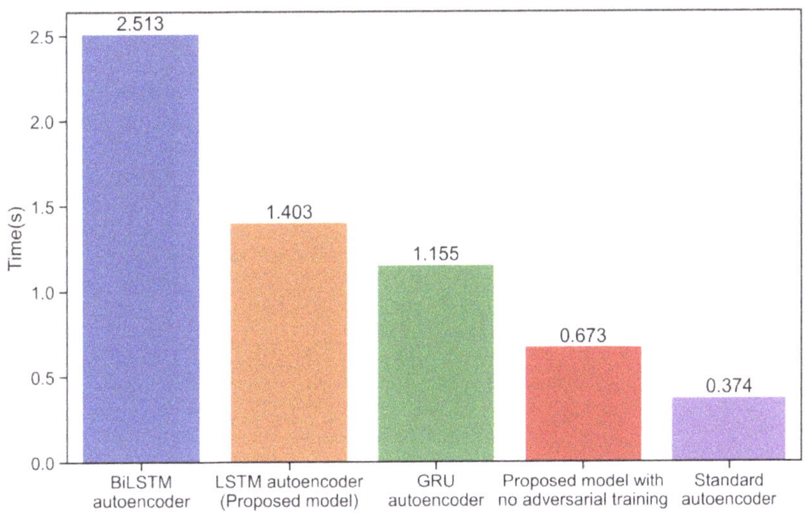

Figure 11. Training time for proposed model and other models.

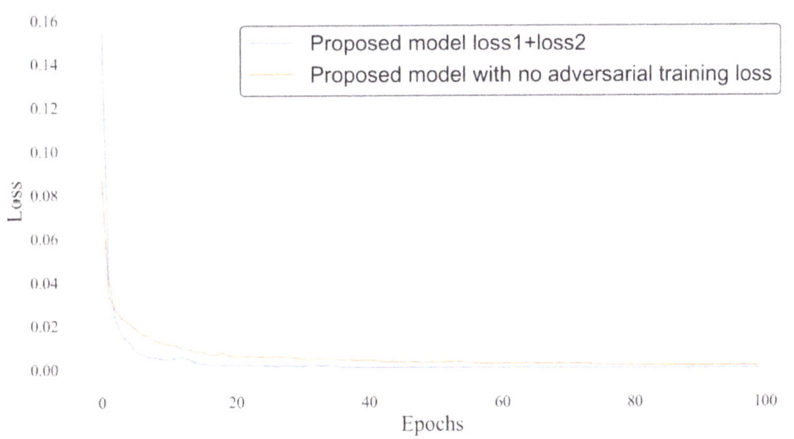

Figure 12. Loss with adversarial training and without adversarial training.

Table 10. Performance comparison of LSTM autoencoder with others.

Category	F1	P	R	A
Standard autoencoder	0.568	0.414	0.903	0.581
BiLSTM autoencoder	0.767	0.843	0.703	0.870
GRU autoencoder	0.729	0.888	0.618	0.860
LSTM autoencoder (proposed model)	0.758	0.800	0.720	0.860
Proposed model with no adversarial training	0.730	0.828	0.652	0.853

6. Conclusions

Given the special characteristics of ICS networks, we designed a method to extract network features. Based on the latest publicly available ICS dataset, the network features are extracted using the previously mentioned method, and then an ICS cyber–physical dataset is created. The anomaly detection algorithm obtained by training with this fused feature has better performance. In addition, we propose an unsupervised anomaly detection method based on LSTM-Autoencoder and GAN. The results of the ablation experiments show that using LSTM as an autoencoder is the optimal choice, and adversarial training based on GAN can also help the model to detect more anomalies.

This paper uses a dataset acquired in ICS using only the Modbus TCP protocol, but other protocols such as S7 and EtherNet/IP exist in the global industry. Our future work will investigate a more effective and compatible method for detecting ICS anomalies based on a more comprehensive dataset.

Author Contributions: Conceptualization, Y.D. and Y.H.; funding acquisition, Y.H. and G.W.; methodology, Y.D. and Y.H.; resources, G.W.; software, Y.D.; validation, Y.H., G.W., and P.H.; writing—original draft, Y.D.; writing—review and editing, G.W. and P.H. All authors have read and agreed to the published version of the manuscript.

Funding: This research was supported by Natural Science Foundation of Sichuan Province (No. 2022NSFSC0557), Foundation of Sichuan Network Culture Research Center (No.WLWH22-18), National Natural Science Foundation of China (No. 62102049, No. 62076042), and Key Research and Development Project of Sichuan (No. 2021YFSY0012, No. 2021YFG0332).

Data Availability Statement: The data presented in this study are openly available in the IEEE DataPort at [10.21227/rbvf-2h90] accessed on 20 November 2022, reference number [37].

Conflicts of Interest: The authors declare no conflict of interest.

References

1. Siniosoglou, I.; Radoglou-Grammatikis, P.; Efstathopoulos, G.; Fouliras, P.; Sarigiannidis, P. A Unified Deep Learning Anomaly Detection and Classification Approach for Smart Grid Environments. *IEEE Trans. Netw. Serv. Manag.* **2021**, *18*, 1137–1151. [CrossRef]
2. Liu, J.; Lin, X.; Chen, X.; Wen, H.; Li, H.; Hu, Y.; Sun, J.; Shi, Z.; Sun, L. ShadowPLCs: A Novel Scheme for Remote Detection of Industrial Process Control Attacks. *IEEE Trans. Dependable Secur. Comput.* **2022**, *19*, 2054–2069. [CrossRef]
3. Khan, R.; Maynard, P.; McLaughlin, K.; Laverty, D.M.; Sezer, S. Threat Analysis of BlackEnergy Malware for Synchrophasor based Real-time Control and Monitoring in Smart Grid. In Proceedings of the 4th International Symposium for ICS & SCADA Cyber Security Research, Swindon, UK, 23–25 August 2016; pp. 53–63. [CrossRef]
4. Alladi, T.; Chamola, V.; Zeadally, S. Industrial Control Systems: Cyberattack trends and countermeasures. *Comput. Commun.* **2020**, *155*, 1–8. [CrossRef]
5. Fahim, M.; Sillitti, A. Anomaly Detection, Analysis and Prediction Techniques in IoT Environment: A Systematic Literature Review. *IEEE Access* **2019**, *7*, 81664–81681. [CrossRef]
6. Ayodeji, A.; Liu, Y.; Chao, N.; Yang, L. A new perspective towards the development of robust data-driven intrusion detection for industrial control systems. *Nucl. Eng. Technol.* **2020**, *52*, 2687–2698. [CrossRef]
7. Zhang, M.; Qu, H.; Belatreche, A.; Chen, Y.; Yi, Z. A highly effective and robust membrane potential-driven supervised learning method for spiking neurons. *IEEE Trans. Neural Netw. Learn. Syst.* **2018**, *30*, 123–137. [CrossRef]

8. Zhang, M.; Wang, J.; Wu, J.; Belatreche, A.; Amornpaisannon, B.; Zhang, Z.; Miriyala, V.; Qu, H.; Chua, Y.; Carlson, T.; et al. Rectified linear postsynaptic potential function for backpropagation in deep spiking neural networks. *IEEE Trans. Neural Netw. Learn. Syst.* **2021**, *33*, 1947–1958. [CrossRef]
9. Huang, Y.; Wang, D.; Sun, Y.; Hang, B. A fast intra coding algorithm for HEVC by jointly utilizing naive Bayesian and SVM. *Multimed. Tools Appl.* **2020**, *79*, 33957–33971. [CrossRef]
10. Gou, J.; Sun, L.; Yu, B.; Wan, S.; Ou, W.; Yi, Z. Multi-Level Attention-Based Sample Correlations for Knowledge Distillation. *IEEE Trans. Ind. Inform.* **2022**, 1–11, (early access). [CrossRef]
11. Huang, Y.; Lu, J.; Tang, H.; Liu, X. A Hybrid Association Rule-Based Method to Detect and Classify Botnets. *Secur. Commun. Netw.* **2021**, *2021*, 1028878. [CrossRef]
12. Amer, M.; Goldstein, M.; Abdennadher, S. Enhancing one-class support vector machines for unsupervised anomaly detection. In Proceedings of the ACM SIGKDD Workshop on Outlier Detection and Description, Chicago, IL, USA, 11 August 2013; pp. 8–15. [CrossRef]
13. Liu, F.T.; Ting, K.M.; Zhou, Z. Isolation Forest. In Proceedings of the 2008 Eighth IEEE International Conference on Data Mining, Washington, DC, USA, 15–19 December 2008; pp. 413–422. [CrossRef]
14. Bank, D.; Koenigstein, N.; Giryes, R. Autoencoders. *arXiv* **2020**, arXiv:2003.05991.
15. Tuli, S.; Casale, G.; Jennings, N.R. TranAD: Deep Transformer Networks for Anomaly Detection in Multivariate Time Series Data. *arXiv* **2022**, arXiv:2201.07284. [CrossRef]
16. Cai, Z.; Xiong, Z.; Xu, H.; Wang, P.; Li, W.; Pan, Y. Generative Adversarial Networks. *ACM Comput. Surv.* **2021**, *54*, 1–38. [CrossRef]
17. Provotar, O.I.; Linder, Y.M.; Veres, M.M. Unsupervised Anomaly Detection in Time Series Using LSTM-Based Autoencoders. In Proceedings of the 2019 IEEE International Conference on Advanced Trends in Information Theory (ATIT), Kyiv, Ukraine, 18–20 December 2019; pp. 513–517. [CrossRef]
18. Ahmed, C.M.; Zhou, J.; Mathur, A.P. Noise matters: Using sensor and process noise fingerprint to detect stealthy cyber attacks and authenticate sensors in cps. In Proceedings of the 34th Annual Computer Security Applications Conference, San Juan, PR, USA, 3–7 December 2018; pp. 566–581. [CrossRef]
19. Lin, Q.; Adepu, S.; Verwer, S.; Mathur, A. TABOR: A graphical model-based approach for anomaly detection in industrial control systems. In Proceedings of the 2018 on Asia Conference on Computer and Communications Security, Incheon, Republic of Korea, 4 June 2018; pp. 525–536. [CrossRef]
20. Nguyen, L.V.; Kapinski, J.; Jin, X.; Deshmukh, J.; Butts, K.; Johnson, T.T. Abnormal Data Classification Using Time-Frequency Temporal Logic. In Proceedings of the 20th International Conference on Hybrid Systems: Computation and Control, Pittsburgh, PA, USA, 18–20 April 2017; pp. 237–242. [CrossRef]
21. Zhao, P.; Kurihara, M.; Tanaka, J.; Noda, T.; Chikuma, S.; Suzuki, T. Advanced correlation-based anomaly detection method for predictive maintenance. In Proceedings of the 2017 IEEE International Conference on Prognostics and Health Management (ICPHM), Dallas, TX, USA, 19–21 June 2017; pp. 78–83. [CrossRef]
22. Liu, H.; Lang, B. Machine Learning and Deep Learning Methods for Intrusion Detection Systems: A Survey. *Appl. Sci.* **2019**, *9*, 4396. [CrossRef]
23. Zhanwei, S.; Zenghui, L. Abnormal detection method of industrial control system based on behavior model. *Comput. Secur.* **2019**, *84*, 166–178. [CrossRef]
24. Lee, J.; Park, K. AE-CGAN Model based High Performance Network Intrusion Detection System. *Appl. Sci.* **2019**, *9*, 4221. [CrossRef]
25. Benaddi, H.; Jouhari, M.; Ibrahimi, K.; Ben Othman, J.; Amhoud, E.M. Anomaly Detection in Industrial IoT Using Distributional Reinforcement Learning and Generative Adversarial Networks. *Sensors* **2022**, *22*, 8085. [CrossRef]
26. Kalech, M. Cyber-attack detection in SCADA systems using temporal pattern recognition techniques. *Comput. Secur.* **2019**, *84*, 225–238. [CrossRef]
27. Feng, C.; Li, T.; Chana, D. Multi-level Anomaly Detection in Industrial Control Systems via Package Signatures and LSTM Networks. In Proceedings of the 2017 47th Annual IEEE/IFIP International Conference on Dependable Systems and Networks (DSN), Denver, CO, USA, 26–29 June 2017; pp. 261–272. [CrossRef]
28. Zhang, Y.; Li, X.; Li, D.; Yang, H. Abnormal flow monitoring of industrial control network based on convolutional neural network. *J. Comput. Appl.* **2019**, *39*, 1512. [CrossRef]
29. Beaver, J.M.; Borges-Hink, R.C.; Buckner, M.A. An Evaluation of Machine Learning Methods to Detect Malicious SCADA Communications. In Proceedings of the 2013 12th International Conference on Machine Learning and Applications, Miami, FL, USA, 4–7 December 2013; pp. 54–59. [CrossRef]
30. Borges Hink, R.C.; Beaver, J.M.; Buckner, M.A.; Morris, T.; Adhikari, U.; Pan, S. Machine learning for power system disturbance and cyber-attack discrimination. In Proceedings of the 2014 7th International Symposium on Resilient Control Systems (ISRCS), Denver, CO, USA, 19–21 August 2013; pp. 1–8. [CrossRef]
31. Kravchik, M.; Shabtai, A. Detecting Cyber Attacks in Industrial Control Systems Using Convolutional Neural Networks. In Proceedings of the 2018 Workshop on Cyber-Physical Systems Security and PrivaCy, Toronto, ON, Canada, 19 October 2018; pp. 72–83. [CrossRef]

32. Chang, C.P.; Hsu, W.C.; Liao, I.E. Anomaly Detection for Industrial Control Systems Using K-Means and Convolutional Autoencoder. In Proceedings of the 2019 International Conference on Software, Telecommunications and Computer Networks (SoftCOM), Split, Croatia, 19–21 September 2019; pp. 1–6. [CrossRef]
33. Audibert, J.; Michiardi, P.; Guyard, F.; Marti, S.; Zuluaga, M.A. USAD: UnSupervised Anomaly Detection on Multivariate Time Series. In Proceedings of the 26th ACM SIGKDD International Conference on Knowledge Discovery & Data Mining, Virtual Event, USA, 6–10 July 2020; pp. 3395–3404. [CrossRef]
34. Lu, H.; Du, M.; Qian, K.; He, X.; Wang, K. GAN-Based Data Augmentation Strategy for Sensor Anomaly Detection in Industrial Robots. *IEEE Sens. J.* **2022**, *22*, 17464–17474. [CrossRef]
35. Li, D.; Chen, D.; Jin, B.; Shi, L.; Goh, J.; Ng, S.K. MAD-GAN: Multivariate Anomaly Detection for Time Series Data with Generative Adversarial Networks. In Proceedings of the 28the International conference on artificial neural networks, Munich, Germany, 17–19 September 2020; pp. 703–716. [CrossRef]
36. Müller, N.; Ziras, C.; Heussen, K. Assessment of Cyber-Physical Intrusion Detection and Classification for Industrial Control Systems. *arXiv* **2022**, arXiv:2202.09352.
37. Faramondi, L.; Flammini, F.; Guarino, S.; Setola, R. A Hardware-in-the-Loop Water Distribution Testbed Dataset for Cyber-Physical Security Testing. *IEEE Access* **2021**, *9*, 122385–122396. [CrossRef]

mathematics

MDPI

Article

Deep Large-Margin Rank Loss for Multi-Label Image Classification

Zhongchen Ma [1,2,*,†], Zongpeng Li [1,2,†] and Yongzhao Zhan [1,2]

1 The School of Computer Science and Communications Engineering, Jiangsu University, Zhenjiang 212013, China
2 Jiangsu Engineering Research Center of Big Data Ubiquitous Perception and Intelligent Agriculture Applications, Zhenjiang 212013, China
* Correspondence: zhongchen_ma@ujs.edu.cn
† These authors contributed equally to this work.

Abstract: The large-margin technique has served as the foundation of several successful theoretical and empirical results in multi-label image classification. However, most large-margin techniques are only suitable to shallow multi-label models with preset feature representations and a few large-margin techniques of neural networks only enforce margins at the output layer, which are not well suitable for deep networks. Based on the large-margin technique, a deep large-margin rank loss function suitable for any network structure is proposed, which is able to impose a margin on any chosen set of layers of a deep network, allows choosing any ℓ_p norm ($p \geq 1$) on the metric measuring the margin between labels and is applicable to any network architecture. Although the complete computation of deep large-margin rank loss function has the $\mathcal{O}(C^2)$ time complexity, where C denotes the size of the label set, which would cause scalability issues when C is large, a negative sampling technique was proposed to make the loss function scale linearly to C. Experimental results on two large-scale datasets, VOC2007 and MS-COCO, show that the deep large-margin ranking function improves the robustness of the model in multi-label image classification tasks while enhancing the model's anti-noise performance.

Keywords: image classification; large-margin technique; deep neural network; robustness; anti-noise performance

MSC: 68T01

Citation: Ma, Z.; Li, Z.; Zhan, Y. Deep Large-Margin Rank Loss for Multi-Label Image Classification. *Mathematics* **2022**, *10*, 4584. https://doi.org/10.3390/math10234584

Academic Editor: Jakub Nalepa

Received: 27 October 2022
Accepted: 29 November 2022
Published: 3 December 2022

1. Introduction

Multi-label image classification (MLiC) aims to predict a set of visual concepts present in an image, which is one of the most important problems in computer vision. It can be widely applied to numerous real-world applications, such as scene recognition [1,2] or medical diagnosis [3,4]. In contrast with single-class or multi-class image classification, which only allows each image associated with a unique class label from a set of disjoint class labels, MLiC allows the images to be associated with more than one class label. MLiC is thus more general and realistic than the other tasks and such a generality makes it more difficult than them.

To cope with this task, one approach is called problem transformation, which transforms the multi-label learning problem into several binary classification problems or multi-class classification problems. Representative algorithms include binary relevance [5] and random k-labelsets [6]. Another approach is called algorithm adaptation, which adapts popular learning techniques to deal with multi-label data directly. Representative algorithms include ML-kNN [7] and Rank-SVM [8]. Conventionally, most of them use handcrafted features for image classification, such as SIFT [9], histogram of oriented gradients [10] and local binary patterns [11]. Inefficient feature representation may limit the performance of traditional methods in multi-label image classification tasks.

Motivated by the success of deep neural networks, some approaches combine deep representation learning and multi-label learning into an end-to-end trainable system. By dividing the original multi-label classification problem into multiple independent binary classification tasks, convolution neural network (CNN) can be applied naturally. However, this kind of method ignores label correlations, which has promoted research into deep learning methods to capture and explore label correlations. RNN-CNN [12] and ML-GCN [13] are two typical representatives of this kind of method. Some new approaches tend to explore label correlations, ref. [14] designed the label correlation term defined on some anchor data, and ref. [15] proposed a novel framework with local feature selection and local label correlation.

For simplicity, most deep MLiC classifiers adopt binary cross-entropy (BCE) loss function for training. Training such a deep multi-label image classifier requires collecting clean multi-label annotations for a large number of images, which is costly or even impossible in real-world applications. Therefore, even slight label perturbations may reduce the performance of traditional deep MLiC classifiers. The large-margin technique, maximizing the distance of each training point to a decision boundary, can effectively solve this problem [16]. Specifically, if the classifier reaches the boundary of γ, that is, the decision boundary is at least γ away from all training images, then any input perturbation less than γ will not flip the predicted label. For deep MLiC classifiers, the conventional definition of the margin is based on output values. However, the input margin is often of more practical interest. For example, a large-margin in the input space implies immunity to input perturbations. However, the margin in the input space is computationally intractable for deep MLiC classifiers.

To address the aforementioned issues, a novel deep large-margin rank loss function (DlmRl) for MLiC task is proposed. By treating the activations at each intermediate layer of the deep MLiC classifier as an intermediate representation of the image, DlmRl is able to impose a margin on any chosen set of layers of a deep network. The margin between labels can be measured by choosing any ℓ_p norm ($p \geq 1$), which applies to any network architecture and provides more practicability. Although the complete computation of DlmRl has the $\mathcal{O}(C^2)$ time complexity, where C denotes the size of the label set, we propose the negative sampling technique to make our loss function scale linearly to C. Experimental results on VOC2007 and MS-COCO show the effectiveness of our approach. Our contributions are three-fold:

(1) In this paper, a novel deep large-margin ranking loss for multi-label image classification tasks is designed, which can be applied between any layers of the deep network, the implementation of which is more flexible and compatible, thus enhancing the universality of the deep network;

(2) The proposed method quantifies the interval by an arbitrary ℓ_p norm ($p \geq 1$) to achieve a measurable margin. The metric enhances the controllability of the labels, improves the confidence of the label data, and therefore strengthens the comprehensibility and trustworthiness of the deep network.

(3) We propose a negative sampling technique applied to the large-margin loss in multi-label image classification tasks. This negative sampling technique greatly reduces the complexity of operations and therefore improves the performance of DlmRl operations.

2. Related Works

2.1. Multi-Label Image Classification

Deep convolutional neural networks have made great progress on the MLiC task. Some works embed label dependencies with the deep model to improve the accuracy of MLiC. A popular method is to use recurrent neural networks (RNNs) [17] or long short-term memory (LSTM) [18] to model the label dependencies. However, its performance depends on the label order. Recent works use graph neural networks (GNNs) to explicitly model label dependencies. For example, the works [13,19,20] utilized GNN to propagate the dependencies to learn inter-dependent classifiers.

Some works mainly focus on learning deep attentional representations for each label by treating an image as multiple images sampled from different regions. For example, ref. [21] introduced a max pooling layer that hypothesizes the possible location of the label in an image. Ref. [22] research on capturing the proximity and geometric structure of k-nearest neighbors. Ref. [23] combined the global average pooling with class activation maps to enable the localization ability of CNN. Ref. [24] proposed a new activation function to output the sparse probabilities of each label. Ref. [25] generated class-specific features for every category by proposing a simple spatial attention score. Ref. [26] unite similarity-based learning and generalized linear models to achieve the best of both worlds.

Recent works exploit the label noise property of the multi-label problem. For example, ref. [27] proposed a robust logistic loss function to train CNNs from user-provided tags. Ref. [28] exploited the potential connections between noisy labels and feature contents to identify the noisy labels. Ref. [29] proposed a curriculum learning strategy to predict missing labels. Ref. [30] proposed a loss function that measures the smoothness of labels and features of images on the data manifold to handle training data with noise labels. Although good performance has been achieved, these methods all add specific noisy-label-processing terms to the traditional multi-label loss function, e.g., BCE with logits loss (bce) [31]. In this paper, we aim to propose a plug and play loss, which performs well on MLiC tasks and is also robust to label noise.

2.2. *Large-Margin Classification*

The large-margin technique plays a key role in many machine learning algorithms. Traditional large-margin algorithms are designed for shallow models and have good interpretability. Support vector machine (SVM) [32] is a well-known large-margin technique, which tries to separate the training examples of different classes with a maximized margin. The margin provides good support to the generalization performance of SVM and has also been extended to interpret the good generalization of many other learning algorithms, such as AdaBoost [33].

In the context of deep neural networks, the large-margin technique has also shown potential performance. Ref. [34] encouraged large-margin solutions of cross-entropy loss by additional terms, however, these terms encourage margins only at the output layer of a deep neural network. Ref. [35] demonstrated that deep networks can attain a max-margin solution by their proposed regularizer, however, the regularizer may not be robust to the deviation of data. Ref. [16] formulated a loss function that directly maximizes the margin at any layer, including input, hidden and output layers. Its formulation is general to margin definitions in different distance metrics (e.g., ℓ_1, ℓ_2, and ℓ_∞ norms), and thus is relatively robust to data disturbances. Inspired by this large-margin loss formulation, we proposed a large-margin rank loss for the MLiC task, which inherits the good properties, and shows the effectiveness on three large scale MLiC datasets.

3. Method

3.1. *Notations*

The goal of MLiC task is to find all labels of an image. Suppose we have N training images $I_1, \dots, I_N$, as well as observe their label vectors $\{\mathbf{y}^i\}_{i=1}^N$, where $\mathbf{y}^k = [y_1^k, \dots, y_C^k] \in \mathcal{Y} \subseteq \{-1, 1\}^C$, C denotes the number of labels. For a given image I_k and label c, $y_c^k = 1(resp. -1)$ indicates the presence (resp. absence) of the label c in image k. Let P_k and N_k denote the positive labels and the negative labels in $\mathbf{y}^k$.

3.2. *Large-Margin Ranking Loss*

The above tasks can be converted to solve optimization problems to learn deep prediction models $f(I;\theta) \in \mathbb{R}^C$ with parameter θ by solving an optimization problem [36].

$$\min_{\theta} \frac{1}{N} \sum_{k=1}^{N} l\left(f(I_k;\theta), \mathbf{y}^k\right) + \mathcal{R}(\theta) \tag{1}$$

where $l\left(f(I_k;\theta), \mathbf{y}^k\right)$ is a loss function and $\mathcal{R}(\theta)$ is a regularization term. Let f_c^i denote the prediction score of a deep network for classifying the image i to label c.

Multi-label pairwise ranking loss aims to produce a label vector for image I_k, whose values for positive labels P_k are greater than those for the negative labels N_k, i.e., $f_u(I_k) > f_v(I_k), \forall u \in P_k, vs. \in N_k$,

$$l_{\text{rank}} = \sum_{v \in N_k} \sum_{u \in P_k} \max(0, \alpha + f_v(I_k) - f_u(I_k)) \tag{2}$$

where α is a hyper-parameter that determines the margin, commonly set to 1 [31].

Although pair-wise ranking loss has achieved state-of-the-art results on various benchmarks of MLiC, it only encourages margins at the output layer of a deep neural network. We propose that the input margin is more robust to input perturbations and is thus often of more practical interest.

Specifically, a model of MLiC with a margin of δ is robust to perturbations $I_k + \delta$, where $sign(f_v(I_k) - f_u(I_k)) = sign(f_v(I_k + \delta) - f_u(I_k + \delta))$, for $\forall u \in P_k, vs. \in N_k$. $sign(\cdot)$ is a sign function, in mathematics and computer operations, which takes the sign (positive or negative) of a number. For instance, the example shown in Figure 1 expresses the goal of our task.

Figure 1. As shown in the above figure, the left side represents the prediction value of image (I_k) obtained through the prediction model, and the right side represents the predicted value of the image with perturbations ($I_k + \delta$) obtained through the prediction model. The positive labels in the clean image include: umbrella, rain coat, car and person; negative labels include trunk and sunglasses. We hope that our model is robust to perturbations $I_k + \delta$. For example, the car is the positive label in the real predicted value. After the perturbations are added, the predicted value of the car is still higher than that of negative labels.

To this end, a deep large-margin ranking loss for MLiC, i.e., DLmRl, is proposed, which is able to impose a margin on any chosen set of layers of a deep network, allowing to choose any ℓ_p norm ($p \geq 1$) on the metric measuring the margin between labels and is applicable to any network architecture. We define the ranking boundary between any pair of labels $\{u, v\}$, where $u \in P_k$, $v \in N_k$, as

$$\mathcal{D}_{\{u,v\}} \triangleq \left\{ I_k \mid f_u^k = f_v^k \right\} \tag{3}$$

Under this definition, the distance of an image I_k to the ranking threshold is defined as the smallest displacement of the point that results in a score tie:

$$\begin{aligned} d_{f,I_k,\{u,v\}} &\triangleq \min_{\delta} \|\delta\|_p \\ \text{s.t.} \quad & f_u(I_k + \delta) = f_v(I_k + \delta) \end{aligned} \tag{4}$$

The exact computation of d is intractable when fs are nonlinear, ref. [16] presented an approximation to d by linearizing f with respect to δ around $\delta = 0$.

$$\tilde{d}_{f,I_k,\{u,v\}} \triangleq \min_{\delta} \|\delta\|_p$$
$$\text{s.t.} \quad f_u^k + \left\langle \delta, \nabla_{I_k} f_u^k \right\rangle = f_v^k + \left\langle \delta, \nabla_{I_k} f_v^k \right\rangle \tag{5}$$

According to [16], this problem then has the following closed form solution:

$$\tilde{d}_{f,I_k,\{u,v\}} = \frac{\left| f_u^k - f_v^k \right|}{\left\| \nabla_{I_k} f_u^k - \nabla_{I_k} f_v^k \right\|_q} \tag{6}$$

where $\|\cdot\|_q$ is the dual-norm of $\|\cdot\|_p$. Specifically, if distances are measured with respect to l_1, l_2, or l_∞ norm, their dual norms will, respectively, be l_∞, l_2, or l_1 norm.

We start with a triple set (I_k, u, v) and penalize the displacement of I_k to satisfy the margin constraint for $f_u^k > f_v^k$. This implies using the following loss function:

$$\max\left\{0, \gamma + d_{f,k,\{u,v\}} sign\left(f_v^k - f_u^k\right)\right\} \tag{7}$$

where the $sign(\cdot)$ adjusts the polarity of the distance. The intuition is that, if the constraint $f_u^k > f_v^k$ is already satisfied, then we only want to ensure it has distance γ from the ranking threshold, and penalize proportional to the distance $d_{f,k,\{u,v\}}$ it falls short, so the penalty is $\max\{0, \gamma - d\}$. However, if it is not satisfied, we also want to penalize the label for not being correctly ranked. Hence, the penalty includes the distance I^k which needs to travel to reach the ranking threshold as well as another γ distance to travel on the correct side of the ranking threshold to attain the γ margin. Therefore, the penalty becomes $\max\{0, \gamma + d\}$. For image I_k, we aggregate individual losses arising from each $u \in P_k$ and $v \in N_k$ to obtain the DlmRl formulation, i.e.,

$$\ell_{DlmRl} = \sum_{u \in P_k, v \in N_k} \max\left\{0, \gamma + d_{f,k,\{u,v\}} sign\left(f_v^k - f_u^k\right)\right\} \tag{8}$$

Plugging (6) into (8), the loss function becomes:

$$\sum_{u \in P_k, v \in N_k} \max\left\{0, \gamma + \frac{\left| f_u^k - f_v^k \right| sign\left(f_v^k - f_u^k\right)}{\left\| \nabla_{I_k} f_u^k - \nabla_{I_k} f_v^k \right\|_q}\right\} \tag{9}$$

This further simplifies into the following loss formulation:

$$\sum_{u \in P_k, v \in N_k} \max\left\{0, \gamma + \frac{f_v^k - f_u^k}{\left\| \nabla_{I_k} f_u^k - \nabla_{I_k} f_v^k \right\|_q}\right\} \tag{10}$$

In deep networks, the activations at each intermediate layer could be interpreted as some intermediate representation of the data. To force the entire representation and ranking thresholds to maintain a large-margin, the loss formulation can be defined based on any intermediate representation and the ultimate ranking thresholds.

Thus, the loss formulation (10) can impose a margin on any chosen set of layers of a deep network (including input and hidden layers) by replacing the input with its intermediate representations. It can be adapted as below to incorporate intermediate margins:

$$\sum_{u \in P_k, v \in N_k} \max\left\{0, \gamma + \frac{f_v^k - f_u^k}{\epsilon + \left\| \nabla_{h_l} f_u^k - \nabla_{h_l} f_v^k \right\|_q}\right\} \tag{11}$$

where h_l denotes the output of the lth layer ($h_0 = I$), γ_l is the margin enforced for its corresponding representation, and ϵ is used to prevent numerical problems.

3.3. Negative Sampling

The complete calculation of the loss involves $P \times N$ pairwise comparisons, thus having the $O(C^2)$ time complexity. This can cause scalability issues when C is large. To make the loss scale linearly to C, we sample at most t pairs from the Cartesian product. Denoting this by $\phi(I_k; t) \subseteq P_k \otimes N_k$, the DlmRl loss formulation becomes

$$\sum_{\phi(I_k;t)} \max\left\{0, \gamma + \frac{f_v^k - f_u^k}{\epsilon + \left\|\nabla_{h_l} f_u^k - \nabla_{h_l} f_v^k\right\|_q}\right\} \tag{12}$$

We set $t = 100$ by default, which achieves a better performance in most cases.

4. Discussion

We evaluate our method on the VOC2007 [37] and the MS-COCO [38] datasets. For each dataset, we use the standard training/test sets. To evaluate the performances, we show the results for the mean average precision (MAP) [39] and the instance-centric mean average precision (MiAP), which are standard multi-label classification metrics. We compare our DlmRl loss against different loss functions in three scenarios: (a) full-image labels, where only a subset of the images are labeled, but the labeled images have the annotations for all the categories; (b) partial labels [29], where all the images are used but a subset of images only have one positive label; (c) noisy labels [40], where the categories of all images are labeled but some labels are wrong. The experiments are carried out on a single NVIDIA V100 GPU.

4.1. Implementation Details and Baselines

All the deep models used in our experiments are implemented in PyTorch. ResNet-101 is employed as our classification network, whose weights were pretrained in ImageNet for single-label image classification as the initialization and fine-tune the weights of all layers. Note that we prefer a suitable CNN to more advanced frameworks to focus on the advantages of DlmRl rather than to show state-of-the-art results. We use a stochastic gradient descent (SGD) optimizer for model training with an initial learning rate of 0.1. When the validation loss stops decreasing for 5 epochs, the learning rate delays to one tenth. We stop training when the learning rate drops to 0.0001, which takes less than 20 epochs in most cases.

Since our loss function can be used in a variety of multi-label scenarios, only the traditional classical loss function without complex regularization terms as a comparison method is fair to us. In the experiments, we compare our Dlrml loss against two classic loss formulations, i.e., BCE with Logits Loss (bce) [31] and MultiLabel SoftMargin Loss (slm) [41], whose formulations are shown below:

$$\ell_{bce} = -\sum_{c}^{C} y_c^k \log \sigma\left(\hat{y}_c^k\right) + \left(1 - y_c^k\right) \log\left(1 - \sigma\left(\hat{y}_c^k\right)\right) \tag{13}$$

and

$$\ell_{slm} = -\sum_{c} y_c^k \log\left((1 + \exp(\hat{y}_c^k))^{-1}\right) + (1 - y_c^k) \log\left(\frac{\exp(-\hat{y}_c^k)}{(1 + \exp(-\hat{y}_c^k))}\right) \tag{14}$$

4.2. Results on VOC2007 Dataset

VOC2007 is a widely used multi-label image classification dataset. It has 9963 images and 20 classes, in which the training set has 5011 images and the test set has 4952 images.

Full labels: We randomly sample a subset of the standard training set for training. The proportion is between 10% (10% of training images are used) and 100% (all training images are used). The results of ResNet-101 using different loss functions are shown in Figures 2 and 3, from which we can see: (1) as the number of training samples increases, the performance of all models improves gradually; (2) Our method performs slightly worse than the bce method when only 10% of the training data are available, but this can be viewed as the cost of learning more robust feature representations. As the training data increase, the performance of the DlmRl method is able to maintain the highest level, which is due to the fact that the margin plays a lesser role when the amount of data is small than when the amount of data is large, illustrating that our method can effectively improve accuracy when dealing with large-scale data, as it can impose the margin in a large amount of data, which is more advantageous compared to other methods in dealing with large amount of data.

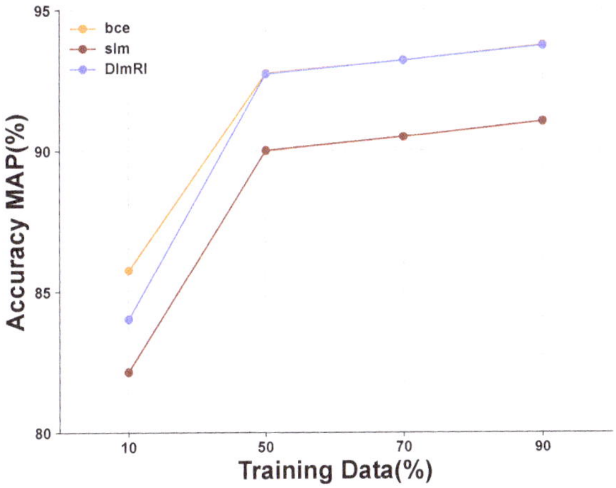

Figure 2. The figure shows the MAP score (%) of three different loss methods on VOC2007 with full labels. The orange line indicates the accuracy rate using BCE with Logits Loss (bce): the red line indicates the accuracy rate using MultiLabel SoftMargin Loss (slm); and the blue line indicates the accuracy rate using our DlmRl.

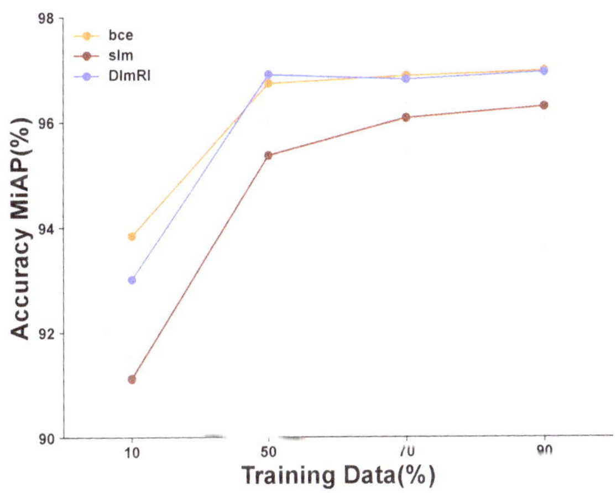

Figure 3. The figure shows the MiAP score (%) of three different loss methods on VOC2007 with full labels. The orange line indicates the accuracy rate using BCE with Logits Loss (bce); the red line indicates the accuracy rate using MultiLabel SoftMargin Loss (slm); and the blue line indicates the accuracy rate using our DlmRl.

Partial labels: We generate an extreme partial dataset by keeping only one positive label per image. The simulation copes with extreme single-label datasets in reality, e.g., ImageNet. If the image has more than one positive label, we randomly select one positive label among the positive labels and switch the other positive labels to negative labels. The proportion of partial images in the standard training set is between 10% (10% of training images only have one positive label) and 90% (90% of the training images only have one positive label). The performances of different loss functions on the partial dataset are shown in Figures 4 and 5, from which we can see that: (i) As the proportion of partial training samples increases, the performance of all loss functions degrade gradually. (ii) The performance of *bce* loss function drops the fastest and the performance degradation of our loss function is the slowest. (iii) When the fraction exceeds 30%, the performance of our loss function is consistently better than other loss functions. This shows that our DlmRl can cope with extreme datasets very well. In a dataset with almost all single labels, our method has an extremely good performance compared to other methods, which shows that DlmRl has excellent robustness in dealing with datasets with sparse labels. Due to the good robustness of DlmRl to extreme datasets, it is possible to only label the main items of the images when labeling them realistically.

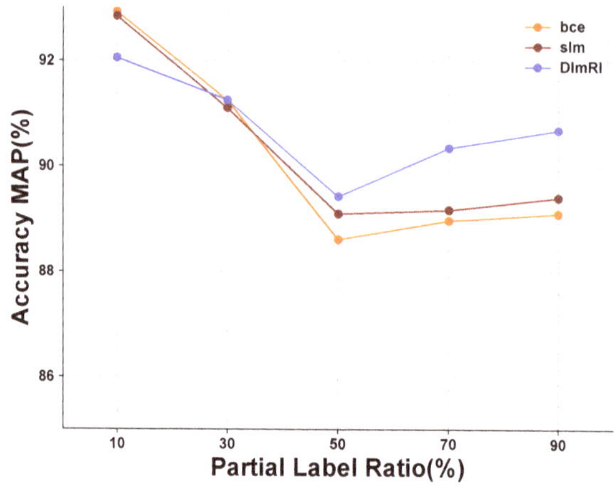

Figure 4. The figure shows the MAP score (%) of three different loss methods on VOC2007 with partial labels. The orange line indicates the accuracy rate using BCE with Logits Loss (bce): the red line indicates the accuracy rate using MultiLabel SoftMargin Loss (slm); and the blue line indicates the accuracy rate using our DlmRl.

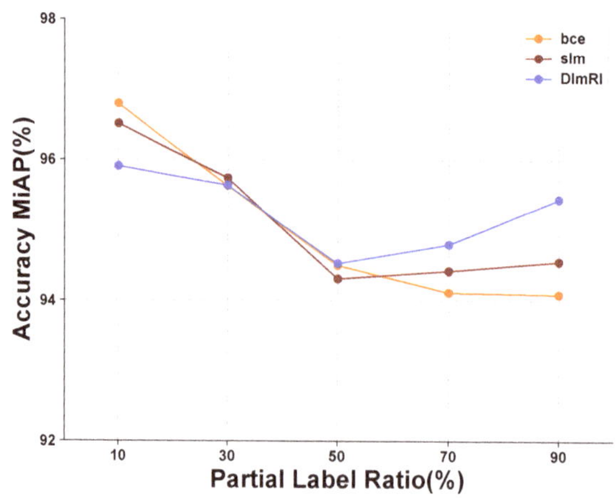

Figure 5. The figure shows the MiAP score (%) of three different loss methods on VOC2007 with partial labels. The orange line indicates the accuracy rate using BCE with Logits Loss (bce): the red line indicates the accuracy rate using MultiLabel SoftMargin Loss (slm); and the blue line indicates the accuracy rate using our DlmRl.

Noisy labels: In this experiment, we randomly choose, for each training image, whether to flip its positive/negative label to the other label. The fraction of such flipped labels range from 5% to 20% in increments of 5%. An increment of 5% means that the 5% of labels are wrong during training, while 95% of other labels are clean. The performance of different loss functions on the partial dataset are shown in Table 1, Compared with bce, we observe a substantial improvement in the MAP of 1.98%, 5.07%, 7.41% and 9.85% for the 5%, 10%, 15% and 20% ratio of noisy labels, respectively. from which we can see that: (i) Under all noise ratios, DlmRl is consistently more robust than other methods. (ii) As the noise ratio increases, the performance of DlmRl only slightly decreases. (iii) As the noise ratio increases, the performance of slm degrades the fastest, which reveals the limitation of the traditional large-margin technique.

Table 1. MAP and MiAP score (%) of different methods on VOC2007.

Methods	Noisy Ratio 5%	Noisy Ratio 10%	Noisy Ratio 15%	Noisy Ratio 20%
bce (MAP) [31]	88.79	85.50	82.83	80.05
slm (MAP) [41]	88.70	85.48	83.13	79.96
DlmRl (MAP)	**90.77**	**90.57**	**90.24**	**89.90**
bce (MiAP) [31]	94.74	93.28	91.69	89.82
slm (MiAP) [41]	94.70	93.19	91.68	89.94
DlmRl (MiAP)	**95.96**	**95.68**	**95.00**	**94.77**

4.3. Results on MS-COCO Dataset

MS-COCO Microsoft is widely used for segmentation, classification, detection and captioning. We use COCO-2014 in our experiments, which has 82,081 training images and 40,137 validation images and 80 object classes. Due to the large scale of this dataset, we conduct only one experiment for each of the three labeled scenarios, i.e., full label, partial label and noisy label. The ratios in the full, partial and noisy label scenarios are randomly set to 10%, 10% and 5%, respectively. From Table 2, we can see that DlmRl can achieve comparable performance against its counterparts on the full labels scenario, but significantly better performance than them on the partial and noisy label scenarios.

Table 2. MAP and MiAP score (%) of different methods on MS-COCO.

Methods	Training Ratio 10%	Particle Ratio 10%	Noisy Ratio 5%
bce (MAP) [31]	**65.53**	74.16	75.90
slm (MAP) [41]	65.29	74.21	75.87
DlmRl (MAP)	65.25	**74.83**	**75.99**
bce (MiAP) [31]	84.12	87.00	88.11
slm (MiAP) [41]	84.05	87.10	88.03
DlmRl (MiAP)	**84.12**	**87.68**	**88.15**

4.4. Ablation Study

In this subsection, we conduct experiments to study the effect of different hyper-parameters or components of our loss function on the VOC2007 dataset. To discuss the effect of one hyper-parameter, we conduct experiments on its different values, but keep other hyper-parameters or components fixed.

Figures 6 and 7 show the effect of γ with values in $\{10^1, 10^2, 10^3, 10^4\}$. The penalty includes the distance that I^k needs to travel to reach the ranking threshold as well as another γ distance to travel on the correct side of the ranking threshold to attain the γ margin. As can be seen, the performance of different values is very similar, so the classification performance is not very sensitive to γ.

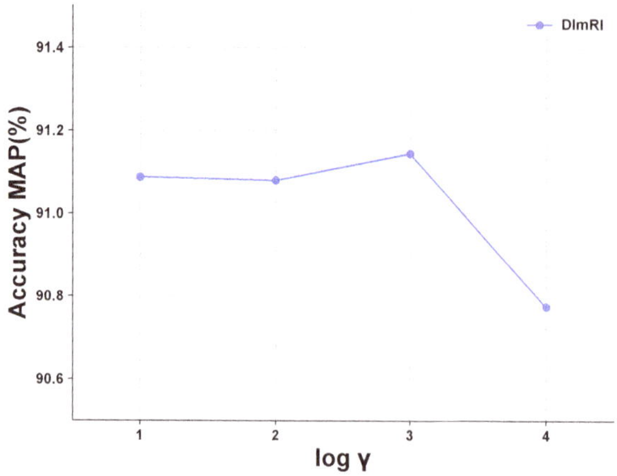

Figure 6. The figure shows the effect of γ on the MAP score using our DlmRl.

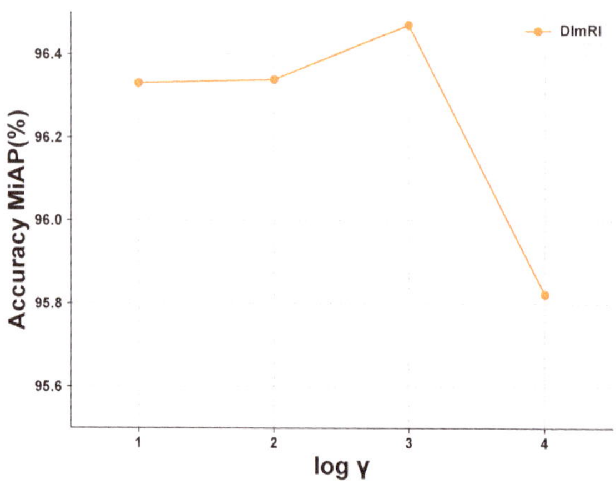

Figure 7. The figure shows the effect of γ on the MiAP score using our DlmRl.

Figures 8 and 9 show the effect of ϵ with values in $\{10^{-1}, 10^{-2}, \ldots, 10^{-6}\}$. As can be seen, a small value of ϵ is very important. When the value is small enough, the classification performance will only change slightly. The ϵ is used to prevent numerical problems. This experimental result is reasonable. When the value of ε is too small, the maximum margin represented by Formula (12) will be too large, and when it exceeds a certain range, the effect of our DlmRl will not be displayed.

The architecture of ResNet-101 consists of four blocks from bottom to up, i.e., Block1, Block2, Block3 and Block4, as well as two fully connected layers. To analyze the effect of imposing a margin on different hidden neural network layers, we conduct experiments on the four different blocks of ResNet-101, respectively. Figures 10 and 11 show the experimental results. As can be seen, it achieves the best MAP score and MiAP score by imposing a margin on Block4.

Figures 12 and 13 show the effect of q with values in $\{1, 2, \infty\}$. As can be seen, the classification performance is sensitive to this parameter and $q = \infty$ is the best.

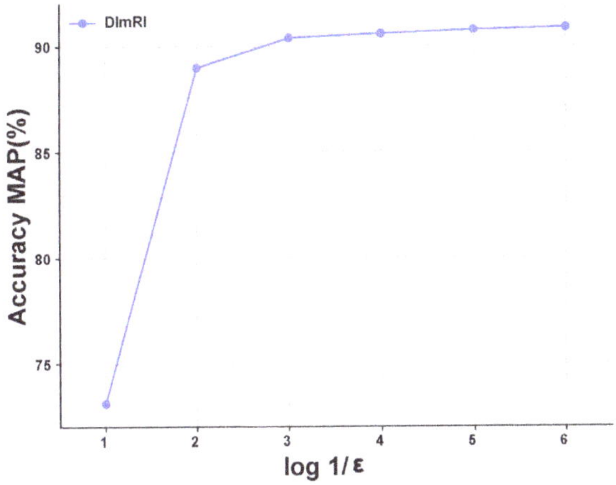

Figure 8. The figure shows the effect of ϵ on the MAP score using our DlmRl.

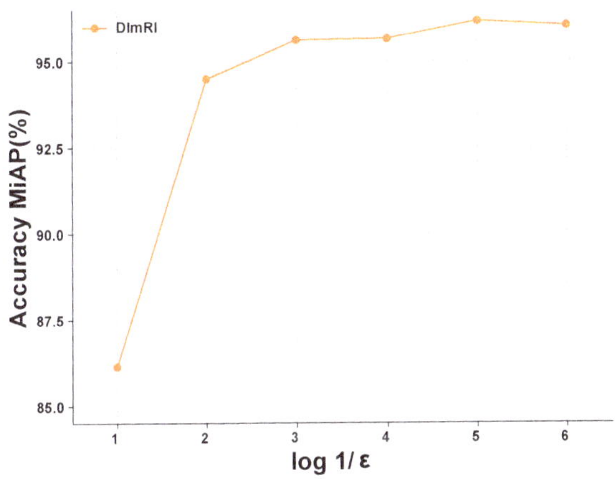

Figure 9. The figure shows the effect of ϵ on the MiAP score using our DlmRl.

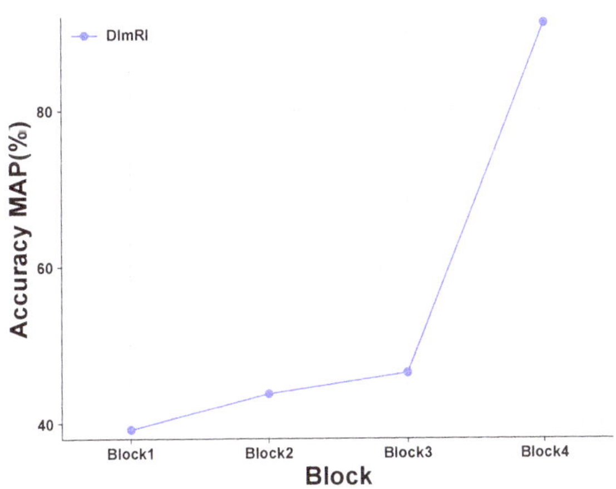

Figure 10. The figure shows the effect of imposing a margin on different blocks on the MAP score using our DlmRl.

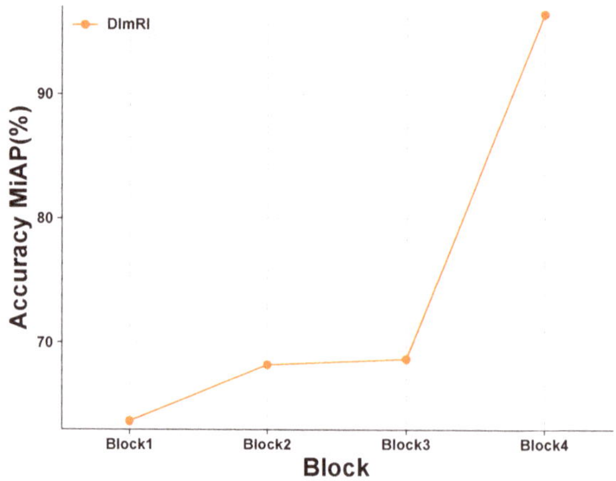

Figure 11. The figure shows the effect of imposing a margin on different blocks on the MiAP score using our DlmRl.

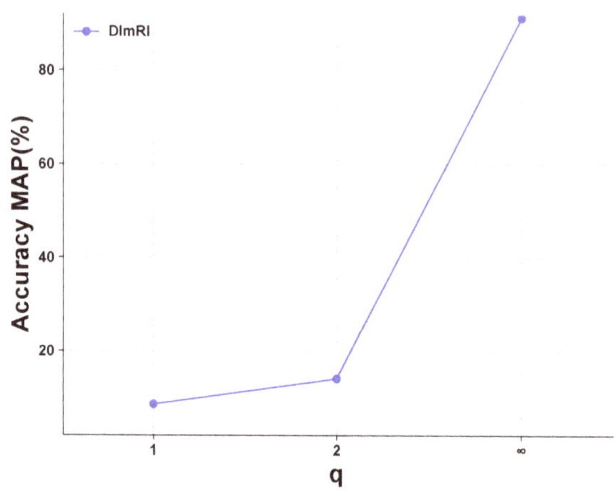

Figure 12. The figure shows the effect of q on the MAP score using our DlmRl.

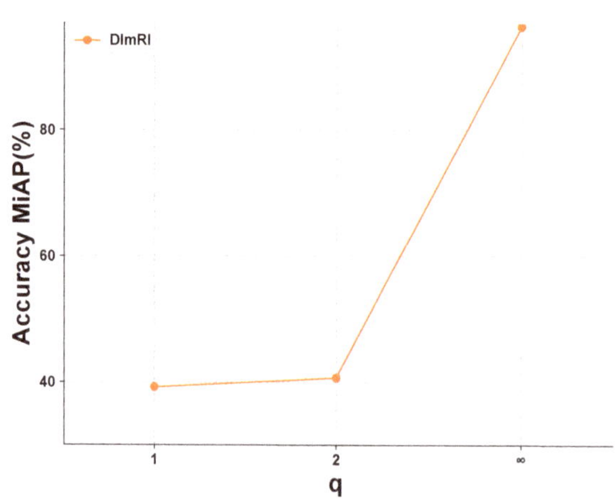

Figure 13. The figure shows the effect of q about MiAP score which using our DlmRl.

According to the above analysis, in the experiments described previously, we set $\gamma = 10^3, \epsilon = 10^{-6}, q = \infty$ and impose large margin on Block4 of ResNet-101 by default.

5. Conclusions

In this paper, we have proposed a novel loss, i.e., DlmRl, for a MLiC task. It is a plug and play loss, and is thus applicable to any network architecture. In contrast to a traditional large margin, the ranking loss encourages only margins at the output layer of a deep neural network, so the proposed loss formulation imposes a margin on any chosen set of layers of a deep network and allows choosing any ℓ_p norm ($p \geq 1$) on the metric measuring the margin between labels— showing a far more flexible and compatible implementation. We design a negative sampling technique to make it more computationally efficient, thus addressing the scalability issues brought by full computation. Experiments on the VOC2007 dataset and the COCO dataset have verified that our DlmRl is better than other methods by applying a margin to the input layer, and our computational efficiency has been greatly improved thanks to the introduction of negative sampling technology. Extensive experiments show that our loss formulation is more robust than traditional loss formulations of MLiC.

Author Contributions: Writing—original draft, Z.L.; Writing—review & editing, Z.M. and Y.Z.; Project administration, Y.Z. All authors have read and agreed to the published version of the manuscript.

Funding: This research was funded by the National Natural Science Foundation of China (NSFC) grant number 62006098, and the Fellowship of China Postdoctoral Science Foundation grant number 2020M681515.

Institutional Review Board Statement: Not applicable.

Informed Consent Statement: Not applicable.

Data Availability Statement: Not applicable.

Conflicts of Interest: The authors declare no conflict of interest.

References

1. Chen, L.; Zhan, W.; Tian, W.; He, Y.; Zou, Q. Deep integration: A multi-label architecture for road scene recognition. *IEEE Trans. Image Process.* **2019**, *28*, 4883–4898. [CrossRef] [PubMed]
2. Chen, B.; Zhang, Z.; Lu, Y.; Chen, F.; Lu, G.; Zhang, D. Semantic-interactive graph convolutional network for multilabel image recognition. *IEEE Trans. Syst. Man Cybern. Syst.* **2021**, *52*, 4887–4899. [CrossRef] [PubMed]
3. Ge, Z.; Mahapatra, D.; Sedai, S.; Garnavi, R.; Chakravorty, R. Chest x-rays classification: A multi-label and fine-grained problem. *arXiv* **2018**, arXiv:1807.07247. [CrossRef]
4. Gérardin, C.; Wajsbürt, P.; Vaillant, P.; Bellamine, A.; Carrat, F.; Tannier, X. Multilabel classification of medical concepts for patient clinical profile identification. *Artif. Intell. Med.* **2022**, *128*, 102311. [CrossRef]
5. Boutell, M.R.; Luo, J.; Shen, X.; Brown, C.M. Learning multi-label scene classification. *Pattern Recognit.* **2004**, *37*, 1757–1771.
6. Tsoumakas, G.; Vlahavas, I. Random k-labelsets: An ensemble method for multilabel classification. In *European Conference on Machine Learning*; Springer: Berlin/Heidelberg, Germany, 2007; pp. 406–417. [CrossRef] [PubMed]
7. Zhang, M.L.; Zhou, Z.H. Ml-knn: A lazy learning approach to multi-label learning. *Pattern Recognit.* **2007**, *40*, 2038–2048 [CrossRef]
8. Elisseeff, A.; Weston, J. A kernel method for multi-labelled classification. *Adv. Neural Inf. Process. Syst.* **2001**, *14*, 681–687.
9. Lowe, D.G. Distinctive image features from scaleinvariant keypoints. *Int. J. Comput. Vis.* **2004**, *60*, 91–110. [CrossRef]
10. Dalal, N.; Triggs, B. Histograms of oriented gradients for human detection. In Proceedings of the 2005 IEEE Computer Society Conference on Computer Vision and Pattern Recognition (CVPR'05), San Diego, CA, USA, 20–26 June 2005; IEEE: Piscataway, NJ, USA, 2005; Volume 1, pp. 886–893.
11. Ojala, T.; Pietikäinen, M.; Harwood, D. A comparative study of texture measures with classification based on featured distributions. *Pattern Recognit.* **1996**, *29*, 51–59. [CrossRef]
12. Wang, J.; Yang, Y.; Mao, J.; Huang, Z.; Huang, C.; Xu, W. Cnn-rnn: A unified framework for multi-label image classification. In Proceedings of the IEEE Conference on Computer Vision and Pattern Recognition, Las Vegas, NV, USA, 27–30 June 2016; pp. 2285–2294.
13. Chen, Z.M.; Wei, X.S.; Wang, P.; Guo, Y. Multi-label image recognition with graph convolutional networks. In Proceedings of the IEEE/CVF Conference on Computer Vision and Pattern Recognition, Long Beach, CA, USA, 15–20 June 2019; pp. 5177–5186. [CrossRef]

14. Xu, Z.; Liu, Y.; Li, C. Distributed information-theoretic semisupervised learning for multilabel classification. *IEEE Trans. Cybern.* **2022**, *52*, 821–835. [CrossRef]
15. Ma, J.; Chiu, B.C.Y.; Chow, T.W.S. Multilabel classification with group-based mapping: A framework with local feature selection and local label correlation. *IEEE Trans. Cybern.* **2020**, *52*, 4596–4610. [CrossRef]
16. Elsayed, G.; Krishnan, D.; Mobahi, H.; Regan, K.; Bengio, S. Large margin deep networks for classification. *Adv. Neural Inf. Process. Syst.* **2018**, *31*, 842–852.
17. Chen, L.; Wang, R.; Yang, J.; Xue, L.; Hu, M. Multi-label image classification with recurrently learning semantic dependencies. *Vis. Comput.* **2019**, *35*, 1361–1371.
18. Liu, F.; Xiang, T.; Hospedales, T.M.; Yang, W.; Sun, C. Semantic regularisation for recurrent image annotation. In Proceedings of the IEEE Conference on Computer Vision and Pattern Recognition, Honolulu, HI, USA, 21–26 July 2017; pp. 2872–2880. [CrossRef]
19. Meng, Q.; Zhang, W. Multilabel image classification with attention mechanism and graph convolutional networks. In Proceedings of the ACM Multimedia Asia, Beijing, China, 16–18 December 2019; pp. 1–6. [CrossRef]
20. Wu, X.; Chen, Q.; Li, W.; Xiao, Y.; Hu, B. Adahgnn: Adaptive hypergraph neural networks for multi-label image classification. In Proceedings of the 28th ACM International Conference on Multimedia, Seattle, WA, USA, 12–16 October 2020; pp. 284–293.
21. Oquab, M.; Bottou, L.; Laptev, I.; Sivic, J. Is object localization for free?-weakly-supervised learning with convolutional neural networks. In Proceedings of the IEEE Conference on Computer Vision and Pattern Recognition, Boston, MA, USA, 7–12 June 2015; pp. 685-694. [CrossRef]
22. Gou, J.; Sun, L.; Du, L.; Ma, H.; Xiong, T.; Ou, W.; Zhan, Y. A representation coefficient-based k-nearest centroid neighbor classifier. *Expert Syst. Appl.* **2022**, *194*, 116529. [CrossRef]
23. Zhou, B.; Khosla, A.; Lapedriza, A.; Oliva, A.; Torralba, A. Learning deep features for discriminative localization. In Proceedings of the IEEE Conference on Computer Vision and Pattern Recognition, Las Vegas, NV, USA, 27–30 June 2016; pp. 2921–2929.
24. Martins, A.; Astudillo, R. From softmax to sparsemax: A sparse model of attention and multilabel classification. In Proceedings of the International Conference on Machine Learning (PMLR 2016), New York, NY, USA, 19–24 June 2016; pp. 1614–1623.
25. Zhu, K.; Wu, J. Residual attention: A simple but effective method for multi-label recognition. In Proceedings of the IEEE/CVF International Conference on Computer Vision, Montreal, QC, Canada, 10–17 October 2021; pp. 184–193.
26. Ma, Z.; Chen, S. A Similarity-based Framework for Classification Task. *IEEE Trans. Knowl. Data Eng.* **2022**. [CrossRef]
27. Izadinia, H.; Russell, B.C.; Farhadi, A.; Hoffman, M.D.; Hertzmann, A. Deep classifiers from image tags in the wild. In Proceedings of the 2015 Workshop on Community-Organized Multimodal Mining: Opportunities for Novel Solutions, Brisbane, Australia, 26–30 October 2015; pp. 13–18.
28. Xie, M.K.; Huang, S.J. Partial multi-label learning with noisy label identification. *IEEE Trans. Pattern Anal. Mach. Intell.* **2021**, *44*, 3676–3689. [CrossRef]
29. Durand, T.; Mehrasa, N.; Mori, G. Learning a deep convnet for multi-label classification with partial labels. In Proceedings of the IEEE/CVF Conference on Computer Vision and Pattern Recognition, Long Beach, CA, USA, 15–20 June 2019; pp. 647–657.
30. Huynh, D.; Elhamifar, E. Interactive multi-label cnn learning with partial labels. In Proceedings of the IEEE/CVF Conference on Computer Vision and Pattern Recognition, Seattle, WA, USA, 13–19 June 2020; pp. 9423–9432.
31. Gong, Y.; Jia, Y.; Leung, T.; Toshev, A.; Ioffe, S. Deep convolutional ranking for multilabel image annotation. *arXiv* **2013**, arXiv:1312.4894.
32. Cortes, C.; Vapnik, V. Support-vector networks. *Mach. Learn.* **1995**, *20*, 273–297. [CrossRef]
33. Freund, Y.; Schapire, R.E. A decision-theoretic generalization of on-line learning and an application to boosting. *J. Comput. Syst. Sci.* **1997**, *55*, 119–139.
34. Sun, S.; Chen, W.; Wang, L.; Liu, T.-Y. Large margin deep neural networks: Theory and algorithms. *arXiv* **2015**, arXiv:1506.05232. [CrossRef]
35. Sokolić, J.; Giryes, R.; Sapiro, G.; Rodrigues, M.R.D. Robust large margin deep neural networks. *IEEE Trans. Signal Process.* **2017**, *65*, 4265–4280.
36. Li, Y.; Song, Y.; Luo, J. Improving pairwise ranking for multi-label image classification. In Proceedings of the IEEE Conference on Computer Vision and Pattern Recognition, Honolulu, HI, USA, 21–26 July 2017; pp. 3617–3625.
37. Everingham, M.; Eslami, S.M.; Van Gool, L.; Williams, C.K.; Winn, J.; Zisserman, A. The pascal visual object classes challenge: A retrospective. *Int. J. Comput. Vis.* **2015**, *111*, 98–136.
38. Lin, T.Y.; Maire, M.; Belongie, S.; Hays, J.; Perona, P.; Ramanan, D.; Dollár, P.; Zitnick, C.L. Microsoft coco: Common objects in context. In *European Conference on Computer Vision*; Springer: Cham, Switzerland, 2014; pp. 740–755.
39. Baeza-Yates, R.; Ribeiro-Neto, B. *Modern Information Retrieval*; ACM Press: New York, NY, USA, 1999; Volume 463. [CrossRef]
40. Xie, M.K.; Huang, S.J. Ccmn: A general framework for learning with class-conditional multi-label noise. *IEEE Trans. Pattern Anal. Mach. Intell.* **2022**. [CrossRef]
41. Imambi, S.; Prakash, K.B.; Kanagachidambaresan, G.R. PyTorch. In *Programming with TensorFlow*; Springer: Cham, Switzerland, 2021; pp. 87–104. [CrossRef]

mathematics

Article

Dual-Word Embedding Model Considering Syntactic Information for Cross-Domain Sentiment Classification

Zihao Lu [1], Xiaohui Hu [2,*] and Yun Xue [2]

[1] School of Physics and Telecommunication Engineering, South China Normal University, Guangzhou 510006, China
[2] School of Electronics and Information Engineering, South China Normal University, Foshan 528225, China
* Correspondence: huxh@scnu.edu.cn

Abstract: The purpose of cross-domain sentiment classification (CDSC) is to fully utilize the rich labeled data in the source domain to help the target domain perform sentiment classification even when labeled data are insufficient. Most of the existing methods focus on obtaining domain transferable semantic information but ignore syntactic information. The performance of BERT may decrease because of domain transfer, and traditional word embeddings, such as word2vec, cannot obtain contextualized word vectors. Therefore, achieving the best results in CDSC is difficult when only BERT or word2vec is used. In this paper, we propose a Dual-word Embedding Model Considering Syntactic Information for Cross-domain Sentiment Classification. Specifically, we obtain dual-word embeddings using BERT and word2vec. After performing BERT embedding, we pay closer attention to semantic information, mainly using self-attention and TextCNN. After word2vec word embedding is obtained, the graph attention network is used to extract the syntactic information of the document, and the attention mechanism is used to focus on the important aspects. Experiments on two real-world datasets show that our model outperforms other strong baselines.

Keywords: cross-domain sentiment classification; word embedding; GAT

MSC: 68T50

Citation: Lu, Z.; Hu, X.; Xue, Y. Dual-Word Embedding Model Considering Syntactic Information for Cross-Domain Sentiment Classification. *Mathematics* **2022**, *10*, 4704. https://doi.org/10.3390/math10244704

Academic Editors: Jianping Gou, Weihua Ou, Shaoning Zeng and Lan Du

Received: 9 November 2022
Accepted: 9 December 2022
Published: 11 December 2022

1. Introduction

Sentiment classification is an important task in natural language processing, and it can help people make better decisions in daily life [1,2]. Over the past few decades, many machine learning methods have been introduced for classification tasks, such as logistic regression, collaborative representation, support vector machines, and neural networks [3–7]. With the development of the internet, a large number of user comments and other texts containing sentiment have been generated from different domains. However, the classical sentiment classification methods require that the training and testing data come from the same domain [8,9]. In addition, the training of deep networks relies on a large amount of labeled data, but texts in many domains lack sufficient labeled data. Cross-domain sentiment classification (CDSC) is a promising direction that can make full use of the rich labeled data in the source domain to assist the target domain with the lack of labeled data for sentiment classification.

Traditional word-level vector representations, such as word2vec [10], glove [11], and fastText [12], can use a single vector to represent all possible meanings of a word. This method results in providing the same representation for words that express different sentiment polarities in various domains. In recent years, pre-trained language models, such as ELMO [13] and BERT [14], have been widely used in natural language processing (NLP) tasks because they can obtain contextualized word embedding. Notably, BERT has achieved state-of-the-art results on many NLP tasks because of its strong language understanding capabilities. In cross-lingual tasks, multilingual BERT (mBERT) can share part of its representation space between languages [15]. In addition, the mBERT language model has the ability to transfer syntactic knowledge cross-lingually, and can embed the dependency parse tree of sentences cross-lingually [16]. This shows that Bert parse trees have a strong ability to perform different tasks. However, some problems occur with directly fine-tuning BERT in CDSC tasks [17]. One of the pre-training tasks of BERT is to randomly MASK off 15% of the words, and when the words are filled back, various domains may fill back different words. In addition, because no labeled data exist in the target domain, fine-tuning only by the labeled data in the source domain reduces the performance because of different training and test distributions. Therefore, using BERT or word2vec only to obtain word vector embeddings in CDSC is insufficient. On the other hand, many current models aim to learn transferable semantic information in CDSC to predict the sentiment polarity of the target domain. However, in addition to semantic information, syntactic information is equally important. Therefore, extracting transferable syntactic information is important for CDSC tasks to better help target domain sentiment classification.

To solve the above problems, we propose a dual-word embedding model considering syntactic information for CDSC. The model performs dual-word embedding through BERT and word2vec to obtain rich word embedding information. Different from most previous models that only consider semantic information, we adopt dual-channel to obtain transferable semantic information and syntactic information. Semantic information is obtained by self-attention and TextCNN. Syntactic information is obtained through the graph attention network so that the aspects in the sentence can obtain syntactic information [18]. Then, the attention mechanism is used to pay attention to important aspects so that the syntactic information of aspects can play a role. Finally, domain-invariant features are obtained through adversarial training. The contributions of our study can be summarized as follows:

- A CDSC method is proposed using BERT and word2vec to obtain dual-word embeddings;
- Dual-channel feature extraction and adversarial training to obtain transferable semantic and syntactic information;
- Extensive experiments are conducted on two real-world datasets, and experimental results show that our model achieves better results compared to other strong baselines.

2. Related Work

2.1. CDSC

CDSC aims to utilize the source domain with rich labeled data to help sentiment classification in the target domain without labeled data. The traditional CDSC method needs to manually select pivots. Blitzer et al. [19] proposed the structural correspondence learning (SCL) method. The most frequently used words in both domains are good predictors of source domain labels, so they select the set of pivot features that appear most frequently in both the source and target domains. Pan et al. [20] proposed spectral feature alignment (SFA) for CDSC. They want to associate the source domain with the target domain by aligning pivots with non-pivots. However, manually obtaining domain-invariant features through these traditional methods is a time-consuming and expensive process. With the rise of neural networks in recent years, many scholars have explored the application of deep learning in CDSC tasks. Among them, the domain adversarial neural network (DANN) [21] is explored to learn domain-invariant features in the min-max game between the domain classifier and the feature extractor through adversarial training. Li et al. [22] proposed a hierarchical attention transfer network (HATN) that can automatically capture pivots and non-pivots through hierarchical attention and auxiliary tasks. Zhang et al. [23] designed an interactive attention transfer network (IATN) that applies interactive attention to CDSC, considering the influence of aspects in sentences. Yang et al. [24] proposed a dual-channel mutual learning domain adaptive model. In recent years, BERT has been gradually applied to CDSC because of the advantages of the BERT pre-training model. Du et al. [17] designed a domain-aware BERT (BERT-DAAT) to apply BERT to unsupervised CDSC tasks. Du et al. [25] designed a Wasserstein-based transfer network (WTN) to obtain rich domain-invariant features. Fu et al. [26] paid closer attention to the intra-domain structure, and they proposed domain adaptation with a contractible difference strategy. The successful application of the attention mechanism improves classification accuracy substantially. However, it is difficult to obtain syntactic information using attention. In this paper, we consider adding a graph attention network to obtain transferable syntactic information.

2.2. *Graph Attention Work*

Graph neural networks have received extensive attention from scholars in recent years because these networks allow the use of deep learning frameworks on graph structure data [27–30]. At present, many mature neural network models can work on regular network structures. Since the graph convolutional neural network (GCN) [31] was proposed as a deep convolutional learning paradigm for graph structure data, it has filled the gap in the development of deep learning for processing such data. To capture the dependencies between discontinuous and long-distance words in a document, Vashishth et al. [32] used GCN to characterize the dependency tree for each sentence in the document. However, the importance of each node in the graph should be different, and a graph convolutional neural network cannot deal with this situation. Therefore, some researchers have introduced the idea of attention mechanism into the graph convolutional neural network. Veličković proposed [33] graph attention network (GAT), which mainly improves GCN by using the attention mechanism to aggregate the characteristics of discriminated neighbor nodes. Therefore, compared with GCN, GAT can better handle dynamic graphs. Huang et al. [18] used GAT to establish dependencies between words. Although it is common to use GCN or GAT to obtain syntactic information in single-domain tasks, few people extract syntactic information in CDSC tasks.

2.3. *Word Embedding*

Word vector representations transform words in natural language into a form that the computer can recognize and understand [34]. We can obtain word vector representations by using word embedding methods, such as word2vec and glove. Nguyen et al. [35] applied a word2vec embedding model to construct a semantic vector for the plot content of each movie. Wang et al. [36] trained their personality classification model on a shared potential feature space by predictive text embedding. Naderalvojoud [37] et al. proposed two methods to create sentiment-aware word embeddings, improving on the pre-trained word embedding of the word2vec and gloVe models.

In recent years, BERT has received a lot of attention because it can learn contextualized word representations. BERT is a bidirectional variant of the multilayer transformer, which further integrates bidirectional representations. Jawahar et al. [38] revealed elements of the English language structure learned by BERT. They also demonstrated that BERT captures phrase-level information at the low layers, syntactic features at the intermediate layers, and semantic features at the high layers. In addition, the information at lower layers is diluted at higher layers. In this paper, we combine word2vec and BERT to obtain rich word vector information. In addition, in order to prevent the low-layer information from being diluted at the high-layer, we use the weighted sum of all layer information of BERT as the input vector.

3. Methodology

In this section, we introduce the framework of DWE in technical detail. First, we describe the problem and provide a model structure. Then, the training strategy is detailed.

3.1. *Problem Definition*

In the task of CDSC, we are given two domains, D_s and D_t, which denote a source domain and a target domain, respectively. A set of labeled data $\{X_s, Y_s\}$ is used in D_s, where $\{X_s, Y_s\} = \{x_i^s, y_i^s\}_{i=1}^{N_s}$ presents N_s labeled samples in D_s. We also have a set of unlabeled data $\{X_t\}$ in D_t, where $\{X_t\} = \{x_i^t\}_{i=1}^{N_t}$ presents N_t unlabeled samples in D_t.

The goal of the CDSC task is to utilize the source domain with rich labeled data to assist the target domain lacking labeled data for sentiment classification.

3.2. Model Structure

As shown in Figure 1, DWE mainly contains three parts: feature extraction module, domain discriminator, and sentiment classifier. The feature extraction module uses dual channels to obtain semantic information and syntactic information. The domain discriminator obtains domain-invariant features. The sentiment classifier uses the softmax activation function to obtain the probability of the sentiment label.

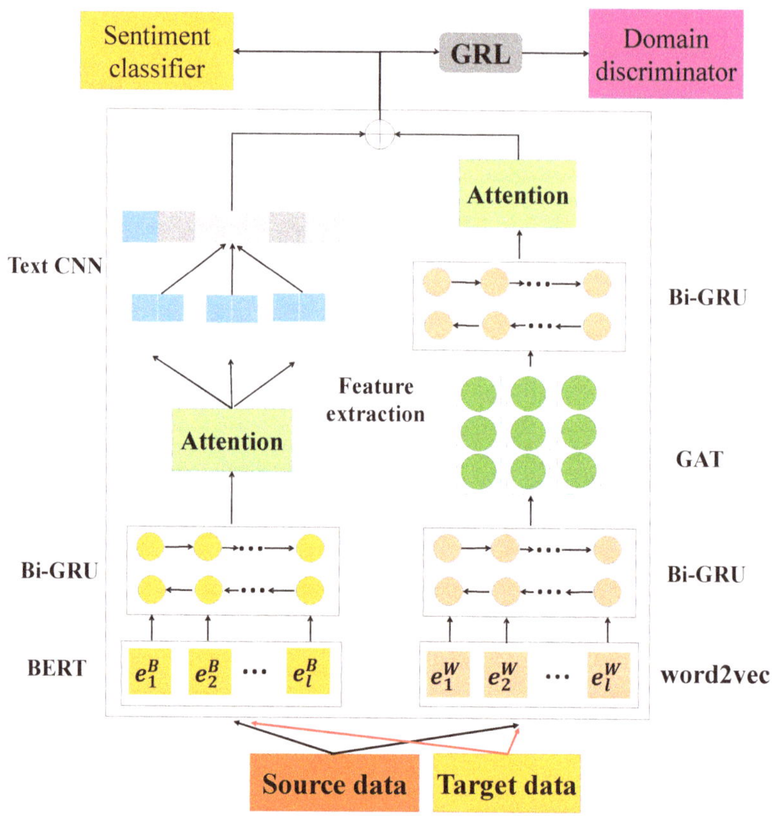

Figure 1. Model architecture.

3.3. Feature Extraction

To get rich word embedding information, we use BERT and word2vec to obtain dual word embedding. After obtaining different word embeddings, a dual channel is formed to extract transferable semantic information and syntactic information.

3.3.1. Bert Semantic Channel

In this channel, we mainly extract semantic information. We first use BERT to obtain word vectors. To prevent the loss of some information, unlike in the general final hidden state using the BERT structure, we apply an approach similar to that by Du et al. [25], using the weighted sum of all hidden states as the input vector. We define the nth hidden state of the mth layer as h_n^m. We suppose that a document contains S sentences with k words, and w_i is the ith word of the input document. w_i is tokenized to q BPE (byte pair encoding) tokens $w_i = \{b_i^1, b_i^2, \ldots, \ldots, b_i^n\}$. The word vector obtained by BERT can be defined as

$$e_i^B = \sum_{m=1}^{L} \alpha_m \cdot \frac{\sum_{n=1}^{q} h_n^m}{q} \tag{1}$$

where α_m and L are the weight coefficients of layer m and the number of hidden state layers of BERT, respectively. BiGRU is the variant of BiLSTM, which has the ability to learn long-term dependencies. We can use BiGRU to build sequential information about words or sentences. Thus, we then input the word vector into BiGRU to obtain the hidden states

$$h_i^B = BiGRU\left(e_i^B\right) \tag{2}$$

Different words in a sentence have different effects on sentence sentiment because these words express different semantic information. The attention mechanism can pay attention to the words that play an important role in sentence sentiment according to attention coefficient. In this paper, we use self-attention to calculate word-to-word associations in sentences, which can focus on words that have a stronger impact on sentence sentiment. Attention scores were calculated as follows:

$$g_i^B = tanh\left(W * h_i^B + b\right) \tag{3}$$

where W and b represent the learnable weight matrix and bias in the network, respectively.

Furthermore, we normalized the attention scores by using the softmax activation function to generate the attention coefficients α_i^B for each word

$$\alpha_i^B = \frac{exp(g_i^B)}{\sum_{i=1}^{n} exp(g_i^B)} \tag{4}$$

The attention coefficient is combined with the hidden state obtained by BiGRU to obtain the sentence vector s^B

$$s^B = \sum_{j=1}^{k} \alpha_j^B \cdot h_j^B \tag{5}$$

where $\cdot$ indicates the element-wise product. After obtaining sentence vectors, TextCNN [39] is used to further extract important semantic information that mainly includes convolution layer and pooling layer. First, we input the sentence vector to the convolution layer and the convolution operation involves the filter w_{cnn}

$$c^B = F\left(w_{cnn} \circ s^B + b_{cnn}\right) \tag{6}$$

where $\circ$ represents the convolution operation, b_{cnn} is the bias term, and F is a nonlinear function such as Relu. Then, max pooling is performed to retain important features. Finally, dropout prevents overfitting to obtain the sentence representation of the semantic channel. The relevant formulas are the following:

$$c_p^B = Maxpooling\left(c^B\right) \tag{7}$$

$$d^B = dropout\left(c_p^B\right) \tag{8}$$

3.3.2. Word2vec Syntax Channel

In this channel, we first use word2vec to obtain the word vector representation

$$e_i^w = word2vec(w_i) \tag{9}$$

Then, input the word vector into BiGRU to extract the sentence representation. The hidden output of BiGRU can be expressed as follows:

$$h_i^w = BiGRU(e_i^w) \tag{10}$$

To obtain syntactic information, the syntax dependency tree of the given sentence is built in advance, and then the tree structure is converted into a graph structure in which each node represents a word. Given a dependency graph with N nodes, the node representation is computed by aggregating the hidden states of the neighborhood. After l layers of GAT, the last layer outputs the syntactic representation. The output of the ith node at layer l is defined as g_i^l, and g_i^0 indicates the initial node status, $g_i^0 = h_i^w$. The node update process is as follows:

$$e_{ij}^l = leakyRelu\left(\alpha^{l^T}\left(W_g^l g_i^l \| W_g^l g_j^l\right)\right) \tag{11}$$

$$\alpha_{ij}^l = \frac{exp\left(e_{ij}^l\right)}{\sum_{k \in N(k)} e_{ik}^l} \tag{12}$$

$$g_i^{l+1} = \sigma\left(\sum_{j \in N(i)} \alpha_{ij}^l W_g^l g_i^l\right) \tag{13}$$

where W_g^l and α^{l^T} are trainable weight matrices and weight vectors, respectively. $\|$ represents vector concatenation. e_{ij}^l is the raw attention score between the ith and jth nodes. $N(i)$ is the set of all adjacent nodes. α_{ij}^l is the normalized attention weight. σ denotes a Relu activation function. For simplicity, we can write such feature propagation process as

$$g_i^{l+1} = GAT\left(g_i^l, A, \theta_l\right) \tag{14}$$

where A is the graph adjacent matrix and θ_l is the set of parameters at layer l. Finally, we input the syntactic representation into BiGRU and Attention. BiGRU can build the long-term dependencies of sentences in a document. Attention mechanism can make the syntactic information of important aspects in syntactic representation play a more critical role. Thus, we obtain the final representation of the syntactic channel:

$$H_i^w = BiGRU(g_i^w) \tag{15}$$

$$\alpha_i^w = \frac{exp(tanh(W_w H_i^w + b_w))}{\sum_{i=1}^n exp(tanh(W_w H_i^w + b_w))} \tag{16}$$

$$d^w = \sum_{j=1}^k \alpha_j^w \cdot H_j^w \tag{17}$$

where α_i^w, $\cdot$, W_w and b_w represent the attention weight, the element-wise product, the learnable weight matrix, and bias in the network, respectively.

3.3.3. Final Document Representation

The final document representation is obtained by concatenating the document representation of the two channels as follows:

$$d = \left[d^B, d^w\right] \tag{18}$$

3.4. Sentiment Classifier

The ultimate goal of our task is to predict sentiment labels. In this module, we use the softmax activation function to obtain the sentiment prediction label for the document

$$y = softmax(W_y d + b_y) \tag{19}$$

where W_y and b_y represent the learnable weight matrix and bias, respectively.

3.5. Domain Discriminator

The purpose of the domain discriminator (D) is to enable the feature extractor (FE) to learn domain-invariant representations. We consider using adversarial training. The domain discriminator tries to find out which domain the document vector comes from, while the feature extractor aims to deceive the domain discriminator so that it cannot distinguish which domain the document comes from and achieve the purpose of domain information transfer. The domain discriminator regards the document representation obtained by the feature extractor as input and outputs the probability that the document comes from the source domain. If a document belongs to the source domain, we set $r_i = 1$. For the target domain, we set $r_i = 0$. To better solve this problem, we introduce a gradient reversal layer (GRL) that can reverse the gradient direction during training. We can treat the gradient reversal layer as a pseudo function $G(x)$. Through the domain discriminator, we can obtain domain-invariant features. Formally, the domain discriminator performs a min-max game to optimize the parameters Θ_{FE} and Θ_D as follows:

$$\tilde{d} = G(d) \tag{20}$$

$$y'_d = softmax(W_d \tilde{d} + b_d) \tag{21}$$

$$\Theta_{FE}, \Theta_D = \underset{\Theta_{FE}}{argmax} \, \underset{\Theta_D}{min} \, L_{dom} \tag{22}$$

$$L_{dom} = -(r_i In y'_d + (1 - r_i) In(1 - y'_d)) \tag{23}$$

where L_{dom}, Θ_{FE}, and Θ_D represent the domain loss, parameters of the feature extractor, and parameters of the domain discriminator, respectively.

3.6. Training Strategy

We apply the cross-entropy loss function to the sentiment classifier to obtain the sentiment classification loss

$$L_{sen} = -(y' In y + (1 - y') In(1 - y)) \tag{24}$$

where y' represents the ground truth of the sentiment label. Furthermore, we obtain our total loss function

$$L_{total} = L_{sen} + L_{dom} + \rho L_{reg} \tag{25}$$

$$L_{reg} = \lambda ||\theta||^2 \tag{26}$$

where L_{reg}, ρ, λ, θ represents the L_2 regularization term which can avoid overfitting, regularization parameter, hyperparameters, and all parameters in the network, respectively. The regularization term can automatically weaken unimportant feature variables, automatically extract important feature variables from many feature variables, and reduce the magnitude of feature variables.

4. Experiment

4.1. Datasets

To verify the effectiveness of the proposed model, we used two datasets which are obtained from Amazon product reviews. Dataset 1 has been widely used in CDSC tasks. It contains reviews from four different domains: Books (B), DVDs (D), Electronics (E), and Kitchen (K). A total of 2000 labeled data are in each domain, consisting of 1000 positive reviews and 1000 negative reviews. We selected 800 positive and 800 negative reviews in the source domain as the training data; 1600 in the target domain for domain classification; and the remaining 200 positive reviews and 200 negative reviews in the target domain as the test data. Table 1 records the details of Dataset 1.

Dataset 2, constructed by He et al. [40], contains data for three sentiment labels, namely, positive, neutral, and negative, so this dataset is more convincing. Dataset 2 also contains data from four domains: Book (BK), Beauty (BT), Music (M), and Electronics (E). Each domain has two types of data: Set 1 and Set 2. Set 1 is balanced, with 2000 data for each sentiment label, while Set 2 is unbalanced. For Dataset 2, we choose processing similar to that used by Du et al. [25], using balanced Set 1 as the training data of the source domain, and using unbalanced data Set 2 as the training data of the target domain. We selected 1200 reviews from the training set of the source domain as the development set. The balanced data Set 1 from the target domain is used as the test set. Table 2 presents an overview of the datasets.

Table 1. Statistics of Dataset 1.

Domain	Positive	Negative	Vocabulary
Books	1000	1000	26,278
DVD	1000	1000	26,940
Electronics	1000	1000	13,256
Kitchen	1000	1000	11,187

Table 2. Statistics of Dataset 2.

Domain		Positive	Negative	Neutral
Book	Set1	2000	2000	2000
	Set2	4824	513	663
Beauty	Set1	2000	2000	2000
	Set2	4709	616	675
Music	Set1	2000	2000	2000
	Set2	4441	785	774
Electronics	Set1	2000	2000	2000
	Set2	4817	694	489

4.2. Experiment Setup

In the experiment, we use the common word2vec and BERT to obtain dual-word embedding. First, we use 300-dimensional word2vec vectors as one of the word embeddings, which are trained on 100 billion words from Google News. Then, we fine-tune it during the training. We use uniform distribution U (−0.25,0.25) to randomly initialize words outside the vocabulary. In addition, we use BERT with 12 layers, 768 hidden units, 12 self-attention heads, and 110 million parameters as another word embedding. The dimension of the attention vector is set to 200. The dimension of the feature representation in each field and the maximum word number of every review are set to 200. The weight matrix in the network is randomly initialized from the uniform distribution U (−0.01,0.01). The dropout rate is 0.5 to prevent overfitting. The number of GAT layers is set to 3, and Adam algorithm is used as the optimizer.

4.3. Experimental Results

Following previous studies, we apply the accuracy rate as the evaluation standard. The accuracy rate is the percentage of correctly classified data in the total data. The best results are highlighted in bold. We compare the proposed model DWE with some classic baselines as follows:

- DANN [21]: The model is trained using the domain adversarial network approach, including GRL for domain obfuscation;
- AuxNN [41]: The model uses auxiliary tasks for CDSC;
- AMN [42]: The model is based on memory network and the adversarial training method to obtain domain-invariant features;
- DAS [40]: It uses feature adaptation and semi-supervised learning to improve classifiers while minimizing domain divergence;
- HATN [22]: The hierarchical attention network is used for CDSC, and pivots and non-pivots features are extracted to assist classification tasks;
- IATN [23]: Interactive attention mechanism is used to connect sentences with important aspects;
- WTN [25]: A Wasserstein-based transfer network is used to obtain domain-invariant features;
- PTASM [43]: The attention-sharing mechanism and parameter transferring method are used for CDSC;
- DWE w/o BERT: The BERT word embedding is removed from our proposed model;
- DWE w/o word2vec: The word2vec word embedding is removed from our proposed model.

Table 3 records the classification accuracy of different models on Dataset 1. The results show that our proposed model DWE achieves the best performance on 11 cross-domain pairs. Our model outperforms DANN by 12.24%, AMN by 9.64%, DAS by 9.44%, HATN by 6.74%, IATN by 5.64%, WTN by 1.14%, and PTASM by 0.44% on average. DAS uses entropy minimization and self-integration methods to refine its classifier, which improves the experimental results compared with DANN and AMN. The addition of attention has greatly improved HATN and IATN compared with DAS, reflecting the effectiveness of the attention mechanism. Both WTN and PTASM have applied BERT to CDSC, which has been greatly improved compared with previous methods. WTN is based on Wasserstein distance as a domain discrepancy learning module, while PTASM uses an attention transfer mechanism and hierarchical attention to improve target domain classification. Different from previous methods, our proposed model uses dual-word embedding to make up for the deficiency of single word embedding. Our model also considers both transferable semantic information and syntactic information, which may be the reason for the improvement of our model.

Table 3. Classification accuracy of various models on Dataset 1.

S → T	DANN	AMN	DAS	HATN	IATN	WTN	PTASM	DWE
B → D	0.8330	0.8450	0.8390	0.8590	0.8680	0.9090	0.9012	**0.9150**
B → K	0.7920	0.8090	0.8220	0.8470	0.8590	0.8840	0.9060	**0.9100**
B → E	0.7730	0.8030	0.8120	0.8490	0.8650	0.8960	0.9010	**0.9075**
D → B	0.8050	0.8360	0.8190	0.8600	0.8700	0.9080	0.8990	**0.9125**
D → E	0.7980	0.8050	0.8160	0.8510	0.8690	**0.9150**	0.9110	**0.9150**
D → K	0.8080	0.8160	0.8140	0.8580	0.8580	0.8910	0.9080	**0.9100**
K → B	0.7490	0.8010	0.8020	0.8260	0.8470	0.9160	0.9210	**0.9250**
K → E	0.8320	0.8540	0.8590	0.8640	0.8760	0.9190	0.9190	**0.9200**
K → D	0.7680	0.8120	0.8150	0.8400	0.8440	0.8890	0.9140	**0.9150**
E → K	0.8380	0.8580	0.8490	0.8760	0.8870	**0.9320**	0.9170	0.9300
E → B	0.7350	0.7740	0.7970	0.8060	0.8180	0.9010	0.9140	**0.9175**
E → D	0.7790	0.8170	0.8020	0.8380	0.8410	0.8920	0.9070	**0.9075**
Average	0.7930	0.8190	0.8210	0.8480	0.8590	0.9040	0.9110	**0.9154**

Furthermore, we also compare our proposed model DWE with other baseline models on Dataset 2 and conduct ablation experiments simultaneously.

Table 4 records the classification accuracy on Dataset 2. We can see that our model DWE has the best performance among all cross-domain pairs. Our model outperforms AuxNN by 9.5%, DAS by 6.5%, and WTN by 3.8% on average, which demonstrates the effectiveness of our proposed model. On the other hand, after removing BERT word embedding and word2vec word embedding, the average performance decreases by 8.9% and 1.9%, respectively, which demonstrates the validation of the proposed dual-word embedding. The possible reason is that the single word embedding causes the model to lose part of the information, especially after removing the BERT word embedding, where a large amount of context-related information is lost.

Table 4. Classification accuracy of various models on Dataset 2.

S → T	AuxNN	DAS	WTN	DWE w/o BERT	DWE w/o word2vec	DWE
BK → BT	0.478	0.547	0.576	0.5160	0.558	**0.588**
BK → E	0.482	0.539	0.579	0.504	0.559	**0.587**
BK → M	0.488	0.535	0.582	0.551	0.587	**0.603**
BT → BK	0.585	0.633	0.640	0.550	0.643	**0.655**
BT → E	0.591	0.598	0.631	0.571	0.650	**0.654**
BT → M	0.536	0.560	0.576	0.534	0.600	**0.615**
M → BK	0.582	0.608	0.623	0.591	0.686	**0.692**
M → BT	0.469	0.497	0.545	0.499	0.588	**0.595**
M → E	0.494	0.529	0.545	0.485	0.583	**0.603**
E → BK	0.577	0.552	0.588	0.570	0.579	**0.646**
E → BT	0.544	0.560	0.590	0.544	0.644	**0.654**
E → M	0.523	0.554	0.561	0.505	0.577	**0.592**
Average	0.529	0.559	0.586	0.535	0.605	**0.624**

4.4. Case Study

To demonstrate the role of the proposed DWE model, we selected a piece of data from BK as our case analysis and compared it with WTN when BT was the source domain and BK was the target domain. Figure 2 shows the attention weights of the DWE and WTN for the sample. The darker the color, the higher the attention weight.

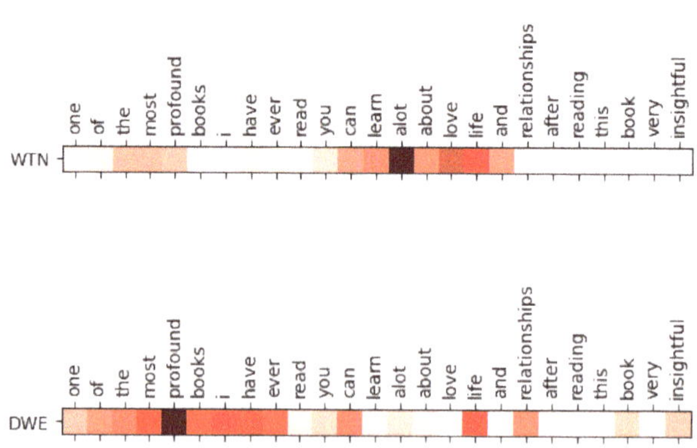

Figure 2. Case Study of Book Domain.

Figure 2 shows that the WTN model focuses more on "alot" and "love," while our proposed DWE model focuses more on the most important sentiment word "profound".

The main reason may be that the syntactic module we added allows "profound" and "book" to establish a syntactic connection, thereby focusing on the more important sentiment word.

4.5. Visualization of Feature Representation

In this section, we visualize the data in two cross-domain pairs, namely, M → BK and BT → E in Dataset 2. Figure 3 shows the feature representation of M as the source domain and BK as the target domain. Figure 4 shows the feature representation of BT as the source domain and E as the target domain.

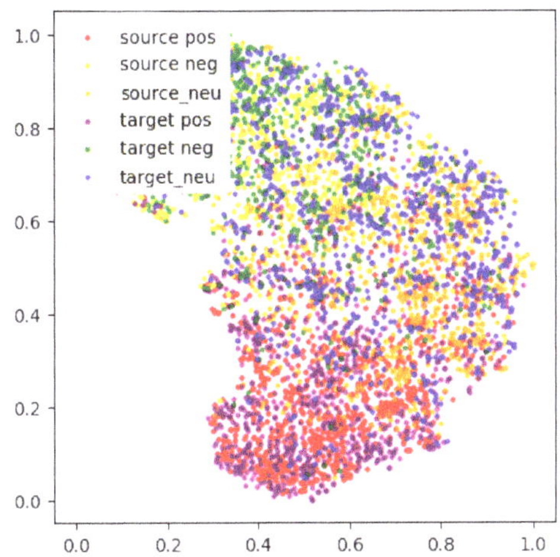

Figure 3. Visualization of feature representation on M → BK.

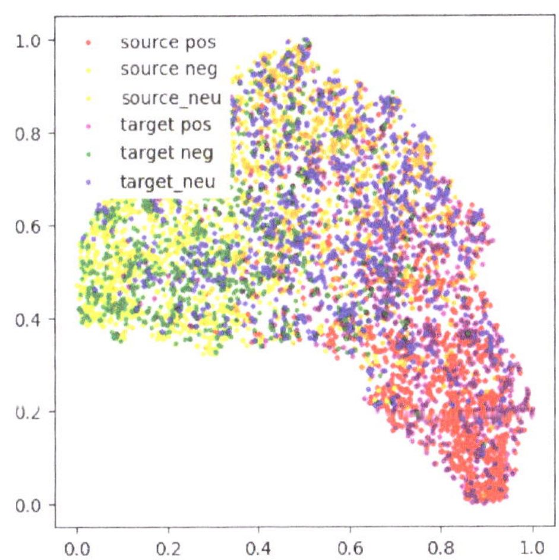

Figure 4. Visualization of feature representation on BT → E.

Figures 3 and 4 show that the sample features of two different domains are aligned. No obvious boundary exists between the two domains, and distinguishing between them is difficult. This condition shows that the two domains can share the learned feature representation, and the information from the source domain can be transferred to the target domain.

5. Conclusions

In this paper, we proposed a dual-word embedding model considering syntactic information for CDSC. The dual-word embedding is obtained through BERT and word2vec; then, the transferable syntactic information and semantic information are obtained by combining dual channel and adversarial training. Experiments showed that our model achieved better results on two real-world datasets. In future work, we will apply the model to cross-domain aspect-based sentiment analysis.

Author Contributions: Conceptualization, Z.L. and Y.X.; methodology, Z.L.; formal analysis, Z.L.; writing—original draft preparation, Z.L.; writing—review and editing, X.H.; supervision, Y.X. and X.H.; funding acquisition, X.H. All authors have read and agreed to the published version of the manuscript.

Funding: This work was supported by the Characteristic Innovation Projects of Guangdong Colleges and Universities (Nos. 2018KTSCX049) and the Science and Technology Plan Project of Guangzhou under Grant Nos. 202102080258 and 201903010013.

Institutional Review Board Statement: Not applicable.

Informed Consent Statement: Not applicable.

Data Availability Statement: Not applicable.

Conflicts of Interest: The authors declare no conflict of interest.

References

1. Liu, B. Sentiment analysis and opinion mining. *Synth. Lect. Hum. Lang. Technol.* **2012**, *5*, 1–167.
2. Tang, D.; Qin, B.; Liu, T. Document modeling with gated recurrent neural network for sentiment classification. In Proceedings of the 2015 Conference on Empirical Methods in Natural Language Processing, Lisbon, Portugal, 17–21 September 2015.
3. Gou, J.; He, X.; Lu, J.; Ma, H.; Ou, W.; Yuan, Y. A class-specific mean vector-based weighted competitive and collaborative representation method for classification. *Neural Netw.* **2022**, *150*, 12–27. [CrossRef] [PubMed]
4. Hu, M.; Liu, B. Mining and summarizing customer reviews. In Proceedings of the Tenth ACM SIGKDD International Conference on Knowledge Discovery and Data Mining, Seattle, WA, USA, 22–25 August 2004.
5. Pang, B.; Lee, L.; Vaithyanathan, S. Thumbs up? Sentiment classification using machine learning techniques. *arXiv* **2002**, arXiv:cs/0205070.
6. Gou, J.; Yuan, X.; Du, L.; Xia, S.; Yi, Z. Hierarchical Graph Augmented Deep Collaborative Dictionary Learning for Classification. *IEEE Trans. Intell. Transp. Syst.* **2022**, *23*, 25308–25322. [CrossRef]
7. Zhang, K.; Zhang, K.; Zhang, M.; Zhao, H.; Liu, Q.; Wu, W.; Chen, E. Incorporating Dynamic Semantics into Pre-Trained Language Model for Aspect-based Sentiment Analysis. *arXiv* **2022**, arXiv:2203.16369.
8. Cambria, E.; Das, D.B.; Yopadhyay, S.; Feraco, A. Affective computing and sentiment analysis. In *A Practical Guide to Sentiment Analysis*; Springer: Cham, Switzerland, 2017; pp. 1–10.
9. Wang, D.; Jing, B.; Lu, C.; Wu, J.; Liu, G.; Du, C.; Zhuang, F. Coarse alignment of topic and sentiment: A unified model for cross-lingual sentiment classification. *IEEE Trans. Neural Networks Learn. Syst.* **2020**, *32*, 736–747. [CrossRef]
10. Mikolov, T.; Sutskever, I.; Chen, K.; Corrado, G.S.; Dean, J. Distributed representations of words and phrases and their compositionality. *Adv. Neural Inf. Process. Syst.* **2013**, *26*, . [CrossRef]
11. Pennington, J.; Socher, R.; Manning, C.D. Glove: Global vectors for word representation. In Proceedings of the 2014 Conference on Empirical Methods in Natural Language Processing (EMNLP), Doha, Qatar, 25–29 October 2014.
12. Bojanowski, P.; Grave, E.; Joulin, A.; Mikolov, T. Enriching word vectors with subword information. *Trans. Assoc. Comput. Linguist.* **2017**, *5*, 135–146. [CrossRef]
13. Peters, M.E.; Neumann, M.; Iyyer, M.; Gardner, M.; Clark, C.; Lee, K.; Zettlemoyer, L. Deep contextualized word representations. *arXiv* **2018**, arXiv:1802.05365.
14. Devlin, J.; Chang, M.W.; Lee, K.; Toutanova, K. Bert: Pre-training of deep bidirectional transformers for language understanding. *arXiv* **2018**, arXiv:1810.04805.
15. Chi, E.A.; Hewitt, J.; Manning, C.D. Finding universal grammatical relations in multilingual BERT. *arXiv* **2020**, arXiv:2005.04511.
16. Guarasci, R.; Silvestri, S.; De Pietro, G.; Fujita, H.; Esposito, M. BERT syntactic transfer: A computational experiment on Italian, French and English languages. *Comput. Speech Lang.* **2022**, *71*, 101261. [CrossRef]
17. Du, C.; Sun, H.; Wang, J.; Qi, Q.; Liao, J. Adversarial and domain-aware bert for cross-domain sentiment analysis. In Proceedings of the 58th Annual Meeting of the Association for Computational Linguistics, Online, 5–10 July 2020.
18. Huang, B.; Carley, K.M. Syntax-aware aspect level sentiment classification with graph attention networks. *arXiv* **2019**, arXiv:1909.02606.

19. Blitzer, J.; Dredze, M.; Pereira, F. Biographies, bollywood, boom-boxes and blenders: Domain adaptation for sentiment classification. In Proceedings of the 45th Annual Meeting of the Association of Computational Linguistics, Prague, Czech Republic, 23–30 June 2007; pp. 440–447.
20. Pan, S.J.; Ni, X.; Sun, J.-T.; Yang, Q.; Chen, Z. Cross-domain sentiment classification via spectral feature alignment. In Proceedings of the 19th International Conference on World Wide Web, Raleigh, NC, USA, 26–30 April 2010.
21. Ganin, Y.; Ustinova, E.; Ajakan, H.; Germain, P.; Larochelle, H.; Laviolette, F.; Marchand, M.; Lempitsky, V. Domain-adversarial training of neural networks. *J. Mach. Learn. Res.* **2016**, *17*, 2096–2030.
22. Zhang, K.; Zhang, H.; Liu, Q.; Zhao, H.; Zhu, H.; Chen, E. Hierarchical Attention Transfer Network for Cross-domain Sentiment Classification. In Proceedings of the AAAI Conference on Artificial Intelligence, New Orleans, LA, USA, 2–7 February 2018.
23. Zhang, K.; Zhang, H.; Liu, Q.; Zhao, H.; Zhu, H.; Chen, E. Interactive attention transfer network for cross-domain sentiment classification. In Proceedings of the AAAI Conference on Artificial Intelligence, Honolulu, HI, USA, 27 January–1 February 2019; Volume 33.
24. Yang, C.; Zhou, B.; Hu, X.; Chen, J.; Cai, Q.; Xue, Y. Dual-Channel Domain Adaptation Model. In Proceedings of the IEEE/WIC/ACM International Conference on Web Intelligence and Intelligent Agent Technology, Melbourne, VIC, Australia, 14–17 December 2021.
25. Du, Y.; He, M.; Wang, L.; Zhang, H. Wasserstein based transfer network for cross-domain sentiment classification. *Knowl.-Based Syst.* **2020**, *204*, 106162. [CrossRef]
26. Fu, Y.; Liu, Y. Domain adaptation with a shrinkable discrepancy strategy for cross-domain sentiment classification. *Neurocomputing* **2022**, *494*, 56–66. [CrossRef]
27. Wu, M.; Pan, S.; Zhu, X.; Zhou, C.; Pan, L. Domain-adversarial graph neural networks for text classification. In Proceedings of the 2019 IEEE International Conference on Data Mining (ICDM), Beijing, China, 8–11 November 2019.
28. Wu, Z.; Pan, S.; Long, G.; Jiang, J.; Zhang, C. Graph wavenet for deep spatial-temporal graph modeling. *arXiv* **2019**, arXiv:1906.00121.
29. Zhu, S.; Zhou, C.; Pan, S.; Zhu, X.; Wang, B. Relation structure-aware heterogeneous graph neural network. In Proceedings of the 2019 IEEE International Conference on Data Mining (ICDM), Beijing, China, 8–11 November 2019.
30. Zhu, S.; Zhou, L.; Pan, S.; Zhou, C.; Yan, G.; Wang, B. GSSNN: Graph smoothing splines neural networks. In Proceedings of the AAAI Conference on Artificial Intelligence, New York, NY, USA, 7–12 February 2020; Volume 34.
31. Kipf, T.N.; Welling, M. Semi-supervised classification with graph convolutional networks. *arXiv* **2016**, arXiv:1609.02907.
32. Vashishth, S.; Dasgupta, S.S.; Ray, S.N.; Talukdar, P. Dating documents using graph convolution networks. *arXiv* **2019**, arXiv:1902.00175.
33. Velickovic, P.; Cucurull, G.; Casanova, A.; Romero, A.; Lio, P.; Bengio, Y. Graph attention networks. *arXiv* **2017**, arXiv:1710.10903.
34. Zhou, M.; Liu, D.; Zheng, Y.; Zhu, Q.; Guo, P. A text sentiment classification model using double word embedding methods. *Multimed. Tools Appl.* **2020**, *81*, 18993–19012. [CrossRef]
35. Vuong Nguyen, L.; Nguyen, T.H.; Jung, J.J.; Camacho, D. Extending collaborative filtering recommendation using word embedding: A hybrid approach. *Concurr. Comput. Pract. Exp.* **2021**, e6232. [CrossRef]
36. Wang, H.; Zuo, Y.; Li, H.; Wu, J. Cross-domain recommendation with user personality. *Knowl.-Based Syst.* **2021**, *213*, 106664. [CrossRef]
37. Naderalvojoud, B.; Sezer, E.A. Sentiment aware word embeddings using refinement and senti-contextualized learning approach. *Neurocomputing* **2020**, *405*, 149–160. [CrossRef]
38. Jawahar, G.; Sagot, B.; Seddah, D. What does BERT learn about the structure of language? In Proceedings of the ACL 2019-57th Annual Meeting of the Association for Computational Linguistics, Florence, Italy, 28 July–2 August 2019.
39. Chen, Y. Convolutional Neural Network for Sentence Classification. Master's Thesis, University of Waterloo, Waterloo, ON, Canada, 2015.
40. He, R.; Lee, W.S.; Ng, H.T.; Dahlmeier, D. Adaptive semi-supervised learning for cross-domain sentiment classification. *arXiv* **2018**, arXiv:1809.00530.
41. Yu, J.; Jiang, J. Learning sentence embeddings with auxiliary tasks for cross-domain sentiment classification. In Proceedings of the 2016 Conference on Empirical Methods in Natural Language Processing, Austin, TX, USA, 1–5 November 2016.
42. Li, Z.; Zhang, Y.; Wei, Y.; Wu, Y.; Yang, Q. End-to-End Adversarial Memory Network for Cross-domain Sentiment Classification. In Proceedings of the Twenty-Sixth International Joint Conference on Artificial Intelligence (IJCAI-17), Melbourne, Australia, 19–25 August 2017.
43. Zhao, C.; Wang, S.; Li, D.; Liu, X.; Yang, X.; Liu, J. Cross-domain sentiment classification via parameter transferring and attention sharing mechanism. *Inf. Sci.* **2021**, *578*, 281–296. [CrossRef]

mathematics

MDPI

Article

Keyword-Enhanced Multi-Expert Framework for Hate Speech Detection

Weiyu Zhong †, Qiaofeng Wu †, Guojun Lu, Yun Xue and Xiaohui Hu *

School of Electronics and Information Engineering, South China Normal University, Foshan 528225, China
* Correspondence: huxh@scnu.edu.cn
† These authors contributed equally to this work.

Abstract: The proliferation of hate speech on the Internet is harmful to the psychological health of individuals and society. Thus, establishing and supporting the development of hate speech detection and deploying evasion techniques is a vital task. However, existing hate speech detection methods tend to ignore the sentiment features of target sentences and have difficulty identifying some implicit types of hate speech. The performance of hate speech detection can be significantly improved by gathering more sentiment features from various sources. In the use of external sentiment information, the key information of the sentences cannot be ignored. Thus, this paper proposes a keyword-enhanced multiexperts framework. To begin, the multi-expert module of multi-task learning is utilized to share parameters and thereby introduce sentiment information. In addition, the critical features of the sentences are highlighted by contrastive learning. This model focuses on both the key information of the sentence and the external sentiment information. The final experimental results on three public datasets demonstrate the effectiveness of the proposed model.

Keywords: hate speech detection; contrastive learning; multi-task learning

MSC: 18C50

Citation: Zhong, W.; Wu, Q.; Lu, G.; Xue, Y.; Hu, X. Keyword-Enhanced Multi-Expert Framework for Hate Speech Detection. *Mathematics* **2022**, *10*, 4706. https://doi.org/10.3390/math10244706

Academic Editors: Jianping Gou, Weihua Ou, Shaoning Zeng and Lan Du

Received: 12 November 2022
Accepted: 8 December 2022
Published: 11 December 2022

1. Introduction

With the widespread use of social media and mobile internet platforms, the increasing speed of online speech and the freedom to publish it have led to the malicious prevalence of hate speech. Exposure to such language may cause negative effects on the mental health of victims [1], which may lead to severe social problems. To prevent further negative effects, authorities need to intervene in detecting hate speech online. Thus, the rapid and accurate automatic detection of hate speech has become a popular topic of research in the field of natural language processing. Hate speech detection has gained attention in recent years.

Figure 1 shows an example in which the first sentence contains the hate term *fucking aids* which is an obvious form of offensive hate speech, while the second sentence without obvious hate words or semantics is a positive sentence.

This guy is giving me fucking aids. ➡ Offensive score:0.792

I'm literally doing the same tonight! ➡ Offensive score:-0.625

Figure 1. An example sentence from the Ruddit dataset. The offensive score ranges between −1 (maximally supportive) and 1 (maximally offensive).

An approach to hate speech detection using deep learning has been the focus of most of the research in recent years [2–5]. However, previous research disregarded the sentiment features of target detection sentences and only used pre-trained models or deeper neural networks to obtain semantic features. Wang, C. [6] showed that the semantics of hate speech bear a strong tendency toward negative sentiment. To overcome this problem, recent studies have proposed the use of multi-task learning (MTL), which improves the performance of hate speech detection by using sentiment information [7]. Transfer learning is the process of transferring generalizable knowledge gained from training data to the target task. MTL is a type of transfer learning that involves learning several related tasks simultaneously, allowing these tasks to share information during the learning process, and utilizing the correlation between various tasks to enhance the model's performance and generalization capacity on each task. Kapil, P. [8] proposed a deep MTL framework to exploit useful information from several related classification tasks to perform hate speech detection; this framework uses a hard parameter-sharing approach that is prone to negative transfer. Zhou, X. [9] used multiple feature extraction units to share multi-task parameters so that the model can perform sentiment knowledge sharing. Then, gated networks were used to fuse features for hate speech detection. This model employed a soft parameter sharing method by dividing a single expert into multiple experts, thereby mitigating the negative transfer problem caused by hard parameters.

Although hate speech detection has achieved good performance in recent years, the following problems remain: (1) The latest multi-task framework used in hate speech detection is soft parameter sharing [9], where all experts share all tasks, but the tasks of hate speech detection and sentiment analysis have both positive and negative correlations. Positive correlations are parameter relationships that are beneficial to the fit of the primary task, and conversely, negative correlations are not beneficial. If the negative correlation parameters between tasks are not separated, some noise occurs as part of the tasks, which leads to negative transfer. Moreover, when using multiple experts, the simple gated networks cannot effectively fuse and filter the different information because the experts have abundant information from different tasks. (2) Current work lacks the ability to extract critical information (e.g., keywords) from sentences [5]. It cannot effectively identify different types of hate words, such as profanities, nor identify the association between certain identity terms and offensive statements. Certain identity terms (especially those involving minority groups) appear mainly in texts that are offensive [10], such as the sentence *"This is also the reason that so many of Obama's policies are being overturned/undone, it's just because the Black Guy did them."* has no conspicuous hate words, but rather racial discrimination through the identity term *Black*.

To solve the aforementioned problems, we propose the following approaches. **(1) For the first problem,** we are inspired by the recent progressive layered extraction (PLE) model [11] and gated network research [12]. We divide feature extraction units (e.g., expert modules) into a shared part and task-specific parts. This approach strengthens the independent features of the tasks themselves and better reduces the negative transfer caused by weakly correlated task-sharing parameters. Moreover, we design a feature-filtering gate that can better fuse and filter the information of multiple expert modules. **(2) To solve the second problem,** we propose a solution inspired by a recent contrastive learning model [13]. Our model applies contrastive learning to English hate speech detection by using a swearing dictionary and an identity term dictionary to construct positive and negative examples. This result allows the model to be more sensitive to the critical words so that it can learn the association between various types of hate words or identity term words and offensive statements. In summary, the contributions of our study are as follows:

- To better examine the interaction between hate and sentiment information, we propose an MTL model that is more suitable for hate speech detection, which uses shared experts and task-specific experts to extract features, and finally employs feature-filtering gates to fuse features.
- Given the lack of use of important word information in previous work, we introduce contrastive learning to the pre-trained model to enable our model to better identify keywords in text.
- Experimental results on three baseline datasets demonstrate that our model is effective in hate speech detection.

2. Related Work

Recently, researchers have widely studied automatic hate speech detection. In this section, we review related work on deep-learning-based methods for hate speech detection, especially MTL-based methods, as well as related work on contrastive learning.

Recently, deep-learning-based approaches have achieved considerable success in hate speech detection. Ref. [14] proposed a transformed word embedding model (TWEM), which balances high performance while achieving a simple structure. Ref. [3] proposed a deep neural network structure (combining CNN and GRU) as a feature extractor to learn the semantic features of hate speech. Ref. [4] built a large-scale dataset using hate speech and its reactions and used the pre-trained language model GPT-2 to detect hate speech. Ref. [5] created the first English Reddit comment dataset with fine-grained, real-valued scores and used the pre-trained model HateBERT to detect hate speech. Clearly, deep learning models can extract underlying semantic features of text, which provide the most direct clues to detect hate speech.

Transfer learning can bring more useful information to hate speech detection, and common transfer learning methods include multi-task learning and knowledge distillation [15]. Knowledge distillation aims at knowledge transfer through a wide network (teachers) to a small network (students). Multi-task learning aims at training multiple related tasks and sharing information between tasks at the same time. In recent years, some results have been achieved in the field of hate speech detection using multi-task learning [7]. Ref. [16] proposed a theoretical framework for hate speech type detection that includes fuzzy multi-task learning. Ref. [17] proposed an MTL approach based on the pre-trained model BERT for hate speech detection. Ref. [8] proposed a deep MTL framework to improve the performance of hate speech detection by exploiting useful information from multiple related classification tasks. Ref. [9] proposed a hate speech detection framework based on sentiment knowledge sharing. The preceding studies show that MTL can exploit the relevance between sentiment analysis tasks and hate speech detection tasks, which improves model performance and generalization in hate speech detection.

In addition, some optimization algorithms [18,19] have recently been proposed to obtain better classification results and semantic representations, and contrastive learning is one of them. Contrastive learning aims to learn effective representations by pulling semantically similar sentences together and pushing dissimilar sentences apart [20]. Several recent approaches use contrastive objectives to obtain different views from data augmentation or different copies of the model [21–24]. For example, [24] proposed ConSERT, a Contrastive Framework for Self-Supervised SEntence Representation Transfer, which employs contrastive learning to fine-tune BERT in an unsupervised manner. SimCSE [25] uses the simplest idea of applying only the standard dropout as noise to obtain different outputs of the same sentence, thereby forming positive instances. We propose the use of contrastive learning for hate speech detection, which increases the sensitivity of the model to key information of the sentence and improves the performance of the task.

3. Methodology

In this section, our model keyword-enhanced multi-expert framework for hate speech detection (KMT) is presented. This model exploits critical information of the sentence and external sentiment information to improve hate speech detection.

The general architecture of KMT is shown in Figure 2. The framework consists of four modules: **(1) Textual input module.** The bottom of the figure shows the textual input module, where the pre-trained model BERT or HateBERT is used to encode the input sentences and generate contextually and semantically integrated input vector x; **(2) Multi-task learning module.** The top left of the figure shows the multi-task learning module, where we use the multi-task learning framework to interact sentiment information and hate information, and learn the shared features and task-specific features to assist hate speech detection using sentiment information; **(3) Feature-filtering module.** Gate of the figure is the feature-filtering module, which is used to filter and fuse the features outputted by expert modules to select the important information of sentiment and hate speech; **(4) Contrastive learning module.** The top right of the figure shows the contrastive learning module, which extracts critical information within the sentences to improve the sensitivity of the model to sentence keywords. Finally, the MTL and contrastive learning modules are jointly trained.

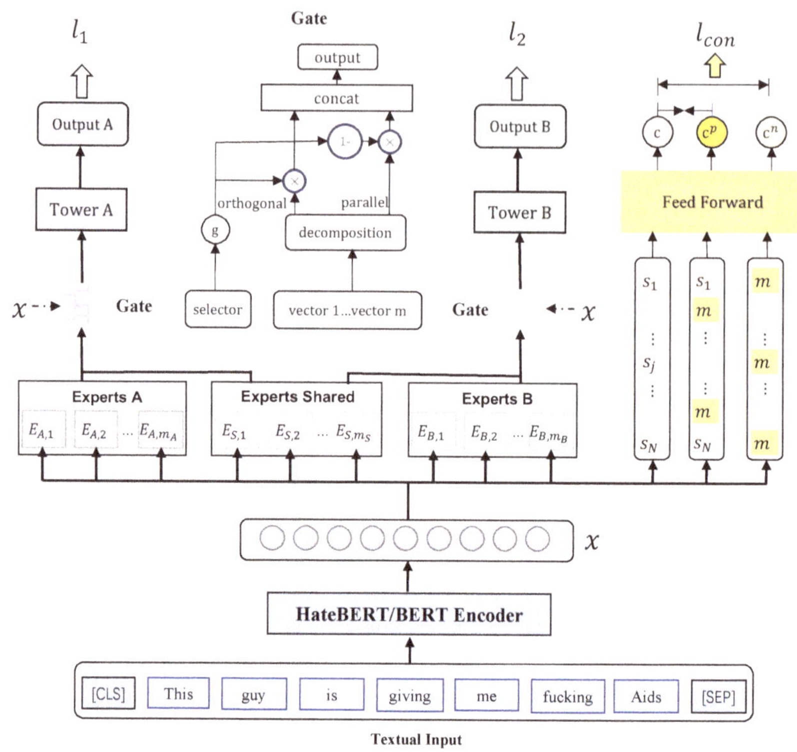

Figure 2. The overall architecture of our proposed Keyword-enhanced Multi-expert Framework for Hate Speech Detection (KMT).

Given the input text $s = \{w_1, w_2, \ldots, w_n\}$, n is the length of the text s. We feed the sequence $[CLS]s[SEP]$ to the BERT or HateBERT encoder in the Textual input module to obtain the input vector x with contextual information. Subsequently, x is taken as input to both multi-task learning module and contrastive learning module. In multi-task learning, the hate information and sentiment information in x are interacted by shared expert and task-specific expert modules, the features are then fused and filtered using a feature-filtering gate, and finally the hate speech detection is performed using the tower containing the classification layer. In the contrastive learning module, positive and negative examples are generated by masking x. Subsequently, the model is enabled to focus on key information in the sentences by bringing x closer to positive examples and away from negative examples. More details of each module are shown as follows.

3.1. Multi-Task Learning Module

Due to the diversity of language, insulting meanings in many sentences are implicit, causing difficulty in determining whether a sentence is offensive or not. For example, the sentence *"These guys are all a bunch of pigs."* does not contain an explicitly hateful word, but the sentence still constitutes hate speech. Although the word *pig* is neutral, most people associate it with foolishness and clumsiness. Thus, likening guys with pigs is demeaning to the former. The secret to effectively judging sentences is grasping emotional common sense. The sentence *"He's a fucking good player."* contains the obvious hate word *fucking*. However, in this case, *fucking* is merely an adverb of level used to indicate excitement; hence, the sentence does not constitute hate speech. From the preceding two examples, we can see that although hate speech tends to contain hate words, achieving better results in detecting it by using only the hate information of the sentence itself is difficult. To introduce external sentiment information, we combine the generic sentiment dataset and then interact the information from the sentiment dataset and the hate dataset using the MTL approach, which improves the performance of hate speech detection.

In MTL frameworks, the problem of overfitting is fundamentally reduced due to extensive use of the shared experts layer structure. However, the effectiveness of the framework may be affected by the seesaw phenomenon and negative migration problem because of the differences between tasks and data distribution [11]. Thus, we use the PLE framework structure [11]. As shown in Figure 2, the model is divided between task-specific tower structures at the top and expert modules at the bottom. The number of Experts in each expert module is the hyperparameter to be tuned. Each expert module comprises numerous sub-networks known as Experts. The shared experts in PLE are responsible for extracting shared features, while the task-specific experts extract task-specific features. Each tower network extracts information from the shared experts and its own task-specific experts. Our expert modules and tower networks consist of feed-forward neural networks. Specifically, when the model performs gradient backpropagation, it changes the parameters in the expert modules. As the output of the task-specific expert modules is only passed to the tower of their own tasks, their parameters are only affected by their own task gradients. By contrast, the shared expert modules have parameters that are affected by the mixed gradients of all tasks because the output is passed to the towers of all tasks.

In the MTL module, features are extracted using the shared experts E_s^T and the task $k's$ specific experts E_k^T. Then, the extracted features are concatenated to form $S^k(x)$ as Equations (1)–(3):

$$E_k^T = \left[E_{(k,1)}^T, E_{(k,2)}^T, \cdots, E_{(k,m_k)}^T\right] \tag{1}$$

$$E_s^T = \left[E_{(s,1)}^T, E_{(s,2)}^T, \cdots, E_{(s,m_s)}^T\right] \tag{2}$$

$$S^k(x) = \left[E_k^T, E_S^T\right]^T \tag{3}$$

where x is the input vector, m_s and m_k are the number of sub-networks in the shared experts E_s^T and task $k's$ specific experts E_k^T, $E_{(k,m_k)}^T$ and $E_{(s,m_s)}^T$ are the sub-networks in task $k's$ specific experts and shared experts, respectively. The features $S^k(x)$ of the shared experts and task $k's$ specific experts are selectively fused through a feature-filtering gate (Gate). The filtered features of task k are formulated as Equation (4):

$$G^k(x) = \text{Gate}\left(x, S^k(x)\right) \tag{4}$$

Lastly, the task k prediction using the tower network is:

$$O^k(x) = f^k\left(G^k(x)\right) \tag{5}$$

where $f^k(\cdot)$ stands for the task $k's$ tower network, which consists of feed-forward neural networks as Equation (5).

3.2. Feature-Filtering Module

The multiple expert setting in MTL enables better interaction of affective and hate information, but because multiple experts have a large amount of information, a structure is needed for selective fusion. Thus, we are inspired by the research on gating modules [12] to design a feature-filtering module that not only better fuses the information between experts but also reduces the noise. As shown in Figure 2, the input vector x is used as a selector to obtain useful information on the selected vector (e.g., the output $S^k(x)$ of the experts) as follows Equations (6)–(9):

$$g^k(x) = W_g^k x \tag{6}$$

$$\text{parallel:} \quad p^k(x) = \frac{S^k(x) \cdot x}{x \cdot x} x \tag{7}$$

$$\text{orthogonal:} \quad o^k(x) = S^k(x) - p^k(x) \tag{8}$$

$$G^k(x) = \text{concat}\left(g^k(x)o^k(x), \left(1 - g^k(x)\right)p^k(x)\right) \tag{9}$$

where $W_g^k \in R^{(m_k+m_s)d}$ is a parameter matrix, d is the dimension of the input vector, and $g^k(x)$ is the weight vector for task k obtained by a linear transformation. $S^k(x)$ is decomposed into an orthogonal component and a parallel component. The parallel component $p^k(x)$ is a projection of $S^k(x)$ onto x, which contains part of the information of x. On the contrary, $o^k(x)$ is orthogonal to x, and therefore contains new information. Specifically, if x is the hate speech input, $p^k(x)$ is the part of $S^k(x)$ that contains hate speech information, and $o^k(x)$ is the part of $S^k(x)$ that contains sentiment information, then $G^k(x)$ represents the fusion of these two components. $g^k(x)$ is used to regulate the composition of both components to obtain the optimal fusion.

3.3. Contrastive Learning Module

As the pre-trained model lacks the ability to grasp critical word information from sentences, it cannot effectively distinguish between different types of hate words and cannot identify the relationship between certain identity terms and offensive statements. Currently, contrastive learning demonstrates excellent ability in acquiring and distinguishing crucial knowledge by focusing on positive examples and comparing negative examples, which has resulted in considerable advances in many tasks. Our goal is to make our model more sensitive to the essential words within a body of text. To this end, we use a contrastive learning module to focus on the positive examples while pushing the negative ones away, allowing the model to more effectively distinguish between important and minor information. To create a positive example x^p, we mask each non-key token representation in the input vector x as a constant vector $m \in R^d$ where this constant is equal to 1e-6. This method allows the sentence to combine key information and eliminate unimportant words. To obtain the negative example x^n, we simultaneously employ a similar method to mask the key token representation in x as m.

Thereafter, we model x, x^p, and x^n separately using the feed-forward neural networks with the following formulation Equations (10)–(12):

$$c = f(x) \tag{10}$$

$$c^p = f(x^p) \tag{11}$$

$$c^n = f(x^n) \tag{12}$$

where $f(\cdot)$ denotes the feed-forward neural networks. We then compute the cosine similarity of the positive and negative examples as follows Equation (13):

$$\text{sim}\left(c^1, c^2\right) = \frac{c_1^T c_2}{||c_1|| \cdot ||c_2||} \tag{13}$$

where $\mathrm{sim}(c^1, c^2)$ denotes as $\mathrm{sim}(c, c^p)$ and $\mathrm{sim}(c, c^n)$. We follow the contrast module training objectives developed by [26] as Equation (14):

$$l_{\mathrm{con}} = -\sum_{k=1}^{K}\sum_{i=1}^{N}\log\frac{e^{\frac{\mathrm{sim}(c_i, c^p)}{\tau}}}{\sum_{j=1}^{N}\left(e^{\frac{\mathrm{sim}(c_j, c^p)}{\tau}} + e^{\frac{\mathrm{sim}(c_j, c^n)}{\tau}}\right)} \tag{14}$$

where N is the length of a sentence, K is the batch size, and τ is a temperature hyperparameter that is set to 1 in our model.

3.4. Loss Function

In the training process, we jointly train the objectives of the multi-task learning module and the contrastive learning module. Our training aims to minimize the following total loss functions as Equation (15):

$$\mathrm{loss} = \sum_{i=1}^{n}\lambda_i l_i + \lambda l_{con} \tag{15}$$

where n represents the number of tasks, l_i is the loss function of each task in the MTL module, and λ and λ_i are hyperparameters.

4. Experiments

4.1. Datasets

In our experiments, we employed two sentiment datasets and three public hate speech datasets. Table 1 displays the statistics of the datasets.

Ruddit [5] It is the first English Reddit comment dataset with fine-grained, real-valued scores ranging between −1 (maximum support) and 1 (maximum offense).

OffensEval 2019 (Offen) [27] This dataset was published in the evaluation exercise for SemEval 2019: Task 6. The dataset contains a total of 14,100 tweets. It is divided into a training set with 13,240 tweets and a test set with 860 tweets. There are 4400 tweets marked as offensive in the training and 240 in the test.

AbusEval (Abuse) [28] To obtain this dataset, the researchers added a layer of abusive language annotation to OffensEval 2019. The dataset is the same size as OffensEval 2019, as well as being divided into a training set of 13,240 texts and a test set of 860 texts.

Reddit Sentiment Analysis (RSA) (https://www.kaggle.com/datasets/cosmos98/twitter-and-reddit-sentimental-analysis-dataset [November 2022]) This dataset was produced as a result of a university study using PySpark to conduct sentiment analysis across multiple social media networks. The dataset also includes a sentimental label and approximately 37,000 comments. Since this dataset is an auxiliary dataset for training the multi-task learning module, we only use the training set.

Tweet Sentiment Analysis (TSA) (https://www.kaggle.com/datasets/dv1453/twitter-sentiment-analysis-analytics-vidya [November 2022]) This is a tweet sentiment dataset from Kaggle 2018. This dataset contains more positive tweets and less negative tweets. This dataset also uses only the training set.

We used Pearson correlation (Pear) and mean square error (MSE) as evaluation metrics for the Ruddit dataset and Macro F1 (F1) as evaluation metrics for the Offen and Abuse datasets.

Table 1. Statistics of three experimental datasets.

Dataset	Total	Classes
Ruddit	5828	Score 0–1 (2514) Score −1–0 (3442)
Offen	14,100	hate (4640) non-hate (9460)
Abuse	14,100	exp-hate (2129) imp-hate (798) non-hate (11,173)
RSA	37,249	neutral (13,142) negative (8277) positive (15,830)
TSA	31,962	negative (2242) positive (29,720)

4.2. Training Details

We use the five-fold cross-validation approach to evaluate the performance of our model on all three datasets. Referring to [5], we separated the original dataset into five equal parts, using one copy for testing and used the remaining data for training. To prevent the problem of data imbalance in multi-task learning, we use the WeightedRandomSampler approach to sample the data according to the weights. In our experiments, in the MTL module, the number of subnetworks in share expert is 2, and the number of sub-networks in the task-specific expert is also 2. Each expert has one layer of dropout, which is 0.1. The dropout used in the tower network is also 0.1. For the contrastive learning module, the temperature parameter τ is set to 1. The optimizer is Adam, the learning rate is 2×10^{-5}, and the batch size is 16.

4.3. Comparison with Baselines

We compare our model (KMT) with a number of reliable baselines. The following is a brief description of the models:

BERT [29] This pre-trained model is mainly used to capture sentence features for the detection of hate speech.

HateBERT [30] It is a BERT variant that has been specially trained to recognize hate speech in English. The big dataset RAL-E, which contains Reddit comments from communities that have been banned because of their hateful or offensive speech, was used to train HateBERT. In the three popular datasets OffensEval 2019 [27], AbusEval [28], and HatEval [31], HateBERT significantly outperforms the BERT model.

KMT It is our proposed hate speech detection model based on sentence critical information and external sentiment information.

The comparison of the entire performance of KMT is shown in Table 2. From the results in this table, the following conclusions can be drawn:

(1) The performance of HateBERT is much better than that of BERT in the three datasets. In particular, the performance is significantly improved on the Abuse dataset, which indicates that HateBERT can better capture the semantic relationships between words in hate speech and better perform hate speech detection.

(2) Our proposed model KMT obtained good performance on all three datasets. Compared with the current best performing model, the Pearson correlation of KMT increases by 0.006 on the Ruddit dataset, the F1 value of KMT improves greatly by nearly 0.028 on the Abuse dataset. These results illustrate the effectiveness of our method.

Table 2. Comparative results of KMT and existing methods. Superscript * indicates data obtained from the literature. The best results for each model are shown in boldface.

Models	Ruddit (Regression)		Abuse (3 Class)	Offen (2 Class)
	Pear ↑	MSE ↓	F1 ↑	F1 ↑
BERT * [5,30]	0.873 ± 0.005	0.027 ± 0.001	0.727 ± 0.008	0.803 ± 0.006
HateBERT * [5,30]	0.886 ± 0.005	0.025 ± 0.001	0.765 ± 0.006	**0.809 ± 0.008**
KMT (BERT)	0.8764 ± 0.007	0.027 ± 0.0007	0.7882 ± 0.01	0.8028 ± 0.02
KMT (HateBERT)	**0.8921 ± 0.006**	**0.0231 ± 0.001**	**0.7929 ± 0.01**	0.8064 ± 0.01

4.4. Ablation Experiments

We analyze the effect of different modules on the performance of our model. The results are shown in Table 3, where *w/o cl* indicates the ablation experiment for contrastive learning; *w/o s* indicates that the MTL module is removed and the sentiment dataset is not used as input to the model; and *w/o gate* indicates that the feature-filtering gate module is replaced with simple feed-forward neural network and a softmax layer.

According to the results in Table 3, we find that:

(1) When the contrastive learning module is removed, the performance of the model on the two datasets decreases the most, indicating that the swear words and certain identity terms in the sentences are highly correlated with hate speech. The results show that the contrastive learning module can improve the sensitivity of the model to keywords and thus improve the performance of hate detection effectively.

(2) When the MTL module is removed, the performance of the model on the three datasets also decreases, indicating that adding sentiment information can effectively assist the detection of hate speech.

(3) When the feature-filtering module is replaced with the basic gating network, the performance also decreases slightly, indicating that our proposed feature-filtering gates can better achieve the fusion of various expert information and reduce the influence of noise.

(4) KMT outperforms other models, which directly demonstrates the importance and effectiveness of sentence critical information and external sentiment information for hate speech detection.

Table 3. Results of ablation experiments. The best results for each model are shown in boldface.

Models	Ruddit (Regression)		Abuse (3 Class)	Offen (2 Class)
	Pear ↑	MSE ↓	F1 ↑	F1 ↑
KMT *w/o cl*	0.8879 ± 0.005	0.0246 ± 0.0005	0.7827 ± 0.02	0.7995 ± 0.024
KMT *w/o s*	0.8907 ± 0.004	0.0234 ± 0.0008	0.7846 ± 0.02	0.7957 ± 0.019
KMT *w/o gate*	0.8892 ± 0.004	0.0249 ± 0.001	0.7886 ± 0.02	0.8035 ± 0.02
KMT	**0.8921 ± 0.006**	**0.0231 ± 0.001**	**0.7929 ± 0.01**	**0.8064 ± 0.01**

4.5. Effect of Number of Experts

Each expert module in the multi-task module consists of multiple sub-networks called Experts. To investigate the effect of the number of respective Experts (e.g., E_s^T and E_k^T) in the shared expert module and task-specific expert module on the performance, we use 1 to 4 Experts on the Ruddit dataset to evaluate our model. As shown in Figure 3, the model performs best when the shared expert module has two Experts and the task-specific expert module has two Experts, which justifies the number of experts we choose in the experimental setup. In addition, the performance of the model is worse when the number of Experts in the shared expert module is three or four. This result indicates that having a larger number of parameters does not improve the performance of the model because too many parameters may cause the model to be more difficult to train and an extremely large number of Experts may cause redundant information.

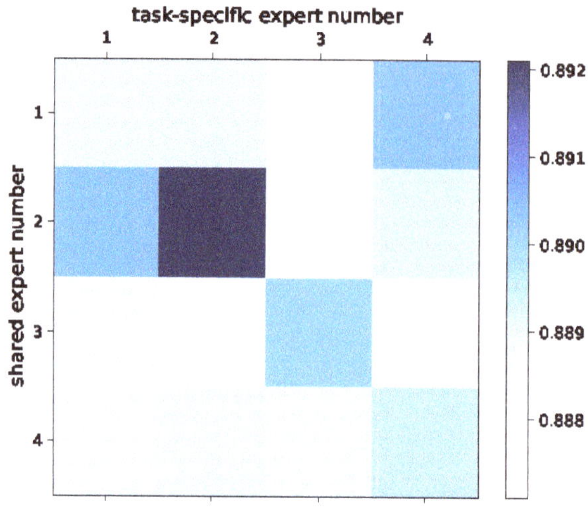

Figure 3. Pear mean value of model with different number of Experts, where the darker color indicates a higher Pear value.

4.6. Effect of Extraction Network Layer Number

Extraction networks are in the multi-tasking module, and each network consists of the expert modules and the feature-filtering module (Gate) in Figure 2, which is mainly used to extract features. To investigate the effect of the number of extraction network layers on performance, we test the effects of one-layer and two-layer extraction networks on our model on the Ruddit dataset. According to experience, the number of training parameters increases with the depth of the network structure. As the results shown in Table 4, the model performs better when the extraction network is one layer. As the depth of the extraction network increases, the model performance decreases because when the model is highly complex, it causes overfitting that the model becomes unstable. Furthermore, we also compare the overall running time of the two models, performed at the 3090 GPU setting, as shown in Figure 4. The results illustrate that the overall performance of the model is improved when the one-layer extraction network is used, besides, the number of parameters is also reduced due to the reduction in the number of network layers, which improves the efficiency of the model.

Table 4. Effect of number of extraction network layers

Models	**Ruddit (Regression)**	
	Pear ↑	**MSE** ↓
1 layer	0.8921 ± 0.006	0.0231 ± 0.001
2 layers	0.8731 ± 0.007	0.0283 ± 0.001

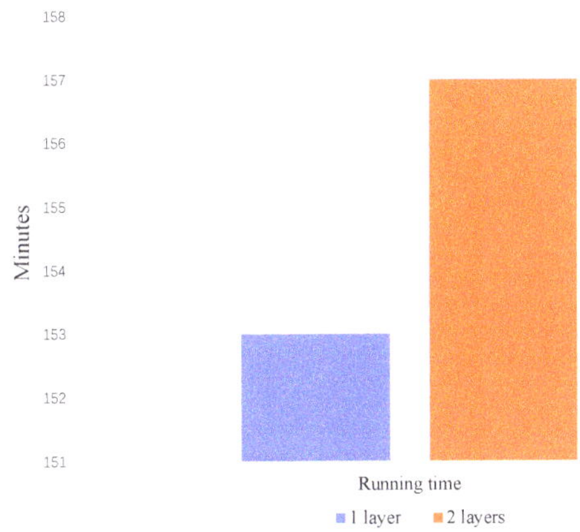

Figure 4. Runtime comparison.

5. Conclusions and Future Work

In this work, we propose a keyword-enhanced multi-expert framework for hate speech detection. This model can leverage both the external sentiment information and critical information of the sentence itself. Moreover, this model mainly uses a shared expert module to share certain parameters of multiple tasks. Through this approach, the model can more effectively share sentiment information and then fuse features by employing a feature-filtering gate to detect hate speech. We use contrastive learning for keyword enhancement, which enables the model to better identify critical information in sentences. Experiments show that our model, keyword-enhanced multi-expert framework, performs better on three datasets. Finally, detailed analysis further demonstrates the effectiveness of our model and the contribution of each module. In future work, we will explore the portability and generalization of the model and conduct portability experiments across datasets. Meanwhile, based on this work, we consider adding image information for multimodal hate detection.

Author Contributions: Conceptualization, W.Z. and G.L.; methodology, W.Z.; formal analysis, W.Z. and Q.W.; writing—original draft preparation, W.Z. and Q.W.; writing—review and editing, Y.X. and X.H.; supervision, Y.X. and X.H.; funding acquisition X.H. All authors have read and agreed to the published version of the manuscript.

Funding: This work was supported by the Characteristic Innovation Projects of Guangdong Colleges and Universities (Nos. 2018KTSCX049), and the Science and Technology Plan Project of Guangzhou under Grant Nos. 202102080258 and 201903010013.

Institutional Review Board Statement: Not applicable.

Informed Consent Statement: Not applicable.

Data Availability Statement: Not applicable.

Conflicts of Interest: The authors declare no conflict of interest.

References

1. Munro, E.R. *The Protection of Children Online: A Brief Scoping Review to Identify Vulnerable Groups*; Childhood Wellbeing Research Centre: London, UK, 2011.
2. Jahan, M.S.; Oussalah, M. A systematic review of hate speech automatic detection using natural language processing. *arXiv* **2021**, arXiv:2106.00742.
3. Zhang, Z.; Luo, L. Hate speech detection: A solved problem? the challenging case of long tail on twitter. *Semant. Web.* **2019**, *10*, 925–945. [CrossRef]
4. Tekiroglu, S.S.; Chung, Y.L.; Guerini, M. Generating counter narratives against online hate speech: Data and strategies. *arXiv* **2020**, arXiv:2004.04216.

5. Hada, R.; Sudhir, S.; Mishra, P.; Yannakoudakis, H.; Mohammad, S.M.; Shutova, E. Ruddit: Norms of offensiveness for English Reddit comments. *arXiv* **2021**, arXiv:2106.05664.
6. Wang, C. Interpreting neural network hate speech classifiers. In Proceedings of the 2nd Workshop on Abusive Language Online (ALW2), Brussels, Belgium, 31 October 2018; pp. 86–92.
7. Chiril, P.; Pamungkas, E.W.; Benamara, F.; Moriceau, V.; Patti, V. Emotionally informed hate speech detection: A multi-target perspective. *Cogn. Comput.* **2022**, *14*, 322–352. [CrossRef] [PubMed]
8. Kapil, P.; Ekbal, A. A deep neural network based multi-task learning approach to hate speech detection. *Knowl. Based Syst.* **2020**, *210*, 106458. [CrossRef]
9. Zhou, X.; Yong, Y.; Fan, X.; Ren, G.; Song, Y.; Diao, Y.; Yang, L.; Lin, H. Hate speech detection based on sentiment knowledge sharing. In Proceedings of the 59th Annual Meeting of the Association for Computational Linguistics and the 11th International Joint Conference on Natural Language Processing (Volume 1: Long Papers), Virtual, 1–6 August 2021; pp. 7158–7166.
10. Sap, M.; Card, D.; Gabriel, S.; Choi, Y.; Smith, N.A. The risk of racial bias in hate speech detection. In Proceedings of the 57th Annual Meeting of the Association for Computational Linguistics, Florence, Italy, 28 July–2 August 2019; pp. 1668–1678.
11. Tang, H.; Liu, J.; Zhao, M.; Gong, X. Progressive layered extraction (ple): A novel multi-task learning (mtl) model for personalized recommendations. In Proceedings of the Fourteenth ACM Conference on Recommender Systems, New York, NY, USA, 22 September 2020; pp. 269–278.
12. Lai, T.; Ji, H.; Bui, T.; Tran, Q.H.; Dernoncourt, F.; Chang, W. A context-dependent gated module for incorporating symbolic semantics into event coreference resolution. *arXiv* **2021**, arXiv:2104.01697.
13. Hu, J.; Li, Z.; Chen, Z.; Li, Z.; Wan, X.; Chang, T.H. Graph Enhanced Contrastive Learning for Radiology Findings Summarization. *arXiv* **2022**, arXiv:2204.00203.
14. Kshirsagar, R.; Cukuvac, T.; McKeown, K.; McGregor, S. Predictive embeddings for hate speech detection on twitter. *arXiv* **2018**, arXiv:1809.10644.
15. Gou, J.; Yu, B.; Maybank, S.J.; Tao, D. Knowledge distillation: A survey. *Int. J. Comput. Vision* **2021**, *129*, 1789–1819. [CrossRef]
16. Liu, H.; Burnap, P.; Alorainy, W.; Williams, M.L. Fuzzy multi-task learning for hate speech type identification. In Proceedings of the The World Wide Web Conference, New York, NY, United States, 13 May 2019; pp. 3006–3012.
17. Ousidhoum, N.; Lin, Z.; Zhang, H.; Song, Y.; Yeung, D.Y. Multilingual and multi-aspect hate speech analysis. *arXiv* **2019**, arXiv:1908.11049.
18. Gou, J.; He, X.; Lu, J.; Ma, H.; Ou, W.; Yuan, Y. A class-specific mean vector-based weighted competitive and collaborative representation method for classification. *Neural Networks.* **2022**, *150*, 12–27. [CrossRef]
19. Gou, J.; Yuan, X.; Du, L.; Xia, S.; Yi, Z. Hierarchical Graph Augmented Deep Collaborative Dictionary Learning for Classification. *IEEE Trans. Intell. Transp. Syst.* **2022**, *23*, 25308–25322. [CrossRef]
20. Hadsell, R.; Chopra, S.; LeCun, Y. Dimensionality reduction by learning an invariant mapping. In Proceedings of the 2006 IEEE Computer Society Conference on Computer Vision and Pattern Recognition (CVPR'06), New York, NY, USA, 17–22 June 2006; IEEE: Piscataway Township, NJ, USA, 2006; Volume 2, pp. 1735–1742.
21. Meng, Y.; Xiong, C.; Bajaj, P.; Bennett, P.; Han, J.; Song, X. Coco-lm: Correcting and contrasting text sequences for language model pretraining. *Adv. Neural Inf. Process. Syst.* **2021**, *34*, 23102–23114.
22. Janson, S.; Gogoulou, E.; Ylipää, E.; Cuba Gyllensten, A.; Sahlgren, M. Semantic re-tuning with contrastive tension. In Proceedings of the International Conference on Learning Representations, Vancouver, BC, Canada, 4 May 2021.
23. Kim, T.; Yoo, K.M.; Lee, S.G. Self-guided contrastive learning for BERT sentence representations. *arXiv* **2021**, arXiv:2106.07345.
24. Yan, Y.; Li, R.; Wang, S.; Zhang, F.; Wu, W.; Xu, W. Consert: A contrastive framework for self-supervised sentence representation transfer. *arXiv* **2021**, arXiv:2105.11741.
25. Gao, T.; Yao, X.; Chen, D. Simcse: Simple contrastive learning of sentence embeddings. *arXiv* **2021**, arXiv:2104.08821.
26. Robinson, J.; Chuang, C.Y.; Sra, S.; Jegelka, S. Contrastive learning with hard negative samples. *arXiv* **2020**, arXiv:2010.04592.
27. Zampieri, M.; Malmasi, S.; Nakov, P.; Rosenthal, S.; Farra, N.; Kumar, R. Semeval-2019 task 6: Identifying and categorizing offensive language in social media (offenseval). *arXiv* **2019**, arXiv:1903.08983.
28. Caselli, T.; Basile, V.; Mitrović, J.; Kartoziya, I.; Granitzer, M. I feel offended, don't be abusive! implicit/explicit messages in offensive and abusive language. In Proceedings of the 12th Language Resources and Evaluation Conference, Marseille, France, 11–16 May 2020; pp. 6193–6202.
29. Devlin, J.; Chang, M.W.; Lee, K.; Toutanova, K. Bert: Pre-training of deep bidirectional transformers for language understanding. *arXiv* **2018**, arXiv:1810.04805.
30. Caselli, T.; Basile, V.; Mitrović, J.; Granitzer, M. Hatebert: Retraining bert for abusive language detection in english. *arXiv* **2020**, arXiv:2010.12472.
31. Basile, V.; Bosco, C.; Fersini, E.; Nozza, D.; Patti, V.; Pardo, F.M.R.; Rosso, P.; Sanguinetti, M. Semeval-2019 task 5: Multilingual detection of hate speech against immigrants and women in twitter. In Proceedings of the 13th International Workshop on Semantic Evaluation, Minneapolis, MN, USA, 6–7 June 2019; pp. 54–63.

mathematics

MDPI

Article

A Novel Deep Reinforcement Learning Based Framework for Gait Adjustment

Ang Li [1,2], Jianping Chen [2,3,*], Qiming Fu [1,2,*], Hongjie Wu [1,2], Yunzhe Wang [1,2] and You Lu [1,2]

1 School of Electronic and Information Engineering, Suzhou University of Science and Technology, Suzhou 215009, China
2 Jiangsu Province Key Laboratory of Intelligent Building Energy Efficiency, Suzhou University of Science and Technology, Suzhou 215009, China
3 School of Architecture and Urban Planning, Suzhou University of Science and Technology, Suzhou 215009, China
* Correspondence: alan@usts.edu.cn (J.C.); fqm_1@mail.usts.edu.cn (Q.F.)

Abstract: Nowadays, millions of patients suffer from physical disabilities, including lower-limb disabilities. Researchers have adopted a variety of physical therapies based on the lower-limb exoskeleton, in which it is difficult to adjust equipment parameters in a timely fashion. Therefore, intelligent control methods, for example, deep reinforcement learning (DRL), have been used to control the medical equipment used in human gait adjustment. In this study, based on the key-value attention mechanism, we reconstructed the agent's observations by capturing the self-dependent feature information for decision-making in regard to each state sampled from the replay buffer. Moreover, based on Softmax Deep Double Deterministic policy gradients (SD3), a novel DRL-based framework, key-value attention-based SD3 (AT_SD3), has been proposed for gait adjustment. We demonstrated the effectiveness of our proposed framework in gait adjustment by comparing different gait trajectories, including the desired trajectory and the adjusted trajectory. The results showed that the simulated trajectories were closer to the desired trajectory, both in their shapes and values. Furthermore, by comparing the results of our experiments with those of other state-of-the-art methods, the results proved that our proposed framework exhibited better performance.

Keywords: deep reinforcement learning; attention mechanism; state reconstruction; gait adjustment

MSC: 03D80; 68Q30

Citation: Li, A.; Chen, J.; Fu, Q.; Wu, H.; Wang, Y.; Lu, Y. A Novel Deep Reinforcement Learning Based Framework for Gait Adjustment. *Mathematics* **2023**, *11*, 178. https://doi.org/10.3390/math11010178

Academic Editor: Jianping Gou, Weihua Ou, Shaoning Zeng and Lan Du

Received: 18 November 2022
Revised: 15 December 2022
Accepted: 21 December 2022
Published: 29 December 2022

1. Introduction

Regaining the ability to walk is a primary goal of recovery for stroke patients. However, patients often experience restrictions on their daily communication and freedom of movement. Therefore, gait rehabilitation is urgently needed for these patients [1]. In the fields of gait rehabilitation and walking assistance, most lower-limb exoskeletons are developed for assisting paraplegic patients with disabilities of both of their legs. Through gait rehabilitation, we can achieve the goal of helping patients with mobility disorders in the rehabilitation of their musculoskeletal strength, motor control, and gait.

In traditional rehabilitation therapies, intensive labor is involved, and physical therapists have to provide patients with highly repetitive training that is usually inefficient and time-consuming [2]. The inherent shortcomings of these therapies include their failure to autonomously adapt to the user's changing needs, as well as the lack of sensory feedback that they provide to the user regarding the states of the limb and of the device. Compared to traditional physical therapies, exoskeleton-assisted rehabilitation has the advantages of reducing the work of therapists, and it is more convenient to use for quantitatively assessing the patient's level of recovery by measuring force and movement patterns [3].

To date, studies on exoskeleton control methods have achieved remarkable results. Mendoza-Crespo, Rafael et al. [4] developed and presented a method to acquire and saliently analyze subject-specific gait data, with the subject donning a passive lower-limb exoskeleton. In [5], a trajectory tracking controller based on the boundary layer augmented sliding control (BASMC) law was implemented to guide the subject's limbs along physiological gait trajectories. However, patients are normally trained to passively follow a predefined gait reference trajectory and their initiatives or motivations are usually not considered in the abovementioned methods. Therefore, adaptive control techniques and deep reinforcement learning (DRL)-based control methods have been proposed. DRL can potentially be used for exoskeleton control, and a predefined gait trajectory is not required. More importantly, interaction between the exoskeleton of the lower extremity and the patient during rehabilitation can be achieved. Thus, in this study, we focused on the control of a lower-limb exoskeleton using DRL.

2. Novelty and Contribution of the Study

In this study, in order to achieve the goal of gait rehabilitation and walking assistance, we simulated an exoskeleton based on the lower-limb musculoskeletal model used in the 2019 NeurIPS "Learning to Move–Walk Around" challenge.

Firstly, we adopted the Markov decision process (MDP) to model the gait adjustment problem, which provided an intelligent policy for the control of the exoskeleton. Secondly, in order to solve the curse of dimensionality caused by the complexity of the musculoskeletal model, we proposed a DRL-based framework named AT_SD3, which incorporated key-value attention-based state reconstruction and Softmax Deep Double Deterministic policy gradients (SD3). Based on the key-value attention mechanism, we presented a novel state reconstruction framework, in which all sampled sates are used in order to be fused proportionally with the initial observations, which enables the model to extract the self-dependent feature information of each sampled state to reconstruct an effective and interpretive state. Then, the DRL agent can select a better action in accordance with the same policy. Moreover, we used the autoencoder to extract features from the reconstructed state to solve the curse of dimensionality. Finally, we compared gait trajectories, including the desired trajectory, the unadjusted trajectory obtained in previous works, and the adjusted trajectory obtained in this work. The results showed that the adjusted trajectory was closer to the desired trajectory, in terms of its shape and value, than the unadjusted trajectory, and the performance of our proposed framework was better than that of other state-of-the-art DRL algorithms.

The related code and dataset are available at https://github.com/li0516/opensim-rl.git (accessed on 17 November 2022).

3. Related Works

3.1. Adaptive Control Techniques

Adaptive control techniques utilize dynamics models for both the user and the exoskeleton. Fatai Sado proposed a control strategy that integrated a dual unscented Kalman Filter (DUKF) for trajectory generation/the prediction of the spatio-temporal features of human walking and used an impedance-cum-supervisory controller to enable the exoskeleton to follow this trajectory in order to synchronize human walking [6]. In order to improve the control performance, the authors introduced a linear quadratic regulator with integral action (LQRi) and an unknown input observer (UIO) to compensate for disturbances [7]. In [8], an adaptive oscillator method named the amplitude omega adaptive iscillator (AωAO), comprising both low-level classifiers (to detect activities) and high-level classifiers to detect transitions between activities, was proposed to provide bilateral hip assistance for human locomotion. Sado, F. et al. [9] proposed a exoskeleton controller, with the design of a low-level linear quadratic gaussian (LQG) torque controller, a middle-level user-input torque estimator based on the use of a dual extended Kalman filter (EKF), and a novel high-level supervisory algorithm for the detection of movement and the synchronization of the exoskeleton with the user.

3.2. DRL-Based Control Methods

As one of learning-based control methods, Deep Reinforcement Learning (DRL), has been used in lower limb exoskeletons control. A human–robot interactive control, designed with Sigmoid function and the reinforcement learning algorithm, was proposed to govern the assistance provided by a lower limb exoskeleton robot to patients in the gait rehabilitation training [10]. In [11], Zhang, Y. et al. proposed a reinforcement-learning-based impedance controller, which actively reshapes the stiffness of the force-field to the subject's performance. In [12], an optimal adaptive compliance control was proposed for a Robotic walk assist device, where the reinforcement-learning-based strategy is a completely dynamic-model-free scheme, and this scheme employed joint position and velocity feedback as well as sensed joint torque (applied by user during walk) for compliance control. In [13], Rose, L. et al. presented for the first time an end-to-end model-free deep reinforcement learning method for an exoskeleton that can learn to follow a desired gait pattern, while considering a user's existing gait pattern and being robust to their perturbations and interactions. Oghogho, Martin et al. [14] employed the Twin Delayed Deep Deterministic Policy Gradient (TD3) method for rapid learning of the appropriate controller's gain values and delivering personalized assistive torques by the exoskeleton to different joints to assist the wearer in a weight handling task. In [15], Kumar, V.C.V. et al. took the Proximal Policy Optimization (PPO) to develop a human locomotion policy which can imitates the human walking reference motion. Based on all these achievements above, DRL-based control is inherently both adaptive and optimal, which can adapt to uncertainty and unforeseen changes in the robot dynamics [12].

Previous studies have shown that DRL is effective in the lower limb exoskeleton control. Moreover, with the concept of strengthening the discrimination among all the similar classes using the specific weights [16], in this paper, we propose a DRL-based framework, which incorporates a novel DRL algorithm SD3 and the key-value attention mechanism. Compared with the previous DRL methods, our framework can deal with the curse of dimensionality caused by the musculoskeletal model with high degree of freedom. From this perpective, our framework can greatly improve the performance of the DRL algrithm when a reinforcement learning (RL) agent observes a high dimensional state, and more importantly, experimental results show that our proposed framework has the state-of-art performance for the gait adjustment.

4. Preliminaries

4.1. Reinforcement Learning

We usually model the reinforcement learning problem as a MDP. A MDP is a quintuple (S, A, R, P, γ), where S is the state space, A is the action space, R is the reward function, P is the transition probability distribution and γ is the discount factor. At time step t, the agent selects and executes an action $a_t \in A$ according to the policy π, which maps from the state s to the probability of an action a. Then, the environment moves to a new state $s_{t+1} \in S$, where s_{t+1} is determined from the transition probability $P(s_{t+1}|s_t, a_t)$. Simultaneously, the agent receives the immediate reward $r_{t+1} \sim R(s_t, a_t)$. The dynamic diagram of the agent interaction with the environment is shown in Figure 1.

In RL, we aim to find an optimal policy which maximizes the return $G_t = \sum_{k=0}^{\infty} \gamma^k r_{t+k+1}$. To achieve this, we evaluate the policy π by estimating the value function, including state-value function V_π and action-value function Q_π. Here, the state-value function V_π is the expected return G_t when starting in state s and following policy π thereafter:

$$V_\pi(s) = E_\pi[G_t \mid s_t = s], \tag{1}$$

where the $E_\pi[\cdot]$ denotes the expected value of the return G_t given that the agent follows policy π. The action-value function, also called Q-value, $Q_\pi(s,a)$, represents the expected return G_t after taking an action a in state s and thereafter following policy π:

$$Q_\pi(s,a) = E_\pi[G_t \mid s_t = s, a_t = a]. \tag{2}$$

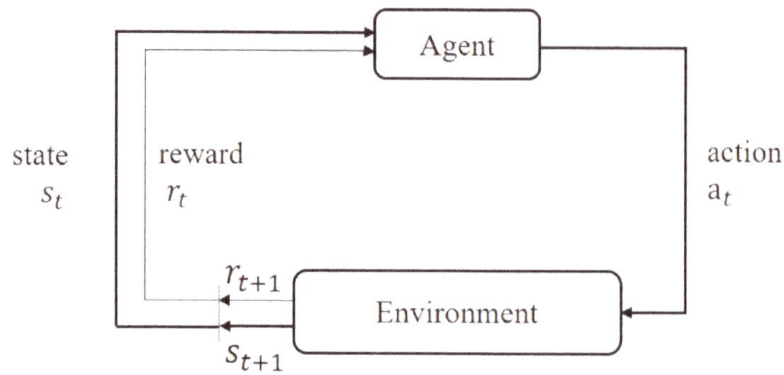

Figure 1. The interaction between the agent and the environment in RL.

Thereafter, the optimal policy π_* can be obtained by maximizing the state-value function or the action-value function, denoted V_* and Q_*, respectively. These two functions can be defined as follows:

$$V_*(s) = \max_\pi V_\pi(s), \tag{3}$$

$$Q_*(s,a) = \max_\pi Q_\pi(s,a) = E\Big[R_{t+1} + \gamma \max_a Q_*(s_{t+1},a) \mid s_t = s, a_t = a\Big]. \tag{4}$$

4.2. *Softmax Deep Double Deterministic Policy Gradients*

DDPG algorithm is often used to solve continuous control problems [17,18]. However, one of the dominant concerns for DDPG is that it suffers from the overestimation problem caused by selecting an action with highest action-value estimates according to the critic network [19]. To reduce the adverse impact of the overestimation, double estimators were proposed for the critic in TD3 [20]. Nevertheless, another problem is the large underestimation bias caused by direct adoption of taking minimum estimation of action-value from the two critics in TD3 [21].

To tackle this problem, Pan, L. [19] proposed a method, called SD3, which combines the softmax operator with the estimation of the action-value based on double critic estimators. In SD3, double actor networks and critic networks are built to select multiple actions and evaluate the corresponding action-values, respectively. To be specific, alternative actions will be selected via different actor networks, and then the minimum action-value can be obtained by calculating and comparing the action value functions of the corresponding actions evaluated by two critic networks:

$$\hat{Q}_{i=1,2}(s',a') = \min(Q_{i=1}(s',a';\theta^-_{i=1}), Q_{i=2}(s',a';\theta^-_{i=2})). \tag{5}$$

Thereafter, the minimum Q-value will be induced by the softmax operator in expectation by the importance sampling, and the specific definition of the softmax Q-value is as follows:

$$\text{softmax}_\beta(Q(s',\cdot;\theta^-)) = \frac{E_{\hat{a}'\sim p}\left[\frac{\exp(\beta Q(s',\hat{a}';\theta^-))Q(s',\hat{a}';\theta^-)}{p(\hat{a}')}\right]}{E_{\hat{a}'\sim p}\left[\frac{\exp(\beta Q(s',\hat{a}';\theta^-))}{p(\hat{a}')}\right]}, \tag{6}$$

where β is the parameter of the softmax operator, and the implication of $p(\hat{a}')$ is the probability density function of the Gaussian distribution for the importance sampling. The $E_{\hat{a}'\sim p}[\cdot]$ denotes the expected value of a random variable given that $\hat{a}'$ are sampled from the Gaussian distribution $p(\hat{a}')$. And $\hat{a}'$ is the action with additional noises for exploration, which are sampled from the Gaussian distribution $p(\hat{a}')$. Finally, the softmax Q-value can be obtained to calculate the target value:

$$y = r + \gamma(1-d)\,\mathrm{softmax}_\beta(Q(s', \cdot; \theta^-)). \tag{7}$$

4.3. Key-Value Attention Mechanism

Attention mechanism [22] in neural networks is introduced to focus on the information which is critical to the current task among the numerous input information. Therefore, the attention mechanism is often used to solve the problem of information overload and improve the efficiency and accuracy of task processing.

However, it is not suitable for some specific problems. So, Vaswani, A. et al. [22] introduced the key-value attention mechanism, which uses the format of a key-value pair to represent input information. The key is used to calculate the attention distribution α_i, and the value is used to calculate aggregate information. As shown in Figure 2, $(K, V) = [(k_1, v_1), \ldots, (k_n, v_n)]$ is used to represent N sets of the input information and the vector q is used to represent the query vector for a given task. Then, the attention function can be defined as follows:

$$\mathrm{att}(X, q) = \sum_{i=1}^{N} \alpha_i x_i = \sum_{i=1}^{N} \frac{\exp(s(k_i, q))}{\sum_j \exp(s(k_i, q))} v_i, \tag{8}$$

where s is the attention evaluation function, and x_i is equal to v_i which is used to represent the value of N sets of the input information. Finally, a weighted average of the input information v_i, the final output a , can be achieved according to the distribution α_i, which is computed based on the function s.

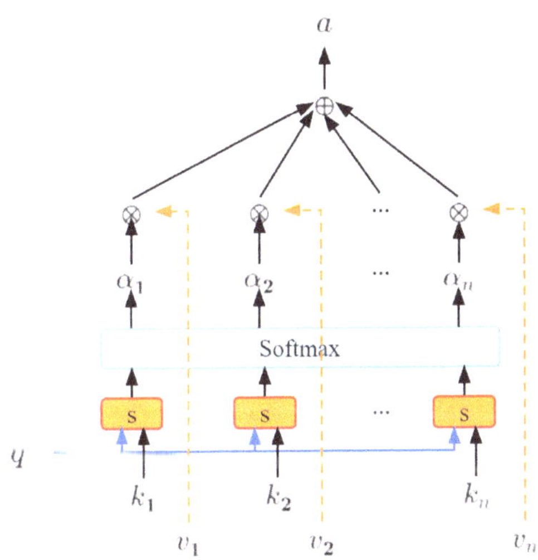

Figure 2. The key-value attention mechanism.

4.4. Parameter Space Noise for Exploration

Traditional RL methods increase exploration by adding noise, for example the Gaussian noise, to the output of the actor network. That is to say, the noise added to the actor network is independent of the state s_t, in other words, state-independent exploration. Hence, even for the same state s_t, a different action a_t will be certainly achieved and even sometimes it has nothing to do with s_t.

Therefore, Fortunato, Meire et al. [23] and Plappert, Matthias et al. [24] proposed to add noise to the agent's parameters. They sampled from a set of policies by adding the noise sampled from the Gaussian noise to the current policy $\pi(s_t)$, and in this case, the same action $a_t = \tilde{\pi}(s_t)$ can be achieved every time the same state s_t is taken as the input to the actor network.

5. Problem Modeling

In the previous work, we conducted gait simulation experiments with DRL algorithms based on the lower limb musculoskeletal model. The experimental results show that DRL algorithm is effective in gait simulation. However, sometimes during the simulation, there will be abnormal gait. In this paper, we adopt MDP to model the gait adjustment problem based on the musculoskeletal model.

5.1. The Lower Limb Musculoskeletal Model

In our work, the simulated environment used for the gait adjustment, named osim-rl, used in 2019 NeurIPS "Learning to Move–Walk Around" challenge, incorporates the lower limb musculoskeletal model and DRL to provide the accurate human movement simulation. The lower limb musculoskeletal model built in OpenSim has 8 internal degrees of freedom (4 per leg) and is actuated by 22 muscles (11 per leg). During the simulation, muscles are driven by muscle activations (the control signals that muscles produce power), and then states of the musculoskeletal model including joint angles, body location and ground reaction forces will be returned. The lower limb musculoskeletal model is shown in Figure 3. More detailed environment description can be found at the page: http://osim-rl.kidzinski.com/docs/nips2019/environment/ (accessed on 17 November 2022).

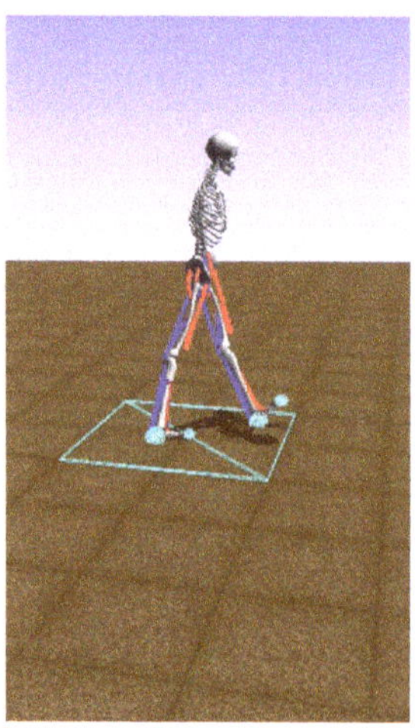

Figure 3. The lower limb musculoskeletal model.

5.2. MDP Modeling

5.2.1. State Space

The observation of the DRL agent consists of two parts: a target velocity map T and a body state S. Firstly, as shown in Figure 4, the target velocity map T is represented as a randomly generated target velocity matrix, which is a 2-dimensional target velocity vector, consisting of the target position and the current position of the model. Then, a target velocity vector can be achieved based on these positions. Secondly, the body state S is expressed by a 97-dimensional vector which consists of the pelvis state, ground reaction forces, joint angles and states of lower limb muscles. To be specific, the varibles of state space is listed in Table 1.

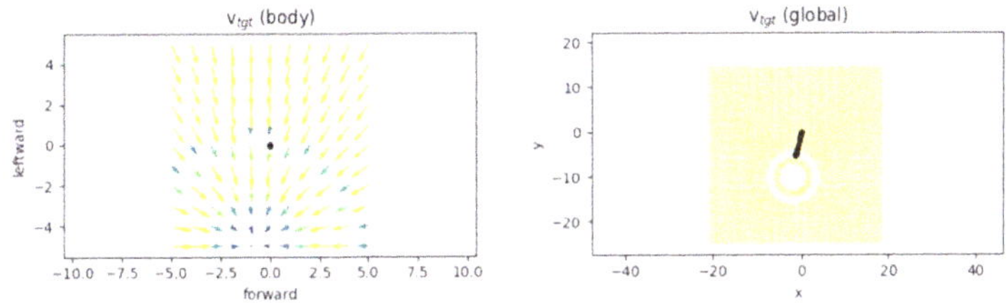

Figure 4. The target velocity map.

Table 1. State space.

	Symbols	Description
Body state S	S_p	pelvis state
	S_g	ground reaction forces
	S_j	joint angles
	S_m	muscle states
Target velocity map T	T_g	target velocity (global)
	T_b	target velocity (body)

5.2.2. Action Space

The action space $[0,1]^{22}$ represents muscle activations of 22 muscles. Muscles responds to these activations and generate forces, and then the model will act accordingly, for example, moving forward. At the same time, states of the model change accordingly.

5.2.3. Reward Function

The DRL agent will obtain a reward $J(\pi)$. The specific definition is as follows:

$$J(\pi) = R_b + R_g, \tag{9}$$

where R_b and R_g refer to the reward for the initial gait simulation and the gait adjustment according to the desired trajectory. To be specific, R_b ensures that a basis human gait can be obtained based on the musculoskeletal. However, during the simulation, deformed gaits sometimes appeared. So R_g is designed to make up for the gait defects, which is reflected in the deviation between the simulated angle and the desired angle of each joint of the lower limb.

Firstly, the specific definition of R_b is as follows:

$$R_b = M_{alive} + M_{step}, \tag{10}$$

where M_{alive} and M_{step} refer to the model remaining standing as long as possible and moving with minimal forces according to the target velocity map, respectively. Here, M_{alive} and M_{step} are defined as follows:

$$M_{alive} = \sum_i m_{alive}, \tag{11}$$

$$M_{step} = \sum_{step_i} \left(w_{step} m_{step} - w_{vel} c_{vel} - w_{eff} c_{eff} \right). \tag{12}$$

In Equation (11), m_{alive} refers to the unit time of "model survival". In addition, in Equation (12), on the one hand, m_{step} is stepping reward which represents the total elapsed time-steps of "model survival" in simulation. c_{vel} and c_{eff} are the velocity and effort costs, respectively. On the other hand, w_{step}, w_{vel} and w_{eff} are weights for the stepping reward, velocity and effort costs. Another point needed to note is that w_{step} is used to avoid getting higher reward by making small steps in human gait simulation.

Secondly, R_g is designed based on the changes of the real-time angle of each joint relative to the desired trajectory, for example, approaching or even exceeding in each episode. The specific definition is as Equation (13):

$$R_g = \sum_{i=0}^{n} (w_h r_{i_h} + w_k r_{i_k} + w_a r_{i_a}), \tag{13}$$

where r_i and w_i are the reward for each of the three joints in the lower limb and the corresponding weight, respectively. The reward r_i for timestep i is defined as follows:

$$r_i = w_F F(q_i) + w_G G(q_i), \tag{14}$$

where w_F and w_G are the weights for the reward $F(q_i)$ and the penalty $G(q_i)$, respectively. Here, on one hand, the function $F(q_i)$, representing the reward for the tendency approaching the desired trajectory, is defined based on the Gaussian function:

$$F(q_i) = \frac{1}{\sigma\sqrt{2\pi}} e^{-\frac{1}{2}\left(\frac{d-\mu}{\sigma}\right)^2}, \tag{15}$$

where μ and σ represent the mean and the SD of the desired joint angle, respectively. In addition, d, the absolute value of the difference between the real-time angle q_i and the desired joint angle q_{d_i} is defined as follows:

$$d = |q_i - q_{d_i}|. \tag{16}$$

On the other hand, the function $G(q_i)$, representing the penalty for exceeding the desired trajectory, is defined as Equation (17).

$$G(q_i) = -M(y_{max}) - M(y_{min}), \tag{17}$$

where $M(\cdot)$ is defined as follows:

$$M(y) = \begin{cases} 0 & y \leq 0 \\ y & y > 0 \end{cases}, \tag{18}$$

and

$$y_{max} = q_i - q_{max}, \tag{19}$$

$$y_{min} = q_{min} - q_i, \tag{20}$$

where q_{max} and q_{min} are the maximum and the minimum joint angle, respectively.

6. Methodology

6.1. Overall Framework

As depicted in Figure 5, the overall framework for gait adjustment consists of two parts: state reconstruct and SD3. First of all, the simulated environment initialization. Secondly, we reconstruct the initial observation via extracting features from existing states based on the attention mechanism, where the states are sampled in pairs with actions from the replay buffer randomly.

In the second part, the reconstructed state is taken as the input of SD3. Then, the actor network selects an action a_i according to the observation where i refers to the serial number of the action corresponding to different actor networks, and following, the critic network evaluates the value of the state action pair $Q(s, a_i)$. Moreover, the final action a depends on the result of comparing action-values which are evaluated by two critic networks. It is worth noting that, we add noise directly to the actor network parameters for a state-dependent exploration, which ensures a dependency between the sampled state and the corresponding selected action.

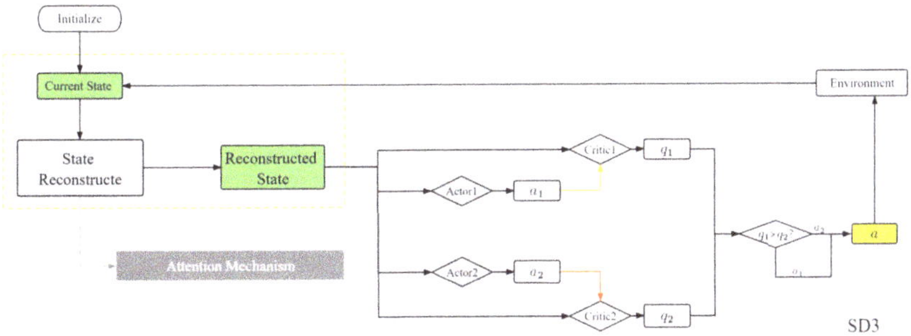

Figure 5. The overall framework for gait adjustment.

6.2. Key-Value Attention-Based State Reconstruction

In this work, the initial observation is a 339-dimensional state which consists of a 97-dimensional body state and a 242-dimensional target velocity map. Therefore, the RL agent cannot extract effective information easily, and then choose better actions due to too much redundant information in this high-dimensional observation. Moreover, in RL, the observed state s and the selected action a of an RL agent often plays a significant role for the training of RL algorithms, and the information in each state usually play an important role in the choice of the action. For example, in the case of the same policy and different states, RL agent takes different actions without active exploration. As shown in Figure 6, the actions taken to reach s_3, s_4 are shown by arrows. Although s_1 and s_2 are very close in space, they are functionally different, and these states contain necessary self-dependent feature information for the agent to perform the corresponding action. In other words, the self-dependent feature information in a state, for example s_1, is different from shared information that exists in all states, and necessary for decision making, for example a_1, which differs to the action a_2. In our work, the musculoskeletal model moves accoring to the target velocity map, if the musculoskeletal model moves to the target position, and then a new target position will be randomly generated. Immediately, the RL agent will make a new action, for example turning right, to move towards another target position. Therefore, in this case, we refer to the specific information contained in the state that signals that the musculoskeletal model has reached the target position as the self-dependent information, which makes the agent makes a specific action.

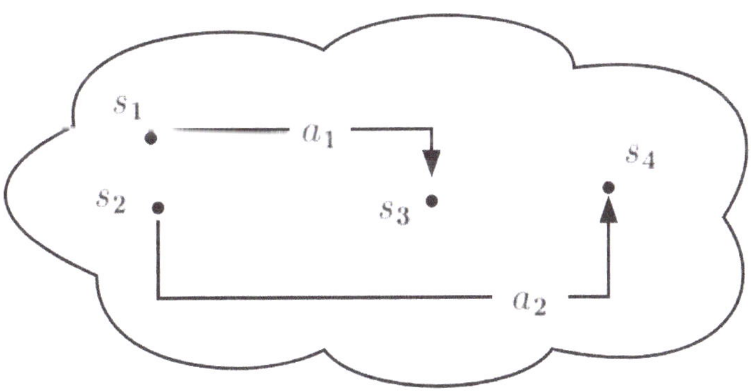

Figure 6. The choice of different actions under the same policy and different states.

The attention mechanism is introduced to focus on the information which is critical to the current task among the input information. Therefore, on one hand, based on the key-value attention mechanism, we try to reconstruct the current observation via capturing self-dependent feature information in each sampled state. To be specific, firstly, we randomly sample n sets of state action pairs $(s_1, a_1), (s_2, a_2), \ldots, (s_n, a_n)$ from the replay buffer. Here, the role of the sampled state action pairs (s_i, a_i) in our proposed framework is equal to (k_i, v_i) in the key-value attention mechanism. The state s_i and the action a_i are used to calculate the attention distribution and aggregate information, respectively. Moreover, we take the state-dependent exploration for the dependency between the sampled state s_i and the sampled action a_i. In other words, in the case of the same policy, the selected action is only related to the state inputted to the policy. Secondly, considering the advantage of the critic network in dealing with continuous action spaces, for example the simulated environment in our work, the critic network is usually used to approximate action-value function [25], so we take the critic network as the attention evaluation function. Thus, we calculate the action-value q_i of the above sampled actions with the critic network which takes the current observation and each sampled action a_i as input.

Based on the above method, a series of action-value q_i for the sampled actions can be achieved, which will serve as a basis for distinguishing the corresponding sampled state and reconstructing the initial observation. Thus, next to this operation, Softmax is used to normalize the corresponding action-value q_i, where the normalized action-value w_i represents the proportion of the sampled state in the reconstructed state. Significantly, the computed proportion w_i can be seen as the attention distribution α_i in key-value attention mechanism. Then, based on the attention distribution w_i, the sampled states s_i will be fused with the initial observation proportionally. In a word, the self-dependent feature information in each sampled state corresponding to the sampled action with higher action-value q_i will account for a larger proportion in reconstructed state. It is worth noting that, the way we perform feature fusion is element-wise addition. Based on this approach, the reconstructed state is influenced by the agent's action, and accordingly the state contains the information necessary to the action. Thus, the RL agent can select the corresponding action based on the information.

On the other hand, notably, autoencoder [26] is a kind of unsupervised neural network, and the goal of dimensionality reduction can be achieved by adjusting the number of hidden layers in both modules including the encoder and the decoder. Therefore, we use autoencoders to overcome the curse of dimensionality caused by the high-dimensional musculoskeletal model. The specific process is depicted as Figure 7.

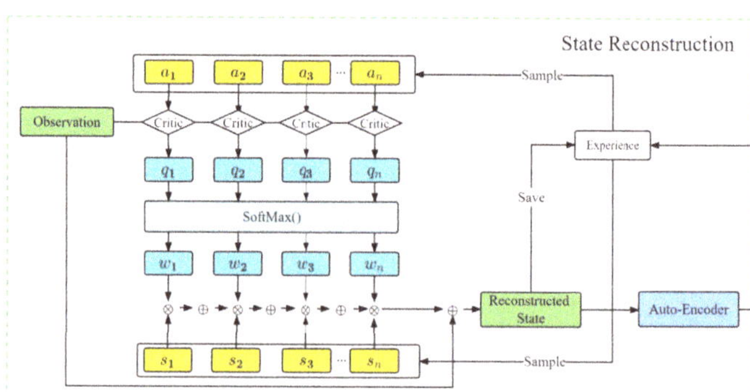

Figure 7. State reconstruction.

6.3. *AT_SD3 for Gait Adjustment*

Algorithm 1 presents the pseudocode of AT_SD3 for the gait adjustment.

Algorithm 1: AT_SD3 for the gait adjustment.

Initialize the simulated musculoskeletal model environment
Initialise critic networks α_1,α_2 and actor networks β_1,β_2 with random parameters θ_1,θ_2,ϕ_1,ϕ_2
Initialise target networks $\theta_1^- \leftarrow \theta_1, \theta_2^- \leftarrow \theta_2, \phi_1^- \leftarrow \phi_1, \phi_2^- \leftarrow \phi_2$
Initialise replay buffer B
Add noise to the actor network β_1, β_2
for t = *1 to T* **do**
    Observe the environmental state s (including the musculoskeletal state S and the target velocity map T)
    if t >*10000* **then**
        n state-action pairs $(s_1, a_1), (s_2, a_2), \ldots, (s_n, a_n)$ from the replay buffer B
        Calculate the action value q_i of the sampled action a_i and the current observation with the critic network
        Get the attention distribution w_i by normalizing the Q-value $(q_1, q_2, \ldots, q_n)$ with Softmax operation
        Get state s' through fusing sampled state s_i according to the w_i
        Fuse the current observation s and the s' to get reconstructed state
        Based on the reconstructed state s'', use auto-encoder to extract state features $\varphi(s'')$
        Store transition tuple ($\varphi(s'')$,a, J,s,d) in B
    else if t <*10000* **then**
        Execute an action a referring to the muscle activations
        Observe reward J using Equation (12), new state s and done flag d
        Store transition tuple (s, a, J, s, d) in B
    for i = *1, 2* **do**
        Sample a batch of N transitions from B
        Sample K noises $\epsilon \sim N(0, \bar{\sigma})$
        Add the additional noises to the action a
        Compute the action value using Equation (5)
        Compute the target value using Equation (7)
        Update actor networks using $1/N \sum_s [\nabla_a \alpha_i(s, a \mid \theta_i) \nabla_{\phi_i} \beta(s \mid \phi_i)]$
        Update critic networks using $1/N \sum_s (y_i - \alpha_i(s, a \mid \theta_i))^2$
        Update target networks using $\theta_i^- \leftarrow \tau\theta_i + (1-\tau)\theta_i^-, \phi_i^- \leftarrow \tau\phi_i + (1-\tau)\phi_i^-$

7. Experiment Analysis

7.1. *Experiment Preparation*

7.1.1. Dataset

To validate the effectiveness of the kinematic and ground reaction forces obtained via the simulation based on DRL algorithms, we compare the simulated data with the experimental data in a public dataset [27], where more details of the experiment refer to Section 7.2.2. The dataset contains a single-source, readily accessible repository of comprehensive gait data for a large group of children walking at a wide variety of speeds including very slow (below average speed), slow, free, fast and very fast (above average speed). Specifically, there are seven kinds of gait data: joint rotations, ground reaction forces, joint moments, joint power, EMG (electromyographic), cycle events and an ANOVA table with results for selected parameters in this dataset.

7.1.2. Evaluation Metrics

In order to compare the similarity between the experimental gait data and the simulated gait data, two evaluation metrics are adopted in this paper, namely mean absolute error (MAE), root mean square error (RMSE). These two metrics are defined as follows:

$$MAE = 1/m \sum_{i=1}^{m} |y_i - y_i'|, \tag{21}$$

$$RMSE = \sqrt{1/m \sum_{i=1}^{m} (y_i - y_i')^2}, \tag{22}$$

where m denotes the total number of gait data, y_i and y_i' represent the simulated and experimental data of the $i-th$ sample, respectively.

7.1.3. Parameter Settings

The hyperparameters of all methods are summarized in Table 2. It can be observed that two hidden layers are used, and the number of neurons in each hidden layer are 128 and 64, respectively. Considering the high-dimensional environment, we set the replay buffer size to 5×10^6 and the batch size is 256. Regarding the learning rate, TD3, AT_SD3, SD3, SD3_AE and PPO methods are all set to 0.0001, while DDPG method is set to 0.01. In addition, the hyperparameters, related to the noise added to the actor network, are also listed in Table 1. Note that all parameters are obtained through extensive numerical experiments.

Table 2. Hyperparameters of TD3 [14], DDPG [13], SD3, SD3_AE, PPO [15] and AT_SD3.

Method	Parameters	Results
Shared hyperparameters	Batch size	256
	Critic network	256 →128→64→1
	Actor network	256 →128→64→22
	Optimizer	Adam
	Replay buffer size	5×10^6
	Discount factor	0.99
	Target update rate	0.01
SD3	Learning rate	0.0001
	TAU	0.005
	Policy noise	0.2
	Sample size	50
	Noise clip	0.5
	Beta	0.05
	Importance sampling	0
PPO	Learning rate	0.0001
	Iteration	8
AT_SD3	Learning rate	0.0001
	Encoder	256→128→64→32→16→3
	Decoder	3→16→32→64→100
	Initial standard deviation (SD)	1.55
	Desired action SD	0.001
	Adaptation coefficient	1.05
DDPG	Learning rate	0.01
TD3	Learning rate	0.0001
	TAU	0.005
SD3_AE	Encoder	256→128→64→32→16→3
	Decoder	3→16→32→64→100
	Learning rate	0.0001

7.2. Results and Analysis

7.2.1. Algorithm Performance

In order to verify the effectiveness of AT_SD3 in the respect of gait adjustment based on the musculoskeletal model, we compare it with other state-of-the-art DRL algorithms, including TD3 [14], DDPG [13], PPO [15], SD3_AE and SD3, on the gait adjustment problem. The result is shown in Figure 8.

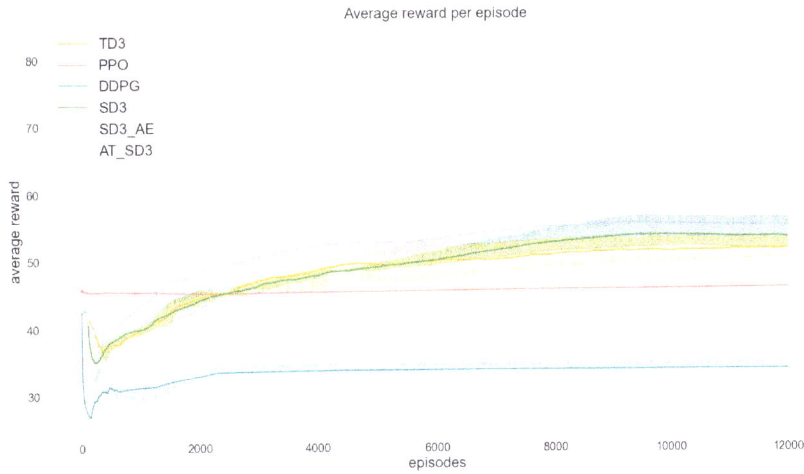

Figure 8. Performance of AT_SD3 and other state-of-the-art DRL algorithms.

Figure 8 shows the performance of AT_SD3 and other state-of-the-art DRL algorithms for the gait adjustment, where the horizontal axis represents the number of episodes and the vertical axis is the average reward. In this figure, each curve indicates the average reward for the gait adjustment using different DRL algorithms over a total of 12,000 episodes. The shaded area represents the SD varying from the mean value of the three independent experiments with same hyperparameters.

It can be noted that, on the one hand, the performance of AT_SD3 outperforms other traditional DRL algorithms after a certain number of episodes, including DDPG, PPO, TD3 and a novel DRL algorithm SD3. On the other hand, the performance of PPO keeps stable throughout the simulation, and the performance of DDPG is always poor compared to other algorithms, which may result from the limited algorithmic power in dealing with the curse of dimensionality in DRL. On the contrary, TD3, with more complex network structure, has better performance than PPO and DDPG. In our work, the current observation is a 339-dimensional musculoskeletal state, which may lead to this phenomenon. So, we introduce SD3 into our work to deal with the difficulty of gait adjustment caused by this problem. Due to the complexity of network structure, SD3 has a relative advantage over other RL algorithms in dealing with 'the curse of dimensionality'. However, as can be seen from Figure 8, after a certain number of episodes, the performance of SD3 keeps stable gradually but the rewards are relatively low. Therefore, an attention mechanism-based framework for gait adjustment is proposed. Based on the reward difference between AT_SD3 and other algorithms observed in Figure 8, we can conclude that AT_SD3 is more efficient than other traditional algorithms for the gait adjustment. Moreover, we provide an ablation experiment, named SD3_AE, to prove the effectiveness of our proposed framework. To be specific, we combine SD3 with the autoencoder for the gait adjustment. As can be seen in Figure 8, the performance of SD3_AE is better than SD3 due to the advantage of feature extraction and solving the curse of dimensionality. More importantly, by comparing the performance of AT_SD3 and SD3_AE, we can conclude that state reconstruction through the key-value attention mechanism is effective in gait adjustment. Through the above groups of comparative experiments, the experimental result demonstrates the effectiveness of fusing the self-dependent feature information necessary for decision making in each sampled state with the current observation.

7.2.2. Gait Adjustment

We compare different gait trajectories including the unadjusted trajectory obtained in previous work, the adjusted trajectory obtained in this work and the desired trajectory obtained in [27].

a. Unadjusted Trajectory and Desired Trajectory

Figure 9 shows the gait trajectories for different joints, including the ankle flexion/extension, the knee flexion/extension, the hip adduction/abduction and the hip flexion/extension corresponding to sub-figure (a) to (d), respectively, where the horizontal axis represents the gait cycle and the vertical axis represents different gait trajectories. In each sub-figure, red curve indicates the desired trajectory and another curve represents the unadjusted trajectory obtained by the human gait simulation in previous work. In terms of RMSE and MSE, Table 3 shows these similarity metrics between the desired trajectory and the unadjusted trajectory simulated in previous work.

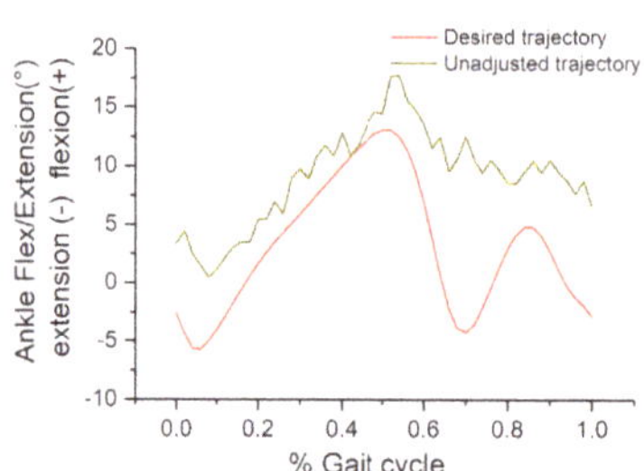

(**a**) Gait trajectories for the ankle flexion/extension

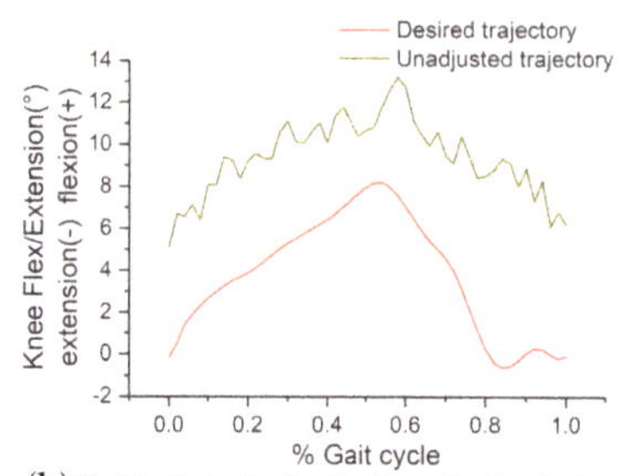

(**b**) Gait trajectories for the knee flexion/extension

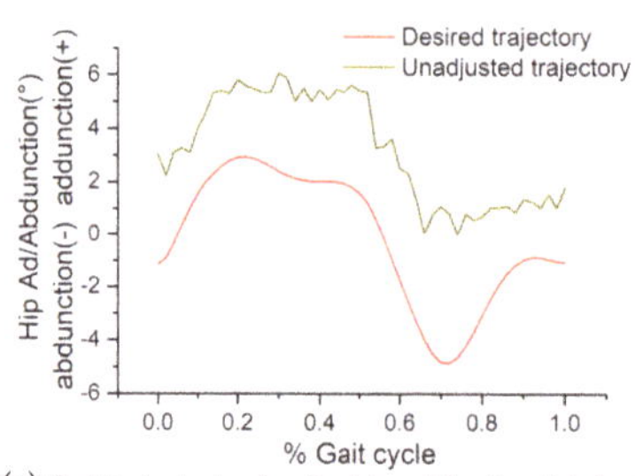

(**c**) Gait trajectories for the hip adduction/abduction

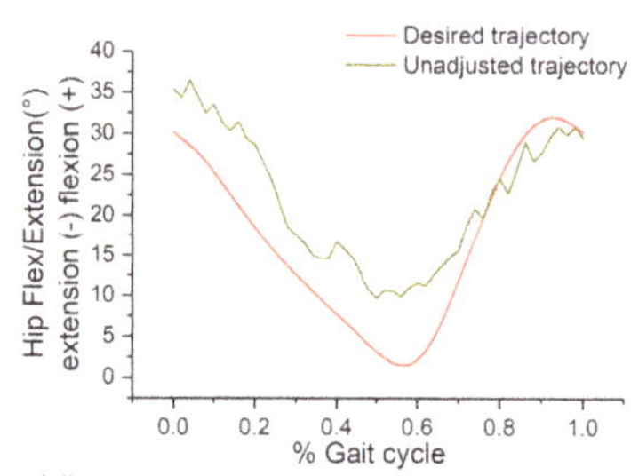

(**d**) Gait trajectories for the hip flexion/extension

Figure 9. The simulated kinematics compared to the experimental data in [27].

As can be seen from Figure 9, the unadjusted trajectory for different joints obtained in previous work are similar in shape to the desired trajectory, which is the mean kinematics calculated from the maximum and minimum value of the kinematics. However, as shown in Table 3 and Figure 9, there is a deviation between the unadjusted trajectory and the desired trajectory, which result from the randomness of the gait simulated by the algorithms in previous work. As can be seen from Table 3, these two kinds of metrics obtained in previous work are no more than 2.64 SD and no less than 1.22 SD.

Table 3. Metrics between desired trajectory and the unadjusted trajectory.

Metrics	Hip Ad/Abduction	Hip Flex/Extension	Knee	Ankle
RMSE	1.66	2.64	1.58	2.13
MAE	1.22	2.19	1.32	1.74

b. Adjusted Trajectory and Desired Trajectory

Figure 10 shows the trajectories for different joints, including the ankle flexion/extension, the knee flexion/extension, the hip adduction/abduction and the hip flexion/extension corresponding to sub-figure (a) to (d), respectively, where the horizontal axis represents the gait cycle and the vertical axis represents the gait trajectory for different joints. In each sub-figure, red curve indicates the desired trajectory and another curve represents the adjusted trajectory obtained in this work. Table 4 summarizes the similarity metrics between the desired trajectory and the adjusted trajectory obtained in this work, in terms of RMSE and MSE.

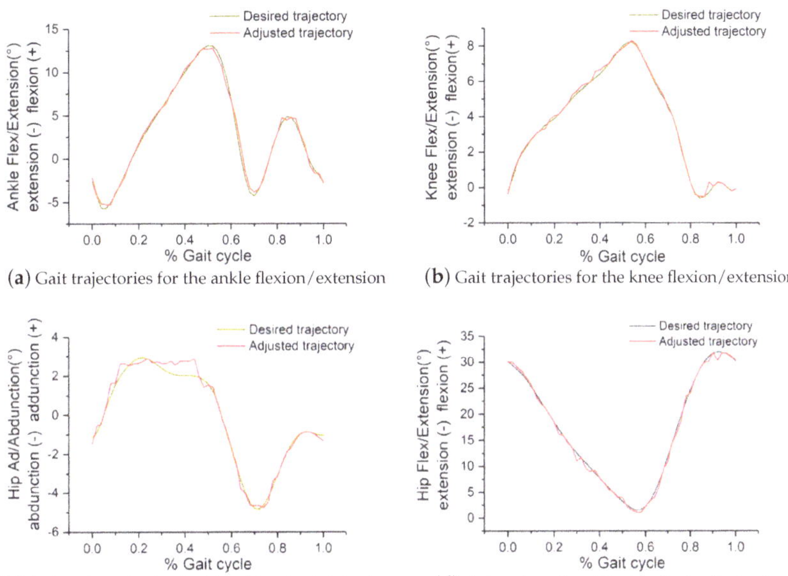

(**a**) Gait trajectories for the ankle flexion/extension (**b**) Gait trajectories for the knee flexion/extension

(**c**) Gait trajectories for the hip adduction/abduction (**d**) Gait trajectories of the hip flexion/extension

Figure 10. Desired trajectory and the adjusted trajectory based on the simulated lower limb exoskeleton.

Table 4. Metrics between desired trajectory and the adjusted trajectory.

Metrics	Hip Ad/Abduction	Hip Flex/Extension	Knee	Ankle
RMSE	0.32	0.18	0.14	0.28
MAE	0.23	0.1	0.1	0.22

As can be found from Figure 10, the gait trajectories for different joints obtained in this work are almost consistent with the desired trajectory in shape and value. This phenomenon demonstrates the effectiveness of gait adjustment with the simulated lower limb exoskeleton, which is modeled as a MDP problem in this work. However, in sub-figure (c), the adjusted trajectory for the hip adduction/abduction deviate from the desired trajectory in part of the gait cycle, which may result from the randomness. As can be found from Table 3, these metrics are no more than 0.32 SD which is much lower the figures in

Table 4, and these figures also demonstrate the effectiveness of the gait adjustment with the simulated exoskeleton.

8. Conclusions and Future Work

In order to verify the effect of gait rehabilitation for patients with mobility disorders, one available approach is to adjust gait without using physical equipment, where the musculoskeletal model is used in 2019 NeurIPS "Learning to Move–Walk Around" challenge. In this paper, we adopt MDP to model the gait adjustment problem. Moreover, based on DRL algorithms and the attention mechanism, a framework named AT_SD3 for the gait adjustment is proposed. Taking advantages of the attention mechanism, the self-dependent feature information for decision making in the sampled states generated by the agent's actions can be captured, with which we can reconstruct the initial observation with more interpretive information. Considering the high dimension of RL state and the advantage of autoencoder, the autoencoder is applied to solve the problem of 'the curse of dimensionality'. To investigate the performance of the proposed framework, the proposed framework and other traditional DRL algorithms are applied to the gait adjustment. The comparison results suggest that the performance of the proposed framework is superior to other traditional RL algorithms. Moreover, we compare different trajectories, including the unadjusted trajectory and adjusted trajectory obtained in previous work and in this paper, respectively, and comparative results suggest the trajectories simulated by using our proposed framework are closer to the desired trajectory in both shape and value, which outperforms the related previous work. In terms of the evaluation metrics of MAE and RMSE, results show the trajectories obtained in this paper are more accurate than those obtained in previous work.

As for the future work, the way to extract the information in each sampled state that is critical to the selected action is still worth studying. Moreover, we will purchase an actual lower limb exoskeleton to verify the effectiveness of the proposed exoskeleton control framework. Therefore, in the process of controlling the actual lower limb exoskeleton, the adjustment of exoskeleton parameters and the RL modeling for the exoskeleton control are worth studying.

Author Contributions: Conceptualization, A.L.; data curation, A.L.; formal analysis, A.L.; funding acquisition, J.C., Q.F. and Y.W.; investigation, H.W., Y.W. and Y.L.; methodology, A.L. and Q.F.; project administration, J.C., H.W., Y.W. and Y.L.; software, A.L.; supervision, J.C., Q.F. and Y.L.; validation, A.L.; writing—original draft, A.L.; writing—review and editing, Q.F. All authors have read and agreed to the published version of the manuscript.

Funding: This work was financially supported by National Key R&D Program of China (No. 2020YFC2006602), National Natural Science Foundation of China (No. 62172324, No. 62072324, No. 61876217, No. 61876121), University Natural Science Foundation of Jiangsu Province (No. 21KJA520005), Primary Research and Development Plan of Jiangsu Province (No. BE2020026), Natural Science Foundation of Jiangsu Province (No. BK20190942).

Data Availability Statement: The data presented in this study are openly available at https://doi.org/10.1016/j.jbiomech.2008.03.015 (accessed on 17 November 2022)

Conflicts of Interest: The authors declare no conflict of interest.

Abbreviations

The following abbreviations are used in this manuscript:

RL	Reinforcement Learning
DRL	Deep Reinforcement Learning
MDP	Markov Decision Process
SD3	Softmax Deep Double Deterministic policy gradients
DDPG	Deep Deterministic policy gradients

TD3	Twin Delayed Deep Deterministic policy gradient
PPO	Proximal Policy Optimization
SD	Standard Deviation
MAE	Mean Absolute Error
RMSE	Root Mean Square Error

References

1. Louie, D.R.; Eng, J.J. Powered robotic exoskeletons in post-stroke rehabilitation of gait: A scoping review. *J. Neuroeng. Rehabil.* **2016**, *13*, 53. [CrossRef] [PubMed]
2. Riener, R.; Lunenburger, L.; Jezernik, S.; Anderschitz, M.; Colombo, G.; Dietz, V. Patient-cooperative strategies for robot-aided treadmill training: First experimental results. *IEEE Trans. Neural Syst. Rehabil. Eng.* **2005**, *13*, 380–394. [CrossRef] [PubMed]
3. Chen, B.; Ma, H.; Qin, L.Y.; Gao, F.; Chan, K.M.; Law, S.W.; Qin, L.; Liao, W.H. Recent developments and challenges of lower extremity exoskeletons. *J. Orthop. Transl.* **2015**, *5*, 26–37. [CrossRef] [PubMed]
4. Mendoza-Crespo, R.; Torricelli, D.; Huegel, J.C.; Gordillo, J.L.; Rovira, J.L.P.; Soto, R. An Adaptable Human-Like Gait Pattern Generator Derived From a Lower Limb Exoskeleton. *Front. Robot. AI* **2019**, *6*, 36. [CrossRef] [PubMed]
5. Hussain, S.; Xie, S.Q.; Jamwal, P.K. Control of a robotic orthosis for gait rehabilitation. *Robot. Auton. Syst.* **2013**, *61*, 911–919. [CrossRef]
6. Sado, F.; Yap, H.J.; Ghazilla, R.A.B.R.; Ahmad, N. Exoskeleton robot control for synchronous walking assistance in repetitive manual handling works based on dual unscented Kalman filter. *PLoS ONE* **2018**, *13*, e0200193. [CrossRef] [PubMed]
7. Castro, D.L.; Zhong, C.H.; Braghin, F.; Liao, W.H. Lower Limb Exoskeleton Control via Linear Quadratic Regulator and Disturbance Observer. In Proceedings of the 2018 IEEE International Conference on Robotics and Biomimetics (ROBIO), Kuala Lumpur, Malaysia, 12–15 December 2018; pp. 1743–1748.
8. Chinimilli, P.T.; Subramanian, S.C.; Redkar, S.; Sugar, T. Human Locomotion Assistance using Two-Dimensional Features Based Adaptive Oscillator. In Proceedings of the 2019 Wearable Robotics Association Conference (WearRAcon), Scottsdale, AZ, USA, 25–27 March 2019; pp. 92–98.
9. Sado, F.; Yap, H.J.; Ghazilla, R.A.B.R.; Ahmad, N. Design and control of a wearable lower-body exoskeleton for squatting and walking assistance in manual handling works. *Mechatronics* **2019**, *63*, 102272. [CrossRef]
10. Bingjing, G.; Jianhai, H.; Xiangpan, L.; Lin, Y.Z. Human–robot interactive control based on reinforcement learning for gait rehabilitation training robot. *Int. J. Adv. Robot. Syst.* **2019**, *16*, 1729881419839584. [CrossRef]
11. Zhang, Y.; Li, S.; Nolan, K.J.; Zanotto, D. Adaptive Assist-as-needed Control Based on Actor-Critic Reinforcement Learning. In Proceedings of the 2019 IEEE/RSJ International Conference on Intelligent Robots and Systems (IROS), Macau, China, 3–8 November 2019; pp. 4066–4071.
12. Khan, S.G.; Tufail, M.; Shah, S.H.; Ullah, I. Reinforcement learning based compliance control of a robotic walk assist device. *Adv. Robot.* **2019**, *33*, 1281–1292. [CrossRef]
13. Rose, L.; Bazzocchi, M.C.F.; Nejat, G. End-to-End Deep Reinforcement Learning for Exoskeleton Control. In Proceedings of the 2020 IEEE International Conference on Systems, Man, and Cybernetics (SMC), Toronto, ON, Canada, 11–14 October 2020; pp. 4294–4301.
14. Oghogho, M.; Sharifi, M.; Vukadin, M.; Chin, C.; Mushahwar, V.K.; Tavakoli, M. Deep Reinforcement Learning for EMG-based Control of Assistance Level in Upper-limb Exoskeletons. In Proceedings of the 2022 International Symposium on Medical Robotics (ISMR), Atlanta, GA, USA, 13–15 April 2022; pp. 1–7.
15. Kumar, V.C.V.; Ha, S.; Sawicki, G.; Liu, C.K. Learning a Control Policy for Fall Prevention on an Assistive Walking Device. In Proceedings of the 2020 IEEE International Conference on Robotics and Automation (ICRA), Paris, France, 31 May–31 August 2019; pp. 4833–4840.
16. Gou, J.; He, X.; Lu, J.; Ma, H.; Ou, W.; Yuan, Y. A class-specific mean vector-based weighted competitive and collaborative representation method for classification. *Neural Netw.* **2022**, *150*, 12–27. [CrossRef] [PubMed]
17. Silver, D.; Lever, G.; Heess, N.M.O.; Degris, T.; Wierstra, D.; Riedmiller, M.A. Deterministic Policy Gradient Algorithms. In Proceedings of the ICML, Beijing, China, 21–26 June 2014.
18. Lillicrap, T.P.; Hunt, J.J.; Pritzel, A.; Heess, N.M.O.; Erez, T.; Tassa, Y.; Silver, D.; Wierstra, D. Continuous control with deep reinforcement learning. *arXiv* **2015**, arXiv:1509.02971.
19. Pan, L.; Cai, Q.; Huang, L. Softmax Deep Double Deterministic Policy Gradients. *arXiv* **2020**, arXiv:2010.09177.
20. Fujimoto, S.; van Hoof, H.; Meger, D. Addressing Function Approximation Error in Actor-Critic Methods. *arXiv* **2018**, arXiv:1802.09477.
21. Ciosek, K.; Vuong, Q.H.; Loftin, R.T.; Hofmann, K. Better Exploration with Optimistic Actor-Critic. In Proceedings of the NeurIPS, Vancouver, BC, Canada, 8–14 December 2019.
22. Vaswani, A.; Shazeer, N.M.; Parmar, N.; Uszkoreit, J.; Jones, L.; Gomez, A.N.; Kaiser, L.; Polosukhin, I. Attention is All you Need. *arXiv* **2017**, arXiv:1706.03762.
23. Fortunato, M.; Azar, M.G.; Piot, B.; Menick, J.; Osband, I.; Graves, A.; Mnih, V.; Munos, R.; Hassabis, D.; Pietquin, O.; et al. Noisy Networks for Exploration. *arXiv* **2017**, arXiv:1706.10295.
24. Plappert, M.; Houthooft, R.; Dhariwal, P.; Sidor, S.; Chen, R.Y.; Chen, X.; Asfour, T.; Abbeel, P.; Andrychowicz, M. Parameter Space Noise for Exploration. *arXiv* **2017**, arXiv:1706.01905.

25. Haarnoja, T.; Zhou, A.; Abbeel, P.; Levine, S. Soft Actor-Critic: Off-Policy Maximum Entropy Deep Reinforcement Learning with a Stochastic Actor. In Proceedings of the International Conference on Machine Learning, Stockholm, Sweden, 10–15 July 2018.
26. Baldi, P. Autoencoders, Unsupervised Learning, and Deep Architectures. In Proceedings of the ICML Unsupervised and Transfer Learning, Bellevue, WA, USA, 2 July 2011.
27. Schwartz, M.H.; Rozumalski, A.; Trost, J.P. The effect of walking speed on the gait of typically developing children. *J. Biomech.* **2008**, *41*, 1639–1650. [CrossRef] [PubMed]

mathematics

MDPI

Article

Embedding Uncertain Temporal Knowledge Graphs

Tongxin Li, Weiping Wang, Xiaobo Li, Tao Wang *, Xin Zhou and Meigen Huang

School of Systems Engineering, National University of Defense Technology, Changsha 410000, China
* Correspondence: wangtao1976@nudt.edu.cn

Abstract: Knowledge graph (KG) embedding for predicting missing relation facts in incomplete knowledge graphs (KGs) has been widely explored. In addition to the benchmark triple structural information such as head entities, tail entities, and the relations between them, there is a large amount of uncertain and temporal information, which is difficult to be exploited in KG embeddings, and there are some embedding models specifically for uncertain KGs and temporal KGs. However, these models either only utilize uncertain information or only temporal information, without integrating both kinds of information into the underlying model that utilizes triple structural information. In this paper, we propose an embedding model for uncertain temporal KGs called the confidence score, time, and ranking information embedded jointly model (CTRIEJ), which aims to preserve the uncertainty, temporal and structural information of relation facts in the embedding space. To further enhance the precision of the CTRIEJ model, we also introduce a self-adversarial negative sampling technique to generate negative samples. We use the embedding vectors obtained from our model to complete the missing relation facts and predict their corresponding confidence scores. Experiments are conducted on an uncertain temporal KG extracted from Wikidata via three tasks, i.e., confidence prediction, link prediction, and relation fact classification. The CTRIEJ model shows effectiveness in capturing uncertain and temporal knowledge by achieving promising results, and it consistently outperforms baselines on the three downstream experimental tasks.

Keywords: uncertain temporal knowledge graph; temporal knowledge graph; knowledge graph embedding; confidence score

MSC: 68T07; 68T30

Citation: Li, T.; Wang, W.; Li, X.; Wang, T.; Zhou, X.; Huang, M. Embedding Uncertain Temporal Knowledge Graphs. *Mathematics* **2023**, *11*, 775. https://doi.org/10.3390/math11030775

Academic Editor: Mikhail Goubko

Received: 30 December 2022
Revised: 31 January 2023
Accepted: 1 February 2023
Published: 3 February 2023

1. Introduction

KGs, which store various relation facts in the real world, are extensively applied in downstream tasks such as natural language processing [1], information retrieval [2], and knowledge question answering [3]. A relation fact (or triple) is composited of two entities (as nodes) and the relation that connects them (as the edge), which can be described as (h, r, t) or (s, p, o) [4]. Although KGs contain millions of such triples, it is known to suffer from incompleteness. This issue gives rise to the task of KG completion, which entails predicting the information missing in KGs. KG embedding, also known as knowledge representation learning, has become the mainstream method for KB completion by building the distributed representations (or vector embeddings) of entities and relations [5].

Specifically, KG embedding represents a symbolic triple (h, r, t) as low-dimensional, dense real-valued vectors $(\boldsymbol{h}, \boldsymbol{r}, \boldsymbol{t})$, each corresponding to the head entity, relation, and tail entity, respectively. Various embedding methods are currently emerging, mainly including translation-distance-based and semantic-matching-based models. TransE [6] is an original model based on translation distance and is known for its effectiveness and simplicity. In the TransE model, the sum of the head entity vector $\boldsymbol{h}$ and its relation vector $\boldsymbol{r}$ is close to its tail entity vector $\boldsymbol{t}$ for each relation fact, i.e., $\boldsymbol{h} + \boldsymbol{r} \approx \boldsymbol{t}$. TransE can effectively capture the structural and semantic information of the KG, but it cannot handle complex relations. To solve this problem, researchers have proposed multifarious models [7–9]. In addition, there are many embedding models based on semantic matching [10–12], which have achieved a high accuracy in link prediction tasks.

The above research methods are all reasoning on deterministic and static KGs without considering the uncertain and temporal information of triples, which leads to some key issues. The first is how to embed the uncertain KG. Uncertain KGs, such as ConceptNet [13] and NELL [14], associate each relation fact with a confidence score representing the likelihood of that fact to be true. During the construction of a KG, many automated methods generate noise and conflict, resulting in a certain degree of uncertainty for each triple. Embedding such uncertain knowledge can critically capture the uncertain nature of reality and provide more precise reasoning. The second is to learn information about the temporal dynamics of the relation facts in KGs. Most relation facts in KGs change over time, for example, the fact Claudio Raineri, coach, Chelsea is only true from 2000 to 2004, and ignoring such temporal information may lead to ambiguity and misunderstanding. The temporal information of relation facts also carries essential causal patterns that can assist the link prediction. To sum up, embedding the uncertain and temporal characteristics of relation facts can help KGs to perform better reasoning.

For the uncertainty of triples, uncertain KG embedding (UKGE) [15] calculates a score function based on the DistMult model and considers a probabilistic soft logic to generate confidence scores for unseen relation facts, but it does not fully exploit the structural information in the KG. Structural and uncertain knowledge embedding (SUKE) [16] employs an evaluator and a confidence generator to embed the confidence scores and structural information simultaneously, but the evaluator and the confidence generator are not combined into a unified framework, which means that the entity and relation vectors generated by the two components are not shared. Chen et al. [17] abandoned the probabilistic soft logic to generate extra training samples and leveraged a pool-based semisupervised learning model PASSLEAF to generate confidence scores for unseen relation facts. This model could partially solve the false-negative problem caused by random negative sampling, but it only considered the knowledge confidence and ignored the rich information contained in the graph structure. For embedding temporal information in KGs, a significant number of temporal KG representation learning models have recently emerged. The models TTransE [18] and HyTE [19] learned the distinct representations on each snapshot, and ATiSE [20] simplified the evolution of a temporal KG as a diachronic entity representation. Lately, most of the models apply neural networks to characterize the structural information and temporal evolution of KGs [21–23]. However, none of the aforementioned studies exploit both uncertainty and temporal information. Chekol et al. [24] explored Markov logic networks and probabilistic soft logic for reasoning on uncertain temporal KGs without utilizing embedding-based approaches and obtained a high computational complexity and low efficiency.

In response to the above issues, we propose the confidence score, time, and ranking information embedded jointly model CTRIEJ for the uncertain temporal KG embedding, which integrates the uncertainty, temporal information, and structural information into a unified framework. The CTRIEJ model first utilizes the sequence model to incorporate temporal information into the embedding of relations and then applies the sum of two loss functions as the objective function for training, one is the square loss function representing the confidence prediction, and the other is the pairwise ranking loss function representing structural information. When evaluating the model on multiple downstream tasks, we still employ the score function based on semantic matching for the confidence prediction and relation fact classification, and we design a score function based on translation distance and semantic matching to predict missing relation facts in the uncertain temporal KG. In addition, we adopt a self-adversarial negative sampling technique to train the model.

The main contributions of this paper can be summarized as follows:

- We leverage a GRU-based sequence model to incorporate temporal information into the embedding of the relation sequence and tie in two score functions on account of semantic matching and translation distance simultaneously to characterize the confidence information and structure information for the uncertain temporal KG in a unified framework.

- We exploit multiple score functions to simultaneously infer the existence of relation facts and the confidence scores of existing facts. We further adopt a self-adversarial negative sampling technique, which utilizes the embedding of current entities and relations to generate negative samples.
- We evaluate our model on the Wikidata dataset wikidata_5k on three typical tasks: confidence prediction, link prediction, and relation fact classification. The results demonstrate that the performance of the CTRIEJ model is better than other benchmarks.

The rest of the paper is organized as follows. We introduce the definition of uncertain temporal KGs and then review related work in Section 2. In the following two Sections, we propose our CTRIEJ model and conduct related experiments. Finally, we draw a conclusion in Section 5.

2. Related Work

As far as we know, there is currently no embedding learning method for the uncertain temporal KG, so we introduce the related work from three aspects: deterministic KG embedding models, temporal KG embedding models, and uncertain KG embedding models. For the sake of understanding, we first define the relevant problems of the uncertain temporal KG.

2.1. Problem Definition

The relevant definitions of the uncertain temporal KG are given as follows.

Definition 1. *Temporal knowledge graph: A temporal KG can be denoted by* $G = (E, R, Q)$, *where* E *and* R *represent the set of entities and relations, respectively, and* Q *represents the set of temporal relation facts. Each relation fact* (h, r, t) *in the graph has a valid time* $[T_s, T_e]$, *which denotes the closed interval from* T_s *to* T_e, *with* $T_s \leq T_e$ *and* $T_s, T_e \in T$, *i.e.,* $f = (h, r, t, [T_s, T_e])$. *We refer to* f *as a temporal fact.*

For a temporal KG G, its snapshot at time T is the graph (the nontemporal KG): $G(T) = \{(h, r, t) | (h, r, t, [T, T]) \in G\}$.

Definition 2. *Uncertain temporal knowledge graph: An uncertain temporal KG consists of temporal relation facts with confidence scores that typically model the inherent uncertainty. We can represent a fact as* $u = \left(f, s_f\right)$, *where* $f = (h, r, t, [T_s, T_e])$ *is a temporal relation fact, and* $s_f \in \mathbb{R}_{[0,1]}$ *is a real-valued weight assigned to* f.

Example 1. *Uncertain temporal knowledge graph: the following uncertain temporal KG represents sport's personality Claudio Raineri's career [24]:*

1. *(Claudio Raineri, bdate,1951) 1.0;*
2. *(Claudio Raineri, playsFor, Palermo, [1984, 1986]) 0.5;*
3. *(Claudio Raineri, coach, Napoli, [2001, 2003]) 0.6;*
4. *(Claudio Raineri, coach, Chelsea, [2000, 2004]) 0.9;*
5. *(Claudio Raineri, coach, Leicester, [2015, 2016]) 0.7.*

Definition 3. *Uncertain temporal knowledge graph embedding: Given an uncertain temporal KG, the embedding can be expressed as a mapping function* $f : h \rightarrow \boldsymbol{h} \in \mathbb{R}^{d_E}$, $r \rightarrow \boldsymbol{r} \in \mathbb{R}^{d_R}$, $t \rightarrow \boldsymbol{t} \in \mathbb{R}^{d_E}$, $T_{token} \rightarrow \boldsymbol{T}_{token} \in \mathbb{R}^{d_T}$, *where* $\boldsymbol{h}, \boldsymbol{r}$, *and* $\boldsymbol{t}$ *are the vector representations of the head entity, relation, and tail entity, respectively,* $\boldsymbol{T}_{token}$ *is the vector representation of the temporal token, which is described in detail in Section 4.2,* d_E, d_R, *and* d_T *represent the dimension of the entity vector, relation vector, and temporal token vector, respectively. In this model, we make* $d_E = d_R = d_T = d$.

2.2. Deterministic Knowledge Graph Embeddings

The deterministic KG contains a series of triples (h, r, t), where $h, t \in E$, $r \in R$. The deterministic KG can be regarded as an uncertain KG with triples whose confidence scores are all one. At present, the deterministic KG embedding models can be mainly divided into three categories: tensor-decomposition-based models, translation-based distance models, and neural-network-based models.

Structured embedding (SE) [25] is one of the earlier knowledge representation methods. For a relation fact, SE projects the head and the tail entity vector into a relation vector space through its two matrices and then calculates the distance between the two projection vectors in this space. This distance reflects the semantic relevance of the two entities under the relation, and the smaller their distance is, the more likely it is that the fact triple is established. In addition, the semantic matching energy model (SME) [26] defines several projection matrices and utilizes bilinear functions to describe the internal relationship between entities and relations. Bilinear functions are also utilized in the latent factor model (LFM) [27], which proposes to employ a relation-based bilinear transformation to characterize the second-order relationship between entities and relations. The DistMult model [11] also explores a simplified form of latent factor, which sets the relation matrix as a diagonal matrix. Based on the LFM, the neural tensor network (NTN) [28] model further employs the bilinear transformation of the relation to characterize the relationship between entities and relations. In addition, some researchers have proposed to apply matrix factorization for knowledge representation learning, and the RESACL model [10] is the representative method in this regard. The basic idea of RESACL is similar to the aforementioned LFM, and the difference lies in that RESACL optimizes all positions in the tensor, including the position with a value of zero, while the LFM only optimizes the triples that exist in the KG.

Bordes et al. were inspired by the translation invariance of the semantic and syntactic relationship in the word vector space and proposed the TransE model [6], which treated the relation in the KG as a translation vector between the head and tail entity. Compared with previous models, TransE has fewer parameters and a low computational complexity, and it can directly establish complex semantic connections between entities and relations. Bordes et al. conducted evaluation tasks such as link prediction on the WordNet and Freebase data sets, and experimental results showed that the performance of TransE was significantly improved, especially on large-scale sparse KGs. However, TransE has difficulty handling one-to-many, many-to-one, and many-to-many relations. To overcome the shortcomings of TransE, TransH [7] introduces a relation hyperplane, which is based on the idea of allowing an entity to have different vector representations in different relation triples. By employing a relation-specific hyperplane, the TransH model distinguishes different roles of the same entity in different triplets. The TransR [8] model also allows entities and relations to be in different dimensional representation spaces and then maps both to the same dimension by exploring the relational-related transformation space. There are many variants based on TransE, including TransM [29], TransF [30], TransA [9], etc., and most of these algorithms were introduced to further solve the defects of TransE and improve the expressive ability of the model. There are not only translation transformations in the representation space, but also rotation transformations. The RotatE [31] model represents the relation in the KG as a rotation operation in complex space based on Euler's formula. Through such a design, RotatE can express symmetric and antisymmetric relations, reciprocal relations, and compositional relations contemporarily, which was not available in previous models.

According to a variety of neural networks, knowledge embedding models of neural networks can generally be divided into five categories: linear/bilinear neural networks, convolutional neural networks (CNNs) [32–34], recurrent neural networks (RNNs) [35–37], graph neural networks (GNNs) [38–41], and generative adversarial networks (GANs) [42].

2.3. Temporal Knowledge Graph Embeddings

Current research in KG embedding focuses on static KGs, where relation facts do not change over time, such as the TransE model, TransH model, RESCAL model, etc., mentioned above. However, KGs are usually dynamic in practical applications, where facts evolve over time and are only valid for a specific period. Previous static KG embedding models completely ignore temporal information, which makes these methods unable to work in practical scenarios. Therefore, a significant number of temporal KG embedding models have emerged.

Know-Evolve [21] updates the embedding representation of entities subject to temporal changes by building an RNN on top of the static KG representation. TTransE [18] utilizes time information to constrain triples and models the time-predicate sequence for inference. TA-TransE and TA-DistMult [22] utilize the temporal information to constrain relation representations and construct temporal relation representations for each knowledge instance with a digital-level long short-term memory (LSTM) model. ATiSE [20] fully mines the impact of time on the evolution of entities, not only including the impact of past time but also mining the impact of future time on entities through the trend, cycle, and randomness of time series. RE-NET [23] converts time into a sequence of events with temporal information, constructs RNN-based encoding of entities in the sequence to capture the influence of their historical information, and finally leverages a relation-aware GCN to aggregate information about the entities within the same time. Chang2vec [43] splits the temporal KGs into multiple static KGs on each snapshot and employs metapath encoding for each KG to recompute the entity representation of nodes that have changed and update their embedding. CyGNet [44] exploits the historical information in KGs by designing a special replication module, while the generation module is designed to predict the knowledge that appears for the first time. xERTE [45] combines low-dimensional static vectors and temporal functions for the embedding representation of entities, not only to represent long-term properties of entities that do not change over time and the characteristics of change affected by time but the model can also visualize the paths interpretably for inference. RE-GCN [46] learns the evolutional representations of entities and relations at each timestamp by modeling the KG sequence recurrently and also incorporates the static properties of entities (such as entity types) via a static graph constraint component to obtain better entity representations.

Most of the above approaches make use of the temporal and structural information in the KG, but all assume that the triples are deterministic, and neither of them considers the confidence score of each relation fact.

2.4. Uncertain Knowledge Graph Embeddings

Some open KGs with uncertain information, such as NELL, ConceptNet, etc., add a confidence score to each triple to describe the uncertainty of this relation fact. Different KGs have different strategies for calculating confidence scores. The confidence level is obtained through the frequency of crowdsourcing annotations in ConceptNet [13], while NELL calculates the confidence value with probabilistic semantics by the EM algorithm [14].

Compared with the deterministic KG, the uncertain KG has additional triple confidence information. Recently, some research has been conducted on the representation and inference of uncertain KGs from different perspectives. GTransE [47] aims to improve the robustness of the representation model in learning noisy data. Specifically, it uses the confidence scores of triples to dynamically adjust intervals in the pairwise ranking loss, so that the higher confidence triples have larger intervals between positive and negative examples, thus making the model more focused on learning higher confidence triples.

UKGE [15] first proposed the task of learning the representation of uncertain KGs and embedding the structural information and confidence information at the same time. Specifically, it calculates the mean square error (MSE) Loss to fit the confidence scores of triples based on the energy function of DistMult. In this way, the confidence information is embedded into the distance of entities and relations, and we can employ the energy function of the triple to predict its confidence score. In addition, UKGE also introduces logic rules as prior knowledge, employs PSL probabilistic soft logic to reason about unseen facts, and applies them as training data to train to embed, thereby preserving the constraints of the rules into the embedding representation.

SUKE [16] still applies the DistMult model as an energy function and explores different logistic functions to transform the energy score into a structural information function and a confidence prediction function. The model consists of two parts: an evaluator and a confidence generator. For unseen triples, the evaluator learns the structural information and uncertain information to evaluate their plausibility and obtains a candidate set. The confidence generator then predicts corresponding confidence scores by learning the uncertain information of triples in the candidate set. However, the embedding vectors of entities and relations generated by the two components are independent of each other, which means that twice as much storage and computational space needs to be allocated.

PASSLEAF [17] argued that if we set the confidence scores of all observed triples to zero, it would cause a false-negative problem. In an uncertain KG, in addition to visible triples with confidence scores, there are more unseen triples that may also have a variety of confidence scores. The model leveraged semi-supervised learning and a sample pool to generate training samples in order to consider confidence scores of unseen triples. Moreover, multiple types of score functions were compared in the experiments of the model.

3. Confidence, Time, and Ranking Information Embedded Jointly

3.1. The Framework Overview

In this section, we propose the CTRIEJ model, which can simultaneously infer the missing relation facts and predict their confidence scores. The overall framework of the model is shown in Figure 1. It consists of three main components: a time-aware embedding model that incorporates time embedding in the relation embedding, a confidence prediction model that characterizes the uncertain information, and a pairwise ranking loss model that represents the structural information. In Section 4.2, a gate recurrent unit (GRU) is employed to process the sequence of the relation and time to obtain the relation embedding incorporating time. In Section 4.3, we describe in detail two functions based on semantic matching and translation distance, which characterize the uncertain information and structural information in the uncertain temporal KG, respectively. Finally, we combine the loss functions of the two components to form a joint embedding model and adopt a self-adversarial negative sampling technique to generate negative samples, which sample the negative triples according to the current embedding vectors. The details are in Section 4.4.

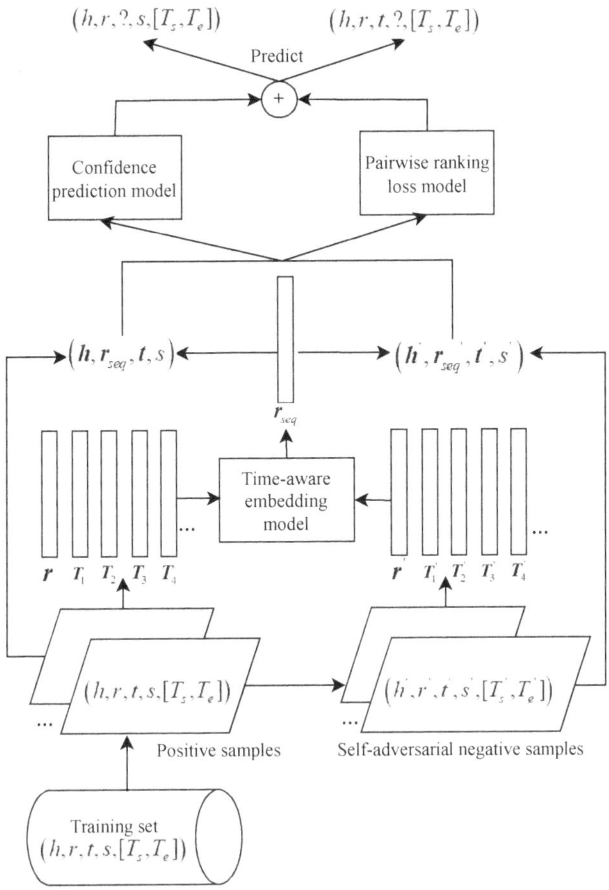

Figure 1. The overall framework of the CTRIEJ model.

3.2. GRU for Time-Aware Embedding Sequences

Contrary to all previous approaches, we encode sequences of temporal tokens with a GRU. A GRU is a neural network architecture particularly suited for modeling sequential data. Given an uncertain temporal KG where some triples are augmented with temporal information, we can decompose a given timestamp into a sequence consisting of some of the following temporal tokens.

As shown in Figure 2, the month and the day are represented by numbers 0 to 9. In addition to these numbers, the year has an extra "-", which is used at the beginning to indicate BC. The year usually consists of 4 digits, the month consists of 2 digits to characterize January to December, and the number of days consists of 2 digits to represent one day in a month. Hence, temporal tokens have a vocabulary size of 31. A complete timestamp should contain a start time T_s and an end time T_e, which we combine as the sequence of temporal tokens. Moreover, for each triple, we refer to the concatenation of the relation and its sequence of temporal tokens as the relation sequence $r_{seq} = \left(r, T_{s_{1y}}, T_{s_{2y}}, T_{s_{3y}}, T_{s_{4y}}, T_{s_{1m}}, T_{s_{2m}}, T_{s_{1d}}, T_{s_{2d}}, T_{e_{1y}}, T_{e_{2y}}, T_{e_{3y}}, T_{e_{4y}}, T_{e_{1m}}, T_{e_{2m}}, T_{e_{1d}}, T_{e_{2d}}\right)$ with length 17, where the suffixes y, m, and d indicate whether the digit corresponds to the year, month, or day information. Now, an uncertain temporal KG can be represented as a set of quadruples of the form (h, r_{seq}, t, s), where the sequence of relation r_{seq} includes the temporal information. These relation token sequences are used as input to a GRU. The equations defining a GRU are as follows:

$$\begin{aligned}
\boldsymbol{\Gamma}_u &= \sigma(\boldsymbol{W}_u \cdot [\boldsymbol{c}_{n-1}, \mathbf{x}_n]) + \boldsymbol{b}_u \\
\boldsymbol{\Gamma}_r &= \sigma(\boldsymbol{W}_r \cdot [\boldsymbol{c}_{n-1}, \mathbf{x}_n]) + \boldsymbol{b}_r \\
\boldsymbol{c}_n &= \boldsymbol{\Gamma}_u * (\tanh(\boldsymbol{W}_c[\boldsymbol{\Gamma}_r * \boldsymbol{c}_{n-1}, \boldsymbol{x}_n]) + \boldsymbol{b}_c) + (1 - \boldsymbol{\Gamma}_u) * \boldsymbol{c}_{n-1}
\end{aligned} \tag{1}$$

where $n = 1, 2, \cdots, 17$, $\boldsymbol{\Gamma}_u$ and $\boldsymbol{\Gamma}_r$ are update and reset gates, respectively, $\boldsymbol{c}$ is the hidden state, $\sigma(\cdot)$ is an activation function, and $\boldsymbol{x}_n \in \mathbb{R}^d$ is the embedding of the nth element of the relation token sequence r_{seq}.

Each token of the input sequence r_{seq} first gets its corresponding d-dimensional embedding by a random initialization, and the resulting embedding sequence is used as the input to the GRU. The relational sequence embedding is the last hidden state representation of the GRU, that is $\boldsymbol{r}_{seq} = \boldsymbol{c}_{17}$. Now that we have the relational sequence embedding, which characterizes temporal information, in the next section, we combine it with the head and tail entity embedding in varied loss functions.

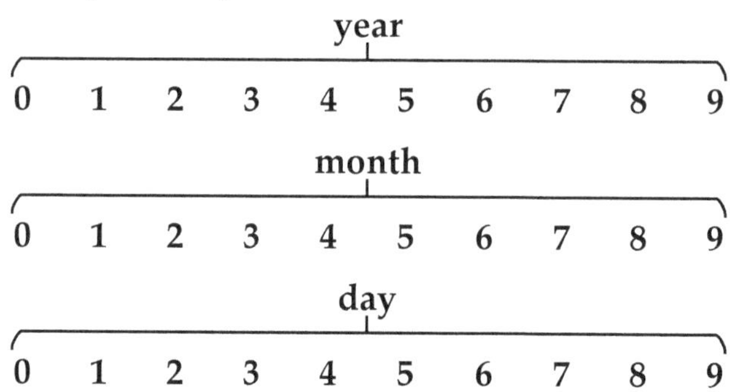

Figure 2. The temporal tokens.

3.3. Incorporating Uncertain Information and Structural Information

We leverage two score functions based on semantic matching and translation distance, namely, $S(h, r_{seq}, t)_{unce}$ and $S(h, r_{seq}, t)_{rank}$, and the corresponding loss function consists of two segments L_{unce} and L_{rank}, where L_{unce} characterizes the confidence prediction and L_{rank} models the graph structure information. The first component of the score function $S(h, r_{seq}, t)_{unce}$ can be employed to predict the confidence scores of triples, and the second one $S(h, r_{seq}, t)_{rank}$ is mainly designed to complete the missing relation facts. The MSE loss function in UKGE treats the semantic-matching-based DistMult model as its energy score function, which shows satisfactory performance, and therefore, our CTRIEJ model preserves the representation of uncertainty information through the MSE loss function. Specifically, we first obtain the energy function based on DistMult:

$$f = \boldsymbol{r}_{seq} \cdot (\boldsymbol{h} \circ \boldsymbol{t}) \tag{2}$$

where $\boldsymbol{h}$ and $\boldsymbol{t}$ represent the head and tail entity embedding of the triple, $\boldsymbol{r}_{seq}$ denotes the relation sequence embedding obtained by the GRU in the previous step, $\circ$ is the elementwise product, and $\cdot$ is the inner product. Then, we still leverage two different conversion functions [15] to transform energy scores into confidence scores in the range of 0 and 1:

$$S(h, r_{seq}, t)^{logi}_{unce} = \frac{1}{1 + e^{-(wf+b)}} \tag{3}$$

$$S(h, r_{seq}, t)^{rect}_{unce} = \min(\max(wf + b, 0), 1) \tag{4}$$

where w is a weight, b is a bias, and r_{seq} is the sequence of relation tokens with time mentioned in the previous section. $S(h, r_{seq}, t)_{unce}^{logi}$ denotes the confidence score function transformed using the logistic function, and $S(h, r_{seq}, t)_{unce}^{rect}$ denotes the confidence score function transformed using the bounded rectifier.

The MSE loss function containing positive samples D_{pos} and negative samples D_{neg} is as follows:

$$L_{unce} = \left|S(h, r_{seq}, t)_{unce} - s\right|^2 + \left|S\left(h', r'_{seq}, t'\right)_{unce}\right|^2 \tag{5}$$

where $(h, r_{seq}, t) \in D_{pos}$ is an observed fact in the data set, s is its confidence score, $\left(h', r'_{seq}, t'\right) \in D_{neg}$ is a corresponding negative sample through random negative sampling, and the function $S(\cdot)_{unce}$ can be either $S(\cdot)_{unce}^{logi}$ or $S(\cdot)_{unce}^{rect}$.

Then, the structural loss of the KG that employs the energy function based on TransE is calculated:

$$S(h, r_{seq}, t)_{rank} = -d(h, r_{seq}, t) = -\|\boldsymbol{h} + \boldsymbol{r}_{seq} - \boldsymbol{t}\|_{l_1/l_2} \tag{6}$$

where $\|\cdot\|_{l_1/l_2}$ represents the l_1 or l_2 norm. The smaller the value of the distance function $d(h, r_{seq}, t)$, the more likely the triple exists.

Following the TransE model, we can acquire a margin-based pairwise ranking loss function. Since the confidence level of each triplet is varied, we employ the confidence score as the weight of the ranking loss for each sample to obtain the following loss function:

$$L_{rank} = s \cdot \max\left(\gamma - S(h, r_{seq}, t)_{rank} + S\left(h', r_{seq}{}', t'\right)_{rank}, 0\right) \tag{7}$$

where $\gamma > 0$ represents a margin hyperparameter. This allows us to focus more on learning those triples with higher confidence scores and cut down on the contribution of those triples with lower confidence scores. To validate the generality of our proposed framework, relatively primitive score functions are employed in both segments above. We can further explore higher performance score functions based on semantic matching and translation distance for integration into our framework in future work.

3.4. Joint Loss Function

Negative sampling has been shown to be quite effective for learning KG embeddings. The commonly applied uniform negative sampling produces poor-quality negative samples and does not contribute much to the training of the model. Utilizing GAN to generate negative samples can effectively improve the efficiency of negative sampling, but it can also enhance the complexity of the model. To improve the quality of negative sampling without introducing additional model parameters, we leverage the idea of the self-adversarial negative sampling technique proposed in the RoTATE model [29] to our proposed model by figuring the scores of negative samples on the ground of the current entity and relation embeddings. The higher the scores, the higher the weights of the negative samples, so that the contribution of high-quality negative samples to the model can be raised.

In calculating the MSE loss function, we first utilize uniform negative sampling for a visible triplet (h, r_{seq}, t) to randomly generate n negative samples, and then we assign varied weights to negative samples based on the score function of the current entity and relation embeddings:

$$w_{unce}\left(\left(h'_i, r'_{seq_i}, t'_i\right) \middle| (h, r_{seq}, t)\right) = \frac{\exp S\left(h'_i, r'_{seq_i}, t'_i\right)_{unce}}{\sum\limits_{j=1}^{n} \exp S\left(h'_j, r'_{seq_j}, t'_j\right)_{unce}} \tag{8}$$

where $i = 1, 2, \cdots, n$, and $w_{unce}\left(\left(h'_i, r'_{seq_i}, t'_i\right) \middle| (h, r_{seq}, t)\right)$ represents the weight of the ith negative sample when computing the MSE loss of the triple (h, r_{seq}, t). In this way, we acquire the MSE loss function with the self-adversarial negative sampling technique.

$$L_{unce} = \left|S(h, r_{seq}, t)_{unce} - s\right|^2 + \sum_{i=1}^{n} w_{unce}\left(\left(h_i', r_{seq_i}', t_i'\right) | (h, r_{seq}, t)\right) \cdot \left|S\left(h_i', r_{seq_i}', t_i'\right)_{unce}\right|^2 \tag{9}$$

Similarly, when computing the pairwise ranking loss function, we also employ this technique to assign different weights to negative samples and obtain the final ranking loss function.

$$w_{rank}\left(\left(h_i', r_{seq_i}', t_i'\right) | (h, r_{seq}, t)\right) = \frac{\exp S\left(h_i', r_{seq_i}', t_i'\right)_{rank}}{\sum_{j=1}^{n} \exp S\left(h_j', r_{seq_j}', t_j'\right)_{rank}} = \frac{\exp -d\left(h_i', r_{seq_i}', t_i'\right)}{\sum_{j=1}^{n} \exp -d\left(h_j', r_{seq_j}', t_j'\right)} \tag{10}$$

$$L_{rank} = s \cdot \max\left(\gamma - S(h, r_{seq}, t)_{rank} + \sum_{i=1}^{n} w_{rank}\left(\left(h_i', r_{seq_i}', t_i'\right) | (h, r_{seq}, t)\right) \cdot S\left(h_i', r_{seq_i}', t_i'\right)_{rank}, 0\right) \tag{11}$$

Combining Equations (9) and (11), we get the final joint loss function with the self-adversarial negative sampling.

$$\begin{aligned} L_{joint} &= L_{unce} + L_{rank} \\ \|h\|_2 \leq 1, &\|r\|_2 \leq 1, \|t\|_2 \leq 1 \end{aligned} \tag{12}$$

We employ two different computational models for scoring $S(h, r, t)_{unce}$, referring to the variant using Equation (3) as CTRIEJ$_{logi}$ and the variant using Equation (4) as CTRIEJ$_{rect}$.

4. Experiments

Our proposed model was evaluated on three tasks: confidence prediction, link prediction, and relation fact classification. Obtaining the confidence scores of existing facts is the goal of confidence prediction, that is, for a given relation fact, with the head and tail entity, relation, and time, the corresponding confidence score should be predicted. The link prediction task aims to forecast the missing relation facts, e.g., given the head entity, relation, and its corresponding time, the missing tail entity should be predicted. Relation fact classification is a binary classification problem. We classified relation facts in wikidata_5k into strong and weak relation facts according to a given threshold τ, and the facts with confidence scores above the threshold were considered strong relation facts, otherwise, they were weak relation facts.

4.1. Datasets

At present, universal uncertain temporal datasets are not available. We applied the datasets extracted from Wikidata mentioned in [24]. Wikidata contains structured temporal information obtained from various sources using open information extraction (OIE). Ref. [24] obtained over 6.3 million temporal facts from Wikidata with confidence scores for various relations including plays for (>4 million facts), educated at (>6K), member of (>23K), occupation (>4.5K), spouse (>20K), and so on. Several of the extracted datasets are similar in composition, so we chose only one of them, named wikidata_5k.

Data preprocessing. We first performed preprocessing operations on this dataset. The initial confidence scores in wikidata_5k range from 1 to 10, where 96.4% are less than or equal to 5.0 in the dataset. For normalization, we first bounded the confidence scores to $s \in [1.0, 5.0]$, and then applied the min-max normalization on s to map them into $[0.0, 1.0]$. After data preprocessing, the wikidata_5k dataset contained 2233 entities, 6 relations, and 4818 uncertain temporal relation facts with a mean confidence score of 0.269 and a variance of 0.225.

4.2. Experimental Setup

We divided the dataset into 85% for training, 7% for validation, and 8% for testing. To test if our model could correctly interpret negative links, we added the same number of negative links as existing relation facts into the test set. We used the Adam optimizer for training and the grid search method to select optimal parameters in the following set: the embedding dimension $d \in \{64, 128, 256, 512\}$ of entities, relations, and time; the training batch size $b \in \{128, 256, 512, 1024\}$; the learning rate $l_r \in \{0.001, 0.005, 0.01\}$; and the margin value $\gamma \in \{1, 2, 10\}$ in the ranking loss. We used the L_2-norm when computing the translation distance. Through experiments, we concluded that in the wikidata_5k dataset, the best parameters for CTRIEJ$_{logi}$ were $\{d = 512; b = 256; l_r = 0.001; \gamma = 2\}$, and the best parameters for CTRIEJ$_{rect}$ were $\{d = 128; b = 256; l_r = 0.001; \gamma = 2\}$. We evaluated the results of all models on the ground of setting the best parameters for each experiment.

4.3. Baselines

We considered three types of baselines in our comparison, which included the deterministic KG embedding models TransE [6] and DistMult [11], the uncertain KG embedding models UKGE$_{rect}$ and UKGE$_{logi}$ [15], and the temporal KG embedding models TA-TransE and TA-DistMult [22].

- The deterministic KG embedding models: We chose TransE and DistMult for deterministic KG embedding models because these models have demonstrated a high performance. In wikidata_5k, we chose the high-confidence temporal relation facts from KGs for training and set a confidence score threshold τ to distinguish the high-confidence temporal relation facts from the low-confidence ones. These models were only applied in the link prediction and relation fact classification tasks since they could not predict confidence scores. We used the same grid search method to choose the best hyperparameters and the same optimizer for training. The best parameters of TransE were $\{d = 128; b = 256; l_r = 0.001; \gamma = 2\}$, and the best parameters of DistMult were $\{d = 128; b = 256; l_r = 0.001\}$.
- The uncertain KG embedding models: UKGE was the first model for embedding uncertain KGs, and it contains two variants, UKGE$_{logi}$ and UKGE$_{rect}$. The hyperparameter search method and optimizer were the same as above. In wikidata_5k, the best parameters of UKGE$_{logi}$ were $\{d = 128; b = 512; l_r = 0.001; \gamma = 2\}$, and the best parameters of UKGE$_{rect}$ were $\{d = 64; b = 256; l_r = 0.001; \gamma = 2\}$.
- The temporal KG embedding models: To incorporate temporal information, TA-TransE and TA-DistMult utilize the LSTM to learn time-aware representations of relation types which can be used in conjunction with the existing deterministic KG embedding methods. Likewise, these models are only suitable for link prediction and relation fact classification tasks. The best parameters of TA-TransE were $\{d = 128; b = 256; l_r = 0.001; \gamma = 2\}$, and the best parameters of TA-DistMult were $\{d = 128; b = 256; l_r = 0.001\}$.

4.4. Confidence Prediction

Evaluation metrics: The goal of confidence prediction is to obtain corresponding confidence scores of the existing relation facts. We acquired the confidence score for each relation fact through Equation (3) or Equation (4) and used the MSE and mean absolute error (MAE) as evaluation metrics for good or bad prediction. The smaller the MSE and MAE, the more accurate the prediction and the better the model performance.

Experimental results: The confidence prediction results are shown in Table 1. The deterministic KG representation learning model could not predict the confidence score, so we only employed the uncertain KG embedding model UKGE as the benchmark model. In general, on the wikidata_5k dataset, both of our variant models outperformed the corresponding UKGE variants, and CTRIEJ$_{rect}$ performed best on both MSE and MAE. Compared with the best-performing benchmark model UKGE$_{rect}$, CTRIEJ$_{rect}$ reduced the MSE by approximately 13.8% and the MAE by approximately 19.6%. Our proposed model outperformed UKGE on the task of confidence prediction, showing that incorporating temporal and structural information into the model could help more accurately predict confidence scores for relation facts.

Table 1. MSE and MAE of relation fact confidence prediction ($\times 10^{-2}$).

Dataset	wikidata_5k	
Metrics	MSE	MAE
$UKGE_{logi}$	5.39	17.54
$UKGE_{rect}$	4.63	15.28
$CTRIEJ_{logi}$	4.38	12.35
$CTRIEJ_{rect}$	3.99	12.28

4.5. Link Prediction

Evaluation metrics: The link prediction is a typical KG embedding evaluation task, i.e., predicting the missing head or tail entities based on known entities and their relations, or sometimes it means predicting the corresponding relations based on known head entities and tail entities. In the experiments of this paper, we forecast the missing tail entities through the known head entities, relations, corresponding temporal information, and uncertainty information. We obtained the plausibility ranking of each candidate tail entity via computing the score function, and then we calculated the evaluation metrics Hit@K and the average rank. Among them, Hit@K denoted the proportion of candidate tail entities ranked in the top K where the correct tail entities existed, and the average rank was the average of the ranking values for the correct tail entities. Since the confidence score of each triple varied, we followed the PASSLEAF model [17] to linearly weight Hit@K and the average rank to obtain WH@K and WMR as follows:

$$WH@K = \frac{\sum\limits_{(h,r_{seq},t,s)\in T_K} s}{\sum\limits_{(h,r_{seq},t,s)\in T} s} \tag{13}$$

$$WMR = \frac{\sum\limits_{(h,r_{seq},t,s)\in T} s \cdot rank_{(h,r_{seq},t)}}{\sum\limits_{(h,r_{seq},t,s)\in T} s} \tag{14}$$

where T represents the test dataset, T_K represents the top K data in the test set, and $rank_{(h,r_{seq},t)}$ represents the ranking value of the triplet (h, r_{seq}, t). We utilized the sum of the energy function through a translation distance and the confidence prediction function through semantic matching as the score function to rank the candidate tail entities. When computing WH@K and WMR with the test set, candidate tail entities may exist in both the training set and validation set, and they cannot be considered wrong. Hence, we removed the candidate tail entities that occurred in the training set and validation set to acquire the filtered WH@K and WMR. The larger the WH@K and the smaller the WMR, the better the model performance. For WH@K, we conducted experiments for $K = 2$ and $K = 10$, respectively.

Experimental results: The results of WMR, WH@2, and WH@10 are reported in Table 2. It can be seen that the CTRIEJ models generally outperformed the benchmark model, $CTRIEJ_{logi}$ performed best on WMR, and $CTRIEJ_{rect}$ performed best on WH@2 and WH@10. The deterministic KG embedding models TransE and DistMult did not perform as well as our proposed model because they did not consider the temporal information and confidence scores. UKGE performed poorly also because it only considered the confidence scores and did not leverage the temporal information and the structural information. TA-TransE and TA-DistMult only embedded temporal information, so the performance was not as good as that of our proposed model. Overall, for the task of link prediction, our model performed the best, followed by the deterministic KG embedding models and the temporal KG embedding models, and finally the UKGE model, which also showed the importance of temporal information and structural information to the model. In this paper, we employed the sum of the energy function based on translation distance and confidence prediction function as the evaluation function, and we can explore better function fusion methods to rank the triples in the future.

Table 2. Tail entity prediction.

Dataset	wikidata_5k		
Metrics	WMR	WH@2	WH@10
TransE	23.46	41.47%	78.32%
DistMult	25.82	47.68%	90.65%
$UKGE_{logi}$	177.69	15.42%	17.90%
$UKGE_{rect}$	36.76	48.22%	85.51%
TA-TransE	21.37	49.64%	79.19%
TA-DistMult	18.41	41.70%	85.68%
$CTRIEJ_{logi}$	13.51	42.74%	88.87%
$CTRIEJ_{rect}$	15.41	51.57%	92.77%

4.6. Relation Fact Classification

Evaluation metrics: We set the confidence score threshold $\tau = 0.3$ to classify the strong and weak relations for uncertain temporal relation facts. Under this setting, 36.03% of the relation facts in wikidata_5k were considered strong relations. By fitting a function between the predicted confidence scores in the training set and their relation categories, we obtained a binary classification model that was applied to classify relation facts in the test set. We used the F-1 score and accuracy to evaluate how well the models classified.

Experimental results: The results are shown in Table 3. Overall, our two variant models outperformed the baseline models. From the perspective of F-1 scores, the results of the baseline models did not have much difference, and our two variant models greatly improved the evaluation results. Among them, $CTRIEJ_{rect}$ had the best result, which was nearly 29.6% higher than the best-performing baseline model TA-TransE. In terms of accuracies, our model slightly outperformed the baseline models, with $CTRIEJ_{logi}$ performing the best, outperforming the best-performing baseline model DistMult by 2.1%. In conclusion, since our model embedded confidence scores, temporal information, and structural information simultaneously, the performance was better than that of the deterministic KG embedding models, the UKGE model, and the temporal KG embedding models.

Table 3. F-1 scores (%) and accuracies (%) of relation fact classification.

Dataset	wikidata_5k	
Metrics	F-1	Accu
TransE	18.1	74.2
DistMult	20.8	77.8
$UKGE_{logi}$	19.6	75.6
$UKGE_{rect}$	20.1	77.5
TA-TransE	27.4	75.6
TA-DistMult	25.6	75.4
$CTRIEJ_{logi}$	31.7	79.4
$CTRIEJ_{rect}$	35.5	75.9

4.7. Ablation Study

To verify the effect of incorporating temporal and structural information, and adopting the self-adversarial negative sampling method in our model, we took the variant $CTRIEJ_{logi}$ as an example and proposed its three simplified versions, called $CTRIEJ_{t-}$, $CTRIEJ_{s-}$, $CTRIEJ_{n-}$. In $CTRIEJ_{t-}$, we only kept the head entity, tail entity, relation, and corresponding confidence score of each relation fact and removed their time information. In $CTRIEJ_{s-}$, we reserved the MSE loss function for confidence prediction and removed the ranking loss function characterizing structural information. In CTRIEJ$_{n-}$, we utilized a uniform negative sampling method to obtain negative samples.

We experimentally tested the four evaluation indicators of MSE, MAE, F-1 score, and accuracy on these three models, and the results are shown in Table 4. It can be seen that the three simplified versions did not perform as well as the source model CTRIEJ$_{logi}$, thus verifying the effectiveness of our proposed model.

Table 4. MSE ($\times 10^{-2}$), MAE ($\times 10^{-2}$), F-1 score (%), and accuracy (%).

Dataset	**wikidata_5k**			
Metrics	MSE	MAE	F-1	Accu
CTRIEJ$_{logi}$	4.38	12.35	31.7	79.4
CTRIEJ$_{t-}$	4.59	13.49	20.8	78.4
CTRIEJ$_{s-}$	4.42	13.19	18.4	78.2
CTRIEJ$_{n-}$	4.51	13.43	23.5	78.0

5. Conclusions and Future Work

In this paper, we proposed an embedding model, the CTRIEJ model, for uncertain temporal KGs. The model leveraged a GRU-based sequence model to incorporate temporal information into the embedding of relation sequences and then tied in semantic-matching-based and translation-distance-based energy functions to integrate the confidence scores and structure information of KGs into a unified framework. Moreover, a self-adversarial negative sampling technique was adopted to generate negative samples for training our model. The CTRIEJ model outperformed other benchmarks in three downstream tasks: confidence prediction, link prediction, and relation fact classification. In future work, we will investigate how to integrate better-performing embedding models into our framework and how to better utilize these score functions for evaluating downstream tasks. In addition, predicting the relation facts and the corresponding confidence scores that exist at future moments in uncertain temporal KGs is another topic worth investigating.

Author Contributions: Conceptualization, T.L. and W.W.; methodology, T.L.; software, T.L.; validation, T.L., T.W. and X.L.; writing—original draft preparation, X.Z.; writing—review and editing, M.H. All authors have read and agreed to the published version of the manuscript.

Funding: This work is supported in part by the National Natural Science Foundation of China under Grant 72101263.

Institutional Review Board Statement: Not applicable.

Informed Consent Statement: Not applicable.

Data Availability Statement: Not applicable.

Acknowledgments: National University of Defense Technology.

Conflicts of Interest: The authors declare no conflict of interest.

References

1. Petroni, F.; Rocktäschel, T.; Lewis, P.; Bakhtin, A.; Wu, Y.; Miller, A.H.; Riedel, S. Language models as knowledge bases? *arXiv* **2019**, arXiv:1909.01066.
2. Wang, Q.; Mao, Z.; Wang, B.; Guo, L. Knowledge graph embedding: A survey of approaches and applications. *IEEE Trans. Knowl. Data Eng.* **2017**, *29*, 2724–2743. [CrossRef]
3. Wang, R.; Wang, M.; Liu, J.; Chen, W.; Cochez, M.; Decker, S. Leveraging knowledge graph embeddings for natural language question answering. In Proceedings of the International Conference on Database Systems for Advanced Applications, Chiang Mai, Thailand, 22–25 April 2019; Springer: Berlin/Heidelberg, Germany, 2019; pp. 659–675.
4. Ji, S.; Pan, S.; Cambria, E.; Marttinen, P.; Philip, S.Y. A survey on knowledge graphs: Representation, acquisition, and applications. *IEEE Trans. Neural Netw. Learn. Syst.* **2021**, *33*, 494–514. [CrossRef] [PubMed]
5. Lin, Y.; Han, X.; Xie, R.; Liu, Z.; Sun, M. Knowledge representation learning: A quantitative review. *arXiv* **2018**, arXiv:1812.10901.

6. Bordes, A.; Usunier, N.; Garcia-Duran, A.; Weston, J.; Yakhnenko, O. Translating embeddings for modeling multi-relational data. *Adv. Neural Inf. Process. Syst.* **2013**, *26*, 2787–2795.
7. Wang, Z.; Zhang, J.; Feng, J.; Chen, Z. Knowledge graph embedding by translating on hyperplanes. In Proceedings of the AAAI Conference on Artificial Intelligence, Quebec City, QC, Canada, 27–31 July 2014; Volume 28.
8. Lin, Y.; Liu, Z.; Sun, M.; Liu, Y.; Zhu, X. Learning entity and relation embeddings for knowledge graph completion. In Proceedings of the Twenty-Ninth AAAI Conference on Artificial Intelligence, Austin, TX, USA, 25–30 January 2015.
9. Xiao, H.; Huang, M.; Hao, Y.; Zhu, X. TransA: An adaptive approach for knowledge graph embedding. *arXiv* **2015**, arXiv:1509.05490.
10. Nickel, M.; Tresp, V.; Kriegel, H.P. A three-way model for collective learning on multi-relational data. In Proceedings of the ICML, Bellevue, WA, USA, 28 June–2 July 2011.
11. Yang, B.; Yih, W.t.; He, X.; Gao, J.; Deng, L. Embedding entities and relations for learning and inference in knowledge bases. *arXiv* **2014**, arXiv:1412.6575.
12. Trouillon, T.; Welbl, J.; Riedel, S.; Gaussier, É.; Bouchard, G. Complex embeddings for simple link prediction. In Proceedings of the International Conference on Machine Learning, PMLR, New York City, NY, USA, 19–24 June 2016; pp. 2071–2080.
13. Speer, R.; Havasi, C. ConceptNet 5: A large semantic network for relational knowledge. In *The People's Web Meets NLP*; Springer: Berlin/Heidelberg, Germany, 2013; pp. 161–176.
14. Mitchell, T.; Cohen, W.; Hruschka, E.; Talukdar, P.; Yang, B.; Betteridge, J.; Carlson, A.; Dalvi, B.; Gardner, M.; Kisiel, B.; et al. Never-ending learning. *Commun. ACM* **2018**, *61*, 103–115. [CrossRef]
15. Chen, X.; Chen, M.; Shi, W.; Sun, Y.; Zaniolo, C. Embedding uncertain knowledge graphs. In Proceedings of the AAAI Conference on Artificial Intelligence, Honolulu, HI, USA, 27 January–1 February 2019; Volume 33, pp. 3363–3370.
16. Wang, J.; Nie, K.; Chen, X.; Lei, J. SUKE: Embedding model for prediction in uncertain knowledge graph. *IEEE Access* **2020**, *9*, 3871–3879. [CrossRef]
17. Chen, Z.M.; Yeh, M.Y.; Kuo, T.W. PASSLEAF: A Pool-bAsed Semi-Supervised LEArning Framework for Uncertain Knowledge Graph Embedding. In Proceedings of the AAAI Conference on Artificial Intelligence, Virtual, 2–9 February 2021; Volume 35, pp. 4019–4026.
18. Leblay, J.; Chekol, M.W. Deriving validity time in knowledge graph. In Proceedings of the Companion Proceedings of the Web Conference 2018, Lyon, France, 23–27 April 2018; pp. 1771–1776.
19. Dasgupta, S.S.; Ray, S.N.; Talukdar, P. Hyte: Hyperplane-based temporally aware knowledge graph embedding. In Proceedings of the 2018 Conference on Empirical Methods in Natural Language Processing, Brussels, Belgium, 31 October–4 November 2018; pp. 2001–2011.
20. Xu, C.; Nayyeri, M.; Alkhoury, F.; Yazdi, H.S.; Lehmann, J. Temporal knowledge graph embedding model based on additive time series decomposition. *arXiv* **2019**, arXiv:1911.07893.
21. Trivedi, R.; Farajtabar, M.; Biswal, P.; Zha, H. Dyrep: Learning representations over dynamic graphs. In Proceedings of the International Conference on Learning Representations, New Orleans, LA, USA, 6–9 May 2019.
22. García-Durán, A.; Dumancic, S.; Niepert, M. Learning Sequence Encoders for Temporal Knowledge Graph Completion. In Proceedings of the EMNLP, Brussels, Belgium, 31 October–4 November 2018.
23. Jin, W.; Jiang, H.; Qu, M.; Chen, T.; Zhang, C.; Szekely, P.; Ren, X. Recurrent Event Network: Global Structure Inference over Temporal Knowledge Graph. 2019. Available online: https://www.semanticscholar.org/paper/Recurrent-Event-Network-%3A-Global-Structure-Over-Jin-Jiang/2474b36db67907dca830e2e4ddea6512e4dd2f5e (accessed on 20 December 2022).
24. Chekol, M.; Pirrò, G.; Schoenfisch, J.; Stuckenschmidt, H. Marrying uncertainty and time in knowledge graphs. In Proceedings of the AAAI Conference on Artificial Intelligence, San Francisco, CA, USA, 4–9 February 2017; Volume 31.
25. Bordes, A.; Weston, J.; Collobert, R.; Bengio, Y. Learning structured embeddings of knowledge bases. In Proceedings of the Twenty-Fifth AAAI Conference on Artificial Intelligence, San Francisco, CA, USA, 7–11 August 2011.
26. Bordes, A.; Glorot, X.; Weston, J.; Bengio, Y. A semantic matching energy function for learning with multi-relational data. *Mach. Learn.* **2014**, *94*, 233–259. [CrossRef]
27. Jenatton, R.; Roux, N.; Bordes, A.; Obozinski, G.R. A latent factor model for highly multi-relational data. *Adv. Neural Inf. Process. Syst.* **2012**, *25*, 3167–3175.
28. Socher, R.; Chen, D.; Manning, C.D.; Ng, A. Reasoning with neural tensor networks for knowledge base completion. *Adv. Neural Inf. Process. Syst.* **2013**, *26*, 926–934.
29. Fan, M.; Zhou, Q.; Chang, E.; Zheng, F. Transition-based knowledge graph embedding with relational mapping properties. In Proceedings of the 28th Pacific Asia Conference on Language, Information and Computing, Phuket, Thailand, 12–14 December 2014; pp. 328–337.
30. Feng, J.; Huang, M.; Wang, M.; Zhou, M.; Hao, Y.; Zhu, X. Knowledge graph embedding by flexible translation. In Proceedings of the Fifteenth International Conference on the Principles of Knowledge Representation and Reasoning, Cape Town, South Africa, 25–29 April 2016.
31. Sun, Z.; Deng, Z.H.; Nie, J.Y.; Tang, J. Rotate: Knowledge graph embedding by relational rotation in complex space. *arXiv* **2019**, arXiv:1902.10197.
32. Dettmers, T.; Minervini, P.; Stenetorp, P.; Riedel, S. Convolutional 2d knowledge graph embeddings. In Proceedings of the AAAI Conference on Artificial Intelligence, New Orleans, LA, USA, 2–7 February 2018; Volume 32.

33. Nguyen, D.Q.; Nguyen, T.D.; Nguyen, D.Q.; Phung, D. A novel embedding model for knowledge base completion based on convolutional neural network. *arXiv* **2017**, arXiv:1712.02121.
34. Balažević, I.; Allen, C.; Hospedales, T.M. Hypernetwork knowledge graph embeddings. In Proceedings of the International Conference on Artificial Neural Networks, Munich, Germany, 17–19 September 2019; Springer: Berlin/Heidelberg, Germany, 2019; pp. 553–565.
35. Gardner, M.; Talukdar, P.; Krishnamurthy, J.; Mitchell, T. Incorporating vector space similarity in random walk inference over knowledge bases. In Proceedings of the 2014 Conference on Empirical Methods in Natural Language Processing (EMNLP), Doha, Qatar, 25–29 October 2014; pp. 397–406.
36. Neelakantan, A.; Roth, B.; McCallum, A. Compositional vector space models for knowledge base completion. *arXiv* **2015**, arXiv:1504.06662.
37. Guo, L.; Sun, Z.; Hu, W. Learning to exploit long-term relational dependencies in knowledge graphs. In Proceedings of the International Conference on Machine Learning, PMLR, Long Beach, CA, USA, 9–15 June 2019; pp. 2505–2514.
38. Schlichtkrull, M.; Kipf, T.N.; Bloem, P.; Berg, R.v.d.; Titov, I.; Welling, M. Modeling relational data with graph convolutional networks. In Proceedings of the European Semantic Web Conference, Anissaras, Greece, 3–7 June 2018; Springer: Berlin/Heidelberg, Germany, 2018; pp. 593–607.
39. Welling, M.; Kipf, T.N. Semi-supervised classification with graph convolutional networks. *arXiv* **2016**, arXiv:1609.02907.
40. Shang, C.; Tang, Y.; Huang, J.; Bi, J.; He, X.; Zhou, B. End-to-end structure-aware convolutional networks for knowledge base completion. In Proceedings of the AAAI Conference on Artificial Intelligence, Honolulu, HI, USA, 27 January–1 February 2019; Volume 33, pp. 3060–3067.
41. Nathani, D.; Chauhan, J.; Sharma, C.; Kaul, M. Learning attention-based embeddings for relation prediction in knowledge graphs. *arXiv* **2019**, arXiv:1906.01195.
42. Cai, L.; Wang, W.Y. KBGAN: Adversarial Learning for Knowledge Graph Embeddings. In Proceedings of the NAACL-HLT, New Orleans, LA, USA, 1–6 June 2018.
43. Bian, R.; Koh, Y.S.; Dobbie, G.; Divoli, A. Network embedding and change modeling in dynamic heterogeneous networks. In Proceedings of the 42nd International ACM SIGIR Conference on Research and Development in Information Retrieval, Paris, France, 21–25 July 2019; pp. 861–864.
44. Zhu, C.; Chen, M.; Fan, C.; Cheng, G.; Zhang, Y. Learning from history: Modeling temporal knowledge graphs with sequential copy-generation networks. In Proceedings of the AAAI Conference on Artificial Intelligence, Virtual, 2–9 February 2021; Volume 35, pp. 4732–4740.
45. Han, Z.; Chen, P.; Ma, Y.; Tresp, V. xerte: Explainable reasoning on temporal knowledge graphs for forecasting future links. *arXiv* **2020**, arXiv:2012.15537.
46. Li, Z.; Jin, X.; Li, W.; Guan, S.; Guo, J.; Shen, H.; Wang, Y.; Cheng, X. Temporal knowledge graph reasoning based on evolutional representation learning. In Proceedings of the 44th International ACM SIGIR Conference on Research and Development in Information Retrieval, Virtual, 11–15 July 2021; pp. 408–417.
47. Kertkeidkachorn, N.; Liu, X.; Ichise, R. GTransE: Generalizing translation-based model on uncertain knowledge graph embedding. In Proceedings of the Annual Conference of the Japanese Society for Artificial Intelligence, Kumamoto-ken, Japan, 9–12 June 2020; Springer: Berlin/Heidelberg, Germany, 2020; pp. 170–178.

MDPI
St. Alban-Anlage 66
4052 Basel
Switzerland
Tel. +41 61 683 77 34
Fax +41 61 302 89 18
www.mdpi.com

Mathematics Editorial Office
E-mail: mathematics@mdpi.com
www.mdpi.com/journal/mathematics

www.ingramcontent.com/pod-product-compliance
Lightning Source LLC
Chambersburg PA
CBHW061457220926
51850CB00004B/108
* 9 7 8 3 0 3 6 5 7 2 6 2 8 *